BUSINESS LAW

BUSINESS LAW

——— SIXTH EDITION ———

EWAN MACINTYRE

PEARSON

Harlow, England • London • New York • Boston • San Francisco • Toronto • Sydney
Auckland • Singapore • Hong Kong • Tokyo • Seoul • Taipei • New Delhi
Cape Town • São Paulo • Mexico City • Madrid • Amsterdam • Munich • Paris • Milan

Pearson Education Limited
Edinburgh Gate
Harlow
Essex CM20 2JE
England

and Associated Companies throughout the world

Visit us on the World Wide Web at:
www.pearson.com/uk

First published in Great Britain in 2001
Second edition published 2005
Third edition published 2007
Fourth edition published 2008
Fifth edition published 2010
Sixth edition published 2012

© Pearson Education Limited 2001, 2005, 2007, 2008, 2010, 2012

The right of Ewan MacIntyre to be identified as author of this work has been asserted by him
in accordance with the Copyright, Designs and Patents Act 1988.

ISBN 978-1-4082-9274-7

British Library Cataloguing-in-Publication Data
A catalogue record for this book is available from the British Library.

Library of Congress Cataloging-in-Publication Data
A catalog record for this book is available from the Library of Congress.

10 9 8 7 6 5 4 3 2 1
15 14 13 12

Typeset in 9/12 Charter by 75
Printed and bound by Rotolito Lombarda, Italy

Brief contents

Detailed contents

Your complete learning package

Visit **www.mylawchamber.co.uk/macintyre** to access a wealth of resources to support your studies and teaching.

 All our premium sites provide access to an **interactive Pearson eText**, an electronic version of *Business Law* which is fully **searchable**. You can **personalise** your Pearson eText with your own notes and bookmarks and extensive **links are provided to all of the resources** below. The eText page presentation mirrors that of your textbook.

 Use the eText to link to **Case Navigator** for help and practise with **case reading and analysis in business law**.

In addition access:
- Interactive multiple-choice questions to test your understanding of each topic
- Weblinks to help you read more widely around the subject and really impress your lecturers
- Glossary to use as a quick reference for legal terms and definitions
- Glossary flashcards to test yourself on legal terms and definitions
- Legal newsfeed to help you read more widely, stay right up to date with the law and impress examiners
- Legal updates to help you stay up to date with the law and impress examiners
- Introductions to each chapter providing a wider understanding of the subject

Use the access card at the back of the book to activate mylawchamber premium. Online purchase is also available at **www.mylawchamber.co.uk/register**.

Teaching support materials
- **Case Navigator** is easy to integrate into any course where case reading and analysis skills are required
- The **business law MyTest testbank** can be used to create print tests or to create tests to **download into your learning environment**. It gives you access to a wide variety of questions designed to be used in formal assessments or to check students' progress throughout the course and includes over **900** questions
- **Instructor's Manual** including ideas for seminars and assessment with handouts for use in class

Also: The regularly maintained mylawchamber premium site provides the following features:
- Search tool to help locate specific items of content.
- Online help and support to assist with website usage and troubleshooting.

Use the access card at the back of the book to activate mylawchamber premium. Online purchase is also available at **www.mylawchamber.co.uk/register**.

Case Navigator access is included with your mylawchamber premium registration. The LexisNexis element of Case Navigator is only available to those who currently subscribe to LexisNexis Butterworths online.

Preface

Changes in the law

In the two years since the fifth edition, the law has continued to develop apace. Chapter 21 has been substantially re-written as the Equality Act 2010 has replaced the old statutes and regulations which outlawed discrimination on the grounds of a personal characteristic. The Bribery Act 2010 is considered in Chapter 22. New cases are included throughout the text. The most important of these, in the order in which they appear in the text, are:

Bloomsbury International Ltd v Sea Fish Industry Authority [2011] UKSC 25, [2011] 1 WLR 1546

R v Magro [2010] EWCA Crim 1575, [2010] 3 WLR 1694

R v Horncastle and others [2009] UKSC 14, [2010] 2 WLR 47

R v Thompson and others [2010] EWCA Crim 1623, [2010] All ER (D) (Sep)

RTS Flexible Systems Ltd v Molkerei Muller GmbH [2010] UKSC 14, [2010] 1 WLR 753

Tekdata Interconnections Ltd v Amphenol Ltd [2009] EWCA Civ 1209, [2010] 1 Lloyd's Rep 357

AG of Belize v Belize Telecom Ltd [2009] UKPC 11, 26 BHRC 578

Mediterranean Salvage and Towage Ltd v Seamar Trading and Commerce Inc: The Reborn [2009] EWCA Civ 531, [2009] All ER (D) 83 (Jun)

Chartbrook Ltd v Persimmon Homes Ltd [2009] UKHL 38, [2009] 1 AC 1101

Tekdata Interconnections Ltd v Amphenol Ltd [2009] EWCA Civ 1209, [2010] 1 Lloyd's Rep 357

UK Housing Alliance (North West) v Francis [2010] EWCA 117, [2010] 3 All ER 519

Sylvia Shipping Co Ltd v Progress Bulk Carriers [2010] EWHC 542, [2010] 2 Lloyd's Rep 81

Joyce v Bowman Law Ltd [2010] EWHC 251, [2010] PNLR 22

Lombard North Central Plc v Automobile World (UK) Ltd [2010] EWCA Civ 20, [2010] All ER (D) 166 (Jan)

Siemens Building Technology FE Ltd v Supershield Ltd [2009] EWHC 927, [2009] 2 All ER (Comm) 900

Fisher v Brooker and others [2009] UKHL 41, [2009] 1 WLR 1764

Kulkarni v Manor Credit (Davenham) Ltd [2010] EWCA Civ 69, [2010] All ER (D) 120 (Feb)

Wittmer v Gebr. Weber GmbH [2011] WLR (D) 210

Knight Frank LLP v Aston Du Haney [2011] EWCA Civ 404

Robinson v PE Jones [2011] EWCA Civ 9, [2011] BLR 206

Harvey v Plymouth City Council [2010] EWCA Civ 860, [2010] NPC 89

Star Energy Weald Basin Ltd v Bocardo SA [2010] UKSC 35, [2010] 3 WLR 654

Stadium Capital Holdings v St Marylebone Properties Co. [2010] EWCA Civ 952, [2010] All ER (D) 83 (Nov)

Co-operative Group (CWS) Ltd v Deborah Pritchard [2011] EWCA Civ 329

Spiller v Joseph [2010] UKSC 53, [2010] 3 WLR 1791

MAGA v Trustees of the Birmingham Archdiocese of the Roman Catholic Church [2010] EWCA Civ 256, [2010] 1 WLR 1441

Online Catering Ltd v Frank Acton [2010] EWCA Civ 58

Tiffin v Lester Aldridge LLP [2010] UKEAT 0255_10_1611, [2011] IRLR 105

Rowlands v Hodson [2009] EWCA Civ 1042, [2010] PNLR 8

Enviroco Ltd v Farstad Supply [2011] UKSC 16, [2011] WLR (D) 126

Stainer v Lee, Elliott and Eldington Holdings Ltd [2010] EWHC 1539 (Ch), [2011] BCC 134

Iesini v Westrip Holdings Ltd [2009] EWHC 2526, [2010] BCC 420

Secretary of State for BERR v Neufeld [2009] EWCA Civ 280, [2009] 3 All ER 790

Southern Cross Healthcare Ltd v Perkins [2010] EWCA Civ 1442, [2011] IRLR 247

Gisda Cyf v Barratt [2010] UKSC 41, [2010] IRLR 1073

Societe Generale v Geys [2011] EWCA Civ 307, [2011] All ER (D) 350 (Mar)

Buckland v Bournemouth University Higher Education Corporation [2010] EWCA Civ 121, [2010] IRLR 445

Tao Herbs & Acupuncture Ltd v Jin [2010] UKEAT 1477–09.

The aim of this book

This book aims to provide a comprehensive treatment of business law in a way which is both interesting and easily understood. The text covers most areas which could be classified as business law in an academically rigorous way. More specifically this text aims to be:

- **Comprehensive** in its scope, covering not only the more traditional business law subjects, but also the English Legal System, Employment, Consumer Credit, Intellectual Property, Trade Descriptions, Misleading Price Indications, Competition Law and Product Safety.
- **Holistic** in its approach. In every chapter there are numerous cross-references to other sections of the text, demonstrating the inter-relationship between the various subject areas.
- **Thorough** in its treatment of the law. Despite the easily readable style of the text, difficult issues are dealt with thoroughly even in areas where the law is highly technical.
- **Easy to read.** The style of the text is straightforward and accessible. The policy behind the law is explained, making comprehension of the law much easier.
- **Well structured**. In every chapter the text frequently reminds the reader of the main issues involved and the context of the particular subject being considered.
- **Up to date** in its treatment of the law. The text reflects the changes made by recent cases, and legislation and above all by EU law. The accompanying web sites will deal with changes to the law and keep the text as up to date as possible.

Who should use this book?

This book is intended to be suitable for a wide variety of students who study Business Law; for example:

- **Undergraduates** who study one or more law modules as part of their accountancy, business studies or business-related degrees.
- Students on **professional courses,** such as ACCA, CIMA, ILEX, ICAEW, IComA and ICSA.
- **HNC/D students**.
- **Postgraduate students** who need a thorough grounding in business law.

Distinctive features

Clear structure

The book is very clearly structured. The text in each chapter is broken up with several sets of 'Test your understanding' questions. These are designed to keep the reader firmly focused on the main issues with which the text deals. 'Key Points' at the end of each chapter have the same aim. The text is detailed, but the reader is frequently reminded of the context and structure of the material.

Study skills section

The study skills section is designed to give students a clear explanation of the skills they should apply when answering legal questions. The technique of answering a problem-style question is considered in some detail. I very much hope that this new section will inspire readers and allow them to see that legal assessments do not require rote learning and reproduction of facts, but do invite evaluation, analysis and application of conflicting principles.

Multiple choice and summary questions

Each chapter ends with a selection of multiple choice and summary questions. These questions are designed to be intellectually demanding and to give the reader the chance to apply the law contained in the preceding chapter to problem situations. The answers to the questions can be found in the Instructor's Manual, which is available to lecturers.

Student and lecturer web sites

Several areas of business law are changing very rapidly. None of the areas remain static. The student web site will point students to important changes in the law. There will be a brief summary of new cases and new legislation, along with an explanation of how these changes fit in with the book. The student web site will also contain a brief overview of each chapter and additional multiple choice questions. The answers to the multiple choice questions are 'justified', so that students can refer to the text and see why the answer is as it is. The lecturers' web site will contain a brief overview of each chapter, PowerPoint slides and more detailed comment on changes in the law and how these changes affect the material in the book.

Selected further readings

At the end of the book there is a short bibliography, suggesting further reading for those who want to know more about a particular subject area.

Guided tour

How can I get the most out of my study?

Use the **study skills** section at the beginning of the book for essential advice on the skills you will need in studying law, from lectures and seminars to coursework and exams.

What are the main facts and decisions arising from cases?

Case summary boxes throughout the chapters highlight the key legal principles and important facts of those essential key cases, making them easier to remember.

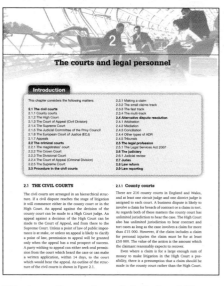

Will difficult concepts in law be presented in a manageable way?

New **bulleted chapter introductions** help students break down each area of the law, whilst the full colour design aids navigation throughout. **Examples, figures and flowcharts** also provide visual learning of those complex legal structures and processes.

What are the main points I should be aware of after reading this chapter?

Key points are listed at the end of every chapter. These pick out the essential information from the chapter you have read.

How can I check I've understood what I've read?

Test your understanding questions appear throughout the chapters to ensure you understand the topics as you read. Answers to these questions are provided at the back of the book.

How can I check I've learnt what I've read?

Summary questions and **multiple-choice questions** extensively test what you have learnt in each chapter.

How can I apply my knowledge of the law?

Tasks at the end of each chapter provide exercises to help you to apply the law you have learnt to scenarios.

Your complete learning package

Visit **www.mylawchamber.co.uk/macintyre** to access an **interactive Pearson eText**, an electronic version of *Business Law* which is fully **searchable**. You can **personalise** your Pearson eText with your **own notes and bookmarks** and extensive **links are provided to all of the self-study resources**:

Pearson eText

- Case Navigator to help improve your case reading and analysis skills
- Interactive multiple-choice questions to test your understanding of each topic
- Weblinks to help you read more widely around the subject and really impress your lecturers
- Glossary to use as a quick reference for legal terms and definitions
- Glossary flashcards to test yourself on legal terms and definitions
- Legal newsfeed to help you read more widely, stay right up to date with the law and impress examiners
- Legal updates to help you stay up to date with the law and impress examiners
- Introductions to each chapter providing a wider understanding of the subject

Table of cases

Visit **www.mylawchamber.co.uk/macintyre** to access unique online support to improve your case reading and analysis skills.

Case Navigator cases are highlighted in **bold** below.

Case Navigator provides:

- **Direct deep links** to the core cases in **business law**.
- **Short introductions** provide guidance on what you should look out for while reading the case.
- **Questions** help you to test your understanding of the case, and provide feedback on what you should have grasped.
- **Summaries** contextualise the case and point you to further reading so that you are fully prepared for seminars and discussions.

Please note that access to Case Navigator is free with the purchase of this book, but you must register with us for access. Full registration instructions are available on the website. The LexisNexis element of Case Navigator is only available to those who currently subscribe to LexisNexis Butterworths online.

Table of statutes

Table of statutory instruments

Table of European legislation

Study skills

Get organised from the start

When you start your course, decide how much time you can afford to devote to your study of each subject. Be realistic when doing this. There will be a lot to learn and that is why your time must be managed as effectively as possible. Listen to your lecturers, who will explain what is expected of you. Having made your decision to devote a certain amount of time per week to a particular subject, stick to what you have decided. If it will help, draw up a weekly chart and tick off each period of study when you complete it. You should attend all your lectures and tutorials, and should always read the pages of this book which are recommended by your lecturer. Steady work throughout the year is the key to success.

Take advantage of what your lecturer tells you

Many lecturers set and mark their students' assessments. Even if the assessment is externally set and marked, your lecturer is likely to have experience of past assessments and to know what the examiners are looking for. Take advantage of this. If you are told that something is not in your syllabus, don't waste time on it. If you are told that something is particularly important, make sure you know it well. If you are told to go away and read something up, make sure that you do. And if you are told to read certain pages of this book, make sure that you read them. You may be told to read this book after you have been taught, so as to reinforce learning. Or you may be told to read it beforehand, so that you can apply what you have read in the classroom. Either way, it is essential that you do the reading.

After the lecture/tutorial

As soon as a lecture or tutorial is over, it is tempting to file your notes away until revision time. You probably understood the ground that was covered and therefore assumed that it would easily be remembered later. However, it is an excellent idea to go over what was covered within 24 hours. This need not take too long. You should check that all the points were understood, and if any were not you should clear them up with the help of your notes and this book. Make more notes as you do this. Give these notes a separate heading, something like 'Follow up notes'. These additional notes should always indicate which aspects of the class seemed important. They should also condense your notes, to give you an overview of the material covered.

In many cases your lecturer will be setting your exam or coursework. If a particular area or topic is flagged up as important, it is more likely to be assessed than one which was not. Even if your assessment is externally set, your lecturer is likely to know which areas are the most important, and thus most likely to be tested. Fifteen minutes should be plenty to go over a one hour class. Each 15 minutes spent doing this is likely to be worth far more time than an extra 15 minutes of revision just before the exam.

Answering questions

What skills are you expected to show?

In 1956 Benjamin Bloom categorised the skills which students are likely to be required to display when being assessed. These skills are shown in Figure 1. Each skill in the pyramid builds upon the one beneath it.

Before deciding which skills you might be required to demonstrate, a brief explanation of the skills, in a legal context, needs to be made.

Knowledge, on its own, is not nearly as important as many students think. On the one hand, knowledge is essential because without knowledge none of the other skills are possible. But mere knowledge is unlikely to score highly in a traditional law assessment. Most assessments require comprehension, analysis and application. An exam question **might** require mere knowledge by asking something such as, *'List the terms implied by the Sale of Goods Act 1979'*. But not many assessments are so limited. Far more likely is a question such as, *'Describe the terms implied by the Sale of Goods Act 1979 and analyse the extent to which they adequately protect buyers of goods'*. This is a very different question. It requires knowledge, of course, but it also requires the higher level skills. It is these later skills which gain the higher marks. In 'open-book' exams especially, mere knowledge is likely to be worth very little.

Comprehension cannot be shown without knowledge. Some questions do require just knowledge and comprehension, for example, *'Explain the effect of the Contracts (Rights of Third Parties) Act 1999'*. But you should make sure that this is all the question requires. For example, if the question had said, *'Consider the extent to which the Contracts (Rights of Third Parties) Act 1999 has changed the law relating to privity of contract'*, most of the marks would be gained for application, for showing how the Act would have affected the pre-Act cases such as **Tweddle v Atkinson** and **Beswick v Beswick**. Knowledge of the Act, and comprehension of it, would be needed in order to achieve this. But if there was no application then the question would not have been answered.

Application of the law is very commonly required by a legal question. There is little point in knowing and understanding the law if you cannot apply it. The typical legal problem question, which sets out some facts and then asks you to advise the parties, always requires application of the law. It is not enough to show that you understand the relevant area of law, although some credit is likely to be given for this, you must then apply the law to advise the parties. These problem questions frequently also allow you to demonstrate analysis, synthesis and evaluation, as we shall see below when we consider how to answer such a question. However, this is not always true. When there is only one relevant case, and where it is obviously applicable, mere application of that case is all that is required.

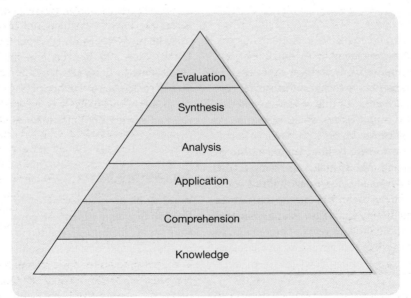

Figure 1 Study skills

Analysis of the law occurs when you recognise patterns and hidden meanings. You break the law down into component parts, differentiating and distinguishing ideas. For example, you might explain how one case (*Adams v Lindsell* on page **70**) introduced the postal rule on acceptance of contracts, and how another case (*Holwell Securities Ltd v Hughes* on page **71**) limited its application. Having made such an analysis of the law you could apply it to a problem question.

Synthesis is the gathering of knowledge from several areas to generalise, predict and draw conclusions; precisely the skill required to deal with the more complex problem questions!

Evaluation of the law requires you to compare ideas and make choices. It is a useful skill in answering problem questions. For example, in a problem question on offer and acceptance you might need to evaluate the applicability of *Adams v Lindsell* and *Holwell Securities Ltd v Hughes*. Evaluation is often asked for in essays, for example, *'Consider the extent to which the Unfair Terms in Consumer Contracts Regulations 1999 add to the protection of consumers conferred by the Unfair Contract Terms Act 1977. Do you think that the combined effect of the Regulations and the Act adequately protect consumers against unfair contract terms?'* When you evaluate you are giving your own opinion, realising that there are no absolutely right and wrong answers. But it is not pure opinion which is required. You must demonstrate the lower level skills described above in order to give some justification for your opinion. You also evaluate when deciding which legal principles are most applicable and should therefore be applied.

When you look at past assessments, try to work out which skills are required. Then make sure that you demonstrate these skills. Do not introduce the higher level skills if they are not expected of you in a particular question. For example, the very simple question, *'List the terms implied by the Sale of Goods Act 1979'*, is looking only for knowledge. No extra marks will be gained for evaluating the effectiveness of the terms. It must be said that such a question would be more suitable to a test than to an exam. But the point is, see what skills the question requires and make sure that you demonstrate those skills.

Answering problem questions

Almost all law exams have some problem questions, such as the end of chapter questions in this book.

These questions require application of the law rather than mere reproduction of legal principles.

You should always make a plan before you answer a problem question. Read the question thoroughly a couple of times, perhaps underlining important words or phrases. Problem questions can be lengthy, but the examiner will have taken this into account and allowed time for thorough reading of the question. So don't panic or read through too hurriedly. Next, see what the question asks you to do. (This is usually spelled out in the first or the last sentence of the question.) Then identify the legal issues which the question raises. Finally, apply the relevant cases to the issues and reach a conclusion.

The following question can be used as an example. It requires knowledge of the law relating to offer and acceptance of contracts. The law in this area is set out on pages **65–72** and **88–90** and it might be a good idea to read these pages before you use the example.

> Acme Supastore advertised its 'price promise' heavily in the *Nottown Evening News*. This promise stated that Acme was the cheapest retailer in the city of Nottown and that it would guarantee that this was true. The advertisement stated: 'We are so confident that we are the cheapest in the area that we guarantee that you cannot buy a television anywhere in Nottown cheaper than from us. We also guarantee that if you buy any television from us and give us notice in writing that you could have bought it cheaper at any other retailer within five miles of our Supastore on the same day we will refund double the price difference. Offer to remain open for the month of December. Any claim to be received in writing within 5 days of purchase.' Belinda saw the advertisement and was persuaded by it to buy a television from Acme Supastore for £299. The contract was made on Monday 3 December. On Saturday 8 December Belinda found that a neighbouring shop was selling an identical model of television for £289 and had been selling at this price for the past six months. Belinda immediately telephoned Acme Supastore to say that she was claiming double the difference in price. She also posted a letter claiming this amount. The letter arrived on Monday 10 December. Acme Supastore are refusing to refund any of the purchase price. Advise Belinda as to whether or not any contract has been made.

The final sentence of the question tells you what you are required to do – advise Belinda as to whether or not a contract has been made. If you have read pages **65–72** and **88–90** you will have seen that the requirements of a contract are an offer, an acceptance, an intention to create legal relations and consideration. So if these are all present a contract will exist. Notice that all the question asks you is whether or not a contract exists. It did not ask what remedies might be available if such a contract did exist and was breached. It might have done this, but it did not. So make sure you answer the question asked.

The first legal issue is whether the advertisement is an offer. So first define an offer as a proposal of a set of terms, with the intention that both parties will be contractually bound if the proposed terms are accepted. Then you apply your legal knowledge in depth. The advertisement might be an invitation to treat. *Partridge v Crittenden* (see page **66**) established that most advertisements are not offers. If advertisements were classed as offers problems with multiple acceptances and limited stock of goods would soon arise. The advertisement here, like the one in *Partridge v Crittenden*, uses the word 'offer'. But this advertisement can be distinguished from the one in *Partridge v Crittenden* because it shows a much more definite willingness to be bound. Nor would possible multiple acceptances cause a problem here. There would be no need for Acme to hold unlimited stock. If many people accepted, Acme would need only to make multiple price refunds, which would probably be small. So the multiple acceptance issue would not indicate a lack of intention to make an offer.

You then compare the advertisement in the question to the one in *Carlill's* case (see page **67**), noting similarities and differences. (Analysis, evaluation and synthesis will be shown in a really good answer.) There is no need to reproduce all the facts of *Carlill's* case. You might point out that the advertisement in the question said that it was guaranteeing that what it said was true, and that this is similar to the Smoke Ball Company's advertisement, which said that money had been deposited in the bank to show that they meant what they said. You would explain that whether or not there is an intention to create legal relations is an objective test and that in this commercial context it would be presumed that there was an intention unless there was evidence to suggest otherwise. Again, a comparison could be made with *Carlill's* case where, as in the question, the advertisement was made in a commercial context. You might explain that, as in *Carlill's* case, the advertisement set out what action was required to accept the offer and that acceptance could be made only by performing the requested act. In both the question and *Carlill's* case a valid acceptance could not be made by merely promising to perform the requested act. It is a feature of an offer of a unilateral contract that acceptance can be made only by performing the act requested. Acme's offer, like the one in *Carlill's* case, seems to be the offer of unilateral contract.

Next you would consider whether the offer had been accepted within the deadline, noting that the terms of the offer ruled out acceptance by telephone. The letter would have been within the deadline only if the postal rule applied. The rule should be explained and analysed, along with the limitations put upon it by *Holwell Securities Ltd v Hughes* (see page **71**). An analysis of this case would probably lead you to conclude that the postal rule would not apply, particularly as the advertisement in the question said that the acceptance had to be received before the deadline. In *Holwell Securities Ltd v Hughes* the Court of Appeal refused to apply the postal rule because acceptance had to be made 'by notice in writing' and it was held that this meant that it had to be received to be effective.

Next we would explain that there could have been consideration from both parties. Acme's consideration would have been their promise to give the refund. Belinda's consideration would have been performing the act requested. You might think it a waste of time to mention consideration. It would be a waste of time to consider it at length. But consideration is a requirement of a valid contract and you were asked to advise whether or not a contract existed. If you were absolutely certain that there was no valid acceptance it might be all right to say that there was therefore no need to consider consideration. But whether or not the postal rule would apply is not a matter of certainty. You might be wrong to say that it would not apply. If this was the case, consideration would be a part of the answer. If you reach a conclusion before the end of a question, which makes further investigation of the question unnecessary, you should conduct that further investigation anyway. It is most unlikely that a question has been set where the first line gives the answer and the rest of the question is irrelevant. For example, you might have decided that Acme's advertisement was definitely an invitation to treat. If this were true then there could have been no contract. (Belinda would have made an offer which was not accepted.) So if you did decide that the advertisement was an invitation to treat, by all means say so. But then explain that it might possibly have been an offer and go on to consider the rest of the question.

You should reach a conclusion when answering a problem question. But your conclusion might be that it is uncertain how the cases would apply and that therefore there might or might not be a valid contract. Do not be afraid of such a conclusion. Often it is the only correct answer. If a definite answer to any legal problem could always be found cases would never go to court.

Finally, do not be on Belinda's side just because you have been asked to advise her. Belinda wants an objective view of the law. A lawyer who tells his or her client what they want to hear does the client no favours at all. The client may well take the case to court, lose the case when the judge gives an impartial decision, and then be saddled with huge costs. If the news is bad for Belinda, as it probably is, then tell her so.

Try to practise past problem questions, but make sure that they are from your exam, and that there is no indication that future questions will be different. It can be very helpful to do this with a friend, or maybe a couple of friends, and to make a bit of a game of it. Find some old questions and give yourselves about ten minutes to make a plan of your answer. Then go through the questions together, awarding points for applying relevant cases or for making good points. It is probably best to keep this light-hearted but perhaps gently criticise each other (and yourself!) if you are missing things out.

Finally, it can be an excellent technique to get together with a small group of friends who all set a problem question for each other. First, you have to define the subject you are considering, perhaps formation of a contract. Then go over all the past questions. Then each try and set a similar question, along with a 'marking plan' showing how you would allocate a set number of marks (maybe 20). In the marking plan make sure that you list the skills which should be shown, analysis, application etc. This will get you thinking like the examiner. It is hoped that it will show you that all of the questions have great similarities and that the same things tend to be important in most answers. Lecturers who set a lot of exams know that most questions on a particular topic are looking for the same issues, that the same cases tend to be important, and that it is very difficult to invent wholly original questions. By the time you have set each other questions in this way the real exam questions should look a lot easier.

Using cases and statutes

Whenever you can, you should use cases and legislation as authority for statements of law. In the section above, on answering problem questions, we saw how *Carlill's* case might be used. Notice how different that use was from writing *Carlill's* case out at great length and then saying that the advertisement in the question is just the same and so *Carlill's* case will be applied. To do that not only wastes a lot of words but, worse, it shows little application of the law. You have recognised that the case might apply, but you have not applied it convincingly. To apply the case well you will need to analyse it, and to evaluate arguments and ideas. As we have seen, these are the skills which score the highest marks.

If a question on satisfactory quality within the Sale of Goods Act 1979 concerned a car sold by a taxi driver, you would want to apply *Stevenson v Rogers* (see page **217**). There would be no point in writing out all of the facts. You might say that *Stevenson v Rogers* established that whenever a business sells anything it does so in the course of a business for the purposes of s.14(2) SGA. Better still, you might say that the taxi driver will have sold the car in the course of a business for the purposes of s.14(2) SGA, because this is essentially the same as the fisherman in *Stevenson v Rogers* selling his boat. In each case what was sold was not an item the business was in business to sell, but a business asset which allowed the business to be carried on.

As for sections of statutes, there is usually little point in reproducing them in full if you can briefly state their effect. But they might be worth reproducing in full if you are going to spend a lot of time analysing them. For example, if a large part of a question was concerned with whether or not a car was of satisfactory quality, you might reproduce the statutory definition of satisfactory quality in full, or at least fairly fully. But you would do this only because you would then go on to analyse the various phrases in it, perhaps devoting a brief paragraph to each relevant phrase. Reproducing a statute is particularly likely to be a bad idea if you can take a statute book into the exam with you.

In this study skills section I have concentrated on how to answer legal questions. I hope that this will be useful to you. I also hope that you enjoy the subject and enjoy reading this book. Above all, I hope that you appreciate that the study of law is not a dry matter of learning facts and reproducing them. Some learning is necessary, but the true fascination of the subject lies in the endlessly different ways in which legal principles might apply to any given situation.

Lastly, I wish you good luck with your assessments. But in doing so I remind you of the famous reply of Gary Player, the champion golfer, when he was accused of winning tournaments because he was lucky. He admitted that he was lucky, but said that the more he practised the luckier he seemed to get. So practise your study skills, put in the work and make yourself lucky!

1

The legal system

1.1 FEATURES OF THE ENGLISH LEGAL SYSTEM

The English legal system is unlike that of any other European country. An outline knowledge of the features which make the English system so distinct is essential to an understanding of English law and the English legal process.

1.1.1 Antiquity and continuity

English law has evolved, without any major upheaval or interruption, over many hundreds of years. The last successful invasion of England occurred in 1066, when King William and his Normans conquered the country. King William did not impose Norman law on the conquered Anglo-Saxons, but allowed them to keep their own laws. These laws were not uniform throughout the kingdom. Anglo-Saxon law was based on custom and in different parts of the country different customs prevailed.

In the second half of the twelfth century King Henry II introduced a central administration for the law and began the process of applying one set of legal rules, 'the common law', throughout England. Since that time, English law has evolved piecemeal. For this reason the English legal system retains a number of peculiarities and anomalies which find their origins in mediaeval England.

The world history of the past few hundred years has been a litany of revolution and conquest. The new rulers of a country tend to start afresh with the law. In the Soviet Union the communists introduced Soviet law, in France Napoleon introduced the Napoleonic code, in the United States the founding fathers wrote the American Constitution. But England is one of the very few countries to have survived the last nine hundred years with no lasting revolution from within or foreign conquest from abroad. Some English laws and legal practices have evolved continuously since the time of King Ethelbert, who became king of Kent in the year 580. The Norman Conquest was a major upheaval, but even that was not a fresh beginning for the law.

English law does not become inoperative merely because of the passage of time. When we study the law of contract we shall see that two ancient cases, *Pinnel's Case* (1602) 5 Co Rep 117a and *Lampleigh v Brathwaite* (1615) Hob 105, are still important precedents. Although these cases have been refined and developed by subsequent cases, there would be no reason why a modern lawyer should not cite them in court. In the same way, statutes remain in force indefinitely or until they are repealed. A statute loses none of its authority merely because it has lain dormant for many years. In *R v Duncan* [1944] KB 713, for example, a defendant was convicted of fortune-telling under the Witchcraft Act 1735, even though the statute had long since fallen into disuse.

Occasionally a litigant springs a major surprise by invoking an ancient law. In 1818 the defendant in *Ashford v Thornton* (1818) 1 B & A 405, claimed the right to have an appeal against his conviction for murder settled by battle. Trial by battle had been a method of resolving disputes shortly after the Norman Conquest but had fallen into disuse before the end of the thirteenth century. In *Ashford v Thornton*, the offer of trial by battle was declined and so the defendant was discharged. The Appeals of Murder Act 1819 was hurriedly passed. Until Parliament passed this Act trial by battle still existed as a possible means of settling some types of legal disputes.

1.1.2 Absence of a legal code

In most European countries the law has been codified. This means that the whole of the law on a particular subject, for example the law of property, can be found in one document or code. Some such codes merely provide a framework for the law, others attempt to provide a complete statement of the law. As we shall see, the bulk of English law has been made by judges in individual cases. Rules of law made by senior judges must be followed in later cases. In the majority of cases brought before an English court a lawyer who is trying to establish a legal principle will cite earlier cases to prove that the principle exists and that it should be applied in the current case. Often a statute, an Act of Parliament, will provide the main legal rules applicable to a particular case. A statute ranks higher as a source of law than the previous decision of any court. But even where a statute does apply to a particular case, the court is likely to be guided as to the meaning of the statute by earlier cases which have considered its meaning.

In general, the important cases on a particular area of law are not reported in one special volume of law reports devoted to a particular area of law, such as the law of contract. (There are exceptions, specialist law reports can be found on some areas of law such as employment law or road traffic law. The system of law reporting is examined in the following chapter at 2.9.) Generally, cases are reported as they are decided and are therefore to be found in the law report volume devoted to the year in which the case was decided. As lawyers and students are only too well aware, it can be very difficult to find all the cases relevant to a particular legal issue.

Occasionally, Parliament codifies an area of law with a statute such as the Partnership Act 1890. Such an Act aims to take all the relevant case law on a particular subject and to codify it into one comprehensible statute. The Law Commission, an important law reform institution set up in 1965, has the codification of appropriate areas of law as one of its objects. But as we shall see, the vast majority of English law remains uncodified. Nor does Britain have a written constitution, as most other democratic countries have.

1.1.3 The law-making role of the judges

In most European countries the judges interpret the legal code. In doing this they do not themselves deliberately set out to create law. Later in this chapter, when we study the doctrine of judicial precedent, we shall see that the English courts are arranged in an hierarchical structure and that courts lower down the hierarchy must follow the previous decisions of courts which are higher up. Senior English judges therefore have a dual role. First, they interpret the existing law, which is to be found in legislation and previous decisions of higher ranking courts. Second, they create the law by making legal principles which courts lower down the hierarchy are bound to follow.

1.1.4 Importance of procedure

In the Middle Ages a legal right could only be enforced by means of a writ (an order signed by the King, requiring a defendant to appear in court to answer the claim being made). There were few types of writ and, if a claim could not be brought within the confines of one of the writs then no remedy was available. To some extent lawyers were people who knew the procedure of obtaining a remedy, rather than people who knew the substantive principles of the law. A person with a perfectly just claim would need a lawyer to fit the claim within the procedures of one of the writs. If the correct procedure was not rigidly adhered to, then the claim would fail, even if the substance of the claim was perfectly valid. To some extent this is still true today. If a litigant fails to follow the correct procedure it is possible that his claim will be struck out. Recent reforms of the judicial process, which we consider in Chapter 2, have attempted to reduce the importance of procedure. However, in cases which involve a substantial claim there is no doubt that procedure remains very important.

1.1.5 **Absence of Roman law**

The Romans occupied England from 55 BC to AD 430. Roman law was extremely sophisticated by the standards of its day. The other European countries which were part of the Roman Empire have retained elements of Roman law. But English law has almost no direct Roman law influence, although Roman law is still taught as an academic subject at some English universities and some areas of law have been indirectly based on Roman law concepts. Scotland was not conquered by the Romans, but Scots law has more of a Roman law influence than English law. This influence has been brought about by the traditional alliance of France and Scotland. During the Renaissance, when the modern European world began to develop, Scotland and Continental Europe saw a revival of interest in Roman law. This interest was largely absent in England.

1.1.6 **The adversarial system of trial**

The English system of trial is adversarial. This means that the lawyers on either side are adversaries, who 'fight' each other in trying to win judgment for their client. The judge supervises the battle between the lawyers, but does not take part. Today the battle is metaphoric, one party's lawyers try to establish that there is a case, the other party's lawyers deny this by whatever means permissible. In the early Middle Ages the battle could be real enough, as certain types of dispute were resolved with a Trial by Battle. In such

a trial the parties would fight each other, both armed with a leather shield and a staff and it was thought that God would grant victory to the righteous litigant. If either of the parties was disabled, too young or too old, he could hire a champion to fight for him. This was no doubt considerably more entertaining than a modern trial, but eventually it came to be realised that it was not the best way to achieve justice. Lawyers therefore replaced the champions. But the idea of a battle survived and a trial is still a battle between the lawyers, even if the shields and staffs have given way to witnesses and precedents.

Most other countries have an **inquisitorial** system of criminal procedure where the judge is the inquisitor, determined to discover the truth. A French investigating judge (juge d'instruction), for example, has enormous powers. He takes over the investigation of a criminal case from the police. He can interrogate whoever he wishes. He can compel witnesses to give evidence and can surprise witnesses with other witnesses, hoping that the confrontation will point the finger of guilt. In a civil case, too, a French judge will take a much more interventionist approach than an English judge and it is the judge, rather than the lawyers, who manages, the case.

When a French case reaches court it is often all but decided. By contrast, no one can ever be certain of the outcome of an English trial. The lawyers will fight for their clients on the day and either side might win. The judge should be disinterested in the outcome, merely ensuring that the lawyers fight by the rules. However, since the introduction of the Civil Procedure Rules in 1999 civil trials have become less adversarial and the judge manages the case to some extent.

An important aspect of the adversarial system of trial is that it is the task of the lawyers to bring the relevant legal rules to the attention of the court. If a lawyer in court makes a perfectly true statement of law, such as the statement that all goods sold in the course of business must be of satisfactory quality, he must provide authority for this statement. This means that the lawyer must quote the case, or in this instance the statute, which made the law. Similarly, students must cite authorities. At all levels of study, a statement of law with no authority to back it up is not regarded highly.

Two other features of the English legal system, both of which are examined in Chapter 2, are worth mentioning here. First, the legal profession is divided, lawyers being either barristers or solicitors. Second, in almost all criminal trials the innocence or guilt of the accused is decided by laymen, rather than by lawyers or judges. If the accused is tried in the Crown Court it will be a jury who decides whether the accused is guilty. If the crime is tried in the magistrates' court it is generally a bench of lay magistrates who make this decision.

Commonwealth and former Commonwealth countries, such as Australia, Canada and New Zealand, have retained the adversarial system of trial and most other features of the English legal system. In the United States of America trials are adversarial and some features of the English legal system have been retained. As we shall see both in this chapter and in Chapter 2, there is now considerable pressure to change many of the traditional features of the English legal system, which are increasingly perceived to be ill-suited to the needs of the twenty-first century.

1.2   CLASSIFICATION OF ENGLISH LAW

English law can be classified in three main ways: as public law or private law; as common law or equity; or as civil law or criminal law. Each of these classifications is worth considering in some detail. It is also worth considering the distinction between **law** and **fact**.

1.2.1   Public law and private law

Public law is concerned with decisions made by bodies which are governmental in nature. Private law is concerned with the legal relationships of individual citizens. Criminal law, for example, is regarded as public law. Citizens are prosecuted by the State. The law of contract, on the other hand, is private law. A person who sues for breach of contract acts as one individual suing another individual. The State provides a framework for such a dispute to be resolved. That is to say, it provides the courts and the judges, but it plays no part in bringing or defending the action.

There are three main areas of public law. Constitutional law is concerned with the workings of the British Constitution, deciding such matters as the powers of Government Ministers. Criminal law makes certain types of behaviour criminal offences, giving the State the power to prosecute and punish those who commit such offences. Administrative law deals with disputes between citizens and Government agencies, such as the Department for Work and Pensions.

Private law is also called civil law and can be broadly broken down into five main areas: contract, tort, property, trusts and family law.

1.2.2   Common law and equity

The term common law is used in three distinct senses. First, it is used to distinguish countries which have adopted the features of the English legal system from those countries which have not. The features of the English legal system were explained at the beginning of this chapter. Countries which adopt these features are said to have a common law system. Countries which adopt the central European system are said to have a civil law system. Second, the term common law denotes that body of law which was made by the judges in the King's (or Queen's) courts, rather than the body of law made by the judges in the courts of equity. Third, common law means judge-made law as distinct from statute law.

It is, perhaps, unfortunate that the term common law is used in three different ways. However, the context in which the term is used will generally make apparent the sense in which the term is used. Here we are considering the difference between the law made by the judges in the King's courts and the law made by the judges in the courts of equity. To understand this distinction and to understand the meaning of equity, we must know something of the historical development of the law.

A hundred years after the Norman Conquest, Henry II began the process of applying one set of legal rules, the common law, throughout the country. The King's representatives travelled from London to the provinces, checking on the procedures in the local courts. Gradually these representatives became judges rather than administrators. When they arrived they would try the cases which had been waiting for them (a system which survived into the 1970s). The decisions of these first travelling judges began to be recorded. Subsequent judges followed the earlier decisions, in order to provide a uniform system of law. Gradually one set of legal rules became common to the whole country and it therefore became known as the common law.

The common law grew to have several defects. First, legal actions could only be commenced through the issuing of a writ. By the middle of the thirteenth century there were around 50 writs, to cover different types of cases. In the reign of Henry III, after political pressure from the barons, the Provisions of Oxford in 1258 ruled that new types of writs should not be created. The development of the common law was very much hindered by this. Sometimes existing writs could be stretched to cover new situations, but more often they could not.

A second defect of the common law was that procedure was extremely hidebound. If a writ contained the slightest defect in its wording it was rendered useless. There were also problems with fictitious defences. Originally the truth of these defences had been checked by the King's knights, but later the defences became very effective delaying tactics. A third major defect of the common law was that it had only one civil remedy at its disposal, the payment of damages. In some cases, such as those where a nuisance was being continually committed, the payment of damages was not much of a remedy. What the litigant really wanted was that the defendant be ordered to stop committing the nuisance.

In the Middle Ages people who could not gain a remedy under the rigid rules of the common law could petition the Chancellor, the highest ranking clergyman, to ask him to intercede.

The Church was the one mediaeval institution where men of ability could better themselves. Generally speaking, only clergymen could read and write. Clergymen were trained in Canon Law. This was based on God's law, and on the laws of conscience, and therefore contained an element of natural justice. The Chancellor could order litigants to appear before him, without the use of writs. There were no complex rules of evidence or procedure and the Chancellor could order justice to be done in various ways. In particular, he could issue injunctions which ordered a person to behave in a certain way. This justice dispensed by the Chancellor became known as equity.

Equity was not designed to be a rival system to the common law system. Originally it was intended to supplement the common law, to fill in the gaps. But gradually equity developed into a rival system and gradually it became just as hidebound as the common law.

For several hundred years, until the Judicature Act 1873 which came into effect in 1875, England had two separate systems of courts and laws. The systems did not always deal with separate matters. In the *Earl of Oxford's Case* (1615) 1 Rep Ch 1 it was decided that if common law and equity conflicted then equity had to prevail.

The Judicature Acts 1873–1875 merged the two systems of law. These Acts created the modern court structure, designed to apply both common law equity side by side in the same courts. This has no meant that equity has ceased to exist. Equity still plays an important part in English law. The administration of common law and equity may have been fused, but the separate rules of each branch of the law have lived on. Equitable remedies remain discretionary and can be withheld from those who have behaved inequitably (unfairly). This was reflected in the maxim, 'He who comes to Equity must come with clean hands'. An example can be seen in *Falcke v Gray* (1859) ER 4 Drew 651 in Chapter 7 at 7.2.4.

Any court can now apply both legal and equitable rules. However, barristers still tend to regard themselves as either common law barristers, dealing with contract, tort or crime, or Chancery barristers, dealing with trusts and property.

1.2.3 Civil law and criminal law

The distinction between civil and criminal liability is fundamental to English law. The courts themselves are divided into civil courts and criminal courts and the two sets of courts have quite different purposes. The civil courts are designed to **compensate** people who have been caused loss or injury by the wrongful acts of other people. The criminal courts are designed to **punish** people who have committed a criminal offence.

Table 1.1 shows the essential differences between civil and criminal law.

Despite the differences shown in Table 1.1, it is quite possible that the same wrongful act will give rise to both civil and criminal liability. For example, if a motorist injures a pedestrian by dangerous driving then both a crime and a tort (a civil wrong) will have been committed.

The State might **prosecute** the driver for the crime of dangerous driving and if found guilty the driver will be punished. (Probably by a driving ban and possibly by a fine or imprisonment.) The **injured pedestrian** might **sue** the driver in the civil courts for the tort of negligence. If the driver is found to have committed this tort then damages will be sought to compensate for the pedestrian's injuries.

The different functions of the civil and criminal courts can be further demonstrated if we consider what would have happened if the driver's behaviour had been much worse.

Let us now assume that the driver was very drunk, driving very badly and had killed the pedestrian.

tial differences between civil and criminal law

	Criminal	Civil
case	To punish a wrongdoer.	To compensate a person who has suffered loss or injury or to prevent unlawful acts.
	The State prosecutes a person (the defendant) e.g. **Regina (Queen) v Smith**.	An individual (the claimant) sues an individual (the defendant) e.g. **Smith v Jones**.
The outcome	The defendant is either acquitted or convicted.	The claimant either wins the case or does not.
The consequences	If convicted, the defendant will be sentenced.	If the claimant wins he will be awarded a remedy.
The courts	The case is first heard in either the magistrates' court or the Crown Court.	The case is first heard in either the county court or the High Court.
The costs	Legal aid is often available to the defendant. If convicted, he must pay towards the costs.	Generally, the loser pays both sides' costs. Insurance against losing is encouraged. Legal aid may be available to the very needy.
The facts	Decided by bench of magistrates (occasionally by a district judge) or by the jury.	Decided by the judge.
The law	Decided and applied by the judge or by the magistrates on the advice of the legally qualified clerk.	Decided and applied by the judge.
Burden and standard of proof	The prosecution must prove the defendant's guilt beyond reasonable doubt.	The claimant must prove his case on a balance of probabilities.
Examples	Murder, theft, committing unfair trade practices, failure to observe health and safety provisions.	Negligence, trespass, breach of contract, disputes as to ownership of property.

Under the criminal law the driver would be charged with the more serious offences of causing death by dangerous driving and of driving with excess alcohol. The purpose of charging the driver with these more serious offences would be to impose a more serious punishment. If convicted the defendant would almost certainly be imprisoned.

However, the civil courts would not order the defendant to pay more damages merely on account of worse behaviour. In fact, if the pedestrian was killed the damages might well be less than for a bad injury. If the pedestrian was injured in such a way that nursing care would be required for life, damages might well exceed a million pounds, as they would take account of the cost of the nursing care, pain and suffering and loss of earnings, if appropriate. If the driver was killed instantly no damages would be paid in respect of nursing care or pain and suffering. A pedestrian who was not injured at all could bring no claim for damages.

This example demonstrates the different purposes which the two sets of courts are trying to achieve. The criminal courts are designed to punish bad behaviour. The worse the behaviour, the more severe the punishment. The civil courts are not concerned with the heinousness of the defendant's behaviour, they are concerned with compensating a person for injuries suffered as a consequence of the defendant's wrongdoing. The more severe the injuries, the higher the compensation. Almost all businesses will insure themselves against incurring civil liability. However, this will not make them indifferent to incurring such liability. Once a claim on an insurance policy has been made, insurance will be more expensive the following year.

As we have seen, crimes which cause injury to a victim will also give rise to a civil action. But 'victimless' crimes will not. Possessing a dangerous drug, for example, is a crime and the possessor of the drug might be prosecuted by the State. But the fact that a person possesses the drug does not directly injure anyone else, and so no one will have any right to sue him. Although the criminal courts have as their purpose the punishment of offenders, rather than the compensation of the injured, they do have the power to make compensation orders. Section 35 of the Powers of Criminal Courts (Sentencing) Act 2000 gives magistrates the power to make compensation orders of up to £5 000 per offence. The compensation is paid by the perpetrator of the crime. The Crown Court is given the power to make a compensation order of any amount, although it is required to have regard to the defendant's means. If a court does not make a compensation order in a case in which it is empowered to do so, it must give reasons for not making the order when passing sentence. An award made in the magistrates' court does not preclude a later civil claim by the victim of the crime. Compensation orders can generally not be ordered when the offence is a motoring offence.

The Criminal Injuries Compensation Authority can also award compensation to victims of violent crime, but any award is reduced by the amount of any compensation ordered by a criminal court. The Authority has reference to a list of suggested awards for various types of injury. For example, the suggested award for the loss of a front tooth is currently £3 300, and for the loss of one eye £27 000. The suggested award for loss of both eyes is £110 000.

Most civil wrongs are not crimes. If a person breaks a contract or trespasses on another's property that person might well be sued, but in general will have committed no crime.

The burden of proof is placed upon the party who must prove the case. In criminal cases the burden is placed upon the prosecution. In civil cases the burden is placed on the claimant. The standard of proof is concerned with the extent to which the case must be proved. In criminal cases the prosecution must prove the guilt of the accused beyond reasonable doubt. In a civil case the claimant must prove the case on a balance of probabilities.

1.2.4 The distinction between law and fact

In general, civil cases require the claimant to prove not only the facts which give rise to the claim, but also the principles of law which provide a remedy in respect of the facts proved. So a pedestrian run over by a car will first need to prove that the defendant did run him over and will also have to prove that the law of negligence provides him with a remedy in respect

of this. Generally, the criminal law also requires the prosecution to prove both fact and law. The prosecution must prove beyond a reasonable doubt that the defendant did the act for which he is being prosecuted and must also prove that such an act amounts to a criminal offence.

It can be important to distinguish law and fact for three main reasons. First, only statements of law can become precedents. (Judicial precedent is examined below at 1.3.2.) Second, in many cases an appeal may only be possible on a point of law. In other cases an appeal on the law would go to one court, whereas an appeal against a finding of fact would go to a different court. Third, in a criminal trial conducted in the Crown Court the jury's function is to determine the facts, whereas the correct application of the law is the function of the judge.

Often it is obvious enough whether or not a question is one of law or fact. The well-known case *Carlill v The Carbolic Smoke Ball Company* [1893] 1 QB 256, which is set out in Chapter 3 at 3.1.2, can be used as an example. Whether or not Mrs Carlill really did use a smoke ball and whether she really did catch flu were questions of fact. Whether or not the advertisement was an offer or an invitation to treat was a question of law.

Sometimes it must be decided whether certain facts fit within a definition made by a statute, or fit within a rule made by the common law. These questions can be regarded as a question of mixed law and fact, or law and degree as they are sometimes known. For example, in *Cozens v Brutus* [1975] AC 854 the defendant was charged with using insulting behaviour whereby a breach of the peace was likely to be occasioned, contrary to s.5 of the Public Order Act 1936. The defendant had interrupted the Wimbledon tennis tournament by blowing a whistle, sitting down on the court and attempting to hand a leaflet to the players. The magistrates held that the defendant's behaviour had not been insulting. The Court of Appeal considered that whether or not the defendant's behaviour was insulting was a question of law and went on to define the meaning of insulting in this context. As they regarded the magistrates' finding as provisional, they sent the case back to the magistrates to continue the hearing. The House of Lords reversed the decision of the Court of Appeal and held that whether or not the defendant's behaviour had been insulting was a question of fact. It had therefore been properly decided by the magistrates and so no appeal against their finding could be made.

The conflicting decisions of the Court of Appeal and the House of Lords demonstrate the difficulty of classifying some questions as either questions of law or questions of fact. In deciding such matters the courts will, of course, try to reach the correct conclusion. However, there is perhaps a tendency to classify such questions as matters of fact to reduce the number of precedents being made and to reduce the number of appeals which will be allowed.

Test your understanding 1.1

1 What is meant by the adversarial system of trial?

2 What is meant by the distinction between common law and equity? Does the distinction still exist?

3 What are the different purposes of a civil and a criminal case?

4 Upon whom is the burden of proof placed in civil and criminal cases? What standard of proof is required?

5 For what three reasons might it become important to distinguish law and fact?

1.3 SOURCES OF ENGLISH LAW

1.3.1 Statutes

Acts of Parliament are called statutes. The theory of Parliamentary sovereignty holds that Parliament has the power to enact, or revoke, any new law it pleases and that the courts cannot question the validity of this law. Even Parliament itself cannot limit the power of a successive Parliament. In *British Railways Board v Pickin* [1974] AC 765, for example, a claimant whose land had been compulsorily purchased under the British Railways Act 1968 tried to argue that the statute was invalid. The 1968 Act was a private Act, which had been passed unopposed and the claimant argued that Parliament had been fraudulently misled into passing it. The House of Lords, then the highest court in the land, ruled that such an argument could not be raised in any court. Several times in recent years Parliament has used a statute to specifically overrule a decision of the House of Lords, thereby demonstrating the supremacy of legislation as a source of law. (See,

for example, s.3 of the Compensation Act 2006, which is considered in Chapter 12 at 12.2.4.2.)

The United Kingdom joined the European Economic Community, now called the European Union, in 1973. It is arguable that membership of the European Union means that the United Kingdom Parliament is no longer truly sovereign. This matter is considered below at 1.4.4.

1.3.1.1 How is a statute passed?

The Government of the day is formed by the political party which wins a majority of the seats in the House of Commons. The Government takes the political decisions as to what legislation should be enacted in each sitting of Parliament. Then Government departments, such as the Department for Business, Innovation and Skills, propose legislation for approval. Parliamentary draftsmen (lawyers who specialise in drafting legislation) then draw a Bill up and the Bill starts its parliamentary journey.

To become a statute the Bill must pass through both Houses of Parliament, that is to say the House of Commons and the House of Lords, and then gain the Royal Assent. Many Bills achieve this without significant alterations. Others have to be amended to gain parliamentary approval and some Bills fail to become statutes at all.

Bills usually start in the House of Commons. The initial stage is the **First Reading**. This merely gives the title of the bill and announces the date of the Second Reading. At the **Second Reading** the principles of the Bill are debated. If the Bill passes this stage, on account of more MPs having voted in favour of it than against it, it is referred to a **standing committee** which considers the details of the Bill and recommends amendments. Any such amendments are considered by the House of Commons at the report stage, after which the Bill then proceeds to the **Third Reading**. Like the First Reading, this is a short stage where only minor amendments to the content of the Bill, rather than amendments to the general principle of the Bill, can be made.

The Bill is then sent to the House of Lords, where the whole process is repeated. The wording of the Bill must be the same for both Houses of Parliament. If the House of Lords disagrees with the wording or refuses to pass the Bill, the Parliament Acts 1911 and 1949 can be invoked. The effect of these Acts will be that the Bill can go ahead without House of Lords approval, after a delay of one year. (This happens very rarely.) A Money Bill, which would contain only financial provisions, can become a statute without being passed by the House of Lords after a delay of only one month.

After passing through both Houses of Parliament, the Bill will then receive the Royal Assent. It is a convention that the Queen does not withhold consent and no monarch has done so since 1707. (The Queen does not give assent personally but through the Lord Commissioners or by notification to both Houses of Parliament.)

Once the Bill has received the Royal Assent it becomes a statute (an Act of Parliament) which the courts must enforce, either from a date agreed by Parliament or when an order is passed by the relevant Secretary of State.

Almost all Bills are introduced into Parliament by the Government of the day. A Government with a large majority has enormous power to ensure that Bills it proposes become enacted. The system is subject to the criticism that the Government can ignore not only the wishes of opposition MPs but, if its majority is large enough, can also ignore the wishes of many of its own MPs. However, not all Bills are introduced by the Government. Every year a ballot is held to identify 20 MPs who may attempt to introduce **Private Member's Bills**. In fact, only an MP who was close to winning the ballot will have a reasonable chance of seeing his Private Member's Bill become the law. The Abortion Act 1967, which liberalised the law on abortion, was introduced as a Private Member's Bill by David Steel MP.

1.3.1.2 Codifying, consolidating and amending Acts

We have seen that, in general, English law is not codified. However, certain areas of law have been the subject of a **codifying Act**. Such an Act attempts to put all the existing law on a particular subject, whether common law or statutory, into one comprehensive statute. In doing this the law may be changed and if the Act is inconsistent with the law which it codified, the Act prevails. The major codifications in English law have been the Bills of Exchange Act 1882, the Partnership Act 1890, the Sale of Goods Act 1893, and the Theft Act 1968.

A **consolidating Act** re-enacts all the law on a given area, so that the law contained in several existing statutes is re-enacted as one new statute. Minor changes to the law may be made, but the purpose of a consolidating Act is not to change the law, but to make it more easily accessible. The Trade Union and Labour Relations (Consolidation) Act 1992, for example, consolidated existing legislation relating to collective labour relations. An **amending Act** changes one or more sections of an existing Act.

Example

The effects of the three types of Act can be considered by looking at the history of sale of goods law. Prior to 1893 sale of goods law was almost entirely common law, that is to say it was made by the courts in innumerable cases. In 1893 the Sale of Goods Act, a codifying Act, codified the common law.

No real changes were made until 1973, when the 1893 Act was amended very slightly to make it more appropriate to the needs of consumers. These minor changes were made by an amending Act, the Supply of Goods (Implied Terms) Act 1973. In 1977 the Unfair Contract Terms Act made more amendments. In 1979 the Sale of Goods Act 1979, a consolidating Act, was passed. This Act, which is the Act currently in force, consolidated the 1893 Act and the amendments which had been made to it. Three amending Acts have been passed since 1979: the Sale of Goods (Amendment) Act 1994; the Sale and Supply of Goods Act 1994; and the Sale of Goods (Amendment) Act 1995. The amendments achieved by these Acts are incorporated into the Sale of Goods Act 1979.

Parliament has the power to repeal any statute. As we saw earlier, a statute remains in force until it is repealed even if it has become obsolete.

1.3.1.3 Delegated legislation

Delegated legislation is the name given to legislation passed otherwise than as a statute. Most delegated legislation is concerned with relatively narrow, technical matters. However, it is arguable that delegated legislation is a more important source of law than statute. This argument is based on the fact that nowadays there is far more delegated legislation than statute law. Once delegated legislation is enacted, it generally has the same force as the statute which enabled it to be enacted.

Delegated legislation can take several forms. The most important form is a **statutory instrument**. This legislation is not passed as a statute. Instead, a statute called an enabling Act is passed and this enabling Act gives a Government Minister the power to introduce the legislation. The statutory instrument will contain a preamble which sets out the authority under which it was passed. It will also contain a statutory note which sets out its purpose and its scope. Statutory instruments are made in the name of a Minister but are drawn up by the legal department of the relevant ministry. The Deregulation and Contracting Out Act 1994 allows Ministers to change certain Acts of Parliament, by way of statutory instrument, without going through the normal parliamentary procedure. The 1994 Act is used to repeal or amend provisions in primary legislation which impose a burden on business or others. In later chapters we shall see that legislation of considerable importance, such as the Commercial Agents (Council Directive) Regulations 1993, takes the form of statutory instrument rather than the form of a statute. Many statutory instruments, such as the 1993 Regulations, are used to implement EU Directives. (Directives are examined later in this chapter at 1.4.2.4.)

Orders in Council are made by the Privy Council. When making such orders the Privy Council is generally made up of four ministers in the presence of the Queen. The Government of the day can use orders in council to introduce legislation without going through the process of enacting a statute. Orders in Council can be used to implement emergency legislation, where there would not be time to have formal debates in the Houses of Parliament. Orders in Council are also used to give effect to provisions of the European Union which do not have direct effect, to shift responsibilities between Government departments or in relation to matters which affect the constitution. Many statutes only become operative when an Order in Council provides that they should, the power exercised by the Order in Council being contained in the statute itself.

Bye-laws made by local authorities and other public bodies are another type of delegated legislation. These are used to introduce local rules of minor importance. The power to enact bye-laws is given by an enabling Act, such as the Local Government Act 1972.

Delegated legislation has certain advantages and disadvantages. The advantages usually claimed are that it can be enacted without using up parliamentary time, that it makes use of particular expertise held by those who enact it, and that it is flexible enough to deal speedily with changing circumstances and emergencies. These claims in general seem to be true. Parliament often does not have time to pass all of its legislative programme, even though the vast majority of this is already contained in statutory instruments. In

2008 over three thousand statutory instruments were passed, but only 33 Public Acts. It is also true that MPs are not particularly knowledgeable about the details of the types of matters which are enacted by statutory instrument. These matters are often extremely technical, dealing with a huge variety of matters, such as the safe storage of hazardous materials, or the intricacies of housing benefit. A separate justification is that if there were to be a true emergency, such as a major leak of radiation, legislation might be needed quickly and there would not be the time to pass a statute and have debates in the Houses of Parliament. Also, the type of matter which arises from time to time, such as financial eligibility for housing benefit, are obviously better dealt with by delegated legislation than by statute. The same is obviously true of local bye-laws. MPs have no real interest in areas other than the areas which they represent, or in which they live, and could not therefore determine whether or not a bye-law was needed.

Delegated legislation is also criticised on several grounds. First, there is the danger that the Government can pass legislation setting out new principles by abusing the process of delegated le-gislation. Second, some delegated legislation gives ministers the power to alter statutes, possibly including the very enabling Act which conferred the power to make the delegated legislation in question. In *Hyde Park Residence Ltd* v *Secretary of State for the Environment, Transport and the Regions* [2000] 1 PLR 85 the Court of Appeal held that although it was possible for one statute to confer a power to amend another statute by delegated legislation, this power should be construed narrowly and strictly. Third, it is possible that the enabling Act states that the delegated legislation should not be subject to judicial review by the courts, or that it is worded so widely that the courts would not be able to say that its powers had been exceeded. (Judicial review is considered in Chapter 2 at 2.6.1.)

Certain controls over delegated legislation do exist. Ministers are often required by the enabling Act to consult various bodies before enacting delegated legislation. Statutory instruments must be published and made available for sale to the public. In addition to these controls, delegated legislation is controlled both by Parliament and by the courts. Although some non-contentious statutory instruments just become law on the date stated in them, most are required by their enabling Acts to be laid before both Houses of Parliament. If this process is subject to the negative resolution procedure the legislation must be laid before both Houses for 40 days, during which time either House can pass an annulment or negative resolution, which will cause the statutory instrument to be rendered ineffective. Any MP can put forward a motion for annulment. The affirmative resolution procedure requires the instrument to be laid before one or both Houses for a specified time, usually 40 days, after which time an affirmative resolution agreeing to the instrument must be passed or the instrument will have no effect. Delegated legislation to deal with politically contentious or emergency matters generally requires this procedure. However, the majority of delegated legislation is subject only to the negative control. It is most unusual for either House of Parliament to have the power to amend a statutory instrument. They either allow it to be passed or annul it.

The courts have the power, through the process of judicial review, to declare a statutory instrument *ultra vires* on the grounds that it tries to exercise a power greater than that conferred by the enabling Act. It is presumed that an enabling Act does not confer the power to raise tax; or to retrospectively alter the law; or to prevent a person from having access to the courts; or to take away civil liberties. However, if the enabling Act was sufficiently clear it could confer these powers. A statutory instrument can be declared invalid on the grounds of being unreasonable only if the objectives of the instrument were so outrageously unreasonable that Parliament could not have intended that the powers created by the enabling Act would be used in the way in which they were used. The courts can also declare a statutory instrument *ultra vires* on the grounds that some mandatory procedure, such as a mandatory duty to consult, was not adhered to.

Below (at 1.4) we examine the effect of European Community legislation, much of which is implemented into UK law by statutory instrument under s.2(2) of the European Communities Act 1972.

1.3.1.4 Interpretation of statutes

The three approaches

When considering the meaning of legislation, the courts are guided by three approaches. These approaches are often called rules – the literal rule, the golden rule and the mischief rule. The rules contradict each other to a certain extent and it cannot be certain which rule a court will apply. In general, the court will tend to use whichever of the approaches seems best suited to achieving justice in the case it is hearing. However, the literal approach is generally used when interpreting criminal or tax legislation, and the purposive approach is preferred when interpreting legislation emanating from the EU.

When the **literal rule** is applied words in a statute which are not ambiguous are given their ordinary, literal meaning, even if this leads to a decision which is unjust or undesirable. An example of this approach can be seen in *Inland Revenue Commissioners v Hinchy* [1960] AC 748, in which the House of Lords was considering the effect of the Income Tax Act 1952. Section 25(3) of the Act stated that a person found guilty of tax avoidance should 'forfeit the sum of £20 and treble the tax which he ought to be charged under this Act'. Hinchy's lawyers argued that this meant a £20 fine and treble the amount of tax which had been avoided. Unfortunately for Hinchy, the House of Lords decided that the literal meaning of s.25(3) was that a tax avoider should pay a £20 fine and treble his whole tax bill for the year.

The outcome of the case was that Hinchy had to pay slightly over £438, even though the amount he had avoided was only £14.25. This was obviously a severe blow for Hinchy. (In 1960, £438 could be a year's pay for an unskilled worker.) But the implications for other tax avoiders were terrifying. Under the system of precedent, all other English courts are bound to follow precedents formulated in the House of Lords. So other tax avoiders appearing before the courts would have to be fined on the same basis as Hinchy had been fined. A court hearing the case of a wealthy businessman, who rightly paid £1 million tax in the year but avoided paying £5, would be bound to fine him £3 000 035!

It is almost certain that the meaning applied by the House of Lords was not what Parliament had in mind when the Income Tax Act was passed. The statute was badly worded. The blame for this must lie with the Parliamentary draftsmen. But at the same time it must be realised that they have a near impossible task. Skilled lawyers though these draftsmen are, they cannot possibly foresee every interpretation of the statutes they prepare. But once the statute has become law, any lawyer in the land might be looking for an interpretation which would suit his client. In *Hinchy's* case the Revenue lawyers, with typical ingenuity, spotted a literal meaning that had not been apparent before. The House of Lords gave the words in the statute their literal meaning, holding that the words of the statute were not ambiguous. When the literal rule is applied the court is seeking not what Parliament meant to say when it enacted the statute, but rather the true meaning of the words which Parliament used.

If Parliament considers that the application of the literal rule by a high-ranking court causes a statute to be interpreted in a way which is contrary to what was intended when the statute was enacted, it can pass an amending Act to rectify the situation.

There has been a movement away from the literal approach in recent years. In *McMonagle* v *Westminster City Council* [1990] 2 AC 716 the House of Lords unanimously indicated that the literal rule would not be applied where to do so would produce an absurd result. In such a case the golden rule, also known as the purposive approach, would be applied. When the golden rule is used a judge gives the words in a statute their ordinary, literal meaning as far as possible, but only to the extent that this would not produce some injustice, absurdity, anomaly or contradiction.

The idea that the court should prefer an outcome which is not absurd to the one which is absurd seems obviously to be correct. An example of the golden rule being used in this way can be seen in *Adler* v *George* [1964] 2 QB 7. The defendant had got into an RAF station, which was classified as a prohibited place by the Official Secrets Act 1920. He was arrested and charged with obstructing a member of the armed forces 'in the vicinity of a prohibited place', contrary to s.3 of the 1920 Act. The defendant argued that as he was actually inside the prohibited place he was not in the vicinity of it and should not therefore be convicted. The Divisional Court rejected this argument and held that the proper construction of s.3 was to read the words 'in the vicinity of' as 'in or in the vicinity of'. Lord Parker CJ gave the only judgment of the court and said that it would be absurd to read the section as the defendant had argued that it should be read.

When the words of the statute are not ambiguous but would, if interpreted literally, produce an absurd result, the golden rule is sometimes seen as an extension of the literal rule. First, the court considers the literal rule. Seeing that the literal rule would lead to a manifestly absurd result and wishing to avoid this result, the court chooses to apply the golden rule and give the statutory words a meaning other than their normal meaning. The following case provides an example. In *R* v *Allen* (1872) LR 1 CCR 376 the

defendant was charged with bigamy. He had married another woman even though his first wife was still alive and he was not divorced from her. Section 57 of the Offences Against the Person Act 1861 provided that a person should be guilty of bigamy if 'being married, [he or she] shall marry any other person during the life of the former husband or wife'. The defendant argued that he was not guilty of the offence as he had not legally married the second wife, because you cannot legally get married if you are already married. He claimed that he had only gone through a ceremony of marriage with the second woman. The court gave the word 'marry' in s.57 the meaning of going through a ceremony of marriage, rather than the meaning of contracting a legal marriage, and therefore convicted the defendant. Had they not done this, bigamy would have been impossible to commit. In *Bloomsbury International Ltd* v *Sea Fish Industry Authority* [2011] UKSC 25 the Supreme Court considered ambiguous words in the Fisheries Act 1981. Lord Mance said that the starting point should not be that words have a natural meaning, an idea which he did not always find very helpful. Rather the starting point should be the statutory purpose of the legislation and the general scheme by which it was to be put into effect. He also said that where an Act has been amended, as the 1981 Act had been, it should not lightly be concluded that Parliament had misunderstood the general scheme of the legislation when making the amendment. Lord Phillips said that if a certain meaning had been given to the ambiguous words for thirty years then this, at the very least, led to a presumption that this meaning was the correct one.

The oldest of the three main rules of statutory interpretation is the mischief rule. In *Heydon's Case* (1584) 3 Co Rep 7a it was established that before applying the mischief rule the court should ask itself four questions. First, what was the common law before the Act was passed? Second, what mischief or problem did the Act seek to rectify? Third, what remedy had Parliament decided upon to cure the mischief? Fourth, what was the reason for providing the remedy? Having considered these four questions, a court would be guided as to how the statute should be interpreted. This rule is only to be used when a statute is ambiguous, it should not be used to deal with a clear, but absurd, meaning. The following case provides an example of the rule.

Smith v Hughes [1960] 1 WLR 830

Two prostitutes, standing either on a balcony or behind the windows of their house, attracted passers-by to invite them into the house. They did this by tapping on the balcony rail or the window panes. They were charged under s.1(1) of the Street Offences Act 1959, which made it an offence to solicit 'in a street or public place' for the purposes of prostitution. The defendants argued that they were not guilty as they had not been in the street or in a public place when they had been soliciting customers.

Held. Applying the mischief rule, the defendants were guilty. It did not matter that they were not literally in the street when soliciting, if the solicitation was projected to and aimed at somebody who was walking in the street.

COMMENT Lord Parker CJ, 'For my part, I approach the matter by considering what is the mischief aimed at by this Act. Everybody knows that this was an Act intended to clean up the streets, to enable people to walk along the streets without being molested or solicited by common prostitutes. Viewed in that way, it can matter little whether the prostitute is soliciting while in the street or is standing in a doorway or on a balcony, or at a window, or whether the window is open or shut or half open; in each case her solicitation is projected to and addressed to somebody walking in the street. For my part, I am content to base my decision on that ground and on that ground alone.'

In *Inco Europe Ltd* v *First Choice Distribution* [2000] 1 WLR 561 Lord Nicholls, giving the only speech of the House of Lords, considered the circumstances in which the court could read words into a statute to correct an obvious drafting error. Lord Nicholls said:

'This power is confined to plain cases of drafting mistakes. The courts are ever mindful that their constitutional role in this field is interpretative. They must abstain from any course which might have the appearance of judicial legislation. A statute is expressed in language approved and enacted by the legislature. So the courts exercise considerable caution before adding or omitting or substituting words. Before interpreting a statute in this way the court must be abundantly sure of three matters:

(1) the intended purpose of the statute or provision in question;

(2) that by inadvertence the draftsman and Parliament failed to give effect to that purpose in the provision in question; and

(3) the substance of the provision Parliament would have made, although not necessarily the precise words Parliament would have used, had the error in the Bill been noticed.

The third of these conditions is of crucial importance. Otherwise any attempt to determine the meaning of the enactment would cross the boundary between construction and legislation.'

Lord Nicholls went on to say that even if the three conditions were satisfied the court might nevertheless sometimes find itself inhibited from interpreting the statutory provision in accordance with what it was satisfied was the underlying intention of Parliament. This might be the case if the alteration in language would be too far-reaching, or if the subject matter of the statutory provision called for strict interpretation of the statutory language, as in penal legislation.

The Court of Appeal recently applied the mischief rule in *Wolman* v *Islington LBC* [2007] EWCA Civ 823, (2007) 104(32) LSG 24. A GLC bye-law made it a criminal offence to park a vehicle with one or more wheels 'on any part of' a pavement. The claimant, a barrister, parked his motorbike on a stand in such a way that its wheels were above the pavement but not actually on it. He therefore claimed not to have committed the offence. Applying the mischief rule, the Court of Appeal held that the offence was committed if one or more of the bike's wheels were either on or over the pavement.

Finally, it should be remembered that the rules relating to statutory interpretation are guiding principles, rather than rules which must be obeyed. In *Maunsell* v *Olins* [1975] AC 373, Lord Reid said: 'They [the rules of construction] are not rules in the ordinary sense of having some binding force. They are our servants, not our masters. They are aids to construction, presumptions or pointers. Not infrequently one "rule" points in one direction, another in a different direction. In each case we must look at all relevant circumstances and decide as a matter of judgment what weight to attach to any particular "rule".'

Minor rules of statutory interpretation

Other, less important, rules of statutory interpretation are applied by the courts. The *ejusdem generis rule* (of the same kind rule) means that general words which follow specific words must be given the same type of meaning as the specific words. For example, the Betting Act 1853 prohibited betting in any 'house, office, room or other place'. In *Powell v Kempton Racecourse Company* [1899] AC 143, the House of Lords held that the Act did not apply to betting at a racecourse. The specific words, 'house, office, room', were all indoor places and so the general words, 'or other place', had to be interpreted as applying only to indoor places.

The rule *expressio unius est exclusio alterius* (to express one thing is to exclude another) means that if the statute lists specific words and these are not followed by any general words, then the statute only applies to the specific words listed. For example, in *R v Inhabitants of Sedgeley* (1831) 2 B & Ad 65, a statute which raised taxes on 'Lands, houses, tithes and coal mines', did not apply to other types of mines such as the mine in question, a limestone mine.

Aids to construction of statutes

When considering the meaning of a statute, a court may consider certain aids to construction. Thse aids are usually labelled either intrinsic aids, which are part of the statute itself, or extrinsic aids, which are not part of the statute itself. Intrinsic aids would include interpretation sections of the Act, which state the meaning of words used in the Act. The Act's title and punctuation are also of relevance as intrinsic aids. It is not clear to what extent marginal notes and headings are to be regarded as aids to construction of the statute. It is probable that both can be considered.

Extrinsic aids to interpretation include dictionaries, previous statutes concerning the same subject matter, and the Interpretation Act 1978. Despite the name of this Act it is concerned with relatively minor matters such as: unless there is an indication to the contrary, the singular includes the plural; and, when a statute refers to the masculine it also includes the feminine.

Until relatively recently, a judge interpreting a statute was not allowed to consider the speeches which MPs made when the statute was being debated. However, in the following case, a landmark decision, the House of Lords held that Hansard could be consulted if this was the only way to solve an ambiguity.

Pepper (Inspector of Taxes) v *Hart*
[1992] AC 593 (House of Lords)

Masters at a fee-paying school were entitled to have their sons educated at the school at one fifth of the usual price. During the years in question the school was never full and so no pupils were turned away in consequence of this right. Section 61 of the Finance Act 1976 provided that masters who took advantage of the scheme should be taxed on the cash equivalent of the benefit they had received. The masters contended that the cash benefit was the marginal cost of admitting their sons and therefore practically nothing. The Revenue argued that the cash equivalent could be found for each pupil by dividing the whole costs of running the school by the number of pupils attending the school. The statute was ambiguous as to which meaning was correct.

Held. The masters should only be taxed at the marginal cost of their sons attending the school. This was the intention of Parliament, as could be discovered by consulting Hansard. The rule that Parliamentary material could not be considered by a court should be relaxed if (i) the legislation was either ambiguous or obscure, or led to absurdity, and (ii) the material relied upon consisted of statements made by the relevant Minister, or promoter of the Bill, or other material such as was necessary, and (iii) the statements relied upon were clear.

Presumptions

There are certain presumptions which a court may make when in doubt as to the meaning of a statute. These are: a presumption against changing the common law (so a statute does not change the common law in any particular way unless it makes clear that it does); a presumption against ousting the jurisdiction of the courts (only if clear language is used is a statute to be read as taking away the right to take a case to court); a presumption that citizens will not have their liberty, property or rights taken away; presumption against criminal liability without *mens rea* (for the meaning of *mens rea* see Chapter 22 at 22.1); a presumption that a statute does not bind the Crown; a presumption that Parliament does not intend a statute to conflict with international law; and a presumption against a statute having retrospective effect. Some statutes clearly state that they are to have retrospective effect. (See, for example, s.3 of the Compensation Act 2006, set out in Chapter 12 at 12.2.4.2.)

Impact of the Human Rights Act 1998

Later in this chapter, at 1.5.1, the Human Rights Act 1998 is considered. As we shall see, s.3(1) of this Act requires that, so far as it is possible to do so, all legislation must be read and given effect in a way which is compatible with the Convention rights. In *R v A* [2001] 2 AC 45 Lord Steyn said that a declaration of incompatibility was a measure of last resort and to be avoided. Such a declar-ation should be made only when it was plainly impossible to avoid making it. In *S (Children) (Care Order: Implementation of Care Plan),* Re [2002] UKHL 10, [2002] 2 AC 291, [2002] 2 WLR 720 Lord Nicholls said that use of s.3(1) was obligatory and that it was not an optional rule of construction. The new approach seems to be first to ask if the Act in question is incompatible with a Convention right. If so, then to ask whether any incompatibility could be avoided by using the purposive approach, the mischief rule or *Pepper v Hart*. Finally, the Act in question must be read in accordance with s.3(1) of the Human Rights Act, unless there was evidence that Parliament had intended to legislate in a way which was contrary to the Act.

Test your understanding 1.2

1 What three procedures must be satisfied before a Bill becomes a statute?

2 What is the meaning of a codifying Act, a consolidating Act and an amending Act?

3 What is delegated legislation? What are the main types of delegated legislation?

4 What are the three main rules of statutory interpretation? What is the effect of these rules?

5 What is the effect of the *ejusdem generis* rule and the rule *expressio unius est exclusio alterius*?

6 What intrinsic and extrinsic aids can be used to assist in interpreting a statute?

1.3.2 Judicial precedent

The doctrine of judicial precedent, or *stare decisis*, holds that judges in lower-ranking courts are bound to follow legal principles previously formulated by judges in higher-ranking courts. As so much of the law in this book is derived from precedent, it seems important to examine the system in some detail.

1.3.2.1 The hierarchy of the courts

The courts are arranged in an hierarchical structure. The structure of the courts is considered in more detail in Chapter 2. Here it is enough to outline the five levels in the hierarchy.

The Supreme Court (formerly The House of Lords)

The Supreme Court is the most senior of the English courts. It replaced the House of Lords on 1 October 2009. The court is comprised of 12 judges, known as Supreme Court justices (Law Lords), five of whom usually sit in any one case. The Supreme Court is not bound to follow any previous precedents. Furthermore, the decisions of the Supreme Court are binding on all courts beneath it. Until 1966 the House of Lords was bound to follow its own previous decisions. However, in 1966 a Practice Statement was made by Lord Gardiner on behalf of the other Law Lords. This statement said that the House of Lords recognised that if the doctrine of precedent was too rigidly adhered to, the development of the law might be hindered and injustice might be caused in a particular case. The House of Lords would therefore normally treat its own decisions as binding, but would depart from them where it appeared right to do so. In doing this the Lords would bear in mind the danger of disturbing agreements previously entered into. The Supreme Court will adopt a similar approach.

In practice, the House of Lords only rarely departed from one of its own previous decisions. In *Horton v Sadler* [2006] UKHL 27, [2006] 2 WLR 1346 Lord Bingham said, 'Over the past 40 years the House has exercised its power to depart from its own precedent rarely and sparingly. It has never been thought enough to justify doing so that a later generation of Law Lords would have resolved an issue or formulated a principle differently from their predecessor ... As made clear in the 1966 *Practice Statement* ([1966] 1 WLR 1234) former decisions of the House are normally binding. But too rigid adherence to precedent may lead to injustice in a particular case and unduly restrict the development of the law. The House will depart from a previous decision where it appears right to do.'

Sometimes seven, or nine, judges sit rather than five. (See, for example, *Kay and others v Lambeth LBC* [2006] UKHL 10, [2006] 2 AC 465 below at 1.3.2.2.) However, a later sitting of the court can still refuse to follow the decision made by the seven or nine-member court.

The Supreme Court justices also hear appeals from the courts in Her Majesty's dominions and from some Commonwealth countries. When they sit in this particular capacity they are known as the Judicial Committee of the Privy Council, commonly shortened to the Privy Council. Countries from which appeals are still heard by the Privy Council include Barbados, Bermuda, the Falkland Islands, Gibraltar and Jamaica. Technically, decisions of the Privy Council are not binding on English courts. However, in practice they are usually regarded as having the same authority as Supreme Court decisions. (An example of this can be seen in Chapter 12 at 12.2.4.3, where the Privy Council decision in *The Wagon Mound* [1961] AC 388 is generally taken to have overruled the long-standing Court of Appeal decision in *Re Polemis* [1921] 3 KB 560.)

The Court of Appeal

The Court of Appeal is the next rung down the ladder. Its decisions are binding on all lower courts. They are also binding on future Court of Appeal judges. In terms of precedent the Court of Appeal is the most important court, hearing many more appeals than the Supreme Court. There are 38 Court of Appeal judges, known as Lord Justices of Appeal. However, the Supreme Court hears cases of greater public importance and there is no doubt that its decisions have the greatest authority.

Following Lord Gardiner's Practice Statement of 1966, the Court of Appeal made several attempts to depart from its own previous decisions. However, the Practice Statement itself stated that it was not meant to apply to any court other than the House of Lords. It is plain, therefore, that the Court of Appeal is bound by its own previous decisions, the only exceptions to this principle having been formulated in *Young v Bristol Aeroplane Co Ltd* [1944] KB 718. In that case it was decided that the Court of Appeal could depart from its own previous decisions in only three circumstances.

(1) Where there were two conflicting earlier Court of Appeal decisions it could decide which one to follow and which one to overrule.
(2) If a previous Court of Appeal decision had later been overruled by the House of Lords the Court of Appeal should not follow it.
(3) A previous Court of Appeal decision should not be followed if it was decided through lack of care, ignoring some statute or other higher-ranking authority such as a previously decided House of Lords case.

Although the principles set out apply to both the Civil and Criminal Divisions of the Court of Appeal, it is generally recognised that the Criminal Division has slightly wider powers to depart from its own previous decisions. It can do so where justice would otherwise be denied to an appellant. In *R* v *Magro* [2010] EWCA Crim 1575, [2010] 3 WLR 1694 the Court of Appeal rejected an argument that a five judge Court of Appeal (Criminal Division) was entitled to disregard the only previous decision of a three judge Court of Appeal (Criminal Division) on a distinct and clearly identified point of law, reached after full argument and close analysis of the relevant legislative provisions. This was particularly the case where the consequences of doing so would be to the disadvantage of the defendant. Generally, the Court of Appeal is comprised of three judges. Sometimes a full court of five judges sit in the Court of Appeal. A full court of the Court of Appeal has no greater power to depart from its own previous decisions than an ordinary court.

Divisional Courts

Each of the three divisions of the High Court has a Divisional Court, staffed by three High Court judges. In certain areas of business law the Queen's Bench Divisional Court makes a large number of significant precedents. This court hears appeals from lower courts, as explained in Chapter 2. Decisions of the Divisional Courts are binding upon other sittings of the Divisional Court (subject to the *Young v Bristol Aeroplane Co Ltd* exceptions), on High Court judges sitting alone and on all inferior courts. Decisions of the Divisional Court are not binding upon the Employment Appeal Tribunal (EAT). (The jurisdiction of the EAT is explained in Chapter 20, Introduction.) Divisional Courts are bound by the decisions of the House of Lords (now the Supreme Court), the Court of Appeal and by previous decisions of Divisional Courts. In criminal cases a Divisional Court may depart from the decision of a previous Divisional Court where it would cause injustice not to do so.

The High Court

Judges sitting in the High Court are bound by decisions of the House of Lords (now the Supreme Court) the Court of Appeal and the Divisional Courts. There are currently 108 High Court judges. High Court decisions are binding upon all lower courts. High Court judges are not bound by the decisions of other High Court judges. However, High Court judges do tend to follow each other's decisions as not to do so can lead to uncertainty, particularly as regards decisions made and agreements reached on the strength of the earlier judgment.

Inferior courts

The decisions of inferior courts (the Crown Court, the county court and the magistrates' court) are not binding on any other courts. Judges sitting in these courts do not make binding precedents.

All English courts must take into consideration decisions made by the European Court of Human Rights. The effect of this is considered below at 1.5. The European Court of Justice, which gives authoritative opinions on matters of EU law, does not use a system of precedent. However, the decisions of this court are binding upon all English courts, a matter considered below at 1.4.

1.3.2.2 **The binding part of the case**

The *ratio decidendi*, loosely translated from the Latin as the reason for the decision, is the part of the judgment which is binding on other courts. The *ratio decidendi* might be described as any statement of law which the judge applied to the facts of the case and upon which the decision in the case is based. The ratio of a case will be decided by future courts when they are considering whether or not they are bound by the ratio. Cases may contain more than one ratio.

Statements of law which did not form the basis of the decision are known as *obiter dicta* (literally, other things said). Obiters can arise as statements of law based on facts which did not exist. It commonly happens that judgments state what the law would have been if the facts had differed in some material way. Statements of law which were wider than was necessary to deal with the facts of the particular case are also *obiter dicta*. Examples of obiters can be found in most cases. Obiters are not binding on lower courts, no matter which court made the *obiter*. However, if the judges in a superior court strongly express an *obiter* then a lower court judge would almost certainly follow this in the absence of a binding precedent.

Courts to which appeals are made (appellate courts) usually have more than one judge sitting. Fortunately, it is an odd number of judges rather than an even number. A majority of judges will therefore decide for one of the parties or for the other. If the decision is unanimous, for instance the Court of Appeal decides 3 : 0 for the defendant, then the ratio of the case can be found in the judgments of any of the three judges. If the Court reaches a decision by a majority of 2 : 1,

then the ratio must be found in the decisions of the two judges in the majority. The decision of the judge in the minority may be persuasive as *obiter*, but it cannot form a ratio which will bind future courts.

> ### Example
>
> If you read the case of **Carlill v The Carbolic Smoke Ball Company** [1893] 1 QB 525 (Court of Appeal), which is set out in Chapter 3 at 3.1.2, you will see that it concerned whether or not an advertisement made by the company was an offer which could be accepted by a member of the public buying a smoke ball, using it and catching flu. The Court of Appeal held that the advertisement was an offer and that the claimant was entitled to the £100 reward as she had accepted the offer and thus created a contract between herself and the company. This famous case can be used to demonstrate several points.
>
> First, the ratio of the case will be decided by later courts. However, it seems fairly safe to say that the ratio is something like: 'Newspaper advertisements offering rewards to members of the public who perform certain well-defined actions can amount to contractual offers, which can be accepted by members of the public who perform those actions, as long as the advertisement was not too vague to be understood by an ordinary member of the public.' Further ratios might be that an offer can be made to the whole world and that the offer of a unilateral contract can be accepted without notification of acceptance, merely by performing the action requested by the offeror. An example made by Bowen LJ, concerning a reward offered for a lost dog, was clearly *obiter dicta* as it was based on facts which did not arise. As this case was decided in the Court of Appeal, the *ratio decidendi* of the case would be binding upon later sittings of the Court of Appeal and upon all inferior courts, but not upon the Supreme Court. Bowen LJ's *obiter* could be persuasive if a court was considering a case concerning a reward for finding a lost dog or more generally by way of analogy.

A higher-ranking court can **overrule** a ratio created by a lower ranking court. The Supreme Court, for instance, could overrule *Carlill's* **case** later this year and hold that newspaper advertisements cannot be offers. (This is most unlikely, it is merely an example.) If the Supreme Court were to overrule the decision then the ratio of *Carlill's* **case** would be deemed to have been wrongly decided. When overruling a case, the superior court specifically names the case and the rule of law being overruled. A statute may overrule the ratio of a particular case, but the statute will not mention the case concerned. (See, for example, s.3 of the Compensation Act 2006, which is considered in Chapter 12 at 12.2.4.2.)

Many cases are **reversed** on appeal. Reversing is of no legal significance. It merely means that a party who appeals against the decision of an inferior court wins the appeal. No rule of law is necessarily changed. For example, in the fictitious case *Smith* v *Jones*, let us assume that Smith wins in the High Court and Jones appeals to the Court of Appeal. If Jones's appeal is allowed, the Court of Appeal have reversed the judgment of the High Court.

Disadvantages of the system of precedent

In addition to the 12 Supreme Court justices, the 38 Lord Justices of Appeal and the 108 High Court judges, there are five Heads of Division. The Heads of Division are: the Lord Chief Justice, who is also Head of Criminal Justice; the Master of the Rolls, who is also Head of Civil Justice; the President of the Queen's Bench Division; the President of the Family Division, who is also Head of Family Justice; and the Chancellor of the High Court. Every sentence of every judgment made by a High Court judge might contain a precedent which would be binding on future judges. Plainly, it is an impossible task for anyone to be aware of all of these potential precedents. In fact, so many High Court judgments are made that most are not even reported in the law reports.

Law reporting is not a Government task but is carried out by private firms. The law reporters are barristers and they weed out the vast number of judgments which they consider to be unimportant. Even so, as students become aware when they step into a law library, the system of precedent does mean that English law is very bulky. There are so many precedents that it can be very hard for a lawyer to find the law he is looking for. The fact that major law reports are now available on the Internet has made them more easily accessible.

Precedent suffers from another disadvantage and that is that bad decisions can live on for a very long time. As we have seen, before 1966 a House of Lords decision was binding on all other courts, including future sittings of the House of Lords. If a bad House of Lords decision was made, then before 1966 it could be changed only by Parliament, which was generally far too busy to interfere unless grave injustice was being caused. So an argument can be made that errors are perpetuated.

A third disadvantage is that the vast number of precedents can take away the very certainty which

the system is said to promote. This is particularly true when appellate courts apply the law creatively to achieve justice in the particular case in front of them.

A fourth disadvantage is that the higher courts cannot choose to hear a case unless the parties appeal that case to the court in question. So the Supreme Court, for example, might wish to overrule or modify an earlier precedent but would be unable to do so until an appropriate case was appealed all the way to the Supreme Court.

It might also be a disadvantage of the system that decisions of precedent-making courts act retrospectively as well as prospectively. That is to say they alter the law not only in the future but also in the past. This can be unfair if a person has relied on the law as it was, only for a precedent-making court to change the law when deciding a case. The House of Lords considered this matter in *Re Spectrum Plus* [2005] UKHL 41, [2005] 3 WLR 58 and rejected an argument that their rulings should be prospective only. There are exceptional circumstances in which retrospective effect would not be appropriate, but generally precedents are effective retrospectively as well as prospectively.

These disadvantages of the system of precedent are thought to be outweighed by the advantages of the system. One final criticism which might be made is that under the system of precedent judges make most of the law. Most laymen might be surprised to find that this is the case and might question whether it ought to be. Some have argued that as regards decisions which might be classed as 'political' the judges are not the most appropriate body to create the law. However, it seems hard to imagine that anyone other than the judiciary could so effectively create law of a technical nature, such as the law of contract, and so effectively allow it to respond to the changing needs of business.

The Supreme Court Justices are careful not to usurp the role of Parliament. In *Gregg* v *Scott* **[2005]** UKHL 2, [2005] 2 AC 176, for example, Lord Hoffmann said that to change the law in a way which a barrister had suggested would be such a radical change as to amount to a legislative act and that if the law was to be changed in this way that was a matter for Parliament. (The case considered whether a person who had lost a chance should be able to sue in the tort of negligence and is considered in Chapter 12 at 12.2.4.2). However, in April 2011 the prime minister, David Cameron, speaking to voters in Luton, said that he was uneasy that privacy law was being developed by the judiciary rather than by Parliament. He said, 'What ought to happen in a parliamentary democracy is Parliament, which you elect and put there, should decide how much protection do we want for individuals and how much freedom of the press and the rest of it. So I am a little uneasy about what is happening…It is an odd situation if the judges are making the law rather than Parliament.' His comments seem apt as regards the creation of law which might be regarded as 'political'.

Advantages of the system of precedent

The first advantage is that the device of **distinguishing** a case means that the system of precedent is not entirely rigid. A judge who is lower down the hierarchy can refuse to follow an apparently binding precedent if he distinguishes it on its facts. This means that the judge will say that the facts of the case he is considering are materially different from the facts of the case by which he appears to be bound. This device of distinguishing gives a degree of flexibility to the system of precedent. It allows judges to escape precedents which they consider inappropriate to the case in front of them.

A second and more important advantage of precedent is that it causes high quality decisions to be applied in all courts. Judges in appellate courts have the time and the experience to make very good decisions, often on extremely complex matters. These decisions can then be applied by much busier and less experienced lower court judges, who do not have to give the same consideration as to whether the principles of law involved are right or wrong.

It must be realised that the House of Lords, the highest English court in England, until it became the Supreme Court, was quite different institution from the Parliamentary House of Lords. Historically, it has been possible for people of no great ability, whether through inheritance or public service, to gain entry to the Parliamentary House of Lords. It is nowadays impossible for any but the very able to become Supreme Court Justices.

The way in which a person might become a Supreme Court justice demonstrates that only those of the highest ability could achieve it. Until recently, judges were chosen only from the ranks of barristers. Now solicitors too can become judges. The Bar is a career, rather like acting, which has extremes of success and very many talented young people enter it. If a barrister gains promotion and becomes a circuit judge he will sit in the Crown Court or the county court. This is an honour and an achievement. Even so, a circuit judge will make no law. He will supervise proceedings, decide who wins civil cases, award damages and sentence those convicted in the Crown Court. But no matter how brilliant a circuit judge's analysis of the law might be, it will not form a precedent.

High Court judges are a different matter. There are only 110 of them and they make the law of England from the very first case in which they sit. Every word they speak is open to scrutiny by the other judges, by lawyers and by academics. If they were not very able, this would soon be noticed.

About 50 judges are promoted beyond the High Court to the Supreme Court or Court of Appeal. These days it seems unthinkable that any but the very able should go this far.

It is not only on the grounds of ability that the Supreme Court ought to come to very high quality decisions. Unlike lower court judges, the Supreme Court justices do not decide a case there and then. They hear the facts and the arguments in the case and then reserve their judgment. They talk to each other informally to see whether there is a consensus of opinion. If there is a consensus one of the judges is chosen to write the judgment. If there is no consensus the minority will write their own dissenting judgments. In a particularly difficult case the process of writing the judgment can take a very long time.

English Commercial Law is very often adopted by businesses of different nationalities when they contract with each other. In the event of a dispute they consult English lawyers and settle their cases in the English courts or in front of English arbitrators. The earnings to the United Kingdom from these disputes amount to a considerable invisible export. English law would not be adopted in this way if it were not thought to be the most suitable system of law for resolving commercial disputes. The main reason why it should be thought the most suitable is that the system of precedent allows for excellent updating of the law in a way which can keep up with changing business trends.

A third major advantage of the system of precedent is that it is consistent and certain. Lawyers can predict the outcome of most cases, as almost any legal problem will have been previously considered by the courts and a precedent made. This certainty enables the vast majority of cases to be settled without the need to go to court. (The practical importance of this is explained in Chapter 2 at 2.4.) In *Broome v Cassell & Co Ltd* [1972] AC 1027 Lord Hailsham said, 'in legal matters, some degree of certainty is at least as valuable a part of justice as perfection'.

Impact of the Human Rights Act 1998

In *Kay and others v Lambeth LBC* [2006] UKHL 10, [2006] 2 AC 465 the House of Lords considered whether or not a lower court should follow a precedent of a higher court if a judgment of the Court of Human Rights, in Strasbourg, made after the precedent contradicted it. Which should be followed, the earlier English precedent or the later Strasbourg ruling? The House of Lords decided that the earlier English precedent should be followed and leave to appeal against this decision should be granted.

Lord Bingham considered the question in some depth. First he noted that s.2(1) of the 1998 Act required domestic courts to take account of judgments at the Court of Human Rights, but it did not strictly bind them in the way that s.3(1) of the European Communities Act 1972 and rulings of superior domestic courts bound them. (Section 3(1) of the ECA 1972 requires English courts to follow decisions of the European Court of Justice, the highest court on matters of EU law.) He also said that s.6(1) HRA 1998 made it unlawful for public authorities, such as courts, to act in a way which is incompatible with a Convention right. Second, he noted that precedent was the cornerstone of our legal system. Third, he rejected an argument that the earlier precedent should be ignored where it was 'plainly inconsistent' with the Strasbourg judgment, pointing out that the appellate courts were often divided in deciding whether or not two such judgments were plainly inconsistent with each other. Fourth, he noted the huge importance of certainty. Fifth, he said that this certainty was best achieved by adhering to the rules of precedent, even in the context of the Convention. Leave to appeal should be granted and leapfrog appeals (see Chapter 2 at 2.1.7) might well be appropriate. Finally, he noted that the Strasbourg court always takes full effect of national authorities and the particular facts of any case:

> 'Thus it is for national authorities, including national courts particularly, to decide in the first instance how the principles expounded in Strasbourg should be applied in the special context of national legislation, law, practice and social and other conditions. It is by the decisions of national courts that the domestic standard must be initially set, and to those decisions the ordinary rules of precedent should apply.'

However, Lord Bingham did accept that a House of Lords decision made before the 1998 Act need not necessarily be followed if the Human Rights Act undermined the policy upon which the decision was made, and if no reference was made to the European Convention in any of the Lords' opinions. Even here though, he thought that the facts of the case which was not being followed would have to be of an 'extreme character' so as to make the case a 'very exceptional case'. All of the other six members of the House of Lords agreed with what Lord Bingham said.

Alternatives to the system of precedent

Most other countries do not use a system of precedent. France, which is fairly typical of European countries, has a codified system of law known as a civil law system. The civil law is contained in the various Civil Codes. French judges, who are civil servants rather than lawyers, do not feel compelled to interpret the Codes according to previous decisions until those decisions have for some time unanimously interpreted the Codes in the same way. Scotland has a mixed legal system. It is based on the civil law system, but has strong common law influences. In Scotland the system of precedent is used, but a precedent does not have quite the same force as in England.

Test your understanding 1.3

1 What is meant by the doctrine of judicial precedent?

2 What are the five main levels of the courts, for the purposes of precedent?

3 What is meant by *ratio decidendi* and *obiter dicta*? What is the significance of the distinction?

4 What is meant by overruling, reversing and distinguishing?

1.4 EUROPEAN UNION LAW

In 1952 the European Coal and Steel Community was set up with the object of preventing any European country from building up stockpiles of steel and coal, the raw materials needed to wage war. Following the success of this, the European Economic Community (the EEC) came into existence in 1957. The six original Member States signed the Treaty of Rome, which was also known as the EEC Treaty, which founded the European Economic Community or the 'common market'. These six original countries were Germany, France, Italy, Belgium, the Netherlands and Luxembourg. Part of the founding philosophy of the Community was to provide an appropriate response to the Soviet Bloc countries to the East, but the motivation was also more pragmatic in that there seemed to be obvious advantages to the creation of a free market in Europe. At the time of writing there are 27 Member States, the original six having been joined by Austria, Bulgaria, Cyprus, the

Czech Republic, Denmark, Estonia, Finland, Greece, Hungary, Ireland, Latvia, Lithuania, Malta, Poland, Portugal, Romania, the Slovak Republic, Slovenia, Spain, Sweden and the United Kingdom. Croatia, Macedonia, Iceland and Turkey are candidate countries, meaning that their application to join has been officially accepted by the European Council. Five other Balkan states are potential candidate countries.

The United Kingdom joined the EEC in 1973. In order to be admitted as a member, the UK Parliament passed the European Communities Act 1972. This statute agreed that Community law should be directly effective in UK courts.

In 1986 the Community consisted of 12 Member States, all of whom signed the Single European Act. This Act, a Treaty rather than a UK Act of Parliament, was designed to remove all barriers to a single market by 1992. In addition, the Act introduced a system of qualified majority voting in the European Council, thereby reducing the power of any single State to block developments. The Act also strengthened the powers of the European Parliament and created a Court of First Instance to work beneath the European Court of Justice.

In 1992 the treaty on European Union, the Maastricht Treaty, was signed by all 15 States which were at that time Member States. The Treaty was more of a statement of political intention than a statement of precise obligations. It proposed cooperation on matters other than purely economic matters, envisaging the creation of a European Union with the three following pillars: the European Community; a common foreign and security policy; and cooperation in the fields of justice and home affairs. Also, the European Parliament was given greater power to legislate and a timetable was set for economic and monetary union. The Treaty envisaged that economic and monetary union would be achieved in three stages. However, the UK and Denmark opted out of the third stage. The UK also opted out of participation in the social chapter, which set out employment and social rights.

The Treaty of Amsterdam was signed in October 1997 and came into force in May 1999. This Treaty aimed for closer political cooperation between Member States. It incorporated much of the Justice and Home Affairs pillar into the EC Treaty and gave Member States a greater power to veto proposals which would affect their vital national interests. It again increased the power of the European Parliament and gave the EU greater power to fight fraud, to prevent discrimination

and to protect the environment. It also renumbered the articles of the EC Treaty.

The Treaty of Lisbon was signed by all EU leaders in December 2007. However, it could not become effective until all Member States ratified it. In June 2008, Irish voters rejected the Treaty in a referendum. In October 2009, at the second time of asking, they voted in favour of the Treaty. The Treaty came into force in December 2009 when the Czech Republic became the last country to ratify it.

The Treaty amended the existing treaties, incorporating them into a new treaty called the Treaty on the Functioning of the European Union. This has four main aims: to make the EU more democratic and transparent; to make it more efficient; to promote rights, values, freedom, solidarity and security; and to make the EU an actor on the global stage.

The first of these aims involves increasing the power of the European Parliament so that it will be placed on an equal footing with the Commission. As regards most EU legislation, the Parliament and the Commission will approve legislation using a co-decision procedure. A greater role in making EU law will be given to national Parliaments in areas where they can achieve better results than the EU. A Citizens' Initiative will allow 1 million citizens from several Member States to ask the Commission to introduce new policies. The relationship between the EU and Member States will be clarified, and States which wish to do so will be allowed to withdraw from the EU.

Great efficiency will be achieved by extending qualified-majority voting. From 2014, a qualified majority will be achieved if a dual majority of 55 per cent of Member States, and Member States representing 65 per cent of the EU's population, vote in favour. The EU Commission will be reduced in size and a new President of the European Council will be elected by national governments for a period of office lasting two and a half years. The European Council will be separate from the Council of Ministers, the leaders of which will continue to be elected on a six-month rotating basis. The European Council will not have legislative powers but will guide policy. The promotion of rights, values, freedom, solidarity and security will be achieved by guaranteeing the principles set out in the Charter of Fundamental Rights, and by giving them legal force. This charter set out principles of human rights to be applied throughout the EU but at present it has no legal force. In addition, the EU will be given a greater role in fighting crime and preventing terrorism. New provisions relating to humanitarian aid, civil protection and public health will enhance the EU's ability to respond to threats to its citizens. The EU will be made a stronger actor on the global stage by creating a High Representative for Foreign Affairs and Security Policy, and by encouraging the EU to act as a single legal personality.

The provisions of the Treaty will be introduced gradually, and may take about ten years to become fully adopted.

1.4.1 The Institutions of the European Union

The original EEC Treaty set up four principal institutions. These institutions are now known as: the Council of the European Communities; the European Commission; the European Parliament; and the European Court of Justice. The first three of these are considered immediately below. The European Court of Justice is considered below at 1.4.3. In addition, there is a Court of Auditors and two advisory bodies: the Economic and Social Committee and the Committee of the Regions. The Court of Auditors monitors the Community's accounts. The Economic and Social Committee gives advisory opinions to the institutions. The Committee of the Regions is a consultative body which promotes the interests of the regions at European level. Both of these committees have 344 members. Each Member State has between six and 24 representatives, depending upon the size of the State.

1.4.1.1 The Council of the European Union

The Council of the European Union, generally known as the Council, is not a permanent body. It consists at any given time of one Minister from the Government of each Member State, and the President of the European Commission. Which Government Ministers will constitute the Council of Ministers depends upon the nature of the measures which the Council is considering. For example, if the measures relate to agriculture then it will be the relevant Ministers of Agriculture. Often the Council is made up of heads of Government or the Member States' Foreign Ministers. Up to four times a year the presidents or prime ministers of all of the countries along with the President of the European Commission, hold meetings as the 'European Council'. At these meetings overall EU policy is set and issues which could not be settled at a lower level are settled.

The Council passes legislation, co-ordinates EU policy, concludes international agreements, approves the EU budget and develops the EU Common Foreign and Security Policy. The Council passes legislation, generally in conjunction with the European Parliament. It does this by means of a system of qualified majority voting. However, a Treaty might require unanimity for votes on certain matters such as the common and foreign security policy, police and judicial cooperation in criminal matters, asylum and immigration policy, economic and social cohesion policy or taxation. Under this system each country is allocated a certain number of votes in relation to its population. The United Kingdom is one of four countries having the maximum voting weighting of 29 votes. Malta has the fewest votes, with just three. There are 345 votes in total. A qualified majority is reached in two circumstances. First, if 255 (73.9 per cent) votes are in favour. This means that 91 votes can defeat a proposal and so at least four countries must vote against. Second, if a simple majority of Member States approve. However, if a matter which was not based on a proposal from the Commission is being voted upon a two-thirds majority of Member States must approve. Additionally, any Member State can require confirmation that votes representing at least 62 per cent of the total population of the EU were in favour. If it is discovered that this figure was not reached then the proposal voted upon will not be regarded as having been accepted.

Article 11 of the Treaty of Amsterdam gives effect to the Luxembourg Accord and allows any Member State to argue that unanimity, rather than a qualified majority vote, should be required on any particular proposal. When such an argument is raised, the Council will delay taking a vote in order to enable the dissenting State to gain the support of other Member States. However, if it is unsuccessful in this the issues will anyway be resolved by a qualified majority vote.

Two committees assist the Council. The Committee of Permanent Representatives (COREPER) prepares the work of the Council and performs other administrative functions. This committee is comprised of senior diplomatic representatives of the Member States. The Economic and Social Committee (ECOSOC) has a consultative role.

1.4.1.2 The European Commission

Twenty-seven individual commissioners are appointed by the Member States to serve in a full-time capacity for a term of five years. When these commissioners act collectively they are known as the European Commission, which is generally abbreviated to the Commission. Commissioners also have individual responsibility for a particular matter, such as agriculture. The Commission is supported by large executive and administrative systems. The commissioners are expected to act completely independently of their Member States but in practice tend to guard the independence of their Member States. They are selected on political grounds, and all UK commissioners have previously played a leading role in UK politics. In 2014 the number of commissioners will be reduced to two-thirds of the number of Member States.

The most powerful position in the EU is the President of the Commission. The President is the figurehead of the EU and has a strong political influence upon it. The Council selects the President and the appointment must then be approved by the European Parliament.

The Commission is involved in broad policy-making. It prepares specific proposals to be submitted to the Council. It also manages and implements EU policies and the EU budget, it acts jointly with the Court of Justice to enforce EU law and it acts as the EU's representative when dealing with other countries. It is politically accountable to the European Parliament which can demand that the whole Commission resigns. Individual commissioners can be forced to resign if the President of the Commission demands this and the other commissioners agree. In addition to its major roles, the Commission also commissions research and prepares reports on matters which concern the Community and negotiates with non-Member States on these matters. It also prepares the draft Community budget.

1.4.1.3 The European Parliament

Members of the European Parliament are elected directly by Member States, using a system of proportional representation. The European Parliament has 736 MEPs, representing the 27 countries in the EU. MEPs do not sit in national state blocks but as members of seven groups which represent different political views. One of the Parliament's most significant powers is to approve or amend the EU budget. The Commission prepares a draft budget, which is submitted to the Council and then to the Parliament. The Parliament must approve, amend or reject the budget within 45 days. When the budget is amended by the Parliament the Council is given 15 days to consider

the amendments. If no challenge is made to the amendments then the budget is deemed to have been accepted as amended. If the Council does challenge the amendments, the budget is resubmitted to the Parliament. The Parliament then has 15 days to amend or reject the modifications made by the Council. This must be done by a 60 per cent majority and a majority of members must vote. If no such vote is passed, the Council's modifications are adopted as the budget.

The Parliament must approve the Commission when it is first appointed and must also approve the new President. It must also approve the accounts of the Commission and new appointments to the Commission. Article 201 of the EC Treaty gives the Parliament the power to pass a vote of censure to dismiss the Commission. Such a vote must be passed by a two-thirds majority. In January 1999 a vote to remove the Commission on account of nepotism and corruption failed: 232 MEPs voted for removal, 293 voted against. However, the whole of the Commission resigned in March 1999, on publication of a report made by an investigative committee.

Initially the Parliament had few real powers. It had to be consulted about EU legislation but had no powers to block any legislation. The EU Parliament still does not have the power to legislate in the way that the UK Parliament has. It passes law by 'co-decision' with the Council. On many matters the Parliament and the Council have equal standing, but on others the Council has the power to legislate after consulting the Parliament. The Parliament also has the power to ask the Commission to put forward proposals for legislation.

1.4.2 Sources of community law

1.4.2.1 Applicability and effect

In order to understand the effect of EU law it is necessary to understand the distinction between the terms 'direct applicability' and 'direct effect'. If EU legislation is directly applicable, it automatically forms part of the domestic law of Member States, without those States needing to legislate to bring the law in. However, this would not necessarily mean that individuals could directly rely upon the legislation in the domestic courts of their own countries. In order for such reliance to be possible, the legislation would have to be capable of having direct effect. Where EU legislation has direct effect an individual can directly rely upon the legislation, either as a cause of action or as a defence, in the domestic courts of his or her country. The Articles of the EC Treaty are always directly applicable, as are Regulations, but as we have seen this does not necessarily mean that they have direct effect.

No EU legislation can have direct effect unless it satisfies the criteria laid down by the European Court of Justice in *Van Gend en Loos v Nederlands Administratie der Belastingen* [1963] ECR 1. These criteria will be satisfied only if the legislation is sufficiently clear, precise and unconditional, and if the legislation intends to confer rights. Many Treaty Articles do not meet these criteria as they are mere statements of aspiration. Even if Community legislation does meet the *Van Gend* criteria, it may have only direct vertical effect, rather than direct horizontal effect. If it has direct vertical effect it can be invoked by an individual only against the State and against emanations of the State, such as health authorities. A provision which has direct horizontal effect can be invoked against other individuals as well as against the State and emanations of the State.

If an EU law does not have direct effect it might nevertheless have indirect effect. An indirectly effective EU law could not be enforced in national courts. However, these courts would be obliged to interpret their own national law, to the extent that this is possible, in such a way that it did not conflict with the indirectly effective EU law.

1.4.2.2 **Treaty Articles**

The Treaty on the Functioning of the European Union has over 350 articles. These are directly applicable. Whether or not a Treaty Article has direct effect depends first upon whether it satisfies the criteria in *Van Gend*. As we have seen, some will not satisfy these criteria as they are merely statements of aspiration. Some of the Articles are much more significant than others. Article 157 of the Treaty on the Functioning of the European Union requires Member States to ensure and subsequently maintain the application of the principle that men and women should receive equal pay for equal work. The effect of this Article has been highly significant, as we shall see in Chapter 21, and has caused the Sex Discrimination Act 1975 to be amended to make sure that the Article is not contradicted. Although Article 157 is addressed to Member States, individuals have successfully invoked it against

other individuals, usually their employers. Article 157 therefore has direct horizontal effect.

Some Treaty Articles, like Article 157, have both direct horizontal and vertical effect, others have only direct vertical effect. Whether or not they have direct horizontal effect will depend upon the wording of the Article and the interpretation of the Article by the ECJ. For example, Article 34 of the TFEU, which prohibits restrictions on the free movement of goods, only has direct vertical effect. It can therefore only be invoked by an individual against the State or against an emanation of the State. One private company could not invoke Article 34 against another private company which was not an emanation of the State.

1.4.2.3 **Regulations**

Regulations are binding in their entirety and are directly applicable in all Member States without any further implementation by Member States. A regulation may specify the date on which it is to come into effect. If it does not do this, it will come into effect 20 days after the date of its publication in the *Official Journal of the European Union*. Regulations may be directly invoked, sometimes both vertically and horizontally, providing the *Van Gend* criteria are satisfied. Even if these criteria are not satisfied, a Regulation may have indirect effect. This means that, although an individual cannot invoke the Regulation, the courts of Member States are bound to take account of it.

1.4.2.4 **Directives**

Directives are addressed to the Governments of Member States and must be published in the *Official Journal of the European Union*. Directives are not directly applicable. It is therefore left to each individual Member State to implement the objectives of the Directive in a manner and form that is best suited to its own particular political and economic culture. All Directives are issued with an implementation date and Member States are under a duty to implement by this date. If the Directive is not implemented by the due date, the Commission has the power to take proceedings against the Member State in question.

Before the implementation date has been reached, Directives have no effect at all. However, in the *Wallonie ASBL* case [1997] ECR I-7411 the European Court of Justice held that a Member State should not enact legislation or implement measures that significantly conflict with the objectives of a Directive that has yet to meet its implementation date. Generally, the UK Government will implement EU Directives by delegated legislation. Several statutory instruments which we consider in this book, such as the Commercial Agents (Council Directive) Regulations 1993, were enacted to give effect to Directives. (It is slightly confusing that these statutory instruments are usually called Regulations, given that EU Regulations are a quite different matter.) Once an EU Directive has been implemented by UK legislation then, obviously, an individual can invoke the domestic legislation against another individual. For example, the Commercial Agents (Council Directive) Regulations 1993 are regularly invoked by individuals against individuals.

There can, however, be a problem if the UK Government either fails to implement a Directive at all, or does not implement the Directive properly. Once the implementation date has been reached, whether or not the Directive has direct effect depends first upon whether the Directive satisfies the *Van Gend* criteria, and second upon the relationship between the parties involved. Where the parties to a legal action are in a vertical relationship (for example, patient and health authority), the Directive is capable of having direct effect. Where the parties are in a horizontal relationship (for example, a consumer suing a shop), the Directive does not have direct effect. In other words, Directives which should have been implemented are capable of having direct vertical effect, but not direct horizontal effect. (This can mean that a person employed by an emanation of the State, such as a worker in the NHS, might have more rights against his employer than a person employed by a person who is not an emanation of the State.) However, when dealing with a case between two individuals the domestic courts are under a duty, by virtue of Article 10 of the EC Treaty, to attempt as far as possible to give indirect effect to the EU Directive which should have been implemented. This means that they have to try, as far as possible, to interpret the domestic legislation so as to give effect indirectly to the objectives of the Directive.

In situations where it is not possible for the domestic court to give direct or indirect effect to an EU Directive, the remedy of last resort is for the aggrieved individual to sue the Member State for failure to implement. If found to be in breach, the Member State could be ordered to pay compensation to the aggrieved individual. This right was set out in the following case.

Francovich and Bonifaci v Republic of Italy
[1993] 2 CMLR 66 (European Court of Justice)

Mr Francovich's employer went into liquidation, while owing money to Mr Francovich and others. A Directive required Member States to set up compensation funds to deal with this type of situation. However, Italy had not set up such a fund. The Directive in question was not sufficiently precise to have direct effect. Mr Francovich asked for damages against Italy to compensate for its failure to set up a fund.

Held. Article 10 impliedly allowed for an individual to be compensated on account of a Directive not having been implemented, but only if three conditions were satisfied. First, the Directive must relate to rights conferred upon an individual. Second, the contents of those rights must be identifiable from the Directive's provisions. Third, a causal link must exist between the State's failure to implement the Directive and the loss suffered by the individual.

In *Brasserie du Pêcheur SA v Germany* [1996] ECR I–1029 the ECJ refined the *Francovich* criteria in the following way. First, the rule of law in question must confer rights upon individuals. Second, the breach must be sufficiently serious. Third, there must be a direct causal link between the breach and the damage. That the breach should have been sufficiently serious, means that the Member State must have 'manifestly and gravely' disregarded the limits on its discretion. In deciding whether or not this had happened, account will be taken of the following matters: the clarity of the legislation in question; whether the rule in question allowed any measure of discretion; whether the failure to implement and the damage caused were deliberate; whether the error had been induced by the acts or words of the Council or the Commission; whether the error was contrary to settled ECJ case law; and the speed with which the error was corrected.

The legal effect of the Treaties, Regulations and Directives is shown in Figure 1.1.

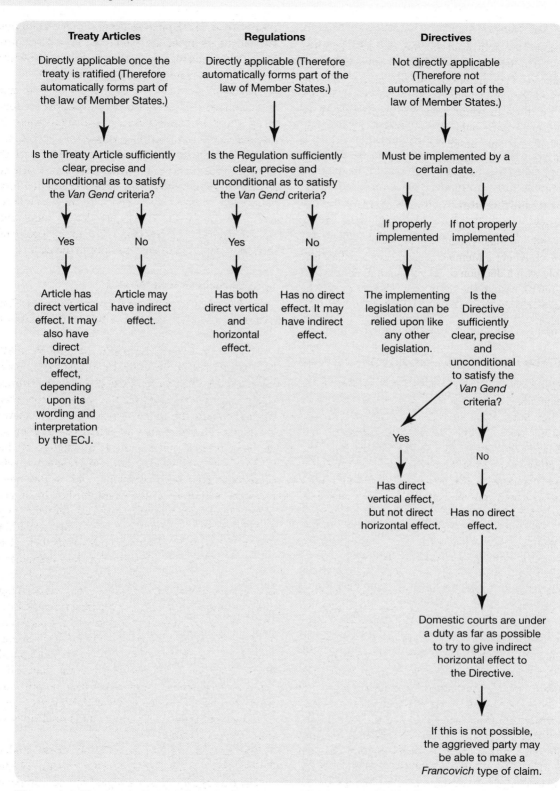

Figure 1.1 The legal effect of Treaty Articles, Regulations and Directives

1.4.2.5 **Decisions**

Decisions are addressed to one or more Member States, to individuals, to categories of individuals or to institutions. They are binding in their entirety, without the need for implementation by Member States, but only on those to whom they were addressed. They do not need to be published in the Official Journal. Decisions can only be invoked against the person to whom they are addressed. In practice, decisions are of little practical importance.

1.4.2.6 **Recommendations and opinions**

The Commission has the power to make recommendations and opinions. These have no binding legal force. However, where a Member State passes legislation to comply with a decision or an opinion a national court may refer a case to the ECJ to see whether or not the decision or opinion applies and how it should be interpreted.

1.4.3 **The European Court of Justice**

The European Court of Justice (ECJ), which sits in Luxembourg, is made up of 27 judges, one from each Member State. These judges are assisted by eight advocates-general. The judges and advocates are appointed by common consent of the Member States and hold office for a six-year term which may be renewed.

The decisions of the court are signed by all the judges, without any indication that some may have dissented. Eighty per cent of cases are referred to one of the six chambers where either three or five judges sit. The Grand Chamber of the court consists of thirteen judges, and disputes involving Member States tend to be heard by a Grand Chamber. The number of judges sitting is always odd, so that a majority decision can always be reached. The more important the issues thought to be involved, the greater the number of judges sitting. The judgments of the court are available free on its website, but cases typically take between 18 months and two years to be heard. The advocates-general must act with complete impartiality and independence, in open court, making reasoned submissions on cases brought before the Court. They do not therefore argue the case for either of the sides involved. Each case has an advocate-general assigned to it. The advocate-general makes a summary of the facts, an analysis of all the relevant Community law and a recommendation as to what the decision of the court should be. The parties cannot comment on this and the judges deliberate upon it in secret. The Court has no obligation to agree with the advocate-general's recommendation but generally do agree.

When ready to vote the most junior judges vote first and then the other judges vote in order of reverse seniority. The court does not use a system of precedent. It can and does depart from its own previous decisions.

Certain matters may be referred to the Court of First Instance rather than to the European Court of Justice. This Court of First Instance operates in a very similar way to the way in which the ECJ operates. Article 51 of the EC Treaty provides an automatic right of appeal on a point of law, but not on a point of fact, from the Court of First Instance to the ECJ.

1.4.3.1 **Jurisdiction of the ECJ**

Apart from hearing appeals from the Court of First Instance, the ECJ has three separate heads of jurisdiction.

First, it can express an authoritative opinion on EU law, if requested to do so by a national court. Once the ruling has been made by the ECJ the case returns to the court which asked for the ruling so that that court can apply the ruling. Article 267 TFEU allows a national court to request an authoritative ruling as to three types of matters: the interpretation of the EU legislation; the validity and interpretation of acts of institutions of the Community; and on the interpretation of statutes of bodies established by an act of the Council, where those statutes so provide. Any national court or tribunal may refer a matter within Article 267 to the ECJ if it thinks this necessary to give judgment. Most of the ECJ's work involves preliminary rulings. In Chapter 20 we shall consider several cases in which a national court sought a preliminary ruling as to the interpretation of EU legislation from the ECJ. The ruling is sought by the court, not by the parties to the case. Although a national court has a discretion to seek a preliminary ruling, a court of final appeal has an obligation to do so where a relevant point of EU law is at issue and where there has been no previous interpretation of the point by the ECJ. However, there is no such obligation where the point is so obvious as not to require a ruling.

The second area of jurisdiction arises under Articles 263 and 264 TFEU, which allows the ECJ to review the legality of acts adopted by the European Parliament or other Community institutions. The ECJ can also review a community institution's failure to act. This review process is similar to the process of judicial review whereby the High Court ensures that the Government and others do not exceed their powers.

The third area of jurisdiction arises under Article 258, which allows the Commission to bring actions against Member States to make sure that they fulfil their Community obligations. Article 259 allows Member States to take other Member States to the ECJ for failure to live up to their Treaty obligations.

1.4.4 Supremacy of EU law

EU law can only be effective if it overrides national law. If every Member State were free to pass legislation which conflicted with EU legislation, the EU would be rendered ineffective. In *Costa v ENEL* [1964] ECR 585 the ECJ stated that the EEC Treaty had become an integral part of the legal systems of Member States and that the courts of Member States were bound to apply the Treaty. It also stated that Member States had, by signing the Treaty, limited their sovereign rights, within limited areas, and created a body of law which bound both their citizens and themselves. The case specifically decided that Italian legislation which was incompatible with Community law, and which had been passed after Italy had signed the Treaty, could have no effect.

In *R v Secretary of State for Transport, ex parte Factortame (No. 2)* [1991] 1 AC 603, Spanish companies sought judicial review of the Merchant Shipping Act 1988, which they claimed breached two Articles of the EC Treaty. The companies asked for an injunction to suspend that part of the Act which was in breach of the relevant Treaty Article. The House of Lords held that injunctions could not be effective against the Crown and refused to grant the injunction. However, the case was referred to the ECJ, under what is now Article 267 TFEU, which held that UK limitations on the availability of remedies should be overruled and that the injunctions should be available. Subsequently, the House of Lords immediately suspended the operation of the offending part of the Act. A few years after *Factortame* in *Equal Opportunities Commission v Secretary of State for Employment* [1994] 1 All ER 110, the House of Lords suspended the operation of a section of the governing employment legislation on the grounds that it was in breach of the EU Equal Treatment legislation. However, it should be noted

that this power of UK courts to suspend conflicting domestic legislation will only be used sparingly in cases involving serious breaches of directly effective EU legislation.

Whilst the United Kingdom remains a member of the EU it is therefore arguable that it has surrendered Parliamentary sovereignty. However, two points should be noted. First, other Treaties such as those which provided that the United States had direct command over US soldiers based in the United Kingdom, have at some time or other meant that the United Kingdom did not have true Parliamentary sovereignty. Second, the UK Parliament could vote to repeal the European Communites Act 1972 and leave the EU. It must be said, however, that this option becomes increasingly unlikely and would become virtually impossible if full monetary union were ever achieved.

Test your understanding 1.4

1 What is the role of the Council of the European Communities?

2 What is the role of the European Commission?

3 What is the role of the European Parliament?

4 What is meant by EU legislation being directly applicable?

5 What is meant by EU legislation having direct effect?

6 What is the difference between direct vertical effect and direct horizontal effect?

7 Are Articles of the EC Treaty and Regulations directly applicable? Do they have direct effect?

8 What is the legal effect of a Directive both before and after implementation?

9 Can an individual sue a Member State on account of a Directive not having been correctly implemented?

10 What is the jurisdiction of the European Court of Justice?

1.5 THE EUROPEAN CONVENTION ON HUMAN RIGHTS

1.5.1 The Human Rights Act 1998

The Human Rights Act 1998 came into effect in October 2000. This Act incorporates the main provisions of the European Convention on Human Rights into UK law. However, the implementation is not complete as Parliamentary sovereignty is preserved. Section 2(1) of the Act states that a court or tribunal which is determining a question which has arisen in connection with a Convention right must take into account both the Convention and decisions of institutions of the Convention, such as the Court of Human Rights.

Section 3(1) of the Act requires that, so far as it is possible to do so, all legislation must be read and given effect in a way which is compatible with the Convention rights. This can be regarded as a new rule of statutory interpretation and it is not to be restricted to statutory provisions which are ambiguous. Section 4 allows any precedent-making courts (the High Court, Court of Appeal and Supreme Court) to make a declaration of incompatibility in any legal proceedings in which a court determines whether or not UK legislation is compatible with a Convention right. This is a last resort and is not an alternative to trying to interpret the legislation in such a way that it is compatible with the Convention. Such a declaration of incompatibility does not affect the validity of the legislation in question, and is not binding on the parties to the litigation. However, where a declaration of incompatibility is made, the relevant Minister has the option to revoke the offending legislation, or amend it so that it is no longer incompatible.

Section 10 gives the Minister power to do this by remedial order so as to achieve the change by a 'fast-track' procedure. However, the Minister will revoke or amend the legislation only if he considers that there are compelling reasons for doing either of these things. As the Minister can leave the incompatible legislation in place, Parliamentary sovereignty is preserved. The relevant Minister has the same power to revoke, amend or leave primary legislation in place following an adverse ruling from the European Court of Human Rights. Primary legislation includes Acts of Parliament and certain Orders in Council. Secondary legislation includes all delegated legislation other than certain Orders in Council. If secondary legislation is found to be incompatible with Convention rights, any domestic court can declare the legislation invalid, unless the Parent Act provides that the secondary legislation is to prevail even if it is incompatible. If the Parent Act does not allow the legislation to be declared invalid, a precedent-making court has the power to make a declaration of incompatibility. The process of judicial review (see Chapter 2 at 2.6.1)

can also cause secondary legislation which is invalid to be declared *ultra vires* the Parent Act (see 1.3.1.3, above).

Since the Act came into effect, positive consideration must be given as to whether new legislation is compatible with the Convention. Before the Second Reading of a Bill in Parliament the relevant Minister will have to make a written statement to Parliament, either stating compatibility with the Convention or stating incompatibility. If stating incompatibility, the Minister will need to state the Government's intention to proceed with the legislation anyway. The Minister does not need to state the way in which the legislation is incompatible. Obviously, stating incompatibility might lead to political difficulties. By mid-2010 there had been 27 declarations of incompatibility which had not been reversed by a higher court.

Section 6(1) provides that it is unlawful for a public authority to act in a way which is incompat-ible with a Convention right. However, this is not the case if the public authority could not have acted differently as a result of primary UK legislation. Section 6(1) will have a considerable impact on many UK businesses, as s.6(3) defines a public authority as including not only a court or a tribunal, but also any person certain of whose functions are functions of a public nature. Therefore, businesses such as private nursing homes, private schools, security firms and housing associations are subject to the effect of s.6(1).

Earlier in this chapter, at 1.3.2.2, *Kay and others v Lambeth LBC* [2006] UKHL 10, [2006] 2 AC 465 was considered. In this case Lord Bingham thoroughly reviewed how the HRA 1998 affected the doctrine of judicial precedent. Section 7 creates a new public tort which allows individuals to bring legal proceedings against public authorities breaching Convention rights. It is only the 'victim' of a breach of Convention rights who has the standing to bring proceedings under s.7. Where proceedings are brought a court may order such remedies as it considers just and appropriate.

Section 13(1) provides that if a court's determination of any question arising under the Act might affect the exercise by a religious organisation of the Convention right to freedom of thought, conscience and religion, it must have particular regard to the importance of that right.

An outline of the effect of the Human Rights Act can be seen in Figure 1.2.

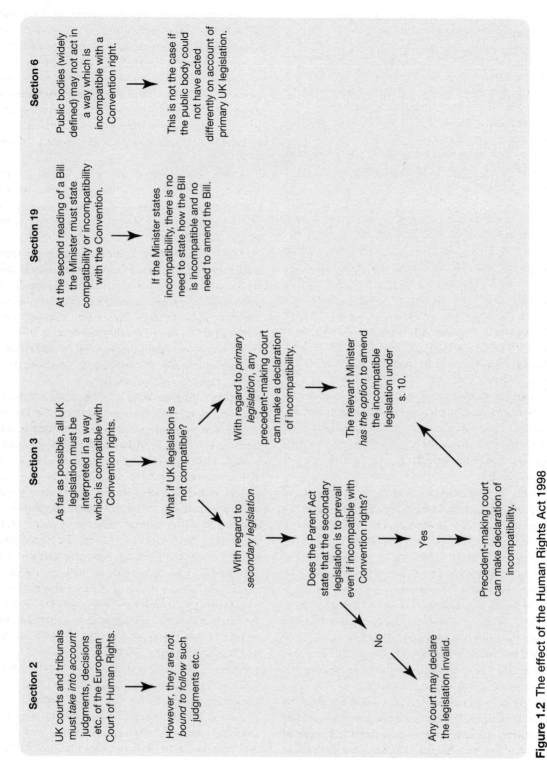

Figure 1.2 The effect of the Human Rights Act 1998

1.5.2 The European Convention on Human Rights

We have seen that the Human Rights Act incorporates the main provisions of the European Convention on Human Rights into UK law. It is therefore necessary to consider the effect of the Convention. The Articles are set out below, but Articles 1 and 13 have not been incorporated into UK law.

Article 2 provides that everyone's right to life shall be preserved by law, except in carrying out a death sentence properly passed by a court.

Article 3 provides that no one shall be subjected to torture or to inhumane or degrading treatment or punishment. In *Ireland* v *UK* (1978) 2 EHRR 25 the Court of Human Rights found that the UK's interrogation of suspected terrorists was inhumane and degrading, although it fell short of being torture. In *D* v *UK* (1997) 24 EHRR 423 it was held that deporting a person with Aids to a country where there would be no treatment and where he would be destitute breached Article 3. In *Tyrer* v *UK* (1978) 2 EHRR 1 it was held that birching on the Isle of Man breached Article 3.

Article 4 provides that no one should be held in slavery or servitude or be required to perform forced or compulsory labour. There are exceptions for prisoners, the military, for work done as part of normal civic obligation, or service required in the case of an emergency or calamity threatening the life or well-being of the community.

Article 5(1) provides that everyone has the right to liberty and security of person. No one is to be deprived of their liberty except in the following circumstances: after conviction by a court; upon arrest; to prevent the spread of infectious diseases; in order to treat the mentally ill; or in the case of alcoholics, drug addicts or vagrants. Article 5(2) gives anyone arrested the right to be informed promptly, in a language which he understands, of the reason for the arrest and the charges against him. Article 5(3) requires that those arrested are brought promptly before a judge. If anyone is arrested in contravention of Article 5 he is given an enforceable right to compensation.

Article 6(1) guarantees the right to a fair trial. The trial must be a public hearing within a reasonable time of arrest by an independent and impartial tribunal established by law. Judgment has to be pronounced publicly. Article 6(2) holds that everyone charged with a criminal offence is presumed innocent until found guilty according to the law. Article 6(3) sets out the minimum rights of those charged with a criminal offence. These include: prompt information as to the details of the charge; adequate time and facilities to prepare a defence; the right to choose a lawyer and to be given free legal assistance if the interests of justice demand this; to have the same rights to require witnesses to attend as is enjoyed by the prosecution; to have the prosecution witnesses cross-examined; and to have the free assistance of an interpreter if one is needed.

Article 7 provides that no one should be guilty of a criminal offence which did not exist at the time when the act was committed, unless the act was criminal according to the general principles of law recognised by civilised nations.

Article 8(1) provides that everyone has the right to respect for his private and family life, his home and his correspondence. However, Article 8(2) provides that public authorities may interfere with this right on the following grounds: in the interests of national security, public safety or the economic well-being of the country; for the prevention of disorder or crime; for the protection of health or morals; or for the protection of the rights and freedoms of others.

Article 9 gives the right to freedom of thought, conscience and religion. However, this right is balanced against the rights of others to free expression, which includes criticism of religious beliefs and practices.

Article 10(1) gives a right to freedom of expression. This does not prevent the State from requiring broadcasters to hold licences, but does insist upon freedom to hold opinions, and to receive and impart information and ideas without interference by public authority. Article 10(2) provides that the freedoms set out in Article 10(1) carry duties and responsibilities and therefore may be subject to formalities, conditions, restrictions or penalties as are prescribed by law and as are necessary in a democratic society for the following reasons: to secure the interests of national security, territorial integrity or public safety; to prevent disorder or crime; to protect public health or morals; to protect the reputation or rights of others; to prevent the disclosure of confidential information; or to maintain the authority and impartiality of the judiciary.

Article 11 gives the right to freedom of peaceful assembly and to freedom of association with others, including the right to form and join a trade union. This right does not apply to the armed forces or the police. Restrictions are also allowed in the interests of national security or public safety, to prevent disorder or crime, to protect health or morals, or for the protection of the rights and freedoms of others.

Article 12 gives members of the opposite sex the right to marry and form a family if they are of marriageable age.

Article 14 provides that the rights set out in the Convention shall be secured without discrimination on any ground. This Article cannot be invoked on its own. The discrimination in question must have taken place in relation to a different Convention right.

Article 15 allows derogation from the Convention in time of war.

Article 16 provides that Articles 10, 11 and 14 do not prevent restrictions on the political activities of aliens.

Article 17 provides that nothing in the Convention allows a person the right to do anything which would deny other rights under the Convention, except to the extent that this is provided for in the Convention. So racist groups could not use the right to freedom of expression to attack other rights such as freedom of religion.

Two Protocols, the First and the Thirteenth, have also been incorporated into UK law by the Human Rights Act 1998.

The First Protocol, Article 1 provides that every natural or legal person is entitled to peaceful enjoyment of his possessions. Nobody should be deprived of his possessions except in the public interest and subject to provisions provided for by law.

The First Protocol, Article 2 provides that no one should be denied the right to education.

The First Protocol, Article 3 provides that States must agree to conduct free elections at regular intervals by secret ballot so as to allow the people to choose freely the legislature.

The Thirteenth Protocol outlaws the death penalty in all circumstances.

The UK has been allowed one derogation from the Convention under Article 15(3) with regard to Article 5 of the Convention. This allows the authorities to detain anyone suspected of terrorist offences in line with the provisions of the Prevention of Terrorism (Temporary Provisions) Act 1989.

1.5.3 **The European Court of Human Rights**

It is important to realise that this court, which sits in Strasbourg, is quite separate from the European Court of Justice, which sits in Luxembourg. The ECJ is the supreme court of the European Community and its decisions are binding upon the Member States of the European Community. The European Court of Human Rights hears cases concerning breach of the Convention on Human Rights. Forty States have signed the Convention and although this includes all of the Member States of the European Union, it also obviously includes other States which are not EU members.

There are 47 judges in the plenary Court of Human Rights. One judge represents each signatory State. The plenary court sets up Chambers to hear complaints against States. These Chambers are made up of seven judges, the President of the Chamber, a judge from the country against which the complaint is being made and five other judges. Each Chamber sets up Committees of three judges to consider applications and to dismiss as early as possible those which are unfounded. Manifestly inadmissible applications can be dismissed by a single judge. An individual with a complaint applies to a judge, known as a rapporteur, who passes the complaint on to a Committee or Chambers. Particularly difficult cases can be passed on to a Grand Chamber of 17 judges. The Grand Chamber also acts as an appeal court. Judges hold office for six years, with half being replaced every three years. Applicants do not need to be legally represented but usually are. All hearings are held in public and are put on the court's web site on the same day. The deliberations of the judges are, however, secret.

Article 35 of the Convention provides that an applicant to the court must prove:

(a) that the complaint involves a breach of the Convention by a country which has ratified it;
(b) that the breach occurred within the jurisdiction of that country; and
(c) that all domestic remedies have been exhausted and that the application to the Court has been made within six months of these remedies having been exhausted (it is possible, however, for the Court to proceed on the basis that domestic remedies are deemed to be exhausted on account of their being unsatisfactory).

It can be seen that the European Court of Human Rights is very much a court of last resort. A person who thinks that his human rights have been abused will generally seek a remedy through the process of judicial review, which is explained in Chapter 2 at 2.6.1. The decisions of the Court are delivered in open court. Although the decision is binding on the State to which it is addressed, the Court cannot enforce it. If a violation is found the procedure is to send details to the Committee of Ministers of the Council of Europe, which confers with the State in violation to see how the judgment should be executed and future violations prevented. The Court can also, however, order 'just satisfaction', which could order the payment of compensation and costs. In *McCann* v *UK* (1995) 21 EHRR 97, which involved IRA members being shot dead by the SAS in Gibraltar, the United Kingdom was ordered to pay the legal costs of the relatives of the dead IRA men. These costs amounted to £38 000.

The Court does not use a system of precedent. It does, however, adhere to a doctrine of proportionality, meaning that every formality, condition, restriction or penalty must be proportionate to the end which is trying to be achieved. In interpreting the law the Court adopts a broad, purposive approach rather than a technical 'letter of the law' approach.

In 2006 the European Court of Human Rights awarded £3 350 damages and £1 340 costs to George Blake, the traitor who escaped from the United Kingdom to the Soviet Union, over the distress and frustration to him caused by the length of time the Government took in its legal action to prevent him benefiting from his autobiography. (The case itself is considered in Chapter 7 at 7.2.7.1.) The legal action took more than nine years to resolve. Part of this delay was the fault of Blake. However, the appeal to the Court of Appeal took 17 months and the appeal from there to the House of Lords took 31 months. These delays breached Blake's right to a fair trial. The European Court of Human Rights took five years and eight months to decide the case.

1.5.4 **The impact of the Human Rights Act**

In March 2009 Lord Hoffmann, the second most senior Law Lord, delivered the Judicial Studies Board Annual Lecture, in which he was highly critical of the European Court of Human Rights. In criticising the Court, Lord Hoffmann made it clear that he has no problem with either the European Convention on Human Rights or with the Human Rights Act 1998. Unlike the European Court of Justice in Luxembourg, the European Court of Human Rights in Strasbourg had no mandate to attempt to unify the laws of Europe. However, Lord Hoffmann said that the Court 'had been unable to resist the temptation to aggran-

dise its jurisdiction and to impose uniform rules on Member States'. In doing so, the Court ignored the fact that the trade-off between individual rights and effective government, and between the rights of one individual and another, would vary from country to country depending upon local circumstances and legal tradition. The European Court of Human Rights does have a 'margin of appreciation' under which Member States are given some latitude in applying the same abstract rights. However, Lord Hoffmann thought that the Court had not taken this nearly far enough. He accused the Court of considering itself to be the equivalent of the Supreme Court of the United States, 'laying down a federal law for Europe'. He thought that the Court did not enjoy the legitimacy which the Supreme Court enjoyed. This lack of legitimacy was caused not only by the Court exceeding its mandate but also by the quality of the judges. Each of the 47 countries contributes one judge. So the four smallest Member States, with a combined population of less than Islington, contribute four judges. Russia, with a population of 140 million, contributes only one judge. Lord Hoffmann also accused the European Court of Human Rights of introducing new concepts, such as environmental protection, into the European Convention on Human Rights when the treaty had not mentioned them. In a final criticism, he noted that the Court had a backlog of 100 000 applications, which would take over four years to clear. In 2008, 95 per cent of applications had been declared inadmissible but there was no summary mechanism for weeding out the hopeless cases.

In *R* v *Horncastle and others* [2009] UKSC 14, [2010] 2 WLR 47 four men who had been convicted of serious offences by the Court of Appeal made an appeal to the Supreme Court, alleging that they had not received a fair trial as required by Article 6 of the Convention. Two of the men were convicted of grievous bodily harm. Their victim had died of another cause by the time of the trial and the men were convicted 'to a decisive degree' upon a statement of the victim which was read at the trial. The two other men had been convicted of kidnapping. This conviction had been secured 'to a decisive extent' by a written statement of the victim, who had been so frightened that she had run away the day before the trial. Both statements were admissible as evidence under the Criminal Justice Act 2003. In January 2009 a decision of one of the Chambers of the ECHR, *Al-Khawaja and Tahery* v *UK* (2009) 49 EHRR 1, held that Article 6 had been breached because statements of a witness who was not present at the trial had been 'the sole or, at least, the decisive basis' of their conviction. The Supreme Court held that the defendants in *Horncastle* had received a fair trial. Even before the Convention had come into force the rule against 'hearsay' evidence had ensured that defendants received a fair trial in the way that Article 6 was designed to ensure. Furthermore, application of the 'sole or decisive rule' would cause practical difficulties if applied in England and *Al-Khawaja* did not establish that it was necessary to apply the rule. Lord Phillips, who gave a judgment with which the other six Supreme Court Justices all agreed, said,

> 'The requirement to "take into account" the Strasbourg jurisprudence will normally result in this Court applying principles that are clearly established by the Strasbourg Court. There will, however, be rare occasions where this Court has concerns as to whether a decision of the Strasbourg Court sufficiently appreciates or accommodates particular aspects of our domestic process. In such circumstances it is open to this Court to decline to follow the Strasbourg decision, giving reasons for adopting this course. This is likely to give the Strasbourg Court the opportunity to reconsider the particular aspect of the decision that is in issue, so that there takes place what may prove to be a valuable dialogue between this Court and the Strasbourg Court. This is such a case.'

Lord Brown distinguished *Secretary of State for the Home Department* v *AF (No.3)* [2009] UKHL 28, [2009] 3 WLR 74. In that case the House of Lords had felt that it had no alternative but to apply a definitive judgment of the Grand Chamber, *A* v *UK* (2009) 49 EHRR 29, on the very point at issue. In *SSHD* v *AF* Lord Rogers had said, 'Strasbourg has spoken, the case is closed.' Lord Hope agreed with this point of view as *SSHD* v *AF* was not only a decision of the Grand Chamber but was much more clearly reasoned than the Chamber's ruling in *Al-Khawaja*.

In a speech given in Jerusalem in March 2011, Lord Judge, the Lord Chief Justice, defended the judiciary against accusations that they were making inappropriate human rights rulings. Explaining that their hands were tied, he said:

> 'What, however, needs to be examined, is the way in which the criticism of "Human rights" and the judgments made by reference to them, is that the incorporation of the Convention, and the statutory requirement that the decisions of the European Court of Justice must be applied (whether we judges in the United Kingdom agree with them or not), and the decisions of the European Court of Human Rights must be taken into account, represents the law of the United Kingdom as decided in Parliament by the ordinary legislative process. Judges are obliged to apply the legislation enacted by our sovereign Parliament, and the European Communities Act 1972 and the Human Rights Act 1998 are two such Acts. No more and no less.'

He criticised lawyers for inappropriately using ECHR authorities and said that ECHR authorities should not be cited if a Supreme Court decision had overruled them. However, he was not, as he made very clear, advocating any particular changes.

Test your understanding 1.5

1. Which courts have the power to make a declaration of incompatibility? What is the effect of such a declaration?
2. Can new UK legislation be passed by Parliament if it is incompatible with the Convention?
3. What is the position of public authorities under the Human Rights Act?
4. In what circumstances can an individual bring a case before the Court of Human Rights?

Key points

General matters
■ Many of the features of the English legal system have their roots in mediaeval England.
■ English law has not been codified to a great extent.

■ The English system of trial is adversarial. The lawyers representing one party try to prove the case. The lawyers representing the other party use whatever means permissible to prevent the case from being proved.

→

■ Law which originated in the King's or Queen's courts is known as common law and is contrasted with law which originated in the courts of equity, which is known as equity.

■ Any court can now apply both common law and equitable principles.

■ The criminal law is designed to punish wrongdoers who have broken the criminal law. The civil law is designed to compensate those who have been caused loss or injury by the wrongdoing of another.

■ In criminal cases the prosecution must prove the accused's guilt beyond reasonable doubt. In civil cases the claimant must prove his case on a balance of probabilities.

■ It can be important to distinguish between law and fact for three reasons: only statements of law can become precedents; an appeal may only be possible against a question of law, or may be required to be made to a different court depending upon whether the appeal is against a finding of law or fact; and, in Crown Court trials the judge decides the law but the jury decide the facts.

Legislation

■ Bills are introduced into Parliament by the Government. (A very small number of Bills are introduced by individual MPs.)

■ To become a statute, a Bill must pass through both Houses of Parliament and gain the Royal Assent. A Bill which does not pass through the House of Lords can be enacted without approval of the House of Lords after a delay of one year.

■ A codifying Act reduces the existing law to one comprehensive statute. A consolidating Act re-enacts as one Act several pieces of legislation which concern the same subject. An amending Act alters some of the sections of an existing Act.

■ Delegated legislation is passed other than as a statute. Once passed it has the same effect as a statute. Statutory instruments are introduced by Government Ministers upon whom power has been conferred by an enabling Act. Orders in Council are introduced by the Privy Council. Bye-laws are passed by local authorities.

■ The literal rule of statutory interpretation requires that unambiguous words in a statute are given their ordinary, literal meaning.

■ The golden rule allows the court to avoid giving the words in a statute a meaning which is manifestly absurd. It also allows a court to prefer the less absurd or undesirable interpretation when the words of a statute are ambiguous.

■ The mischief rule allows a court to be guided by consideration of the problem which the statute sought to rectify.

■ The *ejusdem generis* rule is that where general words in a statute follow specific words the general words must be interpreted as having the same type of meaning as the specific words.

■ The rule *expressio unius est exclusio alterius* means that where a statute lists specific words which are not followed by any general words then the statute applies only to the words listed.

■ In the very limited circumstances set out in **Pepper v Hart** a court may consider Parliamentary material when interpreting a statute.

Judicial precedent

■ The doctrine of judicial precedent holds that the decisions of higher-ranking courts are binding upon lower-ranking courts.

■ The courts are arranged in an hierarchical structure. The decisions of the Supreme Court (formerly House of Lords) bind all inferior courts. Decisions of the Court of Appeal bind all inferior courts and, almost always, future sittings of the Court of Appeal. Decisions of the Divisional Court of the High Court bind other High Court judges sitting alone and all inferior courts. They also generally bind future sittings of the Divisional Court. Decisions of High Court judges sitting alone bind inferior courts but do not bind other High Court judges.

■ The binding element in a case is the *ratio decidendi*, which might be defined as any statement of law which the judge applied to the facts of the case and upon which the decision in the case is based.

■ Statements of law made by a judge which are not part of the *ratio decidendi* are known as *obiter dicta*. These are of persuasive authority only.

■ A statute or a higher court may overrule a decision, in which case the overruled decision ceases to operate as a precedent.

■ A decision is reversed when an appellate court allows an appeal. No rule of law is necessarily changed.

→

■ A judge can refuse to follow a precedent by distinguishing it, that is by saying that the facts of the case in front of him are materially different from the facts of the case which created the precedent.

The European Union

■ The United Kingdom became a member of the EU in 1973. The European Communities Act 1972 provided that Community law should be directly applicable in the UK courts.

■ The Council of the European Communities is the main policy-making body of the EU. Membership of the Council varies, being made up of relevant Ministers of the Member States.

■ Each Member State has one Commissioner and some of the larger States have two. (However, after the Treaty of Nice is fully effective, each Member State will have a maximum of one.) The Commission makes broad EU policy and drafts secondary legislation. It also ensures that Member States adhere to the Treaties.

■ The European Parliament does not pass legislation. It has a consultative role which is becoming increasingly powerful.

■ Treaty Articles and EU Regulations are directly applicable. This means that they automatically form part of the domestic law of Member States.

■ EU legislation can only be relied upon by an individual in a legal action if it has direct effect. It will only have direct effect if it satisfies the *Van Gend* criteria of being sufficiently clear, precise and unconditional.

■ EU legislation which has only direct vertical effect may only be invoked by an individual against the State or against an emanation of the State. Legislation which has direct horizontal effect may be invoked by one individual against another.

■ Before their implementation date, Directives have no effect (subject to the *Wallonie* principle). After their implementation date they can have direct vertical affect but not direct horizontal effect. This is only likely to be of importance where they are not properly implemented by UK legislation.

■ The European Court of Justice expresses authoritative opinions on EU law when requested to do so by the national courts of Member States.

The Human Rights Act 1998

■ The United Kingdom signed the European Convention on Human Rights in 1951.

■ The Human Rights Act 1998 incorporates the Convention into UK law, but preserves Parliamentary sovereignty.

■ When determining a question which has arisen in connection with a Convention right, a UK court must take into account any decisions of the European Court of Human Rights.

■ As far as it is possible to do so, UK legislation must be read and given effect in a way which is compatible with the Convention rights.

■ A precedent-making court can make a declaration that UK legislation is incompatible with a Convention right. The relevant Minister would then have to consider amending or revoking the UK legislation, but would have the power to leave the legislation in place.

■ New legislation requires positive consideration by the relevant Minister as to whether or not it is compatible with the Convention. However, the Government may still introduce legislation which is incompatible with the Convention.

■ A public authority may not act in a way which is incompatible with a Convention right. However, this is not the case if the public authority could not have acted differently on account of UK legislation. Individuals are given the power to sue public authorities which breach this duty.

■ The major rights set out in the Convention are: the right to have one's life preserved by law; the right not to be subject to torture or inhumane or degrading punishment; the right not to be held in slavery or servitude or required to perform forced or compulsory labour; the right to liberty and security of the person; the right to a fair trial; the right not to be made retrospectively guilty of a criminal offence; the right to respect for private and family life; the right to freedom of thought, conscience and religion; the rights to freedom of assembly and freedom of association with others; and, the right to marry a member of the opposite sex.

■ An individual can only bring a case before the Court of Human Rights after all domestic remedies have been exhausted.

■ Protocols have added that every natural or legal person is entitled to peaceful enjoyment of his possessions, that no one should be denied the right to education, that States must agree to conduct free elections at regular intervals by secret ballot so as to allow the people to choose freely the legislature and that the death penalty is outlawed.

Summary questions

1 Explain the process by which a statute is enacted.

2 Using the newspapers or the Internet, find a recent statute, a recent statutory instrument and a recent rule of law made by a court. In each case, outline the process by which the law in question was made.

3 Explain the three main rules of statutory interpretation.

4 Outline the way in which the system of precedent operates. Do you think that the advantages of the system outweigh the disadvantages?

5 Explain the difference between EU law being directly applicable and its being directly effective.

6 Explain the impact of the Human Rights Act 1998 on UK law. Find a case concerning the Act either in a newspaper or on the Internet. Which Articles of the Convention did the case concern? Describe the outcome of the case or, if it has not yet been decided, state what you think the outcome of the case might be.

Multiple choice questions

1 Which one of the following statements is not true?

a Principles of law may still be classified as equitable, but both common law and equitable principles can now be applied by all courts.

b Equitable remedies are discretionary and can be withheld from those who have acted inequitably.

c In a criminal trial the prosecution must prove the accused's guilt beyond reasonable doubt. In a civil trial the claimant must prove his case on a balance of probabilities.

d An act committed by a person cannot give rise to both civil and criminal liability.

2 Which one of the following statements is not true?

a The power to pass a statutory instrument is conferred by an enabling Act.

b Once properly passed, a statutory instrument can give a Minister the power to alter a statute without the need to pass an amending Act.

c The courts have no power to declare either a statute or a statutory instrument void.

d Some Acts of Parliament are introduced as Bills by individual MPs, rather than by the Government of the day.

3 Which one of the following statements is not true?

a All deliberate statements of law made by the Supreme Court when deciding a case will be binding upon all inferior courts.

b The Court of Appeal is almost always bound by its own previous decisions.

c The decisions of the Divisional Court are binding on High Court judges sitting alone, but the decisions of High Court judges sitting alone are not binding upon other High Court judges.

d Circuit judges do not make precedents.

e A court which distinguishes a case refuses to follow an apparently binding precedent on the grounds that the facts of the case which created the precedent are materially different from the facts of the case it is considering.

4 Consider the following statements.

i The European Parliament enacts EU legislation, but its power to do this is very much subject to the control of the European Commission and the European Council.

ii EU legislation which is directly applicable in Member States cannot always be relied upon by an individual in a legal action.

iii Whether EU legislation has direct vertical effect will depend upon whether it is sufficiently clear, precise and unconditional as to satisfy the *Van Gend* criteria.

iv Regulations which are directly applicable will have only direct vertical effect, whereas Treaty Articles which are directly applicable will always have direct vertical and horizontal effect.

v Only the House of Lords can refer a case to the European Court of Justice, which acts as a final court of appeal on issues of EU law.

Which of the above statements are true?

a i, ii and iv only.

b ii and iii only.

c ii, iv and v only.

d ii, iii and v only.

5 Which one of the following statements is not true?

a The European Court of Human Rights is the highest court of the European Union.

→

b New legislation which is incompatible with a Convention right can still be passed by the UK Parliament.

c It is now possible for a person to sue a public authority for breach of a Convention right.

d Even if a precedent-making court makes a declaration of incompatibility, the relevant Minister will not need to ensure that the UK legislation is amended so as to become compatible with Convention rights.

Task 1

Your employer has asked you to draw up a report, briefly explaining the following matters:

a The different senses in which the expression 'common law' is used.

b How statutes and delegated legislation are passed.

c The main rules of statutory interpretation.

d The way in which the system of judicial precedent operates.

e The ways in which EU law is created and the effect of EU law in the UK.

f The effect of the Human Rights Act 1998.

mylawchamber *premium*

Visit **www.mylawchamber.co.uk/macintyre** to access study support resources including interactive multiple-choice questions, weblinks, glossary, glossary flashcards, legal newsfeed, answers to questions in this chapter, legal updates and an overview of this chapter all linked to the **Pearson eText** version of *Business Law* which you can **search**, **highlight** and **personalise** with your **own notes** and **bookmarks**.

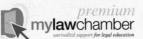

Use **Case Navigator** to read in full some of the key cases referenced in this chapter with commentary and questions:

Carlill v Carbolic Smoke Ball Co. [1893] 1 QB 256
Gregg v Scott [2005] 4 All ER 812

2

The courts and legal personnel

2.1 THE CIVIL COURTS

The civil courts are arranged in an hierarchical structure. If a civil dispute reaches the stage of litigation it will commence either in the county court or in the High Court. An appeal against the decision of the county court can be made to a High Court judge. An appeal against a decision of the High Court can be made to the Court of Appeal, and from there to the Supreme Court. Unless a point of law of public importance is at stake, or unless an appeal is likely to clarify a point of law, permission to appeal will be granted only when the appeal has a real prospect of success. A party wishing to appeal can either seek oral permission from the court which heard the case or can make a written application, within 14 days, to the court which would hear the appeal. An outline of the structure of the civil courts is shown in Figure 2.1.

2.1.1 County courts

There are 216 county courts in England and Wales, and at least one circuit judge and one district judge is assigned to each court. A business dispute is likely to involve a claim for breach of contract or a claim in tort. As regards both of these matters the county court has unlimited jurisdiction to hear the case. The High Court also has unlimited jurisdiction to hear contract and tort cases as long as the case involves a claim for more than £15 000. However, if the claim includes a claim for personal injuries the claim must be for at least £50 000. The value of the action is the amount which the claimant reasonably expects to recover.

Even where a claim is for a large enough sum of money to make litigation in the High Court a possibility, there is a presumption that a claim should be made in the county court rather than the High Court.

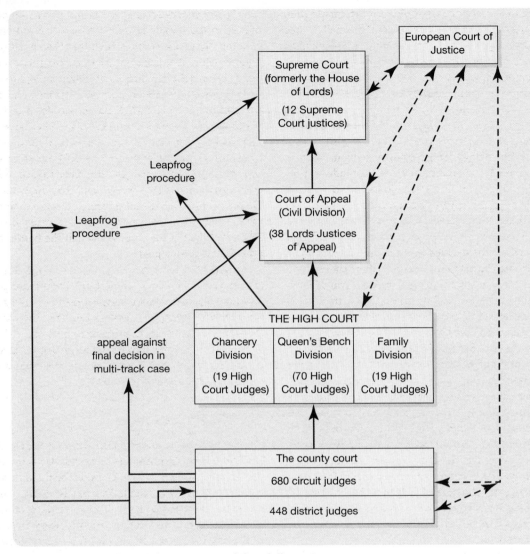

Figure 2.1 An outline of the structure of the civil courts

This presumption might be rebutted on one of three main grounds. First, the claimant believes that the case should be started in the High Court by reason of the amount being claimed. Second, a claim might be brought in the High Court if the claimant believed that the case was sufficiently complex to warrant this. Third, the case might be brought in the High Court if the outcome of the case was of importance to the public in general. (This last reason reflects the fact that the decisions of the High Court can amount to binding judicial precedents, whereas decisions of the county court cannot. See Chapter 1 at 1.3.2.1.)

As well as jurisdiction in contract and tort cases, as described above, the county court can hear equity actions (such as those involving a trust or a will) where the value of the trust or estate is not more than £30 000. It hears claims for salvage which do not exceed £15 000, as well as certain divorce matters, and certain bankruptcy and insolvency matters. Claims to enforce regulated consumer credit agreements must be commenced in the county court. Defamation cases cannot be heard in the county court unless both parties have agreed in writing that they should be.

Generally the district judge, who is junior to the circuit judge, will hear uncontested cases, as well as claims for mortgage repossessions and cases which are allocated to the small claims track. (Below at 2.3.1 we shall see that straightforward claims for not more than £5 000 are generally allocated to the small claims track.) The circuit judge hears the more complex claims and those in which the amount claimed is greater. If the amount claimed is over £25 000 the case should be heard by a circuit judge. If it is between £5 000 and £25 000 the case might be heard by either a district judge or a circuit judge. There are currently 680 circuit judges and 448 district judges. There are also around 800 part-time district judges, known as deputy district judges. Appeals from a district judge are made to a circuit judge. Appeals from a circuit judge are to the High Court. However, in two exceptional circumstances an appeal from a circuit judge can be made to the Court of Appeal. First, where the appeal is a second appeal, that is to say where the decision of the circuit judge is on an appeal from a district judge. Second, where the decision is a final decision (that is to say a decision which determines the entire proceedings) on a multi-track case. (See below at 2.3.) Third, there is a possibility of a leap-frog appeal to the Court of Appeal. (See below at 2.1.3.)

County court judgments are registered with the Registry of County Court Judgments and the register can be inspected by members of the public. A commercial creditor is likely to inspect it before making a loan. Once a county court judgment has been satisfied the judgment debtor's name will be removed from the register. If the judgment was satisfied within one month of judgment the entry on the register is cancelled altogether. If the judgment is satisfied later than one month after the date of judgment it can be noted as satisfied, but an entry will remain on the register. All entries are removed altogether six years after the date of judgment.

The county court does not have the responsibility of enforcing its judgment. It leaves this to the person in whose favour the judgment was given, the judgment creditor. However, the creditor can apply for oral examination of the judgment debtor in which case the debtor may be brought before the court to explain his financial position. Non-attendance is punishable by imprisonment.

County court judgments may be enforced in several ways. A warrant of execution against the debtor's goods allows bailiffs to take those goods, sell them and pay the judgment creditor out of the proceeds. The debtor can prevent this from happening by paying the amount due. A warrant of execution can generally be taken out without the court's permission, by filling in the appropriate form and paying the appropriate fee.

Third party debt orders require a third party who owes money to the judgment debtor to pay the judgment creditor. These proceedings might be taken against an amount held in a bank account. An attachment of earnings order will require the judgment debtor's employer to make regular deductions from his earnings and pay these amounts into court. A charging order over land (including the debtor's house) can sometimes be made and in effect this gives the judgment creditor a mortgage over the judgment debtor's land. The creditor will then be entitled to be paid in preference to most other creditors when the land is sold, and may apply for an order that the land is sold. Despite all these methods of enforcement, many county court judgments are not satisfied. Winning the case is only half the battle. The other half is getting paid.

Judgment debtors have the right to apply for an administration order if their total indebtedness is less than £5 000. Under such an order a list of all the debtor's creditors is drawn up. This list shows the amount owing to each creditor and the debtor is ordered to pay the whole amount owing by instalments. Some 1 879 000 non-family proceedings were started in the county court in 2009.

2.1.2 The High Court

The High Court is divided into three divisions: the Queen's Bench Division, the Chancery Division and the Family Division. Each Division hears different types of actions. The Family Division is, as the name suggests, concerned with family matters and is of little interest in a business context. The Chancery Division deals with matters which originated in equity, such as bankruptcy, mortgages, trusts, wills, company law and partnership law. It also deals with all forms of property and taxation disputes. It includes two specialist courts, the Companies Court and the Patents Court. The Companies Court deals with company liquidation. The Queen's Bench Division deals with common law disputes such as contract and tort cases and includes three specialist courts, the Commercial Court, the Technology and Construction Court and the Admiralty Court. Despite these allocations, any of the three Divisions can transfer a case to another Division. The Commercial Court hears cases involving import and export of goods, banking, insurance and financial services and can hear any case arising out of trade or commerce in general. The Commercial Court has its own specialist procedures, which are set out in a practice direction and in the Commercial Court Guide. These procedures are less formal than those generally used in the High Court, the rules of evidence being somewhat less rigid. The Technology and Construction Court deals with specialist matters relating to building work, engineering work, claims concerning computers and other cases which involve complex scientific or technical questions of fact.

Generally only one judge sits in a High Court case. Slightly junior judges, known as masters, hear some of the less complex High Court cases. Appeals from the High Court go to the Court of Appeal and from there to the Supreme Court. As regards both appeals, permission must be gained. Appeals from a master go first to a High Court judge and then to the Court of Appeal, although it is quite likely that permission for this second appeal will not be granted.

The High Court hears appeals from circuit judges in the county court. It also hears appeals from two criminal courts, the magistrates' court and the Crown Court. When these criminal appeals are heard they are heard by two or three High Court judges, and these courts are known as Divisional Courts. The Queen's Bench Divisional Court is of particular significance in relation to statutes which impose criminal liability on business. The Divisional Court hears appeals by way of case stated from the magistrates' court, tribunals or the Crown Court. An appeal by way of case stated can only be made against a decision of law made by the lower court. These appeals are generally made against decisions taken in the magistrates' court, but can be against decisions of the Crown Court if the case was one which was originally tried in the magistrates' court. The justices' clerk sends a draft case to the parties, and this may be amended after representations from the parties. The case states the facts of the case, the ruling given by the lower court and the question of law for the Divisional Court to consider. The Divisional Court can uphold the decision, reverse it, amend it or send it back to the lower court to make the decision which it thinks fit. The law made in this way is of greater value than the law made by ordinary High Courts. The decisions of ordinary sittings of the High Court are binding upon inferior courts, but not upon other High Courts. The decisions of the Divisional Court are binding upon other Divisional Courts, ordinary sittings of the High Court and inferior courts. The Chancery Divisional Court and the Family Divisional Court also hear appeals, but these are generally less significant in a business context.

We considered the jurisdiction of the High Court when considering the jurisdiction of the county court. There are currently 108 High Court judges, 70 of these sit in the Queen's Bench Division, 19 in the Chancery Division and 19 in the Family Division. The President of the Queen's Bench Division is the head of the Queen's Bench Division. The Vice-Chancellor is the head of the Chancery Division. The head of the Family Division is known as the President of the Family Division.

In 2009, 49 500 proceedings were started in the Chancery Division and 18 600 in the Queen's Bench Division.

2.1.3 The Court of Appeal (Civil Division)

The Court of Appeal is split into two divisions: the Civil Division and the Criminal Division. The Court of Appeal (Civil Division) hears appeals from the High Court, but does not hear appeals from the Divisional Courts. Permission to appeal must be granted. Appeals from a master in the High Court go first on appeal to a High Court judge and only then is there an appeal to the Court of Appeal. Exceptionally, the Court of Appeal may hear a 'leapfrog' appeal from a district judge, a circuit judge or a master. However, this will be possible only if an important point of principle or practice is to be considered, or if there is some other compelling reason for the Court of Appeal to hear the appeal.

A 'leapfrog' appeal can be made direct from the High Court to the Supreme Court if all parties consent, and the Supreme Court gives permission. In addition, the High Court judge must issue a certificate stating that the case involves an important point of law involving the interpretation of legislation or the case concerns a matter which has already been fully considered by the Court of Appeal or Supreme Court. (In which case neither the High Court nor the Court of Appeal would have the power to refuse to follow the earlier decision.) There is also a new leapfrog procedure whereby any appeal to a circuit judge or a High Court judge, from a district judge or a master, can be referred straight to the Court of Appeal. This can be done if the judge who was to hear the appeal, or the Master of the Rolls, considers that it raises an important point of principle or practice, or that there is some other compelling reason why the Court of Appeal should hear it.

There are 38 Lords Justices of Appeal, as Court of Appeal judges are known. Usually three judges sit when an appeal is heard, although sometimes a full court of five judges is invoked. Different batches of three judges sit as the Court of Appeal at the same time. The Master of the Rolls presides over the Civil Division of the Court of Appeal.

In 2009, the Court of Appeal Civil Division disposed of 1 225 appeals; 504 were allowed, 419 were dismissed after a hearing, 159 were dismissed with the consent of the parties and 4 were struck out.

2.1.4 **The Supreme Court**

The Supreme Court is the highest appellate court in Great Britain and Northern Ireland. It replaced the House of Lords on 1 October 2009, when 11 Law Lords became the first Supreme Court justices. The Supreme Court now has its full complement of 12 judges. A sitting of the House of Lords was generally comprised of five of the twelve Law Lords, although in recent years seven or nine judges sat in a number of important cases. (For example, seven judges sat in **Pepper** v **Hart**, which was considered in the previous chapter at 1.3.1.4.) It is envisaged that a panel of seven or nine judges will sit more frequently in the Supreme Court. The justices are known as My Lord or My Lady. They wear robes only for ceremonial events.

The Supreme Court hears appeals from the Court of Appeal. Before such an appeal can be made, leave to appeal is needed. The Court of Appeal hears such an application for leave to appeal and refers it to an Appeal Committee of three Supreme Court justices. This Committee can allow the barrister representing the appellant to make an oral argument. The first President of the Supreme Court, Lord Phillips of Worth Matravers, has indicated that in future he would like all Supreme Court justices to receive synopses of applications for leave to appeal, so that all of them can have some input.

In 2009, 40 appeals were presented to the House of Lords, 31 of these coming from the Civil Division of the Court of Appeal. Like the House of Lords before it, the Supreme Court will also hear appeals from the Scottish Court of Session and, occasionally, from the High Court when the leapfrog procedure is invoked. Typically, a case takes about two days to hear. The Supreme Court justices, like the Law Lords before them, always reserve their judgment, so they do not give a decision at the end of the case but at some later date. Lord Phillips hopes that the Supreme Court will, where possible, give one single judgment. If this is not possible he hopes that there will be one majority judgment and one dissenting one. In many cases the House of Lords gave 3:2 judgments in which all of the judges

said something different. (See, for example, **Shogun Finance Ltd** v **Hudson** at 6.2.3.1.) This made it very difficult to deduce the *ratio decidendi* of the case. Judgments of the Supreme Court are published on the Internet at www.supremecourt.gov.uk.

The main purpose behind the transformation of the House of Lords to the Supreme Court was to free the highest appellate court from the second house of Parliament and to remove the Law Lords from the legislature. The change is seen as increasing the judiciary's independence from both the legislature and the executive. The new court will be the Supreme Court of all of the United Kingdom: England, Wales, Scotland and Northern Ireland. It will sit in a building in Parliament Square, Middlesex Guildhall, rather than in Parliament itself. Although television cameras are not allowed in any other courts, interesting cases will be broadcast. Press summaries are issued about pending and decided cases and the public has access to the Supreme Court building so that they can watch cases. The first case to be heard concerned the power to freeze the assets of suspected terrorists and was deliberately chosen to be one of significant public interest.

The primary purpose of the Supreme Court is to give rulings on difficult points of law. It does not have the power to overturn legislation, as the US Supreme Court has, and will not gain such power unless the UK Constitution is significantly changed.

2.1.5 **The Judicial Committee of the Privy Council**

The Judicial Committee of the Privy Council (generally known as the Privy Council) is the final court of appeal for about 23 Commonwealth territories and 4 independent Republics within the Commonwealth which choose to use it. The origins of this court can be traced back to the Middle Ages, when the King would consult advisors known as the Privy Council. The Judicial Committee Act 1933 created the Judicial Committee of the Privy Council, as a court in which senior judges should hear legal appeals.

The Judicial Committee of the Privy Council is, in effect, made up of Supreme Court justices. Five of these justices sit in a case, sometimes accompanied by a judge from the country where the appeal originated. The judgment of the Council is usually delivered as one opinion. Prior to 1966 dissenting opinions were not allowed. It is still the case today that there will not be more than one dissenting opinion published, even if two of the justices dissent. Although technically of persuasive value only, decisions of the Privy Council are generally treated as Supreme Court decisions. In 2009, 69 appeals were made to the Privy Council and 47 were disposed of.

The Privy Council also has jurisdiction to hear appeals concerning misconduct of doctors, dentists, opticians and vets.

2.1.6 **The European Court of Justice (ECJ)**

In the previous chapter, at 1.4.3.1, we saw that the ECJ can express an authoritative opinion on EU law, if requested to do so by a national court, and that once the ruling has been made by the ECJ the case returns to the court which asked for the ruling so that that court can apply the ruling. We saw that Article 267 of the Treaty on the Functioning of the European Union allows a national court to request an authoritative ruling as to only three types of matters: the interpretation of the EC legislation; the validity and interpretation of acts of institutions of the Community; and the interpretation of statutes of bodies established by an act of the Council, where those statutes so provide. Any national court or tribunal may refer a matter within Article 267 to the ECJ if it thinks this necessary to give judgment. We also saw that a court of final appeal has an obligation to seek a preliminary ruling where a relevant point of EU law is at issue and where there has been no previous interpretation of the point by the ECJ. (Unless the point is so obvious as not to require a ruling.)

2.1.7 **Appeals**

The basic appeal structure is as follows.

From a district judge to a circuit judge and from there to the Court of Appeal. From a circuit judge to a High Court judge. (Unless the decision of the circuit judge was an appeal from a district judge or a final decision on a multi-track case, in which the appeal is to the Court of Appeal rather than to a High Court judge.) The Court of Appeal hears appeals from High Court judges (but not from Divisional Courts of the High Court) although it is possible for a 'leapfrog' appeal to be made direct to the Supreme Court. The Supreme Court hears appeals from the Court of Appeal. The Privy Council hears appeals from the highest courts in 27 Commonwealth territories and independent Republics.

In all but a few exceptional cases, permission to appeal is required. Permission will be granted only where the court considers that the appeal would have a real prospect of success, or there is some other compelling reason why the appeal should be heard. Permission to appeal from a decision of either the county court or the High Court is usually sought orally from the lower court which made the decision or from the court to which an appeal would lie. If the lower court refuses permission, permission may be sought from the court to which the appeal would lie. When the appeal court refuses permission to appeal it gives reasons for the refusal. The appellant can then ask the same court for an oral hearing to reconsider this decision but this may be made to the same judge as refused the appeal. This is almost always the end of the matter. However, the court which heard the appeal has the power to allow a further appeal to the Court of Appeal if the appeal raises an important principle of law or procedure or if there is some other compelling reason for the Court of Appeal to hear it. In exceptional circumstances the Court of Appeal or the High Court, but not the county court, can reopen proceedings if three conditions are satisfied: first, that it is necessary to do this to avoid real injustice; second, the circumstances are exceptional and make it appropriate to reopen the appeal; third, no alternative effective remedy is available. The Court of Appeal hears applications to appeal to the Supreme Court and refers them to an Appeals Committee of three Supreme Court justices.

In all civil cases an appeal is allowed, and the decision of the lower court reversed, only where either the decision was wrong or where the decision was unjust because of a serious procedural or other irregularity in the lower court proceedings.

Generally, the appeal court reviews the case rather than rehears it.

2.2 **THE CRIMINAL COURTS**

Criminal trials are conducted in either the magistrates' court or the Crown Court. Criminal offences are classified into three bands, according to their seriousness. Offences triable only on indictment are the most serious offences, such as murder, and these can be tried only in the Crown Court. The most minor offences, such as the majority of motoring offences, are triable only summarily and must be heard by the magistrates' court. Other offences, such as theft, are 'either way' offences, and may be tried either in the magistrates' court or in the Crown Court. The magistrates will decide whether they think the case should be tried summarily by the magistrates' court or on indictment in the Crown Court. Generally, the magistrates will opt for summary trial unless the offence is so serious that the sentences which could be passed by the magistrates' court would not be sufficiently severe. If the magistrates decide upon summary trial they must then ask the accused whether or not he consents to this or whether he wishes to opt for jury trial. They must explain to the accused that if he opts for summary trial he may nevertheless be sent to the Crown Court for sentence if the accused's character and history are subsequently found to be such that a sentence greater than that which could be passed by the magistrates is justified.

An outline of the structure of the criminal courts is shown in Figures 2.2 and 2.3.

2.2.1 **The magistrates' court**

There are 134 district judges (magistrates' courts) and slightly under 29 000 lay magistrates. The district judges (magistrates' courts) are full-time judges who used to be called stipendiary magistrates; 170 part-time deputy district judges (magistrates' courts) also sit. Magistrates' courts dispose of 98 per cent of criminal cases. Lay magistrates are not legally qualified. They sit as a bench, usually comprising three magistrates, whereas district judges (magistrates' courts) sit on their own. In a criminal case it is the job of the magistrates to decide the facts, that is to say whether the defendant is guilty or not guilty. If the defendant is guilty the magistrates also pass sentence upon him, although sometimes they commit him to the Crown Court for sentence. Lay magistrates should seek the advice of the clerk of the court, also known as a justice's clerk, in order to ascertain matters of law, sentencing or procedure. Magistrates' clerks are lawyers

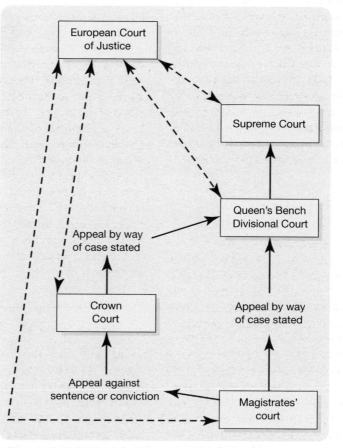

Figure 2.2 Structure of the criminal courts as regards summary offences

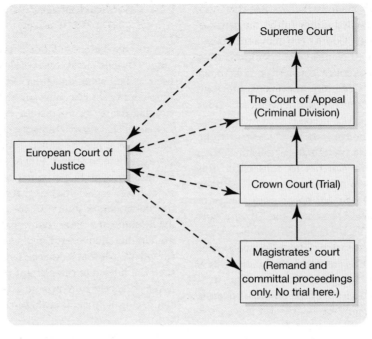

Figure 2.3 Structure of the criminal courts as regards indictable offences

who pursue a career as clerks. They may offer advice to the magistrates even when the magistrates have not sought it.

As well as hearing summary offences and most either way offences, magistrates' courts also have other duties. After a defendant's arrest they decide whether he should be given bail or remanded in custody. They conduct the committal proceedings if the defendant is to be committed to the Crown Court for trial. They have jurisdiction in some civil areas which affect children and families. They hear applications for various types of licences, such as liquor licences, and also deal with some types of civil debts, such as arrears of council tax. The Crime and Disorder Act 1998 empowers them to pass Anti-Social Behaviour Orders (ASBOs) against offenders aged ten or over.

Magistrates may commit those summarily convicted of an either way offence to the Crown Court for sentence if they feel that a punishment which is greater than they can impose is warranted. Magistrates may impose a fine of up to £5 000 and may pass sentences of up to six months in prison in respect of any one offence. Where the offences are triable either way, magistrates can pass two consecutive six month sentences, so that the defendant is sentenced to a total of 12 months in prison.

Defendants have a right to appeal against conviction or sentence to the Crown Court but must be made aware that the Crown Court may increase the sentence passed by the magistrates, as long as this does not exceed the maximum sentence which the magistrates could have passed. If the appeal is against conviction, which is only possible if the defendant pleaded not guilty in the magistrates' court, the case is reheard in the Crown Court. Such an appeal could be against the facts or the law. If the appeal is against sentence the prosecution generally outlines facts admitted or found by the magistrates, although a complete rehearing of the case is possible. However, if the appeal concerns a point of law it may be made to the Divisional Court by way of case stated, which is explained below at 2.2.3.

2.2.2 The Crown Court

The Crown Court sits in 77 centres in England and Wales. As explained earlier, the Crown Court conducts all trials of indictable offences and some trials where the crime was an either way offence. Generally, the Crown Court is staffed by a circuit judge, although sometimes a High Court judge sits. Offences range through four degrees of seriousness.

Class 1 offences, such as murder, are almost always tried by a High Court judge. Class 2 offences, such as rape, are also generally tried by a High Court judge. Class 3 offences, such as causing death by dangerous driving, may be tried by either a High Court judge or by a circuit judge. Class 4 offences, such as grievous bodily harm or an either way offence, are tried by a circuit judge.

The Crown Court may pass sentence on those summarily convicted of an either way offence if the magistrates commit to the Crown Court for sentence. Such a committal would generally be heard, like an appeal from the magistrates' court against sentence or conviction, by a circuit judge and two magistrates.

When a case is tried in the Crown Court the jury decide the facts, that is to say whether the defendant is guilty or not guilty. The judge sums up to the jury the matters which they should take into consideration in reaching their verdict. The judge also supervises the running of the trial, for instance deciding whether or not certain matters are admissible as evidence. If the defendant is found guilty, the judge passes sentence, although there is often a considerable delay while various reports are being made. Appeals against conviction or sentence are made to the Court of Appeal (Criminal Division).

2.2.3 The Divisional Court

The Queen's Bench Divisional Court hears appeals by way of case stated from the magistrates' court. It can also hear appeals by way of case stated from the Crown Court if the case was first tried in the magistrates' court and then appealed to the Crown Court. The appeal can only be on a point of law or on an argument that the magistrates exceeded their powers. Such cases are heard by two or more judges, at least one of whom will usually be the Lord Chief Justice or a Lord Justice of Appeal. If the prosecution appeals, the Divisional Court have the power to order the magistrates' court to convict a defendant who was acquitted by the magistrates. Many cases heard by way of case stated become important precedents. *Partridge* v *Crittenden* [1968] I WLR 1204, considered in Chapter 3 at 3.1.2, provides an example. The appeal to the Divisional Court was made by way of case stated from the magistrates' court. An appeal from a Divisional Court goes to the Supreme Court.

2.2.4 The Court of Appeal (Criminal Division)

The Criminal Division of the Court of Appeal is presided over by the Lord Chief Justice. This court hears appeals from the Crown Court, either against conviction or against sentence. Section 2 of the Criminal Appeal Act 1995 allows an appeal to the Court of Appeal (Criminal Division), against conviction in the Crown Court, on only three grounds: that the jury's verdict should be set aside as having been unsafe and unsatisfactory; that a wrong decision was taken as to a question of law; or that there was a material irregularity in the course of the trial. Appeals against acquittal can be made. These appeals might result in the law being amended, but will not mean that the defendant who was acquitted is subsequently convicted. When an appeal against sentence is made, the Court of Appeal may impose a greater sentence than that imposed by the Crown Court.

2.2.5 The Supreme Court

The Supreme Court hears appeals from the Court of Appeal (Criminal Division) and from the Queen's Bench Divisional Court. The Court of Appeal will need to certify that the case involves a point of law of general public importance. In addition, either the Court of Appeal or the Supreme Court must grant permission for the appeal to be made on the grounds that it is a case which ought to be made to the Supreme Court. The Privy Council's jurisdiction, explained above at 2.1.5, covers criminal appeals as well as civil appeals.

Test your understanding 2.1

1 In which two courts might a civil case be tried?

2 How will it be decided which of the two courts is the appropriate court to try the case?

3 From which courts does the Court of Appeal (Civil Division) hear appeals?

4 From which civil courts does the Supreme Court hear appeals?

5 In which two courts might a criminal case be tried? How will it be decided in which court the case should be tried?

6 What is an appeal by way of case stated?

7 To which court is an appeal against conviction by the magistrates' court, or against the sentence imposed by the magistrates' court, made?

> **8** From which courts do the Court of Appeal (Criminal Division) and the Supreme Court hear criminal appeals?

2.3 PROCEDURE IN THE CIVIL COURTS

In 1999 the Woolf reforms radically overhauled procedure in the civil courts. The reforms were brought about to give effect to the Woolf Report, which was produced by a committee chaired by Lord Woolf, the Master of the Rolls. This report found that the civil justice system was slow, expensive, bound by archaic procedures, excessively complicated and generally ill-suited to the needs of clients. These critical views were shared by a majority of those who had litigated in the courts. The adversarial culture of litigation meant that unnecessary delays and the deliberate running up of expenses were often used as a tactic to defeat the other side. In many types of disputes expensive expert witnesses were routinely produced by each side. Rather than helping the court to resolve a technical problem, these experts were seen as on the side of one or other of the parties and were subjected to partisan pressure by the other party's lawyers.

Lord Woolf's Report concluded that civil justice was in a state of crisis and therefore made recommendations for sweeping change. These changes have been brought about by New Civil Procedure Rules, the overriding objective of which is to enable the court to deal with cases justly.

One of the main features of the reforms is that the management of the case is removed from the hands of the litigants and passes to the judge. Under this new system of judicial case management the judge will first determine which of the three new tracks the case is to be on; the small claims track, the fast track or the multi-track. The judge will also set time scales by which certain procedures must have been completed. The judge's active management of the case requires him to do the following things: encourage cooperation between the parties to the case; encourage the parties to settle the case or part of the case; identify the true points at issue as early as possible and ensure that issues which do not require litigation are disposed of before the case is tried; decide the order in which issues will be resolved; consider whether the taking of any step is justified by the costs which this would involve; and to ensure that the case proceeds quickly and efficiently. Technology should be used wherever appropriate. As many aspects of the case as possible should be dealt with on the same occasion and the case may be dealt with without the parties having to attend court. If the case is to reach court, the judge sets out timetables for the hearing and supervises the control of the case. The courts have the power to decide the issues on which evidence will be allowed. They also have the power to decide the nature of evidence which is to be allowed and the way in which the evidence may be presented.

The judges have been trained to become unsympathetic to the old style of litigation. The court can ask a party to clarify a matter or provide additional information about it. It can shorten the time by which procedures must be completed. The time limits set by the court are rules, not targets. However, in appropriate circumstances the judge can increase time limits. The judge can identify preliminary issues which should be tried first and can dismiss a case or give judgment as soon as a certain preliminary issue has been decided. In many cases the parties will themselves settle the case after one preliminary issue has been decided.

Orders made by the court may be subject to conditions, such as the payment of money into court. If these conditions are not complied with the party in default may have his case struck out. Claims and defences which have no reasonable chance of success can be struck out. They can also be struck out if either a rule, a practice direction or a court order has not been complied with. Lesser sanctions are also available to the court. It may order a party in default to pay all or part of the costs of the case, refuse to allow interest on damages where the claimant is at fault, or order that interest is paid at a higher rate where the defendant is at fault. Procedural errors are not to invalidate any part of the proceedings unless the court exercises its discretion to order that they should. Furthermore, accidental errors or omissions can be corrected at any time and the court may do this on its own initiative.

The parties to a dispute are now actively encouraged to consider alternative dispute resolution (ADR). Moreover, the judge not only encourages the parties to seek ADR, but may also stay (suspend) the proceedings so that the parties can try to resolve their dispute by an alternative method. We examine the various methods of ADR below at 2.4.

Ten pre-action protocols have been drawn up. These protocols require that at the start the parties should identify the issues in dispute, the evidence available and how the disputed points should be resolved. The idea is that litigation is to be a last resort. A party who does not follow the letter and spirit of the protocols can be subject to a sanction. In a business context, three pre-action protocols are of particular significance, relating to professional negligence, clinical negligence and personal injury.

Perhaps the most significant of the new reforms is that cases will be allocated to one of the three tracks. Earlier we considered the jurisdiction of the county court and the High Court. The High Court only takes multi-track cases. The county court takes all fast-track cases and small claims, as well as some multi-track cases. A claim which is being defended will be allocated by the court to either the small claims track, the fast-track or the multi-track. Generally, this allocation will be made by a master or a district judge on the basis of a questionnaire completed by the parties. Each of the three tracks needs to be considered in turn. Before considering them, however, it is worth stressing the point that litigation should always be a last resort for any business. It is expensive, time-consuming, uncertain and very likely to destroy any business relationship which exists with the other party.

2.3.1 Making a claim

Once it has become apparent that a business dispute is not going to be resolved informally, one of the parties may initiate legal proceedings by issuing a claim against the other. First, a final letter should be sent to the other party, warning that a claim will be made if a satisfactory response to the claimant's demands is not received by a certain date. A claim is commenced by filling in a claim form. This is done whether the amount of money claimed is specified or unspecified and whether the claim is for a court order rather than for money. The form will require the claimant to state the value of the amount claimed. The particulars of the claim can either be attached to the claim itself or can be served on the defendant separately. These particulars set out a concise statement of the facts upon which the claimant is relying, and a statement of truth that the claimant believes the facts to be true. It is advisable for the claimant to state the remedy which he is seeking but it is not absolutely necessary to do this as the court may award a successful claimant any remedy to which he would be entitled. The claim, the particulars and a response pack are served

on the defendant, who must generally respond within 14 days or judgment can be given against him. If the defendant does respond, the response might take several forms. First, the defendant might pay the claim in full. Second, the defendant might file an acknowledgement of service if he cannot file a defence within 14 days or wants to dispute the court's jurisdiction to hear the case. The filing of an acknowledgement of service will give the defendant another 14 days in which to respond. Third, the defendant might admit some or all of the claim. If the admission is only partial he will also file a defence. If the claim is for an unspecified amount of money the defendant might offer a certain sum in satisfaction of the claim and might offer to pay this amount by instalments. Where a claim is admitted but the claimant does not accept the amount offered, or the rate at which this amount is to be paid, the claimant may nevertheless ask that judgment is entered in his favour. If this is done, the court will determine the amount of damages at a later hearing. Fourth, the defendant might file a defence. A defence must be specific as to the reason why specific allegations are denied, which allegations the claimant will have to prove, which allegations are admitted and any reason for disputing the value of the claim. The defendant might also make a counterclaim against the claimant, either as part of a defence or while admitting the claim.

The responses which the defendant might make, and the effect of these responses, are shown in Figure 2.4. Once a claim has been filed the court moves on to the process of allocating the claim to one of the three tracks.

2.3.2 The small claims track

Cases other than personal injury cases are likely to be allocated to the small claims track if they satisfy three criteria. First, they must be straightforward claims for not more than £5 000. (This amount can be greater if both parties agree to allocation to the small claims track.) Second, the case should not involve a substantial amount of preparation before the hearing. Third, the case should not be one where large legal costs will be incurred.

The third requirement reflects the fact the small claims procedure has been designed so that the parties have the option of conducting their own case without legal representation. However, litigants on the small claims track can be represented by lawyers if they so wish.

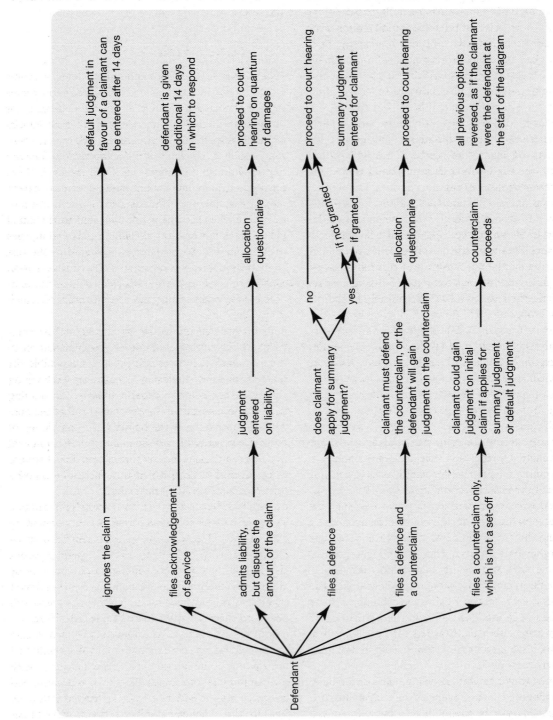

Figure 2.4 An outline of the effect of the defendant's responses to a claim which has been served

Special rules apply to personal injury cases and to landlord and tenant disputes. Personal injury cases will only be allocated to the small claims track where the total amount of the claim is not more than £5 000 and the claim for general damages for personal injuries is not more than £1 000. Claims concerning landlord and tenant are of little significance for the purposes of this book. In broad terms, an allocation will only be made to the small claims track where the tenant is claiming damages of not more than £1 000 or where he is asking that the landlord be ordered to complete repairs which will cost not more than £1 000.

Generally, a small claims case will involve only one hearing in front of a district judge. The parties will be required to file and serve copies of all relevant documents, including any expert's report. However, expert evidence cannot be admitted in a small claim hearing unless the court consents and such consent would not usually be granted. The originals of documents must be brought to the hearing. The judge can hold a preliminary hearing, although this is discouraged. A preliminary hearing might be used to clarify a claim or to dispose of a claim which has no real chance of success. On rare occasions, the judge may decide the case by a 'paper disposal', without any hearing at all.

The district judge has considerable leeway as to the proceedings at the hearing. The hearing is informal and the strict rules of evidence do not apply. The judge will probably appoint each side the same amount of time to present their evidence and give an immediate decision at the conclusion of the case.

Generally each side will pay its own costs. The only costs recoverable will usually be the costs involved in issuing the claim. However, the district judge has a discretion to allow costs for travelling expenses, loss of earnings and an expert's fee. The amount of costs for the expert's fee cannot exceed £200 (and the emphasis is very strongly against experts appearing in small claims hearings) and the amount of costs for lost earnings cannot exceed £50 per day. If a party behaves unreasonably the court can penalise him by ordering him to pay costs.

Appeals against small claims decisions can be made to a circuit judge, but such appeals are most unusual. The appeal cannot be made on fact, but only on the grounds that there was a mistake of law or a serious irregularity in the way in which the case was conducted. Where an appeal is made, the circuit judge will give a decision and will not order a rehearing of the case.

2.3.3 **The fast track**

Cases other than landlord and tenant cases, or claims which include a claim for personal injury, will generally be allocated to the fast track if the claim is for not more than £25 000 and there is not a substantial amount of pre-hearing preparation. However, these cases will not be allocated to the fast track if they are expected to last for longer than one day or if there is likely to be a substantial amount of oral expert evidence at the trial. We saw earlier that a claim of not more than £5 000 is not allocated to the small claims track if it involves a claim for personal injuries of over £1 000. Such cases are allocated to the fast track. We also saw that some claims for less than £1 000 by a tenant against a landlord were not allocated to the small claims track. These too are allocated to the fast track.

It is expected that a fast track case will be completed 30 weeks after allocation. Upon allocation to the fast track the court will set out a timetable for matters such as disclosing documents, exchanging witness statements and expert's reports, the sending of listing questionnaires by the courts so that the date and length of the trial can be fixed, the completing of these questionnaires and the hearing itself. Financial penalties can be imposed on parties who do not adhere to the timetable. Postponement of the trial is a possibility, but is very much a last resort.

A one day fast-track trial actually runs for five hours. The judge will begin with a certain amount of reading time and then brief opening speeches will be made by the lawyers. The majority of the time, perhaps about three hours, will be for examination of witnesses by the two sides. Both the defendant and the claimant will make closing submissions to the judge, who will prepare and deliver judgment and assess the costs.

If extensive oral expert evidence is needed, a case is not suitable for the fast track. In a fast-track trial each party can be allowed one expert per issue, with a maximum of two issues. However, the court will appoint an independent expert, instructed jointly by both parties, wherever possible and will strive to cut down on expert evidence. Generally, expert evidence would be found in written reports rather than given orally at the trial.

2.3.4 **The multi-track**

Claims which are not suitable for the small claims track or the fast track are allocated to the multi-track. This usually means cases where the amount claimed is substantially over £25 000, or cases which are likely to take more than one day in court or in which there will be substantial expert evidence. In addition, a claim will be allocated to the multi-track where the court is likely to have to decide a substantial question of fact. A multi-track case is heard either by a circuit judge or a High Court judge.

As the name suggests, the multi-track allows the court considerable flexibility in dealing with the claim. The case will be judicially managed but there is no standard procedure. Whereas a fast-track case is likely, but not certain, to follow a pre-arranged procedure, multi-track cases adopt the procedure to meet the needs of the case. A party may indicate in the allocation questionnaire that he thinks that it will be necessary to have a case management conference, which is similar to an ordinary business meeting. At such a conference a judge, usually a master or a district judge, will try to identify the issues in dispute. The lawyers attending the meeting must be familiar with the case. They must also have the authority to deal with matters which arise. The court has the power to order the clients to attend. We have already seen that case management would, among other things, encourage the parties to cooperate with each other in the conduct of the proceedings, fix timetables for the case and give directions to ensure the speedy and efficient progress of the trial. The claimant may be asked to provide a case summary, which should generally not be of more than 500 words and which the defendant can be asked to agree to. The summary might set out the issues of fact which are agreed, the issues of fact which are in dispute, and the evidence which will be needed in order to ascertain the facts.

The judge can alter the standard rules on disclosure of documents so as to fit the needs of the particular case. The judge will also determine the extent to which experts are needed. In many multi-track cases it would not be appropriate to insist upon one expert appointed by both sides.

If the case involves complex issues the court may order a pre-trial review. This would usually take place about one or two months before the trial and would be presided over by the trial judge. This review would consider whether any preliminary issues could be sorted out, and then analyse how the trial should run. The order in which issues are to be decided should be set out. Information technology requirements should be set out, as well as the order of witnesses and the way in which the trial documents will be organised. The clients should attend, along with the lawyers who will argue the case.

After the trial itself, the judge may either deliver the judgment, or may reserve judgment until a later date. The assessment of costs will be made after the judgment is given. An appeal from a decided multi-track case goes to the Court of Appeal, whether the case was heard by a circuit judge or a High Court judge.

2.4 ALTERNATIVE DISPUTE RESOLUTION

Litigation should always be a last resort for a business. The disadvantages are manifest. The first and most obvious problem is that the whole process is likely to prove costly. If the case is lost, the loser will have to pay not only his own legal costs but also the costs of the other party. Even if the case is won full legal costs are not always recovered. Costs incurred in attending court as a witness are recoverable, but costs in respect of time spent instructing a solicitor are not. There is also the danger, particularly when the case concerns securing the payment of a debt, that the other side will become insolvent. It is bad enough that even though the case is won the bill is not paid. It is worse still that legal costs have been incurred and these too are not recoverable. In such circumstances it will generally be much better to compromise and get paid something.

A second problem is that litigation is complex. Despite the new rules of procedure the litigants may not always be fully aware of how the case is proceeding. Litigating is also a major worry and the stress involved can mean there are health as well as financial risks. Nor is litigation speedy. It may be quicker than it was before the recent reforms, but a fast track case will only be resolved some six months after allocation and a multi-track is likely to take considerably longer.

A third problem is that litigation creates lasting ill-feeling. If a business sues a customer then, win or lose, this is likely to be the end of the business relationship. If the dispute can be settled amicably the parties may continue to do business with each other.

Yet another disadvantage is that litigation takes place in open court. A typical case might involve a claim for the price of goods, where the buyer alleges that the goods were not of satisfactory quality. The seller will not want the allegations to be aired in open court. Nor will the buyer want it to be publicly claimed that he does not pay his bills. Alternative dispute resolution (ADR) can avoid this bad publicity.

Before considering arbitration, mediation and conciliation, it should be realised that the vast majority of disputes are settled by the parties themselves. Generally, there will be an exchange of correspondence and, perhaps after a period of negotiation, the claimant will agree to withdraw the action in return for the defendant paying a sum of money or agreeing to other conditions.

2.4.1 Arbitration

When the parties to a dispute agree to refer the dispute to arbitration they agree that their dispute should be resolved by an arbitrator rather than by a court. Having made such an agreement the parties are stuck with it. In commercial disputes arbitration may be very similar to litigation, especially if the arbitrator is a judge or a master from the Commercial Court. The rules of procedure may be very similar to those of the High Court and the lawyers representing the parties may be required to act much as they would in the High Court. All of this means that the proceedings might not be much cheaper than litigation, if any cheaper at all. The big advantage is that the case would be resolved in private. The procedure might also be speedier than litigation.

The Arbitration Act 1996 was needed because prior to the Act coming into effect three separate Arbitration Acts, the 1950, 1975 and 1979 Acts, were all in force and it was extremely difficult to know exactly what the law on arbitration was. Arbitrators were also very prone to a challenge by one of the parties, which would bar them from hearing the case. This was particularly the case where arbitrators tried to settle the case in a proactive way. Consequently, the High Court rules of procedure and evidence tended to be followed slavishly to prevent a challenge. Challenges to an arbitrator's jurisdiction to hear the case were an extremely common delaying tactic. The arbitrator could not decide upon his own jurisdiction and so a lengthy referral to a court was necessary.

The new Act has mandatory sections and non-mandatory sections, out of which the parties may contract.

Section 1 of the Arbitration Act 1996 provides that:

'The provisions of this Part are founded on the following principles and shall be construed accordingly–

(a) the object of arbitration is to obtain a fair resolution of disputes by an impartial tribunal without unnecessary delay or expense;

(b) the parties should be free to agree how their disputes are resolved, subject only to such safeguards as are necessary in the public interest;

(c) in matters governed by this Part the court should not intervene except as provided by this Part.'

Section 33(a) requires that the arbitrator should act fairly and impartially as between the parties, giving each party a reasonable opportunity of putting his case and dealing with that of the opponent. Section 33(b) makes it plain that the arbitrator has no need to follow High Court procedures. It requires that the arbitration adopts procedures suitable to the circumstances of the particular case, avoiding unnecessary delay or expense, so as to provide a fair means for the resolution of the matters falling to be determined. Section 33 is mandatory, but s.34, which is non-mandatory, allows the arbitrator to decide all procedural and evidential matters.

There are now fewer challenges to the arbitrator's jurisdiction and unjustified challenges are not dealt with sympathetically. Section 34, a non-mandatory section, allows the arbitrator to decide upon his own jurisdiction to hear the case. It also allows the arbitrator to use an inquisitorial approach to deciding the facts and the law.

A mandatory section, s.40, requires that the parties shall do all things necessary for the proper and expeditious conduct of the arbitral proceedings. This includes complying without delay with procedural and evidential matters and, where it is necessary to gain a preliminary judgment of a question of law from a court, getting such a judgment without delay.

Section 9 allows a party to apply for a stay of the proceedings if the other party brings court proceedings in respect of a matter which it has been agreed should be resolved by arbitration. The court will grant a stay unless satisfied that the arbitration agreement is null and void, inoperative or incapable of being performed.

Section 65, which is non-mandatory, allows the arbitrator to determine that the costs of the proceedings should be limited to a certain amount.

An agreement may be referred to arbitration either by the court, or by an Act of Parliament, or by the parties themselves. The parties may refer the dispute to arbitration by a term of a contract which is in dispute, or by agreement once a dispute has arisen. A court may refer one specific point to arbitration or, if the parties agree or if the case will involve lengthy examination of scientific documents, it may refer the whole case. Several Acts of Parliament refer disputes to arbitration. Legal aid is not available in respect of arbitration proceedings. This may prove a considerable hindrance to those of limited means.

2.4.2 Mediation

As regards litigation and arbitration the dispute is resolved for the parties by an independent body. Mediation is different, in that the parties themselves agree to any resolution of the dispute. The mediator's role is to try and facilitate such an agreement. There are no fixed rules as to how mediation might operate. Generally, however, the parties would first present an outline of their case to each other, in the presence of the mediator and reply to the other party's case. The mediator will set out the rules, trying to keep matters simple and striving to identify the key issues in dispute. Then the two sides will probably repair to different rooms and the mediator will spend time with one group, before passing on the position of that party to the other party. A large number of such visits might need to be made and ideally the parties should move closer to agreement until they finally agree to settle. It is not always the case that those taking part in mediation are genuinely attempting to settle the case. They might merely be trying to find out the strengths and weaknesses of the other party's case. Mediators report that many disputes which are not settled during the mediation are settled shortly afterwards. The Civil Mediation Council has set up a National Mediation Helpline to give civil court users advice and information about mediation. The Helpline does not itself provide mediation but, after having asked about the dispute, is able to pass the details on to a mediation provider who has been approved by the Civil Mediation Council. Such a mediator will provide services for a set fee and for a set time. For a small claim case the fee is £50 plus VAT per hour and the time allowed is one or two hours. For a 'fast track' case it is £300 plus VAT for three hours. For a 'multi-track' case it is £425 for four hours. Additional time is provided at pro rata rates. However, when a claim is for more than £50 000 the parties to the case must agree the fee with the mediator.

The Court of Appeal and the Commercial Court both have mediation schemes. Some county courts have piloted mediation schemes over several years, and one particular scheme, the Manchester Court Mediation Scheme, is to be rolled out to all county courts.

2.4.3 Conciliation

Conciliation is similar to mediation except that the conciliator actually suggests a basis for settlement to the parties. In Chapter 21 we shall see that ACAS attempts to conciliate between the parties before an employment dispute is taken to an employment tribunal.

Both mediation and conciliation suffer from the problem that they may well prove futile in that no settlement will be reached or become any closer.

2.4.4 Other types of ADR

Other types of ADR include: Neutral Evaluation by a third party who gives a non-binding view of the case; Expert Determination, which allows an independent expert to decide an issue; Neutral Fact Finding, whereby a neutral expert comes to a non-binding decision on a complex, technical issue of fact; and Med-arb, which is a combination of mediation and arbitration – first the parties mediate but if this is not successful they take the dispute to arbitration.

2.4.5 Tribunals

Various Acts of Parliament have established tribunals to hear certain types of cases. These tribunals hear very many more cases than are heard by the county court or the High Court. Tribunals might exercise administrative or judicial functions. Those exercising a judicial function act in the same way as a court.

It is not possible to take a dispute to a tribunal unless the dispute concerns the particular type of matter with which the tribunal deals. If the dispute does concern such a matter then a dispute cannot be taken before the ordinary courts, but must be dealt with by the relevant tribunal. The matters with which the major tribunals deal can be deduced from their names.

There are many different types of tribunals, dealing with matters such as social security, child support, asylum and immigration and employment disputes. In the study of business law the tribunals of real significance are the employment tribunals and the

Employment Appeal Tribunal. The nature of these tribunals is explained in Chapter 20. The procedure used in an employment tribunal is examined in Chapter 21 at 21.20.

Typically a tribunal will consist of three members, one of whom, the chairman, will be legally qualified. The two lay members will have some expert knowledge of the area of law with which the tribunal deals and the chairman will tend to specialise in that area of law. For example, in the employment tribunal the two lay members would typically be nominated by a trade union official and by an employer's association, and the chairman would be a lawyer who specialises in employment law.

Several advantages are claimed for tribunals. First, cases can be brought before a tribunal on a certain date and the waiting time for the case to begin is likely to be much shorter than it would be for a court case. Second, the costs in tribunals are likely to be much lower than court costs, as the parties can represent themselves. There are often no court fees and the losers usually do not have to pay the costs of the winner. Third, the proceedings are informal and this allows the parties to express themselves personally or to get a lay person who they feel really understands their case, such as a trade union official, to present the case. Fourth, tribunal members have technical expertise of a practical nature and can bring this to bear on the case. Fifth, it is possible that in certain circumstances a tribunal might sit in private.

These advantages must be viewed in the light of certain disadvantages. First, the lack of court procedure and, perhaps, of legal representation might mean that the high standards of justice which one would expect in court proceedings are not found in tribunal proceedings. Second, an appeal from a tribunal can sometimes be made to another tribunal or to a Minister, rather than to a court of law. Third, the lack of legal aid may mean that some claimants cannot find anyone to represent them effectively.

Tribunals are controlled by the courts and by the Council on Tribunals. A claim of judicial review may be brought before the High Court, arguing that a tribunal has exceeded its powers or has not adhered to the rules of natural justice. The courts also have the power to reverse the decisions of tribunals which did not correctly apply the law. The Council on Tribunals supervises tribunals generally and publishes an annual review in which criticism of tribunals can be made.

Test your understanding 2.2

1 What is the overriding objective of the changes made by the Civil Procedure Act 1997 and the Civil Procedure Rules 1998?

2 To what three tracks might a case be allocated? Who makes this allocation?

3 What are the alternatives open to a defendant upon whom particulars of claim have been served?

4 How does the 'no win, no fee' scheme help to fund personal injury cases?

5 What are the main disadvantages of litigation perceived to be?

6 What is arbitration?

7 What are mediation and conciliation?

8 What is a tribunal?

2.5 THE LEGAL PROFESSION

Unlike other European countries, England has two different types of lawyers – barristers and solicitors. There are currently about 12 240 self-employed practising barristers, about 3 860 of whom are women, and it is their main job to argue cases in court. However, the role of the practising barrister is much wider than merely acting as an advocate. Barristers spend a considerable amount of time giving written opinions, in which they state what they consider the law to be. They also draft statements of case, the formal documents which the parties must exchange before a case is heard in court. Barristers tend to specialise either in criminal law or in a particular branch of civil law. They have rights of audience in all civil and criminal courts. Until 1990 barristers had an exclusive right to be heard in senior courts, but now solicitors may also have rights in such courts.

About 1 250 barristers are known as Queen's Counsel. These senior barristers generally appear in court with a junior barrister assisting them. Queen's Counsel, or QCs as they are usually known, can charge higher fees than other barristers, in recognition of their expertise. Currently only about 11 per cent of QCs are women. In July 2003 the Department for Constitutional Affairs issued a Consultation Paper asking whether the system of Queen's Counsel should be abolished. This has not happened and QCs continue to be appointed by the QC Selection Panel.

Barristers are not allowed to form partnerships. Instead, they operate from chambers, which are offices where several barristers are allocated work by a barrister's clerk, who also negotiates the barrister's fees. A barrister can only be hired by a solicitor and can only meet the client he represents if the client's solicitor is also present. This prevents impropriety and should also mean that the barrister keeps an objective view of the case. Under the 'cab rank' rule a barrister, like a taxi, is supposed to provide his services to any client. Theoretically therefore, any barrister is available to any client whose solicitor asks that the barrister should be engaged. This is not always true as some barristers' fees are beyond the means of many clients and because barrister's clerks, who arrange what cases a barrister can take, are skilled at deflecting unwanted cases. It often happens that when a particular barrister has been engaged he is not available when the case starts because another case in which he is appearing has not finished in time. The client is then allocated a different barrister. Many barristers do not practise, but work in industry or commerce or for local government or the Civil Service.

Barristers must wear wigs and gowns in court, or the judge cannot 'see' or 'hear' them. This, like many other aspects of the Bar, seems somewhat out of date. (It is still part of a barrister's training that he should eat a certain number of dinners at one of the four Inns of Court in London.) In May 2003, the Lord Chancellor's Department (now the Ministry of Justice) issued a working paper seeking views on whether the clothes which barristers and judges wear in court should be made less formal. Complaints against barristers can be made to the Legal Ombudsman. In addition, an independent regulatory body of the Bar Council, the Bar Standards Board, could debar a barrister who was guilty of serious professional misconduct and could thereby prevent him from practising.

There are about 150 000 solicitors, about 118 000 of whom hold a practising certificate. About 45 per cent of solicitors are women, a percentage which is increasing annually. Eleven per cent of solicitors are from ethnic minority backgrounds. In 2007, 60 per cent of newly enrolled solicitors were women and where ethnicity was known, 22 per cent were from ethnic minorities. Solicitors are the first point of contact for a client with a legal problem. Unlike barristers, solicitors can form partnerships and some of the partnerships are very large.

A solicitor in a one-person business should have a good idea of most areas of law and should know where more information could be found if needed.

In the larger firms solicitors would tend to specialise in one particular area of law. Solicitors routinely give their clients legal advice, enter into correspondence on their behalf, draft wills and draw up documents which transfer ownership of land.

Until 1990, solicitors were only allowed to argue cases in the magistrates' court and the county court. Now the barrister's monopoly right to appear in the Crown Court and appellate courts has been removed by statute, and solicitors who have gained the necessary advocacy qualifications can represent clients in any court. About 2 200 have this right and several have become QCs. However, barristers still perform the vast bulk of advocacy work in these courts. Whereas solicitors have gained rights of audience since 1990, they have lost their monopoly rights to perform conveyancing and to obtain grants of probate. The Administration of Justice Act 1985 allowed licensed conveyancers to practise. It was widely predicted that this would be disastrous for many small firms of solicitors, but this does not seem to have been the case.

Complaints against solicitors can be made to the Legal Ombudsman. Complaints about breaches of rules or breaches of the solicitor's code of conduct are dealt with by the Solicitors Disciplinary Tribunal. This tribunal has the power to strike a solicitor off, so that he may no longer practise. The Legal Services Ombudsman has the power to investigate complaints that a professional body relating to a legal professional has not adequately investigated a complaint.

As well as barristers and solicitors, there are over 22 000 legal executives, who are members of the Institute of Legal Executives. If legal executives pass the necessary exams they can have rights of audience in some courts. They generally carry out routine work of a legal nature but increasingly do the type of work formerly carried out by a solicitor.

2.5.1 The Legal Services Act 2007

The Legal Services Act (LSA) received Royal Assent on 30 October 2007. However, it will not fully come into force until 2012. The Act, which sets up a new framework of regulation for legal services in England and Wales, is probably the most significant reform of legal services ever to have been made. Part 1 of the Act sets out the Act's eight regulatory objectives, namely:

(a) protecting and promoting the public interest;
(b) supporting the constitutional principle of the rule of law;

(c) improving access to justice;

(d) protecting and promoting the interests of consumers;

(e) promoting competition in the provision of services;

(f) encouraging an independent, strong, diverse and effective legal profession;

(g) increasing public understanding of the citizen's legal rights and duties; and

(h) promoting and maintaining adherence to the professional principles, which are set out in s.1(3).

The professional principles set out in s.1(3) require 'authorized persons', that is to say those who can offer 'reserved legal services', to act with independence, integrity and confidentiality; to maintain proper standards of work; to act in the best interests of clients; and to act in the best interests of justice when litigating in court.

Part 2 of the Act has created a Legal Services Board (LSB), which aims to maintain and develop standards relating to the regulation, education and training of those who can offer reserved legal services, that is to say of the legal profession. The LSB has a duty to promote the eight regulatory objectives set out in Part 1 of the Act, and to establish a Consumer Panel. It is independent from the Law Society and the Bar Council, which are now called 'front-line' legal regulators.

Part 3 of the Act sets out the 'reserved legal activities' which can be carried out only by lawyers, or in some cases by notaries or commissioners for oaths. The reserved legal activities, set out in s.12(1), are as follows:

(a) the exercise of a right of audience before the courts;

(b) the conduct of litigation, which includes the commencement, prosecution and defence of proceedings before a court;

(c) reserved instrument activities under the Land Registration Act 2002;

(d) probate activities, that is to say charging for the preparation of probate papers which found or oppose either a grant of probate or the grant of letters of administration;

(e) notarial activities which are customarily carried out by a notary;

(f) the administration of oaths by exercising powers conferred on commissioners of oaths.

The matters set out in s.12(1)(e) and (f) can be carried out by notaries and commissioners for oaths respectively. Licensed conveyancers and lawyers will have the right to charge for conveyancing. With very minor exceptions, lawyers will have the exclusive right to carry out the matters set out in s.12(1)(a), (b) and (d). In summary, these matters are advocacy in court, formally conducting litigation, and charging for the preparation of probate papers.

Part 5 of the Act, which came into force in 2009, allows Legal Disciplinary Practices to be set up as companies, partnerships or limited liability partnerships. Within LDPs, solicitors can be in business with non-solicitor partners and non-lawyer managers. (However, managers must be solicitors, barristers, notaries, licensed conveyancers, legal executives, patent agents, trade mark agents or law costs draftsmen.) This allows expertise to be brought into a business, increasing its ability to provide a one-stop service to customers. It also allows non-solicitors to provide capital to businesses which provide legal services. As from September 2012, all LDPs with non-lawyer managers will need to register as Alternative Business Structures (ABS).

Since October 2011 legal service providers have been able to operate as ABS, trading as companies, partnerships or LLPs. In an ABS, lawyers and those without legal qualifications can work together to provide both reserved legal activities and other services. In such businesses non-lawyers are able to exercise professional, management and ownership roles. As long as an ABS has been licensed by an approved regulator, such as the Law Society, it can offer 'reserved legal activities', which need to be carried out by lawyers. However, any other activities can be carried out by those who are not legally qualified. It seems very likely that many non-traditional legal services providers will employ non-lawyers to carry out much of the background work which was traditionally carried out by lawyers. This has caused several distinguished commentators to fear that lawyers, if they are to be able to compete, will have to give up much of the work which they have traditionally done, or accept much reduced salaries for doing it. The legal services market is estimated to be worth about £19 billion annually. It seems very likely that banks, insurance companies and large retailers will try to take over a large share of the market. Lawyers will probably have to change their outlook and their business structures to compete effectively. However, it should be remembered that the LSA does not provide for complete deregulation of legal services providers. Any new ABS still needs to apply for a licence if any non-lawyer has a material interest in the ABS or is able to control it. A licence will be granted only to businesses which are competent to provide legal services. Furthermore, any non-lawyer who owns more than 10 per cent of an ABS is subject to a fitness-to-own test. It should also be remembered that the demise of the legal profession was widely predicted, not least by the profession itself, when in the late 1980s solicitors lost their monopoly rights to write wills and practise conveyancing. Such predictions have been proved spectacularly wrong.

The LSA 2007 is intended to allow non-lawyers to do much of the work currently done by lawyers and thereby to lead to innovation, price reductions and greater access to legal services. The extent to which it will achieve these objectives will not be known for some years.

2.6 THE JUDICIARY

Before 2005 the Lord Chancellor was a cabinet minister, a House of Lords judge and the head of the judiciary. The Lord Chancellor's Department was a Government Department and several Lord Chancellors took a leading political role within the Government of the day. The fact that the head of the judiciary was also the Head of a Government Department and a Cabinet minister meant that the Lord Chancellor was prominent in the legislature, the judicature and the executive. The Lord Chancellor's role therefore breached the theory of the separation of powers. Consequently, the Lord Chancellor's Department became the Department of Constitutional Affairs, which in turn has become the Ministry of Justice. The Lord Chancellor remains a member of the Cabinet but is no longer the head of the judiciary. His role is to defend judicial independence, give the judiciary the support they need to be able to exercise their functions, have regard to the needs of the public interest with regard to matters relating to the judiciary and to ensure that there is an efficient and effective system to support the carrying on of the business of the courts of England and Wales.

The Lord Chief Justice is the head of the judiciary of England and Wales. However, the most senior judge of all is the Head of the Supreme Court. The Lord Chief Justice is responsible for representing the views of the judiciary to Parliament. The Master of the Rolls, who is the second most senior judge, is 'Head of Civil Justice'. The President of the Family Division of the High Court is the 'Head of Family Justice'. The Vice-Chancellor is the 'Chancellor of the High Court'.

Apart from the judicial offices outlined in the previous paragraph, there are five main levels in the judicial hierarchy. Supreme Court justices sit as judges in the Supreme Court, which was formerly the House of Lords. As we saw in the previous chapter, precedents made by the Supreme Court are binding upon all English courts. Lords Justices of Appeal sit in the Court of Appeal. As decisions of the Court of Appeal are generally binding on future sittings of the Court of Appeal, and are binding on all inferior courts, the Court of Appeal is perhaps the most significant court in terms of creating the law. There are currently 38 Lords Justices of Appeal and 12 Law Lords. There are also 108 High Court judges, who sit in the High Court and sometimes in the Crown Court.

It is convenient to consider the judges who sit in the High Court, the Court of Appeal and the Supreme Court as distinct from judges who sit in lower courts. The High Court is generally not an appellate court, but a court of first instance. However, in deciding a case a High Court judge is likely to be very aware of any precedent he is making, as well as being aware of his duty to try the case fairly. The Court of Appeal and Supreme Court do not try cases but only hear appeals. The further up the hierarchy the judge is sitting, the more importance he is likely to attach to the precedent which he is creating.

There are currently 680 circuit judges who try criminal cases in the Crown Court and civil cases in the county court. In the Crown Court these circuit judges are assisted by 1 305 recorders. In the county court they are assisted by 448 district judges and around 800 deputy district judges. Circuit judges, recorders and district judges do not create precedents. Their role is therefore confined to trying the cases which they hear. They supervise the proceedings in court, and in civil cases decide the facts of the case if they are in dispute and award damages and costs. In criminal cases in which a judge sits the facts will be decided by the jury, but the judge will supervise the proceedings. He will also pass sentence if the accused is convicted and sum up the law to the jury, so that they can reach the correct verdict.

Judges are appointed from the ranks of successful lawyers. Prior to 1990 only barristers could become judges, but now solicitors who have acted as advocates in the higher courts are also eligible. Judges are well paid. The Lord Chief Justice currently earns a salary of £239 845, High Court judges earn

£172 753 and circuit judges in the provinces earn £128 296. These salaries are necessary to tempt suitably qualified lawyers to become judges and to ensure that judges maintain their independence when hearing cases.

Judges must now retire at 70 and are subject to training organised by the Judicial Studies Board. However, the retirement age can be extended to the age of 75 on a year-by-year basis. The judgment of any precedent-making judge could well be scrutinised by academics, lawyers and other judges. In the light of this scrutiny, if a senior judge were not up to the high standard required this would soon become apparent.

About 98 per cent of all criminal cases are decided in the magistrates' court, rather than in the Crown Court. Most magistrates are lay magistrates, meaning that they are not legally qualified. However, there are currently 134 district judges (magistrates' courts), formerly known as stipendiary magistrates and over 170 deputy district judges (magistrates' courts). Only lawyers can qualify as district judges (magistrates' courts) and they are paid a salary of £102 921 if they work outside London.

There are around 29 000 lay magistrates, who are not paid a salary. Although they are not legally qualified, upon appointment lay magistrates do receive training on matters such as decision-making, stereotyping and avoiding prejudice. Magistrates generally sit as a bench of three, and are advised about the law by the legally qualified clerk of the court. As well as deciding whether or not a person accused of a crime is granted bail, magistrates try cases, deciding whether an accused is innocent or guilty, and pass sentence on those who are convicted. They also conduct committal proceedings when a defendant is committed for trial to the Crown Court. Lay magistrates must live or work in the area in which they serve, must have a good knowledge of the local community, must be of good character and have personal integrity. Generally, they must be between the ages of 27 and 65. Most people are eligible to become magistrates, but those in the police or the armed forces are not.

2.6.1 Judicial review

Judicial review is a legal procedure which allows the Administrative Court in London to examine whether a public law decision, or the exercise of discretionary power by a public body, is legal. The definition of public body for these purposes is quite wide. It includes Government Ministers and has been held to cover decisions of private bodies which make decisions that affect the public.

An application for judicial review will be subject to an initial filtering process. The applicant (who can be either a person directly affected by a public law decision, or a pressure group representing people who are affected) has first to apply for permission to proceed. On the application for permission to proceed the judge will be checking for the existence of the following criteria:

(a) Whether the decision itself is amenable to judicial review.
(b) Whether there is either express or implied exclusion of judicial review (i.e. whether Parliament has specifically enacted that such a decision should not be reviewed).
(c) Whether the appliant has a sufficient legal interest to sue.
(d) Whether there are grounds for judicial review.

With regard to the last criterion the grounds for judicial review were set out by Lord Diplock in *CCSU v Minister for the Civil Service* [1985] AC 374, commonly referred to as the GCHQ case. Lord Diplock stated that there are three main grounds for review: illegality, irrationality and procedural impropriety. It is important to bear in mind, however, that the grounds are not mutually exclusive.

Where the Administrative Court finds that a decision is not legal (on any one or more of the above grounds) the court can grant one or more of the following remedies:

(a) a quashing order, formerly known as *certiorari* – an order that acts to quash the original decision;
(b) a mandatory order, formerly known as *mandamus* – an order that compels the decision-maker to do something;
(c) a prohibiting order, formerly known as *prohibition* – an order which prevents a decision-maker from embarking on a course of action which is not legal;
(d) *make a declaration* – this is nothing more than the court stating the legal position between the parties;
(e) *award damages* – but only where there are also private law issues involved or it involves a case under the Human Rights Act 1998; and
(f) *issue an injunction* – although an order for *mandamus* is more common in judicial review proceedings.

Judicial review has become increasingly important in recent years as the number of applications has increased dramatically. Businesses are increasingly either applying for judicial review or are subject to judicial review proceedings. A business might apply, for example, on the grounds that a decision taken by a Government Minister affects the running of the business. Even private companies may be subject to judicial review proceedings if their decisions have an effect upon the public. It is important to remember that judicial review is not concerned with the merits of the decision in question, it is concerned with whether or not that decision was legally taken.

2.7 JURIES

In the Crown Court the jury decides whether the accused is guilty or not guilty. This decision is based on the judge's summing up, which explains the relevant law to the jury. It is therefore said that juries decide the facts of the case. A judge can direct a jury to acquit an accused, but cannot direct them to convict. Juries do not give an explanation for their decisions. If a jury acquits, an appeal cannot overturn this acquittal. This enables juries to bring in 'perverse acquittals' if they think that the circumstances of the case so demand. Jurors may sometimes be discharged during a trial if they become ill or otherwise incapable of continuing to serve, but the number of jurors must not fall below nine. Majority verdicts are acceptable, but at least ten out of 11 or 12 jurors must agree, or at least nine out of ten. A jury which falls to nine members cannot give a majority verdict. The judge should not readily accept a majority verdict but should first urge the jury to try to reach a unanimous verdict. If the jury is unable to reach a verdict the case may be retried with a different jury. In the past few years problems have arisen because jurors have used the Internet to help them with their deliberations. In *R v Thompson and others* [2010] EWCA Crim 1623, [2010] All ER (D) (Sep), the Court of Appeal held that, at the beginning of a trial, jurors should be specifically told not to use the Internet but to base their verdict on the evidence presented to them in court. In June 2011 a juror who contacted, via Facebook, a defendant who had already been acquitted, thereby causing a multimillion pound drug trial to collapse, was jailed for eight months for contempt of court.

Citizens between the ages of 18 and 70, who are on the electoral roll and have lived in the United Kingdom for five years, can be required to serve as jurors and can be fined up to £1 000 for failing to serve. However, mentally disordered persons are exempt from jury service. Persons who have been sentenced to a term of imprisonment of more than five years are permanently disqualified. Those who received lesser sentences may be temporarily disqualified. All professionals, including judges and doctors, are now eligible for jury service. However, the court has a discretion to excuse individuals who can provide a good reason why they should not serve. Both the prosecution and the defence have a right to challenge any number of jurors 'with cause', that is to say if it can show that there is a substantial reason why a particular juror should not try a particular case. A juror's race, religion, occupation or politics is not to be regarded as a substantial reason.

Juries play little part in civil cases. This was not always so. In several cases which we consider in this book the appellate court was considering whether or not to overturn the decision of a jury sitting in a civil court. Section 69 of the Supreme Court Act 1981 now limits civil jury trial to cases of defamation, malicious prosecution and false imprisonment and cases where fraud is alleged. The judge has a power to deny the right to jury trial even in these cases if the examination of scientific or technical documents would make a jury inappropriate. Where a jury is used in a civil case the jury also awards damages. The excessive amounts awarded in some defamation cases have led to considerable criticism and the Court of Appeal may now substitute the amount of damages which appears proper for the amount awarded by the jury, without the need for a new trial.

2.8 LAW REFORM

Parliament and the judiciary are, of course, the main reformers of the law. The system of precedent operates in a relatively haphazard way. It depends upon appropriate cases being brought in front of courts which have the power to make new rules of law. For this reason certain law reform bodies have been created. The most significant of these is the Law Commission. Its role is to keep under review all the law with which it is concerned, with a view to its systematic development and reform. In particular it should attempt to codify the law, to eliminate anomalies, to suggest the repeal of outdated and unnecessary Acts, to reduce the number of separate Acts and to generally simplify and modernise the law. The chairman of the Law Commission is a High Court judge and the five full-time commissioners are lawyers seconded for five years at a time. Other lawyers act as part-time commissioners. Reforms suggested by the Law Commission can be enacted by Parliament either in part or in whole. However, many reforms suggested are never enacted at all. The Contracts (Rights of Third Parties) Act 1999, considered in Chapter 4 at 4.2.2.2, provides an example of a statute which enacted a Bill proposed by the Law Commission.

The Law Reform Committee is a part-time body which considers the reform of civil matters referred to it by the Lord Chancellor. The Committee does not meet regularly, but its reports have tended to be very thorough. The Criminal Law Revision Committee examines matters of criminal law when asked to do so by the Home Secretary. It too is part-time, but its reports have led to the passing of significant legislation, such as the Theft Act 1968.

Royal Commissions have been set up to consider various administrative reforms. The Woolf Committee, which proposed the changes to legal procedure outlined above at 2.3, provides a good example. It should also be borne in mind that when the Government is proposing legislation it may first produce its suggestions in a green paper, which invites discussion and comment. After receiving these comments the Government publishes a white paper, in which definite proposals are set out. In this way suggestions as to the reform of the law are invited from a wide body of persons.

2.9 LAW REPORTING

The system of judicial precedent is dependent upon a good system of law reporting. The first law reports are contained in the Year Books, which reported on cases between 1275 and 1535. These reports are very scanty and are never quoted in court. The Private Reports made between 1535 and 1865 vary tremendously in quality, depending upon who the reporter was. Since 1865 the Modern Reports have been published by the Incorporated Council of Law Reporting for England and Wales. The Council is not a Government agency, but a non-profit-making charitable organisation. Since 1891 the Council's reports have been known as the Law Reports, which are divided into four series. A series known as Appeal Cases report the decisions of the House of Lords (now the Supreme Court) and the Privy Council. The other series are known as Queen's Bench, Family Division or Chancery Division. The areas which these reports cover is self-explanatory, although they are not restricted to decisions of the relevant Divisions of the High Court, but may also cover appeals in the Court of Appeal or Supreme Court.

Throughout this book case references are shown. Since 1891 the Law Reports have shown the year in which the case was reported in square brackets. In Chapter 1 we considered *Adler v George* [1964] 2 QB 7. In order to find this law report it is first necessary to find the Queen's Bench Law Reports. Then it is necessary to find volume 2 of the 1964 reports. The case is reported on page 7 of Volume 2. A law report will indicate the court in which the case was heard. (*Adler v George* was heard in the Queen's Bench Division of the High Court.) It will indicate the judges who heard the case (Lord Parker CJ, Paul and Widgery JJ). Then the facts of the case and the decision are set out very briefly. After a fairly detailed description of the facts and the arguments put forward, the judgments of the various judges are set out. The Council also puts out a series of Weekly Law Reports, which appear more quickly than the Law Reports.

Since 1936 Butterworths (now LexisNexis UK) have published the All England Law Reports. These do not set out the arguments put forward by the lawyers. Important cases decided prior to 1936 are set out in 36 other volumes of the All England Law Reports. Specialist reports published by various bodies deal with various specialist matters. There are, for instance, Road Traffic Reports, Industrial Relations Law Reports and Reports on Tax Cases.

Many of the decisions made in the higher courts are not reported. Unreported cases of the Court of Appeal can be found in a Butterworth database known as Lexis. Such cases can only be cited in the Supreme Court with permission from that court. Unreported cases of the House of Lords can be found in the Record Office of the House of Lords. The law reporters decide whether or not a case is worthy of being reported.

Law reporting has been revolutionised in the past few years, as decisions have become available electronically. There is now little need to visit a law library to find a reported case if one has access to online reporting. Some cases, such as Supreme Court and House of Lords decisions, are available on the Internet at www.parliament.uk. Very many decisions are reported electronically by business organisations and are available to private subscribers. Most UK universities subscribe to these private reports and, generally, students have access to them. Electronic law reporting has a further advantage over hard copy reporting in that a person who wants to know if the law in a certain area has changed can type a phrase into a reporting site and the site will then reveal any recent cases which are relevant to that phrase. (It is also possible to search for academic articles relating to the phrase although, technically, this is not law reporting.)

Test your understanding 2.3

1 What are the main roles of practising barristers?
2 What are the main roles of solicitors?
3 Can a member of the public directly engage a barrister to argue a case in court?
4 Which judges make precedents?
5 What is the difference between lay magistrates and district judges (magistrates' courts)?
6 What is judicial review?
7 What is the function of a jury? In which courts are juries used?
8 What are the official law reform bodies?
9 What are the Law Reports?

Key points

The structure of the courts

■ A civil case might be tried in the county court or in the High Court.

■ There is a presumption that a case over which both the county court and the High Court have jurisdiction will be heard in the county court. This presumption can be rebutted if the case is particularly complex or involves issues of importance to the general public.

■ The Court of Appeal (Civil Division) hears appeals from the High Court. The High Court hears most appeals from the county court.

■ The Supreme Court hears appeals from the Court of Appeal (Civil Division). It also very occasionally hears appeals from the High Court when the leapfrog procedure is invoked.

■ Indictable offences are tried in the Crown Court. Summary offences are tried in the magistrates' court. Either way offences can be tried in either the Crown Court or the magistrates' court.

■ When a case is first tried in the magistrates' court appeals on points of law can be made by way of case stated to the Divisional Court. An appeal against sentence or conviction lies from the magistrates' court to the Crown Court.

■ The Court of Appeal (Criminal Division) hears appeals from the Crown Court.

■ The Supreme Court hears appeals from the Divisional Court and from the Court of Appeal (Criminal Division).

Procedure in the courts

■ The Civil Procedure Act 1997 and the Civil Procedure Rules 1998 have radically changed civil procedure, in an attempt to enable the courts to deal with cases justly.

■ The judge has now become the case manager, with wide powers to run the case. Before the reforms the case was to a large extent run by the litigants.

■ Civil cases will be allocated to one of three tracks (the small claims track, the fast track or the multi-track), depending upon the amount of the claim, the complexity of the case and the need for expert evidence.

■ A defendant upon whom a claim has been served may ignore it (and therefore have judgment entered against him), admit the claim in full, admit part of the claim, file an acknowledgement of service (thereby getting an extra 14 days in which to reply), file a defence and/or file a counterclaim.

■ Claims on the small claims track will be heard in the county court, generally by a district judge.

■ Fast-track claims should be decided within 30 weeks of allocation.

■ All cases will be subject to extensive case management by the judge.

Alternative dispute resolution

■ Litigation has several disadvantages. It is costly, slow, complex, worrying and conducted in public. It

→

is also likely to finish any business relationship with the other party.

■ Disputes may be referred to arbitration by the parties, by a court or by an Act of Parliament. If a dispute is referred to arbitration it is resolved by an arbitrator rather than by a court.

■ A mediator communicates between the parties, trying to get them to resolve their dispute.

■ Conciliation involves a conciliator suggesting to the parties the basis on which they might settle their dispute.

■ Tribunals hear disputes on specialist matters, and these types of disputes must be referred to the appropriate tribunal rather than to the ordinary courts. Generally, a tribunal is made up of a legally qualified chairman and two lay members.

Miscellaneous matters

■ The legal profession is split into barristers and solicitors.

■ Barristers act as advocates in all courts, draft opinions and draft statements of case.

■ Solicitors act as general legal advisors. They can act as advocates in the magistrates' court or the county court. If qualified they can act as advocates in higher courts.

■ High Court judges, Court of Appeal judges and Supreme Court justices make precedents. Circuit judges do not.

■ District judges (magistrates' courts) are salaried, legally qualified magistrates. Lay magistrates are not legally qualified and sit as a bench of three.

■ Judicial review is the process by which the Administrative Court considers the legality of decisions of public law and the legality of a discretionary power exercised by a public body.

■ Juries decide whether or not the defendant in a Crown Court trial is guilty or not guilty.

■ The Law Commission is a law reform body with full-time members. The Law Reform Committee and the Criminal Law Revision Committee are part-time law reform bodies.

■ Law reporting is not done by the Government. The most significant law reports are the All England Law Reports and the Law Reports of the Incorporated Council of Law Reporting for England and Wales.

Summary questions

1 A Ltd is suing B Ltd, claiming contract damages of £25 000. B Ltd is contesting the claim. The claim is not in respect of any personal injuries. In which courts might the case be tried? To which courts might an appeal be made, if all possible appeals were made?

2 Explain the considerations which will be taken into account in deciding the appropriate track for the hearing of a case. As regards each track, outline the procedures which are likely to be followed from allocation to conclusion of the case.

3 Explain the way in which a dispute can be referred to arbitration and the powers which an arbitrator has. How do mediation and conciliation differ from arbitration?

4 By scanning the newspapers or the Internet, find a recent case in which an application for judicial review was made. Outline the grounds on which the application was made and the outcome of the application.

Multiple choice questions

1 Which one of the following statements is not true?

a If a claim can be brought in either the county court or the High Court, there is a presumption that it should be heard in the High Court.

b An appeal from a master who is sitting as a High Court judge will be made to a High Court judge, rather than to the Court of Appeal.

c If an offence is classed as triable either way, an accused has the right to insist upon trial in the Crown Court.

→

d Lay magistrates are trained, but they can be appointed even if they have no special knowledge of the law.

2 Which one of the following statements is not true?

a If a defendant upon whom particulars of claim are served does not respond within 14 days, judgment can be entered against him.

b If the defendant files an acknowledgement of service he will be given a further 14 days to respond to the claim.

c An appeal from a district judge's ruling on the small claims track will always be made to the Court of Appeal.

d A fast-track case will generally be concluded within 30 weeks of allocation.

3 Which one of the following statements is not true?

a In a small claims case each side generally pays its own costs.

b If a party tries to bring legal proceedings in respect of a matter which it has been agreed should be resolved by arbitration, the court will stay the proceedings unless the arbitration agreement was either null and void, inoperative or incapable of being performed.

c Tribunals act as specialist courts, hearing certain types of disputes which must be taken to the appropriate tribunal rather than to the ordinary courts.

d A mediator will suggest the basis on which a dispute might be resolved and try to get the parties to agree to be legally bound by the suggested resolution.

4 Consider the following statements.

i A member of the public cannot directly engage a barrister to represent him, but must engage the barrister through a solicitor.

ii Barristers can be appointed judges but solicitors cannot.

iii The process of judicial review allows the Administrative Court to consider the merits of decisions taken by public bodies.

iv Juries can acquit a defendant even if they are sure that he is guilty.

v Not all decisions of the precedent-making courts are reported.

Which of the statements are true?

a i, iii and iv only.

b ii and iii only.

c i, iv and v only.

d All of the statements.

Task 2

Your employer has asked you to write a report, explaining briefly the following matters.

a The different courts in which a civil dispute might start and the courts to which an appeal might subsequently be made.

b The three tracks to which a civil case might be allocated and the principles of case management which the courts will apply.

c The main methods of dispute resolution which can be used as an alternative to going to court.

mylawchamber *premium*

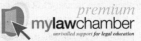

3

Formation of contracts – offer and acceptance

3.1 OFFER

Almost all contracts are made through the process of offer and acceptance. One of the parties (the offeror) makes an offer by proposing a set of terms with the intention that these terms will form a legally binding agreement if they are accepted by the party to whom they are proposed, the offeree. If the offeree accepts, by indicating that he too is willing to be bound by the terms proposed, a contract will result. The offer can be written or spoken, or it can be inferred from the conduct of the offeror. When goods are bought at auction both the offer and the acceptance are made by conduct. The sale of a lot at auction can provide a good initial example of how an offer is made and of how it is accepted.

Let us assume that Mrs Ashley buys an antique vase at an auction conducted by Mr Bower. Mrs Ashley, if she is sensible, will have examined the vase beforehand or at least have seen it described in a catalogue. Neither the examination nor the description in the catalogue amount to an offer.

When the auctioneer comes to the lot in question, let us call it Lot 1, he probably makes a brief description of it to make sure that the bidders know which lot is up for sale. Then the auctioneer asks for bids. He usually suggests a price. None of these actions of the auctioneer amount to an offer.

When one of the bidders signifies that he is making a bid (by raising his hand, or nodding, or making whatever other gesture the auctioneer recognises) this, at last, is an offer. It is the first move of legal significance and as such it is not a move to be made lightly. If the offer is accepted then the bidder will have made a contract to buy Lot 1 and will be legally bound by that contract.

The auctioneer will be in no hurry to accept the first bid. Let us assume that several higher bids are made, but that eventually Mrs Ashley makes a bid of £100 and that this appears to be the highest bid which is going to be made. The auctioneer will probably repeat the figure £100 several times and then, after a slight delay, he will bang his hammer on the table.

At the precise moment that the auctioneer's hammer hits the table the acceptance is made and the contract is concluded.

While the hammer was descending towards the table Lot 1 still belonged to the person who had asked the auctioneer to sell it. But as soon as the hammer hit the table the contract was made. As the contract was for the sale of specific goods in a deliverable state, ownership of Lot 1 would immediately be transferred from the person who put the vase into the auction to Mrs Ashley.

The fact that the contract has now been made has important legal consequences. Mrs Ashley is now free to do as she pleases with Lot 1, but she is no longer free to change her mind and say that she does not want to buy it. (Nor, of course, can the auctioneer say that he no longer wants to sell.) If Lot 1 is damaged **after** the contract has been made then it is Mrs Ashley whose property has been damaged and it is she, not the seller, who would have the right to sue the person causing the damage. If the lot had been damaged **before** the hammer hit the table, no contract would yet have been made and it would have been the seller on whose behalf the auctioneer was acting whose property would have been damaged.

This example of the sale of a lot at an auction is a useful one because the offer and acceptance are well established and easy to recognise. The classical approach to the formation of contracts holds that every other type of contract is made when an offer is accepted. However, it is not always so easy to see what the offer and acceptance were. In exceptional cases a court may hold that a contract existed even though it is not possible to identify a definite offer and a definite acceptance. But this can only happen if the court is satisfied that the parties reached agreement on all material points.

3.1.1 **Invitation to treat**

The word treat has several meanings. In the context of the law relating to offer and acceptance it means to negotiate. An invitation to treat is therefore an invitation to negotiate, or an invitation to make a deal. The main significance of an invitation to treat is that it is not an offer.

Making an offer carries an element of risk. A business, for example, should not offer to sell an asset for £1 000 unless it is quite sure that this is what it wants to do. If the person to whom the offer was made, the offeree, were to accept the offer then the business would have to hand the asset over in return for the money or accept the legal consequences. But it would be quite safe for the business to make an invitation to treat. It might do this by inquiring of another how much he would be prepared to pay for the asset. Whatever the reply, the business could not be forced to sell.

In deciding whether or not one party made an offer to another a court will be guided by the intentions of the parties. These intentions will be deduced from all the circumstances of the case.

3.1.2 **Advertisements**

The legal status of advertisements is of considerable importance. If an advertisement amounts to an offer, then people who respond in such a way that they accept the offer will have made a contract. If an advertisement is only an invitation to treat, as is usually the case, a response to the advertisement cannot form a binding contract. In the following case the court had to decide whether an advertisement which described goods, and the price for which they could be purchased, was an offer or an invitation to treat.

> ### *Partridge v Crittenden* [1968] 1 WLR 1204
>
> The defendant was charged with unlawfully offering for sale a bramblefinch contrary to s.6(1) of the Protection of Birds Act 1954. The defendant had placed an advertisement in the classified section of a magazine. This advertisement had said, 'Quality British ... bramblefinch cocks, bramblefinch hens ... 25 s. each'. The words 'offers for sale' were not directly used in the advertisement. A customer posted a cheque for 25 shillings, requesting a bramblefinch hen. Such a bird was sent to the customer in a box by British Rail.
>
> **Held.** The defendant was not guilty. His advertisement was an invitation to treat, not an offer. The defendant had not therefore 'offered for sale' a wild bird.
>
> **COMMENT** (i) The defendant would have been guilty of a different crime, that of selling a wild bird. Fortunately for him, this was not the crime with which he was charged.
>
> (ii) This case is of course a criminal case, as are several of the cases which follow. In order to decide whether or not a criminal offence has been committed it is often necessary to consider the civil law. This is particularly true of crimes which are committed by selling or offering for sale.

→

(iii) Lord Parker, who gave the leading judgment, indicated that he felt that the defendant ought to be guilty of the offence. However, this had no influence on his decision as to whether or not the advertisement amounted to an offer. Lord Parker's primary concern was with the consequences of the decision he was making. If, in their desire to convict the defendant, Lord Parker and his fellow judge had decided that the advertisement was an offer, then under the doctrine of judicial precedent every junior judge would have become obliged to follow this decision when considering similar advertisements. (The doctrine of judicial precedent is examined in Chapter 1 at 1.3.2.) Lord Parker demonstrated how undesirable the consequences of this might be by quoting with approval the following example concerning a wine merchant sending out a wine list to customers. The example was originally made by Lord Herschell in *Grainger and Son v Gough* [1896] AC 325:

> 'The transmission of such a wine list does not amount to an offer to supply an unlimited quantity of the wine described at the price named, so that as soon as an order is given there is a binding contract ... If it were so, the merchant might find himself involved in any number of contractual obligations to supply wine of a particular description which he would be quite unable to carry out, his stock of wine of that description being necessarily limited.'

Although the advertisement in *Partridge* v *Crittenden* was classified as an invitation to treat, it is possible for an advertisement to amount to an offer. If the general rule that advertisements are only invitations to treat were to be applied rigidly to all advertisements then this would lead to unfairness, as the following case demonstrates.

Carlill v The Carbolic Smoke Ball Company
[1893] 1 QB 525 (Court of Appeal)

The defendant claimed that the smoke balls which they manufactured cured many illnesses and made it impossible to catch flu. They advertised the smoke balls heavily, stating that if anyone could show that they had correctly used a smoke ball yet still caught flu they would be paid £100 reward. The advertisement also stated that the defendant had deposited £1 000 in a Regent Street bank, 'shewing our sincerity in the matter'. The claimant, Mrs Carlill, bought one of the smoke balls on the strength of the advertisement. Despite using the smoke ball properly, the claimant still caught flu. She claimed the £100 reward. The defendants refused to pay on several grounds. First, it was claimed that the advertisement was a mere sales puff rather than an offer. Second, it was contended that a contract could not be made with the whole world. Third, it was argued that the defendant's promises were too vague to be an offer.

Held. The claimant had made a contract with the company and was entitled to the £100 reward. The advertisement constituted an offer of a unilateral contract which was made to the whole world. The offer stipulated that acceptance could be made by using a smoke ball in the correct manner and catching flu. The claimant had fulfilled these requirements and had therefore accepted.

COMMENT (i) A sales puff is a statement which promotes a product in a way which is not intended to be taken to amount to a definite promise. Modern examples can be seen in the claims made by manufacturers of washing powders that their product washes whitest. The defendant's reference to the £1 000 having been deposited in the Regent Street bank indicated to the court that the promise of the reward was not a mere sales puff.

(ii) The case illustrates that an offer can be made to the whole world. In reward cases this is not uncommon. Offers are more usually made to one person or to a group of people. An offer can only be accepted by an offeree, a person to whom it was made (or by an agent acting on an offeree's behalf). The defendant's argument that if the court found for Mrs Carlill this would have meant that a contract was made with the whole world was exposed as a fallacy by Bowen LJ. The offer was made to the whole world but this did not of course mean that a contract was made with the whole world. A contract was only made with that limited portion of the public who accepted the offer.

(iii) The offer was not considered too vague. Bowen LJ reached this conclusion by giving the advertisement its plain meaning as the public would understand it.

3.1.3 Offers of unilateral contracts

Almost all contracts are bilateral (two-sided) because both sides make a contractual promise to the other. If, for example, a farmer telephones a dealer and makes a contract to buy a new combine harvester, this is a bilateral contract. The dealer has promised to transfer ownership of the combine harvester to the farmer and the farmer in return has promised to pay the price agreed.

However, a person who makes an offer of a unilateral contract agrees to be bound if the offeree performs some act, rather than if the offeree promises to perform some act. Although the offeror does not always spell it out so specifically, in effect he says, 'If you do one thing, then I promise that I will definitely do another'. The contracts are called unilateral (one-sided) because only one of the parties, the offeror, makes a promise. The offeree cannot accept by promising to do the act requested, but only by actually doing it. In *Carlill's case*, the Smoke Ball Company promised that if Mrs Carlill, or anyone else, used a smoke ball and caught flu they would be paid the reward. But Mrs Carlill did not promise that she would catch flu, and presumably did not even intend to do so. She accepted by performing the acts requested – using a smoke ball and catching flu.

A further peculiarity of unilateral contracts is that acceptance of the offer does not need to be communicated to the offeror. Mrs Carlill did not need to tell the company that she intended to accept the offer. Indeed, her saying this would not have amounted to acceptance. The only way in which she could accept was by fulfilling the requirements of the offer. That is to say she could only accept by using a smoke ball as directed and catching flu. The company would not have been aware of her acceptance until she claimed the reward. As we shall see later in this chapter, a bilateral contract is generally not legally binding until the acceptance is communicated to the offeror.

3.1.4 Goods in shops

In order to analyse when a contract is concluded by a customer in a shop it is necessary to consider separately those shops which operate a self-service system and those which do not. As regards shops which do not operate a self-service system Somervell LJ, in *Pharmaceutical Society of Great Britain v Boots Cash Chemists (Southern) Ltd* [1953] 1 QB 401, explained the position in the following way:

> 'in the case of an ordinary shop, [one in which there is no self-service] although goods are displayed and it is intended that customers should go and choose what they want, the contract is not completed until, the customer having indicated the articles which he needs, the shopkeeper, or someone on his behalf, accepts that offer.'

The other members of the Court of Appeal seemed to regard this point of view as self-evidently correct, although none of them identified the precise way in which the shopkeeper accepts the offer.

It is well established that the display of goods in a shop window amounts only to an invitation to treat and not to an offer.

Fisher v Bell [1961] 1 QB 394

The defendant displayed a flick knife in his shop window. A ticket behind the knife said, 'Ejector knife – 4s'. The defendant was charged with the criminal offence of offering the knife for sale, contrary to s.1(1) of the Restriction of Offensive Weapons Act 1959.

Held. The defendant was not guilty of the offence. The display of the knife amounted not to an offer to sell, but only to an invitation to treat.

Lord Parker: '. . . the display of an article with a price on it in a shop window is merely an invitation to treat. It is in no sense an offer for sale the acceptance of which constitutes a contract. That is clearly the general law of the country.'

In the following case the Court of Appeal considered the position as regards self-service shops.

Pharmaceutical Society of Great Britain v Boots Cash Chemists (Southern) Ltd [1953] 1 QB 401 (Court of Appeal)

The defendants were charged with the criminal offence of selling a listed drug other than by or under the supervision of a registered pharmacist, contrary to s.18 of the Pharmacy and Poisons Act 1933. The defendants operated a self-service shop where the goods for sale were displayed on shelves around the walls. Customers entering the shop picked up whatever goods they wished to buy and took them to a cashier near the exit. The goods displayed, including listed drugs, were wrapped in packages with the prices marked on them. A registered pharmacist was present near the cash desk and could prevent a customer from buying any listed drug. The prosecution contended that the sale of the displayed goods was completed when the customers put the goods into their baskets. If this contention was correct then the offence would have been committed whenever customers put listed drugs into their baskets because at this stage no pharmacist supervised or made the sale.

Held. The defendants were not guilty. The display of goods on the supermarket shelves amounted to an invitation to treat rather than to an offer to sell. The customers' action in taking the goods from the shelves, placing them in their baskets and taking them to the cash desk constituted an offer to buy. The customers' offer to buy was accepted when the cashier →

took the purchase price. The contract was therefore made under the supervision of a pharmacist and so no offence was committed.

Test your understanding 3.1

1 How does an offeror make an offer?
2 What is the significance of an offer being accepted?
3 What is an invitation to treat?
4 What is a bilateral contract?
5 How is the offer of a unilateral contract made?

3.2 ACCEPTANCE

As soon as an offer is accepted, a contract comes into existence and both sides are legally bound. An acceptance can be made by words or conduct. Unless the offer was of a unilateral contract, or unless the postal rule applies, the acceptance must be communicated to the offeror. These cases apart, the contract is not completed until this communication is received. This important principle is clearly demonstrated by the following case.

Entores Ltd v *Miles Far East Corporation*
[1955] 2 QB 327 (Court of Appeal)

The claimants, in London, telexed an offer to purchase copper cathodes to the defendants in Holland. The defendants telexed acceptance back to London. Later, when sued for breach of contract in England, the defendants argued that the contract was not made in England and was not therefore within the jurisdiction of the English courts. The defendants claimed that the acceptance was effective as soon as it was typed out on the telex machine in Holland and that the contract was therefore made in Holland. The claimants argued that the acceptance was not effective until it was printed out in London, and that the contract was therefore made in England.

Held. English law applied. A contract is complete only when the acceptance is received by the offeror.

Lord Denning: 'Suppose, for instance, that I shout an offer to a man across a river or a courtyard but I do not hear his reply because it is drowned by an aircraft flying overhead. There is no contract at that moment. If he wishes to make a contract, he must wait until the aircraft is gone and then shout back his acceptance so that I can hear what he says. Not till I have heard his answer am I bound.'

COMMENT (i) Lord Denning also explained that an acceptance by telephone would not be effective until it was heard by the offeror, but that this was only the case if the offeree knew that the acceptance had not been heard. He suggested that if the offeror did not make it known that he had not heard the acceptance then a contract would come into existence because the offeror would be estopped (prevented) from saying that he had not received the message. He also thought that this would be the case if the ink ran out on a printer receiving the acceptance and the offeror did not ask for the message to be repeated.

(ii) The decision in *Entores* was approved by the House of Lords in ***Brinkibon Ltd*** v ***Stahag Stahl und Stahlwarenhandelsgesellschaft GmbH*** [1983] 2 AC 34.

(iii) In ***Apple Corps Ltd*** v ***Apple Computer Inc*** [2004] EWHC 768, [2004] All ER (D) 107 (Apr) Mann J held that a contract was created in two different jurisdictions at the same time. The agreement was made between an American corporation and an English company to settle a dispute over a trade mark. Negotiations had taken place over several months but neither side was willing to accept the jurisdiction of the other. The contract therefore contained no clause on which jurisdiction should apply. The agreement was completed by telephone but the evidence did not clearly reveal who said what and in what order. Mann J decided that the contract was made in both the United States and England at the same time. For reasons which are not relevant here, he then decided that English law was the governing law of the contract.

As an acceptance of an offer of a bilateral contract is only effective when it is received, it follows that the acceptance must take the form of some positive action. An acceptance can be made by words or conduct but a person cannot accept a contract by saying nothing and doing nothing, even if the offeror has stipulated that acceptance should be made in this way.

Felthouse v *Bindley* (1862) 11 CBNS 869

The claimant's nephew thought that he had sold a horse to the claimant for 30 guineas (£31.50). The claimant thought that he had bought the horse for £30. Realising that the mistake meant there was no contract, the claimant wrote to his nephew offering to split the difference. The claimant's letter stated, →

'If I hear no more about him, I consider the horse mine at £30 15 shillings.' The nephew wanted to sell at this price so he did not reply. Six weeks later an auctioneer sold the horse by mistake. The claimant sued the auctioneer in tort for selling his property. The auctioneer's defence was that the horse still belonged to the claimant's nephew and that the wrongful sale of the horse was therefore nothing to do with the claimant.

Held. The auctioneer was not liable. The claimant's offer to buy the horse for £30 15 shillings had never been accepted and so the horse still belonged to his nephew.

Some businesses try to sell their goods by sending them to people who have not requested them, and then following up with aggressive demands for payment or the return of the goods. *Felthouse* v *Bindley* makes it plain that the recipients cannot be deemed to have accepted the goods merely because they do not return them. Section 2 of the Unsolicited Goods and Services Act 1971 makes it a criminal offence to demand payment for unsolicited goods sent to a business. (Goods are unsolicited if they are sent to a person who has not made a prior request for them. Furthermore, reg.24 of the Consumer Protection (Distance Selling) Regulations 2000 provides that a consumer recipient of unsolicited goods may treat the goods as an unconditional gift if three conditions are fulfilled. First, the goods must have been sent with a view to the recipient acquiring them. Second, the recipient must have no reasonable cause to believe that the goods were sent with a view to their being acquired for a business purpose. Third, the recipient must have neither agreed to acquire them or return them. The Consumer Protection from Unfair Trading Regulations 2008 also make it a criminal offence to demand payment for such goods.) Surprisingly, this legislation has not eradicated the practice of demanding payment for unsolicited goods. It seems that the basis of such 'selling' is that the goods sent are so worthless and the prices demanded so high, that the sender of the goods makes a profit if even a small percentage of customers pay up. The criminal side of the legislation seems rarely to be enforced. Section 3 of the 1971 Act allows a business to refuse to pay a charge for being included in a trade directory, or to recover any payment made for being included, unless a signed order is made on the stationery of the business to be included in the directory.

3.2.1 The postal rule

As we have already seen, it can be extremely important to know exactly when an acceptance becomes legally effective. Before the acceptance is made the offeror can call the offer off, but once the acceptance has been made this is no longer possible.

When an offer is accepted by posting a letter the effect of the postal rule has to be considered. The rule, which holds that the acceptance of an offer by post is effective as soon as the letter is properly posted, originated in the early nineteenth century. In order to understand the current effect of the rule it is necessary to examine several cases in their historical context.

Adams v Lindsell (1818) 1 B & Ald 681

On Tuesday 2 September 1818 the defendants sent a letter to the claimants, offering to sell wool and requiring an answer by return of post. The defendants misdirected the letter and this caused it to be delivered at 7 pm on Friday 5 September. If the letter had not been misdirected it would have arrived on 3 September. The claimants posted an acceptance on 5 September. As this letter of acceptance was carried via London, it was not received by the defendants until 9 September. If the defendants had not misdirected the letter containing their offer then a reply by return of post would have arrived on 7 September. As they had not received an acceptance by 7 September, the defendants sold the wool to a third party.

Held. There was a good contract on 5 September when the letter of acceptance was posted.

COMMENT (i) To some extent the court was influenced by the fact that it was the defendants' fault that the letter had been misdirected.

(ii) In **Household Fire Insurance Co v Grant** (1879) 4 Ex D 216 the Court of Appeal applied the postal rule in a case where the letter of acceptance was permanently lost in the post. The defendant's letter agreed to buy 100 shares in a company. He paid 5 per cent of the price of £100. A letter accepting his offer was posted but never received. The company went into liquidation. A good contract was formed when the letter was posted and the defendant was therefore obliged to pay the remaining £95.

(iii) In **Henthorn v Fraser** [1892] 2 Ch 27 the Court of Appeal held that the rule would operate not only where the offer was sent by post, but whenever it would reasonably be expected that an acceptance would be made by post. Lord Herschell said that an acceptance

→

would be effective when posted, 'where the circumstances are such that it must have been within the contemplation of the parties that, according to the ordinary usages of mankind, the post might be used as a means of communicating the acceptance of an offer'.

(iv) The rule only ever applies to an acceptance of an offer. A postal revocation of an offer is effective when received.

In order for the rule to apply the letter of acceptance must have been properly addressed and properly posted.

Re London and Northern Bank, ex parte Jones [1900] 1 Ch 220

The claimant applied for shares in a company. On 26 October 1898 he wrote a letter withdrawing his application. This letter of revocation was received by the company at 8.30 am on 27 October and read at 9.30 am. At 7 am on 27 October the company had handed a letter of acceptance to a postman, paying him a small fee for taking this and other letters. This letter of acceptance was delivered to the claimant in Sheffield at 7.30 pm on 27 October. The claimant sued to have his name removed from the company register. He argued that as his offer had been revoked before it was accepted he had never made a contract to buy the shares.

Held. The letter of revocation was received before the letter of acceptance became effective and so there was no binding contract. Postmen are not authorised to take letters for posting and do not do so as agents of the Post Office. Therefore, the company could not prove that the letter of acceptance was properly posted before 9.30 am. Cozens-Hardy J: 'I cannot, therefore, regard the postman as anything better than a boy messenger employed . . . to post the letters, and the mere fact of handing the letter to the postman . . . was not a posting of the letter.'

COMMENT (i) The case also illustrates the well accepted position that letters of revocation are never effective upon posting. The postal rule has never applied to letters of revocation, but only to letters of acceptance.

(ii) Cozens-Hardy J said that the postal rule was made because the Post Office is considered the common agent of both parties. The fact that the rule does not apply to letters of revocation makes this proposition highly dubious.

In *Holwell Securities v Hughes* [1974] 1 WLR 155 the Court of Appeal reviewed the postal rule. On 19

October 1971 Dr Hughes had given Holwell Securities an option to purchase his house for £45 000. The option was said to be exercisable 'by notice in writing' to the defendant within six months. On 14 April 1972 Holwell Securities posted a letter exercising the option, but the letter was never delivered. No further communication was made until the option expired on 19 April. Holwell Securities sued for specific performance (a court order requiring Dr Hughes to sell the house to them). They argued that the postal rule applied, and that a contract was therefore created as soon as their letter was posted. The Court of Appeal held that the rule did not apply and so there was no contract. The express terms of the offer ('by notice in writing') indicated that the acceptance had to reach the offeror to become effective, and so this made the postal rule inappropriate. Lawton LJ also stated that the rule would not apply where it would 'produce manifest inconvenience and absurdity'. He went on to say: 'In my judgment, the factors of inconvenience and absurdity are but illustrations of a wider principle, namely, that the rule does not apply if, having regard to all the circumstances, including the nature of the subject-matter under consideration, the negotiating parties cannot have intended that there should be a binding agreement until the party accepting an offer or exercising an option had in fact communicated the acceptance or exercise to the other.'

If the offeror stipulates that acceptance should be made in a particular manner then any method of acceptance which is equally expeditious is likely to be valid, unless the offeror made it plain that the offer had to be accepted in the precise way stipulated. Even if the offeror does insist that acceptance can only be made in the precise way stipulated, this requirement can be waived by the offeror's conduct.

3.2.2 **Counter offer**

Acceptance of an offer must be unqualified and unconditional. A response which proposes a material alteration of the terms of the offer will amount to a counter offer. The effect of such a counter offer will be to revoke the original offer.

Hyde v Wrench (1840) 3 Beav 334

On 6 June 1840 the defendant offered to sell his farm to the claimant for £1 000. The defendant asked for a reply by return of post as he had another buyer in →

mind. The claimant's agent called on the defendant and offered £950 for the farm on the claimant's behalf. The defendant replied that he would need to think about this and assured the agent that he was not carrying on negotiations to sell to anyone else. On 27 June the defendant wrote to the claimant's agent declining the offer of £950. On 29 June the claimant wrote back accepting the original offer to sell the farm at £1 000. The defendant refused to sell at this price.

Held. There was no contract. The claimant's counter offer of £950 had revoked the defendant's original offer.

COMMENT It might seem strange that the counter offer was held to have revoked the original offer, but this must be the correct decision. If a business offers to sell an asset for a certain price and this offer is rejected by the offeree making a counter offer, the business is likely to sell the asset to someone else. It would be very harsh if the offeree, having refused the original offer, could now accept it and make the offeror liable for breach of contract.

The following case shows a modern example of the counter-offer rule.

Pickfords Ltd v *Celestica Ltd* [2003] EWCA Civ 1741, [2003] All ER (D) 265 Nov (Court of Appeal)

The defendants hired the claimants to move business property from Stoke-on-Trent to Shropshire. On 13 September 2001 the claimants faxed an offer to do the work at a certain price per unit plus additional costs such as insurance. (The first offer.) On 27 September the claimants sent a second offer to do the work for a fixed price, including insurance. On 15 October the defendants faxed a 'confirmation', which stated that the cost of the work would be capped at £10 000. The work was performed and the defendants paid the price based on the first offer. The claimants argued that the price should have been as per the second offer because the defendants had accepted this.

Held. The second offer was materially inconsistent with the first offer and therefore revoked it. It was clear that the defendant intended to accept the first offer because reference to a ceiling price could not mean that they were accepting the second offer, which set a fixed price. However, because the first offer had been revoked the defendant's 'confirmation' fax was a counter offer on the same terms as the first offer, with the additional term that the price should be capped at £10 000. By carrying out the removal work the claimants had accepted this counter offer.

3.2.3 **Auctions**

Earlier in this chapter we saw that when goods are sold by auction the various bidders make a series of offers, and that the auctioneer accepts the highest offer by banging his hammer. Section 57(1) of the Sale of Goods Act 1979 states that each lot is taken to be the subject of a separate contract of sale. Section 57(2) confirms that a sale is complete when the auctioneer announces this by banging his hammer, or by some other customary manner, and that until this time any bid can be retracted.

A sale by auction may be notified to be subject to a reserve price, beneath which the goods will not be sold, and the seller of the goods may also expressly reserve a right to bid for them (s.57(3)). However, if the sale by auction is not notified to be subject to the right to bid by or on behalf of the seller, it is not lawful for the seller to bid, or to employ any person to bid for him, or for the auctioneer to take any such bid (s.57(4)). A sale which contravenes s.57(4) can be treated as fraudulent by the buyer (s.57(5)).

When an auction is advertised as being 'without reserve' this means that if the auction of a particular lot actually starts the auctioneer makes an offer of a unilateral contract, promising that he will sell to the highest genuine bidder, no matter how low that bid might be. This offer of a unilateral contract can be accepted by making the highest bid. Such a bid would not conclude a contract of sale between the bidder and the owner of the goods. It would make the auctioneer liable to the highest bidder on a collateral contract.

In *Barry* v *Davies (T/A Heathcote-Ball & Co)* [2000] 1 WLR 1962 (Court of Appeal) two machines were put up for auction without a reserve price. The machines were each worth about £14 000 and the auctioneer tried to get a bid of £5 000. The claimant bid £400 for the machines but the auctioneer refused to accept the bid. After the auction the machines were sold to a third party for £3 000. It was held that the auctioneer had breached a collateral contract with the claimant and the claimant was awarded damages of £27 600. (This was the difference between what the claimant had bid and the amount he would have had to pay to buy the machines elsewhere.) The auctioneer's promise that the machines would be sold without reserve was the offer of a unilateral contract, given in exchange for the claimant's attending the auction and making the highest bid.

If an auctioneer advertises that goods will be sold 'without reserve' this does not amount to a promise that the goods will be included in the auction or that the auction will definitely take place.

Harris v Nickerson (1873) LR 8 QB 286

An auctioneer advertised in the London newspapers that office furniture was to be sold by auction in Bury St Edmunds. The advertisement stated that the highest bidder would get the goods. The claimant travelled to Bury St Edmunds from London, and bought several lots. However, the office furniture which he intended to buy was not included in the auction. The claimant sued for the expenses which he had incurred.

Held. The claimant had no remedy. The advertisement was merely an invitation to treat and did not amount to a definite offer. It amounted to a declaration of intention rather than a promise to put the goods up for sale.

It must be remembered that most lots at auction do have a reserve price. If this is the case then the auctioneer will take bids in the normal way, but will refuse to sell if the highest bid does not reach the reserve price.

For example, if a painting is put up for auction with a reserve price of £50 then the auctioneer will not sell to the highest bidder unless his bid is £50 or higher.

3.2.4 Tenders

Both goods and services can be bought or sold by tender. As well as being an effective way of contracting at the best price it is a business method particularly favoured by organisations (such as local authorities) which must show that a contract was not gained as a result of favouritism or corruption. The way in which the contract is formed can be understood by reference to an example.

Let us assume that a local authority needs a supply of school desks and that it places advertisements which invite tenders to supply the desks. Whether this advertisement will amount to an offer or an invitation to treat will depend entirely on the words which are used.

If the advertisement merely asks for tenders to supply 1 000 desks of a certain description, then it will amount only to an invitation to treat. A tenderer who responds by submitting a tender to supply the desks at £40 each would be making an offer. The local authority might accept this offer, but it would not be bound to do so.

Sometimes, however, the invitation to tender can itself be an offer. Let us suppose that an invitation to tender invites bids for the sale of certain goods, and states that the highest bid will definitely get the goods. The invitation to tender would amount to the offer of a unilateral contract. The tenderer who submits the highest price would be deemed to have accepted the offer and to have made a contract to buy the goods. These principles are clearly demonstrated by the following case.

Spencer v Harding (1870) LR 5 CP 561

The defendants advertised that they would sell certain goods by tender. The advertisement began, 'We are instructed to offer to the wholesale trade for sale by tender the stock-in-trade of Messrs. G. Eilbeck and Co …' and went on to state where the goods could be viewed, the time at which the tenders would be opened and that payment would have to be in cash. The claimant submitted the highest tender but the defendants refused to sell to him.

Held. The defendants did not have to sell. Their advertisement asking for tenders was only an invitation to treat. The claimant had made an offer but the defendants had no obligation to accept this. However, Willes J stated that the invitation for tenders would have been the offer of a unilateral contract if it had gone on to say, 'and we undertake to sell to the highest bidder'.

Many advertisements invite tenders to supply such goods as the invitor might require within a certain time. A tenderer who puts in a price at which the goods will be supplied for the whole period of time makes what is known as a standing offer.

Such an offer can be accepted many times, and each acceptance leads to a new contract. However, the offer is only accepted when the person who invited tenders actually orders goods, and the offer can be withdrawn before any particular order is made.

Great Northern Railway Company v Witham (1873) LR 9 CP 16

The claimants' advertisement asked for tenders to supply goods 'such as they may think fit to order' in a one year period. The defendant put in a tender stating the price at which he would supply such quantities as the claimants might order within the period. The claimants accepted this tender. After filling several orders the defendant, within the year, refused to fill one. The →

claimants argued that the defendant had made a contract to fill the order.

Held. The defendant had made a contract to fill that particular order. He had made a 'standing offer' and each time the claimants made an order they accepted this offer.

COMMENT The defendant could have withdrawn his offer as regards future orders, even if the orders were made within the one year period. Such a revocation of the standing offer would be effective when it was received. Revocation would be allowed because the defendant had been given no consideration in return for keeping the offer open, that is to say he had been given nothing of any value in return for doing so. (Consideration is considered in detail in Chapter 4.)

In *Harvela Investments Ltd v Royal Trust Co of Canada Ltd* [1986] AC 207 the House of Lords had to consider whether or not to allow 'referential tenders'. Such tenders state their price by reference to other tenders. In the *Harvela* case two people wishing to buy shares were asked to put in a tender indicating the price they would pay. The seller promised that the two tenders would be opened at the same time and that the highest bid would get the shares. The defendant put in a tender agreeing to pay $2 100 000 or $101 000 in excess of any other offer. The other tender was for $2 175 000. The House of Lords held that the referential tender was invalid because it defeated the whole object of fixed competitive tendering, the idea of which is that the amounts tendered are confidential and unknown to the other tenderers. The seller had shown a clear intention to sell and if both sides made a referential bid this intention would have been defeated. The seller was not therefore entitled to accept the referential tender. The tender of $2 175 000 was therefore successful.

In certain circumstances the mere fact of inviting tenders may give rise to a binding contractual obligation to consider tenders properly submitted.

Blackpool & Fylde Aero Club Ltd v Blackpool Borough Council
[1990] 3 All ER 25

The defendants owned and managed an airport. Revenue was raised by letting this out to air operators who conducted pleasure flights. The claimant club had held the concession for several years. The defendants sent invitations to tender for a new con-

cession to the claimant club and to six other parties who were connected with the airport. Tenders were to be submitted in envelopes supplied and were not to bear any mark indicating who the tenderer was. The defendants stated that only tenders received by 12 noon on 17 March 1983 would be considered. The claimants' tender was put into the defendants' letter box at 11 am on 17 March. However, the letter box was not emptied at noon as it should have been. The claimants' tender was regarded as late and was not considered. The claimants sued for damages for breach of contract, arguing that the council had promised that if a tender was received before the deadline it would be considered.

Held. The claimants were entitled to damages. In certain circumstances an invitation to tender could create binding obligations to consider conforming tenders. The circumstances of the case indicated that an offer of a unilateral contract had impliedly been made. This offer was made to the seven potential tenderers and promised that if they submitted their tender in the correct way then in return they would have their tenders opened and considered, along with any other tenders which were considered.

3.3 CERTAINTY

A contract will only come into existence if the offer which is accepted contains all of the essential terms of the contract. A court must be able to identify, with certainty, exactly what has been agreed. It is a well-established principle that a court will not write a contract for the parties. In deciding whether or not an agreement is sufficiently certain to amount to a contract the courts do not consider the subjective views of the offeror and offeree. Rather they take an objective view by asking whether the reasonable person would have thought that the agreement was sufficiently certain.

The advantage of this objective approach can be demonstrated by considering an example. Let us suppose that there is a dispute between X and Y. X made an offer which Y accepted. Later X claims that there is no contract because the meaning of what was agreed is uncertain. Y maintains that the essential terms were agreed with certainty and that there is a contract which X must perform. There is little point in a court considering the subjective opinions of X and Y as to whether or not the agreement was sufficiently certain. Maybe both of the parties genuinely do believe what they maintain. If not, it is perfectly possible that they will be prepared to give evidence in court that they do believe it. Plainly, therefore, many disputes could not be resolved by looking at the subjective opinions of the parties themselves. Instead the courts use the reasonable person to look for the objective meaning of the contract. Reference to the reasonable person allows the court to ask not what the parties to the contract actually meant, but what they appeared to mean. If the contract appeared to the reasonable person to be certain then it will be certain. If it did not appear to the reasonable person to be certain then it will not be.

Scammell and Nephew Ltd v Ouston
[1941] AC 251 (House of Lords)

A firm of furnishers wanted to acquire a new van on hire-purchase. Scammell agreed to supply a van priced at £286, allowing the firm £100 for an old van which was traded in. The agreement stated that 'this order is given on the understanding that the balance of the purchase price can be had on hire purchase terms over a period of two years'. After some disagreements Scammells refused to supply the van, claiming that the agreement was not certain enough to amount to a contract.

Held. There was no contract between the parties. The agreement as to hire-purchase terms was so vague that it could not be given a definite meaning. The parties would need to reach further agreement before there could be a completed contract.

Sudbrook Trading Estate Ltd v Eggleton [1983] AC 444 (House of Lords)

A lease gave the tenant an option to buy the land absolutely, 'at such price, not being less than £12 000, as may be agreed upon by two valuers one to be nominated by the lessor and the other by the lessee and in default of such agreement by an umpire appointed by the . . . valuers . . . '. The tenant exercised the option to purchase but the landlord refused to appoint a valuer.

Held. This was a good contract for sale of the land at a fair and reasonable price which was to be reached by applying objective standards. If the machinery which the parties had set up to ascertain the price broke down the court would substitute its own machinery to find a fair and reasonable price.

If the parties merely agree that they will agree one or more terms in the future this does not create a contract. In **Willis Management (Isle of Man) Ltd v Cable and**

Wireless plc [2005] EWCA Civ 806, [2005] 2 Lloyds Rep 597 CA (Civ Div) Tuckey LJ said, 'An agreement to agree an essential term is not [a binding contract]. The court cannot make for the parties the agreement which they did not make for themselves.' However, in contracts to sell goods or to supply services a contract can exist even if the price has not been agreed. Section 8(1) of the Sale of Goods Act 1979 provides that the price in a contract of sale of goods may be fixed by the contract, or may be left to be fixed in a manner agreed by the contract, or may be determined by the course of dealing between the parties. Section 8(2) provides that where the price is not determined by any of these methods the buyer must pay a reasonable price. Section 15(1) of the Supply of Goods and Services Act 1982 makes a similar provision where the contract is for the supply of a service.

If the parties believe that they have made a contract, a court will not readily hold that they have not. Once an agreement has started to be performed the courts are much more likely to hold that there is a contract. It is not absolutely essential to do this because in the absence of a contract a party who had received valuable benefits could be ordered to pay for them on a *quantum meruit* basis. (This would mean that the person who had supplied the goods or services would be paid a reasonable price or remuneration.) However, the fact of the agreement having been partly performed is a strong indication that the parties intended to create a contract.

Percy Trentham Ltd v Archital Luxfer Ltd
[1993] 1 Lloyd's Rep 25 (Court of Appeal)

The claimants, who were building engineers, were engaged by MMI Ltd as the main contractors to build industrial units in two phases. The defendants were manufacturers and installers of aluminium doors and windows. The defendants did the window work for the claimants in phases 1 and 2, and the claimants paid the defendants for this work. The claimants found defects with the defendants' work in both phase 1 and phase 2. They claimed damages for breach of contract. The defendants denied that their dealings with the claimants ever resulted in concluded contracts.

Held. There was a contract between the two parties as regards both phase 1 and phase 2. This contract was formed by conduct. The parties plainly intended to enter into binding contractual relations. The course of dealing between the parties entitled the claimants to performance of the work and the defendants to be paid. →

Steyn LJ: 'English law generally adopts an objective theory of contract formation. That means that in practice our law generally ignores the subjective expectations and the unexpressed mental reservations of the parties. Instead the governing criterion is the reasonable expectations of … sensible businessmen … The fact that the transaction was performed on both sides will often make it unrealistic to argue that there was no intention to enter into legal relations. It will often make it difficult to submit that the contract is void for vagueness or uncertainty. Specifically, the fact that the transaction is executed makes it easier to imply a term resolving any uncertainty, or, alternatively, it may make it possible to treat a matter not finalised in negotiations as inessential.'

COMMENT Steyn LJ also made the following points. (i) Although the vast majority of contracts would be formed through offer and acceptance this would not necessarily be the case where a contract came into existence by performance.

(ii) If a contract only comes into existence as a result of performance it will frequently be possible to imply that the contract retrospectively covers pre-contractual performance.

(iii) When a transaction has been partly performed this will give rise to similar considerations to those which apply when the contract has been fully performed.

In *RTS Flexible Systems Ltd v Molkerei Muller GmbH* [2010] UKSC 14, [2010] 1 WLR 753, the Supreme Court had to decide whether a contract existed and, if so, on which party's terms. Lord Clark, delivering the judgment of the court, said:

'The general principles are not in doubt. Whether there is a binding contract between the parties and, if so, upon what terms depends upon what they have agreed. It depends not upon their subjective state of mind, but upon a consideration of what was communicated between them by words or conduct, and whether that leads objectively to a conclusion that they intended to create legal relations and had agreed upon all the terms which they regarded or the law requires as essential for the formation of legally binding relations. Even if certain terms of economic or other significance to the parties have not been finalised, an objective appraisal of their words and conduct may lead to the conclusion that they did not intend agreement of such terms to be a pre-condition to a concluded and legally binding agreement … in a case where a contract is being negotiated subject to

contract and work begins before the formal contract is executed, it cannot be said that there will always or even usually be a contract on the terms that were agreed subject to contract. That would be too simplistic and dogmatic an approach. The court should not impose binding contracts on the parties which they have not reached. All will depend upon the circumstances.'

3.3.1 Meaningless terms

Many written contracts contain meaningless terms. As the following case shows, it would be poor policy to allow a person to escape from a contract merely because he had discovered such a term.

Nicolene Ltd v Simmonds
[1953] 1 QB 543 (Court of Appeal)

The claimants wrote to the defendant ordering 3 000 tons of reinforced steel bars and asked for written confirmation of acceptance of the order. The defendant wrote back from his private address thanking the claimants for the contract. However, this letter said 'As you have made the order direct to me, I am unable to confirm on my usual printed form which would have the usual force majeure and war clauses, but I assume that we are in agreement that the usual conditions of acceptance apply.' Later the defendant argued that there was no contract as complete agreement had not been reached with regard to the usual conditions of acceptance.

Held. As there were no usual conditions of acceptance the words were meaningless and could be ignored. There was therefore a complete and enforceable contract between the parties.

Denning LJ: 'In my opinion a distinction must be drawn between a clause which is meaningless and a clause which is yet to be agreed. A clause which is meaningless can often be ignored, whilst still leaving the contract good; whereas a clause which has yet to be agreed may mean that there is no contract at all, because the parties have not agreed on all the essential terms …'

COMMENT Lord Denning pointed out that if meaningless clauses were allowed to negate a contract, 'You would find defaulters all scanning their contracts to find some meaningless clause on which to ride free.'

It should be noted that in this type of case either the previous dealings of the parties or trade custom could have a strong influence on the court's decision.

If, for example, Nicolene Ltd and Simmonds had dealt with each other on several previous occasions there might have been little difficulty in deciding what the usual conditions of acceptance were. Similarly, if Ouston had several times taken vans from Scammell Ltd on hire-purchase then the court might well have decided that 'on hire-purchase terms' was definite enough for the reasonable person to say what had been agreed.

Many agreements, especially those to sell land and houses, are expressed to be made 'subject to contract'. Generally it is accepted that the use of these words means that no contract has yet been concluded.

3.4 OFFER AND ACCEPTANCE WHEN DEALING WITH MACHINES

It has become common for people to buy goods (or tickets which entitle them to services) from machines. At first sight this seems to cause considerable difficulty in finding the offer and the acceptance. The customer cannot make both the offer and the acceptance so the machine, on behalf of the supplier of the goods or services, must make either the offer or the acceptance. In *Thornton v Shoe Lane Parking Ltd* [1971] 2 QB 163 (Court of Appeal) Lord Denning MR analysed the position when a customer in a multi-storey car park is given a ticket by a machine on entry to the car park. He concluded that the contract was completed not when the customer received the ticket, but as soon as the customer became irrevocably committed to the contract, that is to say, as soon as he put his money into the machine.

Lord Denning MR stated:

'The customer pays his money and gets a ticket. He cannot refuse it. He cannot get his money back. He may protest to the machine, even swear at it. But it will remain unmoved. He is committed beyond recall. He was committed at the very moment when he put his money into the machine. The contract was concluded at that time. It can be translated into offer and acceptance in this way: the offer is made when the proprietor of the machine holds it out as being ready to receive the money. The acceptance is made when the customer puts his money into the slot.'

Thornton v Shoe Lane Parking will be considered in more detail in Chapter 5. It will be seen there that the significance of the contract being formed before the ticket was received was that words on the ticket were therefore too late to be incorporated into the contract.

Earlier in this chapter, at 3.2, we considered *Entores v Miles Far East Corporation* [1955] 2 QB 327 (Court of Appeal) and saw that an acceptance by telex is effective when it is received. We also saw that Lord Denning took the view that an acceptance by telex, like a personal communication, will not be effective if the person sending it knows that it has not been received. Lord Denning also indicated that if it was the fault of the offeror that the acceptance was not received, for example if his telex machine had run out of ink, then the acceptance could be regarded as received when it should have been received. In *Brinkibon Ltd v Stahag Stahl und Stahlwarenhandelsgesellschaft GmbH* [1983] 2 AC 34 the House of Lords approved the decision in *Entores*.

Lord Wilberforce, dealing with communication by telex, made it plain that the courts will take a pragmatic, flexible approach.

'The message may not reach, or be intended to reach, the designated recipient immediately: messages may be sent out of office hours, or at night, with the intention, or on the assumption, that they will be read at a later time. There may be some error or default at the recipient's end which prevents receipt at the time contemplated and believed in by the sender . . . And many other variations may occur. No universal rule can cover all such cases; they must be resolved by reference to the intentions of the parties, by sound business practice and in some cases by a judgment where the risks should lie.'

It does seem fairly certain that if an acceptance by telex or fax is received during office hours it is effective when received and not when it is noticed. But what if the recipient machine is turned off? It is not possible to answer such a question with certainty, but in *Brinkibon* Lord Fraser said, 'Once the message has been received on the offeror's telex machine, it is not unreasonable to treat it as delivered to the principal offeror, because it is his responsibility to arrange for prompt handling of messages within his own office.' Lord Fraser also made the point that the acceptor by telex can generally tell if his message has not been received, whereas the offeror would not know that an unsuccessful attempt had been made to send an acceptance.

3.4.1 Offer and acceptance made over the Internet

As yet there have been no significant decisions by the courts as to when a contract is concluded over the Internet. There are two main ways in which such a contract might be formed. First, a contract could be made by exchange of emails. Second, a customer might visit a website and buy goods or services described there.

The position where emails have been exchanged should be catered for by the common law rules already considered in this chapter. The courts will take an objective view of an email and consider whether it was an offer or an invitation to treat. An offer might or might not be of a unilateral contract. In the same way the courts will consider objectively whether an email amounted to acceptance of an offer. The most likely difficulty will arise in deciding precisely when an acceptance by email is effective. The general principles laid down in relation to telex seems likely to be applied. However, email differs from communication by telex in that a person who sends an email does not immediately know whether or not it has been received. In some ways acceptance by email is more similar to acceptance by letter than acceptance by telex. However, it seems very unlikely that the postal rule will apply. The rule is anomalous and the approach of the courts has been to restrict its application rather than to expand it. It seems much more likely that the statement of Lord Wilberforce in **Brinkibon**, set out above, will apply to acceptance by email. This statement does not provide a cast iron answer applicable to all situations. It indicates that the court will be guided by the intentions of the parties, sound business practice and a judgment as to where the risks should lie.

In general, websites which describe goods and services and the prices at which they are available will be making invitations to treat rather than offers. This would be particularly true if the material on the website makes it plain that it is the customer who makes the offer and that his offer might or might not be accepted. The customer might make the offer by clicking on a button. Any acceptance would be effective when the customer was informed that his offer had been accepted. However, there is no reason why a website should not make the offer of a unilateral contract. If this were the case then the contract would be concluded as soon as the customer had performed the stipulated act of acceptance (generally by clicking on an acceptance button).

As we have seen, the key question when dealing with the conclusion of contracts is the time when the acceptance is effective. The Electronic Commerce (EC Directive) Regulations 2002 are concerned with the formalities which must be complied with when a contract is made with an Internet service provider. They do not deal with the time at which the contract is concluded. However, reg.11 provides that an offer made by a consumer to an Internet service provider, and an acknowledgement of having received such an offer, are to be effective when the person to whom they are addressed can access them. The Regulations do not deal with the time at which an acceptance is effective. However, there seems to be no reason why this too should not be when the person to whom it is addressed is able to access it. But this is not explicitly stated. In any event, as we shall see in Chapter 7 at 7.1.5 the question is often of little relevance in consumer contracts because the Consumer Protection (Distance Selling) Regulations 2000 (considered at 7.1.5) give consumers the right to cancel concluded distance contracts. However, the regulations give no such rights to non-consumers.

3.5 ACCEPTANCE OF AN OFFER OF A UNILATERAL CONTRACT

In **Carlill's case** we saw that the offeree's motive for performing the act requested by the offeror is irrelevant. Presumably Mrs Carlill used the smoke ball to avoid catching flu, but this did not mean that she had failed to accept the offer. In **Williams v Carwardine** (1833) 5 C & P 566 a woman gave information leading to the conviction of a murderer. She did this because she thought she was about to die and she wanted to ease her conscience. Nevertheless, she was entitled to the reward which had been offered for the supply of information which led to the murderer's conviction.

Although the situation is not entirely clear, it seems that a person who claims to have accepted an offer of a unilateral contract does not need to have known of the offer at the time when the act which constitutes acceptance was begun. It is sufficient that the offeree has knowledge before the act is completed. So if Mrs Carlill had only heard of the reward shortly before she caught flu she would still have been entitled to claim that she had accepted the offer.

Test your understanding 3.2

1 At what point does an acceptance become effective so as to create a bilateral contract?

2 What is the effect of the postal rule? In what circumstances will the rule not apply?

3 What effect does a counter offer have on the offer to which it is a response?

4 What is the legal effect of advertising that an auction will be held at which goods will be sold without reserve?

5 In what circumstances will an invitation to submit tenders amount to an offer?

6 In ascertaining whether or not an agreement was sufficiently certain to constitute a contract, do the courts consider the objective meaning of what the parties agreed, or do they consider the subjective views of the parties themselves?

7 How will the presence of a meaningless term in a contract affect the validity of the contract?

3.6 TERMINATION OF OFFERS

We have seen that as soon as an offer is accepted a contract results. There are several ways in which an offer which has been made can later cease to exist. Before examining these methods it must be borne in mind that we are not here concerned with whether or not the obligations imposed by a contract have ceased to exist. If an offer ceases to exist, before it has been accepted, then no contract will ever come into existence. The obligations imposed by a contract will cease to exist once the contract has been discharged, a matter considered in Chapter 7.

3.6.1 Revocation

An offer can be revoked at any time before it is accepted. Once revoked, the offer no longer exists and acceptance of it is therefore no longer possible. A revocation is effective only when it is received by the offeree. Earlier in this chapter we saw that, the postal rule and offers of unilateral contracts apart, an acceptance of an offer is only effective when it is received by the offeror. So when an offeree claims to have accepted an offer which the offeror claims to have revoked, the court will need to discover whether or not the acceptance was received before the revocation was received. The following example demonstrates the two possibilities.

Let us suppose that farmer X has offered to sell 100 tons of potatoes to wholesaler Y, who has expressed interest but has not yet accepted. All of the terms of the proposed contract have been clearly identified and if Y were to accept, a contract would immediately be created. Both X and Y go home and watch the news on the television. One of the news items announces that the price of potatoes is likely to increase because of disastrous weather in Europe. X decides that he no longer wants to sell his crop to Y at the price offered and resolves to revoke his offer. Y decides that he wants to make the contract and to let X know that the offer is accepted. Whether or not a contract will come into being will depend upon who communicates first. If Y receives X's revocation before X receives Y's acceptance, then there will be no contract. If X receives Y's acceptance before Y has received the revocation, then a contract will have been created.

Once an offer has been made, if the offeror makes a subsequent inconsistent offer this will revoke the original offer. *Pickfords Ltd v Celestica*, considered earlier in this chapter at 3.2.2, provides an example. In that case the Court of Appeal also stated that acting inconsistently with the original offer, to the knowledge of the offeree, could also revoke the original offer even if no words were used.

Revocation will generally be communicated to the offeree by the offeror or his agent. However, the following shows that an unauthorised third party can also communicate revocation as long as the offeree can regard the third party as reliable.

Dickinson v Dodds
(1876) 2 Ch D 463 (Court of Appeal)

On Wednesday 10 June the defendant delivered a written offer to sell a house and outbuildings to the claimant. The offer stated that, 'This offer to be left over until Friday, 9 o'clock a.m. June 12, 1874.' On Thursday the defendant negotiated to sell the house to one Allan. One Berry found out about the negotiated sale and told the claimant. At 7 am on Friday morning Berry, acting as the claimant's agent, handed the defendant a letter of acceptance and explained its effect to him. The defendant had sold the house to Allan on the Thursday.

Held. There was no contract. As no consideration had been provided to keep the offer open, it could be revoked at any time. At the time when the claimant purported to accept the offer he knew that the defendant had changed his mind. Berry had effectively revoked the offer.

The old postal rule on acceptance of contracts has never applied to revocation of an offer but only to acceptance of an offer. Revocation of an offer is effective when received, whether posted or not, as the following case demonstrates.

Byrne & Co v Van Tienhoven & Co
(1880) 5 CPD 344

On 1 October 1879 the defendants, who carried on business in Cardiff, posted an offer to sell 1 000 boxes of tinplate to the claimants in New York. On 8 October the defendants posted a revocation of their offer. The defendant's offer was received by the claimants on 11 October and a telegram of acceptance was sent the same day. A letter of acceptance was also sent on 15 October. On 20 October the defendant's letter of revocation reached the claimants.

Held. A good contract came into existence on 11 October. The revocation was not effective until it was received on 20 October.

An offer, whether of a unilateral or a bilateral contract, can be revoked at any time before acceptance. However, some difficulty is caused by the fact that acceptance of the offer of a unilateral contract takes the form of performing an action, and frequently the performance of this action will take some considerable time. The following case suggests that the offer of a unilateral contract cannot be revoked once the offeree has started to perform the act which constitutes acceptance.

Errington v Errington & Woods
[1952] 1 KB 290 (Court of Appeal)

A father bought a house for £750, paying £250 cash and borrowing £500 from a building society. The father told his daughter-in-law that if she paid the mortgage instalments she could have the house when the mortgage was paid off. The daughter-in-law did not agree to pay all of the mortgage instalments, but did begin to pay them as they became due. After the daughter-in-law had paid the mortgage instalments for some time, the father died leaving the house in his will to his widow. Soon afterwards the widow claimed possession of the house.

Held. The widow (who was in exactly the same position as her husband would have been in if he had still been alive) could not revoke the offer.

Denning LJ: 'The father's promise was a unilateral contract – a promise of the house in return for their act of paying the instalments. It could not be revoked by him once the couple entered on performance of the act, but it would cease to bind him if they left it incomplete and unperformed, which they have not done. If that was the position during the father's lifetime, so it must be after his death.'

COMMENT This case illustrates a general principle. However, in some circumstances it will be possible to revoke the offer of a unilateral contract even after the commencement of acceptance. (See the House of Lords decision in **Luxor (Eastbourne) Ltd v Cooper** [1941] AC 108 set out in Chapter 11 at 11.5.2.) In **Daulia Ltd v Four Millbank Nominees** [1978] 2 All ER 557 Goff LJ seemed to agree with Denning's view in **Errington v Errington and Woods**: 'there must be an implied obligation on the part of the [unilateral] offeror not to prevent the condition becoming satisfied, which obligation it seems to me must arise as soon as the offeree starts to perform. Until then the offeror can revoke the whole thing, but once the offeree has embarked on performance it is too late for the offeror to revoke his offer.'

Soulsbury v Soulsbury
[2007] EWC A Civ 969, [2008] 2 WLR 834

As part of a divorce settlement, the husband was ordered to pay the wife £12 000 per annum. It was later agreed between the divorced couple that if she did not seek to enforce the award he would leave her £100 000 in his will. After this agreement he stopped making payments and she never attempted to recover arrears. The former husband became ill and on the day he died he remarried. This revoked the will which he had made, under which he had left his former wife £100 000. The deceased's personal representatives refused to pay the former wife the £100 000.

Held. The agreement to pay the £100 000 was valid and could be enforced. Longmore LJ regarded the agreement as a unilateral contract. He said: 'This is a classic unilateral contract of the **Carlill v Carbolic Smoke Ball** [1893] 1 QB 256 or the 'walk to York' kind. Once the promisee acts on the promise by inhaling the smoke ball, by starting the walk to York or (as here) by not suing for the maintenance to which she was entitled, the promisor cannot revoke or withdraw his offer. But there is no obligation on the promisee to continue to inhale, to walk the whole way to York or to refrain from suing. It is just that if she inhales no more, gives up the walk to York or does sue for her maintenance, she is not entitled to claim the promised sum.'

→

COMMENT: (i) Longmore LJ's statement is very clear, but must be regarded as *obiter*. As he acknowledged, the former wife 'had completed all possible performance of the act required for enforcement of [the] promise'. That is to say, she had completed the acceptance of the offer of the unilateral contract. Therefore, the quotation above, which relates to whether the offer could have been revoked before acceptance was complete, was not the basis of the decision. Ward LJ gave a lengthy leading judgment which concentrated on matrimonial law. He did not refer to unilateral contracts. Smith LJ merely said that she agreed with both judgments.

(ii) Offering someone a sum of money if he walked to York has always been the classic example of the offer of a unilateral contract.

The rule that revocation is effective only when it is communicated to the offeree causes some difficulty in reward cases where the offer of a unilateral contract is made to the whole world. It must be possible to revoke such an offer and the legal position seems to be that this can be achieved by advertising the revocation in the same way as the offer was advertised. So the Carbolic Smoke Ball Company's offer to pay the £100 reward could have been revoked by advertising the revocation in the same way as the offer was advertised. This revocation would be effective even as regards a person who had read the offer but had not read the revocation. It would not be effective as regards a person who had already begun to accept the offer by using the smoke ball in the correct way.

3.6.2 **Rejection of offer**

If an offeree communicates rejection of an offer then this terminates the offer. We saw an example in *Hyde* v *Wrench*, above at 3.2.2. The claimant's counter offer of £950 for the farm amounted to a rejection of the defendant's offer to sell for £1 000. It therefore terminated the offer.

A request for more information about an offer does not terminate the offer as it does not imply rejection of it. It can therefore be important to distinguish a request for more information from a counter offer.

Stevenson, Jacques & Co v McLean
(1880) 5 QBD 346

At a time when the market price of iron was extremely volatile, the defendant offered to sell the claimants a quantity of iron for 40 shillings net cash per ton. The offer was made on Sunday 28 September and was to remain open until close of business on Monday 29 September. The claimants would have preferred to take the iron in instalments, paying as each instalment was received. At 9.42 am Monday 29 September the claimants sent a telegram, 'Please wire whether you would accept forty [shillings] for delivery over two months, or if not, longest time you would give'. The defendant did not reply to this telegram but on the same day sold the iron to someone else. At 1.25 pm the defendant telegraphed the claimants to tell them that this had been done. Before this telegram arrived the claimants sent a telegram accepting the defendant's offer. The defendant refused to deliver the iron and the claimants sued for non-delivery.

Held. There was a good contract to sell to the claimants at forty shillings per ton for immediate delivery, as orig-inally offered. The claimants' first telegram had not been a counter offer, it was just a request for more information. Consequently it did not revoke the defendant's offer.

A counter offer attempts to introduce a new term. A request for information does not, rather it merely seeks to clarify what the offer is. When business contracts are made there are often a series of negotiations, proposals and enquiries. It can be very difficult to distinguish those which amount to a counter offer from those which do not.

3.6.3 **Lapse of time**

If an offer is stipulated as being open for a particular time then it will be open for that length of time unless it is revoked. In *Dickinson* v *Dodds*, for example, the offer would have remained open until 9 am on Friday had it not been revoked. Any acceptance before 9 am on Friday would have been effective, but any acceptance after that time would have been too late.

It might seem rather unfair that an offer which has been stipulated as being open for a particular time can then be revoked before the time limit has expired. Revocation is allowed because the person to whom the offer was made has provided no consideration in return for the offer being kept open. This will be better understood after reading the following chapter, in which the meaning of consideration is examined. Put simply, it means that if the offeree had promised any benefit, for example the payment of £10, in return for keeping the offer open then this would have amounted to a contract to keep the offer open and so the offer could not then have been revoked. But because no consideration was given in return for the offer it was just a gratuitous promise and could therefore be revoked. In Chapter 4 we shall see that a promise for which nothing was received in return does not create a binding contractual obligation. *Mountford v Scott* [1975] 1 All ER 198, considered in more detail in Chapter 7 at 7.2.4, provides an example of purchasing an option to keep an offer open. In return for a payment of £1, the defendant promised to keep open for six months an offer to sell his house to the claimant for £10 000. This agreement amounted to a contract and so it was binding on the defendant.

If an offer is not specified as being open for any particular length of time then it will remain open for a **reasonable time** the length of which will depend upon all the circumstances of the case. If, for instance, a businessman made two offers, one to sell a boatload of ripe bananas and the other to sell his business premises, the offers would not remain open for the same length of time. Offers to sell shares in a private company are likely to lapse fairly quickly. In *Ramsgate Victoria Hotel Co v Montefiore* (1866) LR 1 Ex 109, an offer to buy shares made on 8 June was held to have lapsed by the time it was accepted on 23 November.

3.6.4 **Condition not fulfilled**

An offer can be stipulated as remaining in force until the happening of a certain event. When a person offers to buy goods, for example, it is implied that the offer is conditional on the goods remaining in the same condition as when the offer was made until the acceptance is made. If the goods are damaged before acceptance then the offer will cease to exist.

It is also possible to make a contract which will only become operative if a condition is fulfilled. The contract will exist as soon as it is made, but until the condition is fulfilled the rights and obli-gations of the parties do not become operative. For example, it is possible to make a sale of goods on the terms that a third party will fix the price. The contract exists as soon as it is made, and if the third party does fix the price then both sides will be bound to perform their obligations under the contract. But if the third party cannot or does not make the valuation the agreement is frustrated (Sale of Goods Act 1979, s.9).

3.6.5 **Death of offeror or offeree**

The fact that the offeror has died before the offer is accepted will not necessarily prevent the offeree from accepting the offer. If the offer was to supply a personal service, such as to sing at a concert, then the offer cannot be accepted. If the offer was not to supply a personal service, perhaps as an offer to sell a car, then the legal position is less clear. In *Bradbury v Morgan* (1862) 1 H & C 249 it was suggested that the offeree can accept the offer until he has notification of the offeror's death. If this point of view is correct then the offeror's personal representatives would need to perform the contract. The position is different where it is the offeree who has died. Although there is little authority on the matter, it seems likely that the personal representatives of an offeree who has died will not be able to accept any offer.

If one of the parties dies after the contract has been concluded then this will generally not prevent performance of the contract unless the party who died had contracted to supply personal services. This is a separate matter which is examined in Chapter 7 when we look at discharge of contractual obligations.

3.7 **BATTLE OF THE FORMS**

Many businesses use standard form contracts when buying and selling. When a seller believes that the contract was made on his standard form of sale, and the buyer believes the goods were bought on his standard form of purchase, the courts have to decide which form applies. As the following case demonstrates, they do this by applying the ordinary rules of offer and acceptance.

> ### *Butler Machine Tool Co Ltd v Ex-Cell-O Corporation Ltd*
> [1979] 1 All ER 965 (Court of Appeal)
>
> On 23 May 1969 the claimants offered to sell a machine for £75 553, delivery to be made within ten months. The offer was made on the claimants' terms and conditions, which stated that these terms and conditions were to prevail over any terms and conditions in the buyer's order. One of the claimants' terms allowed for an increase in the contract price if the price of manufacture should increase before the date for delivery. On 27 May the defendants ordered a machine, saying that the order was made on their terms and conditions. These terms and conditions →

differed from the claimants' terms and conditions, and did not include a price variation clause. At the foot of the order was a tear-off slip which stated, 'We accept your order on the Terms and Conditions stated thereon'. On 5 June the claimants signed the slip and sent it back to the defendants, adding that the order 'is being entered in accordance with our revised quotation of 23rd May'. The machine was delivered, but the claimants then claimed an extra £2 892 under their price variation clause.

Held. The claimants were not entitled to the extra money as the contract was made on the defendants' terms and conditions. The claimants made an offer on 23 May. The defendants made a counter offer on 27 May. The claimants accepted this counter offer by signing and returning the defendants' acknowledgement slip on 5 June.

COMMENT The decision in this case shows that generally the party who fires the last shot wins, that is to say the person who submits the last counter offer wins as long as the circumstances indicate that the other party accepted this counter offer. Lord Denning MR was critical of the classical offer, counter offer, and acceptance approach. He considered it ill-suited to the needs of modern business. If both sides insist on firing the last shot then a contract will not come into existence at all as agreement will never be reached. In **_Tekdata Interconnections Ltd v Amphenol Ltd_** [2009] EWCA Civ 1209, [2010] 1 Lloyd's Rep 357, the Court of Appeal held that in a 'battle of the forms' case the party who fired the last shot would generally win, but that this would not always be the case. The question would always depend upon what the parties must be taken, objectively, to have intended when the contract was made. This should be determined, objectively, on the basis of a proper interpretation of the documents.

Test your understanding 3.3

1 At what stage will a revocation of an offer be effective?
2 At what stage will revocation of an offer of a unilateral contract no longer be possible?
3 For how long will an offer remain open?
4 How will the courts solve 'battle of the forms' cases?

Key points

Offer

- An offeror makes an offer by proposing a set of terms with the intention that these terms will form a legally binding agreement if they are accepted by the person to whom they are proposed, the offeree.
- An offer can be made by words or by conduct.
- An invitation to treat is an invitation to bargain and is not an offer.
- Advertisements are generally invitations to treat rather than offers. However, an advertisement which makes a definite promise can amount to the offer of a unilateral contract.
- A unilateral contract is offered when one party promises to be bound if the other party performs some specified act. The parties to a bilateral contract exchange promises.
- The display of goods in shop windows or on supermarket shelves does not amount to an offer to sell those goods.

Acceptance

- As soon as an acceptance is received by the offeror a contract will come into existence. When the offer is of a unilateral contract acceptance does not need to be communicated, as acceptance is completed by performing the act requested.
- An offer cannot be accepted by silence and inactivity.
- When the postal rule applies the acceptance of an offer made by posting a letter will be effective from the time when it is posted. The rule will only apply when the letter of acceptance was properly addressed and posted. The rule will not apply where it would cause manifest inconvenience and absurdity. Nor will it apply where the circumstances of the case indicate that the parties cannot have intended that there should be a binding contract until the acceptance was received.
- A counter offer will revoke the original offer.

→

■ If a lot is put up for sale at auction 'without reserve' this amounts to the offer of a unilateral contract by the auctioneer promising that the highest genuine bid will be accepted. Advertising that an auction will be held without reserve does not amount to a definite offer that the auction will be held or that any of the lots will be put up for auction.

■ An invitation to tender is generally only an invitation to treat. However, if the invitation promises that the highest or lowest tender will be successful then it can amount to the offer of a unilateral contract.

■ A standing offer for which no consideration was received can be withdrawn at any time. However, orders placed prior to withdrawal will amount to acceptances of the offer and lead to the creation of contracts.

■ When a seller asks for fixed competitive bids, a referential tender will not be valid and the seller will not be allowed to accept it.

■ A contract will not come into existence unless the offer which is accepted contains all of the essential terms of the contract and the meaning of these terms can be ascertained with certainty.

■ If an accepted offer contains a meaningless term this will not of itself mean that no contract is formed. The meaningless term can generally be ignored.

Termination of offers

■ An offer cannot be accepted after it has terminated.

■ An offer of a bilateral contract can be revoked at any time before it is accepted. The revocation will be effective from the time when it is received by the offeree.

■ In all but exceptional cases it is not possible to revoke an offer of a unilateral contract once the offeree has begun to accept by performing the act requested.

■ An offeree who rejects an offer will not subsequently be able to accept it.

■ If no time limit is stipulated then an offer will remain open for a reasonable time. If no consideration is given for keeping an offer open then it can be revoked at any time, even if the offer was stipulated as being open for a particular time.

Summary questions

1 Which of the following would amount to an offer and which would amount only to an invitation to treat?

a A supermarket advertises that it will give a free chicken to anyone who spends at least £20 in any one visit.

b A business writes to a customer: 'You mentioned that you might want to buy our old fax machine. We have now bought a new machine. I've asked the office manager to put the old machine to one side, and you can have it for £100. If you do want the machine, let me know before the end of the month. If I don't hear from you before then I'll take it you don't want the machine and send it off to an auction.'

c A wholesaler writes to his customers, 'I am selling off all last year's stock. If you place an order before the end of this month I will guarantee 25 per cent discount on any old stock which I still have.'

d A corner shop advertises its biscuits, 'Summer madness! Special offer for the month of June!

Chocolate digestives only 25p! We will not be beaten on price or quality!'

e A manufacturer of electric shavers advertises: 'Shaves as close as your blade or your money back.'

f In a supermarket meat which is nearing its sell-by date bears a 'special offer' label, stating that the original price has been reduced by 25 per cent.

2 If goods on supermarket shelves did generally amount to offers to sell, what undesirable consequences would follow?

3 A motorist drives into a self-service garage and fills his car with petrol. The motorist goes into the office where an attendant asks him for the price of the petrol. The customer pays the price. When was the contract formed?

4 Allen Ltd advertise a second-hand articulated lorry in a trade journal for £6 000. Bernard, a local haulier, phones Allen Ltd and says that he would very much like to look at the lorry but that he is off on a two-day

→

trip to the Continent. The managing director of Allen Ltd says that if another buyer comes forward he will have to sell to that buyer. Bernard then says that he will pay £100 if Allen Ltd promise to keep open for three days an offer to sell the lorry to him for £6 000. The managing director agrees to this. Has any contract been made? If so, what are its terms?

5 A customer in a shop sees a cooker bearing a £56 price tag. The customer says that he will buy the cooker but the shop assistant says that the price tag should read £560. Can the customer insist on buying the cooker for £56?

6 Customers who buy from vending machines make contracts with the owner of the goods which the machines supply. Analyse the offer and acceptance position when a customer buys a can of soft drink from a vending machine. Would it make a difference that the machine did or did not have a coin refund?

7 In **Brogden v Metropolitan Railway** (1877) 2 AC 666 (House of Lords), a dispute arose as to whether a contract existed between a coalman and the railway and, if the contract did exist, what its terms were. The facts of the case can be reduced to the following four statements.

a A company which had taken coal from B for many years sent B a written agreement regarding the future supply of coal.

b B altered the document, signed it, and sent it back.

c The company put the signed document in a drawer, where it stayed for two years.

d The company ordered coal, which B delivered, in accordance with the altered document.

Each of the four statements can be classified as one of the following; an offer, an invitation to treat, a counter-offer, a revocation, a contract, or nothing at all.

Decide which of these each statement is. At least three of the cases quoted in this chapter can be used to justify your decisions. Which cases are they?

8 Company A wants to sell a second-hand machine tool to Company B. Both parties want to make the deal but they cannot agree about the price. Would the agreement be sufficiently certain to be a contract if the price was agreed to be:

a A fair price?

b A price to be fixed by C?

c The price at which a similar machine tool is sold at an auction which is due to take place the following day?

d A price which the parties will agree later?

9 A supermarket has a butchery counter. A customer asks for half a kilo of chuck steak. The assistant weighs a piece of meat and says that it is 480 grams. The customer says that this is all right, and then asks the assistant to mince the meat. The assistant minces it, puts it into a bag and sticks a price label on the bag. The customer pays for the meat at the till. Analyse this transaction in terms of offer and acceptance.

10 In **May and Butcher v R** [1934] 2 KB 17n (House of Lords), M and B agreed to buy tents from the Disposals Board. The price to be paid was described as follows: 'The price or prices to be paid ... shall be agreed upon from time to time between the (Disposals Board) and the purchasers as the quantities of said old tentage become available for disposal.' A further clause said that all disputes arising under the contract should be referred to arbitration. Do you think that this agreement was sufficiently definite to amount to a contract? Would your answer be different if there had been a definite agreement to buy tents with no mention of the price to be paid?

Multiple choice questions

1 Y Co Ltd, a large department store, advertise their price promise which states that if any customer buys from them and, within 28 days, notifies them in writing that the same goods are on sale at a lower price in another local shop they can have all of the purchase price returned to them. On 1 March a shopper buys a camera from the store for £49.99. On 28 March the shopper posts a letter explaining that the same camera is on sale at another shop for £49.89. The letter arrives on 30 March. Which one of the following statements is correct?

a The store's price promise was only an invitation to treat. The shopper made an offer which the store can accept or reject.

b The store's price promise was an offer which the shopper has validly accepted.

c The store's price promise was an offer. However, the shopper's acceptance was too late to be effective.

d The store's price promise was too vague to be an offer and would not apply to a 10p difference in price.

2 At an auction which had been advertised as being 'without reserve' X appears to have made the highest bid for Lot 7. The auctioneer is asking one last time for any higher bids. Assuming that no higher bid is made by anyone else, which one of the following statements is correct?

a X can withdraw his bid. If X does not withdraw his bid the auctioneer can refuse to accept it without being in breach of contract.

b X can withdraw his bid. If X does not withdraw his bid the auctioneer will be in breach of a collateral contract if he refuses to accept it.

c X can withdraw his bid. If X does not withdraw his bid, the auctioneer is bound to accept it and X will then have bought Lot 7.

d X cannot withdraw his bid. If X does not withdraw, the auctioneer has no contractual obligation to accept the bid.

3 Xshire County Council place an advertisement in a newspaper asking for tenders to supply 'such paper as we might require over a 12 month period'. Y puts in a tender stating the price at which he is willing to supply the paper. Xshire County Council write to Y accepting his tender for the whole 12 months. Three months later Xshire County Council place an order which Y refuses to fill. Which one of the following statements is correct?

a Y has made a contract to supply orders for any reasonable amount of paper ordered in the year.

b Y has made a contract to supply any orders for paper placed within the year, no matter how many orders might be placed.

c Y must fill the particular order which has been made. However, Y could then revoke his tender, and refuse to fill any subsequent orders.

d Y has only made an invitation to treat. Each time Xshire County Council place an order this amounts to an offer which Y can either accept or reject.

4 On 20 January X offered to sell his boat to Y. X said that he would have to receive a reply to his offer before 31 January. On 21 January Y telephoned X to ask if X would take a cheque. X replied that he wanted cash. On 29 January X sold the boat to Z, a third party. Y did not know about the sale of the boat and on 30 January he posted a letter, accepting X's offer. The letter did not arrive until 1 February. Which one of the following statements is correct?

a There is no contract between X and Y. Y made a counter offer which revoked X's offer.

b There is no contract between X and Y because the boat had already been sold to Z and this revoked X's offer.

c There is a good contract between X and Y because Y posted the acceptance before the deadline.

d There is no contract between X and Y because Y's acceptance was not received until after the deadline.

5 Consider the following statements.

i In certain circumstances the mere fact of inviting tenders may give rise to a binding contractual obligation to consider tenders properly submitted.

ii Revocation of a unilateral offer will always be effective if it is communicated to the offeror before the offeror has communicated acceptance.

iii The postal rule can mean that acceptances by post, but not revocations, are effective when posted.

iv An advertisement that an auction will take place without reserve does not amount to an offer that the auction will take place or that any particular goods will actually be included in the auction.

Which of the above statements are true?

a i, iii and iv only.

b ii and iii only.

c i and iv only.

d All of the statements.

6 A offers to sell his car to B for £3 000. Which of the following would terminate the offer?

i B offers £2 400 for the car.

ii B inquires if he can have three months' credit.

iii A sells the car to C.

iv B hears from a reliable source that A has sold the car to C.

v B does not reply for two years.

a i, ii, iv and v only.

b i, iv and v only.

c iii and v only.

d All of the alternatives.

Task 3

A friend of yours, a market trader, has always bought his goods from wholesalers. Your friend has heard that goods can sometimes be bought very cheaply at auction or by tender, and would like to know the legal position when buying in these ways.

Write a report, indicating:

a How a contract is made.

b The difference between an offer and an invitation to treat.

c The offer and acceptance position when buying at auctions.

d The offer and acceptance position when buying by tender.

e The extent to which offers can be withdrawn after they have been made.

mylawchamber *premium*

Visit **www.mylawchamber.co.uk/macintyre** to access study support resources including interactive multiple-choice questions, weblinks, glossary, glossary flashcards, legal newsfeed, answers to questions in this chapter, legal updates and an overview of this chapter all linked to the **Pearson eText** version of *Business Law* which you can **search**, **highlight** and **personalise** with your **own notes** and **bookmarks**.

Use **Case Navigator** to read in full some of the key cases referenced in this chapter with commentary and questions:

Carlill v *Carbolic Smoke Ball Co*. [1893] 1 QB 256
Pharmaceutical Society of Great Britain v *Boots Cash Chemists (Southern) Ltd* [1953] 1 QB 401 (CA)

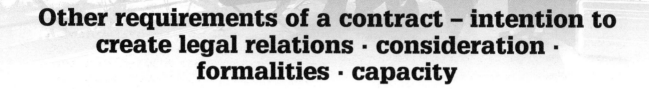

Other requirements of a contract – intention to create legal relations · consideration · formalities · capacity

Introduction

This chapter considers the following matters:

4.1 Intention to create legal relations
4.1.1 Business and commercial agreements
4.1.2 Social and domestic agreements
4.2 Consideration
4.2.1 Executory, executed and past consideration
4.2.2 Sufficiency and adequacy
4.2.3 Part payment of a debt

4.3 Formalities
4.3.1 Contracts which must be made by a deed
4.3.2 Contracts which must be in writing
4.3.3 Contracts which must be evidenced in writing
4.3.4 The Electronic Commerce (EC) Regulations 2002
4.4 Capacity
4.4.1 Minors
4.4.2 Drunkards and mental patients

4.1 INTENTION TO CREATE LEGAL RELATIONS

In Chapter 3 we saw that a contract is made through the medium of offer and acceptance. But the acceptance of an offer will only give rise to a contract if the offeror and the offeree appeared to intend to create legal relations. If the parties did not appear to intend that their agreement should be legally binding then there will be no contract.

Let us assume for example that A says to B, 'I will sell you my shares in X Ltd for £10 000', and that B replies, 'I accept'. There is plainly an offer and plainly an acceptance of it. But whether or not the offer and acceptance would create a contract would depend upon the context in which the words were spoken. If A and B were businessmen, dealing at arm's length in a business context, a court would infer that they did intend to make a contract, and there would therefore be a contract. If A and B were friends, speaking the words lightheartedly, as a long-standing joke, there would be no contract because it would be inferred that they did not intend to make a contract.

In ascertaining whether or not the parties intended that their agreement should be legally enforceable the courts take an objective view of the parties' intentions rather than trying to assess the actual intentions of the offeror and offeree. The question is not whether or not the parties actually did intend to enter into a legal relationship, it is whether they appeared to the reasonable person to have this intention. As Lord Devlin put it in *Parker* v *Clark* [1960] 1 WLR 286: 'The question [whether or not there is a binding contract] must, of course, depend upon the intention of the parties, to be inferred from the language they use and from the circumstances in which they use it.'

4.1.1 Business and commercial agreements

When deciding whether or not there is an intention to create legal relations, the courts divide agreements into two classes; business and commercial agreements on the one hand, and social and domestic agreements on the other. As regards business and commercial agreements, there is a presumption that the parties do intend to make a contract. As regards social and domestic agreements, there is a presumption that they do not. Either of these presumptions can be rebutted by evidence to the contrary.

So if an offer is made and accepted in a business or commercial context a court will start with the strong presumption that the parties did intend to make a contract. An offeror or offeree who wishes to rebut this presumption will need to introduce evidence which shows that there was in fact no intention to create legal relations.

Esso Petroleum Ltd v Commissioners of Customs and Excise
[1976] 1 WLR 1 (House of Lords)

In order to promote their petrol, Esso advertised that they would give a World Cup coin to motorists who bought four gallons of petrol. The coins bore the likeness of one of the 30 footballers in the England squad for the 1970 World Cup. The Customs and Excise Commissioners claimed that the coins were goods on which purchase tax was payable. Schedule 1 to the Purchase Tax Act 1963 made coins of this type liable to purchase tax if they were 'produced in quantity for general sale'.

Held. There was a legally binding contract to supply a World Cup coin to a motorist who bought four gallons of petrol. There was an intention to create legal relations because the advertising took place in a business context and was designed to achieve commercial success.

COMMENT (i) Purchase tax was not payable because the agreement to supply the coin was not a sale. The motorists' consideration for the coins was not the payment of money but rather entering into a contract to buy petrol. (See the definition of a contract of sale of goods in Chapter 8 at 8.1.1.)

(ii) Two of the five Law Lords thought that there was no intention to create legal relations in respect of the coins.

Many claims made in advertisements, although made in a commercial context, do not amount to definite contractual promises because they are either too vague to be capable of being proved true or are too extravagant to be credible. So the claims by various manufacturers of washing powders that their product washes whitest will amount to no more than sales puffs.

If the parties to a commercial agreement make it quite plain that they do not intend their agreement to be a contract, this will override the presumption that they do intend to enter into legal relations.

Rose and Frank Co v Crompton Bros
[1925] AC 445 (House of Lords)

Since 1905 the claimants had been supplied with the defendants' carbonising tissue paper, which the claimants finished and sold in the United States. The business between the two parties was very considerable and very profitable. In 1913 the claimants and the defendants both signed a document which expressed their willingness that the claimants should continue to be supplied with the defendants' products. Under this agreement the claimants were to be the defendants' sole agents in the United States for three years, with an option to extend that period for another three years. An 'Honourable Pledge Clause' stated, 'This arrangement is not entered into ... as a formal or legal agreement, and shall not be subject to legal jurisdiction in the law courts either of the United States or England, but it is only a definite expression and record of the purpose and intention of the ... parties concerned, to which they honourably pledge themselves with the fullest confidence, based on past business with each other, that it will be carried through ...' Later the agreement was extended until March 1920, but in 1919 the defendants terminated the agreement without notice. The claimants sued for breach of contract.

Held. The agreement was not a contract and could not therefore be sued upon. The Honourable Pledge Clause dominated the whole signed document and its ordinary and natural meaning was that the agreement should not be legally enforceable.

A letter of comfort is a letter written to give reassurance to a person who is considering extending credit to a third party. Such a letter may amount to a guarantee, in which case it will provide a definite promise to answer for the debt of the third party. A letter of comfort which does not amount to a guarantee may give rise to a contractual obligation, but this will depend upon whether an intention to create legal relations can be inferred from the language of the letter and all the surrounding circumstances.

Kleinwort Benson Ltd v Malaysia Mining Corporation Bhd
[1988] 1 WLR 379 (Court of Appeal)

The claimant bank was unwilling to lend money to MMC Metals Ltd, a subsidiary of MMC Bhd. The bank was not satisfied with the creditworthiness of MMC Metals Ltd and asked MMC Bhd to guarantee the loan. MMC Bhd replied that it was not their →

policy to guarantee loans made to their subsidiaries. After some negotiations, MMC Bhd issued a letter of comfort which stated that it was MMC Bhd's policy to make sure that MMC Metals Ltd was 'at all times in a position to meet its liabilities to you'. The bank made the loan to MMC Metals Ltd which went into liquidation without repaying the debt. The bank sued MMC Bhd on the letter of comfort.

Held. The letter of comfort did not give rise to any contractual liability. The letter contained no contractual promise intending to give rise to a legal relationship. It was merely a statement of present intention.

COMMENT (i) The letter of comfort was carefully drafted so as not to give rise to a contractual promise. However, care should be taken when considering other letters of comfort. In every case the precise wording is likely to be the deciding factor.

(ii) The Court of Appeal distinguished **Edwards v Skyways** Ltd [1964] 1 All ER 494. In that case the claimant worked for the defendants as a pilot. He was made redundant, along with 15 per cent of the workforce, and given three months' notice of termination of his employment. The claimant had the right either to withdraw pension contributions he had made, or to take the right to a pension which would become payable at retirement age. At a meeting between the defendants and the claimant's trade association, the defendants said that if the redundant employees withdrew their pension contributions the defendants would make *ex gratia* payments which would approximate to the defendant company's pension contributions. (The fact that the payment was *ex gratia* merely meant that it was made voluntarily, without the defendants admitting any legal liability to make it. It did not mean that the agreement should have no effect in law.) On the strength of the defendants' promise the claimant decided to withdraw from the pension fund and take his own contributions and the promised *ex gratia* payment. The defendants got into some financial difficulty and rescinded the promise to make the *ex gratia* payments. It was held that in a business context there was a strong presumption that an agreement was intended to create legal relations and that the defendants had not rebutted this presumption. Therefore the claimant was entitled to the *ex gratia* payment.

4.1.1.1 Terms which exclude the jurisdiction of the courts

In *Rose and Frank Co v Crompton Bros* we saw that it is possible to make a commercial agreement which will not amount to a contract, on account of the parties having expressly stipulated that the agreement should not have any legal effect. However, it is not permissible to make a contract on the basis that the contract will be exempt from the jurisdiction of the courts. Any term in a contract which tries to prevent a party putting an issue of law before a court will be void. (Arbitration, examined in Chapter 2 at 2.4.1, is the one exception to this rule.) An example of a term being held void on account of its attempting to exclude the jurisdiction of the courts can be seen in *Baker v Jones* [1954] 1 WLR 1005. In that case the rules of a weightlifting association made a contract between the association and its members. The association was governed by a central council, made up of officers of the association and certain members. One of the association's rules stated that in any dispute between the association and a member the decision of the association should be final, and neither party should be able to take the dispute to any court. A dispute arose as to whether the central council had improperly used the association's money and it was held that the rule giving the central council the sole right to interpret the rules was against public policy and therefore void. This case differs from a case such as *Rose and Frank Co v Crompton Bros* in that in *Baker v Jones* the rule in question applied to the method of resolving disputes, rather than to the legal effect of the agreement itself. It is permissible to make an agreement and insist that it will have no legal effect. It is not permissible to make a legally binding agreement and say that it should be interpreted by a body other than the ordinary courts.

4.1.2 Social and domestic agreements

When considering whether or not a social or domestic agreement amounted to a contract the courts presume that the parties did not intend to create legal relations. However, this strong presumption can be rebutted by the evidence. All of the circumstances of the case will be examined to deduce the apparent intentions of the parties.

Jones v Padavatton
[1969] 1 WLR 328 (Court of Appeal)

Mrs Padavatton, a 34-year-old divorcee, was working as a secretary at the Indian Embassy In Washington DC, USA. She had a flat in Washington where she lived with her son. Her mother, Mrs Jones, lived in →

Trinidad. The mother agreed to pay her daughter $200 dollars a month if she would go to England and read for the Bar. The daughter left her job and went to England and enrolled as a student at Lincoln's Inn. The mother paid her daughter an allowance of £42 a month, which was the equivalent of 200 West Indian dollars. (The daughter had thought the agreement was for 200 US dollars, worth about £70, a month.) Nothing was agreed as to the duration of the agreement. The agreement was subsequently varied so that the daughter, instead of receiving the allowance, was provided with a house where she could live rent free in part of the house and let the rest out to provide herself with money to live on. After a disagreement the mother gave her daughter notice to quit the house. The daughter maintained that under the varied agreement she had a contractual right to remain in occupation.

Held. The daughter was not entitled to remain in occupation. In family agreements there is a strong presumption that the parties do not intend to create legal relations. The facts of the case indicated that the housing arrangements were not made with the intention of creating a contract but were merely family arrangements.

COMMENT (i) Although the majority of the Court of Appeal, Danckwerts and Fenton Atkinson LJJ thought that there was no intention to create legal relations, Salmon LJ thought that there was. Salmon LJ thought that the initial agreement had been a unilateral offer by the mother but that it was an implied term that the daughter should complete her studies within a reasonable time. As she was not close to completing her Bar exams five years after becoming a student Salmon LJ thought that the offer had lapsed.

(ii) Danckwerts and Fenton Atkinson LJJ also held that the agreement was far too vague and uncertain to amount to a contract.

In *Balfour v Balfour* [1919] 2 KB 571, the Court of Appeal established the principle that agreements between husband and wife are unlikely to be contracts unless there is very clear evidence that this was in fact the intention. In that case Lord Atkin said: '. . . one of the most usual forms of agreement which does not constitute a contract appears to me to be the arrangements which are made between husband and wife . . . they are not contracts because the parties did not intend that they should be attended by legal consequences . . . All I can say is that the small courts of this country would have to be multiplied one

hundredfold if these arrangements were held to result in legal obligations.'

However, the principle set out in the *Balfour* case is very much weakened if the husband and wife are separated or are contemplating separation.

Merritt v *Merritt*
[1970] 1 WLR 1121 (Court of Appeal)

A husband and wife married in 1941 and in 1949 built a house as their home. The house was in the husband's name but in 1966 the couple put the house in their joint names. Soon after this the husband left the wife and went to live with another woman. £180 was left owing on the building society mortgage. The husband and wife held a meeting in the husband's car where the husband agreed to pay the wife £40 a month so that she could keep up the mortgage instalments. The husband gave the wife the building society mortgage book. The wife insisted that the husband sign a statement saying that if she paid all the charges which arose in connection with the house until the mortgage was paid off he would transfer sole ownership of the house to her. The husband signed the agreement. When the wife had paid off the mortgage the husband reduced the payments to £25 a month. The wife applied for a declaration that the house now belonged to her and that the husband should immediately transfer ownership to her.

Held. The agreement which the husband and wife had made was binding upon them. As the couple were no longer living together, the presumption that they did not intend to make a contract was greatly reduced. A reasonable person looking at the agreement would have regarded it as intending to be binding.

COMMENT Lord Denning MR stressed that the courts do not seek the actual intentions of the parties, but their apparent intentions: 'In all these cases the court does not try to discover the intention by looking into the minds of the parties. It looks at the situation in which they were placed and asks itself: would reasonable people regard this agreement as intended to be binding?'

The following case examined whether an agreement between friends, a social agreement, amounted to a contract.

Coward v *MIB*
[1963] 1 QB 359 (Court of Appeal)

In December 1953 Coward and his friend Cole were killed in a motorcycle accident. The motorcycle was →

owned and driven by Cole while Coward rode as a pillion passenger. The accident was caused by Cole's negligence. Coward's widow sued Cole's personal representatives and was awarded £7 850 19s. damages. This sum was not paid because Cole's insurance did not cover pillion passengers and Cole's estate was of no value. Coward's widow therefore sued the Motor Insurers' Bureau who were bound to pay only if the insurance of the pillion passenger was compulsory. If Coward had been carried for 'hire or reward' then insurance of him would have been compulsory, but not otherwise. It was therefore argued by Coward's widow that Cole had made a contract to carry Coward on the bike. Coward had paid Cole a small weekly sum in exchange for being given a lift to work each day.

Held. There was no contract because neither party would have intended to enter into a legal contract.

COMMENT The facts of ***Albert v Motor Insurers' Bureau*** [1971] 3 WLR 291 (House of Lords) were very similar but the outcome was different. Q, the owner of the car in which the passenger was killed, was a docker who had given other dockers a lift to work for eight years. He would carry any docker who would pay and his services were well known although not advertised. The House of Lords decided that these passengers were carried under a contract, the test being whether there was a systematic carrying of passengers which went beyond the bounds of mere social kindness, that is to say whether the agreement was predominantly a business agreement rather than a social one. On the facts of the case this test was satisfied.

In ***Wilson and another v Burnett*** [2007] EWCA Civ 1170, [2007] All ER (D) 372 (Oct) the Court of Appeal considered whether or not three friends had made a contract to share a bingo prize of over £100 000. On the evidence, the Court of Appeal agreed with the trial judge that they had not. May LJ gave the only judgment and said that the case depended upon whether the friends had made a sufficiently certain binding agreement. He was prepared to accept that this might have happened, but said there would always be 'intrinsic problems ... on the question of whether a necessarily casual conversation could be elevated into an agreement binding and enforceable in law.'

In ***Sadler v Reynolds*** [2005] EWHC 309 QB, [2005] All ER (D) 100 (Mar) there was a dispute between the chairman of a football club and a journalist with whom he was friendly. The journalist argued that a contract had been formed under which he was to write the chairman's biography. The chairman denied that a contract had been made. Elizabeth Slade QC held that the agreement fell somewhere between an obviously commercial contract and a social exchange. She found that the burden of proof was on the journalist to prove that the parties had intended to enter into a legal relationship. However, the onus of doing this was less heavy than it would have been if the agreement had been made in a purely social relationship. On the facts, the journalist could discharge the burden of proof and so a contract had been made.

Test your understanding 4.1

1 When an agreement is made in a business or commercial context what presumption do the courts make as to whether or not there was an intention to create legal relations?

2 When an agreement is made in a social or domestic context what presumption do the courts make as to whether or not there was an intention to create legal relations?

3 What is a letter of comfort?

4 What is the effect of a contractual term which excludes the jurisdiction of the courts?

4.2 CONSIDERATION

An agreement cannot amount to a contract unless each party gives some 'consideration' to the other. The word 'consideration' is used here not in its everyday sense, but in the legal sense of a benefit. In bilateral contracts the consideration of both parties takes the form of a promise to do something in the future. The consideration of a person accepting a unilateral offer lies in performing the act specified, rather than in making a promise. In ***Currie v Misa*** (1875) LR 10 Ex 153 the following well-recognised definition of consideration was made: 'A valuable consideration, in the sense of the law, may consist either in some right, interest, profit or benefit accruing to one party, or some forbearance, detriment, loss or responsibility, given, suffered or undertaken by the other.' This definition might be abbreviated to say that consideration consists either in the giving of a benefit or the suffering of a loss. Usually it will amount to both. In a contract of sale of goods, for example, the buyer's consideration is the promise to pay the price. The giving of this promise is a benefit to the seller while at the same time it is a loss to the buyer.

It is the requirement that consideration must move to and from each party which distinguishes contracts from gifts. If a contract is made, each side gives a benefit to the other in return for a benefit received. If a gift is made, only one side gives a benefit.

Let us look at an example. A says to B, 'I will sell you my fax machine for £200', and B accepts. This is a contract, not a gift, because each party has given some consideration to the other. A's consideration is the promise to give B ownership of the fax machine. B's consideration is the promise to pay the money.

If, however, A had said, 'I will give you my fax machine', and B had replied, 'Thank you very much. I accept', there would be no contract. A would have given some consideration to B, but B would not have given any consideration in return.

A contract which is not made by a deed is known as a simple contract and it is in simple contracts that consideration must be given by both parties. An agreement made by deed is enforceable as a specialty contract without the need to prove that consideration was given by both parties. So a promise to make a gift would not be enforceable unless it was made by a deed. The way in which a deed is made is considered below at 4.3.

4.2.1 **Executory, executed and past consideration**

Executory consideration consists of a promise to do something in the future. The consideration is called executory because when the contract is made the promisor has not yet performed (executed) his consideration. If we examine a typical bilateral contract, for example *Nicolene Ltd v Simmonds* at 3.3.1, we see that the consideration of both parties was executory. The defendant promised that he would deliver the 3 000 tons of steel bars, and the claimants promised that they would pay for them.

Executed consideration occurs when one of the parties makes the offer or the acceptance in such a way that he has completely fulfilled his liability under the contract. The only contractual liability remaining is that of the other party. A seller of goods, for example, might offer to sell goods if the buyer sends cash with an order. If the buyer accepts this offer by sending the cash then his consideration is executed. Executed consideration is found in the acceptance of unilateral offers, where the acceptance is made by performing some action rather than by promising to do something in the future. For example, in

Carlill v The Carbolic Smoke Ball Company Mrs Carlill's consideration was executed. She did not promise to use a smoke ball and catch flu, she just did it. The consideration of the smoke ball company, being a promise, was executory.

Past consideration is said to be no consideration. This means that a party cannot give as consideration some act which he has already performed, because to promise to do something which has already been done is to promise nothing at all. In some circumstances the rule can seem rather unfair, but it is a logical consequence of a contract being a bargain under which both parties exchange something of value.

> ### Re McArdle
> [1951] Ch 669 (Court of Appeal)
>
> In 1935 William McArdle died, leaving his estate to his wife for life and then on trust for his five children. One of William's sons, Monty McArdle, lived with his wife Marjorie in a bungalow which formed part of William's estate. In 1943 Monty and Marjorie carried out improvements and repairs to the bungalow which was called Gravel Hill. The cost of this work was £488 and it was paid for by Marjorie. In 1945 Monty and his brothers and sisters signed a document which contained the following terms:' To Mrs Marjorie McArdle ... In consideration of your carrying out certain alterations and improvements to the property known as Gravel Hill ... we the beneficiaries under the will of William Henry McArdle hereby agree that the executors ... shall pay to you ... the sum of £488 in settlement of the amount spent on such improvements.' The money was to be paid when William McArdle's estate was distributed among the five children. When this time came Monty's brothers and sisters refused to pay.
>
> **Held.** The agreement to pay the money was not enforceable as a contract. At the time of executing the agreement all of the work had been completed and so the consideration for the agreement was wholly past consideration.

Similarly, in *Roscorla v Thomas* (1842) 3 QB 324 a promise that a horse was 'sound and free from vice' was given after the contract to buy the horse had been made. The purchaser soon discovered that the horse was very vicious, but the promise was held to have no legal effect. No consideration had been received for the promise, which was made after the contract had been formed.

However, In *Pao On v Lau Yiu Long* [1979] 3 All ER 65 Lord Scarman held that a past act can amount to good consideration for a promise by another person if three conditions are satisfied. First, the act must have been performed at the request of the promisor. Second, both parties must all along have contemplated that payment would be made. Third, the payment given in return for the act would have to have been legally enforceable if it had been given before the act had been performed, that is to say all the requirements to form a contract would have to have been satisfied. The following case shows an early example of seemingly past consideration amounting to good consideration.

Lampleigh v *Brathwaite* (1615) Hob 105

The defendant had killed another man and he asked the claimant to go to the King and obtain a pardon. The claimant managed to get the pardon, a task which involved many days' labour in riding around following the King. Afterwards the defendant was so grateful that he agreed to pay the claimant £100 for the work he had done. Later the defendant refused to pay.

Held. The defendant had to pay the £100 because he had asked the claimant to get the pardon and because both parties would have contemplated that payment would be made.

COMMENT The principle of the case, that there was a good contract, remains unchanged. However, s.15(1) of the Supply of Goods and Services Act 1982 would now imply a term that if no price is fixed when a contract for the supply of a service is made, then the supplier should be paid a reasonable price (see Chapter 8 at 8.3.3.3).

4.2.2 **Sufficiency and adequacy**

It is a general principle of the law of contract that consideration must be 'sufficient' but need not be 'adequate'. In everyday usage the words sufficient and adequate have very similar meanings and this can make the principle seem rather puzzling. However, in this legal context the words 'sufficient' and 'adequate' have distinct meanings. Sufficient means of some recognisable economic value, however small. Adequate means of the same value as the other party's consideration.

By way of example, let us examine a contract to buy a new Ford Focus for its normal selling price of £15 000. The consideration given by the buyer is both sufficient and adequate, and so is the consideration given by the seller. That is to say that the buyer's promise to pay the money is generally thought to be worth

much the same as the seller's promise to transfer ownership of the car.

If the contract had been to sell the new car for £1 then the buyer's consideration would have been sufficient, but would not have been adequate. However, as long as the seller had freely agreed to the deal, and as long as there was an intention to create legal relations, the inadequacy of the buyer's consideration would not matter. The deal would still be a contract. In *Thomas* v *Thomas* (1842) 2 QB 851, for example, the claimant was given a house and premises for life in return for paying £1 a year towards the ground rent and keeping the house in good repair. It was held that this amounted to a contract.

In *White* v *Bluett* (1853) 23 LJ Ex 36 the court had to consider whether a son's promise to his father that he would stop complaining amounted to sufficient consideration. The son had made out a promissory note in favour of his father in respect of money which the father had lent to him. The father had distributed his property in a way which the son considered unfair. The son agreed to stop complaining about this if the father agreed not to enforce the promissory note. The agreement was made but the father later sued the son on the promissory note. It was held that the father could do this because the son's promise to stop complaining could not amount to sufficient consideration. The promise could not be said to be of any economic value.

The rule that consideration does not need to be adequate seems to be based on two principles. The first principle is that it is impossible for the courts to attach definite values to goods and services. The value of a thing at any particular time depends on any number of circumstances. A second reason why the courts have never concerned themselves with the adequacy of consideration is that they have always taken the view that people are free to make any contracts they like. If a business uses this freedom to make bad contracts then the courts will not protect the business from its own stupidity. If the contracts made are sufficiently costly, then it is in the public interest that the business should cease to exist and be replaced by another business which is more astute.

4.2.2.1 **Trivial acts**

Even performing a trivial act is capable of amounting to sufficient consideration, as long as the performance of it can be regarded as conferring an economic benefit. This important principle can be extracted from the following case.

Chappell & Co Ltd v The Nestlé Co Ltd
[1960] AC 87 (House of Lords)

As part of an advertising campaign, the Nestlé company was 'giving away' records to members of the public who sent 1/6d (7.5p) and three chocolate bar wrappers. Nestlé bought the records for 4d each from H. Co and made a slight profit on each sale. The wrappers sent in were thrown away. The records consisted of thin strips of cellulose acetate which were then mounted on cardboard discs which advertised Nestlé's chocolate. The copyright in the record was owned by the claimants, who were most unhappy with Nestlé's scheme because ordinarily records were sold for 6/8d (34p). Section 8 of the Copyright Act 1956 protected retailers against claims for breach of copyright if they paid 6.25 per cent of the 'ordinary retail selling price' of the record to the copyright holders. If the ordinary retail selling price could not be ascertained Nestlé would have been in breach of the Copyright Act. Nestlé claimed that the ordinary retail selling price of the records was 1/6d, arguing that the wrappers were of no value and that sending them was not therefore part of the consideration. The claimants applied for an injunction to prevent further manufacturing of the records.

Held. The sending of the wrappers was part of the consideration. (If customers had sent 1/6d without the wrappers they would not have received a record.) Therefore, the copyright holder could prevent further manufacture and sale of the records.

COMMENT (i) Lord Reid had no doubt that the promotion of the scheme was designed to be an economic benefit to Nestlé Ltd: 'The Nestlé Co's intention can hardly be in doubt. They were not setting out to trade in gramophone records. They were using these records to increase their sales of chocolate ... The requirement that wrappers should be sent was of great importance to the Nestlé Co; there would have been no point in their simply offering records for 1s. 6d each.'

(ii) Lord Somervell made it plain that the adequacy of the consideration was not relevant as long as the consideration conferred some economic benefit: 'It is said that when received the wrappers are of no value to Nestlés. This I would have thought irrelevant. A contracting party can stipulate for what consideration he chooses. A peppercorn does not cease to be good consideration if it is established that the promisee does not like pepper and will throw the corn away ... the whole object of selling the record ... was to increase the sales of chocolate.'

(iii) If sending the wrappers was part of the consideration for the records then it logically follows that sending the wrappers could have been the whole of the consideration.

(iv) Viscount Simmonds and Lord Keith dissented, thinking that sending the wrappers merely qualified a purchaser to buy the record.

4.2.2.2 **Privity of contract**

The common law has always prevented a person who is not a party to a contract from suing on the contract. This is the case even if the contract was expressly made for the benefit of the person trying to sue. The rule is known as privity of contract. The contract is regarded as private between the offeror and the offeree and no other person can become liable under the contract or sue to enforce it. The following case provides a classic example of the rule.

Tweddle v Atkinson (1831) 1 B & S 393

The claimant married the daughter of William Guy. At the time of the marriage William Guy and John Tweddle, the claimant's father, agreed with each other that they would both pay the claimant a sum of money. William Guy promised to pay the claimant £200 and in return for this promise John Tweddle promised to pay the claimant £100. The agreement said that the claimant 'has full power to sue the said parties in any court of law or equity for the aforesaid sums hereby promised and specified'. William Guy died without having paid the £200 he had promised to pay. The claimant sued William Guy's personal representatives for the money.

Held. The claimant could not sue on the contract because he was not a party to it.

COMMENT William Guy had broken the contract which he had made with John Tweddle and John Tweddle could have sued him for breach of contract. However, John Tweddle would only have been awarded nominal damages for the breach of contract as it had caused him no loss. If the case were to arise today, the Contracts (Rights of Third Parties) Act 1999 would allow the claimant to sue and enforce the contract as if he had made it.

In *Jackson v Horizon Holidays Ltd* [1975] 1 WLR 1468 the Court of Appeal appeared to depart from the doctrine of privity. It awarded substantial damages to a man who had booked a holiday for himself and his wife. The holiday was disastrous and the trial judge awarded damages of £1 100 to compensate for the loss of enjoyment suffered by both the husband and his wife. The Court of Appeal allowed this award to stand, but gave different reasons for doing so. Lord Denning MR said that the husband could claim damages on behalf of his wife's vexation and discomfort as the contract was made for her benefit. This decision was severely criticised by the House of Lords in *Woodar Investment Developments Ltd* v *Wimpey Construction UK Ltd* [1980] 1 WLR 277. Lord Keith said that the decision in *Jackson* v *Horizon Holidays* did not 'lay down any rule regarding the recovery of damages for the benefit of third parties'. In the light of the criticism made by the House of Lords, the reasoning of Lord Denning must be regarded as incorrect. Lord Wilberforce, whilst rejecting Lord Denning's reasoning, indicated that the actual decision in *Jackson* v *Horizon Holidays* might well be correct. He said that there were many situations in everyday life which did not fit into neat contractual analysis and that there might be certain types of contracts which called for special treatment. He gave as examples people booking family holidays, or ordering meals in a restaurant or booking a taxi for a group. In the case of package holidays only, the Package Travel, Package Holidays and Package Tours Regulations 1992 now allow damages to be awarded for loss of enjoyment suffered by holidaymakers who did not make the contract. A holiday is a package holiday if it is arranged as a pre-arranged combination of at least two of the following: transport, accommodation and other tourist services.

The privity rule was affirmed by the House of Lords in the following case.

Dunlop Pneumatic Tyre Co Ltd v *Selfridge & Co Ltd*
[1915] AC 847 (House of Lords)

Dunlop sold car tyres to Dew & Co, who were dealers in motor accessories. In return for being given a 10 per cent discount on the price, Dew & Co agreed that they would obtain a written undertaking from any person to whom they resold the tyres that the tyres would not be sold on below a certain price. Dew & Co resold the tyres to Selfridge & Co. Dew & Co gave Selfridge & Co a discount on the price of the tyres in return for the written agreement not to sell the tyres on below the agreed price. Selfridge & Co sold the tyres on below the agreed price and Dunlop sued them on the written agreement not to do this.

Held. Dunlop could not sue Selfridge on the agreement as there was no contract between them. Dunlop had given no consideration to Selfridge & Co in return for the promise not to sell the tyres on below the agreed price. The discount which Selfridge & Co had been given in return for their agreement had been given by Dew & Co and not by Dunlop.

When a contract is made on behalf of a third party it is in some circumstances possible for the contracting party to obtain a decree of specific performance of the contract. If such a decree is obtained the third party may be able to enforce the performance of the contract.

Beswick v *Beswick*
[1968] AC 58 (House of Lords)

A coal merchant assigned his business to his nephew in return for the nephew agreeing to pay the coal merchant £6 10s. for the rest of his life. The agreement also provided that if the coal merchant should predecease his wife the nephew would pay the widow £5 a week for the rest of her life. After the coal merchant died the nephew made only one payment to the widow. Then the nephew refused to make any more payments on the grounds of privity of contract. The widow sued for arrears of £175 and for an order of specific performance requiring future payments to be made. The widow sued not only in her personal capacity, but also as administratrix of her husband's estate.

Held. The widow did not succeed in her personal capacity. However, she did succeed in her capacity as administratrix of her husband's estate, because as administratrix she had the same right to enforce a contract made by her husband as he would have had. The widow could only be awarded nominal damages because her husband's estate had suffered no loss as a consequence of the refusal to make the payments to the widow. However, the widow could have specific performance of the contract as she was, in effect, suing as her husband.

COMMENT This decision achieved justice in the case but is problematic. The remedy of specific performance is examined in Chapter 7 at 7.2.4, where we shall see that it is rarely ordered. In this case it could only be ordered because of the coincidence that the widow happened to be the administratrix of her husband's estate. If someone else had been the administrator they would have been unlikely to risk a legal action on the widow's behalf. Specific performance is not ordered →

to enforce personal service contracts. Nor is it usually ordered to enforce contracts of continuing obligation.

There are several well-established exceptions to the privity rule. Assignment can allow the benefit of a contract to be transferred to another person if certain procedures are followed. Agency allows one person to make a contract on behalf of another (see Chapter 11). When two parties create a contract a collateral contract may arise in favour of a third party (see Chapter 14 at 14.2.2). The privity rule does not apply in the law of trusts where a beneficiary under a trust is entitled to sue to enforce the trust. There are also several statutory exceptions to the rule. Over the years several attempts to evade the doctrine of privity have been made. The Contracts (Rights of Third Parties) Act (CRTPA) 1999 has modified the rule in some circumstances.

The Contracts (Rights of Third Parties) Act 1999

This Act does not abolish the privity rule, but does in some circumstances enable a third party to enforce a term of a contract. Section 1 sets out the two circumstances in which a third party may enforce a term of a contract made by the promisor and the promisee. 'The promisor' is defined by the Act as meaning the party to the contract against whom the term is enforceable by the third party. 'The promisee' is defined as meaning the party to the contract by whom the term is enforceable against the promisor. For example, let us assume that a shop sells a television to X, that the television is not of satisfactory quality, and that the Act operates to allow Y to sue the shop. The shop is the promisor, X is the promisee, and Y is the third party.

Section 1(1)(a) of this Act provides that a third party may enforce a term of a contract if the contract expressly provides that he may. For example, the contract between X and the shop might have expressly stated that Y was to be able to enforce the contract or that he could enforce certain terms of the contract.

Section 1(1)(b) allows a third party to enforce a term of a contract if the term purports to confer a benefit on him. However, s.1(2) provides that this will not be the case if on a proper construction of the contract it appears that the parties did not intend the term to be enforceable by the third party. The Law Commission, whose proposed Bill was enacted as this Act, considered that the effect of s.1(2) was to create a rebuttable presumption that a third party can enforce a term which objectively purports to confer a

contractual benefit on him. If therefore a term in the contract between X and the shop had purported to confer a benefit on Y (for example by stipulating that the television should be delivered to Y at his home address), it would be presumed that Y could enforce the term but this presumption would be rebuttable. This approach was taken in **Nisshin Shipping Co Ltd v Cleaves & Co Ltd** [2003] EWHC 2602 (Comm), [2004] 1 Lloyd's Rep 38. Brokers arranged a charterparty. The contract between the shipowner and the charterer provided that the broker should get 2 per cent commission on the hire paid under the charterparty. The contract was neutral as to whether or not the brokers could enforce the contract. It did not say either that they could or that they could not. Applying s.1(2), the brokers could claim their commission under s.1(1)(b).

Section 1(3) requires that, whether using the s.1(1)(a) route or the s.1(1)(b) route, the third party must be expressly identified in the contract by name, as a member of a class or as answering a particular description. Express identification by name needs no explanation. Express identification by class could arise in many ways, for example if a contractual provision was made for the benefit of all the members of a particular club, or for the benefit of the promisee's brothers and sisters. Express identification of the third party as his or her answering a particular description could also arise in many ways, for example if a contractual provision was made for the benefit of 'my youngest brother' or for the benefit of the Sheriff of Nottingham. Although the third party must be expressly identified, he does not need to be in existence when the contract is entered into (s.1(3)). So enforceable rights could be conferred on unborn children or on companies which had not yet been incorporated.

When a benefit is conferred on a third party by the Act, the third party can avail himself of any remedy which would have been available to him if he had made the contract (s.1(5)). The third party can also avail himself of exclusion or limitation clauses (s.1(6)). Section 4 provides that s.1 does not affect any right of the promisee to enforce any term of the contract. So any rights conferred on the third party are additional to rights conferred on the promisee. However, s.5 protects the promisor from double liability. Section 5(a) provides that where the promisee has recovered any sum in respect of the third party's loss in respect of a term, any award to the third party by the court would be reduced to take account of this. Section 5(b) provides that where the promisee has recovered from the promisor a sum in respect of the expense to the promisee of making good to the third party the default of the promisor, any award to the third party by the court would be reduced to take account of this. So the overall effect of s.5 is that the promisor will not have to compensate twice for a loss to the third party.

Section 2(1) provides that where the third party does gain rights under s.1 to enforce a term of a contract, the parties to the contract may not generally rescind or vary the contract in such a way as to extinguish or alter the third party's rights without his consent. However, this is only the case if the third party has communicated his assent to the contract to the promisor, or if the promisor knows that the third party has relied on the term, or if the promisor should reasonably have foreseen that the third party would rely on the term and the third party has in fact relied upon it. The assent of the third party may be by words or conduct. If it is sent by post it is not to be regarded as communicated to the promisor until received by him (s.2(2)).

The parties to the contract will be able to rescind or vary it without the consent of the third party if an express term of the contract allows them to do this, or if an express term sets out the circumstances in which they will be able to do this (s.2(3)). The assent of the third party can be dispensed with if his whereabouts cannot be reasonably ascertained or if he is mentally incapable of giving his assent (s.2(4)). Section 2(5) allows the court, on application of the parties to a contract, to dispense with the third party's assent if it is satisfied that it cannot reasonably be ascertained whether or not the third party has in fact relied on the term. If the court does dispense with the third party's consent, s.2(6) allows it to impose such conditions as it thinks fit, including a condition requiring the payment of compensation to the third party.

Section 3 provides that if the promisor has any defences, or rights of set-off, arising from or in connection with the contract, these shall be as available against the third party as would have been available against the promisee. For example, a contract is made between B and C. B is to sell 50 bicycles to C, and a term of the contract provides that C should pay the price to D. B delivers only 30 bicycles to C. C accepts the 30 bicycles. C will not need to pay the whole contract price to D, but will only need to pay the price of 30 bicycles. Similarly, if B had induced the contract by making an actionable misrepresentation, or breached the requirement that the goods be of satisfactory quality, C could raise these matters as a defence against D. The promisor will also have available defences, rights of set-off and counterclaims which did not arise in connection with the contract, if these would have been available against the third party if the third party had been a party to the contract. For example, B agrees to sell 50 bicycles to C. A term of the contract provides that C is to pay the price of £5 000 to D. D owes £1 000 to C in connection with a contract made last month. C is entitled to set-off the £1 000 and pay D only £4 000.

Section 6 makes it plain that the Act does not alter the law relating to negotiable instruments. Nor does it confer rights on a third party in the case of any contract binding on a company and its members under s.33(1) of the Companies Act 2006.

Section 7(1) provides that s.1 does not affect any right or remedy of a third party that exists or is available apart from this Act. This allows common law development of third party rights and preserves existing exceptions to the doctrine of privity, whether they be common law or statutory.

Section 7(2) prevents a third party from relying on s.2(2) of the Unfair Contract Terms Act (UCTA) 1977 where the negligence consists of the breach of an obligation arising from a term of a contract. This is somewhat controversial because the third party is put in a worse position than the promisee would have been in. The promisee can use s.2(2) UCTA 1977 to challenge an exclusion or limitation clause on which the promisor intends to rely. The third party cannot use s.2(2) in this way. A third party could rely on s.2(2) UCTA if he was bringing his claim in tort. A third party who is injured or killed by negligence could still rely on s.2(1) UCTA, even where the negligence consists of the breach of an obligation arising from a term of a contract. Section 2(2) UCTA is considered in Chapter 5 at 5.6.1.1.

The limitation periods within which the third party must bring a claim are the same as if he had been the promisee.

4.2.2.3 Performing an existing duty

Whether or not it is good consideration to promise to perform a legal duty which has already arisen depends upon how that duty arose. The existing duty might have arisen under the general law, under a previous contract with a different person or under a previous contract with the same person. Each of the three situations needs to be considered in turn.

The duty was imposed by law

A promise by a person to do something which the general law of the land already obliges him to do will not amount to good consideration.

Collins v Godefroy (1813) 1 B & Ad 950

Godefroy caused Collins to be subpoenaed to go to court and give evidence in a court case which Godefroy was pursuing. (This meant that Collins was legally obliged to attend and give evidence.) Collins attended the court for six days but was not in fact called to give evidence. Collins then demanded 6 guineas (£6.30) as his usual fee for attending in court. Godefroy agreed to pay this, but later a dispute arose.

Held. Collins was not entitled to any payment. As Collins was obliged by the general law to attend and give evidence, he had given Godefroy no consideration for his promise to pay the money.

However, a promise to exceed a duty imposed by the general law will amount to good consideration.

Glasbrook Bros v Glamorgan County Council [1925] AC 270 (House of Lords)

During a coal strike a colliery manager asked the police for extra protection for his colliery and insisted that this could only be provided by billeting policemen on the colliery premises. The police superintendent claimed that this would not be necessary because a mobile force could provide adequate protection. The colliery manager then agreed to pay for extra police at a specified rate if they were billeted on the colliery premises. After the strike the colliery owners refused to pay the bill of £2 300, arguing that no consideration had been provided by the police even though the extra police had been billeted on the colliery premises.

Held. The colliery owners had to pay. The police had a discretion as to how and where best to deploy their forces. If the police believed that adequate protection could have been given by a mobile force then any greater protection could amount to consideration for the manager's promise.

The duty arose under a previous contract with a different person

It is possible for a person to give the same consideration to two different people, thereby creating two valid contracts, as the following case shows.

Shadwell v Shadwell (1860) 9 CB (NS) 159

The claimant was engaged to marry Ellen Nicholl. In those days this was a contract, and if the claimant had broken off the engagement Ellen could have sued him. The claimant's uncle wrote to the claimant in the following way, 'I am glad to hear of your intended marriage with E.N.; and, as I promised to assist you at starting, I am happy to tell you that I will pay to you £150 yearly during my life and until your annual income derived from your profession of a Chancery barrister shall amount to 600 guineas. Your ever affectionate uncle, A.' The claimant married Ellen Nicholl and received the full allowance for 12 of the next 18 years and part of the allowance for one year. The claimant's income from his work as a Chancery barrister never exceeded 600 guineas. The uncle died without having paid five of the yearly sums. The claimant sued the uncle's personal representatives for the payments which had not been made.

Held. The claimant was entitled to the money. His promise to marry Ellen was good consideration in return for the uncle's promise to pay the money, even though he had already given exactly the same promise to Ellen Nicholl in his contract with her.

The principle that the same consideration can be given to two different persons can be important in a business context, as the following case demonstrates.

New Zealand Shipping Co Ltd v A M Satterthwaite & Co Ltd [1974] AC 154 (Privy Council)

Carriers made a contract with the owners of a drilling machine, agreeing to take the machine by sea to New Zealand. The contract provided that the owners of the machine could not sue the carriers, or the stevedores who unloaded the ship, unless the claim was brought within one year. While unloading the machine, the stevedores damaged it. More than one year later, the owners sued the stevedores. The stevedores relied on the agreement between the carriers and the owners. The owners argued that privity of contract meant that the stevedores could not rely on this agreement because they had provided no consideration to the owners.

Held. The owners' promise not to sue if the goods were damaged did form a contract between the owners and the stevedores. The stevedores provided consideration to the owners of the machine by unloading the machine. It was irrelevant that the stevedores had →

already promised someone else, the carriers, that they would unload the machine.

The duty arose under a previous contract with the same person

The position here is less clear. Until recently there was a well-established rule that it is not good consideration for a claimant to promise to perform an existing contractual duty owed to the defendant. Although this might seem unfair, the rule had a logical foundation.

Let us assume that A has promised B that he will service B's boiler for £100. The contract gives rights to B. If A does not perform, B could sue and get damages. Let us now assume that A says that he will not perform and that B, instead of suing, promises to pay an extra £50 if A goes ahead and does perform his contract. If A does service the boiler he can only claim £100. He will not be entitled to the extra £50 because he gave no extra benefit to B in return for the extra £50. This is because if, after the second agreement, A still did not service the boiler, or serviced it improperly, B could only sue him for the same damages as owing under the first agreement. In effect B has been given nothing for the extra £50.

This principle was clearly laid down in the following case.

Stilk v *Myrick* (1809) 2 Camp 317

The claimant signed ship's articles, agreeing to work as a sailor on a voyage for £5 a month. In the course of the voyage, at Crondstat, two of the eleven man crew deserted. The captain agreed that if replacements could not be found, and if the remaining crew worked the rest of the voyage, then the wages of the two deserters would be shared among the remaining crew members. The remaining crew agreed and worked the ship back to London. The captain then refused to pay the extra wages promised.

Held. The men were not entitled to the extra money, but only to the £5 a month originally agreed. They had already promised the captain that they would do their duty when they took their jobs. They could not give the same promise to the same person to create a new contract.

COMMENT In those days there were of course no demarcation roles for sailors. Lord Ellenborough, explaining that the men had given no extra consideration, said: 'There was no consideration for the ulterior pay promised to the mariners who remained

---

with the ship. Before they sailed from London they had undertaken to do all that they could under all the emergencies of the voyage. They had sold all their services till the voyage should be completed.'

If the claimant exceeds the duty owed to the defendant then this can amount to fresh consideration. This was the decision in a very similar case, *Hartley* v *Ponsonby* (1857) 7 E & B 872, where half of a ship's crew deserted and the captain promised extra money to those remaining if they completed the voyage. The jury found as a fact that it was unreasonable to carry on with the voyage with such a diminished crew. Therefore by agreeing to complete the voyage the remaining crew were giving more than they had originally promised and were entitled to the extra money. Lord Ellenborough in *Stilk* v *Myrick* indicated that the men would have been paid the extra money if they had exceeded their duty. He said: 'If they had been at liberty to quit the vessel at Crondstat the case would have been quite different.'

This area of the law was more recently considered by the Court of Appeal in the following case.

Williams v *Roffey Bros Ltd*
[1990] 2 WLR 1153 (Court of Appeal)

The defendants had a contract to refurbish a block of flats. They employed Williams to do the carpentry work on 27 of the flats at a price of £20 000. After doing the carpentry on a few flats Williams realised that he had priced the job too low. He told the defendants that he could not afford to finish the job. The defendants were alarmed because if they did not finish the main contract on time they would have to pay huge penalty clauses to the owner of the block of flats. They therefore orally agreed to pay Williams an extra £575 per flat if he did the carpentry work as originally agreed. Williams did the carpentry work on eight more flats but was not paid all of the extra money which he had been promised. He therefore stopped work on the flats and sued for the amount he had not been paid.

Held. Williams was entitled to the extra money. By carrying on and doing the carpentry work as originally agreed he had helped the defendants avoid the penalty clause. This was a benefit to the defendants because it resulted in their gaining a commercial advantage. It therefore amounted to fresh consideration.

COMMENT (i) If the parties had abandoned their original contract and made a new one then there would have been no doubt that Williams would have been entitled to the extra money. (See Discharge by Agreement in Chapter 7 at 7.1.2.) However, there was no evidence that this is what happened.

(ii) The Court of Appeal did not overrule **Stilk v Myrick**, but claimed to have refined it. However, the principle of the two cases appears to be very similar. All three Court of Appeal judges thought that the defendants had been given a 'practical benefit' when the claimant agreed to carry on with the work. Russell LJ thought that fresh consideration was provided because under the agreement to pay more money per flat completed the 'previous haphazard method of payment' was replaced by a 'more formalised scheme involving the payment of a specified sum on the completion of each flat'. This gave the defendants more control over the carpenter's performance and, along with the fact that the defendants would not need to employ another subcontractor, was an advantage accruing to the defendant. Glidewell LJ thought that the defendants would have needed in practice to obtain a benefit or 'obviate a disbenefit'. He thought that on the facts this condition had been satisfied because: (a) the agreement sought to ensure that the claimant would continue work and not stop in breach of his subcontract; (b) the agreement enabled the defendants to avoid the penalty clause; and (c) the agreement prevented the defendants from having to go to the trouble and expense of finding another carpenter.

(iii) When considering whether or not the performance of an existing duty already owed to the defendant amounts to good consideration, duress, economic duress or fraud might also be relevant. (Duress and economic duress are considered in Chapter 6 at 6.3.) There was no such concept as economic duress when **Stilk v Myrick** was decided. If there had been then the agreement to pay the extra money might have been avoided on the grounds of economic duress rather than invalid for lack of consideration. In **Williams v Roffey Bros Ltd** the agreement was freely entered into by both sides and there was no suggestion of duress. It was significant that it was the defendants who had suggested the extra payments to the claimant.

(iv) In **Re Selectmove** [1995] 2 All ER 534 the Court of Appeal held that the decision in **Williams v Roffey Bros Ltd** could not overrule the decision in **Foakes v Beer** (1884) 9 App Case 605. (Both of these cases are considered below at 4.2.3.) So the principle in **Williams v Roffey** can apply when a person agrees to provide goods or services, and is given extra consideration for doing so, but cannot apply where a person owed a sum of money agrees to accept a lesser sum in complete satisfaction of the debt.

Extent to which performed / How the promise to perform arose	Performed	Exceeded
Duty arose under the general law	No consideration (*Collins* v *Godefroy*)	Good consideration (*Glasbrook Bros* v *G.C.C.*)
Duty arose under a previous contract with a third party	Good consideration (*Shadwell* v *Shadwell*)	Good consideration
Duty arose under a previous contract with the same person	Possibly good consideration (**Williams v R. B. Ltd**) Difficulties with *Stilk* v *Myrick*	Good consideration (*Hartley* v *Ponsonby*)

Figure 4.1 Whether a promise to perform an existing duty amounts to fresh consideration

The current position as to whether or not a promise to perform an existing duty can amount to good consideration is summarised by Figure 4.1.

4.2.2.4 Compositions with creditors

A composition agreement is an agreement between a debtor who is in financial difficulty and participating creditors. Under such an agreement the creditors all agree to accept that their debts will be settled at the same reduced rate. They might, for example, all agree to take 30p for every pound owed. Such agreements are legally binding. However, the legal justification for them is not entirely clear. As we shall see below at 4.2.3, a debtor who agrees to pay a lesser sum of money to extinguish a debt is not regarded as having given the creditor any consideration. The rule is that a lesser sum of money cannot be consideration for a greater sum owed, and so the debt is not extinguished. There would therefore seem to be nothing to prevent a creditor from breaching a composition agreement. However, there is no doubt that composition agreements are legally binding. Two theoretical explanations have been put forward as to why this should be so. First, it is argued that it would be a fraud on the other parties to the agreement if any of the parties were to breach it. Second, it is argued that all the creditors have given each other consideration by promising to take less than what they were owed. This second explanation is plausible as regards agreements between the creditors, but it suffers from the defect that the debtor has given no consideration. So it does not explain why the debtor has the right to hold the creditors to the agreement. The answer may be that the debtor's promise not to file for bankruptcy is regarded as consideration to the creditors.

4.2.2.5 Settling out of court

When a dispute is settled out of court a party who honestly and reasonably believes that he has a right to sue promises to give up that right in return for a payment from the other party. Such an agreement is a perfectly valid contract and there is no need to prove that the legal claim given up would have been successful. The vast majority of legal disputes are settled in this way and it is highly desirable that they should be. (Dispute resolution is considered in Chapter 2 at 2.4.)

For example, let us assume that Firm A's van has run over and injured B, who is demanding £50 000 compensation. Eventually the parties, through their solicitors, settle for a payment of £30 000. This is a contract. Firm A's consideration consists of the promise to pay the money. B's consideration is his promise not to bring proceedings in respect of the accident. No matter how much worse B's injuries might become, or how well he might subsequently recover, neither side can change their minds. (Unless misrepresentation could be proved. See Chapter 6 at 6.1.)

4.2.3 Part payment of a debt

At common law a debt can be extinguished either by paying it in full, or by accord and satisfaction (agreement and consideration). For example, if A owes £10 000 to B the debt is extinguished if A pays £10 000, or if B agrees to accept anything else (perhaps A's delivery van) instead. As we have seen, consideration does not need to be adequate, and so the courts will not enquire whether a thing taken instead of the money was actually worth £10 000.

An ancient case, *Pinnel's Case* (1602) 5 Co Rep 117a, made the rule that payment of a lesser sum of money on the date when a greater sum is due cannot be consideration for the greater sum owed.

Let us assume, for example, that Firm X is owed £10 000 by Firm Y, which is having difficulty in paying. Firm X promises Firm Y that if it pays what it can, say £6 000, the debt will be extinguished. Firm Y accepts this offer and pays the £6 000. Firm X can still sue for the outstanding £4 000 because the lesser sum of money (£6 000) could not be consideration for the greater sum owed (£10 000).

This rule seems somewhat illogical when placed beside the rule that consideration must be sufficient but need not be adequate. In effect, the court is inquiring into the adequacy of the consideration because it is saying that £6 000 cannot be worth £10 000. In *Pinnel's Case* the claimant was owed £8 10 shillings. The defendant paid £5 2 shillings and 2 pence. The Court of Common Pleas held that this could not be consideration for the whole debt, even if both parties had agreed that it should be.

The justification for the rule in *Pinnel's Case* comes from the idea that the only thing which always has a quantifiable monetary value is money itself. We saw earlier in this chapter that the value of goods varies with all the circumstances. However, the one thing which always has a fixed monetary value is money itself, and so a lesser sum of money cannot in any circumstances be worth as much as a greater sum.

The rule in *Pinnel's Case* was approved by the House of Lords in the following case, and this approval gave the rule real authority.

> ### Foakes v Beer
> (1884) 9 App Cas 605 (House of Lords)
>
> Dr Foakes owed Mrs Beer £2 090 and 19 shillings as a result of a court judgment. He could not pay immediately, and Mrs Beer signed a statement that if he paid by instalments she would not 'take any proceedings whatever' on the judgment. Dr Foakes paid, in full, by instalments as agreed. Mrs Beer then remembered that she had forgotten to include the interest which is always payable on a judgment debt and sued for £360 interest.
>
> **Held.** Mrs Foakes was entitled to the £360. The rule in Pinnel's Case was confirmed. The lesser sum (£2 090 by instalments without interest) could not be satisfaction for the greater sum owed (£2 090 by instalments with interest).

The rule in *Pinnel's Case* is subject to certain well-recognised exceptions. If the creditor takes anything other than money in full satisfaction of the debt then the debt will be extinguished. In *Pinnel's Case* the court said that if the claimant had agreed to take a horse, a hawk or a robe in full satisfaction of the debt then the debt would have been extinguished because in certain circumstances these things might be more beneficial to the claimant than the money. It was also said that payment of a lesser sum before the day the greater sum was due would extinguish the debt, but only if this lesser sum was paid early at the creditor's request. Similarly the debt would be extinguished if the creditor requested that a lesser sum of money be paid in some other place. At one time it was thought that payment by cheque, at the creditor's request, could amount to a different form of payment and therefore extinguish the whole debt. It is now accepted that this is not the case. The debt will also be extinguished if the amount owed was uncertain or disputed and the creditor settled for less than he thought he was entitled to. If the creditor accepts a lesser sum in full settlement from a third party this too will extinguish the debt.

The above exceptions to the rule in *Pinnel's Case* are not contentious. The same cannot be said of the final exception, promissory estoppel, which may mean that a person who has promised to accept a lesser sum can, in certain circumstances, be prevented from breaking his promise.

The authority of *Foakes v Beer* (1884) 9 App Cas 605 has been doubted at times. It frustrates the expectations of the parties and makes it difficult to settle debts. In 1937 the Law Revision Committee, chaired by Lord Wright MR, proposed that a statute should be passed to reverse the first rule in *Pinnel's Case*. No such statute has ever been passed. However, the decision protects creditors from unscrupulous debtors, as can be seen in *D & C Builders v Rees*, below. Furthermore, in *Re Selectmove* [1995] 2 All ER 534 the Court of Appeal made it plain that as *Foakes v Beer* was a House of Lords decision, only another House of Lords (now Supreme Court) decision or legislation could change it. It was also made plain that as *Williams v Roffey Bros* (see above at 4.2.2.3) was a Court of Appeal decision it could not change *Foakes v Beer*. The crucial difference between the two cases is that *Williams v Roffey* concerned a promise to pay more than was contractually due, *Foakes v Beer* concerned a promise to accept less. *Foakes v Beer* would therefore seem to be good law as regards part payment of a debt. However, it is possible that promissory estoppel, considered immediately below, can apply to a promise to accept part payment of a debt, as the doctrine may have its origins in *Hughes v Metropolitan Railway* (1877) 2 App Cas 439, a House of Lords case which pre-dated *Foakes v Beer* by seven years.

4.2.3.1 The doctrine of promissory estoppel

The effect of promises which seem to be supported by no consideration must now be viewed in the light of the doctrine of promissory estoppel, which was introduced in the following case.

> ### Central London Property Trust Ltd v High Trees House Ltd [1947] KB 130
>
> In 1937 a block of flats in central London was let to the defendants for £2 500 p.a. During the war years (1939–45) the flats could not be sublet because many people had moved away from central London. In 1940 the claimants therefore agreed to accept rent of £1 250 p.a. but without saying for how long this agreement should last. By the beginning of 1945 the flats were once again fully sublet, but the defendants were still paying the lower rent. In September 1945, in order to regulate the legal position, the claimants sued for the full rent from the time when the flats had become fully sublet and for the future.
>
> **Held.** The claimants won, as both parties had anticipated, because the conditions which had given rise to the agreement no longer applied.

→

COMMENT (i) The actual decision in this case was not at all contentious. But in an *obiter* Denning J stated that if the claimants had sued for the full rent for the war years, as they were thinking of doing, they would not have won because of the doctrine of promissory estoppel. This doctrine would prevent a claimant from insisting on his strict legal rights, even if no consideration were received for the promise, if the following conditions were satisfied: (a) the claimant had made a promise not to insist upon his strict legal rights and this promise was intended to create legal relations; (b) the claimant knew that the promise was going to be acted upon; and (c) the defendant did act upon the promise.

(ii) Denning J suggested that **Foakes v Beer** might have been differently decided if the House of Lords had considered the effect of an earlier House of Lords case, **Hughes v Metropolitan Railway** (1877) 2 App Cas 439. In that case a tenant was obliged to repair the premises he occupied within six months or lose the lease. Shortly after the obligation to repair arose, the landlord began negotiations to buy the lease from the tenant. The tenant therefore did no repairs until the negotiations broke down about ten weeks later, on 31 December 1874. The tenant could not complete the repairs within the original six month time limit but they were completed in June 1875. The landlord claimed the lease but the House of Lords held that the duty to repair was suspended until 31 December 1874. The tenant had completed the repairs within six months of this date and so the lease was not forfeited. Lord Cairns stated: 'It is the first principle on which all Courts of Equity proceed, that if parties who have entered into definite and distinct terms involving certain legal results ... afterwards by their own act or with their own consent enter upon a course of negotiations which has the effect of leading one of the parties to suppose that the strict rights arising under the contract will not be enforced, or will be kept in suspense, or held in abeyance, the person who might otherwise have enforced those rights will not be allowed to enforce them where it would be inequitable having regard to the dealings which have thus taken place between the parties.'

The law on promissory estoppel is still evolving. However, it seems safe to say that promissory estoppel will apply only if the following five conditions are satisfied.

(i) There must have been an existing legal relationship between the claimant and the defendant.

(ii) The claimant must have intended to enter into legal relations, by clearly and unambiguously promising not to insist on his strict legal rights. (Such a promise can be implied.)

(iii) The claimant must have known that the defendant would act upon this promise.

(iv) The defendant must actually have acted upon the promise.

(v) It must be inequitable for the defendant to break his promise and revert to his strict legal rights.

It has long been accepted that estoppel can prevent the claimant from breaking his promise only where it would be inequitable (unfair) of him to do so.

D & C Builders v Rees
[1966] 2 QB 617 (Court of Appeal)

The claimants, a small firm of builders, were owed £482 and 13 shillings for work they had done on the defendant's shop. Knowing that the claimants were in desperate financial difficulty, the defendant's wife intimidated them into accepting £300 in full settlement of the debt, telling them that if they did not take this they would get nothing. The claimants told the defendant's wife that they had no choice but to accept. The claimants took a cheque for £300 'in completion of the account'. Then the claimants sued for the remaining £182 13 shillings.

Held. Applying **Foakes v Beer**, the claimants won.

COMMENT (i) Lord Denning MR by now regarded his own judgment in the **High Trees** case as 'so obviously just that no one could well gainsay it'. (As we have seen, this view is not shared by everyone.) However, Lord Denning thought that promissory estoppel would arise only where it would be inequitable for the claimant to forget the promise he had made and to insist on his strict legal rights. Here it was not inequitable because the claimants had only made the promise as a result of the pressure they were put under.

(ii) The Court of Appeal decided that there was no true accord between the claimants and the defendant and that the agreement was therefore not binding. The law on economic duress (considered at 6.3.1) has advanced very considerably in recent years, and if the case were to arise today the agreement to accept the lesser sum of money would plainly be voidable for economic duress.

(iii) It was in this case that the Court of Appeal emphatically rejected the argument that a payment of a lesser sum by cheque would amount to good consideration for the greater sum owed.

It is often said that promissory estoppel 'is a shield not a sword'. This means that it can be used only as a defence to being sued. It cannot be used to sue somebody with. It would therefore have been no use to the seamen in *Stilk* v *Myrick*. As the captain had never handed over the extra money promised, the seamen would have needed to sue the captain to get it. In the same way it would not have been of any use to the carpenter in *Williams* v *Roffey Bros*.

There is considerable doubt as to whether promissory estoppel acts so as to extinguish rights or whether rights are merely suspended until they are introduced by giving reasonable notice. It seems likely that the doctrine will only suspend the promisor's legal rights unless it would be impossible for the promisee to resume his original position or unless the promisor indicated that he would permanently give up his rights.

Until 1966 the House of Lords was bound by its own previous decisions. The court in *Foakes* v *Beer* would therefore have been bound by the decision in *Hughes* v *Metropolitan Railway*. In the *High Trees case* Denning J seemed to think that the House of Lords in *Foakes* v *Beer* was not familiar with *Hughes* v *Metropolitan Railway*. This seems most unlikely, as the case arose only seven years earlier and two of the Lords sat in both cases. It seems more likely that *Hughes* v *Metropolitan Railway* was not considered relevant as it concerned the temporary suspension of a right whereas *Foakes* v *Beer* concerned the permanent extinction of a right. In *Tool Metal Manufacturing Co* v *Tungsten Electric Company* [1955] 2 All ER 657 the House of Lords held that an estoppel generally suspends rights rather than extinguishes them. But in some cases, such as *D & C Builders* v *Rees*, where the obligation was not a continuing one, a suspension of rights would be of very little use. The answer would seem to be that whether the rights are suspended or are extinguished will depend upon what exactly was promised and the context of the case.

In *Collier* v *Wright* [2007] EWCA Civ 1329, [2008] 1 WLR 643 Lady Justice Arden gave strong support to the idea that promissory estoppel could extinguish a creditor's right to sue for the balance of a debt. She said:

'The facts of this case demonstrate that, if (1) a debtor offers to pay part only of the amount he owes; (2) the creditor voluntarily accepts that offer, and (3) in reliance on the creditor's acceptance the debtor pays that part of the amount he owes in full, the creditor will, by virtue of the doctrine of promissory estoppel, be bound to accept that sum in full and final satisfaction of the whole debt. For him to resile will of itself be inequitable. In addition, in these circumstances, the promissory estoppel has the effect of extinguishing the creditor's right to the balance of the debt. This part of our law originated in the brilliant obiter dictum of Denning J, as he was, in the

High Trees case. To a significant degree it achieves in practical terms the recommendation of the Law Revision Committee chaired by Lord Wright MR in 1937.'

However, this endorsement must be treated with considerable caution. First, it was only an *obiter dictum*. The Court of Appeal had merely been asked to decide, as a preliminary issue, whether there was a real prospect that promissory estoppel could provide a defence when one partner, in a firm of three partners, had settled with a creditor by paying a third of the amount which the firm owed as a result of a court judgment. As all of the partners would be jointly liable for the whole debt, the partner would remain liable for the other two-thirds of the debt unless promissory estoppel provided a defence. The Court of Appeal unanimously held that the defence had a real prospect of success, which is not to say that it would actually succeed, and that the case should be returned to the county court for a trial. Second, the other two judges in the Court of Appeal, Longmore and Mummery LJJ, agreed that there was some prospect of success but did not endorse Lady Justice Arden's statement that the debt would have been extinguished. Longmore LJ thought it arguable that it would be inequitable for the creditor company to resile from its promise but said that there was much to be said on the other side. Mummery LJ merely said that there was a real prospect of success on the promissory estoppel issue. Third, Lady Justice Arden relied rather heavily on an *obiter dictum* of Lord Denning in *D & C Builders* v *Rees*. In this *obiter*, Lord Denning said that if there was a true accord under which the creditor voluntarily accepted a lesser sum in satisfaction, and the debtor acts on that accord by paying the lesser sum and the creditor accepts it, then it would be inequitable for the creditor to insist on the balance. In other words, he said that in such circumstances the debt would be extinguished. Cases decided since 1966 have not tended to regard this *obiter* as decisive.

Test your understanding 4.2

1 What is meant by consideration in the law of contract?

2 What is meant by the rule that past consideration is no consideration? In what circumstances can a past act amount to good consideration?

3 What is meant by the rule that consideration must be sufficient but need not be adequate?

4 What is meant by privity of contract?

5 Can a third party ever sue to enforce a contract made on his behalf?

6 Is it good consideration to promise to perform a duty imposed by the general law?

7 Is it good consideration to promise to perform an existing contractual duty?

8 What is the rule in *Pinnel's Case*?

9 What is promissory estoppel?

4.3 FORMALITIES

In general, contracts do not need to be made in any particular way. Most commercial contracts are made in writing but there is no legal requirement that this should be so. The types of formalities which sometimes are required are as follows.

4.3.1 Contracts which must be made by a deed

(a) A conveyance of a legal estate in land must be made by deed.

(b) The creation of a lease of **over** three years' duration must be made by deed or no legal estate will be created.

(c) A promise of a gift is not enforceable unless made by deed.

The Law of Property (Miscellaneous Provisions) Act 1989 s.1(2) states that an instrument shall not be a deed unless it is made clear on its face that it is intended to be a deed by the party or parties making it, and it is validly executed as a deed. Section 1(3) explains that an instrument is validly executed as a deed by an individual only if:

(i) the instrument is signed by the individual in the presence of a witness who attests the signature; or

(ii) the individual directs someone else to sign the instrument in his presence and in the presence of two witnesses who attest the signature; and

(iii) the instrument is delivered by the individual as a deed or by someone authorised to do so on his behalf. A person attests a document by signing it to show that he has witnessed the signature of another.

The Limitation Act 1980 provides that an action cannot be brought on a simple contract six years after the date when the right to bring the action arose. However, when the contract was made by deed an action cannot be brought 12 years after the right to bring the action arose. (See Time limits on remedies in Chapter 7 at 7.2.8.)

4.3.2 Contracts which must be in writing

Certain types of contracts must be in writing. The most important of these are contracts for the sale or other disposition of land and regulated consumer credit agreements.

4.3.2.1 Contracts for the sale or other disposition of an interest in land

Section 2(1) of the Law of Property (Miscellaneous Provisions) Act 1989 provides that contracts for the sale or other disposition of an interest in land can only be made in writing and only by incorporating all the terms which the parties have expressly agreed in one document or, where contracts are exchanged, in each. Both parties must sign the document. An exception exists for leases of land of three years or less, which can be made orally as long as the lease takes effect immediately. A contract which does not comply with s.2(1) will be void. Before the 1989 Act came into force contracts for the sale or other disposition of land had only to be evidenced in writing. If they were not so evidenced they were unenforceable, rather than void.

4.3.2.2 Regulated consumer credit agreements

Regulated consumer credit agreements are unenforceable without a court order unless they are in writing, and signed by the debtor or hirer. (See the improper execution of regulated agreements in Chapter 14 at 14.1.3.7.)

4.3.3 Contracts which must be evidenced in writing

Section 4 of the Statute of Frauds 1677 requires that contracts of guarantee, under which one person assumes secondary liability to settle the debts or liabilities of another, must be evidenced in writing and signed by the person giving the guarantee or they will be unenforceable. This does not mean that the contract performance of which is being guaranteed must be evidenced in writing. It is only the contract under which the guarantee is given which must be evidenced in writing.

For example, A buys a motorbike from a garage and B guarantees that he will pay the price if A fails to do so. The contract to sell the motorbike does not need to be evidenced in writing, the contract under which B gives the guarantee does.

By evidenced in writing it is meant that there must be some written evidence that the contract has been made. This evidence must contain all the material terms of the contract and must be signed or initialled by the person giving the guarantee. In *Pereira Fernandes SA* v *Mehta* [2006] 1 WLR 1543 it was held that although there was no reason why an email should not be a sufficient note or memorandum to satisfy s.4, it would not be the case that an automatically included email address would be a sufficient signature.

An indemnity must be distinguished from a guarantee, as s.4 does not apply to indemnities. A person who indemnifies another assumes primary liability to settle the obligations of that person. If, in the example about the motorbike, B had told the garage to let A have the motorbike and he (B) would see that the garage was paid, this would have been an indemnity rather than a guarantee.

4.3.4 **The Electronic Commerce (EC) Regulations 2002**

Regulation 9(1) of the Electronic Commerce (EC Directive) Regulations 2002 requires Internet service providers to provide clear, comprehensible and unambiguous information before any offer is made by a recipient of the Internet service. The information must set out: (a) the different technical steps to conclude the contract; (b) whether or not the contract will be filed by the service provider and whether it will be accessible; (c) the technical means of identifying and correcting input errors prior to the placing of the order; and (d) the languages offered for the conclusion of the contract. Regulation 9(2) requires the service provider to indicate relevant codes of practice to which he subscribes and to give information on how these can be consulted electronically. Regulation 9(1) does not apply if the service provider makes the offer. Neither reg.9(1) nor reg.9(2) will apply if the recipient is not a consumer and it has been agreed that the regulation will not apply. A consumer is defined as any natural person who is acting for purposes other than those of his trade, business or profession. Nor will either regulation apply if the contract is concluded exclusively by exchange of email. However, reg.9(3) applies to all contracts concluded by electronic means if the service provider provides terms and conditions which apply to the recipient. In such cases the service provider must make the terms and conditions available to the recipient in such a way that allows him to store and reproduce them.

Regulation 11 deals with placing of the order.

'(1) Unless parties who are not consumers have agreed otherwise, where the recipient of the service places his order through technological means, a service provider shall –

(a) acknowledge receipt of the order to the recipient of the service without due delay and by electronic means; and

(b) make available to the recipient of the service appropriate, effective and accessible technical means allowing him to identify and correct input errors prior to the placing of the order.'

This regulation does not apply where the contract is concluded exclusively by exchange of email. However, it does apply to the typical situation where the web site is an invitation to treat and the consumer makes the offer. The service provider cannot accept the offer without acknowledging receipt of the offer and giving the consumer the chance to correct errors. If the consumer is not given the chance to correct errors then the consumer can rescind the contract (reg.15). If reg.9(1) or 11(1)(a) is breached the recipient can sue for damages for breach of statutory duty (reg.13).

Regulation 11(2) provides that, for the purposes of reg.11(1)(a), an offer, and acknowledgement of receipt of it, will be deemed to be effective when the parties to whom they are addressed are able to access them.

4.4 CAPACITY

Generally speaking, everyone has the capacity to make any contract they please. But minors, mentally disordered persons and drunkards do not have full capacity.

4.4.1 **Minors**

The Family Law Reform Act 1969 s.1 defines a minor as a person who has not yet reached the age of 18. Contracts made by minors fall into three categories.

4.4.1.1 **Valid contracts**

The Sale of Goods Act 1979 s.3(2) provides that where necessaries are delivered to a minor he must pay a reasonable price for them. Section 3(3) defines necessaries as 'goods suitable to the condition in life of the minor or other person concerned and to his actual requirements at the time of sale and delivery'. Three points should be noted. First, the obligation is to pay a reasonable price which may well differ from the price agreed in the contract. Second, the obligation only exists if the goods were sold and delivered to the minor. Third, goods can be necessary goods even though they are not necessities of life. In *Nash v Inman* [1908] 2 KB 1 a Savile Row tailor sued a wealthy Cambridge student for clothes supplied. The clothes included 11 fancy waistcoats. The Court of Appeal held that the clothes were not necessaries and that the minor did not therefore have to pay for them. It was not the case that such clothes could not possibly be necessaries for a wealthy student but rather that the student in question was already adequately supplied with clothes of this type. The provisions of the Sale of Goods Act 1979 apply only to goods. The common law requires minors to pay a reasonable price for necessary services supplied.

A minor can also validly make a contract of employment as long as the contract is overall beneficial to the minor. It is the overall effect of the contract when made which must be considered. A contract which turned out to be against the minor's interests can be binding if it was overall beneficial when made.

Clements v London and North Western Railway Company
[1894] 2 QB 482 (Court of Appeal)

The defendant, a minor, took a job as a railway porter and agreed to become a member of an insurance society formed by the railway employees. Joining this society meant giving up rights against the employer under the Employers' Liability Act 1880. The insurance society gave the members very wide protection against injuries, whether these were caused by the employers' negligence or not and allowed for payment without the need for litigation. However, as regards certain types of claims the amounts payable under the insurance scheme were less than those which could be claimed under the Act. The minor was injured by the employers' negligence and wished to sue under the Act.

Held. The minor could not sue under the Act as he was bound by the agreement he had made. The contract taken as a whole was beneficial to the minor and it was therefore binding upon him.

The same rules apply to contracts which are analogous to contracts of employment. In *Chaplin v Leslie Frewin (Publishers) Ltd* [1966] Ch 71 the Court of Appeal had to decide whether a minor was bound by an agreement he had made to have a book published. The minor was the son of Charlie Chaplin, the famous actor, and when he claimed National Assistance benefits several publishers proposed that he should write

a book about his bohemian life. The minor made contracts to have his life story ghost written and for a publisher to have exclusive rights to publish and sell the book. The minor was paid an initial advance of £300. A further £100 advance was paid when the book was almost ready for publication. The minor then changed his mind about the book and applied for an injunction to prevent publication. The Court of Appeal held that the contract was binding upon the minor because it was analogous to a contract of employment and at the date when the contract was made it was beneficial to him because it would allow him to support his family. Lord Denning MR dissented on the grounds that the contract was not beneficial to the minor as it was scandalous, brought shame on himself and others, invaded family life and exposed the minor to claims for libel.

4.4.1.2 **Voidable contracts**

Contracts giving a minor an interest in property, which also impose a continuing liability on the minor, are voidable by the minor either before he reaches 18 or within a reasonable time of his having done so. By voidable it is meant that the minor has the option to avoid (call off) the contract. If the minor does avoid the contract he is absolved from future liability. Generally, a minor who avoids can be sued for liabilities which had arisen before the contract was avoided. However, this is not the case if there was a total failure of consideration, that is to say if the minor received no benefit at all from the contract.

The main types of contract which are voidable by a minor are:

(a) Contracts of partnership.
(b) Contracts to buy shares.
(c) Contracts to take a lease of land.

4.4.1.3 **Void contracts**

Contracts other than those classed as valid or voidable are not binding on a minor. However, a minor will only be able to recover any money paid or property delivered under such a contract if there has been a total failure of consideration. That is to say only if the minor has received no benefit at all under the contract.

A loan made to a minor will not be enforceable unless the minor, having reached the age of majority, makes a new agreement to pay it. This new agreement does not need to be supported by any consideration.

The Minors' Contracts Act 1987 s.3(1) allows a court to order a minor to return property gained under a void contract, or property representing that gained, if the court considers it just and equitable to do so.

Obviously such an order would not be made if the minor had paid for the property supplied. If the minor no longer has the property supplied, or other property representing that gained, then he will be under no obligation to pay any compensation to the supplier. If the minor sells non-necessary goods on to a third party acting in good faith for value, the third party will gain complete title to the goods and the person who supplied them to the minor will not therefore be able to recover them. Section 2 of the Act allows a person who has guaranteed a contract which is unenforceable against the minor to be sued on the guarantee.

4.4.2 Drunkards and mental patients

Like minors, drunkards must pay a reasonable price for necessary goods delivered and necessary services supplied. Other contracts will be voidable if the drunkard did not know what he was doing when he made the contract, and the person with whom he made the contract was aware of this. If the drunkard ratifies a voidable contract upon becoming sober he will be liable on it. The same rules apply to mentally disordered persons who are not regarded as lacking capacity within the Mental Capacity Act 2005. If a person is protected by the Act then his property becomes controlled by the court and any attempt he makes to dispose of his property will be void.

4.4.2.1 Corporations

The capacity of corporations to make contracts is considered in Chapter 17 at 17.1.8.

Test your understanding 4.3

1 What types of contracts must be made by a deed?

2 Name two classes of contracts which will be void if they are not made in writing.

3 What type of contract must be evidenced in writing?

4 What type of contracts will be binding upon a minor?

5 What type of contracts are voidable if made by a minor?

Key points

Intention to create legal relations

■ A contract will only come into being if it can be objectively inferred that the parties intended to create legal relations.

■ When considering business and commercial agreements the courts will presume that the parties did intend to create legal relations. This presumption can be rebutted by the evidence.

■ When considering social and domestic agreements the courts will presume that the parties did not intend to create legal relations. This presumption can be rebutted by the evidence.

■ A letter of comfort might or might not amount to a contractual promise, depending upon its wording and upon all the surrounding circumstances.

■ A term in a contract which seeks to exclude the jurisdiction of the courts will be void as against public policy. (This is not the case as regards terms which provide for reference of disputes to arbitration.)

Consideration

■ An agreement will only amount to a contract if both parties give some consideration to the other.

■ Consideration consists either in the giving of a benefit or the suffering of a loss.

■ Executory consideration consists of a promise to do something in the future. Executed consideration occurs when one of the parties makes the offer or the acceptance in such a way that he has completely fulfilled his liability under the contract.

■ Past consideration is no consideration for a promise unless the past act was performed at the request of the promisor and both parties all along contemplated that payment would be made.

■ The performance of a trivial act can amount to good consideration if performance of the act conferred an economic benefit on the promisee.

■ The doctrine of privity of contract holds that a person who is not a party to a contract may not sue to enforce the contract or be sued upon the contract. There are several well-established exceptions to the rule.

■ The Contracts (Rights of Third Parties) Act 1999 allows a third party who is expressly identified in a contract to sue to enforce a term of a contract if the term expressly states that he may. An expressly

→

identified third party may also sue to enforce a term which confers a benefit upon him if this is what the parties to the contract intended.

■ It is not good consideration to promise to perform a duty which arose under the general law.

■ The same consideration can be given to two different people, thereby creating two valid contracts.

■ It is possible that it can be good consideration to promise to perform an existing duty which arose under a previous contract with the same person, but only if this promise confers an economic benefit on that person.

■ At common law a lesser sum of money paid on the date due cannot be consideration for a greater sum owed.

■ A lesser sum of money can be good consideration for a greater sum owed if, at the creditor's request, it is paid early or in a different place.

■ Promissory estoppel is an equitable doctrine which will prevent a claimant from breaking a promise not to insist on his strict legal rights if the promise was intended to create legal relations, if the claimant knew that the promise was going to be acted upon and if the defendant did act upon the promise.

■ Promissory estoppel will only prevent a claimant from breaking his promise where it would be inequitable for him to break it.

Formalities

■ Generally, no formalities are needed to make a contract.

■ A conveyance of a legal estate in land must be made by a deed. The creation of a lease of over three years' duration must be made by a deed or no legal estate will be created.

■ Contracts for the sale or other disposition of land must be made in writing or they will be invalid. Regulated consumer credit agreements must be made in writing and signed by the debtor or hirer or they will be unenforceable without a court order.

■ Contracts of guarantee must be evidenced in writing or they will be unenforceable.

Contractual capacity

■ Minors must pay a reasonable price for necessary goods delivered or necessary services supplied.

■ Contracts giving an interest in property, which also impose a continuing liability on a minor, are voidable by the minor.

■ Minors are not bound by contracts to buy non-necessary goods or services. Nor are they bound to repay loans which they took out while minors.

Summary questions

1 Is there likely to be an intention to create legal relations in the following circumstances:

a When a student enrols at a university?

b When magazine readers enter competitions to win prizes?

c When supermarkets promote 'Club Card' schemes, which give customers free spending vouchers for every £100 they spend?

2 In *Appleson v H. Littlewood Ltd* [1939] 1 All ER 464 a punter claimed to have won £4 335 on the football pools but the defendants refused to pay. The pools form which the claimant had completed contained the rules and conditions. Rule 2 said, 'It is a basic condition of the sending in and the acceptance of this coupon that … any agreement entered into or payment made by or under it shall not be attended by or give rise to any legal relationship, rights, duties or consequences whatsoever or be legally enforceable or the subject of litigation, but all such arrangements, agreements and transactions are binding in honour only'. The defendants claimed that the sending in of the coupon and the acceptance of it could not possibly amount to a contract. Do you think that the Court of Appeal agreed?

3 Look again at *Carlill v The Carbolic Smoke Ball Company* (p. **67** above). Analyse the consideration given by Mrs Carlill and by the Smoke Ball Co. When Mrs Carlill claimed the reward, was the consideration of the parties executed or executory?

4 In *Midland Bank Trust Co Ltd v Green* [1981] AC 513 (House of Lords) a farmer, for good reasons of his own, sold his farm to his wife for £500 even though the farm was valued at over £40 000. Was this a good contract?

5 A householder is just about to leave for work when he notices that a pipe in his house has burst. He rings an emergency plumber and arranges for the plumber to pick the keys up from his next-door

→

neighbour and fix the pipe. The plumber repairs the pipe and leaves a bill. Can the householder refuse to pay the plumber on the grounds that the work was already done before any price was mentioned?

6 The president of the local bowls club employs a painter to paint the clubhouse for £600. The painter later finds a job which will pay him more and tells the president that he is not going to do the work. A wealthy club member promises the painter an extra £250 if he goes ahead with the contract, as originally agreed. The painter performs the contract. To how much money, if any, will the painter be entitled?

7 A builder makes a contract with Arthur whereby he is to repair Arthur's house for £500. The builder then decides that he has priced the job too low and tells Arthur that he will not do the work unless he is paid more money. Arthur agrees to pay an extra £250 and the builder carries out the repair. To how much money, if any, will the builder be entitled?

8 John and Mary work together running a seaside tea shop and are paid an hourly wage. One day their employer phones John to tell him that Mary is ill and will be unable to work for the rest of the week. The employer tells John that he will have to run the tea shop single handed. With difficulty, John manages to do this for the rest of the week. At the end of the week the employer tells John that he will be paid double wages for the period when he worked on his own. The employer is now refusing to pay the extra money. Advise John as to whether or not he will be entitled to the extra sum.

9 In *Williams* v *Roffey Bros Ltd* the contractor who had priced the carpentry work too low was entitled to recover the extra money he was promised.

a Is it good policy to allow subcontractors who have priced the job too low to demand more money from the main contractor?
b Would the main contractors, Roffey Bros Ltd, have been able to demand more money if they realised that they had priced the main job, the refurbishment of the flats, too low?

10 George, a builder, owes £36 000 to Builders Merchants Ltd. George explains that he has not been paid by a customer who has become bankrupt and that this means that he cannot pay his bill to Builders Merchants. The manager of Builders Merchants agrees to accept £27 200 in complete satisfaction of the debt. Now the manager of Builders Merchants has heard that George has won £1 million on the National Lottery. Advise Builders Merchants Ltd as to whether or not they will be able to sue for the £8 800 of the original debt which they agreed to forgo.

11 Mary's daughter, Samantha, comes over to England from Australia for Mary's fiftieth birthday. Samantha buys Mary a new television as a birthday present. Mary does not use the television until Samantha has left the country. When Mary does use the television she finds that it does not work. Mary returns the television to the shop from where it was bought, explaining that Samantha bought it as a birthday present. The shop refuses to give Mary any remedy. Samantha will not be returning to England in the foreseeable future. Has Mary any contractual remedy against the shop?

Multiple choice questions

1 A supermarket advertises that any customer who spends £100 on wine will receive a free gallon of petrol. A customer who relied on this promise and who spent £100 on wine is refused the petrol. Which one of the following statements is true?

a There will be no contract as there was no intention to create legal relations.
b There will be no contract as the customer provided no consideration for the petrol.
c The customer will be entitled to the petrol as there was a good contract.
d The customer will not be entitled to the petrol because when he claimed the petrol his consideration was past.

2 A solicitor claims that his wife, an accountant, made a contract to sell him her car for £4 500. Which one of the following statements is true?

a A court would presume that the parties did not intend to make a contract unless the evidence clearly showed that they did.
b A court would presume that the parties did intend to make a contract unless the evidence clearly showed that they did not.
c It is not possible for a husband and wife to make a contract with each other.
d The agreement could not amount to a contract unless it was evidenced in writing.

→

3 A Co Ltd offers a reward of £10 000 to anyone who supplies information which leads to the arrest and conviction of arsonists who set fire to their factory. Bill supplies the necessary information and claims the reward. After Bill has done this, but before A Co Ltd has paid, which one of the following statements is true?

a Bill's consideration is past and therefore amounts to no consideration.

b The consideration given by both sides is executory.

c The consideration given by A Co Ltd is executed, the consideration given by Bill is executory.

d The consideration given by A Co Ltd is executory, the consideration given by Bill is executed.

4 A building firm sells an old lorry for a quarter of its market value. Which one of the following statements is true?

a The buyer's consideration is neither sufficient nor adequate and so there is no contract.

b The buyer's consideration is sufficient and adequate and so there is a contract.

c The buyer's consideration is adequate but not sufficient and so there is no contract.

d The buyer's consideration is sufficient but not adequate and so there is a contract.

5 A joiner agrees with a builder that he will install all the windows in four houses which the builder is constructing for a price of £2 000. The joiner finds that he has priced the job too low and tells the builder that he cannot afford to do the job. The customer for whom the houses are being built tells the joiner that he will pay an extra £1 000 if the joiner performs the job as agreed, which the joiner does. Which one of the following statements is true?

a Neither the builder nor the customer need pay because the joiner broke his contract when he refused to install the windows as originally agreed.

b The builder will need to pay the £2 000, but the customer will not need to pay the £1 000.

c The customer will need to pay the £1 000, but the builder will not need to pay the £2 000.

d The builder will need to pay the £2 000 and the customer will need to pay the £1 000.

6 Which one of the following statements is not true?

a The Contracts (Rights of Third Parties) Act 1999 allows a third party who is expressly identified in the contract to enforce a term of a contract if the term expressly provides that he may enforce it.

b The Contracts (Rights of Third Parties) Act 1999 allows a third party who is expressly identified in the contract to enforce a term of a contract if the term purports to confer a benefit upon him.

c When the Contracts (Rights of Third Parties) Act 1999 allows a third party to enforce a contract, the third party can avail himself of any remedy which would have been available to him if he had made the contract.

d Where a third party does gain rights under s.1 of the Contracts (Rights of Third Parties) Act 1999, the parties to the contract can never alter the contract in such a way as to alter the third party's rights without his consent.

7 A landlord lets a house for one year for a rent of £4 000. The tenant intimidates the landlord into accepting half rent, threatening that if the landlord does not accept this the tenant will refuse to leave when the lease is up. The lease has now expired and the tenant has now left the house. The landlord is suing for the half of the rent which was withheld. Which two of the following statements are true?

a *Foakes* v *Beer* supports the landlord's case.

b *Foakes* v *Beer* supports the tenant's case.

c Promissory estoppel would not prevent the landlord from breaking his promise, as it would not be inequitable for him to break his promise.

d The tenant could not rely on promissory estoppel because it is a shield not a sword.

8 A tenant orally agrees to lease a business unit for one year. The tenant pays two months' rent in advance and takes immediate possession. Which one of the following statements is true?

a The lease is invalid because it was not made by a deed.

b The lease is invalid because it was not in writing.

c The lease is invalid because it was not evidenced in writing.

d The lease was validly formed.

9 Adrian, who is 17, buys a much needed pair of shoes from a mail order catalogue for double their normal price. Adrian has received the shoes but has not yet paid for them. Which one of the following statements is true?

a Adrian must pay the agreed price.

b Adrian must pay a reasonable price for the shoes.

c Adrian can avoid the contract within a reasonable time.

d The contract is void.

Task 4

From Chapter 3, choose three cases in which the court decided that there was a contract. As regards each case, indicate:

a The consideration given by both parties.

b Any formalities with which the parties would have to comply.

c The factors which would have persuaded the court that there was an intention to create legal relations.

mylawchamber *premium*

Visit **www.mylawchamber.co.uk/macintyre** to access study support resources including interactive multiple-choice questions, weblinks, glossary, glossary flashcards, legal newsfeed, answers to questions in this chapter, legal updates and an overview of this chapter all linked to the **Pearson eText** version of *Business Law* which you can **search**, **highlight** and **personalise** with your **own notes** and **bookmarks**.

Use **Case Navigator** to read in full some of the key cases referenced in this chapter with commentary and questions:

Carlill **v** *Carbolic Smoke Ball Co*. [1893] 1 QB 256
Central London Property Trust Ltd **v** *High Trees House Ltd* [1947] KB 130
Williams **v** *Roffey Bros & Nicholls (Contractors) Ltd* [1991] 1 QB 1

5

Contractual terms

5.1 NATURE OF CONTRACTUAL TERMS

The terms of the contract define the contractual promises which the parties exchanged when they made the contract. If any term is breached the injured party will always have a remedy for breach of contract.

Terms are incorporated into contracts in one of two ways; they can either be expressed or implied. Express terms are specifically agreed upon by the parties. Implied terms are put into the contract, either by the courts or by a statute, without the parties needing to express them.

5.2 EXPRESS TERMS DISTINGUISHED FROM REPRESENTATIONS

In Chapter 3 we saw that a contract is formed when an offer is accepted. The express terms of the contract are contained in the offer. By accepting the offer, the offeree agrees to the terms proposed by the offeror. These terms then become contractually binding.

Although it is simple to state that the express terms of the contract are contained in the offer which has been accepted, it can often be very difficult to tell precisely what terms were agreed. When parties negotiate before making a contract, assurances and promises are often made over a period of time. Some of these statements will be incorporated as terms of the contract, but others will amount only to representations. If a representation is subsequently shown to be untrue there is no breach of contract. (In certain circumstances, a remedy for misrepresentation may be available, a matter considered in the following chapter.) In addition, some statements may be neither terms nor representations but mere sales puffs.

The following example may clarify the distinction between terms, representations and sales puffs. Let us assume that X makes an oral contract to buy a car from Y. X asks Y about the car's age, its mileage, and whether it has given any trouble. After receiving satisfactory replies to these questions X offers a price of £6 000 and this offer is accepted by Y. A contract has been made and two express terms are quite evident. X has agreed to pay £6 000 to Y, and Y has agreed to transfer ownership of the car to X. These two matters are terms of the contract because it is evident that X and Y intended them to be contractually binding. But the effect of the assurances given by Y is less clear. If X made it plain that he would only buy the car if it had a valid MOT certificate, and Y assured him that it did, then it would be a term of the contract that the car had a valid MOT certificate. It would have been implicit in X's offer to buy the car for £6 000 that Y's promise that the car had a valid MOT certificate was a part of the bargain. But a statement by Y that he had himself bought the car two years ago for £8 000, which seemed to make little impression on X, would not be a term of the contract. The reasonable person would infer that the parties did not intend the statement to be a part of the contract. Such a statement, being a statement of fact which did not amount to a term of the contract, would merely be a representation. A statement by Y that the car was a bargain at the price would amount to nothing more than a sales puff. The reasonable person would not think that such a statement was intended to amount to a term of the contract. Nor could the statement be taken as a representation, as it did not amount to a statement of definite fact.

In deciding whether or not a statement is a term of a contract, the courts consider whether the parties appeared to intend that the statement should be a term. It is important to realise that the courts are not concerned with the parties' actual intentions but with their apparent intentions. Over the years several tests which assist the courts in determining the parties' intentions have developed.

5.2.1 **The relative degrees of the parties' knowledge**

It is often the case that one of the parties to the contract has considerably more expertise than the other about the subject matter of the contract, so that this expertise will put him in a better position to know whether or not a particular statement is true. A garage owner, for example, will know considerably more about cars than most customers. Statements made by a party with considerably more expertise are likely to be classified by the courts as terms, whereas statements made by a party with considerably less expertise are likely to be classified as representations. The following two cases demonstrate these principles.

Oscar Chess Ltd v *Williams*
[1957] 1 WLR 370 (Court of Appeal)

The defendant, a private motorist, traded in his car to the claimant, a car dealer, in order to acquire a new Hillman Minx. The defendant told the dealer that the car he was trading in was a 1948 model. The defendant believed this to be the case because when he had taken the car on hire-purchase, the previous year, the registration book had shown the year of registration as 1948. The dealer looked the car up in *Glass*'s guide and offered £290 for it, an offer which was accepted by the defendant. Eight months later the dealer discovered that the car was a 1939 model. The dealer sued for breach of contract.

Held. The defendant was not liable for breach of contract because his statement was a representation rather than a term. The defendant knew little about cars whereas the claimant had considerable knowledge and expertise. The defendant could not be taken as having made a definite promise that the car was a 1948 model.

COMMENT (i) In the following chapter we shall see that a representation may become an actionable misrepresentation, thereby providing the injured party with a remedy. The remedy available will depend upon whether the misrepresentation was made fraudulently, negligently or innocently. When a term is breached the state of mind of the party who made the promise is irrelevant. The fact that a term has been breached will amount to breach of contract whether the maker of the term knew that the promise embodied in the term was untrue, whether he ought to have known that it was untrue or whether he could not possibly have known.

(ii) The statement made by the defendant would have amounted to an innocent misrepresentation. Before →

the Misrepresentation Act 1967 came into force a person to whom a non-fraudulent misrepresentation was made could not claim damages. An innocent misrepresentation could give rise to a right to rescind the contract. In this case the claimant could not rescind because his claim to do so came too long after the misrepresentation was made. (Misrepresentation is considered in Chapter 6.)

Dick Bentley Productions Ltd v Harold Smith Motors Ltd
[1965] 1 WLR 623 (Court of Appeal)

The claimant, a wealthy businessman, asked the defendant, a car dealer, to keep his eye open for a 'well vetted' second-hand British car, the history of which was known. The defendant found an apparently suitable car, a Park Ward coupé Bentley, and told the claimant that it had done only 20 000 miles since it had been fitted with a new engine and gearbox. This statement was repeated later the same day when the claimant brought his wife to look at the car. The car soon gave trouble and the claimant discovered that it had done 100 000 miles since the new engine had been fitted.

Held. The defendant was liable for breach of contract as his statement was a term. The defendant, with his greater knowledge of cars, could be taken to have promised that the car had only done 20 000 miles since the new engine had been fitted.

5.2.2 **The reliance shown to be placed on the statement**

If the party to whom the statement was made demonstrated that he considered the statement to be very important to him then the statement is likely to be a term.

Bannerman v White (1861) 10 CB NS 844

The defendant, a hop merchant, bought hops from the claimant, a farmer. The defendant intended to sell the hops to brewers of beer in Burton. These brewers had told the defendant that they would not buy any hops which had been treated with sulphur. The defendant therefore sent a circular to hop growers stating that he would not buy hops which had been treated with sulphur at any price. Before the contract was made the claimant assured the defendant that

the hops which were being sold had not been treated with sulphur. Of the 300 acres of hops sold 5 acres had been treated with sulphur but the claimant had forgotten about this when giving the assurance. When the defendant found that some of the hops had been treated with sulphur he claimed to treat the contract as repudiated and refused to pay the price. The claimant sued for the price. The jury found as a fact that the statement that no sulphur had been used on the hops was intended to be a part of the contract.

Held. The jury's finding was confirmed on appeal. A term of the contract had been broken.

COMMENT (i) The statement was a term of the contract because the defendant had demonstrated how important it was to him. Anybody could later claim that they were thinking that a particular term was very important. The court takes an objective view as to the parties' intentions. This view is reached by considering all of the circumstances.

(ii) As the broken term was a condition of the contract the defendant was entitled to treat the contract as repudiated and therefore had a defence when sued for the price. (The difference between conditions, warranties and innominate terms is considered below at 5.4.3.)

5.2.3 **The strength of the statement**

A statement which is made very strongly is likely to be a term of the contract. A guarded statement is likely to be a representation.

Schawel v Reade
[1913] 2 IR 81 (House of Lords)

The claimant inspected a horse owned by the defendant. The claimant made it plain that he wanted to buy a horse for stud purposes. The defendant told him, 'You need not look for anything; the horse is perfectly sound. If there was anything the matter with the horse I would tell you.' A price for the horse was agreed a few days later and the sale of the horse was concluded about a month later. After the conclusion of the contract the claimant discovered that the horse was quite unsuitable for stud purposes because it had an incurable hereditary eye disease.

Held. The defendant's statement was a term. It was intended to be a part of the transaction and the basis of the sale.

Ecay v Godfrey (1947) 80 Lloyd's Rep 286

The claimant, a Spanish diplomat, bought a boat called the *Tio Pepe* from the defendant for £750. The boat, which had once been a lifeboat, had recently been painted and looked in good condition. In fact the boat was in a very poor condition and barely seaworthy. The defendant said that the boat was sound but he also advised the claimant to have it surveyed before he bought it. The claimant wanted the boat in a hurry and so he bought it without having it surveyed.

Held. The defendant's statement that the boat was sound was a representation rather than a term. The statement was made in such a guarded way that it could not amount to a contractual promise that the boat was sound.

Even a very strong statement will not amount to a term if the parties understood that it was not to be a term. In *Hopkins* v *Tanqueray* (1854) 15 CB 130 the defendant's horse was sold at Tattersall's by public auction. Before the sale the defendant found the claimant looking at the horse's legs and told him, 'You have nothing to look for; I assure you that he is perfectly sound in every respect'. The claimant replied that he was satisfied with this statement and the following day bought the horse at the auction. Later the claimant discovered that the horse was not sound. Despite being a strong statement, it was held that the defendant's assurance could not be a term as both parties were well aware that horses sold at Tattersall's were sold without any terms as to soundness.

5.2.4 The time at which the statement was made

A statement which immediately prompts the making of the contract is more likely to be a term than a statement made a considerable time before the making of the contract. The shorter the delay between the making of the statement and the formation of the contract the more likely it is that the parties intended the statement to be a part of the contract. *Routledge* v *McKay* [1954] 1 All ER 855 provides an example of this test. The vendor of a motorbike told the purchaser that it was a 1942 model, whereas it was in fact a 1930 model. Neither of the parties had any special skill or knowledge. Both parties were private individuals and the vendor had relied on the motorbike's logbook. A written contract was drawn up seven days later, but this made no reference to the age of the motorbike. The Court of Appeal held that the vendor's statement was merely a

representation because it was made some time before the contract was concluded. It must be remembered that this test, like the others, is not conclusive. For example, in *Schawel* v *Reade* the statement was held to be a term even though it was made a month before the contract was finalised. The very similar assurance in *Hopkins* v *Tanqueray* was not a term even though it was made the day before the sale of the horse. Neither are any of the other tests which the courts have evolved conclusive. All of the circumstances must be considered. In all of the post-1913 cases which we have considered the following words of Lord Moulton in *Heilbut, Symons & Co* v *Buckleton* [1913] AC 30 were considered by the various courts to be binding:

'It may well be that [various tests used to tell a term from a representation] may be criteria of value in ... coming to a decision whether or not a [term] was intended; but they cannot be said to furnish decisive tests, because it cannot be said as a matter of law that the presence or absence of these features is conclusive of the intention of the parties. The intention of the parties can only be deduced from the totality of the evidence, and no secondary principles of such a kind can be universally true.'

5.2.5 Written contracts

Where the contract is written the parol evidence rule prevents extrinsic [outside] evidence from being introduced to add to or vary what was written. Consequently, the factors which we have considered above will not apply. The general rule is that what was written will be the entire contract and oral statements will not be included as part of the contract. However, there are a number of exceptions to the rule. The most important of these exceptions are as follows. The equitable remedy of rectification will be allowed to correct a written version of the contract if an oral contract had previously been made and the written version was intended merely to record what had been agreed but had recorded this incorrectly. (Rectification is considered in Chapter 7 at 7.2.6.) Extrinsic evidence will be allowed to show that a contract was rendered invalid by some rule of law. Extrinsic evidence is also allowed to show that the contract was not to operate until a condition was fulfilled. Nor will the parol evidence rule prevent a party from introducing evidence of a custom. Finally, in some circumstances, it may be possible to introduce extrinsic evidence that what was agreed was not the whole contract.

Another matter to be considered is that an oral statement might be part of a collateral contract. Such a contract exists side by side with the main contract which is being made. For example, in *Webster v Higgin* [1948] 2 All ER 127 the defendant took a car on hire-purchase because the supplier said that he would guarantee that the car was in good condition. The written contract of hire-purchase which the defendant signed contained a clause excluding the supplier from liability for the condition of the car. The car was in extremely poor condition. The defendant could not sue on the contract of hire-purchase because the assurance about the condition of the car could not be a term of that written contract and the exclusion clause would probably have prevented him from suing on any implied term as to the quality of the car. However, the defendant succeeded on a collateral contract which existed side by side with the main contract of hire-purchase. The terms of this collateral contract were that the supplier's guarantee about the condition of the car was given in return for the defendant's consideration in entering into the contract of hire-purchase. As the supplier's guarantee was not true he had breached a term of the collateral contract. The defendant was therefore entitled to treat the contract of hire-purchase as terminated and recover all money already paid under it. (*Andrews v Hopkinson* [1957] 1 QB 229, which is set out in Chapter 14 at 14.2.2, provides an example of a collateral contract between one of the parties to the main contract and a third party.)

5.2.6 Statements of opinion

A statement of pure opinion cannot itself amount to either a term or a representation. However, in certain circumstances, as the following case shows, a statement of opinion can nevertheless give rise to a term.

Esso Petroleum Co Ltd v Mardon
[1976] QB 801 (Court of Appeal)

The defendant was persuaded to take over the tenancy of an Esso petrol station because of an assurance that the station would sell about 200 000 gallons of petrol a year within three years. The defendant had indicated that he thought a figure of 100 000 to 150 000 was a more realistic estimate. However, he was persuaded by the fact that the Esso representative who gave the figure of 200 000 gallons had 40 years' experience in the trade. The defendant managed the petrol station well but it became apparent that the station would never come close to selling 200 000 gallons a year. The defendant was sued by the claimants and counterclaimed for breach of warranty.

Held. It was not a term of the contract that the station would sell 200 000 gallons a year because this was only an opinion. However, there was an implied term, in the form of a collateral warranty, that this opinion had been made using reasonable care and skill. This collateral warranty had been broken and so the defendant was en-titled to damages for breach of contract.

COMMENT (i) The statement was made before the Misrepresentation Act 1967 came into force. At that time there could be no claim for damages for a non-fraudulent misrepresentation. If the Act had been in force it would not have been necessary to imply the collateral warranty. (Misrepresentation, and the remedies available, are considered in the following chapter.)

(ii) The Court of Appeal also held that Esso were liable for the tort of negligent misstatement. (This tort is considered in Chapter 12 at 12.3.) However, such a claim would be unlikely to be pursued since the Misrepresentation Act 1967 came into force. Negligent misstatement must be proved by the person alleging it. When negligent misrepresentation is alleged the burden of proof is on the person making the misrepresentation to show that he had reasonable grounds for believing that the statement was true and actually did believe that the statement was true. The statement in this case, although an opinion, implied statements of fact which could amount to a misrepresentation. (See *Smith v Land and House Property Corporation* (1884) 28 ChD 7 in Chapter 6 at 6.1.1.1.)

(iii) Section 1 of the Misrepresentation Act 1967 contemplates that a misrepresentation may later become a term of the contract. If this is the case then remedies will be available for either misrepresentation or for breach of contract. This could be particularly important when a misrepresentation became incorporated as a warranty. Breach of the warranty would not allow the injured party to terminate the contract (see 5.4 below), but the misrepresentation would allow the injured party to rescind the contract (see Chapter 6 at 6.1.3).

Test your understanding 5.1

1 How do express terms arise? How do implied terms arise?

2 Upon what basis will a court decide whether or not an express statement is a term of a contract?

3 In deciding whether or not the parties intended a statement to be a term of the contract the courts are guided by various tests. What do the following matters indicate about the presumed intention of the parties:

   a One of the parties to the contract was much better placed than the other to know whether or not the statement was true?

   b The party to whom the statement was made indicated that the statement was vitally important to him?

   c The statement was made very strongly/ weakly?

   d The contract was concluded a long time after the statement was made?

4 What is the parol evidence rule?

5.3 IMPLIED TERMS

As well as the express terms agreed upon by the parties, most contracts also contain implied terms. These implied terms are inserted into the contract either by a statute or by the courts.

5.3.1 Terms implied by statute

The Sale of Goods Act 1979 implies terms into contracts of sale of goods and these terms are considered in detail in Chapter 8. However, it is important when considering the nature of implied terms to have an outline knowledge of the five major terms implied by the 1979 Act. First, it is implied that the seller has the right to sell the goods. Second, where there is a contract for the sale of goods by description there is an implied term that the goods will correspond with the description. Third, in a contract for the sale of goods by sample it is implied that the goods will match the sample in quality and that the bulk of the goods will not contain defects which were not apparent in the sample. The final major implied terms, which are probably the most important two, are only implied into contracts where the seller sells the goods in the course of a business. The two terms implied into such sales are that the goods sold are of satisfactory quality, and that the goods are reasonably fit for any purpose which the buyer expressly or impliedly made known to the seller.

In Chapter 8 we shall also see that the Supply of Goods (Implied Terms) Act 1973 and the Supply of Goods and Services Act 1982 imply terms into other types of contracts which cannot be classified as contracts of sale of goods. The terms implied into these contracts, under which goods are supplied but not sold, are virtually identical to the terms implied by the Sale of Goods Act. Where a contract is made to supply a service in the course of a business, the Supply of Goods and Services Act 1982 implies an important term that the supplier will carry out the service with reasonable care and skill. This term has no equivalent in the Sale of Goods Act 1979.

Because the three statutes imply the terms outlined above, the parties do not need to mention these terms when they make the contract. The implied terms are automatically put into the contract by the relevant statute. Indeed, when the buyer deals as a consumer the terms implied by the Sale of Goods Act 1979, and the corresponding terms contained in the 1973 and 1982 Acts, cannot be removed from the contract even by an express term which states that they should be. An outline of the statutory implied terms is shown in Figure 8.4 in Chapter 8 at p. **230**.

5.3.2 Terms implied by the courts

The courts imply terms into contracts either as a matter of fact or as a matter of law. Terms are implied as a matter of fact on the grounds that the parties to the contract intended the term to be a part of their agreement even though they did not agree the term verbally. Such terms are implied when it is necessary and obvious that the term should be implied in order to give the agreement 'business efficacy'.

Mackinnon LJ in *Shirlaw v Southern Foundries* [1939] 2 All ER 113 (Court of Appeal) explained the circumstances in which a term will be implied by the courts as a matter of fact: '... that which in any contract is left to be implied and need not be expressed is something so obvious that it goes without saying.' Mackinnon LJ went on to formulate his officious bystander test. Under this test the courts decide whether or not to imply a term by asking how the parties to the contract could be supposed to have reacted if an officious bystander had suggested that the term should be expressly included in their contract. If it could be supposed that the parties would irritably have told the officious bystander that the term was so obviously included that it did not need to be mentioned, then the term would be implied by the courts. If it could not be supposed that the parties would have reacted in this way, then the term would not be implied.

The test can be demonstrated by looking at the following case.

The Moorcock
(1889) 14 PD 64 (Court of Appeal)

The defendants owned a wharf and a jetty on the River Thames. The claimants owned a steamship, the *Moorcock*. An agreement was made that the *Moorcock* should be moored alongside the defendant's jetty so that its cargo could be unloaded and another cargo loaded. If moored at this place the *Moorcock* would inevitably touch the bottom of the river at low tide. No charge was made for the steamship being moored at the jetty. However, the defendant benefited from its being moored there because the claimant paid for the use of cranes and the defendant was entitled to part of this payment as commission. At low tide the *Moorcock* was damaged because it settled on a ridge of hard ground beneath the mud.

Held. The defendants were liable for the damage to the steamship. The steamship would inevitably touch the bottom of the river at low tide, and so the defendants had impliedly promised that they had taken reasonable care to make sure that the bottom of the river adjoining the jetty was in such a condition that it would not damage the steamship.

This case arose half a century before Mackinnon LJ set out his version of the officious bystander test. Even so, we can see that an application of the test would have resulted in the same outcome. If the officious bystander had said to the two parties, 'Hadn't you better include a term that the jetty owner has taken reasonable care to ensure that the jetty is a safe place to moor a steamship?' it can be supposed that they would both irritably have told him that such a term was so obvious that it did not need to be stated.

The officious bystander test will ensure that a term is not implied where one of the parties might not have agreed to the term in question. In *Shell (UK)* v *Lostock Garages* [1976] 1 All ER 481 the defendant made a written contract, agreeing to buy only Shell's petrol in return for a discount on the price. During a price war, Shell supplied all neighbouring garages more cheaply with the consequence that the defendant could only carry on his business at a loss. The defendant claimed an implied term that Shell would not 'abnormally discriminate' against him. The Court of Appeal refused to imply the term not only because it was too vague and uncertain, but also because there was no certainty that Shell would have agreed to it.

Despite having this power to imply terms, the judges have always used it sparingly. They have repeatedly made it plain that they are not prepared to make a contract on behalf of the parties.

As Lord Pearson said in *Trollope* v *NWRHB* [1973] 2 All ER 260 (House of Lords):

'The court does not make a contract for the parties. The court will not even improve the contract which the parties have made for themselves, however desirable the improvement might be ... An unexpressed term can be implied if and only if the court finds the parties must have intended that term to form part of their contract . . . it is not enough for the court to find that such a term would have been adopted by the parties as reasonable men if it had been suggested to them . . . it must have been a term which went without saying, a term necessary to give business efficacy to the contract.'

In *AG of Belize* v *Belize Telecom Ltd* [2009] UKPC 11, 26 BHRC 578 Lord Hoffmann, giving the only judgment of the Supreme Court, considered the process of implication of a term at considerable length. He said:

'The court has no power to improve upon the instrument which it is called upon to construe ... It cannot introduce terms to make it fairer or more reasonable. It is concerned only to discover what the instrument means. However, that meaning is not necessarily or always what the authors or the parties to the document would have intended. It is the meaning which the instrument would convey to a reasonable person having all the background knowledge which would reasonably be available to the audience to whom the instrument is addressed: see *Investors Compensation Scheme Ltd* v *West Bromwich Building Society* [1998] 1 WLR 896, 912–913. It is this objective meaning which is conventionally called the intentions of the parties ... The question of implication arises when the instrument does not expressly provide for what is to happen when some event occurs. The most usual inference in such a case is that nothing is to happen. If the parties had intended something to happen, the instrument would have said so ... In some cases, however, the reasonable addressee would understand the instrument to mean something else. He would consider that the only meaning consistent with the other provisions of the instrument, read against the relevant background, is that something is to happen. The event in question is to affect the rights of the parties. The instrument may not have expressly said so, but this is what it must mean. In such a case, it is said that the court implies a term as to what will happen if the event in question occurs. But the implication of the term is not an addition to the instrument. It only spells out what the instrument means.'

In *Mediterranean Salvage and Towage Ltd v Seamar Trading and Commerce Inc, The Reborn* [2009] EWCA Civ 531, [2009] All ER (D) 83 (Jun) the Court of Appeal indicated that this test was likely to become as well known as the one set out by Lord Hoffmann in *Investors Compensation Scheme Ltd v West Bromwich Building Society* [1998] 1 WLR 896. However, the Court of Appeal stressed the need for necessity to imply a term. Lord Hoffmann also emphasised that the 'officious bystander' test was not concerned with speculation about how the actual parties to the contract would have reacted to the proposed implied term. The test merely emphasised the need for the court to be satisfied that the proposed implied term spelt out what the contract would reasonably be understood to mean.

'Likewise, the requirement that the implied term must "go without saying" is no more than another way of saying that, although the instrument does not expressly say so, that is what a reasonable person would understand it to mean. Any attempt to make more of this requirement runs the risk of diverting attention from the objectivity which informs the whole process of construction into speculation about what the actual parties to the contract or authors (or supposed authors) of the instrument would have thought about the proposed implication.'

As well as implying terms as a matter of fact, the courts also imply terms as a matter of law. These terms are not implied on the basis that the parties to the contract must have intended them to be included in their contract. They are implied if three conditions are satisfied. First, the contract is a sufficiently recognisable type of contract. Second, the parties have not dealt with the issue which the term is concerned with. Third, it is necessary to imply the term to make the contract work.

Liverpool City Council v Irwin
[1977] AC 239 (House of Lords)

Liverpool City Council owned a tower block containing 70 flats. There were two lifts and a staircase. The tenancy agreements imposed a list of obligations on the tenants but did not impose any obligations on the City Council. The condition of the tower block deteriorated very badly because of vandalism and a lack of co-operation from the tenants. The lifts often failed, there was a lack of proper lighting on the stairs and the chutes down which rubbish was deposited were often blocked. Two tenants, a husband and wife, refused to pay rent as a protest. The City Council applied for an order to reclaim possession of their maisonette. The tenants counterclaimed that the City Council had breached an implied term giving the tenants a right to quiet enjoyment of the property.

Held. A term was implied that the City Council should keep the communal facilities in reasonable repair and usability. This term was not implied as a matter of fact, because the City Council would not have agreed to it. It was implied as a matter of law because the three conditions were satisfied.

COMMENT The City Council had not in fact breached the implied term.

5.3.3 Customary terms

Terms will be implied by the courts on the grounds that they are customary in a particular trade, customary in a particular locality or customary between the parties. The courts impose such terms on the grounds that the parties, fully aware of the custom in question, must have intended the term to be a part of the contract.

Many trades have customs, and these customs will be implied into contracts made within the context of that trade. For example, in *British Crane Hire Corporation Ltd v Ipswich Plant Hire Ltd* [1975] QB 303 one of the parties urgently needed to hire a crane from the other. An oral contract was made, and this contract was deemed by the Court of Appeal to include the terms contained in 'the Contractors' Plant Association form'. Both parties were in the business of hiring out heavy earth moving equipment and both knew that whenever heavy plant was hired it was always done so under terms based on the Contractors' Plant Association form.

Similarly, customs of a particular locality will be implied into contracts made within that locality. In *Hutton v Warren* (1836) 1 M & W 466, for example, a Lincolnshire tenant farmer who was given notice to quit the farm had to be paid an allowance for seeds and labour because there was an agricultural custom to that effect in that area.

A particular term can become customary between the parties themselves, if they regularly make contracts which include the term. In *Kendall (Henry) & Sons v William Lillico & Sons Ltd* [1969] 2 AC 31 an oral contract for the sale of animal foodstuffs was made. Over the previous three years the parties had made three or four similar contracts a month with each other. The same written contract note, setting out terms and conditions, was always sent within a day of the oral contract being made. The House of Lords held that the oral contract was made subject to the terms and conditions contained in the written contract note. When the buyers placed an order they did so in the knowledge that the acceptance would be on these terms and conditions.

5.3.4 Exclusion of implied terms

In many circumstances the terms implied by statute cannot be excluded, as we shall see in Chapter 8. But terms implied by the court on the basis that they were obviously what the parties intended can always be excluded by an express term. If, for instance, the lease in *Hutton v Warren* had expressly stated that the tenant farmer would not get an allowance for seeds and labour, then he would not have received such an allowance. Similarly, terms will not be implied by the courts as a matter of law if the parties have expressly agreed that they should not be included.

5.4 TYPES OF TERMS

If any term is broken, the injured party will always be able to claim damages for breach of contract. In addition, the injured party might also be entitled to treat the contract as repudiated and therefore be entitled to refuse performance of the contract. Whether or not the injured party has the right to do this depends upon what type of term was broken.

5.4.1 Conditions and warranties

Traditionally, all contract terms were classified as being either conditions or warranties. A condition is an important term, one which goes 'to the root of the contract'. If a condition is breached then the injured party can not only claim damages but is also entitled to treat the contract as repudiated. This right to treat the contract as repudiated is available even

if the consequences of the breach of condition were trivial.

A warranty is a term which did not seem vitally important when the contract was made. (A term which does not go 'to the root of the contract'.) If a warranty is breached the injured party can only claim damages. He is not entitled to treat the contract as repudiated. If the injured party does treat the contract as repudiated, and refuses to perform his side of the contract, he will himself be in breach of contract.

Two cases decided in 1876, both involving opera singers who had breached their contracts, have traditionally been used to demonstrate the difference between conditions and warranties.

Bettini v Gye (1876) 1 QB 183

Bettini was an opera singer who made a contract to give a series of performances over a three-month period. He fell ill and missed half of the six days' rehearsals which the contract demanded. His employer found a substitute and sacked Bettini. It was a term of Bettini's contract that he should attend all six days of the rehearsals, and there was no doubt that he had breached this term. His employers argued that this term was a condition and that they could therefore terminate the contract. Bettini argued that the term was a warranty and that, while this made him liable in damages, it did not give the employer the right to terminate the contract.

Held. The employer was not entitled to dismiss Bettini. The terms requiring him to attend the rehearsals were only warranties as they did not go to the root of the contract. (So the employer had himself breached a term of the contract, by sacking Bettini unjustifiably, and consequently had to pay damages to Bettini.)

Poussard v Spiers (1876) 1 QB 410

The facts of this case were substantially the same as those of *Bettini v Gye*, except that Madame Poussard became seriously ill five days before the first performance. As a result of this illness, she was unavailable for the first four performances of her three-month contract. The employers found it necessary to sack Madame Poussard because they could only find a replacement if they offered her the whole three months' work.

Held. The employers were entitled to terminate the contract and dismiss Madame Poussard. Missing the opening night amounted to a breach of condition.

5.4.2 Innominate terms

In 1962 Lord Diplock, in the following case, demonstrated that the existing classification of terms into either conditions or warranties could be fundamentally flawed. He invented a new type of term, the innominate term (the term with no name). Innominate terms are sometimes called intermediate terms.

> *Hong Kong Fir Shipping Co Ltd v Kawasaki Kisen Kaisha Ltd*
> [1962] 1 All ER 474 (Court of Appeal)
>
> A ship was chartered to the defendants for a 24-month period. The engines of the ship were in poor condition and the crew were inefficient. Because of these problems five weeks were lost during the first voyage and a further 15 would be lost while repairs were carried out. However, after the repairs were completed and a new crew found the ship was seaworthy in every respect. At this time the ship was still available for the remaining 17 months of the contract. One of the terms said that the ship should be 'in every way fitted for ordinary cargo service'. Both sides agreed that this term had been breached. The defendants argued that the breached term was a condition and that breach of this term therefore entitled them to treat the contract as repudiated. The claimants sued for wrongful repudiation, claiming that the defendants were not entitled to treat the contract as repudiated because the term was only a warranty.
>
> **Held.** The term that the ship should be 'in every way fitted for ordinary cargo service' could not be classified in advance as either a condition or a warranty. The term was an innominate term, and the contract could not be terminated because the defendants had not been deprived of 'substantially the whole benefit which it was the intention of the parties they should obtain'.
>
> **COMMENT** (i) The term that the ship should be in every way fitted for ordinary cargo service covered very minor breaches (such as a rivet being missing) as well as very major breaches (such as the ship sinking). If the term was held to be a condition, this would lead to the absurd result that the whole contract could be terminated because one rivet was missing. If the term was held to be a warranty this would lead to the even more absurd result that the contract could not be terminated even if the ship sunk to the bottom of the ocean.
>
> (ii) Under the charter the ship was hired at 47s per ton. At the time when the defendants claimed to treat the contract as repudiated freight had fallen to 13s 6d per ton. This was almost certainly the defendants' real motive in claiming that they had the right to treat the contract as repudiated. However, the defendants' motive would not have any bearing on the court's decision as to whether or not the contract could be treated as repudiated.

5.4.3 Difference between conditions, warranties and innominate terms

In deciding whether or not a breach of an innominate term allows the injured party to terminate the contract, the court considers the effect of the breach. If the injured party is deprived of substantially the whole benefit of the contract, he can treat the contract as repudiated and claim damages. If he is not deprived of substantially the whole benefit, he can claim damages but not treat the contract as repudiated.

Under the traditional conditions and warranties approach the courts do not wait to see the effect of the breach. Instead they look back to the time when the contract was made, and look at all the circumstances of the case to decide how important the parties would have considered the term to be when they made the contract. If the parties would have intended the term to go to the root of the contract the term was a condition, if they would not have intended the term to go to the root of the contract the term was only a warranty.

Innominate terms have not replaced conditions and warranties. Some terms can now be classed as conditions or warranties, others are innominate terms. In outline, the current position is as follows.

The statutory implied terms are classified by the statutes themselves as either conditions or warranties. The more important statutory implied terms are conditions. Breach of a condition will allow the injured party to treat the contract as repudiated, breach of a warranty will not. However, s.15A of the Sale of Goods Act 1979, s.11A of the Supply of Goods (Implied Terms) Act 1973 and ss.5A and 10A of the Supply of Goods and Services Act 1982 provide that a buyer who does not deal as a consumer will have to treat breach of a statutory implied condition as a breach of warranty if the breach is so slight that it would be unreasonable for the buyer to reject the goods. (See Chapter 8 at 8.3.4.)

Terms other than the statutory implied terms will be treated as innominate terms unless the parties have expressly or impliedly agreed that breach of the term will or will not entitle the injured party to treat the contract as repudiated. If such an intention has been shown then the courts will give it effect and the term will be either a condition or a warranty. (Calling the term a condition or a warranty is not conclusive of such an intention, although it is an indication of it.) Alternatively, a rule of law might indicate that a particular term is to be treated as a condition or a warranty. Where none of the previously mentioned matters classify a term as either a condition or a warranty, the term will be an innominate term. If an innominate term is breached then the injured party can treat the contract as repudiated only if he has been deprived of substantially the whole benefit of the contract.

5.4.4 **Interpretation of contractual terms**

In *Investors Compensation Scheme Ltd v West Bromwich Building Society* [1998] 1 WLR 896, Lord Hoffmann set out the following five principles on the interpretation of contractual documents.

'(1) Interpretation is the ascertainment of the meaning which the document would convey to a reasonable person having all the background knowledge which would reasonably have been available to the parties in the situation in which they were at the time of the contract.

(2) The background was famously referred to by Lord Wilberforce as the "matrix of fact", but this phrase is, if anything, an understated description of what the background may include. Subject to the requirement that it should have been reasonably available to the parties and to the exception to be mentioned next, it includes absolutely anything which would have affected the way in which the language of the document would have been understood by a reasonable man.

(3) The law excludes from the admissible background the previous negotiations of the parties and their declarations of subjective intent. They are admissible only in an action for rectification. The law makes this distinction for reasons of practical policy and, in this respect only, legalinterpretation differs from the way we would interpret utterances in ordinary life. The boundaries of this exception are in some respects unclear. But this is not the occasion on which to explore them.

(4) The meaning which a document (or any other utterance) would convey to a reasonable man is not the same thing as the meaning of its words. The meaning of words is a matter of dictionaries and grammars; the meaning of the document is what the parties using those words against the relevant background would reasonably have been understood to mean. The background may not merely enable the reasonable man to choose between the possible meanings of words which are ambiguous but even (as occasionally happens in ordinary life) to conclude that the parties must, for whatever reason, have used the wrong words or syntax. (See *Mannai Investments Co. Ltd. v Eagle Star Life Assurance Co. Ltd.* [1997] 2 WLR 945.)

(5) The "rule" that words should be given their "natural and ordinary meaning" reflects the common sense proposition that we do not easily accept that people have made linguistic mistakes, particularly in formal documents. On the other hand, if one would nevertheless conclude from the background that something must have gone wrong with the language, the law does not require judges to attribute to the parties an intention which they plainly could not have had. Lord Diplock made this point more vigorously when he said in *The Antaios Compania Naviera S.A. v Salen Rederierna A.B.* [1985] AC 191, 201: "... if detailed semantic and syntactical analysis of words in a commercial contract is going to lead to a conclusion that flouts business common sense, it must be made to yield to business common sense."'

In *Chartbrook Ltd v Persimmon Homes Ltd* [2009] UKHL 38, [2009] 1 AC 1101 the House of Lords held that pre-contractual negotiations could not be used as an aid to construing a contract. If such negotiations could be used this would lead to uncertainty, in that the outcome would be less predictable, and would increase the cost of both litigation and legal advice.

In *Whitworth Street Estates Ltd v Miller* [1970] AC 583 Lord Reid explained that the actions of the parties after the contract was formed might mean that they had made a new contract or that they had discharged the contract. But such actions could not be used to interpret the contract which had been made. If this were possible, a contract might mean one thing one day and a different thing the following day. In *Tekdata Interconnections Ltd v Amphenol Ltd* [2009] EWCA

Civ 1209, [2010] 1 Lloyd's Rep 357 Longmore LJ said that post-contractual correspondence could be used to determine what the terms of a contract are, but could not be relied upon to determine what those terms mean. Dyson LJ said,

'I agree with Longmore LJ that post-contractual behaviour may be admissible to prove the terms of a contract. An obvious example is where there is an issue as to whether a term was orally agreed and in post-contractual correspondence the party who denies the existence of the term admits that it was agreed.'

In *Maggs* v *Marsh* [2006] EWCA Civ 1058, [2006] All ER (D) 95 (Jul) the Court of Appeal held that determining what had been agreed in an oral contract is a matter of fact rather than a question of law. It depended upon recollections of the parties and maybe other witnesses. So things later said and done by the parties might be used to test or throw light upon the accuracy of what the parties and witnesses recollected. These later actions would not alter the way in which the contract should be interpreted, as that is a matter of law. But they might indicate exactly what terms had been agreed at the time of the contract.

Test your understanding 5.2

1 In what circumstances will a court imply a term as a matter of fact?

2 In what circumstances will a court imply a term as a matter of law?

3 In what three circumstances will a term be implied on the grounds of custom?

4 How will a court decide whether or not a term was a condition or a warranty?

5 What are the remedies available for breach of condition and breach of warranty?

6 What remedies are available for breach of an innominate term?

5.5 EXCLUSION CLAUSES

Exclusion clauses, or exemption clauses as they are sometimes known, are contractual clauses which try to exclude or exempt one party's liability. Usually the liability in question will have arisen as a result of an express or implied term of the contract. However, exclusion clauses can also exclude liability arising in tort.

Exclusion clauses have sometimes operated very unfairly, as the following case shows.

L'Estrange v Graucob
[1934] 2 KB 394 (Court of Appeal)

The claimant, a café owner, bought a new cigarette vending machine. She signed an order form which contained the main terms of the contract in ordinary size print. In small print, but still legible, a term stated that, 'Any express or implied, condition, statement or warranty, statutory or otherwise, not stated herein is expressly excluded'. The claimant did not read the order form and did not know of the exclusion clause. The vending machine did not work properly. The claimant sued for damages for breach of the statutory implied term, now contained in s.14(3) of the Sale of Goods Act 1979, that the machine should be fit for the buyer's purpose. There was no doubt that this term, if it was part of the contract, had been broken.

Held. The claimant's claim failed. The claimant had signed the order form and so she was bound by the exclusion clause.

Scrutton LJ: 'When a document containing contractual terms is signed ... the party signing it is bound, and it is wholly immaterial whether he has read the document or not ... The claimant, having put her signature to the document ... cannot be heard to say that she is not bound by the terms of the document because she has not read them.'

The unfair way in which exclusion clauses can operate has been considerably reduced since the Unfair Contract Terms Act 1977 came into force. In addition, the courts may render an exclusion clause invalid, either by holding that the clause was not a term of the contract in question or by finding that the clause did not exclude liability for the particular breach which occurred.

5.5.1 Judicial control of exclusion clauses

The English courts have always been attached to the doctrine of freedom of contract, which holds that sane adults are free to contract on any terms they wish. In *Printing and Numerical Registering Co* v *Samson* (1875) LR 19 Eq 462 Sir George Jessel MR said:

'If there is one thing more than another which public policy requires it is that men of full age and competent understanding shall have the utmost liberty of contracting, and that their contracts when entered into freely and voluntarily shall be held sacred and shall be enforced by Courts of justice. Therefore, you have this paramount public policy to consider – that you are not lightly to interfere with this freedom of contract.'

The courts have traditionally taken the view that if parties to a contract freely agree to an exclusion clause, then it is not the role of any court to interfere with that agreement. However, the assumption that exclusion clauses are freely negotiated rather ignores the reality of the situation. In fact, exclusion clauses are inserted into contracts by the party with the greater bargaining power. In *L'Estrange* v *Graucob*, for example, the café owner would have had little choice but to agree to the exclusion clause. If she had refused to sign the order form then it is likely that she would not have been able to buy the vending machine.

Attached as they were to the notion of freedom of contract, the courts did nevertheless realise the potential unfairness of exclusion clauses and did therefore try to limit the effect of them. There were two main ways in which they might achieve this. First, they might decide that the clause was never incorporated into the contract. Second, they might interpret the clause in such a way that it did not exclude liability for the breach which subsequently occurred. Later in this chapter we will examine the effect of the Unfair Contract Terms Act 1977 and the Unfair Terms in Consumer Contracts Regulations 1999. But first we must examine judicial control of exclusion clauses. If an exclusion clause is not incorporated as a term of a contract then it will not be necessary to consider the effect of the 1977 Act or the 1999 Regulations, as the exclusion clause will not have any contractual effect.

5.5.1.1 Is the exclusion clause a term of the contract?

As we saw in *L'Estrange* v *Graucob*, a person who signs a contract will generally be bound by its contents. This is not the case however if the person signed because the effect of the document was misrepresented to him.

Curtis v *Chemical Cleaning and Dyeing Co* [1951] 1 All ER 631 (Court of Appeal)

The claimant took her white satin wedding dress to a dry cleaners. She was asked to sign a form, headed 'Receipt', and inquired what it said. She was told that the form protected the cleaners against certain specified types of damage, such as damage to beads and sequins. The claimant signed the form which in fact contained a term which stated, 'This article is accepted on condition that the company is not liable for any damage howsoever arising'. The wedding dress was badly stained and the cleaners relied on the exclusion clause.

Held. The cleaners could not rely on the exclusion clause because they had misrepresented its effect.

When both parties sign a written document it is relatively easy to say whether or not an exclusion clause is a term of the contract. If the clause is included in the signed document it is a term, if it is not included it is not. But in contracts which are not written and signed by the parties it is not so easy to say. Case law has decided that a party will be bound by an exclusion clause if it is contained in a document which the reasonable man would have thought to be a contractual document.

Thompson v *London, Midland and Scottish Railway Co* [1930] 1 KB 41 (Court of Appeal)

The claimant's niece bought her a railway ticket. The claimant could not read. If she had been able to read she would have been able to see that the front of the ticket said, 'Excursion. For conditions see back'. On the back of the ticket it was stated that the ticket was issued subject to the defendants' timetables and excursion bills. The excursion bills themselves referred to the conditions in the defendants' time tables. The timetable could be purchased for 6d and one of its conditions excluded liability for injuries caused by the defendants' negligence. While stepping out of the train, the claimant was injured by the defendants' negligence.

Held. The claimant was bound by the exclusion clause in the timetable. Even though she could not read she had sufficient notice of the exclusion clause.

COMMENT (i) The Court of Appeal overruled a jury which had found that passengers had not been given reasonable notice of the exclusion clause.

(ii) What the reasonable man would have thought will depend upon all of the circumstances. The judges emphasised the fact that the ticket was for a special, cheap, 'excursion'. Therefore special conditions, such as limits on liability, might reasonably have been expected.

→

(iii) The Unfair Contract Terms Act 1977 s.2(1) prevents the exclusion of liability for negligence which resulted in personal injury. However, this case is still an authority on the incorporation of exclusion clauses into contracts.

Chapelton v Barry UDC
[1940] 1 KB 532 (Court of Appeal)

Deck chairs belonging to the defendants were piled up on a seaside beach near a notice which read, 'Barry Urban District Council. Cold Knap. Hire of deck chairs 2d per session of 3 hours'. The notice also said that tickets for the deck chairs should be obtained from the attendant and that the tickets should be retained for inspection. The notice did not contain any exclusion clause. The claimant hired two deck chairs from the attendant, paying 4d for two tickets. On the back of the tickets it stated that the defendants could not be liable for any accident or damage arising from the hire of the chair. The defendant did not read the tickets but put them in his pocket. The canvas on one of the chairs came away from the frame of the chair and this caused an accident which injured the claimant.

Held. The exclusion clause was not a part of the contract. The notice board set out the terms on which the deck chairs were hired. The ticket was not a contractual document, it was just a voucher or receipt for the money paid to hire the chair.

COMMENT Although this case appears very similar to **Thompson v LMS Railway**, the essential difference is that in this case the Court of Appeal thought that the ticket was not a document which a reasonable person would expect to contain contractual terms.

To be effective an exclusion clause must be a term of the contract, and as such it must have been agreed before the contract was made. A term cannot later be incorporated into the contract.

Olley v Marlborough Court Hotel Ltd
[1949] 1 KB 532 (Court of Appeal)

A married couple booked into a residential hotel. They paid the bill in advance. Furs belonging to the wife were stolen from the hotel room. When sued for this loss the defendants sought to rely on a notice in the hotel bedroom, which stated, 'The proprietors will not hold themselves responsible for articles lost or stolen, unless handed to the manageress for safe custody. Valuables should be deposited for safe custody in a sealed packet and a receipt obtained'.

Held. The notice was too late to be effective. The contract had already been made before the couple had an opportunity to see the notice.

COMMENT In *Chapelton* the ticket was too late to be a part of the contract. Once a customer had taken a deck chair and sat upon it he had incurred liability to pay for the chair and had therefore already made the contract.

Thornton v Shoe Lane Parking Ltd
[1971] 1 All ER 686 (Court of Appeal)

The claimant was badly injured in a car park operated by the defendants. The accident was partly caused by the defendants' negligence. The claimant had driven into the car park, passing a notice which said, 'All cars parked at owner's risk'. Inside the car park the claimant encountered a red light. When this light changed to green a machine issued the claimant with a ticket. The claimant did not read the ticket, which said that the ticket was issued subject to conditions displayed inside the premises. These conditions excluded liability for damage to goods and for injuries to customers. However, they could only have been discovered by driving into the car park and walking around. The defendants denied liability, relying on the conditions inside the car park to which the ticket referred.

Held. The exclusion clause to which the ticket referred was introduced too late to be a part of the contract. At the time of making the contract the claimant neither knew of the exclusion clause nor had reasonable steps been taken to draw it to his attention.

COMMENT (i) Lord Denning MR analysed that the contract had already been concluded when the customer received the ticket. It was concluded as soon as the customer was irrevocably committed to the contract. (See Chapter 3 at 3.4.)

(ii) The notice outside the car park was incorporated into the contract but it did not exclude liability for personal injuries.

A custom of a particular trade might incorporate an exclusion clause into a contract made within that trade. Similarly a course of dealing between the parties might have the same effect. (See **British Crane Hire Corporation Ltd v Ipswich Plant Hire Ltd** [1975] QB 303 and **Kendall (Henry) & Sons v William Lillico & Sons Ltd** [1969] 2 AC 31 at 5.3.3 above. In both cases exclusion clauses were implied into the contracts.)

In order for a term to be implied on the basis of a course of dealing between the parties the course of dealing must be well established. This is particularly the case where the party against whom the term would operate is a consumer. In *Hollier* v *Rambler Motors Ltd* [1972] 2 QB 71 the claimant had taken his car for repair at the defendants' garage three or four times in the previous five years. Each time a form containing an exclusion clause had been signed. The claimant made an oral contract to have the car repaired. The car was damaged. The Court of Appeal held that a course of dealing had not been clearly established and so the exclusion clause had not been incorporated into the oral contract. Salomon LJ said, 'I am bound to say that, for my part, I do not know of any other case in which it has been decided or even argued that a term could be implied into an oral contract on the strength of a course of dealing (if it can be so called) which consisted at the most of three or four transactions over a period of five years'.

In *McCutcheon* v *David MacBrayne Ltd* [1964] 1 All ER 430 the claimant sued a ferry company for damages when a ferry carrying his car from Islay to the Scottish mainland sank. The contract had been made by the claimant's brother-in-law, one McSporran, and no exclusion clause was signed. However, exclusion clauses had been displayed on the walls of the office where the contract was made and on the ferries. Over the previous years both the claimant and McSporran had used the defendants' ferries to transport sheep, sometimes signing the exclusion clause and sometimes not. The House of Lords held that there was no consistent course of dealing which would have the effect of incorporating an exclusion clause into the contract which McSporran made.

The following case, although not concerned with an exclusion clause, shows a recent example of one party's standard terms being incorporated either by conduct or through a course of dealing.

Photolibrary Group Ltd v *Burda Senator Verlag GmbH* [2008] EWHC 1343 (QB), [2008] 2 All ER (Comm) 881

For some years the claimants had supplied the defendants with non-digital photographic transparencies, along with a delivery note which set out various terms. The defendants sent the transparencies to Germany, where clients of theirs might choose to pay to use them. The defendants lost nearly 2 000 of the claimants' transparencies. The claimants claimed over £1.2 million under a clause in the delivery note. The defendants argued that the delivery note was not part of the contract as they had never signed it. Nor had they signed any of the identical delivery notes which had previously been delivered. On the other hand, they had never done anything to indicate that they did not regard the delivery note as binding.

Held. The delivery note was part of the contract between the claimants and the defendants. This conclusion could be arrived at in three different ways. First, delivery of the transparencies, along with the delivery note, was an offer which was accepted by keeping the transparencies and sending them to Germany. Second, the defendants' act of asking for the transparencies was, in the light of the previous course of dealing between the parties, an offer to have them supplied subject to the terms in the delivery note. This offer was accepted by sending the transparencies and the delivery note. Third, regardless of who made the offer and the acceptance, the terms in the delivery note were simply incorporated through the previous course of dealing between the parties.

If an exclusion clause was accepted only because of an oral undertaking that it would not be enforced then it cannot be enforced.

Evans & Son (Portsmouth) Ltd v *Andrea Merzario Ltd* [1976] 1 WLR 1078 (Court of Appeal)

The claimants imported machines to England from Italy. Since 1959 the claimants had arranged the contracts of carriage with the defendants. The machines were liable to rust and so it was arranged that they would always be carried below deck. In 1967 containerisation was proposed so that in future the machines would be shipped in large containers. The claimants agreed to a new contract only after they were assured that their machines would still be carried below deck. There was nothing in the written contract about carrying the machines below deck. A container carrying one of the claimant's machines fell overboard. The defendants relied on exclusion clauses in their written contract which allowed the containers to be carried on deck.

Held. The oral assurance that the claimants' machines would be carried below deck was contractually binding. The defendants' exclusion clauses could not protect the defendants from liability for breach of the oral term because the printed conditions were repugnant to the oral promise and therefore overridden by it.

Earlier in this chapter we examined *Webster* v *Higgin* and saw that even where an exclusion clause is validly incorporated into a contract there may also exist a collateral contract of which the exclusion clause is no part. We examined the doctrine of privity in the previous chapter and saw that in general only the parties who made a contract will acquire rights under the contract. The doctrine might mean that a person may not be able to rely on an exclusion clause which is expressed to be for his benefit. In *Adler* v *Dickson and Another* [1955] 1 QB 158, for example, a shipping company's exclusion clause stated that the company was excluded from liability for negligence, even if this was caused by the company's employees or other persons directly or indirectly working for the company. The claimant was injured and sued the master and the boatswain of the ship in negligence. Although the clause did not directly confer protection on the company's employees Jenkins LJ held that even if it had done so it would have been ineffective on the grounds of privity of contract. However, in the light of the Contracts (Rights of Third Parties) Act 1999 it would seem that the company's employees could now rely on the exclusion clause. They were expressly identified in the contract and the exclusion clause purported to confer a benefit upon them. (See Chapter 4 at 4.2.2.2.)

5.5.1.2 **Does the exclusion clause cover the breach which occurred?**

Before the Unfair Contract Terms Act 1977 came into force the courts went to considerable lengths to limit the effect of exclusion clauses by interpreting them contra preferentum (strictly against the wishes of the party trying to rely on them). This approach was less strict when the clause limited, rather than excluded, liability. Generally these 'mental gymnastics', as Lord Denning called them, have been made unnecessary by the 1977 Act. However, the Act does not invalidate all exclusion clauses and so the contra preferentum rule can still be important if there is a genuine ambiguity. The following case shows the way in which a court could defeat an exclusion clause by strict interpretation of it.

Andrews Bros Ltd v Singer & Co Ltd
[1934] 1 KB 17 (Court of Appeal)

The claimants agreed to buy 'new Singer cars' from the defendants. One of the cars delivered was not new. Section 13 of the Sale of Goods Act says that when goods are sold by description, 'there is an implied condition that the goods shall correspond with the description'. Relying on this, the claimants claimed damages. The defendants, in turn, relied on an exclusion clause which stated 'All conditions, warranties and liabilities implied by statute, common law or otherwise are excluded'.

Held. The exclusion clause did not apply. It was not an implied term that the cars should be new, it was an express term. The exclusion clause did not limit the effect of express terms.

5.6 THE UNFAIR CONTRACT TERMS ACT 1977

The Unfair Contract Terms Act 1977 was passed because Parliament perceived that the judiciary were not adequately controlling exclusion clauses. The important sections of the Act, ss.2–7, apply only to business liability, which is defined by s.1(3) as:

> 'liability to breach of obligations or duties arising – from things done or to be done by a person in the course of a business (whether his own business or another's): or
>
> from the occupation of premises used for business purposes of the occupier.'

5.6.1 **Section 2 – Liability for negligence**

Section 2(1) provides that a person cannot by reference to a contract term or to a notice exclude or restrict his liability for death or personal injury resulting from negligence.

Section 2(2) provides that liability for other types of loss or damage caused by negligence, such as damage to goods, cannot be excluded except in so far as the term or notice satisfies the Act's requirement of reasonableness. (Later in this chapter we shall examine the requirement of reasonableness.)

'Negligence' is defined by s.1(1) as:

> 'the breach –
> (a) of any obligation, arising from the express or implied terms of a contract, to take reasonable care or exercise reasonable skill in the performance of the contract;
> (b) of any common law duty to take reasonable care or exercise reasonable skill (but not any stricter duty);
> (c) of the common duty of care imposed by the Occupiers' Liability Act 1957.'

It can be seen that in this context 'negligence' means not only the tort of negligence but also negligent performance of a contract and breach of the statutory duty of care which occupiers owe to lawful visitors. (See Chapter 12 at 12.5.)

Smith v Eric S Bush
[1989] 2 All ER 514 (House of Lords)

The claimant applied to a building society for a mortgage to buy a house. The building society employed a firm of surveyors, the defendants, to make a survey of the house. The claimant paid £39 to the building society, who agreed to supply her with a copy of the surveyor's report. A disclaimer said that neither the building society nor the surveyors would be liable for any inaccuracies. The report, which also carried a similar disclaimer, said that the house was worth £16 500 and that no major building work was necessary. Eighteen months later the chimneys fell through the roof because two chimney breasts had been removed without proper supports being fitted. The claimant sued the defendants for negligence. The defendants relied on the disclaimer.

Held. The defendants were liable. The damage to property which had occurred was caused by the defendant's negligence. Section 2(2) therefore applied so that the disclaimer which excluded liability could only be effective in so far as it satisfied the Act's requirement of reasonableness. This requirement of reasonableness had not been satisfied.

COMMENT If the falling chimneys had caused personal injury or death then s.2(1) would have rendered invalid any contract term which tried to exclude liability in respect of this.

Section 2 of the Act is very far reaching in its effect. For example, in most of the cases which we examined when considering judicial control of exclusion clauses the claimant's loss or injury was caused by the defendant's negligence. (This does not mean that the Act renders those cases irrelevant. They are still authorities on the circumstances in which an exclusion clause will be incorporated into a contract. It does show that litigation on exclusion clauses very often involves a claim for loss or injury caused by negligence. In such cases the effect of s.2 of the Act will have to be considered.)

5.6.2 Sections 6 and 7 – Exclusion of statutory implied terms

Earlier in this chapter we considered in outline the terms implied by the Sale of Goods Act (SGA) 1979, the Supply of Goods (Implied Terms) Act (SGITA) 1973 and the Supply of Goods and Services Act (SGSA) 1982. Section 6 of the Unfair Contract Terms Act (UCTA) 1977 deals with exclusion of the terms implied by SGA 1979 and SGITA 1973.

Section 6(1) UCTA provides that the implied terms as to the right to sell which are contained in SGA s.12 and SGITA s.8 cannot be excluded by any contract term.

Section 6(2) UCTA provides that as against a person dealing as a consumer liability for the terms implied by SGA ss.13–15, and liability for breach of the corresponding terms set out in SGITA ss.9–11, cannot be excluded or restricted by reference to any contract term. The terms set out in SGA ss.13–15 and SGITA ss.9–11 can be excluded or restricted where the buyer does not deal as a consumer, but only in so far as the term which excludes or restricts liability satisfies the UCTA's requirement of reasonableness.

Section 7 UCTA 1977 makes similar rules regarding the exclusion of the terms implied by the Supply of Goods and Services Act 1982. The implied terms as to the right to hire or transfer property in goods cannot be excluded by any contract term. Section 7(2) UCTA provides that as regards a person who deals as a consumer the other terms which the Act implies cannot be excluded or restricted by reference to any contract term. Where the person to whom the goods are transferred does not deal as a consumer, the implied terms can be excluded or restricted by a term only in so far as that term meets the UCTA's requirement of reasonableness. The circumstances in which a buyer deals as a consumer are examined below at 5.6.1.3.

Section 13 SGSA 1982 provides that in a contract for the supply of a service where the supplier is acting in the course of a business there is an implied term that the supplier will carry out the service with reasonable care and skill. Sections 6 and 7 UCTA 1977 do not touch exclusion of this implied term. However, s.2(1) and (2) UCTA will apply to attempts to exclude liability for breach of the implied term. Section 1(1) UCTA makes this plain by stating that as regards UCTA 1977 'negligence' means the breach of any obligation, arising from the express or implied terms of a contract, to take reasonable care or exercise reasonable skill in the performance of a contract.

5.6.3 **When does a buyer deal as a consumer?**

In order to fully understand the effect of ss.6 and 7 UCTA we therefore need to know exactly when a person is to be regarded as dealing as a consumer. Section 12(1) UCTA provides the answer:

> 'A party to a contract "deals as a consumer" in relation to another party if –
>
> (a) he neither makes the contract in the course of a business nor holds himself out as doing so; and
>
> (b) the other party does make the contract in the course of a business; and
>
> (c) in the case of a contract governed by the law of sale of goods or hire-purchase, or by s.7 of this Act, the goods passing under or in pursuance of the contract are of a type ordinarily supplied for private use or consumption.
>
> [But if the first party mentioned in subsection 1 is an individual, paragraph (c) of that subsection must be ignored.]'

So when the contracting party is an individual, that is to say a living person rather than a company, only the two requirements in s.12(1)(a) and (b) apply. Where the contracting party is a company s.12(1)(c) must also be satisfied.

By way of example, let us assume that a shop buys a radio from a manufacturer and sells the radio to John, a bus driver, who later sells it to his friend, Mark. The shop does not deal as a consumer because it makes the contract in the course of a business. John does deal as a consumer. Mark does not deal as a consumer because John does not sell the radio in the course of a business of his. John would not have been a consumer if he had held himself out as acting in the course of a business when he had bought the radio.

In *R & B Customs Brokers Ltd v United Dominions Trust Ltd* [1988] 1 All ER 847 the Court of Appeal held that in some circumstances a business can deal as a consumer. The business in question, a company, bought a second-hand car for a director to use both on company business and privately. A term of the contract excluded s.13 SGA 1979. The Court of Appeal held that the term which excluded s.13 SGA could not be effective as the company had dealt as consumer. This decision was reached because, although the company had bought two or three cars previously, the purchase of the car was not made as an integral part of the company's business.

A purchase made by a business will be made as an integral part of the company's business in only three circumstances. First, where the transaction is to buy the type of thing which the business is in business to buy and sell. For example where an electrical goods shop buys in its stock of televisions. Second, where the transaction is to buy something to be sold on at a profit. For example, a market trader trading in cheese would not deal as a consumer if he bought vegetables with the intention of selling them and making a profit. Third, where the business has made the same type of transaction with sufficient regularity. For example, if a car hire firm had regularly bought cars for use in the firm's business, and sold them on after two years, then when it bought another such car it would not be dealing as a consumer. The firm would have been dealing as a consumer when it bought the first car and also when it bought the first few cars if the necessary degree of regularity had not yet been established. (See *Stevenson v Rogers* in Chapter 8 at 8.2.4.) It is very important to remember that the decision in *R & B Customs Brokers* applies only to s.12(1) UCTA definition of dealing as a consumer. The phrase 'in the course of a business' also occurs in s.14 SGA 1979, but in that context it means something quite different.

The decision in *R&B Customs Brokers* increases consumer protection, by including some company purchases, but it was the subject of considerable criticism for two main reasons. First, it makes the concept of dealing as a consumer, which is found in UCTA 1977 and the SGA 1979, quite separate from the concept of being a consumer which is found in most other consumer protection legislation. (See, for example, the definition of a consumer in the Unfair Terms in Consumer Contracts Regulations 1999 at 5.7.1 below.) Second, it adopts a test from the criminal law (the Trade Descriptions Act 1968) and uses it in a civil law context. Despite these criticisms, in *Feldarol Foundries plc v Hermes Leasing Ltd* [2004] EWCA Civ 747, [2004] All ER (D) 138 (May) the Court of Appeal confirmed the decisions in both *R & B Customs Brokers Ltd v United Dominions Trust Ltd* and *Stevenson v Rogers*. The facts of *Feldarol* were similar to those in *R & B Customs Brokers Ltd v United Dominions Trust Ltd* and this time a plc was found to have dealt as a consumer.

Of course, when considering whether *a company* dealt as a consumer UCTA s.12(1)(c) must not be ignored. If in either *R & B Customs Brokers* or *Feldarol* either company had bought an industrial excavator, rather than a car, it would not have dealt as a consumer.

Section 12(2) distinguishes between individuals and companies. Section 12(2)(a) provides that a buyer is not to be regarded as dealing as a consumer if he is an individual (not a company) and the goods are second-hand goods sold at public auction at which individuals have the opportunity of attending the sale in person. Section 12(2)(b) provides that a buyer who is not an individual should never be regarded as dealing as a consumer when he buys goods sold by auction or by competitive tender.

5.6.4 Section 3 – Excluding liability arising in contract

Section 3 UCTA 1977 protects two classes of people:

(a) those who 'deal as a consumer', and
(b) those who deal on the other party's written standard terms of business.

Where a person deals as a consumer it will not be necessary, for the purposes of s.3, to decide whether or not the consumer deals on the other's written standard terms of business. We have already identified the circumstances in which a person deals as a consumer. UCTA 1977 does not define 'written standard terms of business'. However, written terms would seem to be standard where the same terms are used when supplying all customers of the business or where the same terms are always used when the two parties in question make contracts with each other. The Act does not explain when written standard terms are 'the other's'. In *British Fermentation Products Ltd* v *Compair Reavell Ltd* [1999] BLR 352 Judge Bowsher held that a contract made on a model form issued by the Institution of Mechanical Engineers (IME) was not made on 'the other's' (the defendant's) standard terms, even though the defendant introduced them into the contract, because the terms were those of the IME, not those of the defendant. Model forms adopted by one of the parties to the contract would be that party's written standard terms only where they were incorporated as such expressly or by practice. The effect of this decision is that when a person uses a model form created by someone else, s.3 UCTA may not be brought into play. If s.3 UCTA is not brought into play, the terms in the model form would be valid even if they would not pass the UCTA reasonableness test. This seems an unfortunate decision.

As against a person either dealing as a consumer or dealing on the other party's written standard terms, s.3 provides that, except in so far as the contract term satisfies the requirement of reasonableness, the other party cannot by reference to any contract term:

(a) exclude or restrict any liability of his in respect of a breach of contract; or
(b) claim to be entitled to render a contractual performance substantially different from that which was reasonably expected of him; or
(c) claim to be entitled, in respect of the whole or part of his contractual obligation, to render no performance at all.

This section will be useful when the breach of contract does not involve negligence (in which case s.2 provides adequate protection) and does not involve breach of a statutory implied term (in which case ss.6 and 7 provide protection). It might, for example, be useful where Business A contracts to have a building painted on Business B's standard terms, one of these terms stating that Business B cannot be liable if the painting is not completed on time. If the work was completed very late, for reasons other than negligence, then s.3 would only allow the exclusion clause to exclude or restrict the liability of Business B in so far as the term satisfied the Act's requirement of reasonableness.

5.6.5 Section 4 – Indemnity clauses

In the previous chapter, at 4.3.3, we examined the nature of an indemnity. Section 4(1) UCTA 1977 provides that a person dealing as a consumer cannot by reference to any contract term be made to indemnify another person (whether a party to the contract or not) in respect of liability that may be incurred by the other for negligence or breach of contract, except in so far as the contract term satisfies the Act's requirement of reasonableness. In non-consumer contracts indemnity clauses are not touched by the Act, unless they are covered by one of the other sections. The following case shows how this can happen.

> **Phillips Products Ltd v Hyland**
> [1987] 2 All ER 620 (Court of Appeal)
>
> The claimants, who did not deal as consumers, hired an excavator and a driver from a hire company. A term of the contract provided that the claimants had to indemnify the hire company for any damage caused by the   →

driver. The driver damaged the claimants' buildings. The claimants sued the hire company, who relied on the indemnity clause.

Held. If the claimants had dealt as consumers, the indemnity clause would not have applied, under s.4, because it would not have satisfied the Act's requirement of reasonableness. But because the claimants did not deal as consumers s.4 offered no protection. However, the defendant's negligence had damaged the claimants' property. Under s.2(2) a term can only exclude liability for damage to property caused by negligence in so far as the term satisfies the Act's requirement of reasonableness. The term providing that the claimants had to indemnify the hire company did not satisfy the Act's requirement of reasonableness and so it did not apply.

5.6.6 Section 5 – 'Guarantee' of consumer goods

In the context of s.5 'consumer goods' means goods of a type ordinarily supplied for private use or consumption. Section 5(1) provides that in the case of such consumer goods, where loss or damage arises from the goods proving defective while in consumer use, and results from the negligence of a person concerned in the manufacture or distribution of the goods, liability for the loss or damage cannot be excluded or restricted by reference to any contract term or notice contained in or operating by reference to a guarantee of the goods. For the purposes of s.5 consumer goods are in consumer use when a person is using them, or has them in his possession for use, otherwise than exclusively for the purposes of a business (s.5(2)(a)). This section is aimed at manufacturers' 'guarantees' which attempt to exclude liability owed to a consumer in tort. The section is not necessary where a manufacturer's negligence caused death or physical injury, because s.2(1) would not allow the exclusion clause to be effective. Section 5 therefore only covers damage to property caused by the manufacturer's negligence. It does however provide greater protection than s.2(2) in that s.5 applies even if the guarantee's exclusion would have satisfied the Act's requirement of reasonableness. Section 5 does not affect the position between the retailer and the consumer. The Sale and Supply of Goods to Consumers Regulations 2002 provide that a consumer guarantee given by a manufacturer now takes effect as a contractual obligation. The Regulations are considered at the end of this chapter at 5.8.

5.6.7 Section 8 – Excluding liability for misrepresentations

Section 3 of the Misrepresentation Act 1967, as substituted by s.8 UCTA 1977, provides as follows:

'If a contract contains a term which would exclude or restrict—

(a) any liability to which a party to a contract may be subject by reason of any misrepresentation made by him before the contract was made; or

(b) any remedy available to another party to the contract by reason of such a misrepresentation, the term shall be of no effect except in so far as it satisfies the requirement of reasonableness as stated in section 11(1) of the Unfair Contract Terms Act 1977; and it is for those claiming that the term satisfies that requirement to show that it does.'

It should be noticed that this section does not distinguish between those who deal as a consumer and those who do not.

5.6.8 The Act's requirement of reasonableness

We have seen that in several circumstances a term which excludes or restricts liability can be effective only in so far as it satisfies the Act's requirement of reasonableness.

Section 11(1) UCTA states that the requirement of reasonableness in relation to a contract term is 'that the term shall have been a fair and reasonable one to be included having regard to the circumstances which were, or ought reasonably to have been, known to or in the contemplation of the parties when the contract was made'.

The burden of proof is on the party claiming that a contract term or notice satisfies the requirement of reasonableness to show that it does (s.11(5)).

Section 11(2) states that in determining for the purposes of ss.6 and 7 whether a term satisfies the requirement of reasonableness regard shall be had to the particular matters specified in Schedule 2 to the Act. Schedule 2 gives five guidelines for the application of the reasonableness test. Regard should be had to any of these which appear relevant. The matters are:

(a) the strength of the bargaining position of the parties relevant to each other, taking into account (among other things) alternative means by which the customer's requirements could have been met;

(b) whether the customer received an inducement to agree to the term, or in accepting it had an opportunity of entering into a similar contract with other persons, but without having to accept a similar term;

(c) whether the customer knew or ought reasonably to have known of the existence and extent of the term (having regard, among other things, to any custom of the trade and any previous course of dealing between the parties);

(d) where the term excludes or restricts any relevant liability if some condition is not complied with, whether it was reasonable at the time of the contract to expect that compliance with the term would be practicable;

(e) whether the goods were manufactured, processed or adapted to the special order of the customer.

Although Schedule 2 is theoretically only to be used when the contract is to supply goods, the judge considered Schedule 2 in the following case, which concerned a defective service. It is now routine that reference to Schedule 2 will be made whenever a court has to consider the Act's requirement of reasonableness.

Woodman v Photo Trade Processing Ltd (1981) 131 NLJ 933

The defendants were given a reel of film to develop. On account of the defendants' negligence, most of the pictures were lost. The defendants relied on a clause which read: 'All photographic materials are accepted on the basis that their value does not exceed the cost of the material itself. Responsibility is limited to the replacement of the films.' The claimant had taken the pictures at a friend's wedding, where he had been the only photographer.

Held. The exclusion clause did not apply because it was not reasonable. In reaching this decision the judge had regard to the fact that the claimant had little choice but to agree to such a term, as most commercial film developers insisted on a similar term. Consequently, the claimant was awarded damages of £75.

The requirement of reasonableness was recently considered in *Ofir Scheps* v *Fine Art Logistic Ltd* [2007] EWHC 541 (QB). The defendants had been storing a sculpture valued at £600 000, but had allowed binmen to take it away. It was never recovered. The defendants claimed that their liability was limited to £587.13 by the following clause: 'If we are liable for losing damaging or failing to deliver your goods our liability will be limited to a maximum payment in proportion to £350 per cubic meter of the volume of the missing or damaged item even if it forms part of a pair or set or had exceptional value before it was lost or destroyed.' Teare J held that the clause was not part of the contract and could not therefore have effect. He then went on to consider at some length whether or not the clause would have satisfied the UCTA 1977 requirement of reasonableness if it had been part of the contract. He accepted that a clause which limited liability to a fixed sum per weight or volume could have been a fair and reasonable one to have been included, even though the average value of goods stored by the defendants would have been worth around £2 000. The owners knew the value of the goods and could insure them, whereas the defendants would find this very difficult. However, he held that, in this particular case, the clause would not have satisfied the requirement of reasonableness because the evidence showed that the defendants had made no attempt to bring the clause to the claimant's attention, and because other companies in this particular market had similar terms. The claimant could not therefore have made a similar contract on more favourable terms.

5.6.9 **Provisions against evasion of liability**

Section 10 provides that a person is not bound by any contract term prejudicing or taking away rights of his which arose under, or in connection with the performance of, another contract. So if a consumer bought a computer system and also made a second contract under which the system was to be set up, the second contract could not deny the consumer rights which arose under the contract of sale.

Where an earlier section of the Act prevents the exclusion or restriction of liability, s.13 also prevents:

(a) making the liability or its enforcement subject to restrictive or onerous conditions (for example, that defects in garden seeds should be notified within seven days of purchase);

(b) excluding any right or remedy in respect of the liability, or subjecting a person to any prejudice in consequence of his pursuing any such right or remedy (for example, restricting the amount of damages payable to the cost of the goods bought);

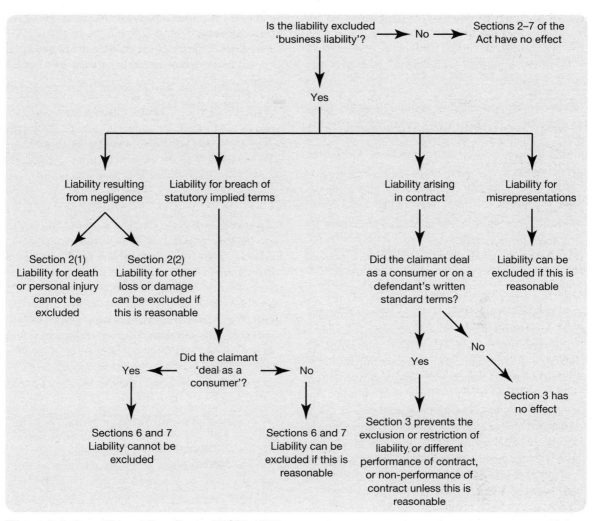

Figure 5.1 An outline of the effect of UCTA 1977

(c) excluding or restricting rules of evidence or procedure (for example, a term would not be able to insist that a buyer's signature would be taken as absolute proof that the goods bought conformed to the contract).

However, s.13(2) provides that an agreement in writing to submit present or future differences to arbitration is not to be treated as excluding or restricting any liability. Such clauses are therefore not affected by UCTA 1977.

An outline of the effect of the main provisions of UCTA 1977 is shown in Figure 5.1.

5.7 THE UNFAIR TERMS IN CONSUMER CONTRACTS REGULATIONS 1999

The Unfair Terms in Consumer Contracts Regulations 1994 were passed to give effect to an EU directive. The regulations did not replace the Unfair Contract Terms Act, but ran alongside it. The 1994 Regulations have been repealed and replaced by the 1999 Regulations. The changes made by the 1999 Regulations were very slight, relating mainly to which bodies were given the power to apply for injunctions to see that the Regulations were complied with.

5.7.1 **Application of the Regulations**

Regulation 4(1) states that the Regulations apply to unfair terms in contracts to supply goods or services if they are concluded between a seller or supplier and a consumer.

A consumer is defined as a natural person (and not therefore a company) who, in contracts covered by the Regulations, is acting for purposes which are outside his trade, business or profession. Notice that this definition is very different from the definition of dealing as a consumer in UCTA 1977. (See 5.6.1.3 above.) In *Evans* v *Cherry Tree Finance Ltd* [2008] EWCA Civ 331, [2008] All ER (D) 86 (Feb) the Court of Appeal held that a loan taken partly for a business purpose and partly for a non-business purpose was covered by the Regulations. The defendant finance company, which was arguing that the Regulations should not apply, had conceded that if any of the purposes for which the loan was taken out were outside the claimant's trade or business, he was a consumer for the purpose of the regulations. The Court of Appeal said that it would not disagree with this, but also indicated that the true meaning of 'consumer' within the Regulations would need to be decided in a future case. Sellers and suppliers are defined as legal persons who, in contracts covered by the Regulations, are acting for purposes relating to their trades, businesses or professions, whether publicly owned or privately owned.

Regulation 4(2) states that the Regulations do not apply to terms which reflect mandatory statutory or regulatory provisions. So it would not be possible to argue that a term such as SGA 1979 s.14(2), which requires goods sold in the course of a business to be of satisfactory quality, was an unfair term within the meaning of the Regulations. In *Baybut* v *Eccle Riggs Country Park Ltd* [2006] All ER (D) 161 (Nov) it was held that it was highly unlikely that a term implied by the common law, on the grounds that it reflected the unspoken intentions of the parties, could be unfair within the meaning of the Regulations. Regulation 6(1) provides that in assessing the fairness of a term all the circumstances should be taken into account. These would include the nature of the goods and services being bought and all the other terms of the contract. Regulation 6(2) provides that the fairness of what have become known as 'core terms' should not be assessed. It says:

'In so far as it is in plain intelligible language, the assessment of fairness of a term shall not relate –

(a) to the definition of the main subject matter of the contract, or
(b) to the adequacy of the price or remuneration, as against the goods or services provided in exchange.'

In the following case the Supreme Court considered Reg.6(2)(b) in great detail.

> ### *Office of Fair Trading* v *Abbey National plc and others*
> [2009] UKSC 6, [2009] 2 WLR 1286
>
> The OFT claimed that certain charges made by the bank should be assessed for fairness under the 1999 Regulations. The bank argued that the charges were exempt from assessment as they were core terms under reg.6(2)(b). The charges in question were of four different types, all of which became payable when the customer had insufficient funds in his account to cover a payment which the bank duly made.
>
> **Held.** The charges in question were core terms within Reg.6(2)(b), and therefore could not be assessed for fairness under the Regulations. Lord Walker gave the leading judgment, with which all of the other Justices agreed. He said that when a package of goods or services were ordered under one contract it was not possible to regard some of the goods or services as more essential to the contract than others. The same approach had to be taken to the price or remuneration paid by the customer. Regulation 6(2)(b) did not indicate that only an 'essential' price was relevant. So any monetary part of the price or remuneration paid by a bank customer would naturally fall within the language of paragraph 6(2)(b). Banking services to current account customers could only be described as a package, as could the consideration which moved from customers to the bank. The customers' consideration consisted of foregoing a high rate of interest on money in their accounts and of overdraft interest and charges for those who did not stay in credit. Lord Phillips said that the banks required their customers to agree to pay the charges as part of the price for the package of services which they received in return. Lord Mance said that there was no reason why the price payable for a package of services should not consist of a contingent liability.

5.7.2 **Unfair terms**

Regulation 5(1) states that: 'A contractual term which has not been individually negotiated shall be regarded as unfair if, contrary to the requirement of good faith, it causes a significant imbalance in the parties' rights and obligations arising under the contract, to the detriment of the consumer.'

Regulation 5(2) states that a term shall always be regarded as not having been individually negotiated where it has been drafted in advance and the consumer has therefore not been able to influence the substance of the term. In *UK Housing Alliance (North West) v Francis* [2010] EWCA 117, [2010] 3 All ER 519, the Court of Appeal considered reg.5(2) in relation to an agreement between a landlord (the supplier) and a tenant (the consumer). The tenant had instructed a solicitor before signing the agreement, which had been drafted by the landlord. However, the term in question was not altered by the tenant or his solicitor. It was held that the term had not been individually negotiated. Longmore LJ said,

> 'It does not follow from the existence of the ability to influence the substance of a term that the term has, in fact been individually negotiated. That is still a matter for the supplier to prove . . .'

So if a supplier drafts a proposed term, and the consumer does not alter it, the term will not have been individually negotiated, even if the consumer had ample opportunity to alter it. Even if a specific term or certain aspects of it has been individually negotiated, the Regulations apply to the rest of the contract if an overall assessment of it indicates that it is a pre-formulated standard contract (reg. 5(3)). The burden of proof is on the seller or supplier to show that a term was individually negotiated (reg. 5(4)).

5.7.3 The requirements of good faith and no significant imbalance

In order to take advantage of the Regulations a consumer will need to show both lack of good faith and a significant imbalance in the parties' rights and obligations arising under the contract to his detriment. A Schedule to the 1994 Regulations sets out a list of matters to be taken into account when assessing whether or not the seller or supplier had acted in good faith. The 1999 Regulations contain no such list as under them a court will consider all relevant matters. In *Director General of Fair Trading v First National Bank plc* [2001] UKHL 52, [2002] 1 AC 481 Lord Bingham said:

> 'The requirement of good faith in this context is one of fair and open dealing. Openness requires that

the terms should be expressed fully, clearly and legibly, containing no concealed pitfalls or traps . . . Fair dealing requires that a supplier should not, deliberately or unconsciously, take advantage of a consumer's necessity, indigence, lack of experience, unfamiliarity with the subject matter of the contract, weak bargaining position . . . Good faith in this context is not an artificial or technical concept . . . it looks to good standards of commercial morality and practice.'

Lord Steyn agreed with Lord Bingham that good faith is an objective criterion which imports the notion of fair and open dealing. He rejected an argument that good faith was concerned only with purely procedural defects when negotiating. Lord Steyn also thought that there was a large overlap between the concepts of 'good faith' and 'significant imbalance in the parties' rights and obligations arising under the contract'. However, he thought that significant imbalance was concerned with the substantive unfairness of the contract, that is to say with whether the terms of the contract actually were unfair to the consumer. As Lord Bingham explained, good faith is concerned with both procedural and substantive unfairness. It does not seem possible to give precise definitions of good faith and significant imbalance, nor to precisely explain the relationship between them. As Lord Steyn said of the Directive which caused the Regulations to be passed, 'The Directive is not an altogether harmonious text. It reflects the pragmatic compromises which were necessary to arrive at practical solutions between Member States with divergent legal systems.'

5.7.4 Assessment of unfair terms

Regulation 6(1) states that: 'Without prejudice to Regulation 12, the unfairness of a contractual term shall be assessed, taking into account the nature of the goods or services for which the contract was concluded and by referring, at the time of the conclusion of the contract, to all the circumstances attending the conclusion of the contract and to all the other terms of the contract or of another contract on which it is dependent.'

Regulation 12 allows the Director General of Fair Trading and other qualifying bodies to apply for an injunction to prevent the use of, or the recommendation of the use of, an unfair term.

5.7.5 Indicative list of terms which may be regarded as unfair

Schedule 2 to the Regulations specifies an indicative and illustrative list of terms which may be regarded as unfair. These include: terms which have the object or effect of excluding liability for death or personal injury caused by negligence (1)(a); making an agreement binding on consumers whereas the seller or supplier's obligations are subject to a condition which he can choose to realise (c); requiring a consumer who fails to fulfil his obligation to pay a disproportionately high sum in compensation (e); authorising the seller or supplier to dissolve the contract on a discretionary basis, where the same facility is not granted to the consumer (f); allowing the seller or supplier to terminate a contract of indeterminate duration without reasonable notice or serious grounds for determination (g); using hidden terms to irrevocably bind the consumer (i); altering the terms of the contract unless there is a valid reason specified in the contract (j, k and l); and requiring the consumer to take disputes to arbitration not covered by legal provisions (q). A complete list of all the indicative and illustrative terms can be found on the Office of Fair Trading's web site.

5.7.6 Effect of unfair term

Regulation 8(1) states that an unfair term in a contract concluded with a consumer by a seller or supplier shall not be binding on the consumer. Regulation 8(2) provides that the contract shall continue to bind the parties if it is capable of continuing in existence without the unfair term. So it seems that a blue pencil test will apply, and the rest of the contract should stand if it could do so unaffected once the unfair term had been crossed out with a blue pencil.

5.7.7 Construction of written contract

Regulation 7 reiterates the contra preferentum rule, providing that if there is a doubt about the meaning of a written term, the interpretation most favourable to the consumer shall prevail.

5.7.8 Prevention of continued use of unfair terms

Regulation 10(1) provides that it is the duty of the Director General of Fair Trading to consider any complaint made to him that any contract term drawn up for general use is unfair. However, the Director does not have to consider the complaint if he considers it frivolous or vexatious. The Director and other qualifying bodies may apply for an injunction to prevent the use of, or the recommendation of the use of, any unfair term drawn up for general use in contracts concluded with consumers (reg.12(1)). Eleven qualifying bodies are listed, and these include the Director Generals of Gas, Electricity, Water and Telecommunications supplies, the Rail Regulator, all British weights and measures authorities and the Consumers' Association. A qualifying body must give the Director General of Fair Trading 14 days' notice of intention to apply for an injunction. However, if given sufficient undertakings about the continued use of an unfair term the Director General may choose not to seek an injunction (reg.10(3)). An injunction may prevent not only the use of the particular unfair term, but also of any term having similar effect (reg.12(4)).

The Office of Fair Trading have taken a very interventionist approach in threatening to apply for injunctions. Almost invariably the business concerned backs down. One unfortunate effect of this success is that there are very few, if any, reported cases on the interpretation of the Regulations, although the Office of Fair Trading do publish reports giving details on the cases in which they have been involved. Under the 1994 Regulations there were no other qualifying bodies which could apply for injunctions. In order to facilitate the investigation of complaints, traders can be ordered by the qualifying bodies or the Director General of Fair Trading to produce copies of their standard contracts and to give information about their use (reg.13(3)).

5.8 CONSUMER GUARANTEES

The Sale and Supply of Goods to Consumers Regulations 2002 have introduced new rules on consumer guarantees. Goods supplied to consumers do not need to come with a guarantee. However, where goods sold or supplied are offered with a consumer guarantee, reg.15(1) provides that the consumer guarantee takes effect at the time the goods are delivered as a contractual obligation. This contractual obligation is owed by the guarantor under the conditions set out in the guarantee statement and the associated advertising. The Regulations have therefore removed the need to prove a contract between the consumer and the manufacturer. (Prior to the Regulations taking effect there was some doubt as to whether or not such a contract could be proved.)

Regulation 2 defines a consumer as any natural person who is acting for purposes which are outside his trade, business or profession. A 'consumer guarantee' is defined as any undertaking to a consumer by a person acting in the course of his business, given without extra charge, to reimburse the price paid or to replace, repair or handle consumer goods in any way if they do not meet the specifications set out in the guarantee statement or in the relevant advertising. It should be noticed that the guarantor only has to do what he promised to do. Many guarantees are restricted to repairing goods and do not promise a refund if the goods are faulty. When a consumer buys defective goods the primary remedy will be against the retailer under the statutory implied terms. (See Chapter 8 at 8.2.) However, a guarantee can be particularly useful if the retailer has become insolvent or if the guarantee period is for several years. SGA 1979, and other equivalent statutes, require goods to be of satisfactory quality at the time of delivery. If the goods prove defective much later it can be difficult to prove that the goods were not of satisfactory quality at the time of delivery. Also, a buyer will be too late to reject, though not too late to claim damages, on account of having accepted the goods if he retains the goods for more than a reasonable time without intimating rejection of them. (See Chapter 10 at 10.4.3.) In the Regulations the 'supply' of goods includes supply by way of sale, lease, hire or hire-purchase.

The guarantee must be written in plain, intelligible English. The name and address of the guarantor must be supplied, along with the extent and duration of the guarantee and how to claim under it. If the consumer so requests the guarantee must, within a reasonable time, be made available to him in writing or in another durable medium which he can access. This obligation to make the guarantee available is placed not only on the guarantor but also on any person who offers the goods to the consumer. Trading standards officers can enforce the rules on supplying the guarantee in the required form by way of injunction.

Test your understanding 5.3

1 In the light of the protection conferred by the Unfair Contract Terms Act 1977 and the Unfair Terms in Consumer Contracts Regulations 1999, why is it still necessary to analyse whether or not an exclusion clause is a term of a contract?

2 An exclusion clause can be incorporated into a contract if it was agreed upon by both parties or if the party affected by the clause had reasonable notice of it. At what time must the clause have been agreed upon or notice of it have been given?

3 As regards business liability, to what extent can a contract term exclude liability for negligence?

4 To what extent can a contract term exclude liability for breach of the terms implied by the Sale of Goods Act 1979 and the corresponding terms implied by the Supply of Goods (Implied Terms) Act 1973 and the Supply of Goods and Services Act 1982?

5 What types of contracts are affected by the Unfair Terms in Consumer Contracts Regulations 1999?

6 What is the main effect of the 1999 Regulations?

Key points

Distinguishing terms and representations

■ Express terms are expressly agreed by the parties. Implied terms are implied either by the courts or by statute.

■ A promise which was intended by the parties to be a part of a contract will be a term of the contract.

■ A representation is not a part of the contract because the parties did not intend that it should be.

■ The courts have devised several tests to help to decide whether or not the parties to the contract intended a particular statement to be a term or not. The tests are not conclusive as the intentions of the parties can only be deduced from all the evidence.

■ The parol evidence rule, to which there are several exceptions, holds that extrinsic (outside) evidence cannot be introduced to add to or vary a written contract.

Implied terms

■ Terms can be implied into contracts either by statute or by the courts.

→

- Important terms are implied into contracts by the Sale of Goods Act 1979, the Supply of Goods (Implied Terms) Act 1973 and the Supply of Goods and Services Act 1982.
- Terms are implied by the courts as a matter of fact on the basis that the parties must have intended the term to be a part of the contract.
- Terms can be implied by the courts as a matter of law on the basis that it is necessary to imply such a term into a contract of this particular type.
- The courts can imply terms on the basis that they are customary in a particular locality, customary in a particular trade, or customary between the parties.

Conditions, warranties and innominate terms

- A condition is a term which the parties intended to be vitally important so that it went to the root of the contract. A warranty is a term which the parties did not intend to be vitally important.
- If a condition is breached the injured party can treat the contract as repudiated and/or claim damages. If a warranty is breached the injured party can claim damages but cannot treat the contract as repudiated.
- Breach of an innominate term will allow the injured party to treat the contract as repudiated only if he was deprived of substantially the whole benefit of the contract. Breach of an innominate term will always allow the injured party to claim damages.

Exclusion clauses

- An exclusion or exemption clause is a term in a contract which tries to exclude or exempt liability for breach of contract. Exclusion clauses may also attempt to exclude liability for breach of a tortious duty.
- An exclusion clause will only be a term of a contract if it was agreed before the contract was made or if the party affected by the clause was given sufficient notice of the clause before the contract was made.
- An exclusion clause will be ineffective to the extent that its effect was misrepresented to the party affected by it.
- An exclusion clause can be incorporated into a contract by a course of dealing between the parties or by a trade custom.
- The important sections of UCTA 1977 apply only to business liability.
- Section 2(1) of UCTA will not allow a contract term to exclude liability for death or personal injury caused by negligence. Section 2(2) allows a term to exclude liability for other types of loss caused by negligence, but only in so far as the term satisfies the UCTA 1977 requirement of reasonableness.
- As against a person dealing as a consumer, s.6 of UCTA prevents liability for breach of the statutory terms implied by SGA 1979 from being excluded by any contract term. As against a person not dealing as a consumer liability for breach of these terms can be excluded by a term which satisfies UCTA's requirement of reasonableness. (However, liability for breach of the term as to the right to sell can never be excluded.) The position is the same as regards the corresponding terms implied by SGITA 1973 and SGSA 1982.
- Section 8 of UCTA 1977 only allows liability for misrepresentation to be excluded by a contract term in so far as the term satisfies the UCTA's requirement of reasonableness.
- The 1999 Regulations apply only to terms in contracts between a consumer and a seller or supplier.
- The 1999 Regulations provide that consumers will not be bound by unfair terms. These are defined as terms which have not been individually negotiated and which, contrary to the requirement of good faith, cause a significant imbalance between the rights and obligations under the contract to the detriment of the consumer.

Summary questions

1 John, a carpenter, sold his van to a small garage on 30 April. On 4 April John drove his van to the garage, where the garage owner gave it a cursory inspection. John said that the van was eight years old but a new engine had been fitted two years ago. In fact no new engine was fitted but John believed

→

that his statement was true because he had been told, when he had bought the van six months ago, that a new engine had been fitted. The garage owner said that he definitely would not buy the van unless a new engine had been fitted. John assured him that it had been. No deal was struck that day. On 30 April John returned to the garage and after five minutes' negotiation about the price the dealer bought the van for £2 500. Before making the contract the dealer told John that if a new engine had not been fitted he would only have paid £1 300. Is John's statement about the new engine having been fitted likely to be a term or a representation?

2 At a typical self-service petrol station the customer drives in, fills his tank, and then pays the cashier. Assuming this to be the series of events, would an exclusion clause be a part of the contract if:

a It was displayed at the entrance to the petrol station?

b It was displayed on the petrol pump?

c It was displayed above the cashier's till?

3 In **Thornton v Shoe Lane Parking** Lord Denning said that the exclusion clause on the ticket did not apply because it came after the contract was made. It follows that the offer and acceptance must have been concluded before the ticket was issued to the driver. What then was the offer, and what was the acceptance?

4 The Unfair Contract Terms Act 1977 and the Unfair Terms in Consumer Contract Regulations 1999 both give special protection to purchasers who deal as consumers. Would the following purchasers be regarded by either the Act or the Regulations as dealing as consumers?

a John, a civil servant, buys a car from Mary, a teacher.

b Mary buys a new car from a garage.

c A garage buys 12 new cars from a motor manufacturer.

d Jack, a self-employed builder, buys a cement mixer from Bill, a retired builder.

e Bill soon regrets having sold his cement mixer. He is bored with retirement and decides to extend his kitchen. He buys a new cement mixer from a builder's merchant, and gets trade discount by pretending that he is still in business.

5 The Unfair Contract Terms Act has not outlawed standard form contracts. Such contracts are very commonly used.

a Identify three types of contracts which are usually made by one party agreeing to the other's written standard terms.

b Is it only consumers who agree to another's written standard terms?

6 Belinda pays £500 to go on a two-week pleasure cruise. Belinda breaks a leg, and her luggage is waterlogged when the captain of the ferry negligently crashes into a pier. In addition, the last four days of her holiday are lost and she has to return home early. Belinda signed a standard form contract when booking the holiday. What would be the effect of:

a A clause in the contract which said that the ferry operator was not to be liable for personal injuries?

b A clause which said that the operator would not be liable for damage to passengers' luggage?

c A clause which said that passengers could not be entitled to any refund or damages if their holiday ended early due to navigational accidents?

7 Assuming that in each case the exclusion clause had been a term of the contract, what would be the outcome of the following cases if they were to arise today?

a **Thompson v London, Midland and Scottish Railway Co**.

b **Chapelton v Barry UDC**.

c **Olley v Marlborough Court Hotel Ltd**.

d **L'Estrange v Graucob**.

Multiple choice questions

1 Which one of the following statements is not true? When reference is made to a statement, assume that the statement was one of fact made by one party to the contract to the other party to the contract.

a In considering whether or not a statement is a term of a contract, the courts will be guided by the apparent intentions of the parties to the contract.

b A very strong statement, made by a party who knows more about the subject matter of the contract than the party to whom the statement was made, will always be a term of the contract.

c If the contract was concluded very shortly after a statement was made, this is an indication that the statement was a term of the contract.

d There are no tests which can be conclusive in determining whether or not the parties to a contract intended a statement to be a term of the contract.

2 By which of the following methods can a term be implied into a contract?

i By a statute.

ii By a court, on the grounds that the term is customary in the locality.

iii By a court, on the grounds that the term would significantly improve the contract.

iv By a court, on the grounds of the previous dealings of the parties to the contract.

v By a court, on the grounds of business efficacy.

a By all of these methods.

b By i, ii, iii and v only.

c By i, ii, iv and v only.

d By i, ii, iii and iv only.

3 In *The Moorcock*, the court implied a term that the jetty was a safe place to moor a boat. On which one of the following grounds was the term implied?

a Because such a term was customary in the locality.

b Because the parties, as reasonable men, would have included the term if it had been suggested to them.

c Because the term was customary in the trade.

d Because the term was necessary to give the contract business efficacy.

4 Which of the following statements are true?

i If a condition is breached then the contract must be terminated.

ii A contract cannot be terminated merely because a warranty has been breached.

iii If an innominate term is breached then the injured party has the choice as to whether or not to terminate.

iv An injured party can terminate a contract if breach of an innominate term deprived him of substantially the whole benefit of the contract.

a i, ii and iii.

b i, ii and iv.

c ii and iv only.

d i and iii only.

5 If *Olley v Marlborough Court Hotel* were to come to court today, which one of the following statements would be true?

a As the notice was not a term of the contract, the case would be decided exactly as it was in 1949.

b As Mrs Olley would now be a consumer, UCTA 1977 would not allow the notice to exclude liability for negligence.

c As Mrs Olley would now be a consumer, the 1999 Regulations would automatically invalidate any term of the contract which would operate to her detriment.

d The effect of the notice was misrepresented and therefore the hotel could not rely on it.

6 If *L'Estrange v Graucob* were to come to court today, the café owner would win the case. On which one of the following grounds would she win?

a Applying the test in *R & B Customs Brokers Ltd v United Dominions Trust Ltd*, the café owner would have dealt as a consumer, because this was the first vending machine which the business had bought. Therefore, liability for breach of the term implied by the SGA could not be excluded.

b The buyer would not be regarded as dealing as a consumer. But in non-consumer sales liability for breach of the terms implied by SGA 1979 can only be excluded if the term seeking to do so would satisfy UCTA 1977 requirement of reasonableness, which the term in question would not.

c The Unfair Terms in Consumer Contracts Regulations 1999 would invalidate the exclusion clause on the grounds that it was not individually negotiated and, contrary to the requirement of good faith, caused a significant imbalance in the parties' rights and obligations under the contract.

d As the buyer dealt on the written standard terms of the seller, the protection conferred by SGA 1979 implied terms could not be excluded under any circumstances.

7 Which one of the following statements is true of the Unfair Terms in Consumer Contracts Regulations 1999?

a The Regulations will invalidate a contract under which a consumer has agreed to pay an exorbitant price for goods or services.

b If a contract to which the Regulations apply contains a term which the Regulations classify as unfair, the whole contract shall not be binding on the consumer.

c The Regulations only apply to contracts concluded between a consumer and a seller or supplier. However, in certain circumstances a company can be classified as a consumer.

d The Regulations define an unfair term as one which has not been individually negotiated, and which, contrary to the requirement of good faith, causes a significant imbalance in the parties' rights and obligations under the contract to the detriment of the consumer.

Task 5

John, a schoolteacher, decides to renovate his house in the summer holidays. John hires an industrial sander for use on the floorboards of his house. Due to an electrical fault, the sander catches fire while in use. John is badly burnt, and the floorboards in his living room catch fire, causing extensive damage to the house. When hiring the sander, John signed a standard 'sales agreement'. This agreement stated that the hire company could not be liable for any loss or damage caused by defects in previously hired goods.

Write a report for John, indicating:

a Whether John deals as a 'consumer', as defined by the Unfair Contract Terms Act 1977.

b The protection given to consumers by the 1977 Act.

c Whether John dealt on the hire company's 'written standard terms', as defined by the 1977 Act.

d The extent to which the Unfair Terms in Consumer Contracts Regulations 1999 would protect John.

e The overall effect of the agreement which John signed.

f The overall effect of the agreement if John had not been a teacher, but had hired the sander for use in his trade as a builder.

mylawchamber *premium*

Visit **www.mylawchamber.co.uk/macintyre** to access study support resources including interactive multiple-choice questions, weblinks, glossary, glossary flashcards, legal newsfeed, answers to questions in this chapter, legal updates and an overview of this chapter all linked to the **Pearson eText** version of *Business Law* which you can **search**, **highlight** and **personalise** with your **own notes** and **bookmarks**.

Use **Case Navigator** to read in full some of the key cases referenced in this chapter with commentary and questions:

Hong Kong Fir Shipping Co. Ltd v *Kawasaki Kisen Kaisha Ltd* [1962] 1 All ER 474
Stevenson v *Rogers* [1999] 1 All ER 613

6

Misrepresentation · mistake · duress and undue influence · illegality

Introduction

This chapter considers the following matters:

6.1 MISREPRESENTATION

In Chapter 5 we examined the difference between terms and representations. We saw that a term is a part of the contract whereas a representation is not.

In some circumstances an untrue representation may amount to an actionable misrepresentation, and if this is the case then the party to whom the misrepresentation was made will have legal remedies. It is important to remember that these remedies are not the same as those available for a breach of contract. A breach of contract occurs whenever a term of the contract is breached. The remedies available for breach of contract are considered in the following chapter. An untrue representation which does not amount to an actionable misrepresentation will not give rise to any legal remedy for misrepresentation. We therefore need to define an actionable misrepresentation.

6.1.1 Definition of an actionable misrepresentation

An actionable misrepresentation is an untrue statement of fact made by one party to a contract which induced the other party to enter into the contract.

We examine the two requirements of this definition in turn. The first requirement is that the untrue statement was one of fact. The second requirement is that this statement induced the other party to enter into the contract. A misrepresentation which does not satisfy these two requirements is not an actionable misrepresentation.

6.1.1.1 **An untrue statement of fact**

A statement of mere opinion, being a statement which is not capable of being objectively proved true or false, cannot amount to a misrepresentation.

Bisset v Wilkinson
[1927] AC 177 (Privy Council)

In May 1919, 2 410 acres of land in the South Island of New Zealand were sold for £13 260. The purchaser knew that no person had ever previously carried on sheep farming on the particular unit of land which was sold. Soon after the land was sold, sheep farming became very unprofitable. Before the contract was made the vendor had told the purchaser that the unit of land could support 2 000 sheep. The purchaser found that the land could not support anything like this number.

→

Held. As the purchaser knew that the unit of land had never been used as a sheep farm, the statement that the farm would support 2 000 sheep was only a statement of opinion and could not amount to a misrepresentation.

In the above case the statement was regarded as being a mere statement of opinion. However, what sounds like a mere statement of opinion may impliedly contain a statement of fact, which is capable of objectively being proved either true or false.

Smith v *Land and House Property Corporation* (1884) 28 ChD 7 (Court of Appeal)

The claimant put a hotel up for auction. The auction particulars stated that the hotel was let to 'F (a most desirable tenant), at a rental of £400 for an unexpired term of 27 and a half years'. The defendant company sent their secretary to the hotel and the secretary thought the hotel was doing little business and that trade in the locality was likely to decline. The defendant company authorised the secretary to bid up to £5 000 for the hotel. The hotel was not sold at the auction. However, immediately after the auction the company secretary bought the hotel on the company's behalf for £4 700. One month later F became insolvent. The defendants refused to complete the purchase. They claimed that the statement which described F as a most desirable tenant was a misrepresentation, because when the statement was made F was badly behind with his rent and the claimants were threatening him with legal action.

Held. The statement was a misrepresentation. It was not a statement of mere opinion, but involved a statement of fact. F was not a most desirable tenant. The statement that he was a most desirable tenant impliedly asserted that the claimant knew of no facts which would lead to the conclusion that he was not. As there had been an actionable misrepresentation the defendants could use this as a defence to being sued on the contract.

COMMENT (i) Bowen LJ explained the circumstances in which a statement of opinion can be a statement of fact in this way: 'It is often fallaciously assumed that a statement of opinion cannot involve a statement of fact. In a case where the facts are equally well known to both parties, what one of them says to the other is frequently nothing but an expression of opinion . . . But if the facts are not equally well known to both sides, then a statement of opinion by one who knows the facts best involves very often a statement of a material fact, for he impliedly states that he knows facts which justify his opinion.'

(ii) Nor would the contract have been void for mistake.

(iii) The decision in this case was approved by the Court of Appeal in *Esso Petroleum Co Ltd* v *Mardon* (1976), which we examined in the previous chapter at 5.2.6.

Generally, a statement of intention cannot amount to a misrepresentation because it cannot amount to a statement of fact. However, when a person makes a statement of intention knowing that it is false, then the statement may be regarded as one of fact. In *Edgington* v *Fitzmaurice* (1885) 29 ChD 476, for example, a company issued a prospectus which invited people to lend money to the company by subscribing for debentures. The prospectus stated that the company intended to use the money raised by the debentures to alter company buildings, to buy horses and vans and to develop the company's trade. In fact the real purpose of issuing the debentures was to raise money to pay off the company's debts. The company argued that their statement in the prospectus could not amount to a misrepresentation as it was a mere statement of their intention, rather than a statement of fact. The Court of Appeal had little difficulty in disposing of this argument. Bowen LJ said that in order for fraudulent misrepresentation to be established, 'There must be a statement of existing fact: but the state of a man's mind is as much a fact as the state of his digestion'.

Until relatively recently, statements of law could not be actionable misrepresentations. However, it seems that this is no longer true, following the Court of Appeal's decision in *Brennan* v *Bolt Burden* [2004] EWCA Civ 1017.

A representation may be made by conduct. In *Spice Girls Ltd* v *Aprilia World Service BV* [2000] EMLR 478 a company which promoted the pop group the 'Spice Girls' made a contract agreeing to advertise Aprilia's scooters. Before the contract was made all of the Spice Girls were filmed in a commercial. At this time they knew that one of the group was about to leave, and this member did leave the group soon after the contract was signed. It was held that a representation was made by the company, to the effect that the company did not know or reasonably believe that any member was about to leave the group. This representation was made by allowing all of the group to take part in the filming. As this representation was untrue, and had induced Aprilia to make the contract, it was an actionable misrepresentation.

6.1.1.2 **Silence as a misrepresentation**

As a general rule, neither party to a contract is under any duty to disclose information to the other party. The old rule *caveat emptor* (let the buyer beware) applies. So remaining silent will generally not amount to making a misrepresentation. This is the case even when the party who remains silent knows that the other party would not have made the contract if aware of all the facts.

Fletcher v Krell (1873) 42 LJ QB 55

The claimant entered into a contract of employment to be a governess in Argentina for three years at a salary of £100 a year. When making the contract she concealed from the defendant the fact that she was divorced. When the employer discovered the truth he refused to employ the claimant.

Held. The claimant was entitled to damages for breach of contract. As she had not been asked whether or not she was divorced, she had no obligation to reveal that she was. Her failure to reveal that she was divorced could not amount to a misrepresentation.

COMMENT (i) In those days both parties would have known that the claimant would have had no chance of getting the job if the employer had discovered that she was divorced.

(ii) In *Smith v Hughes* (1871) LR 6 QB 597 (House of Lords) Cockburn CJ said, 'The passive acquiescence of the seller in the self-deception of the buyer would not entitle the buyer to avoid the contract for mistake.' The facts of this case are set out below at 6.2.3.2.

There are four exceptions to the rule that silence cannot be a misrepresentation. Silence can amount to a misrepresentation if:

(a) there was a change of circumstances; or
(b) the silence concerned a material fact in a contract of insurance; or
(c) a fiduciary relationship existed between the parties; or
(d) the silence made a statement misleading.

These exceptions need to be examined individually.

A change of circumstances

If a person makes a statement which is true at the time when it is made but which, owing to a change of circumstances, becomes untrue before the contract is made, then it may be a misrepresentation not to reveal that the circumstances have changed.

With v O'Flanagan
[1936] Ch 575 (Court of Appeal)

In January 1934 the defendant offered to sell his medical practice to the claimant for £4 000. The defendant stated that the practice had takings of £2 000 per annum. This statement was true when it was made. However, by the time the sale was completed on 1 May the practice was almost non-existent. The defendant had been ill and several locum doctors had stood in for him, but almost all of his patients had deserted the practice.

Held. The statement that the practice had takings of £2 000 per annum had to be treated as continuing until the sale was completed and did therefore amount to an actionable misrepresentation. By failing to correct the statement the defendant continued to make it.

In *Spice Girls Ltd v Aprilia World Service BV*, considered above at 6.1.1.1, the company was liable because it had not corrected the untrue representation it had made by conduct. The representation therefore continued to be made at the time of the contract.

Contracts of insurance

Contracts of insurance are contracts *uberrimae fidei* (of the utmost good faith). In such contracts everything which could influence a prudent insurer as to the price of the premium, or as to whether or not to take the risk, is a material fact. A person taking out insurance must reveal all material facts, whether asked about the matter in question or not.

Lambert v Co-op Insurance Society Ltd
[1975] 2 Lloyd's Rep 485 (Court of Appeal)

In April 1963 the claimant insured her own and her husband's jewellery. There were no questions asked about previous convictions. At the time of taking out the policy the claimant knew that her husband had been convicted some years earlier of receiving 1 730 stolen cigarettes and had been fined £25. In December 1971 the claimant's husband was convicted of offences of conspiracy to steal, and of theft, and was imprisoned for 15 months. The claimant did →

not reveal these convictions to the insurance company either at the time of the conviction or when the policy was renewed in March 1972. In April 1972 the claimant made a claim of £311, representing the value of lost or stolen jewellery.

Held. The insurers could avoid the contract on account of the misrepresentation made by the claimant. The claimant had a duty to disclose the original conviction when applying for the insurance, and to disclose the later conviction when renewing it.

Although insurance contracts are the most important contracts of the utmost good faith, there are other such contracts such as contracts to allot shares in a company.

Where there is a fiduciary relationship between the parties

A fiduciary relationship is a relationship of great trust, where one of the parties can expect to trust the other implicitly. Examples of such relationships would include contracts between partners in a firm, between agent and principal and between promoters or directors of a company and the company. The person of whom the trust is expected must reveal everything to the person with whom he makes the contract. If he does not do so, his silence will amount to a misrepresentation.

A relationship is fiduciary because of the nature of the relationship between the parties. A contract is of the utmost good faith because of the nature of the contract, i.e. that it is a contract of insurance.

When silence makes a statement misleading

Even a statement which is literally true can amount to a misrepresentation if the statement conveys a misleading impression on account of not being the whole truth.

Nottingham Patent Brick and Tile Co v *Butler* (1886) 16 QBD 778 (Court of Appeal)

In 1882 the claimants, a brick manufacturing company, agreed to purchase a plot of land from the defendant and paid a deposit of £610. Some 15 years earlier the land had become the subject of a restrictive covenant which prevented the land from being used to manufacture bricks. The defendant, during the negotiations, made mention of this covenant. The claimants' solicitor asked the defendant's solicitor whether or not any such covenant existed. The defendant's solicitor

replied that he was not aware of any such covenant. The defendant again said that he thought there was a restrictive covenant. The claimants' solicitor asked if this was correct and the defendant's solicitor again said that he was not aware of any such covenant. The defendant's solicitor did not explain that the reason why he was not aware of any such covenant was that he had not read the title deeds and knew nothing of their contents.

Held. The defendant's solicitor's statement, although literally true, was a misrepresentation. It was not the whole truth and it conveyed a misleading statement of fact.

6.1.1.3 **The statement must induce the making of the contract**

A statement can only be an actionable misrepresentation if it was influential in inducing the other party to make the contract on the terms upon which he did make the contract. An untrue statement which did not induce the other party cannot be an actionable misrepresentation. The statement in question does not need to be the sole reason why the claimant made the contract, but it must at least be one of the reasons.

If a person makes a contract without checking the truth of a statement made to him, this suggests that the statement did induce him to make the contract. In *Redgrave* v *Hurd* (1881) 20 ChD 1, for example, a solicitor agreed to become a partner in a firm because he was told that the business had an income of £300 a year. The incoming partner was offered the chance to check the books but declined the offer. If he had checked the books he would have discovered that the income was only £200 a year. Upon discovering the truth, the incoming partner refused to go ahead with the agreement. When sued for breach of contract he successfully raised misrepresentation as a defence. He had no duty to check the truth of the statements made to him, and the fact that he did not check them indicated that they had induced him to enter into the contract.

If a person does check the truth of a statement made to him then he cannot later say that the statement induced him to make a contract. The fact of his checking the statement will prove that he did not rely on it. In *Attwood* v *Small* (1838) 6 Cl & Fin 232, for example, a vendor of a mine exaggerated its capacity. The purchaser got his own experts to check the vendor's statement and these experts mistakenly said that the vendor's statement was correct. Upon finding out that the mine had the reduced capacity, the purchaser claimed to rescind the contract for misrepresentation. He was not allowed to do so. The purchaser had relied on the statement of his own experts, not on the statement of the vendor.

6.1.2 The different types of misrepresentation

Once it has become established that an actionable misrepresentation has been made, it becomes necessary to consider what type of misrepresentation it was. An actionable misrepresentation can be classified as either fraudulent, negligent or wholly innocent. The classification will depend upon the state of mind of the party who made the misrepresentation.

6.1.2.1 Fraudulent misrepresentation

In *Derry* v *Peek* (1889) 14 App Cas 337 the House of Lords defined a fraudulent misrepresentation as one made either knowing that it was false, or without belief in its truth, or recklessly, careless as to whether it was true or false. For example, if X sells a car to Y and makes an actionable misrepresentation that the car has been fitted with a new engine, the misrepresentation would be fraudulent if X knew that the car had not been fitted with a new engine, or if X did not think that it had been, or if X had not the slightest idea whether or not it had been.

Whichever of the three states of mind is held by the maker of the misrepresentation, he must have acted dishonestly. Mere carelessness is not enough to amount to fraudulent misrepresentation. As dishonesty must be proved, the courts require a very strong standard of proof which is closer to the criminal standard (beyond a reasonable doubt) than to the ordinary civil standard (on a balance of probabilities). For this reason many claimants faced with what is probably a fraudulent misrepresentation choose to allege

negligent misrepresentation instead. (See, for example, *Royscot Trust Ltd* v *Rogerson* [1991] 3 All ER 294, which is set out below at 6.1.4.2.)

Fraudulent misrepresentation amounts to the common law tort of deceit. The remedies available are to claim tort damages or to rescind the contract. The remedies available for misrepresentation are examined in detail at 6.1.3 and 6.1.4.

6.1.2.2 Negligent misrepresentation under s.2(1) of the Misrepresentation Act 1967

Section 2(1) of the Misrepresentation Act 1967 provides that damages are available for a negligent misrepresentation. A negligent misrepresentation arises if two steps are satisfied.

First, the injured party must prove that he has suffered a loss because an actionable misrepresentation was made to him, and that this misrepresentation would have entitled him to damages if it had been made fraudulently. Second, the burden of proof is switched to the maker of the misrepresentation. He must prove that the misrepresentation was not made negligently, that is to say that he must prove that he did believe the misrepresentation was true, with reasonable grounds for such a belief, up until the time the contract was made. If the maker of the misrepresentation cannot prove this then negligent misrepresentation is established.

A negligent misrepresentation allows the injured party to rescind the contract and claim damages which will be assessed on a tort basis.

It should also be noticed that when a negligent misrepresentation is committed a common law action for negligent misstatement might also be possible. This action is available whether or not the misrepresentation was an actionable misrepresentation (i.e. whether or not it induced the making of the contract) and is examined in Chapter 12 at 12.3. An action for negligent misstatement is generally not pursued where it is possible to sue for damages under s.2(1) of the Misrepresentation Act because the burden of proof is on the claimant alleging negligent misstatement to prove four things: that a 'special relationship' existed between the parties; that a duty of care was owed; that the duty was breached; and that this caused a foreseeable loss. In the light of the reversed burden of proof which applies when an action is brought under s.2(1) MA 1967, any claimant who had the choice would prefer to sue under that section rather than bring an action for negligent misstatement.

6.1.2.3 **Wholly innocent misrepresentation**

We have seen that a misrepresentation will not be negligent if the party who made it can prove that he did believe that the misrepresentation was true, with reasonable grounds for such a belief, up until the time when the contract was made. If these matters are proved, then a wholly innocent, rather than a negligent, misrepresentation will have been made.

When considering the nature of a fraudulent misrepresentation we considered an example where X sold his car to Y and made a misrepresentation that the car had been fitted with a new engine. We saw the circumstances in which this misrepresentation would be fraudulent. If X honestly believed that the car had been fitted with a new engine then the misrepresentation could not be fraudulent (this is a subjective test). The misrepresentation will be negligent unless X can prove two things: that up until the time of the contract he did believe the car had been fitted with a new engine, and that there were reasonable grounds for this belief. If X can prove these two things then the misrepresentation will have been wholly innocent.

6.1.3 **Rescission of the contract**

All three types of actionable misrepresentation can give rise to the equitable remedy of rescission of the contract. In cases of fraudulent misrepresentation rescission is a right, subject to the rule that any equitable remedy is only available at the discretion of the court. A negligent or wholly innocent misrepresentation almost always allows for rescission, but this is not a right. In cases of negligent or innocent misrepresentation s.2(2) of the Misrepresentation Act 1967 allows the court to award damages in lieu of rescission where it would be equitable to do so. It is most unusual for a court to exercise this power. The circumstances in which it might do so are considered below at 6.1.5.

As all three types of misrepresentation allow for rescission, a contract which has been made because of an actionable misrepresentation is said to be voidable. This means that the person to whom the misrepresentation was made has the option to avoid the contract (to rescind it) within a reasonable time. If the contract is avoided in this way then it is no longer binding and the parties are restored to their pre-contract positions. However, the contract is not rescinded unless the person to whom the misrepresentation was made communicates to the other party that he is rescinding the contract. Once this decision has been made he will

be too late to change his mind. Later in this chapter we shall see that in certain circumstances a contract can be void. There the position is different, a void contract is a nullity.

In cases of fraudulent misrepresentation, especially where a rogue pays for goods with a bad cheque, it may not be possible to communicate rescission. The rogue will generally have disappeared by the time the fraud is discovered. Rescission can still be made in two ways. First, the innocent party might seize the goods which he sold, thus indicating an intention to rescind. Alternatively he might rescind by an overt act which shows an intention to rescind. An example of this can be seen in *Car and Universal Finance Co Ltd* v *Caldwell* [1965] 1 QB 525 in Chapter 9 at 9.3.3.

Misrepresentation may also be raised as a defence by a person being sued on a contract. (An example was seen in *Smith* v *Land and House Property Corporation*, above at 6.1.1.1.)

6.1.3.1 **Losing the right to rescind**

Rescission is an equitable remedy. It can therefore be lost if the person to whom the misrepresentation was made has affirmed the contract, or if it has become impossible to restore the parties to the pre-contract position or if a third party has acquired rights to the subject matter of the contract before it was rescinded. Each of these three bars to rescission needs to be examined in turn.

Affirmation

A person with a right to rescind affirms a contract, and therefore loses the right to rescind it, if he expressly or impliedly indicates that he intends to continue with the contract despite knowledge of his right to rescind. In a commercial contract the right to rescind can be lost through affirmation fairly easily.

> ### *Long* v *Lloyd*
> [1958] 1 WLR 753 (Court of Appeal)
>
> The claimant, a haulage contractor, bought a lorry because of several non-fraudulent misrepresentations, namely that the lorry was in first class condition, that it did 11 miles to the gallon and could be driven at 40 miles per hour. Two days after buying the lorry the claimant took it on a short trip and discovered that the dynamo did not work, that an oil seal was leaking, that one of the wheels was cracked and that the lorry was only doing five miles to the gallon. When the claimant →

complained about these defects the defendant agreed to pay half the cost of putting the dynamo right. The claimant agreed to this and got the dynamo fixed. The next day the claimant's brother took the lorry on a trip from Kent to Middlesbrough. The lorry broke down. The claimant wrote to the defendant rescinding the contract on the grounds that the oil seal leaked, that the lorry was only doing nine miles to the gallon on a long journey and could only do 25 miles per hour when loaded.

Held. The claimant had lost the right to rescind because he had affirmed the contract. He had done this by accepting the agreement to pay half the cost of fixing the dynamo and by sending the lorry to Middlesbrough. The first short journey was not affirmation as it was a reasonable examination of the lorry.

COMMENT (i) This case seemed particularly hard on the claimant as damages for non-fraudulent misrepresentation were not available prior to the Misrepresentation Act 1967.

(ii) The trial judge, Glyn-Jones J, did not find that the defendants had been fraudulent. This seems very surprising, but indicates the high standard of proof required before fraud is proved.

Mere lapse of time may be enough to indicate that a contract has been affirmed.

Leaf v International Galleries
[1950] 2 KB 86 (Court of Appeal)

The claimant bought a painting from a gallery because of a non-fraudulent misrepresentation that the painting was by John Constable. Five years later the claimant discovered that the painting was not by Constable and tried to rescind the contract.

Held. The claimant was too late to rescind. The claimant had affirmed the contract by doing nothing for five years. Rescission for non-fraudulent misrepresentation must take place within a reasonable time.

COMMENT If the misrepresentation had been fraudulent then time would not have started to run against the claimant until he either knew of the misrepresentation or ought to have known of it (Limitation Act 1980 s.32). This is an important practical difference between fraudulent misrepresentation and non-fraudulent. Before the Misrepresentation Act 1967 came into effect there were only two classes of misrepresentations: fraudulent and non-fraudulent.

Inability to restore pre-contract position

In Chapter 5 we examined in outline the remedies available for breach of contract. We saw that a person may treat the contract as repudiated if a condition is breached or if the breach of an innominate term deprived him of substantially the whole benefit of the contract. A contract can be treated as repudiated for breach of condition, or for a breach of an innominate term which deprived of substantially the whole benefit of the contract, even if it is not possible to restore the parties to the positions which they were in before the contract was made. It is future performance that is excused.

When a contract is avoided the parties must be restored to their pre-contract positions. If this is not possible then rescission will generally not be possible. In *Clarke v Dickson* (1858) EB & E 148 Crompton J illustrated this by giving an example of a butcher who bought live cattle because a grazier had made a fraudulent misrepresentation about them. If the butcher only discovered the misrepresentation after the cattle had been slaughtered and butchered rescission would not be possible (although damages for the tort of deceit could be claimed). However, rescission is an equitable remedy and so if the subject matter of the contract cannot be restored in exactly the same condition as it was in before the contract was made the court may order rescission, along with a monetary payment to compensate for the slight change. In *Erlanger v New Sombrero Phosphate Co* (1878) 3 App Cas 1218, for example, the buyer of a phosphate mine had extracted phosphate from the mine by the time he found out that the seller had made a misrepresentation about the mine. The House of Lords did allow rescission and ordered the buyer to compensate the seller for the phosphate he had extracted.

Third party has acquired rights

A contract cannot be rescinded if a third party has acquired an interest in the subject matter of the contract. Section 23 SGA 1979 provides an example. It states that: 'Where the seller of goods has a voidable title to them, but his title has not been avoided at the time of the sale, the buyer acquires a good title to the goods, provided he buys them in good faith and without notice of the seller's defect of title.'

The following case demonstrates the effect of s.23.

Lewis v *Averay*
[1972] 1 QB 198 (Court of Appeal)

The claimant advertised his car for sale for £450. A rogue visited the claimant and agreed to buy the car. When the rogue wrote out a cheque for £450 the claimant demanded proof of identity. The rogue, who had been claiming to be Richard Greene a well known television actor, produced a Pinewood Studios pass. The pass, which was in Richard Greene's name, showed the rogue's photograph, and bore an official looking stamp. The claimant let the rogue take possession of the car and the logbook. In fact the cheque was from a stolen cheque book. The defendant had advertised that he would like to buy a car and the rogue, now in possession of the car which the claimant had sold to him, called upon the defendant. The rogue now pretended to be the claimant and showed the defendant the logbook in the claimant's name and address. The defendant bought the car for £200. The defendant then wrote to the claimant asking for the car's workshop manual and the fraud was discovered. The rogue was never traced.

Held. The contract was voidable for fraudulent misrepresentation. However, once the defendant bought the car in good faith he acquired complete ownership of the car by virtue of s.23 SGA 1979. The claimant could no longer rescind the contract and had lost ownership of the car.

COMMENT (i) If the claimant had avoided the contract before the rogue sold to the defendant then s.23 would have provided no help to the defendant. (See ***Car and Universal Finance Co Ltd* v *Caldwell*** in Chapter 9 at 9.3.3.)

(ii) The contract was not void for mistake. (See below at 6.2.3.)

6.1.4 Damages for misrepresentation

The measure of damages available in respect of an actionable misrepresentation differs according to the type of misrepresentation made.

6.1.4.1 Fraudulent misrepresentation

If a fraudulent misrepresentation is proved then this amounts to the tort of deceit and damages are assessed on a fraud basis. Such damages will attempt to put the parties into the position which they would have been in if the tort had never been committed and so all expenses and losses directly flowing from the tort will be recoverable, even if they were not foreseeable.

Doyle v *Olby*
[1969] 2 QB 158 (Court of Appeal)

The claimant bought an ironmongery business on the strength of a fraudulent misrepresentation that the business achieved its turnover without employing a travelling salesman. The claimant paid £4 500 for the business, the goodwill and the existing lease of the business premises. He paid £5 000 for the stock and took a longer lease of the business premises from the vendor at a greatly increased rent. In fact the vendor of the business had employed a travelling salesman and half of the business had been brought in through this salesman. The claimant could not afford a travelling salesman and so that half of the business was lost. The claimant carried on the business as best he could until the case was heard. The trial judge awarded £1 500 damages. This figure was reached either as the cost of employing a travelling salesman or as the amount by which the goodwill of the business was reduced by the misrepresentation.

Held. £5 500 damages were awarded for the tort of deceit. These damages compensated not only for the money which the claimant had put into the business but also for all losses and expenses which he had subsequently suffered.

Lord Denning MR: 'In contract, the damages are limited to what may reasonably be supposed to have been in the contemplation of the parties. In fraud, they are not so limited. The defendant is bound to make reparation for all the actual damages flowing directly from the fraudulent inducement.'

COMMENT (i) This decision was approved by the House of Lords in ***Smith New Court Securities Ltd* v *Scrimgeour Vickers (Asset Management) Ltd*** [1996] 4 All ER 769.

(ii) The trial judge has assessed damages on the basis of a breach of contract. Fraud damages will generally be higher although this will not always be the case as they do not compensate for loss of the bargain. The quantification of damages for breach of contract, which do take into account the loss of the bargain, is examined in the following Chapter 7 at 7.2.2.2.

(iii) In general, tort damages will be limited by remoteness of damage – damages only being claimable for losses which were reasonably foreseeable. (See Chapter 12 at 12.2.4.) There is no such limitation when damages are awarded for the tort of deceit. Lord Denning LJ in ***Doyle* v *Olby*** said that: 'It does not lie in the mouth of the fraudulent person to say that they [losses actually flowing from the deceit] could not have been reasonably foreseen.'

6.1.4.2 **Negligent misrepresentation**

Before the Misrepresentation Act 1967 came into force misrepresentations were classified as either made fraudulently or made non-fraudulently, and damages were not available for a misrepresentation which was not made fraudulently. (Unless damages could be claimed for the tort of negligent misstatement.) Section 2(1) of the 1967 Act does allow damages for negligent misrepresentation. The section states that where a person has committed a negligent misrepresentation he shall 'be so liable' as if the misrepresentation had been made fraudulently. In the following case the Court of Appeal assessed damages for a negligent misrepresentation on the tort of deceit basis.

Royscot Trust Ltd v *Rogerson*
[1991] 3 All ER 294 (Court of Appeal)

The claimant was a finance company which provided finance for the first defendant (a consumer) to take a car on hire-purchase from the second defendant (a car dealer). The consumer had enough money to put down a deposit of £1 200, this representing 15.8 per cent of the car's price of £7 600. The car dealer knew that the finance company would demand a deposit of 20 per cent. The two defendants therefore falsified the price of the car to £8 000 and the amount of the deposit paid to £1 600. The balance to be paid therefore appeared to be £6 400, which was the true balance the consumer had agreed to pay. The consumer repaid instalments totalling £2 775 and then dishonestly sold the car to an innocent private purchaser. The finance company could not recover ownership of the car and so it sued the car dealer for negligent misrepresentation.

Held. Damages were awarded on the tort of deceit basis. The finance company was therefore able to recover all losses which flowed from their having entered into the contract, even unforeseeable losses, as long as these were not too remote. The finance company was therefore awarded £3 625. This figure was reached by subtracting the amount it had received from the consumer (£2 775) from the amount it had paid the dealer (£6 400).

COMMENT (i) Balcombe LJ said: 'In my judgment the wording of the subsection is clear: the person making the innocent [negligent] misrepresentation shall be "so liable", i.e. liable to damages as if the representation had been made fraudulently.'

(ii) *South Australia Asset Management Corp* v *York Montague Ltd* [1996] 3 All ER 365 was a case decided on negligent misstatement rather than on negligent misrepresentation. However, it has cast some doubt on the correctness of this case. Lord Steyn stated that he could not see why a person who had not behaved immorally should be treated as if he had committed fraud.

(iii) The case seems a clear example of fraudulent misrepresentation. However, the claimant opted for negligent misrepresentation because of the reduced standard of proof and because the burden of proof was thrown on to the defendants to show that they had not made the misrepresentation negligently.

(iv) The innocent private purchaser of the car gained ownership of it by virtue of the Hire Purchase Act 1964 Part III, which is considered in Chapter 9 at 9.3.6.

(v) At first instance the damages were assessed, on the basis of a breach of warranty, at £1 600. This figure was reached by attempting to put the finance company into the position which it would have been in if the dealer had revealed that the true deposit paid was £1 200. The finance company would have regarded this as 20 per cent of the purchase price and would therefore have paid the dealer £4 800. The contract damages would therefore have been the difference between this figure of £4 800 and the actual amount handed over to the dealer (£6 400), which equals £1 600.

6.1.4.3 **Wholly innocent misrepresentation**

There is no right to damages for a wholly innocent misrepresentation. However, the court has a discretion to award damages under s.2(2) of the Misrepresentation Act 1967, the effect of which is considered immediately below.

6.1.5 **Damages under s.2(2) Misrepresentation Act 1967**

Section 2(2) of the Misrepresentation Act 1967 introduced the possibility of damages in lieu of rescission in cases of non-fraudulent misrepresentation (that is to say in cases of negligent or wholly innocent misrepresentation). However, the claimant has no right to such damages, rather the court has a discretion to award damages in lieu of rescission in the following circumstances. First, there must have been a non-fraudulent misrepresentation which would have entitled the claimant to rescind the contract. Second, the claimant must claim that the contract has been or ought to be rescinded. Third, the court must consider it equitable to award damages rather than award rescission. In deciding whether or not it is equitable to award damages the court will consider three matters: the nature of the misrepresentation; the loss which would be caused by the misrepresentation if the contract is upheld; and the loss which would be caused to the misrepresentor if rescission is allowed.

There is some doubt as to whether damages under s.2(2) are still available once the right to rescind has been lost. In **Thomas Witter Ltd v TBP Industries** [1996] 2 All ER 573, it was suggested that damages would still be available even if the right to rescind had been lost. However, in **Governor of Zanzibar v British Aerospace Ltd** [2000] 1 WLR 2333, it was strongly suggested that, if the right to rescind was lost, the right to damages under s.2(2) was also lost. Judge Jack QC thought that damages under s.2(2) should be awarded where this was more equitable than rescission and so an award of damages under s.2(2) was therefore dependent upon the right to rescind still being available. In the case of a negligent misrepresentation, the right to damages under s.2(1) would of course still be available even if the right to rescind had been lost.

It is only very rarely that a court does award damages under s.2(2). When such damages are awarded they will be assessed on a contract basis. That is to say that they will attempt to put the parties into the position which they would have been in if the misrepresentation had not been untrue. They will therefore be the difference in value between the contract price paid and what the price would have been if the misrepresentation had been true. Consequential losses will not be taken into account. In **William Sindell plc v Cambridgeshire County Council** [1994] 3 All ER 932 the Court of Appeal considered s.2(2). In 1988 a building company had bought land from the Council for £5 million. The council had stated that they did not know of any matter likely to affect the use and enjoyment of the land. The sale was concluded in March 1989. Building work started 18 months later but by this time the land was only worth about £2.5 million as the property market had collapsed. In October 1990 the builders found a nine inch foul sewer which had been under the land since 1970. The trial

judge found that there had been a misrepresentation and allowed the builders to rescind the contract. The Court of Appeal (on a matter of land law which does not concern us) found that there had been no misrepresentation. However, the Court of Appeal went on to state that if there had been a wholly innocent misrepresentation then rescission would not have been allowed but instead damages would have been awarded under s.2(2). These damages would either have been the cost of remedying the defect or the lesser amount the land would have been worth at the time of the contract if the defect had been known. In reaching this decision the court considered that rescission would have been inappropriate because it would have meant the Council having to repay £8 million (the purchase price plus interest) for land that was currently worth about £2 million.

When damages are awarded under s.2(2) in a case of negligent misrepresentation these damages should be deducted from any amount awarded under s.2(1).

In the previous chapter, at 5.6.1.7, we examined the circumstances in which liability for misrepresentation can be excluded.

Figure 6.1 shows an outline of the different types of misrepresentations and the different remedies available for each.

Test your understanding 6.2

1 What is the definition of a fraudulent misrepresentation?

2 In what circumstances will a non-fraudulent misrepresentation be (i) negligent and (ii) wholly innocent?

3 What remedies are available in respect of a fraudulent misrepresentation?

4 What remedies are available in respect of a negligent misrepresentation?

5 What remedies are available in respect of a wholly innocent misrepresentation?

6 In what circumstances can damages be awarded under s.2(2) of the Misrepresentation Act 1967? How will these damages be assessed?

7 In what circumstances will the right to rescind the contract for misrepresentation be lost?

	Fraudulent	Negligent	Wholly innocent
Definition	Made (1) Knowing that it was false. (2) Without belief in its truth. (3) Recklessly careless whether true or false (*Derry* v *Peek*). Dishonesty must be proved	Injured party must prove defendant made an actionable misrepresentation The misrepresentation will be negligent *unless* the defendant can prove (i) he did believe misrepresentation was true (ii) with reasonable grounds for such a belief. Misrepresentation Act 1967 s.2(1)	Injured party must prove defendant made an actionable misrepresentation The misrepresentation will be wholly innocent *if* the defendant can prove (i) he did believe misrepresentation was true (ii) with reasonable grounds for such a belief. Misrepresentation Act 1967 s.2(1)
Remedies	A right to rescind. (Time does not run until fraud discovered.) + Damages for the tort of deceit	Usually rescission. (But contract damages might be awarded in lieu – s.2(2) Misrepresentation Act 1967.) + Damages on tort of deceit basis	Usually rescission. (But contract damages might be awarded in lieu – s.2(2) Misrepresentation Act 1967.) No right to damages

Rescission

Contract is affirmed ← lost if → Parties cannot be restored to pre-contract position

Third party has acquired rights

Figure 6.1 The types of actionable misrepresentations and the remedies available

6.2 MISTAKE

In certain circumstances a contract may be void for mistake, in which case it will be a nullity. No legal rights will then be conferred upon the parties. Where goods are sold under a contract void for mistake ownership of the goods will not pass to the buyer. The buyer will therefore be able to recover any of the price paid on the grounds that there has been a total failure of consideration on the part of the seller. When we considered *Lewis* v *Averay*, earlier in this chapter, at 6.1.3.1, we saw that the innocent third party became the absolute owner of the car because he had bought it before the contract with the rogue had been avoided. The claimant, who had sold the car to the rogue, argued that the contract was void for mistake, rather than merely voidable for misrepresentation. If the contract had been void for mistake then the rogue would never have acquired any title to the car at all and he could not therefore have passed any title to the innocent third party. The claimant would have been entitled to regain possession of his car as it would all the time have belonged to him. Nor would it have mattered if the claimant had not realised that the contract was void for some considerable time, or if the car had been damaged and was no longer in the same condition as when sold. The bars to rescission, which apply when a contract is voidable, have no application if the contract is void. As a contract which is void for mistake is a nullity, no contractual obligations arise under it and no property passes as a result of it.

There are several different ways in which the parties to a contract might be labouring under a fundamental mistake. Some of these have no effect at all on the validity of the contract, others make the contract void.

It is convenient when considering mistake to consider first the position where both parties make the same mistake (common mistake), then the position where the offeror thinks the contract is made on one set of terms while the offeree thinks it is made on another (mutual mistake) and finally the position where only one of the parties makes a mistake (unilateral mistake).

6.2.1 Common mistake

When a common mistake occurs the parties to the contract do reach agreement, but they do so while both making the same fundamental mistake. Such a mistake can make the contract void, although it will not necessarily do so. The mistake which the parties make might be about the existence of the subject matter of the contract, the ownership of the subject matter or the quality of the subject matter. Each of these three possibilities needs to be considered in turn.

6.2.1.1 Mistake as to the existence of the subject matter

If, unknown to either of the parties, the subject matter of the contract does not exist at the time when the contract is made then the contract can be void for mistake.

Scott v *Coulson* [1903] 2 Ch 439

A contract for the sale of a life policy of assurance was made. At the time of the sale both parties thought that the assured person was alive. In fact the assured person was dead at the time of the contract.

Held. The contract was void for mistake.

Section 6 of the Sale of Goods Act 1979 provides that where there is a contract for the sale of specific goods and the goods without the knowledge of the seller have perished at the time when the contract is made, the contract is void. There is some doubt about the matter but it seems likely that s.6 would also apply where the goods had never existed. However, this would not be the case if the seller had promised that the goods did exist because the seller would then have assumed the risk of the goods not existing. Section 7 of the Sale of Goods Act 1979 provides that where specific goods cease to exist after the contract was made, but before the risk passes to the buyer, the contract is frustrated and therefore avoided. Both of these sections are examined in some detail at 9.1.1.1.

A contract might well stipulate that one or other party bears the risk of the subject matter not existing, and if this is the case the contract will be valid even if the subject matter did not in fact exist. For example, if X hears that Y's warehouse has suffered a major fire he could validly contract to buy from Y any stock in the warehouse which had survived the fire. If it was later shown that all of the stock had been burnt the contract would not be void for mistake. It might also be possible to find that one party had impliedly assumed the risk of the subject matter not existing. This was emphasised repeatedly in *Great Peace Shipping Ltd* v *Tsavliris Salvage International Ltd* [2002] EWCA Civ 1407, [2002] 3 WLR 1617 (Court of Appeal). Lord Phillips MR, giving the only judgment of the Court of Appeal, said at para. 75: 'Just as the doctrine of frustration only applies if the contract contains no provision that covers the situation, the same should be true of common mistake. If, on true construction of the contract, a party warrants that the subject matter exists, or that it will be possible to perform the contract, there will be no scope to hold the contract void on the ground of common mistake . . .'

6.2.1.2 Mistake as to ownership

If a seller of property does not in fact own the property at the time when it is sold then it is possible that the contract will be void for mistake. First, however, we should notice that the contract will not be void for mistake if the contract is for the sale of goods and the seller expressly or impliedly warrants that he does own the goods. In the previous chapter we mentioned s.12 of the Sale of Goods Act 1979, which states that in a contract of sale of goods there is an implied condition on the part of the seller that he has a right to sell the goods. (This matter is explored further in Chapter 8 at 8.2.1.) We also saw that SGITA 1973 and SGSA 1982 imply similar terms into contracts of hire-purchase, contracts of hire and contracts under which the property in goods is to pass. These terms as to the right to sell cannot be excluded by any contract term, and if they are breached the seller will be in breach of contract. However, these implied terms as to the right to sell do not apply where the terms of the contract, or the circumstances, show an intention that the seller should transfer only such title as he or a third party might have.

Mistake as to ownership is therefore only capable of making the contract void at common law where the contract is not one into which a statute implies a term that the seller has the right to sell. Such situations are relatively rare as one or other of the statutes will imply the term whenever ownership or possession of goods are transferred under a contract. However, an example can be seen in *Cooper v Phibbs* (1867) LR 2 HL 149. A agreed to take a lease of a fishery from B, but unknown to both parties A was already the tenant for life of the fishery and B had no ownership of it at all. The House of Lords held that the contract was voidable in equity. In *Bell v Lever Bros* [1932] AC 161 Lord Atkin thought that the case was correctly decided, except that the contract should have been void rather than voidable and it is now generally accepted that this view of the case is correct.

6.2.1.3 **Mistake as to quality**

It is unlikely that a common mistake as to the quality of what is being sold will have any effect upon the contract.

Bell v Lever Bros
[1932] AC 161 (House of Lords)

In 1926 Lever Bros renewed Bell's contract of employment. The renewed contract was to run for five years and Bell was to be paid £8 000 a year. In 1929 Lever Bros wanted to make Bell redundant. A contract was entered into, giving Bell £30 000 as compensation for the early termination of his contract. In fact Bell could have been dismissed without the payment of any compensation because he had in the past broken his contract of employment by speculating in the employer's business. At the time of the making of the redundancy agreement Lever Bros were not aware that Bell had broken the company rules. The jury found that at the time of making the redundancy agreement Bell had either forgotten that he had broken the company's rules or did not appreciate that this breach could have caused him to be dismissed without paying any compensation.

Held. The mistake did not make the contract void.

Lord Atkin: 'A mistake [as to quality] will not affect assent unless it is the mistake of both parties, and is as to the existence of some quality which makes the thing without the quality essentially different from the thing as it was believed to be. Of course it may appear that the parties contracted that the article should possess the quality which one or other or both mistakenly believed it to possess. But in such cases there is a contract and the inquiry is a different one, being whether the contract as to the quality amounts

to a condition or a warranty, a different branch of the law ... A buys B's horse; he thinks the horse is sound and he pays the price of a sound horse; he would certainly not have bought the horse if he had known, as the fact is, that the horse is unsound. If B has made no representation as to soundness and has not contracted that the horse is sound, A is bound and cannot recover back the price. A buys a picture from B; both A and B believe it to be the work of an old master, and a high price is paid. It turns out to be a modern copy. A has no remedy in the absence of a representation or warranty.'

COMMENT (i) The House of Lords only reached this decision by a majority of 3 : 2. The Court of Appeal had held that the contract was void for mistake.

(ii) What was being bought were Bell's rights under his contract of employment. Both parties were mistaken as to the quality of these rights. They both thought that they were worth somewhere in the region of £30 000. In fact they were worth nothing.

In *Solle v Butcher* [1950] 1 KB 671 the Court of Appeal held that a mistake as to quality could render a contract voidable in certain circumstances. *Solle v Butcher* was overruled by the following case.

Great Peace Shipping Ltd v Tsavliris Salvage International Ltd [2002] EWCA Civ 1407, [2002] 3 WLR 1617 (Court of Appeal)

A ship, the *Cape Providence*, suffered structural damage in the South Indian Ocean. The defendants offered salvage services which were accepted by the ship's owners. The defendants found a salvage tug which would take five or six days to reach the ship. However, it was feared that the ship might have sunk by then so the defendants looked for a ship in the vicinity of the *Cape Providence*. A reliable source told the defendants that the claimant's ship, the *Great Peace*, was the closest and could reach the *Cape Providence* in about 12 hours. The defendants therefore made a contract under which the *Great Peace* was to supply salvage services and save the lives of the crew of the *Cape Providence*. The contract was to run for a minimum of five days. At the time of the contract the defendants thought that the two ships were 35 miles apart, whereas in fact they were 410 miles apart. It would have taken the *Great Peace* 39 hours to reach the *Cape Providence*. When the defendants found out about the mistake they told the claimants that they wanted to cancel the contract but not until they had found out if there was a closer ship which could

→

provide salvage. A few hours later they found such a ship and cancelled the contract with the claimants. At first instance Toulson J found that the defendants were in breach of contract. The defendants appealed on two counts. First, they argued that the contract was void at common law on the grounds of common mistake. Second, they argued that the contract was voidable in equity.

Held. The appeal was dismissed. (i) Contracts cannot be voidable in equity for common mistake. If there was such a rule it would amount to saying that the common law was wrong, rather than of adding to or mitigating the effect of the common law. The role of Equity is to supplement the common law, see Chapter 1 at 1.2.2. (ii) The mistake as to the position of the *Great Peace* did not mean that the services which the *Great Peace* was to provide was something essentially different than what the parties had contracted for. If the closer salvage ship had not been discovered, the defendants would have wanted the contract to be performed. It was not impossible to perform the commercial venture which had been agreed.

Lord Phillips MR, giving the only judgment of the Court of Appeal, classified the mistake in this case as a common mistake such as occurred in **Bell v Lever Brothers**. The decision in **Solle v Butcher** was not reconcilable with **Bell v Lever Bros** and was therefore overruled. There is no equitable doctrine of common mistake. The law on common mistake did not arise on account of an implied term. (That the parties had impliedly agreed that in the circumstances which actually arose the contract should not be binding.) Rather, it arose from a rule of law that if the parties had agreed to do something which is impossible to perform, no contract would arise. However, by impossible to perform this did not mean literally impossible, but rather that 'it was impossible to perform the contractual adventure'. The true question was whether the mistake as to the distance apart of the two ships had the effect that the services which the *Great Peace* was in a position to provide 'were something essentially different from that to which the parties had agreed'. The Court of Appeal decided that they were not, particularly as the contract was not cancelled until a closer salvage ship had been found. Emphasising the common history of common mistake and frustration, Lord Phillips stressed that the doctrine of common mistake could not arise if one of the parties had assumed the risk that the subject matter existed or that it would be possible to perform the commercial venture. Nor could it arise where one of the parties had caused the non-existence of the subject matter or the impossibility of performing the commercial

venture. Generally, construction of the contract would indicate that one of the parties had assumed the risk and this was probably why there were so few cases where a common mistake rendered a contract void.

COMMENT Following this decision contracts will very rarely be void for common mistake. First, the courts will look hard for express or implied terms which allocate the risk. Second, the circumstances in which the contract will be essentially different from what was agreed will be rarely found. This is perhaps fortunate because, once the parties have begun to perform a contract which they take to be valid, the consequences of a court declaring the contract void can be very complicated.

6.2.2 Mutual mistake

The parties are said to have made a mutual mistake when they are at cross purposes, so that there never was any real agreement. The offer relates to one thing and it is accepted in the belief that it relates to a quite different thing. If the reasonable man could not infer that the view of either the offeror or the offeree were objectively what was intended, then the contract can be void for mistake. However, if the reasonable man could objectively infer that either meaning reflected the objective intention of the parties then there will be a good contract on these terms.

Raffles v Wichelhaus (1864) 2 H & C 906

There was a contract for the sale of cotton which was to arrive at Liverpool on the ship *Peerless* from Bombay. In fact two ships called *Peerless* sailed from Bombay to Liverpool. The defendant was thinking of the *Peerless* which set off in October. The claimant was thinking of the *Peerless* which set off in December.

Held. There was no binding contract because there was no *consensus ad idem*, meaning that the parties never reached agreement.

COMMENT (i) If the circumstances had objectively indicated that the parties' intention was that the cotton should be carried on either of the two ships, then there would have been a contract for the sale of cotton to be carried on that ship.

(ii) A modern application of this case can be seen in **South East Windscreens Ltd v Jamshidi and Poor** [2005] EWHC 3322, [2005] All ER (D) 317 (Dec). The →

claimant company sold its windscreen repair business to the defendants. The terms of the agreement were never written down. Both sides had very different views of what had been agreed and it was not possible for the court to decide objectively what had been agreed. As neither side could prove, on a balance of probabilities, that its view of what had been agreed was correct, there was no *consensus ad idem* and no contract.

6.2.3 **Unilateral mistake**

A unilateral mistake occurs where only one of the parties makes a mistake. It is possible that a unilateral mistake as to either the identity of the other contracting party, or as to the terms of the contract, can render an agreement void.

6.2.3.1 **Mistake as to identity**

Mistake as to the identity of the other contracting party is generally important when that party turns out to be a rogue who pays with a bad cheque while pretending to be someone else. Earlier in this chapter, at 6.1.3.1, we examined *Lewis v Averay* (1972) and saw that such contracts are voidable for fraudulent misrepresentation. But we also saw that if the rogue sells the goods on to an innocent third party before the contract is avoided the third party will gain complete ownership of the goods by virtue of s.23 of the Sale of Goods Act 1979. In *Lewis v Averay* the claimant argued that the contract was void for mistake. This argument failed. If it had succeeded the defendant, to whom the rogue sold, would not have gained ownership of the car.

First, we consider the situation where the two contracting parties made a written contract without meeting face to face. Here the contract can be void for mistake, but only if the contracting party claiming mistake was mistaken as to the identity of the other party. It is not enough that he was mistaken merely as to the attributes of the other party. The following two cases demonstrate the difference between a mistake as to identity and a mistake as to attributes.

Cundy v Lindsay
(1878) 3 App Cas 459 (House of Lords)

Blenkarn, a rogue, hired a room at 37 Wood Street, Cheapside. From this address he wrote to the claimants, who were linen manufacturers in Belfast. In the letter Blenkarn ordered handkerchiefs and he disguised his signature so that it looked like Blenkiron & Co., a highly respectable firm which carried on business at 123 Wood Street. The claimants sent a large quantity of linen goods to 'Messrs. Blenkiron & Co, 37, Wood Street, Cheapside'. Blenkarn sold the goods obtained to different purchasers. He sold 250 dozen handkerchiefs to the defendants, who bought them in good faith and who resold them in the ordinary course of their trade. The claimants sued the defendants for the tort of conversion. This action would only be successful if the contract between the claimants and the rogue was void for mistake.

Held. There was no contract between the claimants and the rogue. The contract was void for mistake because the claimants were mistaken as to the identity of the person with whom they were dealing. Consequently, the defendants were liable in the tort of conversion.

Kings Norton Metal Co Ltd v Edridge, Merrett & Co Ltd (1897) 14 TLR 98 (Court of Appeal)

A rogue called Wallis ordered goods from the claimants, who were metal manufacturers in Worcestershire. The letter appeared to come from Hallam & Co, Soho Hackle Pin and Wire Works, Sheffield. No such firm ever existed but the rogue's letter was very impressive. It showed a factory with a large number of chimneys and indicated that there were offices in Belfast, Lille and Ghent. The claimants sent goods to the rogue on credit. The rogue sold the goods which he had obtained on to the defendants, who bought them in good faith. The claimants sued the defendants for the conversion of the goods.

Held. The contract was not void for mistake. The claimants were not mistaken as to the identity of the person with whom they were dealing but only as to his attributes. They made the contract with the writer of the letter. As the contract between the claimants and the rogue was a good one, the defendants were not liable to the claimants in conversion.

COMMENT (i) A person's attributes concern his qualities or features. In this case the claimants thought they were dealing with a creditworthy, respectable buyer. In fact they were dealing with a dishonest rogue. The attributes which they ascribed to the buyer (creditworthiness and respectability) were not in fact held by him. This was not enough to make the contract void. In *Cundy v Lindsay* the claimants had knowledge of Blenkiron & Son. They were convinced that they were dealing with this firm and were therefore mistaken as to the identity of the person with whom they actually dealt. The contract was therefore void for mistake. Not everyone agrees that there is a difference between identity and attributes. Lord Denning, in **Lewis v Averay**, called it 'a distinction without a difference'. Others have argued that a person's name not only identifies him but is also one of his attributes. Despite these arguments, the distinction remains the deciding factor when the parties do not meet face to face.

(ii) The contract, like all the other cases where a rogue buys goods with a bad cheque, would of course have been voidable for fraudulent misrepresentation. But this will not help the party selling to the rogue if the rogue sells the goods on to an innocent third party before the first contract is avoided.

(iii) In all of these cases the rogue could be sued by the innocent party for the tort of deceit. However, rogues are hard to trace and when they are traced they very rarely have the means to pay damages.

(iv) In **Shogun Finance Ltd v Hudson (FC)** [2003] UKHL 62, [2003] 3 WLR 1371 (see below) the two dissenting Law Lords, Lords Millett and Nicholls, thought that **Cundy v Lindsay** should be overruled. The majority, Lords Hobhouse, Phillips and Walker, did not.

Where the parties do meet face to face a mistake as to the person will not make a contract void.

Phillips v Brooks [1919] 2 KB 243

A rogue called North entered the claimant's jeweller's shop and selected pearls at a price of £2 550 and a ring at £450. He wrote a cheque and said, 'You see who I am, Sir George Bullough', and gave an address in St James's Square. The rogue said that he had better not take the pearls until the cheque was cleared but that he would take the ring immediately as it was his wife's birthday the following day. The jeweller checked Sir George's address in a directory and then let the rogue take the ring away. The rogue, now calling himself Firth, pledged the ring to the defendant, a pawnbroker, for £350. The defendant acted in good faith.

Held. The contract was not void for mistake. The jeweller dealt with the person who came into the shop. Consequently, the defendant had a good title to the ring.

COMMENT A 1960 Court of Appeal case, **Ingram v Little** [1961] 1 QB 31, had indicated that in these circumstances a contract could be void for mistake.

In **Lewis v Averay** in 1972 the Court of Appeal confirmed the correctness of the decision in **Phillips v Brooks**. In **Shogun Finance Ltd v Hudson (FC)** (see below) all five Law Lords considered **Phillips v Brooks** and **Lewis v Averay** to be correctly decided.

In the following case the House of Lords gave the authorities on mistake as to the person a very thorough review.

Shogun Finance Ltd v Hudson (FC)
[2003] UKHL 62, [2003] 3 WLR 1371
(House of Lords)

Hudson, the defendant, bought a Mitsubishi Shogun car from a rogue. The rogue had taken the car on hire-purchase from the claimant finance company, Shogun Finance Ltd. He had persuaded the finance company to enter into the hire-purchase agreement by pretending to be one Durlabh Patel, living at an address in Leicester. The rogue had visited a dealer who had the car in his showroom and had produced Durlabh Patel's driving licence, which he had improperly obtained. The dealer got the rogue to fill in one of Shogun Finance Ltd's standard hire-purchase forms, which the rogue did in the name of Durlabh Patel. The dealer then phoned through to Shogun Finance Ltd the details put on the form and also faxed through a copy of the agreement and a copy of Durlabh Patel's driving licence. Having checked the credit rating of Durlabh Patel by computer, the finance company telephoned the dealer and told him to let the rogue have the car. The rogue paid a 10 per cent deposit, only part of which was paid in cash, and drove the car away. If the contract between Shogun Finance Ltd and the rogue was a valid contract of hire-purchase, then the defendant would become owner of the car by virtue of s.27 of the Hire Purchase Act 1964. (The effect of s.27 is set out in Chapter 9 at 9.3.6.) If there was no contract between Shogun Finance Ltd and the rogue, then the defendant could not become owner of the car. The crucial question therefore was whether or not the rogue entered into a valid contract with Shogun Finance Ltd.

Held. (Lords Nicholls and Millett dissenting). There was no contract between the rogue and the finance company and so the defendant had no title to the car. The claimant, Shogun Finance Ltd, had remained owner of the car throughout.

Lord Hobhouse saw significance in the fact that the hire-purchase agreement was a written contract to provide credit. Unlike a sale of goods, where property might well have passed before the time for payment arrived (see Chapter 9 at 9.1.1), in a contract where a credit check is made no contract comes into existence until the credit check has been satisfactorily conducted. The language in the written contract made it plain that Shogun Finance Ltd intended only to make the contract with 'the customer named overleaf'. Therefore, only Durlabh Patel, and not the rogue or anyone else, could have validly made the contract. Durlabh Patel obviously did not make the contract. There was no true agreement between Shogun Finance Ltd and the rogue because Shogun Finance Ltd believed it was accepting an offer from Durlabh Patel, and the rogue had no honest belief or contractual intent whatsoever. The contract was not made face to face because the dealer was not the agent of Shogun Finance Ltd for the purposes of making the contract. Therefore, the principle in **Lewis v Averay** was not applicable. This contract was not a face to face sale of goods, but concerned the construction of a written contract to provide credit.

Lord Phillips approved **Cundy v Lindsay**. He thought that where there was some form of personal contact between parties conducting negotiations there should be a strong presumption that the parties intended to deal with each other. But he thought that there was no need for such a presumption where the dealings were conducted exclusively in writing.

Lord Walker concurred with the speech of Lord Hobhouse. He thought that the face to face principle in **Lewis v Averay** might be extended to the situation where the parties made the contract on the phone. However, he did not think it could cover a case where the contract was formed by written communication by post or email.

Lord Nicholls gave a strong dissenting judgment, indicating that **Cundy v Lindsay** should be overruled, in favour of the approach adopted in **Lewis v Averay**. He did not think that there should be a distinction between cases where the rogue and the seller met face to face and those where they did not. He thought that Shogun Finance Ltd, believing that the person in the dealer's showroom was Durlabh Patel, intended to make the contract with the person in the showroom. If this had not been the case, they would not have let the person in the showroom take the car away.

Lord Millett thought that there should be no distinction between cases where the parties met face to face and those where they did not. He thought that **Cundy v Lindsay** should be overruled and that there was a voidable contract between Shogun Finance Ltd and the rogue.

COMMENT (i) This decision seems to have left the existing authorities unaltered but the fundamental split in the opinions of the Law Lords suggests that the matter has not been finally resolved.

(ii) It might seem surprising that the dealer was not the agent of Shogun Finance Ltd, when making the contract. However, in **Branwhite v Worcester Works Finance Ltd** [1969] 1 AC 552 the House of Lords held that in a triangular transaction such as this (see Chapter 14 at 14.2.2) the dealer is not normally the agent of the finance company when making the contract. However, the dealer does act as the finance company's agent when making delivery of the car to the rogue.

A mistake as to the person can only make the contract void if the mistake was of fundamental importance to the person who made it and if the mistake was known to the other contracting party. In **Mackie v European Assurance Society** (1869) 21 LT 102 the claimant asked a friend to take out an insurance policy on his behalf. The claimant believed that the contract was being made with a certain insurance society but in fact the friend made it with the defendant society. When sued on the policy, the defendants argued that this mistake as to identity meant that the contract was void. The contract was held to be valid because the identity of the insurers did not matter to the claimant.

6.2.3.2 Mistake as to the terms of the contract

If one of the parties knows that the other made the contract on the strength of a fundamental mistake as to the terms of the contract then the contract can be void for mistake.

Hartog v Colin & Shields
[1939] 3 All ER 566

The defendants agreed to sell the claimants 30 000 Argentine hare skins. When selling large quantities, hare skins were either sold per piece (per skin) or per pound, there being roughly three pieces in a pound. The defendants mistakenly offered the skins at a certain price per pound whereas they meant to offer them at this price per piece. The claimants accepted the offer. All the earlier negotiations had been conducted on a per piece basis and Argentine hare skins are generally sold per piece.

Held. There was no contract. The claimants could not reasonably have supposed that the offer expressed the true intention of the defendants and must have known that it was made by mistake.

→

Singleton J: 'I am satisfied that it was a mistake on the part of the defendants or their servants which caused the offer to go forward in that way, and I am satisfied that anyone with knowledge of the trade must have realised that there was a mistake.'

The following case is different because the buyer was not mistaken about the fundamental terms of the contract, but only as to the quality of what he was buying.

Smith v Hughes (1871) LR 6 QB 597

The defendant, a racehorse trainer, bought oats from the defendant, a farmer. The defendant had shown a sample of the oats to the claimant who agreed to pay 34s per quarter. The claimant thought that the oats were old oats, whereas in fact they were new oats. Oats were very scarce at the time, but even so 34s a quarter was a very high price for new oats.

Held. The contract was not void for mistake, even if the claimant knew that the defendant thought he was buying old oats.

Cockburn CJ: 'The question is whether . . . the passive acquiescence of the seller in the self-deception of the buyer will entitle the latter to avoid the contract. I am of opinion that it will not.'

COMMENT If the seller had warranted that the oats were old oats then the outcome would have been different. There would have been a valid contract for the sale of old oats, which could not be performed by delivering new oats. This case differs from *Bell v Lever Bros* and *Great Peace Shipping* in that only one of the parties was mistaken as to the quality of the subject matter of the contract. This was a case of unilateral, not common, mistake.

6.2.4 *Non est factum* (It is not my deed)

If one of the parties signs a document whilst under a complete misapprehension as to its effect then the contract may be void on the grounds of *non est factum*.

Saunders v Anglia Building Society
[1970] AC 1004 (House of Lords)

Mrs Gallie intended to leave her house to her nephew, Parkin, after her death but to remain in the house for the rest of her life. A friend of Parkin's, Lee, visited Mrs Gallie. In Parkin's presence Lee presented a document to Mrs Gallie for signature. Lee told Mrs Gallie that the document gave the house to Parkin. Mrs Gallie

believed this and as her spectacles were broken she signed the document without reading it. In fact the document said that the house had been assigned to Lee and that he had paid for it. Lee then used the document to obtain a mortgage from a building society. Lee did not pay the mortgage instalments and the building society applied to repossess the house.

Held. The plea of *non est factum* was not available to Mrs Gallie because there was not a fundamental difference between what she signed and what she thought she signed. Either way the document was an assignment of her interest in the house.

The plea of *non est factum* will not be available to a person who was careless in signing the document.

A person who signs a blank document is likely to be regarded as having been careless if incorrect figures are subsequently filled in (**United Dominions Trust Ltd v Western** [1976] QB 513 (Court of Appeal)).

A plea of *non est factum* is only rarely successful. An example of a case in which it was successful is provided by **Foster v Mackinnon** (1869) LR 4 CP 704. An old man with feeble eyesight was tricked into signing a bill of exchange because he was told that it was a guarantee. The old man was not liable on the bill because he was completely mistaken as to its effect and he had not been careless in signing.

Test your understanding 6.3

1. What is the effect of a contract being held to be void for mistake?

2. The parties to a contract make a common mistake when they both make the same mistake. As to what three matters might this mistake be made? Could all three matters make the contract void?

3. The parties to a contract make a mutual mistake when they are at cross purposes so that there is never any real agreement. In what circumstances will such a mistake render the contract void?

4. When a unilateral mistake is made only one of the parties makes a mistake. As to what two matters might a unilateral mistake be made?

5. In what circumstances will a mistake as to the identity of the other contracting party make a contract void?

6. In what circumstances will a mistake as to the terms of the contract make a contract void?

7. In what circumstances will *non est factum* make a contract void?

6.3 DURESS AND UNDUE INFLUENCE

Historically, the common law would hold a contract voidable for duress only if the contract was entered into as a result of the threat of unlawful physical violence. A threat to goods was not enough. In recent years a doctrine of economic duress has taken hold, under which a contract becomes voidable by a person who was coerced into making it in such a way that he did not really consent. If one of the parties to the contract exerted undue influence over the other the contract may be voidable in equity. The basis of both duress and undue influence is that one of the parties gave no real consent to the contract.

6.3.1 Duress

Traditionally, the common law only rendered a contract voidable on the grounds of duress if the contract was entered into on account of illegal physical violence or the threat of it. Such cases rarely come before the courts. If the victim is sufficiently frightened to enter a contract against his will, he almost always remains sufficiently frightened not to go to court to argue that the contract is voidable.

In recent years the doctrine of duress has become considerably wider as 'economic duress' has come to be recognised. Many types of economic duress are perfectly valid. For example, if a buyer knows that the seller must sell goods immediately in order to raise cash, then this knowledge might well allow him to buy the goods more cheaply than would otherwise be the case. However, this knowledge would not affect the validity of the contract entered into. In *Occidental Worldwide Investment Corporation* v *Skibs A/S Avanti (The Sibeon and the Sibotre)* [1976] 1 Lloyd's Rep 293 Kerr J rejected a claim of economic duress because, although there was commercial pressure, there was nothing under the law which could be regarded as 'a coercion of will so as to vitiate consent'. This last phrase has been adopted in several later cases as the definition of duress and so its meaning is worth clarifying. A person who is coerced into doing something is pushed into doing it, without regard to his wishes. If consent is vitiated it is destroyed so that consent does not really exist. So we might say that a person has entered a contract on account of duress where he has been pushed into the agreement in such a way that he did not really consent to it. Kerr J was merely putting the matter more succinctly when he said there must have been 'a coercion of will so as to vitiate consent'.

North Ocean Shipping Co Ltd v Hyundai Construction Co Ltd, the Atlantic Baron [1979] QB 705

A shipbuilding company agreed to build a ship for a certain price in US dollars, payment to be made in five instalments. The shipbuilding company agreed to open letters of credit so that the buyers could get their instalments back if the contract was not performed properly. After the first instalment had been paid the US dollar was devalued by 10 per cent. The shipbuilding company demanded that the remaining instalments be increased by 10 per cent. The buyers refused, paying the second and third instalments without the additional 10 per cent. These instalments were returned. The shipbuilding company set a certain date and said that if the extra money was not paid by this date they would terminate the contract. The buyers needed the ship as they were negotiating to charter it out, very profitably, to a third party. They therefore agreed to pay the extra money 'without prejudice' and asked that there should be corresponding increases in the letters of credit. The shipbuilding company agreed to this in June 1973 and so the buyers paid the last instalment, including the extra 10 per cent, without protest. The ship was delivered in November 1974. Only in June 1975 did the shipbuilders know that the buyers were claiming the return of the extra 10 per cent paid in the last four instalments plus interest.

Held. The agreement of June 1973 was voidable for economic duress. However, the buyers had affirmed the contract by making the final payment without protest and by delaying making their claim until July 1975.

COMMENT (i) As duress, economic duress and undue influence can only make a contract voidable, rather than void, the right to avoid can be lost by affirmation, inability to restore the parties to their pre-contract position or the acquisition of rights by third parties. In *Halpern v Halpern* [2006] EWHC 1728 (Comm), [2006] 3 All ER 1139 it was held that, even though duress is a common law action, a party who is unable to substantially restore the pre-contract position cannot avoid the contract. The bars to rescission were considered above, at 6.1.3.1, in relation to misrepresentation. In *Halpern v Halpern (No. 2)* [2007] EWCA Civ 291, [2007] 3 WLR 849, it was argued that a contract could not be avoided for duress by a person who could not give the other party substantial restitution. The Court of Appeal held that this was not necessarily so. Rescission for duress should be the →

same as rescission for misrepresentation, and the extent to which counter restitution was necessary would depend on all the circumstances of the case.

(ii) The case also raised the question of consideration. Had the shipbuilding company provided any additional consideration in return for the extra money? It was held that they had, in that they had increased their letters of credit by 10 per cent, something which the original contract did not require them to do.

In *Pao On v Lau Yiu Long* [1980] AC 614 (Privy Council) Scarman LJ identified four matters to be taken into account in assessing whether or not economic duress had taken place. These four matters are as follows. Did the person claiming to have been coerced protest? Did that person have any other available course of action, such as a legal remedy? Was he independently advised? After entering the contract did he take steps to avoid it?

If the victim protested this would make economic duress more likely, as would the fact that there was no other course of action open to him. If he was independently advised, or if he delayed in taking steps to avoid the contract, these matters would indicate that the contract was not entered into as a result of duress. The effect of the four matters can be seen in the following case.

Universe Tankships of Monrovia v International Transport Workers Federation [1982] 1 AC 366 (House of Lords)

A ship which flew a flag of convenience arrived at Milford Haven. The ITF, a trade union, 'blacked' the ship to prevent it from leaving port because they considered that the wages payable to the crew were too low. The ITF demanded that the shipowners pay $80 000, threatening that if this was not paid the ship could not be allowed to leave port. The owners paid this sum under protest. Part of the $80 000 was paid to a seamen's charity, the Seafarer's International Welfare Fund. Once the ship had sailed out of Milford Haven the shipowners sued to recover the money paid to the charity.

Held. The money was recoverable because the agreement to pay it had been obtained under economic duress.

In general, in order to amount to economic duress the threat must be to do an unlawful act, such as to break a contract, although possibly an immoral lawful act will suffice.

Atlas Express Ltd v Kafco (Importers and Distributors) Ltd [1989] 1 All ER 641

The defendants, Kafco, were a small company which imported basketware and distributed it to retailers. They made a contract with the claimants, a national carrier, under which the claimants were to distribute the basketware to Woolworths shops nationwide. A price of £1.10 per carton was agreed, the claimants' depot manager having estimated that each load would contain a minimum of 400 cartons and maybe as many as 600. The first load contained only 200 cartons and the claimants' depot manager told the defendants that unless they agreed to a minimum payment of £440 per load no more loads would be carried. The defendants agreed to this because they were heavily dependent on the contract with Woolworths and they could find no other carrier. Later the defendants refused to pay the new rate.

Held. The defendants did not have to pay the extra amount. If a person was forced to renegotiate a contract against his will, and had no alternative but to accept the new terms proposed, the consent to the new terms was vitiated by economic duress.

It is possible, although very unlikely, that a threat to perform a lawful act coupled with a demand for payment could amount to economic duress.

CTN Cash and Carry Ltd v Gallagher Ltd [1994] 4 All ER 714 (Court of Appeal)

The claimants, who ran six cash and carry warehouses in the north of England, bought large consignments of cigarettes from the defendants. The defendants arranged credit facilities for the claimants but they were free to withdraw these. By mistake the defendants delivered one consignment of £17 000 worth of cigarettes to the wrong warehouse. It was arranged that the defendants would take the cigarettes to the correct warehouse but before this happened the cigarettes were stolen. The defendants honestly believed that the cigarettes were at the claimants' risk at the time of the theft. (During the trial they discovered that this view was not correct.) The defendants insisted that the claimants pay for the cigarettes. The claimants refused, but then agreed to pay when the defendants made it plain that if they did not do so their credit facilities would be withdrawn. Later the claimants claimed to avoid the agreement to pay the £17 000, on the grounds of economic duress, and sued to get their money back.

Held. The claimants were not entitled to avoid the agreement. Although it is possible that a threat to →

perform a lawful act coupled with a demand for payment might amount to economic duress it would be extremely difficult to succeed in such a claim when the agreement was made between two commercial companies, especially where the person making the demand believed it to be valid.

COMMENT (i) The outcome of the case was described by Steyn LJ as unattractive 'inasmuch as the defendants are allowed to retain a sum which at the trial they became aware was not in truth due to them'. (The rules on the passing of the risk are considered in Chapter 9 at 9.1.4.)

(ii) The Court of Appeal made it plain that it would be highly undesirable if accounts settled in good faith could be reopened once the parties had fallen out with each other.

(iii) In *R v Attorney-General for England and Wales* [2003] UKPC 22, [2003] EMLR 24 considered below, Lord Hoffmann delivered the judgment of the Privy Council and said that the fact that the threat is lawful does not necessarily make the pressure legitimate. He quoted with approval the following example of Lord Atkin's from *Thorne v Motor Trade Association* [1937] AC 797: 'The ordinary blackmailer normally threatens to do what he has a perfect right to do – namely, communicate some compromising conduct to a person whose knowledge is likely to affect the person threatened ... What he has to justify is not the threat, but the demand of money.'

6.3.2 Undue influence

Historically, the limits of duress were very narrow. The courts of equity therefore developed a doctrine of undue influence which can cause either gifts or contracts to be set aside. When considering undue influence a distinction can be drawn between cases where it is presumed and cases where it must be proved.

6.3.2.1 Actual undue influence

A person alleging actual undue influence must prove that he only entered into the contract, or made the gift, on account of undue pressure exerted by the other party. There is no need to prove any type of special relationship or any previous dealings between the parties. In *Williams v Bayley* (1866) LR 1 HL 200, for example, a colliery owner mortgaged his colliery to a bank because the bank indirectly threatened him that if he did not do this his son would be prosecuted for forgery. The House of Lords set the agreement aside because

the colliery owner did not freely and voluntarily enter into it.

The person alleging the undue influence must prove that it was in fact exerted but does not need to show that the agreement consequently entered into was manifestly disadvantageous to him. In *CIBC Mortgages plc v Pitt* [1993] 4 All ER 433 (House of Lords) Lord Browne-Wilkinson said that actual undue influence is a species of fraud and that just as a person who perpetrated a fraud cannot argue that the transaction was beneficial to the person defrauded, so a person exercising actual undue influence cannot argue that the contract was beneficial to the person influenced. The agreement will be set aside (if the wronged party avoids the contract in the correct way) as a matter of justice, because the wrongdoer's conduct prevented the wronged party from exercising free will and a properly informed mind.

Actual undue influence is becoming less important as duress has become easier to establish. The boundaries between duress and actual undue influence are becoming increasingly blurred.

6.3.2.2 Presumed undue influence

Certain types of relationship give rise to an automatic presumption of undue influence. These well-established relationships include those of solicitor and client, doctor and patient, parent and child, guardian and ward, trustee and beneficiary, and religious advisor and disciple. Historically, if the influenced party alleged undue influence and could prove that the contract was manifestly to his disadvantage, the contract would be voidable unless the dominant party could prove that there was no undue influence. In *Allcard v Skinner* (1887) 36 ChD 145, for example, the claimant became a member of a Protestant religious group, the sisterhood of St Mary of the Cross. Over the years the claimant gave £7 000 to the Lady Superior of the Sisterhood. One of the rules of the Sisterhood was that no member should seek outside advice without first getting permission from the Lady Superior. When the claimant left to become a Roman Catholic she would have been able to reclaim such of this money as was left on the grounds of presumed undue influence. (However, the claim was defeated because the claimant did not claim the money until six years after she had left the Sisterhood.)

Following the decision of the House of Lords in *Royal Bank of Scotland v Etridge (No. 2)* [2001] UKHL 44, [2001] 4 All ER 449, the term 'manifest disadvantage' should no longer be used in this context. Instead, the transaction must be one which is not readily explicable by the relationship of the parties. So minor or seemingly normal transactions would not be presumed to have been brought about by undue influence. Lord Nicholls said: 'Something more is needed before the law reverses the burden of proof, something which calls for an explanation. When that something more is present, the greater the disadvantage to the vulnerable person, the more cogent must be the explanation before the presumption will be regarded as rebutted.'

Where the type of relationship is not within those set out in the previous paragraph, undue influence may still be presumed if the influenced party proves as a matter of fact that there existed a relationship of great trust and confidence between himself and the other party. There is no automatic presumption of undue influence between husband and wife, but in several cases a wife has proved that she placed great trust and confidence in her husband. It is also a requirement of presumed undue influence that the victim proves that the contract was not readily explicable by the relationship of the parties. Where a party can prove that the relationship was one of great trust and confidence, and that the contract was not readily explicable by the relationship of the parties, then the court will presume undue influence and it will be up to the other party to disprove that undue influence actually existed. Presumed undue influence can occasionally occur in the relationship between bank and customer, as the following case shows.

Lloyds Bank v Bundy
[1975] QB 326 (Court of Appeal)

The defendant was an elderly farmer. He and his only son had banked with the claimant bank for many years. The son formed a company and opened a company account at the same branch of the bank. In 1966 the farmer mortgaged his farm to the bank for £1 500 in order to guarantee the company's overdraft. The bank's assistant manager and the son visited the defendant and suggested that he sign a further guarantee for £5 000 and a further mortgage of £6 000. After consulting his solicitor the farmer did this in May 1969. In December 1969 the son and the bank's new assistant manager visited the defendant again with a further guarantee of £11 000 and a further charge of £3 500 already written out and ready for the defendant's signature. The defendant signed these because he was told that if he did not his son's business would fail. The son's business did fail and the bank sought to repossess the farmer's only asset, the house which he had mortgaged. The new assistant bank manager said in evidence that the defendant relied on him implicitly to advise him about the transactions as bank manager. The defendant said that he always trusted the assistant manager and sat back and did what the manager said.

Held. The charge and the guarantee executed in December 1969 were set aside. There was such a relationship of confidentiality between the defendant and the bank that the court could intervene to prevent this from being abused. The bank had breached its fiduciary duty of care by not advising the defendant to get independent advice as to the wisdom of what he was doing.

COMMENT Lord Denning MR thought that the contract should be set aside on the grounds of inequality of bargaining power. At one time there did seem to be judicial support for such a theory. In recent years this support has become less marked.

The relationship between banker and customer is not one which usually gives rise to a presumption of undue influence. However, each case must be carefully examined on its facts.

A situation which has come before the courts fairly commonly is that in which a husband exerts undue influence over or makes a misrepresentation to his wife, who then agrees to give the matrimonial home or other assets as a security for a loan which is made to the husband's business. The wife can have the agreement set aside, as against the husband, if either undue influence or misrepresentation is proved. The more difficult question is whether or not she can have the loan set aside against the bank which lent the money.

In *Royal Bank of Scotland* v *Etridge (No. 2)* [2001] UKHL 44, [2001] 4 All ER 449 the House of Lords thoroughly reviewed the situation where a wife charges the matrimonial home by way of security for a loan made to the husband's business. The following points were made.

(1) In undue influence cases the burden of proof will not shift to the dominant party, to prove that there was no undue influence, unless the transaction cannot readily be explained by the relationship of the parties. (The term 'manifest disadvantage' should no longer be used.) Generally, a wife's

guarantee of her husband's business debts should not be regarded as a transaction which, failing proof to the contrary, can be explained only on the basis that it was procured by the husband's undue influence. Such transactions are not to be regarded, as a class, as *prima facie* evidence of the husband having exerted undue influence. However, there will be cases which do call for an explanation.

(2) Where the wife proposes to give her share of the matrimonial home as security for a loan to the husband or his company, the following guidelines apply to the bank and the solicitor acting for the wife:

(i) The bank is put on enquiry whenever a wife stands surety for a husband's debts (or a husband stands surety for a wife's debts). This is the case even if the bank does not know that the parties are cohabiting or that the wife trusts the husband implicitly. If the loan is made to a company it does not matter that the wife is a company officer or shareholder.

(ii) When the bank has been put on enquiry, it only has to take reasonable steps to ensure that the wife understands what she is doing. There is no need for the bank to meet the wife personally. If a solicitor tells the bank that the wife has been properly advised then this will be good enough unless the bank knows that she has not.

(iii) The solicitor should explain why the bank wants the wife to have a solicitor and that this will prevent her from later claiming that her husband pushed her into the agreement or that she did not understand it. As a core minimum the solicitor should make sure that the wife understands: the nature of the documents and their legal effect; the seriousness of the risks involved; that she has a choice not to go ahead; and that she definitely does want to go ahead. All of this should be explained at a face to face meeting without the husband being present and the solicitor should get any information he needs from the bank.

(iv) Except in glaringly obvious cases of the wife being grievously wronged, the solicitor should not refuse to act for the wife because he considers the agreement to be contrary to her best interests.

(v) The solicitor can also act for the bank or the husband, as long as this does not give rise to a conflict of duty or interests.

(vi) Once the bank has been put on enquiry, and is looking for protection from the fact that the wife has been advised by a solicitor, the bank should take the following steps. First, write to the wife telling her to choose a solicitor to act for her and that once she has been legally advised she will not be able to dispute the validity of what she has agreed. She should be told that the solicitor may be the one acting for her husband but that she has the right to choose another. The bank should not proceed until it has received an appropriate response directly from the wife. Second, if the bank does not want to explain the husband's financial affairs directly to the wife, it should make sure that the wife's solicitor has all the financial information to make such an explanation. Third, if the bank suspects that the wife has been misled by the husband or is not entering the transaction of her own free will, it must tell the wife's solicitor why it believes this to be the case. Fourth, the bank should get written confirmation from the wife's solicitor that the previous three matters have been complied with. If the solicitor confirms to the bank that the wife has had explained to her the risks she was running in respect of previous transactions, the bank will be regarded as having discharged its duty regarding these previous transactions.

(3) In future, banks will be put on enquiry every time the relationship between the person providing surety and the debtor is not commercial. The bank must make sure that the guarantor understands the risks of providing surety. If the bank does not do this, it will be deemed to have notice of any claim the guarantor may have that the transaction was entered into on account of undue influence or misrepresentation by the debtor.

Although the judgment talked in terms of husband and wife, it was made plain that it could equally apply to father and daughter, between cohabitees or to any other type of relationship.

In the following case the Privy Council considered both duress and undue influence.

R v Attorney General for England and Wales [2003] UKPC 22, [2003] EMLR 24

R, the appellant, was a former member of the 22 SAS Regiment. He was a member of Bravo Two Zero patrol which had been dropped behind enemy lines during the 1991 Gulf War. Of this patrol three died, one escaped to Syria and four, including R, were captured and tortured. Both the member who escaped and one of the members who had been captured wrote books about the patrol. This angered other members of the patrol and members of the SAS generally, who did not consider the books accurate. It was thought that action should be taken to prevent the future publication of such books. All members of the SAS were balloted on this point and of the 73 per cent who replied 96.8 per cent were in favour of a binding contract to prevent further disclosure. Later all members of the SAS were told that if they did not sign a confidentiality agreement they would be returned to unit, which was generally a punishment for a disciplinary offence or ordered on the grounds of unsuitability for the SAS. In October 1996 R was told to sign the confidentiality agreement or he would be returned to his unit. He asked if he could seek legal representation and was told that he could not. R signed because it was the only way he could stay in the SAS. The contract was straightforward and easy to understand. Two weeks later R decided to leave the Army and he was discharged in April 1997. He went home to New Zealand and in 1998 decided to write his own version of the Bravo Two Zero patrol. The publishers sent a copy of the manuscript to the Ministry of Defence. The Attorney General applied for an injunction to prevent publication and to claim damages and an account of profits. R argued that the agreement he signed was obtained by duress or undue influence, that it was an unconscionable bargain, not supported by consideration and that it was against public policy. The Court of Appeal found that the contract which R had signed was valid and that R was in breach of it. It did not order an injunction preventing publication, but it did order an account of profits and damages. R appealed to the Privy Council.

Held. The Privy Council upheld the Court of Appeal decision. The threat of an unlawful act would generally make a contract voidable for duress. Where, as here, the threatened act was lawful, the contract might yet be voidable for duress, but only if the threat could not be justified. Here the MOD had good reasons for imposing the ban and could regard anyone who would not agree to it as being unsuitable for the SAS. Therefore, the contract was not voidable for duress. (If R had not had a choice, but had been ordered to sign, their Lordships indicated that the outcome might well have been different.) As regards undue influence, and following *Etridge (No. 2)* [1998] 4 All ER 705, the burden of proving that consent was gained by unacceptable means fell on the party alleging this. It was accepted that the Army as an institution, and R's commanding officer as an individual, were able to exercise undue influence over him. But the real question was whether the nature of the transaction was such that it could be inferred that agreement to it had been obtained by an unfair exploitation of that relationship. Their Lordships did not think that the agreement had been so obtained. R's not being able to gain legal advice did not affect the fairness of the transaction. There had been a need to keep matters confidential, R understood the agreement and all a solicitor could have advised him to do was to think about things before signing. He could have made that decision without legal advice.

COMMENT (i) The argument that the agreement was an unconscionable bargain was dismissed in one sentence.

(ii) The Army's consideration was their forbearance from sending him back to his unit, which conferred a practical benefit upon R.

(iii) Lord Scott of Foscote dissented and argued that the contract should have been voidable for undue influence. He thought that the relationship between R and his senior officers meant that undue influence should have been presumed. As no evidence had been introduced to rebut the presumption, and as legal advice had not been available, the contract should have been voidable for undue influence even though none of the senior officers had behaved improperly.

Test your understanding 6.4

1 Historically, in what circumstances would the common law hold a contract voidable for duress?

2 In what circumstances will the common law now hold a contract voidable on account of economic duress?

3 What must a party prove in order to establish actual undue influence? What will be the effect on the contract if this is proved?

4 In what types of relationships is undue influence automatically presumed? What is the effect of this presumption?

5 In what circumstances will undue influence be presumed if the relationship is not one where it is automatically presumed?

6.4 ILLEGAL AND VOID CONTRACTS

A contract may be illegal either at common law or because a statute makes it illegal. The illegality may relate to the nature of the contract itself, or as to the way in which it is performed. If a contract is illegal then it will generally be unenforceable. Certain types of contracts, while not illegal, are void because they contravene public policy.

6.4.1 Contracts illegal at common law

The following types of contracts are illegal at common law because they are contrary to public policy:

6.4.1.1 Contracts tending to promote corruption in public life

An example is provided by *Parkinson* v *College of Ambulance Ltd* [1925] 2 KB 1. The claimant was promised that he would receive a knighthood if he made a donation to a charity. He made the donation but sued for its return when he did not get the knighthood. His action failed because the contract was illegal.

6.4.1.2 Contracts tending to impede the administration of justice

A contract to make sure that a person is not prosecuted would be illegal and void. However, a contract not to pursue a civil action is perfectly valid. (See settling out of court in Chapter 2 at 2.4.)

6.4.1.3 Contracts to trade with enemy nations

In times of war certain nations become enemy nations. A contract to trade with a person voluntarily living in an enemy nation is generally void.

6.4.1.4 Contracts to commit a tort, fraud or crime

A strange example is provided by *Everett* v *Williams* (1725) noted in [1899] 1 QB 826. One highwayman tried to sue another on an agreement to rob a stagecoach. The highwayman failed in this action. (Both the claimant and the defendant were hanged and the solicitors were fined £50 for bringing the case!)

6.4.1.5 Contracts tending to promote sexual immorality

An example is provided by *Pearce* v *Brooks* (1866) LR 1 Ex 213, where a prostitute hired a carriage which the owner knew was to be used for immoral purposes. The prostitute refused to pay for the hire of the carriage but the owner was not allowed to recover the agreed payments.

6.4.1.6 Contracts to defraud the Revenue

If a contract is made to defraud the Revenue then the whole contract is void and a court will not enforce any of its terms.

> ### *Miller* v *Karlinski*
> (1945) 62 TLR 85 (Court of Appeal)
>
> The claimant was employed under an oral contract. He was paid a salary of £10 a week and it was further agreed that the amount of tax which he paid on this salary should be paid to him as 'travelling expenses'. The claimant sued for ten weeks of unpaid wages and also claimed expenses of £21. Of these expenses £4 were genuine travelling expenses, the remaining £17 represented the amount of tax which would have been payable on his wages.
>
> **Held.** The whole agreement was contrary to public policy and the court would therefore enforce no part of it.
>
> **COMMENT** Du Parcq LJ, who gave the only judgment, said that it made no difference whether or not the parties were ignorant that what they were doing was illegal.

6.4.2 Contracts void at common law

Three types of contract are void as contravening public policy. Of the three types, contracts in restraint of trade are far and away the most important. The other two are as follows.

6.4.2.1 Contracts damaging to marriage

Contracts agreeing that one will never marry, and marriage brokage contracts, are void rather than illegal. A marriage brokage contract is one where a third party procures a marriage in return for a consideration.

6.4.2.2 Contracts to oust the jurisdiction of the courts

These contracts are void, rather than illegal. See *Baker v Jones* in Chapter 4 at 4.1.1.1.

6.4.3 Contracts in restraint of trade

It is generally desirable that people should carry on their trade, business or profession without hindrance. Therefore, any contract in restraint of trade is void at common law unless it can be proved to be reasonable between the parties to the contract and reasonable as regards the public interest. The categories of agreements which can be in restraint of trade are not closed, but three particular types of agreement are relatively common.

6.4.3.1 Restraints when a business is sold

It is quite common that the vendor of a business agrees with the purchaser that he will not carry on a competing business after the sale has taken place. Such an agreement will be valid if it is reasonable but will be void if it is unreasonable. Two competing areas of public policy are evident. First, it is public policy that people should work and so in general such agreements should be void. Second, no one is going to buy a business if the vendor would be free to open a competing business next door, so a restraint of trade clause can be valid if it was reasonable. In deciding whether or not the agreed restraint was reasonable the main factors to be considered are the length of time for which the agreement is to run, the geographical area in which the restraint applies, and the types of activity which the contract prohibited.

> **Nordenfelt v *The Maxim Nordenfelt Guns and Ammunition Company Ltd*** [1894] AC 535 (House of Lords)
>
> The defendant had been a manufacturer of military guns and ammunition and had owned patents relating to the business. He sold the patents and the business to the claimants and made a restraint of trade agreement. The agreement was to last for 25 years and prohibited the defendant from trading in or manufacturing guns, gun mountings or carriages, gunpowder, explosives or ammunition. It also prohibited the defendant from working in any business likely to compete with that of the claimant. The defendant later agreed to work for another manufacturer of guns

and ammunition and the claimant sought an injunction to prevent this.

> **Held.** The restraint agreeing not to manufacture guns etc. was valid because it was reasonable. It was not wider than was necessary to protect the claimant company and nor was it detrimental to the interests of the country. The agreement not to work for any business competing with the claimant company was too wide. It was unreasonable and therefore void.

> **COMMENT** It might seem unreasonable to agree not to manufacture guns etc. for such a long period, but a business such as this had very few customers (the Governments of a few wealthy countries).

6.4.3.2 Restraints in a contract of employment

A restraint which prevents an ex-employee from working for competitors will be valid only if it was necessary to protect trade secrets, trade connections or confidential information. Such a restraint will not be upheld merely to prevent the ex-employee from exercising the skills which he learnt in the course of his past employment.

> **Fitch v Dewes** [1921] 2 AC 158 (House of Lords)
>
> The claimant, a solicitor practising at Tamworth, employed the defendant from 1899 to 1914. The defendant worked his way up from junior clerk, to articled clerk to managing clerk. When made managing clerk, on a three year contract, the defendant agreed that he would never 'be engaged or manage or concerned in the office, profession or business of a solicitor, within a radius of seven miles of the Town Hall of Tamworth'. After the termination of his employment the defendant, in 1919, deliberately breached this agreement to test its validity.
>
> **Held.** Even though the agreement was to run for an unlimited period of time it was reasonable. It was not against the public interest and was reasonably necessary to protect the commercial interests of the claimant.

6.4.3.3 Solus agreements

A solus agreement is one by which a person agrees to buy from, or be supplied by, only one supplier. Retailers of petrol commonly make such agreements with the large oil companies. In the leading case, *Esso Petroleum Co Ltd v Harper's Garage (Stourport) Ltd* [1968] AC 269, the claimant, who owned two garages, made a solus agreement with Esso in respect of both garages. In return for a price discount the two garages were to buy only Esso's petrol. As regards the first garage the agreement was to run for four years and five months, as regards the second garage the agreement was to run for 21 years. The House of Lords held that the agreement regarding the first garage was valid because it was reasonable. The agreement regarding the second garage was unreasonable and so it was void.

6.4.3.4 Other situations

There is no closed list of situations in which a contract can be void because it is in restraint of trade. The following case shows that if parties of very unequal bargaining power make a very one-sided agreement, whereby one of them agrees to provide his services exclusively to the other, the contract may well be void.

Schroeder Music Publishing Co Ltd v MacAuley [1974] 1 WLR 1308 (House of Lords)

A 21-year-old unknown songwriter made a contract with a music publishing company on the company's standard terms. The songwriter was to work exclusively for the company for the period of the agreement. The songwriter gave the company the copyright in all of his songs, his remuneration being royalties on the songs published. The agreement was to last for five years but if the total royalties exceeded £5 000 the agreement was automatically extended for another five years. The publisher could end the agreement at any time by giving one month's notice. The songwriter had no right to terminate the agreement. The publishers could assign their rights under the agreement, the songwriter could not do this without the company's agreement. The songwriter sought an application that the agreement was void.

Held. The agreement was unduly restrictive and therefore void. The House of Lords took into account the excessive length of time for which the agreement was to run, the fact that the company could assign their rights, and the fact that the company did not have to publish any of the songwriter's songs and might thus sterilise his talent.

6.4.3.5 The effect of a contract being held to be void

The general rule is that if a contract is void as in restraint of trade a court will not allow either side to sue on it. However, it may be that the whole contract is not void and that the void part can be severed from the remainder of the contract. If severance is allowed then the rest of the contract will be valid and will stand. If severance is not possible then the whole contract is void. Severance will not be allowed where this would alter the whole nature of the contract. Nor will it be allowed if it requires the courts to rewrite the contract. A 'blue pencil' test applies so that severance is only allowed if the offending clauses of the contract could be isolated and clearly crossed out with a blue pencil, leaving behind a valid contract.

The following two cases demonstrate how this test works.

Goldsoll v Goldman [1915] 1 Ch 292 (Court of Appeal)

The claimant and the defendant both carried on businesses selling imitation jewellery. The two businesses were situated very close to each other in London. The defendant sold his business to the claimant and agreed that for two years he would not sell real or imitation jewellery in London, the UK, France, Russia or Spain or within 25 miles of Berlin or Vienna. The defendant breached this agreement and the claimant sought an injunction.

Held. The agreement, in its entirety, covered too wide an area and was therefore unreasonable. However, the unreasonable part could be severed from the rest of the agreement. Once this had been done the agreement not to deal in imitation jewellery in the UK, which was reasonable and necessary for the protection of the claimant's business, could stand.

Attwood v Lamont [1920] 3KB 571 (Court of Appeal)

The claimant was a draper, tailor and general outfitter in Kidderminster. He employed the defendant in the tailoring department of the business. The defendant agreed never to compete as a tailor, dressmaker, general draper, milliner, hatter, haberdasher, gentlemen's, ladies' or children's outfitter within a ten mile radius of Kidderminster. This agreement was contained in one covenant (clause) of the contract.

Held. The agreement was wider than necessary and therefore void as unreasonable. The unreasonable part of the contract could not be severed from the reasonable part without altering the whole nature of the agreement. Severance was not therefore allowed and the whole agreement was void.

→

COMMENT (i) The difference between the two cases is that in **Goldsoll v Goldman** the covenant in restraint of trade was written in such a way that it could be made reasonable, without altering the whole nature of the agreement or the intended effect of it. The way that the covenant was written in *Attwood* meant that severance would not be possible without altering the whole nature of the agreement. The claimant intended the covenant to protect his whole business, not just the tailoring department. When the unreasonable parts of the contract are contained in distinct covenants severance is much more likely.

Younger LJ: 'The doctrine of severance has not, I think, gone further than to make it permissible in a case where the covenant is not really a single covenant but is in effect a combination of several distinct covenants. In that case and where severance can be carried out without the addition or alteration of a word, it is permissible. But in that case only.'

(ii) A majority of the Court of Appeal held that even if severance had been allowed, so as to restrict the covenant to the tailoring business it would still have been void as in restraint of trade.

6.4.4 Contracts made illegal by statute

Many types of contracts are expressly or impliedly made illegal by a statute. There are so many of these, relating to so many different matters, that it is not appropriate to list them in this book. It is worth noting that gaming contracts, while not illegal, are void and unenforceable. A gaming contract is one under which it is agreed that one of the parties shall pay a sum of money to the other, but which of the parties is to pay is dependent upon the outcome of some uncertain event. In order to be a gaming contract both parties must stand to win or to lose. Money paid as a result of a gaming contract is not recoverable. Contracts of insurance are not gaming contracts as the insured has an interest in the non-occurrence of the event insured against.

Test your understanding 6.5

1 What types of contract are illegal at common law?

2 What types of contract are void at common law?

3 In what circumstances will contracts in restraint of trade be valid?

4 What is meant by severance?

Key points

- A voidable contract can be avoided (called off) by one of the parties within a reasonable time of making the contract.
- A void contract is a nullity and confers no legal rights on either party.

Misrepresentation

- An actionable misrepresentation is an untrue statement of fact made by a party to a contract which induced the other party to make the contract.
- Silence is not generally capable of amounting to an actionable misrepresentation. It can however do so if there has been a change of circumstances, if the contract is of the utmost good faith, if the parties were in a fiduciary relationship or if the silence made a statement misleading.

- A fraudulent misrepresentation is one made knowing that it was false, or without belief in its truth or recklessly careless whether it was true or false.
- A non-fraudulent misrepresentation will be a negligent misrepresentation unless its maker can prove that he did believe that the representation was true, with reasonable grounds for such a belief, up until the time of the making of the contract. If this can be proved the misrepresentation will be wholly innocent.
- A fraudulent misrepresentation gives a right to rescind the contract. Damages will be assessed on the tort of deceit basis and will cover any consequential losses, whether foreseeable or not.
- Rescission is available for negligent or wholly innocent misrepresentation. However, under s.2(2) of the Misrepresentation Act 1967 a court may →

award damages in lieu of rescission where it would be equitable to do so. Such damages are calculated on a breach of warranty basis.

■ Damages for negligent misrepresentation can be claimed under s.2(1) of the Misrepresentation Act 1967. Such damages are calculated on the tort of deceit basis.

■ Damages are not available for wholly innocent misrepresentation, unless a court awards them in lieu of rescission under s.2(2) of the Misrepresentation Act 1967. Such awards of damages are very rare.

■ The right to rescind can be lost if the contract is affirmed, if it is impossible to restore the parties to their pre-contract positions or if a third party in good faith has acquired rights in the subject matter of the contract.

■ A contract may be affirmed by mere lapse of time. As regards a fraudulent misrepresentation time starts to run from the time when the fraud was discovered. As regards non-fraudulent misrepresentation time starts to run from the date of the contract.

Mistake

■ The parties make a common mistake when they both make the same mistake. A common mistake as to the existence of the subject matter, or as to the ownership of the subject matter, can render the contract void.

■ The parties make a mutual mistake when they are at cross purposes so that there is no real agreement. Such a mistake will render the contract void if the reasonable man could not infer that the view of one or other of the parties was what was objectively intended.

■ A unilateral mistake as to the identity of the other contracting party can make the contract void if the contract was in writing and the parties did not meet face to face. However, the mistake must have been as to the identity of the other contracting party rather than as to his attributes, and the mistake must have been material.

■ A unilateral mistake as to the terms of the contract will render the contract void only if the person not mistaken could not reasonably have supposed that the other party intended to agree to the terms in question.

■ A party who has signed a document while under a complete misapprehension as to its effect may be able to escape liability on the grounds of *non est factum*. This plea is not open to a party who is careless in signing the document.

Duress and undue influence

■ A contract may be voidable for economic duress if there was commercial pressure which coerced the victim's will so as to vitiate consent.

■ In order for economic duress to arise there must generally have been a threat to perform an unlawful act.

■ A contract or gift can be set aside if it was made as a result of undue influence.

■ In certain relationships undue influence is automatically presumed. These relationships are those of solicitor and client, doctor and patient, parent and child, guardian and ward, trustee and beneficiary, and religious advisor and disciple. Where the parties in such a relationship make a contract which cannot readily be explained by their relationship the contract will be set aside unless the dominant party can prove that there was no undue influence.

■ In relationships other than those where undue influence is automatically presumed, it may still be presumed if the victim can prove the existence of a relationship in which he placed great trust and confidence in the other party and can also prove that the contract cannot readily be explained by their relationship.

Void and illegal contracts

■ The following contracts are illegal at common law: contracts tending to promote corruption in public life; contracts tending to impede the administration of justice; contracts to trade with enemy nations; contracts to commit a tort, fraud or crime; contracts tending to promote sexual immorality; contracts to defraud the Revenue.

■ Three types of contracts are void at common law: contracts damaging to the institution of marriage; to oust the jurisdiction of the courts; or in restraint of trade.

■ A contract in restraint of trade will be void unless it can be proved to be reasonable.

■ If a contract contains unreasonable restraint of trade clauses the whole contract will be void unless the offending clauses could be severed with a blue pencil, leaving the unaffected clauses to stand.

Summary questions

1 A supermarket advertises in the press that, 'In independent tests carried out by *WhatVac* magazine, our own make of XR3 vacuum cleaner outperformed all the big name brands.' Alan was about to buy a Hover vacuum cleaner from a different retailer, but when his friend showed him the supermarket's advertisement he changed his mind and bought an XR3. Alan made no mention of the advertisement when buying the XR3. The vacuum cleaner does not work at all well, and Alan has now discovered that the *WhatVac* magazine tests rated the XR3 vacuum cleaners very poorly as the worst on the market. Has there been an actionable misrepresentation? If an actionable misrepresentation has been made what remedies would be available to Alan?

2 Belinda bought a vase from an antique shop for £500 because the owner of the shop said that the vase was a fine early Victorian antique. Five years later, when Belinda tried to sell the vase, an expert told her that the vase was very modern and that the owner of the antique shop must have known this and must also have known that it was practically worthless. Advise Belinda of any remedies available to her.

3 Charles bought a garage because the vendor said that the garage had a turnover of £120 000 p.a. After the first month Charles' turnover is only £3 000. The written contract made no mention of turnover.

a Is the statement about turnover a term of the contract?

b Has an actionable misrepresentation been made?

c What remedies would be available to Charles?

d In practical terms, what would you advise Charles to do?

4 Dinah bought a painting from a dealer. The dealer said that the painting was worth £700, and Dinah paid £650 for it. Dinah's aunt was sure the painting was extremely valuable. An auction house confirmed this and the following week, with a good deal of publicity, the painting was sold for £1m. The antique dealer saw the publicity and recognised the picture as the one he had sold to Dinah. Advise the dealer of any rights he might have against Dinah.

5 A rogue, by pretending to be a clergyman, induces Edward to take a stolen cheque for his car. Shortly after gaining possession of the car the rogue sells it to Edwina, an innocent third party who pays a reasonable price for the car.

a Will the contract between Edward and the rogue be void for mistake?

b Did the rogue make an actionable misrepresentation to Edward?

c Will Edward get the car back from Edwina?

6 George is a retired bank manager. Fay has agreed to buy George's boat, so that she can sail to the Channel Islands. How would the contract be affected if, unknown to both parties:

a The boat did not belong to George?

b The boat was completely unseaworthy?

c The boat had been destroyed by fire five minutes before the contract was made?

7 Harriett buys a painting from a junk shop for £100. What would the effect on the contract be if:

a Harriett discovered that the painting was utterly worthless?

b The shop owner had untruthfully said that the painting was by the minor Edwardian artist, René Dulux and therefore worth at least £100? (In fact the painting is not by Dulux and so is worthless.)

8 Jim signs a document, believing that it is a contract to buy a new computer system. In fact the computer salesman has tricked Jim into signing a bill of exchange. Jim was in a hurry so he did not read the document. A bank validly takes the bill of exchange for value. The bank now intend to sue Jim on the bill of exchange.

a On what grounds might Jim argue that the signed document is not binding upon him?

b Will the bank be able to hold Jim liable on the bill of exchange?

Multiple choice questions

1 In ***Hands v Simpson, Fawcett & Co Ltd*** (1928) 44 TLR 295 the facts of the case were as follows.

The claimant was employed as a commercial traveller and had to use a car in his work. He was convicted of dangerous driving and banned from driving for three months. His employers dismissed him. The fact that the claimant had been banned was not enough to justify a dismissal, because a

→

substitute could have been used for three months. The employers claimed that the claimant's not having revealed that he had been imprisoned for drunken driving when he took the job amounted to a misrepresentation and that this misrepresentation justified the dismissal. The claimant argued that as the employers had never asked about previous convictions, he had no duty to reveal them.

Which one of the following was the decision of the court?

a   The claimant had not made a misrepresentation because he had no duty to disclose his convictions.

b   The claimant had made a misrepresentation because there was a fiduciary relationship between the employers and the claimant.

c   The claimant had made a misrepresentation because he must have known that the employers would never have given him the job if they had known of his convictions.

d   The claimant had made a misrepresentation because his subsequent conviction amounted to a change of circumstances, as in **With v O'Flanagan**.

2 In **Brown v Raphael** [1958] 2 All ER 79 (Court of Appeal) the facts of the case were as follows.

A buyer bought a trust fund at an auction because the auction particulars stated that the seller did not believe that the fund was subject to estate duty. After buying the fund, the buyer discovered that it was subject to estate duty. The buyer could not easily have discovered this before the sale was made, but the seller should have known it all along. The buyer claimed that the seller's statement, although only an opinion, implied facts which justified the opinion. In particular he claimed that one of these facts (that the seller had reasonable grounds for believing his opinion to be true) amounted to a misrepresentation.

Which of the following was the decision of the court?

a   There had been no actionable misrepresentation because the seller's statement was just an opinion.

b   The seller's statement was an actionable misrepresentation because it implied facts which would justify the seller's opinion.

c   That the fund was not subject to estate duty was a term of the contract because the seller had more knowledge than the buyer.

d   The contract would be void for mistake as both parties proceeded on a mistaken assumption about the quality of what was being sold.

3 On Monday Bob sells his car to a rogue, who calls at his house. The rogue pays with a stolen cheque. Bob only takes the cheque because the rogue produces false identification. On Tuesday the rogue sells the car to Charles, an innocent third party who pays a reasonable price for the car. On Wednesday Bob's bank inform him that the rogue's cheque has bounced, and Bob immediately contacts the local police and the AA. Which one of the following statements is true?

a   Bob will get the car back from Charles. As the rogue's misrepresentation was fraudulent, time will not start to run against Bob until he discovered the fraud.

b   Bob will be too late to avoid for misrepresentation and will have no remedy for mistake.

c   Bob will be too late to avoid for misrepresentation, but the contract will be void for mistake as to the person.

d   The contract will be void for *non est factum*.

4 David, an expert collector of antique clocks, sees an old clock in a dealer's showroom. The dealer assures him that the clock is early eighteenth century, made by Toblerone the Swiss artist, and worth £13 000. David says that he has been looking for a Toblerone clock for some time, but before buying it he would like to check the dealer's valuation. An independent expert assures David that such a price would be fair for a genuine Toblerone clock. David buys the clock under a written contract which makes no mention of the clock's maker or of its value. Three years later when he comes to resell it David discovers that, unknown to the dealer who sold it to him and to the astonishment of several experts, the clock is a fake worth about £2 000. Which one of the following is true?

a   The dealer will be liable for breach of contract because his statement about the clock was a term.

b   The dealer made an innocent misrepresentation and so David can rescind the contract.

c   The dealer made an innocent misrepresentation but David will be too late to avoid the contract. Furthermore, there will be no remedy for mistake.

d   As David relied on his own expert, the dealer made no misrepresentation. Furthermore, there will be no remedy for mistake.

5 Which one of the following statements is not true?

a   Generally, a common mistake as to quality will not make a contract void.

b A unilateral mistake as to the person can make a contract void if the parties did not meet face to face and the mistake was as to the identity of the other party and not merely as to his attributes.

c A unilateral mistake as to the quality of what is being bought will make the contract void if the other contracting party knew at the time of the contract that the mistake was being made.

d A person who signs a document under a complete misapprehension as to its effect, and who was not careless in signing, will not be bound by the contract, on the grounds of *non est factum*.

6 Which one of the following statements is not true?

a If a party to a contract can establish that he made it as a consequence of the threat of physical violence the contract will be void for duress.

b A contract will be voidable for economic duress if it was made as a consequence of unlawful pressure which coerced one party's will so as to vitiate his consent.

c A contract between solicitor and client is one where undue influence is presumed.

d The relationship between husband and wife is not one where undue influence is automatically presumed.

7 Which one of the following statements is not true?

a A contract which involves the evasion of tax is a contract to defraud the Revenue and cannot be sued upon by either party.

b Contracts in restraint of trade will be void unless they can be proved to be reasonable.

c A restraint of trade agreement will not be upheld merely to prevent an ex-employee from exercising the skills which he learnt in the course of his employment.

d If it can be easily done, a court will rewrite a contract to sever the parts which were in restraint of trade. Once this has been done, the rest of the contract will stand.

Task 6

A friend of yours who is a keen collector of antiques has several times bought 'antiques' which turned out to be fakes. He has also on occasion sold antiques in return for stolen cheques. Your friend has asked you to write a report, briefly explaining:

a The nature of an actionable misrepresentation and the remedies available to a person to whom a misrepresentation has been made.

b The circumstances in which a contract can be void for mistake.

c The circumstances in which a contract can be voidable for duress, economic duress or undue influence.

d The types of contracts which can be void or illegal at common law.

mylawchamber *premium*

Visit **www.mylawchamber.co.uk/macintyre** to access study support resources including interactive multiple-choice questions, weblinks, glossary, glossary flashcards, legal newsfeed, answers to questions in this chapter, legal updates and an overview of this chapter all linked to the **Pearson eText** version of *Business Law* which you can **search**, **highlight** and **personalise** with your **own notes** and **bookmarks**.

Use **Case Navigator** to read in full some of the key cases referenced in this chapter with commentary and questions:

Shogun Finance Ltd v Hudson (FC) [2003] UKHL 62, [2004] 1 AC 919

7

Discharge of liability · remedies for breach of contract

7.1 DISCHARGE OF LIABILITY

When a party's contractual liability is discharged it ceases to exist. A party's liability can be discharged by performance of the contract, by agreement, by frustration or by the other party's breach of contract. Each of these methods needs to be considered in some detail.

7.1.1 Discharge by performance of the contract

Once both of the parties to a contract have completely performed all of their contractual obligations, the contract will be discharged and neither party will have any remaining liability under the contract. However, if one of the parties does not completely perform his contractual obligations then he will have breached a term of the contract and the other party will be entitled to claim damages. In addition to claiming damages, the injured party may also be able to treat the contract as repudiated, in which case his own obligation to perform the contract will be discharged. In Chapter 5 we saw that the injured party will be able to treat his further contractual obligation as discharged if the term which was breached can be classified as a condition,

rather than as a warranty, and that whether a term is a condition or a warranty is a matter of construction of the contract. In Chapter 5 we also saw that a term might be classified as an innominate term, in which case the injured party's liability will be discharged only if the breach of the term deprived him of substantially the whole benefit of the contract.

In unilateral contracts terms are not evaluated as conditions, warranties or innominate terms. When an offer of a unilateral contract is made the promise given is dependent on the complete performance of the act requested. If a person is promised £100 if he walks to York, he will not be entitled to any payment if he walks to within one mile of York. The promisor set out what needed to be done in order to create the contract. If it is not done then no contract is created.

In contracts of sale of goods the seller will generally be entitled to treat the contract as repudiated if the buyer breaches one of the terms implied by the Sale of Goods Act 1979. (See for example *Arcos Ltd v E. A. Ronaasen & Son* [1933] AC 470 and *Re Moore & Co Ltd and Landauer & Co Ltd* [1921] 2 KB 519 in Chapter 8 at 8.2.3.) However, in Chapter 8 at 8.3.4 we shall see that s.15A of the Sale of Goods Act 1979 provides that a buyer who does not deal as a consumer will only be able to treat breach of a statutory implied term as a breach of warranty, rather than as breach of a condition, if the breach is so slight that it would be unreasonable for the buyer to reject the goods. The statutory terms implied into sales of goods and other contracts, and the remedies available for their breach, are examined in the following chapter. Here we are concerned with general contract principles, that is to say situations which are not governed by a statutory provision.

Where a bilateral contract imposes on a party an obligation to do one particular thing, the general rule is that the obligation to do that thing is entire, unless the parties have agreed otherwise. If an obligation is entire then it must be completely performed or the other party will be entitled to refuse to perform his side of the contract. Put another way, it is a condition precedent of the other party performing his side of the contract that the entire obligation is completely performed. An example can be seen in the following case.

Cutter v Powell (1756) 6 TR 320

Cutter agreed to be a ship's mate on a voyage from Jamaica to Liverpool for a fee of 30 guineas. The ship's master had given Cutter a note setting out the terms of the contract. The note said, 'Ten days after the ship "Governor Parry", myself master, arrives at Liverpool, I promise to pay Mr. T. Cutter the sum of thirty guineas, provided he proceeds, continues and does his duty as second mate in the said ship from hence to the port of Liverpool.' The voyage from Jamaica to Liverpool would generally have taken about eight weeks and a second mate would generally have been paid about £1 a week. After seven weeks of the journey Cutter died. Cutter's widow sued for a *quantum meruit* payment, that is to say for an amount which made payment for the work he had performed.

Held. The widow was not entitled to any payment. It was a condition precedent of Cutter receiving any payment that he reached Liverpool. His obligation to do this was entire. As it had not been fully performed, the promise given in exchange for it did not have to be performed.

In *Cutter v Powell* the widow claimed to be entitled to a payment on a *quantum meruit* basis. When such a payment is ordered a party who has partly performed his contract is entitled to a payment, the amount he deserves, for work performed. The

court rejected the widow's claim. Whether or not such a party who has not completely performed is entitled to such a payment depends upon the interpretation of the terms of the contract. The court did not think that Cutter should be paid for part performance of the contract. The high rate of pay indicated that it had been agreed that he should be paid 30 guineas if he did work all the way to Liverpool, but nothing if he did not.

7.1.1.1 **Divisible or severable contracts**

If a contract was intended to be divisible or severable then it will consist of a number of separate obligations rather than of one entire obligation. A party who performs only some of these obligations will be entitled to payment for the obligations performed but will be liable in damages in respect of the obligations not performed. If the contract is intended to be entire, consisting of only one obligation, then the intention is that this obligation must be performed or no payment will be due.

Where the terms of a contract to supply goods provide that the goods should be paid for at a certain price per pound or per ton, this is an indication that the parties regarded the contract as severable.

Ritchie v Atkinson (1808) 10 East 295

The master of a ship contracted to carry a complete cargo of hemp and iron from St Petersburg to London. The freight was £5 per ton for the hemp and 5 shillings per ton for the iron. The ship only carried part of the cargo.

Held. Delivery of the complete cargo was not a condition precedent of payment of the freight. The ship's master was paid for the cargo which he did carry, but had to pay damages for the cargo which he did not carry.

A contractual obligation to carry goods to a particular destination is likely to be entire. For example, in *Vierboom v Chapman* (1844) 13 M & W 230 a contract was made to carry a cargo of rice from Jakarta to Rotterdam. The ship only carried the rice as far as Mauritius. The ship owner was not entitled to claim any of the freight.

Even if a contractual obligation is regarded as entire, a party who has very nearly performed in full may be said to have **substantially performed** and may therefore be entitled to payment of the contract price. (Less an amount by way of damages in respect of the part of the obligation which was not performed.) When a contract is substantially performed the breach of the entire obligation is, in effect, treated as breach of warranty.

Hoenig v Isaacs
[1952] 2 All ER 176 (Court of Appeal)

The claimant agreed to furnish and decorate the defendant's flat for £750, 'net cash as the work proceeds, and balance on completion'. £400 was paid but the defendant refused to pay the balance of the contract price, alleging faulty design and bad workmanship. The Official Referee found that there were defects in the claimant's work. A wardrobe door needed replacing, a bookshelf which was too short would have to be replaced, and this replacement would require alterations to a bookcase. The Referee found that these defects would have cost £56 to rectify. He found that the claimant had substantially performed and was therefore entitled to the balance of the contract price, less £56. An appeal was made to the Court of Appeal.

Held. The Referee's decision was upheld. The claimant had substantially performed the contract.

COMMENT (i) Somervell LJ regarded the question as to whether or not substantial performance had been rendered as a matter of fact. He thought that the case was near the borderline and said that if the Referee had decided the case the other way the Court of Appeal would not have interfered with this finding.

(ii) Somervell also made it plain that 'each case turns on the construction of the contract'. He thought that if, in **Cutter v Powell**, Cutter had reached Liverpool but had failed on some occasion in his duty as a ship's mate he would have been entitled to the contract price less an amount in damages.

In the following case the claimant was not regarded as having substantially performed.

Bolton v Mahadeva
[1972] 2 All ER 132 (Court of Appeal)

The claimant agreed to install central heating in the defendant's flat for a lump sum payment of £560. The work was performed in such a way that the gas flue was defective and fumes therefore made the rooms uncomfortable. In addition, the system was inefficient in that it did not distribute heat evenly around the flat. These defects would have cost £174 to rectify.

Held. The claimant had not substantially performed and was not therefore entitled to any of the contract price.

In a contract of employment the fact that wages are to be paid weekly or monthly suggests that the contract is divisible.

7.1.1.2 Acceptance of partial performance of an entire obligation

Below at 7.1.2 we shall see that the parties to a contract are free to make a new contract, thereby discharging the obligations which arose under the first contract. Therefore if the parties make a second contract under which one party agrees to accept partial performance of an entire contractual obligation, the party who has partially performed will be entitled to payment for work done on a *quantum meruit* basis. The Sale of Goods Act 1979 s.30(1) gives a statutory example: 'Where the seller delivers to the buyer a quantity of goods less than he contracted to sell, the buyer may reject them, but if the buyer accepts the goods so delivered he must pay for them at the contract rate.'

The acceptance of partial performance may be express or implied but either way it must have been made as a matter of genuine choice.

Sumpter v Hedges
[1898] 1 QB 673 (Court of Appeal)

The claimant agreed to build two houses and stables on the defendant's land for the sum of £565. After doing work to the value of £333 the claimant said that he had run out of money and could not carry on. The judge found that he had abandoned the contract. The defendant finished the buildings himself, using some of the materials which the claimant had left on the site. The trial judge gave the claimant judgment for the value of the materials used but would allow him nothing for the value of the work which he had done. The claimant appealed to the Court of Appeal.

Held. The claimant was not entitled to any payment for work done. Chitty LJ said, 'There is no evidence from which the inference can be drawn that he [the defendant] entered into a fresh contract to pay for the work done by the plaintiff'.

7.1.1.3 Prevention of performance

If one of the parties prevents the other from performing his contractual obligations then the party prevented may sue for work done on a *quantum meruit*. In **Planché v Colburn** (1831) 5 C & P 58, for example, the claimant had been commissioned by the defendant to write a book. The book was on costumes and armour, part of a series called the Juvenile Library, and the claimant was to be paid £100 on completion. The defendant cancelled the series when the claimant's book was partly written. The claimant was entitled to a *quantum meruit* payment of £50 for the work he had done.

7.1.1.4 **Tender of performance**

A party who tenders performance of a contract offers to perform it in accordance with its terms. If a tender of goods is refused by the buyer the seller is discharged from contractual liability. For example, in **Startup v MacDonald** (1843) 6 Man & G 593 the claimant contracted to sell and deliver ten tons of oil 'within the last 14 days in March'. He tendered performance at 8.30pm on Saturday 31 March. The defendant refused to accept the oil on account of the lateness of the hour, although the oil could have been examined, weighed and received before midnight. The claimant was awarded damages for non-acceptance and was discharged from further obligation to deliver the oil. Although the principle of this case holds good, the case might today be differently decided on its facts. Section 29(5) SGA 1979 now provides that, 'Demand or delivery of tender may be treated as ineffectual unless made at a reasonable hour; and what is a reasonable hour is a question of fact'. A modern court might well hold that 8.30 on a Saturday night is not a reasonable hour to deliver ten tons of oil.

If money is tendered, but not accepted by the seller, the buyer is not discharged from the obligation to pay the price. However, if the buyer pays the money into court this will be a good defence if he is sued by the seller for the price. Bank notes are legal tender for any amount, but coins are only legal tender up to an amount specified for each type of coin. Strictly speaking, payment of the price should be in cash unless the parties have agreed otherwise. In practice cheques are usually accepted, although a payment by cheque is only a good tender if the seller does not object. Once the cheque is honoured and the money transferred to the seller's account this is regarded as payment in cash. If the cheque is dishonoured the recipient can sue either on the cheque or on the original contract.

7.1.1.5 **Time of performance**

In Chapter 10 we shall see that in contracts of sale of goods the time of delivery may be fixed by the express or implied terms of the contract. We shall also see that the time of delivery of the goods is a condition whereas the time of payment for the goods is a warranty. Both of these rules are subject to a contrary intention having been expressed by the parties.

In contracts other than sales of goods, time is generally not of the essence unless the parties have expressly agreed that it should be, or the nature of the contract or the surrounding circumstances indicate that it should be. If there is an unreasonable delay in performance, the party who has been subjected to this can make time of the essence by giving reasonable notice.

7.1.2 **Discharge by agreement**

Once a contract has been made the parties who made it are free to vary the agreement or to discharge each other from their contractual obligations. However, a discharge or variation will only be effective if there is 'accord and satisfaction' amounting to the creation of a new contract.

Accord means agreement. This is obviously essential. One of the parties cannot unilaterally say that he is varying the agreement or discharging his own obligations. Both parties must agree.

Satisfaction means consideration. Just as consideration was an essential element when the contract was being formed, it is also essential when the contract is being called off. This is because the agreement to call the contract off must amount to a second contract. If the agreement to call the contract off is contained in a deed then there is no need for any additional consideration.

An example demonstrates the possibilities.

Example

Let us assume that a contract is made whereby A is to decorate B's office for £2 000. There are five possibilities to be considered.

(i) *Both parties agree to call the contract off before A has started work.* Here the contract is discharged. There is agreement, and there is consideration. (Both parties provide consideration by giving back the rights they gained when the contract was made. →

A lets B off with his obligation to pay the money. B lets A off with his obligation to perform the work.)

(ii) *A begins the work but does not want to finish the job. A says that he is not bothered about getting paid for the work he has done, and B agrees to release him from the contract.* Again the contract is discharged. (A lets B off with the obligation to pay the money. B lets A off with the obligation to finish the job.) If B had agreed to pay A for the work done, then the contract would still have been discharged. (A lets B off with paying the rest of the money, B lets A off with finishing the job.)

(iii) *A completes the work but agrees that B need not pay him.* The contract is not discharged. There is accord, but no satisfaction. (B has given A no consideration in return for being released from his obligation to pay the money.)

(iv) *A completes the work and agrees to take B's car instead of the £2 000.* The contract is discharged. There is accord and satisfaction. Nor will the court be concerned with whether or not B's car was worth £2 000. (Consideration must be sufficient but does not need to be adequate, see Chapter 4 at 4.2.2.)

(v) *A completes the work but agrees that B need only pay £1 500, instead of the £2 000 originally agreed.* The contract is not discharged. There is agreement but no satisfaction. **Foakes v Beer** approved the rule in *Pinnel's Case*, which held that a lesser sum of money cannot be satisfaction for a greater sum owed. (Subject to promissory estoppel – see Chapter 4 at 4.2.3.1.)

The contract itself may provide that it becomes discharged after a certain time, or upon the happening of a certain event. If the time expires or the event occurs the contract is discharged without the need for accord and satisfaction. For example, a contract of hire will usually be for a fixed time and a contract of employment may stipulate the amount of notice which must be given in order to terminate the contract. (There are however statutory minimum periods of notice. See Chapter 20 at 20.3.1.)

Just as contracts can be made orally or in writing, so they can generally be discharged without the need for any formalities. A contract made in writing or by a deed can be rescinded or varied by oral agreement. However, a contract which is required by statute to be in writing, although it can be rescinded by oral agreement, cannot be varied by oral agreement. (Except under the doctrine of promissory estoppel.)

7.1.2.1 **Waiver**

We have seen that the parties may discharge their contractual rights by accord and satisfaction. However, if one of the parties waives his rights and is not given anything in return for doing this then there is no accord and satisfaction as no consideration was provided in return for the waiver.

Let us consider an example where X is to build a garage for Y for £6 000. The contract stipulates that the work is to be completed by 1 November. If Y tells X that it will be all right to finish the job by 1 December he has waived his right to have the job finished by 1 November. What is the legal effect of this?

First, the party who granted the waiver cannot claim that the other party has breached the contract by doing an act allowed for by the waiver.

Levey v Goldberg [1922] 1 KB 688

The claimants claimed damages from the defendant for not accepting cloth which he had agreed to buy. Under the contract delivery was due to be completed by 20 August 1920. During August and September 1920 the defendant asked the claimants if they would extend the time for delivery. The claimants agreed. Later the defendant refused to accept delivery of the goods on the grounds that the delivery had not been made within the contract time.

Held. The defendant had waived his right to delivery by 20 August and was in breach of contract when he refused to accept the goods on the date when they were delivered. The claimants were therefore entitled to damages for non acceptance of the goods.

Second, promissory estoppel may prevent the party who granted the waiver from insisting upon his strict legal rights. We examined promissory estoppel in Chapter 4 at 4.2.3.1 and saw that a party who leads the other party to believe that he is not going to insist on his strict legal rights, intending that the other party will act upon this belief, cannot later insist on his strict legal rights if it would be inequitable for him to do so.

Third, a party who has waived his right to insist upon delivery of goods on time, can reintroduce the right to delivery within a reasonable time by giving notice. (See *Charles Rickards v Oppenheim* in Chapter 10 at 10.1.1.3.)

7.1.3 Discharge by frustration

If the contract which the parties make subsequently becomes illegal or impossible to perform, or becomes radically different from what the parties contemplated when they made it, then the contract may be frustrated. If a contract is frustrated the parties are discharged from further performance of it. However, frustration is a doctrine of last resort. The courts will only reach the conclusion that a contract is frustrated if they cannot help but do so. It is also worth emphasising that frustration only applies where circumstances change so that performance of the contract **becomes** illegal, impossible or radically different from what was contemplated when the contract was made. If the parties make an agreement which is illegal at the outset then the contract will be void. (See Chapter 6 at 6.4.) If one of the parties agrees to something which is plainly impossible then the agreement is void because one cannot give as consideration a plainly impossible act. If, unknown to the parties, the circumstances at the time of formation of the contract were radically different from what they both believed them to be then the contract might or might not be void for common mistake, a subject considered in Chapter 6 at 6.2.1.

There is some dispute as to the theoretical basis of frustration. It may be that a contract is frustrated because the court implies a term to that effect, or it may be that the court regards it as unjust to hold the parties to their original obligations in the light of the changed circumstances. In *Great Peace Shipping Ltd* v *Tsavliris Salvage International Ltd* [2002] EWCA Civ 1407, [2002] 3 WLR 1617 Lord Phillips MR was dismissive of the implied term theory, saying that 'the theory of the implied term is as unrealistic when considering common mistake as when considering frustration'.

7.1.3.1 Circumstances in which a contract will be frustrated

It is possible that a contract can be frustrated on the following grounds: the subject matter of the contract has ceased to exist before the contract is performed; a person who has undertaken to perform the contract personally has become unavailable; an event central to the contract has not occurred; the contract cannot be performed in the manner specified; and the contract becomes illegal to perform. These matters are considered in turn.

The subject matter of the contract ceases to exist

If the subject matter of the contract did exist when the contract was made, but ceases to exist before the contract was performed, then the contract may be frustrated. In *Taylor* v *Caldwell* (1863) 3 B & S 826, for example, the defendant agreed to let the claimant have the use of a music hall for certain specified days, so that concerts could be performed there. The contract made no stipulation as to what should happen if the music hall should be destroyed by fire. The music hall was accidentally burnt down before the specified days came around. The contract was held to be frustrated and consequently the defendant was not in breach of contract.

Section 7 of the Sale of Goods Act 1979 makes a statutory rule which applies only to an agreement to sell specific goods which have perished before the risk has passed to the buyer. It provides that, 'Where there is an agreement to sell specific goods and subsequently the goods, without any fault on the part of the seller or buyer, perish before the risk passes to the buyer, the agreement is avoided.' The effect of this section is examined in Chapter 9 at 9.1.1.1. It should be noted here that when s.7 applies, the Law Reform (Frustrated Contracts) Act 1943, considered below at 7.1.3.3, does not apply. It is important to realise that if a contract to sell unascertained goods is made, and the goods which the seller intended to deliver perish, the contract will not be frustrated either at common law or under s.7 SGA. The seller will have to deliver alternative goods which match the contract description or face being liable for breach of contract.

Unavailability of a person who had undertaken to perform personally

If the terms of the contract were such that a person undertook to perform obligations personally, the contract may become frustrated if that person is incapable of performing the contract. If the person has died, or become permanently incapable then the contract will be frustrated. If the unavailability is only for a very short time then the contract will almost certainly not be frustrated.

Condor v The Barron Knights Ltd
[1966] 1 WLR 87

In December 1962 the claimant, then aged 16, became a drummer with the defendant band. The contract was to last for five years and required the claimant to perform seven nights a week, sometimes giving two performances in one night. In January 1963 the claimant collapsed and was detained in a mental hospital for a few days. On his release doctors ordered him to work no more than four nights a week, saying that if he did he would suffer a more severe breakdown. The claimant claimed to be fit to work seven nights a week but the band refused to accept that he was capable of this. They dismissed him because it was not practical for the claimant to rehearse and drum for four nights a week while a replacement rehearsed and drummed for three nights a week. The claimant sued for damages for wrongful dismissal.

Held. The claimant was not entitled to damages. The contract had become frustrated because it had become impossible for the claimant to perform the terms of the contract.

Non-occurrence of an event central to the contract

If the parties make the contract on the understanding that an event which is central to the contract will happen, the contract may become frustrated if that event does not happen. However, this will only be the case if the non-occurrence of the event was the fault of neither party and if the fact that it did not occur made the contract radically different from what the parties contemplated when they made the contract. The following two cases show the extent to which the contract must have become radically different.

Krell v Henry [1903] 2 KB 740
(Court of Appeal)

The defendant made a written contract, agreeing to pay the claimant £75 for the hire of a flat on Pall Mall on the days of 26 and 27 June 1902. A £25 deposit was paid. Neither the contract nor the parties mentioned the purpose of hiring the flat, but both parties knew that it was hired for these days because the coronation of Edward VII was due to take place and the coronation processions were due to pass down Pall Mall on 26 and 27 June. The coronation was cancelled because the king was ill. The claimant sued for the remainder of the contract price, £50.

Held. The contract was frustrated. It was necessary to infer from the circumstances that the whole purpose of the contract was that the defendant might view the coronation processions. When this became impossible the contract was frustrated.

COMMENT Vaughan Williams LJ said that if a taxi was hired to go to Epsom on the day of the Derby (horserace) and the Derby was cancelled, the contract would not be frustrated. Either party could still insist that the other perform their contractual obligations.

Herne Bay Steamboat Co v Hutton
[1903] 2 KB 683 (Court of Appeal)

The defendant agreed to hire the claimants' steamship, *Cynthia*, on 28 June to take paying passengers from Herne Bay 'for the purpose of viewing the naval review and for a day's cruise round the fleet; also on 29 June for similar purposes: price £250, payable £50 down, balance before ship leaves Herne Bay'. The £50 down was paid but it was then announced that the naval review was cancelled on account of the king's illness. The claimants telegrammed the defendants saying that they were still willing to perform the contract. The claimants received no reply and so used the *Cynthia* on the contract dates to make a profit. They then sued for the balance of the contract price. The defendants claimed that the contract was frustrated.

Held. The contract was not frustrated. The venture was at the defendant's risk and the happening of the naval review was not the sole basis of the contract. It would have still been possible for the defendant to have used the *Cynthia* to take passengers for a day's cruise around the fleet.

COMMENT There seem to be two main differences between these two cases. First, in this case it would

→

still have been worthwhile to have the day's cruise around the fleet even if the naval review did not happen, whereas in *Krell* there would have been no point at all in hiring the room if the coronation procession did not take place. Second, in this case the hirer of the boat intended to take passengers and make a profit. This was a commercial venture and the hirer should have inserted a term dealing with the risk of the naval review not happening.

Contract cannot be performed in manner specified

If the contract specifies that it must be performed in a certain manner then it will become frustrated if it is not possible to perform the contract in the manner specified.

Nickoll and Knight v Ashton, Eldridge & Co [1901] 2 KB 126 (Court of Appeal)

Cotton-seed was to be shipped from Egypt to London. The contract specified that the goods should be shipped on the steamship *Orlando*. The *Orlando* was severely damaged by a peril of the sea and could not be repaired in time to ship the cotton-seed within the contract period. The damage to the ship was not the fault of either of the parties.

Held. The contract was frustrated. The court implied a condition that if the *Orlando* should cease to exist as a ship for the purpose of shipping the cargo the contract should be treated as at an end.

COMMENT The contract was frustrated only because the *Orlando* was named as the ship which should carry the cargo. It would not have been frustrated if the shipowner had merely contemplated that this particular ship would be used.

However, a contract will not be frustrated merely because the cost of performing it has significantly increased.

Tsakiroglou & Co Ltd v Noblee Thorl GmbH [1962] AC 93 (House of Lords)

Under a written contract made on 4 October 1956 sellers agreed to ship Sudanese peanuts to Hamburg during November or December 1956. On 2 November the Suez Canal was blocked and closed to shipping, and was not re-opened for several months. The peanuts could still have been shipped to Hamburg within the contract period but this would have involved a journey around the Cape of Good Hope. Such a journey would have been four times as long as the journey through the Suez Canal and the freight for such a journey would have been double. The shippers did not perform the contract, claiming that it was frustrated. The longer time at sea would not have damaged the peanuts.

Held. The contract was not frustrated. The court could not imply a term that the cargo should be carried via the Suez Canal. Carrying the cargo via the Cape of Good Hope was a change in the method of performing the contract but it was not such a fundamental change that the sellers could claim that the contract was frustrated.

Davis Contractors Ltd v Fareham UDC [1956] 2 All ER 145 (House of Lords)

In March 1946 the claimants agreed to build 78 houses for the defendants in eight months. Owing to a shortage of skilled labour the contract took 22 months to perform. The claimants were paid the contract price but they claimed to be paid more on account of the contract having been frustrated.

Held. The contract was not frustrated.

Lord Radcliffe: '... it is not hardship or inconvenience or material loss itself which calls the principle of frustration into play. There must be as well such a change in the significance of the obligation that the thing undertaken would, if performed, be a different thing from that contracted for.'

COMMENT In this case Lord Radcliffe criticised the implied term theory of frustration as artificial. He went on to say: 'So perhaps it would be simpler to say at the outset that frustration occurs whenever the law recognises that without default of either party a contractual obligation has become incapable of being performed because the circumstances in which performance is called for would render it a thing radically different from that which was undertaken by the contract ... It was not this that I promised to do.'

Supervening illegality

If a contract becomes illegal to perform then it will be frustrated. An example can be seen in *Fibrosa Spolka Akcyjna* v *Fairbairn Lawson Combe Barbour Ltd* [1943] AC 32. In July 1939 an English company agreed to supply machinery to a Polish company. In September 1939 Germany occupied Poland. The contract was frustrated because it is illegal to trade with an enemy occupied country.

7.1.3.2 **Limits on frustration**

Even if a contract does become impossible to perform, illegal to perform or fundamentally different from what the parties contemplated, it will nevertheless not be frustrated in certain circumstances.

Fault of either party

If the 'frustrating' event is the fault of either party, the party at fault cannot claim that the contract is frustrated. Whether the 'frustrating' event was caused deliberately or negligently, self-induced frustration is no frustration.

Maritime National Fish Ltd v *Ocean Trawlers Ltd* [1935] AC 524 (Privy Council)

The claimants owned a steam trawler, the *St Cuthbert*, which was fitted with a type of fishing net known as an otter trawl. The *St Cuthbert* was chartered out to the defendants, it being a term that the trawler could only be used in the fishing industry. In 1932 the contract was renewed for one year. Both parties knew that it would be illegal for a trawler fitted with an otter trawl to leave a Canadian port if it had not first obtained a licence from a Canadian Minister. The defendants had four other boats fitted with otter trawls and applied for five licences. They were granted only three licences and had freedom to assign these to whichever boats they pleased. The defendants assigned the licences to three of their own boats. When sued for the contract price, they claimed that their contract with the claimants was frustrated.

Held. The contract was not frustrated. The absence of a licence had been caused by the defendants' own actions and could not therefore be a frustrating event.

J Lauritzen AS v *Wijsmuller BV* *(The Super Servant Two)* [1990] 1 Lloyd's Rep 1 (Court of Appeal)

The defendants contracted to transport the claimants' drilling rig by sea. The defendants had two vessels capable of doing this, the *Super Servant One* and the *Super Servant Two*. The contract gave the defendants the choice as to which of these to use. The drilling rig was to be delivered in the summer of 1981. The *Super Servant Two* sank in January 1981. Before this time the defendants had decided to use *Super Servant Two* to carry the claimants' drilling rig and had entered into another contract which they intended to perform using the *Super Servant One*.

Held. The contract was not frustrated. When the *Super Servant Two* sank the defendants could still have performed their contract with the claimants by using the *Super Servant One*.

COMMENT The Court of Appeal thought that the defendants had a choice as to whether or not to perform their contract with the claimants. This was the case even though they had no real choice. Bingham LJ said that frustration should not 'depend on any decision, however reasonable and commercial, of the party seeking to rely on it.'

Force majeure clauses

If the parties to the contract foresee the 'frustrating' event and make provision for it in their contract, the clause doing this is known as a '*force majeure*' clause. Such clauses will be given effect so that the contract will not be frustrated and the parties' rights and obligations will be those specified in the contract. The doctrine of frustration is concerned with the allocation of the risk of the frustrating event happening. As a doctrine of last resort it will be applied only where the parties have not specifically allocated the risk. However, a *force majeure* clause will only prevent frustration if this was its intention (rather than to exclude one of the parties from liability for breach) and if the frustrating event which subsequently occurred would have been within the contemplation of the parties as within the *force majeure* clause.

Jackson v *The Union Marine Insurance Co Ltd* (1874) LR 10 CP 125

The claimant's ship was chartered to proceed with all possible despatch 'dangers and accidents of navigation excepted' from Liverpool to Newport and from there to take iron rails to San Francisco. The claimant took out insurance on the chartered freight. On 2 January the ship set out from Liverpool, but on 3 January it ran aground. The ship was not both freed and repaired until the end of August. On 15 February the charterers had engaged a different ship to take the rails to San Francisco. The claimant sued the insurance company for the lost freight. The insurance company denied liability, arguing that the claimant should have sued on the charterparty, in which case he would not have suffered a loss of the freight. The jury found that the time necessary to get the ship ready again put an end, in a commercial sense, to the common speculation which the claimant and the charterer had entered into.

Held. The claimant could claim on his insurance. The charterparty was frustrated, despite the *force majeure* →

clause. The charterers had therefore been entitled to hire a different ship and refuse to pay the freight to the claimant. Literally interpreted, the delay was within the *force majeure* clause. But the clause had never been designed to cater for such a long delay.

Frustrating event foreseen by one of the parties

If only one of the parties either foresaw, or ought to have foreseen, the frustrating event then that party cannot claim that the contract was frustrated.

Walton Harvey Ltd v *Walker & Homfrays Ltd* [1931] 1 Ch 274

A hotel owner made two contracts under which an advertising agency was to be entitled to put electronically illuminated advertisements on the roof of his hotel. Before the contract was due to expire the local authority compulsorily purchased the hotel and demolished it. The advertising agents claimed damages for breach of contract. The hotel owner argued that the contract was frustrated.

Held. The hotel owners were liable on the contract. They could not claim that the compulsory purchase and demolition of the hotel was a frustrating event because at the time of the contract they knew that this might happen and the advertising agency did not.

If both of the parties foresee the frustrating event then it seems likely that the contract can be frustrated.

If one of the parties gives an absolute undertaking that an act will be performed then that party cannot claim that the contract is frustrated.

Peter Cassidy Seed Co Ltd v *Osuustukkuk-Auppa Ltd* [1957] 1 WLR 273

Sellers in Finland agreed to sell an English company a large quantity of ants' eggs, 'Delivery: prompt, as soon as export licence granted'. The sellers had admitted that it was their responsibility to apply for an export licence and had assured the buyers that this would be a 'pure formality'. In fact, the Finnish authorities refused to grant the sellers an export licence.

Held. The contract was not frustrated and the sellers were liable in damages. On the true construction of the contract the sellers had warranted that they would get an export licence, rather than warranted that they would use all due diligence to try to get a licence.

Leases

For some time it was thought that frustration could not apply to a lease because a lease created an interest in land. In *National Carriers Ltd* v *Panalpina (Northern) Ltd* [1981] AC 675, the House of Lords accepted that a lease could be frustrated but indicated that it would be very rare for this to happen.

7.1.3.3 **The effect of frustration**

If a contract is frustrated the common law holds that it comes to an end as soon as the frustrating event occurs. In addition, the Law Reform (Frustrated Contracts) Act 1943 makes the following provisions:

(a) All money still owing under the contract ceases to be due (s.1(2)).
(b) Money already paid under the contract is recoverable. However, the court does have a discretion to allow a party, who has incurred expenses, before the contract was frustrated, to recover their expenses. However, the amount recoverable cannot exceed the amouth paid or payable before the contract was frustrated. The court will allow money to be recovered if it considers it just to do so, having regard to the circumstances of the case. The amount given to cover expenses cannot exceed the amount paid or payable at the time of the frustrating event (s.1(2)).
(c) Whether or not any money was paid or payable at the time of the frustrating event, a party who had already received a valuable benefit under the contract (other than the payment of money) can be ordered by the court to pay whatever amount is fair to compensate for this. This amount should be the amount which the court considers just, having regard to the circumstances of the case, but cannot exceed the value of the benefit received (s.1(3)).

An example might make the effect of the Act clearer. Let us assume that Firm X has agreed to supply Firm Y with 1 000 imitation rifles. The contract price was £50 000, half payable in advance and half payable on delivery. After 200 of the rifles have been made and delivered, the Government outlaws the sale of such rifles. The contract will have become frustrated on the grounds that it has become illegal to perform. Applying the Act:

(a) Firm Y will cease to owe the amount unpaid, £25 000.
(b) Firm Y will be entitled to a refund of the £25 000 already paid. However, Firm X might be able to

keep some of the money to cover expenses already incurred. (Such matters as administration, rifles which have been part produced, etc.) The court has a wide discretion in allowing such expenses and it is never possible to predict accurately what sum a court might allow.

(c) Firm X may receive an amount to compensate for the valuable benefit received, the 200 rifles already delivered. If the payment was on a proportional basis, it would amount to one fifth of the total price, £10 000. (However, the amount payable is at the court's discretion.)

When the frustrating event destroys, or makes worthless, work performed under the contract s.1(3) causes difficulty. Has the party who ordered the work received a valuable benefit or not? For example, in *Appleby* v *Myers* (1867) LR 2 CP 651 the contract was to install machinery on the defendant's premises. A fire destroyed both the premises and machinery already installed under the contract before the work was completed. The contract was frustrated by the fire. But had the defendant received a valuable benefit or not? This depends upon whether the valuable benefit is assessed immediately before or immediately after the frustrating event. Of course the case arose long before the LR(FC)A 1943 was passed and it was decided under the old law. However, in *BP Exploration Ltd* v *Hunt (No. 2)* [1982] 1 All ER 925 Goff J indicated that there would have been no valuable benefit as the correct time of assessment was immediately after the frustrating event.

Finally, it should be noted that the provisions of the Act will not apply if the parties make their own provisions for the effects of frustration (s.2(3)). So if, in the example above, the contract had stated that in the event of frustration the loss should lie where it fell, then this is what would happen.

The Act does not apply to charterparties, contracts of insurance or to contracts to which s.7 of the Sale of Goods Act 1979 applies.

7.1.4 **Discharge by acceptance of breach**

When considering discharge by performance we saw that if one of the parties breaches a condition, rather than a warranty, the injured party may elect to treat the contract as discharged and that if an entire obligation is not completely performed then the consideration promised in return for it need not be performed. We also saw that breach of an innominate term will allow the injured party to treat the contract as repudiated only if the injured party was deprived of substantially the whole benefit of the contract.

Furthermore, if one of the parties repudiates the contract, that is to say shows an intention not to be bound by the contract, then the other party may accept this repudiation and treat his own obligations as discharged. Where the repudiation occurs before the time for performance of the contract has become due this is known as an anticipatory breach. However, it is not only by committing an anticipatory breach that a party can show an intention to repudiate the contract. Such an intention can also be shown during performance of the contract.

7.1.4.1 **Anticipatory breach**

If one of the parties, before the time of performance becomes due, expressly or impliedly lets the other party know that he does not intend to perform the contract then this is an anticipatory breach. The party faced with the anticipatory breach has two options. He can either accept the breach and treat the contract as repudiated (as well as having a right to sue for damages) or can wait until the time when the contract should be performed. If the contract is then not performed he can sue for actual breach of contract.

Hochster v _De La Tour_ (1853) 2 E & B 678

On 12 April 1852 the defendant contracted to employ the claimant as a courier for a three month period, beginning on 1 June. On 11 May the defendant informed the claimant that he had changed his mind and no longer required the claimant's services. The claimant sued for damages on 22 May. The defendants argued that there could be no breach before 1 June.

Held. An anticipatory breach had been committed on 11 May, and this entitled the claimant to sue before 1 June.

COMMENT The injured party has a duty to mitigate his loss (take all reasonable steps to reduce it). This duty arises as soon as the anticipatory breach is accepted as terminating the contract. In this case the claimant managed to mitigate by getting an equally good position which started on 4 July. The fact of the →

claimant accepting this position reduced the amount of his damages because it reduced his actual loss. However, if it could be shown that he had refused the new position his damages would have been reduced anyway on the grounds that he should have mitigated his loss.

Frost v Knight (1872) LR 7 Exch 111

The defendant promised the claimant that he would marry her as soon as his father died. While his father was still alive, the defendant announced that he would not be marrying the claimant and he married someone else. While the defendant's father was still alive, the claimant sued for breach of contract (breach of promise to marry).

Held. An anticipatory breach of contract had been committed and so the claimant was immediately entitled to sue.

In both of these cases there was a repudiation of the contract because the anticipatory breach showed beyond reasonable doubt that the party committing the breach did not intend to be bound by the contract. If the party committing the anticipatory breach does not show an absolute refusal to perform the contract there will not have been a repudiation of the contract.

A party who treats the contract as repudiated on account of an anticipatory breach which did not show an absolute intention not to be bound by the contract will himself be in anticipatory breach. Let us assume, for example, that X has contracted to service Y's photocopiers for a fee of £400. X lets Y know that he might not be able to fully perform the contract on time. If this anticipatory breach shows an absolute intention not to be bound by the contract, Y can treat the contract as repudiated. (He can therefore refuse to pay the contract price and claim damages.) If X's anticipatory breach does not show an absolute intention not to be bound by the contract, then if Y treats the contract as repudiated Y will himself be in breach of contract. (X will therefore be entitled to refuse to perform the contract and be entitled to damages.)

The damages for an anticipatory breach will be the same as they would have been for an actual breach. However, if it can be proved that the party claiming anticipatory breach would not himself have been able to perform the contract then no damages will be available.

If one of the parties shows an intention to repudiate the contract then the other party has the option

to accept this and treat the contract as repudiated. However, the contract is not repudiated until the innocent party clearly and unequivocally indicates that he accepts the repudiation. In *Howard v Pickford Tool Co* [1951] 1 KB 417 Lord Asquith LJ said: 'An unaccepted repudiation is a thing writ in water and of no value to anybody; it affords no legal rights of any sort or kind.' A party who affirms an anticipatory breach cannot later rely on the anticipatory breach and claim to be absolved from performing his side of the contract. Lord Ackner clearly explained this in *Fercometal SARL v Mediterranean Shipping Co SA, The Simona* [1989] AC 788:

> 'When A wrongfully repudiates his contractual obligations in anticipation of the time for their performance, he presents the innocent party B with two choices. He may either affirm the contract by treating it as still in force or he may treat it as finally and conclusively discharged. There is no third choice, as a sort of *via media*, to affirm the contract and yet be absolved from tendering further performance unless and until A gives reasonable notice that he is once again able and willing to perform.'

If the repudiation is not accepted then the repudiating party may yet perform the contract. However, there is always the risk that some outside event might frustrate the contract.

Avery v Bowden (1856) 5 E & B 714

The defendant agreed to supply the claimant's ship with a cargo at Odessa within 45 days. The claimant's ship arrived in Odessa. The defendant repeatedly told the claimant that he would not be able to supply the cargo and advised the claimant to sail away. The claimant did not do this but stayed in Odessa, hoping that the defendant would after all be able to supply a cargo. Before the 45 days had expired the Crimean War broke out.

Held. The contract had become frustrated because Odessa had become an enemy port and it would be illegal to load there. The claimant had therefore lost the right to sue for breach. If the claimant had accepted the anticipatory breach and sailed away then he would have been entitled to damages for breach of contract.

In the following case the anticipatory breach was not accepted, and the injured party continued to perform the contract. The case was unusual in that the injured party could do this without the cooperation of the party who committed the anticipatory breach.

White and Carter (Councils) v MacGregor
[1962] 2 WLR 713 (House of Lords)

The claimants were advertising agents who agreed to advertise the defendant's garage for a three year period. On the same day that the contract was made the defendants wrote to the claimants asking them to cancel the contract. The claimants did not accept this anticipatory breach but began to advertise the defendants' business as agreed. One of the terms of the contract said that if any of the instalments which the defendants were required to pay became four weeks overdue, then the claimants could sue for the whole contract price. The defendants refused to pay any of the instalments. The claimants advertised the defendants' garage as agreed for the whole three year period and then sued for the whole contract price.

Held. The claimants were entitled to perform the contract and sue for the whole contract price. They were not bound to accept the repudiation and sue for damages.

COMMENT (i) Where a party accepts an anticipatory breach he will not be able to claim for a loss which he should have mitigated. (As we saw when considering **Hochster v De La Tour**.) Where the party does not accept the anticipatory breach, as in this case, he may be able to claim for losses which could have been mitigated. (However, the majority of the House of Lords stressed that the action was to recover a debt and so mitigation could not apply. See below at 7.2.3.)

(ii) Lord Reid thought that a party who has no legitimate interest in performing the contract, other than claiming damages, ought not to be allowed to saddle the other party with a burden with no benefit to himself. Subsequent cases have limited the decision of this case in this way. An example can be seen in **Clea Shipping Corp v Bulk Oil International Ltd (The Alaskan Trader)** [1984] 1 All ER 129. After 12 months of a two-year charterparty the ship needed to be repaired. The owners repaired the ship and kept both it and the crew available for the full two-year period. After the repairs were done the charterers committed an anticipatory breach by refusing to give any instructions regarding the ship. The owners continued to wait for instructions. It was held that the owners had no legitimate interest in keeping the contract open and should instead have claimed damages. So they could not retain the full contract price which the charterers had paid. Subsequent cases have held that the innocent party will not be able to keep the contract open and recover the price if this would be 'wholly unreasonable'.

(iii) The advertising contract was unusual in that it could be performed without the cooperation of the other party. The decision will not apply in cases where such cooperation is required.

A person who has the right to terminate a contract on account of a repudiatory breach can lose the right by waiving it. Lord Goff set out how this might be done in *The Kanchenjunga* [1990] 1 Lloyd's Rep 391:

> 'Where with knowledge of the relevant facts a party has acted in a manner which is consistent only with his having chosen one of the two alternative and inconsistent courses of action then open to him, for example, to determine a contract or alternatively to affirm it, he is held to have made his election accordingly ... perhaps because a party who elects not to exercise a right which has become available to him is abandoning that right, he will only be held to have done so if he has communicated his election to the other party in clear and unequivocal terms ... Moreover, it does not require consideration to support it, and so it is to be distinguished from an express or implied agreement, such as a variation of the relevant contract, which traditionally requires consideration to render it binding in English law.'

7.1.5 Discharge under a statutory right

Once a contract has been concluded then the common law approach is that both sides are bound by it. However, several statutes give consumers the right to cancel concluded contracts. **The Consumer Credit Act 1974** gives such a right, in circumstances which are considered in Chapter 14 at 14.1.4. The **Timeshare Act 1992** gives consumers who have entered into a timeshare agreement a 14 day period in which to cancel the contract.

The **Cancellation of Contracts made in a Consumer's Home or Place of Work etc. Regulations 2008** allow consumers to cancel contracts if they were made during a visit by a trader to a consumer's home or place of work, or to the home of another individual. The regulations apply whether the visit was solicited by the consumer or not. They also apply if the contract was made during an excursion organised by the trader away from his business premises, or after an offer made by the consumer during such a home visit or excursion. The Regulations apply to contracts to provide goods or services as long as they have a price of more than £35. The trader cannot enforce the contract unless, at the time of the contract, the consumer was given written notice of the right to cancel the contract within seven days. The consumer must also have been given a statutory cancellation form. The consumer does not need to use this form to cancel. However, the notice of cancellation must be in writing. Once written notice of cancellation has been given, goods supplied to the consumer must be made available for collection by the trader. The consumer gets back any money already paid and does not have to pay any money remaining due under the cancelled contract.

The **Consumer Protection (Distance Selling) Regulations 2000** seek to protect consumers who buy goods or services from a supplier by means of a 'distance contract'. Significant obligations are imposed on suppliers, who must supply the consumer with information about the goods or services sold. The Regulations also give the consumer a seven-day cooling-off period.

A 'distance contract' is defined as 'any contract concerning goods or services concluded between a supplier and a consumer under an organised distance sales or service provision run by the supplier who, for the purposes of the contract, makes exclusive use of one or more means of distance communication up to and including the moment at which the contract is concluded'. It can be seen that the Regulations only protect consumers dealing with suppliers who operate an organised distance sales or service provision. The Regulations would therefore not apply to a one-off supply of goods or services which was made in response to a request from a customer. However, if several such customers were supplied the seller would then probably be regarded as operating an organised provision. Consumers are only protected, whether buying goods or services, if the supplier makes exclusive use of one or more means of distance communication up to and including the moment at which the contract is concluded. If the consumer visits the supplier's showroom, or if a door-to-door salesman visits the consumer, the Regulations will not apply.

Regulation 3 defines 'means of distance communication' as any means which, without the simultaneous presence of the supplier and the consumer, may be used for the conclusion of a contract between those parties. So a contract is made by means of distance communication if it is made without the seller and the supplier being in each other's physical presence. Schedule 1 to the Regulations gives an indicative list of 13 means of distance communication which includes letter, press advertising with order form, catalogue, telephone, radio, television, computer, email, fax and television shopping. Home deliveries by regular roundsmen (such as milkmen) and contracts to provide accommodation, transport, catering and leisure, are excluded from the main provisions of the Regulations.

Regulation 8(2)(b) requires that the supplier provides information about how the right to cancel can be exercised. Unless a term of the contract requires the consumer to do so, a consumer who cancels the contract under the Regulations will not have to return the goods to the supplier. If a term does require the consumer to return the goods, reg.8(2)(b) requires that the consumer is notified of this and who would be responsible for the cost of returning the goods.

It is possible for the consumer to agree that a service may be begun before the end of the cooling-off period and that the consumer will not be able to cancel once performance of the service has begun. If this is the case, reg.8(3) requires the supplier to inform the consumer, in writing or other durable medium, that the consumer will not be able to cancel such a contract once the performance of the services has begun with the consumer's agreement.

If a consumer serves a notice of cancellation then the contract will be treated as if it had never been made (reg.10(2)). Notice of cancellation must be made in writing or in some other durable medium available and accessible to the supplier. However expressed, it must indicate an intention to cancel the contract (reg.10(3)). Regulation 10(4) provides that a notice of cancellation is to be treated as having been properly given if it is left at the supplier's address, posted to the supplier, sent by fax or sent by email. Regulation 10(5) provides that in the case of a company the notice of cancellation can be left at the address of the company or sent to the company secretary or company clerk. In the case of a partnership the notice can be left with or sent to a partner or a person having control or management of the partnership business.

In contracts for the supply of goods the cancellation period begins with the day on which the contract is concluded. The time when the cooling-off period ends varies, depending upon whether reg.8 was or was not complied with. If reg.8 was complied with the cancellation period ends after seven working days have expired, beginning with the day after the day on which the consumer receives the goods (reg.11(2)). If reg.8 is never complied with then an additional three months are added to the cooling-off period (reg.11(4)). If reg.8 is complied with late, but within three months of the day on which the consumer received the goods, the time period expires after seven working days, beginning with the day after the day on which the consumer receives the information.

If the contract is to supply services the time periods are the same except that the cooling-off period begins to reduce on the day after the day on which the contract was concluded. Where an unauthorised payment transaction in connection with a distance contract is made under a regulated agreement within the Consumer Credit Act 1974, the consumer will not be liable for any losses incurred as long as the transaction was covered by the Distance Selling Regulations (CCA 1974 s.83(1) and 84(3A)). If a debit card, or some other method of payment which is not made under a regulated agreement within the CCA 1974, is used reg.62(3)(c) of the Payment Services Regulations 2009 has the same effect.

There are in reg.13 important exceptions to the right to cancel. First, there is no right to cancel in a contract to supply a service where the supplier complied with reg.8(3) by informing the consumer before the conclusion of the contract that the consumer would not be able to cancel once the performance of the contract had begun with his agreement. Second, there is no right to cancel if the price of the goods or services supplied is dependent upon fluctuations in the financial market which cannot be controlled by the supplier (for example, if the contract was to supply Krugerrands). Third, there is no right to cancel if the goods were made to the consumer's specifications or are clearly personalised or were goods which by reason of their nature cannot be returned or are liable to deteriorate or expire rapidly. Fourth, a consumer will not be able to cancel a contract to buy audio or video recordings or computer software once he has broken the seal on the goods. Fifth, contracts for the supply of newspapers or magazines or for gaming, lottery or betting services cannot be cancelled.

Car hire has also been held by the European Court of Justice to be exempt from the provisions of the Regulations. This was the decision in Case C-336/03 *EasyCar (UK) Ltd v OFT* [2005]. The ECJ decided that car hire was within an exemption covering contracts for the provision of transport services.

If the contract is cancelled the supplier must return any money paid by the consumer within 30 days. Any security provided by the consumer shall be treated as if it had never taken effect.

A supplier can make a charge in respect of returned goods only if the goods were the goods ordered (not substituted goods) and a term of the contract provided that the consumer must return any goods supplied if he cancels the contract under reg.10. The charge can then be made only if the consumer does not return the goods or returns the goods at the expense of the supplier. Any such charge made must not exceed the costs of recovering any goods supplied under the contract (reg.14(5)). The supplier's right to make a charge does not apply where any express or implied term of the contract gives the consumer a right to reject. Nor does it apply if any term requiring the consumer to return any goods supplied if he cancels the contract is an 'unfair term' within the meaning of the Unfair Terms in Consumer Contracts Regulations 1999.

If the consumer does cancel a contract any related credit agreement is automatically cancelled (reg.15(1)).

Regulation 17(2) imposes duties on a consumer who cancels the contract under reg.10. The consumer must retain possession of the goods and take reasonable care of them. A consumer who cancels also has a duty to restore the goods to the supplier (reg.17(3)). Restoration does not involve returning the goods to the supplier, but rather making them available for collection by the supplier. The consumer has no duty to deliver the goods except at his own premises. Even then a request to do so must have been made in writing, or some other durable medium accessible to the consumer, and have been given to the consumer either before, or at the time when, the goods are collected from the premises (reg.17(4)). When the consumer delivers the goods to the supplier, or sends the goods back to the supplier at his own expense, he is discharged from any obligation to retain possession of the goods or to restore them to the supplier. The consumer's duties to retain possession of the goods and take reasonable care of them lasts for 21 days, beginning with the day on which notice of cancellation was given. However, if within the 21-day period the consumer receives a request to deliver the goods at his own premises, which is in writing or some other durable medium, and unreasonably either refuses or fails to comply with it, the duties to retain possession of the goods and take reasonable care of them continue until the consumer does deliver the goods (at his own premises or elsewhere) or does, at his own expense, send them back to the supplier.

The Regulations do not provide that if the consumer cancels the contract he must return the goods to the supplier. However, as we have seen, a term of the contract may provide that the consumer must do this. If there is such a term a consumer who cancels must retain the goods and take reasonable care of them for a six-month period. If the supplier makes a written request for the return of the goods this time period is extended until the consumer does send the goods back.

If the consumer traded in goods in part exchange then these goods must be returned to the consumer upon cancellation of the contract in a condition substantially as good as they were when they were delivered to the supplier. If this is not done the supplier must pay a sum equal to the part-exchange allowance (reg. 18(2)). Upon paying such a sum the supplier becomes the owner of the part-exchanged goods.

Unless the parties agree otherwise, the supplier must perform the contract within 30 days, beginning with the day after the day the consumer sent his order to the supplier (reg.19(1)). If the goods or services are unavailable the supplier must inform the consumer and reimburse any sum paid (reg.19(2)). The contract is then treated as never having been made, except for any rights or remedies for non-performance which the consumer might have.

It is not possible to contract out of the provisions of the Regulations.

Test your understanding 7.2

1 In what circumstances can a contract be frustrated?

2 What is the effect of the 'frustrating' event being the fault of one of the parties?

3 What is a *force majeure* clause? Are such clauses given legal effect?

4 Can a contract be frustrated if one of the parties foresaw the frustrating event?

5 How does the Law Reform (Frustrated Contracts) Act 1943 apportion loss in cases of frustration?

6 How does an anticipatory breach of contract arise?

7 What options are open to a party faced with a repudiatory anticipatory breach?

7.2 REMEDIES FOR BREACH OF CONTRACT

Whenever a contract is breached, one or more remedies will be available to the injured party.

7.2.1 Refusal to further perform the contract

Earlier in this chapter we considered discharge by breach and discharge by performance. We saw that the innocent party will be able to treat his obligations as discharged, and therefore be entitled to refuse to perform the contract further, in the following circumstances: if the other party repudiates the contract; or if a non-repudiatory breach amounts to breach of condition rather than to breach of warranty; or if a non-repudiatory breach amounts to breach of an innominate term which deprived of substantially the whole intended benefit of the contract.

As well as treating his further obligations as discharged, the injured party may also be entitled to claim damages. However, when assessing these damages account will be taken of any benefit which the injured party has received.

7.2.1.1 Rescission distinguished

It should be remembered that treating the contract as repudiated on account of a breach of contract by the other party is not the same as rescinding a contract for misrepresentation, duress or undue influence. Rescission, an equitable remedy considered in Chapter 6 at 6.1.3, is not a remedy for breach of contract. Unfortunately, some confusion has been caused over the years because at times both writers and judges have used the word rescission to mean treating a contract as repudiated on account of breach of contract. (It is also unfortunate that in ss.48A–F of the SGA 1979, considered in Chapter 10 at 10.4.6, the word 'rescind' is given a completely different meaning which is limited to those particular sections.)

When we considered misrepresentation we saw that rescission will only be allowed if the parties can be restored to their pre-contract positions. This is because the contract is regarded as having never existed. This requirement is not present when a contract is treated as repudiated for breach. In that case it is further performance of the contract which is discharged. Therefore the fact that the party treating the contract as repudiated cannot restore the parties to their pre-contract positions will not prevent him from treating the contract as repudiated.

7.2.2 Damages

Any breach of contract will entitle the injured party to damages. However, if the injured party has suffered no real loss these damages will be nominal only, perhaps 5p or £1, and costs may not be recoverable. The primary purpose of contract damages is to put the injured party in the financial position he would have been in if the contract had been properly performed. Two steps are necessary to achieve this. First, it must be asked whether or not the loss is too remote for damages in respect of it to be recoverable at all. Then, if the loss is not too remote, damages must be quantified.

7.2.2.1 Remoteness of damage

The injured party cannot claim damages for every loss which was caused by the breach of contract. Damages can only be recovered for losses which were caused by the breach of contract and which fit within one of the two rules in **Hadley v Baxendale** (1854) 9 Exch 341. These rules are a very important limitation on damages which can be claimed for a breach of contract. If there were no such limitation, damages could be claimed for any consequence of a breach of contract, no matter how unforeseeable. This potential liability would deter many people from making contracts if they could possibly avoid it.

Rule 1 states that damages are recoverable for a loss which arose naturally from the breach, according to the usual course of things. Rule 2 states that damages are recoverable for a loss which may reasonably be supposed to have been in the contemplation of both parties, as not unlikely to result, at the time when they made the contract. The following case shows how the two rules work.

Victoria Laundry v Newman Industries
[1949] 1 All ER 997 (Court of Appeal)

The defendants agreed to sell a second-hand boiler to the claimants, a company of launderers and dyers. At the time of the contract the defendants knew that the claimants wanted the boiler for immediate use. The defendants breached the contract by delivering the boiler 20 weeks late. The claimants claimed £16 a week, representing the increased ordinary profit which they could have made with the boiler which the defendants were to supply. They also claimed £262 a week, representing the value of an exceptionally lucrative contract to dye army uniforms. The unavailability of the new boiler had caused the claimants to lose this contract.

Held. The loss of £16 was recoverable within the first rule in **Hadley v Baxendale**. The loss of £262 was neither within the first nor the second rule and was therefore not recoverable.

COMMENT If the claimants had told the defendants about the lucrative dyeing contract, and that the boiler which the defendants were to supply would be needed in time or the dyeing contract would be lost, then the £262 a week would have been recoverable under the second rule.

Koufos v C. Czarnikow Ltd, The Heron II
[1967] 1 AC 350 (House of Lords)

The defendants contracted to deliver 3 000 tons of sugar to Basrah by 22 November 1960. The ship did not arrive until 2 December. During the ten days by which the delivery was late the market price of sugar had fallen from £32 10s per ton to £31 2s 9d per ton. The buyers claimed the difference in price, £4 183. The sellers knew that the buyers were sugar merchants, and also knew that there was a sugar market in Basrah. They did not know that the sellers had intended to resell the sugar as soon as they got it.

Held. The buyers were entitled to the £4 183 under the first rule in **Hadley v Baxendale**.

COMMENT Lord Reid thought the loss should be recoverable because it was 'not unlikely' or 'quite likely' to occur. He thought such a test was preferable to one of reasonable foreseeability, which is the test for remoteness of damage in tort. The contract test is whether the loss could reasonably have been contemplated, not whether it could reasonably have been foreseen.

When applying the two rules in **Hadley v Baxendale** it is important to remember that they are concerned with remoteness at the time of the contract and not at the time of breach.

When the parties make a contract it is assumed that they are aware of the risks of breaching the contract. For this reason the remoteness test is concerned with what losses were foreseeable at this time.

In the following case the House of Lords considered the extent to which the parties' unexpressed intentions should be taken into account when applying the rules in **Hadley v Baxendale**.

Transfield Shipping Inc v Mercator Shipping Inc (The Achilleas) [2008] UKHL 48, [2009] 1 AC 61 (House of Lords)

A ship owner, M, chartered a ship to T. T was to redeliver the ship to M by 2 May 2004. On 20 April M chartered the ship out to another person, X, for about five months at $39 500 a day. Under this second contract, if the ship was not delivered to X by 8 May, X had the right to cancel the contract. T breached the first contract by redelivering the ship nine days late. This meant that X could refuse to be bound by its contract with M. Shipping rates had suddenly collapsed and M had to renegotiate the contract with X, so that X would pay only $31 500 a day. X took the ship from M for about five months at this price. T agreed to pay damages for the nine days that the ship was late. M also claimed the difference between the price which X had first agreed to pay, and the price which X actually paid, for the whole five months when X had the ship. This came to $1 364 584.

Held. T did not have to pay the extra $1 364 584, even though it was 'not unlikely' that M would charter the ship to another person, and that the market rates would collapse. The potential liability of a charterer if such liability were to exist would be completely unquantifiable. The new contract might be for a week, a month or for several years. There was no legal precedent on the matter, but the evidence showed that everyone in the chartering business thought that a charterer did not assume liability to pay damages for this type of loss. All contractual liability is voluntarily undertaken, and the objective intention of the parties was that T would not have assumed this liability.

COMMENT (i) The decision of the House of Lords was unanimous and reversed the decision of the Court of Appeal.

(ii) Lord Hoffmann gave the leading judgment. He said that the case raised a fundamental point of principle. Was the rule that a party could recover losses which were foreseeable an external rule of law which would always be imposed on the parties? Or was it merely a *prima facie* presumption which could be rebutted by the context of the contract, the surrounding circumstances and the general understanding in the relevant market? He thought that as all contractual liability is voluntarily undertaken, liability for damages should be based on the (objectively assessed) intentions of the parties. It would be wrong to hold a contracting party liable for a risk which he would not reasonably be considered to have undertaken, even if the risk was foreseeable. The contract price would be determined by the risk taken, and if a party were made liable for a risk which he did not think he had undertaken, this would give the other party something for nothing. Also, if a charterer were to be liable for loss of a subsequent contract, this would expose him to almost unlimited liability. When the courts imply a term, they

consider the contract, as a whole in its commercial context, to see what obligations the parties can reasonably be expected to have assumed and paid for. The same approach should be taken when implying the limits of damages liability. Lord Hope agreed with this broader approach.

(iii) Lord Rodger and Baroness Hale decided the case on the orthodox approach. Lord Rodger thought that the parties would not reasonably have contemplated that an overrun of nine days would 'in the ordinary course of things' have caused the loss for which damages were claimed. Baroness Hale said that the loss arose only because of the unusual volatility of the market at the time. She thought that it could not be said that the extremely volatile conditions were within the parties' contemplation as 'not unlikely'.

(iv) Lord Walker gave a judgment which included elements of both the broader and the orthodox approach. This made the *ratio decidendi* of the case very hard to discern.

In *Sylvia Shipping Co Ltd* v *Progress Bulk Carriers* [2010] EWHC 542, [2010] 2 Lloyd's Rep 81 Hamblen J considered *The Achilleas* in some detail. Having considered subsequent authorities which had considered the case, he said:

'In my judgment, the decision in *The Achilleas* results in an amalgam of the orthodox and the broader approach. The orthodox approach remains the general test of remoteness applicable in the great majority of cases. However, there may be "unusual" cases, such as *The Achilleas* itself, in which the context, surrounding circumstances or general understanding in the relevant market make it necessary specifically to consider whether there has been an assumption of responsibility. This is most likely to be in those relatively rare cases where the application of the general test leads or may lead to an unquantifiable, unpredictable, uncontrollable or disproportionate liability or where there is clear evidence that such a liability would be contrary to market understanding and expectations. In the great majority of cases it will not be necessary specifically to address the issue of assumption of responsibility. Usually the fact that the type of loss arises in the ordinary course of things or out of special known circumstances will carry with it the necessary assumption of responsibility ... The orthodox approach therefore remains the "standard rule" and it is only in relatively unusual cases, such as *The Achilleas* itself, where a consideration of assumption of responsibility may be required.'

7.2.2.2 **Quantification of damages**

The purpose of contract damages is to put the injured party, as regards foreseeable losses, in the financial position which he would have been in if the contract had not been breached. Contract damages are not designed to penalise the party in breach and should not put the injured party in a better financial position than he would have been in if the contract had been properly performed. Therefore, a party who has suffered no loss as a result of the breach of contract will ordinarily not be entitled to more than nominal damages.

Loss of the bargain

Where the seller commits a breach of contract by failing to deliver goods, the Sale of Goods Act 1979 lays down statutory rules in assessing the buyer's damages. These rules are examined in Chapter 10 at 10.4.1. Where the buyer in a contract of sale of goods refuses to accept and pay for the goods or refuses to take delivery of them the seller will be entitled to damages. Again, statutory rules are set out in the Sale of Goods Act 1979. These rules are examined in Chapter 10 at 10.3.2.2. These statutory rules reflect common law principles that a party faced with a breach of contract should be compensated for the loss of the bargain he had made.

If the breach of contract consisted of improperly performing a contract other than a sale of goods then the loss of the bargain damages will usually be the cost of rectifying the defect and an amount to compensate for other foreseeable consequential losses. However, this will not be the case where it would be unreasonable to assess damages in this way.

Ruxley Electronics and Construction Ltd v Forsyth
[1995] 3 All ER 268 (House of Lords)

The defendant agreed that the claimants should build a swimming pool in his garden for a price of £70 178. The contract expressly stated that the maximum depth of the pool should be 7 feet 6 inches. When the work was completed the defendant discovered that the maximum depth was only 6 feet 9 inches, and that at a point where people were likely to dive in it was only 6 feet. The defendant paid various amounts but the balance due still amounted to £39 000. The claimants sued for this balance and the defendant counterclaimed for breach of contract. The trial judge awarded the defendant damages of £2 500 for loss of amenity. Despite the fact that the shortfall in depth did not decrease the value of the swimming pool, the Court of Appeal nevertheless awarded the defendant £21 560 damages. This figure was based on the cost of making good the breach of contract by re-digging the swimming pool. The claimants appealed to the House of Lords.

Held. The defendant's damages should not be the cost of re-digging the swimming pool to make it conform to the contract specifications. It would be unreasonable for the defendant to insist on this and out of all proportion to the benefit which he would obtain. The defendant was therefore only entitled to damages for the difference in value between the pool as it was and the pool as it ought to have been. However, even where there had been no diminished value modest damages could be awarded for loss of expectation of performance, loss of a pleasurable amenity or failure to satisfy a personal preference. The trial judge's award of £2 500 was restored.

As well as damages generally being available for the cost of remedying a defect, they would also be available for other foreseeable consequential losses. Let us assume that Y Ltd is a small bakery and that X contracts to service the bakery's oven, knowing that it is the bakery's only oven. If X's service is badly performed and renders the oven useless then Y Ltd will be able to claim damages not only for the cost of remedying the defect but also for profits lost until the oven could be repaired or replaced. An example of this sort of situation was seen in *Victoria Laundry v Newman Industries*, where the £16 per week ordinary business profit was claimable from the date when the boiler should have been supplied until the date when it was actually supplied.

Where a loss suffered by the injured party would be subject to taxation (for example, lost earnings) the amount of damages should be the amount which the injured party would have received after tax had been paid. This is a logical consequence of contract damages being designed to put the injured party in the position he would have been in if the contract had been performed.

Damages paid by the injured party

It commonly happens that a business buyer who is supplied with defective goods finds himself in breach of contract when such goods are sold on. Damages paid to the second buyer will be recoverable by the first buyer if the selling on was within one of the two rules in *Hadley v Baxendale*.

Pinnock Bros v Lewis & Peat Ltd
[1923] 1 KB 690

The defendants sold copra cake, which was to be used as cattle food, to the claimant. The claimant resold the cake to B, who resold it to C, who resold it to farmers, who used it for feeding cattle. The cake was poisonous to cattle. The claimant sought damages from the defendants.

Held. The claimant was entitled to recover damages to cover the damages and costs he had himself had to pay out, because it was within the contemplation of the parties that such a loss would arise.

Damages which are difficult to quantify

The fact that damages are hard to quantify will not prevent an award of damages.

Chaplin v Hicks
[1911] 2 KB 786 (Court of Appeal)

The defendants had advertised a beauty contest in their newspaper. There were 6 000 entrants and these were whittled down to 50, one of whom was the claimant. There were to be 12 winners, and their prizes were that they would be employed as actresses for three years. The first four winners were to be paid £5 a week, the next four £4 a week and the last four £3 a week. The defendants breached the contract by not allowing the claimant the chance to become one of the winners. The other 49 women did proceed and 12 were selected as winners. The jury awarded the claimant £100 damages and an appeal was made to the Court of Appeal.

Held. The claimant was entitled to damages for loss of opportunity to win one of the prizes and the jury's award was allowed to stand.

COMMENT This case was considered to be correct by the House of Lords in *Gregg v Scott* [2005] UKHL 2, considered in Chapter 12 at 12.2.2.

Joyce v Bowman Law Ltd
[2010] EWHC 251, [2010] PNLR 22

A licensed conveyancer negligently breached a contract, in that he failed to include an option giving a house buyer the right to buy additional, adjoining land for £20 000. This option was to be available to the buyer only if the seller of the property failed to get planning permission to develop the additional land within 12 months. The buyer of the house

accepted that the house he bought was worth no less than he had paid for it. Nor did he argue that the adjoining land was inherently valuable and worth more than £20 000. Instead he claimed the profit which he could have made by exercising the option, knocking down the house he bought, and building a large house on the combined plots of land. The claimant's profit, if his plan had gone ahead, would have been £375 000. However, he could have mitigated his loss by building a new house on the original plot of land which he bought. If he had done this his profit would have been £245 000. Mitigation was required because the claimant always intended to demolish the old house, which was dilapidated, and develop the property to the greatest possible extent.

Held. In order to make the additional profit of £130 000 four hurdles would need to have been overcome. The judge thought that there was a real and substantial chance of these becoming overcome, rather than a mere speculative chance and awarded a percentage chance to each. First, the claimant would need to have been granted a watertight option which he could have exercised after one year if the seller had not obtained planning permission. (85 per cent.) Second, the claimant would have needed to exercise that option. (100 per cent.) Third, the claimant would have needed planning permission for the new house on the combined plots. (40 per cent.) Finally, the claimant would have needed to get funding to build a large house on the combined plots. (85 per cent.) The combined chance of all of these things happening was 28.9 per cent (85% × 100% × 40% × 85%), which the judge rounded up to 29 per cent. The claimant was therefore awarded damages of 29 per cent of £130 000, which came to £37 700.

Damages for injured feelings and disappointment

As a general rule damages are not recoverable for loss of enjoyment, although they clearly can be recoverable for physical injury or physical or mental illness.

However, in exceptional cases damages are recoverable for loss of enjoyment, particularly where the object of the contract was to provide the claimant with enjoyment and relaxation. In *Jarvis v Swans Tours Ltd* [1973] 1 QB 233 (Court of Appeal), for example, the claimant was awarded damages for disappointment and distress caused by a skiing holiday being particularly disastrous. In *Watts v Morrow* [1991] 4 All ER 97 Bingham LJ said that damages were not generally available for distress, frustration, anxiety, displeasure, tension or aggravation. However, he recognised two exceptions. First, where the very object of the contract was to provide pleasure, relaxation, peace of mind or freedom from molestation and the contract did not succeed in achieving that. (A contract to survey a house for a prospective purchaser was not an example of such a contract.) Second, damages could be recovered for physical inconvenience and discomfort caused by a breach of contract and also for mental suffering which was directly related to that physical inconvenience or discomfort. These views were approved by the House of Lords in the following case.

Farley v Skinner
[2001] UKHL 49, [2002] 2 AC 732 (House of Lords)

A surveyor was employed by a potential house purchaser to survey a house and particularly to find out if there were any problems with noise from aircraft. The surveyor breached the contract by stating that there was no problem with aircraft noise. In fact there was, as aircraft were 'stacked' above the house before coming in to land. This noise materially affected the use and enjoyment of the house, particularly at weekends. Relying on the survey, the potential purchaser bought the house. The county court judge thought that the noise did not affect the value of the house but nevertheless awarded damages of £10 000. The Court of Appeal overturned this award. Applying **Watts v Morrow**, it thought that the very object of the contract was not to provide pleasure and that the noise did not amount to physical inconvenience. An appeal was made to the House of Lords.

Held. The judge's award of £10 000 was restored. The case came within the first category set out in **Watts v Morrow**. The contract was not one designed principally to provide pleasure, relaxation or peace of mind but it was enough that a major object of the contract was to do this.

COMMENT Lords Scott and Steyn also thought that damages could be recovered under the second category set out in **Watts v Morrow**. Stressing that it can be very difficult to decide when inconvenience is 'physical', Lord Scott thought that the distinction should be based on the cause of the inconvenience, not on a distinction between different types of inconvenience. He said: 'If the cause is no more than disappointment that the contractual obligation

has been broken, damages are not recoverable even if the disappointment has led to a complete mental breakdown. But if the cause of the inconvenience or discomfort is a sensory (sight, touch, hearing, smell etc.) experience, damages can, subject to the remoteness rule, be recovered.'

The following case provides an interesting example of a claim, amongst other things, for injured feelings.

Wiseman v Virgin Atlantic Airways Ltd
[2006] EWHC 1566, [2006] All ER (D) 344 (Jun)

The defendants refused to let the claimant board a plane back from Nigeria even though he had a return ticket. This was because he would not pay a bribe. The defendants also ridiculed him in front of his church friends and accused him of having a fake passport. The defendants admitted that they were in breach of contract. The claimant made strenuous efforts to return to the United Kingdom and managed to do so after 12 days, during which time he was attacked by robbers.

Held. The defendant could recover damages for legitimate expenses caused by the breach. These damages included the cost of reasonable accommodation, food, transport, phone calls and postage. He was not entitled to damages for the following things:

(i) Expenses which his fiancée in England incurred while he was in Nigeria. These expenses did not flow from the breach and were anyway too remote.

(ii) The breakdown in his relationship with his fiancée, whom he was going to meet at the airport on his return. The court did not accept that the defendants' breach caused this breakdown, but even if it had damages for distress could not be claimed, applying **Watts v Morrow**.

(iii) Expenses incurred by his church friends. These expenses were too remote.

(iv) W's breakdown in health. This was too remote because at the time of the contract the parties would not have considered it a 'not unlikely consequence' of the breach.

(v) The robbery, because the breach of contract was not the cause of the robbery.

Damages for losses caused to third parties
This subject was considered under the heading Privity of contract in Chapter 4 at 4.2.2.2.

Damages for expenses incurred in reliance on the contract

Instead of claiming damages to compensate for the lost bargain, the injured party may instead claim damages for expenditure wasted in reliance on the contract.

Anglia Television Ltd v Reed
[1972] 1 QB 60

Robert Reed, a well-known actor, agreed to play the lead part in a television play which the claimants were producing. Shortly after making the contract the defendant repudiated it. The claimants, who could not get a substitute at short notice, accepted the repudiation. The claimants claimed all of their wasted expenditure, which amounted to £2 750. The defendant argued that they should only get the amount of expenditure wasted after the contract had been concluded, £854.

Held. The claimants could choose to claim their wasted expenditure instead of their lost profits. Furthermore, they could recover £2 750 because when the contract was made this was the amount which would reasonably be in the parties' contemplation as the amount wasted if the contract were broken.

COMMENT Although the injured party may generally elect to claim either on the basis of the loss of the bargain or on the basis of wasted expenditure, this is not always the case. The court may force the injured party to claim on the loss of the bargain basis where he has made a bad bargain and where the circumstances show that the wasted expenditure would not have been recovered anyway (*C & P Haulage v Middleton* [1983] 3 All ER 94).

7.2.2.3 Mitigation of loss

A party faced with a breach of contract will not be able to claim for losses which could have been mitigated by taking reasonable steps. Whether or not a loss would have been avoided by the taking of reasonable steps is a question of fact, depending upon the circumstances of the case.

Brace v Calder
[1895] 2 QB 253 (Court of Appeal)

On 23 December 1892 a partnership of four partners appointed the claimant their office manager for a two year period at £300 a year. In May 1893 the partnership was dissolved when two of the partners retired. The two remaining partners carried on business in the firm's name and the claimant did not find out that the original partnership had been dissolved until the end of July 1893. The dissolution was a breach of the claimant's contract of employment and, technically, meant that he had been wrongfully dismissed. When the claimant did find out about the dissolution the two remaining partners agreed to honour the contract he had made. The claimant sued for breach of contract.

Held. A breach of contract had occurred, but the claimant should have mitigated his loss by accepting the offer of alternative employment. He was therefore only entitled to nominal damages from the original partners.

The burden of proof is on the party in breach of contract who is alleging a failure to mitigate. In *Lombard North Central Plc v Automobile World (UK) Ltd* [2010] EWCA Civ 20, [2010] All ER (D) 166 (Jan) Rix LJ said:

'it is well recognised that the duty to mitigate is not a demanding one ... it is the party in breach which has placed the other party in a difficult situation. The burden of proof is therefore on the party in breach to demonstrate a failure to mitigate. The other party only has to do what is reasonable in the circumstances.'

Earlier in this chapter we examined *White and Carter (Councils) v MacGregor* and saw that a party faced with an anticipatory breach, who chooses to keep the contract alive, and who can perform the contract without the assistance of the other party, whilst having a legitimate interest in doing so, may be able to claim damages even in respect of losses which could have been mitigated.

7.2.2.4 Causation and contributory negligence

A defendant will be liable for a loss only if his breach of contract caused the loss. However, the defendant's breach does not need to be the sole cause of the loss. Causation is a matter of fact. In *Siemens Building Technology FE Ltd v Supershield Ltd* [2009] EWHC 927, [2009] 2 All ER (Comm) 900 the defendants caused a building to be flooded when water overflowed from a sprinkler tank. A valve should have turned the water off but it did not do so because the defendants had not tightened a nut and bolt properly. Drains, alarms and maintenance systems, for which the defendants were not responsible, failed. If they had worked properly they might have prevented the flood. The defendants were liable for the loss caused by the flood because their failure to tighten the nuts and bolts was an effective cause of the flood. The Law Reform (Contributory Negligence) Act 1945 is considered in Chapter 12 at 12.2.7.1. The Act is concerned mainly with liability in tort. It provides that a claimant's damages should be reduced where the loss arose partly as a result of his own fault. The Act will not apply in contract cases where the defendant's liability is strict, that is to say where liability does not depend upon negligence on the part of the defendant. It will apply in cases where the defendant's breach of contractual duty to take care would also amount to a tort. There is some doubt as to whether or not it would apply to an intermediate situation, where the contract required the defendant to take care but where there would be no common law duty to do so.

7.2.2.5 Agreed damages

Generally, the damages for breach of contract will be unliquidated, meaning that they will be fixed by the court rather than by the parties. Sometimes, however, a term of the contract provides exactly what the damages should be in the event of breach. These agreed damages may be one of two things; liquidated damages or penalties.

Liquidated damages

Liquidated damages are a **genuine pre-estimate of the loss** and will be applied no matter what the actual loss.

Penalties

Penalties are not a genuine pre-estimate of the loss, but are designed to warn a party against breaking his contract. The courts will ignore penalty clauses completely and calculate damages in the usual way. Figure 7.1 shows an outline of the law relating to damages for breach of contract.

An example will show how penalties and liquidated damages operate.

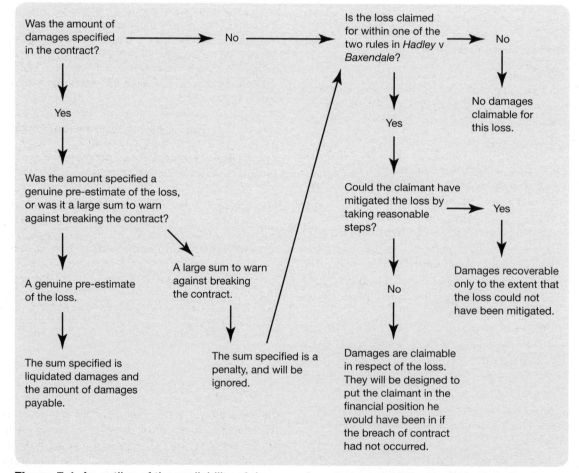

Figure 7.1 An outline of the availability of damages for a loss caused by a breach of contract

Example

Let us assume that a builder agrees to build a new shop, and that a term of the contract provides that if the shop is not ready on time the builder will pay £1 000 damages for every week that completion is late.

If the court considered that this sum of £1 000 a week was what the parties genuinely thought the loss to the shop owner would be, when the contract was made, then the term would be liquidated damages and the builder would have to pay at the rate of £1 000 a week no matter what the actual loss which the shop suffered. (The £1 000 a week would have been a 'genuine pre-estimate of the loss'.)

If the court considered that the figure of £1 000 a week was not what the parties thought the loss would be, but was designed to warn the builder against breaking the contract, then the term would be a penalty and would be ignored. Damages would then be calculated in the usual way.

In *Dunlop Pneumatic Tyre Co Ltd v New Garage Ltd* [1915] AC 79 (House of Lords) Lord Dunedin laid down five rules for distinguishing penalties and liquidated damages:

(1) If the stipulated damages are greater than could conceivably flow from the breach then the clause providing for such damages will be a penalty.
(2) 'It is no obstacle to the sum stipulated being a genuine prc-estimate of damage, that the consequences of breach are such as to make precise pre-estimation almost an impossibility. On the contrary, that is just the situation where it is probable that pre-estimated damage was the true bargain between the parties.'
(3) The clause will be presumed to be a penalty if it makes the same sum payable as damages for several different breaches which are likely to cause different amounts of loss.
(4) If the breach of contract consists solely of not paying a fixed sum of money, and the clause provides that in the event of breach a greater sum shall be payable as damages, this will invariably be a penalty.
(5) Calling the clause a 'penalty' or 'liquidated damages' is relevant in deciding its status but is not decisive.

A sum of money which becomes payable for a reason other than breach of contract cannot be a penalty.

Euro London Appointments Ltd v Claessens International Ltd
[2006] EWCA Civ 385, [2006] 2 Lloyd's Rep 436

An agency provided staff to an employer for a certain price. A term, clause 4.1, provided that if this price was paid in full within seven days of receipt of the invoice, it would be refunded on a sliding scale in the event of the staff proving unsuitable within 12 weeks. The staff provided did prove unsuitable within 12 weeks. However, the employer had not paid the full price within seven days of receipt of the invoice and was therefore refused the rebate.

Held. The term was not a penalty, it was just a condition precedent to claiming the rebate. As clause 4.1 was merely a condition precedent to getting the rebate, the employer did not breach the contract by not paying in time. The clause could not therefore be a penalty because penalties arise only where the excessive sum of money becomes payable on account of a breach of contract. If one term had said that the employer must pay within seven days, and that if he did not he would lose the rebate, then this would have been a penalty as the breach in not paying on time would have caused the full, excessive sum to be paid even though the staff provided were unsuitable. So the employer could not get the rebate and had to pay the full contract price.

COMMENT (i) A different term, clause 3.1(c), said the employer should pay within seven days of receipt of the invoice. However, this did not make clause 4.1 a penalty because the two clauses were not interdependent.

(ii) Chadwick LJ approved Lord Diplock's summary of what a penalty is, taken from *Philip Bernstein Ltd v Lydiate Textiles Ltd* [1962] CA Transcript 238. 'In the ordinary way a penalty is a sum which, by the terms of the contract, a promisor agrees to pay to the promisee in the event of a non-performance by the promisor of one or more of the obligations and which is in excess of the damage caused by such non-performance.'

7.2.2.6 Interest

A court is allowed to order the payment of interest on all claims for judgment or damages. The interest is payable from the date when the claim arose. In addition, the parties may expressly or impliedly agree to pay interest at a certain rate.

7.2.3 An action for an agreed sum

A person who brings an action for an amount agreed in the contract, perhaps for the price in a contract of sale of goods, is not suing for damages. For example, if X agrees to buy Y's car for £3 500 but then refuses to pay the price Y might bring an action for the price. Because such a claim would not be for damages the rules on remoteness, quantification and mitigation of damages would not be relevant. The seller's action for the price in a contract of sale of goods is examined in Chapter 10 at 10.3.2.

Earlier in this chapter, when considering discharge of obligations by performance, we saw that the general rule is that, unless a contract is divisible, a party will only be able to sue for the contract price when he had completely discharged his own obligations. We also saw that there are several exceptions to this general rule.

7.2.4 Specific performance

As we have seen, the usual remedy for a breach of contract is an award of damages. However, in certain circumstances such an award does not adequately achieve justice. Equity therefore developed the remedies of specific performance and injunction to cater for these situations.

Specific performance is a court order requiring a person to perform his contract. If the party disobeys this order he will be in contempt of court. For example, if A agrees to sell a painting to B but then refuses to hand it over, a decree of specific performance would order A to hand the painting over. If A still refused to do so he would be in contempt of court and would be liable to a fine or imprisonment.

The courts are somewhat reluctant to order specific performance, and there are many circumstances in which it will not be ordered.

First, specific performance will not be ordered where damages would be an adequate remedy, unless the court considers specific performance the more appropriate remedy. Therefore it will not normally be ordered where a seller refuses to deliver mass-produced goods, because generally the buyer will be able to use his damages to buy similar goods elsewhere.

However, if a seller refuses to deliver unique goods then damages will not be an adequate remedy. If a person agreed to sell a painting by Picasso, for example, and then went back on his contract it is quite likely that specific performance would be ordered. Damages would not adequately compensate the buyer because he would not be able to use the damages to buy a similar painting.

All plots of land are regarded as unique and if a seller of land refuses to go through with the sale specific performance will generally be ordered. The Courts of Equity thought it only fair that if specific performance could be ordered in favour of one party then, as a general principle, it should also be available to the other party. Therefore if a buyer of land refuses to complete, specific performance will generally be ordered against him.

A second limitation on the awarding of specific performance is that, being an equitable remedy, it will not be ordered in favour of a party who has behaved unfairly. An ancient equitable maxim expressed this by saying *'He who comes to Equity must come with clean hands'*. In the following case the claimant did not have *'clean hands'* and so equity would not help him.

Falcke v Gray (1859) ER 4 Drew 651

A landlady let a room to the claimant, an antique dealer. It was agreed that when the six-month lease had expired the dealer could buy a pair of china vases from the landlady for £20 each. The dealer told the landlady that he thought this a fair price. Shortly afterwards the landlady began to have her doubts. She asked another dealer for a valuation. This dealer offered £200 for the vases. The landlady accepted this offer and the second dealer took the vases away. The claimant claimed specific performance against the landlady and that the second dealer should be ordered to hand the vases over to him.

Held. Although this was not a contract where damages would be an adequate remedy, specific performance was not granted because the claimant had behaved inequitably. The parties were not on an equal footing and the claimant knew that the price he had agreed to pay was grossly inadequate.

However, a party will not be protected against specific performance merely because he has made a bad deal. As long as the other party has behaved fairly specific performance can be ordered, as the following case demonstrates.

Mountford v Scott
[1975] 1 All ER 198 (Court of Appeal)

In December 1971 the defendant sold an option for £1. The option gave the claimant the right to buy the defendant's house for £10 000, if he so wished, at any time within the next six months. The claimant had taken options on three other houses because he was considering developing the land on which the four houses stood. In January 1972 the defendant tried to call the option off. In March the claimant exercised the option. The defendant refused to vacate the house, saying that with the £10 000 he could not find another suitable house. The claimant sued for specific performance.

Held. Specific performance was granted.

Russell LJ: 'If the owner of a house contracts with his eyes open ... it cannot in my eyes be right to deny specific performance to the purchaser because the vendor then finds it difficult to find a house to buy that suits him and his family ...'

COMMENT (i) It was suggested that £1 was insufficient consideration for the granting of the option. This was rejected as 'a startling proposition' by Russell LJ.

(ii) The bargain was not in any way unconscionable. At the time of the contract the house was not worth more than £10 000. The defendant had in fact successfully held out for £1 000 more than his neighbours.

Equitable remedies are only awarded at the court's discretion. There are many circumstances in which the courts use their discretion and refuse to order specific performance. For example, a court will not order specific performance where to do so would cause undue hardship to the defendant. Similarly, specific performance will not be ordered for on-going contracts which would require constant supervision because of the rule that 'Equity does nothing in vain'. Specific performance will not therefore be ordered in contracts of employment. To order specific performance of employment contracts would be in vain, because the court would find it impossible to check that the employer and employee were fulfilling their respective duties. Nor

will specific performance be awarded in favour of or against a minor.

It should be noted that despite this an employer can be ordered to reinstate an unfairly dismissed employee under the Employment Rights Act 1996 s.112. This is not specific performance, it is merely a statutory provision. If the employer refuses to obey the order he will not be in contempt of court but will have to pay greater compensation. (See Chapter 20 at 20.4.4.1.)

7.2.5 Injunction

An injunction is a court order requiring a person to do or not to do a certain thing. A person who refuses to obey an injunction will be in contempt of court. The granting of an injunction, to prevent an action which would deliberately cause a breach of contract, is an equitable remedy for breach of contract. It is, however, not ordered where damages would be an adequate remedy.

It is possible that an injunction which would amount to specific performance will be ordered in a contract to supply generic goods. In *Sky Petroleum v VIP Petroleum* [1974] 1 All ER 954 the defendants had a ten-year contract to supply the claimants with petrol. During an oil crisis oil became exceedingly difficult to get. The defendants threatened to terminate the agreement, claiming a breach of contract by the claimants. The court granted the claimants an injunction which prevented the defendants from withholding supplies of petrol, even though in effect this amounted to specific performance of the contract.

Specific performance of a personal service contract will not be ordered, as we have seen. In the following case the claimant applied for an injunction to prevent a breach of a personal service contract.

Lumley v Wagner (1853) 1 De GM & G 604

The defendant agreed to sing at the claimant's theatres twice a week for three months, and not to perform elsewhere during this period. She decided to break the contract and sing elsewhere.

Held. An injunction was granted, ordering her not to perform elsewhere until the three months were up.

However, an injunction will not be granted if its effect would amount to an order of specific performance of a personal service contract.

Page One Records Ltd v Britton
[1968] 1 WLR 157

A pop group, the Troggs, made a written agreement with the claimant in 1967. The agreement provided that the claimant should be the group's manager for a five-year period, and that the group would not appoint anyone else as manager. Shortly afterwards the Troggs wanted to replace the claimant as their manager. The claimant could not have asked for specific performance because this will not be ordered in personal service contracts. Instead the claimant asked for an injunction to prevent the Troggs from employing anyone else as their manager.

Held. This injunction could not be granted. It would amount to specific performance. The Troggs definitely needed a manager. If they could not employ anyone else they would be compelled to employ the claimant or to disband. Stamp J: 'Indeed, it is the claimant's own case that the Troggs are simple persons, of no business experience, and could not survive without the services of a manager.'

However, there is no reason why an injunction should not be granted if it merely persuades, rather than compels, a person to honour a contract of employment.

Warner Bros Pictures Inc v Nelson
[1936] 1 KB 209

The defendant, better known as the actress Bette Davis, made a two-year contract with the claimants. Under this contract, which was made in the United States, she agreed to act for the claimants and not to act for anyone else. The defendant came to the United Kingdom with the intention of appearing in a film not made by the claimants. The claimants sought an injunction to prevent her from doing this.

Held. The injunction was granted. It did not compel the defendant to act for the claimants because she could earn a living performing other jobs. It was however very likely to persuade her to act for the claimants as this paid far more than any other types of work she was likely to obtain.

The injunctions which we have so far considered have been prohibitory injunctions, that is to say that they have been sought to prevent a person from breaching the terms of a contract. A mandatory injunction orders a person to commit some positive act to prevent a further breach of contract. Such an injunction is very rarely granted as a remedy for breach of contract.

7.2.5.1 Freezing injunction (formerly known as *Mareva injunction*)

A person who knows that an injunction against himself is about to be sought might attempt to pre-empt the effect of this by moving assets out of the jurisdiction of the English courts. A freezing injunction prevents specified assets from being moved out of the court's jurisdiction. It is an interlocutory injunction, meaning that it can only be ordered once court proceedings have commenced, and that it is not the final outcome of the dispute in question. The injunction was first used in *Mareva Compania Naviera SA v International Bulk Carriers SA* [1975] 2 Lloyd's Rep 509 and its use is now provided for by Supreme Court Act 1981 s.37(3).

The party seeking the injunction will normally do so without the other party being present. The court has a discretion as to whether or not to grant the injunction and will try to balance the interests of the parties. The claimant will have to prove not only that he is likely to win the case, but also that the defendant has assets which may well be moved out of the jurisdiction. The claimant must specify over precisely which assets the injunction is being sought, and may be asked to provide an indemnity against the injunction turning out not to have been justified.

7.2.5.2 Search order (formerly known as *Anton Pillar order*)

This injunction allows the claimant to inspect, photocopy or take away documents belonging to another party. It is sought without the other party being present and it must be necessary to prevent the other party from destroying or removing the documents. Because of the drastic nature of the injunction it is only ordered in very exceptional circumstances. The injunction was first used in the case immediately below, but is now granted by virtue of Supreme Court Act 1981 s.33.

Anton Pillar KG v Manufacturing Processes Ltd [1976] 1 All ER 779 (Court of Appeal)

The defendants were an English company who acted as agents for the claimants, a German company who manufactured frequency converters for computers. The claimants claimed that the defendants were passing on confidential information about their products to other German companies. The claimants applied for an interim injunction to prevent the defendants from infringing →

their copyrights and disclosing confidential information. They wanted permission to enter the defendants' premises to inspect all such documents and to allow the claimants' solicitor to have custody of them.

Held. An injunction was granted, allowing the claimants' solicitor to enter the defendants' premises and to remove the confidential material. This was allowed only because the claimants seemed to have a very strong case, because the actual or potential damage to the claimants was very serious, and because there was clear evidence that the defendants possessed vital material which they might destroy or dispose of so as to defeat the doing of justice.

In enforcing rights granted under a search order the claimants must act carefully and with full respect for the defendants' rights.

7.2.6 **Rectification**

Rectification is an equitable remedy which allows a written document to be corrected if it does not accurately reflect the terms of an oral contract which the parties subsequently decided to reduce to writing. It is not a remedy for breach of contract.

Rectification will only be ordered if the following conditions are satisfied: the parties did reach a definite oral agreement as to the terms of the contract; this agreement did not change up until the time when the contract was written down; and what was written down did not accurately record what had been agreed. An example of rectification can be seen in *Craddock Brothers Ltd* **v** *Hunt* [1923] 2 Ch 136. In that case there was a verbal agreement for the sale of land. When this agreement was reduced into writing there was a mutual mistake so that the written agreement did not accurately reflect what the parties had agreed. The mistake was embodied in a deed of conveyance, but the Court of Appeal ordered that the conveyance be rectified to reflect the true intentions of the parties.

7.2.7 *Quantum meruit*

A party to a contract may occasionally claim for payment on a *quantum meruit*. Such a claim will be for work done, paying the amount that is deserved. A *quantum meruit* can only be claimed in the following circumstances: if the other party prevented completion of the contract (see *Planché* **v** *Colburn* above at 7.1.1.3); or if work has been done and

accepted under a void or partially performed contract; or if the contract did not expressly provide what the remuneration should be. If it were not for the possibility of a claim on a *quantum meruit* one of the parties to the contract might become unjustly enriched.

7.2.7.1 **Restitution**

Restitution is not a remedy for breach of contract, but allows a party to recover money which has been paid. In relation to the law of contract, restitution can arise in two circumstances. First, where there has been a total failure of consideration (see *Rowland* **v** *Divall* [1923] 2 KB 500 in Chapter 8 at 8.2.1). Second, where money was paid under a common mistake as to fact which avoided the contract (see *Scott* **v** *Coulson* in the previous chapter at 6.2.1.1).

Restitution, in the form of accounting for profits made while acting in breach of contract, also arose in the following case.

Attorney General v Blake (Jonathan Cape Ltd, third party) [2001] 1 AC 268 (House of Lords)

In 1961 a spy, George Blake, was sentenced to 41 years' imprisonment. He escaped from prison in 1966 and went to live in Moscow. In 1990 he published his autobiography, in which he described his life as a spy. This was a breach of contract because when he joined the secret services he had signed an agreement that he would never reveal anything about this work. The case was brought because Blake's British publishers had £90 000 which they intended to pay to Blake.

Held. Blake had to account to the Government, the other contracting party, for the profits he had made by doing the very thing he had contracted not to do. Such a remedy would arise only in very exceptional circumstances and only where the claimant had a legitimate interest in preventing the defendant's profit-making activity and of depriving him of his profit.

COMMENT (i) Lord Hobhouse dissented, believing that the court had sacrificed general contract principles in their desire to prevent Blake from benefiting from his deplorable criminal behaviour.

(ii) In the somewhat similar case of *R* **v** *Attorney General for England and Wales* [2003] UKPC 22, set out in detail in Chapter 6 at 6.3.2.2, the Privy Council upheld an order for an account of profits.

7.2.8 **Time limits on remedies**

A person sued on a contract may be able to plead the Limitation Act 1980 as a defence.

A simple contract, that is to say one not made by a deed, cannot be sued upon after six years have expired from the date when the right to sue arose (Limitation Act 1980 s.5). It should be noted that this is not necessarily six years from the making of the contract. It is six years from the breach. If the claim is for personal injuries then the time limit is reduced to three years after the time when the right to sue arose or from the date when the injured person knew of the injury, but the court has a discretion to extend this period. Section 8(1) of the Act provides that a contract made by deed cannot be sued upon when more than 12 years have expired from the time when the right to sue arose.

Where a party is suffering from a legal disability the time limits do not run until the disability has been removed. They do not therefore run against minors until they reach the age of 18 and do not run against mentally disordered persons until they cease to be mentally disordered. Where a party is the victim of fraud the time limits will not start to run until the fraud is discovered or ought to have been discovered.

Where the claim is for a debt or is otherwise a liquidated claim, then the time limits will begin again if a person acknowledges the debt in writing. (There is no need for an agreement to pay it.) It also begins again with every payment made in respect of the debt. Where the amount claimed is unliquidated, and therefore cannot be quantified in figures, acknowledgement of it or a payment will not cause the time limits to start again.

The statutory time limits do not apply to equitable remedies, but these are lost much more quickly through 'laches' or unreasonable delay in pursuing them. In *Fisher v Brooker and others* [2009] UKHL 41, [2009] 1 WLR 1764 the House of Lords held that a member of the band Procol Harum could bring a claim for a future share in the musical copyright in the band's hit song 'A Whiter Shade of Pale' thirty-eight years after the song was released. No statutory limitation applies to a claim for copyright in English law. The claim was not defeated by laches for two reasons. First, laches can only defeat a claim to equitable relief. What was being claimed here was not equitable relief, but a declaration as to the existence of a long-term property right. Second, the doctrine of laches would have applied only if the claimant had done some acts during the period of delay and if these acts had resulted in a 'balance of justice' which would justify refusing his claim. However, the defendants had suffered no prejudice on account of the delay and even if they had this would have been far outweighed by the benefits which the delay had conferred on them.

Test your understanding 7.4

1 Is an action for an agreed sum the same as an action for damages?

2 What is a claim on a *quantum meruit*? In what circumstances can such a claim be made?

3 What is specific performance?

4 What is an injunction?

Key points

Discharge of liability by performance

■ A party will be entitled to treat his further obligation to perform the contract as discharged if the other party breached a condition rather than a warranty, or if the other party breached an innominate term in such a way that this breach deprived of substantially the whole benefit of the contract.

■ The general rule is that if a contract consists of one entire obligation then that obligation must be completely performed or the other party will have no obligation to perform the contract.

■ If a contract is divisible or severable then it will consist of several obligations. If only some of the obligations are performed this will not necessarily discharge the other party from performing the contract. However, damages will have to be paid as regards the parts of the contract which were not performed.

■ A party can receive payment for an entire obligation which was not completely performed if the other contracting party genuinely accepted the partial performance, or if the obligation was substantially performed or if the other party prevented complete performance.

■ A seller who properly tenders the delivery of goods discharges himself from further obligation

→

and can sue for damages for non-acceptance if the tender is not accepted.

■ A buyer who tenders the price cannot be sued on the contract if he pays the sum tendered into court.

Discharge of liability by agreement

■ A contract can be discharged or varied by accord and satisfaction (agreement and consideration). The accord and satisfaction must amount to a new contract.

■ A party who waives a strict legal right will not later be able to claim breach of contract on account of the right waived not being adhered to. However, the right waived may be reintroduced by reasonable notice.

Frustration

■ A contract can be frustrated if after the contract has been created, but before it has been performed, any of the following circumstances arise: the subject matter of the contract ceases to exist; a person who was to perform personally has become unavailable; an event which was central to the contract has not occurred; the contract cannot be performed in the manner agreed in the contract; or the contract has become illegal to perform.

■ Frustration cannot be claimed by a party if the 'frustrating' event was his own fault, or if he was the only party who foresaw the event or should have foreseen it.

■ A *force majeure* clause spells out what should happen if an event which would ordinarily frustrate a contract arises. Such clauses are given legal effect.

■ The Law Reform (Frustrated Contracts) Act 1943 provides that when a contract is frustrated the following provisions apply: money owing ceases to be due; money paid is recoverable, although the court has a power to allow some money paid or payable to be retained to cover expenses; a party who has received a valuable benefit may be ordered to pay a just amount to compensate for this.

Discharge by breach

■ An anticipatory breach occurs when, before the time when performance of the contract was due, one of the parties lets the other know that he does not intend to be bound by the contract.

■ A party faced with an anticipatory breach may sue at once for breach of contract or keep the contract alive. If the contract is kept alive but not performed as agreed an actual breach of contract will then have occurred.

Damages

■ Contract damages are designed to put the injured party in the financial position which he would have been in if the contract had been properly performed.

■ Damages will not be awarded to compensate for losses which were too remote from the breach.

■ A loss arising from a breach of contract will be too remote unless it is within one of the two rules in *Hadley* v *Baxendale*. The first rule is that damages can be claimed for a loss if the loss arose naturally from the breach according to the usual course of things. The second rule is that damages can be claimed for a loss if both of the parties would have contemplated that the loss would be the probable result of breach, at the time when they made the contract.

■ Losses cannot be claimed in respect of a loss which could have been mitigated by the taking of reasonable steps.

■ If damages agreed in the contract were a genuine pre-estimate of loss they will be classified as liquidated damages and the amount specified will be the amount recoverable no matter what the actual loss. If the sum set out is a large sum designed to warn the other party against breaking the contract it will be a penalty clause. Such a clause will be ignored and damages will be calculated as if the clause had not existed.

Other remedies

■ An action for an agreed sum is an action in debt. Therefore the rules on remoteness, quantification and mitigation of damage do not need to be considered.

■ A party claiming on a *quantum meruit* claims for reasonable remuneration for work performed. Such a claim can be made if: the other party prevented completion of the contract; or if work has been done and accepted under a void or partially performed contract; or where the contract does not expressly provide what the remuneration should be.

■ Specific performance is a discretionary equitable remedy. When specific performance is granted a party is ordered to perform his contract. Failure to comply will put the party in contempt of court.

→

■ An injunction can be granted to prevent a person from breaking the terms of his contract. The remedy is equitable and discretionary.

■ A simple contract cannot be sued upon more than six years after the right to sue arose. If personal injuries are claimed these must generally be claimed within three years of the injuries arising. If the contract is made by deed the claim must be brought within 12 years of the right to sue arising.

■ The Limitation Act does not apply to the remedies of specific performance or injunction. These equitable remedies are lost if there is an unreasonable delay in pursuing them.

Summary questions

1 Arthur agrees to sell his car to Brian for £5 000. Thinking that he has won the lottery, Arthur delivers the car and tells Brian that he will accept a compact disc instead of the money. Brian happily gives Arthur the disc. Arthur has now discovered that he has not won the lottery. Advise Arthur as to whether or not:

i   He can give the disc back and insist on receiving the £5 000?

ii He could insist that Brian pays the remainder of the money if Arthur had promised to take £5 (rather than the compact disc) in full settlement of the debt.

2 Firm X has two contracts, one to supply pipes to Iran and the other to supply pipes to Iraq. During the Gulf War Britain declares war on Iraq and outlaws the export of goods to that country. It is still possible to supply the pipes to Iran but it means taking a much longer route. Advise Firm X as to whether or not either of these contracts would be frustrated.

3 In the **Davis Contractors** case Lord Radcliffe said: 'So, perhaps it would be simpler to say at the outset that frustration occurs whenever the law recognises that, without default of either party, a contractual obligation has become incapable of being performed because the circumstances in which performance is called for would render it a thing radically different from that which was undertaken by the contract.'

It can be useful to examine other cases in the light of this statement, asking whether the contractual obligation was incapable of being performed because the circumstances in which performance is called for would render it radically different from what was agreed in the contract.

For example, in **Krell v Henry** to have had the use of the room on a day when the procession did not take place would have been a radically different thing than what was envisaged when the contract was made.

Analyse the following cases in this way. In which of the cases would the circumstances have changed matters so that performance of the contract would be radically different from what was agreed in the contract?

a   **Herne Bay Steamboat Co v Hutton** (the day's cruise around the fleet).

b   **Davis Contractors v Fareham UDC** (building the 78 houses in eight months).

c   **Tsakiroglou v Noblee Thorl** (carrying the peanuts from Sudan to Germany).

Does the use of Lord Radcliffe's test in each case provide the same result as the actual decision of the court?

4 How would **Taylor v Caldwell** have been decided if:

a   The defendant had deliberately burnt down his own music hall?

b   The defendant's own negligence had caused a fire which destroyed the music hall?

5 How would **Maritime National Fish Ltd v Ocean Trawlers Ltd** have been decided if the Canadian Government had issued no licences to the defendants?

6 A taxi driver orders a new car, asking the garage to adapt the car for use as a taxi. The taxi is to be delivered the following week, but due to a shortage of labour, the garage cannot deliver on time. As soon as he had made the contract, the taxi driver sold his old taxi and went on holiday for a week. On his return the taxi driver loses business until he can acquire another taxi. The stress of this causes him to suffer a nervous breakdown and he consequently spends several thousand pounds on alternative medicines. Advise the taxi driver of the amount of damages he is likely to be able to recover from the garage.

7 On Grand National day a customer hires a car to take him to Aintree. The car does not turn up. Could the customer claim damages for having missed a day at the races?

Multiple choice questions

1 A builder agreed to build a house for £150 000. The builder completed all of the work. However, he failed to glaze the windows properly, with the result that the glass is likely to fall out of the windows in a moderate to strong wind. The builder found that he had no time to replace the glass, because he had started another job at the other end of the country. The owner of the house could not move into the house until the glass was replaced, so he hired a glazier to reglaze the windows, at a cost of £500.

Which one of the following statements is likely to reflect the legal position?

a The builder will not be entitled to any payment as he did not fully perform his contract.

b The builder substantially performed and therefore will be entitled to £149 500.

c The contract was frustrated and the builder will receive an amount calculated by reference to the Law Reform (Frustrated Contracts) Act 1943.

d The builder will be entitled to the full contract price. The owner, by employing the glazier to finish the job, impliedly accepted the work the builder had done.

2 Alice decides to have her house decorated and makes a contract under which Jackie is to do the work. The contract price is £2 000, which is to be payable on completion of the work. Shortly after the contract is made Alice decides that she would rather not have the work done. Jackie has plenty of work on and agrees that Alice can pull out of the contract if she pays £50 for materials which Jackie had bought especially for this job. Alice agrees to this. The following day Jackie loses a big contract to work elsewhere. Jackie now wants to hold Alice to the original agreement.

Which one of the following statements is true?

a The original contract is discharged. Alice will therefore have to pay the £50 for materials but no more.

b Jackie's obligation to do the work is discharged. Alice is completely discharged from any obligation to pay any money.

c Jackie has discharged her obligations by being willing to do the work. She can therefore insist on full payment of the £2 000.

d Jackie can insist that the contract goes ahead. She will be entitled to full payment, but only if she decorates Alice's house as originally agreed.

3 Cilla books a room in the Granchester Hilton for the first week in August, paying her bill in advance.

The price of a room in the Hilton varies throughout the year, depending on the tourist trade. The Granchester Festival takes place in the first week in August. During the first week in August the rooms in the Granchester Hilton are 10 per cent more expensive than in other summertime weeks. Because of a protest by local residents, the Granchester Festival is cancelled. Hearing of the Festival's cancellation, Cilla phones the Hilton to say that she no longer wishes to have the room for the week and that she wants a return of her money. The Hilton refuse to return any of the money. No mention of the Granchester Festival was made when Cilla booked the room, but as it happened the whole purpose of Cilla's holiday was to attend the Festival.

Which one of the following statements is true?

a Cilla will not be entitled to any refund.

b Cilla will be entitled to a full refund. The contract has become frustrated because it has become radically different.

c Cilla will be entitled to a full refund. The contract has become frustrated because it has become impossible to perform.

d The hotel has committed an anticipatory breach of contract. Cilla will be able to reclaim her money and perhaps also claim damages.

4 X Ltd orders 10 000 widgets from Y Ltd. The price is £10 000 and £5 000 is payable in advance and actually paid. After Y Ltd have manufactured 5 000 widgets, and delivered 1 000 of them to X Ltd, the Government outlaws the manufacture and sale of widgets.

Which one of the following statements is true?

a The contract is frustrated. The loss will lie where it falls. Y Ltd will therefore keep the £5 000 already paid, but be entitled to no more. X Ltd can keep the widgets already delivered.

b The contract is not frustrated because it was not X Ltd's fault that the production and sale of widgets became illegal.

c The contract is frustrated. The £5 000 paid to Y Ltd is returnable and the £5 000 owed is no longer due. However, X Ltd will have to return the widgets already delivered.

d The contract is frustrated. The £5 000 paid to Y Ltd is returnable and the £5 000 owed is no longer due. In addition, Y Ltd may be awarded expenses, up to the amount of £5 000, and X Ltd may have to pay an amount which is fair in respect to compensate for the benefit of the widgets already delivered.

→

5 Which one of the following statements is not true?

a Damages in respect of a loss arising from a breach of contract can be recovered if the loss arose naturally from the breach.

b Damages in respect of a loss arising from a breach of contract can be recovered if the loss would have been contemplated by both of the parties when they made the contract.

c A party cannot recover damages for a loss arising from a breach of contract if he could have avoided the loss by taking reasonable steps.

d A party can recover damages for a loss caused by a breach of contract as long as he can definitely prove that the loss would not have arisen if the contract had been properly performed.

6 A roofer agrees to put a new roof on a shop by 1 December for a price of £3 000. The shop owner explains that in December last year the shop made a profit of £300 per day. The roofer assures the shop owner that the job can be done on time. As the parties agree that the shop owner is likely to lose £300 a day for every day on which the shop cannot be opened, a term of the contract states that in the event of the roofer not performing the contract on time he will pay £300 damages for every day that he is late. The job turns out to be more difficult than the roofer had envisaged. The roofer does his best but cannot finish the job until 6 December. The shopkeeper admits that trade in the area has been well down on last year as a new supermarket has opened nearby. The profits made by neighbouring small shops indicate that this year the shop would only have made £150 profit per day.

Which one of the following statements is likely to reflect the true legal position?

a The contract is frustrated and the roofer is absolved from all liability. As the shop has received a valuable benefit worth £3 000, it will have to pay for this.

b The roofer will be entitled to the contract price, but will have to compensate the shop for the actual loss suffered. The roofer will therefore have to pay £150 per day damages.

c The roofer will be entitled to the contract price but will have to pay £300 damages per day, even though the shop did not suffer such a loss.

d The roofer will not be entitled to any payment. He did not perform his contractual obligations in accordance with the terms of the contract.

7 Which of the following contracts might be specifically enforceable?

i Arthur has agreed to sell his house to Bill, but no longer wishes to sell.

ii Charles has agreed to buy Duncan's house, but no longer wishes to buy it.

iii Edward has agreed to buy a new Ford Ka from a garage, but the garage is now refusing to go ahead with the contract.

iv Georgina has agreed to buy from Harold a painting by Rembrandt. Harold later changes his mind and refuses to hand the painting over.

v Luciano Pavadomingo has agreed to perform a concert at Julian's theatre. Luciano has a better engagement elsewhere and therefore does not intend to perform his contract with Julian.

vi A confused World War II veteran has agreed to sell his unique medal collection to a dealer for a quarter of its real value.

a All of the agreements.

b i, iii, v and vi only.

c i, ii and iv only.

d i, ii, iv and v only.

Task 7

Last year your company, Amcafe, made a contract to buy 10 000 tons of coffee beans from a coffee wholesaler. Due to a terrible frost in South America, there is now a world shortage of coffee. The wholesaler has managed to get only 10 000 tons of coffee beans, rather than the 50 000 tons he was expecting. The price of coffee beans has increased fourfold. The wholesaler intends to sell the 10 000 tons of beans to a new customer at the current higher price.

Your employer has asked you to draft a preliminary report, indicating:

1 Whether Amcafe will be able to force the wholesaler to deliver the 10 000 tons of beans, as agreed in the contract.

2 Whether Amcafe will be able to prevent the wholesaler from selling the beans to the new customer.

→

3 If Amcafe do not get the beans they will have to close their factory and will also be in breach of several contracts to supply supermarkets. Assuming that they do not get the beans, and that this is a breach of contract, would they be able to claim damages against the wholesaler in respect of:

   a The cost of closing their factory?

   b The damages which they themselves will have to pay to the supermarkets?

   c Profits they would lose by not making and selling coffee?

   d Health care required by the managing director, who had a heart attack when he heard that the contract had been breached?

mylawchamber *premium*

Visit **www.mylawchamber.co.uk/macintyre** to access study support resources including interactive multiple-choice questions, weblinks, glossary, glossary flashcards, legal newsfeed, answers to questions in this chapter, legal updates and an overview of this chapter all linked to the **Pearson eText** version of *Business Law* which you can **search**, **highlight** and **personalise** with your **own notes** and **bookmarks**.

Use **Case Navigator** to read in full some of the key cases referenced in this chapter with commentary and questions:

Transfield Shipping Inc v Mercator Shipping Inc, The Achilleas [2008] UKHL 48, [2009] AC 61
Ruxley Electronics and Construction Ltd v Forsyth [1996] AC 344
Gregg v Scott [2005] 4 All ER 812
AG v Blake [2001] 1 AC 268 (HL)

Terms implied by statute

Introduction

This chapter considers the following matters:

8.1 THE SALE OF GOODS ACT 1979

8.1.1 The definition of a contract of sale of goods

If a contract can be classified as a contract of sale of goods then it is the Sale of Goods Act (SGA) 1979 which implies the relevant terms into the contract in question. Our first task is therefore to examine the definition of a contract of sale of goods. This definition is to be found in SGA 1979 s.2(1), which states:

'A contract of sale of goods is a contract by which the seller transfers or agrees to transfer the property in goods to the buyer for a money consideration, called the price.'

There are then three requirements which must be satisfied before a contract can be classified as a contract of sale of goods. First, the buyer's obligation under the contract must be to pay a money consideration called the price. Second, the subject matter of the contract must be goods. Third, the seller's obligation under the contract must be transferring or agreeing to transfer the property in the goods to the buyer. Each of these three matters needs to be considered in turn.

8.1.1.1 A money consideration, called the price

In order for a transaction to be classified as a contract of sale of goods the buyer's consideration must consist of money. It does not matter whether the buyer pays the price in cash, or by cheque or by credit card. But a free gift, where the buyer pays no money, cannot be a sale. As well as excluding gifts, the requirement that the buyer's consideration be money rules out several types of contracts, such as contracts of barter or contracts where the buyer's consideration consists of performing some action.

It can be difficult to say whether or not a contract of part-exchange coupled with a payment of money is a sale of goods. In **Aldridge v Johnson** (1857) 7 El & Bl 885 the claimant gave the defendant 32 bullocks and £23 cash in return for 100 quarters of barley. The Court of Queen's Bench held that the parties intended this to be two contracts of sale of goods as the parties had valued the barley and the bullocks in monetary terms. The court was helped in reaching this conclusion because the contract stated that the barley was valued at £215 and the bullocks at £192. If the goods had not been given a price in this way then the contract would not have been a sale of goods but a contract of barter.

8.1.1.2 Sale and agreement to sell

Where the contract takes effect to immediately pass ownership to the buyer this is called a sale. Where the contract takes effect so that ownership is passed at some future time or when some condition is fulfilled this is called an agreement to sell. The time at which ownership passes from seller to buyer is considered in Chapter 9 at 9.1. Both sales and agreements to sell are covered by the provisions of SGA 1979. However, as we shall see, some very few sections apply only to sales and not to agreements to sell.

8.1.1.3 The meaning of goods

Section 61(1) of the Act defines goods as 'all personal chattels other than things in action'.

A **personal chattel** is a physical thing which can be **touched** and **moved**, for example a bicycle, a bed or a book.

A **thing in action** is a right which can only be enforced by suing (bringing a legal action). A guarantee, for example, is a thing in action. A guarantee may be written on a piece of paper but the paper is not the property. The property is the right which the guarantee gives and, ultimately, that right can only be enforced by suing the person who gave it. (See legal concepts of property in Chapter 23 at 23.1.)

Contracts to sell land or an interest in land are not included as goods, but s.61(1) tells us that emblements, which are annual crops cultivated by human labour, are included. Section 61(1) also includes as goods things attached to or forming part of the land if they are to be severed before sale or under the contract of sale.

Contracts to supply a service are not governed by the Sale of Goods Act 1979. A person who sells a service agrees to perform some action and does not 'agree to transfer the property in goods to the buyer', as required by s.2(1)'s definition. A contract of work and materials is not a sale of goods. For example, if a sculptor agrees to make a sculpture for a fixed price this is a contract of work and materials. If a sculptor sold a finished sculpture this would be a sale of goods. In making this distinction a court will try to ascertain the substance of the contract. The extent to which computer software can be classed as goods has yet to be authoritatively decided. Personal chattels which are made useful only by the software they contain, such as computers, are undoubtedly goods. In *Kingsway Hall Hotel Ltd* v *Red Sky IT Ltd* [2010] EWHC 965, (2010) 26 Const LJ 542 it was accepted without argument that an 'off the shelf' software package, which would allow a hotel to make reservations and book customers in and out, was goods. It may be the case that software which is downloaded from the Internet, rather than bought on a disk, cannot be classified as goods as the software is not contained on a personal chattel. If this is the case neither the Sale of Goods Act 1979 nor the Supply of Goods and Services Act 1982 would apply to the contract. So liability would not be strict but rather in the tort of negligence and therefore based on fault. However, it must be said that it would seem very strange to have different legal regimes applying to two contracts which are, in effect, virtually identical. It may also be the case that a contract to supply 'bespoke' software, which is written specifically for the buyer's needs, will be classed as the provision of a service rather than a sale of goods. Again, this would mean that liability would be based on fault rather than being strict.

Goods can be existing or future. Existing goods are either owned or possessed by the seller at the time of the contract of sale. Future goods are to be manufactured or acquired by the seller after the contract of sale. There can also be a sale of goods when it is not certain that the seller will be able to acquire the goods. When future goods are sold this is, technically, an agreement to sell rather than a sale. The important point is that the agreement is governed by the Act.

8.1.1.4 Transfer of the property in goods to the buyer

When the Sale of Goods Act 1979 talks of transferring the property in goods it means that the seller must transfer the ownership of the goods. So a contract will only be a sale of goods if the seller has transferred or agreed to transfer the ownership of the goods to the buyer. This requirement rules out contracts to hire or to lease, where possession of the goods is transferred but ownership is not. Nor is a contract of hire-purchase a sale of goods. Under a contract of hire-purchase the hirer has an option to buy the goods at the end of the period of hire, but has no obligation to buy. Therefore, until the hirer exercises the option to buy, it cannot be said that the seller has transferred or agreed to transfer the property in the goods to the buyer (*Helby* v *Mathews* [1895] AC 471).

1 What is the definition of a contract of sale of goods?

2 How are goods defined by the SGA 1979?

3 Which of the following contracts could be classified as contracts of sale of goods?

  a Having the windows of a house cleaned in return for £6 cash.

  b A purchase of the patent on a new invention for £12 000.

  c A purchase of a new car, paid for with a cheque for £14 000.

  d A purchase of a trolley of groceries, paid for with a credit card.

  e A 'free chicken' to customers who spend £20 in a supermarket.

  f A house bought for £95 000.

  g The sale by a farmer of 100 tons of potatoes for £6 000. The potatoes have not been grown yet, but the delivery date is fixed at 30 June next year.

  h A purchase of the copyright in a song for £100 cash.

  i A pen is bought in a shop for £19.99 cash.

  j A bicycle is exchanged for a personal stereo. Neither item is given a price.

  k A landscape painting is commissioned at a price of £200.

  l A ticket to the cinema is bought for £6 cash.

  m A television is hire-purchased over three years, at £20 a month.

  n 1 000 shares in a company purchased for £2 000.

8.2 THE TERMS IMPLIED BY THE SALE OF GOODS ACT 1979

Sections 12–15 of the Sale of Goods Act 1979 imply terms which favour the buyer into contracts of sale of goods. These terms do not need to be mentioned by the buyer or the seller, as the Act will automatically imply them. However, the terms as to satisfactory quality and fitness for the buyer's purpose are implied only into sales which are made in the course of a business.

- **Section 12(1)** implies a condition that the **seller has the right to sell the goods.**
- **Section 12(2)** implies warranties that the goods are **free from encumbrances** and that the buyer will enjoy **quiet possession of the goods.**

- **Section 13(1)** implies a condition that where goods are sold by description they will **correspond with the description.**
- **Section 14(2)** implies a condition that goods sold in the course of a business are of **satisfactory quality.**
- **Section 14(3)** implies a condition that goods sold in the course of a business are **fit for the buyer's purpose.**
- **Section 15(2)** implies two conditions when goods are sold by sample. First it is implied that the **bulk will match the sample in quality.** Second it is implied that the goods will be **free from defects** which would make their quality unsatisfactory if these defects would not be apparent on a reasonable examination of the sample.

These implied terms are important, and each one must be examined closely. It should also be realised that Part 5A SGA gives significant new remedies to consumer buyers where the goods do not conform to the contract of sale. Goods do not conform to the contract of sale if there is in relation to them a breach of ss.13–15. (Part 5A is considered in detail at 10.4.6.)

8.2.1 The right to sell (s.12(1))

Section 12(1) of the Act provides that:

> 'There is an implied [condition] on the part of the seller that in the case of a sale he has a right to sell the goods, and in the case of an agreement to sell that he will have such a right at the time when the property is to pass.'

This term is the most fundamental of the implied terms. We have seen that the seller's obligation under a contract of sale is to transfer, or agree to transfer, the ownership of the goods to the buyer. A seller who does not have the right to sell the goods will not be able to transfer ownership to the buyer.

Section 12(3) prevents the application of s.12(1) where there appears from the contract, or is to be inferred from the circumstances, an intention that the seller should transfer only such title as he or a third person may have.

Section 12(5A) states that the term set out in s.12(1) is a **condition**, and in Chapter 5 we saw that if a condition is breached the injured party can treat the contract as repudiated and claim damages. A buyer who treats a contract as repudiated is entitled to a refund of the purchase price. As breach of s.12(1) is seen as a total failure of consideration, a buyer can claim back all of the purchase price even if he has enjoyed the use of the goods for some time, and even if the goods cannot be returned to the seller.

Rowland v Divall
[1923] 2 KB 500 (Court of Appeal)

A thief stole a car from its owner and sold the car to the defendant. The claimant, a motor dealer, bought the car from the defendant for £334. The claimant painted the car and displayed it in his showroom for two months before selling it to a customer, Colonel Railsdon, for £400. Two months after this sale the police discovered that the car had been stolen. The police took the car from Colonel Railsdon and returned it to its original owner. Colonel Railsdon went back to the claimant, who returned the £400 he had paid. The claimant then sued the defendant for the return of the £334 which he had paid, arguing that there had been a total failure of consideration.

Held. The claimant was entitled to all of his money back, as there had been a total failure of consideration. Section 12(1) says that the seller must have the right to sell, and when the defendant sold the car to the claimant he did not have this right because he did not own the car. The thief never owned the car and therefore could not pass ownership to the defendant, who could not pass ownership to the claimant, etc. None of the parties except the original owner ever had the right to sell the car.

Atkin LJ: 'It seems to me that in this case there has been a total failure of consideration, that is to say that the buyer has not got any part of that for which he paid the purchase price. He paid the money in order that he might get the property, and he has not got it. It is true that the seller delivered to him the de facto [actual] possession, but the seller had not got the right to possession and consequently could not give it to the buyer. Therefore the buyer, during the time that he had the car in his actual possession, had no right to it, and was at all times liable to the true owner for its conversion.'

COMMENT If the breach had been of ss.13, 14 or 15, rather than of s.12(1), the buyer would not have been entitled to reject the car and get all of his money back because he would have 'accepted' the car. He would have done this by keeping the car for more than a reasonable time without intimating to the seller that he was rejecting it. The Court of Appeal held that acceptance, which is considered in detail at 10.4.3, could have no application when s.12(1) was breached because such a breach would amount to a total failure of consideration.

In **Rowland v Divall** the claimant and his customer between them had the use of the car for about four months. The case has been criticised on the grounds that in effect they got these four months' use for nothing. It has been argued that the defendant should get an allowance to cover the use of the car which the claimant had. The Law Commission examined this problem in 1987 and decided that as the defendant never had the right to sell in the first place he therefore had no right to an allowance for use of the car by the claimant or the claimant's customer. To change the law would have meant changing the law of conversion and this would have been very difficult. (The tort of conversion is examined briefly in Chapter 13 at 13.6.)

When a thief steals a car which is then sold along a chain of innocent buyers the loser will generally be the person who bought from the thief, as in **Rowland v Divall** (see Figure 8.1). Of course this person could successfully sue the thief, but in practical terms this would be a waste of money as it is most unlikely that the thief could be found and would have the money to pay.

However, if any of the sellers in the chain has become insolvent then the person who bought from the insolvent seller will be the one with no practical remedy.

Figure 8.1

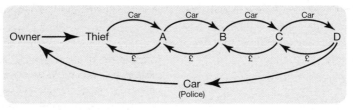

Figure 8.2

For example, let us assume that a thief steals a car from its owner and then sells the car to A, who sells it to B, who sells it to C, who sells it to D. As can be seen from Figure 8.2, A is likely to be the loser.

But now let us further assume that B has become insolvent. D can recover from C, but C cannot recover from B. Nor can C leapfrog B and sue A – there is no contract between the two of them.

The goods will always be returned to the owner because he has owned them all along. Others might have had possession of the goods, and believed that they owned them, but ownership remained throughout with the person from whom the thief stole the goods.

It is not only on account of the seller of goods not owning them that s.12(1) can be breached. In **Niblett Ltd v Confectioners' Materials Co Ltd** [1921] 3 KB 387 (Court of Appeal), 3 000 tins of condensed milk were sold; 1 000 of the tins were labelled 'Nissly Brand'. Nestlés warned the buyers of the milk that the word 'Nissly' was too similar to their trademark [Nestlé], and that if they attempted to sell the milk they would be prevented from doing so by an injunction. The buyers accepted that this was the legal position, and that they would be unable to resell the milk without removing the labels. They therefore sued the sellers for damages on the grounds that the sellers had breached s.12(1). The Court of Appeal held that s.12(1) had been breached. The sellers did own the milk when they sold it, but they had no right to sell the milk because they could have been restrained by an injunction from doing so.

8.2.2 Implied warranties about title (s.12(2))

Section 12(2) implies two terms about title. Section 12(5A) makes it plain that these terms are warranties, so if they are breached the buyer will not be entitled to treat the contract as repudiated but will be entitled to damages.

Section 12(2)(a) implies a term that the goods are free from any charge or encumbrance which is not disclosed or known to the buyer before the contract is made.

Section 12(2)(b) implies a warranty that the buyer will enjoy quiet possession of the goods, except as regards rights of others which were disclosed or known to the buyer before the contract.

The first of these terms means that the seller warrants that at the time when ownership of the goods is to pass to the buyer nobody else has any ownership rights regarding the goods. The second warranty is an ongoing assurance that no one will interfere with the buyer's right to possess the goods. An example of breach of s.12(2)(b) can be seen in **Microbeads AG v Vinhurst Road Markings** [1975] 1 WLR 218. The sellers sold road marking machines. Unknown to the buyers or sellers a third party was applying for a patent which would affect these machines. The patent was granted and became effective shortly after the contract was made. The third party then brought an action against the buyers for breach of patent. The buyers sued the sellers for breach of s.12(1) and s.12(2). It was held that s.12(1) had not been breached because the buyers had the right to sell the machines at the time of the sale. However, s.12(2)(b) had been breached because the buyers could not continue to enjoy quiet possession of the machines.

Section 12(3) allows a seller to make a contract to transfer only such ownership as he or another person may have. For example, a seller who does not know if he owns certain goods (perhaps because of an ongoing legal dispute about the ownership of the goods) can contract to sell only such ownership as he may have. When a seller takes advantage of s.12(3) the terms implied by ss.12(1) and 12(2) do not apply. However, two warranties, contained in sections 12(4) and 12(5), require the seller to disclose to the buyer all charges and encumbrances which the seller knows about and to warrant that the buyer's quiet possession will not be disturbed.

1 What term is implied by SGA s.12(1)?

2 What terms are implied by SGA s.12(2)?

3 Read s.12(1) of the Sale of Goods Act 1979 on page 242. Does it provide that the seller must have the right to sell the goods or does it say that the seller must think that he has the right to sell the goods?

4 A grain merchant agrees to sell 1 000 tons of grain to a buyer, delivery to be made next November. The merchant intends to buy the grain from a Canadian exporter, but as yet this contract has not been made and so the merchant does not yet own the grain. Does this mean that the merchant breaches s.12(1)?

5 In *Rowland v Divall*, Lord Atkin stated that the seller did deliver de facto [actual] possession of the car. Why then was the buyer entitled to all of his money back?

6 A thief steals a consignment of batteries and, after the batteries have passed through a succession of buyers, a shopkeeper buys them in good faith. The shopkeeper sells the batteries to a customer who uses them until their power is exhausted.

   a Did the customer ever have ownership of the batteries?

   b Did the customer ever have de facto [actual] possession of them?

   c Did the customer ever have legal possession?

   d Ought the customer be able to claim all of his money back from the shop?

8.2.3 Correspondence with description (s.13(1))

Section 13(1) of the Act provides that:

> 'Where there is a contract for the sale of goods by description, there is an implied [term] that the goods will correspond with the description.'

The starting point with this section must be to consider the circumstances in which goods are sold **by description**. If the goods are not sold by description then s.13 will not help the buyer. As we shall see, the fact that there has been some description of the goods does not necessarily mean that they have been sold by description.

First we need to distinguish unascertained, future and specific goods. Specific goods are identified and agreed upon at the time of the contract, whereas unascertained goods are not. As we saw earlier in this chapter, future goods had yet to be manufactured or acquired by the seller at the time of the contract. Unascertained and future goods are always sold by description, otherwise the parties could not identify what was being sold. Furthermore, in contracts for the sale of unascertained future goods all descriptive words are likely to be part of the description by which the goods were sold. In *Reardon Smith Line v Hansen Tangen* [1976] 1 WLR 989 Lord Wilberforce indicated that in other contracts of sale of goods the sale will only be 'by description' if the descriptive words are a substantial part of the identity of what is being bought, a matter which will depend upon the intentions of the parties.

As regards specific goods, the mere fact of the seller describing specific goods to the buyer does not necessarily mean that the goods are sold by description, even if the descriptive words were identifying what was being bought. It is also necessary that the buyer relies on the description and that the description is an essential term of the contract.

Harlingdon & Leinster Enterprises Ltd v Christopher Hull Fine Art Ltd
[1991] 1 QB 564

The sellers sold two oil paintings for £6 000, saying that the paintings were by Gabriele Munter (1877–1962), a German expressionist painter. Both the sellers and the buyers were London art dealers. The buyers were specialists in German expressionistic painting, the sellers were not. In 1980 auction particulars had attributed the paintings to Munter. The sellers had also taken the paintings to Christies who had shown an interest in them. The sellers phoned the buyers, knowing that they were specialists in German expressionist art, and asked if they might be interested in the paintings. The buyers sent round an employee to view the paintings, and the employee was told that the sellers knew nothing about the paintings and nothing about Munter. It later came to light that the paintings were a fake and were worth under £100. The buyers rejected the paintings under s.13(1).

Held. The buyers could not reject the paintings under s.13(1). The sellers had clearly made a description, but the buyers had not relied on this description when deciding to buy the paintings. The description was not an essential term of the contract and so the sale was not made by description.

Section 13(2) envisages that a sale might be made by sample as well as a sale by description and states that if this is the case then not only must the bulk of the goods correspond with the sample, but the bulk must also correspond with the description. In **Nichol v Godts** [1854] 10 Exch 191 oil was bought by sample, the oil being described as 'foreign refined rape oil'. The bulk of the oil did correspond with the sample, but neither the bulk nor the sample matched the description as the oil was in fact a mixture of rape and hemp oil. It was held that the buyer could reject the oil, a conclusion which would nowadays be reached by applying s.13(2).

Section 13(3) states that a sale of goods is not prevented from being a sale by description by reason only that, being exposed for sale or hire, they are selected by the buyer. So the mere fact that a shopper in a supermarket has selected the goods which are to be bought will not automatically prevent the sale from being by description.

Descriptions which do not come within s.13 may still be terms of the contract. However, they might be innominate terms or warranties rather than conditions. (The difference between conditions, warranties and innominate terms is explained in Chapter 5 at 5.4.) The true significance of s.13 is that it is a condition and so it allows the buyer to treat the contract as repudiated without having to prove that the breach has deprived him of substantially the whole benefit of the contract. Descriptions which do not amount to a term at all may be actionable misrepresentations if they were untrue statements of fact which induced the buyer to make the contract. (See Chapter 6 at 6.1.)

Having decided that a sale is made by description we then need to consider how closely the goods must correspond with the description. The old cases suggest that the required degree of correspondence is very high. Only if the description could be regarded as a trifle would s.13 not have been breached. (*De minimis non curat lex* – the law is not concerned with trifles.)

Arcos Ltd v E. A. Ronaasen & Son [1933] AC 470 (House of Lords)

The sellers contracted to sell a quantity of wooden staves. The staves, which were to be shipped to England, were to be of Russian wood and the sellers knew that the buyers intended to use them to make cement barrels. The contract described the length and breadth of the staves and allowed for some deviation in these matters. However, there was no allowance for deviation in the thickness of the staves, the contract describing the staves as $\frac{1}{2}$ an inch thick. When the staves were delivered the buyers discov-

ered that 6.4 per cent were $\frac{1}{2}$ an inch thick, 75.3 per cent were between $\frac{1}{2}$ an inch and $\frac{9}{16}$, and 18.3 per cent were over $\frac{9}{16}$. None of the staves was over $\frac{5}{8}$ of an inch thick. The buyers rejected all of the staves, even though they were of merchantable (now satisfactory) quality and perfectly fit for making barrels.

Held. The buyers could reject all of the staves, as they did not correspond with the description by which they had been sold.

Lord Atkin: 'It was contended that in all commercial contracts ... there must always be some margin ... I cannot agree. If the written contract specifies conditions of weight, measurement and the like, these conditions must be complied with. A ton does not mean about a ton, or a yard about a yard. Still less when you descend to minute measurements does $\frac{1}{2}$ inch mean about $\frac{1}{2}$ inch. If the seller wants a margin he must and in my experience does stipulate for it. Of course by recognised trade usage particular figures may be given a different meaning, as in a baker's dozen ...

'If a condition is not performed the buyer has a right to reject ... No doubt, in business, men often find it unnecessary or inexpedient to insist on their strict legal rights. In a normal market if they get something substantially like the specified goods they may take them with or without grumbling and claim for an allowance. But in a falling market I find that buyers are often as eager to insist on their legal rights as courts of law are ready to maintain them.'

Re Moore & Co Ltd and Landauer & Co Ltd [1921] 2 KB 519 (Court of Appeal)

The sellers, who were in Australia, sold a consignment of 3100 tins of peaches which were to be sent to the buyers in London. The buyers rejected the consignment because the peaches had been described in the contract as packed 30 tins to a case, whereas in fact about half of the tins were packed 24 to a case instead of 30. The correct number of tins was delivered. The market value of the goods would have been the same whether they were packed 24 or 30 tins to the case.

Held. The buyers could reject all of the tins, as they did not correspond with the description by which they had been sold.

In both of these cases the buyer was a commercial buyer rather than a consumer. In holding that s.13 had been breached, and that the two buyers could therefore treat the contract as repudiated, the courts were influenced by two factors. First, commercial buyers do not include descriptions in their contracts if they do not consider them important. Second, a commercial buyer might well have sold the goods under the same description, and the easiest way to nip this ongoing problem in the bud is to hold that the first seller has breached s.13.

These two cases also demonstrate that s.13 is not concerned with the quality of the goods. In *Arcos* v *Ronaasen* there was nothing wrong with the quality of the staves, in *Re Moore & Co Ltd and Landauer & Co Ltd* there was nothing wrong with the quality of the tins of peaches.

It might be thought unfair that such a slight breach as occurred in each of the above two cases should be classified as a condition of the contract and therefore entitle the buyer to treat the contract as repudiated. The House of Lords considered this matter in *Reardon Smith Line* v *Hansen Tangen* [1976] 1 WLR 989 and suggested that some of the old decisions on s.13 might be ready for a fresh examination. However, since that case was heard the remedies available for breach of the term implied by s.13(1) have been changed. Since the amendments made by the Sale and Supply of Goods Act 1994, s.15A of the Sale of Goods Act 1979 has altered the status of s.13(1) so that it is no longer always a condition. The term remains a condition where the buyer deals as a consumer. But if the buyer does not deal as a consumer the term is not a condition where the breach of it is so slight that it would be unreasonable for the buyer to reject the goods. So if *Re Moore & Co Ltd and Landauer & Co Ltd* were to arise today the buyer would not be able to treat the contract as repudiated and reject the goods, even if s.13(1) had been breached. The buyer would of course be able to claim damages for breach of warranty. The complex definition of dealing as a consumer is examined in detail in Chapter 5 at 5.6.1.3.

Test your understanding 8.3

1 What term is implied by SGA s.13(1)?

2 Are unascertained future goods always sold by description?

3 In what circumstances are specific goods sold by description?

4 If a supermarket shopper does buy goods which are sold by description, s.13(1) will imply a term that the goods must correspond with the description. What remedies would be available to the shopper if s.13(1) was breached? Assuming that the supermarket bought the goods under the same description as that under which it sold the goods, and that s.13(1) had again been breached, would the same remedies always be available to the supermarket?

8.2.4 **Satisfactory quality (s.14(2))**

Section 14(2) provides that:

> 'Where the seller sells goods in the course of a business, there is an implied [condition] that the goods supplied under the contract are of satisfactory quality.'

This is the most significant of the statutory implied terms, but it is important to begin by considering the circumstances in which the term will not be implied.

First, the term as to satisfactory quality will not be implied unless the seller sells the goods in the course of a business. Section 61(5) SGA, the Act's definition section, tells us that business includes professions and the activities of public departments and local or public authorities. But is everything which a business sells sold in the course of a business? Until relatively recently this matter was in some doubt, but the following case has now provided an authoritative answer.

Stevenson v Rogers
[1999] 1 All ER 613 (Court of Appeal)

The defendant, who had been in business as a fisherman for 20 years, sold a fishing boat to the claimant. The boat was not being used as part of the defendant's stock in trade at the time of the sale. Subsequently the claimant argued that the boat was not of merchantable quality (the case having arisen before the requirement of merchantable quality was changed to a requirement of satisfactory quality). The trial judge ruled that s.14(2) SGA 1979 did not apply because the boat was not sold in the course of the defendant's business. An appeal was made to the Court of Appeal.

Held. The boat was sold in the course of the defendant's business. Consequently, s.14(2) implied a term that the boat was of merchantable quality. For the purposes of s.14(2) SGA 1979 the words 'in the course of a business' should be taken at face value. Any sale made in the course of a business is within s.14(2), without the need to prove any degree of regularity of such sales. Therefore sporadic sales which are no more than incidental to the seller's business are included. By contrast, purely private sales which are →

outside the confines of the business carried on by the seller are not within s.14(2).

COMMENT In Chapter 5 at 5.6.1.3 we considered the meaning of 'deals as a consumer' for the purposes of UCTA 1977. We saw that in the context of deciding whether or not a person deals as a consumer a business can deal as a consumer when buying goods. This happens when the business buys goods which are not an integral part of the business, because the business is then regarded as not having bought the goods in the course of its business. The SGA adopts the UCTA 1977 definition of dealing as a consumer (s.61(5A) SGA) and several important sections of the SGA apply only where a person does deal as a consumer. So the unfortunate position is that the phrase 'in the course of a business' means one thing when considering s.14 SGA, and means a quite different thing when considering whether a business dealt as a consumer for the purposes of the SGA and UCTA 1977. This unfortunate state of affairs was confirmed by the Court of Appeal in **Feldarol Foundries plc v Hermes Leasing Ltd** [2004] EWCA Civ 747 on the grounds that it increases consumer protection.

If an agent, acting in the course of a business, makes a sale of goods on behalf of a principal then the principal will be liable if the goods are not of satisfactory quality and fit for the buyer's purpose. However, if the buyer is aware that the principal is not selling the goods in the course of a business, or if reasonable steps have been taken to bring this to the buyer's attention, then neither the term as to satisfactory quality nor as to fitness for the buyer's purpose is implied.

The seller's liability under s.14(2) is strict. It is immaterial whether or not it is the seller's fault that the goods are not of satisfactory quality. Often, as in the case of a retailer selling pre-packaged goods, a seller in breach of s.14(2) will have had no opportunity to discover the defect which renders the goods unsatisfactory. In such cases the seller in breach of the implied term can in turn sue the person from whom the goods were ordered. If goods are manufactured in such a way that their quality is defective, and later sold down the line to a succession of buyers who do not examine the goods or have the defect specifically pointed out to them, then every seller of the goods in the course of a business can be sued by their buyer under s.14(2).

Section 14(2C) lists two circumstances in which the term as to satisfactory quality will not be implied.

First, s.14(2C)(a) provides that there is no requirement of satisfactory quality as regards defects which are **specifically** drawn to the buyer's attention before the contract is made. This is the case even if the cost of repairing these defects turns out to be considerably greater than the buyer envisaged.

Bartlett v Sidney Marcus Ltd
[1965] 1 WLR 1013 (Court of Appeal)

The sellers, who were motor dealers, sold a second-hand Jaguar. A sales executive employed by the sellers had told the buyer that the clutch was defective and that he thought this would be a minor repair, costing £2 or £3. The buyer traded in his old car and agreed to pay £550 cash. The buyer had chosen this option rather than pay £575 and letting the sellers repair the clutch. Two weeks later the buyer arranged for his own garage to repair the clutch. The total cost of this repair came to slightly over £84. The buyer claimed damages for breach of s.14(2).

Held. B could not claim damages under s.14(2). The defect in the clutch had been drawn to B's attention, and could not therefore render the car of unmerchantable (now unsatisfactory) quality.

Second, s.14(2C)(b) provides that **if** the buyer examines the goods before the contract is made there is no requirement of satisfactory quality as regards defects which the examination ought to reveal. However, it is important to note that the buyer has no obligation to examine the goods. If the buyer chooses not to examine the goods before the contract is made then even highly apparent defects can render the goods of unsatisfactory quality.

The requirement of satisfactory quality extends not only to the goods bought but also to any other things supplied under the contract. In **Geddling v Marsh** [1920] 1 KB 668 the claimant bought a bottle of mineral water. Although the mineral water was sold, the bottle itself was not, as it remained throughout the property of the manufacturer of the mineral water. (Customers were expected to return the empty bottles to the shop and to reclaim a deposit.) The bottle exploded and injured the claimant, who was able to recover damages under s.14(2) even though the bottle itself was not sold. The bottle was supplied under the contract.

8.2.4.1 **The meaning of satisfactory quality**

The requirement that the goods be of satisfactory quality (rather than merchantable quality) is fairly recent, having been added to the 1979 Act by the Sale and Supply of Goods Act 1994. Section 14(2A) SGA 1979 provides the definition of satisfactory quality:

'For the purposes of this Act, goods are of satisfactory quality if they meet the standard that a reasonable person would regard as satisfactory, taking account of any description of the goods, the price (if relevant) and all the other relevant circumstances'.

It can be seen that goods will be of satisfactory quality if they meet an objective standard, that which a reasonable person would regard as satisfactory. Although the description, the price (if relevant) and all the other relevant circumstances have to be taken into account, it is important to notice that the word description here is much more general than the meaning of the word under s.13. Here there is no need for the sale to be made by description. Any description of the goods will be taken into account in deciding whether the goods meet the standard which a reasonable person would regard as satisfactory. Section 14(2B) amplifies the meaning of the quality of goods, listing five aspects of quality to be taken into account in appropriate cases:

'For the purposes of this Act, the quality of goods includes their state and condition and the following (among others) are in appropriate cases aspects of the quality of goods –

(a) fitness for all the purposes for which goods of the kind in question are commonly supplied,
(b) appearance and finish,
(c) freedom from minor defects,
(d) safety, and
(e) durability.'

It is important to note that these five matters listed are not hard and fast requirements, the absence of which will mean that goods are not of satisfactory quality. They are only aspects of the quality of goods in appropriate cases. In a consumer sale of a new product all of the aspects are likely to be appropriate.

Sections 14(2A) and 14(2B) were enacted to give effect to the proposals set out by the Law Commission Report 160, 'Sale and Supply of Goods' (1987). The requirement of satisfactory quality replaced a requirement that goods sold in the course of a business should be of merchantable quality. Merchantable quality was defined by s.14(6) of the Act in the following way:

'Goods . . . are of merchantable quality . . . if they are as fit for the purpose or purposes for which goods of that kind are commonly bought as it is reasonable to

expect having regard to any description applied to them, the price (if relevant) and all the other relevant circumstances.'

The Law Commission found the term merchantable quality gave rise to various problems. First, the courts adopted two different tests, the acceptability test and the usability test, to decide whether or not goods were of merchantable quality. The acceptability test regarded goods as merchantable if their condition was such that a reasonable buyer would still have bought the goods at the same price, and without any special terms, if he had known of the actual condition of the goods, including any defects, when making the purchase. The usability test regarded the goods as merchantable if a reasonable buyer could have used the goods for any of the purposes for which goods of that contract description were commonly used. The acceptability test, which tends to be more favourable to the buyer, was used more in consumer cases whereas the usability test was used more in commercial cases. Second, the word 'merchantable' suggested contracts between merchants and was therefore not suitable for consumer sales. Third, the definition concentrated too heavily on the goods' fitness for their purpose and did not consider sufficiently their other characteristics. Fourth, the definition did not specify that the goods should be reasonably durable, although the case law would indicate that if they were not reasonably durable then they were not merchantable. The Law Commission accepted that it was not possible to have a single formula defining the quality required of goods sold in the course of a business. The possible circumstances in which goods might be sold in the course of a business are so varied that no single formula could possibly define the required quality in every case. Feeling that it would be wrong to apply a qualitative adjective such as 'good' (because sometimes the buyer and seller did not expect the quality of the goods to be good) the Commission considered several neutral adjectives, before settling for 'satisfactory'. It was suggested that the standard should be assessed by reference to that expected by the reasonable person, rather than that expected by a reasonable buyer, because the Commission thought that standards would drop if that test of a reasonable buyer was applied. Sellers might argue that goods of a certain type often had minor defects and that such defects would not therefore amount to a breach of contract as a reasonable buyer would be expecting them.

The views of the Law Commission on the aspects of the quality of the goods in appropriate cases are also worth considering. The Commission envisaged that all or any of the aspects might be taken into account in any particular case. Other factors might also be relevant, but the five aspects listed were commonly found to be important aspects of the quality of goods. The first aspect, fitness for all the purposes for which goods of the kind in question are commonly supplied, applies unless there is an indication to the contrary. The second and third aspects, appearance and finish and freedom from minor defects, were considered particularly appropriate to new goods and particularly to new consumer goods. As regards new consumer goods, even very minor blemishes would mean that the implied term as to quality was breached, unless the blemishes were so trifling as to be quite negligible and not breaches of contract at all. The fourth aspect, safety, was considered to be an important aspect of the quality of many consumer goods such as electrical appliances and cars. It was recognised that inherently unsafe goods which required safety precautions to be taken might not be of satisfactory quality if appropriate warnings were not given. The fifth requirement, durability, is that the goods should last for a reasonable time. The Commission did not think it possible to lay down a certain time (a week, a month or a year) for which all goods should last, as goods are so varied in their nature. The Commission considered that the requirement of durability should bite at the time of supply. At that time, the goods should be reasonably durable. If the goods subsequently break down this will be strong evidence that they were not reasonably durable at the time of supply. However, it will not be conclusive proof. All the evidence will need to be examined, particularly the way in which the goods were treated after the time of supply.

The change to satisfactory quality has resulted in the old body of case law on the meaning of merchantable quality becoming lost. Most Commonwealth countries have not made the change and so judgments from the higher courts of these countries will no longer be available to the English courts. It was generally thought that these problems would be of little importance by now as the English courts would have illustrated the meaning of satisfactory quality. However, there is as yet little significant case law on the meaning of satisfactory quality, although the following cases have given us some insights.

Bramhill v Edwards [2004] EWCA Civ 403, [2004] 2 Lloyd's Rep 653 (Court of Appeal)

E was a specialist dealer in motor homes imported from the United States. He imported a 'Dolphin' motor home which was 102 inches wide. Regulation 8 of the Road Vehicles (Construction and Use) Regulations 1986 provides that vehicles over 100 inches wide cannot legally be used on UK roads. B and his wife, enthusiasts who knew that vehicles over 100 inches wide could not legally be used, saw the Dolphin at a show in Malvern where E was displaying it. Shortly afterwards, after living in the Dolphin for a few days, B bought it for £61 000. B had ample opportunity to measure the width of the Dolphin before purchasing it but there was no evidence that he actually did this. After some seven months using the vehicle, B measured it and found it to be 102 inches wide. B complained to E about this. E said that the width would not cause a problem and B continued to use the Dolphin. After another four months B complained to E that he thought he had bought a 100 inch-wide vehicle, not an illegal 102 inch-wide one. Two months later still, B informed the Vehicle Inspectorate of the vehicle's width, and they told him that continued use of the Dolphin 'could result in prosecution'. B asked E to take the Dolphin back in part exchange for one of two other vehicles, one of which was also 102 inches wide, and when these requests were refused he sued E.

Held. (i) B had not proved that s.14(2A) had been breached on account of the vehicle being too wide. There was plenty of evidence that the authorities turned a blind eye to the use of vehicles which were 102 inches wide and enthusiasts for such vehicles knew this. Consequently, B had not proved, on a balance of probabilities, that a reasonable person would regard the vehicle as unsatisfactory. (ii) An argument that the excessive width made the vehicle uninsurable did not succeed. The evidence showed that if the width was disclosed to insurance companies it was not a problem to get insurance. (iii) Even if s.14(2A) had been breached, s.14(2C) would have given E a defence. (iv) Even if there had been a breach of s.14(2A), and no defence under s.14(2C), B's damages would have been nominal because B had not proved that the excessive width reduced the vehicle's value. (B had obviously accepted the vehicle and so would have lost the right to reject it.)

COMMENT (i) Auld LJ gave the only judgment. When considering the excessive width of the vehicle, he said that the test of satisfactory quality was an objective →

test which focused on the attitude of the reasonable person. But he went on to say that this meant the reasonable person in the position of the buyer with the buyer's know-ledge, and that it would not be appropriate to consider a reasonable third party observer who was not acquainted with the background of the transaction. Auld LJ:

> 'The reasonable buyer must be attributed with knowledge of all background facts ... such facts in this case would include that: ... a significant number of vehicles of greater width than permitted in this country were in use on its roads; and the authorities were turning a blind eye to that illegal use.'

Recognising that there were arguments both for and against a reasonable person thinking that the Dolphin was of satisfactory quality, Auld LJ set aside the judge's finding because B had failed to prove that the reasonable person would think that the Dolphin was not of satisfactory quality. B had therefore not discharged his obligation to prove his case on a balance of probabilities. (ii) The trial judge had heard evidence that insurability was not a problem and Auld LJ was not prepared to overturn this. (iii) Auld LJ agreed with the trial judge's finding that E had made a representation to B that the interior of the Dolphin was 100 inches wide and that this meant that he had specifically drawn to B's attention that the exterior was more than 102 inches wide, which B knew would make the vehicle illegal for use. This gave a defence under s.14(2C)(a). Auld LJ also thought that there was a defence under s.14(2C)(b) because B examined the vehicle several times before buying it and, in the light of E's representation as to its internal width, should have realised that it was over 102 inches wide. He also said that he would have upheld the judge's finding that the examination of the Dolphin before purchase ought to have revealed its width even though the width was not actually measured. (Section 14(2C) was considered above at 8.2.4.)

In *Jewson Ltd v Kelly* [2003] EWCA Civ 1030, [2004] 1 Lloyd's Rep 505, which is considered below in relation to s.14(3), the Court of Appeal held that boilers supplied to a property developer were of satisfactory quality because there was nothing inherently wrong with the boilers. The property developer had claimed that they were not of satisfactory quality because they did not work well in the flats in which he had installed them. There had been discussions about the boilers' suitability between the property developer and the

sellers but the developer did not rely upon the skill and judgment of the sellers as to whether the boilers were suitable for the flats in question. Clarke LJ held that in these circumstances it would be 'a startling result' if the sellers were in breach of s.14(2) when they were not in breach of s.14(3). Sedley LJ said:

> 'Section 14(2) is directed principally to the sale of substandard goods. This means that the court's principal concern is to look at their intrinsic quality, using the tests indicated in subsection (2A)(2B) and (2C). Of these, it can be seen that the tests postulated in paragraphs (a) and (d) of subsection (2B), and perhaps others too, may well require regard to be had to extrinsic factors. These will typically have to do with the predictable use of the goods. But the issue is still their quality: neither these provisions nor the residual category of "all the other relevant circumstances" at the end of subsection (2A) make it legitimate, as a general rule, to introduce factors peculiar to the purposes of the particular buyer. It is section 14(3) which is concerned with these.'

He then went on to use a soft toy as an example. The safety and durability of such a toy would ordinarily be evaluated in relation to how a toddler might handle it. If it harmed the toddler when it got into his mouth s.14(2) might well have been breached. But if it was given to a dog, and harmed the dog's mouth, the claim would have to be brought under s.14(3) or fail. (Unless the toy was bought in a pet shop, in which case this would be a relevant circumstance for the purposes of s.14(2A).)

A Scottish case, *Thain v Anniesland Trade Centre* 1997 SLT 102 Sh Ct considered whether a second-hand car which soon developed a major fault could be rejected on the grounds that it was not of satisfactory quality. The car was a five- or six-year-old Renault 19, which had done 80 000 miles. To buy such a car new would have cost about £11 000. The claimant had bought the car from a dealer for £2 995, declining to take out a three-month warranty. Some two weeks after the car was purchased a differential bearing in the automatic gearbox began to make a noise. This noise became worse as the claimant continued to use the car and it soon became apparent that the gearbox would need to be replaced. This would have been uneconomic in a car of this age. The sheriff principal held that the action failed. The problem with the gearbox was one which had to be expected and one which could happen at any time, as the claimant should have been aware. The car had been examined by several knowledgeable drivers before it had been purchased, and they had found nothing wrong with it. At the time of sale the car had met the standard which a reasonable person would regard as satisfactory because there had been no noise from the gearbox, and it could reasonably be inferred that there was no defect present. As it was well known that the gearbox on a car such as this could fail at any time, the reasonable person would accept that the risk of its failing, and the need for an expensive repair, could arise at any time. It was a matter of luck when this would happen. The claimant had been unlucky. But in all the circumstances of the case durability was not a quality that a reasonable person would have demanded of this particular car. If the car had been new, one could reasonably have expected to use it for at least the guarantee period without an important component or system failing.

In *Clegg* v *Andersson* **[2003]** EWCA Civ 320, [2003] 2 Lloyd's Rep 32 Lady Justice Hale stated that a customer buying a high-priced quality product 'may be entitled to expect that it is free from even minor defects, in other words perfect or nearly so.' The facts of the case are set out in detail in Chapter 10 at 10.4.3, as the case is mainly concerned with how the right to reject for breach of ss.13–15 can be lost on account of the buyer having accepted the goods.

In *Egan* v *Motor Services (Bath) Ltd* [2007] EWCA Civ 1002, [2008] 1 WLR 1589 Lady Justice Ward, giving the only significant judgment of the Court of Appeal, considered the extent to which a minor defect would make an expensive new car of unsatisfactory quality. She said:

'[It was] argued that a buyer should be entitled to reject the car because, under section 14(2B)(c), goods may be of unsatisfactory quality by reason of minor defects. That I accept is so, but the overall test of whether goods are of satisfactory quality is to be found in section 14(2A). Goods are of satisfactory quality if they meet the standard that a reasonable person would regard as satisfactory, taking account of any description of the goods, the price (if relevant) and all other relevant circumstances. This is an objective test and is a matter of judgment for the judge on the individual facts of each case. However, it seems to me unlikely that a buyer will be entitled to reject goods simply because he can point to a minor defect. He must also persuade the judge that a reasonable person would think that the minor defect was of sufficient consequence to make the goods unsatisfactory. Of course, if

a car is not handling correctly, one would expect any reasonable person to say that it is not of satisfactory quality ... But, the mere fact that a setting is outside the manufacturer's specification will not necessarily render the vehicle objectively unsatisfactory. The reasonable person may think that the minor defect is of no consequence.'

In *Hazlewood Grocery Ltd* v *Lion Foods Ltd* [2007] EWHC 1887, [2007] All ER (D) 433 (Jul) chilli powder which was slightly contaminated with a prohibited red dye, Para Red, was sold to a food manufacturer. The contamination was only very slight and the chilli powder posed no risk to health. However, at the time of sale the Food Standards Agency (FSA) adopted a zero tolerance approach. It required the manufacturer to recall all affected food and to publish a list of affected products on a website. It was predictable that the FSA would take this approach. One month after the sale, the FSA published new guidelines which allowed considerably higher levels of Para Red than were found in the chilli powder sold. It was held that the chilli powder was not of satisfactory quality. The reasonable person would not have regarded it as satisfactory at the date of sale if its use would cause products to be recalled and details of affected foods to be publicised. (Section 14(3) of the Sale of Goods Act 1979 was also breached, as the chilli powder was not fit for its purpose.)

8.2.4.2 Public statements on the specific characteristics of the goods

In 2002, SGA 1979 was amended by the Sale and Supply of Goods to Consumers Regulations 2002 and ss.14(2D), (2E) and (2F) were inserted. Section 14(2D) provides that where the buyer deals as a consumer, the relevant circumstances mentioned in s.14(2A) include any public statements on the specific characteristics of the goods made about them by the seller, the producer or his representatives, particularly in advertising or labelling. (Producer means the manufacturer of the goods, or the person who imported them into the EC or a person who put his own name, trade mark or other distinctive mark on the goods.) However, s.14(2E) provides that a public statement is not by virtue of s.14(2D) to be considered a relevant circumstance if the seller can show one of three things. First, that at the time of the contract the seller was not, and could not reasonably have been, aware of the statement. Second, that the statement had been withdrawn in public or corrected in public before the contract was made.

Third, that the decision to buy the goods could not have been influenced by the statement. Section 14(2F) provides that ss.14(2D) and 14(2E) do not prevent any public statement from being a relevant circumstance for the purposes of s.14(2A) if the statement could have been a relevant circumstance regardless of ss.14(2D) and 14(2E). For the circumstances in which a buyer deals as a consumer, the SGA adopts the test set out in s.12(1) UCTA 1977 (see 8.5 below).

A breach of s.14(2) will always be regarded as a breach of condition where the buyer deals as a consumer. Where the buyer does not deal as a consumer breach will be a breach of condition unless the breach is so slight that it would be unreasonable for the buyer to reject the goods. In such cases breach of s.14(2) will be regarded as breach of warranty, entitling the buyer to damages but not to reject the goods. (Section 15A.)

8.2.5 Fitness for purpose (s.14(3))

Section 14(3) of the Act provides that:

'Where the seller sells goods in the course of a business and the buyer, expressly or by implication, makes known ... to the seller ... any particular purpose for which the goods are being bought, there is an implied [condition] that the goods supplied under the contract are reasonably fit for that purpose, whether or not that is a purpose for which such goods are commonly supplied, except where the circumstances show that the buyer does not rely, or that it is unreasonable for him to rely, on the skill or judgment of the seller.'

Before we examine the liability which this term imposes on the seller, we should be aware of the four circumstances in which the term will not be implied.

First, like s.14(2), the term will not be implied unless the seller sells the goods in the course of a business. The test set out in **Stevenson v Rogers** (see above at 8.2.4) is used in deciding this. Second, the term will not be implied unless the buyer expressly or impliedly makes known to the seller the particular purpose for which the goods are being bought. Third, the term will not be implied where the buyer does not rely on the skill and judgment of the seller. Fourth, the term will not be implied where it is unreasonable for the buyer to rely on the skill and judgment of the seller.

The buyer does not need to indicate expressly the particular purpose for which the goods are being bought, or make plain that he is relying on the seller's skill and judgment. Both of these matters can be implied. When consumers buy goods which they put

to their usual purpose it will be implied that they had made known the purpose for which the goods were being bought, and that they relied on the seller's skill and judgment to supply goods which are fit for that usual purpose. However, s.14(3) does not require the goods to be fit for an unusual purpose which the buyer did not make known to the seller.

Grant v Australian Knitting Mills Ltd
[1936] AC 85 (Privy Council)

While in the defendant's shop, Dr Grant selected and bought a pair of long woollen underpants. The underpants had been badly manufactured in that a chemical had not been rinsed out properly. The presence of this chemical caused Dr Grant to suffer dermatitis which hospitalised him for several months.

Held. The terms as to merchantable (now satisfactory) quality and fitness for purpose had both been breached.

Lord Wright: '[Section 14(3) SGA 1979] entitles the buyer to the benefit of an implied condition that the goods are reasonably fit for the purpose for which the goods are supplied, but only if that purpose is made known to the seller "so as to show that the buyer relies on the seller's skill and judgment". It is clear that the reliance must be brought home to the mind of the seller, expressly or by implication. The reliance will seldom be express: it will usually arise by implication from the circumstances: thus to take a case like the one in question, of a purchase from a retailer, the reliance will in general be inferred from the fact that a buyer goes to the shop in the confidence that the tradesman has selected his stock with care and skill.'

The buyer's purpose is often made known by the circumstances of the case. In **Manchester Liners Ltd v Rea Ltd** [1922] 2 AC 74 (House of Lords), for example, the seller was a coal merchant in Liverpool, who regularly supplied coal as fuel for steamships. The buyers contracted to buy 500 tons of South Wales coal to be used as fuel on the Manchester Importer, a steamship on the Manchester Ship Canal. The coal supplied was as described, but was unfit for use on this type of steamship. As a consequence the ship had to return to port after it had set off. The coal merchant was held liable under what is now s.14(3) of the Sale of Goods Act because the circumstances showed that the buyers had relied on the seller's skill and judgment to supply a type of coal which was fit for the buyer's purpose when placing the order. However, s.14(3) will not protect a buyer who fails to make known, either expressly or impliedly, the particular purpose for which the goods are bought. In *Griffiths v Peter Conway Ltd* [1939] 1 All ER 685 (Court of Appeal) the buyer bought a Harris tweed coat, which was specially made for her by the seller. Shortly after beginning to wear the coat, the buyer contracted dermatitis. The buyer had abnormally sensitive skin, but had not made this fact known to the seller. The coat would not have caused anyone with normal skin to contract dermatitis. The Court of Appeal held that the sellers were not in breach of either s.14(2) or s.14(3).

It is also possible that the buyer makes a partial reliance on the skill and judgment of the seller.

Ashington Piggeries Ltd v Christopher Hill Ltd [1971] 1 All ER 847 (House of Lords)

The buyers, who were manufacturers of animal feedstuffs, were asked to make food for mink, according to a certain formula. As this formula included herring meal, the buyers agreed to buy herring meal from the sellers. The sellers knew that the herring meal was going to be used to feed mink, but had never previously made mink food. The meal was contaminated with a chemical (DMNA) which reacted with the meal so that it became poisonous. The meal would have been poisonous to all animals, but it was only fatally poisonous to mink. At the time the state of scientific and technical knowledge was such that this contamination of the foodstuff could not have been suspected.

Held. Section 14(3) had been breached. The buyers had made a partial reliance on the seller's skill and judgment. The buyers might have supplied the formula, but still relied on the seller's skill and judgment to use wholesome materials.

Jewson Ltd v Kelly [2003] EWCA Civ 1030, [2004] 1 Lloyd's Rep 505

Jewsons of Bideford, builders' merchants, sold 12 boilers to a property developer, Kelly, who was converting a former convent school building into 13 self-contained flats. Kelly wanted each flat to have a separate boiler. Having decided that oil, gas and solid fuel were all unsuitable, he realised that he had to go for electric boilers. One of the flats, however, already had an oil burning boiler so he needed only 12 more boilers. Kelly described his needs to an employee of Jewsons', who said that he would look into the problem of finding suitable boilers. The employee later told Kelly that he had been in touch with a boiler manufacturer, Amptec, and that their boilers seemed ideal. Kelly knew that the employee was only passing on what he had been told by Amptec. A meeting was held at the premises to be converted. At the meeting were Kelly, his electrician, his plumber, an employee from Jewsons and an employee from Amptec. Kelly was given a leaflet extolling the virtues of Amptec's boilers. In reliance upon what he was told at this meeting, Kelly bought the boilers from Jewsons. However, when they were installed the boilers gave very low SAP readings. (These readings are the Government's way of giving home energy ratings to individual residences.) The readings were low in respect of the flats because electricity is an expensive way of heating a residence and because the flats were poorly insulated. These low ratings caused some purchasers of the flats to be put off, as the readings meant that they could not get mortgages to buy the flats. The trial judge found that Jewsons were in breach of s.14(3) of the Act. Jewsons appealed to the Court of Appeal.

Held. Section 14(3) was not breached. Kelly did make known to the seller the purpose for which the boilers were being bought. The boilers were not fit for that purpose as they increased the risk of a delayed sale of the flats. It would be up to the sellers to show that the buyer did not rely on their skill and judgment or that, if he did, it was unreasonable for him to have done so. However, Kelly did not rely on the skill and judgment of the sellers that the boilers would be suitable for the particular flats in question. The effect of the boilers on the flats' SAP ratings was within the expertise of Kelly and his advisors, it was not within the expertise of Jewsons or Amptec.

COMMENT Clarke LJ said that the case provided an example of the principle stated by Lord Steyn in *Slater v Fleming Ltd* [1997] AC 471 at 486: 'After all, if the buyer's purpose is insufficiently communicated, the buyer cannot reasonably rely on the seller's skill and judgment to ensure that the goods answer that purpose.'

In *Grant v Australian Knitting Mills Ltd* we saw that the goods sold were neither of satisfactory quality nor fit for the buyer's purpose. The seller was therefore in breach of both s.14(2) and s.14(3). Where unsatisfactory goods are bought and used for their usual purpose it will commonly be the case that the seller will be in breach of both of the implied terms. However, it is important to notice the different circumstances in which the terms are implied. Section 14(2) does not require any reliance on the seller's skill and judgment. However, it does not apply where the buyer examined the goods and ought to have noticed the defect or where the defect was specifically pointed out to the buyer. Section 14(3) does require reliance on the seller's skill and judgment, although this can be implied from the circumstances, and it does require that this reliance is reasonable. Section 14(3) can help a buyer as regards defects which were specifically pointed out, or which the buyer ought to have noticed while examining the goods. This would be unusual, but would be the case if the buyer relied on assurances from the seller that the defect pointed out or discovered would not affect the fitness of the goods for the buyer's purpose.

An overview of ss.14(2) and 14(3) is shown in Figure 8.3.

The following case shows that even when highly defective goods are bought for their usual purpose it is not necessarily true that both s.14(2) and s.14(3) have been breached.

Wren v Holt [1903] 1 KB 610

A customer bought beer from a pub. The beer made the customer ill because it was contaminated with arsenic. The seller's pub was a tied house, selling only Holden's beer. The customer knew this and had sought the pub out because he particularly liked Holden's beer.

Held. The beer was plainly not of merchantable (now satisfactory) quality and so s.14(2) had been breached. However, s.14(3) had not been breached. The customer had not relied on the the seller's skill and judgment to supply goods which were fit for his purpose in that he knew that the pub only sold the one type of beer.

When the term as to fitness for purpose is implied the standard required of the goods is that they must be fit for the particular purpose which the buyer expressly or impliedly made known to the seller. The seller's liability is strict and if an unusual purpose was made known by the buyer the standard required can be well in excess of the standard of satisfactory quality. Let us suppose for example that a customer buys an ordinary road bicycle from a shop, having been assured by the seller that the bicycle is fit for off road use. When used on a country path one of the bicycle's wheels buckles. The seller will be in breach of s.14(3) even if the bicycle was of satisfactory quality and perfectly fit for use on roads.

Section 15A applies to a breach of s.14(3) so that the breach is always regarded as a condition, unless the buyer dealt otherwise than as a consumer and the breach was so slight as to make rejection of the goods unreasonable.

Test your understanding 8.4

1 To what extent will the term as to satisfactory quality be implied into the following contracts?

a Adam, a postman, sells his car to Brian, a builder.

b Adam buys a second-hand car from a garage for £8 000 after giving the exterior of the car a thorough visual examination. The car's brakes are totally unsafe (because the car's brake cylinders are worn out) and the car is very rusty underneath. Adam did not notice the rust and did not give the car a test drive as he was not insured to drive it at the time.

c Charlene buys a new motorbike from a garage. The garage point out that the bike's fuel tank is slightly damaged and £50 is knocked off the price to take account of this. The repair to the fuel tank costs £150, three times as much as Charlene had anticipated that it would.

d David buys a new bicycle from a shop. The seller explains that some of the bicycles have been damaged in transit and so 10 per cent is knocked off the price 'to take account of any defects'. David does not examine the bicycle before the contract is made. The bicycle's gears will not work as they have been knocked out of shape.

2 What term is implied by SGA s.14(3)?

3 Generally second-hand cars are more expensive to buy from a garage than they are to buy privately. Why might a customer who knows little about cars be better off buying from a garage?

4 David, who knows little about cars, feels that he will get a better price from a garage if he appears to have some mechanical expertise. Before buying a car he therefore kicks the tyres, looks underneath the chassis, and examines the engine. Why might these be unwise moves?

8.2.6 Sale by sample (s.15(2))

Section 15(2) SGA gives the following definition of a sale by sample:

'A contract of sale is a contract for sale by sample where there is an express or implied term to that effect.'

Where there is an express term stating that the sale is by sample then this is straightforward enough. A sale will impliedly be by sample where all of the circumstances would suggest that this is what the parties intended. In **Drummond v Van Ingen**

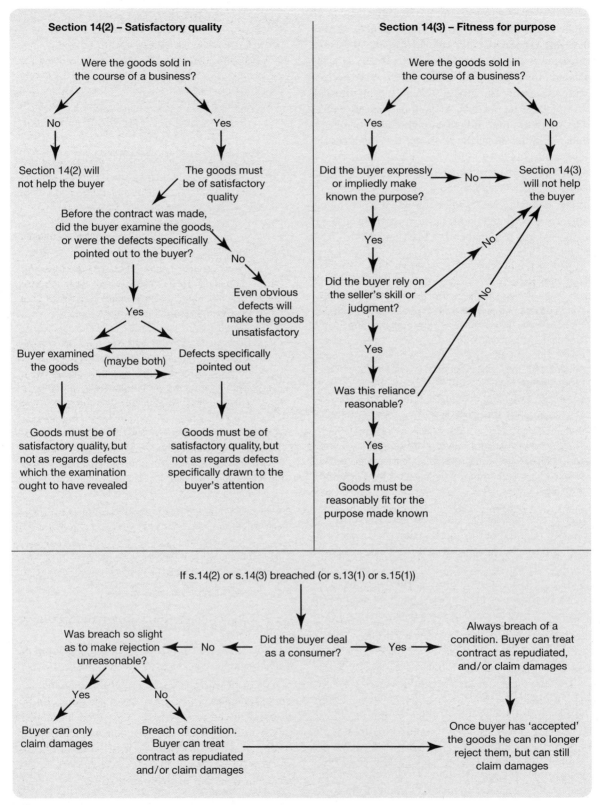

Figure 8.3 An overview of ss.14(2) and 14(3) SGA 1979

(1887) 12 App Cas 284 Lord MacNaghten described the purpose of a sample. 'The office [function] of a sample is to present to the eye the real meaning and intention of the parties with regard to the subject matter of the contract which, owing to the imperfection of language, it may be difficult or impossible to express in words. The sample speaks for itself.' However, it is important to remember that not everything shown to the buyer in advance of the contract will be a sample. The parties must intend the contract to be a sale by sample.

Section 15(2) implies two terms into contracts of sale by sample:

'In the case of a contract for sale by sample there is an implied [condition] –

(a) that the bulk will correspond with the sample in quality; ...

(b) that the goods will be free from any defect, making their quality unsatisfactory, which would not be apparent on reasonable examination of the sample.'

These terms are implied into all sales by sample, whether made in the course of a business or not. Section 15(2)(a)'s requirement that the bulk should correspond with the sample in quality is similar to the requirement of s.13 that when goods are sold by description they should correspond with the description. In effect the sample is the description. As we saw earlier in this chapter, it is possible that goods are sold by sample and by description, in which case they must correspond with both the sample and the description.

We have already seen that where goods are sold in the course of a business then they will have to be of satisfactory quality and that the buyer will have no obligation to examine the goods before the contract is made. But when goods are sold by sample s.14(2C)(c) makes it plain that s.15(2)(c) prevails over the s.14(2) requirement of satisfactory quality and imposes on the buyer an obligation to examine the sample. If goods are sold by sample and the bulk of the goods are of unsatisfactory quality, and if this defect could have been discovered by making a reasonable examination of the sample, then the buyer will have no remedy on the grounds of unsatisfactory quality or under s.15. If the defect could not have been discovered by making a reasonable examination of the sample then s.15(2)(c) will have been breached.

Godley v Perry [1960] 1 All ER 36

A small newsagent, who also sold toys, sold a catapult to a boy aged six for 6d. The boy was using the catapult in the normal way when it snapped and caused him to lose his left eye. The newsagent had bought several catapults from a wholesaler with whom he had dealt previously. The sale between the newsagent and the wholesaler had been a sale by sample. The newsagent's wife had tested a sample catapult, by pulling the elastic back, and had then ordered two dozen. The testing of the sample had not revealed the defect which was in all of the catapults. The defect could only have been discovered by snapping a catapult or testing it to destruction. The newsagent was sued by the injured boy and himself claimed against the wholesaler.

Held. The wholesaler was liable to the newsagent for breach of s.15(2)(c). The defect which made the bulk of the catapults unsatisfactory was not apparent on a reasonable examination of the sample.

COMMENT If the defect which rendered the goods of unsatisfactory quality would have been apparent on a reasonable examination of the sample then the shopkeeper would have noticed it and would, presumably, have refused to buy the catapults. But if the defect would have been apparent on a reasonable examination of the sample, and the shopkeeper either did not examine the sample or did not notice the defect, then neither s.14(2) nor s.15(2)(c) would have been breached.

Section 15A applies to the terms implied into a contract for sale by sample. So if either of the two terms implied by s.15 are breached then this will be a breach of condition, unless the buyer did not deal as a consumer and the breach was so slight as to make rejection of the goods unreasonable.

8.2.6.1 Additional rights of buyer in consumer cases

When there is a breach of ss.13–15 of the Act and the buyer deals as a consumer then Part 5A of the Act, ss.48A–F, gives important new additional remedies. These remedies, which arise when the goods do not conform to the contract, are considered in detail in Chapter 10 at 10.4.6, as they are available not only when one of the statutory implied terms in SGA ss. 13–15 is breached, but also whenever an express term of a contract of sale of goods is breached.

Test your understanding 8.5

1 Which of the following sales are likely to be sales by sample?

   a A grain merchant buys 100 tons of wheat which is lying in another merchant's store.

   b A shopper examines a square metre of carpet in a shop and then orders 16 square metres of this type of carpet.

   c After test driving a demonstration model, a motorist buys a new car.

   d A shop agrees to stock a new type of pen.

   e A householder orders a three piece suite which he saw described in a magazine advertisement.

2 What two terms are implied into a sale by sample?

3 In *Godley v Perry* the boy sued the shopkeeper and won. Under which section(s) would the boy have sued?

8.3 IMPLIED TERMS IN CONTRACTS OTHER THAN SALES OF GOODS

As we have seen, the terms implied by the Sale of Goods Act have protected buyers of goods since 1893. However, the Act has never applied to contracts which do not fit within the definition of a contract of sale of goods (considered above at 8.1.1). In the 1970s Parliament passed several statutes which extended the Sale of Goods Act implied terms into other types of contract.

8.3.1 Terms implied into contracts of hire-purchase

The Supply of Goods (Implied Terms) Act (SGITA) 1973 extended the statutory implied terms into contracts of **hire-purchase**. The terms are virtually identical in effect to the terms implied by ss.12–15 of the Sale of Goods Act, and are contained in the following sections.

- **Section 8(1)(a) – The right to sell** (When the property is to pass)
- **Section 8(1)(b) – Quiet possession and freedom from encumbrances**
- **Section 9(1) – Correspondence with description**
- **Section 10(2) – Satisfactory quality** (Where goods hired in the course of a business)

- **Section 10(3) – Fitness for buyer's purpose** (Where goods hired in the course of a business)
- **Section 11(1) – Correspondence with sample**

As the terms implied are so similar to the SGA implied terms we do not need to examine them in any detail. Case law on the Sale of Goods Act will be applicable to the terms implied by SGITA 1973. Although SGITA 1973 s.8(1)(a) does not imply a term that the bailor owns the goods at the commencement of the hire-purchase contract, such a term is implied at common law. It is well settled that if this term is breached the bailor is entitled to a full refund of all payments made and to claim damages for additional expenses incurred.

A contract of hire-purchase is one whereby a person (the bailee) agrees to hire goods for a fixed period, and is given an option to purchase the goods for a nominal sum at the end of that period. Let us look, for example, at Mrs Smith who takes a car on hire-purchase from a garage. The car would have cost £7 000 to buy, but Mrs Smith takes it on hire-purchase for three years at £340 a month. Until the final payment is made Mrs Smith is merely hiring the car. If she continues to hire the car for the full three year period her final instalment will contain a nominal purchase price and she will have bought the car. The nature of a contract of hire-purchase is examined in more detail in Chapter 14 at 14.2.2. Here we are concerned with the statutory terms implied into such contracts.

When we consider the Consumer Credit Act 1974, in Chapter 14, we shall see that it gives many other rights to hire-purchasers. But it is ss.8–11 SGITA 1973 which imply terms as to title, corres-pondence with description, quality and correspondence with sample. Section 10 SGITA 1973, which implies the terms as to satisfactory quality and fitness for purpose, applies only if the owner of the goods makes the hire-purchase agreement in the course of a business. The other sections apply to all contracts of hire-purchase. In almost all hire-purchase agreements the owner of the goods will make the agreement in the course of a business. Earlier in this chapter, at 8.2.4.2 we saw that the recently introduced SGA 1979 ss.14(2D)–14(2F) set out the circumstances in which public statements made about the specific characteristics of the goods can be relevant circumstances for the purposes of determining whether the goods meet the standard which a reasonable person would regard as satisfactory. These sections are reproduced in relation to contracts of hire-purchase as SGITA 1973 ss.10(2D)–10(2F).

8.3.2 Terms implied into contracts for the transfer of property in goods and contracts of hire

Part 1 of the Supply of Goods and Services Act 1982 implies terms into contracts for the **transfer of property in goods**, and into contracts for the **hire of goods**. The terms are contained in the following sections.

Contracts for the transfer of property in goods

- **Section 2(1) – The right to transfer the property**
- **Section 2(2) – Quiet possession and freedom from encumbrances**
- **Section 3(2) – Correspondence with description**
- **Section 4(2) – Satisfactory quality** (Where the property is transferred in the course of business)
- **Section 4(5) – Fitness for buyer's purpose** (Where the property is transferred in the course of business)
- **Section 5(2) – Correspondence with sample**

Contracts of hire

- **Section 7(1) – The right to hire**
- **Section 7(2) – Quiet possession and freedom from encumbrances**
- **Section 8(2) – Correspondence with description**
- **Section 9(2) – Satisfactory quality** (Where goods are supplied in course of business)
- **Section 9(5) – Fitness for buyer's purpose** (Where goods are supplied in course of business)
- **Section 10(2) – Correspondence with sample**

A contract for the transfer of property in goods includes any contract which involves ownership of the goods passing, unless such a contract is a sale of goods, a hire-purchase agreement, or is made by redeeming trading stamps. The types of contracts which are excluded do not need SGSA 1982 to imply the terms as other pre-existing statutes already do this. A contract to have central heating put in a house would be a contract for the transfer of property in goods, as regards the materials supplied, and the terms implied by SGSA 1982 ss.2–5 would therefore be implied into it. The contract would also be a contract for the supply of a service, and so s.13(1) SGSA 1982 (which is explained below at 8.4.3) would also imply a term that the service was carried out using reasonable care and skill. If goods supplied to a consumer do not conform to the contract then SGSA 1982 ss.11M–S give important new remedies to the consumer (see Chapter 10 at 10.4.6).

A contract of hire is not a contract to transfer the property in goods as the customer never acquires ownership of the goods hired, but only temporary possession. The Sale of Goods Act does not therefore apply to contracts of hire and so ss.7–10 SGSA 1982 are needed to cater for contracts of hire. Earlier in this chapter, at 8.2.4.2 we saw that the recently introduced SGA 1979 ss.14(2D)–14(2F) set out the circumstances in which public statements made about the specific characteristics of the goods can be relevant circumstances for the purposes of determining whether the goods meet the standard which a reasonable person would regard as satisfactory. These sections are reproduced as ss.4(2B)–4(2D) SGSA 1982 (in relation to contracts for the transfer of property in goods) and ss.9(2B)–9(2D) SGSA (in relation to contracts of hire).

Figure 8.4 shows which sections of which statutes imply the terms into the various types of contracts under which the ownership or possession of goods are passed.

8.3.2.1 Additional rights of buyer in consumer cases

When there is a breach of any of the terms in Figure 8.4 (other than a term as to the right to sell, hire etc.) additional new rights will be available to a buyer who dealt as a consumer. These rights are examined in detail in Chapter 10 at 10.4.6.

8.3.3 Terms implied into contracts for the supply of a service

All of the terms which we have so far considered are implied only into contracts under which the ownership or possession of **goods** is transferred. Part II of the Supply of Goods and Services Act 1982 codified the common law to imply three terms into contracts for the supply of a service. These terms are implied by the following sections:

- **Section 13(1) – Implies a term that the supplier should exercise reasonable care and skill** (Where supplier is acting in the course of a business)
- **Section 14(1) – Implies a term about time of performance** (Where supplier is acting in the course of a business)
- **Section 15(1) – Implies a term about consideration**

Type of contract / Term implied	Sale of goods	Hire-purchase	Transfer of the property in goods	Hire
Right to sell	SGA 1979 s.12(1)	SGITA 1973 s.8(1)(a)	SGSA 1982 s.2(1)	SGSA 1982 s.7(1)
Quiet possession and freedom from encumbrances	SGA 1979 s.12(2)	SGITA 1973 s.8(1)(b)	SGSA 1982 s.2(2)	SGSA 1982 s.7(2)
Correspondence with description	SGA 1979 s.13(1)	SGITA 1973 s.9(1)	SGSA 1982 s.3(2)	SGSA 1982 s.8(2)
Satisfactory quality in business sales	SGA 1979 s.14(2)	SGITA 1973 s.10(2)	SGSA 1982 s.4(2)	SGSA 1982 s.9(2)
Fitness for purpose in business sales	SGA 1979 s.14(3)	SGITA 1973 s.10(3)	SGSA 1982 s.4(5)	SGSA 1982 s.9(5)
Correspondence with sample	SGA 1979 s.15(2)	SGITA 1973 s.11(1)	SGSA 1982 s.5(2)	SGSA 1982 s.10(2)

Figure 8.4 The terms implied by SGA 1979, SGITA 1973 and SGSA 1982

As there are no such equivalent terms implied by the Sale of Goods Act, we need to consider the effect of these three terms in some detail.

8.3.3.1 Reasonable care and skill (s.13)

Section 13 of the Supply of Goods and Services Act 1982 provides that:

'In a contract for the supply of a service where the supplier is acting in the course of a business, there is an implied term that the supplier will carry out the service with reasonable care and skill.'

This term is implied only where the supplier of the service is acting in the course of a business. It might therefore be thought that the term is similar in effect to the SGA implied terms as to satisfactory quality and fitness for purpose. However, the term as to carrying out the service with reasonable care and skill is very different in that it implies a tort standard of reasonable care rather than the strict liability standard of satisfactory quality. In *Greaves & Co Contractors Ltd v Baynham, Meickle & Partners* [1975] 3 All ER 99

Lord Denning MR contrasted the different standards required of a surgeon agreeing to provide a service and a dentist agreeing to sell goods, 'The surgeon does not warrant that he will cure the patient. Nor does the solicitor warrant that he will win the case. But, when a dentist agrees to make a set of false teeth for a patient, there is an implied warranty that they will fit his gums.'

The standard required of a person providing a service in the course of a business was considered in the following case. Although the case pre-dates the Supply of Goods and Services Act 1982, that Act codified the law and so the case is still relevant in determining the standard required.

> **Bolam v Friern Hospital Management Committee** [1957] 2 All ER 118
>
> The claimant was suffering from a mental illness. On the advice of a consultant he attended the defendant hospital for electro-convulsive therapy. He signed a consent form which did not warn him that this →

treatment involved a 1 in 10 000 risk of fractures. The claimant suffered fractures while undergoing the treatment. The risk of fractures could have been greatly reduced by the use of relaxant drugs. At the time there were two prevailing bodies of medical opinion about the use of relaxant drugs and manual control while undergoing the treatment. One body of opinion, which had subsequently become accepted as correct, was that relaxant drugs should be used unless there was a reason why they would be considered inappropriate. The alternative view was that relaxant drugs might discourage mentally ill patients from undergoing the treatment. The claimant argued that the defendants had been negligent in administering the treatment without either relaxant drugs or manual control and in not warning him of the risks of the treatment.

Held. The hospital had not been negligent. A doctor who acts in accordance with the opinion of skilled medical men is not negligent merely because there are other skilled medical men who take a contrary view.

However, in **Bolitho v City & Hackney Health Authority** [1998] AC 232 the House of Lords held that the mere fact that some distinguished experts would agree with the actions taken by a defendant doctor would not necessarily mean that the defendant doctor had not been negligent. (See Chapter 12 at 12.2.2.)

It may of course be the case that the supplier of the service does guarantee that the service will have the desired effect. If this is the case then breach of this express term will result in strict contractual liability. In **Thake and another v Maurice** [1986] 1 All ER 497 a surgeon carried out a vasectomy which did not have the desired effect. The surgeon had performed the operation successfully, but the effect of a very few vasectomies can be reversed naturally. The doctor was not liable to the patient, although he would have been if he had expressly and clearly guaranteed that the operation would be successful.

The yardstick by which those who supply services is measured is that of reasonable care and skill. However, this is an objective assessment. It is no defence to a person who has only recently begun to supply a service that he is not quite up to scratch yet. In **Nettleship v Weston** [1971] 2 QB 691 a learner driver crashed the car and this injured the person who was teaching her

to drive. The Court of Appeal held that the duty of care which the driver owed to passengers and the public was the same objective and impersonal standard as every other driver owed, even though she was a learner.

This term implied by s.13 is an innominate term rather than a condition or a warranty. The customer will therefore only be entitled to treat the contract as repudiated if the breach of the term deprived him of substantially the whole benefit of the contract. (Innominate terms were considered in Chapter 5 at 5.4.2.) If a service is supplied other than in the course of a business s.13 will not apply. However, the common law would imply a term that the service be supplied using reasonable care and skill, as was demonstrated by **Nettleship v Weston**. The degree of care and skill expected would be that of a competent amateur rather than that of a competent tradesperson.

Contracts can be classified as contracts for the supply of a service even though the possession or ownership of goods is also to be transferred. So a contract to buy tyres from a garage, where the garage is to fit the tyres, would be a contract of sale of goods as well as a contract for the supply of a service. Sections 13–15 of SGSA 1982 would imply terms into the contract, but so would ss.12–15 of SGA 1979. If the tyres were not of satisfactory quality the buyer would sue under SGA s.14(2). If the tyres were not fitted properly the buyer would sue under s.13(1) SGSA 1982. If a contract was made to service a car then this would be a contract to provide services. If the car owner was injured as a result of the service being negligently performed he would sue under SGSA s.13. If he was injured because a spare part fitted as part of the service was not of satisfactory quality he would sue under SGSA s.4(2).

8.3.3.2 Time of performance (s.14(1))

Section 14(1) of the Supply of Goods and Services Act 1982 provides that:

'Where, under a contract for the supply of a service by a supplier acting in the course of a business, the time for the service to be carried out is not fixed by the contract, left to be fixed in a manner agreed by the contract or determined by the course of dealing between the parties, there is an implied term that the supplier will carry out the service within a reasonable time.'

Again this term is implied only into contracts for the supply of a service where the supplier is acting in the course of a business. It is important to note that the term will only be implied where the time for the service to be carried out is not fixed by the contract, left to be fixed in a manner agreed by the contract or determined by a course of dealing between the parties. Section 14(2) tells us that what is a reasonable time is a question of fact.

8.3.3.3 Reasonable price (s.15(1))

Section 15(1) SGSA 1982 provides that:

> 'Where, under a contract for the supply of a service, the consideration for the service is not determined by the contract, left to be determined in a manner agreed by the contract or determined by the course of dealing between the parties, there is an implied term that the party contracting with the supplier will pay a reasonable charge.'

Unlike the other two terms implied into contracts to supply a service, this term is implied whether the supplier is acting in the course of a business or not. The term is not implied where the consideration for the service has been determined by the contract, or left to be determined in a manner agreed by the contract, or has been determined by a course of dealing between the parties. Difficulties can arise when a customer is given a price in advance but it is not made clear whether this is definitely the contract price. A quotation is regarded as a definite price at which the contract will be performed, whereas an estimate is only an indication of what the price is likely to be. When s.15(1) takes effect, s.15(2) tells us that what is a reasonable charge is a question of fact.

8.4 THE STATUS OF THE STATUTORY IMPLIED TERMS

The terms as to the right to sell goods contained in SGA 1979 s.12(1), and the equivalent terms contained in SGITA 1973 s.8(1)(a) and SGSA 1982 ss.2(1) and 7(1) are conditions. Breach of these terms will always give the buyer the right to treat the contract as repudiated and reclaim all of the price because if the seller or owner does not have the right to sell or hire the goods this amounts to a total failure of consideration.

The terms as to freedom from encumbrances and quiet possession are classified by the various statutes as warranties. Breach of these terms will therefore entitle the buyer or hirer to damages but will not give the right to treat the contract as repudiated.

Section 15A SGA 1979 deals with the status of the SGA terms as to correspondence with description, satisfactory quality, fitness for purpose and correspondence with sample. It tells us that although these terms are conditions, a buyer who does not deal as a consumer will be compelled to treat breach of them as a breach of warranty if the breach is so slight that it would be unreasonable for the buyer to reject the goods. This is the case unless a contrary intention appears in the contract or can be implied from it. The section does not state that a buyer who deals as a consumer will always be able to reject the goods for breach of the implied terms, but it does imply this. The complex definition of dealing as a consumer is examined in detail in Chapter 5 at 5.6.3.

So when the implied terms in SGA 1979 ss.13–15 are breached the buyer is always given a right to reject the goods unless: (i) the buyer does not deal as a consumer; and (ii) the breach is so slight that it would be unreasonable for the buyer to reject; and (iii) the contract has not expressly or impliedly given the buyer a right to reject even as regards a breach which is so slight that it would be unreasonable for him to reject. However, s.11(4) SGA 1979 provides that where a buyer has accepted goods, or part of them, he can only treat a breach of condition by the seller as a breach of warranty. The ways in which goods are accepted are rather technical and are dealt with in Chapter 10 at 10.4.3.

Terms which are the direct equivalent of SGA 1979 s.15A are contained in the SGITA 1973 s.11A and SGSA 1982 ss.5A and 10A.

The term implied by s.13 SGSA 1982 is not classified by the Act as either a condition or a warranty and is therefore an innominate term. The buyer can therefore treat the contract as repudiated only if the breach substantially deprives the whole intended benefit of the contract.

Test your understanding 8.6

1 By which section of which statute are the following terms implied? If the term is implied only where the seller/hirer is acting in the course of a business indicate that this is so.

→

a Satisfactory quality in contracts of hire?

b The right to sell in contracts for the transfer of property in goods?

c Correspondence with description in sales of goods?

d That reasonable care and skill will be used when a service is supplied?

e Fitness for the buyer's purpose in contracts of hire-purchase?

2 Are the following statutory implied terms conditions, warranties or innominate terms? What is the significance of the distinction?

a The implied term as to satisfactory quality in contracts of hire-purchase.

b The implied terms as to freedom from encumbrances and quiet possession in contracts of sale of goods.

c The implied term that reasonable care and skill will be used in the supply of a business service.

8.5 EXCLUSION OF THE STATUTORY IMPLIED TERMS

We saw in Chapter 5 that an exclusion clause is a contractual term which tries to limit or exclude liability. Until relatively recently exclusion clauses could take away a customer's statutory rights, and this severely limited the effect of the terms implied by the Sale of Goods Act. We saw an example of this in *L'Estrange* v *Graucob* [1934] 2 KB 394. It might be remembered that in that case a café owner who bought a cigarette vending machine signed a sales agreement without reading it. The sales agreement said, in regrettably small print, that the café owner gave up all of her statutory rights. The machine did not work properly and was not therefore fit for the buyer's purpose. Even so, there was nothing the café owner could do. She had unwittingly agreed that the implied terms as to merchantable (now satisfactory) quality and fitness for purpose should be excluded from the contract which she was making.

In Chapter 5 at 5.6 we considered the Unfair Contract Terms Act 1977 in some detail. We saw that UCTA specifically mentions the terms implied by ss.12–15 of the Sale of Goods Act, and that subsequent legislation has extended the protection conferred by UCTA to cover the terms implied by SGITA 1973 and SGSA 1982. It is worth repeating this protection, in outline, here.

In the context of excluding the statutory implied terms under which the ownership or possession of

goods is to pass, the Unfair Contract Terms Act makes a distinction between a person who 'deals as a consumer' and one who does not.

This distinction is vitally important here because ss.6 and 7 UCTA provide that:

(a) When the buyer deals as a consumer the terms as to correspondence with description, satisfactory quality, fitness for purpose or correspondence with sample cannot be excluded or restricted by any contract term.

(b) When the buyer does not deal as a consumer these terms can be excluded or restricted, but only by a term which satisfies the Act's requirement of reasonableness.

Section 6 UCTA 1977 deals with exclusion of the terms implied by the Sale of Goods Act 1979 and the Supply of Goods (Implied Terms) Act 1973. Section 7 UCTA 1977 deals with exclusion of the terms implied by the Supply of Goods and Services Act 1982.

It will be remembered that s.12(1) UCTA provides that a person deals as a consumer if:

(a) he neither makes the contract in the course of a business nor holds himself out as doing so; and

(b) the other party does make the contract in the course of a business; and

(c) (which applies only in cases where the potential consumer is a company rather than an individual) the goods supplied under the contract are of a type ordinarily supplied for private use or consumption.

For example, when a customer buys a television from a shop for his own personal use the customer deals as a consumer. He is not in the business of buying televisions, whereas the shop is in the business of selling televisions. When the shop orders a new consignment of televisions from the manufacturer the shop does not deal as a consumer because the shop is buying the televisions in the course of business. In Chapter 5, at 5.6.3, we saw that in *R & B Customs Brokers Ltd* v *United Dominions Trust Ltd* [1988] 1 All ER 847 the Court of Appeal held that a business, even a company, can in some circumstances deal as a consumer when buying goods. The complex definition of dealing as a consumer was considered in detail.

However, if a company does deal as a consumer this will bring in the requirement in UCTA s.12(1)(c) that the goods are of a type ordinarily supplied for private use or consumption (such as a television).

Section 12(2)(b) provides that companies who buy goods at auction or by competitive tender are never to be regarded as consumers. Section 12(2)(a) provides that individuals who buy goods at public auctions are not to be regarded as consumers if the goods were second-hand and the individuals had the opportunity of attending the auction in person. When a person claims to deal as a consumer the burden of proof is on the other party to show that he does not deal as a consumer.

Sections 6 and 7 UCTA provide that as regards a person who is not dealing as a consumer the terms implied by the various statutes are excludable only to the extent that the term excluding li-ability satisfies the Act's requirement of reasonableness. Schedule 2 to the Unfair Contract Terms Act describes the factors which a court will consider in assessing whether or not the exclusion clause was reasonable. It might be remembered that these factors are:

(a) The relative strength of the parties' bargaining position, which will include whether or not the customer could find another supplier.
(b) Whether the customer was given any inducement to agree to the term, or could have agreed a similar contract with another person without having to agree to a similar term.
(c) Whether the customer knew or ought reasonably to have known of the existence and extent of the term.
(d) Where the term excludes liability unless some condition is complied with, whether or not it was reasonably practicable to comply with that condition.
(e) Whether the goods were manufactured, altered or adapted to the special order of the customer.

It should also be remembered that the Unfair Terms in Consumer Contracts Regulations 1999, considered in Chapter 5 at 5.7, might provide additional protection as regards terms made between a supplier and a consumer if these terms were not individually negotiated.

Sections 6 and 7 UCTA provide that the implied terms as to title cannot be excluded by any contract term. If the supplier does not have title to what he supplies under the contract then there has been a total failure of consideration, and no term can protect against this. Sections 6 and 7 UCTA were considered in more detail in Chapter 5 at 5.6.2.

UCTA applies to the term implied by s.13 SGSA (that a service supplied in the course of a business will be supplied using reasonable care and skill), in a rather different way. Sections 6 and 7 UCTA do not apply to the term implied by s.13 SGSA. However, s.2 UCTA will apply. In Chapter 5 we saw that s.2(1) UCTA provides that a person cannot by reference to any contract term exclude or restrict liability for death or personal injury caused by negligence. Section 2(2) UCTA allows a term to exclude or restrict liability for other loss or damage caused by negligence in so far as the term satisfies the requirement of reasonableness. A supplier in breach of s.13 SGSA 1982 will have been negligent for the purposes of UCTA. Section 2 UCTA was considered in more detail in Chapter 5 at 5.6.1.

Test your understanding 8.7

1 How does s.12(1) UCTA 1977 define dealing as a consumer?

2 To what extent will UCTA 1977 allow a term to exclude liability for breach of the following statutory implied terms?

   a Section 9(2) SGSA 1982 is breached when a car hire business hires a car which is not of satisfactory quality to Jemima, a shop assistant.

   b Section 14(2) and 14(3) SGA 1979 are breached when bicycles sold to a shop by the manufacturer prove not to be of satisfactory quality or fit for the buyer's purpose.

   c Section 13 SGSA 1982 is breached when a plumber repairs a burst water pipe in a negligent manner, so that it soon begins to leak.

Key points

Terms implied by the Sale of Goods Act 1979

■ The Sale of Goods Act 1979 implies terms only into contracts of sale of goods.

■ A contract of sale of goods is a contract by which the seller transfers or agrees to transfer the property in goods to the buyer for a money consideration, called the price.

■ Section 12(1) implies a condition that the seller has the right to sell the goods. If this term is breached the buyer will be entitled to a full refund →

of the price even if he has had the use of the goods for some time.

■ Section 12(2) implies warranties that the goods are free from encumbrances and that the buyer will enjoy quiet possession of the goods.

■ Section 13(1) implies a condition that goods will correspond with any description by which they were sold.

■ Unascertained future goods are always sold by description. In other contracts of sale of goods the sale will only be 'by description' if the descriptive words are a substantial part of the identity of what is being bought and if the description is an essential term of the contract.

■ Section 14(2) implies a condition that goods sold in the course of a business are of satisfactory quality.

■ The seller's liability under s.14(2) is strict. However, there is no requirement of satisfactory quality as regards defects which are specifically drawn to the buyer's attention before the contract is made.

■ If the buyer examines the goods before the contract is made, which he has no obligation to do, there is no requirement of satisfactory quality as regards defects which the examination ought to have revealed.

■ Goods are of satisfactory quality if they meet the standard which a reasonable person would regard as satisfactory, taking account of any description of the goods, the price (if relevant) and all the other relevant circumstances.

■ If the buyer deals as a consumer, public statements about the specific characteristics of the goods can be a relevant circumstance for deciding whether or not the goods meet the standard which a reasonable person would regard as satisfactory.

■ In appropriate cases the following matters, among others, are aspects of the quality of goods: (a) fitness for all the purposes for which goods of the kind in question are commonly supplied; (b) appearance and finish; (c) freedom from minor defects; (d) safety; and (e) durability.

■ Section 14(3) implies a condition that goods sold in the course of a business will be fit for the buyer's purpose.

■ The term implied by s.14(3) will not be implied unless the buyer expressly or impliedly makes known to the seller the particular purpose for which the goods are being bought. Nor will it be implied where the buyer does not rely on the skill and judgment of the seller. Nor where it is unreasonable for the buyer to rely on the skill and judgment of the seller.

■ Section 15(2) implies two conditions when goods are sold by sample. First, it is implied that the bulk of the goods will match the sample in quality. Second, it is implied that the goods will be free from defects which would make their quality unsatisfactory if these defects would not be apparent on a reasonable examination of the sample.

Terms implied by other statutes

■ Terms which are virtually identical to those implied by SGA 1979 are implied by SGITA 1973 into contracts of hire-purchase, and by SGSA 1982 into both contracts for the transfer of property in goods and into contracts of hire.

■ Section 13 SGSA 1982 provides that in a contract for the supply of a service where the supplier is acting in the course of a business, there is an implied term that the supplier will carry out the service with reasonable care and skill. This term imposes a tort standard of reasonable care rather than the strict liability standard of satisfactory quality.

■ Where no time is fixed for the provision of a service which is to be supplied in the course of a business, s.14(1) SGSA 1982 implies a term that the supplier will carry out the service within a reasonable time.

■ Where the consideration is not fixed in a contract for the supply of a service, s.15(1) SGSA implies a term that the price will be a reasonable price.

Exclusion of the statutory implied terms

■ The statutory terms as to the right to sell/hire/transfer the property cannot be excluded by any contract term.

■ Where the customer deals as a consumer liability for breach of the statutory implied terms as to correspondence with description, satisfactory quality, fitness for purpose and correspondence with sample cannot be excluded by any contract term. Where the customer does not deal as a consumer liability for breach of these terms can only be excluded in so

→

far as the term which excludes liability satisfies the UCTA 1977 requirement of reasonableness.

■ A supplier in breach of s.13 SGSA 1982 will, for the purposes of UCTA 1977, be regarded as having been negligent. Section 2(1) UCTA provides that a person cannot by reference to any contract term exclude or restrict liability for death or personal injury caused by negligence. Section 2(2) UCTA allows a term to exclude or restrict liability for other loss or damage caused by negligence in so far as the term satisfies UCTA's requirement of reasonableness.

Summary questions

1 Naseem, who has begun to work as a market trader, bought several items from Rashid, a market trader who is retiring. Naseem has experienced several problems with the items bought. These problems might be summarised as follows.

a The van which Rashid sold for £2 000 has proved to be totally unroadworthy. Rashid said that the van had a steering problem and 10 per cent was knocked off the price to take account of this. When Naseem took the van to the garage he was told that the steering would cost £500 to put right and that to fix the brakes, the clutch and the bodywork would cost another £500, which is more than the van would be worth.

b A tarpaulin which Naseem bought has been seized by the police because, unknown to Rashid, it was one of a consignment stolen from the manufacturer. Naseem has been using the tarpaulin for several months.

c Naseem bought Rashid's stock, including a box of digital watches. Several customers have returned these watches claiming that they do not work. Rashid says that he never had any such problems, and that as the watches are still in the manufacturer's packing this cannot be his fault.

Advise Naseem of any rights he might have against Rashid under the Sale of Goods Act 1979.

2 In *Godley v Perry* there was a chain of buyers, as follows.

Manufacturer → importer → wholesaler 1 → wholesaler 2 → shopkeeper → boy

a Who was the eventual loser likely to be?

b How would the bankruptcy of wholesaler 1 have affected the position?

3 Gerald, a teacher, buys a car at a car auction. The car was put into the auction by Acme Finance Ltd. At the auction a prominently displayed notice states that all cars are to be sold without any guarantee, and that the terms implied by ss.13–15 are expressly excluded. The notice also says that bidders should satisfy themselves as to the quality of any cars before making a bid. The auctioneer reads this notice out before the sale starts. Gerald paid £2 000 for a four-year-old Ford Granada. The car's brakes are very poor, the bodywork is badly corroded and the engine is virtually worn out. Advise Gerald of his legal position.

4 Mrs Smith buys a new computer as a wedding present for her niece. When she gets the computer home she notices that the mouse has been damaged and cannot be used. She returns the computer to the shop who say that they can easily supply another mouse immediately and that the computer is otherwise perfect.

a Can Mrs Smith reject the goods and demand her money back?

b Could the shop reject the computer and return it to the manufacturer from whom they bought it?

5 A motorist buys a new car from a garage but the car has a serious defect in the steering system. No mention of the steering was made when the contract was formed. Which section(s) of which statute gives the motorist a remedy?

6 How would your answer to question 6 be different if

a The motorist had hired the car?

b The motorist had bought the car from his friend, an accountant who is employed by the city council?

7 Hugh decides to have his garden landscaped. Gardener and Son agree to do the job for £1 200. Soon after he starts work, Mr Gardener arrives at Hugh's house with a load of Tarmac. He says that this is left over from another job and that the original contract could easily be extended to include

Tarmacking Hugh's small driveway. Hugh is pleased to agree to this, although no price is mentioned. The landscaping work turned out to be unsatisfactory. The lawn has not been levelled, as Hugh was assured that it would be, and the grass on the lawn is of very poor quality. Gardener and Son are demanding that Hugh pay the full price, and have also submitted a bill of another £2 050 for Tarmacking the drive. Hugh had thought that the additional cost for Tarmacking might be about £50. Advise Hugh of his statutory rights.

8 In the following contracts which of the buyers would be regarded as dealing as a consumer, as defined by the Unfair Contract Terms Act 1977?

a A motor dealer orders a dozen new cars from Ford.

b A manufacturing company buys a new car for one of its salesmen.

c A salesman fills his company car with petrol at a filling station.

d A lady who has inherited an extremely valuable painting sells it to a gallery.

e A postman sells his old television to his neighbour.

f An amateur DIY enthusiast orders a reinforced steel joist from a builder's merchant.

Multiple choice questions

1 A firm of builders hire a JCB digging machine from a hire company for a three week period. The builders asked the hire company whether the machine supplied would be capable of digging through rock. The hire company assured the builders that the machine was suitable and so the builders made the contract. The digger is a small model which is unable to dig through rock, but is perfectly adequate for smaller jobs. The builders have to hire a more powerful machine from another company. Under which one of the following will the builders have a remedy against the hire company?

a Sections 13(1) and 14(3) of the Sale of Goods Act 1979.

b Sections 13(1) and 14(2) of the Sale of Goods Act 1979.

c Sections 8(2) and 9(5) of the Supply of Goods and Services Act 1982.

d Sections 9(1) and 10(3) of the Supply of Goods (Implied Terms) Act 1973.

2 For many years a fish and chip shop has bought potatoes from a local farmer. The quality of the potatoes was never formally described, but the potatoes supplied were always large enough to be cut into chips. The latest consignment consisted of small potatoes, which cannot be turned into chips. Which one of the following statements is true?

a The chip shop has no remedy.

b The chip shop can reject the potatoes under s.14(2) of the Sale of Goods Act 1979.

c The chip shop can reject the potatoes under s.14(3) of the Sale of Goods Act 1979.

d The chip shop can reject the potatoes under s.15(2) of the Sale of Goods Act 1979.

3 A farmer buys a large quantity of seed potatoes from a local seed merchant. The merchant tells the farmer that the potatoes in question are for export to Egypt because they do not grow well in English conditions. The farmer says that his farmland is most untypical and will grow any sort of potatoes. The farmer, as usual, signs an invoice which says that the seed merchant cannot be responsible for any defect in goods supplied. The potatoes do not grow at all well and the farmer consequently loses a great deal of money. The potatoes would have grown well enough in Egypt. Which one of the following statements is true?

a The seed merchant will have incurred no liability.

b The seed merchant will be liable under s.14(2) and (3) of the Sale of Goods Act. This liability cannot be excluded or restricted by any contract term.

c The seed merchant will be liable under s.14(2) and (3) of the Sale of Goods Act unless the exclusion clause satisfied UCTA 1977's requirement of reasonableness.

d The seed merchant will be liable under s.13(1) of the Sale of Goods Act unless the exclusion clause satisfied UCTA 1977's requirement of reasonableness.

4 Buildo Ltd, a firm of builders, hire a JCB digging machine from Hire Co Ltd. Buildo's manager signs a contract, without reading it, which contains a clause, 'All terms expressed or implied by statute or otherwise are hereby expressly excluded'. The JCB will not excavate due to a mechanical fault. Hire Co refuse to repair it, exchange it for another machine or return Buildo's money. Which of the following is true?

a Buildo will win under s.14(2) and (3) of the Sale of Goods Act, unless the exclusion clause satisfied UCTA 1977's requirement of reasonableness.

b Buildo will win under s.9(2) and (5) of the Supply of Goods and Services Act, unless the exclusion clause satisfied UCTA 1977's requirement of reasonableness.

c Hire Co Ltd will be liable under s.14(2) and (3) of the Sale of Goods Act. This liability cannot be excluded or restricted by any contract term.

d Hire Co Ltd will be liable under under s.9(2) and (5) of the Supply of Goods and Services Act. This liability cannot be excluded or restricted by any contract term.

5 Anjana, the managing director of Anjana Enterprises Ltd, hires a professional magician for the staff Christmas party. The magician arrives very drunk and is unable to perform any tricks. Which one of the following will provide a remedy?

a Sections 9(2) and (3) of the Supply of Goods and Services Act 1982.

b Section 4(2) and (5) of the Supply of Goods and Services Act 1982.

c Section 10(2) and (3) of the Supply of Goods (Implied Terms) Act 1973.

d Section 13 of the Supply of Goods and Services Act 1982.

6 Geraldine bought a pair of shoes at half price in the January sale. Above the till was a sign which clearly stated, 'No refunds on sale goods'. The shop assistant pointed the sign out to Geraldine when the sale was made. Within a week the heel fell off one of the shoes. Which one of the following statements is true?

a Geraldine has no remedy.

b Geraldine can get her money back unless the exclusion clause satisfied UCTA 1977's requirement of reasonableness.

c Geraldine can get her money back because the sign cannot exclude or restrict liability to her for breach of ss.13–15 of the Sale of Goods Act 1979.

d Geraldine cannot get her money back but is entitled to exchange the shoes for another pair.

7 Arthur bought a bicycle from Bill's shop. The bicycle frame was defective and snapped in half, injuring Arthur. At Arthur's request Bill had ordered the bicycle from Charles's wholesale company, which in turn had bought it from the manufacturer. Which of the following is true?

a Section 14(2) of the Sale of Goods Act will protect only Arthur.

b Section 14(2) of the Sale of Goods Act will impose liability on Bill, Charles's company and the manufacturer.

c Bill will not be able to sue Charles under the Sale of Goods Act. It was his business to know about bicycles and he should have spotted the fault.

d Bill will be liable under s.13 of the Supply of Goods and Services Act because he should have serviced the bicycle before selling it.

Task 8

You work for a firm which installs double-glazing in houses. Your firm buys most of its materials, but occasionally hires machinery. Your employer has asked you to write a report, briefly indicating:

a What statutory protection is given to your firm when it buys materials from suppliers.

b What statutory protection is given to customers for whom your firm works.

c The extent to which liability for breach of the statutory implied terms can be excluded by the contract under which goods and services are provided.

d To what extent the Unfair Contract Terms Act 1977 and the Unfair Terms in Consumer Contracts Regulations 1999 adequately protect consumers.

mylawchamber *premium*

Visit **www.mylawchamber.co.uk/macintyre** to access study support resources including interactive multiple choice questions, weblinks, glossary, glossary flashcards, legal newsfeed, answers to questions in this chapter, legal updates and an overview of this chapter all linked to the **Pearson eText** version of *Business Law* which you can **search**, **highlight** and **personalise** with your **own notes** and **bookmarks**.

Use **Case Navigator** to read in full some of the key cases referenced in this chapter with commentary and questions:

Jewson Ltd v *Kelly* [2003] All ER (D) 470 (Jul)
Stevenson v *Rogers* [1999] 1 All ER 613

Sale of goods – the passing of ownership

Introduction

This chapter considers the following matters:

9.1 THE PASSING OF THE PROPERTY AND THE RISK

The purpose of a contract of sale of goods is to pass the property in the goods (ownership of the goods) to the buyer in return for payment of the price. There are several circumstances in which it can be important to know exactly when the property passes. It might be thought that the property would pass either upon delivery of the goods or upon payment of the price. As we shall see, the property does not generally pass at either of these times.

A dispute over whether or not the property has passed from the seller to the buyer will usually arise if either of the parties has become insolvent, or if the goods have become damaged, lost or destroyed. However, it can also be important to know whether or not the property has passed because generally the seller only has a right to sue for the price once the property has passed.

First, let us consider the position where the seller of the goods, having made the contract of sale, becomes insolvent. If the seller becomes insolvent before the property in the goods passes to the buyer, then

the buyer will not own the goods and will not therefore be entitled to claim possession of the goods from the seller's liquidator. If the buyer already has possession of the goods then the liquidator will be entitled to reclaim the goods from the buyer. This is the case even if the buyer has paid for the goods, although the buyer will be able to bring a claim as an unsecured creditor for the return of money he has paid. However, if the property does pass to the buyer before the seller becomes insolvent then the buyer will be entitled to claim the goods from the seller's liquidator or to retain the goods if they have already been delivered. The buyer owns the goods and is therefore entitled to possession of them. (The buyer will of course have to pay for the goods if payment has not already been made.) As the seller's insolvency necessarily means that all those to whom the seller owes money are not going to be paid in full, if they are paid at all, a buyer would obviously be in a far better position claiming ownership of the goods bought rather than claiming damages for breach of contract as an unsecured creditor.

Next, we consider the position where the buyer has become insolvent after the contract of sale was made. If the buyer has already paid the full price then there will be no problem. The buyer (or his liquidator) will either have received possession of the goods if they have already been delivered or will be entitled to demand possession from the seller if they have not. But if the full price has not been paid then the seller will want to know whether or not the property in the goods had passed at the time of the insolvency. If the property had passed, then the seller could claim the price only as an unsecured creditor. (However, if the unpaid seller exercises his real remedies (see Chapter 10 at 10.3.1) he can resell the goods to a second buyer and pass a good title to that second buyer.) If the property in the goods had not passed, the seller could reclaim the goods if they have been delivered or refuse to deliver them if they have not. A seller who did this would of course have to refund to the buyer's liquidator any part of the price already paid. If the property had not passed, the buyer's liquidator could elect to enforce the contract but would then have to pay the full price in return for ownership of the goods.

Finally, we consider the position where the goods have become lost, damaged or destroyed after the contract of sale was made. Generally, as we shall see below at 9.1.4, the risk of damage to or deterioration of the goods passes at the same time as the property. Therefore if the goods were damaged etc. before the property had passed to the buyer, the seller would have to bear this loss as the goods belonged to him at the time of the damage. If the damage meant that the goods were of unsatisfactory quality then the buyer would be entitled to refuse to accept and pay for the goods. If the goods were specific the seller would be in breach of contract, if the goods were unascertained the seller could deliver other goods matching the contract description. If the goods were damaged after the property had passed to the buyer then the loss would fall on the buyer, as the buyer would have been the owner of the goods at the time when the damage occurred.

It is possible that the buyer and seller agree that the risk of the goods being lost, damaged or destroyed should not pass with the property in the goods. If this is expressly or impliedly agreed then the party who has accepted the risk will bear the loss when the goods are damaged etc. However, this is not the usual position. Unless there is an express or implied agreement to the contrary, the risk passes at the same time as the property in the goods.

Sections 16–20 SGA 1979 lay down rules as to when the property in the goods is to pass. These rules make a distinction between specific goods and unascertained goods. Specific goods are defined by s.61 as goods which are identified and agreed on at the time a contract of sale is made. The Act does not define unascertained goods, but any goods which are not specific are unascertained. Future goods, that is goods which have yet to be acquired or manufactured by the seller, are always regarded as unascertained in this context. This is the case even if the buyer and seller identify the particular goods which the seller is to acquire and sell.

This distinction between specific and unascertained goods is vital when considering the passing of property. You must first decide whether the goods are specific or unascertained because if they are specific one set of sections of the SGA will govern the passing of property whereas if they are unascertained a different set of sections will do this. It is also essential to realise that you are concerned with whether or not the goods were specific or unascertained at the time of the contract. Having made that decision, you decide which set of SGA sections are applicable and stick to using these sections. As will be seen, unascertained goods may become ascertained, but they never become specific.

Test your understanding 9.1

1 What is meant by the passing of the property in the goods?

2 What is meant by the risk?

3 How are specific goods defined?

4 What is the definition of unascertained goods?

5 What is the meaning of future goods? Are future goods regarded as specific or unascertained?

6 Are the following contracts sales of specific or unascertained goods?

   a Arthur, who has owned a bicycle for six years, agrees to sell it to Bill.

   b Arthur telephones Charles's shop and orders a new Raleigh Super Tourer Mark 2 bicycle. Charles has several such bicycles in stock.

   c Charles knows that David is thinking of selling his antique penny-farthing bicycle, which is in Charles's shop to be repaired. Charles agrees with Edward that if he can buy the bicycle from David he will then sell it to Edward. (Consider both the sale from David to Charles and the sale from Charles to Edward.)

9.1.1 **Specific goods**

Section 17 of the Sale of Goods Act 1979 provides that the property in specific goods passes when the parties to the contract intend it to pass, and this intention can either be a term of the contract or can be inferred from the conduct of the parties and the circumstances of the case. (In this Chapter all references to 'the Act' are references to the Sale of Goods Act 1979 unless it is made clear that they are not.)

If the parties' intentions cannot be found, then s.18 Rules 1–4 will apply. Rule 1 provides that:

'Where there is an unconditional contract for the sale of specific goods in a deliverable state the property in the goods passes to the buyer when the contract is made, and it is immaterial whether the time of payment or the time of delivery, or both, be postponed.'

Before considering the meaning of s.18 Rule 1 it is essential to understand that this Rule is to be applied only if s.17 does not apply. All the five Rules in s.18 are subservient to s.17. Section 18 itself makes this quite clear. Before setting out any of its five Rules, s.18 begins, 'Unless a different intention appears, the following are rules for ascertaining the intention of the parties as to the time at which the property in the goods is to pass to the buyer...' As a practical matter it can be very difficult to say whether or not the parties have sufficiently shown an intention for s.17 to apply.

In order for Rule 1 to apply the contract must be unconditional, meaning that the passing of the property must not have been made subject to any condition.

Section 61(5) states that goods are in a deliverable state when they are in such a state that the buyer would, under the contract, be bound to take delivery of them. However, this definition does not mean that goods are not in a deliverable state just because the buyer could refuse to take delivery of them. If that were so, property would never pass in goods which were not of satisfactory quality. In fact, property in goods which are not of satisfactory quality does pass to the buyer, but the buyer has the option to reject the goods for breach of the condition set out in s.14(2). The following case suggests that goods are in a deliverable state where the seller has no more obligation to do anything to the goods.

Underwood Ltd v Burgh Castle Sand and Cement Syndicate
[1922] 1 KB 343 (Court of Appeal)

On 20 February 1920 the claimants agreed to sell a horizontal condensing engine to the defendants, to be delivered 'free on rail'. The engine weighed 30 tons. It was bolted to a concrete floor and had become embedded in the floor by its own weight. The machine had to be taken from the floor and dismantled before it could be delivered free on rail. The unfastening would take two days, the dismantling about two weeks. The machine was damaged while it was being loaded onto the railway wagon.

Held. Section 18 Rule 1 did not apply because at the time of the contract the machine was not in a deliverable state. As the parties had agreed that the machine was to be delivered free on rail they had shown an intention that the property was not to pass until the machine was loaded onto the train. If no intention had been shown the contract would have been governed by s.18 Rule 2 (see immediately below) and the property would not have passed as the buyer had not been informed that the goods were in a deliverable state.

COMMENT In this case Rowlatt J explained that a full-size billiard (snooker) table could be in a deliverable state despite its size and that the need to pack goods would not prevent them from being in a deliverable state. He said that in order for an item to be in a deliverable state 'it must have everything done to it that the sellers had to do to it as an article'.

In *Kulkarni v Manor Credit (Davenham) Ltd* [2010] EWCA Civ 69, [2010] All ER (D) 120 (Feb) the Court of Appeal held that a new car which had been sold to a consumer was not in a deliverable state if it did not have its registration number plates attached to it. Without the plates the consumer could not have driven the car. He would therefore not have been bound to have taken delivery of it. (The contract was for the sale of unascertained goods and so the case concerned s.18 Rule 5, considered below at 9.1.2. Rule 5 can apply only when the goods are in a deliverable state.)

Rule 2 applies where the contract is for the sale of specific goods which the seller is bound to put into a deliverable state:

'Where there is a contract for the sale of specific goods and the seller is bound to do something to the goods for the purpose of putting them into a deliverable state, the property does not pass until the thing is done and the buyer has notice that it has been done.'

Rule 2 would have been applied in *Underwood Ltd* v *Burgh,* if the parties had not shown an intention as to when the property was to pass. If Rule 2 had been applied the property in the goods would not have already passed at the time of the damage as the goods would not at that time have been put into a deliverable state. Even if the goods had been put into a deliverable state the property would not have passed until the buyer had received notice of this.

Rule 3 applies to contracts for the sale of specific goods which the seller must weigh, measure, test etc. to find the price:

'Where there is a contract for the sale of specific goods in a deliverable state but the seller is bound to weigh, measure, test, or do some other act or thing with reference to the goods for the purpose of ascertaining the price, the property does not pass until the act or thing is done and the buyer has notice that it has been done.'

This Rule is of limited effect. It only applies where the seller is the person doing the weighing etc. and it only applies where this is being done in order to ascertain the price. When the Rule does apply the property passes only when the buyer has notice that the weighing etc. has been done.

Rule 4 applies when goods are delivered to the buyer on approval or sale or return or other similar terms:

'When goods are delivered to the buyer on approval or on sale or return or other similar terms the property in the goods passes to the buyer –

(a) when he signifies his approval or acceptance to the seller or does any other act adopting the transaction;

(b) if he does not signify his approval or acceptance to the seller but retains the goods without giving notice of rejection, then, if a time has been fixed for the return of the goods, on the expiration of that time, and, if no time has been fixed, on the expiration of a reasonable time.'

Goods are delivered on approval when the buyer has the choice as to whether or not to approve the contract. Goods are delivered on sale or return when the buyer has the option to return the goods to the seller if he

cannot himself sell them. In either of these circumstances, or if the goods are sold on similar terms, Rule 4 sets out four circumstances in which the property will pass. First, the property will pass when the buyer signifies his approval. Second, when the buyer does an act adopting the transaction. (Any act which would prevent the buyer from returning the goods to the seller, such as selling the goods on, will be regarded as an act adopting the transaction.) Third, if the contract fixes a time by which the goods must be returned to the seller then the property will pass if the goods are not returned by this time. Fourth, if there is no such time limit then the property will pass once the buyer has retained the goods for more than a reasonable time.

9.1.1.1 Mistake and frustration

In Chapter 6 we examined the circumstances in which the common law will render a contract frustrated or void for mistake. Sections 6 and 7 SGA 1979 make two further rules which apply only to contracts for the sale of specific goods.

Section 6 states that:

'Where there is a contract for the sale of specific goods, and the goods without the knowledge of the seller have perished at the time when a contract is made, the contract is void.'

Not only is this section restricted to contracts for the sale of specific goods, it is also necessary that the goods must have perished at the time of the contract and that the seller was not aware of this when the contract was made. If the seller was aware that the goods had perished then he cannot take advantage of s.6 and will be liable for breach of contract. Section 6 only applies where the goods have perished. Goods which have been stolen will be regarded as having perished. The following case considered whether goods which had become damaged could be regarded as having perished. When s.6 makes a contract void, the seller will not be in breach of contract for failure to deliver the goods. The buyer need not pay the price and can recover any amount of the price which has already been paid.

Asfar & Co Ltd v *Blundell*
[1896] 1 QB 123 (Court of Appeal)

Dates which were on board a ship were sold. The ship sank on the river Thames, but later it was raised. Although the dates still looked like dates, and although →

they were still worth a good deal for the purposes of distilling into spirit, the dates were covered in sewage and had begun to ferment. The dates were clearly no longer of merchantable (now satisfactory) quality but they were of some value as they could be distilled into spirit.

Held. For insurance purposes, the cargo could be regarded as a total loss.

COMMENT There is no direct authority on the meaning of perish under ss.6 and 7 SGA. It would seem that if the dates could be regarded as a total loss for insurance purposes then they would surely have perished for the purposes of ss.6 and 7.

Section 7 deals with the frustration of an agreement to sell specific goods:

'Where there is an agreement to sell specific goods and subsequently the goods, without any fault on the part of the seller or buyer, perish before the risk passes to the buyer, the agreement is avoided.'

Here the specific goods which have been agreed to be sold must perish after the agreement to sell has been made but before the risk has passed to the buyer. It is possible to separate risk and the passing of the property, as we shall see below at 9.1.4. When the buyer does not deal as a consumer, and the parties have not agreed to separate the passing of the property and the passing of the risk, s.7 can only apply to contracts governed by s.18 Rules 2 and 3, it cannot apply to contracts governed by Rules 1 or 4. If Rule 1 operates there will be no time gap between the agreement to sell and the passing of the risk. Under Rule 4 there is no agreement to sell until the buyer signifies his approval or otherwise causes the property in the goods to pass. If s.7 is to frustrate the contract, the perishing of the goods must not be the fault of either party. If the buyer does deal as a consumer, s.20(4) provides that the risk does not pass until the goods are delivered to the buyer. (See 9.1.4.1.) Therefore, s.7 could apply to a consumer contract governed by Rules 1, 2 or 3.

Earlier in this chapter we saw that future goods cannot be classified as specific goods when applying ss.16–18. It seems likely that some future goods can be classified as specific goods for the purposes of ss.6

and 7. Let us assume, for example, that a car dealer has agreed to buy a second-hand Lexus car from A, and that before acquiring the car he has agreed to sell it to B. The sale to B is one of future goods because the seller, the car dealer, has yet to acquire the goods. If the car were to perish before the car dealer acquired it, then it is likely that the contract between the car dealer and B would be frustrated under s.7. The car fits within the definition of specific goods as it was identified and agreed upon at the time of sale. The application of s.7 would not cause any difficulty and would result in a fair outcome.

When s.7 applies the contract is avoided. The seller will have no obligation to deliver the goods. The buyer will have no obligation to pay the price and will be able to recover any part of the price already paid. Other losses will lie where they fall. The Law Reform (Frustrated Contracts) Act 1943, which we considered in Chapter 7 at 7.1.3.3, does not apply where s.7 SGA does apply. The courts will not therefore be empowered to apportion the loss between buyer and seller.

Test your understanding 9.2

1 What rule does s.17 make about the passing of the property in specific goods?

2 When considering the time at which the property in specific goods passes, does s.17 take precedence over s.18, or does s.18 take precedence over s.17?

3 In **Tarling v Baxter** [1827] 6 B & C 360 a haystack was sold. Before the price had been paid, and before the contract allowed the haystack to be moved, the haystack was accidentally destroyed by fire. The parties did not show an intention as to when the property or the risk was to pass. Applying SGA 1979 to the facts of this case, what would the outcome now be?

4 What is the test for deciding whether or not specific goods are in a deliverable state, for the purposes of s.18 SGA 1979?

5 Specific goods which the seller has yet to put into a deliverable state are sold. At what time will the property pass to the buyer?

Figure 9.1 summarises the situation regarding mistake and frustration.

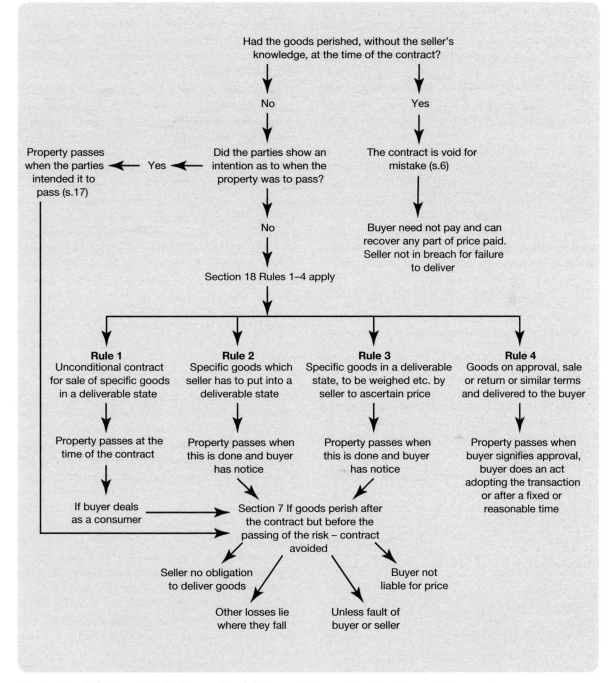

Figure 9.1 The passing of the property in specific goods mistake and frustration

9.1.2 **Unascertained goods**

Several sections of SGA 1979 apply to the passing of the property in unascertained goods. These sections are hierarchical and must be applied in the correct order. The starting point is s.16, which states that:

'[Subject to section 20A below] Where there is a contract for the sale of unascertained goods no property in the goods is transferred to the buyer unless and until the goods are ascertained.'

The goods will become ascertained when they are identified in accordance with the agreement after the contract of sale has been made. Until this has happened the property in unascertained goods cannot pass to the buyer. (Subject to s.20A, which only applies in very limited circumstances and which it is convenient to ignore until the usual rules have been explained.) Ascertainment requires that the goods be identified in accordance with the agreement. It is highly significant in that property cannot pass until it has happened. But it is important to remember that mere ascertainment does not pass property: it only operates to make it possible for property to pass under s.17 or s.18.

Once the goods have become ascertained, s.17 will pass the property to the buyer at such time as is indicated by the terms of the contract, the conduct of the parties or the circumstances of the case.

If s.17 does not help, s.18 Rule 5(1) provides as follows:

> 'Where there is a contract for the sale of unascertained or future goods by description, and goods of that description and in a deliverable state are unconditionally appropriated to the contract, either by the seller with the assent of the buyer or by the buyer with the assent of the seller, the property in the goods then passes to the buyer; and the assent may be express or implied, and may be given either before or after the appropriation is made.'

In order for the property in the goods to pass under Rule 5, several conditions must be fulfilled. First, the goods in question must match the contract description. Second, the goods must be in a deliverable state. Third, the goods must be unconditionally appropriated to the contract. Fourth, the unconditional appropriation must be made either by the seller with the assent of the buyer or by the buyer with the assent of the seller. (However, the assent to the appropriation is easily inferred. When a buyer makes a contract for goods to be delivered to him it will be inferred that he assented to the seller unconditionally appropriating the goods to the contract.)

The meaning of 'in a deliverable state' was considered above at 9.1.1, in relation to s.18 Rules 1 and 2.

Pearson J in *Carlos Federspiel & Co SA* v *Charles Twigg & Co Ltd* [1957] 1 Lloyd's Rep 240 explained what is meant by appropriating the goods to the contract: 'To constitute an appropriation of the goods to the contract, the parties must have had, or be reasonably supposed to have had, an intention to attach the contract irrevocably to those goods, so that those goods and no others are the subject of the sale and become the property of the buyer.'

So merely sorting out goods which match the contract description, or separating such goods from other goods, or even attaching the buyer's name to such goods is not enough. The intention must be to attach the goods irrevocably to the contract so that they become the property of the buyer. The seller will generally be taken to have done this at the point when it becomes out of his control to change his mind and use the goods for some other purpose. When considering the passing of the property in unascertained goods it is important to remember that you do not change s.18 Rules once the goods become ascertained. If the contract was for the sale of unascertained goods then ss.16, 17 and 18 Rule 5 will determine when the property passes. Rules 1–4 will be of no relevance. Unascertained goods may become ascertained, but they never become specific.

By way of example, let us assume that B orders ten bicycles from a manufacturer, S. The bicycles were described as being of a certain type. The contract was for the sale of unascertained goods because the parties did not identify any particular ten bicycles which were to be the subject matter of the contract. S was merely to find ten corresponding bicycles from his stock. On Monday, S put ten bicycles in a crate bearing B's name. On Tuesday S loaded this crate onto B's lorry. The goods were ascertained on Monday and so property could have passed then if, for example, B had telephoned S and agreed that the property would pass then. In the absence of any agreement as to when the property was to pass, it would have passed on Tuesday when the goods were loaded onto B's lorry. This loading would have been an unconditional appropriation of the goods to the contract, because it would have shown an irrevocable intention that only those goods were to be the subject matter of the contract. Put another way, once S had loaded those bicycles onto B's lorry he could not have changed his mind and used them for some other purpose.

Section 18 mentions two special circumstances in which goods will be regarded as having been unconditionally appropriated to the contract. (It is important to remember that these two rules are in s.18 and are therefore subservient to ss.16 and 17. They cannot therefore apply to pass property in unascertained goods and will not apply if the parties showed an intention as to when property was to pass.) Section 18 Rule 5(2) states that where the seller in pursuance of the contract delivers goods to the buyer or to a carrier or other bailee for the purpose of transmission to the buyer, and does not reserve the right of disposal, he is to be taken to have unconditionally appropriated the goods to the contract. A carrier in this context would be an independent carrier, not one of the seller's employees. Section 18 Rule 5(3) provides that where a specified quantity of unascertained goods in a deliverable state forming part of a bulk has been sold to a particular buyer then if the bulk is reduced to that quantity (or to less than that quantity) the remaining goods are to be taken as having been unconditionally appropriated to the contract. The following conditions must be satisfied:

(1) A specified quantity of unascertained goods which forms part of a bulk must have been bought. The definition of a bulk is considered below at 9.1.3.
(2) These goods must form part of a bulk which is identified either in the contract or by subsequent agreement between the parties. It is not enough that the seller happens to have a bulk of goods out of which the specified quantity might be delivered.
(3) The bulk must have been reduced to the buyer's share or to less than the buyer's share.

So if Buyer A agreed to buy 600 tons of wheat, out of an identified cargo of 1 000 tons aboard a certain ship, and the seller delivered 400 tons to a different buyer, the 600 tons remaining would be regarded as having been unconditionally appropriated to Buyer A's contract by exhaustion under s.18 Rule 5(3).

The following case provides an example of a dispute as to whether or not the property in unascertained goods which had deteriorated had passed at the time of the deterioration.

Healy v Howlett and Sons [1917] 1 KB 337

The claimants, who were fish exporters in Ireland, agreed to sell 20 boxes of mackerel to the defendant, a fish merchant in London. The claimants sent 190 boxes of mackerel to their agents at Holyhead. The fish were consigned to the claimants' own order, but the claimants sent a telegram instructing their agents at Holyhead to deliver 20 boxes to the defendant, 20 boxes to C and 150 boxes to D. The train on which the 190 boxes were carried to Dublin was delayed and consequently a boat to Holyhead was missed. At Holyhead the agents picked out and earmarked 20 boxes for the defendant, 20 for C and 150 for D. The mackerel were not of merchantable (now satisfactory) quality when they reached the defendant. The defendant refused to accept the goods and the claimants sued for the price. The claimants argued that when the goods had been sent to the agents in Holyhead, along with the instructions, the goods had been unconditionally appropriated.

Held. There was no appropriation of the goods to the defendant until the agents at Holyhead earmarked and picked out the 20 boxes which were to be delivered to the defendant. (By this time the fish had already become unmerchantable.) The defendant was therefore entitled to reject the goods because at the time when the property and the risk passed to him the goods were unmerchantable.

9.1.3 Undivided shares in goods forming part of a bulk

Sections 20A and 20B were introduced into the Sale of Goods Act 1979 by the Sale of Goods (Amendment) Act 1995. Section 20A allows a person who has bought a specified quantity of unascertained goods which form part of a bulk to become an owner in common of the bulk even though his share of the bulk has not been ascertained. The following conditions must be satisfied:

(1) A specified quantity of unascertained goods which form part of a bulk must have been bought.
(2) These goods must form part of a bulk which is identified either in the contract or by subsequent agreement between the parties. It is not enough that the seller happens to have a bulk of goods out of which the specified quantity might be delivered.
(3) The buyer must have paid the price for some or all of the goods which are the subject of the contract and which form part of the bulk.

The buyer does not become owner of his share of the goods. He becomes a co-owner of the bulk. Only when goods are unconditionally appropriated to the buyer will he become owner of those goods.

A 'bulk' is defined by s.61 SGA 1979 in the following way:

'a mass or collection of goods of the same kind which –

(a) is contained in a defined space or area; and
(b) is such that any goods in the bulk are interchangeable with any other goods therein of the same number and quantity.'

Where these conditions are met, property in an undivided share in the bulk is transferred to the buyer and the buyer becomes an owner in common of the bulk. Section 20A(3) provides that the buyer's share of the bulk will be such share as the quantity of goods paid for and due to the buyer out of the bulk bears to the quantity of goods in the bulk at that time.

Let us suppose for example, that B examines 100 identical bicycles in S's warehouse and agrees to buy 30 of these bicycles. B pays the price in advance. Upon payment B becomes a $\frac{3}{10}$ co-owner of the bulk of 100 bicycles. B is therefore immediately protected against the prospect of S becoming insolvent. However, if all of the bicycles were to be accidentally damaged B might have to take his share of the loss, depending upon whether or not the risk had passed to him.

Now let us assume that S sells 1 000 tons of wheat, from an identified bulk, to three buyers who pay the full price in advance. A buys 400 tons, B buys 300 tons and C buys 300 tons. A, B and C own the wheat in common, A having $\frac{2}{5}$ ownership, while B and C have $\frac{3}{10}$ ownership. If it transpired that the identified wheat amounted to only 500 tons rather than 1 000 tons then s.20A(4) would apply and the proportions of the bulk owned by the three buyers would remain the same, so that A would still be a $\frac{2}{5}$ co-owner of the 500 tons, whilst B and C would both be a $\frac{3}{10}$ owner of it. The three buyers could sue the seller for non-delivery of the shortfall.

Section 20A(3) implies that if the goods are partially destroyed then the loss should first fall on the seller, unless there has been an agreement to the contrary. It does this by stating that the undivided share of a buyer in a bulk at any time shall be such share as the quantity of goods paid for and due to the buyer out of the bulk bears to the quantity of goods in the bulk at that time. So if X had bought 300 tons of potatoes from a specified bulk of 1 000 tons and paid in advance, while Y had similarly bought and paid for 200 tons, the seller would still have 500 tons unsold. X would be a 3/10 owner of the 1 000 ton bulk, Y would be a 2/10 (or 1/5) owner and the seller would be a 5/10 (or 1/2) owner. If 500 tons were damaged there would be 500 tons left. Applying s.20A(3), X would be 3/5 owner of this remaining bulk,

while Y would be a 2/5 owner. Therefore, the loss of the other 500 tons would have fallen on the seller. If 950 tons were destroyed X and Y would have their shares reduced proportionately, so that X would be a $\frac{3}{5}$ owner of the remaining 50 tons while Y would be a $\frac{2}{5}$ owner. Whether or not they could sue the seller for non-delivery of the remaining goods due under their contracts would depend upon whether the risk had passed to them at the time of destruction.

Section 20B(1)(a) provides that a person who has become an owner in common by virtue of s.20A is deemed to have consented to any delivery of the goods out of the bulk to any other owner in common of the bulk, being goods which are *due to him under his contract*. So let us assume that A has bought and paid for 40 computers out of a specified bulk of 100 computers while B has bought 50 of these computers and paid 20 per cent of the price. (A is therefore a $\frac{4}{10}$ owner of the bulk and B is $\frac{1}{10}$ owner.) A is deemed to consent to B removing 50 computers from the bulk, even though B has only a $\frac{1}{10}$ ownership of the bulk. This is because s.20B(1)(a) specifies that a co-owner under s.20A consents to any other co-owner removing goods 'due to him under his contract' and not just to goods representing his co-ownership. When B removed the 50 computers, 50 would remain and, applying s.20A(3), A would become a $\frac{4}{5}$ owner of this remaining bulk. If B had bought 60 computers and removed 60 then A would become complete owner of the remaining 40 computers. When B removed the 60, the property in the remaining 40 would have passed to A by virtue of s.18 Rule 5(3) (considered above at 9.1.2). Section 20B(1)(b) provides that a person who has become an owner in common by virtue of s.20A is deemed to have consented to any removal, deaing with or delivery of goods in the bulk by any other person who is a co-owner of the bulk (including the seller) in so far as the goods fall within that co-owner's share at the time of the delivery etc.

Sections 20A and 20B do not specify when the risk should pass to a co-owner. As we have seen, s.20A(3) implies that if the seller is still a co-owner of the bulk then the risk of damage to goods forming the bulk first falls on the seller. This aside, it might be thought that s.20(1) would apply, placing a share of the risk on the buyer in proportion to his share of the bulk. Against this must be weighed s.20B(3)(c), which states that nothing under s.20A shall affect the rights of any buyer under his contract. This suggests that even if the whole bulk is destroyed a buyer who has become a co-owner under s.20A can still sue the seller for non-delivery.

The parties may contract out of ss.20A and 20B and provide that property in an undivided share of a bulk of goods shall pass to B at some time after payment.

Section 19 allows the seller to retain ownership of specific goods, or of goods which have subsequently been appropriated to the contract, until the payment of the price or until some other condition has been fulfilled. A seller can reserve title to the goods even though they may have been delivered to the buyer. This matter is explored in more detail below at 9.2.

The overall position regarding the passing of property in unascertained goods is shown in Figure 9.2.

9.1.4 The passing of the risk

If the risk has passed to the buyer at the time when the goods become damaged or suffer from deterioration then the buyer will need to pay the full price of the goods. This is the case even if the goods are destroyed. Furthermore, the fact of the goods having been damaged etc. will not give the buyer a right to sue the seller for non-delivery or for damages for breach of s.14(2). If the risk is with the seller at the time of deterioration etc then the position depends upon whether the goods were specific or unascertained. If the goods were specific the seller will not be able to perform the contract, without being in breach of the s.14(2) requirement of satisfactory quality, unless the goods can be repaired. If the goods were unascertained the seller can perform the contract by delivering replacement goods which match the contract description. The party with whom the risk lies ought to insure the goods.

Section 20 lays down the general rule on the passing of the risk:

'Unless otherwise agreed, the goods remain at the seller's risk until the property in them is transferred to the buyer, but when the property in them is transferred to the buyer the goods are at the buyer's risk whether delivery has been made or not.'

So although the risk will generally pass at the same time as the property in the goods, the parties may expressly or impliedly agree that this is not to be the case. For example in international sales of goods made on CIF terms the property and the risk do not pass at the same time. (International sales are examined in Chapter 10 at 10.5.) The case of

Sterns v *Vickers* provides an example of an implied agreement that the risk should not pass at the same time as the property.

Sterns Ltd v *Vickers Ltd*
[1922] All ER 126 (Court of Appeal)

The sellers sold 120 000 gallons of white spirit, which was part of a larger consignment of spirit lying in a tank at a storage company. The storage company was to select the spirit to be delivered. The buyers took a delivery order from the storage company and this would have entitled them to demand delivery of the spirit. The buyers sold the spirit on to sub-buyers. As the delivery order was indorsed to the sub-buyers they could have demanded immediate delivery. However, the sub-buyers did not take delivery of the spirit for several months. When the sub-buyers did take delivery of the spirit they found that it had deteriorated in quality. The buyers sued the sellers for damages.

Held. The property in the goods had not passed to the buyers as the sale was of unascertained goods. (No equivalent to what is now s.20A of the 1979 Act was in force at the time and so the buyers did not become co-owners of the bulk.) However, the risk passed to the buyer at the time they took the delivery order as the sellers then no longer had any control over the spirit and had done everything they had undertaken to do. The buyers therefore could not sue for damages.

COMMENT This case differs from *Healy v Howlett and Sons* because in this case the buyer had a right to possession of the goods at the time of the deterioration.

The risk is not concerned with damage to the goods which is caused by the fault of either of the parties, but only with accidental damage or destruction. Section 20(2) provides that where the delivery of the goods is delayed through the fault of either the buyer or the seller the goods are at the risk of the party at fault as regards any loss which would not have occurred but for such fault.

Section 20(3) states that: 'Nothing in this section affects the duties or liabilities of either seller or buyer as a bailee or custodier of the goods of the other party.'

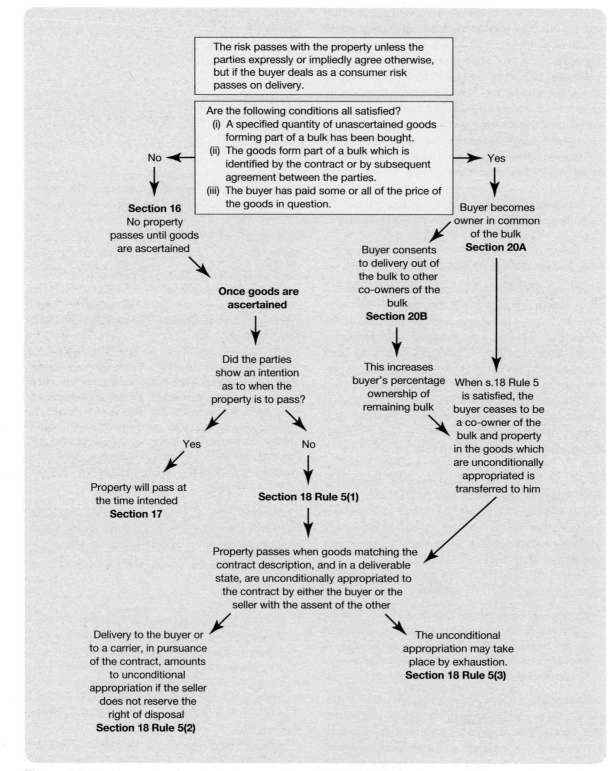

The risk passes with the property unless the parties expressly or impliedly agree otherwise, but if the buyer deals as a consumer risk passes on delivery.

Are the following conditions all satisfied?
(i) A specified quantity of unascertained goods forming part of a bulk has been bought.
(ii) The goods form part of a bulk which is identified by the contract or by subsequent agreement between the parties.
(iii) The buyer has paid some or all of the price of the goods in question.

No

Section 16
No property passes until goods are ascertained

Once goods are ascertained

Did the parties show an intention as to when the property is to pass?

Yes

Property will pass at the time intended
Section 17

No

Section 18 Rule 5(1)

Property passes when goods matching the contract description, and in a deliverable state, are unconditionally appropriated to the contract by either the buyer or the seller with the assent of the other

Delivery to the buyer or to a carrier, in pursuance of the contract, amounts to unconditional appropriation if the seller does not reserve the right of disposal
Section 18 Rule 5(2)

The unconditional appropriation may take place by exhaustion.
Section 18 Rule 5(3)

Yes

Buyer becomes owner in common of the bulk
Section 20A

Buyer consents to delivery out of the bulk to other co-owners of the bulk
Section 20B

This increases buyer's percentage ownership of remaining bulk

When s.18 Rule 5 is satisfied, the buyer ceases to be a co-owner of the bulk and property in the goods which are unconditionally appropriated is transferred to him

Figure 9.2 The passing of the property in unascertained goods

A bailee consents to take possession of goods which he does not own. The main duties of a bailee are to take reasonable care of the goods and to be ready to return them to the owner if asked to do so. Bailment is common and often arises informally. For example, when a seller sells specific goods in a deliverable state then, unless there has been an agreement to the contrary, both risk and the property will pass to the buyer immediately. So if the seller retains possession of the goods for any time then he will become a bailee of the goods and s.20(3) will place on him a duty to look after the goods. If the seller does not take reasonable care of the goods then the buyer will be able to sue the seller for breach of a duty of a bailee. Sometimes the buyer will be a bailee of the seller's goods. For example, when s.18 Rule 4 operates the buyer will be a bailee of the seller's goods until the property passes. If the buyer fails to take reasonable care of the goods the seller will be able to sue him for breaching a duty of a bailee.

9.1.4.1 Passing of risk in consumer sales

Section 20(4) provides that in a case where the buyer deals as a consumer, sub-ss.20(1)–(3) must be ignored and the goods remain at the seller's risk until they are delivered to the consumer. Section 32(1) has also been amended by s.32(4), which provides that where the buyer deals as a consumer the general rule that delivery to the carrier is delivery to the buyer (see Chapter 10 at 10.1.1.1) is changed. Instead, s.32(4) specifically states that where the buyer deals as a consumer delivery of the goods to a carrier is not delivery to the buyer. So if, for example, a consumer ordered a book which was to be posted to him by the seller, the book would remain at the seller's risk until the book was delivered to the consumer, that is to say delivered to his home. The complex definition of dealing as a consumer was considered in Chapter 5 at 5.6.3.

Test your understanding 9.3

1 Is it possible for the property in unascertained goods to pass to the buyer before the goods have become ascertained?

2 How do unascertained goods become ascertained?

3 If the parties show an intention as to when the property in unascertained goods is to pass, what will the effect of this be?

4 Assuming that s.18 Rule 5 applies, at what time will it operate so as to pass the property in unascertained goods to the buyer?

5 What three conditions must be satisfied for s.20A to operate so as to make a buyer of unascertained goods forming a bulk the owner in common of the bulk?

6 What is meant by the risk in this context?

7 In what circumstances will the risk not pass with the property in the goods?

8 What is a bailee? What are the two main duties of a bailee?

9.2 RESERVATION OF TITLE CLAUSES

When goods are sold in a commercial context, particularly when large quantities of manufactured goods are sold, it is often the case that the seller reserves title to the goods. This means that the seller lets the buyer have possession of the goods, but the terms of the contract stipulate that the property in the goods is not to pass to the buyer until the full price of the goods has been paid. Reservation of title clauses will be particularly useful where the buyer has become insolvent. If the property in the goods has not passed to the buyer then the seller, as owner, will be able to reclaim the goods from the buyer's liquidator. Without a reservation of title clause the seller would be restricted to making a claim as an unsecured creditor. Unsecured creditors of insolvent companies will not receive all that they are owed and often receive very little. See Chapter 19 at 19.1.3.

Section 19(1) SGA plainly allows for reservation of title clauses:

> 'Where there is a contract for the sale of specific goods or where goods are subsequently appropriated to the contract, the seller may, by the terms of the contract or appropriation, reserve the right of disposal of the goods until certain conditions are fulfilled; and in such a case, notwithstanding the delivery of the goods to the buyer…the property in the goods does not pass to the buyer until the conditions imposed by the seller are fulfilled.'

It is important to realise that s.19 merely allows for reservation of title clauses, it does not provide that there will be such a clause. A reservation of title clause can only be effective if it was incorporated into the contract as a term. The incorporation of terms was considered in relation to exclusion clauses in Chapter 5 at 5.5.1.1. There it was seen that a term can be incorporated by a consistent course of dealing between the parties. The following case provides an example of an effective reservation of title clause.

Clough Mill Ltd v *Geoffrey Martin*
[1985] 1 WLR 111 (Court of Appeal)

The claimant company entered into four contracts to sell yarn to a company which manufactured fabric. Each of the contracts contained a reservation of title clause which provided as follows: the claimants retained ownership of the yarn until they received full payment for all the yarn supplied under the particular contract in question; if payment became overdue the claimants could enter the buyers' premises to reclaim the yarn; if insolvency proceedings were commenced against the buyers payment should become due immediately; and that if the yarn was incorporated into other goods the claimants should own these other goods unless the buyers had sold the goods on to a bona fide purchaser. The defendant was appointed the buyers' liquidator. The claimants wrote to the defendant saying that they wished to collect unused yarn and that the buyers should stop being allowed to continue to use the yarn sold in their manufacturing process. The defendant did not pay the purchase price or prevent the buyers from continuing to use the yarn in their manufacturing process. The claimants, who had been refused permission to enter the buyers' premises, sued the defendant for conversion of the yarn.

Held. The claimants were entitled to reclaim the unused yarn, as the property in this yarn never passed to the buyer. (The Court of Appeal stated *obiter* that ownership of the manufactured product would depend upon the intentions of the parties. It would generally be taken that they intended the product to belong to the buyer. Any clause which provided that the seller owned the manufactured product would give the seller a windfall profit and involve assets being transferred to him and would therefore be void as an unregistered charge.)

Although there is no doubt that reservation of title clauses can be effective, there are a variety of situations where they are not effective or where their effect is not clear. At the heart of many failed reservation of title clauses is the reasoning that the clause is an unregistered charge. Section 874 of the Companies Act 2006 provides that a charge issued by a company will be invalid if it is not registered with the Registrar of Companies within 21 days of being created. Unfortunately, the CA 2006 does not define a charge. Slade J in *Re Bond Worth* [1980] Ch 228 said that whenever a company granted a security interest

to secure a debt, and this interest would cease to exist if the debt was paid, then this amounts to a charge. A simple reservation of title clause will not be a charge. Section 19 provides that a simple reservation of title clause operates so as to prevent the property passing to the buyer. A company buyer can grant a charge only over property it owns, but if property ever does pass to the buyer and is then given back to the seller, or if the seller is given some other property interest of the buyer, then a charge can arise. According to Slade J it will do so if the buyer's property or property interest was given to the seller to secure a debt, and if the security would cease to exist if the buyer paid the debt. So when the claimant in *Clough Mill* claimed to be entitled to products manufactured out of the yarn which was sold, it was claiming some of the buyer's property as security for a debt. As this security would disappear if the debt was paid, this was a charge and void. There are two reasons why sellers do not register their retention of title clauses as charges. The first is that it would not be practical to do this every time goods were sold. The second is that any charge which was created would rank behind existing charges. Companies which become insolvent have generally charged all of their assets to a bank to secure a loan.

9.2.1 All moneys clauses

A simple reservation of title clause provides that the title in the goods sold is not to pass until those particular goods have been paid for. An all moneys clause states that the title is not to pass until all sums owing to the seller, whether under the contract in question or under previous contracts, have been paid. If such clauses are effective they can mean that the buyer will never own any of the goods which he has bought from the seller. For example, let us suppose that a motor manufacturer supplies a car dealer with new cars every six weeks under a contract containing an all moneys reservation of title clause. The car dealer pays for each delivery of cars two months after delivery and so never completely settles his debts to the manufacturer. If the clause is effective the dealer will not own any of the cars he has ever bought from the manufacturer. (As we shall see at 9.2.2, this would not generally affect customers who bought the cars from the dealer.)

Where the buyer is a company, an all moneys clause might be ineffective as an unregistered company charge. In *Clough Mill Ltd* v *Geoffrey Martin* it was held that if the seller retains 'equitable and beneficial ownership' in the goods sold a charge is created. The logic was that if legal ownership was not retained then the buyer must have acquired this, and any security the seller had over the goods must therefore have been transferred back to the seller by the buyer, thus creating a charge. However, in a Scottish case *Armour* v *Thyssen Edelstahlwerke AG* [1990] 3 All ER 481 the House of Lords held that an all moneys clause did not create a charge and that the clause was therefore valid. The logic was that if the clause was effective then it prevented any property from ever passing to the buyer. As the buyer never owned the property it could not issue a charge in respect of it. But this case considered only one contract: there had not been a series of contracts between the parties all containing an all moneys clause.

If the seller does reclaim goods sold under a previous contract it seems likely that the all moneys clause will be a charge. If the seller makes any windfall profit then he is being given the buyer's property to secure a debt. If the debt is paid then the seller would lose any right to take the buyer's property in this way. If the buyer sells the reclaimed goods and deducts only the amount he is owed, then he is admitting that he only wants the goods reclaimed to secure his debt. The only way around this would be to hold that no goods ever passed to the buyer, and so it was not the buyer's property which the seller was taking as security for the debt. Where there is a long series of contracts and the seller is never fully paid this seems to ignore the reality of the situation.

9.2.2 **The position where the buyer resells the goods**

If the buyer of the goods which are the subject of a reservation of title clause resells the goods to a second buyer who takes delivery of the goods, the property in the goods will pass to the second buyer as long as the second buyer did not know of the reservation of title clause when making the contract and as long as he acted in good faith. (Section 25 SGA 1979, considered below at 9.3.5.)

Often the original seller knows that the buyer intends to resell the goods and so the reservation of title clause may stipulate that the seller is entitled to the proceeds of sale. In the following case such a claim was successful.

Aluminium Industrie Vaasen BV* v *Romalpa Aluminium Ltd
[1976] 1 WLR 676 (Court of Appeal)

The claimants, a Dutch company which manufactured aluminium foil, sold foil to the defendants, an English company. Clause 13 of the terms and conditions on which the foil was sold contained a complex retention of title clause which provided that: ownership of the foil would only pass to the defendants when they had paid all money owing to the claimants; until the date of payment the defendants could be required to store the foil in such a way that it was clearly the claimants' property; if the foil was mixed with other materials to produce new goods, the ownership of the new goods was to be transferred to the claimants as surety for the full payment of the price; until the full payment of the price the defendants were to hold the mixed goods for the claimants as fiduciary owner of them; the defendants could sell mixed goods but if the full price had not been paid to the claimants the defendants were to assign to the claimants the benefit of any claim against sub-purchasers. The defendants got into financial difficulties and a receiver was appointed. At this time the defendants owed the claimants £122 000. The receiver certified that he was holding £35 151 which represented the proceeds of sale of unmixed aluminium foil supplied by the claimants and sold on to sub-purchasers. The claimants claimed this money.

Held. As it was the intention of the parties that the defendants should have the power to sell unmixed foil, and that they should account for the proceeds of such a sale until all the money owed to the claimants had been paid, terms were implied to give effect to these intentions. The claimants could trace the proceeds of sale of the unmixed foil because the defendants, as between themselves and the claimants, sold the foil in their fiduciary capacity as agents and bailees of the claimants. (If the goods are traced they are followed and the proceeds of sale taken when the fiduciary sells the goods.) As between the defendants and the sub-purchasers the defendants sold the foil as principals, on their own account.

Although the claim to the proceeds of sale was successful in the *Romalpa* case, this outcome has not been reached in any subsequent case. In *Romalpa* the Court of Appeal did not even consider the possibility that a charge had been created and that such a charge would be void for non-registration. The court's decision that the defendants resold the foil in a fiduciary capacity also causes considerable difficulty. If this were the case then all of the proceeds of sale should have been paid into the separate bank account and even the profit made on the resale of the aluminium should have been the property of the claimants. The parties clearly did not contemplate this happening and so it is very hard to see how such a term could be implied. Furthermore, in the *Romalpa* case the defendants conceded that they were bailees of the goods. In fact it is highly likely that they were not bailees as a bailee has a duty to return the goods, something the parties did not contemplate. Subsequent courts have avoided following the decision on this ground. If the reservation of title clause only allows the seller to reclaim the proceeds of sale to the extent that he is owed the price of the goods by the buyer, it will be void as an unregistered charge.

In *Pfeiffer GmbH* v *Arbuthnot Factors* [1988] 1 WLR 150 it was held that where the terms of a contract allowed the buyer to resell the goods in the normal course of his business before paying the seller for them, it would normally be implied that the buyer did so on his own account rather than as a fiduciary who would have to account to the seller for the proceeds. However, even if the buyer did sell the goods on as a fiduciary of the original seller then the parties would have intended that the seller was only entitled to what he was owed, rather than the whole proceeds of sale. The retention of title clause would not therefore have retained complete ownership in the goods sold, but only have created an interest by way of security for the amount owed. It would therefore be void as an unregistered charge.

9.2.3 Claims to goods manufactured out of the goods sold

Where the goods sold are to be used in a manufacturing process a reservation of title clause often states that the seller should be entitled to any goods manufactured out of the original goods sold. It may be possible for the seller to reclaim the goods sold if they are still recognisable, despite the manufacturing process, and if they could easily be detached from other goods used in the process and returned to their original state. However, once the goods have become altered beyond this point then the right to reclaim the goods will be lost.

Borden (UK) Ltd v *Scottish Timber Products Ltd* [1981] Ch 25 (Court of Appeal)

The claimants supplied resin to the defendants. The resin was to be used in the creation of chipboard and it was clearly contemplated that it would be used in this way before it had been paid for. Once the resin had been mixed with other materials it could not physically be recovered. A reservation of title clause stipulated that the property in the resin was to pass to the defendants only when all goods supplied under the contract had been paid for in full. A receiver was appointed and the claimants argued that they were entitled to claim the chipboard and the proceeds of sale of chipboard which had been manufactured using the resin.

Held. The resin had ceased to exist once it was manufactured into chipboard and so the claimants could not trace it into the chipboard. They could not therefore claim either the chipboard or the proceeds of sale.

Re Peachdart Ltd [1983] 3 WLR 878

The claimants supplied a company with leather, which the company was to use to manufacture into handbags. A reservation of title clause provided that: the claimants retained ownership of the leather until they were paid in full; that until they were paid the claimants owned any products made from the leather until these were sold by the company; and that when products made from the leather were sold by the company the claimants were entitled to trace the proceeds of sale of the handbags. The company got into financial difficulties and a receiver was appointed. It was conceded that the claimants had the right to leather which remained unmanufactured. However, the claimants also claimed the proceeds of sale of handbags and ownership of partly manufactured handbags.

Held. The parties intended that once the leather was manufactured into handbags it was no longer the exclusive property of the claimants. If the claimants did have any rights over the handbags or the proceeds of sale this must have been given to them by the company. Therefore any such rights would be by way of a charge and void as the charge had not been registered.

If the goods sold are not manufactured into other goods, but merely altered in such a way that no value is added to them, then the seller should be able to recover them. This was the case in *Armour* v *Thyssen* where steel was sold and cut into lengths by the buyer. There is no charge because the seller is not claiming any of the buyer's property as security and is not making a windfall profit. But if the alteration in the goods means that the goods increase in value then the seller would make a windfall profit if he reclaimed them and a charge would be created. An example can be seen in *Modelboard Ltd v Outer Box Ltd* [1993] BCLC 623 where cardboard which was sold was manufactured into cardboard boxes.

The law on reservation of title clauses is not particularly clear. All of the decisions result from a consideration of the complex facts of each case. The courts have tended to solve the difficulties presented by the case in front of them rather than to lay down any definite policy. The wording of reservation of title clauses is often at odds with the intentions of the parties. Where the clauses have been upheld, the courts have tended to give effect to the wording. Where they have not been upheld they have tended to give effect to the intentions of the parties.

Test your understanding 9.4

1 What is meant by a reservation of title clause?

2 If a reservation of title clause is in fact a company charge how might this cause problems for the seller of the goods?

3 Susan sells goods to Brain. The contract of sales states that Susan is reserving title to the goods until the full price has been paid. Brain takes possession of the good's and sells them to Belinda, who did not know about Susan's reservation of title clauses. Can Susan recover the goods from Belinda?

9.3 SALE BY A PERSON WHO IS NOT THE OWNER

It is almost always the case that a person who does not own goods cannot pass ownership to anyone else unless he sells the goods as the agent of the owner. This rule, which is often expressed in the Latin maxim *nemo dat quod non habet* (nobody gives what they do not have), is contained in s.21 SGA 1979, which provides as follows:

'Subject to this Act, where goods are sold by a person who is not their owner, and who does not sell them

under the authority or with the consent of the owner, the buyer acquires no better title to the goods than the seller had, unless the owner of the goods is by his conduct precluded from denying the seller's authority to sell.'

So the general position is that if a seller of goods does not own the goods a person who buys from the seller will not own the goods either. The true owner of the goods will be able to reclaim the goods from the person who bought the goods and sue the seller or the buyer for the tort of conversion of the goods. This is true not only where the goods were stolen by the person who later sells them, but also where the owner is tricked or defrauded into parting with possession. Although it was not the point at issue in the case, we saw an example of the *nemo dat* rule in *Rowland v Divall* in Chapter 8 at 8.2.1. The thief did not own the car which he sold. Therefore, none of the three subsequent buyers acquired ownership. All three of these buyers, and the thief, could have been liable in conversion to the true owner, who was entitled to reclaim the car.

Despite the logic of this rule there are six exceptions to it, which we now examine in turn. All of these exceptions can only apply in favour of a person who acquires the goods in good faith, without notice that the seller does not have the right to sell. Good faith is a subjective matter, as is made clear by s.61(3) of the Sale of Goods Act 1979: 'A thing is deemed to be done in good faith within the meaning of this Act when it is in fact done honestly, whether it is done negligently or not.' In this context notice means actual notice, not constructive notice. The final exception which we consider is contained in the Hire Purchase Act 1964, rather than in the Sale of Goods Act, but again whether or not the person in favour of whom the exception operates is in good faith is a subjective matter.

As regards ownership of the goods the law takes an all or nothing approach. The loss is never apportioned between the innocent parties.

9.3.1 Mercantile agency

Agency is an obvious exception to the *nemo dat* rule. When an agent sells the principal's goods the whole point of the contract is that the agent (who does not own the goods) passes ownership to the purchaser.

Section 21(1) impliedly recognises agency with the words 'and who does not sell them under the authority or with the consent of the owner'.

When the agency is disclosed the third party will know that the agent is acting as an agent and will know that he is creating a legal relationship with the principal rather than with the agent. But even where the agency is undisclosed, so that the third party thinks he is contracting with the agent rather than with the principal, s.21(1) recognises that the agent passes a good title to the principal's goods to the third party. (Undisclosed agency is considered in some detail in Chapter 11 at 11.3.)

Section 2(1) of the Factors Act 1889 provides a statutory exception to the *nemo dat* rule. It provides that a mercantile agent can pass ownership of goods to a third party, even if the mercantile agent did not have the authority of the owner to do this. Ownership can be passed if the mercantile agent sells the goods, or pledges them as security or makes any other disposition of the goods. Section 21(2) SGA recognises this by saying that nothing in SGA affects the provisions of the Factors Acts.

Section 1 of the Factors Act 1889 defines a mercantile agent as an agent 'having in the customary course of his business as such agent authority either to sell goods or to consign goods for the purpose of sale, or to buy goods, or to raise money on the security of goods'.

Note the requirements to this exception to the *nemo dat* principle:

(a) The agent must be a mercantile agent, that is to say a professional agent who is in business and who sells or deals with other people's goods as part of that business.

(b) The agent must either be in possession of the goods or of documents of title at the time when the goods are sold or disposed of. A bill of lading is a document of title but a car log book is not.

(c) This possession must have been gained with the consent of the owner, even if this consent was obtained by means of deception.

(d) Possession must have been acquired by the mercantile agent for some purpose connected with his business as a mercantile agent. So if the mercantile agent had possession so that he could repair the goods this would not be enough. Possession must be granted for the purpose of sale, or receiving offers, or display or something of that kind.

(e) The sale or disposition of the goods must have been made in the ordinary course of business as a mercantile agent. (During business hours, from a proper place of business and not in such a way as to make the third party think that there was anything wrong.) Also, an agreement to sell will not be within s.2(1) of the Factors Act. For the difference between a sale and an agreement to sell see Chapter 8 at 8.1.1.2.

(f) The person taking the goods must have done so in good faith, without notice of the agent's lack of authority and it is up to him to prove this.

Example

Customers have for some time been in the habit of leaving jewellery at a jeweller's shop so that the jeweller could sell the jewellery. The jeweller is therefore a mercantile agent. Oswald left his diamond ring at the jeweller's shop, asking the jeweller to try to get offers for it. Oswald tells the jeweller that he must not sell the ring without express permission to do so. If the jeweller sold the ring to a customer who bought it in good faith then s.2(1) of the Factors Act 1889 would pass ownership to that customer. Oswald could not reclaim the ring but could sue the jeweller for damages.

In *Folkes v King* [1923] 1 KB 282 a mercantile agent gained possession of a car by deception. The owner had given the car to the mercantile agent but had expressly instructed him not to sell it for less than £575. The mercantile agent immediately sold the car to A, who bought it in good faith, for £340. The car passed to several other buyers before passing to K. The owner sued K to recover the car but could not do so. A good title had passed to A under s.2(1) of the Factors Act, and this title had passed through the other buyers to K.

If a mercantile agent sells a car without the registration book then generally this will not be a sale in the ordinary course of business of a mercantile agent and so title will not be passed to the purchaser. Furthermore, the owner of the car must have consented to the mercantile agent's possession of the registration book. In *Pearson v Rose and Young Ltd* [1951] 2 All ER 1027 a mercantile agent received possession of a car with the consent of the owner. The mercantile agent also tricked the owner into handing over the registration book, claiming that he wanted to have a look at it. Then when the owner was distracted by a trick the mercantile agent kept hold of the registration book and the same day sold the car with the registration book. The purchaser of the car did not receive good title. The owner had consented to the mercantile agent having possession of the car, but had not consented to him having possession of the registration book.

When all of the conditions are met, the title passed by a mercantile agent is the title of the principal who gave possession of the goods to the agent. This may seem somewhat hard on the principal, but the principal must have consented to the mercantile agent having possession of the goods or the documents of title to the goods. If ownership is passed without the consent of the principal, the principal can sue the mercantile agent for damages. If the principal who entrusted the goods to the mercantile agent has no title to the goods, then the mercantile agent will not be able to pass any better title to anyone else.

When a mercantile agent sells goods with the consent of the owner then he will pass good title under general agency principles. In such cases there will therefore be no need to consider the detailed requirements of s.2(1) Factors Act 1889.

9.3.2 **Estoppel**

A person who is estopped from denying that someone else is the owner of goods is prevented from denying it. The Sale of Goods Act does not expressly mention estoppel as an exception to the *nemo dat* principle, but s.21 impliedly recognises estoppel with the words 'unless the owner of the goods is by his conduct precluded [prevented] from denying the seller's authority to sell'.

So if the owner of goods makes a representation to a third party that a seller of goods has the right to sell the goods, either as agent or owner, the owner will be estopped (prevented) from denying the truth of the representation later. The following case provides an example of this.

Eastern Distributors Ltd v *Goldring*
[1957] 2 All ER 525 (Court of Appeal)

M wanted to take a car from C, a motor dealer, on hire-purchase but did not have enough money to pay the deposit. As part of a complex fraud to finance the deal, M authorised C to sell his (M's) van to a finance company, the claimants. The finance company was then to pass the van to M on hire-purchase terms and the proceeds of the sale of the van were to pay the deposits on the hire-purchase of both the van and the car. C only had authority to sell the van if he went along with the whole scheme. M signed blank hire-purchase documents and left them with C to complete. The forms stated that C was the absolute owner of the van. C sold the van to the claimants, the finance company, as if it were his own even though the proposal to take the car on hire-purchase did not go through. The claimants then took M's proposal to take the van on hire-purchase at face value and sent M a copy of the agreement. Upon finding out that the deal to take the car on hire-purchase was not going ahead, M told C that the whole deal was off. M then sold the van to the defendant, Goldring, who bought it in good faith and with no knowledge that it did not belong to M. M did not pay the hire-purchase instalments and so the claimants claimed the van or its value from Goldring.

Held. The claimants were entitled to recover the van. C had no actual authority to sell the van. However, M was estopped from denying that C had authority to sell it. M's title to the van therefore passed to the claimants and so M had no title to pass when he sold the van to the defendant.

In order for the estoppel to arise the owner of the goods must make a representation to the third party. Mere negligent behaviour by the owner will not be enough to amount to a representation unless the owner owes the third party a duty of care. Lord MacNaghten in *Farquharson Bros and Co* v *C. King & Co* [1902] AC 325 gave the following example: 'If a person leaves a watch or a ring on a seat in the park or on a table at a cafe and it ultimately gets into the hands of a bona fide purchaser, it is no answer to the true owner to say that it was his carelessness and nothing else that enabled the finder to pass it off as his own.' As regards mere economic loss a duty of care will only be owed in very exceptional circumstances.

Generally, only the person who represented that the seller had the right to sell the goods is estopped from denying that the seller had this right. If the person making this representation had good title to the goods, then the third party who buys the goods on the strength of it will acquire complete title. But if the person who made the representation did not have title to the goods then no title will be passed.

9.3.3 **Sale under a voidable title**

In Chapter 6 we saw that a seller who is induced to make a contract by a misrepresentation has the right to rescind the contract. A contract which is capable of being rescinded is said to be voidable (capable of being made void). So a person who makes a misrepresentation when buying goods does not acquire a complete title to the goods, but only a voidable title. (One which can be avoided by the seller within a reasonable time, as explained in Chapter 6 at 6.1.3.) We also saw that duress or undue influence might make a contract voidable.

Section 23 SGA provides that: 'When the seller of goods has a voidable title to them, but his title has not been avoided at the time of the sale, the buyer acquires a good title to the goods, provided he buys them in good faith and without notice of the seller's defect of title.'

So if a person with only a voidable title to goods sells the goods *before* the contract was avoided then a new buyer who acts in good faith will get complete ownership of the goods. This is an exception to the *nemo dat* principle because a seller with only a voidable title is giving more than he has got; he is giving a complete title. (And, of course, the seller's voidable title would become worthless once the contract was avoided.) If the seller with only the voidable title resells the goods *after* the contract has been avoided then the third party acting in good faith will acquire no title at all under s.23. Once the contract was avoided the seller's voidable title had been extinguished and the seller no longer had any title to pass on.

Two cases, both considered in Chapter 6, demonstrate the way in which s.23 works. In *Lewis v Averay* [1971] 3 All ER 907 a rogue bought a car with a bad cheque, pretending to be Richard Greene, the television actor. As this was a fraudulent misrepresentation, the rogue therefore had only a voidable title to the car. In the long run this voidable title would have been worth very little to him as the owner would surely have avoided the contract as soon as he discovered that the cheque was worthless. Before the owner discovered this, the rogue sold the car to the defendant, who bought the car in good faith. The Court of Appeal held that the defendant had a complete title to the car as he had bought it before the owner avoided the contract with the rogue.

In *Car and Universal Finance Co Ltd v Caldwell* [1964] 1 All ER 290 another rogue bought a car with a bad cheque. As this was again a fraudulent misrepresentation, it again made the contract voidable. The rogue sold the car to a company called Motobella, but before he did this the owner of the car informed the police and the AA that the car had been stolen. Motobella did not buy the car in good faith but three days after acquiring the car they sold it to a buyer in good faith. After passing through the hands of sev-eral purchasers the car ended up with the claimants, who had bought it in good faith. The Court of Appeal held that the contract had been avoided by inform-ing the police and the relevant authorities. So the original owner did get the car back and the innocent third party was left with nothing but the worthless right to sue the rogue. (Although the Court of Appeal decided that telling the police and the AA was enough to avoid the contract in the circumstances where the rogue had behaved fraudulently and was subsequently impossible to contact, it left open the question whether or not such actions would have been enough to avoid in the case of a non-fraudulent misrepresentation.)

All of the exceptions to the *nemo dat* principle require that the person claiming that a good title passed to him must have acted in good faith. The s.23 exception differs from all the others in that the burden of proof as regards good faith is on the original owner, who is denying that s.23 passes a good title. The original owner must prove that the buyer did not act in good faith. As regards all the other exceptions, the person claiming to have acquired a good title must prove that he did act in good faith.

It is possible that a rogue who acquired possession of a car under a voidable contract which has been avoided might nevertheless pass title as a buyer in possession of the goods. (See *Newtons of Wembley Ltd v Williams* [1964] 3 All ER 532 below at 9.3.5.) If this is the case then the effect of *Car and Universal Finance* will be of limited practical importance.

9.3.4 Sale by a seller in possession after a sale

Section 24, a very lengthy section of the Sale of Goods Act, provides that if a seller sells goods to one buyer, but keeps possession of the goods or of documents of title to the goods, and then sells or disposes of the same goods to a second buyer, who takes delivery of the goods or the documents of title, then the second buyer will get ownership of the goods. Section 8 of the Factors Act 1889 is virtually identical to s.24 SGA.

This is an exception to the *nemo dat* rule in circumstances in which the first buyer would have got ownership of the goods before the sale to the second buyer. (As we saw earlier in this chapter this would generally be the case where the contract was for the sale of specific goods in a deliverable state. Applying s.18 Rule 1 ownership would pass to the first buyer as soon as the contract was made.) When s.24 takes effect the first buyer can of course sue the seller for damages in conversion or for breach of contract.

Example

A shop has a grand piano in its New Year Sale. X makes a contract to buy the piano and pays the full price. As we saw earlier in this chapter, this means that X is now owner of the piano, by virtue of SGA s.18 Rule 1. By mistake, another shop assistant later sells the same piano to Y, who takes it away. Y will get title to the piano. X can sue the shop for damages.

The rule set out in s.24 seems to be based on convenience. In the above example either X or Y will get ownership of the piano and the other will be left with the right to sue the shop for damages. X and Y have behaved identically, and justice does not favour either one of them more than the other. It is more convenient to let Y keep the piano, as he already has possession of it, than to say that X has ownership of the piano.

The title passed is only the title which originally passed from the seller to the first buyer. If at the outset the seller in possession did not have complete title to the goods then complete title will not be passed to either the first or the second buyer.

The following New South Wales case shows the operation of the seller in possession exception in a commercial context.

Pacific Motor Auctions Pty Ltd v *Motor Credits (Hire Finance) Ltd*
[1965] AC 867 (Privy Council)

M Ltd, a company dealing in cars, had an arrangement with a finance company called Motor Credits Ltd. Under the agreement M bought cars and then sold them to Motor Credits for 90 per cent of the price which they had paid. M then sold the cars as the agents of Motor Credits. (The purpose of this arrangement was to allow M to have money available for future trading.) The cars were never physically transferred to Motor Credits, but were continuously in the possession of M. Knowing that M was in financial difficulty, Motor Credits revoked M's agency to sell the cars. Despite this, M sold 29 cars to Pacific Motors which Pacific Motors took away. Pacific Motors were ignorant of the fact that these cars had previously been sold to Motor Credits and acted in good faith.

Held. Pacific Motors became the owners of the cars under s.28 of the Sale of Goods Act 1923 of New South Wales (which is identical to s.24 SGA 1979).

9.3.5 Sale by a buyer in possession

Section 25(1) applies where a person who has bought or agreed to buy goods obtains the goods, or documents of title to the goods, with the seller's consent. If such a buyer in possession delivers the goods or the documents of title to a third party acting in good faith as part of a contract of sale or other disposition of the goods, title to the goods is passed to the third party as if the buyer in possession had been a mercantile agent acting on behalf of the owner. Section 9 of the Factors Act 1889 is virtually identical to s.25(1) SGA except that it allows the buyer in possession to pass the goods on under an agreement to sell.

Example

S owns goods and sells them to B, who has not yet paid the price. Under the terms of the contract ownership of the goods is not to pass to B until the full price has been paid. If B gets possession of the goods and sells them to C (who does not know that ownership has not yet passed to B) then C will own the goods as soon as they are delivered to him.

Section 25(1) will not apply if 'the first buyer' took the goods on hire-purchase, or on sale or return. In neither of these cases will the first buyer have bought or agreed to buy the goods. Section 25(2) provides that s.25(1) does not apply where the first buyer has taken the goods on a conditional sale agreement, payable by instalments, which is regulated by the Consumer Credit Act 1974. A conditional sale agreement is virtually identical to a hire-purchase agreement except that the buyer is committed at the outset to paying all of the instalments. Property in the goods will not pass to the buyer until this has been done. The circumstances in which such agreements are governed by the CCA 1974 are considered in Chapter 14 at 14.2.3.

There is considerable uncertainty about the circumstances in which s.25 will apply. In one of the leading cases, *Newtons of Wembley Ltd* v *Williams* [1964] 3 All ER 532 the Court of Appeal decided that s.25 would only apply in cases where the buyer in possession resold the goods in the manner in which a mercantile agent would have sold them.

(The requirements for a person to be acting as a mercantile agent were set out above at 9.3.1.) In **Newtons of Wembley Ltd v Williams** a rogue bought a car with a bad cheque. The owner of the car successfully avoided the contract before the rogue resold the car. The rogue could not therefore pass good title under s.23 of the Act. The rogue then resold the car at a streetside market. The Court of Appeal held that the rogue did pass a good title to the purchaser under s.25, but only because the rogue had sold the car in the way in which he would have sold it if he had been a mercantile agent. (In business hours, from business premises, etc.) This requirement that the buyer in possession should act as a notional mercantile agent would seem to make the effect of s.25 very limited.

Section 25 will only operate to pass the title which the person who sold to the buyer in possession had. If that person did not own the goods, perhaps because he had bought them from a thief, then ownership will not be passed to the buyer in possession or to the third party buying from the buyer in possession. In **National Employers Mutual General Insurance Association Ltd v Jones** [1988] 2 WLR 952 a thief stole a van and sold it to A. The van passed through several more hands before being acquired by Jones, who bought it in good faith. The original owner sued Jones for the return of the van. Jones claimed to be the owner of the van under s.25. The House of Lords held that Jones was not the owner. Section 25 operates to pass good title as if the buyer in possession was a mercantile agent. We saw above at 9.3.1.1 that a mercantile agent only passes the title of the person who entrusted him with possession of the goods. Neither the thief nor any of the subsequent purchasers had a good title to the van. In **Car and Universal Finance Co Ltd v Caldwell** the claimants could not claim to have title to the car as a buyer in possession because the person who bought from the rogue, Motobella, did not act in good faith and did not therefore acquire title as a buyer in possession. It followed that no later buyer in the chain could claim title as a buyer in possession. Also, no title would have passed under s.25 because the rogue, the buyer in possession, did not resell the goods in the same way as a mercantile agent would have sold them. Therefore the **Newtons of Wembley** criteria were not satisfied.

In **Re Highway Foods Ltd** [1995] BCLC 209 the owner of goods sold them to B1 under a retention of title clause. B1 sold the goods to B2, again under a retention of title clause. As the goods were resold under a retention of title clause this was an agreement to sell by B1, the buyer in possession. We saw earlier that s.9 of the Factors Act is wider than s.25 SGA in that it encompasses an agreement to sell by the buyer in possession. Nevertheless, it was held that no title was passed. The reasoning was that an agreement to sell never passes property until the conditions set out in the agreement are fulfilled. As B2 had not paid B1 in full, the conditions set out in the reservation of title clause had not been fulfilled. Therefore property could not have passed to B2.

9.3.6 **Motor vehicles on hire-purchase**

A person who takes goods on hire-purchase does not own the goods until all of the hire-purchase instalments have been paid. It follows that if such a person sells the goods before all of the instalments have been paid the buyer of the goods will not own them. Ownership will remain with the finance company who let the goods out on hire-purchase.

The Hire Purchase Act (HPA) 1964 Part III makes an exception where a motor vehicle on hire-purchase is sold to a private purchaser who takes it in good faith, without notice of the hire-purchase agreement. In such circumstances the title of the creditor (the finance company) will pass to the third party. The exception also applies where the goods are the subject of a conditional sale agreement. (The conditional sale agreement here does not need to be a regulated agreement within the CCA 1974.) It applies only to motor vehicles. Section 29(1)(a)(iii) defines a motor vehicle as 'a mechanically propelled vehicle intended or adapted for use on roads to which the public has access'.

> **Example**
>
> A takes a car on hire-purchase. (A does not therefore own the car.) A sells the car to B, a dealer in cars. B sells the car to C, a private purchaser who takes it without knowing about the hire-purchase agreement. C will own the car, even though A and B did not. (If A had sold the car directly to C, then again C would own the car.)

Note the requirements:

(a) The Act only applies in favour of the first private purchaser, that is to say a purchaser who is not in business as a motor dealer or a finance company.

If the first private purchaser acts in good faith he gains a good title under HPA 1964. He becomes the owner of the motorised vehicle and can pass ownership on to subsequent buyers. If the first private purchaser does not act in good faith then no subsequent purchaser, private or not, can gain ownership under the HPA. In *Stevenson v Beverley Bentinck Ltd* [1976] 2 All ER 606 it was held that a person who dealt in cars as a hobby, and who bought a car privately for his personal use, was not a private purchaser. In *GE Capital Bank Ltd v Stephen Rushton* [2005] EWCA Civ 1556, [2006] 1 WLR 899 the Court of Appeal held that a person, who had not previously been a motor dealer, was not a private purchaser within the meaning of the Act because he had bought cars as a business venture with a view to selling them at a profit. The person in question had bought 13 second-hand vehicles for £64 500. The vehicles were stored in a barn with the intention that they would be sold on to private purchasers or dealers as the opportunity arose.

(b) The first private purchaser must act in good faith and in ignorance of the hire-purchase agreement. If the first private purchaser acts otherwise than in good faith then no subsequent purchaser, private or otherwise, is protected.

(c) The protection only applies to motor vehicles on hire-purchase. It does not apply to other goods on hire-purchase.

(d) To be protected, the third party must either agree to buy the motor vehicle or must agree to take it on hire-purchase.

The title passed under the Act is only the title which the creditor had. If the creditor had no title then no title can be passed.

9.3.7 Special powers of sale

Section 21(2) of the Act states that:

'Nothing in this Act affects –

(a) the provisions of the Factors Acts...

(b) the validity of any contract of sale under any special common law or statutory power of sale or under the order of a court of competent jurisdiction.'

This section allows for a variety of situations in which it is recognised that a non-owner has the right to sell goods. Examples would include pawnbrokers selling unredeemed pledges, repairers selling unclaimed goods, and bailiffs selling goods seized under writs or warrants of execution.

9.3.8 Market overt

This exception to the *nemo dat* rule, which used to be contained in s.22 SGA 1979, was abolished by the Sale of Goods (Amendment) Act 1994 with effect from 3 January 1995. The exception can still apply as regards goods sold before that date. This was the only exception to the *nemo dat* rule which allowed a thief to pass a good title. It allowed a seller of goods to pass a good title if the goods were sold at an established market, according to the normal usage of the market, between the hours of sunrise and sunset, to a buyer who acted in good faith and without notice that the seller had a defective title to the goods. The exception also applied if goods were sold in the city of London.

Test your understanding 9.5

1 What is meant by the maxim *nemo dat quod non habet*?

2 What is a mercantile agent?

3 In what circumstances can a mercantile agent pass title to another person's goods without that person's consent?

4 In what circumstances will s.21 SGA regard a person as estopped?

5 What provision does s.23 make regarding a seller who has a voidable title to goods?

6 In what circumstances can a seller in possession after a sale pass a good title to goods?

7 In what circumstances does s.25 allow a buyer in possession to pass title to goods?

8 What exception to the *nemo dat* rule is set out in the Hire Purchase Act 1964?

Key points

The passing of the property and the risk

- Once the property in goods sold passes to the buyer he will own the goods. Until the property passes the buyer will not own the goods.

- The property in specific goods passes when the parties to the contract intend it to pass, and this intention can either be a term of the contract or can be inferred from the conduct of the parties and the circumstances of the case (s.17).

- The Rules in s.18 apply only if the parties have not shown an intention as to when the property is to pass.

- Section 18 Rule 1 provides that where there is an unconditional contract for the sale of specific goods in a deliverable state the property in the goods passes to the buyer when the contract is made.

- Section 18 Rule 2 provides that where there is a contract for the sale of specific goods and the seller is bound to do something to the goods for the purpose of putting them into a deliverable state, the property does not pass until the thing is done and the buyer has notice that it has been done.

- Where there is a contract for the sale of specific goods, and the goods without the knowledge of the seller have perished at the time when a contract is made, the contract is void (s.6).

- Where there is an agreement to sell specific goods and subsequently the goods, without any fault on the part of the seller or buyer, perish before the risk passes to the buyer, the agreement is avoided (s.7).

- Subject to s.20A, where there is a contract for the sale of unascertained goods no property in the goods is transferred to the buyer unless and until the goods are ascertained (s.16).

- Section 18 Rule 5 provides that where there is a contract for the sale of unascertained or future goods by description, and goods of that description and in a deliverable state are unconditionally appropriated to the contract, either by the seller with the assent of the buyer or by the buyer with the assent of the seller, the property in the goods then passes to the buyer; and the assent may be express or implied, and may be given either before or after the appropriation is made.

- Section 20A makes it possible for a person who has bought a specified quantity of unascertained goods which form part of a bulk to become an owner in common of the bulk even though his share of the bulk has not been ascertained.

- Unless otherwise agreed, the goods remain at the seller's risk until the property in them is transferred to the buyer, but when the property in them is transferred to the buyer the goods are at the buyer's risk whether delivery has been made or not (s.20).

Reservation of title

- When goods are sold subject to a reservation of title clause the seller lets the buyer have possession of the goods, but the terms of the contract stipulate that the property in the goods is not to pass to the buyer until the full price of the goods has been paid.

- An all moneys clause states that the title is not to pass until all sums owing to the creditor, whether under the contract in question or under previous contracts, have been paid. When the buyer is a company, it is unclear whether such clauses are void as unregistered company charges.

- If the buyer of the goods which are the subject of a reservation of title clause resells the goods to a second buyer who takes delivery of the goods, the property in the goods will pass to the second buyer as long as the second buyer did not know of the reservation of title clause when making the contract and acted in good faith. It is possible, but very unlikely, that a reservation of title clause may entitle the original seller to the proceeds of sale.

Sale by a non-owner

- Subject to certain exceptions, a person who is not the owner of goods cannot pass ownership to anyone else. This rule is known by the Latin maxim *nemo dat quod non habet*.

- In certain circumstances a mercantile agent can pass ownership of goods to a third party, even if the mercantile agent did not have the authority of the owner to do this.

- If the owner of goods makes a representation to a third party that a seller of goods has the right to sell the goods, either as agent or owner, the owner can be prevented from denying the truth of the representation later.

→

■ When the seller of goods has a voidable title to them, but his title has not been avoided at the time of the sale, the buyer acquires a good title to the goods, provided he buys them in good faith and without notice of the seller's defect of title (s.23).

■ If a seller sells goods to one buyer, but keeps possession of the goods or of documents of title to the goods, and then sells or disposes of the same goods to a second buyer, who takes delivery of the goods or the documents of title, then the second buyer will get ownership of the goods (s.24).

■ A person who has bought or agreed to buy goods can pass ownership of those goods to a sub-buyer, even if he had not himself acquired ownership. The goods, or documents of title to them, must be delivered to the sub-buyer as part of a contract of sale or other disposition of the goods (s.25).

■ Where a motor vehicle on hire-purchase is sold to a private purchaser who takes it in good faith, without notice of the hire-purchase agreement, the title of the creditor (the finance company) can pass to the private purchaser (Hire Purchase Act 1964 Part III).

Summary questions

1 S Ltd sell goods to B Ltd for £1 000. B Ltd pays £400 in advance. The parties do not agree to separate the property from the risk. Why would it be important to know whether or not the property had passed if:

a S Ltd had become insolvent after the contract had been made?

b B Ltd had become insolvent after the contract had been made?

c The goods had become accidentally damaged, to the extent of making them of unsatisfactory quality, after the contract had been made?

2 Adam, a builder, visits a wood yard and makes contracts to buy the following goods. A large industrial planing machine which is attached to the ground, an extremely heavy slab of slate which is lying in the wood yard and a heap of '3 by 2' timber. The timber is sold at 20p a foot and the seller is to measure it to see how many feet there are so that the price can be calculated. That night, before any of the goods have been paid for or taken away, the wood yard is burnt down by a fire caused by a stray firework and all of the goods are destroyed. Advise Adam of his legal position.

3 Belinda makes leather belts and bags which she sells to shops. Belinda leaves 20 bags at Cedric's shop on a sale or return basis. In what four ways might the property in the bags pass to Cedric?

4 David phones Edward's house and contracts to buy Edward's bench saw, which is embedded in the floor of Edward's workshop. No mention is made of the passing of the property or the risk.

a At what time would the property in the saw pass to David?

b What would be the legal position if, unknown to either party, the saw had been destroyed by fire one hour before the contract was made?

c What would be the legal position if the saw was destroyed by fire one hour after the contract was made?

5 Look again at the facts of *Tarling v Baxter,* set out at page **244** in the 'Test your understanding' questions in this chapter. What would the legal position have been if it had been the seller's fault that the haystack was burnt down?

6 S Co Ltd, a company which sold china and pottery by mail order, has gone into liquidation. Brian had ordered and paid for ten china plates depicting England's World Cup winning rugby squad. At the time of the order S Co Ltd had 200 cases of these plates. Billy had ordered two dozen Coronation tea cups and saucers. Unknown to Billy, S Co Ltd happened to have just two dozen such cups and saucers in their warehouse, but more would probably have been obtained by S Co Ltd fairly shortly. Bert had asked if S Co Ltd had any reject Coronation plates. S Co's manager had told Bert that there was a consignment of 50 such plates sitting in the warehouse, that this consignment had been bought at auction and that this was a one-off chance to buy as much of the consignment as Bert liked. Bert agreed to buy ten of these plates. All of the buyers paid the full price for the goods which they ordered. At the time of liquidation S Co Ltd had packed the orders for the three buyers and attached the buyers' names to the orders. Advise the three buyers of their legal positions.

7 S sold 100 gearboxes to B Co Ltd, a car manufacturer. B Co Ltd have now gone into liquidation.

→

The contract of sale stated that S retained equitable and beneficial ownership of the gearboxes until B Co Ltd paid the price of the goods and also paid any other moneys owing to S. Over the years many such contracts had been made between the two parties and B Co Ltd had never entirely cleared its debts to S. The contract also stated that if B Co Ltd sold the gearboxes on to another buyer the gearboxes still remained the property of S and could be recovered from the sub-buyer; that if the gearboxes were sold while in finished cars S would own the cars until the cars were sold by B Co Ltd; and that if B Co Ltd sold the cars S would be entitled to the proceeds of sale. Ten of the gearboxes sold are lying in B Co Ltd's warehouse and can be identified. Fifty of the gearboxes have been fitted as components of finished cars which are waiting to be sold by B Co Ltd. Twenty of the gearboxes have been sold on to sub-buyers. These last 20 could be identified and have not been altered or mixed with other goods. Advise S of the likely effect of his reservation of title clause.

8 Work out who will own the goods in the following examples.

i   A has agreed that B can borrow his bicycle while A goes on a month's holiday. Without permission or authority, B sells the bicycle to C, who believes that B is the owner of the bicycle. A did not know B well and made no attempt to check whether or not he was honest.

ii   D buys a car from a garage, paying with a bad cheque. The following day the garage owner discovers that the cheque has bounced and tells the police and the AA to look out for the car. One week later D sells the car to E, an innocent purchaser who paid a reasonable price for the car.

iii   F has taken a car on hire-purchase from a finance company. F sells the car to G, a dealer in cars who does not know that the car is the subject of a hire-purchase agreement. G sells the car to H, another dealer in cars. I, a carpenter, buys the car from H in good faith and then sells it on to J.

iv   An art dealer who often sells paintings on behalf of clients is asked to renovate a painting by K, so that K can sell it at auction. L visits the art dealer's shop while the art dealer is having his lunch and the art dealer's shop assistant, M, sells the painting to L.

v   N visits an art dealer's shop and examines a painting for some considerable time. Later N phones the shop and makes a definite agreement to buy the painting for £2 000. The dealer is to deliver the painting to N's house the following day. Later, by mistake, a shop assistant sells the same painting to O, who takes it away.

vi   P buys a machine from Q for £4 000. Ownership is not to pass to P until the full price has been paid. P takes possession of the machine and, without Q's permission or knowledge, sells the machine to R. P has now become insolvent.

Multiple choice questions

1 On Thursday Alice, a dealer in fine art, visited Belinda's shop where she agreed to buy a large vase for £400. Alice gives Belinda a cheque for £400 and Belinda agrees to deliver the vase to Alice's house the following day. Later on Thursday Belinda takes the vase to her van, but she accidentally drops it and the vase is destroyed. Which one of the following is true?

a   No property passed to Alice and so she will not have to pay the price.

b   The property in the vase did pass to Alice. However, Belinda broke a duty of a bailee and will therefore be liable for destroying Alice's property.

c   The property in the vase would have passed at the time of the contract. However, the risk would have stayed with Belinda and so she would have to bear the loss.

d   The property in the vase would not have passed to Alice because the vase would not have been in a deliverable state until Belinda took it to her van.

2 Cedric agrees to buy 1 000 tons of Canadian wheat from David Ltd. David Ltd happens to have 5 000 tons of such wheat in his warehouse, although Cedric is not aware of this. Cedric pays the price immediately. Before the wheat is delivered David Ltd goes into liquidation. Which one of the following is true?

a   As the contract was for the sale of unascertained goods no property can have passed to Cedric. Cedric can only claim as an unsecured creditor of David Ltd.

b   Under s.20A SGA 1979, Cedric will have become a $\frac{1}{5}$ owner of the 5 000 tons in David Ltd's warehouse. Cedric will therefore be able to claim his 1 000 tons from David Ltd's liquidator.

c   The contract would have become frustrated when David Ltd became insolvent. Under s.7 SGA 1979 Cedric would therefore be able to claim back the money which he paid.

→

d If at the time of liquidation David Ltd had delivered 4 000 of the 5 000 tons of wheat in the warehouse to other buyers, Cedric's 1 000 tons would have become ascertained and would have become unconditionally appropriated to the contract by virtue of s.18 Rule 5(3). Cedric would therefore own the 1 000 tons remaining.

3 On Monday a private college agrees to buy all of a school's old whiteboards, which are attached to the walls of the school. On Tuesday the school detaches the whiteboards from the walls. On Wednesday the school phones the college to say that the whiteboards have been detached and that the college can pick them up during school hours. On Thursday the college collects the whiteboards from the school. The parties did not expressly or impliedly indicate when ownership was to pass. On which day will ownership of the whiteboards have passed to the college?

a On Monday.
b On Tuesday.
c On Wednesday.
d On Thursday.

4 Consider the following statements:

i The only circumstance in which any property in unascertained goods can pass from seller to buyer is by the operation of SGA s.20A.
ii Section 20A will operate to pass the property in the goods to the buyer whenever the buyer agrees to buy a specified quantity of an unidentified bulk.
iii Section 20A can only operate to pass the property in the goods to the buyer if the bulk of goods is identified either by the contract or by subsequent agreement between the parties.
iv Section 20A will operate in favour of any buyer who has agreed to pay some or all of the price.
v Section 20B provides that a person who becomes an owner in common of the bulk by virtue of s.20A is deemed to have consented to a delivery out of the bulk to any other owner in common of the bulk.

Which one of the following statements is correct?

a All of the above statements are true.
b i, iii and v only are true.
c i, ii, iv and v only are true.
d ii, iii, iv and v only are true.

5 Which one of the following statements is not true?

a If a charge on company assets is not registered with the Registrar of Companies it will be invalid.

b Once goods which are the subject of a retention of title clause have been manufactured into other goods, so that they have lost their identity, then the seller's right to reclaim the goods sold will be lost.
c Goods may be sold subject to a retention of title clause. But once the buyer takes delivery of the goods the seller's title will always be extinguished.
d A retention of title clause will be ineffective against a sub-buyer who buys the goods in good faith and who takes delivery of the goods.

6 On Friday Alice advertises her car for sale in the evening newspaper. A rogue, pretending to be Wayne Rooney the international footballer, persuades Alice to part with the car in exchange for a stolen cheque. Alice later wonders whether she should have taken the cheque. On Monday she presents the cheque to her bank and asks for quick clearance. The bank ring Alice to tell her that the cheque was stolen. Alice contacts the police and the large motoring organisations to report the deception and to ask them to keep a look out for the car. The police trace the car to Mr Smith, who bought it from the rogue at a second-hand car dealership which the rogue used to operate before he fled.

Which one of the following statements is not true?

a The rogue only had a voidable title to the car, but as long as Mr Smith bought the car in good faith before Alice told the police and the motoring organisations Mr Smith will get a complete title to the car under s.23 SGA 1979.
b The rogue only had a voidable title to the car. If Alice had avoided the contract before the rogue sold the car to Mr Smith then s.23 will not operate so as to pass a good title to Mr Smith.
c Regardless of s.23 of the Act, Mr Smith might have gained ownership of the car as the rogue could possibly have passed title under s.25 as a buyer in possession after a sale.
d Regardless of s.23 of the Act, Mr Smith might have gained ownership of the car as the rogue could possibly have passed title under s.24 as a seller in possession after a sale.

7 Mr Bibliophile discovers an antique book in his attic. Knowing that his local book dealer often sells goods on behalf of customers, he takes the book to his shop to find out the value of the book. The dealer tells Mr Bibliophile that the book is worth at least £2 000 and, if the prints are originals, could be worth much more. Mr Bibliophile agrees to pay the dealer

5 per cent of the selling price if he finds out the value of the book and places it in a suitable auction. It is agreed that the dealer is not to sell the book without express permission from Mr Bibliophile. The dealer says that he will need to take the book to London to show it to an expert. While in his local pub the dealer gets drunk and sells the book to a wealthy collector. Which one of the following statements is true?

a The wealthy collector will own the book because the dealer was a buyer in possession after a sale.
b The wealthy collector will own the book because the dealer was a seller in possession after a sale.
c The wealthy collector will own the book because the dealer sold it as a mercantile agent.
d Mr Bibliophile will still own the book and will be able to sue the wealthy collector for its return.

8 A rogue takes a car, a car radio and a trailer on hire-purchase from three different suppliers. The rogue sells all three items to Fred, who does not suspect that the rogue does not own the goods and who knows nothing of the hire-purchase agreements.

Which one of the following statements is true?

a As the rogue owned none of the goods, Fred cannot own any of them either.
b The rogue had a voidable title to the goods, and so Fred will have a complete title as long as he bought the goods before the various hirers discover the rogue's fraud and avoided the various contracts.
c Fred will have a complete title to all of the goods.
d Fred will have a complete title to the car, but no title to the radio or the trailer.

Task 9

A market trader friend of yours has recently bought several car battery chargers which, unbeknown to him, had been stolen six months ago. The police took the battery chargers from your friend and returned them to the owner. Your friend also bought tyre pumps from a company which went into liquidation before the pumps were delivered. So far none of the price of the pumps which your friend paid has been refunded by the company's liquidator. Your friend has asked you to write a report dealing with the following matters. In order that the report should be easy to understand you should include examples which relate to the business of a market trader wherever possible.

1 At what time does ownership of goods which have been bought pass to the buyer? What is the significance of ownership passing?
2 In what circumstances will a contract for the sale of specific goods become frustrated or void for mistake? What will be the effect of the contract becoming frustrated or void for mistake?
3 To what extent is it possible to sell goods but to retain ownership of them until the full price is paid?
4 Outline the circumstances in which a person who is not the owner of goods can nevertheless pass ownership to someone else.

mylawchamber *premium*

Visit **www.mylawchamber.co.uk/macintyre** to access study support resources including interactive multiple-choice questions, weblinks, glossary, glossary flashcards, legal newsfeed, answers to questions in this chapter, legal updates and an overview of this chapter all linked to the **Pearson eText** version of *Business Law* which you can **search, highlight** and **personalise** with your **own notes** and **bookmarks**.

10

Sale of goods – duties of the parties · remedies · international sales

Introduction

This chapter considers the following matters:

10.1 Duties of the seller
10.1.1 The seller's duty to deliver
10.2 Duties of the buyer
10.2.1 The duty to pay the price
10.2.2 The duty to accept the goods
10.2.3 The duty to take delivery of the goods
10.3 Remedies of the seller
10.3.1 Real remedies of the unpaid seller
10.3.2 Personal remedies of the seller

10.4 Remedies of the buyer
10.4.1 The buyer's right to damages
10.4.2 The right to reject the goods
10.4.3 Acceptance of the goods
10.4.4 Rejection in other supply contracts
10.4.5 Specific performance
10.4.6 Additional rights of buyers in consumer cases
10.5 Auction sales
10.6 International sales
10.6.1 The bill of lading
10.6.2 Fob (free on board) contracts
10.6.3 Cif (cost, insurance and freight) contracts

10.1 DUTIES OF THE SELLER

Section 27 of the SGA 1979 states that:

'It is the duty of the seller to deliver the goods, and of the buyer to accept and pay for them in accordance with the terms of the contract of sale.'

It can be seen from this that whereas the seller has only the one duty, the duty to deliver the goods, s.27 imposes two duties on the buyer, to accept the goods and to pay for them. The buyer has an additional duty to take delivery of the goods when requested to do so (s.37(1)).

The seller's duty to deliver the goods and the buyer's duty to pay for them are said by s.28 to be 'concurrent conditions', unless otherwise agreed. This does not mean that delivery and payment must necessarily take place simultaneously but rather that, unless otherwise agreed, the seller must be ready and willing to deliver the goods and the buyer must be ready and willing to pay for them. If the seller indicates that he is not ready and willing to deliver, then the buyer can sue for damages without having actually paid the price, as long as he can show that he was ready and

willing to pay. If the buyer indicates that he is not ready and willing to pay the price, then the seller can sue for damages without having actually delivered the goods, as long as he can show that he was ready and willing to deliver. In many business contracts the rule in s.28 is varied as credit is given to the buyer. In most retail contracts payment of the price and delivery of the goods do take place at the same time.

10.1.1 The seller's duty to deliver

Section 27 states that the seller must deliver the goods 'in accordance with the terms of the contract'. If the contract was for the sale of specific goods, then the buyer must deliver the goods specified. If the contract was for the sale of unascertained goods, then the seller must deliver goods which match the contract description.

If the seller should fail to deliver as required the buyer can sue for damages for non-delivery and refuse to pay the price. If any part of the price has already been paid this can be recovered.

Section 61 defines delivery as 'voluntary transfer of possession from one person to another'. This does not necessarily mean that the seller must physically bring the goods to the buyer. Depending on the terms of the contract, it may mean only that the seller allows the buyer to come and collect the goods. It should be remembered that delivery concerns the transfer of possession of the goods, not the transfer of ownership.

10.1.1.1 Ways of effecting delivery

Delivery will usually take the form of physical delivery of the goods. However, delivery can also be achieved by:

(a) Delivering the means to control the goods. (For example, giving the buyer the keys to a car or the keys to a warehouse where the goods are stored.)
(b) Getting a third party who holds the goods, such as a warehouseman, to acknowledge (attorn) that he now holds the goods for the buyer rather than for the seller.
(c) Delivering a document of title, such as a bill of lading, to the buyer. (In the previous chapter we saw that a car registration book is not a document of title. The legal status of a bill of lading is explained below at 10.5.1.)
(d) A buyer who has possession of the goods as a bailee retaining possession of the goods. For example, in hire-purchase contracts such a notional delivery will usually take place when the buyer pays the final instalment.
(e) Delivering the goods to a carrier. This is regarded as delivery to the buyer if the seller is authorised or required by the contract to send the goods to the buyer, as long as the carrier is not the seller's employee or agent (s.32(1)). The seller must make a reasonable contract with the carrier (s.32(2)). If the seller fails to make a reasonable contract the buyer may decline to treat delivery to the carrier as delivery to himself, or may hold the seller responsible in damages (s.32(2)). However, where the buyer deals as a consumer s.32(4) provides that s.32(1) and (2) must be ignored. If in pursuance of a contract of sale the seller is authorised or required to send the goods to a buyer who deals as a consumer, delivery of the goods to a carrier is not delivery of the goods to the buyer. (As we saw in the previous chapter, s.20(4) also provides that where the buyer deals as a consumer the goods remain at the seller's risk until they are delivered to the consumer.)

10.1.1.2 The place of delivery

Section 29 deals with the place of delivery:

(1) Whether it is for the buyer to take possession of the goods or for the seller to send them to the buyer is a question depending in each case on the contract, express or implied, between the parties.
(2) Apart from any such contract, express or implied, the place of delivery is the seller's place of business if he has one, and if not, his residence; except that, if the contract is for the sale of specific goods, which to the knowledge of the parties when the contract is made are in some other place, then that place is the place of delivery.

If the express or implied terms of the contract stipulate that the seller is to take the goods to the buyer or that the buyer is to go and pick the goods up from the seller then the place of delivery is agreed by the parties. If there is no such agreement then as regards unascertained goods the place of delivery is the seller's place of business or, if he has not got a place of business, his home. The place of delivery will also be the seller's place of business or his home as regards specific goods the whereabouts of which are not known to both parties. But when the contract is for the sale of specific goods which both parties know to be at some other place then that place is the place of delivery.

So unless the parties have shown a contrary intention it is up to the buyer to go and collect the goods. The seller fulfils the duty to deliver by making the goods available to the buyer. Very often the parties do show a contrary intention. The contract might stipulate, for example, that the goods are to be delivered to the buyer's house or place of business.

10.1.1.3 Time of delivery

If no time of delivery is fixed by the contract then delivery must be made within a reasonable time (s.29(3)). A tender of delivery must be made at a reasonable time of day and what amounts to a reasonable time of day is a question of fact (s.29(5)). A seller makes a tender of delivery by showing a willingness and readiness to deliver.

Any late or early delivery of the goods will amount to a breach of contract and so the buyer will always be entitled to damages for breach of warranty. In many cases however the buyer will want to go further and treat the contract as repudiated, as well as or instead of claiming damages. Whether or not the buyer will have this right will depend upon whether or not the term which the seller has breached by delivering late can be classified as a condition of the contract. Section 10(2) makes it plain that no general rule can be laid down by stating that whether or not the time of delivery is of the essence (a condition of the contract) depends upon the intentions of the parties. Case law has established that in commercial contracts any time of delivery fixed by the contract is presumed to be of the essence, and that this presumption is particularly strong where the goods are to be carried by sea.

Bowes v Shand (1877) 2 App Cas 455 (House of Lords)

A cargo of rice was sold on terms that the rice was to be shipped on board the *Rajah of Cochin* during the months of March or April 1874. Seven-eighths of the rice was loaded on board in February 1874. The buyer refused to accept the rice as it had not been shipped at the correct time.

Held. The buyer was entitled to reject the cargo. Even though the early shipment did not affect the value of the rice, a condition had been broken.

If late delivery does amount to breach of condition the buyer may waive his right to treat the contract as breached if his conduct leads the seller to believe that he intends to carry on with the contract. Once the right to repudiate has been waived the buyer can only reintroduce it by giving the seller reasonable notice of his intention to do so.

Charles Rickards v Oppenheim [1950] 1 All ER 420 (Court of Appeal)

The claimants agreed to supply the defendant with a specialist car. The car was to be finished within seven months and a term of the contract stated that time was to be of the essence. The car was not completed on time but the defendant waived the original stipulation as to time by continuing to press for delivery on later dates. Three months after the original delivery date the defendant was told that the car would be ready within two weeks. The defendant then gave written notice that if it was not ready within one month he would refuse to take delivery of it. The car was not completed for another 15 weeks, at which time the defendant refused to take delivery of it.

Held. The defendant was entitled to refuse to take delivery. Having waived the initial stipulation that time was of the essence, the defendant had re-introduced it by giving reasonable notice.

If no time is initially fixed for delivery, so that delivery within a reasonable time is implied, this implied term is not initially a condition. However, the buyer can make the term a condition by giving the seller reasonable notice of his intention to do so. Even if the buyer does not do this the mere fact that more than a reasonable time has elapsed will entitle the buyer to treat the contract as repudiated.

McDougall v Aeromarine of Emsworth Ltd [1958] 3 All ER 431

The defendants contracted to build a yacht for the claimant, the yacht to comply with the claimant's specifications. The defendants agreed to try to finish the yacht by 1 May 1957, but this delivery date could not be guaranteed. The defendant paid the first instalment of the price in November 1956. The yacht was presented for a trial run on 3 June 1957. However, the yacht was not fit for its purpose. Negotiations took place between the claimant and the defendants, but by the beginning of September 1957 the yacht was still four or five weeks away from being ready for delivery. Four-fifths of the 1957 yachting season was by now over. The claimant therefore terminated the contract and demanded the repayment of his first instalment.

Held. The contract obliged the defendants to deliver the yacht within a reasonable time after 1 May 1957. This time had expired by September 1957. Applying s.10 SGA, the obligation as to time of delivery was a condition of the contract. The claimant was therefore entitled to repudiate the contract and get his money back.

10.1.1.4 **Delivery of wrong quantity**

Where the seller delivers to the buyer a quantity of goods which is less than the quantity he contracted to sell, the buyer may reject the goods, but if the buyer accepts the goods delivered he must pay for them at the contract rate (s.30(1)). So if, for example, a buyer of coal ordered ten tons of coal at a price of £1 000 and the seller delivered only nine tons the buyer could either reject the lot or pay £900 for the nine tons delivered. If the buyer rejected the lot, he could recover any of the price paid and make a claim for damages for non-delivery. If he accepted the nine tons he could recover part of the price and claim damages for non-delivery of the shortfall.

Where the seller delivers to the buyer a quantity of goods larger than he contracted to sell, the buyer may accept the quantity of goods which should have been delivered and reject the rest, or he may reject the whole (s.30(2)). Alternatively, the buyer may accept the whole of the goods delivered and pay for them at the contract rate (s.30(3)). So if in the above example the seller delivered 11 tons of coal, the buyer could either keep ten tons and pay £1 000, or reject the lot and sue for damages for non-delivery, or keep the lot and pay £1 100.

The rules in s.30 are subject to any usage of trade, special agreement or course of dealing between the parties (s.30(5)). They are also subject to the rule *de minimis non curat lex* – the law is not concerned with trifles. So if the extra quantity delivered amounted to a trifle then the seller will not have breached the contract.

Shipton Anderson & Co v Weil Bros
[1912] 1 KB 574

A cargo of wheat was sold. The cargo was to weigh 10 per cent more or less than 4 500 tons. The maximum quantity would therefore have been 4 950 tons. The sellers delivered 55 lb more than 4 950 tons. The buyers rejected the cargo on the grounds that the quantity delivered was in excess of the contract quantity. The sellers did not demand any extra payment for the extra 55 lb, which would have been worth about four shillings (20p).

Held. The excess delivered was a trifle and so the sellers had not breached the contract.

Section 30(2A), an amendment introduced by the Sale and Supply of Goods Act 1994, provides that a buyer who does not deal as a consumer cannot reject the goods on account of delivery of the wrong quantity if the seller can show that the shortfall or excess is so slight as to make rejection unreasonable. The rights of consumer buyers are not affected by this amendment. Consumers will be entitled to reject for delivery of the wrong quantity, subject to the *de minimis* rule.

10.1.1.5 Delivery by instalments

Unless otherwise agreed, a buyer of goods is not bound to accept delivery of them by instalments (s.31(1)). When the contract does allow for delivery by instalments problems can arise when the delivery of one or more instalments amounts to a breach of condition by the seller. Is the buyer entitled to terminate the whole contract, or is he only entitled to reject the defective instalment?

If the instalment contract can be regarded as entire, that is to say as one indivisible obligation, then a breach

of condition as regards any of the instalments will entitle the buyer to treat the whole contract as repudiated. The buyer will therefore be entitled to return instalments already delivered and demand all of his money back.

If the contract is not entire, then s.31(2) will apply. It states that:

'Where there is a contract for the sale of goods to be delivered by stated instalments, which are to be separately paid for, and the seller makes defective deliveries in respect of one or more instalments, or the buyer neglects or refuses to take delivery of or pay for one or more instalments, it is a question in each case depending on the terms of the contract and the circumstances of the case whether the breach of contract is a repudiation of the whole contract or whether it is a severable breach giving rise to a claim for compensation but not a right to treat the whole contract as repudiated.'

Section 31(2) tells us that when considering whether the breach of a severable instalment contract amounts to a repudiation of the whole contract regard must be had to the terms of the contract and the circumstances of the case. That regard should be had to the terms of the contract is obvious enough; if the parties agree to a solution the courts will apply it. The following cases show that when the courts look to the circumstances of the case the two most important circumstances to be considered are: (i) the ratio of the breach to the contract as a whole; and (ii) the likelihood of the breach being repeated.

Maple Flock Co Ltd v Universal Furniture Products (Wembley) Ltd [1934] 1 KB 148
(Court of Appeal)

100 tons of rag flock (waste wool) were sold. The flock was to be delivered in three loads a week, each load weighing one and a half tons and each to be separately paid for. The contract contained a written guarantee that the flock would conform to Government standards, which permitted 30 parts of chlorine to 100 000 parts flock. It was a criminal offence to use flock containing more chlorine than this. The sixteenth load delivered contained 250 parts chlorine. The defendants did not realise this until two further loads had been delivered. On discovering that the sixteenth load was defective the defendants claimed to treat the contract as repudiated.

Held. The claimant's breach of contract did not amount to a repudiation of the whole contract. The breach affected only a small ratio of the contract and was unlikely to be repeated.

By contrast, in **Robert A. Munro & Co Ltd** v **Meyer** [1930] 2 KB 312 the buyers were entitled to treat the whole contract as repudiated. The contract was for the sale of 1 500 tons of bone and meal by instalments. The first 651 tons delivered had been adulterated with cocoa husks and this amounted to a repudiation of the whole contract by the sellers. The buyers were not therefore obliged to take future instalments and were entitled to damages in respect of the deliveries already received. They could have refused to accept these deliveries if they had discovered the defect in time to do so.

10.1.1.6 **The importance of delivery**

Delivery is concerned with possession of the goods rather than with ownership. It is however important because once delivery has been made or tendered:

(i) the buyer must accept the goods or face the prospect of paying damages for non-acceptance;
(ii) the seller can demand payment (although it is possible that he may not be able to sue for the price);
(iii) it will no longer be possible for an unpaid seller to have a lien over the goods. (The unpaid seller's lien is considered below at 10.3.1.)

If the seller breaches the duty to deliver, the buyer will be able to sue for damages for non-delivery. The buyer may also have a right to treat the contract as repudiated or to bring an action for specific performance. (The buyer's remedies are considered later in this chapter at 10.4.)

Test your understanding 10.1

1 A buyer of goods has indicated to the seller that he is not ready and willing to pay for the goods. Must the seller deliver the goods in accordance with the contract before he can sue for damages for non-acceptance?

2 If the contract does not contain a term fixing the place of delivery, where will this place be as regards

  a Unascertained goods?
  b Specific goods, the whereabouts of which are not known to both of the parties?
  c Specific goods, the whereabouts of which are known to both of the parties?

3 What is the significance of the time of delivery being of the essence in a contract of sale of goods? How will a court decide whether or not time was of the essence?

4 What options are open to the buyer if

  a the seller delivers too large a quantity of goods?
  b the seller delivers too small a quantity?

5 In a severable instalment contract, a buyer wishes to terminate the whole contract on account of a breach of condition as regards one instalment. How will it be decided whether or not the buyer can do this?

10.2 DUTIES OF THE BUYER

The buyer has three duties: to pay the price, to accept the goods, and to take delivery of the goods.

10.2.1 **The duty to pay the price**

Unless otherwise agreed, payment of the price and delivery of the goods are concurrent conditions. As we have seen, this means that the seller must be ready to give possession of the goods to the buyer in exchange for the price, and the buyer must be ready and willing to pay the price in exchange for possession of the goods (s.28). If one of the parties shows an unwillingness to perform the contract then the other party is entitled to withhold performance. Late payment of the price, unlike late delivery of the goods, amounts only to a breach of warranty unless a different intention appears from the terms of the contract (s.10(1)).

Section 8 explains how the price is to be fixed:

'(1) The price in a contract of sale may be fixed by the contract, or may be left to be fixed in a manner agreed by the contract, or may be determined by the course of dealing between the parties.

(2) When the price is not determined as mentioned in subsection (1) above the buyer must pay a reasonable price.

(3) What is a reasonable price is a question of fact dependent on the circumstances of each particular case.'

To illustrate the effect of s.8, let us assume that Firm A orders goods from Firm B. It would usually be the case that the price would be expressly agreed in the contract. However, the contract might instead specify the manner in which the price is to be fixed. It might, for instance, state that the price will be fixed by an independent third party. If the contract neither fixed the price nor agreed the manner of fixing it, the court would look at previous dealings between Firm A and Firm B. If it discovered that the same price was always paid for goods of the type sold then, in the absence of any indication to the contrary, this would be taken to be the price. If none of the above methods helped, Firm A would have to pay a reasonable price, which would depend upon the circumstances of the particular case. If the parties agree that they will themselves fix the price at some future date then there will be no concluded contract. (See *Willis Management (Isle of Man) Ltd* v *Cable and Wireless plc* [2005] EWCA Civ 806, [2005] 2 Lloyd's Rep 597 in Chapter 3 at 3.3.)

10.2.2 The duty to accept the goods

The word 'accept' is not used here in its everyday sense of taking possession of the goods. Rather it means that the buyer must not wrongfully reject the goods. If the buyer does wrongfully reject the goods then this will constitute a repudiatory breach. The seller will therefore be entitled to terminate the contract and to sue the buyer for damages for non-acceptance.

10.2.3 The duty to take delivery of the goods

The buyer has a duty to take delivery of the goods. Where the seller is ready and willing to deliver the goods, and requests the buyer to take delivery, and the buyer does not within a reasonable time after such request take delivery of the goods, he is liable to the seller for any loss occasioned by his neglect or refusal to take delivery, and also for a reasonable charge for the care and custody of the goods (s.37(1)). Above at 10.1.1.5 we set out s.31(2) which relates to breach of an instalment contract which is not entire. This section states that if the buyer neglects or refuses to take delivery of one or more instalments, the terms of the contract and the circumstances of the case will determine whether this is a repudiation of the whole contract or whether it is a severable breach which merely gives a right to damages.

10.3 REMEDIES OF THE SELLER

Whenever the buyer breaches the contract the seller will be entitled to a remedy. The remedies available to the seller can be classified as real remedies or personal remedies. Real remedies are taken against the goods, personal remedies are taken against the buyer.

10.3.1 Real remedies of the unpaid seller

The real remedies against the goods are only available to an unpaid seller. Section 38 defines a seller as an unpaid seller –

(a) when the whole of the price has not been paid or tendered;
(b) when a bill of exchange or other negotiable instrument has been received as conditional payment, and the condition on which it was received has not been fulfilled by reason of dishonour of the instrument or otherwise.

Section 38(a) allows a seller to be classed as an unpaid seller even if the buyer has been granted credit. Where the buyer pays by cheque, s.38(b) makes the seller an unpaid seller if the buyer's cheque is dishonoured.

There are three real remedies which the unpaid seller might have: a lien on the goods; the right to stop them in transit; or the right to resell them. These remedies are available even though the property in the goods has already passed to the buyer.

10.3.1.1 Lien

Section 41(1) explains the seller's right to a lien:

'(1) Subject to this Act, the unpaid seller of goods who is in possession of them is entitled to retain possession of them until payment or tender of the price in the following cases:–

(a) where the goods have been sold without any stipulation as to credit;
(b) where the goods have been sold on credit but the term of credit has expired;
(c) where the buyer becomes insolvent.'

Example

Farmer A visits farmer B's farm and agrees to buy a second-hand tractor for £3 000. There is no mention of credit and the parties do not discuss when the property or the risk are to pass. As the tractor is →

specific goods in a deliverable state, the property in the goods would pass to farmer A upon the making of the contract (s.18 Rule 1). However, farmer B would be entitled to keep possession of the tractor until the full £3 000 had been paid or tendered. If farmer A gave farmer B a cheque farmer B would still be entitled to exercise his right of lien. Offering a cheque as payment does not amount to a tender of the price, the exact sum of money in cash would have to be offered.

A seller who exercises his right of lien and retains possession of the goods does not thereby terminate the contract (s.48(1)). If the price is later paid by the buyer, or by the buyer's liquidator, then the seller will have to hand possession of the goods to the buyer. The right to a lien is excluded when the seller has granted credit to the buyer, unless the credit has expired. A lien is most likely to be useful where goods have been sold to a buyer without granting any credit and the buyer has become insolvent before paying the full price of the goods.

Section 43 sets out three ways in which an unpaid seller will lose the lien:

'(a) when he delivers the goods to a carrier or other bailee or custodier for the purpose of transmission to the buyer without reserving the right of disposal of the goods;
(b) when the buyer or his agent lawfully obtains possession of the goods;
(c) by waiver of the lien or right of retention.'

Section 43 makes it clear that retention of possession by the seller is the key to the lien.

10.3.1.2 Stoppage in transit

Once the seller has delivered the goods to a carrier or other bailee for transmission to the buyer he has waived his lien by giving up possession of the goods. However, if the buyer is insolvent, the seller can stop the goods while they are still in transit. The carrier must then redeliver the goods as directed by the seller and the seller must pay the expenses of this (s.46(4)). If the seller does not stop the goods while they are in transit the buyer's trustee in bankruptcy or liquidator will regard the goods as just another asset, to be applied in paying off all the creditors. The exercise of stoppage in transit does not of itself terminate the contract (s.48(1)). The trustee in bankruptcy or

liquidator may choose to tender the price and enforce the contract.

An actual physical stopping of the goods is not necessary. The seller merely needs to give the carrier notice that he is exercising his right. However, once the goods have been delivered to the buyer the seller will be too late. The carrier must be a common carrier and not the agent of either the buyer or the seller. (If the carrier is the seller's agent, the seller can exercise the right of lien; if the carrier is the buyer's agent, the right of stoppage in transit will be ended when the carrier receives the goods.)

Example

S Ltd has sold 100 garden tables to B Ltd. S has delivered the tables to a common carrier for delivery to B Ltd. The property in the goods has therefore passed to B Ltd. S Ltd hears on the local news that B Ltd has become insolvent. S Ltd contacts the carrier to give notice that they are effecting stoppage in transit. The carrier must redeliver the goods to S Ltd, who must pay the costs of this redelivery. B Ltd's liquidator could still choose to pay for the goods as the contract of sale is not terminated.

Stoppage in transit was a more potent right in the last century when delivery of goods was a much slower process.

Neither the unpaid seller's lien nor the right of stoppage in transit are affected by any sale or other disposition of the goods which the buyer may have made, unless the seller has assented to it (s.47(1)). However, if the buyer is given a document of title, and if he transfers this to a third party acting in good faith and for valuable consideration, then the unpaid seller's rights of lien and stoppage in transit are lost or can only be exercised subject to the rights of the transferee (s.47(2)). Where an unpaid seller who has exercised his right of lien or retention or stoppage in transit resells the goods, the second buyer acquires good title to them against the original buyer (s.48(2)).

The unpaid seller's lien and right to stop the goods in transit apply where the property in the goods has already passed to the buyer. Where the property in the goods has not passed to the buyer the unpaid seller has (in addition to his other remedies) a right of withholding delivery similar to and coextensive with his rights of lien or retention and stoppage in transit where the property has passed to the buyer (s.39(2)).

10.3.1.3 **The right to resell the goods**

The purpose of a contract of sale of goods is to pass ownership of the goods from the seller to the buyer. Once ownership has passed the seller therefore has no right to resell the goods to anyone else because the goods are no longer his to sell. You should notice that here we are talking about the right to resell, not the power to do so. Section 24 SGA (considered in the previous chapter at 9.3.4) would give a seller in possession the power to pass ownership to a second buyer. However, this would generally amount to a breach of the contract made with the original buyer. When the seller has a right of resale he commits no breach of contract by exercising it and can recover damages from the original buyer. Section 48(1) provides that a contract of sale is not rescinded merely because the seller exercises his right of lien or stoppage in transit. Section 48(2) and (3) give the seller a right to resell the goods to a second buyer in three circumstances:

(a) where the goods are of a perishable nature and the buyer does not pay or tender the price within a reasonable time;

(b) where the unpaid seller gives the buyer notice of an intention to resell the goods and the buyer does not pay or tender the price within a reasonable time;

(c) where the contract expressly allows for a right of resale.

An unpaid seller would also have a right to resell where the first buyer repudiates the contract, that is to say where the buyer expressly or impliedly makes known to the seller that he no longer regards himself as bound by the contract.

If the seller exercises his right of resale this terminates the contract with the original buyer. As long as the resale was justified, the seller can sue the original buyer for damages if he has to resell at a lower price. He can keep any extra profit if he resells at a higher price. The seller will of course not be able to sue for the price and will have to refund any part of the price already paid. The insolvency of the buyer is not enough to give the unpaid seller the right to resell, as the liquidator has the option of paying the price and enforcing the contract.

10.3.2 **Personal remedies of the seller**

The seller has two personal remedies against the buyer: to sue for the price, or to sue for damages for non-acceptance.

10.3.2.1 **An action for the price**

Section 49 stipulates that the seller can only sue for the price if the property in the goods has passed to the buyer or if the contract fixed a definite date for payment.

> ### *Colley v Overseas Exporters Ltd*
> [1921] 3 KB 302
>
> A quantity of unascertained leather goods were sold on fob terms. (Fob is explained below at 10.5.2.) The buyer had a duty to nominate an effective ship on to which the goods could be loaded. The buyer breached the contract because, despite five attempts, he could not secure an effective ship. The goods were left lying on the docks. The sellers sued for the contract price.
>
> **Held.** The sellers could not sue for the price because the contract did not fix a definite date for payment and the property in the goods had not passed to the buyer. (In an fob contract the property in the goods passes to the buyer when the goods are passed over the ship's rail.)
>
> **COMMENT** At first sight this seems particularly harsh on the seller. However, the seller would be able to claim damages for non-acceptance (see immediately below).

If the seller sues for the price then questions of mitigation or remoteness of damage will not arise. The seller will be suing for a debt, not suing for damages. (See Chapter 7 at 7.2.3.)

10.3.2.2 **Damages for non-acceptance**

If the buyer has refused to accept and pay for the goods the seller will be able to sue for damages for non-acceptance. This remedy is available whether the property in the goods has passed to the buyer or not. A seller who has the right to sue for the price might elect to sue for damages for non-acceptance instead.

Section 50 states that:

'(1) Where the buyer wrongfully neglects or refuses to accept and pay for the goods, the seller may maintain an action against him for damages for non-acceptance.

(2) The measure of damages is the estimated loss directly and naturally resulting in the ordinary course of events, from the buyer's breach of contract.

(3) Where there is an available market for the goods in question the measure of damages is *prima facie* to be ascertained by the difference between the contract price and the market or current price at the time or times when the goods ought to have been accepted or (if no time was fixed for acceptance) at the time of the refusal to accept.'

Section 50(3) applies if there is an available market for the goods, s.50(2) applies if there is not. Section 50(2) reiterates the first Rule in **Hadley v Baxendale** (which we considered in Chapter 7 at 7.2.2.1). It would cater for the seller recovering any foreseeable losses caused by the buyer's breach, such as profit which the seller would have made on the sale. The second Rule in **Hadley v Baxendale** is not mentioned by the Act but it would be applied under the common law. Where there is an available market for the goods s.50(3) explains how the courts will assess the loss directly and naturally flowing from the breach. There will be an available market if the goods were not unique, if a different buyer of the goods could be found, and if the price of the goods could be fixed by the prevailing conditions of supply and demand. There is no available market for second-hand cars as they are regarded as unique.

Where there is such an available market the *prima facie* measure of damages will be the difference between the contract price and the price at the time when the goods ought to have been accepted or, if the time for acceptance was not fixed, at the time when the buyer refused to accept. If the market price of the goods has risen or remained the same, then the seller ought to mitigate his loss by reselling the goods to another buyer. If the seller does not do this then he will not be entitled to damages for loss of profit on the sale. If the market price of the goods has fallen, then generally the seller's lost profit will be calculated as the contract price minus the market price at the time when the goods ought to have been accepted.

Example

On 1 April A sells a ton of wheat to B at a price of £1 000, delivery to be made on 20 April. On 20 April B refuses to accept the wheat. If on 20 April the market price of a ton of this type of wheat was £1 200 then the seller will not be entitled to damages for any loss of profit. He could have mitigated his loss by selling the wheat to another buyer. If on 20 April the price of wheat was £800 then prima facie the seller's damages for loss of profit will be £200. If on 20 April the price of wheat was £1 000 then the seller will not be entitled to any damages for loss of profit.

It should be noticed that the seller does not have to sell in the available market. He can, instead, take a gamble and hold on to the goods, hoping that the market price will rise. However, the damages will still be assessed by reference to the market price at the time when the goods ought to have been accepted, even if the seller does not try to resell the goods in the market.

Section 54 states that:

'Nothing in this Act affects the right of the buyer or seller to recover interest or special damage in any case where by law interest or special damage may be recoverable, or to recover money paid where the consideration for the payment has failed.'

This section preserves the common law rules on damages and allows the seller to claim for other expenses reasonably incurred if they can reasonably be supposed to have been in the contemplation of the parties at the time of the contract. In the light of s.37, considered immediately below, it is unusual for these special damages to be claimed.

10.3.2.3 Damages for refusing to take delivery

If the buyer accepts the goods late then damages for refusing to take delivery can be recovered under s.37, which states that:

'(1) When the seller is ready and willing to deliver the goods, and requests the buyer to take delivery, and the buyer does not within a reasonable time after such request take delivery of the goods, he is liable to the seller for any loss occasioned by his neglect or refusal to take delivery, and also for a reasonable charge for the care and custody of the goods.

(2) Nothing in this section affects the rights of the seller where the neglect or refusal of the buyer to take delivery amounts to a repudiation of the contract.'

These damages are not designed to compensate for loss of bargain, but only for delay in taking delivery. Although s.37(1) mentions a reasonable charge for care and custody of the goods, other expenses, such as extra insurance, or the costs involved in attempting to deliver, might also be recoverable. Sellers suing for damages for non-acceptance would include the losses mentioned in s.37(1) as part of their claim for damages under s.50.

10.3.2.4 The seller's right to terminate the contract

If the buyer has repudiated the contract the seller may accept the repudiation and treat the contract as terminated. The seller will then have no further obligation to perform the contract and may sue for the price or for damages. Whether or not the buyer's behaviour can be taken as repudiating the contract will be decided upon general contract principles.

> ### Test your understanding 10.2
>
> 1 By what methods can the price of goods in a contract of sale be fixed?
>
> 2 What is the definition of an unpaid seller?
>
> 3 What three remedies are available only to an unpaid seller?
>
> 4 In what two circumstances does a seller of goods have a right to sue for the price?
>
> 5 As far as the market rule in s.50(3) is concerned, what is the meaning of an available market for the goods? Where there is such an available market how will the courts assess the loss directly and naturally flowing from the breach?

10.4 REMEDIES OF THE BUYER

Any breach of contract by the seller will entitle the buyer to damages. These damages will be available either for non-delivery of the goods, or for late delivery or for breach of warranty. Where the seller has breached a condition, or where the breach of an innominate term has deprived the buyer of substantially the whole benefit of the contract, the buyer will also be entitled to treat the contract as repudiated and reject the goods. The buyer will lose the right to reject the goods once the goods have been accepted, although the right to damages will remain.

10.4.1 The buyer's right to damages

A buyer might sue the seller for damages for non-delivery, for breach of warranty or for late delivery.

Section 51(1) gives the buyer the right to sue for damages for **non-delivery** where the seller wrongfully neglects or refuses to deliver the goods. This right would also be available if the seller breached a condition and the buyer treated the contract as repudiated. The measure of damages depends upon whether or not there was an available market for the goods in question. If there was no available market, the measure of damages is the estimated loss directly and naturally resulting in the ordinary course of events from the seller's breach of contract (s.51(2)).

Section 51(3) states that where there is an available market for the goods in question the measure of damages is *prima facie* to be ascertained by the difference between the contract price and the market price of the goods at the time or times when they ought to have been delivered or (if no time was fixed) at the time of the refusal to deliver. This 'market price' rule is the inverse of s.50(3). The principles set out in s.51 are very similar to the principles in s.50. In addition special damages might be available under s.54.

> ### Example
>
> On 1 September S agrees to sell a ton of wheat to B for £10 000. The date of delivery is fixed as 20 September but S does not deliver on that date. If there was an available market for the goods in question, then under s.51(3) B's right to damages would prima facie be as follows: (a) if the market price of this type of wheat was £9 500 on 20 September then B will be entitled to no damages; (b) if the market price had gone up to £11 000 then *prima facie* B will be entitled to damages of £1 000; (c) if the market price had remained at £10 000 B will be entitled to no damages. Whatever B's entitlement under s.51, special damages which were in the seller's contemplation at the time of the contract, such as additional transport costs, might be recoverable under s.54. If there is no available market then under s.51(2) B would be entitled to claim damages for foreseeable losses or losses which can reasonably be supposed to have been contemplated by S at the time of the contract, on ordinary contract principles. These damages might be in respect of profit lost by B, or the expenses of finding another seller of wheat.

Section 53 deals with damages where there has been a **breach of warranty**, or where the **buyer elects (or is compelled) to treat a breach of condition as a breach of warranty**. In these circumstances the buyer cannot reject the goods, but can either sue the seller for damages for breach of warranty or can deduct damages which would be payable for breach of warranty from the price the seller is to be paid (s.53(1)). The measure of damages is to be calculated under *Hadley v Baxendale* Rule 1 (s.53(2)). In the case of a breach of warranty of quality the buyer's loss is *prima facie* the difference between the value of the goods in the state they were in and the value which they would have had if the warranty had not been breached (s.53(3)).

In the following case the Court of Appeal did not apply the *prima facie* rule set out in s.53(3).

Bence Graphics International Ltd v *Fasson UK Ltd* [1997] 1 All ER 979 (Court of Appeal)

The defendants supplied cast vinyl film to the value of £564 328 to the claimants. This film was used by the claimants to manufacture decals, the purpose of which was to identify bulk containers in the shipping industry. A term of the contract provided that the film should remain in good legible condition for at least five years. In fact the film degraded prematurely and many of the decals became illegible. As a consequence the claimants were unable to sell on about £22 000 worth of film. Although the claimants received several complaints from customers, very few actual claims were made against the claimants. When the claimants sued for breach of warranty the defendants admitted liability. Applying s.53(3) the judge awarded damages of £564 328, plus interest as the amount of damages. He regarded this as the amount which the parties would have thought would have been recoverable for breach of warranty when the contract was made.

Held. Where goods containing a latent defect were sold, and the defect only became apparent after the goods were converted in a manner contemplated by both parties and then sold on, the measure of damages should be the actual loss suffered by the buyer under or arising from a breach of contract for onward sales. In these circumstances the prima facie rule was displaced. At the time of making the contract the parties were aware of facts which indicated to both of them that the loss would not be that set out in the prima facie rule in s.53(3). The parties would have contemplated the measure of damages as the claimants' liability to the ultimate user. The defendants knew that the claimants sold the film on and therefore knew that a breach of warranty would result in the claimants having to pay damages.

The Sale of Goods Act makes no special rules on damages when the goods are delivered late and the buyer accepts them. Damages for **late delivery** will therefore be assessed on ordinary contract principles. If time is of the essence and the buyer chooses to treat the late delivery as a breach of condition then damages will be available for non-delivery and quantified under s.51.

10.4.2 **The right to reject the goods**

The buyer will have the right to reject the goods in four circumstances. First, if the seller has breached a condition of the contract or delivered the wrong quantity of goods. Second, if the seller has breached an innominate term and this breach has deprived the buyer of substantially the whole benefit of the contract. Third, if the express or implied terms of the contract conferred upon the buyer a right to reject. Fourth, if the seller has repudiated the contract. However, a buyer who does not deal as a consumer cannot always reject for breach of condition or on account of the wrong quantity having been delivered. Section 15A provides that a buyer who does not deal as a consumer cannot reject on account of a breach of ss.13–15 if the breach was so slight as to make rejection unreasonable. Section 30(2A) provides that a buyer who does not deal as a consumer cannot reject on account of the wrong quantity having been delivered if the shortfall or excess is so slight as to make rejection unreasonable. As regards both sections the burden of proof is on the seller to show that the breach was so slight as to make rejection unreasonable. The complex definition of dealing as a consumer was considered in Chapter 5 at 5.6.1.3.

The buyer can reject the goods after they have been delivered and after ownership of the goods has passed to him, as long as he has not accepted the goods. When the buyer rightfully refuses to accept the goods he does not have to return them physically to the seller, it is enough that he lets the seller know that he is refusing to accept them (s.36). Having rightfully rejected the goods, the buyer can sue for damages for non-delivery. The buyer can also refuse to pay the price and recover any amount of the price which has already been paid.

If the buyer wrongfully rejects then the seller can treat the contract as repudiated. The seller will then be able to treat the contract as discharged and sue for damages for non-acceptance.

A buyer faced with a breach of condition does not have to reject the goods. The buyer may elect to treat the breach of condition as a breach of warranty and sue for damages instead (s.11(2)).

10.4.3 **Acceptance of the goods**

Acceptance of the goods by the buyer is highly significant because once goods sold under a non-severable contract have been accepted, a breach of condition by the seller can only be treated by the buyer as a breach of warranty. The buyer will therefore be able to claim damages for the breach of warranty but will not be able to reject the goods and treat the contract as repudiated (s.11(4)).

Under s.35 a buyer is deemed to have accepted the goods when:

(a) he intimates to the seller that he has accepted them (s.35(1)(a));

(b) when the goods have been delivered to him and he does any act in relation to them which is inconsistent with the ownership of the seller (s.35(1)(b));

(c) when after the lapse of a reasonable time the buyer retains the goods without intimating to the seller that he is rejecting them (s.35(4)).

The buyer would intimate to the seller that he is accepting the goods by letting the seller know that the goods have been accepted or by giving the seller the impression that they have been accepted. Where goods are delivered to the buyer and he has not previously examined them, the buyer will not be deemed to have accepted the goods by intimating acceptance to the seller unless he has had a reasonable opportunity to examine the goods to see whether they are in conformity with the contract (s.35(2)). If the buyer deals as a consumer he cannot lose this right conferred by s.35(2) (s.35(3)).

A buyer will be deemed to have accepted goods delivered to him when in relation to the goods he does an act which is inconsistent with the seller's continuing ownership. Such an act would be inconsistent with the seller's right to have the goods returned in much the same condition as they were in when delivered. It might, for example, take the form of selling the goods on, or using them or asking for them to be repaired. (Although s.35(6), which was added by the Sale and Supply of Goods Act 1994, tells us that neither asking the seller to repair the goods nor delivering the goods to a sub-buyer are necessarily to be taken as acceptance of the goods.) However, a buyer will not be deemed to have accepted the goods in this way unless he has had a reasonable opportunity to examine the goods to see whether they are in conformity with the contract (s.35(2)). A buyer who deals as a consumer cannot lose this right (s.35(3)).

A buyer who retains the goods for more than a reasonable time, whether dealing as a consumer or not, can be deemed to have accepted the goods even though he has not had a chance to examine the goods to see whether they are in conformity with the contract. However, whether or not the buyer has had a reasonable opportunity of examining the goods to see whether they are in conformity with the contract is material in deciding what amounts to a reasonable time (s.35(5)). A term of the contract which fixed a date for rejection would be held to be effective, as long as it was not an exclusion clause. If it was an exclusion clause then it could be effective against a buyer who did not deal as a consumer as long as it satisfied the UCTA 1977 requirement of reasonableness, but could not be effective against a buyer who did deal as a consumer.

The meaning of s.35 was considered in the following cases.

Truk (UK) Ltd v Tokmakidis GmbH
[2000] 1 Lloyd's Rep 543

The claimants, an English company, contracted to supply and fit towing and lifting equipment to a chassis supplied by the defendants, a German company. This was a sale of goods. The essence of the contract was the delivery and sale of the lifting and towing equipment, which would allow broken down HGV vehicles to be recovered. The claimants delivered the vehicle on 14 June 1996. However, the contract was breached in that the vehicle did not comply with certain guidelines specified in the contract. The defendants had bought the goods for resale. The contract envisaged that the resale of the vehicle might take more than six months, in that it provided that the price should be paid six months after delivery or on resale, whichever was sooner. The claimants had not intimated that they were rejecting until they discovered, in December 1996, that the vehicle did not comply with the contract specifications. (A potential buyer had pointed this out.) The parties then entered into negotiations which lasted until July 1997, when the defendants rejected the goods and refused to accept redelivery of a repaired vehicle.

Held. A reasonable time in which to intimate rejection had not passed. When goods are sold for resale, defects in the goods are often only discovered when the sub-buyer examines the goods. Therefore, a reasonable time in which to intimate rejection of the goods would usually be the time which it would be expected would be needed to resell the goods plus an additional period in which the sub-purchaser →

might inspect them and try them out. (If the vehicle had not been for resale, a month or two might have been a reasonable time on these facts, although discussions about remedying defects might have extended this period.) In July 1997 the defendants were still entitled to reject because they had done nothing to affirm the contract. Nor were they deemed to have accepted the goods by failing to reject them within a reasonable time. They had reserved their position while they were discovering what was wrong and negotiating, and they were allowed a reasonable time for that.

Clegg v Andersson [2003] EWCA Civ 320, [2003] 2 Lloyd's Rep 32 (Court of Appeal)

In December 1999 Clegg agreed to buy a new Malo 42 yacht from Andersson for £236 000. The shoal draught keel was to be in accordance with Malo's specification. Malo delivered the yacht to Andersson on 25 July 2000 and he delivered the yacht to Clegg on 12 August 2000. At the time of delivery Andersson told Clegg that the yacht's keel was considerably heavier than the weight prescribed by Malo's specification. This extra weight caused the yacht to sit low in the water. Having taken the yacht on an eight-day cruise to Falmouth and Alderney, Clegg returned it to Andersson, saying that he liked the yacht and the way it sailed. Later Clegg complained about the extra weight, which gave the yacht too much stability, a matter which affected sailing performance and the rig loads. Andersson wrote to Clegg saying that Malo would reduce the weight of the keel. Clegg asked to delay this work until after the Southampton boat show, adding that he wanted time to discuss the problem with his legal advisors and others. After considerable correspondence between Andersson and Clegg, about the overweight keel, its consequences and possible remedies, Clegg rejected the yacht on 6 March 2001. The trial judge found that there was no breach of s.14(2) SGA and that even if there had been Clegg would be deemed to have accepted the yacht, and therefore lost the right to reject in all three ways set out in s.35 SGA. An appeal was made to the Court of Appeal.

Held. (i) The yacht was not of satisfactory quality. The reasonable person would not regard it as satisfactory because its overweight keel affected its safety and would need considerable remedial work.

(ii) Clegg had not intimated his acceptance of the yacht under s.35(1)(a). First, Clegg's statement of late August 2000 that he liked the yacht was counter-

balanced by his requests for further information. Nor did a letter of 13 January 2001, informing Andersson that Clegg intended to move the yacht to Portugal or Gibraltar in early May, intimate acceptance. The letter did not indicate that this would be done if the results of the testing of the yacht were unsatisfactory. Finally, leaving personal possessions on the yacht could not intimate acceptance in the light of the outstanding request for further information.

(iii) Clegg had not accepted the yacht under s.35(1)(b). Property in the yacht had passed to Clegg and he had done nothing which would be inconsistent with the ownership of the seller. (The reversionary interest of the seller should the yacht be rejected.) Insuring the yacht would not affect Anderson's reversionary interest. Furthermore, he had to insure the yacht because the loan agreement under which Clegg borrowed the money to buy the yacht required him to insure it.

(iv) Clegg had not accepted the yacht under s.35(4) by keeping it for more than a reasonable time without intimating his rejection of it. Section 59 SGA provides that what is a reasonable time is a question of fact. Section 35(5) provides that whether or not the buyer has had a reasonable time to inspect the goods is only one of the questions to be answered in deciding whether there has been acceptance under s.35(4) and that s.35(6) shows that time taken by Clegg requesting or agreeing to repairs, and for carrying them out, should not be counted. As Clegg had not received all the information about modification or repair until 15 February 2001, only three weeks had elapsed before he rejected on 6 March 2001 and this did not exceed a reasonable time for the purposes of s.35(4).

(v) Lady Justice Hale said, 'If a buyer is seeking information which the seller has agreed to supply which will enable the buyer to make a properly informed choice between acceptance, rejection or cure, and if cure in what way, he cannot have lost his right to reject.'

Jones v Gallagher [2004] EWCA Civ 10, [2004] WL 62087 (Court of Appeal) considered this statement too wide. The case concerned kitchen units which had a patent defect in that they plainly did not match the colour of the existing units, as the contract specified that they should. The buyer did not finally reject for some months, and by this time had lost the right to reject under s.35(4). The buyer could therefore receive damages but could not reject and recover the whole contract price. Buxton LJ said that s.35(6) provides that the right to reject is not lost merely because repair is requested. It did not say that it was impossible to lose the right to reject during a period of complaint and request for remuneration. Commenting on Hale LJ's statement in *Clegg*, he said, 'I am sure that Hale LJ did not intend to go so far as to say that it was generally impossible to lose the right to reject while a buyer was still seeking information.' It seems likely that Hale LJ's statement should be restricted to s.35(4), so that time would not run against a buyer, for the purposes of s.35(4), while the buyer was seeking the type of information to which she referred.

In the following case, the House of Lords considered whether a buyer who had requested that faulty goods be repaired could later reject the repaired goods on account of the seller refusing to disclose what had been wrong with them.

J & H Ritchie Ltd v *Lloyd Ltd* [2007] UKHL 9

A farmer bought equipment made up of a seed drill and harrow for slightly over £14 000. He knew that the goods had been repossessed from another farmer. The goods were modified slightly to suit the second farmer's requirements. On the first day of use the farmer noticed that the harrow was vibrating but he could not see why. After two more days' use he realised that the problem was serious and stopped using the equipment. With the farmer's agreement, the sellers detached the harrow from the equipment and replaced it with a second-hand harrow so that the farmer could carry on planting his crops. The sellers discovered that the problem was due to missing bearings – a major defect. The sellers repaired the harrow, although the consequences of repair had never been agreed with the farmer. When the harrow was ready for collection the buyer asked what had been wrong with it. The sellers' workshop supervisor refused to tell him, but merely said that the harrow had been repaired to 'factory gate specification'. The buyer then asked for an engineer's report but the sellers refused to provide one. Informally, the farmer was told by those who had been repairing the harrow that the problem was caused by missing bearings. The farmer was unsure what problems this might cause, as he had used the harrow for three days without the missing bearings. He was also concerned that any problems caused would not become apparent until the following spring, when the equipment would be used again. The farmer therefore rejected the goods on the grounds that he had not been given the information which he had asked for.

Held. The farmer had not accepted the goods and so he could reject them.

Lord Hope said that although s.35(6)(a) of the Sale of Goods Act 1979 provided that merely asking for a repair did not necessarily amount to acceptance, the Act did not set out what the position would be after a buyer had asked for or agreed to a repair. He thought that the contract under which the equipment was sold contained an implied condition that the sellers would tell the buyer what the problem had been. This term had been breached and so the farmer was not in a position to make an informed judgment as to whether or not he should accept the repaired goods. The implied term arose because, in the circumstances of the case, every buyer would have sought it and no reasonable seller could refuse it. However, if the nature of the defect and the expense of correcting it had been obvious, a buyer who allowed the seller to repair the goods would have impliedly agreed that he would accept and pay for the goods once they had been repaired. Lord Scott said that he was in complete agreement with Lord Hope's judgment.

Lord Rodger, like Lord Hope, began by noting the effect of s.35(6)(a) of the Sale of Goods Act 1979. He thought that a second contract to have the harrow repaired had been created. He noted several terms which would be implied into this second contract. First, a term would be implied requiring the buyer to accept the goods once they had been properly repaired. If, on the other hand, the sellers did not perform the repair, the farmer could regard this as a repudiatory breach of the repair contract and consequently rescind the contract of sale. Significantly, he also thought that the repair contract contained an implied term that the sellers would tell the buyer what the fault had been. As this term had been breached, the repair contract had been breached and the farmer could refuse to collect the harrow. While the repairs were being carried out, the repair contract would have prevented the farmer from terminating the contract of sale. But the breach of the repair contract freed the farmer from this limitation and entitled him to terminate the contract of sale. Lord Brown also thought that the sellers breached a term of the repair contract and that this meant that they could not compel the buyers to take delivery for a second time. Lord Mance's judgment was similar to that of Lord Rodger.

COMMENT This case strongly suggests that, by asking for a repair, a buyer would impliedly agree not to reject while the repair was being carried out, and also agree not to reject if the repair was properly carried ➜

out and the buyer was told what the problem had been. This is likely to be the most important aspect of the case. The actual decision will rarely be applied, as few sellers are likely to conduct a repair and then refuse to say what the original fault was.

A proposed EC Directive on Consumer Sales will require the current law on acceptance to be changed when the buyer is a consumer. The proposals, and the way in which the Law Commission thinks they should be implemented, are explored below at 10.4.6.7.

Prior to amendments to the Sale of Goods Act made in 1994, a buyer who accepted part of the goods could not reject any of the goods. (This was not the case where the contract was severable or where the buyer was rejecting on account of the seller having delivered too large a quantity.) Section 35A now deals with the position where the seller commits a breach of contract by delivering goods which are not in conformity with the contract. If this breach only affects some of the goods but would give the buyer the right to reject all of the goods, the buyer can:

(i) reject all of the goods,
(ii) accept the goods which do conform to the contract and reject those which do not, or
(iii) accept all of the goods which do conform to the contract as well as some of those which do not.

What the buyer cannot do is reject some of the goods which are unaffected by the breach once other unaffected goods have been accepted. If the breach affects all of the goods the buyer can reject all of the goods or reject some while accepting others.

However, this right of partial rejection will not apply where the goods form one commercial unit as s.35(7) provides that:

'Where the contract is for the sale of goods making one or more commercial units, a buyer accepting any goods included in a unit is deemed to have accepted all the goods making the unit; and in this subsection "commercial unit" means a unit division of which would materially impair the value of the goods or the character of the unit.'

The Law Commission, at whose suggestion the subsection was included, gave as examples of a commercial unit, a pair of shoes, a set of encyclopedias, or a component in a car. So a buyer who had bought a set of encyclopedias, and who had accepted the first

volume, would be deemed to have accepted the later volumes, even if their pages were blank. Although this acceptance would prevent the buyer from rejecting the later volumes it would not of course prevent him from suing for damages for breach of warranty.

Earlier in this chapter we saw that if an instalment contract was severable a buyer could in certain circumstances reject later instalments even if he had already accepted some earlier instalments. Prior to the amendments made by the Sale and Supply of Goods Act 1994, a buyer who accepted one instalment of an indivisible contract could not reject later deliveries even for breach of condition. Now, unless the contract is for the sale of a commercial unit, even a buyer under an indivisible contract can have the right to reject later instalments despite having accepted earlier ones.

10.4.4 Rejection in other supply contracts

The rules on acceptance of the goods which we have just considered apply only to contracts which can be classified as contracts of sale of goods. Where the contract is one of hire, hire-purchase or for the transfer of the property in goods then the provisions of the SGA 1979 will not apply. In these contracts the right to treat the contract as repudiated will be lost once the contract has been affirmed. (However, in *Jones v Gallagher* the Court of Appeal applied s.35 SGA 1979 to a breach of ss.3 and 4 SGSA 1982. This appears to have been no more than a mistake.) There are no statutory rules on the meaning of affirmation. General common law principles regard affirmation as a matter of choice so that a person only affirms a contract when, knowing of the breach, his conduct indicates that he intends to go on with the contract. When a customer in a contract other than a sale of goods does rightfully treat the contract as repudiated there is no automatic right to regain all money paid. The customer will only be entitled to a full refund of the price if there has been a total failure of consideration. (See *Yeoman Credit Ltd v Waragowski* in Chapter 14 at 14.1.9.6.)

A proposed EU Directive on Consumer Sales will require the current law on affirmation to be changed when the buyer is a consumer. The proposals, and the way in which the Law Commission thinks they should be implemented, are explored below at 10.4.6.7.

10.4.5 Specific performance

Where the seller is in breach of an obligation to deliver specific or ascertained goods, s.52 allows the court to order specific performance of the contract. However, the court will only order this if it thinks fit to do so. In Chapter 7 at 7.2.4 we examined the circumstances in which specific performance will not be ordered.

10.4.6 Additional rights of buyers in consumer cases

In March 2002 the SGA 1979 was amended to introduce Part 5A of the Act, ss.48A–48F. Before examining the details of these sections, it is very important to note that the rights which they confer are **additional** to any other rights which the Act might confer. The new Part 5A does not therefore diminish any existing rights gained under the Act.

Section 48A sets out the two requirements for Part 5A to apply. First, the buyer must deal as a consumer. Second, the goods must not conform to the contract of sale at the time of delivery.

10.4.6.1 Dealing as a consumer

Section 61(5A) of the Act refers us to Part 1 of the Unfair Contract Terms Act 1977 to find the meaning of dealing as a consumer. In Chapter 5 at 5.6.1.3 we saw that s.12(1) UCTA 1977 provides that a person deals as a consumer if: (a) he neither makes the contract in the course of a business nor holds himself out as doing so; and (b) the other party does make the contract in the course of a business. We also saw that if a company (rather than an individual) is to be regarded as dealing as a consumer the goods passing under or in pursuance of the contract must be of a type ordinarily supplied for private use or consumption. The circumstances in which a business can deal as a consumer are complex and were examined in greater detail at 5.6.3.

10.4.6.2 Lack of conformity with the contract

Section 48F provides that the goods do not conform to a contract of sale if there is, in relation to the goods, a breach of an express term of the contract or a term implied by ss.13–15 of the Act. Section 48A(3) provides that goods which do not conform to the contract at any time within the period of six months starting with the date on which the goods were delivered to the buyer must be taken not to have conformed at that date. So when there is a lack of conformity within six months of the date of delivery there is a presumption that they did not conform at the date of delivery. However, s.48A(4) provides that this presumption can be rebutted in two circumstances: (a) if it is established that the goods did conform to the contract at the date of delivery; or (b) if the presumption is incompatible with the nature of the goods or the nature of the lack of conformity.

10.4.6.3 The hierarchy of rights

Having established that the buyer dealt as a consumer and that the goods did not conform to the contract, ss.48A–48F set out a hierarchy of rights.

Repair or replacement of the goods

Section 48B(1) provides that the buyer may require the seller to repair or replace the goods. If the buyer does request either of these remedies then s.48B(2) provides that the seller must: (a) repair or replace the goods within a reasonable time but without causing significant inconvenience to the buyer; and (b) bear any necessary costs incurred in so doing (including in particular the cost of labour, materials or postage). Repair is defined by s.61(1) as meaning bringing the goods into conformity with the contract. In *Wittmer v Gebr. Weber GmbH* [2011] WLR (D) 210 the First Chamber of the Court of European Justice held that where consumer goods, installed in good faith by the consumer, were not in conformity with the contract under which the consumer had purchased them and were restored to conformity by way of replacement, the seller was obliged pursuant to [Directive 1999/44/EC which required Part 5A to be implemented] either to remove the goods from where they had been installed and to install the replacement goods there or else to bear the costs of that removal and installation. The seller could not refuse to replace the defective goods on the ground that the costs were disproportionate but it could limit the payment to a proportionate amount.

However, the right to repair or replacement is not absolute. Section 48B(3) provides that the buyer must not require the seller to repair or replace the goods in three circumstances: (a) if this would be impossible; (b) if this would be disproportionate in relation to the other of those remedies (that is to say, if repair was requested and this would be disproportionate to replacement, and vice versa); (c) if it would be disproportionate in comparison with either of the lower level remedies, reduction in the purchase price or rescission. Section 48B(4) tells us that one remedy is disproportionate in comparison to another if it imposes costs on the seller which, in comparison to the costs imposed by the other remedy, are unreasonable, taking into account: (a) the value which the goods would have if they conformed to the contract of sale; (b) the significance of the lack of conformity: and (c) whether the other remedy could be effected without significant inconvenience to the buyer. Section 59 provides that what is a reasonable time is a question of fact. Section 48B(5) provides that any question as to what is a reasonable time or as to what is significant inconvenience is to be determined by reference to: (a) the nature of the goods; and (b) the purpose for which the goods were acquired.

Section 48D provides that if the buyer requires the seller to repair or replace the goods he must give the seller a reasonable time in which to do this before rejecting the goods and terminating the contract for breach of condition. So if the lack of conformity was caused by a breach of s.14(2), a buyer who has requested repair or replacement can no longer reject the goods under s.14(2) until the seller has been given a reasonable time in which to repair or replace the goods as requested. Nor can a buyer who has requested repair or replacement request the other of these two remedies (repair or replacement) until the seller has had a reasonable time in which to effect the remedy requested.

Reduction of the price or rescission of the contract

Section 48C(1) sets out the secondary remedies of the buyer, namely: (a) requiring the seller to reduce the purchase price of the goods in question by an appropriate amount; and (b) rescinding the contract with regard to those goods. However, s.48C(2) provides that these secondary remedies are available in only two circumstances: (a) that the buyer can require neither repair nor replacement because the remedies are either impossible or disproportionate in relation to one of the secondary remedies; or (b) the buyer has required the seller to repair or replace the goods, but the seller is in breach of the s.48B(2)(a) requirement to do so within a reasonable time and without significant inconvenience to the buyer.

In Chapter 6 at 6.1.3 we examined the meaning of rescission in relation to misrepresentation, and

the ways in which the right to rescind can be lost. It should be stressed that rescission has a different, statutory, meaning here and that the right to rescind will not be lost in the ways explained at 6.1.3.1. The meaning of rescission in ss.48A–48F is much closer to treating the contract as repudiated for breach of condition. However, s.48C(3) provides a very significant difference. It provides that if the buyer rescinds under s.48C(1)(b) any reimbursement to him may be reduced to take account of the use he has had of the goods since they were delivered to him. There is no such concept when a contract is treated as repudiated for breach of condition or breach of an innominate term. However, as we saw at 10.4.3, where a condition is breached in a contract of sale, s.11(4) will apply to prevent a buyer who has accepted the goods from rejecting the goods and treating the contract as terminated. Section 11(4) will not apply to ss.48A–48F because lack of conformity with the contract is not a condition. Indeed, the main use of Part 5A may be to allow a consumer to rescind the contract even after he would have been deemed to have accepted the goods.

10.4.6.4 **Powers of the court**

Section 48E sets out additional powers of the court where proceedings have been brought under ss.48A–48F. Section 48E(2) allows, if the buyer applies for it, specific performance of the seller's obligation to repair or replace as requested under s.48B. Section 48E(4) applies if the buyer asks for any of the four remedies set out in ss.48B and 48C but the court decides that another ss.48B or 48C remedy is more appropriate. The court may then award the other remedy instead. Section 48E(6) allows the court to grant any ss.48B or 48C remedy unconditionally or on such terms and conditions as to damages, payment of the price or otherwise as it thinks just.

10.4.6.5 **Likely effect of Part 5A of the Act**

The effect of Part 5A is likely to be limited. First, as we have seen, the rights which it confers are additional rights in consumer cases. These rights will not apply in non-consumer cases. Furthermore, the existing rights to terminate the contract and reject the goods for breach of condition will remain a consumer's strongest remedies where a breach of ss.13–15 of the Act has occurred. Even if a consumer buyer is prevented from rejecting the goods because the goods have been accepted the right to damages will remain. The Part 5A remedies might be most useful where a consumer wants to reject the goods but can no longer do so for breach of a condition on account of having accepted the goods. Part 5A might provide a backdoor means of rejecting the goods. However, it does not seem easy for a consumer to get to rescission under s.48C, as this is a secondary remedy. Furthermore, even if rescission is allowed under s.48C the reimbursement of the price to the buyer will take account of any use he has had of the goods. Perhaps courts will, in some cases, award an equal amount of damages to put rescission under ss.48A–48F on a par with rejecting the goods for breach of condition. (Although, of course, damages can be awarded in addition to rejection for breach of a condition.)

Part 5A is also likely to cause difficulties in that it raises many uncertainties. When the buyer rescinds under s.48C, how will the extent to which the reimbursement should be reduced be decided? If the buyer and seller cannot agree then more cases are likely to be taken to court. Similar difficulties are likely to arise in relation to the other secondary remedy, reduction of the purchase price. By how much will the price be reduced? The answer given by s.48C(1)(a) is by 'an appropriate amount'. But how is this to be calculated?

Example

Asif, a teacher, buys a car from a garage. After re-spraying the car and replacing the seats, Asif discovers that the car was not of satisfactory quality when sold because it had been rebuilt after being in a serious accident. Section 14(2) has clearly been breached. However, s.11(4) would prevent rejection for breach of condition if Asif had accepted the car. Asif would have been deemed to have accepted the car under s.35(1)(b). Damages would still be available to Asif but he would no longer be able to reject. Asif dealt as a consumer, and the car did not conform to the contract because s.14(2) was breached. Therefore, s.48A(1) and (2) would allow Asif the primary s.48B(1) remedies of repair and replacement. However, neither of these remedies is possible. (The car could not be replaced as it was specific goods. Repair would have to remove the lack of conformity, which would not be possible as the lack of conformity was caused by the car having been rebuilt after an accident.) Therefore, s.48C(2)(a) would allow Asif to choose between reduction of the purchase price

and rescission. Reduction of the price would put him in no better position than would damages for breach of s.14(2), to which he remains entitled. Asif could choose to rescind under s.48C(1)(b). The purchase price might be reduced to take account of any use of the car which he had had (s.48C(3)). However, the court could award Asif damages under s.48E(6).

10.4.6.6 Conformity with the contract in contracts other than sales of goods

The Supply of Goods and Services Act 1982 has been amended to include rules which are virtually identical to those contained in ss.48A–48F of the SGA 1979. However, these amendments do not apply to contracts of hire, but only to contracts for the transfer of property in goods. (For the different ways in which the SGSA 1982 classifies these contracts, see Chapter 8 at 8.3.) The new rules are contained in SGSA 1982 ss.11M–11S. Section 11S sets out the two circumstances in which goods do not conform to a contract for the supply or transfer of property in goods. The first is that there has been a breach of an express term or of one of the statutory implied terms as to correspondence with description, satisfactory quality, fitness for purpose or correspondence with sample. (These statutory implied terms are contained in ss.3–5 of the SGSA, see Chapter 8 at 8.3.2.) The second circumstance is that installation of the goods forms part of the contract for the transfer of goods, and the goods were installed in breach of s.13 SGSA or in breach of any term implied by any rule of law as to the manner in which the installation is carried out. (Section 13 SGSA is considered in Chapter 8 at 8.3.3.1.)

We saw above that in a sale of goods the new rules on conformity with the contract are most likely to be useful when a consumer buyer cannot reject the goods for breach of condition because he has accepted the goods. In a contract for the transfer of property in goods it is probably affirmation, rather than acceptance, which would prevent rejection for breach of condition. (See above at 10.4.4.) The new rules on lack of conformity are therefore most likely to be useful once the consumer has affirmed the contract.

Figure 10.1 shows an overview of the effect of Part V SGA.

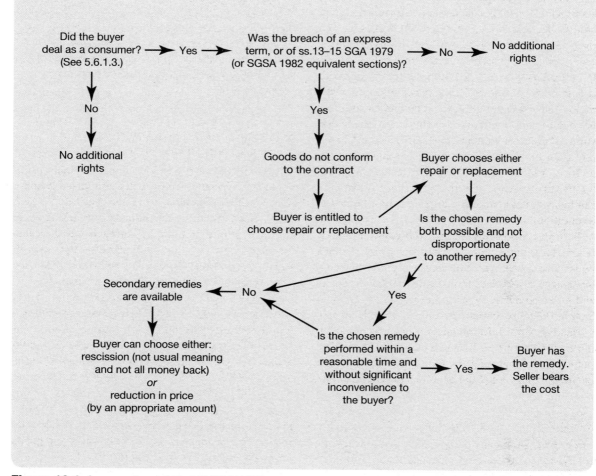

Figure 10.1 An overview of Part V SGA 1979

10.4.6.7 **Reform of consumer remedies**

Part 5A of the Sale of Goods Act 1979 was introduced in order to implement the EC 1999 Consumer Sales Directive (CSD). In October 2008 the European Commission published a proposal for a new directive on consumer rights. When the new CSD is finalised, it will have to be implemented by Member States in such a way that consumers in all EU countries have exactly the same rights in respect of faulty goods. The European Commission wants to harmonise consumer law across the EU and so it will not be possible for a Member State to give consumers more rights, or fewer rights, than those which will be contained in the CSD. As the new CSD is at present only a set of proposals, the precise rights which will have to be implemented

have not yet been finalised. The Law Commission has issued a consultation paper, Consultation Paper No. 188 Consumer Remedies for Faulty Goods, asking for views on what the new Directive should require and on how best to implement those requirements.

The Law Commission consultation paper recommends that consumers should retain a short-term right to reject. However, as some EU countries have such a right and others do not, this right might be lost if the new Directive considers the right to be inappropriate. The Law Commission also suggests that the normal period for rejection of goods, whether the goods were supplied under a contract of sale of goods or a contract for work and materials, should be 30 days from the date of delivery. However, this period might be increased or decreased, depending upon the circumstances. It might, for example, be increased if goods were bought in October as a Christmas present. It might be decreased if the goods were perishable or if the consumer carried out an act inconsistent with the seller's continuing ownership after noticing a defect. In its current form the CSD proposes that a consumer should not be able to reject the goods on account of a minor defect, but should instead be limited to repair or replacement of the goods. The Law Commission strongly proposes that the right of rejection should remain, even for minor defects.

Part 5A of the Sale of Goods Act 1979, as we have seen, sets out two first tier remedies (repair and replacement) and two second tier remedies (reduction of the purchase price and 'rescission'). A consumer can move from a first tier remedy to a second tier remedy where the seller has failed to conduct a repair within a reasonable time and without causing significant inconvenience to the buyer. In the context of failed repairs or replacements, there is little agreement as to what amounts to a reasonable time or significant inconvenience. The European Commission has proposed that a second tier remedy should be available if 'the same defect has reappeared more than once within a short period of time'. The Law Commission would prefer a second tier remedy to be available after two failed repairs or one failed replacement. Both the European Commission and the Law Commission thought that if the second tier remedy of 'rescission' was reached the refund of the purchase price should not be reduced to take account of the consumer's use of the goods. The Law Commission also wanted the six-month reversal of the burden of proof, which currently applies only when a remedy is being sought under Part 5A SGA, to apply to remedies not set out in Part 5A. It also thought that if the goods were repaired or replaced, the six-month time period should start again.

In conclusion, the Law Commission report proposed that consumers who bought defective goods should have three remedies available to them. First, the right to reject within 30 days and claim a full refund of the price. Second, the right to choose either repair or replacement. Third, the right to be able to move on to the second tier remedies of 'rescission' and reduction of the price after two failed repairs or one failed replacement. There is no doubt that the law in this area will have to change in order to implement the new CSD. However, at the time of writing it has not yet been decided what the finalised CSD will require.

10.5 AUCTION SALES

Section 57 of the Sale of Goods Act lays down the following rules about auction sales.

'(1) Where goods are put up for sale by auction in lots, each lot is *prima facie* deemed to be the subject of a separate contract of sale.

(2) A sale by auction is complete when the auctioneer announces its completion by the fall of the hammer, or in other customary manner, and until the announcement is made any bidder may retract his bid.

(3) A sale by auction may be notified to be subject to a reserve or upset price, and a right to bid may also be reserved expressly by or on behalf of the seller.

(4) Where a sale by auction is not notified to be subject to a right to bid by or on behalf of the seller, it is not lawful for the seller to bid himself or to employ any person to bid at the sale, or for the auctioneer knowingly to take any bid from the seller or any such person.

(5) A sale contravening (4) above may be treated as fraudulent by the buyer.

(6) Where, in respect of a sale by auction, a right to bid is expressly reserved (but not otherwise) the seller or any one person on his behalf may bid at the auction.'

As the property in the lot passes to the buyer at the fall of the hammer, it will then be too late for the auctioneer later to insist on conditions to be fulfilled before the buyer becomes the owner of the lot.

Dennant and Skinner v Collom
[1948] 2 All ER 29

A rogue bought several cars at an auction. After the sale the auctioneer allowed the rogue to take the cars away in return for a cheque. The auctioneer only did this when the rogue gave him a certificate which said that the property in the vehicles would not pass until the cheque was cleared. The rogue's cheque was dishonoured. The rogue sold one of the cars to a third party who sold it to the defendant. The auctioneer sued to get the car back.

Held. The auctioneer failed. The purchaser gained the property in the car at the fall of the hammer.

An auctioneer is, of course, an agent and as such he warrants his authority to sell the goods and that he does not know of any defects in the principal's title. (The agent's liability for breach of warranty of authority is considered in Chapter 11 at 11.3.1.) The auctioneer also undertakes to give possession of the goods in exchange for the price and that this possession will not be disturbed by either himself or the principal.

Where an auctioneer sells specific goods, without disclosing the name of the principal, he does not warrant that the principal owns the goods.

Benton v Campbell, Parker & Co Ltd
[1925] 2 KB 410

The defendants sold cars at auction. The claimant bought a car which had been put into the auction by S Co. The defendants did not reveal the name of S Co. The claimant paid the price to the defendants and after deducting their commission the defendants paid S Co for the car. It later transpired that S Co had not owned the car at the time of the auction as they had taken it on hire-purchase from B. B saw the car being driven by T, to whom the claimant had sold it, and claimed it back. The claimant refunded to T the price he had paid for the car and then sued the defendants for the price he had paid.

Held. The claimant did not succeed as he knew that the defendant was an auctioneer and that the sale was of specific goods. The defendant did not therefore warrant that the principal owned the goods.

The auctioneer has a right to sue the purchaser for the price, even if the purchaser has paid the principal directly. He also has a lien over the proceeds of sale to safeguard his commission and other charges. However, both of these rights can be excluded by agreement.

The auction particulars, or notices, may contain exclusion clauses. These clauses can be overridden by the auctioneer making an oral warranty. Exclusion clauses would also be subject to the Unfair Contract Terms Act 1977. In Chapter 8 we saw that a person who buys goods at an auction or by competitive tender is not in any circumstances to be regarded as dealing as a consumer for the purposes of the UCTA (UCTA s.12(2)).

The Auction (Bidding Agreements) Act 1969 makes it an offence for a dealer to give any person any consideration in return for not bidding at an auction. Both the dealer and the person who took the consideration can be banned from attending auctions for up to three years. The seller of the goods can avoid the contract and if it is not possible to reclaim the goods may recover any loss he has suffered (the difference between the sale price and the true price) from any party to the prohibited agreement.

Test your understanding 10.3

1 How will the buyer's damages for non-delivery by the seller be assessed **(a)** where there is no available market for the goods, and **(b)** where there is an available market for the goods?

2 How are damages for breach of warranty of quality of the goods to be assessed?

3 In what four circumstances will the buyer have a right to reject the goods?

4 What is the significance of the buyer having accepted the goods?

5 In what three ways can the buyer be deemed to have accepted the goods?

6 At an auction sale at what time does the property in the goods pass to the buyer?

10.6 INTERNATIONAL SALES

International sales of goods are usually made on special terms. The two most important sets of terms are fob (free on board) and cif (cost insurance and freight). An outline meaning of these special terms is set out below, but before we examine them we need to understand the legal significance of a bill of lading.

10.6.1 The bill of lading

A bill of lading is a document issued to a shipper of goods by the shipowner which states that certain goods have been delivered on board ship. It is signed by or on behalf of the shipowner and sets out the terms on which the goods are to be carried. Generally, a mate's receipt is issued when the goods are first loaded on board. The mate's receipt will note the condition of the goods loaded on board and these details will then be transferred to a bill of lading, which will be issued to the shipper when the ship leaves port.

A bill of lading has legal significance in three different ways. It is evidence of the contract of carriage, it is a receipt for the goods shipped and it is a document of title. Each of these matters needs to be considered in outline.

Although a bill of lading sets out the terms of the contract of carriage it is not the contract itself. The contract of carriage will be made when the ship is booked, and the bill of lading is not issued until the goods have been loaded on board. The bill of lading usually contains the terms of the contract of carriage and so, between the shipper of the goods and the shipowner, the bill of lading is very strong evidence of the contract of carriage. Once the bill of lading is transferred by the shipper to a third party, the third party will take over the contract of carriage and the bill of lading. The bill of lading then becomes conclusive evidence of the contract of carriage.

The bill of lading is a receipt for the goods shipped. If the bill is a **clean bill** it will state that the correct quantity of goods are shipped in apparent good order and condition. If the bill is '**claused**' or '**dirty**' it will specify the ways in which the goods did not appear to be in apparent good order or condition. It might for example state that some packages were broken or waterlogged. By issuing a clean bill of lading the shipper is not guaranteeing that the goods conform to the contract, but merely saying that the goods loaded on board outwardly appear to conform to the contract.

The Hague-Visby Rules, which govern most international sales of carriage by sea involving the United Kingdom, require a clean bill of lading to show four things: the 'leading marks' by which the goods can be identified; the quantity of goods shipped; the apparent order and condition of the goods; and the date on which the goods were shipped. If, upon arrival, the holder of the bill finds that the goods do not outwardly conform to the contract then the shipowner will be liable for issuing a clean bill of lading. If the goods do outwardly conform to the contract, but are found to have some defect which was not outwardly apparent, the shipowner will have no liability in respect of this defect. Between the shipper and the shipowner the bill of lading is only *prima facie* evidence of the quantity and apparent condition of the goods. Once the bill has been transferred to a third party it becomes conclusive evidence of these matters. The third party will take over the rights under the contract of carriage by virtue of s.2(1) of the Carriage of Goods by Sea Act 1992.

A bill of lading is said to be a document of title. This does not mean that the holder of the bill definitely has ownership of the goods to which the bill relates. It does mean that the holder has constructive possession of the goods and that the shipowner will acknowledge that the goods are now held on behalf of the holder of the bill. Mustill LJ in *Enichem Anic SpA v Ampelos Shipping Co Ltd, the Delfini* [1990] 1 Lloyd's Rep 252 said 'It [the bill of lading] is a symbol of constructive possession of the goods which (unlike many such symbols) can transfer constructive possession by endorsement and transfer: it is a transferable "key to the warehouse"'. The holder of the bill will therefore be entitled to take the goods from the ship and the shipowner should only allow the holder of the bill to do this. Very commonly the property in the goods passes to the buyer along with the bill of lading as this is what the parties intended. If the bill of lading is negotiable the buyer can transfer it to a third party. However, a bill of lading is not a negotiable instrument and so the description of a bill of lading as negotiable does not mean that a subsequent holder can have a better title than the person from whom he took the bill.

Section 19(2) provides that where the goods are shipped, and by the bill of lading the goods are deliverable to the order of the seller or his agent, the seller is *prima facie* taken to reserve the right of disposal. So where a bill of lading is made out to the order of the seller, the shipowner will only allow the seller or his agent to collect the goods. This would therefore show an intention that property was not to pass to the buyer. Property will not pass to the buyer until the seller has been paid the full price.

10.6.2 Fob (free on board) contracts

Where a contract is made on fob terms, the seller contracts to deliver the goods free on board a ship nominated by the buyer. Although such contracts are generally international sales this is not always the case. Under an fob contract it is the duty of the buyer to nominate an effective ship, and traditionally it is also the buyer's duty to make the contract of carriage with the shipowner. If the buyer wants the goods to be insured whilst they are being shipped then it is up to the buyer to arrange insurance. However, s.32(3) provides that, unless otherwise agreed, where goods are sent by the seller to the buyer by a route involving sea transit, under circumstances in which it is usual to insure, the seller must give such notice to the buyer as may enable him to insure them during sea transit. If the seller does not do this then the goods are at his risk during the period of sea transit. As a minimum the seller would need to tell the buyer the details of the cargo, the name of the ship and the ports of loading and destination. It is the seller's duty to deliver the goods on board ship by passing them over the ship's rail and also to pay the loading charges.

Once the goods have been put on board the ship, delivery of the goods is completed. The port identified in an fob contract is the port at which the goods are to be loaded.

It is not always the case that it is the buyer's duty to make the contract of carriage. In **Pyrene & Co Ltd v Scindia Steam Navigation Co Ltd** [1954] 2 All ER 158 Devlin J identified three types of fob contracts. Under Devlin's 'classic' fob contract the seller makes the contract of carriage, booking a ship nominated by the buyer. When the seller delivers the goods on board the ship he is given a bill of lading by the shipowner and he forwards this to the buyer. The bill of lading will give the buyer constructive possession of the goods. Under Devlin's 'fob with additional services' the seller again makes the contract of carriage, booking a ship nominated by the buyer, and possibly arranges insurance. The seller has the bill of lading made out in his own name. This indicates a presumption that the property in the goods is not to pass to the buyer upon shipment of the goods (s.19(2) SGA). If the carriage costs increase the buyer must pay the extra amount. In Devlin's third category, 'strict fob', the buyer makes the contract of carriage. The seller puts the goods on board and gets a mate's receipt for them. The seller sends the mate's receipt to the buyer who uses it to get a bill of lading.

When the seller does make the contract of carriage s.32(2) SGA requires him to make a reasonable contract, having regard to the nature of the goods and the circumstances of the case. If, for example, the goods were of a type which would be needed to be kept at a certain temperature, the seller would have to make a contract which ensured that the shipowner would keep the goods at this temperature.

Unless the parties agree otherwise it is the buyer's duty to nominate an effective ship, that is to say a ship which is both physically capable of carrying the goods and ready and willing to do so. The nominated ship must arrive in time to allow the seller to load the goods on board within the contract period. This duty is a condition and so if an effective ship is not nominated in time the seller can treat the contract as repudiated. The buyer can nominate an alternative ship as long as this is done in time. Once the nominated ship arrives at the port, it is the seller's duty to load the goods on board within the shipment period. Failure to load on time will be a breach of condition entitling the buyer to treat the contract as repudiated.

Example

Goods are sold on strict fob terms Hull, September shipment. The parties have therefore agreed that: the buyer is to make the contract of carriage; the port named, Hull, is the port where the goods are to be loaded; the buyer must nominate an effective ship which will arrive at Hull in time for the seller to load the goods before the end of September; the seller must load the goods on board before the end of September. As the buyer made the contract of carriage, the seller takes a mate's receipt for the goods once they are loaded on board. The seller will probably send the mate's receipt to the buyer, who will then have a duty to pay the price of the goods. The buyer will use the mate's receipt to obtain a bill of lading, which will give the buyer the right to take possession of the goods at the port of arrival.

When the goods are not loaded within the shipment period disputes commonly arise as to whose fault this was.

Bunge & Co Ltd v Tradax England Ltd
[1975] 2 Lloyd's Rep 235

One thousand tons of barley were sold on fob terms. The buyers nominated a ship in due time but the ship was delayed and so they nominated another ship. Delivery of the goods was to be made between the 1 and 20 January 1973, both dates inclusive. The second ship nominated was expected to be ready to load on Friday 19 January. The sellers protested that this would not give them time to load all of the goods within the shipment period, which ended at midnight on Saturday 20 January. The ship arrived at 1500 hours on Friday 19 January and only 110 tons could be loaded that day as the normal working hours ended at 1700 hours. The buyers agreed to pay overtime rates so that the barley could be loaded on Saturday 20 January but it rained all day and nothing more was loaded.

Held. The sellers had an obligation to begin loading as soon as the ship arrived but they had no obligation to continue loading after the expiry of the shipment time. Both the obligation to deliver and the obligation to accept delivery were strictly confined to the contract time. The buyers had no right to demand shipment outside this time.

When the contract is governed by English law then the SGA 1979 will apply. In an international contract almost any description of the goods is likely to be regarded as a condition. The goods will of course have to be of satisfactory quality if they are sold in the course of a business. In an international sale it is not, as it is in a domestic sale of goods, at the time of delivery that the goods must be of satisfactory quality. The goods must remain satisfactory until they arrive at the port of destination and are disposed of.

Mash & Murrell Ltd v Joseph I Emanuel Ltd [1961] 1 All ER 485 (Court of Appeal)

The defendants sold the claimants 2 000 bags of spring crop potatoes. The potatoes had been exported from Cyprus and were due to be delivered to Liverpool. The defendants knew that the claimants would sell the potatoes on for human consumption. Upon arrival the potatoes were not of merchantable (now satisfactory) quality.

Held. Diplock J held that in an international sale the goods must remain of merchantable quality until a reasonable time has elapsed for their disposal at the port of arrival.

COMMENT This was not an fob contract. However, the principle of the case applies to fob contracts so that the seller must put the goods on board ship in such a state that they will remain of satisfactory quality until a reasonable time after their arrival. The Court of Appeal approved Diplock's judgment. However, the case was reversed on its facts. The Court of Appeal found that the potatoes were loaded in good condition but that they had deteriorated because of excessive heat and poor ventilation on the voyage. The buyer therefore did not succeed against the seller although he would have been able to succeed against the shipowner.

The SGA rules on the passing of the property and the risk, which we examined in the previous chapter, will apply to fob contracts. Subject to s.20A, no property can pass until the goods are ascertained. We saw that once goods have become ascertained the property in them will pass when the parties intend it to pass under s.17, but that if the parties do not express an intention then the five rules of presumed intention contained in s.18 will determine when the property in the goods is to pass. When a contract is made on fob terms the s.18 rules of presumed intention are not needed. If the parties have not expressly indicated otherwise, it is taken that they intend the property in the goods to pass when the goods pass over the ship's rail. However, if the seller has the bill of lading made out in his own name, rather than in the buyer's name, then it is presumed that the seller is reserving title to

the goods until the price has been paid (s.19(2) SGA). Under s.20 SGA the risk will pass at the same time as the property in the goods. However, in fob contracts risk passes when the goods go over the ship's rail even in circumstances where the property did not pass as this is taken to be the intention of the parties.

10.6.3 Cif (cost, insurance and freight) contracts

Under a cif contract it is the seller's duty to make the shipping contract, insure the goods and pay the freight. Having done this the seller must then deliver to the buyer three documents: the bill of lading, a policy of insurance and an invoice for the goods. The buyer must accept and pay for these documents if they are in order, even if the goods have been lost or damaged. The named port is the port of destination, not the port of loading. A cif contract is always an international sale.

Example

One thousand tons of wheat are sold cif New York. The seller makes the shipping contract and pays all the costs of this. Once the goods are loaded the seller will be given a bill of lading. The seller insures the goods, acquiring a policy of insurance. The seller sends the bill of lading, the policy of insurance and an invoice for the goods to the buyer. The buyer must accept the three documents and pay for them, if they are in order. Once the goods arrive in New York the bill of lading will entitle the buyer to gain possession of them.

If the shipping documents are not in order, then the buyer has no duty to accept them and can treat the contract as repudiated. The bill of lading must therefore be clean and must show the date on which the goods were shipped. A policy of insurance rather than a certificate of insurance must be delivered. Even if the buyer knows that the goods have been lost before their arrival, there is no right to refuse to accept and pay for the documents.

Manbre Sacharine Co Ltd v Corn Products Co Ltd [1919] 1 KB 198

The claimants claimed damages for failure to deliver goods. The defendants had made two cif contracts to sell starch and syrup. The price included war risk insurance. One of the ships carrying the goods which had been appropriated to the contract was sunk by a

→

German submarine and some of the goods were not delivered. Both parties knew of the ship's loss at the time when the seller presented the documents. The buyer refused to take the documents.

Held. The buyers were in breach of contract by not taking the documents and paying the price. The seller's obligation was to deliver the documents rather than the goods. All the buyers could call for was the delivery of the documents.

Although this case seems particularly hard on the buyer, it should not ordinarily cause any inconvenience. The goods have been insured by the seller, and the buyer takes over the policy of insurance and the contract of carriage. If the goods are damaged or lost due to the negligence of the shipowner, then the buyer will sue the shipowner on the contract of carriage. If the goods are lost or damaged in some other way then the buyer will claim on the policy of insurance.

The buyer's right to reject the documents if they are not in order is quite distinct from his right to reject the goods if they do not conform to the contract. The shipowner who issues a bill of lading will merely be stating that the goods which were loaded on board outwardly appeared to conform to the contract. The shipowner would therefore indicate, for example, that the right number of boxes were delivered and that the boxes were labelled and not damaged. If the buyer later discovers that the goods shipped are not of satisfactory quality, or do not match the contract description, the shipowner will have no liability for this unless the breach was outwardly apparent. However, the buyer will be able to treat the contract as repudiated and reject the goods, even though the property in the goods may have passed to the buyer when he discovers the seller's breach.

In a cif contract the property in ascertained goods will pass when the parties intend that it should under s.17 SGA 1979. The parties might well express an intention. However, if they do not then the property will pass when the shipping documents are delivered to the buyer and the price is paid. Property in unascertained goods cannot pass, subject to s.20A SGA 1979, until the goods are ascertained (SGA 1979 s.16). When unascertained goods are sold on cif terms the seller has to appropriate goods matching the description to the contract, so that the buyer knows it is only these goods which can be delivered. In a domestic sale this would pass property under s.18 Rule 5, but in a cif contract this will not be the case. Section 17 will apply as the parties will have shown an intention

that the property is to pass when the price is paid in return for the documents. No matter when the property in the goods passes, the risk passes to the buyer as soon as the goods are delivered on board ship. This is because from that time the buyer has taken over the contract of carriage and the rights under the policy of insurance. Cif buyers commonly buy goods which are afloat, having already begun their journey. When this happens the risk passes to the buyer retrospectively from the time of loading. As the rights under the contract of carriage and the policy of insurance also pass retrospectively this should not cause the buyer any problems.

The property in the goods is likely to have passed to the buyer by the time that he gets physical possession of the goods and the right to examine them. However, if a condition relating to the description or the quality of the goods has been breached the buyer can still reject the goods, even if he appears to have accepted them. (The buyer will commonly have done an act inconsistent with the seller's continuing ownership, by pledging the documents with a bank to raise money to finance the purchase of the goods, and therefore seem to be deemed to have accepted the goods. See above at 10.4.3.) However, the property passed to the buyer only conditionally on the goods conforming to the contract. If the goods do not conform to the contract then the buyer can reject the goods and pass the property back to the seller (*Kwei Tek Chao v British Traders and Shippers Ltd* [1954] 2 QB 459).

Cif contracts are more attractive to small buyers who do not want to do anything other than pay the price for the goods. Fob contracts are generally preferred by large-scale importers who can arrange favourable shipping terms or carry the goods on their own ships.

Test your understanding 10.4

1 To what extent can a bill of lading be taken as representing the contract of carriage?

2 What is meant by the bill of lading being a document of title?

3 What is meant by (a) a clean bill of lading? (b) a claused bill of lading?

4 What are the duties of the buyer and the seller under an fob contract?

5 What are the duties of the buyer and the seller under a cif contract?

Key points

Duties of the parties

■ The seller has a duty to deliver the goods. The buyer has duties to accept and pay for the goods and to take delivery of them.

■ Unless otherwise agreed, the seller's duty to deliver the goods and the buyer's duty to pay for them are concurrent conditions. This means that the seller must be ready and willing to deliver and in return the buyer must be ready and willing to pay.

■ Delivery is concerned with the transfer of possession of the goods, not with the transfer of ownership. It can be achieved in various ways and does not necessarily mean the seller taking or sending the goods to the buyer.

■ Unless otherwise agreed the place of delivery is the seller's place of business or, if he has not got a place of business, his home. However, if the contract is for the sale of specific goods which both of the parties know to be in some other place that place is the place of delivery.

■ A term fixing the time of delivery may be either a condition or a warranty, depending upon the intentions of the parties. In commercial contracts it is presumed that the parties intended such a term to be a condition.

■ If too small a quantity of goods is delivered the buyer can either reject the lot or accept the goods delivered and pay at the contract rate.

■ If too large a quantity of goods is delivered the buyer can either reject the lot, or accept the correct quantity and reject the excess, or accept the lot and pay for the excess at the contract rate.

■ In a severable instalment contract, whether a breach of condition by the seller as regards one or more instalments amounts to a repudiation of the whole contract will depend upon the terms of the contract and the circumstances of the case. The two most important circumstances will be the ratio of the breach to the contract as a whole and the likelihood of the breach being repeated.

Remedies of the seller

■ An unpaid seller is a seller to whom the whole of the purchase price has not been paid or tendered.

■ An unpaid seller may have three real remedies (remedies which can be taken against the goods rather than against the buyer); a lien, stoppage in transit and the right of resale.

■ The lien gives the unpaid seller the right to retain possession of the goods even though the property in the goods has passed to the buyer.

■ Stoppage in transit allows the seller to reclaim the goods from a carrier who is not the agent of the buyer up until the time when the goods are delivered to the buyer.

■ The right of resale allows the seller, in certain circumstances, to sell the goods to a different buyer without being in breach of the contract made with the original buyer.

■ The seller may sue for the price only if the contract fixed a definite date for payment or if the property in the goods had passed to the buyer.

■ If the buyer refuses to accept and pay for the goods the seller can sue for damages for non-acceptance. The measure of damages will be the estimated loss directly and naturally resulting, in the ordinary course of events, from the buyer's breach of contract.

■ Where there is an available market for the goods in question the measure of the seller's damages for non-acceptance is *prima facie* to be ascertained by the difference between the contract price and the market or current price at the time or times when the goods ought to have been accepted or (if no time was fixed for acceptance) at the time of the refusal to accept.

■ The seller will have a right to terminate the contract if the buyer has repudiated the contract.

The buyer's remedies

■ The buyer will have the right to sue for damages for non-delivery where the seller wrongfully neglects or refuses to deliver the goods.

■ The measure of the buyer's damages is the estimated loss directly and naturally resulting in the ordinary course of events from the seller's breach of contract. Where there is an available market for the goods this loss will generally be ascertained by using the market rule.

→

- The buyer may also claim damages to compensate for breach of warranty or for late delivery.
- Once the buyer has accepted the goods then rejection of the goods will no longer be possible. However, the right to sue for damages will remain.
- The buyer can be deemed to have accepted the goods: (a) when he intimates to the seller that he has accepted them; (b) when he does an act which is inconsistent with the seller's continuing ownership; or (c) where he retains the goods for more than a reasonable time without letting the seller know that he is rejecting them.
- At a sale by auction the property in each lot passes at the fall of the hammer.

International sales

- A bill of lading is evidence of the contract of carriage, a receipt for the goods shipped and a document of title.
- A clean bill of lading indicates that the goods shipped outwardly appeared to be in good order and condition.

- Under an fob contract the seller's duty is to pass the goods over the ship's rail within the shipment period. The buyer must nominate a ship which will arrive in time for the seller to do this.
- Unless otherwise agreed, the property in ascertained goods, and the risk, will pass to the buyer under an fob contract when the goods pass over the ship's rail.
- Under a cif contract the seller must deliver to the buyer a clean bill of lading, a policy of insurance and an invoice for the goods. The buyer must accept and pay for these documents if they are in order.
- Unless otherwise agreed, the property in ascertained goods sold on cif terms will pass to the buyer when the buyer accepts the documents and pays for them. The risk will pass to the buyer from the time when the goods were loaded on board ship.
- Even though the property may have passed to the buyer under a cif contract, he can still reject the goods (although not the documents) if he discovers that the goods do not conform to the contract.

Summary questions

1 In November Ken ordered a new customised surfboard from HiSurf Ltd, who manufacture surfboards. Ken paid a 20 per cent deposit. The contract stated that the board was to be ready by 1 April and that Ken would take delivery of the board and pay for it within one week of this date. The surfboard was not ready by 1 April, but Ken was told that it would be ready within two weeks. Ken agreed to this. On 15 April Ken was told that the board was still not ready but would be within one more week. Ken begrudgingly agreed to wait for another week. When told, on 22 April, that the board was still not ready Ken said that if it was not ready within one more week then he would refuse to take it and buy a surfboard elsewhere. On 22 April Ken was told that although the board was not finished it would be within two days. Advise Ken as to whether or not he can refuse to be bound by the contract and claim the return of his deposit.

2 Jane entered into a contract under which she agreed to buy 600 boxes of candles from Candle Co Ltd. The candles are to be delivered to Jane's

shop in 12 instalments of 50 each. Each instalment is to be comprised of 25 white candles and 25 gold candles. The first three instalments present no problem. The candles delivered in the fourth instalment cannot be lit as their wicks have not been sufficiently trimmed. Jane receives complaints from several customers. She contacts Candle Co who assure her that the problem will not recur as it was caused by a technical problem which has since been fixed. The fourth instalment contains only 20 white and 20 gold candles. Jane finds that demand for candles has fallen away. Can she reject the fourth instalment? Can she terminate the whole contract?

3 In July Bill ordered 100 tons of corn from Sid Suppliers Ltd. A contract was signed and the corn was to be delivered on 1 August. The day after signing the contract Bill explained that he had changed his mind and intended to buy corn from elsewhere. Sid Suppliers Ltd had ordered the corn from a Canadian exporter but are likely to have little trouble in selling it to a different customer. Advise Sid Suppliers Ltd of their legal position. How would your answer be different if Bill had

→

ordered a second-hand combine harvester, and not the corn, for delivery on 1 August and had made it plain that he would refuse to be bound by the contract?

4 Six months ago Arthur's business sold a new car to David for £9 995, which was paid in full. Yesterday David had the car towed back to Arthur's garage, claiming that he was rejecting it and wanted a return of the purchase price. The car had only travelled 2 250 miles but its engine had then seized up because the oil had leaked from the engine due to an oil seal leaking. This problem was caused by negligence when the car was manufactured. Arthur offers to repair the car under the manufacturer's warranty. David refuses to accept this and says that he wants all of his money back. Advise David of his legal position.

5 Pelham Products Ltd, which manufacture garden furniture, have contracted to sell 200 garden tables to Sunny Garden Centres Ltd. None of the price was paid, although no mention of credit was made. After handing over the garden chairs to a carrier, who was to transport them to Sunny Garden Centres Ltd, the manager of Pelham Products hears that Sunny Garden Centres Ltd have gone into liquidation. Pelham Products Ltd could easily find another buyer for the chairs. Advise them of their legal position.

6 Exporters Ltd buy 1 000 tons of barley from Grain Supply Ltd, fob Lowestoft. Under the contract Exporters Ltd have a duty to nominate the ship. Delivery of the goods is to be made in March. Exporters Ltd nominate a ship, the Hulk, which arrives on Thursday 26 March. The barley is loaded on board the Hulk on Friday 27 March. On Saturday 28 March the barley is infested by a swarm of locusts. Advise Exporters Ltd of their legal position.

7 Importers Ltd bought 1 000 tons of wheat, cif London, from Exporters Ltd. After they have made the contract Importers Ltd discover that the wheat is not of satisfactory quality. Exporters Ltd present to Importers Ltd a clean bill of lading, an invoice for the wheat and a policy of insurance covering the wheat. Advise Importers Ltd of their legal position.

Multiple choice questions

1 Bill examines an ex-demonstration model television at Super Stores Ltd. Bill buys the television, paying the full price cash. No mention of delivery is made, although Bill is asked to give his name and address. Bill lives within one mile of the store. Bill does not take the television with him when he leaves the store.

Consider the following statements.

i It is up to Bill to collect the television from Super Stores Ltd, who will have to make it available for collection.

ii Super Stores Ltd will have to deliver the television to Bill's house. Bill will have to ensure that someone is in to take delivery.

iii Until delivery is made Super Stores Ltd will have a lien over the television.

iv As the times of delivery and payment are concurrent conditions, Super Stores Ltd are in breach of contract as they did not deliver the television at the same time as payment was made.

Which of the statements are true?

a i and iii only.

b ii and iii only.

c ii and iv only.

d i only.

2 S Ltd sells to B 1 000 tons of wheat. The wheat is unascertained goods. The parties do not expressly or impliedly agree upon a place of delivery.

Consider the following statements.

i The place of delivery will be S Ltd's place of business.

ii Once S Ltd has separated 1 000 tons of wheat to be used to perform the contract, and told B where that wheat is, the place of delivery will be the place where both of the parties know the wheat to be.

iii If S Ltd deliver too much wheat, B can accept the correct quantity, accept the lot and pay for the excess at the contract rate or reject the lot.

→

iv Delivery of the goods to a carrier would amount to delivery of the goods to B if S Ltd were authorised or required by the contract to send the goods to B.

Which of the following statements are true?

a i, iii and iv only.

b ii, iii and iv only.

c ii and iii only.

d All of the statements.

3 Which one of the statements is true?

a If the seller breaches the contract and the buyer consequently rightfully rejects goods which have been delivered, the buyer can bring an action against the seller for non-delivery.

b The seller can always sue for the contract price once the goods have been delivered to the buyer.

c If there is an available market for the goods, then the seller's damages for non-acceptance will be calculated according to the market rule, but only if the seller actually sells the goods in the available market.

d A seller will not be able to sue for the price unless he can show that he has mitigated his loss.

4 Which one of the following statements is not true?

a A buyer who rightfully refuses to accept the goods does not need to physically return the goods to the seller, but only to let the seller know that he is rejecting them.

b Once the buyer has accepted, or has been deemed to have accepted, the goods then he will not be able to reject them, even for breach of condition.

c A buyer, whether a consumer buyer or not, can be deemed to have accepted the goods if he retains the goods for more than a reasonable time. This is the case even if he has not had a reasonable opportunity to examine the goods.

d If a buyer sells the goods on to a sub-buyer this will amount to performing an act which is inconsistent with the seller's continuing owner-ship. Therefore the buyer will always be deemed to have accepted the goods.

5 Which one of the following statements is true?

a The issue of a clean bill of lading amounts to a representation by the shipowner that the goods shipped conform to the contract absolutely when shipped.

b A buyer of goods sold on cif terms must accept and pay for the documents even if he knows that the goods themselves have been destroyed.

c As between the shipper and the shipowner, the bill of lading is conclusive evidence of the contract of carriage.

d As the bill of lading is a document of title, the holder of the bill will always own the goods to which the bill relates.

6 Which one of the following statements is not true?

a In an fob contract the named port is the port of loading, whereas in a cif contract the named port is the port of arrival.

b If a seller of goods on fob terms has the bill of lading made out in his own name then it is pre-sumed that he is reserving title to the goods until payment of the price.

c If goods which are already afloat are bought on cif terms, the property in the goods will usually pass to the buyer when the documents are taken and paid for. However, the risk will pass as from the time when the contract was made.

d Under a cif contract the property in the goods will usually pass to the buyer when the documents are taken and paid for. However, the risk will have passed retrospectively from the time when the goods were loaded aboard the ship.

Task 10

As a consequence of a supplier not delivering components on time your employer has had to find alternative supplies of these components at a higher price. Your employer has asked you to write a report, briefly dealing with the following matters.

a To explain the duties of the buyer and the seller under a contract of sale of goods.

b To explain the remedies available to a buyer or seller when a contract of sale of goods has been breached.

c The meaning of the terms fob and cif in international contracts of sale.

mylawchamber *premium*

Visit **www.mylawchamber.co.uk/macintyre** to access study support resources
including interactive multiple-choice questions, weblinks, glossary, glossary
flashcards, legal newsfeed, answers to questions in this chapter, legal updates
and an overview of this chapter all linked to the **Pearson eText** version of
Business Law which you can **search**, **highlight** and **personalise** with your
own notes and **bookmarks**.

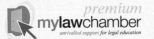

11

Agency

11.1 THE CONCEPT OF AGENCY

An agent has the power to alter the legal position of another person, known as the principal. Generally, an agent will have the power to make contracts on the principal's behalf, and this is the particular aspect of agency on which we concentrate. If an agent with the necessary authority makes a contract on the principal's behalf then the principal will be bound by the contract.

Auctioneers provide an easily understood example of agency. When an auctioneer sells a Lot it is not his own property which he is selling but the property of his principal, the person who put the goods into the auction. If X instructs an auctioneer to auction a painting, and the painting is knocked down to a third party for £100, then the contract of sale takes effect between X (the principal) and the third party. However, the contract was actually formed by the agent, and the third party.

No economy could function effectively without agency. If every person wishing to enter into a contract

had to make the contract personally then the business world would come to a standstill. Boards of Directors act as agents of their companies. Partners act as agents of the firm and of their fellow partners for the purpose of the business of the partnership. These types of agency are recognised by most people, but few people realise how common agency is. Shop assistants, for example, are agents. The goods which they sell belong not to themselves but to the shop owners who employ them. Strangely, many people who call themselves agents are not in fact agents in the legal sense. Retailers of motor vehicles, for example, commonly call themselves sole agent of a particular manufacturer in a particular locality. However, these retailers are not agents in the legal sense. They do not sell the cars on behalf of the manufacturer, rather they buy the cars from the manufacturers and sell them on their own behalf. They might be more accurately described as sole distributors rather than as sole agents.

Agents are usually employed to buy or to sell. Commonly they also have the power to dispose of the principal's property or to receive property on the principal's behalf. For example, shop assistants have the power to receive payment for goods sold on the principal's behalf. If a dishonest shop assistant pockets money paid by a customer, rather than putting it into the till, this is not the concern of the customer. Having paid the price in good faith to the shop assistant, the customer is regarded as having paid the price to the shop owner. Some agents act for more than one principal, and thereby offer customers a wide choice of services or products. Others provide a specialist service which their principals would find hard to provide themselves.

11.2 CREATION OF AGENCY

An agent can only act to alter the principal's legal position if he has authority to do so. There are several ways in which an agent may acquire this authority. As many legal disputes are concerned with whether or not an agent had the power to alter a principal's legal position, we need to examine each method by which authority might be acquired in some detail.

11.2.1 Express actual authority

Actual authority, whether express or implied, arises from an agreement between principal and agent. An agent has express actual authority when the principal and agent agree in words that the agent will have authority to act for the principal. The agreement may be made orally or in writing and will usually be a contract, although this is not necessary. An agent who agrees to act for no reward is known as a gratuitous agent. An agreement to act gratuitously will not amount to a contract as the agent is given no consideration for his services.

11.2.2 Implied actual authority

An agent has implied actual authority to act for the principal where the principal and agent agree, otherwise than in words, that the agent should have such authority. Implied actual authority arises from the principal and agent's relationship to each other or from their conduct. It is often an extension of express actual authority, but in the following case the agent's actual authority was entirely implied.

Hely-Hutchinson v Brayhead Ltd
[1968] 1 QB 549 (Court of Appeal)

The directors of a company allowed the company chairman to act as if he was the managing director of the company. In fact the chairman had never been appointed managing director and so had no express authority to bind the company. The chairman made a contract with a third party on the company's behalf.

Held. The chairman had implied actual authority to bind the company and so the company was bound by the contract which the chairman had made. The company, by its conduct, had impliedly agreed with the chairman that he should have the same authority as if he had actually been appointed managing director.

COMMENT In this case Lord Denning MR explained the difference between express actual authority and implied actual authority in the following way: '... actual authority may be express or implied. It is *express* when it is given by express words, such as when a board of directors pass a resolution which authorises two of their number to sign cheques. It is *implied* when it is inferred from the conduct of the parties and the circumstances of the case, such as when the board of directors appoint one of their number to be managing director. They thereby impliedly authorise him to do all such things as fall within the usual scope of that office.'

The whole of an agent's actual authority can be entirely implied. More commonly, implied authority can add to an agent's express authority, extending it beyond the powers expressly conferred. The courts can imply terms into contracts (as we saw in Chapter 5 at 5.3.2) on the grounds that it is necessary to do so to make the contract work as the parties intended, or on the grounds of custom. Contracts of agency are no different in this respect. An agent's authority is often implied on the grounds that the actions which the agent took are customarily taken on the principal's behalf. For example, a solicitor who has been given express authority to sue also has implied authority to abandon the action and reach a settlement. However, the implied actual authority of an agent can never contradict a limitation on authority which has been expressly agreed. In *Waugh v HB Clifford and Sons Ltd* [1982] 2 WLR 679 a firm of builders who had negligently built houses employed a firm of solicitors to defend proceedings brought against them. The solicitors suggested a compromise to the builders, but the builders ordered the solicitors not to compromise on this basis. The solicitors ignored these instructions and did compromise. The Court of Appeal recognised that generally solicitors employed to defend proceedings would have implied actual authority to enter into a compromise. This could not be the case, however, when they had been expressly ordered not to do this. Terms implied by the court on the basis that they were obviously what the parties intended can always be excluded by an express term.

11.2.3 Apparent (or ostensible) authority

We have seen that actual authority, whether express or implied, arises from an agreement between principal and agent. Apparent authority is quite different. It arises not from any agreement between principal and agent, but on account of the principal having made a representation to a third party that the agent has the authority to act on his behalf. If a principal's words or actions represent that he has consented to a person acting as his agent, then the principal may be estopped (prevented) from denying this once the third party has acted upon the representation. Generally the third party acts upon the representation by entering into a contract.

Three requirements are necessary to give rise to such an estoppel:

(i) there must have been a representation that the person was an agent;

(ii) this representation must have been made by the principal or by someone authorised to make it on his behalf;

(iii) the third party must have relied on the representation.

In ***Freeman & Lockyer (a firm)* v *Buckhurst Park Properties Ltd*** [1964] 2 QB 480 the directors of a company allowed one director, Kapoor, to act as if he had been appointed managing director of the company. Kapoor engaged a firm of architects to act on the company's behalf. The company later refused to pay the architects, arguing that Kapoor was not managing director and had no power to make contracts on the company's behalf. The Court of Appeal held that the company were bound by the contract. They had given the impression that Kapoor had the power to bind the company and so the company was liable on the contract to the architects who had relied on this representation by making the contract.

This case is somewhat similar to ***Hely-Hutchinson* v *Brayhead Ltd***. In that case the chairman was held to have implied actual authority to bind the company. In ***Freeman & Lockyer*** Kapoor was held to have apparent authority to do so. The two types of authority often overlap, as Lord Denning MR explained in ***Hely-Hutchinson* v *Brayhead Ltd***:

'Ostensible or apparent authority is the authority of an agent as it *appears* to others. It often coincides with actual authority. Thus, when the board appoint one of their number to be managing director, they invest him not only with implied [actual] authority, but also with ostensible authority to do all such things as fall within the usual scope of that office. Other people who see him acting as managing director are entitled to assume that he has the usual authority of a managing director. But sometimes ostensible authority exceeds actual authority. For instance, when the board appoint the managing director, they may expressly limit his authority by saying he is not to order goods worth more than £500 without the sanction of the board. In that case his *actual* authority is subject to the £500 limitation, but his *ostensible* authority includes all the usual authority of a managing director. The company is bound by his ostensible authority in his dealings with those who do not know of the limitation. He may himself do the "holding out". Thus, if he orders goods worth £1 000 and signs himself "Managing Director, for and on behalf of the company", the company is bound to the other party who does not know of the £500 limitation . . .'

Lord Denning recognised that in ***Hely-Hutchinson* v *Brayhead Ltd*** the chairman who was allowed to act as if he had been appointed managing director had apparent authority as well as implied actual authority.

The principal will be bound to the third party whether the agent had either actual or apparent authority. However, if an agent acts with apparent authority, but without actual authority, the principal cannot sue the third party on the contract, unless he ratifies the contract. (The principal has represented to the third party that the agent has authority, but the third party has made no representation to the principal.) However, the principal would be able to counterclaim and raise appropriate defences if sued on the contract by the third party. As regards the rights between principal and agent it also matters whether or not the agent had actual authority. If the agent had actual authority to do what he did then the agent will not become liable to the principal for so doing. Furthermore, if the agent has a contractual right to payment for his services then he will have a right to be paid for executing his actual authority. On the other hand an agent without actual authority, but with apparent authority, can be liable to the principal for acting in contravention of his instructions. In **Waugh v HB Clifford and Sons Ltd** we saw that the solicitors did not have implied actual authority to make the compromise on behalf of the builders. They did, however, have apparent authority to do so. Therefore, although the builders were bound by the compromise which the solicitors had made, the solicitors would have been liable to the builders for acting without actual authority. An agent without actual authority can also become liable to a third party for breach of warranty of authority, as explained below at 11.3.1.

The representation which gives rise to apparent authority must be made by the principal, or by a person who has been given authority to make it, and not by the agent. Where the principal is a company the board of directors will almost invariably be given actual authority to exercise all the powers of the company by the company's articles of association. Using this actual authority the board can confer actual authority on others, such as salesmen. Furthermore, if the board appoint a person to a certain position within the company then they may confer actual or apparent authority on that person to do certain things. In deciding whether or not a person within a company had apparent authority to do a certain act the courts will consider what representation the company has made to a third party, either by appointing the person to the position in question or otherwise. In **Armagas Ltd v Mundogas SA** [1986] AC 717 the House of Lords held that if the third party knows that the agent does not have authority to do a certain thing, or should have known this, then the agent cannot have apparent authority to do that thing because the third party cannot be said to have relied upon the representation. This is the case even if the employee is employed in a senior position. In **Criterion Properties plc v Stratford UK Properties LLC** [2004] UKHL 28, [2004] 1 WLR 1846 Lord Scott explained the position where an agent makes a contract which is against the principal's commercial interests:

'If a person dealing with an agent knows that the agent does not have actual authority to conclude the contract or transaction in question, the person cannot rely on apparent authority. Apparent authority can only be relied upon by someone who does not know that the agent has no actual authority. And if a person dealing with an agent knows or has reason to believe that the contract or transaction is contrary to the commercial interests of the agent's principal, it is likely to be very difficult for the person to assert with any credibility that he believed that the agent did have actual authority. Lack of such a belief would be fatal to a claim that the agent had apparent authority.'

In **First Energy (UK) Ltd v Hungarian International Bank Ltd** [1993] 2 Lloyd's Rep 194 the Court of Appeal had to decide whether or not the defendant bank was bound by an offer to provide credit to the claimants. The claimants had dealt with one Jamison, the senior manager of the Manchester branch of the bank. Jamison had made it plain that he himself did not have authority to grant the credit facilities. Later Jamison informed the claimants that the credit facility had been approved by the bank's head office, although no such approval had in fact been given. It was held that the bank was bound by the offer to provide the credit. Jamison would not have had apparent authority to grant the credit himself, as the claimants knew that he did not have such authority. However, Jamison did have authority to communicate decisions of the bank. By appointing Jamison to a senior position the defendants had represented to those with whom he dealt that he had such authority.

It will almost always be the case that the representation which gives rise to apparent authority will be made before the third party makes the contract. However, the following case shows that it is the possible for the representation to be made after the contract has been concluded.

Spiro v Lintern [1973] 1 WLR 1002
(Court of Appeal)

The defendant owned a house and asked his wife to find a buyer. Through a firm of estate agents the defendant's wife found a buyer, the claimant, who made an unconditional offer to buy the house for £25 000. A written contract was drawn up and signed by the claimant and by the estate agent acting on instructions from the defendant's wife. However, the defendant had not authorised his wife to make a binding contract and so she had no authority to do so or to enable the estate agents to do so. The defendant was advised by his solicitor that the sale was probably binding upon him. Later the claimant sent an architect to the house and some days later the claimant visited the house and was introduced to the defendant as the new owner. The defendant did not dispute this in any →

way. The defendant then allowed a builder to work on the house on behalf of the claimant. The defendant then went abroad, instructing his wife to complete the sale to the claimant. Instead the defendant's wife sold the house to a third party for £30 000. The claimant sued for specific performance.

Held. The claimant was granted specific performance. By failing to correct the claimant's belief that the defendant was under an obligation to sell the house, the defendant represented that such an obligation did in fact exist.

11.2.4 **Agency by operation of law**

It is possible that an **agency of necessity** will be implied in circumstances where one person acts to safeguard the property of another. This will only be the case if the following requirements are satisfied:

(i)   The agent must have been in control of the principal's property.

(ii) It must have been impossible for the agent to obtain the principal's instructions.

(iii) There must have been a commercial emergency which made it necessary for the agent to act as he did.

(iv) The agent must have acted in good faith as regards all parties.

Such agency of necessity is usually found in maritime emergencies. Established cases have given the captains of ships the power to sell cargoes which were perishing and to borrow money on the shipowner's behalf.

Occasionally, agencies of necessity can be found on dry land, but only if the four conditions are satisfied. In *Springer* v *Great Western Railway* [1921] 1 KB 257 carriers of tomatoes which had been imported from Jersey were delayed first by bad weather and then by a dock strike. The tomatoes were rapidly going bad and so the carriers took the decision to sell them locally. The carriers were liable to the owners of the tomatoes for doing this, even though the court was sure that the owners would have consented to it. No agency of necessity arose because the carriers could have communicated with the owners and asked them if this is what they wanted them to do.

Agency can also arise by cohabitation. A person cohabiting with another may have authority to pledge that other's credit to buy necessary goods and services.

Agency is occasionally imposed by statute. In Chapter 14, for example, we shall see that a person who conducts negotiations on behalf of a creditor can in certain circumstances be deemed to do so as the agent of the creditor, by virtue of s.56(2) of the Consumer Credit Act 1974.

11.2.5 **Usual authority**

The following, difficult, case does not easily fit within any of the established ways in which agency can be created, but nevertheless it was held that an agency did exist. Some writers analyse the case by saying that the agent in the case had usual authority. However, this term should be used with care because usual authority can be used in quite distinct senses, as is explained in the paragraph following the case.

Watteau v Fenwick [1893] 1 QB 346

A pub owner (the principal) let a manager (the agent) run a pub. The owner authorised the manager to buy only bottled drinks and expressly forbade him to buy tobacco on credit. Acting against these instructions, the manager bought cigars on credit. The tobacco salesman had no idea that the manager was an agent. He thought that the manager owned the pub because the manager had previously owned the pub and his name was still painted above the door. When the manager could not pay for the cigars the seller sued the owner claiming that the owner was liable on the contract.

Held. The owner was liable on the contract.

COMMENT The manager had no express or implied actual authority to buy the cigars. (On the contrary, he had been forbidden to do this.) Nor did the manager have apparent authority because the principal never represented to the third party that the manager did have such authority. (The third party did not believe the manager to be an agent, and did not therefore even know of the principal's existence.) The case is perhaps best explained by saying that the manager had usual authority. The owner of the pub did make the manager an agent and so the agent was clothed with all the authority which one would usually expect an agent of this type to have. There is some doubt about the correctness of this case, but until it has been overruled it will operate as a precedent. However, the circumstances in which it will apply are fairly limited. First, the third party must think that the agent is acting on his own behalf. Second, the agent must make a contract which an agent in his position would usually have actual authority to make. Third, there must be no actual authority because the agent has been forbidden by the principal to make such a contract.

There is considerable uncertainty about the way in which the term usual authority should be used. It can not only be used to describe the situation in **Watteau v Fenwick**, but can also be used to describe a particular type of either implied actual authority or apparent authority. Implied actual authority may give an agent the power to do whatever is usual in the context of his trade, profession or position in order to execute his actual authority. Some writers call this usual authority. An agent who is appointed to a position in which he would usually have authority to do a certain act can have apparent authority to do that act, even if the principal has forbidden him to do it, and some writers call this authority usual authority. The terminology is used in a very confusing way and whenever the term usual authority is used it is best to make clear the sense in which it is used.

11.2.6 Agency by ratification

Agency by ratification occurs when an agent acts for a principal either without any authority at all, or in excess of the authority which he does have. If the principal ratifies the contract (later agrees to adopt it), either expressly or impliedly, then he retrospectively confers actual authority on the agent. The principal and third party will therefore become contractually bound to each other, just as if the agent had been given prior actual authority, and so the agent will not be liable to the third party on the contract or for breach of warranty of authority. (Breach of warranty of authority is explained below at 11.3.2.) The agent will not be liable to the principal for having exceeded his authority and may have a claim against the principal for reasonable remuneration or an indemnity. The principal has no obligation to ratify and may choose not to do so.

Example

X sees a bargain which he is sure that Y would want to buy. X therefore buys the bargain on Y's behalf, even though Y has given X no authority to do this. Y is not bound by the contract as he gave X no authority to buy the goods and has made no representation that X has such authority. But if Y later ratifies the contract then he will retrospectively give X actual authority. This will mean that there is now a good contract between Y and the seller of the goods and that X will be absolved from liability on the contract.

It might be thought that ratification would be as simple as the example given. However, five conditions must be satisfied for the ratification to be effective, and these are set out below.

(1) The agent must have purported to act as an agent

The principal cannot ratify the contract unless the agent purported to make the contract as an agent. Only the principal who was either named or capable of being ascertained can sue. An undisclosed principal cannot ratify.

Keighley Maxted & Co v Durant
[1901] AC 240 (House of Lords)

An agent was authorised to buy wheat on behalf of a partnership at a certain price. He bought wheat at a greater price, by telegram, intending it to be for the partnership. He did not tell the corn merchant that he was buying the wheat for the partnership, but this was always his intention. The partnership ratified the contract the following day. Later the partnership refused to accept delivery of the wheat.

Held. The ratification was not effective because the agent had not made it plain that he was acting as an agent when he bought the wheat. Therefore, the partnership was not bound by the contract.

Similarly, in **Watteau v Fenwick** the owner of the hotel could not have ratified the contract which the manager made. At the time of the contract the tobacco salesman did not even know of the principal's existence. (However, when sued by the tobacco salesman the hotel owner could counterclaim for the price and raise any appropriate defences.)

(2) The principal must have had full capacity to make the contract both when the agent made the contract and when it was ratified

Kelner v Baxter (1866) LR 2 CP 174

A, B and C were intending to form a company. Before the company was formed, they bought £900 worth of wine on behalf of the company. The company was formed as planned and the wine was consumed. The company went into liquidation before paying for the wine. The supplier sued A, B and C, who argued that as the company had ratified the contract they were no longer personally liable on it.

→

Held. The ratification was not effective because the company did not have the capacity to make the contract when the agents made it. (Because the company had not yet been formed it had no capacity.)

COMMENT This case illustrates a general rule on the need for the principal to have capacity. In *Kelner* v *Baxter* A, B and C were personally liable on the contract because they intended to contract personally. However, as regards companies, s.51(1) of the Companies Act 2006 must now be considered. This makes the promoters of a company personally liable on pre-incorporation contracts made on the company's behalf unless there has been an agreement to the contrary between the supplier and the promoters. (See Chapter 16 at 16.8.)

(3) At the time of ratification the principal must either have known all of the material facts or intended to ratify no matter what they were

The principal can adopt an action which another person fraudulently claimed to be making on his behalf. However, the ratification will only be effective if, at the time of the ratification, either:

(i) the principal knew of all the material facts and made an unequivocal adoption of the actions; or
(ii) the circumstances showed a clear inference that the principal was adopting the actions of the purported agent whatever the nature of the actions (*Marsh* v *Joseph* [1897] 1 Ch 213).

(4) A void contract cannot be ratified

(5) Ratification must take place within a reasonable time, and will not be allowed where third parties have acquired property rights which would be adversely affected by ratification

11.2.6.1 Effect of ratification

If a contract is successfully ratified then it is effective as if the agent had had actual authority at the time the contract was made.

Bolton Partners v *Lambert*
(1889) 41 ChD 295 (Court of Appeal)

On 8 December 1886 the defendant wrote to the managing director of a company, offering to buy the company. On 13 December a works committee

decided to accept the offer, although it did not have the authority to do this. The managing director wrote to the defendant that the Board of Directors of the company had accepted the offer. On 13 January the defendant said that he was revoking his offer. On 17 January the Board of Directors issued a writ claiming specific performance of the agreement and on 28 January the Board ratified the acceptance made by the managing director.

Held. As soon as the Board of Directors ratified the contract it became effective from 13 December. The defendant could not therefore revoke his offer on 13 January.

Although the rule in *Bolton Partners* v *Lambert* seems somewhat unfair to the third party, it is modified by the requirement that ratification must take place within a reasonable time, and will not be allowed where third parties have acquired property rights which would be adversely affected by ratification. In *Metropolitan Asylums Board* v *Kingham and Sons* 1890) 6 TLR 217, there was a delay of ten days between an agent's unauthorised acceptance of the defendant's offer to supply eggs and the principal's ratification of that unauthorised act. During the ten-day period, the defendant revoked his offer. It was held that the ratification was ineffective, as it had not been made within a reasonable time of the unauthorised acceptance. Nor does the rule apply where the third party knew that the agent's authority was limited or that the contract would have to be ratified.

The principal will generally ratify by informing the third party that he is doing so. However, ratification can be implied from the principal's conduct and even silence or inactivity can amount to ratification in some circumstances. What is important is that the principal unequivocally shows that he is adopting the agent's actions. Rowlatt J gave the classic description of what is required for ratification in *Harrisons & Crossfield Ltd* v *LNW Railway Company* [1917] KBD 755:

'Now, ratification does not rest upon estoppel. It need not be communicated to the party alleging it. Ratification is a unilateral act of the will, namely, the approval after the event of the assumption of an authority which did not exist at the time. It may be expressed in words or implied from or involved in acts. It is implied from or involved in acts when you cannot logically analyse the act without imputing such approval to the party, whether his mind in fact approved or disapproved or wholly disregarded the question.'

11.3 LIABILITY ON CONTRACTS MADE BY AGENTS

The rights of a third party to sue on a contract made by an agent with actual authority differ, depending upon whether the agency was disclosed or undisclosed.

11.3.1 Disclosed and undisclosed principals

Agency is disclosed when the agent indicates that he is acting as an agent, whether or not the principal for whom he is acting is actually identified.

If an agent with actual authority makes a contract for a disclosed principal then generally the agent incurs no liability on the contract. By disclosing that he was acting for a principal, the agent will be taken to have shown the third party that he did not intend to become personally liable on the contract. If the circumstances show otherwise, however, the agent can incur personal liability. The principal will be liable on the contract just as if he had made it personally.

If an agent with actual authority acts for an undisclosed principal (i.e. the agent did not reveal that he was acting for a principal) then the contract first takes effect between the agent and the third party. So the agent will be liable to the third party on the contract and the third party will be liable to the agent on the contract. Once the principal is revealed, the third party ceases to be liable to the agent and becomes liable to the principal. Initially, both the principal and the agent will be liable to the third party on the contract. Where such joint liability arises, the third party can choose to sue either the agent or the principal.

However, having made an unequivocal election to hold one or other liable on the contract, the third party will not be able to change his mind. If the agent did not have actual authority to make the contract then the principal will not be liable on the contract. (Unless the case can be brought within the requirements set out in *Watteau v Fenwick*.) Nor can the principal ratify the contract because ratification is only permissible where the agent purported to act as an agent.

There are three situations where an undisclosed principal cannot sue on the contract, even if the agent did have actual authority to make the contract. These situations are:

(i) that a term of the contract excluded agency;

(ii) that the third party would have refused to contract with the undisclosed principal;

(iii) that the third party made the contract with the agent because he particularly wanted to contract with the agent personally.

Said v Butt [1920] 3 KB 497

The claimant, a theatre critic, wanted to attend the first night of a play at a certain theatre. He knew that the theatre owners would refuse to supply him with a ticket, as he had made serious unfounded allegations against members of the theatre. He therefore asked his friend to buy him a ticket, but not to state who the ticket was for. The defendant, the managing director of the theatre, refused to let the claimant use the ticket to gain entry to the theatre. The claimant sued the defendant for maliciously procuring the theatre owners to breach a contract.

Held. The defendant was not liable as there was no contract between the claimant and the theatre owners. The identity of the claimant was a material element in the formation of the contract.

COMMENT This case provides an example of a case where the third party would have refused to have contracted with the undisclosed principal. McCardie J said that in this case the personal element was 'strikingly present' as the reviews of a play's first night could make or break the play. If the ticket had said that it was not transferable, as many nowadays do, then a term of the contract would have excluded agency. In *Shogun Finance Ltd v Hudson* (*FC*) [2003] UKHL 62, [2003] 3 WLR 1371 Lord Millett indicated that the evidence showed that the theatre ticket was not transferable and so an undisclosed principal could not intervene on a contract intended to be made with the agent personally.

Dyster v Randall [1926] Ch 932

The claimant wanted to buy two plots of land from the defendants. The claimant used to work for the defendants but had been dismissed by them. He knew that the defendants profoundly distrusted him and would not sell him the land. The claimant therefore asked one Crossley to buy the land for him, asking Crossley not to reveal for whom he was acting. Crossley bought the land as requested. When the defendants discovered that Crossley had been acting for the claimant they refused to be bound by the contract. The claimant sued for specific performance.

Held. The claimant was granted specific performance. There was no personal element strikingly present and so there was no reason why an undisclosed principal should not buy the land on behalf of the claimant.

The position is different if an agent is asked whether or not he is acting for a particular principal and deliberately misrepresents that he is not. In *Archer v Stone* (1898) 78 LT 34 the third party asked the agent if he was acting for a particular principal. The agent said that he was not, although in fact he was. It was held that the principal could not enforce the contract against the third party.

Greer v Downs Supply Co [1927] 2 KB 28 provides an example of undisclosed agency not being allowed because the third party particularly wanted to contract with the agent personally. The agent owed the third party £17. The third party contracted to buy timber from the agent for £29, it being a term of the contract that the third party could set the £17 off against the price. The agent had dishonestly told the third party that he was not selling the wood on behalf of an undisclosed principal, but in fact he was. The Court of Appeal held that the undisclosed principal could not sue on the contract. The third party had particularly wanted to contract with the agent so that he could deduct the £17 from the price of £29.

If the third party is sued on the contract by an undisclosed principal, he will be able to take advantage of defences which he would have had against the agent.

In *Siu Yin Kwan v Eastern Insurance Co* [1994] 1 All ER 213 Lord Lloyd of Berwick summarised the law as regards undisclosed principals as follows:

(1) An undisclosed principal may sue and be sued on a contract made by an agent on his behalf, acting within the scope of his actual authority.

(2) In entering into the contract the agent must intend to act on the principal's behalf.

(3) The agent of an undisclosed principal may also sue and be sued on the contract.

(4) Any defence which the third party may have against the agent is available against his principal.

(5) The terms of the contract may, expressly or by implication, exclude the principal's right to sue, and his liability to be sued. The contract itself, or the circumstances surrounding the contract, may show that the agent is the true and only principal.

11.3.2 **Breach of warranty of authority**

We have seen that an agent will generally incur no liability on a contract made for a disclosed principal. However, if an agent makes a representation to a third party, warranting that he has authority to act for a principal when he does not in fact have such authority, and if the third party acts on this representation to his detriment, then the agent will be strictly liable to the third party for breach of this warranty of authority. It is an essential requirement that the agent's representation of his own authority causes the third party to act in a way in which he otherwise would not have acted. Usually, the third party will act upon the warranty by making the contract with the principal. The agent can also become liable for breach of warranty of authority where he exceeds the authority which he does have. Liability for breach of warranty of authority is independent of liability on the contract made on the principal's behalf, and can arise even if the agent could not have known that his authority had been revoked. This is because the agent is regarded as having made the offer of a unilateral contract by warranting his authority. The agent's consideration to the third party is promising that he does have the authority claimed. The third party's consideration to the agent is entering into the contract.

Yonge v Toynbee
[1910] 1 KB 215 (Court of Appeal)

A client (the principal) instructed a solicitor (the agent) to defend a case. The client became certifiably insane and this automatically terminated the solicitor's authority to act for him. The solicitor did not know that the client had become insane and continued to act for him.

→

Held. As soon as the client was certified insane the solicitor lost his authority to act for the client. All proceedings taken after this date were therefore struck out, and the solicitor had to pay all the other party's costs which were incurred after this date.

If the principal ratifies the agent's actions then the agent will not be liable for breach of warranty of authority. Nor will the agent be liable for breach of warranty of authority if the third party knew, or should have known, that the agent did not have the authority warranted. Damages for breach of warranty of authority are calculated by reference to the two rules in *Hadley v Baxendale*. These damages are designed to put the third party in the position which he would have been if the warranty had not been breached. This does not make the agent liable on the contract between third party and principal.

An example of damages for breach of warranty of authority is provided by *Simons v Patchett* (1857) 7 E & B 568. A bought a ship from T claiming to have authority from P. In fact A had exceeded his limited authority in doing this. The contract price was £6 000. P refused to be bound by the contract. T therefore sold the ship to another buyer, X, for £5 500. This was the best price T could get, and was a fair price at the time. T sued A for breach of warranty of authority. It was held that A had to pay £500 damages. If the agent's warranty of authority had not been breached, T would either have received the full price of £6 000 from P, or would have been able to sue P for breach of contract. If sued for breach of contract, P would (under *Hadley v Baxendale*) have had to pay damages of £500. Either way, A's breach of warranty of authority had cost T £500, representing the difference between the £6 000 originally agreed and the £5 500 actually received. P was, therefore, entitled to £500 damages from A.

The following case shows that the claimant can recover damages greater than the normal measure for breach of warranty of authority as long as the damages claimed are within *Hadley v Baxendale*.

Habton Farms (an unlimited company) v Nimmo and another [2003] EWCA Civ 68, [2003] 3 WLR 633 (Court of Appeal)

In October 1998 the defendant purported to buy a racehorse from the claimant, on behalf of one Williamson, for £70 000. The defendant warranted that he had authority to do this as Williamson's agent. The purchase was subject to the horse being inspected by a vet and X-rays being approved. The defendant later told the claimant that the vet's inspection and the X-rays were satisfactory and arranged for the horse to be collected on 2 or 3 November. On one of these ates the claimant was told that Williamson would not buy the horse. The claimant was not told that defendant had no actual or apparent authority to act for Williamson. The claimant continued to ask for the price and refrained from selling the horse to anyone else. At the end of November the horse contracted peritonitis, from which it died on 2 December. The claimant then discovered that the defendant had no authority to act for Williamson and sued for damages for breach of warranty of authority. The judge ordered the defendant to pay damages of £70 000. An appeal was made to the Court of Appeal.

Held. The Court of Appeal dismissed the appeal. The defendant had warranted his authority to act for Williamson both when he made the contract and when he indicated that the vet's inspection and the X-rays were satisfactory. If this warranty had been true the claimant would have received the purchase price of £70 000. The ordinary measure of damages for breach of warranty of authority was the difference between the contract price and the market price on the day when the contract was concluded. On this basis, the damages would have been nominal only. However, the warranty of authority had caused the claimant not to sell the horse to anyone else and to try to enforce the contract of sale. This meant that it was inappropriate to deduct the market price from the contract price and so the defendant was liable to pay £70 000 damages.

An agent acting with only apparent authority can be liable for breach of warranty of authority. However, as the principal is liable on the contract which has been made, the third party is usually likely to have suffered no loss as a consequence of the breach and will therefore be entitled to no damages.

In *Halbot v Lens* [1901] 1 Ch 344 it was established that an agent will not be liable for breach of warranty of authority if he specifically denies having authority, or if the third party did not rely on the existence of his authority. In *Knight Frank LLP v Aston Du Haney* [2011] EWCA Civ 404 the Court of Appeal held that if a person falsely represented that another person was his principal, and then later said that his principal might have been someone else, he should be treated as having no principal and therefore be liable for breach of warranty of authority, rather than being liable on the contract as a principal. However, liability for breach of warranty of authority would arise only if the agent's representation caused the third party to act in a way in which he would otherwise not have acted.

Test your understanding 11.2

1 In what circumstances is agency undisclosed?

2 Where agency is disclosed:

   a In what circumstances will the principal be liable on the contract?

   b What liability might the agent have towards the third party?

3 Where agency is undisclosed, what is the liability on the contract to the third party of:

   a The principal?

   b The agent?

4 In what circumstances can the undisclosed principal not sue on the contract?

11.4 DUTIES OF THE AGENT

Agents owe several duties to their principals. These duties arise either from the agreement made between principal and agent, whether a contract or not, or from the fiduciary nature of agency. The fiduciary duties are imposed by the law because the nature of agency is such that a principal has to be able to place great trust and confidence in the agent.

11.4.1 To obey instructions

An agent with actual authority will have agreed to act for the principal. If this agreement amounts to a contract, as will generally be the case, then the agent can be liable for failure to perform the contract. Furthermore, an agent must obey lawful instructions, even if he thinks he is helping the principal by not doing so. For example, in *Bertram Armstrong and Co v Godfrey* (1830) 1 Kn 381 an agent was ordered to sell shares as soon as they reached a certain price. The shares did reach the appropriate price, but the agent did not sell because he thought they would go higher. In fact the price of the shares fell. The agent was held liable, and had to pay damages for not obeying his instructions.

11.4.2 Care and skill

An agent must exercise care and skill when performing his duties. The precise degree of care and skill required will depend upon several factors, including any expertise which the agent has expressly or impliedly claimed to have. For example, if a professional person such as a solicitor is employed as an agent he should show the degree of care and skill which one could reasonably expect from a solicitor. Where the agency is to provide a service in the course of a business s.13 SGSA 1982 requires that the agent provides the service using reasonable care and skill. Where the agent was not acting in the course of a business the common law would impose a similar duty to that imposed by s.13 SGSA. If there is no contract between principal and agent the duty to use reasonable care and skill may arise in tort.

Chaudry v Prabhakar [1988] 3 All ER 718 (Court of Appeal)

The claimant, who had recently passed her driving test and knew nothing about cars, asked a friend, the first defendant, to find her a suitable second-hand car. The defendant was not a mechanic but had some knowledge of cars. The claimant stipulated that she did not want any car which had been in an accident. The first defendant found a car being sold by the second defendant, a car sprayer and panel beater. The first defendant noticed that the bonnet had been crumpled and straightened but thought the car was in good condition. He therefore recommended that the claimant buy the car, which she did at a price of £4 500. Some months later the claimant discovered that the car had been in a very bad accident, that it had been badly repaired and that it was quite unroadworthy. The judge found the second defendant liable for breach of the 1979 Sale of Goods Act implied term that the car was of merchantable (now satisfactory) quality and the first defendant liable for breach of his duty to take reasonable care. The first defendant appealed.

Held. The first defendant was liable. A gratuitous agent owes a duty to show the degree of care and skill which could be expected of him in all the circumstances. This standard is assessed objectively.

COMMENT In this case counsel for the first defendant conceded that a duty of care was owed. May LJ indicated that he thought that this concession should not have been made and that it was inappropriate to impose a duty of care when a person gratuitously did a favour for a friend in a social context. If the concession had not been made then the first defendant might well not have been liable.

11.4.3 Personal performance

Generally, the agent must perform personally and must not delegate his authority. This is sometimes expressed by the Latin maxim, *delegare non potest delegare* (a delegate must not sub-delegate).

There are four exceptions to this rule. An agent is allowed to delegate his duties in the following circumstances:

(i) If the principal expressly authorises delegation.
(ii) If the agent can imply a power to delegate from the circumstances.
(iii) If the delegation is of an act requiring no care and skill.
(iv) If the delegation became necessary due to unforeseen circumstances.

In *John McCann & Co v Pow* [1975] 1 All ER 129 (Court of Appeal) it was held that an estate agent who had been given the task of selling a house, and who described himself in his advertisements as 'sole agent', could not delegate the task. Therefore, the agent's claim to commission, on the basis that he had delegated to a different estate agent who actually sold the property, failed.

11.4.4 Fiduciary duties

As agency is a fiduciary relationship, having its origins in equity, fiduciary duties are placed upon the agent. Although we consider four fiduciary duties it is important to realise that these duties often overlap, so that a breach of one involves a breach of another. The fiduciary duties are as follows:

11.4.4.1 To avoid any conflict of interest

An agent must avoid a conflict between his own interests and those of his principal. For example, an agent who is employed to sell the principal's property cannot buy it himself unless he makes full disclosure of this to the principal. Similarly, an agent employed by the principal to buy cannot perform the contract by selling his own property to the principal without full disclosure. So in *Armstrong v Jackson* [1917] 2 KB 822 a stockbroker who had been asked to buy 600 shares in a certain company had a conflict of interest when he sold the principal 600 shares which he himself owned in the company. The agent had been a promoter of the company in question and pretended that he had bought the shares in the open market. Some years later the principal discovered what had happened and the court set the agreement aside. McCardie J said: 'It matters not that the agent sells at the market price, or that he acts without intent to defraud . . . The prohibition of the law is absolute. It will not allow an agent to place himself in a situation which, under ordinary circumstances, would tempt a man to do that which is not the best for his principal.'

Imageview Management Ltd v Jack [2009] EWCA Civ 63, [2009] 1 Lloyd's Rep 436

Mr Jack was a professional footballer who played goalkeeper for Trinidad and Tobago. He contacted Dundee United football club with a view to playing for them. He asked Mr Berry to act as his agent in negotiations with the club. Jack entered into a two-year contract with Berry's company, Imageview. Under this agreement the company was to represent him in connection with any contract, or the renewal of any contract, with a UK club. In return, Imageview was to get 10 per cent of Jack's monthly salary. Berry negotiated a contract under which Jack was to play for Dundee United for two years. Whilst doing this, Berry also agreed that Dundee United would pay Imageview £3 000 for getting the claimant the work permit which he would need in order to play in the United Kingdom. The trial judge found that the actual value of getting such a permit was £750. A year later, Jack found out about the £3 000 payment. He asked Berry about it and was told that it was none of his business. Jack therefore stopped making the 10 per cent payment to Imageview. Imageview sued for the unpaid agency fees. Jack retaliated by claiming back all the fees he had already paid. He also claimed the £3 000 which had been paid to Imageview or, alternatively, the 'excess' of £2 250 above the real value of the work done.

Held. Imageview had a clear conflict of interest. The more it got for itself, the less it got for Jack. Furthermore, Imageview had an interest in Jack signing for Dundee United, rather than for any other club. There would have been no such conflict if Jack had been told about the £3 000 deal before it was made. Jack could recover the commission already paid, had no liability to pay the commission unpaid and could recover the £3 000 secret profit paid to Imageview.

Jacob LJ, who gave the only significant judgment, said:

'The law imposes on agents high standards. Footballers' agents are not exempt from these. An agent's own personal interests come entirely second to the interest of his client. If you undertake to

→

act for a man you must act 100%, body and soul, for him. You must act as if you were him. You must not allow your own interest to get in the way without telling him. An undisclosed but realistic possibility of a conflict of interest is a breach of your duty of good faith to your client. That duty should not cause an agent any problem. All he or she has to do to avoid being in breach of duty is to make full disclosure.'

He also said that the strictness of the rule was founded in policy. It might be thought unfair that Jack had gained the agent's services at no cost. But here the remedy was concerned with betrayal of trust, which brought equity and conscience into play. Such betrayals of trust were not always discovered. If the penalty was merely to pay damages when found out, this would encourage betrayal of trust. The strict rules were there as a deterrent to betrayal.

11.4.4.2 **Not to make a secret profit**

The agent must not make any profit other than that which has been agreed with the principal. In the following case Lord Denning MR identified that such a profit might arise from the agent's use of the principal's property, from the use of his position of authority, or from information or knowledge which he had acquired in the course of his agency.

Boardman v Phipps [1967] 2 AC 46
(House of Lords)

The defendant acted as a solicitor to a trust. The trust owned shares in a certain company and the solicitor advised the trust to buy more of these shares. Despite being repeatedly advised to buy more shares, the trust did not do so. The solicitor himself bought shares in the company. This meant that the solicitor and the trust between them controlled the company and it enabled both the solicitor and the trust to make large profits. The trust sued the solicitor, claiming the profits he had made.

Held. The solicitor had to account to the trust for the profit he had made and hold these profits on constructive trust for the trust. The solicitor had used knowledge which he had acquired in the course of his agency to make the profit.

COMMENT (i) Although this case seems rather unfair to the solicitor he was awarded very generous payment, on a *quantum meruit* basis, for the work he had done on the company's behalf. The case illustrates

---

that the fiduciary duties are enforced even where their breach causes no loss to the principal.

(ii) Lord Denning, when the case was heard in the Court of Appeal, explained the rule that an agent must not make a secret profit in the following way: 'It is quite clear that if an agent uses *property*, with which he has been entrusted by his principal, so as to make a profit for himself out of it, without his principal's consent, then he is accountable for it to his principal ... So, also, if he uses a *position of authority,* to which he has been appointed by his principal, so as to gain money by means of it for himself, then also he is accountable to his principal for it ... Likewise with *information or knowledge* which he has been employed by his principal to collect or discover, *or which he has otherwise acquired,* for the use of this principal, then again if he turns it to his own use, so as to make a profit by means of it for himself, he is accountable ... for such information or knowledge is the property of the principal, just as much as an invention is.'

(iii) In **Imageview Management Ltd v Jack**, considered above in relation to conflict of interests, the agent was ordered to pay back the secret profit made.

11.4.4.3 **Not to take a bribe**

In this context a bribe does not necessarily indicate corruption. In **Anangel Atlas Compania Naviera SA v Ishikawajima-Harima Heavy Industries Co Ltd** [1990] 1 Lloyd's Rep 167 Leggatt J gave the following definition: 'a bribe consists in a commission or other inducement, which is given by a third party to an agent as such, and which is secret from his principal'. For example, if a firm's buyer is given inducements to favour a particular supplier a court will almost certainly regard this as a bribe. Much of 'corporate hospitality' and the giving of 'free samples' to people who buy on behalf of others is potentially a bribe.

If an agent does take a bribe the principal has the following remedies: dismiss the agent and recover commission or salary paid to the agent; recover the bribe from either the agent or the person who paid it, or alternatively regard the bribe as held on trust for the principal; as an alternative to recovering the bribe, sue the agent or the person who paid the bribe for losses sustained as a result of the bribe; rescind the contract made with the third party.

11.4.4.4 **The duty to account**

This duty requires that the agent keeps his own property separate from the principal's property. If the agent mixes the two up, the principal will be entitled to all of the property unless the agent can clearly show what property belonged to him. The agent will also be obliged to keep a record of his dealings on the principal's behalf, which the principal can ask to inspect. The principal might have a right to inspect records held on computer. In *Yasuda Ltd* v *Orion Underwriting Ltd* [1995] QB 174 the claimants were entitled by an express clause of the contract to inspect 'all necessary books accounts records and other documentation'. It was held that this clearly included all computer material. If the defendants could not reasonably quickly separate material on the computer which did not relate to the claimants' business then they would have to allow the claimants access to all material which included reference to the claimants' business.

11.4.4.5 Duty of confidentiality

An agent owes a duty of confidentiality as regards information gained as a result of being an agent. In *Bolkiah* v *KPMG* [1999] 2 WLR 215 the House of Lords held that this duty could continue after the agency had been terminated.

11.4.4.6 Remedies for breach of fiduciary duties

The possible remedies for breach of fiduciary duty include the following:

  (i) Recover a secret profit from the agent.
 (ii) Refuse to pay the agent's commission or salary.
(iii) Dismiss the agent without notice.
 (iv) Terminate the contract with the third party.
  (v) Recover the amount of any bribe or, alternatively, claim damages for fraud.

Attorney General for Hong Kong v Reid and others [1994] 1 AC 324
(Privy Council)

The agent was a customs officer who breached his fiduciary duties by taking bribes. He used some of the money gained to buy properties conveyed to himself, his wife and his solicitor. On being discovered the agent was jailed for eight years and ordered to repay the amount of the bribes taken.

Held. The principal, the Crown, could choose between recovering the amount of the bribes or requiring that the property acquired with the bribes be held on constructive trust for the principal.

It is not always easy to say which remedies will be granted as the court has a wide discretion. In several cases where an agent has made a secret profit without dishonesty the only remedy awarded has been to hand over the profit. In other cases, such as the one which follows, the remedies have been more draconian.

11.4.5 Additional duties of commercial agents

The Commercial Agents (Council Directive) Regulations 1993 reg.2(1) define a commercial agent as:

'a self-employed intermediary who has continuing authority to negotiate the sale or purchase of goods on behalf of another person (the "principal"), or to negotiate and conclude the sale or purchase of goods on behalf of and in the name of that principal.'

This definition is considered more fully below at 11.6.2.

Regulation 3(1) imposes on a commercial agent the duties to look after the interest of the principal, to act dutifully, and to act in good faith. These duties seem similar to a combination of the common law fiduciary duties and duty to obey instructions. However, the duty to act in good faith is expressed in a positive way whereas the duty not to breach the various fiduciary duties is expressed in a negative way. Regulation 3(2) amplifies the three duties somewhat by stating that, in particular, a commercial agent must:

(a) make proper efforts to negotiate and, where appropriate, conclude the transactions he is instructed to take care of;
(b) communicate to his principal all the necessary information available to him;
(c) comply with reasonable instructions given by the principal.

Regulation 5(1) provides that the parties cannot contract out of these duties.

11.4.6 The agent's liability in tort

When the agent is an employee of the principal, the principal will be vicariously liable for torts of the agent which are committed during the course of his employment. Vicarious liability is considered in detail in Chapter 13 at 13.8.

As regards agents who are not employees, an untrue representation by the agent can make the principal liable for the tort of deceit, or under s.2(1) of the Misrepresentation Act 1967, or for negligent misstatement. Deceit and s.2(1) MA 1967 are considered in Chapter 6 at 6.1.2. Negligent misstatement is considered in Chapter 12 at 12.3. As regards torts other than those committed by making an untrue representation, the general position is that the principal will not be liable for torts committed by an agent who was not an employee of the principal. The principal will however be jointly and severally liable with the agent if he gave the agent actual authority to commit the tort.

11.5 THE RIGHTS OF THE AGENT

An agent may have any of the following rights: a right to an indemnity for expenses incurred, a right to the remuneration agreed in the contract, a right to a lien over the principal's goods. We examine the three rights in turn.

11.5.1 Indemnity

Unless the contract which created the agency provides otherwise, an agent will be entitled to an indemnity from his principal for liability incurred or money spent in the performance of the agency. This means that the principal must repay any expenses which the agent has properly incurred. For example, in *Rhodes* v *Fielder, Jones and Harrison* (1919) 89 LJ KB 15 a country solicitor had to indemnify a firm of London solicitors who had paid barrister's fees on behalf of the country solicitor. The country solicitor had asked the London firm to engage a barrister to act for them, but had later instructed the London firm not to pay the barrister's fees. The London firm had paid the barrister's fees because, although they had no legal duty to do so, they had a very strong moral duty to do so.

The right to an indemnity can be lost if the agent exceeds his duty or acts negligently.

11.5.2 Remuneration

The agent's contract with the principal may expressly provide that the agent should be paid and may fix the amount of remuneration. Many professional agents offer to act only on their standard terms and conditions, leaving their principals with a take it or leave it choice.

> **Re Richmond Gate Property Co Ltd**
> [1965] 1 WLR 335
>
> The articles of association of a company set out the remuneration of the managing director. The relevant article provided that the managing director should receive 'such remuneration (whether by way of salary, commission or participation in profits, or partly in one way and partly in another) as the directors may determine'. The company went into liquidation nine months after incorporation. The managing director had been paid nothing during this time and claimed £400.
>
> **Held.** The managing director was not entitled to any payment. An express term of the contract determined what he should be paid. An implied term could not contradict this and nor could more be paid on a *quantum meruit*.

If there is no agreement as to remuneration then the agent must rely on an implied term in order to get paid. Such a term will be implied on the same basis as any other term implied by the courts.

> **Luxor (Eastbourne) Ltd v Cooper**
> [1941] AC 108 (House of Lords)
>
> Estate agents were offered £10 000 commission for selling two cinemas, the commission to be paid on completion. The estate agents found buyers for the cinemas, but the cinema owners changed their minds and refused to sell. The estate agents asked for an implied term that the cinema owners would not refuse to complete the sale to a suitable buyer.
>
> **Held.** No such term could be implied. The commission was so huge that the contract was in the nature of a gamble. If the whole deal went through the estate agents would get their commission. But if anything went wrong, they would not.
>
> Lord Russell: 'I can find no safe ground on which to base the introduction of any such implied term. Implied terms, as we all know, can only be justified under the compulsion of some necessity. No such compulsion or necessity exists in the case under consideration ... The chances are largely in favour of the deal going through, if a purchaser is introduced. The agent takes the risk in the hope of a substantial remuneration for comparatively small exertion.'

(The factors which the court will consider were examined in Chapter 5 at 5.3.) Section 15 SGSA 1982 states that where under a contract for the supply of a service the consideration for the supply of a service is not determined by the contract, left to be determined by a manner agreed by the contract or determined by the course of dealing between the parties, there is an implied term that the party contracting with the supplier will pay a reasonable charge. Where an express term deals with the amount of remuneration the agent will not be able to argue that an implied term entitles him to more, and nor will s.15 SGSA apply (*Richmond Gate*).

Even if the contract does provide that the agent should be paid, it is often difficult to decide whether or not he has done enough to be entitled to the payment. (*Luxor v Cooper*).

Some estate agents nowadays ensure that the contract with the customer provides that if a buyer is found, the agents will be paid whether the seller proceeds with the sale or not.

11.5.3 Lien

A lien is a right to hold onto goods until a claim is satisfied. An agent to whom the principal owes money may have a lien over the principal's goods. The lien of an agent is a particular lien and so it can only allow the agent to retain possession of goods until debts which relate to those particular goods, or to related transactions, are satisfied. (A general lien gives the right to hold onto any of the debtor's goods until a debt is satisfied.) A lien can only arise if the agent has possession of the goods. Furthermore, the lien must not be excluded by the contract. For example, a salesman who has not been paid by his employer might have a lien over the goods he was employed to sell until he does get paid. An agent may lose a lien by waiving it. (By voluntarily parting with possession of the goods or otherwise indicating that he intends to abandon the lien.)

To exercise the lien, the agent must have lawfully come into possession of the goods in his capacity as an agent. The lien only gives a right to possession of the goods over which it is exercised. It does not give a right to sell or dispose of the goods.

The rights conferred on commercial agents by the Commercial Agents (Council Directive) Regulations 1993 are considered below at 11.6.2.

11.6 TERMINATION OF AGENCY

An agent acts for a principal on account of having the principal's actual authority to do so (although an agent can make a principal liable on account of having apparent authority or under *Watteau v Fenwick*). Apart from some exceptional circumstances which make an agency irrevoc-able, the principal can withdraw the agent's authority at any time. However, unless third parties are informed of this, the agent might still be able to bind the principal on account of having apparent authority. For example, in *Trueman and others v Loder* (1840) 11 Ad & El 589 it was well known that an agent in London represented a principal in St Petersburg and that the agent conducted no business on his own account. The principal withdrew the agent's authority, but the agent went on to buy tallow from a third party who believed that the agent was, as usual, acting on behalf of the principal. It was held that the principal was bound by the contract as the agent still had apparent authority to act for the principal. To make sure that such apparent authority does not continue, the principal should inform third parties to whom it has been represented that the agent has authority that the authority has been terminated.

If the principal does withdraw the agent's authority then this might or might not be a breach of contract, depending upon what was agreed between principal and agent. Employees gain a statutory right to a minimum period of notice after one month's continuous employment. (See Chapter 20 at 20.3.1.) In *Martin Baker Aircraft Co Ltd v Canadian Flight Equipment Ltd* [1955] 2 QB 556 it was held that contracts other than those of employment can be terminated by giving reasonable notice and that what amounts to reasonable notice is a question of fact depending upon all of the circumstances. Similarly, an agent who terminates the agreement early may be liable for breach of contract. If the parties agree to end the agency there can be no question of breach of contract. Specific performance will not be ordered to compel a party to continue to act as agent, as it will not be ordered to enforce personal service contracts. (See Chapter 7 at 7.2.4.) Nor will an injunction be ordered if it would, in effect, amount to specific performance of an agency contract. So in *Warren v Mendy* [1989] 3 All ER 103 a professional boxer who had agreed to employ the claimant as his manager, and not to employ any other manager, for a three-year period could not be restrained by injunction from employing another manager before the end of the period.

A fixed term agency ends when the term is up. If the agency is for an indeterminate term either party can end it by giving a reasonable amount of notice of his intention to do so, subject to minimum requirements where the Commercial Agents Regulations apply. If the principal unilaterally ends a contract of agency under which the agent was an employee there may be a claim for unfair dismissal (see Chapter 20 at 20.4) or for damages for breach of contract.

11.6.1 **Termination by operation of law**

Agency is terminated automatically in the following ways:

(i) By frustration. (This will occur for the usual reasons: that performance of the contract becomes impossible, illegal or radically different.)
(ii) By the death of either party.
(iii) By the insanity of either party.
(iv) By the bankruptcy of the principal.
(v) By bankruptcy of the agent if this would render him unfit to perform his duties.

If either principal or agent terminates the agency in breach of contract, damages will be assessed on normal contract principles under the two rules in *Hadley* v *Baxendale*.

11.6.2 **Termination under the Commercial Agents (Council Directive) Regulations 1993**

11.6.2.1 **Definition of a commercial agent**

Earlier in this chapter we saw that the Commercial Agents (Council Directive) Regulations 1993 reg.2(1) define a commercial agent as:

'a self-employed intermediary who has continuing authority to negotiate the sale or purchase of goods on behalf of another person (the "principal"), or to negotiate and conclude the sale or purchase of goods on behalf of and in the name of that principal.'

Now we examine this definition in more detail before going on to consider the rights which may accrue to a commercial agent when the agency is terminated.

First, it should be noted that the commercial agent must buy or sell goods rather than services. It is also necessary that the commercial agent is self-employed, rather than an employee. Limited companies have been held to be commercial agents and a partnership could also be a commercial agent.

A commercial agent must be paid (reg.2(2)(a)) but does not need to be paid on commission. (However, if the agent is not paid on commission several of the regulations, which deal with commission, do not apply.)

Earlier in this chapter, at 11.1, we saw that some retailers call themselves agents when in fact they are not. The example given was of motor retailers calling themselves sole agents of manufacturers in a certain area, when in fact these retailers bought from the manufacturers and sold on their own behalf, rather than selling on behalf of the manufacturers. Such retailers would clearly not be commercial agents as the definition in reg.2(1) requires a commercial agent to sell 'on behalf' of the principal. There is also a requirement that they negotiate and conclude the contract 'in the name of the principal'. So undisclosed agents cannot be commercial agents. An agent who is employed to make only one contract cannot be a commercial agent as the authority of the agent must be 'continuing'. Partners in firms, company officers and dealers in commodity exchanges or commodity markets are all excluded from being commercial agents.

Regulations 2(3) and (4) provide that the Regulations do not apply to persons whose activities as commercial agents are to be considered 'secondary'. The Schedule to the Regulations attempts to clarify the meaning of this. Paragraph 2 of the Schedule says that activities are not to be secondary if: (a) the principal's business is the sale of goods of a particular kind; and (b) the goods concerned are such that (i) transactions are normally individually negotiated and concluded on a commercial basis, and (ii) procuring a transaction on one occasion is likely to lead to more transactions with that person or with other people in the same geographical area or among the same group of customers. In addition, it must be in the commercial interests of the principal to appoint someone to use his own effort, skill and expense to develop the market. Paragraph 3 lists five indications that a commercial agency does exist. These are that:

(a) the principal is the manufacturer, importer or distributor of the goods;
(b) the goods are specifically identified with the principal in the market;
(c) the agent devotes substantially the whole of his time to his agency duties, for one or more principal whose interests do not conflict;
(d) the goods are not normally available otherwise than through the agent;
(e) the arrangement is described as commercial agency.

Paragraph 4 lists three indications that there is no commercial agency, as follows:

(a) promotional material is supplied direct to potential customers;
(b) persons are granted agencies without reference to existing agencies in a particular area or in relation to a particular group;
(c) customers normally select the goods for themselves and merely place their orders through the agent.

Paragraph 5 provides that consumer credit agents and mail order catalogue agents for consumer goods are presumed not to be commercial agents.

11.6.2.2 **Minimum notice periods**

Regulation 16 provides that the Regulations do not apply if the agency agreement is justifiably immediately terminated on account of one of the parties having failed to carry out all or part of his obligations under the contract, or where exceptional circumstances apply.

Where the agency agreement is for an indefinite period, reg.15 sets out minimum notice periods, as follows. In the first year of the agency contract the minimum period is one month. In the second year it is two months. After two years it is three months. The parties cannot agree to shorter notice periods. They can agree to longer periods, as long as the notice to be observed by the principal is not less than that to be observed by the agent. Unless the parties agree otherwise, the notice period must end at the end of a calendar month.

If the agency agreement was for a fixed period but it continues to be performed by both sides after the notice has expired, reg.14 provides that it is deemed to have been converted into an agreement for an indefinite period. The notice periods set out in reg.15 will then apply and, in calculating the required notice, the earlier fixed notice period is taken into account.

11.6.2.3 **Compensation and indemnity payments**

Regulations 17 and 18 entitle the commercial agent to indemnity or compensation on termination of the agency contract. Furthermore, reg.19 provides that these two regulations cannot be contracted out of to the detriment of the agent. However, the agent will lose the rights to indemnity or compensation if he does not inform the principal, within one year of termination of the agency contract, that he intends pursuing his entitlement (reg.17(8)).

Indemnity and compensation are not the same things, and the agent is entitled to be compensated rather than indemnified, unless the agency contract provides otherwise (reg.17(2)). So compensation is the usual remedy and we consider it before considering indemnity.

Compensation

Regulation 17(6) provides that the commercial agent shall be entitled to compensation for the damage he suffers as a result of the termination of his relations with the principal. The agent must therefore have suffered a loss but there is no requirement that this should be the principal's fault.

Regulation 17(7) then states that such damage to the agent shall be deemed to occur particularly when the termination takes place in either or both of two circumstances. First, circumstances which deprive the commercial agent of the commission which proper performance of the agency contract would have procured for him whilst providing his principal with substantial benefits linked to the activities of the commercial agent. Second, circumstances which have not enabled the commercial agent to recoup the costs and expenses that he had incurred in the agency contract on the advice of his principal.

Lord Hoffmann thoroughly reviewed the rights of compensation and indemnity in *Lonsdale v Howard & Hallam Ltd* [2007] UKHL 32, [2007] 1 WLR 2055. The claimant was a commercial agent for a shoe manufacturer, H & H. H & H ceased trading, having given the claimant six months' notice, and sold the goodwill in the business to a competitor. The agency was terminated by reasonable notice and so the claimant had no more contractual entitlement. He was, however, entitled to compensation under the Regulations. Lord Hoffmann analysed how this compensation should be valued. He noted that the right to indemnity came from German law, whilst the right to compensation was derived from French law. In this case compensation was the appropriate remedy because the contract had not agreed upon indemnity. The French courts had tended to value the compensation as twice the average gross commission over the previous three years. However, Lord Hoffmann declined to adopt this approach, as it was not what the Regulations required. The language of the Regulations suggested that the agent should be compensated for having lost something of value as a result of the termination. French law regarded the agent as having a share in the goodwill of that part of the principal's business which he had built up. The principal retains the goodwill after the agency is terminated and so the agent has to be compensated for this. The amount of compensation should be the amount which the agent has lost by not continuing to be agent, that is to say the amount of future commission lost. This can be assessed by asking for how much the agent could have sold the right to be agent to a willing purchaser, assuming that the agency would have continued. If the market was declining, or if earning the commission would have involved expense, then obviously this would reduce the compensation. Lord Hoffmann also noted that if the appropriate right had been an indemnity, rather than compensation, no indemnity would have been payable. This was because the principal, having gone out of business, would not have continued to enjoy any benefit from the customers introduced by the agent. The trial judge had considered valuing the compensation at nothing, even though in the final year the agent's net commission had been about £8 000. He did not think that there was much evidence that anyone would have bought the agent's rights for anything, in view of the declining market and the costs involved in running the agency. However, he thought that this analysis might be over rigorous and awarded £5 000. The Court of Appeal and the House of Lords agreed that this award should stand. Lord Hoffmann thought that relatively few cases would in future be brought to court, once it became understood that the compensation is for the loss in value of the agency. If cases did go to court then often the judge could do the necessary valuation without the help of expert valuers.

Indemnity

The two requirements for an indemnity are: (a) that the agent has brought the principal new customers or has significantly increased the volume of business with existing customers and the principal continues to derive substantial benefits from the business with such customers; and (b) the payment of the indemnity is

equitable, having regard to all of the circumstances and, in particular, the commission lost by the commercial agent on the business transacted with such customers (reg.17(3)).

Regulation 17(4) provides that the amount of the indemnity cannot be more than a figure equivalent to an indemnity for one year, calculated by reference to the agent's actual pay over the previous five years or, if the agent has not worked for five years, such time as he has worked.

The grant of an indemnity does not prevent the agent from seeking common law damages (reg.17(5)).

Loss of indemnity and compensation

Regulation 18 sets out three circumstances in which neither indemnity nor compensation are payable, as follows.

(a) Where the principal has justifiably terminated the contract on account of the agent's breach of contract.
(b) Where the agent has himself terminated the contract. (Unless this was justified by circumstances attributable to the principal, or unless the agent had become so old, ill or infirm that he could not reasonably be required to carry on with his activities.)
(c) Where the commercial agent, with the agreement of the principal, has assigned his rights to a third party.

11.6.2.4 Other duties of the principal

If the agent's remuneration is not fixed, reg.6(1) provides that the agent should receive the remuneration which a commercial agent selling the type of goods sold, in the place where they are sold, would customarily receive. If there is no such customary practice he should be paid a reasonable amount.

Regulation 4(2) imposes two duties on the principal. First, the principal must provide the commercial agent with the necessary documentation relating to the goods concerned. Second, he must obtain for the commercial agent the information necessary for the performance of the agency contract, and in particular notify the agent within a reasonable time if he anticipates that the volume of commercial transactions will be significantly lower than that which the commercial agent could normally have expected.

Regulation 4(3) requires the principal to inform his commercial agent, within a reasonable time, of any acceptance, refusal or non-execution of a commercial transaction which the commercial agent procured for him. The duties set out in reg.4 cannot be excluded by agreement between the parties.

Test your understanding 11.3

1 What non-fiduciary duties are imposed on an agent?

2 What fiduciary duties are imposed on an agent? Why are these fiduciary duties imposed?

3 What rights against the principal might an agent have?

4 Once a principal has withdrawn an agent's authority, is it possible for the agent to continue to make contracts which bind the principal?

5 In what ways may agency be terminated by operation of law?

Key points

■ An agent has the power to alter the legal position of his principal. Most agents do this by making contracts on the principal's behalf.

Creation of authority

■ An agent has actual authority when the principal and agent agree that he should have such authority. If this agreement is made in words the authority is express actual authority. If the agreement is made otherwise than in words, the authority is implied actual authority.

■ An agent has apparent or ostensible authority when a third party acts upon a representation made by the principal that the agent had authority to act on the principal's behalf. Once the third party has acted upon the representation the principal will be estopped from denying it.

■ Agency may arise by operation of law. In an emergency there may be an agency of necessity, and various statutes impose agency.

■ Agency by ratification arises where a principal later agrees to adopt a transaction entered into on his behalf by an agent who did not have the necessary authority. Once the contract has been ratified it takes effect as if the agent had had actual authority from the outset.

Liability on contracts made by agents

■ Agency is disclosed when the agent indicates that he is acting as an agent, whether or not the principal for whom he is acting is actually identified.

■ If an agent makes a contract for a disclosed principal then generally the agent incurs no liability on the contract.

■ If an agent makes a contract for an undisclosed principal then the agent will be liable to the third party on the contract.

■ A principal will be bound by an agent's actions on his behalf only if the agent had some type of authority to act for the principal.

■ Where both agent and principal are liable on the contract the third party may sue either agent or principal. However, once an unequivocal election has been made to hold either agent or principal liable on the contract the third party will not be able to change his mind.

■ An undisclosed principal can sue on a contract made on his behalf as long as the agent acted within his actual authority. However, the undisclosed principal will not be able to sue on the contract: where a term of the contract excluded agency; where the third party would have refused to contract with the undisclosed principal; where the third party made the contract with the agent because he particularly wanted to contract with the agent personally.

■ An agent can be liable for breach of warranty of authority if he warrants to a third party that he possessed authority which he does not in fact possess. The third party's damages will be calculated on general contract principles under *Hadley v Baxendale*, being designed to put the third party

→

in the position which he would have been in if the warranty had not been breached.

Rights and duties of the agent

- Agents have non-fiduciary duties to obey the principal's instructions, to use an appropriate amount of care and skill and to perform their duties personally.
- Agents also have fiduciary duties to avoid a conflict of interest with the principal, to avoid making a secret profit, not to take bribes and to account to the principal.
- The Commercial Agents (Council Directive) Regulations 1993 impose additional duties on self-employed commercial agents as follows: to look after the interests of the principal, to act dutifully, and to act in good faith.
- Unless the contract provides otherwise, an agent will be entitled to an indemnity to cover expenses necessarily incurred in the execution of the agency.

- The express or implied terms of the contract between principal and agent will govern the amount of remuneration to which the agent is entitled.
- The agent may have a particular lien over the principal's goods until some claim is satisfied.

Termination of agency

- Unless the agency is irrevocable, the principal can withdraw authority from the agent at any time. This might amount to breach of a contract with the agent.
- Even if the principal has withdrawn the agent's authority, the agent may still have apparent authority to bind the principal.
- Agency will be terminated automatically by: frustration; death of either party; insanity of either party; bankruptcy of the principal; or bankruptcy of the agent if this would render him unfit to perform his duties.
- Upon termination of the agency self-employed commercial agents may be entitled to an indemnity or to compensation under the Commercial Agents (Council Directive) Regulations 1993.

Summary questions

1 Peter runs and owns a shop which sells second-hand hi-fi equipment. When Peter booked his two weeks annual holiday, he arranged that his friend Alec should run the shop while he was away. Alec is told that he can sell any equipment in stock, as long as he gets at least 75 per cent of the price displayed on it. He is told that under no circumstances should he buy any equipment.

While Peter is away Alec sells an amplifier to Keith for 70 per cent of the price shown on it. Keith thinks that Alec owns the business. Louise, who regularly does business with Peter, buys a stereo system for 60 per cent of the price shown on it. She knows that Peter usually insists on at least 80 per cent of the price shown, even as regards a trade buyer such as herself. Alec buys a stereo system from Harry because he is sure that it is such a bargain that Peter would want it. On his return, Peter discovers that the stereo system bought from Harry is in very bad condition and worth nothing like the price which Alec paid.

Advise Peter as to whether or not he will be bound by the contracts which Alec made.

2 Hangpaper Ltd is a company which buys and sells wallpaper and decorating materials. Hangpaper Ltd's articles of association allow for the appointment of a managing director, but none had ever been appointed. Adrian, a director of Hangpaper Ltd, has for the past three years been allowed by the other directors to act as if he had been appointed managing director. Without the authority of his fellow directors, Adrian buys a large consignment of wallpaper paste from Glueit and Co. When the paste ordered is delivered, it is found to be of a type which is unsuitable for Hangpaper's purposes. Hangpaper Ltd phone Glueit to say that Adrian had no authority to buy the paste. Glueit insist that the contract must stand as they believed that, as managing director, Adrian would have had authority. Advise Hangpaper Ltd as to whether or not they will be bound by the contract with Glueit and Co, and of any rights they might have or might acquire against either Adrian or Glueit and Co.

3 Anthony has been given actual authority by Pedro to buy up to 1 000 gallons of spirit, as long as the price does not exceed £20 a gallon. The type of

→

spirit in question has become hard to obtain and Anthony can only manage to buy it from Toby at £24 a gallon. Anthony buys the spirit from Toby, saying that he is acting as Pedro's agent and has authority to make the purchase. Toby has heard of Pedro but has never had any dealings with him. However, Anthony's intention at the time of the contract was to buy the spirit for himself so that he could use it in an industrial process. Anthony then finds that he will not need the spirit as he had thought that he would. When Pedro finds out that the spirit was purchased at the higher price he tells Anthony that he will pay the higher price. Now Pedro has found out about Anthony's dishonesty and is refusing to take delivery of the spirit from Toby. Advise the parties of their legal positions.

4 Anita works for Pamela as a buyer of second-hand cars. Anita has been expressly forbidden to buy any cars for more than £1 000 each, but she can buy several cars for less than this price as long as she does not spend more than £15 000 in any one month. Acting in contravention of her instructions, Anita buys a car from Tina for £1 750.

a Explain the circumstances in which this contract could be ratified by Pamela and how such a ratification would be made.

b If there is an effective ratification of the contract, how would this affect the rights of Pamela against Anita and Tina?

5 Phil and Ted are antique dealers who used to be good friends but have fallen out to the extent that they absolutely refuse to have any dealings with each other. Phil employs an agent, Alphonse, to buy antiques. Alphonse buys at auctions, antique fairs and from other dealers. Alphonse also deals in antiques on his own account. Alphonse has had several business dealings with Ted. Phil asked Alphonse to try and sell a silver salver and to keep his eyes out for any old barometers. He gave Alphonse authority to sell the silver salver for a price of at least £4 000 and to pay up to £2 000 for a good Victorian barometer. Alphonse finds that Ted has a good Victorian barometer for sale and buys it for £1 500. Alphonse also manages to sell Phil's silver salver to Ted for £5 000, being slightly surprised to get such a good price. Alphonse does not know that Phil and Ted refuse to have any dealings with each other. He does not think it worth mentioning to Ted that he is buying and selling the barometer and the silver salver for Phil. When Phil asks Ted for delivery of the barometer, Ted says that he would never have sold it if he had known that Alphonse was buying on behalf of Phil and that he is therefore refusing to be bound by the contract. Phil claims that Ted will have to deliver and to pay the £5 000 for the silver salver. Ted refuses to be bound by this contract either, saying that he would never have bought the silver salver if he had known that it was Phil's and that he only bought it from Alphonse because Alphonse owed him £3 000 and this seemed to be the best way of getting the money. Advise Phil and Ted of their rights and obligations in respect of the two contracts.

6 Alfred is employed by Polish Co Ltd as a buyer of materials at a salary of £26 000 p.a. Alfred's job requires him to visit various manufacturers of solvents and to buy solvents which can be used in the manufacture of polish. Recently Alfred placed a large order with Madeit Ltd, a company with which Polish Co Ltd had not previously dealt. The solvent delivered by Madeit is slightly more expensive than that delivered by the previous supplier, but Alfred insists that it is definitely of higher quality. Alfred also switched a regular order to SolvCo Ltd, a small company with which Polish Co Ltd had not previously dealt. The solvent delivered by SolvCo Ltd is slightly cheaper than that delivered by the previous supplier. It appears to be of exactly the same quality. The managing director of Polish Co Ltd was watching the FA Cup Final on television when he noticed Alfred sitting in the crowd. The managing director has now discovered that Alfred went to the Cup Final by courtesy of corporate hospitality supplied by Madeit Ltd. The managing director has also discovered that Alfred has a significant shareholding in SolvCo Ltd, and that the solvent supplied by Madeit is of no higher quality than that previously supplied.

Advise Polish Co Ltd of any rights which they may have against either Alfred, Madeit Ltd or SolvCo Ltd.

Multiple choice questions

1 Mr Phillips asks an auctioneer to auction his old computers. The auctioneer says that the computers might fetch between £5 000 and £9 000. Mr Phillips says that he wants a reserve of £5 000 on the computers and that he will be pleased to get £7 500. The auctioneer is to get a commission of 10 per cent of the selling price. The computers do not attract a bid of £5 000 and are not therefore sold at the auction. After the auction is finished, a dealer agrees to pay £5 000 for the computers and the auctioneer sells at this price. Mr Phillips has sold goods through this auctioneer previously and on several occasions his goods have been sold after the auction for the reserve price. Mr Phillips never objected to this, and always paid the auctioneer's commission, but he never expressly agreed to it either. Which one of the following statements is true?

a The auctioneer had no authority to sell other than at the auction. Mr Phillips can therefore claim damages from the auctioneer and get the computers back from the dealer.

b The auctioneer originally had no authority to sell other than at the auction. However, the auctioneer ratified the contract by selling later. The auctioneer will therefore be entitled to keep his commission and Mr Phillips will have no remedy.

c The auctioneer had implied actual authority to sell the computers. Mr Phillips will be bound by the contract with the third party and will have to pay the auctioneer's commission.

d The auctioneer would have had usual authority to sell the computers, as in **Watteau v Fenwick**. Therefore, Mr Phillips will be bound by the contract with the third party and will have to pay the auctioneer's commission.

2 Which one of the following statements is not true?

a Both express actual authority and implied actual authority arise by virtue of an agreement between principal and agent.

b Apparent authority arises where the agent makes a representation to a third party that he (the agent) has authority to act for the principal.

c When a principal effectively ratifies a contract, the contract takes effect from the time when the agent made it, not from the time of the ratification.

d Apparent authority can arise on account of a representation made after the agent has made the contract with the third party.

3 Andrew visits a car showroom and buys a second-hand car for £4 000. Andrew intends to purchase the car on behalf of Peter. Consider the following statements.

i If Andrew claimed that he was acting for Peter, when the contract was made, then the contract will always take effect between Peter and the owner of the car showroom.

ii If Andrew claimed that he was acting for Peter, when the contract was made, then the owners of the car showroom will be able to enforce the contract against Peter only if Andrew had prior actual authority to act for Peter, or if Andrew had apparent authority, or if Peter ratified the contract.

iii If Andrew did not disclose that he was acting for Peter, then Peter will not be bound by the contract but Peter could ratify the contract anyway, in which case a contract will then exist between him and the car showroom owner.

iv If Andrew did not disclose that he was acting for Peter then Peter will be bound by the contract as long as Andrew had actual authority to act for Peter and intended to act for him.

Which two of the following statements are not true?

a i and iii only.

b ii and iv only.

c i and iv only.

d ii and iii only.

4 Boy Billy, a struggling musical artiste, appoints Frank King as his agent for a five-year period. Due to Frank King's efforts Boy Billy becomes very successful, earning over £1 million in the first year. It was agreed that King should take 40 per cent of any earnings over £25 000 p.a. Two years into the agreement Boy Billy wishes to get rid of King as his agent as he feels that he can negotiate a better deal with another agent. Which one of the following statements is true?

a Boy Billy can terminate the agency. Frank King has made a great deal of money from the agency and must accept the risk of the agency being ended, as in **Luxor (Eastbourne) Ltd v Cooper**.

b Under no circumstances can Boy Billy terminate the agency before the end of the five-year period.

c Boy Billy can terminate the agency but will be committing a breach of contract. He will have to pay damages to Frank, these damages being calculated under the rules in **Hadley v Baxendale**.

→

d Boy Billy can terminate the agency but Frank will be entitled to an indemnity or to compensation under the Commercial Agents (Council Directive) Regulations 1993.

5 Which one of the following statements is not true?

a A gratuitous agent can be liable for failure to use an appropriate amount of care and skill.

b An agent must obey the principal's instructions even though he thinks it would be more beneficial to the principal not to do so.

c Any payment made to the agent by the third party with whom the agent was contracting will constitute a bribe if it was kept secret from the principal.

d If the contract between principal and agent fixes the agent's remuneration, but contrary to the expectation of both parties this remuneration is very low, then the agent can be paid more under an implied term of the contract.

6 Which one of the following statements is true?

a Bankruptcy of either the principal or the agent will automatically end the agency.

b If no other agent could be found, a decree of specific performance could be ordered, requiring an agent to continue as agent until the end of the agreed agency period.

c Unless the agency is irrevocable the principal can withdraw the agent's authority at any time.

d An agent will never have the power to bind the principal once the principal has revoked the agent's authority.

Task 11

Read the following case study and then write a brief report, answering the questions which follow.

Each summer Arthur is employed by Peter to sell saddles and riding equipment at horse shows and fairs. Peter makes the saddles by hand, and in the winter months Arthur helps out in the workshop.

Peter pays all of the expenses of sale. He books a stand at the horse shows and pays all the travelling expenses, including putting Arthur up at bed and breakfast accommodation while he is away.

For the past two years Arthur has taken his unemployed son along to the horse shows. Peter has heard about this from customers. He suspects that the son does a good deal of Arthur's selling for him, and is sure that Arthur and his son sleep in the van. Arthur never mentions that his son goes with him. Peter does not mind reimbursing Arthur for his fictitious payment on accommodation as this is a tax-free expense, and he just regards it as part of Arthur's wages.

Last month things went badly wrong. Peter had spent a lot of time in the winter making a new design of saddle. He asked Arthur to show it around to customers, but definitely not to sell it. While Arthur was away at the pub, his son sold the saddle to Harvey Jones, a leading show jumper. When Peter heard what had happened he travelled to the horse show, but Harvey Jones absolutely refused to return the saddle, saying that he had paid for it and was keeping it.

Peter also noticed that Arthur was selling his own leather work on the stall. Arthur's son had spent the winter making this and it was displayed more prominently than Peter's wares. Peter told Arthur's son that Arthur was sacked and would not receive any more wages or expenses at all. Arthur responded by driving away Peter's van and all of Peter's unsold goods.

Arthur refuses to return anything to Peter, who is not only refusing to pay future wages and expenses, but claiming back all sums paid to Arthur that summer.

1 Is Arthur Peter's agent?

2 Does Arthur have authority to get his son to perform some of his duties? If so, what type of duties?

3 Does Harvey Jones own the newly designed saddle, or must he return it to Peter?

4 When Arthur sells his own leather goods on Peter's stall does he break a duty to Peter? If so, which one(s)? What remedies would Peter have?

5 On what basis might Arthur possibly have a right to take the van and the unsold goods?

6 What do you think the outcome of this dispute would be?

mylawchamber *premium*

Visit **www.mylawchamber.co.uk/macintyre** to access study support resources including interactive multiple-choice questions, weblinks, glossary, glossary flashcards, legal newsfeed, answers to questions in this chapter, legal updates and an overview of this chapter all linked to the **Pearson eText** version of *Business Law* which you can **search**, **highlight** and **personalise** with your **own notes** and **bookmarks**.

premium
mylawchamber
unrivalled support for legal education

Use **Case Navigator** to read in full some of the key cases referenced in this chapter with commentary and questions:

Freeman & Lockyer (a firm) v *Buckhurst Park Properties (Mangal) Ltd* [1964] 1 All ER 630
Hely-Hutchinson v *Brayhead Ltd* [1967] 3 All ER 98

12

The law of torts 1

12.1 NATURE OF TORTIOUS LIABILITY

It is notoriously difficult to define a tort, but a possible definition would be that a tort is a civil wrong other than a breach of contract. This definition makes it plain that civil liability can arise in two ways; either on account of a breach of contract or on account of a tort having been committed. Before considering individual torts, we need to examine the fundamental differences between contractual and tortious liability.

In earlier chapters we have seen that contractual liability is voluntarily assumed, and that it is assumed in return for the benefits promised by the other contracting party. For example, if Company A makes a contract to buy a computer system from a retailer, Company B, then both the decision to buy and the decision to sell will have been freely made. Both sides will have chosen to make the bargain and to give some consideration to the other. The liabilities assumed under the contract will have been given in exchange for the rights gained under the contract.

Liability in tort is not undertaken voluntarily. It is imposed by the courts on the basis that certain types of behaviour warrant the imposition of tortious liability. If a person injures another by such behaviour the injured person may bring a legal action in order to gain compensation. If, for example, a driver injures a pedestrian by driving badly then the injured pedestrian will be able to bring an action against the driver. The driver has no choice about whether or not to accept such liability, the courts will impose it. Nor will the driver have received any benefit in return for accepting the liability. It will have arisen not as a result of a bargain, but as a consequence of a tort (the tort of negligence) having been committed.

Another difference between the two types of liability is that liability in contract is generally strict, whereas liability in tort is based on fault. In Chapter 8, at 8.2.4, we considered the nature of the contractual term that goods sold in the course of a business should be of satisfactory quality. As we saw, retailers are liable for breach of this term even if they could not possibly have known that the goods which they sold were not of satisfactory quality. But in almost all circumstances a person will only incur tortious liability if his conduct does not match up to an objective, reasonable standard.

To extend the earlier examples, once Company B has made the contract to supply the new computer system to Company A, it will have to do so or face the legal consequences. It will be no excuse for Company B to show that it was unable to deliver on time because vital components became more expensive, or to argue that although the computer was not of satisfactory quality they could not possibly have known this because the computer was sold in unopened packaging. But the driver who injured the pedestrian will only be liable if it can be shown that he drove badly and failed to take reasonable care. If it cannot be shown that the driver drove badly then he will not be liable, no matter how severe the pedestrian's injuries.

Both the breaching of a contract and the commission of a tort give rise to liability in damages. However, the purpose of contract damages is not the same as the purpose of tort damages. Both of course are designed to compensate. But contract damages achieve this by putting the injured party in the position he would have been in if the contract had been performed. Tort damages achieve it by putting the injured party in the position he would have been in if the tort had never been committed.

To once again extend the earlier example, if the computer system which Company B agreed to sell to Company A was delivered one month late, then Company A would be entitled to damages. Subject to the test of foreseeability laid down in *Hadley v Baxendale*, these damages would be assessed by reference to the amount it had cost Company A that the computer system was not delivered on time. Such damages might include an amount for business lost as a result of the computers not being available, or for the cost of employing extra workers who were needed to do the work which the computers were meant to do. (Contract damages are examined in Chapter 7 at 7.2.2.)

As long as a pedestrian run over by a driver could establish that his injuries were caused by the driver having committed the tort of negligence, he too would be awarded damages. The purpose of these damages would be to put him in the position he would have been in if he had not been run over, subject to the loss being of a type which was a foreseeable consequence of the tort. He might be awarded an amount for pain and suffering, for lost wages and perhaps for damage to his clothes. These losses would be recoverable because if the tort had not been committed, none of the losses would have arisen.

Often a person affected by a tort which is ongoing seeks an injunction rather than damages. If the injunction is granted, the person committing the tort will be restrained from continuing to do so, on pain of a fine or imprisonment. As we saw in Chapter 7 at 7.2.5, injunctions can also be ordered to prevent a person from breaking a contract. Such injunctions are, however, very rarely granted.

In this book several chapters have been devoted to the law of contract and the particular rules which apply to contracts of sale of goods. Contractual rights and obligations have always been the heart of any book on Business Law. But the law of tort is becoming increasingly important in a business context. The English courts are showing a willingness to extend tortious liability to an ever increasing number of situations. Even if the parties have a contractual relationship with each other, this will not necessarily prevent one of the parties from suing the other in tort if this would produce a better remedy. In *Henderson and others v Merrett Syndicates Ltd* [1994] 3 All ER 506 the House of Lords held that an existing contractual relationship would only preclude the possibility of an action in tort where the contract so provided. In *Commissioners of Customs and Excise v Barclays Bank plc* [2006] UKHL 28, [2006] 3 WLR 1 considered below at 12.2.1.2, Lord Bingham said that a duty of care in tort can co-exist with a similar duty in contract. However, the duties are not identical. In *Robinson v PE Jones* [2011] EWCA Civ 9 Stanley Burnton LJ said,

'It is important to note that a person who assumes a contractual duty of care does not thereby assume an identical duty of care in tort to the other contracting party. The duty of care in contract extends to any defect in the building, goods or service supplied under the contract, as well as to loss or damage caused by such a defect to another building or goods. The duty of care in tort, although said to arise from an assumption of liability, is imposed by the law ... The duty of care in tort applies to damage to other property than that supplied, or to personal injury or death, caused by a defect in the property supplied.'

12.2 NEGLIGENCE

Negligence is the most important tort, covering an enormous number of situations. To a certain extent, negligence fills the gaps left by the more strictly defined torts.

In order to establish the tort of negligence the claimant must prove three things:

(a) that the defendant owed him a duty of care;
(b) that the defendant breached this duty; and
(c) that a reasonably foreseeable type of damage was caused by the breach.

We need to examine each of these three matters in turn. However, it is important to realise that the three matters often overlap. As we shall see when considering the cases, the courts do not always regard them as separate matters to be established one after the other. But in understanding the tort of negligence this is the easiest approach to take.

12.2.1 That the defendant owed the claimant a duty of care

The case which follows created the modern law of negligence. As we shall see, it concerned the liability of a manufacturer to an eventual user of his product. However, the language used by the House of Lords' judges was so broad that it became possible to extend the tort of negligence to other situations in which one person had failed to take sufficient care to see that another was not injured.

Donoghue v Stevenson
[1932] AC 562 (House of Lords)

The claimant and her friend visited a café in Glasgow. The claimant's friend ordered a 'ginger beer float' for the claimant. This consisted of ice-cream in a glass, along with a bottle of ginger beer to pour over the top of it. The ginger beer arrived in an opaque stone bottle. Having poured some of the ginger beer over the ice cream, the claimant ate some of the ginger beer float. The claimant's friend poured the remainder of the ginger beer into her own glass. A nauseating substance, which might have been a decomposed snail, fell out of the bottle. The claimant became ill. She might have been poisoned by the ginger beer, or made ill by the sight of the foreign body, or made ill by a combination of poisoning and the sight of the foreign body. The claimant sued the manufacturer of the ginger beer, Stevenson, arguing that he owed a duty of care to her. Stevenson argued that there was no case to answer, even if all the facts alleged by the claimant were true. This issue was appealed all the way to the House of Lords.

Held. (By a majority of 3 to 2) Manufacturers owe a duty of care to see that the ultimate users of their products are not injured by these products.

Lord Atkin: 'You must take reasonable care to avoid acts and omissions which you can reasonably foresee would be likely to injure your neighbour. Who, then, in law is my neighbour? The answer seems to be – persons who are so closely and directly affected by my act that I ought reasonably to have them in contemplation as being so affected when I am directing my mind to the acts or omissions which are called in question.'

COMMENT (i) If the claimant had herself ordered the ginger beer she would have sued the café rather than the manufacturer. Liability would have been strict, being contractual. There would be a statutory requirement that the ginger beer should be of satisfactory quality, and a contractual claim would proceed on the basis that this term had been breached.

(ii) If the case were to arise today, on precisely the facts alleged by the claimant, the possible effect of the Contracts (Rights of Third Parties) Act 1999, which is set out in Chapter 4 at 4.2.2.2, would also have to be considered.

(iii) As the claimant's injury was caused by the ginger beer not being safe the manufacturer could nowadays be made liable, without the need to prove fault, under the Consumer Protection Act Part 1. This Act is considered at 12.4.

(iv) The claimant never took the case to trial.

Donoghue v Stevenson was particularly important, not only because it established that manufacturers could owe a duty of care to the eventual users of their products, but also because it demonstrated that the tort of negligence could be expanded to cover new situations to which it had never previously been applied.

Lord Atkin's neighbour speech was obviously *obiter dicta*, rather than the *ratio decidendi* of the case, as it was a far wider statement of law than was needed to deal with the facts of the case. (For the meaning of *ratio decidendi* and *obiter dicta* see Chapter 1 at 1.3.2.2.) However, the courts have subsequently tended to treat the statement as *ratio decidendi*, so that claimants who can show that their relationship with the defendant satisfied the 'neighbour test' are presumed to have shown that the defendant owed them a duty of care in the particular circumstances of the case.

In certain types of situations case law has established that a duty of care will be owed. For example, it is now established that duties are owed by repairers to their customers, by professional persons to their clients and of course by manufacturers to their customers. When a new situation arises the courts tend to develop the law of negligence incrementally and by analogy with earlier precedents. The court will consider the relationship between the parties, the type of risk involved and whether or not it would be in the public interest to find that a duty of care existed. In *Caparo Industries plc v Dickman* [1990] 2 AC 605 (House of Lords), the facts of which are set out in Chapter 17 at 17.3.3, Lord Roskill said: 'I agree with your Lordships that it now has to be accepted that there is no simple formula or touchstone to which recourse can be had in order to provide in every case a ready answer to the questions whether, given certain facts, the law will or will not impose liability for negligence or in cases where such liability can be shown to exist, determine the extent of that liability.' Lord Roskill went on to say that he thought it infinitely preferable that there should be a return to the traditional categorisation of cases pointing to the existence and scope of any duty of care, rather than a duty being imposed by recourse to wide generalisations which leave their practical application matters of difficulty and uncertainty. The other Law Lords expressed much the same opinion and cases decided since *Caparo* have tended to adopt the incremental approach to deciding whether or not a duty of care is owed. Under this approach new categories of negligence will be created incrementally and by analogy with established categories. This incremental approach is adopted more in cases of pure economic loss and psychiatric injury than in cases of physical injury, damage to property and consequential economic loss.

It is now established that the mere fact that harm is foreseeable is not enough to give rise to a duty of care. Rather, it might be regarded as the first necessary step. A second step is 'proximity of relationship' between the claimant and the defendant. This proximity can be present only if it was foreseeable that harm would be caused to the claimant, but often it goes further than mere foreseeability. What amounts to the necessary proximity will depend upon the facts of the case. For example, if a driver runs over a pedestrian, causing physical injury, then the necessary proximity is established merely because the injury was foreseeable. But if a second claimant suffered nervous shock as a result of seeing the accident, whether there was the necessary proximity would depend upon matters such as how far from the accident the second

claimant was and also how close the relationship between the first and second claimants was. The third and final step is that it must be fair, just and reasonable to impose a duty of care. Ultimately, this will depend upon whether the court thinks that it needs to protect the claimant by imposing liability. Where the claimant has suffered physical injury, the courts are much more likely to find it just and reasonable to impose a duty than where the defendant has suffered only economic loss or nervous shock. Although these three steps sound logical enough, it must be said that in many cases they are hard to find as separate concepts. As Lord Oliver said in *Caparo Industries plc v Dickman* [1990] 2 AC 605.

> 'Indeed it is difficult to resist a conclusion that what have been treated as three separate requirements are, at least in most cases, in fact merely facets of the same thing, for in some cases the degree of foreseeability is such that it is from that alone that the requisite proximity can be deduced, whilst in others the absence of that essential relationship can most rationally be attributed simply to the court's view that it would not be fair and reasonable to hold the defendant responsible. "Proximity" is, no doubt, a convenient expression so long as it is realised that it is no more than a label which embraces not a definable concept but merely a description of circumstances from which, pragmatically, the courts conclude that a duty of care exists.'

The cases set out above were thoroughly reviewed by the House of Lords in *Commissioners of Customs and Excise v Barclays Bank plc* [2006] UKHL 28, [2006] 3 WLR 1. The leading cases were approved and recognised as the appropriate ones to be used in deciding whether or not a duty of care is owed. All of the leading cases had led to a sensible and just outcome, however the tests used to discover whether a duty of care was owed were expressed. Lord Hoffmann warned against using phrases such as 'proximate' and 'fair, just and reasonable' as slogans. The case is considered in detail below at 12.2.1.2, as it concerned liability for pure economic loss.

Although Lord Atkin's neighbour speech referred to omissions as well as to acts, it is a general principal of English law that a person is not to be made liable for mere failure to act. This is the case even where it is apparent that failure to act will result in another person suffering injury. However, omissions can give rise to a duty of care where the defendant has undertaken to do something which he later fails to do or where he has led someone else to believe that he has done something which he has not in fact done. The ownership or occupation of land might also create a duty to do something for the benefit of those coming onto the land or for the benefit of neighbours. Also, once it is established that a duty is owed, for example that a driver owes a duty to a pedestrian, it would not matter that the duty was breached by a failure to act, such as not applying the brakes.

12.2.1.1 Liability for psychiatric injury

A claimant who suffers psychiatric injury as a result of negligence may well be able to claim damages for this. However, the courts have restricted the circumstances in which there is a duty not to cause psychiatric injury. Damages cannot be claimed in respect of sorrow, grief or anxiety. Many of the older cases classify psychiatric injury caused by a tort as 'nervous shock'. Partly because psychiatric injuries are much more easily feigned than physical injuries, the courts have adopted a cautious approach to finding liability for causing nervous shock. Over the years the courts have made a distinction between 'primary victims', who suffer nervous shock as a result of themselves being physically endangered, and 'secondary victims', who suffer nervous shock as a result of witnessing the death or injury of another person. In *Page* v *Smith* [1995] UKHL 7, [1996] AC 155 the House of Lords considered nervous shock suffered by a primary victim. The defendant had negligently driven into the claimant's car. The claimant had not suffered physical injury but he claimed that the accident worsened his ME, a debilitating condition from which he had been recovering. Reversing the Court of Appeal, and by a majority of 3:2, the House of Lords held that, where physical injury to the claimant was foreseeable, he was a primary victim and could therefore recover for psychiatric injury which was caused. This was so even though no physical injury had in fact been caused, and even if the psychiatric injury had not been reasonably foreseeable because a person of reasonable fortitude and courage would not have suffered psychiatric injury. In effect, the majority of the House of Lords held that, where physical injury is foreseeable, physical and psychiatric injury should be regarded as the same type of injury. This reasoning has suffered considerable criticism. However, in *Corr* v *IBC Vehicles Ltd* [2008] UKHL 13, [2008] 1 AC 884 the House of Lords affirmed the decision. The claimant had suffered a severe head injury at work as a result of the employer's negligence. This caused him to become depressed and he later committed suicide. The House of Lords held that he was a primary victim and that the employer was liable for his psychiatric illness as it was the same type of injury as his physical injuries. In *Rothwell* v *Chemical Insulating Co Ltd* [2007] UKHL 39, [2007] 3 WLR 876 the House of Lords distinguished *Page* v *Smith*. The case concerned claimants who had suffered psychiatric illness after being informed that they had suffered changes to lung tissue (known as pleural plaques) after being exposed to asbestos by their employer. The existence of the pleural plaques meant that the claimants were at risk of more serious disease in the future. The fear of this caused them to suffer psychiatric harm. The House of Lords held that the principle in *Page* v *Smith* should be confined to victims of psychiatric injury who had been at risk of immediate physical injury. Lord Hoffmann confined the principle to events which had actually occurred. It could not apply to psychiatric illness caused by apprehension of the possibility of an unfavourable event which had not actually happened.

In the following case, the House of Lords considered the position of secondary victims in some detail.

Alcock v *Chief Constable of South Yorkshire Police* [1991] 4 All ER 907

Ninety-five people died, and many more were severely injured, as a consequence of the defendant's negligent policing of a football match. The disaster was seen by a variety of claimants, who were all relatives or friends of those involved. These claimants were not primary victims, as they were never themselves in danger. Some claimants saw the events from the other side of the stadium, others saw them on television or heard them described on the radio. All of the claimants suffered psychiatric illness and claimed in respect of this against the defendant.

Held. A duty of care will be owed to a secondary victim who suffers psychiatric illness only if the following conditions are satisfied. First, the relationship between the claimant and those injured would have to be sufficiently proximate. It is not possible to make a closed list of relationships, such as husband and wife or parent and child, which will be regarded as sufficiently proximate. Rather, the necessary proximity will exist if there was a close enough relationship of love and affection to make it reasonably foreseeable that the claimant would suffer nervous shock if they apprehended that the primary victim had been or might be injured. Whether or not such closeness existed would require careful scrutiny in every case. Second, it is →

also necessary that the claimant prove closeness to the accident or its aftermath in terms of both time and space. Third, the nervous shock must have been suffered on account of seeing or hearing the accident or its immediate aftermath. Applying these principles, the claims of those who saw the accident on television failed. Two claimants who were inside the football ground failed in their claim because they were not in a sufficiently proximate relationship to the victims of the disaster.

In *Alcock,* two of the Law Lords said that, if an event was sufficiently horrific, even a mere bystander might be able to claim. An example was given of a bystander witnessing a petrol tanker catching fire in a school playground and causing serious injuries to children. However, in **McFarlane v EE Caledonia Ltd** [1994] 1 All ER 1, the Court of Appeal refused to allow a claim by a bystander who had suffered nervous shock. The claimant, a painter on an oil rig, had witnessed a catastrophic explosion and fire on the oil rig. This had caused the deaths of 164 people. The claimant had been evacuated to a boat less than 100 yards from the burning rig and had been forced to watch the incident for almost two hours. However, it was held that a duty of care would be found only if there was a sufficient degree of proximity, which requires nearness in time and place and a close relationship of love and affection, between claimant and victim. In this case the sufficient degree of proximity was found to be absent.

Damages will not be awarded for trauma suffered immediately before death by a claimant who is killed by the defendant's breach of duty. It is also the case that the nervous shock must be caused by witnessing a sudden horrific event and not by witnessing a gradual process, such as death from a wasting disease.

In **French v Chief Constable of Sussex Police** [2006] EWCA Civ 312, [2006] All ER (D) 407 (Mar) Lord Phillips CJ summarised the law on psychiatric injury in the following way:

'(i) There is a duty to exercise reasonable care not to cause psychiatric injury by putting the claimant in fear for his or her physical safety ...

(ii) A defendant who breaches his duty of care not to endanger the physical safety of a claimant will be liable if the breach causes not physical but psychiatric injury, even if it was not reasonably foreseeable that psychiatric injury alone might result ...

(iii) There is no general duty to exercise reasonable care not to cause psychiatric injury as a result of causing the death or injury of someone ("the primary victim") which is witnessed by the claimant ("the secondary victim") ...

(iv) Proposition (iii) applies equally where the claimant is employed by the defendant ...

(v) As an exception to proposition (iii) there is a duty of care not to cause psychiatric injury to a claimant as a result of causing the death or injury of someone loved by the claimant in circumstances where the claimant sees or hears the accident or its aftermath ...

Turning to the duties owed by an employer to an employee, an employer is usually entitled to expect that an employee will be capable of withstanding the stresses inherent in his or her employment. Where, however, an employer knows or ought to know that these stresses are putting a particular employee at risk of psychiatric injury, the employer will come under a duty to take reasonable steps to protect the employee against that risk.'

In **Hatton v Sutherland; Barber v Somerset County Council** [2002] EWCA Civ 76, [2004] 1 WLR 1089 Hale LJ comprehensively set out the approach which should be taken when considering psychiatric injury caused by stress at work:

'(1) ... The ordinary principles of employer's liability apply.

(2) The threshold question is whether this kind of harm to this particular employee was reasonably foreseeable: this has two components (a) an injury to health (as distinct from occupational stress) which (b) is attributable to stress at work (as distinct from other factors).

(3) Foreseeability depends upon what the employer knows (or ought reasonably to know) about the individual employee ... An employer is usually entitled to assume that the employee can withstand the normal pressures of the job unless he knows of some particular problem or vulnerability.

(4) The test is the same whatever the employment: there are no occupations which should be regarded as intrinsically dangerous to mental health.

(5) Factors likely to be relevant in answering the threshold question include: (a) The nature and extent of the work done by the employee ... (b) Signs from the employee of impending harm to health.

(6) The employer is generally entitled to take what he is told by his employee at face value, unless he has good reason to think to the contrary.

(7) To trigger a duty to take steps, the indications of impending harm to health arising from stress at work must be plain enough for any reasonable

employer to realise that he should do something about it.

(8) The employer is only in breach of duty if he has failed to take the steps which are reasonable in the circumstances, bearing in mind the magnitude of the risk of harm occurring, the gravity of the harm which may occur, the costs and practicability of preventing it, and the justifications for running the risk.

(9) The size and scope of the employer's operation, its resources and the demands it faces are relevant in deciding what is reasonable.

(10) An employer can only reasonably be expected to take steps which are likely to do some good: the court is likely to need expert evidence on this.

(11) An employer who offers a confidential advice service, with referral to appropriate counselling or treatment services, is unlikely to be found in breach of duty.

(12) If the only reasonable and effective step would have been to dismiss or demote the employee, the employer will not be in breach of duty in allowing a willing employee to continue in the job.

(13) In all cases, therefore, it is necessary to identify the steps which the employer both could and should have taken before finding him in breach of his duty of care.

(14) The claimant must show that that breach of duty has caused or materially contributed to the harm suffered. It is not enough to show that occupational stress has caused the harm.

(15) Where the harm suffered has more than one cause, the employer should only pay for that proportion of the harm suffered which is attributable to his wrongdoing, unless the harm is truly indivisible.

(16) The assessment of damages will take account of any pre-existing disorder or vulnerability and of the chance that the claimant would have succumbed to a stress related disorder in any event.'

These principles were applied in the following case.

Intel Corp (UK) Ltd v Daw
[2007] EWCA Civ 70, [2007] 2 All ER 126

Intel is a very large company which employed D, a hard-working and conscientious payroll analyst. D had twice suffered from post-natal depression. When D returned to work after the second episode, she was given a greater workload and made accountable to a larger number of managers. Her work was sensitive and complex. D complained to her managers at least 14 times that she had too much work to do, and that she had to stay at work for too long in order to try and do what was expected of her. Intel had merely assured D that she would be given some help, although she never was. D, who had worked for Intel for 13 years, had a serious breakdown and became permanently unable to work.

Held. Intel were liable to D in negligence for failing to reduce the risk of D suffering depression on account of her overwork. Even if Intel had not been aware that D was susceptible to work-related depression, D's managers were aware of her excessive workload. Intel's failures of management had caused the breakdown and her injury had been foreseeable enough to require immediate attention. Intel should have reduced her workload. Furthermore, D was not at fault for failing to use Intel's internal counselling services. The only way to reduce the risk to D was to reduce her workload.

12.2.1.2 Pure economic loss

In Chapter 7 we saw that a claim for economic loss is often the basis of a claim for damages for breach of contract. The law of tort is generally concerned with liability for injury to the person and damage to property. However, damages may also be recoverable in respect of economic loss which is a direct consequence of physical injury or damage to the claimant's own property. (For example, lost earnings if a claimant is injured and unable to work.) An example of such claimable economic loss can be seen in **British Celanese v A H Hunt (Capacitors) Ltd** [1969] 1 WLR 959. The defendants negligently caused the claimant's factory to suffer a loss of power by allowing foil strips to blow onto a power line. This caused damage to the claimant's machines. The Court of Appeal held that the resulting economic loss of not being able to use the machines was fully recoverable. **Spartan Steel and Alloys Ltd v Martin & Co (Contractors) Ltd** [1973] QB 27 provides a contrast. Here the defendant's power shovel negligently cut a cable belonging to the utility company. This caused the defendant's factory to be without electricity for 14 hours. Damages could be recovered for the reduction in value of metal which had to be removed from a furnace and for the profit which would have been made on that particular 'melt' of metal. However, the Court of Appeal did not award damages for four other lost 'melts' which would have been produced but for the power cut. This loss was economic loss which did not flow directly from the claimant's own physical loss and so no duty of care was owed in respect of it.

In *Weller v Foot and Mouth Research Institute* [1966] 1 QB 569, a firm of auctioneers were not able to claim damages in respect of lost profits caused by the defendants' negligently allowing foot and mouth disease to escape from their laboratory. The ensuing outbreak caused the claimants to be prevented from holding auctions but the defendants owed them no duty in respect of their lost profits. This principle is necessary to limit the number of persons who might have a claim. If the auctioneers had been able to claim in respect of their economic loss then a similar claim could have been made by a large number of other businesses, such as pubs and cafés, which had also been caused economic loss. It may, however, be possible for the claimant to succeed in an action for damages for pure economic loss if he can bring himself within one of several exceptions to the general rule. These exceptions would include liability for negligent misstatement, which is considered below at 12.3.

In the following case the House of Lords thoroughly reviewed the circumstances in which liability for causing mere economic loss might arise.

Commissioners of Customs and Excise v Barclays Bank plc
[2006] UKHL 28, [2006] 3 WLR 1

B Ltd and D Ltd owed large sums of money to Customs and Excise in respect of unpaid VAT. Customs and Excise were granted freezing injunctions against both companies. The freezing injunction against B Ltd was for £1 800 000, the one against D Ltd was for £3 928 130. These freezing injunctions would prevent the companies' assets from being moved out of the jurisdiction of the English courts. (See Chapter 7 at 7.2.5.1.) Both B Ltd and D Ltd had accounts with Barclays. The freezing orders were served on Barclays, who sent back a standard letter saying that they would abide by them and would claim back any costs incurred in doing so. Within three hours of each order being served, Barclays allowed B Ltd to withdraw £1 240 570 and D Ltd to withdraw £1 064 289. Customs and Excise never recovered the money which B Ltd and D Ltd owed them, so they sued Barclays in negligence.

Held. Barclays were not liable for the economic loss which Customs and Excise had suffered. They owed no duty of care to Customs and Excise. Liability for pure economic loss will arise in only three situations: first, where a person has, or can be taken to have, assumed responsibility for what he said and did vis-à-vis the claimant; second, under the threefold test considered above at 12.2.1 in relation to the general existence of a duty of care (reasonable foreseeability, proximity and whether it is fair, just and reasonable to impose a duty of care); third, under the incremental test as set out in *Caparo* (again, see above at 12.2.1).

COMMENT (1) Lord Bingham made several important points. (i) The assumption of responsibility test is to be applied objectively and is not concerned with what the defendant thought or intended. (ii) The threefold test does not tend to give straightforward answers to the vexed question as to whether or not a duty of care should be imposed in a novel situation. (iii) The incremental test is little use in itself. It needs to be combined with a test which identifies the legally significant features of a situation. However, the closer the case in question to one in which a duty of care has been held to be owed the more likely it is that a duty will have been owed, and vice versa. (iv) A duty of care in tort can co-exist with a similar duty in contract or with a statutory duty. (v) It would have been unjust and unreasonable to hold Barclays liable, particularly as they stood to gain no reward.

(2) Lord Hoffmann made the following points. (i) In cases of personal or physical injury reasonable foreseeability is usually enough to give rise to a duty of care, but in cases of economic loss something more is needed. (ii) Whether it is fair, just and reasonable to impose a duty is not just a question of fact, questions of fairness and policy also enter into the decision. (iii) The law of negligence does not generally impose liability for mere omissions. (iv) The question of whether a duty of care had arisen in this case was comparable with the question as to whether a statutory duty created a common law duty of care. A statutory duty cannot generate a common law duty of care. The statute either creates a statutory duty or it does not.

(3) Lord Mance said: 'The review of authority confirms that there is no single common denominator, even in cases of economic loss, by which liability may be determined. In my view the threefold test of foreseeability, proximity and fairness, justice and reasonableness provides a convenient framework although it operates at a high level of abstraction.' He also said that the key factor in the case was that Barclays had no real choice as to whether or not they would be involved with the freezing injunction.

Economic loss is of course recoverable for breach of contract. In *Robinson v PE Jones* [2011] EWCA Civ 9 the claimant had bought a defectively built house from the defendants who had built it. The defect, defective flues, did not cause personal injury or damage to other property and did not become apparent until some time after the contract was made. The claimant was too late to sue for breach of contract but not too late to bring an action for negligence. (See s.14A Limitation Act 1980 in Chapter 12 at 12.6.) The Court of Appeal had to decide whether in such circumstances the defendant owed a duty of care regarding pure economic loss. It was held that as regards a contract between a manufacturer (or a builder) and a client the law of contract governed the parties' liabilities. As ever, such contractual liability would have been assumed by the parties themselves. The law of tort would also impose a duty of care as regards personal injury or damage to property. However, the law of tort would not impose a duty of care as regards economic loss, unless one of the parties had assumed a duty regarding such loss, to run co-extensively with his contractual liabilities.

Jackson LJ summarised the law by saying that:

'(i) When A assumes responsibility to B in the *Hedley Byrne* sense, A comes under a tortious duty to B, which may extend to protecting B against economic loss.

(ii) The existence of a contract between A and B does not prevent such a duty from arising.

(iii) In contracts of professional retainer, [where a client pays for advice, a report or plans,] there is commonly an assumption of responsibility which generates a duty of care to protect the client against economic loss.'

Every case had to be looked at in the light of all the surrounding circumstances. However, in this case there was nothing to suggest that the defendants had assumed responsibility for pure economic loss in the *Hedley Byrne* sense and the claimants had not paid for the preparation of advice, reports or plans. This was a normal building contract where the builder was building a house according to a specified plan.

Stanley Burnton LJ saw the crucial distinction as being between a person who supplies something which is defective, thereby becoming liable only in contract, and a person who supplies something (whether a building, goods or a service) which because of its defects causes loss or damage to something else, thereby becoming liable in tort as well. He said that a client could not sue his solicitor or accountant in tort just because the professional advice given was incorrect, and therefore worth less than what was paid for it. But the client could sue in tort if he relied on the advice and lost money as a consequence.

12.2.2 **Breaching the duty**

Merely owing a duty of care is not enough to give rise to liability for the tort of negligence. Every time a person drives across a town he owes a duty of care to many people. He is not liable to be sued by any of these people unless he injures them by breaching the duty of care which he owes them.

A duty of care will be breached if the defendant does not take the care which a reasonable person would have taken in all the circumstances of the case. This is an **objective** standard. It is no defence that the defendant was doing his incompetent best. For example, in **Nettleship v Weston** [1971] 2 QB 691 the Court of Appeal held that the duty of care which a learner driver owed to passengers and the public was the same objective and impersonal standard as every other driver owed. (Notice the contrast with criminal law here. The *mens rea* of most serious crimes require an intention to do the act which a statute or the common law made illegal. See Chapter 22 at 22.1.)

A higher standard of care is expected of professional people and those who claim to have some special competence. Professional people must show the degree of care which a reasonably competent person in that profession would show. Failure to show this standard will amount to breach of duty. In Chapter 8 at 8.3.3.1 we considered **Bolam v Friern Hospital Management Committee** [1957] 1 WLR 582. In that case McNair J said:

'Where you get a situation which involves the use of some special skill or competence ... the test is the standard of the ordinary skilled man exercising and professing to have that special skill.'

In *Bolam* the Court of Appeal held that a doctor who acts in accordance with the opinion of skilled medical professionals will not be negligent merely because other skilled medical professionals would have taken a contrary view. However, in **Bolitho v City & Hackney Health Authority** [1998] AC 232 the House of Lords held that the mere fact that some distinguished experts would agree with the actions taken by a defendant doctor would not necessarily mean that the defendant doctor had not been negligent. It would be very likely to mean this, but it was still up to the court to decide, in the light of all the circumstances, whether or not the defendant doctor had acted reasonably. The court had to be satisfied that the expert opinion upon which the defendant relied had a logical basis and in particular that those holding the opinion had directed their minds, where appropriate, to the question of comparative risks and benefits and, having done so, had reached a defensible conclusion. It would be possible that in rare cases the expert opinion could not stand up to logical analysis. In such cases the court could hold that the opinion did not provide the benchmark by which the doctor's conduct should be assessed.

In deciding whether or not a duty of care was breached, the state of scientific and technical knowledge which prevailed at the time may be an important consideration.

Roe v Minister of Health
[1954] 2 All ER 131 (Court of Appeal)

In 1947 two claimants underwent operations in hospital for relatively minor complaints. Each of the claimants was given a spinal injection of Nupercaine, which was administered by a specialist anaesthetist. The Nupercaine had been contained in glass ampoules which were stored in a solution of phenol. After the operations both claimants were paralysed from the waist downwards. This paralysis was caused by phenol having seeped through invisible cracks in the glass ampoules. The cracks had developed when the container moving the ampoules was moved, but nobody had become aware of the cracks. The anaesthetist had examined the ampoules for cracks prior to administering the injection. Nobody had been aware that there might be a crack which an ordinary visual inspection would not reveal.

Held. The defendant was not liable because in 1947 competent anaesthetists generally did not appreciate that glass ampoules of Nupercaine stored in phenol could become contaminated through invisible cracks. Neither the anaesthetist nor any member of the hospital staff had been negligent.

Of course a hospital would have been liable if a similar accident had occurred after this fact had become known. But, as Denning LJ said, the court, 'must not look at the 1947 accident with 1954 spectacles'.

In deciding whether or not a duty has been breached the following four factors are likely to be of considerable importance:

(a) the likelihood of harm being caused to the claimant;

(b) the potential seriousness of injury which was likely to be caused;

(c) the cost of making sure that injury was not caused; and

(d) the usefulness of the objective which the defendant's actions were trying to achieve.

The first two factors tend to be weighed against the second two. If it is highly likely that injury would be caused to the claimant then this is an indication that the duty of care was breached. This is especially true in cases in which the injury is likely to be serious. However, if the defendant was trying to achieve some particularly valuable objective, or if the cost of making sure that no injury was caused was exceptionally high, then these are indications that the duty was not breached. The following three cases show these considerations being given weight by the courts. However, it would be wrong to think that they form an exhaustive check list. Rather it would be true to say that an overall appreciation of all the relevant cases would tend to indicate that the four matters specified are, consciously or subconsciously, weighed against each other by the courts.

Bolton v Stone [1951] AC 850 (House of Lords)

The claimant was standing in the road outside her house when she was hit by a cricket ball. A game of cricket was in progress at the Cheetham Cricket Club and a batsman had hit the ball for six, striking it right out of the Club's grounds. Cricket had been played on these grounds since 1864 and the nearby houses had been built long after this date. It was most unusual for a ball to be hit out of the ground. The evidence suggested that this had happened about six times in the previous 28 years. The ball which hit the claimant had travelled over 100 yards, clearing a fence which was 78 yards from the pitch and 17 feet higher than the pitch. The claimant sued the committee and members of the Cheetham Cricket Club in both negligence and nuisance.

Held. The duty of care was not breached and so the claim did not succeed.

COMMENT In this case the cost of making sure that no injury occurred was enormous (erecting a much higher fence around the relevant part of the ground) and so the defendants did not breach the duty by continuing to play cricket on the ground. It was also most unlikely that anyone would be injured, although it was foreseeable to some extent because balls had previously been hit out of the ground and people did walk up and down the road. The usefulness of playing cricket →

was not much of a factor in this case. However, it was accepted that people need to take recreation and that cricket is a traditional type of English recreation.

Paris v *Stepney Borough Council*
[1951] 1 All ER 42 (House of Lords)

The claimant, a fitter who had the use of only one eye, was told by his employers to hammer and grind the underneath of a vehicle. He was not given protective goggles and lost the use of his good eye when this was pierced by a shard of metal which flew off when he was hammering a bolt in order to remove it.

Held. The duty of care owed by the employers was breached. The likelihood of harm and the potential seriousness of damage were very considerable, especially as the employers knew that the claimant had the use of only one eye. The cost of making sure that the accident did not happen, by providing goggles, was minimal.

The usefulness of the defendant's actions tends to be an important factor in cases where the defendant acted in an emergency.

Watt v *Hertfordshire CC*
[1954] 2 All ER 268 (Court of Appeal)

A fire station received a call that a woman was trapped under a heavy vehicle about 250 yards away from the station. The officer in charge of the station set off immediately, ordering that a lorry should be loaded with a large jack for lifting heavy weights and that this lorry should follow as soon as possible. The jack, which weighed two or three hundredweight and had four small wheels, was loaded onto the back of the lorry. The jack could not be lashed down so the men in the back of the lorry were meant to hold it steady. When the lorry driver suddenly applied the brakes one of the firemen travelling with the jack was severely injured. If the standard procedures had been followed another fire station would have been contacted to provide a safe means of carrying the jack. This would have caused a delay of at least ten minutes.

Held. The fire authorities had not breached the duty of care which they owed to the injured fireman. The risk to the firemen had to be balanced against the end to be achieved.

Denning LJ: 'If this accident had happened in a commercial enterprise without any emergency, there could be no doubt that the [injured fireman] would succeed.

But the commercial end to make profit is very different from the human end to save life and limb. The saving of life and limb justifies the taking of considerable risk.'

Section 1 of the Compensation Act 2006 provides as follows:

'Deterrent effect of potential liability

A court considering a claim in negligence or breach of statutory duty may, in determining whether the defendant should have taken particular steps to meet a standard of care (whether by taking precautions against a risk or otherwise), have regard to whether a requirement to take those steps might –

(a) prevent a desirable activity from being undertaken at all, to a particular extent or in a particular way, or

(b) discourage persons from undertaking functions in connection with a desirable activity.'

This section codified the existing common law. It is not meant to change the standard of care expected, but is concerned solely with whether, on the facts of any particular case, reasonable care has been taken to avoid breaching the duty of care owed. The law was codified to counter the 'compensation culture' view that some desirable activities should not be undertaken for fear of litigation.

Section 2 of the Act is very straightforward and provides that

'An apology, an offer of treatment or other redress, shall not of itself amount to an admission of negligence or breach of statutory duty.'

In the following case the Court of Appeal considered the standard of care expected of a parent who had hired a bouncy castle for children to play on.

Harris v *Perry*
[2008] EWCA Civ 907, [2009] 1 WLR 19

The defendants, Mr and Mrs Perry, hired a bouncy castle for their triplets' tenth birthday party. The claimant, an 11-year-old who had not been invited to the party, was injured before the party had begun. Mrs Perry had given permission for the claimant to use the castle and her barrister conceded that this meant that she owed him a duty of care. Mrs Perry turned her back on the castle briefly to help a child strap some equipment around himself. Three children each then did a somersault on the castle. The bare foot of the →

third of these children, a gentle boy who was 15 years old and 5 feet 9 inches tall, hit the claimant on the head and caused him extremely severe injuries. The claimant's case was that the defendants had failed to maintain an appropriate level of supervision, and that they should have kept a constant watch of the bouncy castle.

Held. The duty of care had not been breached and so the defendants were not liable.

Lord Phillips CJ gave the only judgment of the Court of Appeal. He said that all risk could not be precluded when children play together and that it would be against the public interest to require parents to keep them under constant surveillance. However, some activities did require supervision or even constant surveillance. The court's task was to decide 'what precautions the defendant [Mrs Perry] should reasonably have taken to protect against risks which she knew, or ought to have known, children playing on the castle would be exposed'. The required standard of care would be identified on the basis of the facts which the defendant knew or ought to have known. The defendant had read a hire agreement and should have had regard to relevant information which that document contained. However, it was inappropriate to have regard to two other documents which the defendant had not read, a health and safety information sheet and the British Inflatable Hirers Association standard conditions of hire. Although the claimant had suffered injuries of horrifying severity, the chance of even severe injury had not been reasonably foreseeable. The standard of care required was 'that appropriate to protect children against a foreseeable risk of physical harm that fell short of serious injury'. Constant surveillance was not therefore required.

12.2.3 The burden of proof

As a claim in negligence is a civil action, the burden of proof is generally upon the claimant to prove the case. However, the Civil Evidence Act 1995 s.11 provides that a defendant who has been convicted of a crime can be taken in civil proceedings to have committed that crime unless he can prove that he did not. In such cases the burden of proof is therefore reversed.

A difficulty which claimants often face is that, although the evidence seems to suggest that the defendant did breach a duty of care, the claimant cannot prove exactly how the injury was caused or who caused it. In such cases the claimant might be able to claim that 'the thing speaks for itself' (formerly known

by the Latin maxim *res ipsa loquitur*). If the claimant can claim that the thing speaks for itself the defendant will be taken to have breached the duty of care unless he can show that he did not in fact breach it.

When the claimant is able to say that 'the thing speaks for itself' the burden of proof is, in effect, reversed and put upon the defendant. However, this will only happen if the following three conditions are satisfied:

(a) the defendant must have been in exclusive control of the thing or the situation which caused the damage;
(b) the accident must be of a kind which would not normally happen without negligence on the part of some person; and
(c) the precise cause of the accident must not be capable of being ascertained by the court.

An example can be seen in **Ward v Tesco Stores** [1976] All ER 219, in which a shopper in a supermarket slipped on yoghourt on the supermarket floor. The customer did not know how long the yoghourt had been there. Tesco would only have been liable if the yoghourt had been there for an unreasonable time and there was no evidence as to how long it had been there. By a majority the Court of Appeal found for the claimant, even though Tesco showed that they normally swept the floor five or six times a day.

Megaw LJ said:

'It is for the [claimant] to show that there occurred an event which is unusual and which, in the absence of explanation, is more consistent with fault on the part of the defendants than on the absence of fault ... When the [claimant] has established that, the defendants can still escape from liability ... if they could show that the accident must have happened, or even on balance of probability would have been likely to have happened, irrespective of the existence of a proper and adequate system, in relation to the circumstances, to provide for the safety of customers.'

Ward v Tesco Stores was distinguished by the Court of Appeal in **Tedstone v Bourne Leisure Ltd** [2008] EWCA Civ 654, [2008] All ER (D) 74 (May). The claimant was badly injured when she slipped on a pool of water near a jacuzzi at the defendants' hotel. Water had not gathered in this area before, and had not been there five minutes before the accident. No reasonable system of the defendants could have dealt with the water in such a short time. Therefore, the claimant's argument that the accident would not have happened if the defendants had not been negligent failed. So no burden of proof passed to the defendants.

12.2.4 Causation

A claimant can only recover damages if he can prove that he suffered a loss and that the defendant's breach of duty caused this loss. Furthermore, he must prove that the loss in question was of a type which would reasonably foreseeably follow from the defendant's breach.

A defendant who has suffered no loss cannot claim. But even where the defendant's negligence has caused a loss to the claimant the courts may choose not to regard this loss as damage. An example can be seen in *McFarlane and another* v *Tayside Health Board* [1999] 4 All ER 961 where a man who had had a vasectomy, and been told that it was successful, impregnated his wife. The couple already had four children and wanted no more but chose not to terminate the pregnancy. The House of Lords held that where a healthy child was born as a result of medical negligence damages could not be recovered for the cost of rearing the child. It was not fair, just or reasonable to impose liability for such economic loss on the negligent doctor and his employer. However, damages were allowed for the pain and distress suffered during pregnancy and birth, and for financial losses which were associated with the pregnancy. (This approach was followed by the House of Lords in *Rees* v *Darlington Memorial Hospital NHS Trust* [2003] UKHL 52, [2004] 1 AC 309.)

12.2.4.1 The 'but for' test

The claimant can only recover damages in respect of a loss which he can prove was caused by the defendant's breach of duty. This is a factual matter, which is generally assessed on a 'but for' test; that is to say but for the defendant having breached the duty, the claimant would not have suffered the injury in respect of which he is claiming.

If, therefore, the claimant would have suffered exactly the same loss even if the defendant had not breached his duty, the defendant will generally not be liable in respect of that loss. For example, in *Barnett* v *Chelsea Hospital* [1969] 1 All ER 428 a doctor at a hospital negligently failed to diagnose a patient who had been admitted with vomiting as having been poisoned with arsenic. The patient was turned away

and died. However, as the patient would have died anyway, regardless of whether he had been admitted to the hospital or not, the hospital was not liable for his death.

Where several people cause the loss in circumstances such that the loss would have occurred on account of the actions of any one of them, common sense is applied and the 'but for' test does not exonerate all of the causers of the loss from liability. Rather, they will all be liable on a proportional basis. So if driver A and driver B both drive negligently, and this causes an accident in which a pedestrian is injured, both A and B will be liable to the pedestrian. Responsibility will be apportioned between A and B, who will be liable accordingly. This is the case even if the accident would not have happened unless both drivers had driven negligently.

As the following case shows, the 'but for' test is not always appropriate.

Chester v *Afshar*
[2004] UKHL 41, [2005] 1 AC 134

The claimant saw a surgeon about her severe back pain. He advised her to have an operation. However, he did not explain to her, as he should have done, that the operation carried a 1–2 per cent chance of severe neurological damage. The claimant had the operation three days later and did suffer the feared neurological damage. This was not caused by the surgeon's negligence in performing the operation. If the claimant had been warned of the risk she would not have had the operation straightaway. She would have sought further advice. The trial judge could not decide whether or not she would have had the operation at some later date if she had been given the warning. If she had decided to have the operation at a later date the same risk would have been present.

Held (3:2). Even though she would not succeed on the 'but for' test, the claimant could succeed in negligence against the surgeon.

Lord Hope, in the majority, said:

'To leave the patient who would find the decision difficult without a remedy, as the normal approach to causation would indicate, would render the duty useless in the cases where it may be needed most. This would discriminate against those who cannot honestly say that they would have declined the operation once and for all if they had been warned. I would find that result unacceptable. The function of the law is to enable rights to be vindicated and to provide remedies when duties have been breached. →

Unless this is done the duty is a hollow one, stripped of all practical force and devoid of all content. It will have lost its ability to protect the patient and thus to fulfil the only purpose which brought it into existence. On policy grounds therefore I would hold that the test of causation is satisfied in this case. The injury was intimately involved with the duty to warn. The duty was owed by the doctor who performed the surgery that Miss Chester consented to. It was the product of the very risk that she should have been warned about when she gave her consent. So I would hold that it can be regarded as having been caused, in the legal sense, by the breach of that duty.'

Lord Walker substantially agreed with this approach.

Lord Steyn, in the majority, thought that the claimant should succeed. He thought that the law existed to right wrongs, and that 'the decision arrived at by the House today reflects the reasonable expectations of the public in contemporary society'.

Lord Bingham dissented. He recognised that the 'but for' test was not always suitable, as for example in the *Fairchild* exception, considered below at 12.2.4.3. However, he said, 'A defendant is not bound to compensate the claimant for damage not caused by the negligence complained of'.

Lord Hoffmann, in a very dismissive judgment, said that the claimant should not succeed because she had not proved that the defendant's breach of duty caused her damage. To do this she would have had to have proved that she would not have had the operation if she had been informed of the risk.

12.2.4.2 Breaking the chain of causation

The claimant must prove that the defendant's breach caused the loss for which he is claiming. To do this he will need to show that there was a chain of causation between breach of a duty of care and the loss which the claimant suffered. This chain must not be broken by a new act intervening (formerly known as *novus actus interveniens*). Actions taken by third parties may break the chain of causation, but they will generally not do so if it was foreseeable that such actions might be taken.

> **The Oropesa**
> [1943] 1 All ER 211 (Court of Appeal)
>
> The *Oropesa* collided with another ship, the *Manchester Regiment*. Both ships were negligently navigated and both were badly damaged. The *Manchester Regiment* had a crew of 74, 50 of whom travelled to the safety of the *Oropesa* in a lifeboat. More than an hour later the captain of the *Manchester Regiment,* with the remaining 24 crew, decided to travel in a lifeboat to the *Oropesa* to discuss a salvage claim. The *Oropesa* was by this time more than a mile away. The captain of the *Manchester Regiment* was persuaded to row to the *Oropesa* by the fact that his ship was a dead weight in the water and the seas were becoming increasingly rough. The lifeboat capsized in the heavy sea. The claimants' son was one of nine crew who were drowned. The other 15 crew members were saved by the *Oropesa*.
>
> **Held.** The owners of the *Oropesa* were liable to the claimants in respect of the death of their son. The actions of the captain of the *Manchester Regiment* did not break the chain of causation because they were reasonable under the circumstances.

Unreasonable actions will usually break the chain. This is particularly true if the action was both unreasonable and unforeseeable. So if one of the first lifeboat's crew had drowned after deciding to swim to the *Oropesa* then the chain would have been broken and the owners of the *Oropesa* would not have been liable for his death.

We shall see that a claimant has a duty to mitigate the loss caused by the breach of duty. If the claimant takes action which attempts to mitigate loss then it is likely that this will not cause the chain of causation to be broken. Nor will reflex actions break the chain of causation. In *Carmarthenshire CC v Lewis* [1955] AC 549 the House of Lords held that a primary school was liable for the death of a lorry driver who had killed himself when swerving to avoid a four-year-old boy whom the school had negligently allowed to get on to the road.

In *Corr v IBC Vehicles* [2006] EWCA Civ 331, [2006] 2 All ER 929 the claimant suffered head injuries at work on account of the defendants' negligence. After a long period of post traumatic stress and depression he committed suicide. The Court of Appeal held, by a majority of two to one, that the defendants were liable for the claimant's death, as the act of committing suicide did not break the chain of causation. The act of committing suicide was a foreseeable consequence of the accident and resulted from the depression.

12.2.4.3 Multiple causes and loss of a chance

Difficulties arise where the claimant's loss was caused not only by the defendant's negligence but also by other causes as well.

McGhee v National Coal Board
[1972] 3 All ER 1008 (House of Lords)

The claimant's employers asked him to clean out brick kilns. No washing facilities were provided even though the work was hot and dirty and exposed the claimant to clouds of brick dust. The claimant used to ride his bicycle home while caked with sweat and grime. The claimant soon developed dermatitis. This was caused by working in the kiln, but the risk of dermatitis was materially increased by the claimant cycling home without washing. The Court of Session held that the employers were in breach of duty by not providing washing facilities. However, the claimant failed in his action because it could not be shown that this breach of duty caused the dermatitis. There was no positive evidence that he would not have contracted dermatitis anyway, even if proper washing facilities had been provided. The claimant appealed to the House of Lords.

Held. The claimant won. A defendant was liable to a claimant if his breach of duty had caused, or had materially contributed to, the claimant's injury. This was the case even if there were other factors which contributed to the injury. If the court found that the defendant's breach of duty had materially increased the risk of injury this amounted to a finding that the breach had materially contributed to the injury (unless the defendant could positively prove the contrary).

In *Hotson v East Berkshire Health Authority* [1987] AC 750 the defendant's negligence had a 25 per cent chance of having caused the claimant's injury. The House of Lords held that to prove causation on a balance of probabilities what was required was at least a 51 per cent probability that the negligence caused the injury. Consequently, the claim failed.

In *Wilsher v Essex Area Health Authority* [1988] AC 1074 the House of Lords considered the case of a prematurely born baby who was negligently given too much oxygen whilst in hospital. The baby developed retrolental fibroplasia which eventually caused him to go blind. Although retrolenta fibroplasia can be caused by being given too much oxygen, there were in this case five other possible causes. The trial judge held that the burden of proof was shifted so that the hospital had to prove that it was not their breach of duty which caused retrolental fibroplasia. The House of Lords rejected this approach and insisted that it was up to the claimant to prove that the hospital's negligence was a material cause of the injury. (A retrial was ordered so that the

medical evidence could be assessed in the light of this ruling.)

The House of Lords considered multiple causation again, in the following case.

Fairchild v Glenhaven Funeral Services Ltd [2002] UKHL 22, [2003] 1 AC 32 (House of Lords)

The case was brought by several claimants who had contracted mesothelioma, a type of lung cancer which is invariably fatal. Mesothelioma is caused by inhaling a single strand of asbestos dust. It is not caused by cumulative exposure and once it has been contracted further exposure will not make it worse. The claimants had been employed at different times, and at different places, by various employers who had negligently exposed them to the risk of inhaling asbestos dust. However, none of the claimants could prove, on a balance of probabilities, that they had inhaled the strand of asbestos dust while working for any particular employer. Furthermore, some of the employers could not be sued as they had ceased to carry on business. Applying the 'but for' test, the Court of Appeal held that the claimants could not succeed against employers who were still in business.

Held. The claimants could succeed, and recover full damages, against any of the employers who had been negligent. (The employer who had to pay the damages could gain a contribution from the other employers.) To apply the 'but for' test would yield unfair results. In special circumstances the 'but for' test could be departed from and a lesser degree of causal connection would then be sufficient. This lesser degree would be that the defendant's breach of duty had materially contributed to causing the claimant's injury by materially increasing his risk of contracting the disease. All the employers who had negligently exposed the claimants to the risk made a material contribution to the claimants contracting the disease. Any injustice which might be caused to the employers by this approach was heavily outweighed by the injustice which would be caused to the claimants if this approach were not taken.

COMMENT (i) The principle in this case has now been given statutory effect by s.3 of the Compensation Act 2006, considered below.

(ii) In *Fairchild* the *McGhee* principle was approved, so materially increasing the risk is to be regarded as materially contributing to the risk. *Wilsher* was not overruled but approved on its own facts. *Wilsher* differs from *McGhee* in that in *Wilsher* there were several →

different ways in which the injury could have arisen whereas in *McGhee* there was only one, exposure to brick dust.

(iii) In **Grace Sanderson v Donna Marie Hull** [2008] EWCA Civ 1211, [2009] CP Rep 12 the Court of Appeal allowed for the possibility of developing the exceptions to the 'but for' test, but said that great caution should be exercised in doing so. The **Fairchild** conditions which applied to mesothelioma might be applied to other diseases, but only if it was impossible, rather than merely difficult, for the claimant to prove enough to satisfy the 'but for' test.

Section 3 of the Compensation Act 2006 provides that where a person has contracted mesothelioma as a result of negligent exposure to asbestos, any person responsible is liable to the claimant for the whole of the damage caused by the disease. Any person jointly and severally liable in this way can seek a contribution from any other person (including the claimant) who negligently exposed the claimant to asbestos. Unless the parties agree otherwise, in assessing the contributions due from the parties the court will consider the lengths of time for which each person exposed the claimant to asbestos. Section 16(3) of the Act gives retrospective effect to s.3 by providing that 'Section 3 shall be treated as having always had effect'.

The following example illustrates how s.3 will work.

Example

X has contracted mesothelioma due to negligent exposure to asbestos. Employers A, B, C and D exposed X to asbestos. X worked for A for 20 years, and for B, C and D respectively for 5 years. He also worked for himself, negligently exposing himself to asbestos, for 5 years. Employers A, B and C have gone into liquidation. X can sue D for all of his loss. However, X's contributory negligence will reduce his damages by 12.5 per cent. If none of his ex-employers had gone into liquidation, X could have sued any of them for his full loss, subject to the deduction for contributory negligence. The party who paid would then be able to seek a contribution from the others. If X's loss was £1 000 000, his contributory negligence would reduce his damages to £875 000. If X sued C, C would have to pay all of this amount to X. C could then seek a contribution of £500 000 from A and of £125 000 each from B, C and D.

In the following case the House of Lords thoroughly reviewed the law relating to loss of a chance in medical cases.

Gregg v Scott
[2005] UKHL 2, [2005] 2 WLR 268

Mr Gregg developed a cancerous lump under his left arm. He visited his GP, Dr Scott, who concluded that the lump was a collection of fatty tissues. The trial judge found that this amounted to negligence because Dr Scott should have suspected something sinister and had the lump investigated. After a nine month delay Mr Gregg visited another GP who sent him for urgent tests. A biopsy was done. This did not show that the cancer had spread. While awaiting treatment Mr Gregg was admitted to hospital, as an emergency, with intense chest pain. This was caused by the cancer having spread to his left pectoral region. Mr Gregg was given high dose chemotherapy. He was told that he could not be cured, a patient being regarded as cured if he goes 10 years without a relapse. Two years later Mr Gregg had a relapse. In the three subsequent years up to the date of the trial he was very anxious and preoccupied with thoughts of his death. At the time of visiting Dr Scott, Mr Gregg's chance of survival for 10 years was 42 per cent. At the time of the trial it was 25 per cent.

Held (3:2). Mr Gregg had not established the tort of negligence because he had not established, on a balance of probabilities, that Dr Scott's failure to send him for tests had caused his loss. In order to prove causation in medical negligence cases the claimant will need to prove that, before the alleged negligence, he had at least a 50 per cent chance of survival.

Lord Hoffmann, in the majority, dismissed the claim. He accepted that there were cases, such as *Chaplin* v *Hicks* (considered in Chapter 7 at 7.2.2.2) where damages could be claimed for loss of a chance. However, he did not think that damages for loss of a chance could be recovered in a case like this. He regarded himself as bound by *Hotson*, *Wilsher* and *Fairchild*, and said that the present case was clearly not within the *Fairchild* exception. He thought that to change the law in this area would be so radical as to 'amount to a legislative act'. He also thought that it would have enormous consequences for the Health Service and insurance companies.

Lord Phillips, in the majority, considered several different situations. First, he thought that, subject to the *Fairchild* exception, a claim that negligence has caused a discrete injury would succeed only if the claimant could prove that there was a probability that →

this was so. Second, where there was a claim that an injury caused by negligence might cause further injury, the claimant might make a claim for the original injury and leave open the claim for the further injury. To succeed in either case the claimant would need to prove that the injury in question was caused by the defendant on a balance of probability. Usually, however, if the original injury was proved to have been caused the court would make a single award which took account of the chance of future injury. Third, he considered that in the type of claim in front of him, that negligence had reduced the prospect of the cure of a fatal illness. He thought that because the claimant's prospect of survival had not been as high as 50 per cent at the time of seeing Dr Scott, Dr Scott's negligence had not altered the course of his illness or his prospect of survival.

Baroness Hale, in the majority, thought that the claim was not for the loss of an outcome, in this case the cure of a disease, which the claimant would have enjoyed but for the negligence. The claim was for the reduced chance of achieving that outcome. She thought that in many cases a doctor could probably have improved a patient's chances if he had done what he ought to have done, because the very reason he ought to have done the thing was to improve the patient's chances. If this led to liability, there would be liability in almost every case. She thought, however, that the all-or-nothing approach led to some injustice. A claimant who can prove a 51 per cent chance that the defendant caused his injury gets 100 per cent of damages for his loss. A claimant who can prove only a 49 per cent chance gets nothing. But to award damages on the percentage chance of the loss (so that in the example above, one claimant would get 51 per cent of his full damages and the other 49 per cent) would be a retrograde step in most personal injury cases.

Lord Nicholls gave a strong dissenting judgment. He said

'2 This is the type of case under consideration. A patient is suffering from cancer. His prospects are uncertain. He has a 45 per cent chance of recovery. Unfortunately his doctor negligently misdiagnoses his condition as benign. So the necessary treatment is delayed for months. As a result the patient's prospects of recovery become nil or almost nil. Has the patient a claim for damages against the doctor? No, the House was told. The patient could recover damages if his initial prospects of recovery had been more than 50 per cent. But because they were less than 50 per cent he can recover nothing.

3 This surely cannot be the state of the law today. It would be irrational and indefensible. The loss of

a 45 per cent prospect of recovery is just as much a real loss for a patient as the loss of a 55 per cent prospect of recovery. In both cases the doctor was in breach of his duty to his patient. In both cases the patient was worse off. He lost something of importance and value. But, it is said, in one case the patient has a remedy, in the other he does not.

4 This would make no sort of sense. It would mean that in the 45 per cent case the doctor's duty would be hollow. The duty would be empty of content ... The common law does not compel courts to proceed in such an unreal fashion. I would hold that a patient has a right to a remedy as much where his prospects of recovery were less than 50–50 as where they exceeded 50–50.'

He also said that he thought that the patient's loss was the loss of a chance of a favourable outcome, rather than the loss of the outcome itself.

Lord Hope dissented. He thought that the case was not a loss of a chance case. He thought that loss of a chance applied to cases where the claim was for an economic loss or for something to which a claimant had a right, as was the case in *Chaplin* v *Hicks*. He thought that the case should be distinguished from cases where the claim was for a disease from which the claimant was not currently suffering. If there was a less than 50 per cent chance that the claimant ever would suffer from such a disease his claim was speculative. He also thought that it should be distinguished from cases, such as *Barnett* v *Chelsea Hospital,* where the claimant would have suffered the same loss even without the defendant's negligent act. *Scott* v *Gregg* was different because the claimant was already suffering from cancer and he claimed that the doctor's negligence diminished his prospect of a successful recovery.

12.2.5 Remoteness of damage

The damage suffered by the claimant must be a **type of damage** which was reasonably foreseeable, otherwise it will be regarded as too remote. However, the extent of the damage does not need to be foreseeable, nor does the precise way in which it arose.

The Wagon Mound
[1961] AC 388 (Privy Council)

The defendant's negligence caused a large quantity of furnace oil to spill into the bay of Sydney harbour. The oil spread on the water to the claimant's wharf, some 600 feet away. The claimants stopped welding →

on their wharf until they were assured by the wharf manager that it was safe to continue. When they resumed welding a spark from a welding torch ignited a piece of cotton waste which was floating in the water. The cotton ignited the oil and considerable damage was caused to the claimant's wharf. The defendants did not know that furnace oil could be ignited when floating on water and could not reasonably have been expected to know this.

Held. The defendants were not liable for the fire, even though they had been negligent in spilling the oil on the water. The test on remoteness of damage is whether the damage in question is of a type which was reasonably foreseeable. In this case a fire was not a reasonably foreseeable type of damage and so the defendants were not liable for any fire damage. If a claim for general fouling by oil had been made it would have been successful as this was a foreseeable type of damage.

COMMENT (i) This case overturned the decision set out in **Re Polemis** [1921] 3 KB 560. In that case the Court of Appeal had held that the test was whether or not the claimant's loss was a direct consequence of the defendant's tort. The defendant would be liable if the loss was a direct consequence, even if the loss was not a foreseeable type of damage.

(ii) This is an interesting example of a decision of the Judicial Committee of the Privy Council being taken to overrule a long-standing decision of the Court of Appeal. (See the hierarchy of the courts in Chapter 1 at 1.3.2.1.)

In the following case the House of Lords held that the complete series of events which caused the injury does not need to be foreseeable.

Hughes v Lord Advocate
[1963] 1 All ER 705 (House of Lords)

Workmen had dug a hole in the road. They left it unattended with a tent on top of it and paraffin lamps around about it. Two young boys took a lamp into the manhole. When one of them dropped the lamp an explosion was caused. This injured one of the boys. An injury by burning was foreseeable but an injury by explosion was not. The explosion had been caused by the paraffin vaporising, an unusual occurrence.

Held. The claimant could recover. The distinction between burning and explosion was too fine a distinction to mean that the danger was not of a reasonably foreseeable type. It was not necessary that the whole series of events satisfied the foreseeability test.

COMMENT (i) In this case the *Wagon Mound* was not considered by the House of Lords.

(ii) The Law Lords strongly made the point that each case must depend upon its own particular facts.

In **Doughty v Turner Manufacturing Co** [1964] 1 All ER 98 the Court of Appeal took the *Wagon Mound* approach rather than the approach taken in **Hughes v Lord Advocate**. A workman dislodged an asbestos cover into a furnace of very hot liquid sodium cyanide. Some minutes later the presence of the asbestos in the liquid caused an explosion in which the workman was severely injured. The workman, however, could not recover damages against his employers. A splash of molten metal was foreseeable but an explosion was not. Diplock LJ said that in the light of the *Wagon Mound,* the decision in *Re Polemis* was no longer the law. He also stated that the House of Lords in **Hughes v Lord Advocate** treated the *Wagon Mound* as correctly stating the law, but distinguished the case on its facts.

Once it has become established that a particular type of damage was a foreseeable consequence of the defendant's breach the defendant will be liable for all damage of that type, no matter what the extent of this.

The 'egg-shell skull' rule is concerned with the extent of the injury caused, in circumstances in which a certain amount of injury was inevitable. The defendant must take his victim as he finds him. So if a certain amount of damage of a particular type was inevitable, the defendant will be liable for all damage of this type caused to a particularly sensitive claimant. For example, in **Smith v Leech Brain** [1962] 2 QB 405 a worker had the task of removing galvanised objects from a tank of molten metal. As a consequence of the defendant's negligence, the worker was injured when a drop of molten metal splashed onto his lip. The worker was particularly susceptible to cancer and consequently the burn became malignant and caused him to die of cancer. Those who were not particularly susceptible would not have suffered cancer as a consequence of the burn. Nevertheless, the defendants were liable for the cancer.

12.2.6 Damages

If the defendant's negligence destroys or damages the claimant's property or goods, the measure of damages will ordinarily be the cost of restoration of the goods. This cost will generally be assessed by reference to the market value. A claim might also be made for loss of the use of the goods if replacement goods could not easily be obtained. Such a claim could take account of profit lost on account of the goods not being available.

Claims in respect of damages for personal injuries might be made in respect of pecuniary losses or non-pecuniary losses. Damages in respect of pain and suffering are awarded, and so are damages for loss of amenity, that is to say loss of the ability to enjoy life. Loss of earnings and the costs of health care are also recoverable. Damages are not subject to tax, and so when a claim for loss of earnings is made the claimant is only to be compensated in respect of the amount of earnings he would have received after tax had been deducted. The fact that the claimant has taken out insurance will not reduce his damages.

If the claimant is killed then damages will necessarily not include some heads of damage which are recoverable in cases of personal injury. First, funeral expenses are payable. No claim for the personal injuries of the deceased will be claimable unless there was a significant period of time between the injury and the death. Section 1A of the Fatal Accidents Act 1976 allows bereaved spouses and the parents of a deceased minor to make a statutory claim of £11 800. Dependants of the deceased may also be able to claim damages in respect of lost earnings of the deceased, but only if they can show that the deceased was supporting them.

As tort damages are compensatory in nature, aggravated and exemplary damages are not awarded.

A claimant is expected to take reasonable steps to **mitigate** his loss. Damages will not be recoverable in respect of losses which the claimant brought upon himself by his own careless actions after the tort had been committed by the defendant. If a reasonable attempt to mitigate in fact increases the loss to the claimant, he will be able to claim in respect of this increased loss.

12.2.7 Defences to negligence

12.2.7.1 Contributory negligence

Contributory negligence is not a complete defence, but reduces the damages payable to the claimant. In extreme cases individual damages for personal injuries can run to several million pounds, and any percentage reduction can amount to a good deal of money.

The Law Reform (Contributory Negligence) Act 1945 s.1 provides that:

'Where any person suffers damage as the result partly of his own fault and partly of the fault of any other person or persons, a claim in respect of that damage shall not be defeated by reason of the fault of the person suffering the damage, but the damages recoverable in respect thereof shall be reduced to such extent as the court thinks just and equitable having regard to the claimant's share in responsibility for the damage.'

Capps v Miller [1989] 2 All ER 333 provides an example of how this works. A motorcyclist suffered head injuries when the defendant negligently crashed into him. The motorcyclist was wearing a safety helmet, but had not fastened the strap properly. He suffered head injuries as a result of the crash and these were increased by his helmet coming off. The Court of Appeal reduced his damages by 10 per cent as it considered this reduction to be just and equitable having regard to the claimant's share in responsibility for his injuries.

In order for the Act to apply, the claimant must have been to some extent responsible for his injuries. It is not necessary that he must have been responsible to some extent for the accident itself. (In *Capps v Miller*, for example, he was not.) The Act is not limited to damages for personal injuries but also covers claims for damage to property.

It is possible for a claimant who is more than 50 percent to blame for his own injuries to succeed in a claim for negligence, as the following case shows.

> **Green v Bannister** [2003] EWCA Civ 1819, [2003] All ER (D) 279 (Dec) (Court of Appeal)
>
> The defendant reversed along a road. It was dark but the road was lit by a single sodium lamp. The defendant looked over her right shoulder to make sure that she did not reverse into parked cars. After reversing for about 35 yards the defendant ran over the claimant, who was lying in the road in a drunken stupor. The trial judge found that the defendant had not been negligent merely on account of having been reversing down the road, but that she had been negligent in not looking in her mirror or over her left shoulder. The judge also apportioned blame 60 per cent to the claimant and 40 per cent to the defendant. The defendant appealed against both of these findings.
>
> **Held.** Both findings were upheld by the Court of Appeal. If the defendant had looked over her left shoulder and in her mirror she would probably have seen the claimant lying in the road. Her not having done these things was negligent and caused the →

accident. The apportionment of liability made by the trial judge was correct and so the claimant was entitled to damages for his injuries, subject to a reduction of 60 per cent.

In *Ehrari v Curry* [2006] EWHC 1319, [2007] All ER (D) 258 (Feb) the High Court held a child of nearly 14, who walked into a a road without first looking for traffic, to be 70 per cent responsible for the accident. She was hit by a truck driving at 20 mph. The truck driver was negligent in that he had not seen the child at all even though he knew that children were in the area.

In *Badger v Ministry of Defence* [2005] EWHC 2941, [2006] 3 All ER 173 an award to a widow in respect of her husband's death from lung cancer was reduced by 20 per cent because he had not given up smoking despite warnings that this was harming his health. The husband had died at 63. Exposure to asbestos at work was the main cause of death but smoking was a contributory factor.

In *St George v The Home Office* [2008] EWCA 1068, [2009] 1 WLR 1670 a prisoner aged 29 was injured and suffered brain damage when he suffered a seizure and fell from a top bunk bed. He had told prison officers that he was a heroin addict who drank heavily and that he had previously had seizures. The trial judge reduced the claimant's damages by 15 per cent on the grounds of contributory negligence. The Court of Appeal reversed this finding. The claimant was 'at fault' in becoming addicted to drugs. However, this fault was too remote in time, place and circumstance to be connected with the negligence of the prison staff, and so it could not properly be regarded as having caused his injury.

12.2.7.2 *Volenti non fit injuria*

Literally translated, *volenti non fit injuria* means 'to one who volunteers, no harm is done'. *Volenti* can act as a complete defence. There are two elements to the rule. First, that the claimant knows of the risk. Second, that he consents to accept the risk.

The consent which gives rise to the defence may be express or implied. The following case shows an example of implied consent.

Morris v Murray
[1990] 3 All ER 801 (Court of Appeal)

The claimant met his friend at a pub where they had a few drinks. After several more drinks the friend suggested that they go for a joy ride in the friend's light aircraft. Conditions were poor and flying at the aerodrome had been suspended. The plane did manage to get into the air briefly but then crashed. The claimant was badly injured, the friend was killed. An autopsy showed that the deceased friend was three times over the drink-driving alcohol limit. The claimant sued the deceased friend's estate.

Held. The claimant was defeated by *volenti non fit injuria*. By his actions the claimant had implicitly waived his right to damages.

Volenti can also provide a complete defence where the claimant has agreed not to sue, or where the defendant has excluded liability by means of a contractual term or a notice. However, as we saw in Chapter 5 at 5.6.1, the Unfair Contract Terms Act 1977 s.2(1) would not allow a business to exclude liability for death or personal injury caused by negligence by reference to any contract term or notice. We also saw that s.2(2) of the 1977 Act would not allow a business to exclude liability for other types of loss or damage caused by negligence unless the term or notice so doing satisfied the Act's requirement of reasonableness. It would also be the case that the defendant would have had to have taken reasonable steps to bring the term or notice to the attention of the claimant before the claimant could be said to have agreed to it.

In employment cases the consent of the employee is not easily proved, as employees often have very little true choice about whether or not to agree to conditions imposed or suggested by the employer. However, it is possible for the defence to be successfully invoked by the employer. (See *ICI Ltd v Shatwell* [1965] AC 656 in Chapter 21 at 21.11.7.4.) Also, the Road Traffic Act 1988 s.149 provides that *volenti* is not available as a defence where a passenger in a car sues a driver who should be compulsorily insured. The fact that the passenger has willingly accepted the risk of negligence on the driver's part does not negate any such liability of the driver.

A claimant who is making an effort to effect a rescue will not be defeated by *volenti*. So in *Haynes v Harwood* [1935] 1 KB 146 (Court of Appeal) a policeman who suffered injury when he stopped a runaway horse which was pulling a van was able to claim for his injuries. The policeman had been on duty inside a police station when he saw the horses coming down the street. At the time the police station had contained a large number of people, including children.

12.2.7.3 Illegality

A claimant who is injured whilst committing an illegal act with the defendant may be debarred from making a claim against him. However, the outcome will depend upon the seriousness of the illegal act, and the degree of connection with the harm which the claimant suffers.

Ashton v Turner [1981] QB 137

Three young men committed a burglary after an evening drinking together. They tried to escape in a car driven by the defendant. The defendant crashed the car and the claimant was severely injured.

Held. The defendant did not owe a duty of care to the claimant. As a matter of policy the law will not in certain circumstances allow a perpetrator of a crime to bring an action against a fellow perpetrator in respect of actions done in the course of committing the crime. (*Volenti non fit injuria* would also have prevented the claimant from succeeding.)

Test your understanding 12.1

1. What are the three main differences between contractual and tortious liability?

2. What three things will the claimant need to prove in order to succeed in an action for negligence?

3. In what circumstances will a breach of duty owed by a defendant to a claimant have been breached?

4. What four factors have emerged from the case law as being of significance when deciding whether or not a defendant breached a duty of care?

5. What is the effect of the 'but for' test, which can be used to assess whether or not the defendant's breach of duty caused the claimant's loss?

6. To what extent does the injury suffered by the claimant have to have been a foreseeable consequence of the defendant's breach of duty?

7. In what circumstances can damages for psychiatric injury caused by witnessing an accident to a loved one be claimed?

8. Can damages be claimed for pure economic loss caused by the defendant's negligence?

9. What is meant by contributory negligence?

10. What is meant by *volenti non fit injuria*?

12.3 NEGLIGENT MISSTATEMENT

Negligent misstatement is not a tort in its own right, but is merely an aspect of the tort of negligence. However, it is convenient to consider liability for negligent misstatements separately from general liability for negligence.

Liability for negligent misstatements can arise in relation to pure economic loss. Such liability was considered by the House of Lords in the following case.

Hedley Byrne & Co Ltd v Heller and Partners Ltd [1963] 2 All ER 575
(House of Lords)

A bank asked the defendants, who were merchant bankers, about the financial position of E Ltd, one of their customers. The bank asked in confidence, and without responsibility on the defendants' part, whether E Ltd were sound as regards an advertising contract worth between £8 000 and £9 000. A few months later the bank made a similar request, this time asking whether E Ltd were trustworthy in the way of business to the amount of £100 000 a year. The defendants replied, in a letter headed 'For your private use and without responsibility on the part of the bank or its officials', that E Ltd were respectably constituted and considered good for their normal business engagements. This information was passed on to the claimants, advertising agents, who placed advertising orders on E Ltd's behalf. These deals were made in such a way that the claimants made themselves personally liable on them. E Ltd went into liquidation without paying the claimants some £17 000 owing in respect of the advertisements placed. The claimants sued the defendants for this money, claiming that the defendants had been negligent by giving a misleading indication as to E Ltd's creditworthiness.

Held. The defendants were not liable because their disclaimer that the advice was given without responsibility prevented a duty of care from arising. However, but for the disclaimer a duty of care might have arisen. Such a duty of care arises where there is a special relationship between the parties, on account of the very close proximity between them.

This case was highly significant in that it recognised that a duty of care could be owed in respect of negligent misstatements, even as regards pure economic loss. However, mere foreseeability of loss would not be enough to give rise to liability. A claim for pure economic loss caused by a negligent misstatement can be made only if the following four conditions are satisfied: first, there must be a special relationship of trust and confidence between the parties; second, the party preparing the advice or information must, expressly or impliedly, have voluntarily assumed risk; third, the claimant must rely on the advice or information; fourth, this reliance must have been reasonable in all of the circumstances. The special relationship can possibly arise even where the relationship is purely gratuitous. (See *Chaudry* v *Prabhakar* [1988] 3 All ER 718 (Court of Appeal) which is set out in Chapter 11 at 11.4.2.)

In *Caparo Industries plc* v *Dickman* [1990] 1 All ER 568, the House of Lords held that a very proximate relationship must exist between claimant and defendant before liability in negligent misstatement will arise. The claimants were shareholders in a company who had relied upon the audited accounts of the company when deciding to make a take-over bid for the company. After the take-over had been successfully completed the claimants discovered that the company accounts, which had been audited by the defendants, showed a pre-tax profit of £1.2 million, whereas they should have shown a loss of £0.4 million. The House of Lords held that the defendants owed no duty of care to the claimants as their relationship was not sufficiently proximate. Lord Oliver put forward criteria which could be used to establish the necessary relationship of proximity:

'What can be deduced from the *Hedley Byrne* case, therefore, is that the necessary relationship between the maker of a statement or giver of advice ("the adviser") and the recipient who acts in reliance upon it ("the advisee") may typically be held to exist where: (1) the advice is required for a purpose, whether particularly specified or generally described, which is made known, either actually or inferentially, to the adviser at the time when the advice is given; (2) the adviser knows, either actually or inferentially, that his advice will be communicated to the advisee, either specifically or as a member of an ascertainable class, in order that it should be used by the advisee for that purpose; (3) it is known either actually or inferentially, that the advice so communicated is likely to be acted upon by the advisee for that purpose without independent inquiry, and (4) it is so acted upon by the advisee to his detriment. That is not, of course, to suggest that these conditions are either conclusive or exclusive, but merely that the actual decision in the case does not warrant any broader propositions.'

The auditors owed a duty of care to the company and to the shareholders of the company as a body, but not to individual shareholders or to members of the public. The Law Lords also emphasised that the tort of negligence should be developed incrementally, and not by means of one broad general principle.

In Chapter 6, at 6.1.2.2, we saw that a person to whom an actionable negligent misrepresentation has been made can sue to rescind the contract or claim damages under s.2(1) of the Misrepresentation Act 1967, and that damages might be more easily gained under the 1967 Act than under negligent misstatement. In addition, it is worth noticing that the Financial Services Act 1986 can make promoters of companies liable for misstatements when shares, debentures or securities are issued. In Chapter 20 at 20.2.4.7 the case *Spring* v *Guardian Assurance plc* [1994] 3 All ER 129 is set out. The case shows that an employer who carelessly or inaccurately prepares a reference for an employee can be liable for negligent misstatement.

In *Commissioners of Customs and Excise* v *Barclays Bank plc* [2006] UKHL 28, [2006] 3 WLR 1 considered above at 12.2.1.2, the House of Lords, [2006] 3 WLR 1 considered *Hedley Byrne*, *Caparo* and *Spring* and considered all of them to be binding decisions which had achieved justice on their respective facts.

12.4 THE CONSUMER PROTECTION ACT 1987 PART I

Part I of the Consumer Protection Act 1987 imposes civil liability, allowing a claimant who is injured by an unsafe product to sue the manufacturer of the product (and possibly others) without having to prove the tort of negligence. Liability under Part I of the Act is strict. This means that, in the absence of one of the defences listed in the Act, injured consumers will be entitled to damages if they show that they were injured by a product which was less safe than could reasonably be expected. The defences available are, as we shall see, narrow and specific.

12.4.1 Who may sue?

The Act gives the right to sue to any person who is injured by a product, the safety of which was 'not such as persons generally are entitled to expect'.

For over a hundred years the Sale of Goods Act required that goods sold by a business were of merchantable quality. As we have seen, this requirement has been replaced by a requirement that the goods must be of satisfactory quality. They must also be fit for the buyer's purpose and must correspond with any description by which they were sold. If a buyer of goods is injured because goods sold by a business were not of satisfactory quality the Sale of Goods Act 1979 will provide the buyer with a remedy against the seller. But privity of contract restricts the remedies offered by the Sale of Goods Act to the buyer of the goods. (Subject to the Contracts (Rights of Third Parties) Act 1999, the effect of which is considered in Chapter 4 at 4.2.2.2.) The Consumer Protection Act now gives a similarly high level of protection to anyone injured by the goods. Claims such as the one in **Donoghue v Stevenson**, which are made against a manufacturer by a person injured by one of the manufacturer's products, would now be more easily established under the Consumer Protection Act Part I rather than in the tort of negligence.

12.4.2 Who is liable?

Section 1 of the Act defines a 'producer' of a product as meaning:

'(a) the person who manufactured it;
(b) in the case of a substance which has not been manufactured but has been won or abstracted, the person who won or abstracted it;
(c) in the case of a product which has not been manufactured, won or abstracted but essential characteristics of which are attributable to an industrial or other process, having been carried out (for example, in relation to agricultural produce) the person who carried out that process.'

Section 2 makes producers of products liable under the Act. It also makes 'own branders', who add their label to products which they did not produce, and anyone who imports the product into the European Union liable. Any of the classes of people who can be liable are liable where damage is caused wholly or in part by a defect in a product. (The meaning of 'defect' is considered below.)

Ide v ATB Sales Ltd [2007] EWHC 1667, [2007] All ER (D) 238 (Jul) provides an illustration of an importer into the EU being strictly liable under the Consumer Protection Act 1987 Part 1. The defendant had imported mountain bikes into the EU and the claimant had bought one of these bikes. The bike in question had been defective in that its handlebar had suddenly snapped while the claimant was riding it. As the defendant had imported the bike into the EU, he was strictly liable for the claimant's injuries.

Anyone involved in the chain of supply can also be liable if he does not, upon request, name a party who would be primarily liable (s.2(3)). If more than one of these people are liable they are jointly and severally liable. Each person is therefore liable for the full amount of the damage suffered. The retailer of the product is not liable unless he is an own-brander. An own-brander uses distinguishing marks to hold himself out as the producer of the product. Most supermarkets, for example, have their own brands of foods such as baked beans. (Retailers are of course liable to the purchasers of any defective goods under the Sale of Goods Act 1979.) A third party might also be able to sue on the contract if the contract expressly provided that he could or if a term of the contract which he is seeking to enforce purported to confer a benefit upon him. (See the Contracts (Rights of Third Parties) Act 1999 at 4.2.2.2.)

12.4.3 Defective products

The Act imposes liability in respect of defective products. Section 3 of the Act says that products can be regarded as defective if their safety is not such as persons are generally entitled to expect, and that safety embraces not only risks of death or personal injury, but also the risk of damage to property. Products include any goods or electricity, and also include a product which is comprised in another product, whether by virtue of being a component part or raw material or otherwise. So a car is a product, the car tyres are a product and the rubber from which the tyres are manufactured is a product.

The court will consider all the circumstances when deciding whether or not this objective standard has been breached. Section 3(2) mentions a number of factors to be considered, including:

Section 3(2) mentions a number of factors to be considered, including:

'(a) The manner in which, and purposes for which, the product has been marketed, its get-up, the use of any mark in relation to the product and any instructions for, or warnings with respect to, doing or refraining from doing anything with or in relation to the product;

(b) what might reasonably be expected to be done with or in relation to the product; and

(c) the time when the product was supplied by its producer to another.'

This last factor is designed to give some protection to manufacturers producing new products. These are not to be considered unsafe just because later products were safer. (This is linked to the controversial 'development risks' defence, which is considered below.) Warnings may not only make an unsafe product safe, if they are inappropriate they might also make a safe product unsafe. Advertisements and their context might also affect the safety or otherwise of a product.

The burden of proof is on the consumer to prove that the product was defective (unsafe).

The Court of Appeal considered the meaning of a defective product in the following case.

> ### Abouzaid v Mothercare (UK) Ltd
> [2000] EWCA Civ 348, [2000] All ER (D) 2436 (Court of Appeal)
>
>
>
> A 12-year-old boy was injured while fitting a child's sleeping bag to a pushchair. The sleeping bag, which was manufactured by the defendants, was designed to be attached to pushchairs by elasticated straps. A metal buckle attached to one of the straps was to be used to attach the elasticated straps to each other. While trying to attach the straps the boy let go of one of them. This caused the metal buckle to hit him in the eye, severely damaging his retina.
>
> **Held.** The product was defective. It was designed in such a way that an accident such as this could happen. There was no need for the straps to be elasticated and instructions could have warned of the dangers. The risk of injury to the eye, and the seriousness of such injuries, meant that the safety of the product was not such as persons generally are entitled to expect.

In *Tesco Stores Ltd v Pollard* [2006] EWCA Civ 393, [2006] All ER (D) 186 (Apr) the Court of Appeal again considered the meaning of defective. A 13-month-old toddler had been injured on account of ingesting dishwasher powder. The Court of Appeal accepted the judge's finding that the toddler's mother had not negligently left the bottle open, but did not seem entirely to believe this. A product is defective under the Act if its safety is not such as persons generally are entitled to expect. The dishwasher powder had been in a bottle with a child resistant closure cap, which was more difficult to open than an ordinary screw top bottle.

However, the bottle top did not comply with the British Standard torque measure. The Court of Appeal held that the product was not defective. The public would expect the bottle top to be more difficult to open than an ordinary screw top, which it was. Members of the public were unlikely even to know about the existence of the British Standard, never mind what it required.

12.4.4 Damage suffered

Section 5 allows a claimant to claim for death or any personal injury caused by the unsafety of the goods. Damage to property is only claimable if it causes an individual to suffer a loss of more than £275. The loss may be made up of damage to several items.

Damage to the product in question is not recoverable. Nor is damage to other products supplied with the product in question. So if a car battery caught fire and destroyed both the car and the battery the Act would provide no remedy for either loss. (However, the purchaser of the car could gain a remedy against the vendor of the car, under s.14(2) of the Sale of Goods Act 1979, as long as the vendor sold the car in the course of a business.)

> ### Example
>
> John buys a microwave oven as a wedding present for Mr and Mrs Smith. The oven is defective and this causes it to catch fire and burn Mr Smith's hand. The kitchen work surface is damaged and the oven itself is destroyed. Under the Act, damages could be claimed for the injury to Mr Smith and for all the damage to the work surface as long as this amounted to at least £275. Damage to the oven itself could not be claimed under the Act. John could claim for damage to the oven under the Sale of Goods Act 1979 s.14(2), as the oven was not of satisfactory quality. If John had told the retailer that the oven was a present for Mr and Mrs Smith, and had sufficiently identified them, the Contracts (Rights of Third Parties) Act 1999 would have allowed Mr and Mrs Smith to claim under s.14(2) SGA for all loss and damage suffered.

Compensation for injury, death and damage to goods must be claimed within three years of the loss becoming apparent. In addition, there is an absolute time limit of ten years after the date when the product was put into circulation by the producer. This date begins when the producer voluntarily relinquishes control over the product, for commercial reasons, to a person who is not so closely associated with the producer that the two can be regarded as the same person.

Contributory negligence on the part of the claimant can reduce the damages. So if in the above example the court considered that Mr Smith was 25 per cent to blame for his injuries, perhaps because his injuries worsened on account of his not seeking medical help, then his damages would be reduced by 25 per cent.

Section 5(3) excludes liability for loss or damage to business property. At the time of the loss or damage, the property must be 'of a description of property ordinarily intended for private use, occupation or consumption; and intended by the person suffering the loss or damage mainly for his own use, occupation or consumption.'

12.4.5 Defences

Liability is strict and this means that the claimant does not need to prove fault. Nor can liability be excluded by any contract term, notice or other provision. There are however certain defences available, the burden of proving them being on the defendant. These defences are as follows:

'(a) that the defect was caused by complying with EU or UK legislation;

(b) that the accused did not at any time supply the product to another;

(c) that the accused did not supply the product in the course of a business or with a view to profit. For example, a person who made jam as a hobby would not be liable under this Act if he gave the jam away and it poisoned a person who consumed it;

(d) that the defect in the product did not exist when the product was supplied by the defendant to another;

(e) that the state of scientific and technical knowledge was not such that a producer of products of the same description as the product in question might be expected to have discovered the defect if it had existed in his products while they were still under his control;

(f) that the defect constituted a defect in a 'subsequent product' in which the product in question had been comprised and was wholly attributable to the design of the subsequent product or to compliance by the producer of the product in question with instructions given by the producer of the subsequent product.'

The 'development risks' defence set out in (d) is controversial. It would have meant that the victims of the drug Thalidomide would not have had a remedy because when the drug was created scientists were not aware of its danger. (For the same reason the drug manufacturers would not have been liable in negligence.) The Government included the development risk defence because it thought that not to do so would make the manufacture of drugs and certain other products so hazardous as to be economically impractical.

Ultimately, the balance to be struck between the interests of drug manufacturers and drug users is a matter of politics. However, the wording of the Directive which gave rise to the Act is wider in respect of this defence than the wording of the Act. The Directive requires the defendant to prove that 'the state of scientific and technical knowledge at the time when he put the product into circulation was not such as to enable the existence of the defect to be discovered'. This wording concentrates on not only whether the state of scientific and technical knowledge was such that the producer of the product could have discovered the defect, but whether it was such that anybody could have discovered it. (For the circumstances in which an incorrectly implemented Directive can be relied upon see Chapter 1 at 1.4.2.4.)

The development risks defence was raised in *Abouzaid* v *Mothercare (UK) Ltd*. The defendants argued that they could rely on the defence because there was no record of a similar accident having occurred before, and there was no research which showed that the elasticated straps could cause injury. The Court of Appeal rejected these arguments because they did not show that the defect was not discoverable at the time when the product was manufactured.

The Act does not replace the common law but supplements it.

12.5 THE OCCUPIERS' LIABILITY ACTS 1957 AND 1984

Occupiers of premises owe a duty of care to all lawful visitors, and a separate duty of care to trespassers. The Occupiers' Liability Act 1957 sets out the duty owed to lawful visitors. The 1984 Act sets out the duty owed to trespassers. Almost all businesses must occupy some premises, and so almost all are potentially liable.

Section 1(2) of the 1957 Act provides that the common law definition of an occupier should apply when considering liability under the Act. The common law also provides the definition of an occupier for the purposes of the 1984 Act. The common law shows us that the person who has control over the premises is the occupier and this might include an independent contractor, such as a builder. In the leading case, **Wheat v Lacon** [1966] AC 552 (House of Lords), Lord Denning stated that any person with any degree of control over the state of the premises would be an occupier. It is obvious from this that there might be more than one occupier. Section 1(3) of the 1957 Act makes it plain that liability can be imposed not only on the occupier of premises, but also on the occupier of any fixed or moveable structure, including any vessel, vehicle or aircraft. This is a wide area of liability and ladders, for example, have been held to be a moveable structure within the meaning of the Act. However, the Acts are to be used only for problems arising from structures and not for activities that happen to take place in or on these. As regards these activities, **Fairchild v Glenhaven Funeral Services Ltd** indicated that the common law of negligence is more appropriate.

12.5.1 Lawful visitors

Any person who comes on to premises with either express or implied permission of the occupier will be a lawful visitor. Express permission is simply a question of fact. Whether implied permission has been granted is more problematic. It is a matter which must be proved on a balance of probabilities by the person claiming to be a lawful visitor. The fact that the defendant tolerates persons to be on his premises does not necessarily mean that he has granted them implied permission to be there, although it could have this effect. In the following case the Court of Appeal considered whether a man running across land at night was a 'visitor' for the purposes of the 1957 Act.

Harvey v Plymouth City Council
[2010] EWCA Civ 860, [2010] NPC 89

In the early hours of the morning the claimant, who was aged 21, suffered serious injuries when he fell five and a half metres down a sheer drop from land owned by the defendant. The claimant had been drunk at the time and had been running away from a taxi without having paid the fare. As he ran, he tripped over a chain link fence which had been pushed down to a height of about 14 inches. The land had been used for informal recreation for some years. Evidence was accepted that children had been in the habit of making dens on the land. There was also evidence of bonfires, smoking, drinking and sexual activity by adults and teenagers at night-time. It was argued for the claimant that he was an 'implied licensee' on the defendant's land. The trial judge found that the claimant had left the taxi and gone onto the land in youthful high spirits and not with dishonest intent. He had left a friend behind in the taxi, feeling that the friend had not paid his fair share earlier in the evening.

Held. The claimant was not a licensee because the City Council had not impliedly assented to his activities on the land. This was the case even if his activities, or similar activities, could have been foreseen. He was not therefore a 'visitor' and so was not covered by the 1957 Act. Carnwath LJ, who gave the only judgment, said:

'When a council invites the public to use its land for recreational purposes, it is consenting to normal recreational activities, carrying normal risks. An implied licence for general recreational activity cannot, in my view, be stretched to cover any form of activity, however reckless.'

Even when a person is invited onto premises he is not necessarily invited onto the whole of the premises and is not invited to abuse the part of the premises to which he is invited. A person who wrongfully uses premises onto which he has been invited becomes a trespasser. It is possible, where there are several occupiers, that a person on the premises might be a lawful visitor as regards some occupiers and a trespasser as regards others. People who enter the premises as of right, such as the postman, will be lawful visitors whether invited onto the premises or not.

Section 2(2) of the Occupiers' Liability Act (OLA) 1957 defines the common duty of care which is owed to all lawful visitors.

'The common duty of care is a duty to take such care as in all the circumstances of the case is reasonable to see that the visitor will be reasonably safe in using the premises for the purposes for which he is invited or permitted by the occupier to be there.'

As the duty is to provide such care as is reasonable, different occupiers might find themselves liable to provide different standards of care. In ascertaining whether or not an occupier has satisfied the common duty of care a court will consider all the circumstances of the case, including the likelihood of injury, the type of danger and the steps which would need to be taken to prevent injury. Sections 1 and 2 of the Compensation Act 2006, considered above at 12.2.2, will both apply when a court is considering whether a duty of care has been breached.

Section 2(3) of the 1957 Act provides that an occupier must be prepared for children to be less careful than adults. It also provides that an occupier may expect that a person, in the exercise of his trade or profession, will appreciate and guard against any special risks ordinarily incident to the trade or profession, so far as the occupier leaves him free to do so.

Section 2(4)(a) deals with warnings provided by the occupier. Whilst the section recognises that warnings may mean that the occupier has discharged his common duty of care, it also provides that a warning is not to be treated, without more, as absolving the occupier from liability. It will only have this effect if in all the circumstances it was enough to enable the visitor to be reasonably safe.

Section 2(4)(b) provides that an occupier who has properly entrusted work to an independent contractor should not necessarily be liable for damage caused to a visitor by the faulty execution of that work. The occupier should not be liable if he acted reasonably in entrusting the work to the contractor, and if he had taken such steps as he reasonably ought to have done to satisfy himself that the contractor was competent and that the work had been properly done.

Mere warning notices will not be subject to the Unfair Contract Terms Act 1977, but notices which attempt to exclude or restrict liability will. We have already examined the UCTA 1977 in Chapter 5 at 5.6. There we saw that the Act only applies to business liability, which can include liability arising from the occupation of business premises. Section 2(1) and (2) of the 1977 Act will prevent the restriction of liability for negligence. S.1(1)(c) UCTA 1977 defines negligence as including the common duty of care imposed by the Occupiers' Liability Act 1977. As we have seen, s.2(1) UCTA 1977 does not allow any contract term or notice to exclude liability for death or personal injury caused by negligence. We have also seen that s.2(2) UCTA 1977 does allow liability for damage other than death or personal injury caused

by negligence to be excluded, but only by a term or notice which satisfies the 1977 Act's requirement of reasonableness. Subject to the provisions of UCTA 1977, a non-contractual notice can be enough to exclude or restrict liability. This is made plain by the final two words of s.2(1) OLA 1957 which states that: 'An occupier of premises owes the same duty, the "common duty of care", to all his visitors, except in so far as he is free to and does extend, restrict, modify or exclude his duty to any visitor or visitors by agreement or otherwise.'

Damages can be claimed in respect of personal injury, or damage to property or financial loss, but only if the loss was of a type which was reasonably foreseeable. *Volenti non fit injuria* is a defence. However the defence must be considered in the light of s.2(3) UCTA 1977, which states: 'Where a contract term or notice purports to exclude or restrict liability for negligence a person's agreement to or awareness of it is not of itself to be taken as indicating his voluntary acceptance of any risk.'

Contributory negligence may be raised as a defence in the same way as it may be raised as a defence to the tort of negligence.

12.5.2 **Non-visitors**

Any person who enters the premises other than as a lawful visitor will do so as a non-visitor. Trespassers are the most common type of non-visitor. Frequently, such trespassers will be children, and the courts have recognised that even trespassers need considerable protection from inherently dangerous things such as live railway lines. In *British Railways Board* v *Herrington* [1972] AC 877 the House of Lords held that the general common law duty towards trespassers was not to deliberately or recklessly harm them. However, it also held that where the occupier knew that the condition of his land or the activities of the trespasser meant that the trespasser was likely to be injured, the duty of 'common humanity' required the occupier to ensure that the trespasser avoided the danger. The Railways Board was held liable to young children who were electrocuted by a live railway line. The children had gained entry through a broken down fence and the Railways Board had been warned that children were in the habit of trespassing through the fence and playing near the live line.

The Occupiers' Liability Act 1984 has replaced the common law duty owed to trespassers.

Section 1(3) of the 1984 Act states that a person owes a duty of care to a person other than a lawful visitor if:

(a) he is aware of the danger or has reasonable grounds to believe that it exists;

(b) he knows or has reasonable grounds to believe that the other is in the vicinity of the danger concerned, or that he may come into the vicinity of the danger . . . and

(c) the risk is one against which, in all the circumstances of the case, he may reasonably be expected to offer the other some protection.

Section 1(4) of the 1984 Act states that: 'Where, by virtue of this section, an occupier of premises owes a duty to another in respect of such a risk, the duty is to take such care as is reasonable in all the circumstances of the case to see that he does not suffer injury on the premises by reason of the danger concerned.' As was the case with the 1957 Act, ss.1 and 2 of the Compensation Act 2006, considered above at 12.2.2, will apply when a court is considering whether a duty of care has been breached.

Volenti non fit injuria can provide a defence. Section 1(6) of the 1984 Act provides that: 'No duty is owed by virtue of this section to any person in respect of risks willingly accepted as his by that person (the question whether a risk was accepted to be decided on the same principles as in other cases in which one person owes a duty of care to another).'

Section 1(5) deals with the effect of warnings: 'Any duty owed by virtue of this section in respect of a risk may, in an appropriate case, be discharged by taking such steps as are reasonable in all the circumstances of the case to give warning of the danger concerned or to discourage persons from incurring the risk.'

The Unfair Contract Terms Act 1977 does not apply to the duty created by OLA 1984. Section 1 of the 1977 Act states that, as far as the 1977 Act is concerned, 'negligence' means: (a) the breach of any obligation, arising under the express or implied terms of a contract, to take reasonable care or exercise reasonable skill in the performance of the contract; or (b) breach of any common law duty to take reasonable care or exercise reasonable skill (but not any stricter duty); or (c) breach of the common duty of care imposed by the Occupiers' Liability Act 1957.

Liability under OLA 1984 is limited to personal injury. Section 1(8) of the 1984 Act states that: 'Where a person owes a duty by virtue of this section, he does not, by reason of any breach of that duty, incur any liability in respect of any loss or damage to property.'

12.6 TIME LIMITS

Earlier in this chapter we saw that when a claim is brought under the Consumer Protection Act Part I compensation for injury, death and damage to goods must be claimed within three years of the loss becoming apparent. We also saw that there is an absolute time limit of ten years from the date when the product was put into circulation by the producer.

As regards common law actions, s.2 of the Limitation Act 1980 provides that an action in tort, other than an action for personal injuries, must be brought within six years of the date when the right to sue accrued. As regards latent damage, s.14A provides an alternative period of three years from the date when the claimant knew the following: that the damage was serious enough to justify proceedings; that it was capable of being attributed to the defendant's negligence; and the identity of the defendant. Latent damage is damage which does not become apparent for some time after it was caused. There is a longstop period of 15 years from the act or omission which is alleged to have caused the claimant's damage, after which no action can be brought (s.14B Limitation Act 1980).

In the case of a claim for personal injuries the limitation period is three years either from the date on which the right of action accrued or from the date on which the claimant had knowledge of his injury (s.11 Limitation Act 1980). A person is regarded as having knowledge of his injury when he knows that the injury was significant; that it was capable of being attributed to the defendant's negligence, nuisance or breach of duty; and the identity of the defendant (s.14 Limitation Act 1980). If personal representatives claim on behalf of a deceased person the claim must be brought within three years of the date of the death or three years from the date on which they had knowledge (ss.11(5) and 12 Limitation Act 1980). In exceptional cases, s.33 allows the court to override the limits on bringing claims in respect of personal injuries or death if it would be equitable to do so. In *Horton v Sadler* [2006] UKHL 27 the House of Lords held that the s.11 time limit on bringing a case for personal injury could be disapplied by the court where it appeared equitable to do this.

Time does not run against minors (persons under 18) until they become 18. Nor does time run against a person who is suffering from a mental disorder, within the meaning of the Mental Health Act 1983, to the extent of being incapable of managing and administering his property and affairs. Where a claim is based upon the defendant's fraud, such as a claim under the tort of deceit, time does not run against the claimant until he discovered the fraud or could with reasonable diligence have done so (s.32(1)(a) Limitation Act 1980). Similarly, time does not run if the defendant has deliberately concealed the claimant's right of action (s.32(1)(b)).

Section 36(1) of the Limitation Act provides that the usual limitation periods do not apply where the claimant is seeking an equitable remedy, such as an injunction. Such remedies will be defeated by the equitable doctrine of laches or acquiescence. The court has a wide power to allow or refuse a claim for an equitable remedy and it is not possible to state a maximum time period within which such a remedy must be claimed.

Test your understanding 12.2

1 In what circumstances can a defendant be liable for negligent misstatements?

2 What is the main effect of the Consumer Protection Act 1987 Part I?

3 As regards what type of damage can a claim be made under the 1987 Act?

4 Who is an occupier of premises for the purposes of the two Occupiers' Liability Acts 1957 and 1984?

5 What duty does an occupier of premises owe to a lawful visitor?

6 What duty does an occupier of premises owe to a trespasser?

Key points

The nature of tortious liability

■ Tortious liability is imposed by the courts and is generally based on fault. Tort damages are designed to put the claimant in the position in which he would have been if the tort had never been committed.

Negligence

■ In order to establish that the tort of negligence has been committed the claimant will need to prove three matters: that the defendant owed him a duty of care; that the defendant breached this duty; and that the claimant suffered a foreseeable type of damage caused as a consequence of this breach.

■ Claims in respect of psychiatric injury, often known as 'nervous shock', have been restricted by the courts.

■ A claimant will not generally be awarded damages in respect of pure economic loss.

■ A duty of care will have been breached if the defendant does not take the care which a reasonable person would have taken in all the circumstances.

■ In an action for negligence the claimant can only succeed in respect of a type of damage which was a foreseeable consequence of the defendant's breach. The extent of the damage does not need to be foreseeable.

■ The claimant will only succeed if there is an unbroken chain of causation between the defendant's breach of duty and the damage suffered by the claimant.

■ The Law Reform (Contributory Negligence) Act 1945 allows the court to reduce the claimant's damages to the extent that it considers this just and equitable, having regard to the claimant's responsibility for the damage which he suffered.

■ A claimant who, expressly or impliedly, voluntarily consents to running a risk may be defeated by *volenti non fit injuria*.

Negligent misstatement

■ A negligent misstatement can give rise to liability in negligence if there is a sufficiently proximate special relationship between the claimant and the defendant.

■ A suitably worded disclaimer can prevent a duty of care in respect of negligent misstatements from arising.

■ Liability for negligent misstatement can arise in respect of pure economic loss.

The Consumer Protection Act 1987 Part I

■ The Consumer Protection Act 1987 Part I allows a person injured by an unsafe product to sue the manufacturer of the product, the extractor of raw materials, the person who imported the product into the EC, processors of the product, own-branders or, possibly, others in the chain of supply. A claiOm can only be made in respect of death or personal injury, or in respect of damage to non-business property which amounted to more than £275.

→

- The Act does provide limited defences. However, liability is strict and is not therefore based on fault.

Occupiers' liability

- An occupier of premises has a degree of control over the state of the premises.
- An occupier of premises owes the common duty of care to visitors, under the Occupiers' Liability Act 1957, to take such care as in all the circumstances of the case is reasonable to see that they are reasonably safe in using the premises for the purposes for which they are invited or permitted by the occupier to be there.
- Under the Occupiers' Liability Act 1984, occupiers of premises owe a duty to trespassers if they are aware of a danger or have reasonable grounds to believe it exists, and know or have reasonable grounds to believe that the trespasser is or might come into the vicinity of the danger. The duty of care is to take such care as is reasonable in all the circumstances of the case to see that the trespasser does not suffer injury on the premises by reason of the danger concerned.

Summary questions

1 In *Haley v London Electricity Board* [1965] 3 All ER 185 (House of Lords) the facts of the case were as follows. Electricity Board workers dug a 60 foot trench in the pavement and left warning signs at both ends of the trench. They also placed a long-handled hammer across one end of the trench and picks and shovels across the other. One end of the hammer lay on the pavement, the other was hooked on to some railings. These precautions would have been quite sufficient for ordinarily sighted people. But the claimant, who was blind, tripped over the hammer and banged his head on the pavement. The claimant often walked along the pavement in question. As a result of this accident he became almost totally deaf and was forced to retire early from his job. The claimant was not himself negligent, his white stick passed over the hammer. He sued the Electricity Board for the tort of negligence. Government figures showed that at the time of the case about 1 in 500 people were blind.

a Do you think that the defendants owed a duty of care to the claimant?

b Assuming that a duty of care was owed to the claimant, do you think that the defendants breached the duty?

c If a duty was owed and was broken, would the type of damage suffered by the claimant have been sufficiently foreseeable for the claimant to be awarded damages in respect of it?

d Assuming that a duty was owed, that it was broken and that the type of injury suffered was sufficiently foreseeable, would any defence be available to the Electricity Board?

2 In the school holidays Martha took her two young children, Bill and Jack, to a play-day run by the local authority. After dropping the children off Martha picked up her friend Jill as the two of them intended to go shopping. As Martha's car drove past the play event a large explosion occurred. This was caused because a local authority employee negligently allowed gas to escape from a large container. Martha and Jill rushed towards the scene but were prevented from getting closer than 100 yards by the police who swiftly cordoned off the area. Bill and Jack were both badly burnt in the explosion and died before they reached hospital. Martha, who had always been a cheerful person, suffered post-traumatic stress disorder as a consequence of seeing the accident. She also suffered debilitating grief and sorrow. As a consequence she was unable to continue in her job as a teacher. Jill had a long history of nervous disorders. She suffered severe depression which left her unable to go to work or look after her family. Martha's mother, Mary, watched the local television news and suffered extreme anxiety when she saw the accident. She had not been warned by anyone that the accident had occurred. Since suffering this attack of anxiety, Mary has become agoraphobic and unable to leave her house. Advise the local authority of any liability they might have in respect of Martha, Jill and Mary's problems.

3 John buys a second-hand electric lawn mower from his neighbour. The lawn mower was bought by the neighbour from SupaStores Unlimited one year ago. SupaStores Unlimited bought it from a wholesaler, who bought it from the manufacturer, Supamowers Ltd. The lawn mower catches fire when John is using it. John is badly burnt and so are his clothes. The lawn mower itself is destroyed and John's garden shed, containing all of his tools, is burnt down. Advise John of any claim which he might have against SupaStores Unlimited or

→

Supamowers Ltd. How would your answer be different if John had himself bought the lawn mower from SupaStores Unlimited?

4 Cedric hosts a party at his house to celebrate his 40th birthday. Cedric is a keen amateur inventor. He absent-mindedly leaves his soldering iron turned on in a bedroom when he answers the door to the first guest. Later in the evening one of the newly arrived guests, Cecilia, is told by Cedric to leave her coat upstairs in the bedroom. The light bulb in the bedroom expires as Cecilia switches it on and so the bedroom is in darkness. Cecilia does not see the soldering iron and her hand is badly burnt when it comes into contact with it. Jimmy, who was not invited to the party, decides to try and get in via an unlocked window at the rear of the house. The room into which Jimmy gains entry is locked, so Jimmy cannot get into the party. Jimmy turns on the light in this room but is severely electrocuted as Cedric was in the process of rewiring this room and had forgotten to isolate the supply of electricity to it. Advise Cedric of any liability he might have towards either Cecilia or Jimmy.

Multiple choice questions

1 Consider the following statements. Apart from the first one, the statements apply to the tort of negligence.

i Liability in contract is generally strict, whereas liability in tort is generally based on fault.

ii A duty of care will be breached if the defendant did not take the care which a reasonable person would have taken in all the circumstances.

iii If the defendant caused the claimant's injury while trying to achieve some particularly useful objective, this makes it less likely that a duty of care owed was breached.

iv If it can be shown that the claimant would have suffered the loss in respect of which he is claiming even if the defendant had not breached a duty of care owed, then generally the defendant will not be liable for the claimant's loss.

v Neither reflex actions, nor reasonable attempts to mitigate loss, will generally break the chain of causation which must link the defendant's breach of duty and the claimant's loss.

Which of the above statements are true?

a All of the statements.
b i, iii and v only.
c i, ii and iv only.
d ii, iv and v only.

2 Which one of the following statements is not true?

a The 'egg-shell skull' rule means that a claimant can claim in respect of a loss which was not a foreseeable type of loss if he was particularly susceptible to such losses.

b A claim for psychiatric injury caused by witnessing injury to another can be successful if the claimant loved the victim and witnessed the accident which caused the injury.

c In an action for negligence, damages can be recovered in respect of economic loss which was a direct consequence of a foreseeable type of physical injury or a foreseeable type of damage to property.

d If a claimant's reasonable attempt to mitigate loss in fact increases his loss, the claimant will be able to recover damages for the increased loss.

3 Which one of the following statements is not true?

a *Volenti non fit injuria* can be a complete defence. Contributory negligence can reduce the amount of damages to which the claimant is entitled.

b A claimant's damages can only be reduced on account of contributory negligence if the claimant had some responsibility for the initial breach of duty which caused his injuries.

c A claimant will not be defeated by *volenti non fit injuria* if he is injured while making a reasonable attempt to effect a rescue.

d In certain circumstances the law will, as a matter of public policy, prevent a perpetrator of a crime from suing a fellow perpetrator in respect of actions done while committing the crime.

4 Which one of the following statements is not true?

a Liability for negligent misstatements is a branch of the tort of negligence, rather than a tort in its own right.

b Liability for negligent misstatements can only arise where there is a special relationship between the parties.

c A suitably worded disclaimer can prevent liability for negligent misstatements from arising.

d A person who acts entirely gratuitously, and who is not even in business on his own account, cannot become personally liable on account of a negligent misstatement.

→

5 Consider the following statements, which are made in relation to the Consumer Protection Act 1987 Part I.

 i Liability under the Act is strict. A manufacturer of a product can therefore become liable under the Act even if he has not been negligent.

 ii Liability under the Act can arise in respect of any product the quality of which is not such as persons are generally entitled to expect.

 iii A claim for damages under the Act can be made in respect of either personal injury or damage to property, but in either case only if the claim is for more than £275.

 iv A claim in respect of damage to business property cannot be made under the Act.

 v Contributory negligence on the part of the claimant can reduce the damages to which he is entitled under the Act.

Which of the above statements are true?

 a All of the statements.

 b i, iv and v only.

 c ii, iii and iv only.

 d i, iii and v only.

6 Which one of the following statements is not true?

 a Any person with any degree of control over the state of the premises can be an occupier, for the purposes of the Occupiers' Liability Acts 1957 and 1984.

 b An occupier who has entrusted work to an independent contractor cannot become liable for damage caused to a visitor by the faulty execution of that work.

 c The Unfair Contract Terms Act 1977 does not apply to the duty of care created by the Occupiers' Liability Act 1984.

 d Subject to the effect of the Unfair Contract Terms Act 1977, even a non-contractual notice can be enough to restrict or exclude liability of the common duty of care owed by occupiers to lawful visitors to their premises.

Task 12

A group of American students who are visiting your University wish to know how the different English torts can be committed. Using a local business as an example, write a report giving details of the following:

a The meaning of owing a duty of care and breach of duty in the tort of negligence.

b The extent to which damage caused by a breach of a duty of care must be foreseeable in order to be recoverable.

c The extent to which a person can become liable for negligent misstatements.

d The outline effect of the Consumer Protection Act 1987 Part I.

e The extent to which an occupier of land owes a duty of care to lawful visitors and to trespassers.

mylawchamber *premium*

Visit **www.mylawchamber.co.uk/macintyre** to access study support resources including interactive multiple-choice questions, weblinks, glossary, glossary flashcards, legal newsfeed, answers to questions in this chapter, legal updates and an overview of this chapter all linked to the **Pearson eText** version of *Business Law* which you can **search**, **highlight** and **personalise** with your **own notes** and **bookmarks**.

Use **Case Navigator** to read in full some of the key cases referenced in this chapter with commentary and questions:

Abouzaid v Mothercare (UK) Ltd [2000] All ER (D) 2436
Caparo Industries plc v Dickman and others [1990] 1 All ER 568
Fairchild v Glenhaven Funeral Services Ltd and others [2002] 3 All ER 305
Gregg v Scott [2005] 4 All ER 812
Henderson v Merrett Syndicates Ltd [1994] 3 All ER 506
Barber v Somerset County Council [2004] 2 All ER 385

13

The law of torts 2

13.1 PRIVATE NUISANCE

A private nuisance is an indirect unlawful interference with another person's land or his use or enjoyment of his land. For example, if a manufacturing company makes persistent unreasonable noise in a residential area this would be a private nuisance. There is nothing unlawful in the company making a noise. What makes it unlawful, and therefore a private nuisance, is that it unreasonably prevents others from enjoying the use of their property.

As private nuisance is an interference with the use and enjoyment of land, only the owner or occupier of land, with a recognised legal or equitable interest in the property, can sue. The House of Lords confirmed this in ***Hunter* v *Canary Wharf Ltd*** [1997] AC 655, holding that a person who merely occupied the premises as a home, without a recognised legal or equitable interest, could not sue. However, this ruling may have to be changed in the light of the Human Rights Act 1998.

In Chapter 1, at 1.5.1 we saw that s.6(1) of the 1998 Act makes it unlawful for a court to act in a way which is inconsistent with a Convention right. We also saw that Article 8(1) gives all citizens the right to respect for their private and family life and their home. This probably means that anyone who occupies a house as their home will now also be able to claim.

A direct interference with a person's land, such as dumping rubbish onto it, would amount to the tort of trespass to land. Indirect interferences, such as noise, are nuisance. However, nuisance is by no means limited to noise. Vibrations, noxious fumes, encroaching roots from trees and even the use of premises as a sex shop have all been held to amount to a private nuisance.

A claimant can only bring an action if he suffers some damage. This need not necessarily involve physical injury or damage to property, it can also include the damage suffered by not being able to enjoy using the land.

Leeman v Montagu [1936] 2 All ER 1677

The claimant bought a house in a residential area which bordered on open countryside. The defendant, a poultry breeder, kept a flock of 750 cockerels in an orchard about 100 yards from the claimant's house. These cockerels crowed from 2 am to 7 am. The claimant and his wife had to sleep with cotton wool in their ears and with the windows shut. Even when adopting these measures it was very difficult to sleep. The claimant asked the court for an injunction to prevent the defendant from keeping the cockerels on his land. The defendant claimed that he could not rearrange his farm so as to move the cockerels further from the claimant's house, although there was some expert evidence that this could be done without much difficulty.

Held. The defendant had committed a nuisance and so the injunction was granted. However, the injunction was suspended for one month to give the defendant a chance to reduce the noise.

The law attempts to strike a balance between the different interests of people trying to enjoy the use of their land. Furthermore, to amount to nuisance the interference must be substantial. All users of land must make a certain amount of noise etc. The question is whether this unreasonably prevents neighbours from enjoying the use of their land. What is reasonable will depend upon the area in which the alleged nuisance was committed. In *Sturges v Bridgman* (1879) 11 Ch D 852 Thesiger LJ famously said: 'What would be a nuisance in Belgrave Square would not necessarily be so in Bermondsey.'

Noisy manufacturing operations have to be carried on somewhere. If they are carried on in an industrial estate the noise (as well as the smell, vibrations etc.) are unlikely to constitute a nuisance. Similarly, if the defendant in *Leeman v Montagu* had kept his cockerels in a completely rural area, the noise they made would not have constituted a nuisance. The frequency with which the interference is caused is also relevant. If a manufacturer conducted a noisy cleaning process once a year this would be more likely to be reasonable than if he conducted it every day.

Claimants who suffer damage only because they are abnormally sensitive are not protected. The interference must be such that it would prevent an ordinary person from using and enjoying his property. In *Robinson v Kilvert* (1889) 41 Ch D 88 (Court of Appeal) Lopes LJ said: 'a man who carries on an

exceptionally delicate trade cannot complain because it is injured by his neighbour doing something lawful on his property, if it is something which would not injure anything but an exceptionally delicate trade'.

The motive of the defendant may be relevant. If a defendant causes the interference maliciously then this is much more likely to be a nuisance.

Christie v Davey [1893] 1 Ch 316

Much to the defendant's annoyance, the claimant, his next door neighbour, gave music lessons and held musical parties. The music lessons were held for about 17 hours a week and besides the lessons there was often singing and practising on the violin and the piano. Practice on the cello often continued until 11 pm. The defendant's house was semi-detached from the claimant's. The defendant retaliated by blowing whistles, shrieking, shouting, banging trays and hammering whenever there was music played in the claimant's house. This noise often imitated what was being played in the claimant's house. The defendant said that he made the noises solely for his own musical entertainment. The claimant asked the court to grant an injunction to prevent the defendant from continuing to make the malicious noises.

Held. The defendant's actions amounted to a nuisance because they were done maliciously. Therefore, an injunction was granted restraining the defendant from making sounds or noises designed to vex or annoy the claimant.

The tort of private nuisance was considered in depth by the House of Lords in the following case.

Cambridge Water Co v Eastern Counties Leather [1994] 1 All ER 53 (House of Lords)

Cambridge Water Co (CWC) claimed damages in respect of the contamination of water available for extraction from their borehole. This contamination was caused by Eastern Counties Leather (ECL) using a solvent while tanning leather about 1.3 miles away from the borehole. The solvent seeped through the ground and was carried by water into the borehole. ECL had carried on business for over a hundred years and generally ran the business well. The particular solvent had been in common use in the tanning of leather since the early 1950s. The solvent had found its way into the borehole as a consequence of regular small spillages. It was not foreseeable by

→

a reasonable supervisor that these spillages would pollute a borehole. Although water from the borehole could not be used as drinking water because it was 'unwholesome' under EC Regulations, it was not in fact injurious to health.

Held. ECL were not liable in either private nuisance or under the rule in **Rylands v Fletcher** (which is considered later in this chapter at 13.3).

In the above case, Lord Goff, who gave the only speech, said that the fact that the defendant had taken all reasonable care would not necessarily exonerate him from liability. However, he also said that the defendant would only be liable in nuisance for damage of a type which he could reasonably foresee. This makes liability strict but not absolute.

In **Dobson v Thames Water Utilities** [2009] EWCA Civ 28, [2009] 3 All ER 319 the Court of Appeal held that **Hunter v Canary Wharf** had established that damages for nuisance were to compensate for injury to the property and not for injury to the sensibilities of the occupiers. Where the nuisance was transitory, in that it interfered with the comfort and enjoyment of the land, the actual impact upon the occupiers of the land might be relevant in assessing the damages. However, the person who had the right to sue had no right to recover damages on behalf of other occupants of the property. It was also held that damages for breach of Article 8 of the European Convention on Human Rights, the right to respect for private and family life, home and correspondence, would be very unlikely to exceed the amount of damages for nuisance. Nor should extra damages for breach of Article 8 be paid. The court declined to state whether or not a non-property owner member of the affected household could claim damages personally.

13.1.1 Remedies

13.1.1.1 Damages

Damages for private nuisance are designed to compensate only for diminution in the value of the land or diminution of the benefits of using and enjoying the land. These damages can cater for lost business. As we have seen, damages will only be awarded in respect of a type of loss which is foreseeable. In **Cambridge Water Co Ltd v Eastern Counties Leather plc** the House of Lords held that the *Wagon Mound* test of reasonable foreseeability applied, so that the type of damage in respect of which a claim was made must have been a reasonably foreseeable type of damage. However, if the type of damage was reasonably foreseeable then even a defendant who had taken all reasonable care could be liable. In **Loftus-Brigham and another v Ealing London Borough Council** [2003] EWCA Civ 1490, (2004) Const LJ 82 the Court of Appeal held that the rules relating to causation were the same in nuisance and negligence.

13.1.1.2 Injunction

In addition to, or as an alternative to, seeking damages the claimant may seek an injunction to restrain the defendant from continuing to commit the nuisance. As an injunction is a discretionary equitable remedy, it may be refused by the courts even if a nuisance is being committed. It is often the case than an injunction is suspended, to give the defendant a chance to stop committing the nuisance. We saw an example of this in **Leeman v Montagu**.

13.1.1.3 Abatement

This is a self-help remedy whereby the victim removes the nuisance himself. It is generally only allowed if it does not involve entering onto the defendant's land. An example is provided by **Lemmon v Webb** [1895] AC 1, in which the Court of Appeal held that an owner of land was en-titled to trim overhanging branches of mature trees on his neighbour's land, as long as he did not trespass on the neighbour's land and as long as he only trimmed the branches to the extent that they were overhanging his own land. In **Burton v Winters** [1993] 3 All ER 631 the Court of Appeal held that the right of abatement could only arise where legal proceedings were inappropriate or where it was necessary to take urgent action.

13.1.2 Defences

13.1.2.1 Statutory authority

If a statute merely permits something to be done, it is presumed that the statute does not absolve a person from liability in private nuisance for doing the thing which the statute permitted. If the statute authorises the act which is alleged to be a nuisance then the statute must be interpreted to see whether liability in nuisance can still arise.

Allen v Gulf Oil Refining Ltd
[1981] 1 All ER 353 (House of Lords)

The Gulf Refining Act 1965 gave Gulf Oil the right to compulsorily purchase land and build an oil refinery on it. The preamble to the Act stated that: 'it is essential that further facilities for the importation of crude oil and petroleum products and for their refinement should be made available'. The statute also conferred powers to compulsorily purchase land. Once the refinery was running a nearby resident said that its noise, smell and vibrations amounted to a nuisance.

Held. The preamble indicated that Parliament had intended that the refinery should be built and had not merely allowed for such a refinery to be built. The statute also expressly or impliedly gave a right to operate the refinery once it was built. Therefore, Gulf Oil were entitled to the defence of statutory authority.

13.1.2.2 **Prescription**

If a person has committed a nuisance continuously for 20 years, prescription might give him a right to continue committing the nuisance as an easement without redress. (An easement is a property right allowing the land of another person to be used in a certain way, or a right which restricts the way in which another person's land can be used.) It is not enough that the defendant has been committing the act complained of continuously for 20 years. It must also have amounted to a nuisance for 20 years. It must also have been done without force, openly and without permission.

Sturges v Bridgman [1879] 11 ChD 852
(Court of Appeal)

A confectionery manufacturer occupied premises next door to a doctor. For more than 20 years the confectioner had operated heavy pestles and mortars which were noisy and caused vibrations. This did not bother the doctor until he built a consulting room which adjoined the room where the pestles and mortars were used. The doctor then applied for an injunction to stop the use of the pestles and mortars.

Held. The noise and vibration were a nuisance and the injunction was granted. Prescription was not available as a defence because although the noise had been committed for 20 years, the nuisance had not.

13.1.2.3 **Consent of the claimant (*volenti non fit injuria*)**

Consent of the claimant is a defence to private nuisance. In *Leakey v National Trust* [1980] 1 All ER 17 Megaw LJ said: 'While it is no defence to a claim in nuisance that the [claimant] has "come to the nuisance", it would have been a properly pleadable defence . . . that the [claimants], knowing of the danger to their property, by word or deed, had shown their willingness to accept that danger.'

So if the claimant consents to the commission of the nuisance then this will give the defendant a complete defence. However, the claimant does not consent merely by occupying or buying land with the knowledge that a nuisance is being committed.

13.2 PUBLIC NUISANCE

The following definition of public nuisance was given by Romer LJ in *Attorney-General v PYA Quarries* [1957] 1 All ER 894:

> 'Any nuisance is "public" which materially affects the reasonable comfort and convenience of life of a class of Her Majesty's subjects. The sphere of the nuisance may be described generally as "the neighbourhood", but the question whether the local community within that sphere comprises a sufficient number of persons to constitute a class of the public is a question of fact in every case. It is not necessary, in my judgment, to prove that every member of the class has been injuriously affected; it is sufficient to show that a representative cross-section of the class has been so affected.'

To commit such a public nuisance is a crime. It will also give rise to liability in tort to an individual who has suffered particular damage, that is to say damage of a higher degree than that generally suffered by the class. Physical injury and loss of trade will suffice, but the loss must be more than mere inconvenience. The local council has the power to seek an injunction to prevent a public nuisance under s.221 of the Local Government Act 1971. Individuals have the power to apply for an injunction to prevent a public nuisance, bringing an action in the name of the Attorney General.

Obstructing the highway is perhaps the most common type of public nuisance. Other, more unusual, examples where a public nuisance has been held to have been committed include: permitting travellers to camp near a residential neighbourhood; making many obscene phone calls to a number of women in a particular area; and quarrying to an extent which caused personal discomfort and dust.

A claimant does not need any property interest in order to bring a claim for public nuisance. Nor need the public nuisance arise from the defendant's use of his land. Prescription is a defence to public nuisance. A claim for public nuisance can be for pure economic loss. The defences of contributory negligence and *volenti non fit injuria* are both available.

13.3 STRICT LIABILITY (THE RULE IN RYLANDS V FLETCHER)

Rylands v *Fletcher* is best understood as a special branch of private nuisance. The basis of the tort was explained by Blackburn J in the case itself, which is set out below.

Rylands v *Fletcher* (1866) LR 1 Ex 265
(House of Lords)

The defendant, Mr Rylands, wanted to improve the water supply to his mill. One Lord Wilton agreed that a reservoir could be built on his land. Reputable engineers, acting as independent contractors, were taken on to build the reservoir. The engineers came across disused mine shafts which they failed to seal properly. As a consequence water from the reservoir flooded the claimant's coal mine. The engineers had failed to take reasonable care but the defendant had not.

Held. The defendant was liable for the flooding even though he was not vicariously liable and had not been negligent.

Blackburn J: 'We think that the true rule of law is, that the person who for his own purposes brings on his lands and collects and keeps there anything likely to do mischief if it escapes, must keep it at his peril, and, if he does not do so, is prima facie answerable for all the damage which is the natural consequence of its escape.'

In *Claimants on the Register of the Corby Group Litigation* v *Corby BC* [2008] EWCA Civ 463, [2009] QB 335, the Court of Appeal held that the cases which rule out a claim for personal injury in private nuisance or under *Rylands* v *Fletcher* (*Hunter* v *Canary Wharf* and *Transco*) did not rule out such a claim in public nuisance.

13.3.1 Requirements of the tort

The defendant must bring something on to his land or deliberately let it accumulate there
The tort would not apply as regards things, such as rainfall or weeds, which are on the land without any action

on the defendant's part. In *Transco plc* v *Stockport Metropolitan Borough Council* [2003] UKHL 61, [2003] 3 WLR 1467 considered below, Lord Walker said that the gradual and invisible saturation of the adjacent ground by a water pipe which was not known to be burst could not be described as an accumulation made by human design and so the conditions for strict liability had not been fulfilled. He contrasted the behaviour of Mr Rylands, who had planned, constructed and started to fill his reservoir.

The bringing of the thing onto the land, or the allowing it to accumulate there, must be a non-natural use of the land
In *Transco plc* v *Stockport Metropolitan Borough Council* Lord Bingham said: 'I think it clear that ordinary user is a preferable test to natural user, making it clear that the rule in *Rylands* v *Fletcher* is engaged only where the defendant's use is shown to be extraordinary and unusual.' He rejected a test of reasonable user because a user could be quite out of the ordinary but not unreasonable: 'The question is whether the defendant has done something which he recognises, or ought to recognise, as being quite out of the ordinary in the place and time when he does it.' Lord Hoffmann said: 'A useful guide in deciding whether the risk has been created by a "non-natural" user of land is therefore to ask whether the damage which eventuated was something against which the occupier could reasonably be expected to have insured himself.'

The thing must be likely to do mischief if it escapes
Water, petrol, gas, fumes and explosives have all been held to be hazardous things, which are likely to do mischief if they escape. In *Transco plc* v *Stockport Metropolitan Borough Council* Lord Bingham thought that the mischief test should not be easily satisfied. 'It must be showed that the defendant has done something which he recognised, or judged by the standards appropriate at the relevant place and time, he ought reasonably to have recognised, as giving rise to an exceptionally high risk of danger or mischief if there should be an escape, however unlikely an escape may have been thought to be.'

The thing must escape and cause damage
For example, in *Read* v *J Lyons & Co* [1947] AC 146 (House of Lords) a factory inspector killed by an explosion at a war-time munitions factory did not succeed in an action under *Rylands* v *Fletcher*. The dangerous

munitions exploded, but they did not escape from the defendant's premises.

Earlier in this chapter we considered *Cambridge Water Co Ltd v Eastern Counties Leather plc* [1994] 1 All ER 53. In this case the House of Lords decided that, as regards *Rylands v Fletcher*, the appropriate test on foreseeability is the *Wagon Mound No. 1* test: i.e. was the damage which subsequently occurred of a type and extent which was reasonably foreseeable? If it was not, then damages cannot be claimed in respect of the damage. However, if the type of damage caused was foreseeable then the defendant can be liable for this even if he acted without fault. The case also went some way to classifying *Rylands v Fletcher* liability as type of nuisance, rather than as a tort in its own right. In *Transco plc v Stockport Metropolitan Borough Council* Lord Hoffmann said that the defendant could be liable even if he could not reasonably have foreseen that there would be an escape but that he should be liable only for foreseeable consequences of that escape.

In *Transco plc v Stockport Metropolitan Borough Council* the House of Lords thoroughly reviewed the rule in *Rylands v Fletcher* and held that it did exist as a tort in its own right. Lord Bingham, who gave the leading judgment, categorised it as a sub-species of nuisance. (Lord Hobhouse as an 'aspect' of the law of private nuisance.) Lord Bingham also said that a claim under *Rylands v Fletcher* cannot include a claim for death or personal injury because such a claim does not relate to any right in or enjoyment of land. Following *Transco,* the tort is likely to apply only in respect of ultra-hazardous activities for which a statutory defence is not provided.

The case arose because a local authority was piping a supply of water from a mains supply to a block of flats which it owned when the pipe burst. The local authority had not been negligent. The burst in the pipe was not immediately detectable and this caused a great deal of water to escape so that an embankment became flooded and collapsed. This meant that a gas pipe belonging to the claimant became unsupported, and a claim was made for the cost of carrying out remedial work. The claim under *Rylands v Fletcher* failed because the local authority had not brought onto its land something likely to do mischief if it escaped, rather they were making an ordinary use of the land and they had never accumulated any water. Lord Hoffmann noted that counsel in the case could not find a single case since the Second World War in which anyone had succeeded under the rule. Lord

Scott said that the essential element of escape was also absent. The water 'began its "escape" on the council's property, accumulated on the council's property and eventually damaged the embankment, also the council's property. It is in respect of damage to the embankment that Transco seek damages.'

The rules on who can sue are the same as those for private nuisance. This should mean that as well as those with an interest in the land, anyone who occupies a house as a home will probably be able to claim, now that the Human Rights Act 1998 is in force. Damages for personal injuries may be recovered only by an occupier of land.

13.3.2 Defences

There are defences to the tort created by *Rylands v Fletcher*. However, as we have seen, the defendant can be liable without having been negligent although the type of damage caused must have been foreseeable.

The defences are:

(a) That the claimant consented to the defendant bringing the dangerous thing onto his land, or that it was the claimant's fault that the thing escaped.
(b) That the escape was caused by an act of God (i.e. such an extraordinary event that it could not possibly be foreseen and provided against).
(c) That the escape was caused by the act of a stranger. The stranger must not be an employee of, or an independent contractor working for, the defendant.
(d) Statutory authority.
(e) Contributory negligence.

13.4 TRESPASS TO LAND

Any unauthorised direct interference with land which another person possesses or has the right to possess will amount to trespass to land. This is the case whether the interference was intentional or negligent. The tort can be committed not only by persons entering another's land, but also by depositing things onto it. If, for example, a business deposits rubbish onto someone else's land this will be a direct invasion of the land and will therefore amount to trespass to land.

Trespass can be committed underneath the ground or in the airspace above the land. For example, in *Star*

Energy Weald Basin Ltd v *Bocardo SA* [2010] UKSC 35, [2010] 3 WLR 654 an owner of land was able to sue an oil company which had built oil wells at a depth of 800 to 2 900 feet below his land. It was held that the owner of the surface of land owned the strata beneath it, including the minerals, unless there had been an alienation of them to someone else, either by a conveyance, or at common law or by statute. There would be a stopping point where the physical features, such as temperature and pressure, made the whole concept of the strata belonging to anyone absurd. However, the oil wells in the case were a long way from such a stopping point. Without the defence given by statutory authority, aeroplanes would commit trespass when they flew above a person's land and mining companies would commit a trespass when they mined underneath it.

Trespass is actionable without proof of damage. However, unless some damage has been caused the amount of damages will be nominal. In *Stadium Capital Holdings* v *St Marylebone Properties Co* [2010] EWCA Civ 952, [2010] All ER (D) 83 (Nov) the Court of Appeal held that the amount of damages should generally be assessed as a reasonable fee to be paid by the trespasser for the occupation of the land. However, in the most serious cases, damages could be assessed on the basis of what the trespasser had gained by using the land. An injunction could be gained to prevent repeated trespass from continuing. The landowner may use reasonable force to eject a trespasser, but not once the trespasser has secured occupation of the land.

Statutory authority and permission to enter the land are both defences to trespass to land.

The distinctions between trespass to land, private nuisance and *Rylands* v *Fletcher* are somewhat arbitrary. To summarise, to be liable under *Rylands* v *Fletcher* a dangerous thing brought on to the land, or allowed to accumulate there, must **escape** from the land. Private nuisance is an **indirect** interference with another's use and enjoyment of his land. Trespass to land is a **direct** invasion of another person's land.

13.5 TRESPASS TO THE PERSON

There are three forms of trespass to the person.

Battery is the direct infliction of unlawful force on another person, without that person's consent. The force must be inflicted intentionally. So if a night club

bouncer unlawfully punched a customer this would amount to battery.

Assault occurs when a person is directly and reasonably made to feel frightened that he is about to be immediately battered. This must be done intentionally. For example, it would be an assault for a security guard to point a loaded gun at a person, making the person believe that he was about to be shot. An assault can be committed by words alone. On the other hand, words may prevent an assault from having been committed. For example, in *Tuberville* v *Savage* (1669) 1 Mod Rep 3 the defendant put his hand on his sword in a way that might well have constituted assault. However, as he said, 'If it were not Assize time I would not take such words from you,' no assault was committed.

False imprisonment consists of wrongfully depriving another person of his personal liberty, either intentionally or negligently. It is not necessary that the claimant is locked up. If a shop prevents a customer from leaving the premises, in the mistaken belief that the customer has been shoplifting, this would amount to false imprisonment. In *Thompson* v *Metropolitan Police Commissioner* [1998] QB 498 the Court of Appeal indicated that, as a rough guide, the first hour of false imprisonment might give rise to damages of £500, the first 24 hours might give rise to £3 000 and that the amount payable for subsequent days should reduce progressively. *Volenti non fit injuria* is a defence to trespass to the person. However, in *Co-operative Group (CWS) Ltd* v *Deborah Pritchard* [2011] EWCA Civ 329 the Court of Appeal held that as a matter of law contributory negligence could not be a defence to the intentional torts, such as assault and battery.

Assault and battery are also crimes; false imprisonment is not. These torts are of little significance in a business context.

13.6 TRESPASS TO GOODS

A person commits **conversion**, a form of trespass to goods, if he intentionally deals with goods in a way which is inconsistent with the right of another to possess those goods. Usually the person suing will be the owner of the goods. A person whose goods are damaged or destroyed can sue the perpetrator for conversion.

A person can be liable for conversion even though he has acted innocently. He must intend to deal with the goods, but does not need to know that this is denying another the lawful right to possession of the goods. For example, if a thief steals a car and sells it to an innocent purchaser, this innocent purchaser will be liable in conversion even though he did not know that the car was stolen. He will therefore have to return the car to its owner and might also be liable in damages. In Chapter 8 at 8.2.1 we considered the case of **Rowland v Divall** and saw that Lord Atkin explained that a person innocently coming into possession of a stolen car would be liable in conversion to its true owner.

Section 2(2) of the Torts (Interference with Goods) Act 1977 provides that a bailee is to be regarded as having committed conversion in respect of loss or damage to goods which he has allowed to happen in breach of his duty to his bailor. As we saw in Chapter 9 at 9.1.4, a bailee consents to take possession of goods which he does not own. So a person who borrows a book from a library is a bailee. If such a person allows the book to be damaged he will be liable to the library in conversion.

Conversion may be committed in various other ways, such as destroying or damaging goods, wrongfully using goods, wrongfully taking possession of them, wrongfully disposing of them or wrongfully refusing to surrender them to the person entitled to possession of them. In **Vine v Waltham Forest London Borough Council** [2000] 1 WLR 2383 the Court of Appeal held that wheel-clamping a car amounted to trespass to goods unless it could be proved that the owner of the car had consented to the risk of the car being clamped or willingly assumed that risk. The person doing the clamping would be liable to the owner of the car unless he could show that the owner both saw and understood a notice warning that the car might be clamped. This was the case even where the car was committing an act of trespass to land. In the case the recorder had found that the owner of the car had not seen the signs warning that cars might be clamped because the signs were not particularly well displayed and the car owner had been in a very distressed condition at the time. The Court of Appeal found that if notices were displayed where they were bound to be seen the normal inference would be that they had been seen. The claimant had had to pay £105 for the release of her car and a £3.68 administration fee for the use of her credit card. She was awarded damages of £108.68 plus interest, and £5 in respect of the loss of use of her car. However, she was not awarded the exemplary damages she had claimed.

Damages are available for conversion, generally being the market value of the goods or, if the goods are returned, the loss caused to the claimant by not having had possession of the goods. It is also possible that a restitutionary claim can be made in respect of the advantage which the defendant gained by his possession of the goods. Consequential losses are also recoverable.

Section 3 of the Torts (Interference with Goods) Act 1977 allows the court to make an order for delivery of the goods to the person entitled to possession, either instead of or in addition to the payment of damages.

> ### Test your understanding 13.1
>
> 1 What is the tort of private nuisance?
>
> 2 As regards private nuisance, to what extent does the defendant have to have been negligent and to what extent does the damage caused have to have been foreseeable?
>
> 3 What remedies are available in respect of private nuisance?
>
> 4 What is the tort of public nuisance?
>
> 5 What is the tort of strict liability, as set out in **Rylands v Fletcher**?
>
> 6 What is trespass to land?
>
> 7 What are the three forms of trespass to the person and how might they be defined?
>
> 8 What is the tort of conversion?

13.7 DEFAMATION

Defamation occurs when the defendant publishes a statement which either lowers the claimant in the estimation of right-thinking people generally or causes the claimant to be shunned and avoided.

If the publication is in some permanent form, such as writing, the defamation will be libel. If the publication has no permanent form, as in the case of mere spoken words, the defamation will be slander. In **Monson v Tussauds Ltd** [1894] 1 QB 671 at 692 Lopes LJ said: 'Libels are generally in writing or printing, but this is not necessary; the defamatory matter may be conveyed in some other permanent form. For instance, a statue, a caricature, an effigy, chalk marks on a wall, signs or pictures may constitute a libel.'

Statements of opinion can amount to defamation. Both trading companies and living people can be defamed. A statement which does not directly cause people to think less of the claimant can be defamatory if reasonable people would infer something against the claimant. Sometimes the claimant can establish that the statement, although not defamatory to most reasonable people, was defamatory to those with special knowledge. When the claimant pleads this type of special knowledge this is known as innuendo. The drawback to pleading innuendo is that the damages are likely to be reduced because the claimant has been defamed only as regards people who understood the innuendo.

In defamation cases in which there is a jury, the judge first decides whether or not the defendant's statement is capable of being defamatory and the jury then decide whether or not it actually is defamatory. However, many cases are tried without a jury as this substantially reduces costs. In defamation proceedings Legal Aid is not available to either defendant or claimant.

The defendant does not need to intend to defame or even know that his statement is defamatory. Although the claimant does not need to be mentioned in the statement, words can be defamatory only if they are understood to be published about the claimant. A statement cannot be defamatory unless it was published. However, in this context publishing merely means making the statement known to one person other than the claimant. This could be done, for example, by dictating a letter to a typist. As regards the creator of the statement, liability is strict and neither a worthy motive nor a belief that the statement was true are relevant.

Libel is the more serious form of defamation and is always actionable without proof of actual damage (actionable *per se*). Slander is generally not actionable unless actual damage can be proved. However, slander is actionable *per se* in the following circumstances: where it clearly and unambiguously imputes that the claimant has committed an imprisonable crime; if it disparages (damages the reputation of) the claimant in any office, profession, calling, trade or business held by the claimant at the time of publication; if it imputes that the claimant is currently suffering from a contagious disease to which a stigma is attached; or if it imputes that a woman is not chaste or has committed adultery. The last two of these exceptions are in modern times of much reduced significance. Where it is necessary to prove actual damage the *Wagon Mound* test on remoteness of damage applies. Therefore, the claimant can claim only for a type of loss which was

a reasonably foreseeable consequence of the defendant's act.

13.7.1 Defences

13.7.1.1 Consent of the claimant

A claimant who consented to the publication, expressly or impliedly, cannot sue for defamation.

13.7.1.2 Justification

It is a complete defence for the defendant to prove that the statement was true. This is the case even if the statement was made maliciously.

13.7.1.3 Innocent publication

Section 1 of the Defamation Act 1996 provides a defence to a distributor, who was not the author, editor or publisher of the defamatory statement, if he took reasonable care in relation to its publication and did not have reason to believe that his actions caused or contributed to the publication of the defamatory matter. For the purposes of s.1 of the Act, organisations which sell access to the Internet are not 'publishers' of material posted on the Internet by their customers.

Godfrey v Demon Internet Ltd
[2001] QB 201

The defendants, Internet service providers, received and stored on their news server an article which defamed the claimant. The defendants did not know who had posted the article. The claimants told the defendants that the article was defamatory and asked them to remove it. The defendants did not remove the article and so it remained on the Internet until it automatically expired ten days later. When sued for libel, the defendants relied on s.1 of the Defamation Act 1996.

Held. The defence was not available because once the defendants had been informed of the defamatory material, and had chosen not to remove it, they could no longer claim that they had taken all reasonable care in relation to the publication. Nor could they claim that their actions did not cause or contribute to the defamatory matter.

So once it has been pointed out to an Internet service provider that material which they publish is defamatory, they will have to remove the material immediately in order to escape liability.

13.7.1.4 **Offer of amends**

Sections 2–4 of the Defamation Act 1996 allow a defendant who did not know, and had no reason to believe, that his statement referred to the claimant and defamed him to offer to make amends. There are four requirements:

(a) the offer must be in writing;
(b) it must correct and apologise for the original statement;
(c) it must offer to publish the correction and apology; and
(d) it must also offer to compensate the claimant and pay his legal expenses.

If the claimant accepts the offer of amends then no action can later be brought in respect of the defamatory statement. If the claimant does not accept the defendant can raise the offer of amends as a defence.

13.7.1.5 **Absolute privilege**

Absolute privilege allows for statements made in certain contexts to be immune from liability for defamation. The contexts are: Parliamentary proceedings; communications between high ranking civil servants; statements made in court cases; fair and accurate reports of court proceedings; and some solicitor–client communications.

13.7.1.6 **Qualified privilege**

Qualified privilege is not an absolute defence but it can be a defence as long as the statement was not published with malice. The defence applies where the defendant has a duty or an interest to pass on information about the claimant to a third party and the third party has a duty or an interest to receive the information. An example would be passing information to the police to help detect a crime.

13.7.1.7 **Honest comment**

In *Spiller* v *Joseph* [2010] UKSC 53, [2010] 3 WLR 1791 the House of Lords set out the four requirements of this defence: first, the matter in respect of which the comment is made must be a matter of public interest; second, the comment must be recognisable as comment, as distinct from an imputation of fact; third, the comment must be based on facts which are true or protected by privilege; fourth, the comment must explicitly or implicitly indicate, at least in general terms, the facts on which it is based.

13.7.2 **Remedies**

13.7.2.1 **Damages**

Damages for defamation are designed to compensate the claimant for loss of reputation. It follows that a defendant who already had a poor reputation is unlikely to receive as much in damages as a person who had a good reputation. In cases heard before a jury it is the jury which sets the level of damages and this has led to some very high awards being made. (However, the Court of Appeal has the power to reduce any award to the amount which seems proper.) The way in which the statement was published and the extent of the publication will be relevant factors in quantifying damages.

13.7.2.2 **Injunction**

A defendant may seek an injunction to prevent further publication of a defamatory statement.

13.8 **VICARIOUS LIABILITY**

A person who is vicariously liable takes the blame for the fault of someone else. The concept is an ancient one. In the Middle Ages if a royal schoolboy misbehaved, his 'whipping boy' was punished.

These days vicarious liability is placed on employers. They are vicariously liable for employees who commit torts during the course of their employment. So if an employee, while performing his work, injures another person then both the employee and his employer will be liable. The employee will be personally liable and the employer will be vicariously liable.

The injured person is likely to sue the employer rather than the employee. (The employer ought to be insured, and should therefore have the assets to pay any damages awarded.)

Vicarious liability will only arise if two conditions are satisfied:

(a) the relationship between the worker and the person for whom the work was done was that of employer and employee; and
(b) the employee committed the tort during the course of his employment.

The distinction between employees and independent contractors is essentially a matter of employment law and is considered in Chapter 20 at 20.1. Here, therefore, we need only consider the circumstances in which an employee can be taken to have been acting in the course of his employment. One point which is not considered in Chapter 20 is which of the employers will be vicariously liable when one employer 'lends' an employee to another employer. In *Mersey Docks & Harbour Board* v *Coggins and Griffiths (Liverpool) Ltd* [1946] 2 All ER 345 the House of Lords held that there is a strong presumption that the lending employer will retain liability. This presumption can be displaced if it can be shown that the employer to whom the employee was lent did in fact have sufficient control of the employee.

In *Viasystems Ltd* v *Thermal Transfer Ltd and Darwell Ltd* [2005] EWCA Civ 1151, [2006] QB 510 the Court of Appeal found two employers vicariously liable for the negligence of an employee as both of them could have prevented the employee's negligent act.

In *Hawley* v *Luminar Leisure Ltd* [2006] EWCA Civ 18, [2006] IRLR 817 a nightclub was held vicariously liable for a doorman who assaulted a customer. The doorman had been supplied under a contract to provide security services. The nightclub was the doorman's 'temporary deemed employer' because it had detailed control not only of what he did but also of the way in which he did it.

13.8.1 When is an employee acting in the course of his employment?

Employers are only liable for the torts of their employees if these torts were committed in the course of the employee's employment. If a bus driver, for example, crashes a bus while at work, the bus company will be liable to people who are injured. If the same driver crashes his own car while driving to the supermarket the bus company will not be liable.

In many cases, as with the bus driver in the example above, it is easy to tell whether or not an employee is acting in the course of his employment. In other cases it is not so easy, and over the years the courts have developed the following rules.

An employee will be acting in the course of his employment when he is doing what he is expressly or impliedly authorised to do

Poland v *John Parr and Sons* [1927] 1 KB 236 (Court of Appeal)

A carter who was employed by the defendants was on his way home for his dinner at midday. He was walking close behind a wagon carrying five tons of bagged sugar which was being driven by one of his employers. A boy was walking beside the wagon and had one of his hands on a bag of sugar. The carter thought that the boy was stealing sugar and hit him on the back of his neck. The boy fell beneath the wheel of the wagon and his foot was injured.

Held. The employer was vicariously liable. The employee had implied authorisation to take reasonable actions to protect the employer's property.

If an employee is authorised to do an act properly then the employer will be liable if the employee performs the act negligently

This is obviously the case. If all employees performed their duties properly then it would be most unusual for cases of vicarious liability ever to arise. It is when employees perform their duties negligently that accidents happen.

Century Insurance Co v *Northern Ireland Road Traffic Board* [1942] AC 509 (House of Lords)

The driver of a petrol tanker, while emptying his tanker, lit a cigarette and threw away the match. The match set fire to material on the ground and the fire spread to a manhole into which the petrol was being emptied. The owner of the garage used a fire extinguisher to try to put the fire out. The delivery driver drove the tanker out into the street, without turning off the stop-cock. The fire ran along the trail of petrol until it reached the tanker, which exploded causing damage to the garage owner's car and neighbouring houses.

Held. The employer was liable. The driver was employed to empty his tanker and that was what he was doing, badly, when he caused the explosion.

If an employee commits the tort while doing some act which is designed to help the employer then the employer will be liable

Kay v *ITW Ltd* [1967] 3 All ER 22 (Court of Appeal)

O, a general assistant in the defendant's warehouse, was authorised to drive trucks and small vans. O was driving a fork lift truck when he found that he could not get into a warehouse because the entrance was blocked by a five ton diesel lorry. This lorry did not belong to the defendants, O's employers. The lorry driver was in the back of the lorry with the claimant, stacking cases. O climbed into the lorry and started →

the engine so that he could move it and get into the warehouse. O did not appreciate that the lorry had been parked in reverse gear. He did not warn the driver or the claimant of what he did. The lorry jerked backwards and the claimant was injured.

Held. The employers were liable for O's actions. O had been moving the lorry so that he could get the fork lift truck into the warehouse, an act which was clearly within the scope of his employment. He was therefore acting within the scope of his employment when reversing the lorry because his conduct was not so gross and extreme as to take him outside the scope of his employment.

If the employee does something entirely for his own benefit

If the employee does something which is entirely for his own benefit he may be said to be 'on a frolic of his own', in which case the employer will not be liable. (See, however, *Lister v Hesley Hall* [2001] UKHL 22, [2001] 1 AC 215 at 13.8.3 below.)

Hilton v Thomas Burton (Rhodes) Ltd
[1961] 1 WLR 705

The deceased and H were employed demolition contractors. They were driven in the employer's van to their place of work, arriving at 7.30 am and leaving at 5.30 pm. Any of the men were allowed to use the van for purposes such as going to get refreshment while at work. On the day of the accident seven men were working about 30 miles from the employer's place of business. At 12.20 the deceased, H and a third man went to a pub for about an hour. At 3.30 the same three men decided to go to a cafe some seven miles distant for tea. As they got near the cafe the three realised that they would not have time to go in because they had to pick up the other workers to return to the employer's premises. On the return journey the deceased was killed, the accident being caused by H's negligent driving. The deceased's widow claimed against the employer.

Held. The employer was not liable because at the time of the accident H was not doing anything which he was employed to do. The men were on a frolic of their own.

13.8.2 **Liability for prohibited acts**

If the employer prohibits the employee from performing certain acts then generally he will not be liable if the employee ignores the prohibition. But if the employer's prohibition is only as to the manner of performing an authorised act then he will remain liable. Two cases illustrate this distinction. In *Rose v Plenty* [1976] 1 WLR 141 (Court of Appeal) a milk roundsman used a 13-year-old boy to help him on his milk round. The employers had expressly prohibited roundsmen from using young people to help them. The boy was injured as a consequence of the roundsman's negligence and brought an action against the employer. The Court of Appeal held that the employer was liable to the boy. The prohibition was only as to the manner in which the roundsman should deliver the milk and collect the bottles. In *Iqbal v London Transport Executive* [1973] KIR 329 a bus conductor who had been prohibited from driving buses ignored the prohibition and negligently caused an accident while driving a bus. The employers were not liable because the conductor was not authorised to drive buses at all.

If a prohibition as to the manner of performing authorised duties could be used to escape vicarious liability then all transport firms could avoid easily liability for accidents caused by their drivers. They would merely need frequently to order the drivers to obey the highway code at all times.

Several cases have considered the position where drivers are ordered by their employers not to give lifts to people. If the driver does give a lift to a passenger, who is injured when the driver negligently causes a crash, can the passenger sue the employer? In *Conway v George Wimpey & Co Ltd* [1951] 2 KB 266 the defendants employed drivers to give their own employees a lift to work and ordered the drivers not to carry any other employer's workers. The defendants were not liable when their drivers ignored this order because the prohibition was not as to the manner of what they were doing but as to the scope. The drivers were doing something (giving a lift to the workers of other employers) which they had been forbidden to do. However, as we have seen, in *Rose v Plenty* the employers of a milk roundsman were liable when, in contravention of his instructions, the roundsman gave a lift on his milk float to a boy who helped deliver the milk. The Court of Appeal held that the prohibition was only as to the way in which the roundsman should deliver the milk. It must be said that it is hard to find a great deal of difference between these cases. Perhaps the difference is that in *Rose v Plenty* the driver's act of giving a lift to the boy was for a purpose which helped the employer whereas in *Conway v George Wimpey & Co Ltd* the giving of the lift did not help the employer at all.

13.8.3 **Overtly criminal acts**

For most of the last century it was thought that an employer would not be vicariously liable for serious criminal acts committed by an employee. In *Warren v Henlys Ltd* [1948] 1 All ER 935, for example, a petrol pump attendant battered a customer whom he thought was trying to drive away without paying and the employer was not vicariously liable. This was because the act was one of personal vengeance rather than one done within the course of the employment.

The House of Lords considered this matter recently in *Lister v Hesley Hall* [2001] UKHL 22, [2001] 1 AC 215 where a warden at a boarding school for children with emotional and behavioural difficulties sexually abused some of the children while they were in his care. The Court of Appeal found that the employer was not liable because the warden's acts could not be regarded as an unauthorised way of doing what he was authorised to do. The House of Lords rejected this and found the employer liable. The abuse of the boys had been inextricably interwoven with the task the warden was employed to do and was so closely connected with what the warden was employed to do that it was fair and just to hold the employers vicariously liable. It was also relevant that the employers should have realised that the risk of sexual abuse by wardens was inherent in the nature of their business. The employer would not have been liable if the abuse had been committed by an employee, such as a gardener, whose work merely gave him the opportunity to be on the premises.

In *MAGA v Trustees of the Birmingham Archdiocese of the Roman Catholic Church* [2010] EWCA Civ 256, [2010] 1 WLR 1441 the Court of Appeal held an archdiocese of the Roman Catholic Church vicariously liable for a priest who had sexually abused a non-catholic boy. Following the authoritative judgment in *Hester Hall,* the test was whether the employee's torts were so closely connected with his employment that it would be fair and just to hold the employer liable. The claimant's case was weakened by the fact that he was not a Catholic. However, a number of factors pointed to it being fair and just to impose liability. These included: that the priest had been dressed in clerical garb when he committed the torts and was in a sense never off duty; the priest had a duty to evangelise and so was performing his duty by getting to know the claimant; the priest had a special responsibility for youth work at the church and so when he was 'grooming' the claimant he was ostensibly carrying out one of the tasks he had been specifically assigned to perform; and the abuse was made possible only because he had priestly status and authority which allowed progressive stages of intimacy to become possible, and meant that no-one would question him being alone with the claimant. So the priest's employment had significantly contributed to the occurrence of the harm and his employer was held to be vicariously liable.

Until recently liability for the fraud of an employee would fall on the employer only if all aspects of the fraud occurred within the course of the employment. So in *Lloyd v Grace, Smith & Co* [1912] AC 716 a firm of solicitors were held vicariously liable for the act of their managing clerk who, while conducting a conveyancing transaction, fraudulently induced a customer to sign documents in such a way that she transferred her property to the clerk. By contrast, in *Credit Lyonnaise Bank Nederland NV v Export Credits Guarantee Department* [1999] 1 All ER 929 a fraud was committed partly by an employee and partly by a third party. The employee had committed some aspects of the fraud whilst he was at work and other aspects while he was not. The House of Lords refused to hold the employer vicariously liable because not all of the acts which amounted to the tort occurred during the course of the employee's employment. However, in *Dubai Aluminium Co Ltd v Salaam and others* [2002] UKHL 48, [2003] 2 AC 366 the House of Lords indicated that this approach was incorrect. Lord Nicholls said that when deciding whether or not an act was done in the ordinary course of an employee's employment the relevant question was not simply whether the employee was authorised by the employer to do the act he did: 'Perhaps the best general answer is that the wrongful conduct must be so closely connected with acts the ... employee was authorised to do that, for the purpose of liability of the ... employer to third parties, the wrongful conduct *may fairly and properly be regarded* as done by the [employee] while acting in the ordinary course of the [employer's] business.' The question whether or not this actually happened is a question of law, not fact, to be decided with regard to all of the circumstances of the case and previous decisions. Lord Nicholls thought it wrong to say that an employer could not be liable unless all of the acts or omissions which made the employee personally liable took place within the course of his employment. He thought that 'vicarious liability is not imposed unless all the acts or omissions which *are necessary* to make the employee personally liable took place within the course of his employment'. If this were the case, it would not matter that other acts which would have made the employee personally liable were done while acting outside the ordinary course of his employment.

13.8.4 Defences

Both *volenti non fit injuria* and contributory negligence will be available to an employer who is sued on the grounds of vicarious liability. An employer may also be able to claim a contribution to indemnify him for his loss from the employee who caused the accident, under the Civil Liability (Contribution) Act 1978. In practice, such claims are rare.

13.8.5 Liability for independent contractors

In general, a person who uses the services of an independent contractor will not be liable for any torts committed by the contractor. However, liability can arise if the 'employer' authorises the contractor to commit the tort or if the tort is one which can be committed without negligence. We saw an ex-ample of such liability earlier in this chapter in the case of *Rylands v Fletcher* (1866) LR 3 HL 330. As regards torts where negligence does need to be proved, the 'employer' of an independent contractor will not be liable unless he is himself negligent, for example by appointing an obviously incompetent contractor, or unless the duty delegated was a kind of duty where responsibility cannot be delegated. Statute creates several non-delegable duties which are generally rather technical. In *Biffa Waste Services Ltd v Maschinenfabrik Ernst Hese GmbH* [2008] EWCA Civ 1257, [2009] QB 725, [2009] 3 WLR 324 the Court of Appeal held that a person who employs an independent contractor will be liable for the negligence of that independent contractor where the independent contractor is engaged to carry out 'extra-hazardous or dangerous operations'. These operations, by their very nature, involve special danger to others, for example removing support from adjoining houses, doing dangerous work on the highway, or creating fire or explosion. Because these operations are inherently dangerous, the 'employer' is under a non-delegable duty to see that all reasonable precautions are observed. If he does not he will be responsible for the consequences, even if he has stipulated that all reasonable precautions should be taken by the independent contractor.

13.9 THE TORT OF BREACH OF STATUTORY DUTY

In some cases a statute may impose duties without mentioning sanctions or while mentioning only criminal sanctions. In such a situation a person who has suffered harm as a result of the breach of duty will try to sue in tort. He could either sue in negligence or for the tort of breach of statutory duty. To show the latter he must show that Parliament intended liability in tort to ensue, despite its not having mentioned such liability in the statute.

The principles here are based on a series of presumptions. First, it is essential that the legislation in question imposes an obligation upon the defendant. Second, if the statute provides for some special remedy then it is taken that this excludes the possibility of other tortious remedies. Third, the claimant must show that he was within a class which was intended to benefit from the statute. It is also necessary that the statute indicates that Parliament intended to give a right to sue if the statute was breached.

13.10 ECONOMIC TORTS

It may be tortious intentionally to harm the business interest of another by an unlawful act. Several 'economic torts' exist to protect business interests. These torts could take the form of interfering with a subsisting contract, intimidation, conspiracy, interference with trade by unlawful means or passing-off. Passing-off is considered in Chapter 15 at 15.4.1.3. Here we need to consider briefly the other economic torts.

13.10.1 Interfering with a subsisting contract

If X intentionally persuades Y to breach his contract with Z, to the detriment of Z, then Z will have an action against X. Liability will arise only if X knows of the existence of the contract between Y and Z and either knows that he is interfering with Z's contractual rights or is reckless as to whether or not he is doing so. Generally, X would commit the tort by persuading Y to breach the contract. However, the tort could also be committed by X entering into a contract with Y in the knowledge that this contract makes Y's performance of his contract with Z impossible. No right of action would arise if X merely persuaded Y not to enter into a contract with Z. Nor would there be a right of action if X's actions merely made a contract between Y and Z less valuable to Z. Z will only be able to bring an action in respect of damage suffered as a result of the interference.

13.10.2 Intimidation

The tort of intimidation might be three-party intimidation or two-party intimidation. If X intimidates Y and intentionally causes him to act to Z's detriment then this is three-party intimidation and Z can have a right of action against X. If X intimidated Y into acting to his own detriment this would be two-party intimidation. Intimidation must involve the threat to do some unlawful act and the threat must be coercive in effect.

13.10.3 Conspiracy

Conspiracy is committed when two or more persons agree to do something with the intention of harming the claimant's business interests. If what the defendants agreed to do was unlawful then they will be liable for harm so caused even if their primary intention was to benefit themselves. If the defendants conspired to harm the claimant by lawful means then the defence of justification will be available if their main aim was to advance their own legitimate interests.

13.10.4 Interference with trade by unlawful means

It can be a tort to inflict harm on the trade or business of another by unlawful means in such a way that the situation is not covered by one of the other economic torts. It seems likely that the tort can protect only identifiable legal rights.

The economic torts are often concerned with the effects of strikes and other activities of trade unions. The law relating to these torts is not particularly clear and it is beyond the scope of this book to examine the torts in any detail.

Test your understanding 13.2

1 How is defamation committed?
2 What is the difference between libel and slander?
3 What is meant by vicarious liability of employers?
4 What are the four 'economic torts'?

Key points

Nuisance
- A private nuisance is an indirect interference with another person's use and enjoyment of his land.
- Only a person with a legal or equitable interest in land can sue in private nuisance.
- Damages for private nuisance are designed to compensate for the reduction in the value of the land or the diminution of the benefits of using and enjoying the land.
- A public nuisance is a nuisance which materially affects the comfort and convenience of a class of Her Majesty's subjects. Public nuisance is also a crime.

Rylands v Fletcher
- A person who brings on to his land, or allows to accumulate there, something which is likely to do harm if it escapes is liable without negligence if the thing does escape and does cause harm. However, damages can only be claimed in respect of a type of loss which was a foreseeable consequence.

Trespass to land
- Trespass to land is a direct unauthorised interference with another person's land.

Trespass to the person
- There are three forms of trespass to the person. **Battery** is the direct infliction of unlawful force on another person. **Assault** is directly making another person reasonably fear that he is about to be immediately battered. **False imprisonment** is wrongfully depriving another person of his personal liberty.

Trespass to goods
- Conversion is committed by intentionally dealing with goods in a way which is inconsistent with the right of another to possess those goods. It can be committed innocently, in that the defendant can

→

be liable even if he did not know of the other's right to possess the goods.

Defamation

■ Defamation is committed by publishing a statement which lowers the claimant in the estimation of right-thinking people generally or which causes the claimant to be shunned and avoided.

■ If the publication is in a permanent form the defamation will be libel, if in a non-permanent form it will be slander. Libel is actionable without proof of damage.

Vicarious liability

■ An employer will be vicariously liable for the torts of employees which are committed during the course of the employment.

■ An employer can be vicariously liable for prohibited acts if the prohibition was as to the way in which the act should be performed rather than as to the scope of the act itself.

■ It is possible for an employer to be vicariously liable for an overtly criminal act of an employee.

■ Generally, a person who uses the services of an independent contractor will not be vicariously liable for torts committed by the contractor while performing the services.

Breach of statutory duty

■ It is possible, if certain conditions are fulfilled, to bring a civil claim on the grounds that breach of a statute caused loss.

Economic torts

■ The torts of interfering with a subsisting contract, intimidation, conspiracy and interference with trade by unlawful means are known as economic torts.

Summary questions

1 The Smalltown Sports Centre was taken over by new owners two years ago. The new owners have considerably expanded the Centre's activities and the Centre now has three times the number of members it used to have. The Centre's car park is not sufficiently large to cater for all the cars of the new members and so they park around the local streets (where parking is permitted). For the past 12 months the Centre has run a monthly football competition which has proved remarkably popular. Generally, about 16 teams take part in these competitions which run from midday until 11 pm on a Saturday. Local residents have complained about the noise of these competitions, as several of the teams bring large numbers of rowdy supporters. The buses of these teams have often parked in such a way that they cut off vehicular access to a small group of shops. One of these shops, a small builders' merchant, claims that their trade is well down on days when football competitions are held as customers cannot drive into their car park and the builders' merchants delivery vans have been prevented from making deliveries. Advise the owners of the Sports Centre as to any liability they might have in respect of these facts.

2 Dirty Ltd manufacture pesticides. Six months ago Clean Ltd, a manufacturer of wholefood products, moved to premises adjacent to those of Dirty Ltd.

Clean Ltd have encountered the following two problems. First, a barrel containing a toxic chemical rolled downhill from the premises of Dirty Ltd onto the premises of Clean Ltd. The chemical has contaminated a consignment of wholemeal flour. Dirty Ltd claim that they were not negligent in allowing the chemical to escape from their premises, as the accident was caused by a squirrel eating through a cable which secured the barrel in place. Second, Clean Ltd claim that fumes from Dirty Ltd's furnace are being blown towards the warehouse in which they store their raw materials and that if their customers discovered this they might not buy their products. Dirty Ltd reply that they have been emitting the same fumes for 30 years and that any contamination would be so slight as to be incapable of being detected, even by chemical analysis. Advise Clean Ltd of any rights which they might have in respect of these facts.

3 Jim works as a security guard for X Ltd. One night, whilst guarding X Ltd's premises, Jim comes across an intruder. The intruder says that he has accidentally walked on to the premises and offers to leave. Jim is convinced that the intruder is the person who stole X Ltd's safe three months ago. Jim threatens to attack the intruder with a crowbar if he tries to leave. This frightens the intruder who runs away. Jim rugby tackles the intruder and punches him several times. Jim then locks him in a store room while the police are summoned. When the police arrive, an hour later, it is established that the intruder had been acting innocently throughout. The intruder has suffered a broken nose and his clothes are ripped. What torts might Jim have committed? (You should explain the essential requirements of these torts.) Will Jim's employer be vicariously liable for any torts committed?

4 At the Christmas Dinner of Office Ltd Jan is asked to give a speech celebrating the career of the managing director, Keith, who is retiring. Halfway through the speech Jan breaks into speaking Dutch, a language which the managing director speaks fluently, and says that any success which the managing director has enjoyed has been achieved by personal meanness and by spying on the activities of competing firms. Later that day Keith posts an article on the Internet which says that Jan is incapable of telling the truth and that this condition has been brought about because he is suffering from AIDS. Jan's friend, Lenny, tells Jan about this article. Jan contacted the Internet service provider on whose news server this article had appeared and the provider immediately

removed the article. Advise the parties of any torts which might have been committed in respect of the above facts.

5 Mick is employed by Noreen, a business advisor, as an office administrator. Noreen has told Mick that he must never give advice to clients, and in particular must not advise clients on the suitability of investments as he is not qualified to do this. In contravention of this instruction, Mick advises Oliver to invest heavily in Z plc. Oliver immediately does so but loses a great deal of money as a consequence because, as was well known in financial circles, Z Ltd had suddenly been faced with difficulties which looked bound to lead to its liquidation. Mick also cheated Parveen out of her life savings by getting her to sign her house over to Mick as security for a loan. Parveen was at first reluctant to do this but did so after Mick took her to the pub, where an accomplice of Mick's lied to her. Satisfied with what she had heard Parveen returned to Noreen's premises and signed her house over to Mick. Mick, who would have had authority to take Parveen's house as security for a loan made by Noreen, has now disappeared. Advise Oliver and Parveen of any rights which they might have against Noreen.

Multiple choice questions

1 Which one of the following statements is not true?

a A direct invasion of land would be trespass to land rather than nuisance.

b The fact that a defendant has taken all reasonable care will not necessarily protect him from liability for private nuisance.

c A person who takes possession of property knowing that a nuisance is being committed there cannot bring an action in respect of continuation of that nuisance.

d A nuisance can only be a public nuisance if it affects the comfort and convenience of life of a class of Her Majesty's subjects.

2 Which one of the following statements is not true?

a A person who has taken all reasonable care can be liable in private nuisance as long as a reasonably foreseeable type of damage is caused.

b A person affected by private nuisance may always take steps to abate the nuisance, as long as

this does not involve the commission of a tort or breaking the criminal law.

c A person who has committed a private nuisance continuously for 20 years may gain the right to continue committing the nuisance in the future.

d A claimant in private nuisance must have some interest in land but a claimant in public nuisance need not have an interest in land.

3 Which one of the following statements is not true?

a A defendant can be liable under the rule in *Rylands* v *Fletcher* only if he brings a thing onto his land or allows it to accumulate there.

b A defendant can be liable under the rule in *Rylands* v *Fletcher* only if the thing brought onto the land escapes and causes damage.

c A defendant cannot be liable under the rule in *Rylands* v *Fletcher* if he acted without fault.

d Trespass to land could be committed by depositing rubbish onto another's land.

→

4 Which one of the following statements is not true?

a A person can be assaulted without being touched or in any way physically molested.

b A person can be falsely imprisoned without being locked up.

c Wheel-clamping a car could amount to the tort of conversion.

d A person who innocently bought stolen goods would not commit conversion.

5 Which one of the following statements is not true?

a Defamation can be committed only if a defamatory statement is published commercially.

b Libel is actionable without proof of actual damage.

c A claimant who has consented to the publication of a defamatory statement cannot sue in respect of it.

d A person sued for defamation can have a defence if he acted without malice when commenting on matters of public interest.

6 Which one of the following statements is not true?

a An employer can be vicariously liable for the tort of an employee even if the employee was acting in a way in which he had been forbidden to act.

b A employer cannot be liable for an overtly criminal act committed by an employee.

c An employer cannot be vicariously liable unless all the acts or omissions which made the employee personally liable took place within the course of his employment.

d Generally, a person using the services of an independent contractor will not be liable for torts committed by the contractor while performing those services.

7 Which one of the following statements is not true?

a It is possible that a statute which imposes liability, without mentioning sanctions, can be relied upon to bring a civil claim.

b If two or more people agree to do something to harm the business interests of another then they can be liable for the tort of conspiracy.

c A person who persuades another not to make a contract with a third party can be liable to the third party.

d A person who intimidates another into acting to the detriment of a third party can be liable to the third party.

Task 13

A group of American students, who are visiting your University, wish to know how the different English torts can be committed. Using a local business as an example, write a report giving details of the following:

a The meaning of owing a duty of care and breach of duty in the tort of negligence.

b The extent to which damage caused by a breach of a duty of care must be foreseeable in order to be recoverable.

c The extent to which a person can become liable for negligent misstatements.

d The outline effect of the Consumer Protection Act 1987 Part 1.

e The essentials of the torts of private nuisance, public nuisance and strict liability as imposed by the rule in *Rylands v Fletcher*.

f The extent to which an occupier of land owes a duty of care to lawful visitors and to trespassers.

g The essence of the tort of conversion.

h The circumstances in which an employer can be vicariously liable for torts committed by his employees.

mylaw**chamber** *premium*

Visit **www.mylawchamber.co.uk/macintyre** to access study support resources including interactive multiple-choice questions, weblinks, glossary, glossary flashcards, legal newsfeed, answers to questions in this chapter, legal updates and an overview of this chapter all linked to the **Pearson eText** version of *Business Law* which you can **search**, **highlight** and **personalise** with your **own notes** and **bookmarks**.

Use **Case Navigator** to read in full some of the key cases referenced in this chapter with commentary and questions:

Cambridge Water Co Ltd v *Eastern Counties Leather plc* [1994] 1 All ER 53
Hunter v *Canary Wharf Ltd* [1997] 2 All ER 426
Transco plc v *Stockport Metropolitan Borough Council* [2004] 1 All ER 589

14

Credit transactions

14.1 THE CONSUMER CREDIT ACTS 1974 AND 2006

The Consumer Credit Act 1974 provides a framework of the law, leaving the details to be filled in by delegated legislation. As well as regulating the civil law on credit, the Act creates a number of criminal offences relating to the provision of credit. Despite its name, the Act is not restricted to protecting consumers. It can also help those who are provided with credit in the course of a business. The Consumer Credit Act 2006 has significantly amended the 1974 Act. In this chapter all sections to which reference is made are sections of the 1974 Act, unless there is an indication to the contrary. In 2011 several new sets of regulations came into force. These regulations implement the 2008 Consumer Credit Directive, which requires maximum harmonisation of credit laws throughout the EU.

Section 189(1), the definition section, defines over 100 words and phrases used in the Act. Certain key definitions must be mastered before the Act can be understood.

14.1.1 The key definitions contained in the Act

The key definitions which the Act uses are complex. The most important definition is that of a regulated agreement but, as we shall see, this definition requires us to understand the definitions of three other types of agreements. If the main provisions of the Act are to be understood, the definitions of different types of credit and different types of credit agreements must also be understood. Despite the difficulty involved, mastery of these key definitions is essential to understanding the Act.

14.1.1.1 Regulated agreements

In general, the Consumer Credit Act exercises direct control only over agreements which can be classified as regulated agreements. (The rules on unfair relationships between debtors and creditors, considered below at 14.1.7.7, apply whether the agreement is regulated or not.)

Section 189(1) gives the following definition:

> '"regulated agreement" means a consumer credit agreement, or consumer hire agreement, other than an exempt agreement, and "regulated" and "unregulated" shall be construed accordingly.'

Before this definition can have any real meaning, we need to define consumer credit agreements, consumer hire agreements and exempt agreements.

14.1.1.2 Consumer credit agreements

Section 8(1) defines a consumer credit agreement as 'an agreement between an individual (the "debtor") and any other person (the "creditor") by which the creditor provides the debtor with credit of any amount'.

In this context an individual is either a living person, an unincorporated association or a partnership of two or three people. Larger partnerships cannot be individuals and nor can companies. The creditor can either be a company, a partnership or a living person and does not need to be in business. However, if the credit is not supplied in the course of a business the agreement may be a non-commercial agreement. If this is the case then, as we shall see, certain sections of the Act will not apply to it.

As regards agreements created before 6 April 2008, an agreement can be a consumer credit agreement only if the credit provided was not more than £25 000. As regards agreements created on or after 6 April 2008, this financial limit is generally removed, so that agreements can be consumer credit agreements no matter how much credit is provided. However, if a debtor or hirer is given credit of more than £25 000, the agreement will be an exempt agreement if the agreement was entered into wholly or predominantly for the purposes of a business carried on, or to be carried on, by him. (Exempt agreements are considered below at 14.1.1.4 and 14.1.1.5.) The £25 000 limit relates solely to credit provided. It would not include any deposit or any interest on the credit. For example, if a farmer takes a combine harvester under a hire purchase agreement which requires total payments of £35 000 to be made, and puts down a deposit of £5 000 and pays a total of £5 000 interest, the credit provided to the farmer is £25 000. Credit is defined by s.9(1) as including 'a cash loan and any other form of financial accommodation'. However, to be within the Act, the deferment of payment must have been contractual and so some consideration must have been given in return for it.

In *Dimond* v *Lovell* [2000] 2 All ER 897, the House of Lords held that a form of short-term car hire, which was available to motorists whose cars had been damaged by the fault of another, was a consumer credit agreement because the hirer did not have to pay anything when the period of hire ended. The hirer had been given credit because she had been given the hire of the car, and if there had been no credit she would have been required to pay for it during the contract of hire or at the end of that contract. The House of Lords held that, generally, credit will have been provided whenever a contract gives a debtor the right, or the option, to pay at a later time than would have otherwise been the case. However, Lord Hobhouse of Woodborough made the point that the fact that payment under a contract has been deferred will not necessarily mean that credit has been granted. In commercial contracts payment might be deferred for reasons other than providing credit, for example as security for the performance of some other obligation by the creditor.

In *Williams* v *Range* [2004] EWCA Civ 294, [2004] 1 WLR 1858 an employee who was given an advance against future commission which she might earn argued that the advance was a regulated agreement. She further argued that it was unenforceable because it had not been executed in line with the formalities required by the CCA. The employee, a solicitor, was to be paid on commission only, keeping one third of all of her paid bills. However, for the first two years of employment she was to be paid a salary of £22 000 as an advance against commission. She resigned some 18 months later, having never earned the £66 000 per annum which would have justified the £22 000 salary. The employer, under the terms of the contract, claimed back £18 333 in overpaid commission. The Court of Appeal held that the agreement fell outside the Act. The correct time to decide whether or not credit was being provided was when the agreement was made. At this time it was not possible to say whether the employee would end up being the debtor or the creditor. The essence of the contract was that it was a contract of payment of remuneration in advance and did not involve the idea of credit.

14.1.1.3 Consumer hire agreements

Section 15 provides us with the following definition:

> '(1) A consumer hire agreement is an agreement made by a person with an individual (the "hirer") for the bailment of goods to the hirer, being an agreement which –

(a) is not a hire-purchase agreement, and

(b) is capable of subsisting for more than three months, and

(c) [if the agreement was made before 6 April 2008] does not require the hirer to make payments exceeding [£25 000].

(2) A consumer hire agreement is a regulated agreement if it is not an exempt agreement.'

To qualify as a consumer hire agreement the agreement must be **capable** of running for more than three months. However, there is no minimum time for which the agreement must actually run. The agreement in *Dimond v Lovell* could not run for more than 28 days and so was not a consumer hire agreement. As regards agreements made before 6 April 2008, the hirer might end up paying more than £25 000 and yet the agreement still qualify as a consumer hire agreement. However, if the hirer is **required** to pay more than £25 000 the agreement cannot be a consumer hire agreement. From 6 April 2008 an agreement can be a consumer hire agreement no matter how much the hirer is **required** to pay. An exempt agreement can be a consumer hire agreement, but it cannot be a regulated agreement. Hire-purchase agreements are not consumer hire agreements because they are consumer credit agreements.

In *TRM Copy Centres Ltd v Lanwall Services Ltd* [2009] UKHL 35, [2009] 4 All ER 33 photocopiers were installed by their owner in the premises of various retailers. The retailers did not pay for the hire of the photocopiers. Instead, they took a commission on the money paid by customers who used the photocopiers, and handed over the rest of the money to the owner of the photocopiers. It was held by the House of Lords that this was not a consumer hire agreement for the purposes of s.15 because the retailers were not required to pay anything, either in cash or in kind, for the hire of the photocopiers. If nobody used one of the photocopiers then there was no obligation to pay anything. As the agreements were not consumer hire agreements, they were not regulated agreements and so there was no right of early termination. (The right to early termination is explained at 14.8.1.2.)

14.1.1.4 **Exempt agreements**

An exempt agreement will not be a regulated agreement. Exempt agreements are defined by the very lengthy s.16 of the Act and by delegated legislation. We can summarise the combined effect of s.16 and the delegated legislation by saying that the following types of agreements would be exempt agreements.

(a) Mortgages given on land, provided that they are given by a local authority or by a non-profit making organisation, such as a building society or by one of the major High Street banks.

(b) Debtor–creditor agreements where the rate of interest is either lower than 13 per cent or lower than 1 per cent above the base rate of the London Clearing Banks and the credit is offered to only a limited class of individuals, such as employees, and not to the public generally.

(c) Fixed-sum debtor–creditor–supplier agreements, other than conditional sale or hire-purchase agreements, where the number of payments within 12 months of the date of the agreement does not exceed four, where these payments are required to be made within a 12-month period from the date of the agreement.

(d) Purchases made on a credit card which require the debtor to settle the account in full with one payment within a certain time. A purchase with some American Express credit cards would therefore be exempt as this is the way that some American Express cards operate. However, a purchase made with an Access card or a Barclaycard would not be an exempt agreement because the holders of Access cards and Barclaycards do not have an obligation to settle the account with one payment within a given period.

Figure 14.1 might be helpful in understanding the undoubted complexity of the definition of a regulated agreement.

14.1.1.5 **High-net-worth debtors and business exemptions**

As regards agreements created after 6 April 2008, agreements made by high-net-worth debtors and agreements relating to businesses can be exempted from almost all of the provisions of the Act. However, even these agreements will be protected by the provisions relating to unfair relationships between creditors and debtors. (See 14.1.7.7.)

Section 16A(1) provides that, as **regards agreements created after 6 April 2008**, a consumer credit agreement or a consumer hire agreement will not be regulated by the Act where:

(a) the debtor is a natural person (not a partnership or company);

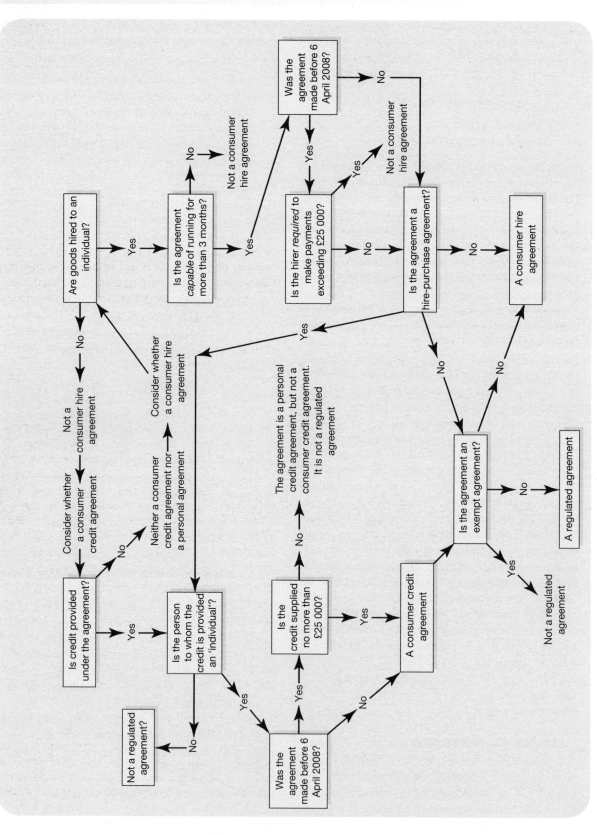

Figure 14.1 The definition of a regulated agreement

(b) the agreement includes a declaration made by him to the effect that he agrees to forgo the protection and remedies that would be available under the Act if the agreement were a regulated agreement;

(c) a statement of high-net-worth has been made in relation to him; and

(d) that statement is current in relation to the agreement and a copy of it was sent to the creditor or owner before the agreement was made.

The statement of high-net-worth cannot be made by the person to whom it relates. It must be made by the creditor or owner, or by an accountant. The Consumer Credit (Exempt Agreements) Order 2007 Schedule 2 contains a standard form statement of high net worth. Such a statement remains current for a period of one year.

A statement of high-net-worth will state that, in the opinion of the person making it, the natural person in relation to whom it is made either:

(a) had net income totalling £150 000 in the previous financial year; or

(b) throughout the previous financial year had net assets of a specified description with a total value of not less than £500 000. Pensions, insurance policies and the debtor's main residence are excluded.

Example

The following example illustrates how s.16A might apply. John, who has retired early in May 2012, owns a house worth £2 million and a holiday home worth £1 million. John has little income until he claims his pension in September 2012 when he reaches the age of 60. John wants to borrow £8 000 to live on. A local business will lend John the money, at a favourable rate of interest, but does not want the agreement to be regulated by the CCA 1974. So the business agrees to lend the money if a high-net-worth exemption is made. John makes a declaration in the specified way that he is giving up the protection and remedies afforded by the Act. John's accountant makes a statement that John's net assets were in the previous financial year worth more than the specified amount. The money is lent, probably secured against John's holiday home. John will have to repay it on the terms agreed and will have no rights or remedies under the Act, except those relating to unfair relationships between creditor and debtor.

Section 16B makes a separate exemption in relation to business borrowing. It provides that as regards agreements entered into on or after 6 April 2008 the Act does not regulate

(a) a consumer credit agreement by which the creditor provides the debtor with credit exceeding £25 000; or

(b) a consumer hire agreement that requires the hirer to make payments exceeding £25 000

if the agreement is entered into by the debtor or hirer wholly or predominantly for the purposes of a business carried on, or intended to be carried on, by him.

If the agreement includes a declaration by the debtor or hirer that the agreement is entered into for business purposes then it will be presumed that it is entered into for business purposes. However, this presumption will not apply if the creditor, or any person acting on his behalf in connection with the entering of the agreement, knows or has reasonable cause to suspect that the agreement is not entered into for business purposes.

14.1.1.6 **Running-account credit and fixed-sum credit**

Fixed-sum credit differs from running-account credit in that the amount of credit is either fixed at the beginning of the agreement or can be calculated by reference to the agreement. A bank loan of £1 000 would be a fixed sum credit agreement. A fixed-sum credit agreement will be discharged once the credit has been repaid.

Running-account credit is provided under a master agreement which is made at the outset. This master agreement allows for separate contracts to be made under it. Running-account credit can continue indefinitely. A credit limit will be agreed, but as the contracts are separate the rate of interest cannot be determined in advance. The debtor will make payments periodically, which will be deducted from the amount of credit outstanding. A bank credit card, such as an Access card or a Barclaycard, provides running-account credit. All credit other than running-account credit is fixed-sum credit.

As regards agreements made before the £25 000 limit was removed on 6 April 2008, the position is as follows. A fixed-sum credit agreement will be regulated if the credit fixed is less than £25 000. A running-account credit agreement will be regulated if the credit limit is fixed at £25 000 or less. The fact that a term of a running-account credit agreement allows the maximum credit to exceed £25 000 will not prevent the agreement from being a regulated agreement if the agreement only allows for this to happen temporarily (s.10(2)). Where there is no credit limit, or where the credit limit is over £25 000, a running-account credit agreement will still be a regulated agreement if:

(a) it is not possible for the debtor to draw an amount exceeding £25 000 at any one time; or
(b) the rate of interest goes up, or some other condition favourable to the creditor comes into operation, on account of the credit balance having exceeded a figure of £25 000 or less; or
(c) at the time the agreement is made it is probable that the amount of credit will not at any time exceed £25 000. (Section 10(3).)

As regards agreements created after 6 April 2008 the £25 000 limit is removed.

14.1.1.7 Restricted-use credit and unrestricted-use credit

Credit is restricted-use where it is transferred directly from the creditor to the supplier of the goods or services being acquired by the debtor. The credit is also restricted-use if the creditor and the legal supplier of the goods or services are the same person. For example, in *Dimond* v *Lovell* 1st Automotive Services Ltd provided Mrs Dimond with both the hired car and the credit so this was restricted-use credit. Contracts of hire-purchase, conditional sale agreements and credit card transactions provide other examples of restricted-use credit. If the money is actually received by the debtor personally the credit is not restricted use. This is so even if the credit has been granted for some definite purpose and even if the debtor would be in breach of contract if he did not use it for this particular purpose (s.11(3)).

14.1.1.8 Debtor–creditor–supplier agreements and debtor–creditor agreements

When there is no connection between the creditor and the person who supplies the goods or services to the debtor then there is no reason why the Consumer Credit Act should interfere with the contract between the supplier and the debtor. Where there is a connection then the contract of supply is influenced to some extent by the provision of credit and therefore comes within the ambit of the Act. What used to be known as a connected loan is now known as a debtor–creditor–supplier

agreement, meaning that either the creditor is the legal supplier of the goods or services, or the creditor has an existing or contemplated future business connection with the supplier. A debtor–creditor agreement is any agreement other than a debtor–creditor–supplier agreement.

Section 12 defines three types of debtor–creditor–supplier agreements. The first definition, set out in s.12(a), covers agreements where the creditor and the supplier are the same person. Examples would be a contract of hire-purchase where the goods are taken directly from the finance company, credit sales, conditional sales and store 'charge cards' under which retailers themselves provide the credit.

Types of regulated agreements are summarised in Figure 14.2.

Section 12(b) and (c) embrace loans to the debtor (or payments to the supplier at the debtor's request) made under a pre-existing arrangement, or in contemplation of future arrangements, between the creditor and the supplier. Here there are of course three parties: the debtor, the creditor, and the supplier with whom the creditor has or will have a connection. The main difference between the two is that s.12(b) applies to restricted use agreements, whereas s.12(c) applies to unrestricted-use agreements. Payment for goods with a credit card would be an example of a s.12(b) debtor–creditor–supplier agreement. Examples of s.12(c) debtor–creditor–supplier agreements are uncommon. One example would be the case where a debtor actually receives a loan from a finance company to purchase from a supplier, the finance company having a pre-existing arrangement with the supplier and knowing that the loan is to finance a transaction with the supplier. Generally, though, in this type of situation the finance company would hand the money direct to the supplier, making the credit restricted-use and therefore within s.12(b).

14.1.1.9 Non-commercial and small agreements

A non-commercial agreement is defined by s.189 as 'a consumer credit agreement or consumer hire agreement not made by the creditor or owner in the course of a business carried on by him'. The definition does not specify that the business carried on by the creditor or owner must be a consumer credit business. However, in *Hare* v *Schurek* [1993] CCLR 47 the Court of Appeal held that only consumer credit or consumer hire businesses were included in the definition.

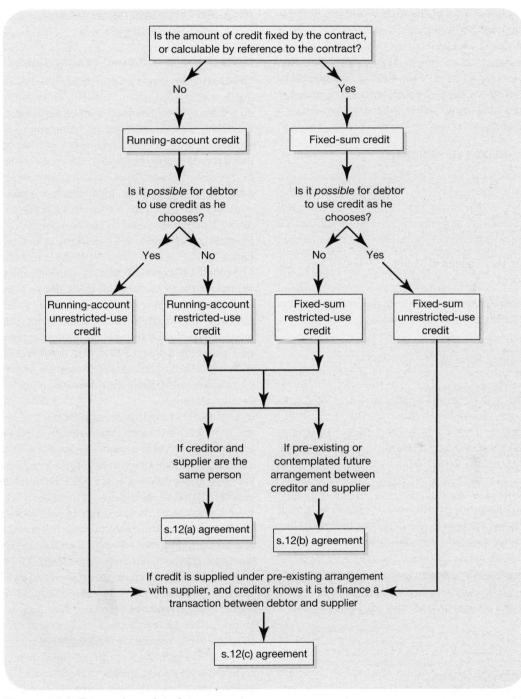

Figure 14.2 Types of regulated agreements

A 'small agreement' is either a regulated consumer credit agreement for credit not exceeding £50, other than a hire-purchase or conditional sale agreement, or a regulated consumer hire agreement which does not require the hirer to make payments exceeding £50. The agreement must be either unsecured or secured only by a guarantee or an indemnity (s.17(1)). Non-commercial and small agreements are exempt from certain of the Act's provisions, occupying a half-way house between regulated and exempt agreements. If the same parties make two or more small agreements, where it appears probable that their intention in doing so was to avoid the provisions of the Act, then the small agreements are regarded as regulated agreements other than small agreements (s.17(3)(b)).

14.1.1.10 Linked transactions

Linked transactions can be taken into account when calculating the total charge for credit. They are also important in respect of the debtor's right to cancel or terminate an agreement. Section 19 of the Act provides a very complex definition. The section could be summarised by saying that a linked transaction is one entered into by the debtor or by a relative of the debtor in relation to an actual or prospective regulated agreement, known as the principal agreement, if any one of the three following conditions is fulfilled:

(a) the transaction is entered into in compliance with a term of the principal agreement, or
(b) the principal agreement is a debtor–creditor–supplier agreement and the transaction is financed, or to be financed, by the principal agreement, or
(c) either the creditor, or the owner or the negotiator initiates the transaction by suggesting it to the debtor or hirer, who enters into it for a purpose related to the principal agreement.

A linked transaction entered into before the making of the principal agreement has no effect until such time (if any) as the agreement is made (s.19(3)).

Test your understanding 14.1

1 What is the definition of a regulated agreement?
2 Why is it necessary to know whether or not an agreement is a regulated agreement?
3 What is the difference between running-account credit and fixed-sum credit?
4 What is the difference between restricted-use and unrestricted-use credit?
5 What is the difference between a debtor–creditor–supplier agreement and a debtor–creditor agreement?
6 What are non-commercial agreements and small agreements?

14.1.2 Advertising, canvassing and licensing

14.1.2.1 Form and content of advertisements

The Consumer Credit (Advertisements) Regulations 2010 cover advertisements made in any medium, but do not apply to agreements secured on land. Nor do they apply if credit is offered to a company, or an LLP, or offered only for business purposes. They require that a representative example of the credit be included in the advertisement, as standard information, if the advertisement includes an interest rate or any amount relating to the cost of the credit (such as a fee, a charge or any repayment of credit). The representative example must reflect at least 51 per cent of the business which is expected to result from the advertisement. Additional standard information comprising the rate of interest, the total charge for credit, the total amount of credit, the cash price and the amount of any advance payment, the duration of the agreement, the total amount payable and the amount of each repayment of credit must be displayed alongside the representative APR. All standard information must be given equal prominence, so the representative APR cannot be given greater prominence.

However, certain advertisements need show only the representative APR. These advertisements either indicate that credit is available to people who would generally find themselves unable to get credit; or indicate that the credit terms are more favourable than would be available elsewhere; or include an incentive to apply for credit. In such advertisements the representative APR must include the word 'representative' and be more prominent than the three matters which have brought the requirement into effect.

As the regulations apply to television and radio, and must be clearly legible or audible, standard information cannot be read out at greater speed, or at lower volume, than the rest of the advertisement. An advertisement in the form of a text message cannot refer the recipient to another source to get some or all of the standard information. Internet advertisements have to make the way in which the standard information could be accessed immediately obvious.

14.1.2.2 Criminal offences relating to advertisements

If there is no cash price for goods supplied on credit then it is not possible to ascertain whether or not a stated rate of credit is true. Consequently, s.45 makes it an offence for an advertiser to indicate that he is willing to provide credit under a restricted-use credit agreement relating to goods or services to be supplied by any person if at the time when the advertisement is published that person is not holding himself out as prepared to sell the goods or services for cash. This offence relates to most advertisements but some mail order firms are exempted.

Section 46 makes it an offence for an advertiser of credit to convey information which is false or misleading in a material respect. Information stating or implying an intention on the advertiser's part is false if he has not got that intention.

If a person offering to provide credit commits an offence under ss.44–46, then publishers, devisers and procurers of the advertisement are guilty of a like offence (s.47). A person charged with an offence under ss.44–46 could rely on the general defence set out in s.168. The person charged would have to prove that he exercised all due diligence and took all reasonable precautions to prevent the commission of the offence. It would also be necessary for him to prove that his act or omission was due to a mistake, or to reliance on information supplied to him, or to an act or omission by another person, or to an accident or some other cause beyond his control. An additional defence is available to publishers, devisers of advertisements and those who procure advertisements if they published the advertisement in the course of a business and did not know and had no reason to suspect that it would be contrary to the provisions of the Act (s.47).

The fact that an advertising regulation has been breached does not affect the validity of any agreement entered into by a consumer (s.170(1)). Nor does it rule out the possibility of an action by the debtor for misrepresentation or breach of contract.

14.1.2.3 Canvassing

Canvassing of regulated agreements off trade premises is defined by s.48 as the soliciting of an individual to enter into a regulated agreement by making oral representations during a visit by the canvasser to a place other than the place of business of the creditor, owner, a supplier, the canvasser or the consumer. However, if the oral representations were made in response to a request made on a previous occasion they will not amount to canvassing.

Section 49(1) makes it an offence to canvass debtor–creditor agreements off trade premises. Section 49(2) makes it an offence to solicit entry into a debtor–credit agreement during a visit requested by the debtor on a previous occasion unless the request by the debtor was in writing and signed. It is not an offence to canvass a debtor–creditor–supplier agreement, or a consumer hire agreement. However, a debtor would be able to get out of such an agreement under the 'cooling off period' (considered below at 14.1.4.1).

The commission of either of the s.49 offences does not affect the validity of an agreement which was canvassed or solicited (s.170(1)).

Section 50 makes it an offence to send circulars offering any form of credit or the hire of goods to minors. Breach of the section does not automatically render an agreement which the minor subsequently enters into unenforceable (s.170(1)).

14.1.2.4 Licensing

The Act lays down comprehensive rules on the licensing of businesses which provide consumer credit or consumer hire and ancillary businesses. The Office of Fair Trading (OFT) administers the system. It is a criminal offence for a person to carry on a business which requires a licence if no licence has been obtained. Regulated credit agreements made by an unlicensed business may be unenforceable without an order from the OFT. The 2006 Act amended the 1974 Act to give the OFT further powers to regulate the conduct of licensees, and the power to require more information from applicants and licensees. Defaulters can be ordered to pay a civil penalty of up to £50 000. The new licences will be more closely targeted to certain types of business and licences will be able to remain in force indefinitely, rather than having to be renewed each year.

14.1.3 Entry into credit or hire agreements

14.1.3.1 Pre-contract information and creditworthiness check

The EU Directive Regulations 2010 have introduced a new section 55A(1) into the Consumer Credit Act. Under s.55A(1) the creditor must:

'(a) provide the debtor with an adequate explanation of the matters set out in s.55A(2);
(b) advise the debtor to consider the information which is required to be disclosed under the Disclosure of Information Regulations 2010 and

where this information is disclosed in person to the debtor, advise the debtor that he is able to take it away;

(c) provide the debtor with an opportunity to ask questions about the agreement, and

(d) advise the debtor how to ask the creditor for further information and explanation.

(2) The matters referred to in subsection (1)(a) are–

(a) the features of the agreement which may make the credit to be provided under the agreement unsuitable for particular types of use;

(b) how much the debtor will have to pay periodically and, where the amount can be determined, in total under the agreement;

(c) the features of the agreement which may operate in a manner which would have a significant adverse effect on the debtor in a way which the debtor is unlikely to foresee;

(d) the principal consequences for the debtor arising from a failure to make payments under the agreement at the times required by the agreement including legal proceedings and, where this is a possibility, repossession of the debtor's home; and

(e) the effect of the exercise of any right to withdraw from the agreement and how and when this right may be exercised.'

The advice and explanation may be given orally or in writing.

The Regulations have also introduced a new section 55B into the Consumer Credit Act. Section 55B requires creditors to assess a debtor's creditworthiness in three situations: first, before entering into a regulated consumer credit agreement; second, if the amount of credit under an existing regulated agreement is significantly increased; or third, if the credit limit under a running-account agreement is significantly increased. The assessment must be based on information obtained from the debtor, where appropriate, and from a credit reference agency where necessary. It is for the creditor to decide exactly what information should be obtained. Section 55B does not apply to an agreement secured on land or where an article is pawned.

Section 55C allows the debtor to request a copy of a proposed credit agreement, in which case the creditor must provide a copy without delay.

The Consumer Credit (Disclosure of Information) Regulations 2010 require certain information to be given to the debtor in good time so that he can pause and consider whether he wishes to proceed with the transaction. The information which must be given is much the same as that which must be given in the credit agreement itself. In addition the debtor must be informed of three other matters. First, the particulars of the Credit Reference Agency if a decision not to proceed is based on information supplied by a CRA. Second, that he has a right to request a copy of the draft credit agreement. Third, the period of time during which the debtor is bound by the pre-contractual information.

14.1.3.2 Antecedent negotiations

Antecedent negotiations, which are defined by s.56, can be important in two ways. First, the negotiations may be deemed to have been conducted as the agent of a creditor. This statutory agency is considered below at 14.1.5. Second, antecedent negotiations are important in the context of cancellable agreements (considered below at 14.1.4).

Section 56(1) defines antecedent negotiations as:

'any negotiations with the debtor or hirer –
(a) conducted by the creditor or owner in relation to the making of any regulated agreement, or
(b) conducted by a credit-broker in relation to goods sold or proposed to be sold by the credit-broker to the creditor before forming the subject-matter of a debtor–creditor–supplier agreement within section 12(a), or
(c) conducted by the supplier in relation to a transaction financed or proposed to be financed by a debtor–creditor–supplier agreement within section 12(b) or (c), and "negotiator" means the person by whom negotiations are so conducted with the debtor or hirer.'

Section 56(1)(a), which has significance only in relation to cancellable agreements, is relatively straightforward. The only two parties involved are the creditor (or owner) and the debtor, and the only requirement is that the agreement is a regulated agreement.

A credit broker is defined as a person who introduces individuals desiring to obtain credit to those who carry on a consumer credit or a consumer hire business (ss.189(1) and 145(2)). Section 56(1)(b) includes as antecedent negotiations any negotiations conducted by a credit broker where the credit broker sells or proposes to sell the goods to the creditor, so that the goods can become the subject of a debtor–creditor–supplier agreement within s.12(a). A debtor–creditor–supplier agreement is within s.12(a) where the creditor and the supplier are the same person. An example of such an agreement would be a hire-purchase contract where the debtor, having conducted negotiations with the dealer (the credit broker), takes the goods from a finance company introduced by the dealer.

Section 56(1)(c) makes negotiations antecedent negotiations where the supplier makes the negotiations and where the transaction is to be financed by a debtor–creditor–supplier agreement within s.12(b) or (c). Section 12(b) and (c) encompass loans to the debtor (or payments to the supplier at the debtor's request) made under a pre-existing arrangement, or in contemplation of future arrangements, between the creditor and the supplier. There are three parties involved, the debtor, the creditor, and the supplier with whom the creditor has or will have a connection. Section 12(b) applies to restricted-use agreements, whereas s.12(c) applies to unrestricted-use agreements. An example of s.56(1)(c) negotiations would be a shopkeeper describing goods which the customer then bought with a Barclaycard.

Antecedent negotiations are taken to begin when the negotiator and the debtor or hirer first enter into communication (including communication by advertisement) and include any representations made by the negotiator to the debtor or hirer and other dealings between them (s.56(4)).

14.1.3.3 Withdrawal from prospective agreements

At common law a person can withdraw from a prospective agreement at any time before the contract has been concluded. In the case of a prospective regulated agreement, this common law right is extended by s.57, which provides that if a party does withdraw from a prospective regulated agreement not only is that agreement cancelled, but so are any linked transactions or any other things done in anticipation of the making of the agreement (s.57(1)). A written or oral withdrawal notice indicating an intention to withdraw, however expressed, may be given to the creditor or owner at any time before the agreement is concluded (s.57(2)). A credit-broker or supplier who acted as a negotiator, or any other person who negotiated the agreement in the course of a business is deemed to be the agent of the creditor or owner for the purposes of receiving the notice (s.57(3)). The rights conferred by s.57 apply to all agreements,

whether cancellable agreements or not (s.57(4)). The Consumer Credit (EU Directive) Regulations 2010 have introduced a new section, s. 66A, which allows a debtor to withdraw from a credit agreement within 14 days of making it. Any credit accrued must be repaid with interest. The right to withdraw does not allow the debtor to cancel contracts for goods or services which were to be financed by the credit. However, insurance connected to the credit would also be cancelled. Section 66A does not apply if the credit was more than £60 260 or if the agreement was secured on land.

14.1.3.4 Making the agreement

The Consumer Credit (Agreements) Regulations 2010 set out in great detail the information which must be included in relevant documents. Among other matters, the credit agreement must include the nature of the agreement, the parties to the agreement, how and when the credit is to be provided, the rate of interest, the total amount payable, the number and frequency of repayments, other charges, the right to withdraw from the agreement, early settlement rights, the debtor's right to terminate, information about the Ombudsman scheme and a statement that the OFT is the relevant supervisory authority. It is beyond the scope of this book to consider these requirements. Section 61(1) provides that a regulated agreement is not properly executed unless a document containing all the prescribed terms and conforming to regulations made under s.60(1) is signed by the debtor or hirer and by or on behalf of the creditor or owner. The document must embody all the terms of the agreement, other than implied terms, and all the terms must be readily legible.

14.1.3.5 Duty to supply copies of agreements

Section 61A provides that where a regulated consumer credit agreement has been made the creditor must give a copy of the executed agreement, and any other document referred to in it, to the debtor. This does not apply if a copy of the unexecuted agreement (and of any other document referred to in it) has already been given to the debtor, and the unexecuted agreement is in identical terms to the executed agreement. However, the creditor must then inform the debtor in writing that the agreement has been executed, that the executed agreement is in identical terms to the unexecuted agreement a copy of which has already been given to the debtor, and that the debtor has the right to receive a copy of the executed agreement if the debtor makes a request for it. If the requirements of this section are not observed, the agreement is not properly executed and cannot be enforced against the debtor without a court order.

If an unexecuted document is presented personally to the debtor or hirer for signature he must there and then be given a copy of the agreement and of any document referred to in it (s.62(1)). Later, within seven days of the making of the agreement the creditor or owner must send a copy of the executed agreement, and of any other document referred to in it, to the debtor or hirer (s.63(2)). The agreement will be made once the debtor or hirer has notice that the creditor or owner has signed it. However, if this notice is sent by post then the postal rule will apply to make it effective from the date of posting.

Section 62(2) deals with the situation where the unexecuted document is sent to the debtor, and it has not yet been signed by the creditor. It requires that a copy of the agreement and of any document referred to in it, must also be sent at the same time. Again the agreement will be made once the debtor or hirer has notice that the creditor or owner has signed it, and again s.63(2) will require that within seven days of the making of the agreement the creditor or owner must send a copy of the executed agreement, and of any other document referred to in it, to the debtor or hirer.

If the creditor has already signed a document which is presented personally to the debtor for signature then the debtor or hirer must there and then be given a copy of the executed agreement and any documents referred to in it (s.63(1)). There is no need to send another copy later (s.63(2)(a)). If the document was sent to the debtor or hirer for signature, having already been signed by the creditor, then a copy of the unexecuted agreement and of any document referred to in it must be sent to the debtor or hirer at the same time (s.62(2)). Again, there is no need to send another copy later.

If any of these requirements as to sending copies of agreements are not met then a regulated agreement is not properly executed (ss.62(3) and 63(5)). This can be a serious consequence as an improperly executed agreement is not enforceable without a court order.

Sections 62 and 63 are designed to ensure that a debtor knows the terms of the agreement, and is aware of the right to revoke the agreement and the right to cancel the agreement.

14.1.3.6 Duty to give notice of cancellation rights

In the case of a cancellable agreement (see 14.1.4), a notice in the prescribed form indicating the right of the debtor or hirer to cancel the agreement, how and when that right is exercisable, and the name and address of a person to whom notice of cancellation must be given must be included in every copy which is required to be given or sent to the debtor or hirer (s.64(1)(a)). Such a notice must also be sent by post to the debtor or hirer within seven days of making a cancellable agreement in cases where there is no need to send further copies of the agreement itself (s.64(1)(b)). If s.64(1) is not complied with then the agreement is enforceable only at the court's discretion (s.127(1)(2)). The rules relating to copies of agreements and to notice of cancellation rights do not apply to non-commercial agreements, overdrafts on current accounts, small debtor–creditor–supplier agreements for restricted-use credit or certain payments arising on or connected with a person's death.

14.1.3.7 The consequences of improper execution

An improperly executed regulated agreement can only be enforced against the debtor or hirer by order of the court (s.65(1)). In an application to enforce an improperly executed agreement the court shall dismiss the application if, and only if, it considers it just to do so, having regard to (i) prejudice caused to any person by the contravention in question, and the degree of culpability for it, and (ii) the powers conferred on the court to discharge or reduce any sum payable by the debtor, and its power to impose conditions and vary agreements (s.127(1)). Section 127(2) allows a court to order enforcement whilst reducing or discharging any sums payable by the debtor, so as to compensate him for prejudice suffered as a result of the contravention which occurred.

Earlier we saw in **Dimond v Lovell** that the car hire agreement entered into by Mrs Dimond was improperly executed, and therefore unenforceable, even though this meant that Mrs Dimond was unjustly enriched. The House of Lords considered that the document was improperly executed (there was no real argument against this point of view) because the requirements of s.61(1) had not been complied with. A document containing all the prescribed terms and conforming to regulations made under s.60(1) had not been signed by both parties. One of these terms (under regulations made by the Secretary of State) would have been 'a term stating the amount of the credit, which may be expressed as the total cash price of the ... services'.

Prior to the amendments made by the 2006 Act, some improperly executed agreements could not be enforced at all, not even by order of the court. Now, however, a court always has the power to enforce an agreement under s.127(1) and (2). In **Wilson v First County Trust Ltd** [2003] UKHL 40, [2003] 3 WLR 568 the House of Lords allowed a debtor who had taken a loan from a pawnbroker, and pledged her car as security for the loan, to avoid repaying the loan because the pawnbroker had inadvertently misstated the amount of credit. This was a mere technicality, as can be seen from the fact that the first instance judge agreed that the pawnbroker had correctly stated the total amount of credit. If the case were to arise today the court could always order enforcement under s.127(1) and (2).

14.1.4 Cancellable agreements

Section 67 provides that a regulated agreement may be cancelled by the debtor or hirer if the antecedent negotiations included oral representations made when in the presence of the debtor or hirer by an individual acting on behalf of the negotiator unless:

(a) the agreement is secured on land, or a bridging loan to purchase land or a restricted-use credit agreement to finance the purchase of land; or

(b) the unexecuted agreement is signed by the debtor or hirer at the business premises of either the creditor or hirer, or a linked party or the negotiator. (It is where the debtor signed, rather than where the negotiations took place, that is important here.)

Negotiations will not be made in the presence of the debtor or hirer if they are made entirely by telephone. As we saw above at 14.1.3.3, s.66A allows a debtor to withdraw from a credit agreement within 14 days of making it. Section 67 does not apply where s.66A applies.

14.1.4.1 The cooling-off period

Section 68 allows a debtor to cancel a cancellable agreement within 14 days of receiving a copy of the agreement under s.61A. Notice of cancellation can be served on (a) the creditor or owner, (b) the person specified in the notice under s.64(1), or (c) the agent of the owner or creditor, or a person who carried on antecedent negotiations on behalf of the creditor or owner in the course of a business carried on by him (s.69(1)). Whoever the notice is served upon, it must be in writing (s.189(1)). It can be expressed in any way as long as it indicates an intention to withdraw from the agreement (s.69(1)).

Whether or not it is actually received by him, a notice of cancellation sent by post to a person shall be deemed to be served on him at the time of posting (s.69(7)).

An agreement which is cancelled shall be treated as an agreement which was never entered into (s.69(4)).

14.1.4.2 The effect of cancellation

Once a regulated agreement, or any linked agreement, is cancelled the effect of this is as follows:

(a) Any sum paid by the debtor or hirer, or by his relative, under or in contemplation of the agreement or transaction, including any item in the total charge for credit, becomes repayable (s.70(1)(a)).

(b) Any sum payable by the creditor or hirer or by his relative, including any item in the total charge for credit, ceases to be due. This includes any item on the total charge for credit which would have been payable had the agreement not been cancelled (s.70(1)(b)).

(c) In the case of a debtor–creditor–supplier agreement falling within s.12(b), any sum paid on the debtor's behalf by the creditor to the supplier becomes repayable to the creditor (s.70(1)(c)).

(d) If, under the terms of the cancelled agreement or transaction, the debtor or hirer or his relative is in possession of any goods, he shall have a lien over them for any sum repayable to him under s.70(1) in respect of that agreement or transaction, or any other linked transaction (s.70(2)).

(e) A sum repayable under s.70(1) is repayable by the person to whom it was originally paid. However, in the case of a debtor–creditor–supplier agreement falling within s.12(b) the creditor and the supplier are jointly and severally liable to repay the sum (s.70(3)).

(f) Linked agreements are also cancelled (s.69(1)).

(g) If the total charge for credit included a fee or commission charged by a credit-broker, the credit-broker can retain £5, but must return any excess (s.70(6)).

(h) When a regulated agreement is cancelled, other than a debtor–creditor–supplier agreement for restricted-use credit, the agreement shall continue in force so far as it relates to repayment of credit and payment of interest (s.71(1)). (Where the agreement was a debtor–creditor–supplier agreement for restricted-use credit then the debtor would never have received any money. Obviously in such a case therefore he would not have to repay anything to the creditor.) However, if the debtor repays all or some of the credit either before the expiry of one month following service of the notice of cancellation, or before the date on which the first instalment is due, no interest is payable on the amount repaid (s.71(2)). If the whole of a credit repayable by instalments is not repaid before the first instalment, the debtor only has to repay the amount outstanding on receipt of a request in writing in the prescribed form, signed by the creditor or on his behalf, stating the amounts of the remaining instalments, but excluding any sum other than principal and interest (s.71(3)).

(i) Any person who possesses goods acquired under a cancelled agreement has a duty to restore the goods to the other party, and meanwhile to retain possession of the goods and to take reasonable care of them (s.72(4)). The possessor of goods does not have to return them but only to make them available for collection. The duty to take reasonable care of the goods ends after 21 days unless a written request for their return is received within that period (s.72(8)). Section 72 does not apply to perishable goods, goods which by their nature are for consumption and which have been consumed, goods supplied to meet an emergency, or goods which before cancellation have become incorporated into land or into some thing not comprised in the agreement (s.72(9)).

(j) If the debtor or hirer gave goods in part exchange then these must be returned to him in substantially the same condition as that in which they were taken within ten days of cancellation, or the debtor or hirer can recover from the negotiator the amount of the part-exchange allowance given (s.73(2)). In the case of a debtor–creditor–supplier agreement within s.12(b) the creditor and the negotiator are under a joint and several liability to pay this sum (s.73(3)). Until the debtor or hirer receives part-exchanged goods, or the amount allowed in part-exchange, he will have a lien on the goods supplied under the cancelled agreement (s.73(5)). This will enable the debtor or hirer to keep possession of the goods until he has received all that he is due.

(k) Any term in any agreement which attempts to evade the provisions protecting the debtor or hirer is void (s.173(1)).

Test your understanding 14.2

1　If an unexecuted agreement is presented personally to a debtor or hirer, what is the position as regards the duty to supply copies of the agreement?

2　What is the position as regards copies of the agreement where an unexecuted agreement is sent to the debtor or hirer for signature?

3　What is the position as regards copies of the agreement where an agreement which has already been signed by the creditor is presented personally to the debtor or hirer for signature?

4　What is the position as regards copies of the agreement where an agreement which has already been signed by the creditor is sent to the debtor or hirer for signature?

5　What is the effect of the debtor or hirer not being given his cancellation rights as required by s.64?

14.1.5 Liability of creditor for breaches by supplier

Often a debtor entering into a credit deal does not have any contact with the creditor. Section 56(2) helps the debtor by providing that in two and three party debtor–creditor–supplier agreements a person who conducts negotiations on behalf of the creditor is deemed to do so as the agent of the creditor. Section 75(1) provides that in debtor–creditor–supplier agreements where the creditor is not also the supplier of the goods the creditor assumes joint and several liability for breaches of contract or misrepresentations made by the supplier. Both s.56(2) and s.75(1) can provide the debtor with important rights against the creditor.

14.1.5.1 Antecedent negotiations made as agent of creditor

In Chapter 11 we examined the nature of agency and saw that an agent has the power to alter the legal position of his principal. Section 56(2) of the Consumer Credit Act makes a credit-broker or supplier the agent of a creditor in certain circumstances.

Earlier in this chapter we examined s.56(1), which defines antecedent negotiations. Section 56(2) states that:

'Negotiations with the debtor in a case falling within subsection (1)(b) or (c) shall be deemed to be conducted by the negotiator in the capacity of agent of the creditor as well as in his actual capacity.'

So this statutory agency only arises as a consequence of antecedent negotiations which were made within s.56(1)(b) and (c), not within antecedent negotiations made within s.56(1)(a). When examining the definition of antecedent negotiations we saw that s.56(1)(a) deals with the situation where the negotiations are made by the creditor or owner. Obviously there is no need for s.56(2) in these situations.

Negotiations conducted by a credit-broker with a debtor are antecedent negotiations within s.56(1)(b) where they relate to goods sold or proposed to be sold by the credit-broker to the creditor before forming the subject matter of a debtor–creditor–supplier agreement within s.12(a). That is to say, debtor–creditor–supplier agreements where the creditor and legal supplier are the same person. A common example arises when a dealer in goods sells the goods to a finance company which then arranges a contract of hire-purchase or conditional sale with a debtor, who was introduced to the finance company by the dealer.

Negotiations would be antecedent negotiations within s.56(1)(c) if they were conducted with the debtor by the supplier in relation to a transaction financed or proposed to be financed by a debtor–creditor–supplier agreement within s.12(b) or (c). Common examples of this would be a supplier accepting payment for goods by a credit card issued by a third party, or a dealer in goods selling the goods to a debtor for cash which the debtor had taken on loan from a finance company introduced by the dealer. A supplier accepting payment by debit card would not be included, whether or not the customer's account was in credit (s.187(3)(b)).

Section 56(2) only applies to regulated agreements, because the types of debtor–creditor–supplier agreements set out in s.12(a), (b) and (c) are defined as being regulated agreements. Section 56(2) does not apply to consumer hire agreements, even if they are regulated agreements. Nor does it apply to debtor-credit agreements, even if a credit-broker conducted negotiations for the creditor. (Because the credit-broker would be the agent of the creditor at common law.) It is important to remember that in order for s.56(2) to apply there must be existing or contemplated connection between negotiator and creditor or the supplier and the creditor must be the same person.

Liability arising under s.56(2) is additional to any personal liability of the credit-broker or supplier.

Any agreement which purports to avoid the statutory agency created by s.56(2) is void (s.56(3)). Section 56(2) will only create a statutory agency as regards antecedent negotiations which either relate to the goods sold or proposed to be sold by the credit-broker, or which relate to the transaction financed or to be financed by a s.12(b) or (c) debtor–creditor–supplier agreement.

The effect of the statutory agency is that the creditor is liable for any misrepresentations made by the negotiator, the creditor is liable for breach of contract if the negotiator's statements become terms of the agreement, money paid to the negotiator will be regarded as paid to the creditor, and notice given to the negotiator will be regarded as having been given to the creditor.

14.1.5.2 Liability where creditor and supplier are not the same person

Where the creditor and the legal supplier are not the same person s.75 provides that a debtor who has a claim for breach of contract or misrepresentation against the supplier has a like claim against the creditor. (It does not apply in cases of hire-purchase where the creditor and the legal supplier are the same person.)

Section 75(1) states that:

'If the debtor under a debtor–creditor–supplier agreement falling within section 12(b) or (c) has, in relation to a transaction financed by the agreement, any claim against the supplier in respect of a misrepresentation or breach of contract, he shall have a like claim against the creditor, who, with the supplier, shall accordingly be jointly and severally liable to the debtor.'

Between them s.12(b) and (c) encompass debtor–creditor–supplier agreements where the supplier and the creditor are not the same person, but have an existing or contemplated future connection.

Section 75(3) limits the effect of s.75(1) slightly:

'Subsection (1) does not apply to a claim –
(a) under a non-commercial agreement, or
(b) so far as the claim relates to any single item to which the supplier has attached a price not exceeding [£100] or more than [£30 000].'

Points to note about s.75(1):

(a) In order for the section to apply the creditor and supplier must be different persons. So where a finance company supplies goods on hire-purchase it will not apply. (This is unlikely to matter much to the debtor. First, s.56(2) of the Consumer Credit Act will help the debtor if the dealer made antecedent negotiations. Second, the Supply of Goods (Implied Terms) Act 1973 will impose liability directly on the finance company if it breaches a term as to correspondence with description.) (See Chapter 8 at 8.3.1.)

(b) The section only applies to debtor–creditor–supplier agreements which are regulated agreements. (Because the debtor–creditor–supplier agreements which fall within s.12(b) and (c) are defined as being regulated agreements.)

(c) Section 75 only makes the creditor liable for the misrepresentations and breaches of contract of the supplier if the supplier would himself have been liable. If an effective exclusion clause prevents the supplier from incurring liability for misrepresentation or breach of contract, then no liability will be incurred by the creditor under s.75.

(d) The creditor and supplier are made jointly and severally liable, so the debtor can sue the supplier or the creditor or both. Gaining judgment against one does not prevent an action from being taken against the other. (Civil Liability (Contribution) Act 1978 s.3.)

(e) In order for liability to arise under s.75 the transaction as regards which the debtor is claiming must be the same transaction as is financed by the debtor–creditor–supplier agreement.

(f) Section 75 does not apply to non-commercial agreements.

(g) Section 75 will apply where goods are bought with a credit card, but not where goods are bought with a debit card or with a cheque guarantee card. This is the case even if the use of a debit or cheque guarantee card causes an account to become overdrawn. However, a purchase made with some American Express credit cards would not be covered because such a purchase would be an exempt agreement. (See 14.1.1.4.)

(h) Section 75 only applies to claims which are in respect of a single item to which the supplier has attached a price of between £100 and £30 000. If several items costing less than £100 are bought under the same debtor–creditor–supplier agreement s.75 will not apply, even if the total price of all the items is well over £100.

(i) The fact that the debtor, in entering into the transaction, exceeded the credit limit or otherwise contravened any term of the agreement will not prevent the application of s.75 (s.75(4)).

(j) The creditor's liability under s.75 is not restricted to the amount of credit given. For example, let us assume that goods costing £10 000 are bought from a supplier. The purchaser pays £9 500 cash and £500 with an Access credit card. Before delivery of the goods the supplier goes into liquidation. The creditor is liable to refund the full £10 000. The creditor could also incur heavy damages if the goods had been delivered, but had proved defective and had caused serious injury to the debtor. The creditor would be liable to pay contract damages to compensate for the injury.

(k) It is not possible to contract out of s.75's provisions (s.173(1)).

(l) It is the credit agreement which needs to be a regulated agreement, not the contract of supply. The contract of supply could be hire, conditional sale, credit sale or cash sale. However, the creditor and supplier must be separate people.

(m) A creditor who becomes liable under s.75 may have a right of indemnity against the supplier. This indemnity could cover costs reasonably incurred in defending proceedings brought by the debtor. It is possible for the creditor and supplier to contract out of this indemnity.

(n) In *OFT v Lloyds TSB Bank Plc* [2006] 2 All ER 821 the Court of Appeal held that s.75 does apply when a credit card issued in the UK is used abroad. The House of Lords has confirmed this decision. Before this decision the UK banks had strongly argued that s.75 did not apply in this situation.

14.1.5.3 Section 75A–Linked credit transactions

In limited circumstances, a new s.75A gives a debtor the right to pursue a creditor where a supplier has breached a contract to supply goods or services with a cash value of over £30 000, if a regulated consumer credit agreement was used specifically to finance the contract. (Generally, it will not therefore apply where a credit card is used.) Even if s.75A does apply, the debtor must first pursue the supplier for a remedy. (This is not the case with s.75.) Section 75A can apply only where s.75 does not apply. Section 75A provides that:

(1) If the debtor under a linked credit agreement has a claim against the supplier in respect of a breach of contract the debtor may pursue that claim against the creditor where any of the conditions in subsection (2) are met.

(2) The conditions in subsection (1) are –

    (a) that the supplier cannot be traced,

    (b) that the debtor has contacted the supplier but the supplier has not responded,

    (c) that the supplier is insolvent, or

    (d) that the debtor has taken reasonable steps to pursue his claim against the supplier but has not obtained satisfaction for his claim.

(3) The steps referred to in subsection (2)(d) need not include litigation.

(4) For the purposes of subsection (2)(d) a debtor is to be deemed to have obtained satisfaction where he has accepted a replacement product or service or other compensation from the supplier in settlement of his claim.

(5) In this section "linked credit agreement" means a regulated consumer credit agreement which serves exclusively to finance an agreement for the supply of specific goods or the provision of a specific service and where –

    (a) the creditor uses the services of the supplier in connection with the preparation or making of the credit agreement, or

    (b) the specific goods or provision of a specific service are explicitly specified in the credit agreement.

(6) This section does not apply where –

    (a) the cash value of the goods or service is £30 000 or less,

    (b) the linked credit agreement is for credit which exceeds £60 260, or

    (c) the linked credit agreement is entered into by the debtor wholly or predominantly for the purposes of a business carried on, or intended to be carried on, by him.'

14.1.6 Credit tokens and credit-token agreements

The Act does not use the term 'credit card' but makes rules about credit tokens. Section 14(1) defines a credit token:

'A credit token is a card, check, voucher, coupon, stamp, form, booklet or other document or thing given to an individual by a person carrying on a consumer credit business, who undertakes –

(a) that on the production of it (whether or not some other action is also required) he will supply cash, goods and services (or any of them) on credit, or

(b) that where, on the production of it to a third party (whether or not any other action is also required), the third party supplies cash, goods and services (or any of them), he will pay the third party for them (whether or not deducting any discount or commission), in return for payment to him by the individual.'

A credit-token agreement is a regulated agreement for the provision of credit in connection with the use of a credit token (s.14(2)).

Some cards which are generally known as credit cards fit within this definition and their use will therefore give rise to a credit-token agreement. However, this is not true of all such cards.

(a) **Credit cards**, such as Access cards and Barclaycards, are credit tokens because in return for payment by the debtor the bank agrees to pay third parties for cash, goods or services supplied. As the agreement under which the credit is provided in connection with the credit token is a regulated agreement, it is therefore a credit-token agreement.

(b) **Bank cash cards** are not normally credit tokens, as they do not provide credit nor do they guarantee payment by the bank to a third party. However, if a bank cash card allows the holder to go overdrawn, then it will be a credit token by virtue of s.14(4).

(c) **Cheque guarantee cards** are not credit tokens. These cards do not involve the bank providing the holder with credit or paying for goods or services supplied. The bank merely guarantees that the holder's cheque will be honoured.

(d) **American Express cards** are credit tokens. In return for payment by the card holder, the bank agrees to pay third parties for cash, goods or services supplied. However, the agreement under which the card is supplied is not always a regulated agreement as it may be an exempt agreement. (This is because with some American Express cards the account must be settled by the making of a single payment at the end of each month, as explained at 14.1.1.4 above.) Therefore the agreement is not a credit-token agreement.

(e) **Store cards** are credit tokens. On production of such a card, goods or services are provided on credit. The agreement under which the credit is provided in connection with such a card is a regulated agreement, and is therefore a credit-token agreement.

(f) **Debit cards**, such as Visa cards, are credit tokens because they can be used to pay third parties for goods and services, Visa paying the third party in return for payment by the card holder. However, the agreement under which a debit card is supplied is not a credit-token agreement, as no credit is provided in connection with the credit token.

14.1.6.1 **Prohibition of unsolicited credit tokens**

It is an offence to supply a credit token to a person who has not asked for it in a signed document (s.51). Where the credit-token agreement is a small debtor–creditor–supplier agreement there must still be a request, but it does not need to be in a signed document (s.51(2)). No offence is committed when previously accepted credit tokens are renewed or replaced, nor if the credit token is supplied under a credit-token agreement previously made (s.51(3)).

If s.51 is breached, the agreement will be improperly executed. The effect of this was considered above at 14.1.3.

14.1.6.2 **Sections 56 and 75 as they relate to credit tokens**

The use of a credit token to acquire goods or services constitutes a three party debtor–creditor–supplier agreement (the three parties being the issuer of the card, the card holder and the supplier of the goods or services bought with the card). Consequently, the issuer of the credit token can be jointly and severally liable with the supplier of the goods or services under s.75(1) of the Act. In *OFT v Lloyds TSB Bank Plc* [2006] 2 All ER 821, [2006] 2 All ER 821 the Court of Appeal held that if there was a fourth party,

a 'merchant acquirer', between the card issuer and the supplier then this would be an agreement within s.12(b) and s.75 would still apply. In that case the role of the 'merchant acquirer' was to recruit suppliers willing to accept the card. Section 56(2) might also make a negotiator the agent of the creditor. Negotiations with the debtor which were conducted by the supplier in relation to a transaction financed or proposed to be financed by a debtor–creditor–supplier agreement are within s.56(1)(c). The use of credit cards at approved outlets would be within this definition.

Where a debtor buys goods by using an American Express card, and the account has to be settled in full periodically by making a single payment, American Express would not be liable under s.56(2) or under s.75(1), as the agreement under which the card was supplied would be an exempt agreement. If the goods had been bought by the use of an Access card Access could become liable under either s.56(2) or s.75(1). If a debtor took money from a cash machine, thereby going overdrawn, so as to be able to buy goods, the bank would not be liable under s.56(2) as there is no connection between the bank and the retailer. Nor would the bank be liable under s.75(1), as there would be no debtor–creditor–supplier agreement within s.12(b) or (c). Payment for goods or services with a debit card would not bring either s.56(2) or s.75(1) into play, whether or not the customer's account was overdrawn.

14.1.6.3 **Duty on issue of new credit tokens**

Section 85(1) provides that:

> 'Whenever, in connection with a credit-token agreement, a credit token (other than the first) is given by the creditor to the debtor, the creditor shall give the debtor a copy of the executed agreement (if any) and of any other document referred to in it.'

Failure to comply with this means that the creditor cannot enforce the agreement while the default continues, and that he commits an offence if the default continues for more than one month (s.85(2)). However, s.85 does not apply to small agreements (s.85(3)).

Section 85 does not apply to the first credit token as the rules in ss.60–66 apply.

14.1.6.4 **Liability for misuse of credit and debit cards**

The Lending Code 2011 sets out protections available to credit card-holders when their cards are misused.

All major UK lenders subscribe to the Code and compliance with it is monitored and enforced by the Lending Standards Board. Paragraph 138 of the Code provides that any interest charged in respect of an unauthorised credit card transaction will be refunded unless the card-holder has acted fraudulently or with gross negligence. Paragraph 139 sets out the limits for credit card misuse where the card-holder has not been fraudulent or grossly negligent, the burden of proof being on the creditor to prove fraud or negligence. First, if someone misuses the card before the card-holder informs the creditor that the card has been lost or stolen, or that someone else knows the PIN, the card-holder will not have to pay more than £50, even if the card was misused several times. Second, if someone uses the card details without the card-holder's permission, and the card has not been lost or stolen, the card-holder will not have to pay anything. Third, the card-holder will not need to pay anything if someone uses the card details without the card-holder's permission to conclude a contract which would be governed by the Consumer Protection (Distance Selling) Regulations 2000. (See Chapter 7 at 7.1.5.). Fourth, the card-holder will not need to pay anything if the card is misused before he receives it. Furthermore, para. 143 requires creditors to make card-holders aware of the protections which are available to them when their cards are misused.

The rules contained in the Lending Code apply only to credit cards. However, the Payment Services Regulations 2009 give protection when a debit card is misused. Regulation 61 sets out the payment service provider's liability for unauthorised payment transactions. It provides that if the card-holder has not authorised a payment transaction the payment service provider must immediately refund the amount of the unauthorised payment transaction to him and restore his account to the position it would have been in if the unauthorised transaction had not taken place. However, this is subject to reg.59, which requires the card-holder to notify the payment service provider, without undue delay, on becoming aware of any unauthorised or incorrectly executed payment transaction. Failure to do this means that the protection conferred by reg.61 is lost. Regulation 62 sets out the card-holder's liability for unauthorised payment transactions. Regulation 62(1) makes the card-holder liable up to a maximum of £50 in respect of an unauthorised transaction arising from the use of a lost or stolen card, or where the card-holder has failed to keep his PIN number safe. Regulation 62(2) makes the card-holder liable for all losses where he has acted fraudulently. It also makes the card-holder liable for all losses where he has, intentionally or grossly negligently, used the card in an unauthorised way or failed to notify the payment service provider without undue delay that the card has been lost, stolen or misused. Regulation 62(3) says that the card-holder who has not acted fraudulently is not liable for any losses incurred in respect of an unauthorised transaction in three circumstances: first, where the card-holder has already notified the payment service provider that the card has been lost, stolen or misused; second, where the payment service provider has failed to provide appropriate means of notifying loss, theft or misuse; third, where the card has been used in connection with a 'distance contract' within the Consumer Protection (Distance Selling) Regulations 2000. Regulation 63 can give a payer a full refund where a payment transaction is initiated by or through a payee under a framework contract. However, this will apply only if the authorisation by the payee did not specify the exact amount to be paid and the amount exceeded what the payer could reasonably have expected, taking into account the payer's previous spending pattern, the conditions of the framework contract and the circumstances of the case. Any refund must be requested within eight weeks of the account being debited.

Examples

(1) A thief steals a debit card and uses it in a shop to obtain goods to the value of £1 000. If this reduced the card-holder's credit from £1 900 to £900 then PSR reg.61 would require the payment service provider to refund the stolen £1 000 and restore the account balance to £1 900. If the thief used the card before the card-holder informed the payment service provider of its loss the card-holder would, however, be liable for £50 of the loss under reg.62(1), so the balance would be reduced to £1 850. If the card-holder acted fraudulently or had failed to notify the payment service provider of the theft of the card, without undue delay, he would be liable under reg.62(2) for the whole loss and so the account balance would remain at £900. If the thief used the card after the card-holder informed the payment service provider of its loss reg.62(3) would require that the balance be restored to £1 900, as the card-holder would not be liable for any of the loss.

→

(2) A thief steals a credit card and uses it in a shop to obtain goods worth £500. This increases the card-holder's debit from £100 to £600. Paragraph 139 of the Lending Code would limit the card-holder's liability to £50. If the card-holder had informed the card issuer of the theft before the thief used the card then the card-holder would not be liable for any of the £500 loss.

(3) A debtor's flatmate discovers the debtor's credit card details and uses them to order several items from various web sites. This increases the card-holder's debit from £600 to £1 500. As long as the card-holder was a 'consumer' within the Consumer Protection (Distance Selling) Regulations 2000, para. 139 of the Lending Code would absolve the card-holder from liability for any of the losses.

(4) A fraudster discovers a consumer's debit card details and uses them to order goods over the Internet. This reduces the card-holder's balance from £480 to £150. PSR reg.62(3)(c) would absolve the card-holder from any losses.

14.1.6.5 Additional rights of credit card-holders

The Lending Code 2011 gives several rights to credit card-holders. Card-holders must be given pre-sale and point of contact information about matters such as how interest is calculated and charged. They must also be given details of day-to-day charges for the running of the account. Interest rates must be made available to card-holders by at least one of the following methods: a telephone helpline, a web site, notices in branches or by asking staff (para.113). Card-holders must be informed about interest rate changes (para.114). Card-holders must be given a monthly statement for their credit card (para.115). Monthly payments must cover more than that month's interest (para.129). Card-holders must be given written notice of any interest rate increases (para.145). Card-holders must also be told that they can reject any interest rate increase within 60 days if they close the account and repay any outstanding balance (para.150). Card-holders can request that their existing credit limit is increased or decreased (para.156). Card-holders' repayments will apply first to the most expensive parts of the credit card balance (para.158). As regards agreements entered into on or after 31 March 2011, the minimum repayments must cover at least 1 per cent of the principal owing (para.160). Card-holders must be given an online capability to set up automated payments to reduce their balances. The customer can choose to reduce by any amount between the minimum payment and full payment (para.162).

Test your understanding 14.3

1 How can s.56(2) help a debtor?
2 How can s.75(1) help a debtor?
3 What is a credit token?
4 What is a credit-token agreement?
5 How is a debtor protected against misuse of a stolen credit token?

14.1.7 Enforcement of the agreement

14.1.7.1 Duty to give notice before taking certain action

Where the debtor has not breached the agreement, s.76(1) prohibits the creditor from enforcing a term of a regulated agreement in three ways without giving seven days' notice of his intention to do so. The three ways are to:

(a) demand earlier payment of any sum, or
(b) recover possession of any goods or land, or
(c) treat any right conferred on the debtor or hirer by the agreement as terminated, restricted or deferred.

Section 76(1) will only apply where the agreement is for a fixed time, although either party might be able to terminate it before that time has expired (s.76(2)(a)). So, for example, it would apply to hire-purchase but not to a bank overdraft.

Where a regulated agreement is for a fixed time which is specified in the agreement, the creditor or owner is not entitled to end the agreement early unless seven days' notice of the termination is given to the debtor or hirer (s.98). This section does not prevent a creditor from treating the right to draw on any credit as restricted or deferred or from taking such steps as may be necessary to make the restriction or deferment effective (s.98(1)).

It might be thought odd that the creditor can terminate the agreement or demand early payment even though the debtor is not in breach of the agreement. However, many agreements give the creditor such rights if the debtor becomes unemployed or bankrupt or changes his address.

14.1.7.2 **The duty to give information**

Sections 77–79 require the creditor or owner to give either copies of agreements or statements of account to the debtor or hirer, who must pay 50p for each agreement requested. The copy of the agreement or the statement of account must then be provided within 12 working days of its being requested in writing or the creditor cannot enforce the agreement while the default continues, and if the default continues for more than one month he commits a criminal offence. Section 77A requires a creditor under a fixed-sum regulated agreement to give the debtor annual statements, as long as some sum is payable under the agreement. The form of these statements will be set out by the Secretary of State. No charge can be made for doing this. Whilst this requirement is not being complied with the creditor cannot enforce the agreement. Furthermore, no interest accrues during the period of non-compliance and the debtor cannot be required to pay any default sum which would have become payable during the period of non-compliance. Section 77B allows a debtor to request a statement of account which shows details of instalments payable in table form. Such a request can be made only in respect of an agreement for fixed sum credit, which is of fixed duration and where the credit is repayable in instalments. The information must be provided by the creditor free of charge and as soon as is reasonably practicable. A request can be made at any time unless the creditor has complied with a previous request within one month.

Where, under a regulated agreement other than a non-commercial agreement, a debtor or hirer is required to keep goods under his possession or control then upon receiving a written request from the creditor or owner the debtor or hirer must tell the creditor or owner where the goods are within seven working days (s.80(1)). If the debtor or hirer fails to comply with s.80(1), and the default continues for 14 days, he commits a criminal offence (s.80(2)).

14.1.7.3 **Appropriation of payments**

If a debtor or hirer is liable to make payments to the same person under two or more regulated agreements, and sends less than the total sums due, he can allocate the payments towards one or more of the agreements as he sees fit (s.81(1)). If the debtor makes no such appropriation then the sum sent is allocated between the various agreements in proportion to the amount due under each (s.81(2)). The right to appropriate payments can be important when the creditor is attempting to repossess goods. (See Repossession of the goods below at 14.1.9.8.)

14.1.7.4 **Death of debtor or hirer**

If the agreement is fully secured, s.86(1) prevents the creditor or owner from doing the following things on the death of the debtor or hirer:

(a) terminating the agreement; or
(b) demanding earlier payment of any sum; or
(c) recovering possession of any goods or land; or
(d) treating any right conferred on the debtor or hirer by the agreement as terminated, restricted or deferred; or
(e) enforcing any security.

If the agreement was only partly secured at the time of the death then the creditor or hirer cannot do any of the above five things without a court order.

14.1.7.5 **Default notices**

Section 86A requires the OFT to publish information sheets about arrears and default. These information sheets must be sent to a debtor or hirer when a default notice is sent. Sections 86B and C require the creditor to give the debtor notice of sums which are in arrears. Failure to do so will mean that during the period of non-compliance the agreement is unenforceable, interest does not arise and default sums do not become payable (s.86D). Section 86E requires a creditor or owner to give a debtor or hirer notice in a specified way when breach of an agreement leads to a default sum becoming payable. Only simple interest is payable in respect of default sums (s.86F). A default sum is defined by s.187A as a sum (other than interest) which is payable by a debtor or hirer under the agreement in connection with a breach of the agreement by him. So this would include matters such as charges for late payment and fees for going over a credit card limit. If a breach means that a sum merely causes a sum to become payable earlier than it would otherwise have become due the sum is not a default sum.

Section 87 requires the creditor or owner to serve a default notice on a debtor or hirer who is in breach of a regulated agreement before doing any of the following:

(a) terminating the agreement; or
(b) demanding earlier payment of any sum; or

(c) recovering possession of any goods or land; or

(d) treating any right conferred on the debtor or hirer by the agreement as terminated, restricted or deferred; or

(e) enforcing any security.

The default notice must be in the form prescribed by the Consumer Credit (Enforcement, Default and Termination) Regulations 1983. Section 88(1) requires a default notice to specify:

(a) the nature of the alleged breach;

(b) if the breach is capable of remedy, what action is required to remedy it and the date before which that action is to be taken; and

(c) if the breach is not capable of remedy, the sum (if any) required to be paid as compensation for the breach, and the date before which it is to be paid.

If a date is specified it must be at least 14 days after the date of service of the default notice. The creditor or owner cannot take any action before the 14 days have expired (s.88(2)). The debtor or hirer can take the action required before the date specified, in which case the breach shall be treated as not having occurred (s.89). A default notice is not needed to prevent the debtor from having any further credit (s.87(2)). Nor is a default notice necessary where a creditor or owner is suing for arrears, as this is not demanding early payment of any sum. Where a debtor is in breach of a regulated consumer credit agreement, the rate of interest is not to be increased on default (s.93).

14.1.7.6 **Protection orders**

On application to the court by a creditor or owner under a regulated agreement, the court may make such order as it thinks fit for protecting any property belonging to the creditor or owner from damage or depreciation pending court proceedings. Such an order can restrict or prohibit the use of the property or give directions as to its custody (s.131).

14.1.7.7 **Unfair relationships**

The Consumer Credit Act 2006 introduced new rules which apply when there is an 'unfair relationship' between the creditor and the debtor. These rules, contained in ss.140A and 140B, replace the old law which applied to 'extortionate credit bargains'. Section 140A(1) allows a court to make an order under s.140B

if the relationship between the creditor and debtor is unfair to the debtor for one of the following reasons:

(a) any of the terms of the agreement or of any related agreement;

(b) the way in which the creditor has exercised or enforced any of his rights under the agreement or any related agreement;

(c) any other thing done (or not done) by, or on behalf of, the creditor (either before or after the making of the agreement or of any related agreement).

In assessing whether or not to make such an order the court should consider all relevant matters, including matters relating to the creditor or the debtor (s.140A(2)). If the debtor alleges that the relationship is unfair then the burden of proof is upon the creditor to show that it was not. An order may be made even after the relationship between the creditor and the debtor has ended.

If a relationship is unfair, s.140B allows the court to:

(a) order repayment of any sum paid by the debtor or by a surety (person who assumes responsibility for another person's debts);

(b) require the creditor to do, or not to do, anything specified in the order in connection with the agreement;

(c) reduce or discharge any sum payable by the debtor or by a surety;

(d) direct the return of any property provided by a surety as security;

(e) set aside, wholly or partly, any duty imposed on the debtor or on a surety;

(f) alter the terms of the agreement or of any related agreement;

(g) direct accounts to be taken between any persons.

The debtor must apply to the county court for a s.140B order to be made. Even unregulated agreements are covered by ss.140A and B.

14.1.8 **Termination by the debtor or hirer**

14.1.8.1 **Early payment by debtor**

The debtor under a regulated consumer credit agreement is entitled to discharge the debt at any time by giving the creditor notice and by repaying the whole debt (s.94(1)). The debtor may also make one or more partial early settlements at any time under s.94(3). Notice of an intention to do this can be made orally or in writing and the partial settlement must be made within 28 days of the notice. If the debtor is in arrears, any payment will first be used to pay off the arrears. Section 95A allows a creditor, in some limited circumstances, to claim compensation for costs incurred by full or partial early settlement if the rate of interest is fixed and the amount of credit repaid exceeds £8 000. The amount of compensation must be fair and objectively justified. Section 95A does not apply if an overdraft is repaid. If the agreement had more than a year to run the amount of compensation cannot be more than 1 per cent of the amount repaid. If it had less than a year to run it cannot be more than 0.5 per cent. If the debtor does this he will be entitled to a rebate of charges for credit (s.95(1)). Where the debtor terminates a hire-purchase or conditional sale agreement there is no right to a rebate as ss.99 and 100 deal with the debtor's liability. (The effect of ss.99 and 100 is considered immediately below.) Nor is there any right to a rebate where the debtor terminates a hire agreement. (The effect of a consumer terminating a consumer hire agreement early is considered below.)

Where for any reason a debt under a regulated consumer credit agreement is discharged early, the debtor is also discharged from any liability under a linked transaction, other than a debt which has already become payable (s.96(1)).

The Consumer Credit (Early Settlement) Regulations 2004 require creditors to give notice of how much would be needed to pay off the debt and how this figure was calculated. However, they allow lenders to postpone the settlement date by 28 days so that they can calculate the interest and also to recover an extra month's interest if the loan was for more than one year.

14.1.8.2 Termination by the debtor of hire-purchase and conditional sale agreements

Section 99(1) provides that:

> 'At any time before the final payment by the debtor under a regulated hire-purchase or regulated conditional sale agreement falls due, the debtor shall be entitled to terminate the agreement by giving notice to any person entitled or authorised to receive the sums payable under the agreement.'

If the debtor does choose to terminate under s.99(1) this does not affect any liability which has already accrued under the agreement, so arrears continue to be due (s.99(2)). If the debtor has been served with

notice (under s.76(1) or s.87) of the activation of an accelerated payments clause the right to terminate under s.99(1) will be lost when the final payment falls due. This would be the time when the notice expired. (Accelerated payments clauses are considered below at 14.1.9.4.)

This right to terminate will not apply where the debtor is deemed to have repudiated the agreement. (See *Yeoman Credit Ltd* v *Waragowski* below at 14.1.9.6.)

When a debtor terminates a hire-purchase or conditional sale agreement early, the financial position is calculated as follows. First, arrears are payable (s.99(2)). Second, unless the agreement provided that a lower sum be payable or that no sum be payable, the debtor can be required to bring payments made up to half of the total price (s.100(1)). Third, if the debtor has failed to take reasonable care of the goods, the amount payable should be increased to compensate the creditor for this (s.100(4)).

Example

Dudley made an agreement to buy a television under a regulated conditional sale agreement. He paid a deposit of £100 and then committed himself to paying £20 a month for 24 months. At the time of cancellation, four months after making the agreement, he was two monthly payments in arrears. The goods have been kept in good condition. Ownership of the goods will never pass to Dudley and the creditor may repossess the television as the conditional sale agreement has been terminated. First, Dudley must pay the arrears of £40. Even when the arrears had been paid, Dudley would only have paid £100 deposit, £40 in monthly payments, and £40 arrears, making a total of £180. Dudley could be required to pay an additional amount of £110 to bring the payments up to £290, half of the total payments of £580. So in total Dudley would need to pay £150 (£40 arrears and the additional £110). As the goods were kept in good condition no compensation will be added.

Where the debtor gives goods in part-exchange, then the allowance given on the part-exchanged goods is counted as a payment made. Section 100(3) allows the court to reduce the amount payable under s.100(1) to the actual loss suffered by the creditor as a result of the debtor's early termination. A debtor who terminates a hire-purchase or conditional sale agreement must of course return the goods to the creditor.

14.1.8.3 Right to terminate regulated consumer hire agreement

Section 101 allows a consumer who is locked into a long term hire agreement to terminate the agreement early, whatever the length of the agreement. Notice must be given to any person entitled or authorised to receive the sums payable under the agreement, but the notice cannot expire earlier than 18 months after the making of the agreement. Termination does not affect any liability under the agreement which has already accrued before the termination. The hirer must either give three months' notice, or the shortest interval between payments, whichever is the shorter period of time. (Subject to the rule that the notice cannot expire earlier than 18 months after making the agreement.) There is no right to terminate early under s.101 if the hirer has to make total payments exceeding £1 500 a year, or if the goods are bailed to the hirer for business purposes, or if the hirer chooses goods which the owner subsequently acquires from another person at the hirer's request. Nor can s.101 apply where the hirer is a company, because in such circumstances the agreement would not be a regulated agreement. It is not possible to contract out of s.101, so any additional payments or penalties will be void.

14.1.9 Remedies of the creditor

If a debtor breaches a credit agreement the creditor might possibly have four rights as follows: to bring an action for arrears, to terminate the contract, to bring an action for damages or to bring an action to repossess the goods. We need to consider each of these matters in turn.

14.1.9.1 An action for arrears

A creditor has a common law right to sue a debtor for arrears which have accrued. However, four of the Act's provisions might be relevant. First, as we have seen, s.93 provides that the rate of interest payable on arrears should not be higher than the interest rate specified in the total charge for credit. Second, the court may make a time order under s.129. (The effect of this is explained immediately below.) Third, as we saw above, the creditor must give the debtor notice (under either s.76(1) or s.87(1)) before demanding early payment of any sum. Fourth, the court might have the power to make an order under s.140B if the creditor and debtor were in an unfair relationship. (This power was considered above at 14.1.7.)

14.1.9.2 Time orders

A court may make a time order under s.129 in certain circumstances, including those where the creditor has brought an action to enforce a regulated agreement, or any security, or recover possession of any goods or land to which a regulated agreement relates. The time order would make sums due under a regulated agreement payable by instalments at intervals which the court would set, having regard to the means of the debtor or hirer and any surety given. A debtor or hirer can apply for a time order upon receipt of a default notice, notice of a sum in arrears or notice under ss.76(1) or 98(1). (Section 129.) Section 129A provides that a debtor or hirer who has been given notice under s.86 B or C (see 14.1.7.5) must give the creditor or owner 14 days notice that he is applying for a time order. Generally, a time order only relates to sums actually owed. However, in the case of hire-purchase and conditional sale agreements it can also apply to sums which would become payable if the agreement remained in force (s.130(2)).

14.1.9.3 Termination of the agreement

At common law a creditor will be entitled to terminate a credit agreement if the terms of the agreement allowed him to do so, or if the breach by the debtor was such that it amounted to a repudiation of the contract. The Act does not prevent the creditor from terminating the agreement. However, the provisions of ss.87–89 and s.98 (considered above at 14.1.7.5) would have to be observed.

14.1.9.4 Accelerated payment clauses

Many credit agreements which are repayable by instalments contain a term stating that all future instalments become payable immediately if the debtor defaults. Such a term is known as an accelerated payment clause. These clauses are particularly useful to the creditor where the debtor's breach does not amount to a repudiation of the contract or where goods which might be repossessed have become worth much less than the value of future instalments.

Accelerated payment clauses are valid as long as they do not amount to penalties. (See Chapter 7 at 7.2.2.4.) However, an accelerated payment clause in a regulated agreement cannot be activated unless a default notice is served under s.87 or, where the debtor is not in default, notice is given under s.76(1). The debtor could then apply to the court for a time order under s.129. (See above at 14.1.9.2.) If granted, the time order would set the intervals at which the instalments should be paid and, in effect, defeat the accelerated payment clause. The Unfair Terms in Consumer Contracts Regulations 1999 might provide additional protection. (See Chapter 5 at 5.7.)

14.1.9.5 Damages

If a hire-purchase or conditional sale agreement is breached by the debtor then the creditor can sue for damages. (Breach of a loan or credit sale will consist of not repaying the instalments and the creditor can sue to recover payment of the unpaid instalments plus interest. This would be an action for an agreed sum rather than an action for damages. See Chapter 7 at 7.2.3.)

Under the common law the damages will be assessed, under the rule in *Hadley* v *Baxendale,* to put the creditor in the position which he would have been in if the contract had been performed as agreed. (See *Yeoman Credit Ltd* v *Waragowski* [1961] 3 All ER 145 below.) If the breach consists of early termination of a hire-purchase or conditional sale agreement by the debtor then the damages will be calculated according to s.100(1), as explained above at 14.1.8.2.

The measure of damages differs depending upon whether the debtor repudiated the agreement or whether the creditor terminated on account of a breach by the debtor which did not amount to a repudiation.

14.1.9.6 Damages where the debtor repudiated the agreement

The following case represented the position before the Act came into force.

Yeoman Credit Ltd v Waragowski
[1961] 3 All ER 145 (Court of Appeal)

The claimants made a hire-purchase agreement with the defendant in respect of a second-hand van. The agreement required the defendant to pay £72 down and to make 36 monthly instalments of £10 0s 9d. The sale price of the van was £360, but the total price including interest and charges was £434 7s 0d. The defendant did not pay any of the monthly instalments. Six months into the agreement the claimants terminated the agreement and repossessed the van. The claimants sold the van for £205 and then sued for arrears of £60 4s 6d and damages.

Held. The claimants were entitled to damages for breach of contract as well as arrears of £60 4s 6d. The

---

damages were assessed as the difference between the amount of money which the claimants had actually received and the amount which they would have received if the defendant had continued with the agreement for the full three years. The damages were therefore £97 2s 6d. (£434 7s 0d − (£72 + £205 + £60 4s 6d))

COMMENT It is not certain whether the debtor's right to escape paying the whole of the agreed price (under ss.99 and 100) would now have to be taken into account. If it would, damages should be based on the maximum amount which might be recovered under s.100(1) less any payments actually made.

If the agreement was a regulated agreement then upon payment of the amount due, the debtor would be entitled to a rebate of charges for credit for early settlement under s.95.

14.1.9.7 Termination by creditor where debtor does not repudiate

If the creditor terminates when the debtor has breached the contract but has not repudiated, then it is the creditor who is bringing it to an end, rather than the debtor. Consequently the creditor will only be entitled to claim arrears and interest plus any amount to compensate for the defendant having failed to take reasonable care of the goods. There will be no damages for the loss of the bargain.

In *Financings Ltd* v *Baldock* [1963] 2 QB 104 (Court of Appeal) a debtor took a truck on hire-purchase, paying a deposit and agreeing to pay monthly instalments for two years. The defendant missed making the first two payments. The creditor used a term of the agreement to repossess the truck and then sold it. It was held that the debtor's behaviour did not amount to repudiation of the contract. A term of the agreement stated that if the debtor defaulted and the creditor repossessed the debtor would pay as damages an amount equal to two-thirds of total payments as compensation for depreciation of the goods. This term was void as a penalty and the debtor was ordered to pay the two instalments in arrears + 10 per cent interest up to the date of judgment. (In Chapter 7 at 7.2.2.4 we saw that where the damages are fixed in advance this will amount either to liquidated damages or to a penalty. If the amount fixed is a 'genuine pre-estimate of the loss' then it will be liquidated damages and the amount fixed will be the amount of damages payable. If the amount fixed is not a genuine pre-estimate of the loss then it will be a penalty, which the courts will ignore. Damages will then be calculated according to ordinary common law principles.)

In *Lombard North Central* v *Butterworth* [1987] 1 All ER 267 (Court of Appeal) a term in a hire contract stated that prompt payment of all instalments was of the essence of the contract. The defendant made several late payments, which would not ordinarily have amounted to a repudiation of the contract. However, the term making prompt payment of the essence was a condition of the contract. Therefore the creditor could terminate the contract and recover damages for the loss of the whole bargain. It is now common for hire-purchase and conditional sale agreements to include a term that prompt payment of all instalments is of the essence.

14.1.9.8 Repossession of the goods

A creditor may terminate a hire-purchase or conditional sale agreement, and repossess the goods, if the debtor does not make all of the payments. However, the Act protects a debtor in three ways, as without this protection a debtor who had made substantial payments before defaulting could suddenly lose all rights when the creditor 'snatched-back' the goods.

First, the creditor will not be able to repossess goods without giving notice and observing the provisions of ss.76, 87–89 and 98. Second, the creditor or owner is not entitled to enter premises to retake possession of the goods without a court order, unless the debtor agrees to this (s.92(1)). Most important though, the goods may become protected goods as explained by s.90(1):

'At any time when –

(a) the debtor is in breach of a regulated hire-purchase or a regulated conditional sale agreement relating to goods, and

(b) the debtor has paid to the creditor one-third or more of the total price of the goods and

(c) the property in the goods remains in the creditor,

the creditor is not entitled to recover possession of the goods from the debtor except on an order of the court.'

If an installation charge is included in the total price for the goods, the amount which the debtor must have paid is the whole of the installation charge and a third of the remainder of the total price (s.90(2)).

Section 90(1) shall not apply, or shall cease to apply, to an agreement if the debtor has termin-ated, or terminates, the agreement (s.90(5)).

The consequences of the creditor breaching s.90 are severe, as s.91 makes plain:

'If goods are recovered by the creditor in breach of s.90 –

(a) the regulated agreement, if not previously termi-nated, shall terminate, and

(b) the debtor shall be released from all liability under the agreement, and shall be entitled to recover from the creditor all sums paid by the debtor under the agreement.'

Examples

(1) Dave takes a motorbike on hire-purchase from Bikes Ltd. Dave pays a deposit of £1 000 and commits himself to paying £100 a month for 36 months. After ten monthly payments Dave defaults on his next payment. Bikes Ltd immediately repossess the motorbike. If Bikes Ltd repossessed the motorbike without a court order then they would be in breach of s.90. Section 91 would therefore terminate the agreement, and entitle Dave to recover all sums paid under the agreement. As the agreement would be terminated, Bikes Ltd would be entitled to possession of the motorbike. Dave, however, would be entitled to the return of the £1 000 deposit and the ten instalments of £100 already paid.

(2) If after ten monthly payments Dave had written to say that he no longer wanted the motorbike he would appear to have terminated the agreement under s.99. Therefore, applying s.90(5), s.90(1) would not apply. As owners of the motorbike, Bikes Ltd would have the right to repossess it. Dave would not be able to recover money already paid. Dave would, under s.100(1), have to make his payments up to half the total price. As Dave has paid £2 000 and the total price was £4 600, he would have to pay a further £300. However, if the court was satisfied that Bikes Ltd's loss was less than £300 then Dave would not have to pay this extra £300 (s.100(3)).

Although it is possible for the debtor to consent to the repossession of protected goods, if a term of the contract states that the debtor gives such consent then the term will be void under s.173(1). The creditor can repossess the goods which have been abandoned, as this is not recovery of goods from the debtor.

14.1.9.9 Provisions protecting hirers of goods

Section 132 gives financial relief to a hirer of goods under a regulated consumer hire agreement where the owner takes the goods back without taking court action. The hirer can apply for a court order that:

(a) the whole or part of any sum paid by the hirer to the owner in respect of the goods shall be repaid, and

(b) the obligation to pay the whole or part of any sum owed by the hirer to the owner in respect of the goods shall cease.

The court will only grant the order if it appears just to do so, having regard to the extent of the enjoyment of the goods by the hirer.

14.1.9.10 The court's powers in hire-purchase and conditional sale agreements

Section 133 applies to regulated hire-purchase and conditional sale agreements, enabling the court to make a return order or a transfer order when the creditor sues to recover goods or when there is an application for an enforcement order or a time order. A return order requires that goods to which the agreement relates are returned to the creditor. A transfer order allows for the transfer to the debtor of the creditor's title to some of the goods to which the agreement relates, while the remainder of the goods are returned to the creditor.

Section 135 gives the court the power to impose conditions in any regulated agreement. Section 136 gives the court the power to amend or vary any agreement when it makes an order under the Act. If the debtor contravenes a return order or a transfer order it can be revoked by the court (s.133(6)).

14.1.10 Dispute resolution

Section 226A of the Financial Services and Markets Act 2000 allows the Financial Services Ombudsman to hear complaints against people licensed under the CCA 1974. A new ombudsman scheme was set up in April 2007. This scheme is funded by a levy taken from licensees and is free to consumers. Under the scheme, businesses that hold consumer credit licences will have to have formal complaints handling procedures. Early indications are that most disputes will be resolved by mediation or by adjudicators, with the Ombudsman needing to decide fewer than 10 per cent. However, either the business or the creditor can ask the Ombudsman to change an adjudicator's decision. As mediation is often used, there are not always clear winners and losers. The ombudsman scheme

does not investigate complaints about the rate of interest charged but does assess complaints under the new rules on unfair relationships between creditors and debtors. It assesses complaints under s.75 unless difficulties about evidence would make the case more suitable for a court. This might occasionally be the case, for example, if the dispute involved assessment of whether goods supplied were of satisfactory quality.

> ### Test your understanding 14.4
>
> 1 What is the debtor's right to appropriate payments to a creditor? In what circumstances might appropriation of payments help a debtor?
>
> 2 What rights of early payment does a debtor have?
>
> 3 What payments must be made by a debtor who terminates a hire-purchase or conditional sale agreement?
>
> 4 How are the creditor's damages for loss of the bargain affected if a debtor's breach of a hire-purchase agreement does or does not amount to a repudiation of the agreement?

14.2 TYPES OF CREDIT TRANSACTIONS

Credit is an underlying fact of commercial and consumer business. It is not usual for commercial organisations to pay cash, or to pay in advance, when making a business deal. Whenever payment for goods or services is deferred some sort of credit will have been provided. There are many different ways of providing credit, and the principal methods are now considered in outline.

14.2.1 Loans

A loan is the most fundamental form of credit. If a loan is made a creditor lends money to a debtor so that the debtor can buy goods or services. The debtor agrees to repay the money, with interest, over a period of time.

The creditor is often not connected with the transaction he is financing. A bank, for example, may lend money to enable a business to buy new machinery. If the bank has no existing or contemplated future connection with the supplier, the contract between the business and the supplier of the machinery is nothing to do with the bank. The bank merely lends the money. As we saw earlier in this chapter at 14.1, this would be regarded by the CCA 1974 as a debtor–creditor

nt. If the bank did have an existing or
uplated future connection with the supplier the
ement would be regarded as a debtor–creditor–
supplier agreement.

Creditors are, however, likely to want **security**
for the money they lend. If the debtor is a company
the creditor will probably register a **charge** over the
company's assets. The effects of this are considered in
detail in Chapter 18 at 18.9. Essentially, a charge is a
mortgage over some of the company's property. The
company is free to continue to use the property but
not to pass ownership to anyone else or do anything
which would reduce its value. If the company does not
repay the debt as agreed, the bank can order the sale
of the assets over which it has a charge and take what
it is owed. To preserve the rights granted, a chargeholder should register the charge with the Registrar
of Companies.

If the debtor is a partnership or a sole trader the
creditor may take a **mortgage** of property. The property mortgaged does not need to be business property,
it might well be the house of the sole trader or of one
of the partners. If the loan is not repaid the creditor
will be able to repossess the property. (Sell it and take
the amount still owed.) Where an individual or a partnership gives goods as security for a loan, but retains
possession of the goods, the security interest must be
registered under the Bills of Sale Act 1878 and the Bills
of Sale (1878) (Amendment) Act 1882. If the documents relating to the security interest are not attested
and registered within seven days, the security becomes
unenforceable. The registrar with whom the documents must be registered is a master of the Supreme
Court. As registration does not amount to notice to
third parties, a subsequent purchaser of the goods who
does not know of the security interest may take title
free from security interest. If a non-possessory security
over the same goods is given to two different creditors,
the date of registration decides which creditor has priority. Registration requires a detailed inventory of the
goods given as security. For this reason individuals and
partnerships cannot grant the equivalent of a floating
charge where a class of assets, both present and future,
are given as security for a loan. In **Online Catering
Ltd** v **Frank Acton** [2010] EWCA Civ 58 the Court of
Appeal confirmed that the Bills of Sale Acts apply only
to individuals and partnerships and not to companies.
Nor will the Acts apply to LLPs.

Alternatively the creditor may be willing to accept
a **third party guarantee** of the loan. The guarantor

would then be liable to repay the loan if the debtor
defaulted. For example, in **Lloyds Bank** v **Bundy**
which is set out in Chapter 6 at 6.3.2.2 the father guaranteed the loans made to his son's business, promising
that he would repay the loans if his son failed to do so.
Such guarantees are effective as long as they are evidenced in writing and as long as they were not made
as a consequence of duress or undue influence.

Security for a loan is not always necessary.
Sometimes a bank will allow an **overdraft** without
requiring security. An overdraft is a form of loan
whereby customers can overdraw their bank accounts
(take more money out of the account than has been
deposited into it) on the understanding that money
will be deposited later. There will be a limit above
which the customer may not overdraw.

The rate of interest on an overdraft is usually higher
than on a bank loan. However, the customer can clear
his overdraft as soon as he wishes, and if the account
is overdrawn for only a short time he might not pay
much interest. Large overdrafts are a risky way for a
small business to borrow money as the bank can insist
that they be repaid at any time.

14.2.2 Hire-purchase

Under a hire-purchase agreement a debtor hires
goods for a fixed period, and has an option to buy
the goods for a nominal sum at the end of that
period. Payment for the hire of the goods is usually
made by regular instalments. As there is no agreement to carry on with the agreement and pay all
of the instalments there is no agreement to sell and
the Sale of Goods Act 1979 will not apply until the
final payment is made, at which time the agreement
becomes a contract of sale.

This can be demonstrated by considering the case of
Yeoman Credit Ltd v **Waragowski,** the facts of which
are set out above at 14.1.9.6. The defendant paid a
deposit and this was to be followed by the payment of
36 monthly instalments. If the agreement had run its full
course then the defendant would have acquired ownership of the van upon making the final payment. Up until
the time of the final payment the defendant would have
been hiring the van which would have remained the
property of the finance company. The defendant would
not have made a commitment to continue with the
agreement for the full 36 months. (The consequences
of not continuing with the agreement until it had run its
course were considered above at 14.1.8.2.)

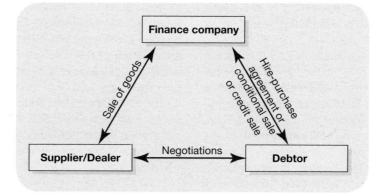

Figure 14.3 Triangular transactions

Usually a finance company, rather than the dealer in the goods, makes the hire-purchase agreement with the debtor. Many debtors under hire-purchase agreements are not aware of this. If the finance is provided by a third party, the hire-purchase agreement takes the form of a triangular transaction as shown in Figure 14.3.

(1) The dealer sells the goods to the finance company.
(2) The finance company makes the hire-purchase agreement with the customer.
(3) There may be a collateral contract between the dealer and the customer. (The meaning of this is considered shortly.)

When the agreement is a regulated agreement within the Consumer Credit Act 1974 s.56(2) will provide the debtor with a remedy against the finance company if the dealer makes a misrepresentation, or a statement which becomes a term of the credit agreement, when conducting antecedent negotiations. (See above at 14.1.5.) In *Branwhite* **v** *Worcester Works Finance Ltd* [1969] 1 AC 552 the House of Lords held that the dealer is not normally the agent of the finance company at common law. However, when the agreement is unregulated a court might be willing to find a collateral contract between the dealer and the customer. If no such **collateral contract** could be found then the dealer would not have any contractual liability to a debtor who made a triangular transaction. The dealer might, however, be liable for fraud or negligent misstatement but these types of liability are hard to establish.

The following case, decided before the Consumer Credit Act was enacted, shows an example of a collateral contract in a triangular transaction.

Andrews v Hopkinson [1957] 1 QB 229

The claimant visited a motor dealer to look at second-hand cars. He took a vehicle on hire-purchase, through a finance company, because the dealer told him 'It's a good little bus. I would stake my life on it. You will have no trouble with it.' In fact the vehicle had defective steering. This caused an accident in which the claimant was badly injured.

Held. The dealer was liable on the collateral contract which he made with the claimant. This collateral contract was created when the claimant agreed to take the vehicle on hire-purchase (thus benefiting the defendant) and the defendant promised that it was 'a good little bus' (thus benefiting the claimant).

To some extent collateral contracts are a fiction, invented by the court to do justice in a particular case. However, they can be useful when no other remedy is available. Since the Consumer Credit Act came into force the court will only need to find a collateral contract if the hire-purchase agreement is not regulated by the Act.

The Supply of Goods (Implied Terms) Act 1973 ss.8–11 imply into hire-purchase contracts terms very similar to those which ss.12–15 SGA imply into contracts for the sale of goods. (See Chapter 8 at 8.3.1.)

14.2.3 **Conditional sales**

A conditional sale agreement is a sale of goods in which ownership of the goods stays with the seller until all of the price has been paid. The buyer usually takes immediate possession of the goods and commits himself to making full payment, often by instalments.

For example, a garage might make a conditional sale of a delivery van to a butcher. The terms of the contract might provide that the butcher is to pay for the van in 36 monthly instalments. The butcher will take immediate possession of the van, but the van will remain the property of the garage until all the instalments have been paid.

Where the payment is to be made in regular instalments a conditional sale agreement appears very similar indeed to a hire-purchase agreement. The difference is that under a hire-purchase agreement the buyer does not commit himself to completing the payments, whereas under a conditional sale agreement he does. An important consequence of this is that the Sale of Goods Act applies **immediately** in the case of a conditional sale, as there is an agreement to sell. The Sale of Goods Act will not apply to hire-purchase until the sale is actually made with payment of the final instalment. (However, in Chapter 9 at 9.3.5 we saw that s.25 SGA, which applies to a sale of goods by a 'buyer in possession', does not apply where the first buyer has taken the goods on a conditional sale agreement, payable by instalments, which is regulated by the Consumer Credit Act 1974.) Conditional sale agreements often involve a finance company in a triangular transaction. A regulated conditional sale agreement is classified by the Consumer Credit Act as a debtor–creditor– supplier agreement for restricted-use credit within s.12(a).

14.2.4 Credit sales

Under a credit sale ownership of the goods passes to the buyer immediately, either upon the making of the contract or upon the delivery of the goods, and the seller extends credit to the buyer.

For example, a mail order catalogue firm might sell a coat to a customer under a credit sale. The coat becomes the customer's property as soon as goods matching the contract description are unconditionally appropriated to the contract by the seller with the assent of the buyer. (This will generally be when the coat is posted to the customer, see Chapter 9 at 9.1.2.) The mail order firm gives the customer credit, and the customer is obliged to pay the price of the coat under the credit terms specified in the contract.

Credit sales are commonly used where the goods supplied have a low second-hand value, there being no point in the seller retaining ownership if the goods are worth very little. The Sale of Goods Act applies to credit sales. If a finance company finances a credit sale then there may well be a triangular transaction, the debtor buying the goods from the finance company rather than from the dealer. A regulated credit sale is classified by the Consumer Credit Act as a debtor–creditor– supplier agreement for restricted use credit within s.12(a).

14.2.5 **Hire and rental agreements**

A person who rents goods to another gives possession of the goods in return for regular payments. He does not agree to sell the goods. Hire is very similar, but is usually for a longer period.

The Sale of Goods Act does not apply to hire agreements, but the Supply of Goods and Services Act ss.7–10 imply terms very similar to those implied by SGA ss.12–15. (See Chapter 8 at 8.3.2.) As we saw at 14.1.1, a consumer hire agreement (within the definition given by s.15 of the Consumer Credit Act 1974) will be a regulated consumer credit agreement as long as it is not an exempt agreement.

14.2.6 **Pawn**

Goods are pawned when possession of them is given to a lender as security for a loan. When the debtor repays the loan he is given the goods back. If the debtor does not repay, the creditor can sell the goods. A pawn differs from a mortgage in that the debtor does not retain possession of the se-curity. Easily transportable goods of high value are suitable to pledge, often to a pawnbroker.

For example, a person who wanted to borrow £100 might pledge a camera worth £1 000 to a pawnbroker. As long as the debtor repays the £100 with interest within a certain time the pawn-broker will return the camera. If the debtor does not repay the debt then eventually the pawnbroker will be able to sell the camera and take what he is owed from the proceeds.

Neither the Sale of Goods Act nor the Supply of Goods and Services Act apply to pawns, but the Consumer Credit Act does.

14.2.7 **Payment by credit card**

When a supplier accepts payment by credit card, the customer/cardholder signs the voucher and this entitles the supplier to a payment which fully discharges the customer's liability for the price of the goods or services. The credit card company will pay the price to the supplier, deducting commission. The supplier knows that when the cardholder/customer signs the voucher he renders himself liable to the credit card company to pay the price of the goods or services. Both the supplier and the cardholder would previously have made contracts with the credit card company. The supplier accepts the payment by credit card in substitution of payment in cash, i.e. as an unconditional discharge of the price. (*Re Charge Card Services Ltd* [1989] Ch 497.) Payment by credit card is classified by the Consumer Credit Act 1974 as a debtor–creditor–supplier agreement for restricted use credit within s.12(b).

14.2.8 **Trade credit**

Trade credit arises when payment for goods or services is informally deferred. Immediate payment for goods is not the norm in commercial life. Just as the newsagent delivers newspapers before he is paid for them, so businesses informally accept deferred payment for goods and services which they supply. For policy reasons this type of informal credit is largely unregulated by the Consumer Credit Act.

14.3 **INTEREST ON TRADE DEBTS**

Businesses which supply goods or services on credit to others might insist that a term is included in the contract making interest payable on the money owed. However, many suppliers are reluctant to do this for fear of losing future contracts with the person to whom credit is provided.

The Late Payment of Commercial Debts (Interest) Act 1998 gives all businesses a statutory right, by way of an implied term, to claim interest on late payment of commercial debts for the supply of goods or services. Such a claim can be made against another business or a public sector body. A debt is a commercial debt for the supply of goods and services if both the supplier and the purchaser are acting in the course of business.

Interest becomes payable under the Act from the day after the relevant date for the debt. This date can be fixed in various ways. It can be the date for payment which the supplier and purchaser agreed, or can be fixed by trade custom or a course of dealing between the parties. If the relevant date is not fixed in one of these ways it is set at 30 days after the supplier performed his obligations under the contract, or at 30 days after the purchaser is given notice of the debt, whichever is the later. So payment would generally become due 30 days after goods or an invoice were delivered. However, there is no need for the notice of the debt to be written and it could be given in person or over the telephone.

The rate of interest is currently set at 8 per cent above the base rate. The interest on the debt can be claimed for as a separate claim from the principal debt and can be assigned to a third party, such as a debt collector.

The effect of the Act cannot be avoided by means of a contractual term unless there is a 'substantial' remedy available for the late payment of the debt. A remedy is not regarded as substantial if it is insufficient for compensating the supplier, or if it would not be fair to allow the remedy to oust or vary the statutory interest payable under the Act. In deciding whether or not a remedy is substantial the court will consider all the circumstances at the time when the debt was agreed. It is only possible for a contractual term to postpone the time at which a debt is created to the extent that the term satisfies the UCTA 1977 requirement of reasonableness. (The UCTA requirement of reasonableness is examined in Chapter 5 at 5.6.1.)

It has been widely reported in the media that the Act has not yet made a significant impact. There is nothing wrong with the drafting of the Act, but it seems that most businesses are reluctant to use it for fear of offending their customers.

In addition to court fees, a successful creditor can claim reasonable compensation for the cost of collecting the debt. The Late Payments of Commercial Debts Regulations 2002 fix this compensation at £40 if the debt was under £1 000, £70 if the debt was at least £1 000 but under £10 000 and £100 if the debt was £10 000 or more.

The late payment interest rate is calculated by adding the current statutory rate to the Bank of England base rate. For example, if the current statutory rate is 8 per cent and the Bank of England base rate is 3.75 per cent then the late payment interest rate is 11.75 per cent.

Example

Five months ago Company A ordered goods to the value of £1 000 from Company B. The relevant date for payment was not fixed. The goods were delivered, along with an invoice, 130 days ago. A commercial debt of £1 000 has been payable for 100 days since the relevant date for the debt. The daily interest rate is calculated as:

$$\frac{£1000 \times 11.75\%}{365} = 0.32\text{p per day}$$

Therefore, £32.00 interest is already owed and the interest will increase by 0.32p per day until the debt is paid. In addition a fixed fee of £70 could be charged.

Any part payment made will first be set off against interest owed and then against the original debt.

The 2002 Regulations allow established representative bodies to apply for injunctions to prevent the use of written standard terms which try to oust or vary the right to statutory interest. The representative bodies must represent either a particular business sector or small and medium sized businesses in general.

In *Ruttle Plant Hire Ltd* v *Secretary of State for Environment Food and Rural Affairs (No. 3)* [2009] EWCA Civ 97, the Court of Appeal held that the increased rate of interest was payable under the Act even if the amount of debt claimed was inaccurate. The defendant had argued that any error in the invoice, other than one which the debtor could obviously see, would mean that the Act did not apply. This argument failed for two reasons. First, because the Act allowed for remission of overpaid interest where the interests of justice demanded this. Second, because if the argument were upheld then debtors would be searching through invoices for the smallest detail of error so as to render the Act inapplicable. The court did, however, recognise that a debtor who did not pay an amount which was reasonably in doubt, or not properly settled, would not have to pay interest under the Act.

Test your understanding 14.5

1   What is a hire-purchase agreement?

2   In what way is a conditional sale agreement different from a hire-purchase agreement?

Key points

Regulated agreements and other definitions

■ A regulated agreement is a consumer credit agreement, or consumer hire agreement, other than an exempt agreement.

■ The definition of a regulated agreement is significant because most of the Act's provisions apply only to regulated agreements.

■ Running-account credit is given under a master agreement which allows for separate credit agreements to be made under it. Fixed-sum credit fixes the amount of credit in the agreement or allows the amount of credit to be calculated by reference to the agreement.

■ Restricted-use credit is transferred directly from the creditor to the supplier of the goods or services being acquired by the debtor, or is provided by the supplier. Any credit actually received by the debtor is unrestricted-use credit.

■ Under a debtor–creditor–supplier agreement the creditor is either the legal supplier of the goods or services or has an existing or future contemplated connection with the legal supplier. Any agreement other than a debtor–creditor–supplier agreement is a debtor–creditor agreement.

■ A non-commercial agreement is one made by the creditor or owner otherwise than in the course of a business carried on by him. A small agreement is one where the credit extended is less than £50 or one where the hirer does not need to make payments exceeding £50.

Cancellation and copies of regulated agreements

■ If the rules concerning the supply of copies of credit agreements are not complied with the agreements are only enforceable by court order and may be unenforceable.

■ If the debtor or hirer is not given notice of cancellation rights, as required by s.64, the agreement may be unenforceable.

Statutory liability of creditor

■ Section 56(2) provides that in two and three party debtor–creditor–supplier agreements a person

→

who conducts negotiations on behalf of the creditor is deemed to do so as the agent of the creditor.

■ Section 75(1) provides that in debtor–creditor–supplier agreements where the creditor is not also the supplier of the goods the creditor assumes joint and several liability for breaches of contract or misrepresentations made by the supplier.

Credit tokens

■ A credit token is a card etc. provided by a person carrying on a consumer credit business who undertakes that on production of it he will supply cash, goods or services on credit or that on production of it to a third party he will pay the third party for cash, goods or services in return for payment to him by the individual.

■ A credit-token agreement is a regulated agreement for the provision of credit in connection with the use of a credit token.

■ A debtor whose credit token is stolen is not liable to the creditor for loss of more than £50 arising from unauthorised misuse of the credit card.

■ If a consumer's card is misused in connection with a distance contract the card holder will suffer no loss.

Enforcement and termination of the agreement

■ If a debtor or hirer is liable to make payments to the same person under two or more regulated agreements, and sends less than the total sums due, he can allocate the payments towards one or more of the agreements as he sees fit (s.81(1)).

■ If there is an unfair relationship between creditor and debtor the court has wide powers to alter the agreement and order the creditor to repay money received.

■ The debtor under a regulated consumer credit agreement is entitled to discharge the debt at any time by giving the creditor notice in writing and by repaying the whole debt (s.94(1)).

■ If a debtor terminates a regulated hire-purchase or conditional sale agreement early, arrears must be paid. The debtor may also be required to bring payments made (including arrears) up to half of the total price. If the debtor has failed to take reasonable care of the goods, the amount payable should be increased to compensate the creditor for this.

■ If a debtor repudiates a hire-purchase agreement the creditor will be able to sue for arrears and for damages for loss of the bargain.

■ If the creditor terminates a hire-purchase agreement on account of a breach by the debtor which did not amount to a repudiation, the creditor will be entitled to arrears (plus interest) but not to damages for the loss of the bargain.

■ A hire-purchase agreement is an agreement under which a debtor hires goods for a fixed period, and has an option to buy the goods for a nominal sum at the end of that period. The debtor has no obligation to continue with the agreement for the whole of the fixed period.

■ Under a conditional sale a buyer agrees to buy goods but the ownership of the goods is not to pass to the buyer until all of the price has been paid. There is an agreement to sell from the outset and the buyer agrees to make all of the payments.

Summary questions

1 Are the following agreements regulated agreements within the meaning given by the Consumer Credit Act 1974? If not, why not?

  a Acme Ltd buys a new van on conditional sale from Ace Finance Ltd. Acme is to make 24 monthly payments of £600. The total interest to be paid, at a rate of 15 per cent, is £2 500.

  b Bill, a self-employed carpenter, hires a van for one year. Bill agrees to pay £200 a month in hire charges.

  c Charlene borrows £2 000 from the bank at which she works so that she can go on an expensive holiday. The loan is to be repaid over 12 months at an APR of 6 per cent, a rate available only to the bank's employees.

  d David, a postman, sells his car to Edward, a plumber. Edward agrees to pay £200 a month for 12 months. This figure includes interest at an APR of 15 per cent.

  e Felicity takes a car on hire-purchase from Ace Finance Ltd. The agreement provides for 24 monthly payments of £200. The APR is 24 per cent.

  f Gerald, one of two partners in a firm of builders, takes a JCB digger on hire-purchase from Ace Finance Ltd, on behalf of the

→

firm. Gerald pays a deposit of £3 000. 36 instalments of £1 000 are to be paid. The APR is 14 per cent, and the total interest payable if the agreement runs its course will be £7 500.

2 Jim goes to an electrical retailer to buy a new stereo system. A salesman explains which system he considers the best buy and Jim is persuaded to take such a system under a regulated hire-purchase agreement. Jim signs an unexecuted copy of the agreement while in the shop. What copies, if any, must be sent to Jim? What cancellation rights, if any, does Jim have?

3 Jim went to a local garage because he was thinking of buying a car. A salesman explained which car he thought would best suit Jim's needs. The next day Jim phoned the garage to say that he was thinking of buying the recommended car. The garage sent Jim a copy of an unexecuted regulated conditional sale agreement. Jim signs this and sends it back. What copies or notices must Jim be supplied with? Is there a cooling-off period?

4 Tony visits Ace Computers Ltd's shop where a salesman persuades him that a particular model of computer will be perfect for his needs. As Tony cannot afford to pay cash, the salesman arranges a hire-purchase agreement under which Tony takes the recommended computer from Acme Finance Ltd. Tony soon discovers that the computer is totally unsuitable for his needs. Ace Computers Ltd has gone into liquidation. Advise Tony of any way in which the Consumer Credit Act 1974 might help him.

5 Mary bought a new bed from Sleepy Stores Ltd, paying the price with her Access card. Before the bed was delivered, Sleepy Stores Ltd went into liquidation. Advise Mary of any way in which the Consumer Credit Act 1974 might help her.

6 Delia takes a new cooker on hire-purchase from Acme Finance Ltd, paying a £50 deposit. The agreement is to run for 36 months and ownership of the cooker is to pass to Delia when she has paid 36 monthly instalments of £50. Delia pays the first ten instalments but she defaults on the eleventh payment. Acme repossess the cooker immediately,

without a court order. Explain Delia's legal position. How would your answer be different if after paying ten monthly instalments Delia had written to Acme Finance Ltd saying that she could not make any more payments?

7 In the transactions described below, company A has agreed to supply machinery to company B. The seven transactions described provide one example of each of the following types of credit: trade credit; a loan; hire-purchase; a conditional sale; a contract of hire; a credit sale; and an overdraft. Match the transactions to the various types of credit. You might, for example, think that (a) was an example of a hire-purchase.

a Company B takes possession of the machinery, but ownership is not to pass to company B until they have paid all 36 instalments of the price. At the outset company B commits itself to making all 36 payments.

b Company B takes possession of the machinery, but ownership is not to pass to company B until they have paid all 36 instalments of the price. Company B does not commit itself to making all 36 payments.

c Along with the machinery, company A sends an invoice which requests payment in full within 28 days.

d Company B has agreed to pay £1 000 a month for the use of the machinery until it has filled an order. After that the machinery will be returned to company A.

e Company B's bank has agreed that company B can pay for the machinery by writing a cheque for £10 000. The company bank balance stands at £2 300.

f Company B's bank has credited the company account with £10 000 so that the machinery can be bought. Company B are to repay this money by paying £560 a month for two years.

g Company B takes immediate possession of the machinery and gets immediate ownership of it. The contract of sale says that the price is to be paid by 12 monthly instalments of £1 000 each.

Multiple choice questions

1 Mary bought a new bed and a bedside lamp from a large department store. The bed cost £650 and the lamp £22. Mary paid for both items with her credit card. Before the goods were delivered the department store went into liquidation. Which one of the following statements is true?

a Mary will have no remedy, other than to claim against the department store as an unsecured creditor.

b As Mary had paid for the goods she would have a charge over them and would therefore be entitled to delivery of them.

c The credit card company will have to recredit Mary's account with both the price of the bed and of the lamp.

d The credit card company will have to recredit Mary's account with the price of the bed. It will not have to recredit the account with the price of the lamp.

2 Which one of the following statements is true?

a A credit agreement with an APR of 130 per cent is automatically void.

b A credit agreement can be a debtor–creditor–supplier agreement even if there are only two parties involved – the creditor (who is also the legal supplier of the goods or services) and the debtor.

c All credit agreements where the credit is less than £25 000 will be regulated agreements, for the purposes of the Consumer Credit Act.

d The Consumer Credit Act protects only consumers, that is to say people who take the credit other than in the course of a business.

3 Gerald is a policeman. Gerald's debit card is stolen from his wallet. Before Gerald notices the theft, the thief uses the card to order goods over the Internet. This reduces Gerald's credit balance from £1 200 to £950. Gerald then phones the bank to tell them of the theft. The bank ask for written confirmation which Gerald sends the following day. Just before the letter was posted the thief reduced Gerald's bank balance to £700 by using the card to buy goods in a shop. By the time the letter arrived Gerald's balance had been reduced by the thief to £500 as the thief had used the card to buy more goods over the Internet. Applying the CCA 1974 and the Banking Code, which one of the following statements is true?

a The bank will have no liability to recredit Gerald's account with any of the stolen money.

b The bank will have to recredit Gerald's account with £250.

c The bank will have to recredit Gerald's account with £450.

d The bank will have to recredit Gerald's account with £700.

4 MacNavvy Ltd need a new steamroller in order to complete a lucrative contract. MacNavvy have not got enough money to pay the full price outright. Steamrollers Ltd deliver a new steamroller to MacNavvy. The contract states that MacNavvy are to have immediate possession of the steamroller and that they commit themselves to paying for it in 24 equal instalments. Ownership of the steamroller is not to pass until MacNavvy have paid all of the instalments. Is this contract an example of:

a Hire-purchase?

b Conditional sale?

c Credit sale?

d Trade credit?

5 John visits a car dealer's showroom and selects a new car. A triangular transaction is entered into and John takes the car on hire-purchase from the finance company. Which one of the following statements reflects the legal position?

a John owns the car. He has committed himself to paying all of the instalments due under the hire-purchase agreement. If John fails to pay all of these instalments then the finance company will be able to repossess the car.

b John owns the car. He has not committed himself to paying all of the instalments due under the hire-purchase agreement. However, if John fails to pay all of these instalments then the finance company will be able to repossess the car.

c The finance company own the car. John has not committed himself to paying all of the instalments due under the hire-purchase agreement. However, if John fails to pay the instalments then the finance company will be entitled to take possession of the car from him.

d The dealer owns the car. John has not committed himself to paying all of the instalments due under the hire-purchase agreement. However, if John fails to pay the instalments then the dealer will be entitled to take possession of the car from him.

Task 14

MacThomson Roadworks is a partnership which repairs roads and drives. The partners decide that they would like to buy a new steamroller, but the firm does not have the money to make such a purchase.

Write a report for the partners, indicating:

a The various ways in which the steamroller might be acquired without paying the full price immediately.

b The main provisions of the Consumer Credit Act 1974.

mylawchamber *premium*

Visit **www.mylawchamber.co.uk/macintyre** to access study support resources including interactive multiple-choice questions, weblinks, glossary, glossary flashcards, legal newsfeed, answers to questions in this chapter, legal updates and an overview of this chapter all linked to the **Pearson eText** version of Business Law which you can **search, highlight** and **personalise** with your **own notes** and **bookmarks**.

Use **Case Navigator** to read in full some of the key cases referenced in this chapter with commentary and questions:

Wilson **v** *First County Trust Ltd* [2003] 4 All ER 97

15

Partnership

15.1 THE NATURE OF PARTNERSHIP

Partnership is a contractual relationship. The partners make a contract with each other and, as regards their relationship with each other, partners are generally free to agree whatever terms they wish. In the absence of agreement to the contrary, s.24 of the Partnership Act 1890 sets out nine terms which are implied into the contract which the partners make. As we shall see, these terms can be expressly excluded by a formal partnership agreement.

In addition to the s.24 implied terms, ss.28–30 of the Act set out three fiduciary duties which partners owe to each other. These duties have their origins in equity and are aspects of the wider fiduciary duties which partners owe to each other. Although the fiduciary duties cannot be contracted out of, it can be a defence to breach of a fiduciary duty to show that the other partners consented to the breach.

The liability of partners to those outside the firm is based on the law of agency. The partners have wide authority to bind the firm. This authority might be actual, apparent or usual. (As we saw in Chapter 11 at 11.2, actual authority would be created by agreement between the principal and agent, apparent authority would be created by a representation made by the principal to the third party with whom the agent contracted, and usual authority would exist on account of the agent occupying a certain role or position.) These types of authority often overlap. It can be important to distinguish between them because actual authority can only arise by agreement between the partners, whereas apparent and usual authority arises regardless of agreement that it should arise, and can give a partner authority to do an act which he has been forbidden to do.

In Chapter 19 at 19.2 we shall see that it is possible to register a business at Companies House as a limited liability partnership (LLP). LLPs are quite different from ordinary partnerships. They have a legal existence of their own, as companies do. However, an ordinary partnership, a firm, has no legal existence of its own. Partnership is a relationship, not a legal entity.

15.2 THE DEFINITION OF A PARTNERSHIP

The Partnership Act 1890 s.1(1) gives the following definition: 'Partnership is the relation which subsists between persons carrying on a business in common with a view of profit.' Although this definition is short, it is a matter of some complexity. It is most easily understood if broken down into its constituent parts.

Before analysing the definition, it is important to realise that, for several reasons, the question as to whether or not a partnership exists can be a matter of considerable significance. Perhaps the most important of these reasons is that if a partnership does exist the actions of an individual partner can make all of the partners liable to outsiders. Another important reason is that if a partnership exists an individual partner will have rights against the other partners, such as the right to share profits or the right to have the other partners share losses. Revenue & Customs will also take an interest in whether or not a business constitutes a partnership. A person who operates as a partner will be taxed accordingly.

15.2.1 Partnership is the relation which subsists between persons

This opening phrase of the definition is important because it shows that partnership is merely a relationship. A partnership is not a separate legal identity (as a company and a limited liability partnership are) with a legal existence of its own. It follows from this that a partnership cannot, as an entity separate from the partners, employ staff or own property. (As we shall see below, at 15.6, it is convenient to talk of partnership property. However, this property is not owned by the partnership, but owned by the partners who hold it on trust for each other.) When in Chapter 19 at 19.2 we examine LLPs we shall see that LLPs do have a separate legal identity of their own. However, LLPs can be created only by registration with Companies House and are, as yet, relatively uncommon. Throughout this chapter when reference to a partnership is made it is reference to an ordinary partnership and not to an LLP.

The relationship which constitutes a partnership is based on a contract, as the following statement of Jessel MR in *Pooley* v *Driver* (1876) 5 ChD 458 makes clear:

'But it [partnership] is a contract of some kind undoubtedly – a contract, like all contracts, involving the mutual consent of the parties: and it is undoubtedly a contract for the purpose of carrying on a commercial business – that is, a business bringing profit, and dividing the profit in some shape or other between the partners. That certainly partnership is.'

Although a partnership is a contract of some kind, it is important to realise that what must be agreed in the contract is that the partners should carry on a business together with a view of making a profit. Whether or not a partnership exists is not a matter of asking whether or not the parties agreed with each other that they should be in partnership. We shall see below at 15.3 that there is no need for the partners to agree that they are in partnership with each other, and that people can be partners even without realising that they are.

By stating that a partnership is the relation which subsists between persons, s.1(1) of the Act also makes it plain that a person who trades solely on his own account, a sole trader, cannot be a partnership. As we shall see in Chapter 16, it is possible for a person trading without others to form a registered company in which he is the sole shareholder and sole director, and to trade through the company.

As a company is regarded by the law as a legal person, it is possible for a company to be a member of a partnership. Companies can go into partnership with each other, or they can go into partnership with a natural person. A company which does become a partner will be liable for the firm's debts in the same way as any other partner. However, if the company is limited its shareholders cannot become personally liable for company debts incurred as a consequence of the company being a partner. Although a company can go into partnership with other people, s.1(2) of the Act provides that a company cannot itself be a partnership.

15.2.2 Carrying on a business

Section 45 of the Partnership Act defines 'business' as including 'every trade, occupation or profession'. However, some professions, such as the Bar, have rules which prevent their members from operating as partnerships. Other professions might prevent partnership with unqualified persons.

Although a partnership can only exist if a business is carried on, this does not necessarily prevent persons engaging in a one-off commercial enterprise from being in partnership. In *Mann* v *D'Arcy and others* [1968] 2 All ER 172 a partner in a firm of produce merchants made a one-off agreement with the claimant, whereby the firm and the claimant were to make a single purchase of 350 tons of potatoes to sell at a profit. It was held that this did create a partnership between the firm of produce merchants and the claimant, but only as regards this one deal.

We have seen that s.1(2) of the Act provides that a registered company cannot itself be a partnership, although it could be a member of a partnership. In the following case the Court of Appeal had to decide whether the promoters of a company were in partnership with each other.

Keith Spicer Ltd v *Mansell* [1970] 1 All ER 462 (Court of Appeal)

The defendant and B agreed to go into business together. They intended to form a limited company, which was to run the defendant's restaurant. Before the company was formed B ordered goods from the claimants. These goods were intended to be used by the company. The defendant and B also opened a bank account in the name of the proposed company, but without the word 'Limited'. The claimant was not paid for the goods which B ordered. He sued the defendant for the price, alleging that B and the defendant were in partnership.

Held. B and the defendant were not in partnership and so the claimant's claim failed. B and the defendant were not carrying on a business in common with a view of profit, they were merely working together to form a company. They did not intend to carry on a partnership prior to incorporation.

In the following case the House of Lords had to consider whether persons intending to trade as a partnership could be partners before the business actually began to trade.

Khan v *Mia* [2000] 1 WLR 2123 (House of Lords)

The two claimants and the three defendants proposed to open a restaurant. One of the parties was to be the restaurant manager, two were to be chefs and the other two were to provide capital. The proposed manager took a lease on suitable premises and he and one of the chefs opened a bank account, describing themselves as 'partners' in a business which was to be created at the beginning of December 1993. Furniture, laundry services and equipment were purchased and the business was advertised in the local press. The freehold of the restaurant premises was bought at auction but completion did not take place until January 1994. There were then delays in the building work and in one party finding capital and this caused the parties' relationship to break down. The relationship between the parties was ended by a solicitor's letter in January. In order to sort out the rights of the parties it became necessary to know whether or not a partnership had ever existed. The trial judge found that there had been a partnership, the Court of Appeal reversed this ruling and an appeal was made to the House of Lords.

Held. The parties had been in partnership. There was no rule of law that parties could not become partners until trading actually began. People who agreed to carry on a business as a joint venture became partners when they embarked on the agreed activity and made contracts on behalf of the joint venture. The purchasing of the freehold, and the purchasing of the goods and the services were all part of the joint venture which the parties had undertaken with a view of profit and so they formed part of the business which the parties had been carrying on as partners.

COMMENT (i) It would not be enough that the parties had merely agreed to become partners in the future. According to Lord Millett, who gave the leading judgment, it depended upon whether they had 'actually transacted any business of the joint venture'.

(ii) Lord Millett made it plain that whether or not parties who proposed to enter into a business venture had actually entered into it would be a question of fact for the trial judge. The House of Lords heard this case to refute the Court of Appeal's finding that there was a rule of law that parties to a joint venture cannot become partners until trading actually begins.

(iii) In the somewhat similar case of *Rowlands* v *Hodson* [2009] EWCA Civ 1042, [2010] PNLR 8 the Court of Appeal held that a solicitor working with an unqualified solicitor, in order to satisfy the Solicitor's Practice Rules, was a partner. The qualified solicitor had been entitled to only 1 per cent of the firm's profits and had not collected her share for two accounting periods. Nevertheless she was a partner for these two periods. During these periods the qualified solicitor had done occasional work for the firm, used

→

the firm's bank account, assumed liability for the firm's overdraft, taken the benefit of the firm's insurance and described herself as a partner on the firm's notepaper and elsewhere. She also intended to play, and did play, an important role in supervising the practice, without which no business could have been carried on.

15.2.3 **In common**

A person will not become a partner in a firm merely on account of working for the firm. In order to become a partner a person must carry on a business in common with the other partners. The following case gives an indication as to what is required.

Saywell v Pope (1979) 53 TC 40

Since 1960 Mr P and Mr S had been partners in a firm which repaired and sold agricultural machinery. When the firm was created there was no written partnership agreement. Mrs P and Mrs S were employed by the firm and were paid small salaries. A partnership agreement was drawn up in 1975, on an accountant's advice. The agreement said that the four parties had gone into partnership on 6 April 1973, and the accounts credited the wives with a share of the profits from April 1973. Neither of the wives ever drew any profits from the firm. The wives contributed no capital to the business. The wives could not write cheques or draw upon the firm's bank account, but they were warned of the risk of becoming partners. Neither the firm's bank, its creditors or its customers were told that the wives had become partners. The Revenue decided that the wives were not partners in the tax years from 1973 to 1975, and an appeal against this decision was made to the High Court.

Held. The wives were not partners during the relevant tax years as they did nothing in their capacities as partners during those years. The written agreement could not operate retrospectively to make the wives partners. The decision as to whether or not the wives were partners at any particular time could only be made by examining all the facts of the case.

An employee of a business will not become a partner merely on account of receiving a share of the business profits. Something more is required, namely that the business is carried on together (that is to say carried on in common). Similarly, a person who supplies goods or services to a business will not be in partnership with the business merely because payment is taken in the form of a share of the profits. In **Strathearn Gordon**

Associates Ltd v *Commissioners of Customs and Excise* [1985] VATTR 79 a limited company, SGA Ltd, acted as a management consultant for seven companies involved in property developments. SGA Ltd did not charge a flat fee, but agreed to take a share of the various companies' profits as payment. The VAT tribunal unanimously decided that SGA Ltd was not in partnership with the seven companies. SGA Ltd were not carrying on a business in common with the seven companies. The taking of a share of the profits was merely a way of SGA Ltd getting paid for services provided to the companies.

In *Tiffin* v *Lester Aldridge LLP* [2010] UKEAT 0255_10_1611, [2011] IRLR 105 Silber J held a salaried partner in a partnership (which had become an LLP) to be a partner in the firm even though his right to manage was very limited. He said,

'There is no statutory provision or authority, which states that for a person to be a partner, he or she has to have a certain minimum number or a certain minimum types of rights to vote or to participate in management decisions. Indeed the members of this Tribunal are aware that in many large professional partnerships, all but very few of the partners have any right to participate in the overwhelming range of decisions made by the firm and yet they are clearly partners.'

15.2.4 **With a view of profit**

It is not necessary that a profit must be made before a partnership can exist. Many of the cases concerned with whether or not a partnership exists arise precisely because the business did not make a profit. What is required is that the partners should intend to make a profit. It is this requirement of an intention to make a profit which distinguishes partnerships from unincorporated associations, such as members' clubs. The members of an unincorporated association might talk of having made a profit or a loss, but what is really meant is that they have run a surplus or gone into debt. A distinguishing feature of a partnership is that the partners must have intended that the firm should make a profit which could be shared by the partners. Unincorporated associations are not set up with this purpose. They are set up with other purposes, such as to provide recreational facilities for their members.

Pitreavie Golf Club v *Penman* 1934 SLT 247

The Pitreavie Golf Club was an unincorporated association, set up for the purposes of playing golf. A person →

who was owed money by the club's council of members had not been paid, and wanted to make the club bankrupt. Under Scots law this would only have been possible if the club was either a partnership or a company. As the club was clearly not a company, it was argued that it was a partnership.

Held. The club was not a partnership. The club's motivation was to allow its members to play golf, not to make a profit to be shared amongst the members.

15.3 SPECIFIC INDICATIONS AS TO WHETHER OR NOT A PARTNERSHIP EXISTS

Whether or not a partnership exists will always depend upon whether or not the definition of partnership which is set out in s.1(1) of the Act has been fulfilled. However, s.2 of the Act lays down rules which can help determine whether or not a partnership exists. It is important to remember that these rules are no more than indications.

15.3.1 Joint or common ownership of property

Section 2(1): 'Joint tenancy, tenancy in common, joint property, common property, or part ownership does not of itself create a partnership as to anything so held or owned, whether the tenants or owners do or do not share any profits made by the use thereof.'

This section was considered in the following case.

Davis v Davis [1894] 1 Ch 393

Under his will, a testator left property to his two sons, as tenants in common. At the time of inheriting the property, which was comprised of a business and three houses, the sons were not in partnership. The sons carried on the business and both usually took £3 a week from it. Whenever one son took more than this, the other took an identical amount. One of the three houses was rented out, and the rent was used to enlarge workshops attached to the other two houses.

Held. The sons were in partnership as regards the business because their conduct suggested partnership. The fact of drawing out identical sums of money inferred that they had agreed to share the profits. They were not in partnership as regards the three houses, as their conduct did not show anything to overturn the presumption contained in s.2(1). Consequently the workshops did not become partnership property.

15.3.2 Sharing of gross returns

Section 2(2): 'The sharing of gross returns does not of itself create a partnership, whether the persons sharing such returns have or have not a joint or common right or interest in any property from which or from the use of which the returns are derived.'

Gross returns might today be referred to more commonly as gross takings. They would consist of all the money which the firm took in. Gross profits are quite different, consisting of any surplus which remains after all liabilities have been discharged.

Cox v Coulson
[1916] 2 KB 177 (Court of Appeal)

The defendant, who leased and managed a theatre, agreed to stage a play with the manager of a touring theatrical company. The defendant was to provide the use of the theatre and the lighting. The manager of the theatrical company was to provide the actors and the scenery. The defendant was to get 60 per cent of the gross takings, the manager of the touring theatre company was to get 40 per cent. During a performance of the play an actor had to shoot a gun which should have been loaded with a blank. Somehow the gun contained a live bullet. When the gun was fired the claimant, a member of the audience, was hit in the wrist and suffered a severe injury. The claimant claimed damages from the defendant on the grounds that the defendant was in partnership with the manager of the touring company.

Held. There was no partnership and so the defendant was not liable. There was nothing in the behaviour of the two managers to contradict the presumption in s.2(2). Neither of them was the agent of the other, and it would have been possible for one of them to have made a profit while the other made a loss.

15.3.3 The receipt of a share of the profits

Section 2(3) begins by stating that: 'The receipt by a person of a share of the profits of a business is *prima facie* evidence that he is a partner in the business, but the receipt of such a share, or of a payment contingent on or varying with the profits of a business, does not of itself make him a partner in the business; . . .' The subsection goes on to list situations, examined below, in which there is a presumption against a person who receives a share of the profits being a partner. In the absence of evidence to the contrary, though, a person who receives a share of the profits will be a partner. If there is other evidence, it must be considered.

The five situations listed in s.2(3), where it is presumed that a person is not a partner merely on account of receiving a share of the profits, are as follows:

(i) where a share of the profits is taken as the payment of a debt, whether taken by instalments or not;

(ii) where a share of the profits is taken as a salary;

(iii) where a widow or a child of a deceased partner receives a share of the profits by way of an annuity;

(iv) where a written contract makes the interest on a loan vary according to the profits of the business;

(v) where a share of the profits is taken as payment for the goodwill of a business.

The following case demonstrates the working of this last exception.

Pratt v Strick (1932) 17 TC 459

One doctor sold his practice and the goodwill to another doctor. Part of the price was paid. The selling doctor agreed to remain at the practice for three months to introduce the new doctor to his patients and to help him generally. For these three months the profits of the business were split equally. The Revenue argued that for these three months the two doctors were in partnership. An appeal was made against this decision.

Held. The doctors were never in partnership. The practice was sold and after this the selling doctor agreed to help the other in return for payment.

It should be remembered that s.2(3) only provides that a receipt of a share of the profits is *prima facie* evidence that a person is a partner. It does not provide conclusive evidence of this, even as regards situations other than the five listed by s.2(3). Shortly after the Act was passed, North J in *Davis v Davis* said: 'by sect.2, sub-sect 3, of the Act, the receipt by a person of a share of the profits of a business is *prima facie* evidence that he is a partner in it, and, if the matter stops there, it is evidence upon which the Court must act. But, if there are other circumstances to be considered, they ought to be considered fairly together – taking all the circumstances together, not attaching undue weight to any of them but drawing an inference from the whole.' In fact there must always be other evidence to be considered. Otherwise the agreement would have consisted solely of an agreement to share profits.

In the following case the Court of Appeal continuously stressed the need to consider all of the evidence in deciding whether or not a person was a partner.

Young Legal Associates Ltd v Zahid (a firm) [2006] EWCA Civ 613, [2006] 1 WLR 2562 (Court of Appeal)

L was solicitor who had been qualified since 1968. L agreed with B that he would join a firm which B was setting up. B had been qualified as a solicitor for only two years and needed to practise with a more experienced solicitor to satisfy Rule 13 of the Solicitors' Practice Rules. It was orally agreed that L should be paid a fixed sum each month and that the firm should exist for only eight months. By then B would have been qualified for long enough to go into partnership with S and satisfy Rule 13, without needing L to be a partner. But when the eight months expired L agreed to remain in his position with the firm. L did not contribute any capital to the firm. L visited the firm in a supervisory capacity for a few hours a day, on a few days a week. He was willing to provide assistance if asked but was rarely asked to do so. An outsider sued the firm and it became necessary to decide whether or not L was a partner in it. The trial judge found that B and L were a two-man firm, set up to comply with Rule 13.

Held. There was a partnership between B and L, even though L was paid a fixed sum per annum. It was significant that both B and L knew that they had to be a partnership in order to satisfy Rule 13 and that they entered into the agreement in order to satisfy Rule 13.

COMMENT (i) Wilson LJ said: 'An agreement for a person to be paid a specified sum for work to be done by him on behalf of a firm does not preclude thereby his becoming a partner of it ... the words of [s.1(1) PA 1890] are wide enough to render the recipient of payments in a fixed sum a partner provided that there is a business, that it is carried on with a view to profit, and, crucially for present purposes, that he is carrying it on in common with another or others.'

(ii) Hughes LJ said: 'The words of s.1 ... refer to the making of a profit as an aim, but studiously abstain from reference to any necessity that it be shared. On principle it seems to me that if there is any essential element of partnership it is the carrying on of business in common, that is to say in such a manner as to make each the agent of the other for all acts done in the course of the business. Having thus constituted themselves, the partners are free under the Act to arrange for the remuneration of themselves in any manner they choose, including by agreement that one or more shall receive specific sums, or that one or more may receive nothing, in either case irrespective of profits.'

15.4 THE PARTNERSHIP AGREEMENT

Although there is no need to have a formal partnership agreement, the vast majority of partnerships do draw such an agreement up. However, before examining the terms which are likely to be found in such agreements, we should remember that a partnership can be created informally and that people can be partners without realising that this is the case.

Earlier in this chapter, at 15.2.1, we saw that partnership is based upon a contractual agreement. Therefore a partnership is only created if all of the requirements of a contract are fulfilled. There must be an offer, an acceptance, an intention to create legal relations and consideration. The contract must not be void for mistake or illegality, and it might be rendered voidable by misrepresentation, duress or undue influence. The contract might become frustrated if it subsequently becomes impossible to perform, or illegal to perform, or if it can be performed only in a manner which is radically different from what the parties contemplated when they made it.

Where the terms of the agreement are not expressed by the partners they might either be implied by the Partnership Act or implied as a matter of general construction of contracts. (The circumstances in which terms will be implied into a contract were considered in Chapter 5 at 5.3.)

15.4.1 Formal partnership agreements

Formal partnership agreements are often known as articles of partnership. Such agreements are com-monly set out as a deed, although there is no requirement that they should be. There are 13 or so matters which would be dealt with by almost any formal partnership agreement. We therefore make a brief consideration of these 13 'universal' articles.

15.4.1.1 The parties to the agreement

The agreement should clearly set out who is a partner and who is not. However, as we saw in *Saywell* v *Pope*, the final decision as to whether or not a person is a partner can only be made in the light of all of the evidence. It should also be realised that the fact that a person is not included in the agreement as a partner will not prevent him from being liable as a partner if he is, with his knowledge, held out as a partner to third parties. (Liability by holding out is considered below at 15.8.3.)

15.4.1.2 The nature of the business

There are three principal reasons why it is important to clearly set out the nature of the partnership business. First, s.5 of the Act makes partners agents of the firm and of their fellow partners for the purposes of the firm's business, but not for other purposes. Second, s.30 imposes a fiduciary duty preventing partners from carrying on a business which competes with the business of the firm or is of the same nature as the business of the firm. (It is however a defence to breach of this duty that the other partners consented to the competition.) Third, having been defined, the nature of the partnership business can only be varied by the consent of all of the partners (s.24(8)). However, this consent can be inferred from the partners' behaviour (s.19).

15.4.1.3 The name of the firm

The name of the firm should be clearly identified. Partners commonly choose to be known by their collective surnames, although they can in general choose to be known by any other name. There is no need to register the firm's name. There is a register of company names and LLP names but there is no central registry of partnership names. However, two factors should be borne in mind when choosing a name. First, the name must comply with the requirements of the Companies Act 2006. Second, the name must not be designed to deceive the public by causing confusion with another business.

Business names

Sections 1192–1199 of the Companies Act 2006 prohibit or restrict the use of certain names by any type of business. Sections 1200–1206 require individuals and partnerships to make certain disclosures.

Section 1192 provides that nothing in the Act prevents an individual from carrying on business under his own surname without any addition other than a 'permitted addition'. If the business is a partnership, nothing prevents the partners from carrying on the business under a name consisting of all of their surnames without any addition other than a permitted addition. The permitted additions are: the first names and initials of the sole trader or of the partners; or, where two or more partners have the same surname, the addition of 's' at the end of that surname; or an addition which merely indicates that the business is carried on in succession to a former owner of that business. The use of any other name, even the use of partners' surnames along with '& Co', will mean that the name used must comply with the provisions, ss.1192–1206. All companies must comply with the provisions, as must all partnerships which have a company as a member.

Section 1193 makes it a criminal offence to use certain names unless the written approval of the Secretary of State for Trade and Industry is granted. The names in question are those which would suggest a connection with Government or with any local authority or with certain public authorities, as defined in Regulations made by the Secretary of State. Section 1194 makes it a separate offence to include sensitive words or expressions which are contained in the Company and Business Names Regulations 1981, as amended. About 100 words are specified, including authority, charity, chartered, dental, English, European, institute, Irish, nursing, police, Royal, Scottish, society and Welsh. Section 1195 allows the Secretary of State to grant permission for such names to be used, after a request has been made to the relevant body specified in the Regulations. For example, to use the word 'dental', the applicant would first need to write to the relevant body, the General Dental Council, and send a copy of the letter and the written response to the Secretary of State, who could then grant permission.

Section 1197 allows the Secretary of State to make Regulations prohibiting a person from carrying on a business consisting of words or expressions which are associated with a particular type of company or organisation. So 'plc', 'Ltd', 'LLP' and similar words or expressions could not be inappropriately used.

Despite the offences created by ss.1192–1197, s.1199 allows a business to carry on using a name which had been lawful under the Business Names Act 1985. It also allows a person who has taken over a business to carry on using such a name for 12 months after the transfer.

Section 1198 makes it a criminal offence to carry on a business under a name which gives so misleading an indication of the nature of the activities of the business as to be likely to cause harm to the public.

Sections 1200–1208, which apply only to individuals and partnerships, require disclosure of certain information when the business is carried on under a business name. The purpose is to allow third parties dealing with the business to identify who the owners are and how documents can be served on them. A name is a business name unless it consists only of the name or names of the trader or partners, along with any of the permitted additions set out in s.1192. The information which must be disclosed, unless the business is a large partnership which is exempt, is the name of the sole trader, or the names of all of the partners, as well as a UK address at which business documents can be served. Section 1202 requires the information to be stated on business documents, s.1204 requires it to be displayed at business premises. Section 1202 requires the information to be stated on: all business letters; written orders for goods or services; invoices and receipts; and written demands for payment of business debts. Partnerships with more than 20 partners are exempt from the requirements of s.1202, in so far as they apply to written documents, if they fulfil the three requirements set out in s.1203. These requirements are that: (a) the partnership keep a list of all the partners' names and addresses at the firm's principal place of business; (b) no partner's name appears in the document except as a signatory; and (c) the document states in legible characters the address of the partnership's principal place of business and that a list of the partners' names is open to inspection there. Any person may inspect the list during office hours. Any partner who unreasonably refuses such a request commits an offence.

Section 1204 requires a sole trader or any partnership to prominently display the names and addresses required by the Act, and an address for service of documents, at any business premises to which the customers or suppliers have access.

Failure to comply with ss.1202 or 1204 is a criminal offence. In addition, s.1206 provides that a party who breaches either of these two sections may not be able to enforce contracts made while they were being breached. However, this will be the case only if the defendant can show that he could not pursue a claim against the firm because of the breach, or can show that he has suffered financial loss in connection with the contract by reason of the claimant's breach.

Confusion with other businesses

As long as the provisions of the Companies Act are complied with, and as long as the intention is not to deceive the public, partners can trade under any name they like. However, if a name is likely to cause confusion with another business, or to deceive the public, an action for the tort of passing-off might be brought. If successful, such an action could result in an injunction preventing the further use of the name or in the payment of damages. James LJ put the position as follows in *Levy* v *Walker* (1879) 10 ChD 436:

> 'It should never be forgotten in these cases that the sole right to restrain anybody from using any name that he likes in the course of any business he chooses to carry on is a right in the nature of a trade mark, that is to say, a man has a right to say "You must not use a name, whether fictitious or real, you must not use a description, whether true or not, which is intended to represent, or calculated to represent, to the world that your business is my business, and so, by a fraudulent misstatement, deprive me of the profits of the business which would otherwise come to me."'

The following case provides a clear example of passing-off.

Croft v *Day* (1843) 7 Beav 84

A well-established firm had for a long time carried on business selling lampblack as Day and Martin at 97 High Holborn. (Lampblack could be used to give a black finish to shoes or metal.) A certain Mr Day, having obtained permission from one Martin to use his name, set up in the same trade at 90 High Holborn. This new outfit sold lampblack, in bottles which resembled those of the old firm, under the name Day and Martin 90 High Holborn.

Held. An injunction was granted preventing the new firm from trading under the name Day and Martin. The intention of the new firm was to deceive the public.

The tort of passing-off is not limited to the use of the name or trade mark of a business. In *Cadbury Schweppes Ltd* v *Pub Squash Co Ltd* [1981] 1 WLR 193 the Privy Council held that passing-off was wide enough to encompass other descriptive materials, such as slogans or visual images associated with the claimant's product by means of an advertising campaign. However, it is still required that the public must be deceived or misled into thinking that the defendant's product was the claimant's product. As long as the public is not deceived in this way, the tort of passing-off will not prevent one business from taking advantage of an advertising campaign conducted by another business. A partnership can make a complaint to a company names adjudicator, under s.69(1) of the Companies Act 2006, if the name of a registered company is the same as a name in which the partnership has goodwill, or is sufficiently similar as to be likely to mislead by suggesting a connection between the company and the partnership. Such objections are considered more fully in Chapter 16 at 16.9.2.

15.4.1.4 Dates of commencement and dissolution

A formal partnership agreement will almost always state the date on which the partnership is to commence. However, as we saw in *Saywell* v *Pope*, this is not conclusive evidence as to whether or not the partnership did in fact commence on that date. The date at which a partnership commenced is a matter of fact, which will be determined by examining all of the evidence. However, the fact that a partnership agreement states a date of commencement is likely to be very strong evidence of a partnership having existed from that date.

A formal partnership agreement might or might not give a date on which the partnership is to end. If such a date is specified then the partnership can only be ended in advance of that date by one of the matters specified in the Partnership Act or by a court order. (These matters are examined below at 15.9.2 and 15.9.3.) So if a date for dissolution is fixed no single partner will be able to dissolve the firm by giving notice before that date.

If no date for dissolution is fixed, the partnership is known as a partnership at will, and any one of the partners can dissolve the firm by giving notice. Section 26(1) provides that: 'Where no fixed term has been agreed upon for the duration of the partnership, any partner may determine the partnership at any time on giving notice of his intention so to do to all the other partners.' This section is not as straightforward as it might appear, and has to be considered in conjunction with s.32(c), which states: 'Subject to any agreement between the partners a partnership is dissolved ... if entered into for an undefined time, by any partner giving notice to the other or others of his intention to dissolve the partnership.' The effect of these two provisions was considered in the following case.

Moss v Elphick [1910] 1 KB 846 (Court of Appeal)

In 1907 the claimant and the defendant made a written agreement to be partners in a tobacconist's business in Brighton. Clause 4 of the agreement stated that 'This agreement shall be terminated by mutual agreement only.' In 1909 one of the partners gave the other a fortnight's notice in writing to dissolve the partnership. The other partner argued that this could not be done as the termination had not been mutually agreed.

Held. The partnership could not be ended by the one partner giving notice. Section 32(c) did not apply because it begins with the words, 'Subject to any agreement between the partners . . .' Clause 4 was such an agreement. Section 26(1) did not apply either. It is to apply only where no fixed term has been agreed for the duration of the partnership. This was interpreted as meaning in cases where the partnership agreement was silent as to the duration of the partnership. Fletcher Moulton LJ explained that the parties had made an agreement for the duration of the joint lives of the parties, unless they both agreed otherwise. He regarded this as for a fixed (i.e. defined) term. He did not think that s.26(1) was intended to interfere with freedom of contract.

The partners do not have to end the partnership upon expiry of a fixed term. Section 27 provides that if all the partners carry the firm on then, unless they agree to the contrary, it is presumed that they carry on under the terms of the agreement which has expired.

15.4.1.5 The capital of the firm and of the individual partners

Section 24(1) provides that 'All the partners are entitled to share equally in the capital and the profits of the business, and must contribute equally towards the losses, whether of capital or otherwise sustained by the firm.'

This presumption that partners will contribute capital equally, and be entitled to equal repayment of capital on dissolution, is very commonly varied. In many partnerships one partner provides the capital while the others provide business skills. The repayment of capital on dissolution is examined below at 15.9.6, where we shall see that the provisions of the Act apply unless there has been a contrary agreement. For the sake of certainty, the partnership agreement should clearly spell out the intentions of the parties.

Section 24(4) provides that, 'A partner is not entitled, before the ascertainment of profits, to interest on the capital subscribed by him.' This implied term is commonly varied so that partners are paid interest on their capital, as if capital contributed were a loan to the firm.

Partnership property is an important concept which is examined below at 15.6. Here it is enough to say that as well as dealing with capital contributions the agreement should make it plain whether property which is used by the firm is partnership property or remains the property of the individual partners.

15.4.1.6 The salary and profit entitlement of the partners

Very commonly, partners do not share equally in the profits of the firm. We have already seen that s.24(1) rules that profits and losses are to be shared equally unless the partners agree otherwise. Obviously, the partnership agreement is the most appropriate place for unequal share in profits to be spelled out. Sometimes the partnership agreement provides for the payment of a notional salary to a partner. This is no more than a way of distributing the profits amongst the partners and does not make the recipient an employee.

15.4.1.7 The management of the business

Section 24(5) states that 'Every partner may take part in the management of the partnership business.' As all of s.24 applies only if no contrary agreement is expressly or impliedly made, it is possible to have a dormant or sleeping partner who has no right to manage the business. Such a partner will normally take advantage of the Limited Partnerships Act 1907, which is examined below at 15.10.

The partnership agreement should set out the duties of the various partners, how majority decisions should be taken, and whether or not some partners are excluded from the right to do certain things. It is commonly the case that partners do not have equal voting or management rights. If a partner is excluded from the management of the firm without having agreed to this, the courts will regard this as a reason to dissolve the firm.

15.4.1.8 Banking arrangements and the right to draw cheques

The partnership agreement should name the firm's bank and specify whether or not individual partners have the right to draw cheques on the partnership account. It is commonly agreed that the signatures of two partners are required on cheques to the value of more than a specified amount. The bank will not be bound by the partnership agreement but has a duty to obey the mandate given by the customer. Therefore if the provisions of the partnership agreement are reproduced in the mandate given to the bank, the bank will not be entitled to debit the firm's account if the provisions of the partnership agreement are not observed.

15.4.1.9 The firm's accounts

The agreement will generally arrange for accounts to be drawn up on certain dates. By reference to these accounts the partners will know how they stand as regards each other, and the firm will know how it stands as regards outsiders.

15.4.1.10 Admission and expulsion of partners

The agreement should set out the grounds on which a partner can be expelled from the partnership. It is also sensible to set out the circumstances in which new partners can be admitted. If there is no express or implied agreement to the contrary, a new partner can only be admitted by the consent of all of the existing partners (s.24(7)). Very often partnership agreements do agree otherwise, so that a new partner can be admitted without the consent of all the existing partners.

15.4.1.11 Death or retirement of partners

Section 33(1) provides that the death of a partner dissolves the firm unless the partners agree otherwise. It would be usual in a commercial firm for the partnership agreement to state that the firm should be carried on after the death of a partner, and to provide a right for a partner to retire from the firm after giving a stated period of notice. (Technically, the firm would still have been dissolved. Section 33(1) deals with whether the firm should continue or be wound up.) In addition, it is important to set out the financial arrangements to be applied when a partner dies or retires. The partnership agreement might also contain a restraint of trade clause preventing a partner from competing with the firm after retirement. In Chapter 6 at 6.4.3 we examined the circumstances in which such a clause will be valid.

15.4.1.12 Valuation of the goodwill

The goodwill is considered below at 15.9.5.1. The agreements should set out how the goodwill should be valued and the entitlement, in respect of the goodwill, of partners who die or retire.

15.4.1.13 Arbitration

One of the most important provisions of a partnership agreement is that disputes should be referred to arbitration. If there is no such provision then disputes between partners could become the subject of litigation. The publicity which this might generate could be very damaging to the firm, and perhaps to the future prospects of the partners as individuals.

15.4.1.14 Variation of partnership agreement

Having been made, a partnership agreement can be altered by the consent of all of the partners, but this consent can be inferred from a course of dealing (s.19). Lord Eldon gave an example of how this might happen in *Const v Harris* (1824) 37 ER 1191: 'If in a common partnership, the parties agree that no one of them shall draw or accept a bill of exchange in his own name, without the concurrence of all the others, yet, if they afterwards slide into a habit of permitting one of them to draw or accept bills, without the concurrence of the others, this Court will hold that they have varied the terms of the original agreement in that respect.'

Simple partnership agreement

This partnership agreement is made on (*date*)...........................
between (*name 1*)............................of (*address*)

(*1*)...

and (*name 2*)................................. of (*address*)

(*2*)..

and (*name 3*).................................of (*address*)

(*3*)...

It is agreed as follows:

(1) The partners shall carry on business in partnership as (*nature of business*)
....
under the firm name of (*partnership name*)...
....
of (*partnership address*)...
....
....

(2) The partnership will commence on the date of this agreement and shall continue in existence for five years.

(3) The partnership capital shall be contributed by the partners in equal shares and the partners
shall be entitled to the profits arising from the partnership in equal shares.

(4) The bankers of the firm shall be
(*name*)... of
(*address*)...
....
Cheques drawn in the name of the firm must be signed by all of the partners.

(5) Each partner shall devote his or her whole time to the business of the partnership.

(6) Each partner shall be entitled to (*number*).................................weeks' holiday each year.

(7) None of the partners shall without the consent of the other: engage in any business other
than partnership business; or employ or dismiss any partnership employee.

(8) Each partner shall be entitled to draw (*amount*).......................as salary from the partnership bank account each month.

(9) All matters relating to the management of the affairs of the partnership shall be decided by
votes taken at a meeting of the partners. At such meetings each partner shall be entitled to
one vote and resolutions shall be passed by a simple majority vote.

(10) The accounts of the firm shall be made up on the close of business on the 4th of April each
year.

(11) No majority of the partners shall be entitled to expel any partner. New partners may only be admitted with the consent of all existing partners.

(12) If any disputes should arise as to the meaning of this partnership deed, or as to the rights and liabilities of the partners under it, such disputes shall be referred to an arbitrator to be appointed by the President of the Chartered Institute of Arbitrators. The decision of the arbitrator shall be binding on all of the partners.

Signed as a deed by (*name 1*)...in the presence of (*witness*)

....

Signed as a deed by (*name 2*)...in the presence of (*witness*)

....

Signed as a deed by (*name 3*)...in the presence of (*witness*)

....

A very simple model partnership agreement is set out above. Such an agreement could be adapted to suit the requirements of a very small firm starting up in business. More complicated partnership deeds can run to several thousand words. They cover the same matters as the simple deed in very much more detail. In addition, they might contain articles dealing with matters such as leasing premises, payment of private debts, negative covenants, banking arrangements, provisions for retiring partners, options to purchase the share of outgoing partners, income tax and retirement annuities.

15.4.1.15 **Numbers of partners**

Until recently most firms were not allowed to have more than 20 partners. This prohibition has now been lifted so that there is no upper limit on the number of partners any firm may have.

15.4.1.16 **Capacity of partners**

It is possible for a minor (a person under 18 years of age) to become a partner. However, the partnership agreement is voidable, at the minor's option, until he reaches the age of 18 and for a reasonable time thereafter. If the minor does avoid the agreement it will no longer bind him and he will not be liable for debts incurred by the firm. If the minor does not avoid the agreement within a reasonable time of becoming 18 he will be bound by future debts of the firm, but not by debts incurred whilst he was a minor. So whether the minor avoids the agreement or not, he cannot be made liable for partnership debts incurred while he was a minor. However, adult partners are en-titled to insist that the partnership assets, including capital contributed by a minor partner, shall be applied in payment of the liabilities of the partnership. Furthermore, the adult partners can insist that any losses suffered by the firm are settled before the minor receives any profit.

A mentally disordered partner can set aside a partnership agreement if he can prove that at the time of making the agreement he was of unsound mind so as not to understand what he was doing, and that the other partners were aware of this.

Test your understanding 15.2

1 Can people be in partnership if they do not make a formal partnership agreement?

2 What are the 13 'universal' matters which all formal partnership agreements are likely to deal with?

3 What are the main provisions of the Companies Act 2006, as they apply to use of business names by partnerships?

4 What is a passing-off action?

5 In what circumstances can a partner terminate the partnership by giving notice?

6 How can a formal partnership agreement be varied?

7 Can minors (persons under 18 years of age) become partners?

15.5 PARTNERS' RELATIONSHIP WITH EACH OTHER

As we have already seen, the partners make a contract with each other and the Partnership Act implies certain terms into this contract. We therefore need to examine these terms and the extent to which partners can exclude the terms by express or implied agreement. In addition, partners owe each other fiduciary duties which arise independently of any contractual agreement. These fiduciary duties are examined at 15.7.

15.5.1 The terms implied by the Partnership Act 1890

Section 24 implies nine terms. When considering the clauses which should be contained in a formal partnership agreement, we examined three of these: the right to share equally in capital and profits (s.24(1)); the right to take part in the management of the business (s.24(5)); and that a new partner can only be admitted by unanimous consent of existing partners (s.24(7)). Before examining the other terms implied by s.24 it is worth reiterating that all of the terms contained in s.24 are implied only if the partners do not make any express or implied agreement to the contrary. For this reason they are often referred to as default provisions.

15.5.1.1 The right to an indemnity

Section 24(2) provides that:

> 'The firm must indemnify every partner in respect of payments made and personal liabilities incurred by him–
>
> (a) In the ordinary and proper conduct of the business of the firm; or,
>
> (b) In or about anything necessarily done for the preservation of the business or property of the firm.'

A right to an indemnity gives a right to be reimbursed for expenses properly incurred. In Chapter 11 at 11.5.1 we examined an agent's right of indemnity. This section merely summarises those common law rules.

15.5.1.2 Advances given to the firm

When considering the articles of partnership, we saw that s.24(4) provides that a partner is not entitled to interest on capital which he subscribes to the firm. If nothing is agreed to the contrary, a partner is entitled

to interest at 5 per cent per annum on a loan (an advance) made to the firm. Section 24(3) provides: 'A partner making, for the purpose of the partnership, any actual payment or advance beyond the amount of capital which he has agreed to subscribe, is entitled to interest at the rate of five per cent per annum from the date of the payment or advance.' Many partnership agreements specify a rate of interest other than 5 per cent per annum.

15.5.1.3 Right to a salary

Section 24(6): 'No partner shall be entitled to remuneration for acting in the partnership business.' First, it should be realised that when a partner is paid a salary this is really just a way of apportioning the profits of the firm. Second, we should realise that in very many cases profits are apportioned by the payment of a salary to a partner.

It is also worth noting that 'salaried partners' in large firms may or may not in fact have the full rights and obligations of partners, depending upon all the facts of the case, and may be held to be merely employees, especially for taxation purposes. In *Young Legal Associates Ltd v Zahid (a firm)* [2006] EWCA Civ 613, [2006] 1 WLR 2562 considered above at 15.3.3, Wilson LJ agreed with Counsel's view that the term 'salaried partner' should be avoided because it has no single meaning, and that whether or not a person called a 'salaried partner' was in fact a partner would depend upon all of the facts of the case. Whether a partner or not, a 'salaried partner' will have the liability of a partner to outsiders to whom he has been held out to be a partner. (Liability by holding out is considered below at 15.8.3.)

15.5.1.4 Introduction of new partners

When considering the articles of partnership we set out s.24(7), which states that no partner can be admitted as a partner without the consent of all existing partners. We also saw that such consent is commonly given in the partnership agreement. The following case shows that the consent given can be very wide.

> **Byrne v Reid** (1902) 87 LTR 507 (Court of Appeal)
>
> The claimant had contributed most of the capital to a firm of five partners, and was entitled to three quarters of the profits. Article 29 of the partnership agreement provided that the claimant could introduce any of his →

sons, or other person whom he considered fit, as a partner as long as the person was over 21 years old. Any such partner introduced could take over all or part of the claimant's profit entitlement. The claimant introduced his son, to take one twelfth of the firm's profits. The other partners refused to consent to this.

Held. The other partners could not refuse to admit the claimant's son as a partner. Section 24(7) was to apply only if there was no agreement to the contrary. In this case there clearly was such an agreement.

15.5.1.5 **Resolving differences**

Section 24(8) deals with resolving differences, but makes a distinction between differences on ordinary matters and changes made in the nature of the partnership business: 'Any difference arising as to ordinary matters connected with the partnership business may be decided by a majority of the partners, but no change may be made in the nature of the partnership business without the consent of all existing partners.'

The Act provides no help in resolving whether a matter is an ordinary matter or a change in the nature of the partnership business. The essential difference is that an ordinary matter is concerned with the day-to-day running of the business whereas a change in the nature of the business would change the business fundamentally.

15.5.1.6 **The partnership books**

Section 24(9) provides: 'The partnership books are to be kept at the place of business of the partnership (or the principal place, if there is more than one), and every partner may, when he thinks fit, have access to and inspect and copy any of them.'

The partners will want access to the partnership books so that they can understand the financial position of the firm. A partner who suspects that he is being unfairly treated will need to inspect the books to find out if his suspicions are well founded. An agent may be needed to assess the books, and the right to inspect the books can be delegated to an agent as long as the agent is not a person to whom the other partners might reasonably object.

15.5.1.7 **The right to expel a partner**

This right is contained in s.25, which states that: 'No majority of partners can expel any partner unless a power to do so has been conferred by express agreement

between the partners.' It is significant that this section was not incorporated into s.24. All the provisions of s.24 can be excluded by implied agreement between the partners. The rule preventing the majority from expelling a partner can only be contradicted by express agreement between all of the partners.

Even when acting under an express agreement which enables them to expel a partner, the partners doing the expelling must observe the rules of natural justice and act in good faith. They must also act strictly within the terms of the partnership agreement.

If a partner is wrongly expelled he may sue for reinstatement as well as for contract damages.

15.6 **PARTNERSHIP PROPERTY**

Partnership property belongs to all of the partners as partners. This is achieved by the partners holding it in trust for each other. If the property consists of land then there can be a maximum of four trustees. As partnership property belongs to all of the partners, no partner can claim complete ownership of any specific item of it. Upon dissolution, however, a partner may become sole owner of certain items of partnership property.

Partnership property must be distinguished from property belonging to the individual partners for three main reasons. First, if the property increases in value this increase will belong to the firm rather than to any individual partner. Second, partnership property should be used exclusively for the purposes of the partnership, as defined by the partnership agreement. Third, on dissolution creditors are first paid out of partnership property.

Section 20(1) sets out three ways in which property can become partnership property. It can either be originally brought into the partnership, or property acquired on behalf of the firm, or property acquired for the purposes of and in the course of the partnership business.

Section 21 provides that, unless the contrary intention appears, property bought with money belonging to the firm is deemed to have been bought on account of the firm (that is to say, bought as partnership property).

It is always a question of fact whether any particular property is partnership property. An express agreement that property is to be partnership property will be conclusive. In the absence of an express agreement property will be partnership property if there is an implied agreement to that effect.

Miles v Clarke [1953] 1 All ER 779

A and B went into partnership as photographers. A had a lease of the premises from which the business operated but had no skill as a photographer. B was a successful freelance photographer and he introduced his considerable business connections. All that was agreed was that profits should be shared equally and that B should be able to draw £125 a month on account of his share of the profits. After flourishing for some time, the business was wound up when the partners fell out. A dispute arose as to what property, if any, had become partnership property.

Held. The consumable stock in trade of the business should be treated as partnership property, even though it was bought by A. All the other property (the lease, equipment and personal goodwill) should be treated as the property of the partner who brought it in. As the partners had made no express agreement, the court would only imply a term that property was partnership property if this was necessary on the grounds of business efficacy.

COMMENT The implying of a term on the grounds of business efficacy is examined in Chapter 5 at 5.3.2.

In the following case the Court of Appeal considered s.20.

Don King Productions Inc v Warren [1999] 2 All ER 218 (Court of Appeal)

The leading American boxing promoter, K, went into partnership with the leading British boxing promoter, W, to promote boxing in Europe. W assigned to the firm all the benefits and burdens of all of his management agreements with boxers. In fact, these agreements were incapable of being assigned because they were for personal services and some of them had express terms forbidding assignment. A second agreement required all agreements relating to the business of the firm to be held for the benefit of the firm absolutely. Later W made a multi-fight agreement for his own benefit. K insisted that W had no right to do this and ended the partnership.

Held. W had breached the partnership agreement by entering into the multi-fight agreement for his own benefit. Even property which was not assignable could be partnership property within s.20. The agreements indicated that each partner held the entire benefit of any management agreement made with a European boxer on trust for the firm, from the time of the first agreement. These benefits continued to

be held on trust after the dissolution of the firm right up until the time when the firm was wound up. Even such agreements entered into after dissolution but before the winding up of the firm were held on trust for the firm, as long as they were renewing contracts with boxers who had previously had a contract with W during the partnership.

15.7 PARTNERS' FIDUCIARY DUTIES TO EACH OTHER

Partners owe each other fiduciary duties out of which they cannot contract. Three of these duties are set out in ss.28–30 of the Act. These three duties often overlap and are not meant to be exhaustive, merely being part of the wider equitable duties which partners owe to each other. As these duties are equitable, they are fluid in nature. Although the partners cannot contract out of their fiduciary duties, it is a defence to a breach of fiduciary duty that the breach was consented to by the other partners. Nor is there any reason why such consent should not be contained in the articles of partnership. (In *Bentley v Craven*, set out below, the partnership agreement allowed one partner who acted as the firm's buyer to buy on his own account. As consent had been given, the other partners would not have been able to claim that the partner's buying on his own account had breached a fiduciary duty.) We now need to look at the three duties set out in the Partnership Act.

15.7.1 Duty to render accounts

Section 28 states that: 'Partners are bound to render true accounts and full information of all things affecting the partnership to any partner or his legal representatives.'

This is a strict, positive duty. It reflects the fact that partnership is a relationship of the utmost good faith.

Law v Law [1905] 1 Ch 140

Four sons were in partnership with their father as manufacturers of woollen clothes in Halifax. After the father died the four sons carried on the business. There was no formal partnership agreement and the sons had equal shares in the business. Two of the sons died, both in turn leaving their share of the business to their remaining brothers in equal shares. The two surviving brothers, W and J carried the firm on, each having an equal share in the partnership. →

W lived in London and ceased to take an active part in the firm's management. W was paid £600 a month but never asked for any account. J agreed to buy W out for £21 000. After this agreement was made, W discovered that there were partnership assets which J had never revealed to him. The money was to be paid in two instalments. Four days after receiving the second instalment, W commenced legal action to have the agreement set aside.

Held. The agreement to buy W's share was voidable, at W's option.

Cozens-Hardy LJ: 'Now it is clear that, in a transaction between co-partners for the sale by one to the other of a share in the partnership business, there is a duty resting upon the purchaser who knows, and is aware that he knows, more about the partnership accounts than the vendor, to put the vendor in possession of all material facts with reference to the partnership assets, and not to conceal what he alone knows; and that, unless such information has been furnished, the sale is voidable and may be set aside.'

COMMENT On the facts of the case W had lost the right to avoid the contract as he had elected not to insist on his right to full disclosure of the firm's assets. He had done this by taking the money while knowing that full disclosure had not been made.

Hogar Estates Ltd v *Shebron Holdings Ltd* (1980) 101 DLR (3d) 509 (High Court of Ontario)

H and S were in partnership to develop a piece of land. It was agreed that the partnership should be ended by S buying H's share. S, who suggested this, told H that the authorities had refused to give planning permission to develop the land. This was true when S said it, but S knew that it had become untrue by the time the dissolution agreement was made.

Held. The agreement to dissolve the firm could be set aside, even though there was no misrepresentation and no proof of dishonesty. S had breached his fiduciary duty to disclose the true state of affairs to H.

15.7.2 **Accounting for profits**

Section 29(1) states that: 'Every partner must account to the firm for any benefit derived by him without the consent of the other partners from any transaction concerning the partnership, or from any use by him of the partnership property name or business connection.'

Bentley v *Craven* (1853) 18 Beav 75

C and three others were in partnership as sugar refiners in Southampton. C was the firm's buyer. C was very skilled at buying sugar and he was authorised by the other partners to carry on his own business as an independent dealer in sugar. On several occasions C bought a consignment of sugar very cheaply and sold it to the firm at the going wholesale rate.

Held. C could not retain the profit which he made from these transactions. The profit had to be handed over to the firm. C had used a partnership asset, his position in the firm, to make the profit from the deals.

The strictness of the duty imposed by s.29 can be demonstrated by *Pathirana* v *Pathirana* [1967] 1 AC 233 (Privy Council). Two brothers, R and A, carried on a partnership running a service station owned by Caltex. They fell out and A gave R three months' notice to dissolve the firm. R informed Caltex that the firm was dissolved and asked Caltex to transfer the service station to his sole management. Caltex did this and R carried on the business as before without accounting to A for his share of the capital and profits. The Privy Council held that under s.29 A was entitled to a share of the profits which R made. Until the notice dissolving the partnership took effect the new agreement, which enabled the firm to build up a profitable business, was treated as a partnership asset. R was also entitled to a share of the profits made since the dissolution of the firm under s.29 because A had used R's share of the capital and profits without accounting for them.

Generally, no fiduciary duty will be broken if information gained in the capacity of a partner is used for purposes wholly outside of, and not competing with, the partnership. In *Aas* v *Benham* [1891] 2 Ch 244 (Court of Appeal), for example, a partner in a firm of shipbrokers helped to form a company, the purpose of which was to build ships. The partner used information gained as a partner and occasionally used the firm's notepaper. He was paid a fee for setting up the company and was also made a director of it. The Court of Appeal held that because the business of the company was beyond the scope of the business of the partnership, the partner did not have to account for benefits received in connection with the new company.

However, in the light of two House of Lords cases, the authority of *Aas* v *Benham* is in some doubt. Lord Hodgson, when delivering the leading judgment in

Boardman v *Phipps* (the facts of which are set out in Chapter 11 at 11.4.4.2) indicated that he was not confident that the decision in *Aas* v *Benham* was correct. The House of Lords decision in *Regal (Hastings) Ltd* v *Gulliver* [1942] 1 All ER 378 also appears to conflict with the decision in *Aas* v *Benham*.

Doubts as to the correctness of *Aas* v *Benham* look better founded in the light of the following recent Court of Appeal decision.

John Taylors v *Masons and Wilsons* [2001] EWCA Civ 2106, [2001] All ER (D) 381 (Nov) (Court of Appeal)

A partnership at will had five partners. The firm were in business as livestock auctioneers. On 4 December 1998 two partners (A and B) gave notice to dissolve the firm with effect from 31 December. The other three partners (C, D and E) carried the firm on. The firm had used premises licensed by the local council since 1947. A ten-year licence was due to expire on 31 December 1998. On 4 December A and B wrote to the local council asking that the licence on the premises be granted to them. C, D and E protested to the council, which wanted to remain neutral. However, C, D and E were not ready to take over the premises on 1 January 1999 so the council granted a provisional licence to A and B, who had formed a new firm. Aware that a dispute had arisen, the local council invited tenders for a new licence. There were three applications; one from A and B; one from C, D and E; and one from a third party. In their application A and B stressed their wealth of experience and their long association with the market. Their tender was successful. C, D and E made a claim for breach of fiduciary duty and under s.29 of the Act.

Held. The opportunity to renew the licence or to get a new licence was a partnership asset. The relationship between the original firm and the local council was a 'business connection', within the meaning of s.29. The goodwill of the original firm, its general business connections, were partnership property. The duty to account can cover assets which were acquired after dissolution but before the winding up was completed. So, under s.29, A and B were accountable for the benefit of the goodwill which they had taken for themselves and for profits and benefits derived from any use of the original partnership's assets. This would include profits made under the provisional and the 1999 licences. Both A and B had also breached the very strict general fiduciary duty imposed on all trustees. The provisional licence and the 1999 licence were obtained whilst there was a conflict of interest, or a possible conflict of interest, between A and B and the original firm. Liability for breach of fiduciary duty was not based on bad faith, but merely on account of a trustee having made a profit from his trust.

In *Don King Productions Inc* v *Warren* (see above at 15.6) the Court of Appeal similarly held that a partner's general fiduciary duty continued after dissolution until the firm was wound up. On the facts of the case, which were set out above, W was in breach of his fiduciary duty to his partner. He should not have taken out the multi-fight agreement for his own benefit when he knew that the firm could have benefited from having it until the firm was wound up. Nor should he have renewed any boxer's contract after dissolution but before the firm was wound up. To do so was an obvious conflict of interest. Furthermore, the multi-fight agreement and the renewed contracts were obtained by reason of W's fiduciary position or by reason of an opportunity or knowledge resulting from such a position.

15.7.3 Competing with the firm

Section 30 provides: 'If a partner, without the consent of the other partners, carries on any business of the same nature as and competing with that of the firm, he must account for and pay over to the firm all profits made by him in that business.'

There is a considerable overlap between this section and s.29. However, their effect is not the same. Under s.30 a partner can be liable merely by competing with the firm, whether or not he used the firm's assets. Under s.29 the partner is liable for using the firm's assets, whether or not he is also competing with the firm.

Trimble v *Goldberg* (1906) 95 LTR 163 (Privy Council)

G, T and B were in partnership together. The three agreed to buy property belonging to one Hollard, this consisting of land and 5 500 shares in a company, Sigma Syndicate. T bought the property on behalf of the firm, but he also took an option to buy other property belonging to Sigma Syndicate. T invited B to share in this deal. When G found out about it, a year later, he sued for a share of the profits.

Held. B and T did not need to share the profits with G. The purchase of the option was not within the scope of the partnership's business. It was not competing with the firm or the carrying on of a rival business. Nor

→

did T gain the information upon which he acted in his capacity as a partner in the firm.

15.8 PARTNERS' RELATIONSHIP WITH OUTSIDERS

Partners are agents of the firm and of their fellow partners for the purpose of the business of the partnership. They may also incur liability for torts which were committed in the ordinary course of the firm's business, or which the other partners authorised them to commit. In addition, a person who is not a partner can be liable as if he were a partner on account of his having allowed himself to be held out (represented) as a partner. These important matters need to be examined in some detail.

15.8.1 Partners as agents

Section 5 of the Act states that:

'Every partner is an agent of the firm and his other partners for the purpose of the business of the partnership; and the acts of every partner who does any act for carrying on in the usual way business of the kind carried on by the firm of which he is a member bind the firm and his partners, unless the partner so acting has in fact no authority to act for the firm in the particular matter, and the person with whom he is dealing either knows that he has no authority, or does not know or believe him to be a partner.'

In Chapter 11 we studied the different types of authority which an agent might have to bind his principal. We saw that if an agent does have actual authority to bind his principal then the principal will be liable on the contract which the agent made. (If you have not read, or have forgotten, Chapter 11 it might pay to have a look at the Key Points at the end of Chapter 11.) Section 5 is merely reflecting common law principles, as the following analysis shows.

If a partner (A) makes a contract with a third party (T), with the express or implied agreement of his fellow partners (B and C) then A will have actual authority and consequently B and C will be bound by the contract.

If A did not have actual authority to enter into a contract which he has made, B and C will nevertheless be liable on the contract if A had apparent authority to make it. This apparent authority would have arisen on account of B and C having made a representation to T, that A had authority to make the contract, and on account of T having acted upon the representation by making the contract.

If A has no actual authority or apparent authority to make the contract, we need to consider whether or not A had what might be called 'usual authority' to make it. The lack of actual authority is likely to have arisen because it has been agreed between the partners (generally in the articles of partnership) that A should not have authority to make certain types of contract on behalf of the firm. We then need to consider whether or not the contract made by A was done in relation to the activities of the partnership business, and 'for carrying on in the usual way business of the kind carried on by the firm'. If not, then B and C will not be liable on the contract in the absence of actual or apparent authority.

Now we consider the position where A makes a contract 'for carrying on in the usual way business of the kind carried on by the firm', but where A has been forbidden by B and C from making such a contract on behalf of the firm. Section 5 tells us that B and C will nevertheless be bound by the contract which A made unless either T did not know or believe A to be a partner in the firm, or unless T knew that A had no authority from B and C to make such a contract. (In Chapter 11 at 11.2.5 we considered the meaning of an agent's 'usual authority' and saw that the term could be used in several different senses and that it is always best to make clear the sense in which it is being used, if the sense is not apparent from the context.)

The various scenarios and outcomes of the above text are summarised in Figure 15.1.

Figure 15.1 The liability of fellow partners (B and C) on a contract which A (a partner) made with T

It is important to remember that s.5 only makes a partner the agent of the firm and his fellow partners as regards 'any act for carrying on in the usual way business of the kind carried on by the firm of which he is a member'. The meaning of this was considered in the following two cases.

Mercantile Credit Co v Garrod [1962] 3 All ER 1103

P and G were partners in a firm, the main business of which was repairing cars and letting lock-up garages.

G was a sleeping partner and therefore took no part in the management of the firm. The partnership agreement prohibited the buying and selling of cars. Without G's knowledge, P contracted to sell a car to a finance company. P did not own this car and so his act was a clear breach of contract. The finance company wanted to make G liable on the contract. The finance company had previously made several similar contracts with P, each time believing that they were dealing with the partnership. The finance company did not know of the prohibitions in the partnership agreement.

→

Held. G was bound by the contract by virtue of s.5. Making the contract was the doing of an 'act for carrying on in the usual way business of the kind carried on by the firm'.

JJ Coughlan Ltd v Ruparelia and others
[2003] EWCA Civ 1057, [2003] All ER (D) 344 (Jul) (Court of Appeal)

The claimant company had £1 million cash which it wanted to invest. As part of an incredible scheme the firm was induced to pay $500 000 to a solicitor, R, who was acting for some fraudsters. R and the fraudsters were present at meetings at which the claimant company was fraudulently induced to part with the money and R was a party to the fraud. R was in partnership with one other solicitor, T. In return for the $500 000, the claimants were meant to receive a risk-free annualised return of 6 000 per cent. A contract made by the claimants with both R and the fraudsters guaranteed that the $500 000 would be returned if the claimants did not receive $2.5 million from a bank within one month. The $500 000 was paid into R's solicitor's account. There was in fact no intention ever to return this money. The claimants sued for breach of contract and in the tort of deceit. The claim in tort arose because R guaranteed the claimants that their funds were protected and that there was no risk to their money. It was claimed that R's firm would be liable on the contract under s.5 of the Partnership Act and for the tort of deceit under s.10.

Held. There is no difference between the words the 'ordinary course of the business' in s.10 Partnership Act 1890 and the words 'the usual way of business of the kind carried on' in s.5. The key question was whether R's acts were the kind or class of acts that are carried out by solicitors in the ordinary course of their business. In answering this, the starting point was to consider whether the general description of the act falls within the scope of the ordinary course of business of solicitors. This requirement has to be satisfied. So a solicitor selling double-glazing would not bind his partners under s.5 or make the firm vicariously liable under s.10. The solicitor's motive, or the fact that he was acting honestly or dishonestly, was not relevant. Then it would be necessary to look at the substance of the transaction to see whether, viewed fairly and properly, it is the kind of transaction which forms part of the ordinary business of a solicitor. This would require the details of the transaction to be examined, including its nature and characteristics, and the court should not be too ready to find the ordinary business requirement unsatisfied. In this case the firm was not

liable under s.5. The scheme proposed by R and the confidence tricksters gave a risk-free annual return of 6 000 per cent. There was nothing normal about the transaction. The scheme was preposterous and what R did in connection with it could not objectively be viewed as being within the ordinary course of a solicitor's business. Nor was there liability under s.10 (see below at 15.8.2) for the same reasons. The nature of the incredible scheme was so far from what R was authorised to do that it could not be regarded as having been done in the ordinary course of his business as a solicitor. Therefore, R's firm could not be liable under s.5 or s.10.

COMMENT (i) Dyson LJ, who gave the only significant judgment, said the fact that the R made a number of false statements to the claimants is not something which it is in the ordinary course of a solicitor's business to do. But if the scheme had been otherwise unremarkable the defendant firm could not have escaped liability. But engaging in a preposterous investment scheme of this kind, which was not at all a normal transaction, was not, viewed objectively, part of a solicitor's business. Therefore R's acts were not carried out in the ordinary course of business of the defendant firm.

(ii) The important question is how the facts reasonably appeared to the third party, not what was actually going on. As Lord Glidewell said in **United Bank of Kuwait v Hammoud** [1988] 1 WLR 105, the test was: 'On the facts represented to the [third party] would a reasonably careful and competent person [such as the third party] have concluded that there was an underlying transaction of a kind which was part of the usual business of a solicitor?' In answering this question both the nature of the act and the way in which it was carried out would need to be considered in turn.

15.8.1.1 Trading and non-trading firms

There has been much case law on whether a particular act is carried on 'in the usual way' of the firm's business. These decisions have tended to recognise that partners in all firms have usual authority to do certain types of acts, and that partners in trading firms have usual authority to do additional types of acts. A trading firm is one which necessarily buys and sells goods.

In all firms an individual partner has usual authority to do the following: buy goods for the partnership to use; sell any goods belonging to the firm; employ and dismiss employees on the firm's behalf; receive payments on the firm's behalf, and by so doing release the payer from further obligation; employ an agent to act for the firm; employ a solicitor to take legal action on the firm's behalf; sign or endorse cheques in the firm's name.

In a trading firm an individual partner will have additional usual authority to: borrow money on the firm's behalf; give the firm's goods as security for a loan; accept and issue all types of negotiable instruments on behalf of the firm.

In neither trading nor non-trading firms will a partner have usual authority to execute deeds in the firm's name; or give guarantees in the firm's name; or submit a dispute to arbitration.

Although a partner, whether in a trading firm or a non-trading firm, would not normally have usual authority to execute a deed on the firm's behalf, the firm will be bound by a deed executed by one partner if the other partners gave that partner actual or apparent authority to execute the deed.

Section 7 of the Act is concerned with contracts which were not made in the ordinary course of the firm's business. It states that:

'Where one partner pledges the credit of the firm for a purpose apparently not connected with the firm's ordinary course of business, the firm is not bound, unless he is in fact specially authorised by the other partners; but this section does not affect any personal liability incurred by an individual partner.'

A partner will pledge the firm's credit if he orders goods or services in the firm's name and indicates to the supplier that the firm will pay the price. If the partner has been authorised to do this by his fellow partners then he has actual authority and obviously the firm and fellow partners are liable to pay the price to the supplier. Section 7 seems to suggest that if the partner has no actual authority then the fellow partners will not be bound to pay the price to the supplier. However, under common law principles the fellow partners would be liable if they had represented to the supplier that the partner had authority, and had thereby given him apparent authority. The partner making the contract will be personally liable on it whether or not the firm and the fellow partners are also liable.

It is possible to sue the firm in the firm name. If judgment is gained against the firm all of the partners become liable to pay the debt if the firm does not have enough assets to pay it. A partner who pays will be entitled to a contribution from his fellow partners. The contribution made by each partner will generally be equal, although the court can order unequal contribution where it considers this just and equitable. Partners also have the right to sue in the firm name. The fact that a firm can sue and be sued in the firm name does not indicate that the firm has a separate legal existence of its own. The rule is merely one of convenience.

15.8.2 Liability by holding out

A person holds himself out as being a partner if he represents himself as being a partner or allows himself to be so represented. Any person who holds himself out as being a partner will become liable as if he really was a partner, as regards a third party who gave credit to the firm as a consequence of the holding out. This provision is set out in s.14(1) of the Act, and is a form of estoppel. The person represented as a partner will be estopped from denying that he is a partner as regards a third party who has given credit to the firm as a consequence of the representation. The representation can be made by words or conduct. An example of holding out can be seen in *D & H Bunny Ltd v Atkins* [1961] VLR 31, where the credit manager of a company let N have goods on credit because A and N told him that they had decided to go into partnership together. A was liable for the price of the goods, even though no partnership was ever formed.

A person cannot become liable in tort as a consequence of s.14(1). The section is concerned only with those outsiders who gave credit to the firm. The representation does not need to be made directly to the outsider who consequently gave credit to the firm. If A represents to B that he (A) is a partner in a firm and B tells C, who relies on the representation, A can be liable to C. However, what is required is that at some stage the person made liable either represents himself to be a partner or knowingly allows himself to be represented as a partner.

> *Tower Cabinet Co Ltd v Ingram* [1949] 1 All ER 1033
>
> The claimant, Tower Cabinet Company Ltd, sued a firm for six suites of furniture sold and delivered. Having gained judgment, the claimant sought to enforce this against a retired partner, Ingram. Upon retiring, Ingram had informed persons with whom the firm had previously dealt that he had retired. However, he did not advertise the fact of his retirement in the *London Gazette*. The remaining partner, now in business →

on his own, had ordered the goods from the claimant on partnership notepaper which indicated that Ingram was a partner. Ingram did not know that this had been done.

Held. Ingram was not liable to the claimants. He had neither represented himself as a partner or knowingly allowed himself to be represented as a partner.

Lynskey J: 'Before the company can succeed in making Mr Ingram liable under this section [section 14(1)], they have to satisfy the court that Mr Ingram, by words spoken or written or by conduct, represented himself as a partner. There is no evidence of that. Alternatively, they must prove that he knowingly suffered himself to be represented as a partner . . . it is impossible to say that Mr Ingram knowingly suffered himself to be so represented.'

Section 14(2) provides that the continued use of the firm's name after a partner's death does not automatically make the deceased partner's estate liable for any partnership debts incurred after his death.

In *Revenue and Customs Commissioners* v *Pal* [2006] EWHC 2016 (Ch), [2006] All ER (D) 480 (Jul) it was held that a person who was not a partner could not incur liability for VAT by signing a VAT registration form and claiming to be a partner. Section 14(1) applies only where credit is given and registering for VAT did not involve the firm being given credit. Section 14(1) is concerned with private law transactions where credit is given in direct or indirect reliance on the representation.

15.8.3 Liability for a partner's torts and other wrongful acts

Section 10 provides that:

'Where, by any wrongful act or omission of any partner acting in the ordinary course of the business of the firm, or with the authority of his co-partners, loss or injury is caused to any person not being a partner in the firm, or any penalty is incurred, the firm is liable therefore to the same extent as the partner so acting or omitting to act.'

This section is somewhat similar to s.5, except that it deals with liability in tort rather than with liability in contract. In effect it states that fellow partners will be vicariously liable for the torts of an individual partner if the individual partner had actual, apparent or usual authority to commit the act which gave rise to the tortious liability.

In *Blyth* v *Fladgate* [1891] 1 Ch 337, for example, a partner in a firm of solicitors made a loan on behalf of a client, the loan being secured by a mortgage on a house. The solicitor was negligent in that he did not check that the house was worth at least as much as the loan. The client lost money as a consequence and all of the partners were held vicariously liable because the solicitor had committed the tort while doing an act which was in the usual course of the firm's business. In *Arbuckle* v *Taylor* (1815) 3 Dow 160 a partner in a firm thought that an outsider had stolen from the firm. He brought a private prosecution which failed. The outsider then sued the firm for the torts of malicious prosecution and false imprisonment. The other partners were not liable for these torts because the act which gave rise to the tort (bringing criminal proceedings against an outsider) was not an act which was within the usual course of the firm's business.

Section 10 will not apply where the tort of one partner injures only another partner. Obviously the partner who committed the tort will be personally liable. Although the position is unclear, it seems likely that the other partners will not incur liability under the common law.

In *Dubai Aluminium Co Ltd* v *Salaam and others* [2002] UKHL 48, [2003] 2 AC 366 the House of Lords fairly recently considered the scope of s.10 in detail. The case concerned the liability of fellow partners for a solicitor who had acted dishonestly. The errant solicitor had set up sham contracts under which the claimant company had been defrauded out of $50m. Although the errant solicitor had knowingly assisted in the fraud, he had benefited only by earning relatively modest fees for the work he did. His co-partners were innocent of any dishonesty. The Court of Appeal had held that the co-partners were not vicariously liable for the errant solicitor because it was not in the ordinary course of the business of a solicitor's firm to plan, draft and sign sham contracts. The House of Lords reversed this judgment and held the co-partners liable. The following points can be taken from the judgment.

(1) Lord Nicholls held that the errant solicitor did not commit a common law tort, such as deceit or negligence, but that did not prevent him from having committed a 'wrongful act or omission' within the meaning of s.10 of the Partnership Act. When deciding whether or not an act was done in the ordinary course of a firm's business the relevant question was not simply whether the partner was

authorised by his co-partners to do the act he did. This would ignore the policy behind vicarious liability of partners – that being in partnership carries the risk of liability for the wrongful acts of the agents who carry the business on. 'Perhaps the best general answer is that the wrongful conduct must be so closely connected with acts the partner or employee was authorised to do that, for the purpose of liability of the firm or the employer to third parties, the wrongful conduct *may fairly and properly be regarded* as done by the partner while acting in the ordinary course of the firm's business.' The question whether or not this actually happened is a question of law, not fact, to be decided with regard to all of the circumstances of the case and previous decisions. Applying this test to the facts, the firm was liable for the errant solicitor because his acts in drawing up the sham contracts were so closely connected with acts which he was authorised to do that they *could fairly and properly be regarded* as done by him while acting in the ordinary course of the firm's business. He drew up the sham contracts while 'acting in his capacity as a partner' because he was acting on behalf of the firm, not on behalf of himself or a third party. He was trying to promote the firm's business.

(2) The errant solicitor committed some of the acts which made him personally liable while acting as a director of the fraudulent companies. He did not therefore commit all such acts while acting within the course of his employment as a partner. Lord Nicholls said that this did not prevent his co-partners from being vicariously liable because the solicitor had committed enough acts to make himself personally liable while acting within the course of his employment.

(3) Lord Hobhouse thought that on the facts the errant solicitor had committed the tort of deceit in the course of the partnership business and so the other partners were plainly vicariously liable under s.10 of the Partnership Act.

(4) Lord Millett said that s.10 of the Partnership Act was not restricted to common law torts. The section is concerned with fault based liability but this could arise under the common law, a statute or an equitable wrong. He also said that whether or not a partner was acting 'in the ordinary course of the business of the firm' was a question of fact, once it had been legally established that

the act in question was legally capable of being performed in this way. (He was the only one of the Lords who saw the question as one of fact.) He saw vicarious liability as a loss distribution device. A partner or employer ought to be liable for all the torts which could fairly be regarded as reasonably incidental risks to the type of business carried on.

(5) Lord Millett also cleared up confusion about the meaning of ss.9, 11 and 13 of the Act. Section 9 is not concerned with the firm's liability but with the individual liability of each partner. It makes each partner jointly liable with the other partners for any debts and obligations of the firm which were incurred while he was a partner. Section 11 makes the firm liable to account for money which was properly received by the firm but which one of the partners later misappropriated. Section 13 deals with the situation where a partner who is also a trustee misuses trust money. All of the partners are made liable to restore the money. Neither s.11 nor s.13 is concerned with vicarious liability, as it would not be in the ordinary course of the firm's business to misappropriate money in the ways which the sections envisage. But this does not prevent the firm from being liable to account for the money misused.

In *JJ Coughlan Ltd v Ruparelia and others* (see above at 15.8.1.1) there was no liability under s.10 of the Partnership Act. In reaching this conclusion regarding s.10 Dyson LJ, who gave the only significant judgment of the Court of Appeal, relied on the extract from Lord Nicholls' speech from *Dubai Aluminium Co Ltd v Salaam* which is set out in (1) above.

Admissions and representations by partners

An admission or representation made by any partner concerning the partnership affairs, and in the ordinary course of its business, is evidence against the firm. However, this is only the case where the admission or representation was made with actual, apparent or usual authority (s.15).

Section 16 states that if an outsider gives a partner notice of a matter relating to the firm's affairs this is regarded as notice to the firm. There are, however, two exceptions. Notice to a dormant or sleeping partner would not be notice to the firm. And notice of a fraud would not be notice to the firm if the notice was given to the very partner who was committing the fraud.

Liability of incoming and outgoing partners

Section 17 provides that a partner coming into a firm is not liable for the pre-existing debts of the firm. It also provides that a partner retiring from a firm remains liable for debts which were incurred before his retirement. A retiring partner can only be discharged from existing liabilities if a contract to that effect is made between himself, the newly constituted members of the firm and the creditors. Such a contract is known as a novation. It can either be made expressly or it can be inferred from a course of dealing between the creditors and the firm as newly constituted. Such a novation can be inferred from conduct fairly easily, but it is not enough that a creditor adopts the newly constituted firm as a debtor.

Section 36(1) provides that an outsider dealing with the firm after a change in the firm's constitution is entitled to regard all apparent members of the old firm as still being members of the firm until he has notice of the change. Apparent authority will continue as regards outsiders who had previously dealt with the firm until they are given actual notice of the change. As regards those who had not previously dealt with the firm a notice in the *London Gazette* is sufficient notice (s.36(2)).

A retiring partner will generally be liable for debts incurred before his retirement. A partner who has retired is not liable for debts incurred after his retirement if the person dealing with the firm did not know that he was a partner. Nor is the estate of a dead or bankrupt partner liable for debts incurred after the death or bankruptcy if the person dealing with the firm had not known the deceased to be a partner (s.36(3)).

Guarantees of the firm given by outsiders

If an outsider gives a guarantee to a firm, or guarantees a third party that he will pay the firm's debts, either guarantee will normally be revoked if a partner leaves or joins the firm. This provision is set out in s.18 and is to apply unless there is any agreement to the contrary.

15.9 DISSOLUTION AND WINDING UP

When a partnership is dissolved it comes to an end. Often this can be little more than a technicality. A firm is dissolved each time there is a change in the membership, although in a commercial firm the remaining partners are likely to carry on in very much the same way as before. Where the firm is dissolved and not carried on much as before there will be a winding up.

This will involve the firm's assets being realised, creditors being paid off and any remaining surplus being divided amongst the partners. A partnership can be dissolved either by the partners themselves, or under one of the provisions of the Partnership Act 1890.

15.9.1 Dissolution by the partners

Earlier in this chapter, at 15.2.1, we saw that partnership arises on account of a contract having been made by the partners. The general common law of contract might allow one or more of the partners to terminate this contract. For example, all of the partners might make a new contract, agreeing to end the partnership, or a formal partnership agreement might set out the circumstances on which the partnership can be ended. In addition, a partner can rescind the contract if he made it in consequence of a misrepresentation, and a partner may apply to the court to terminate the contract if the other partners commit a repudiatory breach of contract.

In *Rowlands* v *Hodson* [2009] EWCA Civ 1042, [2010] PNLR 8, considered above at 15.3.3, the Court of Appeal rejected an argument that a partnership was dissolved because one of the two partners' activity in the firm became no more than nominal. Rimer LJ said:

'That [dissolution of the partnership] could only have been achieved by an agreement to that effect by the two partners, but there was none. If, for example, a partner, whether because of wilfulness, idleness or illness, ceases to attend the partnership office and to carry out any of the partnership business, he will not automatically cease to be a partner, any more than an employee who stops performing his duties because of illness will cease to be an employee. Partnership is a contractual relationship carrying with it both benefits and burdens, including a responsibility jointly and severally for the firm's liabilities. The partnership deed or agreement (if, as here, there is one) will usually provide bases on which a partnership relationship can be terminated . . .'

At 15.5.1.7 we saw that s.25 provides that no majority of the partners can expel any partner unless a power to do this has been conferred by express agreement between the partners. If a partner is expelled then the firm is dissolved. Although this might be little more than a technicality in a large firm, if there were only two partners the expulsion would lead to a winding up of the firm.

15.9.2 Dissolution under a provision of the Act

The Partnership Act lays down that a partnership is dissolved in the following circumstances.

(1) If the partnership was entered into for a fixed term or for a single purpose, it is dissolved by the expiry of that term or the termination of that purpose. (The common law would regard the contract as discharged by performance.)

(2) The firm is dissolved by the death or bankruptcy of a partner, unless the partners have agreed otherwise. Although the partners can agree that the firm should not be wound up upon the death or bankruptcy of a partner, the firm would technically be dissolved anyway. However, if the remaining partners carried on this might be of little practical importance.

(3) A firm may be dissolved, at the option of the partners, if a partner assigns his share of the partnership assets to a creditor so as to satisfy a private debt. This may happen involuntarily, in that a creditor who has gained judgment against a partner in a matter not connected with the partnership can be granted a charging order against the partner's interest in partnership property, up to the amount of the debt. A creditor who does become an assignee of a partner's share in the partnership assets gains no rights to manage the firm.

(4) Section 34 states that in every case a firm is automatically dissolved on the happening of an event which makes it unlawful for the business of the firm to be carried on or for the the members of the firm to carry on the business in partnership.

15.9.3 Dissolution by court order

Section 35 gives a partner the right to apply to the court for dissolution on five grounds, as follows:

(1) That a partner has become permanently incapable of performing his part of the partnership contract.

(2) That the court considers, having regard to the nature of the business, that a partner has been guilty of such conduct as is calculated to prejudicially affect the carrying on of the business.

(3) That a partner wilfully or persistently breaches the partnership agreement, or otherwise conducts himself in matters relating to the partnership business in such a way that it is not reasonably practicable for the other partners to carry on in business with him.

(4) That the business of the partnership can only be carried on at a loss.

(5) That the court considers it just and equitable that the partnership should be dissolved.

It is also possible for a court to dissolve a partnership under the Mental Capacity Act 2005. A court will do this if it is satisfied that a partner is, by reason of mental disorder, incapable of managing his property or affairs.

15.9.4 Winding up

After the dissolution of a partnership the authority of each partner to bind the firm, and the other rights and obligations of the partners, may continue despite the dissolution. However, this authority continues only to the extent that this may be necessary in order to wind up the affairs of the partnership, and to complete transactions begun but unfinished at the time of the dissolution (s.38). In *Re Bourne* [1906] 2 Ch 427, for example, a partnership of two was dissolved when one of the partners died. The surviving partner mortgaged partnership land in order to get an overdraft to temporarily carry the business on. It was held that this act was validly done as it was done in order to wind up the affairs of the firm. The executors of the deceased partner were therefore bound by the mortgage.

After dissolution the firm is not bound by the acts of a bankrupt partner. In addition, any partner can apply to the court to have a receiver appointed. If the court does appoint a receiver the continuing authority of partners to bind the firm will cease. Partners do not need to appoint a receiver to wind a firm up. Partners can themselves generally wind the firm up in a shorter time, more cheaply and with less publicity. A court order may also take away a partner's continuing authority to bind the firm.

15.9.5 Realisation of the firm's assets

On dissolution any of the partners is entitled to have the partnership property applied in payment of the debts and liabilities of the firm (s.39). We saw earlier, at 15.6, that this was one of the most important reasons to identify partnership property in the partnership agreement.

15.9.5.1 **The goodwill**

The goodwill of the firm may be one of the firm's most valuable assets. Accountants might define the goodwill as the excess of the market value of a business over the value of its individual assets. Various legal definitions have been put forward.

In *Trego* v *Hunt* [1896] AC 7 Lord MacNachten defined goodwill as 'the whole advantage, whatever it may be, of the reputation and connection of the firm, which may have been built up by years of honest work or gained by lavish expenditure of money'.

In *Hill* v *Fearis* [1905] 1 Ch 466 Warrington J said that the goodwill was 'the advantage, whatever it may be, which a person gets by continuing to carry on, and being entitled to represent to the outside world that he is carrying on, a business which has been carried on for some time previously'.

Once the goodwill has been sold for the benefit of all of the partners, those partners will not be able to use the firm's name or solicit its customers. There is no reason why they should not otherwise carry on a rival business, unless a valid restraint of trade clause forbids this. Lord MacNachten, in *Trego* v *Hunt*, explained the position in this way:

> 'A person who has sold the goodwill of his business is under no obligation to retire altogether from the field. Trade he undoubtedly may, and in the very same line of business. If he has not bound himself by special stipulation he is free to set up business wherever he chooses. But, then, how far may he go? He may do everything that a stranger to the business, in ordinary course, would be in a position to do. He may set up where he will. He may push his wares as much as he pleases. He may thus interfere with the custom of his neighbour as a stranger and outsider might do; but he must not, I think, avail himself of his special knowledge of the old customers to regain, without consideration, that which he has parted with for value. He must not make his approaches from the vantage ground of his former position. He may not sell the custom and steal away the customers.'

In *Gorne* v *Scales* [2006] EWCA Civ 311, [2006] All ER (D) 426 (Mar) two partners, the defendants, removed a card index of customers and their history when the firm collapsed. (The similarity with data held on a computer is obvious.) These cards provided the defendants with 40–45 per cent of their new firm's business during its first year. The innocent partner chose to claim damages rather than an account of profits. The Court of Appeal held, with Lady Justice Arden dissenting, that the correct valuation for damages was the amount which a willing third party, or the other partners, would have paid for the card index on dissolution. The value of the index in the defendants' new business was not relevant in assessing damages.

15.9.6 **Distribution of the firm's assets**

Once the firm's assets have been sold, a set of realisation accounts will be produced. Then the position will depend upon whether or not the firm was solvent and whether or not there were any losses.

15.9.6.1 **Losses where the firm is solvent**

If the firm is solvent, that is to say where it has enough money to pay all of its debts, then outsiders are guaranteed to receive all that the firm owes them. However, even where the firm is solvent it may have made a loss. For example, if A, B and C went into partnership, each contributing £10 000 capital, the firm might only have £20 000 of capital left once the assets have been realised. The firm is solvent, but there has been a loss of £10 000 capital.

First, it is important to realise that the partners may themselves have agreed how this loss should be borne. If they have made such an agreement this will apply. If there is no agreement between the partners on this matter, s.44 spells out how the assets should be distributed.

Section 44(a) provides that 'Losses, including losses and deficiencies of capital, shall be paid first out of profits, next out of capital, and lastly, if necessary, by the partners individually in the proportion in which they were entitled to share profits.'

It is perhaps best to illustrate this by way of an example. Let us assume that firm X, Y, Z has three partners who are to share profits equally. X contributed £15 000 capital, Y £10 000 and Z £5 000. The total capital was therefore £30 000. If, after realisation of the assets, there is only £24 000 capital left the firm will have suffered a loss of capital of £6 000. Each partner would have to contribute to this loss equally and pay £2 000.

Consequently, X would receive a net £13 000 (£15 000 capital originally contributed minus £2 000); Y would receive £8 000 (£10 000 capital originally contributed minus £2 000); Z would receive £3 000 (£5 000 capital originally contributed minus £2 000).

If the partners had agreed that each loss would be borne according to capital contributions then the position would have been different. The £24 000 of capital remaining is equal to 80 per cent of the original capital. Each partner would therefore be entitled to 80 per cent of his original capital contribution. X would therefore be entitled to £12 000, Y to £8 000 and Z to £4 000.

15.9.6.2 Applying the firm's assets

When producing the final accounts the partnership must discharge its various obligations. Section 44(b) tells us that these obligations must be discharged in the following order.

(1) First, outsiders are paid what they are owed in full.
(2) Second, each partner is paid rateably what he is owed in respect of loans made to the firm.
(3) Third, each partner is paid rateably the capital he contributed to the firm.
(4) Finally any residue is divided amongst the partners in the proportion in which they were entitled to share profits.

If there is not enough money to discharge each class of obligation, then any deficiency is treated as a loss and s.44(a) will apply unless there has been an agreement to the contrary.

Example

Let us assume that in firm PQR there were three partners, who were to share profits equally. The realisation accounts show that the firm has assets of £100 000. £8 000 is owed to the Revenue & Customs. P loaned the firm £10 000. P also contributed £10 000 capital and Q contributed £6 000 capital. First, Revenue & Customs is paid the £8 000 which it is owed. Then P is paid the £10 000 which he loaned to the firm. Then P is repaid his £10 000 capital and Q is repaid his £6 000 capital. The remaining £66 000 is divided amongst the three partners equally, as they were to share profits equally.

Consequently, Revenue & Customs receives £8 000, P receives £42 000, Q receives £28 000 and R receives £22 000.

If there had only been £25 000 of assets remaining, the position would have been as follows. First, the Revenue & Customs would receive full payment of the £8 000 they were owed. Then P would have received full payment of his £10 000 loan. The fact that there was only £7 000 remaining would mean that there

was a shortfall of £9 000 in capital. This loss would be borne equally by the three partners under s.44(a). Each partner would therefore have to contribute £3 000 towards this. P would therefore receive an additional £7 000 (capital contribution of £10 000 minus £3 000). Q would receive £3 000 (capital contribution of £6 000 minus £3 000). R would have to make a further contribution of £3 000.

The rule in *Garner v Murray* [1904] 1 Ch 57 applies where the loss in capital is attributable to the insolvency of one or more of the partners. In such a case the solvent partners are not liable to make good the insolvent partner's contribution to capital. First the solvent partners contribute to lost capital according to their profit-sharing ratio (but they only contribute their own share). Second, the solvent partners share whatever capital is accumulated in the ratio of their original capital contributions.

Example

Let us assume that firm DEF had three partners who were to share profits equally. D contributed £6 000 capital, E contributed £3 000 and F contributed £1 000. There was therefore a total capital contribution of £10 000. When the firm is wound up F has become insolvent and there has been a capital loss of £6 000. D and E must pay towards the lost capital. However, they only pay their own share, in accordance with their profit-sharing ratio. They both therefore pay one third, £2 000, as both were entitled to one third of the firm's profits. After these payments have been made the capital is up to £8 000. D and E share this in the ratio of their capital contributions, that is to say in the ratio 2:1. D therefore receives £5 333, suffering a capital loss of £667. E receives £2 667, suffering a capital loss of £333.

The rule in *Garner v Murray* does not apply where there is an agreement to the contrary and does not affect outside creditors in any way.

Section 42(1) deals with the use of partnership property after a partner has left the firm. 'Where any member of a firm has died or otherwise ceased to be a partner, and the surviving or continuing partners carry on the business of the firm with its capital or assets without any final settlement of accounts as between the firm and the outgoing partner or his estate, then, in the absence of any agreement to the contrary, the outgoing partner or his estate is entitled at the option of himself or his representatives to such share of the profits made since the dissolution as the court may find to be attributable to the use of his share of the partnership assets, or to interest at the rate of 5 per cent per annum on the amount of his share of the partnership assets.'

In *Sandhu v Gill* [2005] EWCA Civ 1297 the Court of Appeal held that 'the partnership assets' towards the end of s.42(1) meant the net partnership assets: that is to say what remained out of gross assets for distribution between the partners after all debts and liabilities of the partnership had been met. Furthermore, the partner's 'share' of the partnership assets was the actual share of those assets, calculated by reference to what the partner in question would have been entitled to receive at the end of a winding up under s.44(b). So the presumption that each partner would share in the assets equally would come into play only as regards assets which would remain after all partners had had their loans and capital repaid.

15.9.6.3 **The position where the firm is insolvent**

The firm will be insolvent if it does not have enough assets to pay its debts. In such a situation it may well be that one or more of the partners remain solvent. All of the solvent partners will be jointly liable to pay creditors whose debts have not been fully satisfied. Section 44(a) of the Act will require the solvent partners to repay the firm's debts in the proportion in which they were going to share profits, unless there has been an agreement to the contrary.

An insolvent firm can be compulsorily wound up as an unregistered company under the Insolvency Act 1986. Either a partner or a creditor may petition the court for such a winding up. (The winding up of companies is considered in Chapter 19 at 19.1.) It is possible for an insolvent partnership to come to a voluntary arrangement with creditors. As long as the correct procedure is followed, such an arrangement will even bind creditors who did not agree to it.If bankruptcy proceedings are also brought against one or more of the partners these will be heard by the same court at the same time.

Small insolvent partnerships can apply for a moratorium during which the firm cannot be wound up, securities cannot be enforced against the firm and legal proceedings against the firm are stayed. A partnership is small for this purpose if it has a turnover of

not more than £5.6 million, assets of not more than £2.8 million and no more than 50 employees. The moratorium can last for up to 28 days.

Insolvent partnerships can also apply for a partnership administration order, but only if all of the partners are solvent. While the order is in force the partnership is protected while it considers restructuring, refinancing or sale of the firm.

15.10 **LIMITED PARTNERS**

It is possible for one or more of the partners to have limited liability for the firm's debts under the Limited Partnerships Act 1907. However, the Act requires that there must always be at least one general partner who has unlimited liability.

Every limited partnership must be registered with the Registrar of Companies. All of the partners must sign a statement, giving the following information:

(a) The firm name. As regards firms registered on or after 1 October 2009, the name must end with the words 'limited partnership' or the abbreviation 'LP'. (Upper or lower case, or any combination of the two, may be used.)
(b) The general nature of the business.
(c) The principal place of business.
(d) The full name of each of the partners.
(e) The date of commencement and the length of time for which the business is entered into.
(f) A statement that the partnership is limited, and the description of every limited partner.
(g) The sum contributed by every limited partner, and whether paid in cash or otherwise.

Limited partners contribute a certain amount of capital and are not liable beyond this amount. However, limited partners are not allowed to take part in the management of the business and are not agents of the firm. A limited partner who does take part in management will lose his limited liability.

The Limited Partnerships Act has not been much of a success. There are few firms which have both general and limited partners. Limited liability partnerships, where all of the partners have limited liability, are a quite different matter and are considered in Chapter 19.

Early in 2009, BERR proposed that the Limited Partnership Act 1907 should be repealed, and its provisions incorporated into the Partnership Act 1890, in accordance with recommendations made by the Law Commission. However, the Government considered that more time was needed to consider the responses which have been made to this proposal. At the time of writing the Act is still in force.

Test your understanding 15.4

1 To what extent does s.5 of the Partnership Act make a partner who acts without actual or apparent authority an agent of the firm and fellow partners?

2 In what circumstances will fellow partners be liable for the torts of an individual partner?

3 How can a person become liable by holding out?

4 Is an incoming partner liable for debts of the firm which have previously arisen?

5 How can a retiring partner cease to be liable for debts which arose prior to his retirement?

6 On what four grounds may a partnership be dissolved under a provision of the Partnership Act 1890?

7 On what five grounds can a partnership be dissolved by court order?

8 How are losses of a solvent partnership to be borne?

9 In what order are the assets of a solvent firm distributed?

10 Can one partner have limited liability for the firm's debts? Can all of the partners have limited liability?

Key points

Definition and nature of a partnership

■ Partnership is the relation which subsists between persons carrying on a business in common with a view of profit.

■ A partnership, unlike a company, has no separate legal identity of its own. It is merely a relationship between the partners. (Limited liability partnerships, which can only be created by registration with Companies House, do have a legal identity of their own.)

■ A partnership can be created only if the partners intended to make a profit to share amongst themselves. It is not necessary that any such profit actually was made.

■ Being a joint owner of property, or sharing the gross takings of a business, do not necessarily create a partnership.

■ Taking a share of the net profits of a business is *prima facie* evidence of being a partner. However, this will not be the case if the other circumstances indicate that there was no partnership.

The partnership agreement

■ Although there is no need for partners to have a formal partnership agreement, most firms do have such an agreement.

■ Certain sections of the Companies Act 2006 make rules applicable to partnerships if they carry on business in a name other than the surnames of all of the partners. These sections make it a criminal offence to use certain words in the firm's name, or to use specified words without having gained permission from a relevant body and the Secretary of State. They also require that the names of all of the partners, and an address at which documents can be served on them, must be displayed on the firm's documents and at the firm's main place of business.

■ A passing off action may prevent the use of a name which is likely to cause confusion with another business, or likely to deceive the public, so as to divert trade from the other business.

■ A partnership agreement can be varied by the consent of all of the partners, and this consent can be inferred from the partners' course of dealing.

■ Minors can become partners but cannot be made liable for partnership debts incurred while they were minors.

Partners' relationship with each other

■ Section 24 of the Partnership Act implies nine terms which govern the partners' relationship with each other. These terms are implied only if the partners do not expressly or impliedly agree that they should not be.

■ A majority of partners cannot expel a partner unless all of the partners have made an express agreement allowing for expulsion.

■ Partnership property is held on trust by the partners for each other.

→

■ Property will be partnership property if the partners have expressly or impliedly agreed that it should be. The Partnership Act s.20(1) provides that partnership property consists of property originally brought into the partnership, or property acquired on behalf of the firm, or property acquired for and in the course of the firm's business. Section 21 provides that unless a contrary intention appears, property bought with money belonging to the firm is also deemed to be partnership property.

■ Partners owe each other fiduciary duties. Three fiduciary duties are mentioned in the Act. These duties, which are not exhaustive, are: to render accounts, to account for profits and not to compete with the firm. It is a defence to breach of fiduciary duty that the other partners consented to the act complained of.

Partners' relationship with outsiders

■ Partners can be agents of the firm even where they have no actual or apparent authority. This agency would arise as regards an act which was done as a partner if the act was the type of act which would ordinarily be done by a partner in the firm, and the act was done in the way in which it ordinarily would be done. However, there is no liability if the outsider either knows that the partner had no authority to do the act, or did not know or believe him to be a partner.

■ All of the partners will be liable for the torts of an individual partner if the tort was committed while the partner was doing an act which he had actual, apparent or usual authority to do.

■ A person who is not a partner can be made liable as if he was a partner if he represented himself as a partner, or if he knowingly allowed himself to be represented as a partner. The liability only arises in respect of a person who gave credit to the firm on the strength of the representation.

Dissolution of the firm

■ A partnership can be dissolved by the partners themselves, or under a provision of the Partnership Act, or by a court order.

■ Where the firm is solvent, losses are paid by the partners in the same ratio as profits would have been shared, unless there was an agreement to the contrary.

■ Where the firm is solvent, the partnership assets are distributed in the following order: first outsiders are paid, then partners are repaid loans made to the firm, then partners are repaid their capital contributions. Any surplus is divided amongst the partners in the proportion in which they were entitled to share profits.

■ An individual partner can register under the Limited Partnerships Act 1907 and thereby acquire limited liability for the firm's debts. However the 1907 Act requires that at least one general partner should have unlimited liability. A limited partner will lose his protection under the 1907 Act if he takes any part in the firm's management.

Summary questions

1 What must partners agree with each other in order for a partnership to be formed? What matters are specified by the Partnership Act 1890 as indicating that a partnership either does or does not exist?

2 Amanda, Beryl and Claire intend to go into partnership together as fashion designers as soon as they graduate from university. Amanda is to work full-time in the business and is to be entitled to 40 per cent of the profits. Beryl, who is to work only one day a week, and who is to contribute all of the firm's capital of £5 000, is to be entitled to 40 per cent of the firm's profits. Claire is to work two and a half days a week and be entitled to 20 per cent of the firm's profits. Claire has applied for a job as a stewardess on an ocean-going liner, as it has always been her ambition to follow such a career. She has been told that she has little chance of getting the job but that she will be interviewed for the job two months after her graduation. If Claire is given the job she intends to take it up two weeks after the interview. Beryl is to buy materials for the firm. She might occasionally need to write a cheque for up to £1 000 if she is offered a bargain. It is not envisaged that Amanda and Claire would write cheques for more than £50. If the venture is a success one year from commencement, the partners intend to take professional advice and to have a detailed partnership deed drawn up on their behalf. However, they do not want to incur any unnecessary costs

→

at the outset and intend to make their own partnership agreement.

Examine the model partnership agreement set out on pp. **420–421** and indicate how the agreement might be amended so that it would become suitable for the proposed firm.

3 X, Y and Z have gone into partnership. Their partnership agreement said that the firm could only be terminated by the partners themselves if two of the three partners agree to this. Would this agreement be given legal effect, or could one of the partners terminate the partnership by giving notice?

4 In a firm of doctors there is some dispute as to whether or not the premises from which the firm operates is partnership property.

a What is the significance of the premises either being or not being partnership property?

b How does property become partnership property?

5 a The partnership deed of a firm of builders says that goods can only be bought on the firm's behalf if all of the partners agree to the purchase. One of the partners in the firm orders a new pneumatic drill, without the knowledge or permission of his fellow partners, saying that it is for the firm. Advise the other partners as to whether or not they will be bound by the contract.

b Would your advice differ if one of the other partners had told the supplier of the drill that the partner who ordered the drill had no authority to order such goods on behalf of the partnership?

c Would the firm of builders be bound if one of the partners, without authority, ordered a new snooker table for the partnership?

6 a As part of his everyday work, a partner in a firm of medical practitioners performs a minor operation to remove a skin cancer on a patient's nose. The operation is performed negligently, and this causes the patient to become permanently disfigured. Advise the other partners as to whether or not the partners as a whole could incur liability for the negligence of the doctor who performed the operation.

b Advise a partner in a firm of doctors as to the circumstances in which the partnership might be liable for a partner in the firm who caused injury to a patient while negligently removing one of the patient's wisdom teeth.

7 In a firm of six partners, five partners want the partnership agreement to be changed and one partner does not. In what circumstances could the partnership agreement be changed by the majority? Can a partnership agreement ever be changed without the partners expressly agreeing that it should be?

8 A firm had three partners, G, H and I. The three partners were to share profits equally. G contributed £25 000 capital, H contributed £14 000 and I contributed £11 000. On dissolution, after all outside creditors have been paid, only £20 000 of capital remains. How would this loss be borne by the partners?

9 Explain the circumstances in which it might be possible for:

a One of the partners in a firm to have limited liability for the firm's debts;

b All of the partners in a firm to have limited liability for the firm's debts.

Multiple choice questions

1 A partner in a firm of general medical practitioners orders a new carpet for the surgery. The two other partners are furious about this because they ordered a new carpet, from a different shop, two days earlier. Which one of the following statements is true?

a The firm is liable on the contract under s.5.

b The firm is not liable on the contract, but the partner who ordered the carpet is, under s.7.

c The firm is not liable on the contract under s.5 or s.7 because only one partner, without the authority of the others, made the contract.

d The firm is liable on the contract under s.10.

2 A partner in a firm of solicitors orders a very expensive telescope, saying that it is for the partnership. His fellow partners did not authorise him to make the contract, or make any representation that he had authority to make it, and are refusing to be bound by it. Which one of the following statements is true?

a The firm is liable on the contract under s.5.

b The firm is liable on the contract under s.7.

c The firm is not liable on the contract under s.5 or s.7, but the partner who made the order is personally liable.

d The firm is liable on the contract under s.10.

3 A partner in a firm of builders, while drunk, drives a van through a customer's greenhouse. Which two of the following statements are true?

a The firm is liable if the partner was driving the van in the ordinary course of the firm's business when he drove through the greenhouse.

b If the van in question belonged to the firm, the firm will be liable even if the partner was not driving the van in the ordinary course of the firm's business when he had the accident.

c The firm is not liable under any circumstances. It would never be within the ordinary course of the firm's business to drive vans through greenhouses.

d Even if the partner had not been driving the van in the ordinary course of the firm's business, the other partners would be liable if they had egged him on to see how close to the greenhouse he could drive.

4 A, B and C are in partnership. No agreement has been made as to how profits or capital are to be shared. At the outset A contributed £10 000 capital, B £5 000 and C £1 000. B also loaned £1 000 to the firm. (When the answers refer to dissolution it should be assumed that the firm is solvent and has enough assets to pay all of its debts.) Which one of the following is true?

a Profits should be shared equally and (on dissolution) so should capital.

b Profits should be shared equally and the partners should be paid interest on the capital advanced.

c Profits and capital should be shared in the proportion to which capital was contributed.

d Profits should be shared equally, but (on dissolution) capital should be shared unequally.

5 D, a partner in DEF Wholesale Fruit and Vegetables, impulsively makes the following contracts in the firm's name. E and F make no representations to any of the suppliers. By which of the contracts would his partners be bound?

i He takes out an unnecessary, bank loan on the firm's behalf.

ii He orders a new computer game for F's son's 21st birthday.

iii He orders a top of the range computer to help with the firm's accounts.

iv He orders a new, and unnecessary, delivery van.

v He orders a ton of ripe bananas.

a By all of the contracts.

b By i, iii, iv and v only.

c By i, iv and v only.

d By i, ii and v only.

6 Consider the following statements.

i A company can be a partner in a firm, although it cannot itself be a partnership.

ii A person who is entitled to a share of the profits of a business venture will inevitably be in partnership with others who are entitled to a share of the profits.

iii No partnership agreement can contradict the nine terms implied by s.24 of the Partnership Act 1890.

iv Minors can become partners, but cannot be made liable for the firm's debts if these arose before the minor became 18 years old.

v If, in contravention of specific instructions given by all of his fellow partners, a partner makes a contract with a third party, that contract cannot be binding on any partner except the one who made it.

vi A person who allows himself to be represented as a partner can become liable as if he really was a partner to a third party who gave the firm credit on the strength of the representation.

Which of the above statements is true?

a i, iv and vi only.

b i, ii, v and vi only.

c ii, iii, iv and v only.

d i, v and vi only.

7 H, a partner in a firm of property developers, is sent to Scotland to bid for a smallholding. All of his expenses are paid by the firm. H bids as high as he was authorised, but does not secure the smallholding. After the auction, a farmer who is desperate for cash offers to sell his Land-Rover to H personally at a very low price. H goes to a local bank and withdraws the cash from his personal account. The following week H sells the Land-Rover at a good profit. Which one of the following is true?

a H will not have to share the profit made with his fellow partners.

b H will have to share the profit under s.28.

c H will have to share the profit under s.29.

d H will have to share the profit under s.30.

→

8 Consider the following statements.

i Individual partners may register as limited partners under the Limited Partnerships Act 1907, but the number of limited partners must not outnumber the number of general partners.

ii Partners registered as limited partners under the Limited Partnerships Act 1907 may not take part in the management of the firm.

iii Limited partners are agents of the firm for contracts made in the ordinary course of the firm's business.

iv A limited liability partnership can be set up, but only by registration with Companies House.

v The members of limited liability partnerships all have limited liability for the firm's debts.

Which of the above statements are true?

a i, ii and iii only.

b i, ii and iv only.

c ii, iv and v only.

d ii and iv only.

Task 15

Three friends of yours are considering going into business together to run a garage. Using a firm of builders as an example, write a report indicating:

a The extent to which one partner can be liable for goods ordered by another partner.

b The extent to which a partner can be liable for another partner's torts.

c The duties which partners owe to each other.

d The extent to which an individual partner can limit his potential liability.

e In what order, and by whom, the assets of a solvent firm will be applied in settling the firm's debts.

mylawchamber *premium*

Visit **www.mylawchamber.co.uk/macintyre** to access study support resources including interactive multiple-choice questions, weblinks, glossary, glossary flashcards, legal newsfeed, answers to questions in this chapter, legal updates and an overview of this chapter all linked to the **Pearson eText** version of *Business Law* which you can **search**, **highlight** and **personalise** with your **own notes** and **bookmarks**.

Use **Case Navigator** to read in full some of the key cases referenced in this chapter with commentary and questions:

Regal (Hastings) Ltd v *Gulliver and others* [1942] 1 All ER 378

The nature of a company and formation of a company

Introduction

16.1 THE COMPANIES ACT 2006

The Companies Act 2006 was introduced to improve the UK's competitiveness. It seeks to do this by providing a sound, flexible framework for UK company law. It was enacted to give effect to the recommendations of a report by the Company Law Review, after very extensive consultation with business and investors. The Act restates most provisions of the earlier Companies Acts, but it has also made significant changes. The ultimate goal of the Act is to introduce a framework for UK company law which is suitable for a competitive economy in the twenty-first century.

The 2006 Act has four main objectives. First, to enhance shareholder engagement and to foster a long-term approach to investment. Second, to adopt a 'Think Small First' approach and to ensure that companies are better regulated. Third, to make it easier to create and run a company. Fourth, to provide flexibility for the future.

Enhancing shareholder engagement and fostering a long-term approach to investment

One of the main objectives of the Act is to create a good understanding between directors and shareholders. Their roles should be clearly defined and they should find it easy to communicate with each other. Directors are to be encouraged to take an approach which promotes long-term investment rather than concentrating merely on short-term profit. These principles are known as 'Enlightened Shareholder Value' and they are enshrined in the Act. Directors now have to consider a variety of matters, such as their duties to the environment and their employees. However, these goals are to be achieved without imposing additional paperwork on directors. Rather, directors need to bear the goals in mind continuously and have regard to them as a matter of sound business practice. Directors of quoted companies need to report on a variety of matters (environmental, social, community, contractual, employee and other relationships) in their Business Review. This will enable shareholders to understand clearly how the company is performing and developing.

Directors are now liable for inaccuracies in their company reports and it will be easier for a shareholder to claim damages if false or misleading statements are made, either recklessly or intentionally. If the directors breach their duties, it is easier for minority shareholders to sue on the company's behalf by means of a derivative action.

The Act allows much required information to be communicated electronically. It is hoped that this will not only save money but also encourage more shareholders to be involved in a dialogue with the company. The Act also gives the Government the power to introduce regulations which will enable shareholders to see how institutional investors have voted with their shares. However, it is hoped that institutions will regulate themselves, using a voluntary disclosure regime, so that the Government will not need to introduce the regulations.

The 'Think Small First' approach and better regulation

Ninety per cent of companies have five or fewer shareholders. However, the earlier Companies Acts were written mainly with large companies in mind. The 2006 Act takes a new approach with its 'Think Small First' approach. New model articles of association have been created. These will apply to a newly registered company by default unless alternative articles are registered. One set of new model articles is much more suitable for small private companies than the old 'Table A' articles, which could previously be adopted. If the model articles are subsequently changed, this will not affect companies which had adopted them prior to the change.

Technical rules which used to prevent private companies from giving financial assistance for the purchase of their own shares have been abolished. These complex rules were of very little significance to most private companies.

The decision-making process used by small companies has been simplified. Private companies will not need to hold a meeting of shareholders in order to pass a resolution. It is envisaged that most resolutions will be passed using the written resolution procedure. Under this procedure, shareholders vote in favour of a resolution merely by signing it.

Private companies no longer need to have a company secretary. It is therefore possible for one person

to be the sole shareholder and the sole director, and to run a company without help from any other person.

The 2006 Act envisages three tiers of companies: private companies; public companies which are not quoted on a stock exchange; and public companies which are quoted. Private companies are presumed to be small and so a 'default position' is often used, whereby they will have minimal regulation imposed on them if they do not positively introduce more extensive rules. If a private company is large, as many are, it can opt for its own more extensive regulation.

Ease of formation and flexibility

As we shall see later in this chapter, the Act has made it easier and quicker to register a new company. In the following two chapters we shall see that it has also become easier to run a small company.

The Act has been written in such a way that it will be relatively easy to amend it in the light of changing circumstances, thus allowing for flexibility in the future.

16.2 THE NATURE OF A COMPANY

When most people think of a company, they think of a vast public company, with hundreds or thousands of employees. But many more companies are very small, often owned and run by just one person, and often having a share capital of less than £100. All companies, no matter what their size, have certain characteristics in common. To some extent these characteristics are interconnected, but they are easier to understand if considered individually.

16.2.1 The company is a separate legal entity

The most important consequence of incorporation is that a company is regarded as being a legal person in its own right. This means that a company has a legal identity of its own, which is quite separate from the legal identity of its owners. It follows that if a wrong is done to a company, it is the company, and not those who own the company's shares, who have the right to sue. Conversely, a person who is injured by a company will have the right to sue the company, but will not have the right to sue the company's shareholders or its officers. This well-established principle, that a company is a legal person in its own right, was laid down by the House of Lords in the following case.

Salomon v Salomon and Co Ltd
[1897] AC 22 (House of Lords)

For several years Salomon had carried on a business as a boot repairer and manufacturer. He formed a limited company and sold his business to the company for slightly over £39 000. The company paid the purchase price by issuing Salomon with 20 000 £1 shares, by regarding him as having loaned the company £10 000, by paying off the existing debts of the business at the time of incorporation and by making up the balance in cash. Salomon's wife and five children each took one £1 share. Salomon took a debenture, secured by a charge on all of the company's assets, as security for the £10 000 loan which he had made to the company. Unsecured creditors later loaned the company further substantial sums of money. Shortly after the company was incorporated it got into financial difficulty. A fresh debenture was issued to B, in return for a further loan. Not long afterwards B appointed a liquidator. Creditors who have taken a charge to secure a loan are entitled to be repaid before unsecured creditors. However, there was not enough money to pay even B in full. The company liquidator claimed that Salomon should personally be liable to pay all of the company's debts, in the same way as he would have been liable to pay all of the business debts if he had carried on his business as a sole trader.

Held. The company had been formed properly and without any fraud. Although Salomon owned all but six of the issued shares he was one person and the company was another. Salomon therefore had no obligation to pay the company's debts.

COMMENT (i) When the High Court heard the case, Salomon was held liable for the company's debts, on the grounds that the company had acted as Salomon's agent. In the Court of Appeal Salomon was held liable on the grounds that the company had run the business as a trustee for Salomon. Both of these arguments were rejected by the House of Lords.

Lord MacNachten said:

'The company is at law a different person altogether from the subscribers to the memorandum [the people who take the first shares]; and, though it may be that after incorporation the business is precisely the same as it was before, and the same persons are managers, and the same hands receive the profits, the company is not in law the agent of the subscribers or trustee for them. Nor are the subscribers as members

liable, in any shape or form, except to the extent and in the manner provided by the Act.'

(ii) **Salomon's case** is regarded as one of the most important in English law, mainly because of the protection which it offers to the shareholders and the officers of companies. However, the decision that a company has a legal identity of its own has many other consequences, as the following two cases show.

(iii) The value of Salomon's unincorporated business, which was sold to the company, was overvalued. Lord MacNaghten said: 'The price on paper was extravagant. It amounted to over 39 000 [pounds], a sum which represented the sanguine expectations of a fond owner rather than anything that could be called a businesslike or reasonable expectation of value.' However, there was no fraud and the unsecured creditors knew that they were lending the money to a limited company. They should either have taken debentures to secure their loans or have insisted that Salomon personally guaranteed that the loans would be repaid.

Macaura v Northern Assurance Ltd
[1925] AC 619 (House of Lords)

Macaura owned a timber estate. He sold all of the timber in the estate to a company in return for fully paid-up shares in the company. Macaura and his nominees were the only shareholders in the company. (They could also have been described as the only members. The members of the company are the shareholders.) The company owed money to Macaura, but not to anyone else. After the company was formed, Macaura insured the timber in his own name with several insurance companies. Most of the timber was destroyed in a fire and Macaura claimed on his insurance policies.

Held. Macaura could not claim on the insurance policies because he had no insurable interest in the timber. (A person has an insurable interest only if he is likely to suffer some monetary loss or be subject to a claim made by another person who has suffered a loss. A person without an insurable interest cannot enforce a contract of insurance.) Macaura had no insurable interest in the timber because he did not own the timber or own any part of it. Macaura might have owned the vast majority of the company's shares, and the company might have owed Macaura a great deal of money, but this did not escape the fact that it was the company, not Macaura, which owned the timber. The company had an insurable interest in the timber, but Macaura did not.

Tunstall v Steigmann
[1962] 2 All ER 417 (Court of Appeal)

Mrs Steigmann ran a pork butcher's shop and leased the shop next door to Mrs Tunstall. Mrs Steigmann wanted to end the lease. Under the Landlord and Tenant Act 1954 Mrs Steigmann could order Mrs Tunstall to leave only if she intended to occupy the building herself, to carry on a business there. Mrs Steigmann did intend to occupy the shop herself to carry on her butchery business. But before the case came to court she turned her business into a company. Mrs Steigmann claimed that as she owned all but two of the shares in the company, she was still the person who wanted to take over the premises.

Held. Mrs Steigmann was not entitled to end the lease. It was not Mrs Steigmann who wanted to occupy and run a business from the leased shop. It was Mrs Steigmann's company which wanted to do this.

Willmer LJ: 'There is no escape from the fact that a company is a legal entity entirely separate from its corporators – see *Salomon v Salomon and Co*. Here the landlord and her company are entirely separate entities. This is no matter of form; it is a matter of substance and reality. Each can sue and be sued in his own right; indeed, there is nothing to prevent the one suing the other. Even the holder of 100 per cent of the shares in a company does not by such holding become so identified with the company that he or she can be said to carry on the business of the company.'

In *Secretary of State for BERR v Neufeld* [2009] EWCA Civ 280, [2009] 3 All ER 790 the Court of Appeal confirmed that there is no reason why a shareholder or a director of a company should not also be an employee of the company, even if the person in question controlled the company. Generally, an employer will exercise some control over how an employee performs his job. (See Chapter 20 at 20.1.) However, even if this element of control was lacking a controller of a company could also be an employee of it, as long as the contract of employment was not a sham. Although a company is regarded as a legal person, it does not have human characteristics. For example, a company does not feel human emotions. In *Firsteel Products Ltd v Anaco Ltd* (1994) *Times*, 21 November, Owen J decided that a company could not sue for 'stress and aggravation', which it claimed to have suffered as a result of a breach of contract: 'This [claim] alleges that "generally the defendant has been put to a considerable amount of inconvenience, stress and difficulty …" The defendant is a limited company, in respect of which the language used is inappropriate.'

Similarly, in *Collins Stewart Ltd v Financial Times Ltd* [2005] EWHC 262, [2006] STC 100 it was held that a company cannot claim aggravated damages. Such damages are designed to compensate for injured feelings and are payable on account of the way in which a wrong was committed. A company has no feelings which can be injured and so cannot claim aggravated damages. In *Richmond London Borough Council v Pinn and Wheeler Ltd* [1989] RTR 354 the Divisional Court held that a company cannot drive a lorry. Pill J said: 'The act of driving a lorry is a physical act which can be performed only by natural persons.'

Despite not having human characteristics, companies do have certain fundamental rights, such as the right to peaceable enjoyment of property, under the European Convention on Human Rights.

16.2.2 Limited liability

In *Salomon*'s case we saw that Salomon was not personally liable for the debts of the company. The vast majority of companies are registered as limited companies, as was Salomon and Co Ltd. (Below at 16.4.2 we shall see that some very few companies are unlimited, and that the shareholders in such companies do not have limited liability in respect of the company's debts.) When people buy shares in a limited company the only commitment which they make is that they agree with the company that they will pay the price of the shares. Generally, these days, the full price is paid immediately but this is not necessarily the case. For example, when the public utilities were privatised, investors were often required to pay half of the share price when subscribing for their shares and remained liable for the other half. If one of these privatised companies had gone into liquidation before shareholders had paid their second instalment, the shareholders would have been liable to pay the amount outstanding to the company liquidator. None of the companies did go into immediate liquidation. The shareholders therefore became liable to pay the amount outstanding on their shares to the company when payment became due under the terms of the contract which they made with the company. If the shares were transferred to another person before their full price had been paid to the company, the person taking the shares would have taken over liability to pay the rest of the price. None of the shareholders would have assumed liability to pay the debts of the company. In Chapter 19 we examine the respective advantages and disadvantages of trading as a company, a partnership or a limited liability partnership. For many business owners limited liability is the main advantage attached to trading as a company.

It must, of course, be emphasised that although a shareholder in a limited company will have limited liability, the company itself will not. If a company has debts, it must pay them, even if this means selling all of its assets and going into liquidation.

16.2.3 Perpetual succession

A three-quarters majority of the members of a company can decide to liquidate it at any time. If they do liquidate the company, it will cease to exist. However, companies can continue in existence indefinitely, and therefore it is said that they have perpetual succession.

Shareholders, of course, must die. But even if all the shareholders in a company die, their shares will be inherited by others and the company will continue in existence. The Hudson's Bay Company is the oldest corporation in the world, having been in existence since 2 May 1670. Generations of its shareholders have died, but the company still exists.

As we saw in Chapter 15, the death of a partner always ends the partnership. The partners may have agreed that, in the event of the death of a partner, the remaining partners will carry the firm on. Even so, technically at least, the death of a partner will dissolve the firm and a set of dissolution accounts will need to be drawn up.

16.2.4 Ownership of property

A company can own property, and this property will continue to be owned by the company regardless of who owns the shares in the company (as was demonstrated in *Macaura* v *Northern Assurance Ltd*). This can be important when a company is trying to borrow money, because the company can give its own property, both present and future assets, as security for a loan. This matter is considered in more detail in Chapter 18.

16.2.5 Contractual capacity

A company has the power to make contracts and can sue and be sued on these contracts. This power must obviously be delegated to human agents, and it is the company directors, or persons who have been authorised by the directors, who actually go through the process of forming the contracts. But the important point is that it is the company itself which assumes the rights and liabilities which the contract creates. As well as being able to make contracts, companies can also sue and be sued in tort.

16.2.6 Criminal liability

As a general principle, a defendant can only be convicted of a crime if it can be proved that he committed a guilty act (*actus reus*) while having a guilty mind (*mens rea*). (The nature of a crime is analysed in Chapter 22 at 22.1.) At first sight it would seem that companies cannot commit crimes because they have not got minds of their own. The point was made as long ago as 1768, when Lord Blackstone said: 'A corporation cannot commit treason, or felony, or other crime, in its corporate capacity; though its members may in their distinct individual capacities.'

However, these days the courts can find companies guilty of crimes if they are prepared to regard the controllers of the company as the minds of the company. In *Tesco Supermarkets* v *Nattrass* [1971] 2 All ER 127 (House of Lords) Lord Reid said: 'A living person has a mind which can have knowledge or intention or be negligent and he has hands to carry out his intention. A corporation has none of these; it must act through living persons, though not always one or the same person. Then the person who acts is not speaking or acting for the company. He is acting as the company and his mind which directs his acts is the mind of the company … If it is a guilty mind then that guilt is the guilt of the company. It must be a question of law whether, once the facts have been ascertained, a person in doing particular things is to be regarded as the company or merely as the company's servant or agent.' In addition, a large number of statutes, such as the Health and Safety at Work etc. Act 1974, specifically impose liability on both companies and company officers.

In 1994 a company called OLL Ltd, and its managing director, were both found guilty of manslaughter after four sixth-form students died as a result of grossly inadequate safety measures while on a canoe trip across Lyme Bay. The *mens rea* of the managing director was attributed to the company. The managing director was sentenced to three years' imprisonment, reduced on appeal to two years, the company was fined £60 000, which represented all of its assets. This case was the first one in which a company had been convicted of manslaughter. Such convictions were very difficult to secure and this led to the passage of the Corporate Manslaughter and Corporate Homicide Act 2007. Now that the 2007 Act is in force, the common law offence of corporate manslaughter has ceased to exist.

16.2.6.1 The Corporate Manslaughter and Corporate Homicide Act 2007

The Corporate Manslaughter and Corporate Homicide Act 2007 has created a new offence of corporate manslaughter (corporate homicide in Scotland). The offence can be committed by companies and by other incorporated bodies, such as LLPs, as well as by some types of unincorporated associations, such as partnerships. The Director of Public Prosecutions must consent to a prosecution being brought.

Section 1(1) provides that the indictable offence of corporate manslaughter is committed by a relevant organisation if the way in which its activities are managed and organised (a) causes a person's death, and (b) amounts to a gross breach of a relevant duty of care owed by the organisation to the deceased. However, s.1(3) provides that an organisation is guilty of the s.1(1) offence only if the way in which its activities are managed or organised by its senior management is a substantial element in the breach to which s.1(1) refers. A breach is a 'gross breach' only if it falls far below what can reasonably be expected of the organisation in the circumstances (s.1(4)(b)). Section 1(4)(c) defines 'senior management', in relation to an organisation, as the persons who play significant roles in (i) the making of decisions about how the whole or a substantial part of its activities are to be managed or organised, or (ii) the actual managing or organising of the whole or a substantial part of those activities. It is important to notice that the emphasis is on organisational failure, rather than on attaching the guilt of an individual to the company. The penalty for commission of the offence is a fine.

Section 2(1) sets out the following comprehensive definition of 'relevant duty of care':

'(1) A "relevant duty of care", in relation to an organisation, means any of the following duties owed by it under the law of negligence –

(a) a duty owed to its employees or to other persons working for the organisation or performing services for it;

(b) a duty owed as occupier of premises;

(c) a duty owed in connection with –

(i) the supply by the organisation of goods or services (whether for consideration or not),

(ii) the carrying on by the organisation of any construction or maintenance operations,

(iii) the carrying on by the organisation of any other activity on a commercial basis, or

(iv) the use or keeping by the organisation of any plant, vehicle or other thing.'

Whether or not a duty of care was owed is a question of law for the judge, not a question of fact for the jury (s.2(5)). Whether there was a gross breach of that duty is a question for the jury. In deciding this, the jury should consider all relevant matters. However, s.8 highlights several issues. Section 8(2) provides that the jury must consider whether the evidence shows that the organisation failed to comply with any health and safety legislation that relates to the alleged breach and, if so, (a) how serious that failure was; and (b) how much of a risk of death it posed. Section 8(3) provides that the jury may also: (a) consider the extent to which the evidence shows that there were attitudes, policies, systems or accepted practices within the organisation that were likely to have encouraged any such failure as is mentioned in s.8(2), or to have produced tolerance of it; and (b) have regard to any health and safety guidance that relates to the alleged breach.

Section 9 allows a court to make a remedial order requiring a breach of s.1(1) to be remedied. Section 10 allows a court to order a convicted organisation to publicise the conviction in a specified manner. This may prove to have a significant deterrent effect.

It is not possible for an individual to be guilty of aiding and abetting corporate manslaughter. An individual could however be guilty of the common law offence of manslaughter by gross negligence. The fact that a company has been convicted of corporate manslaughter does not preclude another prosecution under other health and safety legislation.

16.3 THE CORPORATE VEIL

We have seen that a company has a legal identity of its own. A natural consequence of this is that only the company itself can be liable in respect of a wrong done by the company. The owners of the company will normally be free of any liability. They are said to be protected by the 'veil of incorporation'. This metaphor regards the company's artificial legal personality as a veil, which separates the company and the members of the company.

As we have already seen, this idea is very well established. But there are circumstances in which a court or a statute will lift the corporate veil so that the members of the company are not protected by the company's artificial legal personality. The law in this area was thoroughly reviewed by the Court of Appeal in the following case.

Adams v Cape Industries plc
[1991] 1 All ER 929 (Court of Appeal)

The defendants were two associated English companies which owned South African companies and an American company. The South African companies mined asbestos and the American company marketed the asbestos in the United States. The American company was successfully sued by 250 claimants who had been injured by asbestos marketed in the United States by the American company. Having gained judgment in the United States, the claimants sought to enforce these judgments in the United Kingdom against the two defendants. (The American company had gone into liquidation.) This claim depended upon the defendant companies having been present in the United States when proceedings were commenced. The judge held that the presence of the defendants' subsidiary American company could not be regarded as the presence of the defendant companies themselves.

Held. The corporate veil could not be lifted. The presence of the subsidiary could not be treated as the presence of the defendant companies. There was no reason why the defendant companies should not use their corporate structure to ensure that liabilities fell on subsidiary companies rather than on themselves. The defendants and the subsidiary company could not be treated as one economic unit even if the subsidiary had been set up to reduce tortious liability in the United States.

Adams v Cape Industries plc is regarded as the leading case on lifting the corporate veil because the court considered in some detail the possible circumstances in which the veil might be lifted. First, the idea that groups of companies might be regarded as one single economic unit was regarded as generally very unlikely. Members of the public might think it quite wrong that companies could use subsidiary companies to absolve themselves of risk but, in general, subsidiary companies would be treated as separate legal entities with separate

legal rights and liabilities. However, the wording of a statute or a contract might allow a court to treat a parent company and a subsidiary as one economic unit for some purposes. Second, there is a well-accepted exception where a subsidiary company is a mere façade or sham. *Jones v Lipman* [1962] 1 WLR 832 provides an example. Lipman had sold some land but wanted to escape from the contract. He therefore transferred the land to a company in which he owned nearly all of the shares. The court regarded the company as a mere façade and made an order of specific performance against both Lipman and the company. The subsidiary was not a mere façade or sham in *Cape*, and the court seemed to regard the parent company as able to arrange its affairs in whatever way best reduced potential liability. Third, an argument that subsidiaries acted as agents of their parent companies was thought very unlikely to succeed unless there was an express agreement to this effect. Fourth, it is possible that the veil might be lifted 'in the interests of justice' but it was very hard to find cases where this had actually happened. Fifth, the court recognised that the veil could be lifted in cases of impropriety, as happened in *Jones v Lipman* and in the following case.

Gilford Motor Co Ltd v Horne
[1933] Ch 935 (Court of Appeal)

Mr Horne was employed as managing director of GMC Ltd. In his contract of employment Horne agreed that, after leaving GMC, he would not solicit its customers. When his contract was terminated Horne did begin to solicit GMC's customers. He knew that GMC would not allow him to get away with this, so he formed a company, the sole purpose of which was to employ him while he continued to solicit the customers. Horne's defence, when sued by GMC, was that his promise in his contract of employment was binding only on himself, not on the new company.

Held. An injunction was granted preventing either Horne or the company from soliciting GMC's customers.

Hanworth MR: 'I am quite satisfied that this company was formed as a device, a stratagem, in order to mask the effective carrying on of a business of Mr E. B. Horne. The purpose of it was to try to enable him, under what is a cloak or a sham, to engage in business ... in respect of which he had a fear that the plaintiffs might intervene and object.'

The idea that a subsidiary company was a mere façade was again considered in **Creasey v Breachwood**

Motors Ltd (1992) BCC 638. The manager of a company, Breachwood Motors Ltd, was dismissed and wanted to bring a claim of wrongful dismissal against the company. To avoid liability, the controllers of the company transferred all the assets of the company to another company which they controlled, Breachwood Welwyn Ltd, and then had Breachwood Motors Ltd struck off the register of companies. It was held that the manager could pursue his claim directly against Breachwood Welwyn Ltd. In the following case this decision was held to be wrong by the Court of Appeal.

Ord and another v Belhaven Pubs
(1998) BCC 607 (Court of Appeal)

The claimants took a 20-year lease from the defendant company in 1989. In 1991 the claimants sued, alleging misrepresentation and breach of warranty. In 1997 the action was still continuing and the claimants asked to substitute the defendant's holding company for the defendant company as the defendant company no longer had substantial assets owing to restructuring of the group of companies between 1992 and 1995.

Held. The holding company could not be substituted for the defendant company as the defendant company was not a mere façade for the holding company. No facts had been concealed, all the transactions had been overt and no fraud had been alleged. The companies had operated as trading companies without any sham or ulterior motive. To make the holding company liable would be at odds with the decision of **Salomon v Salomon & Co Ltd**. The claimants could not bring themselves within any principle which would allow the corporate veil to be pierced.

COMMENT Hobhouse LJ, giving the only judgment of the Court of Appeal, said: 'But it seems to me inescapable that the case in **Creasey v Breachwood** as it appears to the court cannot be sustained. It represents a wrong adoption of the principle of piercing the corporate veil and an issue of the power ... to substitute one party for the other following death or succession. Therefore in my judgment the case of **Creasey v Breachwood** should no longer be treated as authoritative.' He did not accept that there had been asset stripping in *Creasey*. If, in *Creasey*, there had been impropriety in the restructuring of the group then s.423 of the Insolvency Act 1986 (examined in Chapter 19 at 19.1.4.3) could have provided a remedy.

The veil can be lifted if the company can be regarded as an enemy in time of war. Also, it may be lifted so that quasi-partnership companies can be wound up as partnerships rather than as companies. In *Ebrahimi* v *Westbourne Galleries* [1972] 2 All ER 492, for example, the House of Lords wound up a small company on the just and equitable ground by treating it as if it were a partnership. The business had originally been a partnership and was founded on a personal relationship. (The circumstances in which a partnership can be wound up by a court order were examined in Chapter 15 at 15.9.3.)

Various statutory provisions may lift the veil. For example, the Income and Corporation Taxes Act 1988 will not allow a company to escape UK tax by registering itself abroad, if the management and control of the company is exercised within the United Kingdom. In addition, s.214 of the Insolvency Act 1986 allows a court to make directors liable for wrongful trading (a matter considered in Chapter 19 at 19.1.4.1). This liability arises only in respect of the liquidation of insolvent companies where directors have continued to run the company when they knew, or should have known, that there was no reasonable prospect of avoiding insolvency. Directors cannot become liable for wrongful trading unless they have been negligent, but if they have been negligent they can become liable to make such contribution to the company's assets as the court thinks proper. We shall see in this chapter, at 16.3.1, that the directors of public companies can become liable on transactions made by the company while the share capital requirements set out in s.761 have not been complied with. Strictly speaking, these matters are not a lifting of the corporate veil because when the veil is lifted it is the members who become liable. In many cases, however, the directors will also be members of the company.

Test your understanding 16.1

1 Is it true to state that a company has a separate legal identity of its own, or is this merely a matter of convenience?

2 What is meant by limited liability in the context of limited companies?

3 What is meant by perpetual succession?

4 Can a company itself own property and make contracts?

5 Can a company commit a crime which requires a *mens rea*?

6 What is meant by the corporate veil? In what circumstances can the veil be lifted?

16.4 CLASSIFICATION OF COMPANIES

Companies can be classified in several different ways, but from a business perspective only the following classifications are useful.

16.4.1 Public companies and private companies

When promoters apply to register a company the application for registration must state whether it is to be registered as a public company or a private company. (Before the 2006 Act came into force, the old-style memorandum of association was required to state this.) Public companies can offer shares and debentures for sale to the public and these shares can be listed on a stock market such as the London Stock Exchange. There is no requirement that shares should be listed. In fact, only the securities of some 2 000 public companies are listed, as it is a requirement of the Listing Rules that a class of listed shares must have a minimum value and only the largest public companies can comply with this requirement. The securities of many more public companies are bought and sold on the Alternative Investment Market, where there is no requirement as to the minimum value of the class of shares in question. The articles of private companies usually restrict the sale of the companies' shares. The most common restrictions are either that the shares must first be offered to other members of the company, or that the shares can only be sold to persons of whom the directors approve. Whatever the articles of association might say, a private company must not offer shares or debentures to members of the public (s.755 of the 2006 Act). Doing so is no longer a criminal offence. However, if a private company proposes to offer shares or debentures to members of the public any company member, or the Secretary of State, can get a prohibition order to prevent the offer. If the sale has already been completed, the court can order the company to re-register as a public company, as long as the company meets the financial requirements of a public company. Alternatively, it can make a remedial order or wind the company up. In addition, any company member, or the Secretary of State, can apply for a remedial order, which has the effect of undoing the transaction (ss.757–759).

Public companies cannot be unlimited companies whereas private companies can. Private companies do not have a lower limit on the amount of contributed capital. A public company must have an allotted share capital of £50 000, or the equivalent amount in Euros, (that is to say, at least £50 000 of shares must have been allotted to members) and a quarter of the value of each share must have been paid up before the company is allowed to conduct any business or borrow any money. The company must therefore have £12 500 contributed capital and a right to call a further £37 500. Section 761 of the Act prevents the issue of a certificate to commence business until a director or the company secretary has sent a form to the Registrar of Companies, stating that the allotted share capital is at least £50 000. If such a certificate is not obtained within one year of incorporation, then an application can be made for a compulsory winding up of the company. Furthermore, s.767(3) provides that if a company enters into a transaction in contravention of s.761, and fails to comply with its obligations arising under the transaction within 21 days of being called upon to do so, the directors of the company are jointly and severally liable to the other contracting party in respect of any loss or damage caused by the company's failure to comply with the obligations in question. In addition, s.767(1) provides that if a company does business or exercises any borrowing powers in contravention of s.761, both the company and every company officer who is in default commits an offence. Payment for shares allotted by a public company must either be in cash or the assets given as payment must be valued. This valuation must be done by a person qualified to act as an auditor of the company, or by someone appointed by a person qualified to act as an auditor of the company.

The names of public companies must end with the words 'public limited company' or its abbreviation, 'plc'. The name of a private limited company must end with the word 'limited' or its abbreviation, 'Ltd'.

Public companies must have at least two directors. Before October 2009 public companies also needed to have at least two members. However, this is no longer the case and a public company, like a private company, can have only one member. The company will also need a company secretary, who must be suitably qualified. By suitably qualified it is meant that he must be a lawyer or an accountant, or have been the secretary of a public company for at least three of the previous five years. The company secretary of a public company may also hold office as a director. There is no requirement that a private company has a company secretary.

Private companies have, in the past decade or so, become increasingly deregulated. Since the 2006 Act came into force, the default position is that the members of a private company do not need to hold an Annual General Meeting, and that resolutions of the members will be passed by the written resolution procedure, without the need to actually hold a meeting. (These matters are considered in detail in Chapter 18.) Public companies must hold an Annual General Meeting at least once each calendar year and cannot pass resolutions other than at company meetings.

There are other minor differences between public and private companies, but Table 16.1 shows the major differences.

Although public companies, such as Marks and Spencer and ICI, make up only about 0.6 per cent of all companies, they tend to be very much larger than most private companies. The assets of the 0.6 per cent of companies which are public would far outweigh the assets of the 99.4 per cent of companies which are private.

It is possible for a public company to re-register as a private one and vice versa. If this is successfully done then a new certificate of incorporation will be issued. Section 97 allows a public company to re-register as a private company by passing a special resolution. (A special resolution would only be passed if three-quarters of company members who vote on the resolution vote in favour.) The company must make such changes to its name and articles as the circumstances require. The application for re-registration must contain a copy of the special resolution, a copy of the amended articles and a statement of compliance, indicating that the requirements for re-registration have been complied with. Section 98 allows shareholders who hold at least 5 per cent of the nominal value of the plc's issued share capital or any class of share capital, or any 50 members of the plc, to apply for a court order cancelling the special resolution as long as they did not vote in favour of it. The application must be made within 28 days, and the court can either confirm the resolution, or cancel it. This safeguard is necessary because shareholders in the company may find their shares very difficult to sell once the company has become a private company. Section 109 allows a public company to re-register as an unlimited company, but only if all of the members agree to this and the company has not previously been re-registered as limited or unlimited. Section 90

allows a private limited company to re-register as a public company by passing a special resolution. The company will also need to make such changes to its articles and its name as are necessary in connection with becoming a public limited company. In addition, the company will need to fulfil the following requirements. First, the company will have to fulfil the share capital requirements which apply to plcs. Second, it will need to produce both a balance sheet and an auditor's report which show that the amount of the company's net assets is not less than the aggregate of its called-up share capital and undistributable reserves of capital. Third, if the private company had no company secretary, its application for re-registration must make a statement giving particulars of the person who is to be the suitably qualified secretary of the plc. Fourth, the application for re-registration must contain a statement of compliance, the proposed name of the plc, a statement of the proposed company secretary (where appropriate), a copy of the special resolution, a copy of the amended company articles and a copy of the required balance sheet and auditor's report. If the Registrar is satisfied that the company is entitled to be re-registered he issues the company with a certificate of incorporation stating that the company is a public company. (He would not be satisfied if the company did not have at least two directors.) Whenever a company is re-registered, a £20 fee is payable, or a £50 fee for same day re-registration.

16.4.2 **Limited and unlimited companies**

16.4.2.1 **Unlimited companies**

Fewer than half of 1 per cent of companies are registered as unlimited companies. These companies do have a legal personality distinct from that of the company members, but the members have agreed with the company that they will have unlimited liability for the debts of the company. This liability only arises if the company is wound up; it is not direct liability to creditors of the company. But if the company, on winding up, has insufficient assets to pay all of its debts the members of an unlimited company will have unlimited liability to supply the company with money so that it can pay its debts. If the company has a share capital, the liability of members to contribute to the debts of the company, and to the costs of winding up, is in proportion to the nominal value of the shares

Table 16.1 Differences between public and private companies

Public companies	Private companies
Name must end with the words 'Public Limited Company' or 'plc'	Name must end with 'Limited' or 'Ltd' (unless the company is unlimited)
Must have £50 000 allotted share capital, or Euro equivalent, one quarter of which must be paid up	No limit on share capital
Shares can be listed on stock exchange (no requirement that they should be listed)	Shares cannot be listed on stock exchange, or advertised for sale
Must have at least two directors	Need have only one director
Shares allotted by the company must be paid for in cash (or qualified auditor must value assets given as payment)	Shares can be given away by the company
Must have a company secretary, who must be suitably qualified	No need to have a company secretary. If there is one, does not need to be qualified.
Must hold AGM every calendar year	No AGM unless positive decision taken to hold one
Cannot pass written resolutions	Can pass written resolutions

held. If there is no share capital then the members are obliged to contribute equally. If one member is unable to pay his share, the other members assume liability to pay it.

The names of unlimited companies must not contain the words 'limited' or 'Ltd'. Public companies may not register as unlimited companies.

Unlimited companies enjoy some advantages over limited companies. For example, their accounts need not be published or delivered to the Registrar of Companies, and it is possible to repay capital to members without following a statutory procedure. However, these advantages have become increasingly insignificant as companies have become deregulated. The advantages are generally considered to be far outweighed by the unlimited liability of the members, and very few unlimited companies are nowadays created. Throughout this book reference to a company should be taken as reference to a limited company.

16.4.2.2 **Limited companies**

Limited companies can themselves be classified into two types.

Companies limited by shares

The vast majority of companies are limited by shares. As we have seen, this means that in the event of liquidation a member's liability is limited to paying off any amount unpaid on his shares. Each share must be for a fixed amount, known as the 'nominal' value or the 'par' value. A person who takes a share from a company agrees to pay the nominal value of the share to the

company. In addition, the shareholder may agree with the company that he will pay an additional amount, known as a premium.

The board of directors can pass a resolution to create new shares and to allot these to new or existing members. Section 561 of the 2006 Act requires that any newly allotted shares are first offered to existing members who hold ordinary shares, in proportion to the nominal value of shares which they already hold. This is to protect existing members from having their percentage ownership of the company's shares diluted by the issue of new shares.

Until October 2009, the total amount of the shares which a company could issue had to be stated in the old-style memorandum of association, which had to be registered with the Registrar of Companies when the company was formed. This amount was known as the 'authorised' share capital, the 'nominal' capital or the 'registered' capital. The 2006 Act has abolished the requirement to have an authorised share capital. The old-style memorandum also had to state the total number of shares issued and the nominal value of each. For example, Ace Ltd might have been registered as a company with an authorised share capital of £10 000, made up of 10 000 shares with a nominal value of £1 each. It should be borne in mind that the nominal value of the shares might well not reflect the true value of the shares. Provisions contained in an old-style memorandum of association have as from October 2009, been put into the articles of association. However, existing companies have not needed to do this immediately. The Government has proposed that there will be transitional provisions which will apply until companies have amended their articles. Under these transitional provisions, existing companies which have not put the provisions of their old-style memorandum into the articles will not be allowed to allot shares beyond the authorised share capital set out in the memorandum.

Often shares are in fact worth more than their nominal value and sometimes those taking shares agree with the company that they will pay an additional amount on each share, known as a share premium. When a share is sold at a premium, the company can enforce the contract it has made with a member and insist that any amount owing, as regards either the nominal value of issued shares or the share premium, must be paid. However, if the company goes into liquidation, only the amount owing on the nominal value of the issued shares must be paid. The share premium is a matter between the company and the members.

Example

Ace Ltd has a share capital of £100. There are 100 shares, each having a nominal value of £1. X took 50 shares when the company was formed. Y was later issued with the other 50 shares, and agreed to pay a premium of £5 per share. Both members have paid only 20p per share so far. Ace Ltd can call upon X to pay the 80p per share which he has not yet paid and call upon Y to pay the £5.80 per share which he has not yet paid. If the company went into liquidation before X and Y had paid more than 20p per share, the liquidator could only require each member to pay the remaining 80p of each share's nominal value.

The original members of the company, the subscribers to the memorandum, must take at least one share each. The new-style memorandum of association must show how many shares each subscriber has taken. Section 28, which came into effect in October 2009, provides that other matters which used to be in the old-style memorandum, but which do not need to be in the new-style memorandum, will be treated as provisions of the articles. (The memorandum and articles are considered below at 16.5.) The subscribers to the memorandum are the original members of the company. We have already seen that a public company must have at least £50 000 allotted share capital, but that there is no such requirement for a private company.

When shares are transferred from one member to another, the new holder of the shares takes over the rights and obligations attaching to the shares.

Companies limited by guarantee

The liability of members of companies limited by guarantee is limited to paying an amount which they have agreed to contribute in payment of the company's debts in the event of the company being wound up. This amount is usually small, typically £5, and is spelled out in the application for registration as a company. It may also be included in the articles of association. A company limited by guarantee has no right to ask for the amount guaranteed while the company is a going concern. If the amount guaranteed by those who are members at the time of liquidation is insufficient to pay the debts of the company, the liquidator can ask those who have ceased to be members within one year to pay the amount they guaranteed. However, these ex-members can only be asked to contribute in so far as this is necessary to cover liabilities which arose while they were members.

Before the Companies Act 1980, a company could be registered as limited by shares and by guarantee, in which case the members were liable to pay both the amount guaranteed and the amount unpaid on their shares. Some such companies, formed before 22 December 1980, continue to exist and are known as hybrid companies. However, since that date a newly formed company must either be registered as limited by shares or be limited by guarantee.

Most companies limited by guarantee are educational or charitable. Guarantee companies are not a suitable medium for trading companies. Public companies cannot be limited solely by guarantee, even if they were formed before 22 December 1980. They must always have a share capital of at least £50 000.

16.4.3 Method of creation

Companies can be created by registration under the Companies Acts, by statute, or by Royal Charter.

16.4.3.1 By registration under the Companies Acts

Almost all companies currently in existence were created by registration under the Companies Acts. Registration is quick and cheap, and it is generally understood that when people speak of a company this is the type of company which they mean. The process of registration is considered below at 16.5.

16.4.3.2 **By statute**

When most of the public utilities (such as the gas, electricity and water boards) were set up they needed special powers to enable them to compulsorily purchase land, and to prevent competition. These powers could only be granted by Parliament and so the companies were created by various statutes. When the utilities were nationalised, by other Acts of Parliament, they became corporations. Many of these utilities have now been privatised. In effect, this means that other statutes have changed their status so that they became registered public limited companies.

16.4.3.3 **By Royal Charter**

A company can be created by Royal Charter. The Hudson's Bay Company was given its Royal Charter by King Charles II. Unless created a very long time ago, such companies will not be trading companies. It is far easier to register under the Companies Act than to gain a Royal Charter.

If an institution is granted a Royal Charter, this is usually seen as conferring a special prestige. The BBC, Oxford and Cambridge Universities, the Law Society and the Institute of Chartered Accountants were all created by Royal Charter.

16.4.3.4 **Corporations sole**

Certain types of office or position are regarded as having a legal personality of their own and are known as corporations sole because only one person could hold that office at any particular time. Bishops, for example, are regarded as corporations sole. Other types of corporation are known as corporations aggregate. The Public Trustee, a civil service position, is a corporation sole. This is convenient, as the corporation can become the legal holder of the land with which the Public Trustee has to deal. It was similarly convenient, historically, for bishops to be capable of holding the legal title to church land. Single member companies, which are considered immediately below, are not regarded as corporations sole.

16.4.3.5 **Single member companies**

The 2006 Act allows both private and public companies to have only one member. New companies can be created with only one subscriber to the memorandum, or an existing company can allow its membership to fall to one. If the membership of an existing company falls to one, then s.123(2) requires that a statement that this has happened be entered into the company's register of members, along with the date on which the company became a company with only one member. Conversely, if the membership of a single member company increases, then s.123(3) requires a statement that this has happened to be entered into the company's register of members, along with the date when this happened.

As we have seen, private companies no longer need to hold an Annual General Meeting or need to lay accounts before a general meeting. Single member companies are most unlikely to hold a meeting. The written resolution procedure allows the single member of a company to pass resolutions without holding a meeting. (Written resolutions are considered in Chapter 18 at 18.4.1.) If a single member company makes a contract with the single member, no formalities are required as long as the contract is made in the ordinary course of business. However, in other circumstances s.231 requires the terms of the contract to be written, or set out in a written memorandum, or recorded in the minutes of the first board meeting held after the contract was made. Failure to do this will not invalidate the contract but it will mean that every company officer who is in default will commit a criminal offence.

16.4.4 **Small companies**

Companies which can be classified as small can submit abbreviated accounts to the Registrar of Companies, although full accounts will still have to be delivered to the members. (This matter is examined in the following chapter at 17.6.2.) In addition, certain small companies are exempt from having to have their accounts audited (see 17.3.1).

Section 382 defines small companies. A company is regarded as a small company if it meets two out of the following three requirements:

(i) The company's annual turnover is £5.6 million or less.

(ii) The total assets of the company are £2.8 million or less.

(iii) The company has 50 or fewer employees.

16.4.5 European Public Limited-Liability Companies

A European Public Limited-Liability Company can be registered in the EU Member State in which it has its head office. Such a company is known as an SE (*Societas Europaea*). Once formed, an SE has to be treated by all Member States as if it were a plc registered in that Member State. SEs are formed in the same way as plcs, except that they must be formed by an existing SE (as a subsidiary) or by existing companies, at least two of which are registered in different Member States. SEs must either begin or end their name with the abbreviation SE. For this reason, companies created after 8 October 2004, and which are not SEs, may not use the abbreviation SE in their name.

Test your understanding 16.2

1 What are the main differences between public companies and private companies?

2 Is an unlimited company regarded by the law as having a legal personality of its own?

3 What is a share premium?

4 What is the liability of the members of a company which is limited by guarantee?

5 Almost all companies are created by registration under the Companies Acts. In what other ways is it possible for a company to be created?

6 What is a corporation sole?

16.5 FORMATION OF REGISTERED COMPANIES

16.5.1 Registration under the Companies Act 2006

A registered company is formed by promoters, who must pay a fee and register certain documents with the Registrar of Companies. If the Registrar is satisfied with the documents, he will issue a certificate of incorporation, and the company will then exist as a corporate body.

The rate of incorporation of new companies has increased by over 60 per cent since 1997. A World Bank Survey conducted in 2006 found that it was easier and cheaper to form a company in the United Kingdom than in any other EU country. Companies House claims to be registering 120 new companies every working hour. The Government encourages this growth in the number of companies, as it believes that this makes the United Kingdom a more attractive place in which to do business.

In October 2009 the process for registering a company changed. Companies which registered before October 2009 used a different procedure. Companies which were registered under the old procedure will not need to re-register. Almost all companies currently in existence were registered under the old procedure. It is therefore necessary to describe that old procedure and the legal effect of the old-style memorandum and articles of association which had to be registered under the old procedure. First, the new registration procedure is described.

16.5.1.1 The new-style memorandum of association

A company is formed by one or more persons subscribing their names to a memorandum of association and by complying with the 2006 Act's registration requirements.

A company may not be formed for an unlawful purpose. It is not the case that a purpose must involve the commission of a criminal offence or a tort to be regarded as unlawful. For example, it is not a criminal offence to trade as a prostitute but in *R v Registrar of Companies, ex parte Attorney General* [1991] BCLC 476 it was held that the Registrar did not have to register a company set up to engage in prostitution. If the Registrar refuses to register a company then this decision can be challenged by judicial review. (Judicial review is examined in Chapter 2 at 2.6.1.)

The new style of memorandum is quite different from the old style of memorandum (considered below at 16.5.3.) It merely states that the subscribers, the people who sign it, wish to form a company under the Act and that they agree to become members of the company by taking at least one share each. This memorandum will not be capable of being changed later. It gives a 'historical snapshot' of the company members on formation of the company. It does seem somewhat unfortunate that the registration document is called a memorandum of association. This is bound to cause confusion between it and an old-style memorandum, which was an altogether different type of document. It might have been better to call a new-style memorandum something different, perhaps 'registration document' or 'incorporation document'.

16.5.1.2 **New-style registration documents**

Section 9(1) provides that the memorandum of association must be sent to the Registrar together with an application for registration of the company, the documents which s.9 requires and a statement of compliance. A £20 fee is also payable.

Section 9(2) requires that the **application for registration** must state:

(a) the company's proposed name;

(b) whether the company's registered office is to be situated in England and Wales (or in Wales), in Scotland or in Northern Ireland;

(c) whether the liability of the members of the company is to be limited, and if so whether it is to be limited by shares or guarantee; and

(d) whether the company is to be a public company or a private company.

Sections 9(4) and(5) also require the application to contain:

(a) a statement of share capital and initial shareholdings, or a statement of guarantee if the company is to be limited by guarantee;

(b) a statement of the company's proposed officers;

(c) a statement of the intended address of the company's registered office; and

(d) a statement of any proposed articles of association, to the extent that default articles are not being used.

The application must be delivered to the Registrar of Companies, along with the memorandum of association.

A company can change its address within its jurisdiction by giving notice in the prescribed form to the Registrar of Companies. The Registrar will publish notice of the altered address in the *Gazette*. The address of a company's registered office is particularly important because under s.1139 a person can serve a document on the company by leaving it at, or sending it by post to, the registered office.

The **statement of capital and initial shareholdings** is required by s.10(2) to state the following:

(a) the total number of shares to be taken on formation by the subscribers to the memorandum;

(b) the aggregate nominal value of those shares;

(c) for each class of shares –

    (i) prescribed particulars of the rights attached to the shares;

    (ii) the total number of shares of that class; and

    (iii) the aggregate nominal value of shares of that class; and

(d) the amount to be paid up and the amount (if any) to be unpaid on each share (whether on account of the nominal value of the share or by way of premium).

If the company has more than one class of shares then this information must be given in respect of each class of shares.

A **statement of guarantee** is necessary only if the company is limited by guarantee. It must identify the guarantors who subscribe to the memorandum and state what contribution they have each agreed to make. These contributions are payable if the company is wound up while a guarantor is a member or within a year of his ceasing to be a member.

The **statement of proposed officers** must give the names and addresses of the first directors and the first company secretary (if the company is to have a company secretary). The statement must also include such information as would be required to be in the register of directors, the register of directors' residential addresses and in the register of company secretaries. The residential addresses of directors will not be disclosed. Directors can give a service address, which can be the address of the company's registered office. The need for this arose because pressure groups, such as those involved in animal liberation, had discovered the addresses of directors of companies involved in vivisection and targeted them personally. Unless a director gives permission, his residential address is not to be disclosed to anyone except the Registrar. Also, the Registrar must omit directors' residential addresses from material that is available for public inspection. However, the Registrar can communicate a director's residential address to public authorities or in compliance with a court order.

The statement must also contain a consent by each person named as a director or secretary to act in the relevant capacity. Upon registration they are deemed to have been appointed.

The **statement of compliance** merely states that the Act's requirements as to registration have been complied with. All of the requirements relating to formation of a company can be complied with by filling in a form, Form IN01, which can be downloaded free from the Companies House web site.

If the Registrar is satisfied that the requirements of the Act have been complied with he registers the documents delivered to him and issues a certificate of incorporation.

16.5.1.3 The effect of registration

A **certificate of incorporation** is conclusive evidence that the requirements of registration have been complied with and that the company has been duly registered under the Act.

Section 15(2) provides that the certificate must state –

(a) the name and registered number of the company;
(b) the date of its incorporation;
(c) whether it is a limited or unlimited company, and if it is limited whether it is limited by shares or limited by guarantee;
(d) whether it is a private or a public company; and
(e) whether the company's registered office is situated in England and Wales (or in Wales), in Scotland or in Northern Ireland.

From the date of incorporation, the company is capable of exercising all the powers of a registered company. The subscribers to the memorandum become members of the company and become holders of the shares set out in the statement of capital and initial shareholdings. The proposed directors and secretary are deemed to have been appointed.

16.5.2 Old-style registration

Companies which registered before the 2006 Act new-style registration came into force will not need to re-register. Obviously, for some years to come almost all companies will have completed an old-style registration. This has important consequences for the constitution of those companies. Therefore, it is necessary to know the procedure required for an old-style registration.

Under the old-style registration the documents which had to be sent to the Registrar were:

(1) The company's memorandum of association.
(2) The company's articles of association.
(3) A statement giving the names of the company's first directors and of the company secretary. (Companies House issued a form, Form 10, on which this information had to be set out.)

(4) A statement that all the statutory requirements of registration had been complied with. (Again, Companies House issued a form on which this statement had to be made, Form 12.)

If the company was to be registered in either England or Wales, the documents had to be sent to the Registrar of Companies in Cardiff. A £20 fee for registration was payable.

The Registrar had to issue a certificate of incorporation if satisfied that all the requirements had been complied with.

16.5.3 Old-style memorandum of association

An old-style memorandum of association was of considerable importance. The constitution of a company registered before the 2006 Act came into force was contained in its memorandum and articles of association. The memorandum set out the structure of the company. Those who did business with a company had constructive notice of the company's memorandum. This notice arose because the memorandum of a company was a registered document which was available for inspection.

Section 2 of the Companies Act 1985 stated that the memorandum of a company limited by shares had to contain five obligatory clauses.

16.5.3.1 The company name (Clause 1)

This clause set out the rules relating to the name of the company. These rules have not been changed by the 2006 Act and are considered below at 16.9.

16.5.3.2 The registered office (Clause 2)

This clause had to state whether the company's registered office was in England and Wales, Wales or Scotland. The address did not need to be given here because it had to be declared in Form 10.

16.5.3.3 The objects (Clause 3)

The objects clause stated the purposes for which the company was being formed and set out the contractual capacity of the company. (That is to say, it set out the contracts which the company could validly make.) At common law any contract which a company makes is *ultra vires* and therefore void if in making the contract the company acts in excess of its contractual capacity, as defined by the objects clause. For this reason most companies tended to have extremely long objects clauses, often running to several pages. Such clauses became unnecessary as long ago as 1985, when s.3A Companies Act 1985 allowed a company to register its objects as to carry on business as a general commercial company. As we shall see, below at 17.1.8.1, s.31(1) of the 2006 Act states that unless a company's articles specifically restrict the objects of the company, its objects are unrestricted. However, many companies may choose specifically to restrict the objects of the company. The problems caused by the *ultra vires* rule, and the extent to which these problems have been resolved, are considered more fully in Chapter 17 at 17.1.8.

16.5.3.4 Limited liability (Clause 4)

If the liability of the members was to be limited then this clause had to state that this was the case.

16.5.3.5 Share capital (Clause 5)

The company had to state the amount of share capital with which it was to be registered and the way in which this capital was to be divided into shares. For example, a company might have stated that it had a share capital of £100, divided into 100 shares of £1 each. This authorised share capital was the maximum amount of shares which a company could validly issue. However, as from October 2009 the 2006 Act abolished the concept of authorised share capital.

16.5.3.6 Additional clauses

As well as the five compulsory clauses, there could have been additional clauses. If an additional clause was stated to be unalterable, then it could not be altered by the members. This is not the case now because s.28(1) of the 2006 Act provides that all provisions of an old-style memorandum, except the basic provisions which would need to be contained in a new-style memorandum, are to be treated as provisions of the company's articles. The articles of a company can generally be altered by a special resolution of the members. However, as from October 2009 some articles may be entrenched. Such articles can be altered only by a specified procedure which is more onerous than the passing of a special resolution, as we shall see below at 16.6.1.1.

The memorandum also had to have an association and subscription clause. Those who signed the association clause indicated that they wished to be formed into a company and that they agreed to take shares in the company. The subscription clause indicated how many shares each subscriber was taking.

16.6 THE CONSTITUTION OF A COMPANY

Before the 2006 Act came into force, a company's constitution, generally regarded as its old-style memorandum and articles, was not defined by statute.

Section 17 of the 2006 Act now provides that a company's constitution includes the company's articles of association and certain types of resolutions. Other matters can be included in the constitution. For example, a company's incorporation certificate will state whether the company is public or private and will therefore be constitutionally relevant.

Shareholder agreements, considered in Chapter 18 at 18.5.3, are not part of a company's constitution.

16.6.1 The articles of association

The articles of association are the rules of the company and they bind both the company and the members of the company. (This is considered more fully in Chapter 18 at 18.5.) Before the 2006 Act came into force, the rules of the company could be found in the memorandum and the articles. The articles were the internal rules of the company, whereas the memorandum set out the structure of the company. People dealing with the company were deemed to have constructive notice of the company's memorandum. As we have seen, as regards companies formed under the 2006 Act, the memorandum will be a mere historical snapshot giving information about the company when it was formed. The rules of the company will be set out in the articles. As regards companies formed before the 2006 Act came into force, s.28(1) provides that provisions of old-style memorandums are to be treated as provisions of the company's articles. This is the case with all provisions of old-style memorandums except those provisions which would be found in a new-style memorandum.

Section 18 provides that a company must have articles of association and that these must be contained in a single document which is divided into paragraphs which are numbered consecutively. Different types of model articles, suitable for different types of companies, have been drafted by the Secretary of State.

Section 20(1) provides that these articles will apply by default to all companies formed after 1 October 2009, unless alternative articles are registered. It also provides that if other articles are registered, the model articles will still apply to the extent that they are not excluded or modified by the articles which are registered. If a company wishes to ensure that the relevant model articles will not apply at all, it should include an article which specifically excludes the model articles. The model articles are designed to allow companies to be formed and do business even if they have not registered suitable articles. Existing companies will not be subject to the new default articles, although they will be able to adopt them either wholly or partially. If a company was registered using the old Table A model articles, which could be adopted before the 2006 Act came into force, they will continue to be governed by Table A.

Section 25 provides that an alteration of the articles which increases the liability of a member since he became a member is invalid against that member unless he has given express written consent to it.

16.6.1.1 Amendment of articles

Section 21(1) provides that a company's articles may generally be amended by special resolution. Case law has established that a company's articles cannot remove this right to alter the articles. However, s.22(1) allows the articles to contain 'provision for entrenchment'. Under such a provision certain **entrenched articles** can be amended or repealed only if conditions are met, or procedures complied with, that are more restrictive than those applicable in the case of a special resolution. The Act does not specify what these conditions might be. However, since a special resolution can be passed only by a 75 per cent majority of those voting on it, the procedures might require procedures such as a unanimous vote or a vote passed by a 90 per cent majority of all company members. Section 22(2) provides that provision for entrenchment can be made only in the company's articles on formation, or by an amendment of the articles agreed to by all the members of the company.

It is not possible to make entrenched articles unalterable. Section 22(3) provides that provision for entrenchment does not prevent alteration of the company's articles by agreement of all the members of a company or by court order. Where a company's articles are amended so as to include or remove provision for entrenchment, s.23 requires the company to give notice of this to the Registrar. Where a company's articles are subject to provision for entrenchment, and the company amends its articles, s.24 requires that a document showing the amendment be sent to the Registrar along with a statement of compliance. This statement will certify that the amendment has been made in accordance with the company's articles. So both the Registrar and any person searching the public register of companies will be able to see whether or not any articles are entrenched and, if they are, how they can be altered.

Before the 2006 Act came into force articles could not be entrenched. They could always have been altered by special resolution. However, provisions which might have been in the articles could have been made unalterable by putting them in the old-style memorandum and stating that they were unalterable.

Whenever a company's articles are amended, whether there is provision for entrenchment or not, s.26(1) provides that the company must send the Registrar a copy of the amended articles within 15 days of the amendment taking effect. If a company does not send altered articles or a document making an alteration in the articles as required, the Registrar can demand compliance within 28 days. If this is not forthcoming, the company is liable to a civil penalty of £200 and may also be liable to prosecution. The officers and the company are also liable to a daily default fine if they continue to fail to send the articles in their altered state. The Registrar must notify the *Gazette* of the receipt of any document which makes or evidences an alteration of a company's articles.

If an authority to give, vary, revoke or renew authority to allot shares is given by ordinary resolution, and is contrary to a provision in the articles, the articles will then be regarded as having been altered even though no special resolution has been passed (s.551(8)).

If something cannot be done by a company unless the articles authorise it, then a special resolution authorising the thing will not be effective because the articles will not be impliedly changed. But if the resolution states that it is doing the thing 'notwithstanding anything in the articles' then the thing will be validly done.

Section 25(1) provides that a member is not bound by any alteration of the articles which requires him to take or subscribe for more shares, or become more liable to contribute to the company's share capital or otherwise pay money to the company, unless the member has expressly agreed to this in writing. Nothing in the articles can exclude the effect of this section.

An alteration of the articles must not include an illegal article or deprive members of rights given to them by the court.

When the members do alter the articles, they must exercise this power *bona fide* for the benefit of the members of the company as a whole, that is to say for the benefit of the company in its capacity as a separate legal person.

16.6.2 Resolutions and agreements affecting a company's constitution

Section 17 provides that a company's constitution is comprised of its articles and Chapter 3 resolutions, which are set out in s.29 of the Act:

'**Section 29 Resolutions and agreements affecting a company's constitution**
(1) This Chapter [Chapter 3] applies to –
   (a) any special resolution;
   (b) any resolution or agreement agreed to by all the members of a company that, if not so agreed to, would not have been effective for its purpose unless passed as a special resolution;
   (c) any resolution or agreement agreed to by all the members of a class of shareholders that, if not so agreed to, would not have been effective for its purpose unless passed by some particular majority or otherwise in some particular manner;
   (d) any resolution or agreement that effectively binds all members of a class of shareholders though not agreed to by all those members; ...
   (f) any other resolution or agreement to which this Chapter applies by virtue of any enactment.'

Broadly speaking, these resolutions are special resolutions, or resolutions or agreements which would have needed to have been passed as special resolutions. Section 30 requires that copies of these constitutional resolutions must be sent to the Registrar within 15 days of their being passed. Section 32 requires an up-to-date copy of the constitutional documents to be sent to members on request.

16.7 OFF-THE-SHELF COMPANIES

An alternative to the promoters themselves forming a company is for them to buy an 'off-the-shelf' company. Some businesses form companies in large numbers, in the hope that customers will wish to buy the companies. Those who form such companies register themselves as the company's first director and company secretary and take one share. Then, when a customer wishes to buy an off-the-shelf company, the share is transferred to whoever the customer nominates, and the original director and secretary resign and, having first procured the appointment of a new director and secretary, notify Companies House that they have resigned. Before the 2006 Act came into force, the risk involved in this could be substantial, in that a company's articles must be suitable for that particular company. Many businesses, in too much of a hurry to become incorporated, adopted unsuitable articles, either by buying an off-the-shelf company or by adopting Table A without considering its effect. Of course, it is always possible to alter these articles while the promoters or the creators of the company hold all the shares in it. But all too often the members were too impatient to set the company up to realise the importance of ensuring that the articles suited their needs. Promoters of off-the-shelf companies are now likely to use the new model default articles. These are far more likely to be suitable for the company than the old Table A articles. However, the purchasers of the company should still ensure that the articles are tailored to their needs.

Test your understanding 16.3

1 What documents must a promoter send to the Registrar of Companies in order to form a company?

2 Before the 2006 Act came into force, what documents had to be sent to the Registrar of Companies in order to form a company?

3 What is the significance of a certificate of incorporation being issued?

4 What will a new-style memorandum of association state?

5 What obligatory clauses did an old-style memorandum of association have to contain?

6 What is the purpose of a company's articles of association?

16.8 CONTRACTS MADE BEFORE THE COMPANY IS FORMED

A company does not come into existence until the Registrar of Companies issues its certificate of incorporation. It follows that until the certificate is issued the company has no capacity to make contracts.

However, the promoters might want to make contracts on the company's behalf in advance of incorporation. For example, if a shop intended to begin trading, as a company, on 1 September then the promoters would need to buy stock in advance of that date.

It might be thought that the easiest way to do this would be for the promoters to make the contract personally, and for the company to ratify the contract as soon as the company is formed. (A person ratifies a contract if he agrees to be bound by it after it has been made (see Chapter 11 at 11.2.6).) Such a ratification would not be effective, as *Kelner v Baxter* (1866) LR 2 CP 174, already considered in Chapter 11, shows. It might be remembered that in that case promoters of a company ordered wine on the company's behalf before the company was formed. The company was successfully formed, the company ratified the contract and the wine was consumed. The company went into liquidation before paying for the wine. The promoters were personally liable to pay for the wine, but only because the wording of their contract with the supplier would have suggested to the reasonable man that they should be liable. The ratification by the company was ineffective.

If the promoters in *Kelner v Baxter* had worded the contract in such a way that the reasonable man would not have thought that they should be personally liable on the contract then they would not have been personally liable, and the supplier of the wine would never have been paid.

Such a situation is now covered by s.51(1) of the 2006 Act, which provides:

'A contract which purports to be made by or on behalf of a company at a time when the company has not been formed has effect, subject to any agreement to the contrary, as one made with the person purporting to act for the company or as agent for it, and he is personally liable on the contract accordingly.'

Section 51(1) says that the person purporting to act on behalf of the company can be personally liable on the contract made on the company's behalf but does not state that this person can also enforce the contract

on the company's behalf. However, the section does state that the contract 'has effect' as one made with such a person. In *Braymist Ltd v Wise Finance Co Ltd* [2002] EWCA Civ 127, [2002] Ch 273 it was held that this section (which is identical to s.36C(1) of the 1985 Act) also entitles the person who made the contract on behalf of the company to enforce the contract against the other contracting party.

The Contracts (Rights of Third Parties) Act 1999, considered in Chapter 4 at 4.2.2.2, can allow companies to enforce contracts which were made before the company was formed, if the contract expressly provided that the company could enforce it or if the contract purported to confer a benefit on the company. However, the promoter who made the contract would also be liable on the contract, along with the company.

The easiest ways to get around the problem of pre-incorporation contracts would seem to be either to wait until the company is formed before getting the company to make the contract, or to make the contract as agent for an off-the-shelf company which, being in existence at the time of the contract, could ratify it later.

It will be noticed that s.51(1) applies 'subject to any agreement to the contrary'. It is therefore possible for the promoters to disclaim personal liability when they make the contract on the company's behalf. However, it would be inadvisable for the other contracting party to deal with the promoters on this basis. In effect, they would be making contracts which could be enforced against them but which they themselves might not be able to enforce.

Promoters who are personally liable on contracts made on the company's behalf can later escape personal liability by novation. This would be achieved by the company, after it is formed, making a second contract with the supplier on the same terms as the pre-incorporation contract. The supplier agrees in this contract that the promoters cease to be liable on the pre-incorporation contract in return for the company assuming liability. The novation can be made expressly or impliedly, but will be effective only if the supplier and the company agree to it.

16.8.1 Duties of promoters

Promoters of a company are fiduciaries and owe duties of loyalty and good faith to the company. So if a promoter buys property and sells it to the company at a profit he will have breached his fiduciary duty.

However, a promoter will not be liable in this way if the profit was disclosed to the company's independent board of directors and the board went ahead and bought the promoter's property. If, as is often the case, there is no board of directors to whom disclosure could be made, a promoter will escape liability by making disclosure to prospective shareholders. This would generally be done in a prospectus. If the shareholders subsequently invested in the company they would be taken to have consented to the promoter's profit and there would then be no breach of fiduciary duty.

If the promoter had acquired the property sold to the company before becoming a promoter the company can rescind the contract, unless one of the bars to rescission applies. (See Chapter 6 at 6.1.3.1.) The profit made by the promoter cannot be recovered. However, the promoter could be sued in the tort of negligence if the company had suffered a foreseeable loss, as would happen when the property was bought in excess of the market price. The promoter might also be liable for the tort of deceit or for negligent misrepresentation under s.2(1) Misrepresentation Act 1967.

If the promoter acquired the property sold to the company after he became a promoter the company can either rescind the contract, if this is possible, or recover the profit which the promoter made. The promoter will have been an agent of the company and will therefore be liable to account to the company for any profit.

There is no legal definition of a promoter which is recognised universally. The term promoter is a business one rather than a legal one. A promoter does not need to see the formation of the company through from conception of the idea to incorporation. A promoter might be involved only at some stage or other, performing tasks such as finding investors or directors, buying property for the proposed company or making business contracts on its behalf.

16.9 THE COMPANY NAME

Earlier in this chapter we saw that the promoters must include the company's proposed name in the application for registration. The name of a company is important because it is the means by which the company, a legal person, can be identified. The word 'Company' is not often included in the names of companies. Strangely, the word appears in the names of partnerships more frequently than in the names of companies. Although, in general, a company is free to choose any name it pleases there are some restrictions on the choice of name.

16.9.1 Prohibited names

Sections 53–56 prohibit the use of certain names, as follows:

(i) The Registrar will refuse to register a name the use of which would, in the opinion of the Secretary of State, constitute a criminal offence or be offensive (s.53).

(ii) Regulations made by the Secretary of State prohibit the use of certain words which suggest a connection with the Government or with local authorities. The Registrar can register such a name but permission from an appropriate body may be required. Certain other sensitive words and expressions (such as 'British', 'charity' and 'university') can be used only if the Secretary of State gives permission. The protected names are set out in the Company and Business Names Regulations 1981, as amended (ss.54–56).

Section 57 allows the Secretary of State to make regulations setting out what letters, signs, punctuation marks and symbols may or may not be used in a company name. For the purposes of registration, the regulations may also specify a standard style or format for the name of a company. So, for example, subscript and superscript might be banned.

Section 58 provides that if the company is a public company then the name must end with the words 'public limited company' or the abbreviation 'plc'. Section 59 provides that if the company is a private limited company then its name must end with the word 'limited' or the abbreviation 'Ltd'. If the company is registered in Wales, the Welsh equivalents of these words and abbreviations may be used instead. Thus, a public company with a registered office in Wales may end the company name with 'cwmni cyfyngedig cyhoeddus' or the abbreviation 'c.c.c.', instead of with 'public limited company'. A private limited company registered in Wales may end the company name with 'cyfyngedig' or the abbreviation 'cyf.' instead of with 'limited'. These specified words and abbreviations must only be used at the end of the name.

Section 65(1) allows the Secretary of State to make regulations prohibiting the use in a company name of specified words, expressions or other indications that are associated with a particular type of company or form of organisation. Similar words may also be prohibited. Section 65(2) prohibits the use in a company name of specified words, expressions or other indications in any part of a company name. The regulations may also stipulate that certain words etc. must be or cannot be used in conjunction with other words etc. (For example, the use of 'plc' or 'community interest company' might be inappropriate and prohibited by regulations made under s.65.)

Section 66(1) provides that a company must not be registered under a name which is identical to the name of another company already on the register. (It is therefore essential to check whether the proposed name has already been registered. This can be done quickly and easily by phoning Companies House or by accessing the Companies House website: www.companieshouse.gov.uk.) The Secretary of State can make regulations on: what matters may be disregarded; the extent to which words, expressions, signs and symbols are to be regarded as the same (e.g. '£' and 'Pound', '1' and 'one' etc.); and the circumstances in which otherwise prohibited names may be used.

Under s.67 of the Act the Secretary of State can order a company to change its name. Such an order can be made within 12 months of the company's registration. If misleading information was given at the time of registration, s.75 allows the Registrar to order the company to change its name within five years of registration. If the name gives such a misleading indication of the nature of the company's activities that harm is likely to be caused to the public the Registrar can order a change of name at any time (s.76(1)).

16.9.2 Objection to a company name

Section 69(1) allows any person to object to a company's registered name on the ground: (a) that it is the same as a name associated with the applicant in which he has goodwill; or (b) that it is sufficiently similar to such a name that its use in the United Kingdom would be likely to mislead by suggesting a connection between the company and the applicant. If the matters set out in s.69(1) are proved by the applicant then the respondent can set up various defences under s.69(4). These include that the name was registered before the commencement of activities in which the applicant is claiming goodwill; that the name was adopted in good faith; or that the interests of the applicant are not adversely affected to any significant extent.

Even if these matters are proved by the respondent, s.69(5) provides that the complaint will nevertheless be upheld if the main purpose in registering the name was to obtain money (or other consideration) from the applicant or to prevent him registering the name. The applicant must make the objection to a company names adjudicator. The Secretary of State is to appoint company names adjudicators and a Chief Adjudicator. An adjudicator can order that a name be changed. A right of appeal will lie to the courts.

A business might also bring a passing-off action to prevent a company registering a name which is so similar as to be likely to divert trade away from the business. The 2006 Act has not removed the common-law right to bring a passing-off action. Such an action would still appear to be the best way forward where an unincorporated business seeks damages on account of a company having traded under a name which diverts business away from it. It would also be appropriate where a company is trying to prevent an unincorporated business from trading under a name which is likely to divert business from the company. A passing-off action will be successful only if the use of the name is likely to divert customers away from the established business or cause confusion between the two businesses. (*Croft v Day* (1843) 7 Beav 84, an example of a partnership bringing a successful passing-off action, was considered in the previous chapter at 15.4.1.3.)

A passing-off action may be brought whether the name was deliberately made similar or was done so accidentally. But the fact that it was done deliberately is likely to influence the court's decision against the new name.

Ewing v Buttercup Margarine Co Ltd
[1917] 2 Ch 1 (Court of Appeal)

The claimant carried on an unincorporated business under the name Buttercup Dairy Company. The business was substantial, with 150 shops, and sold margarine, tea and similar products. The business was carried on mainly in Scotland, but also in the North of England. The defendant company was registered under the name the Buttercup Margarine Company Limited. It intended to manufacture and sell margarine, but in the south of England. The claimant brought a passing-off action. The defendants argued that there would be no confusion between the two businesses as they were wholesalers and the claimant was a retailer and because they only intended to carry on business in and around London. There was →

nothing in the defendants' memorandum of association to prevent them from retailing margarine.

Held. The claimant's action was successful. The defendant company was prohibited from continuing to trade under its registered name. The public might have thought that there was a connection between the two businesses.

Cozens-Hardy MR: 'In my opinion it is a perfectly plain and clear case, not very near the line, but well over the line . . . I can see no principle which withholds us from preventing injury to the plaintiff in his business as a trader by a confusion which will lead people to conclude that the defendants are really connected in some way with the plaintiff or are carrying on a branch of the plaintiff's business.'

COMMENT Now a complaint to a company names adjudicator would seem an easier and more appropriate way to prevent the company from trading under the offending name. However, the case is still useful in demonstrating a successful passing-off action.

The Insolvency Act 1986 s.216 makes it a criminal offence for a person who was a director or a shadow director of an insolvent company within 12 months of the company's liquidation to be a director of a company using the name of the insolvent company or of a company using a name which is so similar as to suggest a connection with the insolvent company. It is also prohibited for the ex-director to take part in the promotion, formation or management of a new company using the same or a similar name. The prohibition lasts for five years from the date of insolvency. A person in breach of s.216 not only commits a criminal offence of strict liability for which he could be fined or imprisoned, but can also become personally responsible for all the debts of the new company. This liability is joint and several with that of the company and any other person who could become liable under s.216. A person who is involved in the management of the new company under the instructions of a director or shadow director who could be liable under s.216 becomes jointly and severally liable for the new company's debts along with the company and any other person who is liable.

Miscellaneous other prohibitions include the inappropriate use of names which would indicate matters such as a connection with charitable organisations or that the company is a bank or a building society.

The abbreviation 'SE' cannot be used by a company created after 8 October 2004 if the company is not a European Public Limited-Liability Company.

16.9.3 Change of name

Section 77 provides that a company may change its name by special resolution, or by an ordinary resolution following a direction from the Secretary of State or a decision from the company names adjudicator, or by other means provided for by the company's articles. Where a name is changed by special resolution, the company must give notice to the Registrar (s.78). This is in addition to the obligation to forward a copy of the resolution to the Registrar. Where a change of a company's name has been made by other means provided for by its articles, the company must give notice to the Registrar, and the notice must be accompanied by a statement that the change of name has been made by means provided for by the company's articles.

The same prohibitions will apply to a change of name as applied to the use of a name on formation of a company. The Registrar has the same powers to refuse to register the changed name. Where the Registrar receives notice of a change of a company's name, and is satisfied that the requirements of the Act have been complied with, the Registrar must issue a new certificate of incorporation. A change of a company's name has effect from the date on which the new certificate of incorporation is issued. The change does not affect any rights or obligations of the company.

16.9.4 Publication of name and address

All companies must publish their names legibly and conspicuously:

(a) Outside the registered office and all places of business (s.82).
(b) On all letters, invoices, notices, cheques, orders for goods and receipts (ss.82 and 84).
(c) On the company seal, if it has a seal (s.45(2)).

If the company does not publish its name as required then every one of its officers is liable to be fined. Section 82 provides that company letters and orders for goods must also show the company number, the address of the registered office and the place (i.e. England and Wales, Wales or Scotland) where the company is registered. For the purposes of ss.82 and 84, s.85 allows the displayed name to differ in the case of the letters, the punctuation, the format or the style. However, this is only the case if there is no real likelihood of the name being taken to be a different name.

16.10 THE REGISTRAR OF COMPANIES

The Registrar of Companies is an official of the Department for Business, Enterprise and Regulatory Reform and is the head of an agency known as Companies House. The Registrar has many other duties besides registering newly formed companies. The main duties of the Registrar are:

(a) To issue a certificate of incorporation when a company is first registered. This is conclusive evidence that the company has been formed and, if appropriate, that it is limited.
(b) To issue a certificate of incorporation on change of company name. (Although a new certificate is issued the company remains the same legal person and its registered number remains the same.)
(c) To keep a list of the names of all UK registered companies, Limited Partnerships and Limited Liability Partnerships. This list is published on microfiche.
(d) To issue certificates of re-registration when a private company changes to a public one, or vice versa, or from unlimited to limited, or vice versa.
(e) To receive the annual return and the annual financial statements of companies.
(f) To register and keep safe the documents which statutes require him to hold.
(g) To issue certificates which register mortgages and charges.
(h) To strike companies off the register when they are dissolved.
(i) To allow any member of the public to see the file of a particular company.
(j) To register special resolutions.
(k) To publish in the *London Gazette* the fact of receipt of various documents.

Section 1075 gives the Registrar the power to correct a document informally, if it appears incomplete or inconsistent with itself. However, the company must consent and give instructions in response to an enquiry from the Registrar. So in some cases the Registrar might contact the company and take instructions over the phone. Section 1081 allows the Registrar to make certain annotations to registers, showing such things as the date a document was received, corrections which were made to it or materials which were removed from it.

Test your understanding 16.4

1 Once formed, can a company ratify a contract made on the company's behalf before the company was incorporated?

2 Will a promoter of a company be personally liable on a pre-incorporation contract which he made on the company's behalf?

3 In what circumstances will the Registrar refuse to register a company under the name proposed?

4 What is meant by a passing-off action?

5 In what places and documents must the name of a company be publicised?

6 What are the main duties of the Registrar of Companies?

Key points

The nature and characteristics of a company
- A company is a legal person.
- Members of limited companies are not liable to pay the companies' debts.
- A company can continue in existence indefinitely. It can also own property.
- A company can make contracts in its own name.
- A company can be guilty of a crime. If the crime requires *mens rea*, the *mens rea* of a person senior enough to be regarded as the mind of the company can be attributed to the company.

- The corporate veil is said to separate a company and its members. The veil can be lifted in a variety of situations, including: if the company was formed for a fraudulent purpose; if the company can be characterised as an enemy in time of war; in exceptional circumstances groups of companies may be regarded as one; small companies which are like

→

partnerships may be wound up as partnerships; in line with various statutory provisions.

Classification of companies

■ The shares of public companies can be listed on a stock market, such as the London Stock Exchange. The shares and debentures of private companies cannot be offered to the public.

■ Public companies must have an allotted share capital of at least £50 000 and at least one quarter of this must be paid up. There is no minimum amount of share capital for private companies.

■ When an unlimited company is wound up, its members have unlimited liability to pay the company's debts.

■ The liability of members of a company limited by shares is limited to paying any amount of the nominal value of the shares which has not yet been paid. The company can require the members to pay this amount before winding up or a liquidator can insist that they pay it upon a winding up.

■ The liability of members of a company limited by guarantee is to contribute the amount which they have guaranteed. This amount only becomes payable if it is needed to pay the company's debts when the company is wound up.

■ It is possible for companies to be created by statute or Royal Charter, but almost all companies were created by registration under the Companies Acts.

Formation of registered companies

■ A registered company is formed by registration with the Registrar of Companies.

■ The Registrar will register a company upon receiving a memorandum of association, an application for registration and a £20 fee.

■ A new-style memorandum of association will merely state that the subscribers, the people who sign it, wish to form a company under the Act and that they agree to become members of the company by taking at least one share each.

■ An old-style memorandum of association had to contain five obligatory clauses, setting out: (i) the name of the company; (ii) the jurisdiction of the registered office; (iii) the objects of the company; (iv) that the liability of the members of the company was limited (if it was); and (v) the amount of share capital and how it was divided into shares.

■ The articles of association set out the rules of the company. Together with certain types of resolutions, the articles form the constitution of a company.

■ To the extent that a company does not register its own articles, it will be taken to have adopted a default set of model articles.

■ A company cannot validly ratify a contract which was made before the company was formed.

■ A promoter who makes a contract on behalf of a company which has not been formed will be personally liable on the contract, unless there is an agreement to the contrary.

The company name

■ The Registrar will not register a company under a name which is identical to the name of a company already on the register, or under a name which the Secretary of State would consider would constitute a criminal offence. Certain words may only be used in a company name if permission is gained from the Secretary of State.

■ Any person may object to a company's registered name on the ground that it is the same as a name associated with the applicant in which he has goodwill, or that it is sufficiently similar to such a name that its use in the United Kingdom would be likely to mislead by suggesting a connection between the company and the applicant. Such an objection is made by making an application to a company names adjudicator.

■ The Registrar of Companies is an official of the Department for Business, Enterprise and Regulatory Reform, who heads a government agency known as Companies House.

Summary questions

1 Explain the main differences between public and private companies.

2 Y Co Ltd allotted 100 shares to Arthur. The shares had a nominal value of £1 each and Arthur agreed to pay a premium of £4 per share. Arthur has only paid Y Co Ltd 30p per share.

a What liability does Arthur have to Y Co Ltd in respect of the shares?

→

b If the company became insolvent before Arthur had paid any more money, how much would Arthur have to contribute towards the company's debts?

3 Explain what is meant by the corporate veil and the circumstances in which the veil can be lifted.

4 X Co Ltd was incorporated in 1993 with X as the sole member and sole director. X's husband, a solicitor, is the company secretary. X Co Ltd has been extremely successful and now operates a successful dot.com business. X has decided that she would like to turn X Co Ltd into a public company. Outline the changes which will need to be made before the

Registrar of Companies will re-register the company as a public company.

5 Your firm has been approached to refurbish a restaurant on behalf of a company which is soon to be incorporated. The contract is lucrative and you know that the promoter who approached you to make the contract is financially sound. The promoter does not want to remain personally liable on the contract. Can the contract be made in such a way that the promoter is not personally liable on it? Assuming that the promoter is personally liable on the contract, can he ensure that this liability should cease once the company comes into existence?

Multiple choice questions

1 A business is registered under the name Acme Trading Ltd. Which one of the following must the business be?

a A public limited company.
b A partnership.
c A private limited company.
d Either a private limited company or a private unlimited company.

2 David owns 100 shares in a private limited company which has debts which amount to 50 times its assets. The company has no prospect of paying the debts. David has paid half the nominal price of his shares. Which one of the following statements is true?

a As the company is limited it need not pay its debts.
b Limited liability will mean that David has to pay nothing towards the company's debts.
c The amount of the company's debts must be paid by all shareholders in proportion to their shareholding.
d David must pay the other half of the nominal price of his shares. Beyond that he need pay no more.

3 Consider the following statements.

i A public company need have only one member.
ii A public company cannot be unlimited.
iii A public company's shares must be quoted on the stock exchange.
iv A public company must have at least £50 000 of allotted, fully paid up, capital.
v A private company will need to pass an ordinary resolution in order to convert to a public company.

Which of the above statements are true?

a i and ii only.
b i, iii and iv only.
c ii and iv only.
d All of the statements.

4 Which one of the following is not a legal person?

a A small family company.
b A public limited company.
c The BBC.
d A partnership of chartered accountants.

5 Consider the following statements.

i A private company will continue in existence indefinitely unless it is liquidated.
ii The members of an unlimited company have unlimited liability to contribute money to the company if the company, acting in good faith, asks them to do this.
iii The members of a company limited by guarantee can at any time be asked by the company to contribute the amount guaranteed.
iv It is no longer possible for a company to be created by Royal Charter. However, some companies created in this way still exist.
v A corporation sole is any company with only one member.

Which of the above statements are true?

a i, ii and iv only.
b ii, iii and v only.
c iii, iv and v only.
d i only.

→

6 Consider the following statements.

i A company's articles of association bind all the members of the company as if they had all signed them.

ii Upon registration a public or private company which does not wish to register its own individual articles will by default be regarded as having adopted a model set of articles.

iii Some or all of a company's articles of association can be entrenched, in which case those articles can be changed only if certain conditions are met, or procedures complied with, that are more restrictive than those applicable in the case of a special resolution.

iv The Registrar can refuse to register a company on the grounds that it is being formed for an unlawful purpose, even if that purpose does not amount to the commission of a criminal offence.

Which of the above statements are true?

a i, ii and iv only.

b ii, iii and iv only.

c iii and iv only.

d All of the statements.

7 Which one of the following statements is not true?

a A promoter of a company will be liable on a pre-incorporation contract made on the company's behalf, unless there is an agreement to the contrary.

b If a company named Acme Company Limited is already registered, the Registrar will refuse to register a company under the name The Acme Company Limited.

c A complaint to a company names adjudicator will be successful only if the claimant can show an intention to deceive the public.

d Either a public or a private company may change its name by special resolution.

Task 16

A friend of yours, currently running his car repair business as a sole trader, wants to form a company. Draft a report explaining the following matters.

a The steps which must be taken in order for a company to be formed.

b The nature and essential content of a company's articles and memorandum of association.

c The extent to which a shareholder can be liable for the debts of a company.

d The restrictions on the choice of name with which a company may be registered.

mylawchamber *premium*

Visit **www.mylawchamber.co.uk/macintyre** to access study support resources including interactive multiple-choice questions, weblinks, glossary, glossary flashcards, legal newsfeed, answers to questions in this chapter, legal updates and an overview of this chapter all linked to the **Pearson eText** version of *Business Law* which you can **search**, **highlight** and **personalise** with your **own notes** and **bookmarks**.

Use **Case Navigator** to read in full some of the key cases referenced in this chapter with commentary and questions:

Adams **v** *Cape Industries plc* [1991] 1 All ER 929

Salomon **v** *Salomon* [1895–99] All ER Rep 33

17

The management of a company

Introduction

17.1 DIRECTORS

We saw in the previous chapter that every company is regarded by the law as a legal person in its own right. However, it is obvious that companies can function only through the actions of living people. The task of managing a company is therefore entrusted to the board of directors, who act as agents of the company. Ultimately, control of a company lies with the shareholders. They have the power to appoint and remove the directors or to alter the company's articles to take away some of the directors' powers. But while the directors hold office it is the board of directors, and not the shareholders, who run a company. Section 250(1) provides that the use of the term 'director' in the Act includes any person occupying the position of director, whether he calls himself a director or not. This section was needed because sometimes those who act as directors of a company call themselves managers, governors or some other title.

A 'shadow director' is defined by s.251(1) as a person in accordance with whose directions or instructions the directors of a company are accustomed to act. However, s.251(2) provides that a person is not to be regarded as a shadow director merely because the directors act on advice given by him in a professional capacity. Most of the statutory provisions which apply to directors apply equally to shadow directors.

As a company will need to have directors, it is not possible to register a company without specifying who the first directors should be. As we saw in the previous chapter, this is done in the statement of proposed officers which must be sent to the Registrar when the company is formed. Generally, there is no requirement that the directors of a company should also be shareholders, although they very commonly are.

Section 154(1) requires a private company to have at least one director and s.154(2) requires public companies to have at least two. Section 155(1) requires all companies to have at least one director who is a natural person. So although one company can be a director of another company, it cannot be the only director. If the number of directors falls below the statutory minimum, s.156 gives the Secretary of State the power to order that the necessary appointments are made. Although statute requires a private company to have a minimum of one director, the articles of association of many private companies require that there be at least two directors. For example, article 64 of Table A states that the company must have at least two directors unless the members by ordinary resolution determine otherwise. It also states that there is no maximum number of directors. However, the Model Articles for Private Companies Limited by Shares has no requirement that there should be at least two directors. The Model Articles for Public Companies sets the quorum at a board meeting at two directors.

Executive directors devote substantially the whole of their working time to performing their duties and derive most of their income from their connection with the company. They are usually employees of the company exercising substantial powers delegated by the board of directors. Non-executive directors do not devote their whole time to performing their duties. They are usually paid a small fee for their services and so they do not generally derive most of their income from the company.

17.1.1 **Appointment of directors**

In Chapter 16 we saw that the promoters of a company must send a statement of proposed officers to the Registrar of Companies giving the names and addresses of the company's first directors and the first company secretary. In the statement the proposed directors must indicate their consent to acting as directors. Upon registration of the company the persons named as directors will become the first directors of the company.

A company's articles of association will almost always set out how subsequent directors are to be appointed. New directors may need to be appointed either to increase the number of directors or to fill a vacancy created by the retirement of a director. If the articles do not deal with the matter, directors will be appointed by ordinary resolution of the members. (An ordinary resolution is passed by a simple majority of company members who vote at a company meeting.) The articles of most companies would anyway generally contain an article saying that directors would be

elected by ordinary resolution. In a private company an ordinary resolution would generally be passed by the written resolution procedure rather than at a company meeting. (The written resolution procedure is examined in Chapter 18 at 18.4.1. It allows the members of a private company to pass a resolution without the need to hold a meeting.) Commonly, the articles allow the board of directors to appoint a director. A person can be appointed as a director only if he consents to being appointed, and the appointment must be exercised for the benefit of the company as a whole. The Model Articles for Private Companies Limited by Shares, like the Model Articles for Public Companies, allow for appointment either by ordinary resolution or by a decision of the directors.

As regards public companies, s.160(1) disallows the appointment of two or more directors by a single resolution, unless there has been a unanimous vote at the meeting to allow such a resolution. So the appointment of each director must be voted on individually. If this section is contravened the appointment of the directors is void, even if no one voted against the resolution at the time (s.160(2)). However, s.161 provides that the acts of a person acting as a director are valid even if it is later discovered that s.160 was breached. The acts are likewise valid under s.161 even if there was some other defect in the director's appointment, if he was disqualified from holding office, if he had ceased to hold office or if he was not entitled to vote on the matter in question.

The dates of birth of the first directors will have been included in the statement of proposed officers delivered to the Registrar of Companies on formation of the company. The dates of birth of directors currently holding office can be found in the register of directors which every company must keep. Section 157 has introduced a new rule that no person can be appointed a director unless he is at least 16 years old. Existing directors who were under 16 at the time ceased to be directors when the 2006 Act came into force (s.159). There is no maximum age for directors.

17.1.2 **Retirement and removal of directors**

A director may give notice of his resignation of office at any time, and the company is obliged to accept such a resignation. The articles of association may also set out circumstances in which a director is deemed to have resigned. The articles may also provide that directors shall retire by rotation. For example, in Table A articles 73 and 74 provide for one third of the directors, those who have held office for the longest, to retire by rotation at the company's annual general meeting. The retiring directors can offer themselves for re-election and can be automatically re-elected if no one else stands to fill the vacancy. Article 21 of the Model Articles for Public Companies requires every director who has been appointed by the directors since the last general meeting, and every director who was not appointed at one of the preceding two annual general meetings, to retire at the general meeting. Such retiring directors can offer themselves for reappointment by the members. The Model Articles for Private Companies Limited by Shares do not contain a similar article.

No matter what a company's articles might say, and no matter what might have been agreed between the director and the company, s.168(1) provides that a director can always be removed by an ordinary resolution of which the company has been given special notice (28 days) as long as the resolution is passed at a meeting of the company members. Section 168(1) is necessary only where the company's articles do not allow a director to be removed by ordinary resolution. A written resolution cannot be used to remove a director under s.168(1) because the director is entitled to be heard at the meeting, However, a company's articles might well allow a director to be removed by an ordinary written resolution.

If a company receives special notice of a resolution to remove a director under s.168(1), s.169(1) provides that the company must immediately send a copy of the notice to the director concerned. Even if he is not a member of the company, the director whose dismissal is proposed has a right to speak at the meeting (s.169(2)). Section 169(3) also allows the director to make written representations, of a reasonable length, to the members. If the company receives these representations in time, it must send them out to members along with notice of the meeting. If it is not reasonably practicable to do this, s.312(3) requires the company to give its members notice, at least 14 days before the meeting, either by advertisement in a newspaper having an appropriate circulation or in any other manner allowed by the company's articles. If the representations are not received in time, the director has the right to require them to be read out at the meeting (as well as the right to be heard orally). There are no rights to be heard or to have written representations circu-

lated if an application is made to a court and the court is satisfied that s.169 is being abused (s.169(5)).

Although s.168 always allows a director to be dismissed by ordinary resolution passed at a meeting of the company members, the shares of the director whose removal is proposed might have enhanced voting power. In some companies these enhanced voting rights might make removal of a director against his will an impossibility.

Bushell v Faith
[1970] AC 1099 (House of Lords)

The 300 shares in a company were owned equally by a brother and two sisters. The brother and one of the sisters were the only directors. The articles provided that on any resolution to remove a director that director's shares should carry three votes per share. The two sisters wanted to remove their brother as a director. At a general meeting the sisters voted for removal, the brother voted against. The sisters claimed that the resolution had been passed by 200–100. The brother claimed that it had been defeated by 200–300. Section 303(1) Companies Act 1985, the precursor to s.168(1) of the 2006 Act, provided that: 'A company may by ordinary resolution remove a director before the expiration of his period of office, notwithstanding anything in its articles or in any agreement between it and him.'

Held. The article giving the enhanced voting rights was perfectly valid. Therefore, the resolution to remove the brother from the board had been defeated by 200 votes to 300.

COMMENT (i) There is no reason why a member's votes should not carry 1 000 or 1 000 000 votes per share in a vote to remove that person as a director. Nevertheless, those with three-quarters of the voting shares might pass a special resolution to change the articles to remove these weighted voting rights. However, if the article in question was entrenched and the director whose removal was proposed was also a shareholder, it could be made impossible to change without his consent.

(ii) Some commentators think that this decision is justified only because the company was a quasi-partnership. However, the wording of s.168 does seem quite clear. The only pertinent difference between it and s.303 Companies Act 1985 is that the words 'anything in its articles', contained in s.303, have been removed. However, a plc could not gain listing on the London Stock Exchange if it had such an article, which would be quite unsuitable for a large company.

Another obstacle to the removal of a director might be that the directors would not call a general meeting or would not include the resolution proposing the director's removal on the agenda of a general meeting. Sections 303(1) and (2) of the 2006 Act allows members holding at least 5 per cent of the paid-up shares to require the directors to call a meeting. The request, which can be sent electronically, must state the general nature of the business to be dealt with at the meeting and may contain the text of any proposed resolution to be moved at the meeting s.303(4)). If the directors are required to hold a meeting under s.303 then s.304 requires them to call the meeting within 21 days of receiving the request. The meeting must actually be held within 28 days of the notice convening the meeting. If the request for the meeting contained a proposed resolution, notice of the meeting must contain notice of the resolution. If the directors are requested under s.303 to call a meeting but do not do so in accordance with s.304 then s.305 allows the members who requested the meeting to call a meeting at the company's expense. In *Pedley v Inland Waterways Association Ltd* [1977] 1 All ER 209 Slade J held that a member or members who did not satisfy the requirements of s.376 Companies Act 1985, the precursor of s.303 of the 2006 Act, could not compel the directors to put a resolution to remove a director on the agenda of the annual general meeting, even if they gave notice of the resolution to the company in the proper way.

When a director is removed under s.168(1), a replacement director cannot be voted in at the same meeting unless special notice of the resolution proposing the appointment has been given (s.168(2)).

Directors can be removed otherwise than under s.168(1) if the articles allow this. In a private company the articles might provide that the director whose removal is proposed had no right to speak at the meeting, or that special notice of a resolution to dismiss a director was not needed, or that removal could be achieved by written resolution. The articles of many companies provide that a director can be removed if all the other directors request this in writing. When the articles do allow other ways to dismiss a director, the members may choose whether to remove the director under s.168(1) or under the other power. However, if they elect to use s.168(1) they must comply with all the necessary formalities.

When a director is removed from office this might amount to breach of contract by the company. If the director is an employee of the company there might be a claim for unfair or wrongful dismissal. Section 168(5) provides that nothing in s.168 is to be taken as depriving a person removed under s.168 of compensation or damages payable in respect of the termination of his appointment as director.

17.1.3 **Disqualification of directors**

There are no special qualifications needed to hold office as a director, other than being at least 16 years old. Even a person who has held office in several companies which have gone into liquidation is free to become the director, or even the sole director, of another company. However, in certain circumstances a person will be disqualified from directing or managing a company. A person who is disqualified automatically ceases to hold office as a director.

Section 11 of the Company Directors Disqualification Act (CDDA) 1986 makes it a criminal offence of strict liability for an undischarged bankrupt to be concerned in the management of a company, without permission from the court which made the bankruptcy order. This applies not only to directors, but to those who act as directors without calling themselves directors.

A separate matter is that a person may be made the subject of a disqualification order, in which case he may not take part in the management of a company, or promote a company, or act as an insolvency practitioner. Both individuals and companies may be the subject of a disqualification order. Not only is it a criminal offence to ignore such an order, but a person who does ignore it can be made personally liable for all debts and liabilities incurred while acting in contravention.

A disqualification order may be made under CDDA 1986 on the following grounds:

(i) Conviction of an indictable offence in connection with the promotion, formation, management, or liquidation of a company, or with the receivership or management of a company's property. Although the offence must be indictable, disqualification under s.2 is still possible if the offence was in fact tried in the magistrates' court (CDDA 1986 s.2).

(ii) Persistent default in sending annual returns, accounts or other documents which have to be filed with the Registrar of Companies. Three convictions within five years is conclusive evidence of persistent default (CDDA 1986 s.3).

(iii) If an officer or receiver of a company which is in liquidation has been guilty of fraud in relation to the company, or has been in breach of his duty as a company officer, or has committed an offence of knowingly being a party to fraudulent trading (a criminal conviction for this is not necessary) (CDDA 1986 s.4).

(iv) Conviction in the magistrates' court, of an offence only triable summarily, of failing to provide the Registrar of Companies with information required to be provided. However, it must also be shown that this is the third conviction for doing this within the past five years (CDDA 1986 s.5).

(v) If a person acting as a director or shadow director of a company which has become insolvent, has engaged in conduct which makes him unfit to be concerned with the management of a company (CDDA 1986 s.6).

(vi) If the Trade Secretary concludes from an inspector's report that the person's conduct makes him unfit to be concerned in the management of a company, or that a disqualification order should be made in the public interest (CDDA 1986 s.8).

(vii) If a director has breached competition law and this breach makes him unfit to be concerned in the management of a company (CDDA 1986 s.9A).

(viii) If the person has been held by a court to be responsible to contribute to the assets of a liquidated company on the grounds of fraudulent or wrongful trading, which are considered in Chapter 19 at 19.1.4 (CDDA 1986 s.10).

Orders made on the ground of (ii) above may not be for longer than five years. Nor may an order on the grounds of (i) and (iv), if made by a magistrates' court. As regards the other grounds, the maximum period is 15 years, and if the order is made on ground (v) it may not be for less than two years.

A register of disqualification orders is kept at Companies House and members of the public may inspect this free of charge.

17.1.4 **The register of directors**

Section 162(1) of the Act requires every company to keep a register of its directors. Section 163(1) provides that this register must give the following information about each director who is an individual:

(a) his name (first name, other forenames and surname) and any former name (a name by which the individual was formerly known for business purposes, including a married woman's former name);

(b) a service address;

(c) the country or state (or part of the UK – England, Scotland etc.) in which he is usually resident;

(d) his nationality;

(e) his business occupation (if any); and

(f) his date of birth.

The service address is defined by s.1141(1) as an address at which documents may be effectively served on that person. Section 163(5) allows the service address to be stated to be 'the company's registered office'. However, the company must also keep a register of directors' residential addresses. If another company or a firm is a director then s.164 requires that the particulars given include: the name of the company which is a director; its registered or principal office; the legal form of the company or firm; the law by which it is governed; and, if applicable, the register in which it is entered and its registration number in that register.

The register of directors must be kept available for inspection at the company's registered office or at a place specified in Regulations made by the Secretary of State (s.162(3)). If the register is not kept at the company's registered office, s.162(4) requires the company to give notice to the Registrar of the place where it is kept and of any change in that place. The members of the company are entitled to inspect the register of directors free of charge. Non-members are entitled to inspect it upon payment of a small fee (s.162(5)). If the register is not open to inspection, the company and its officers commit an offence and may be fined (s.162(6)and (7)) and the court may order immediate inspection to be allowed (s.162(8)). If a person is responsible for refusing to allow the register to be inspected, a court must have regard to this when considering if such a person is unfit to be concerned in the management of a company (CDDA 1986 s.9).

Section 167(1)) provides that if there is a change in the directors of a company, or in the particulars contained in the register of directors, the Registrar of Companies must be informed within 14 days. The Registrar will publicise the change in the *Gazette* (s.1077) and until this has happened the company cannot rely on the change of directors (s.1079.) This does not mean that a person cannot act as a director until his appointment is notified. But it does mean that a person is held out as a director until notification of his having left office is published in the *Gazette*. (The meaning of holding out was considered in Chapter 15 at 15.8.3.)

When a company is listed on the Stock Exchange, the Listing Rules require that the register also gives the following information about each director: details of management experience; unspent convictions; details of personal insolvencies or of insolvencies of companies in which they acted as an executive director; details of public criticism by statutory authorities; and whether they have ever been disqualified as a director.

17.1.4.1 Protection from disclosure of residential address

The 2006 Act introduced measures to prevent disclosure of the residential addresses of directors. Before the Act came into force, any person could inspect a company's register of directors and discover the residential addresses of the directors. This information was misused by some political activists who, being opposed to the activities of certain companies, targeted the directors personally at their homes.

Section 240 now provides that a director's residential address is 'protected information', even after he has left the company. Section 241 prevents the company from using or disclosing this protected information unless it does so for one of three purposes: communicating with the director in question; or sending required particulars to the Registrar of Companies; or under a court order. However, the protected information can be used or disclosed in other circumstances if the director in question consents (s.241(2)). The Registrar must omit protected information from material on the register which is available for public inspection (s.242). However, the Registrar may use protected information for the purpose of communicating with the director himself. Disclosure may also be made to credit reference agencies, to public authorities and to other people as specified by the Secretary of State (s.243). Disclosure may also be made by the Registrar if a court orders it to be made (s.244). Section 245 allows the Registrar to put a director's residential address on the public record in two circumstances; first, if communications sent by the Registrar and requiring a response within a specified period remain unanswered; second, if there is evidence that service of documents at a service address provided in place of the director's usual residential address is not effective to bring them to the notice of the director. However,

the Registrar must first give notice of the proposal to the director and to every company of which he is a director. This notice must state the grounds for the proposal and specify a period within which representations may be made before the address is put on the public record. The notice is sent to the director's usual residential address. But if it appears to the Registrar that service at that address may be ineffective to bring it to the director's notice, it may be sent to any service address provided in place of the usual residential address. If any representations are received within the specified period, the Registrar must take account of them. If the Registrar does put the director's residential address on the register of directors, this address will also be given as his service address (s.246(1)). The Registrar must inform both the director and the company that this has been done (s.246(2)). The company must alter both the register of directors and the register of directors' residential addresses accordingly or it will commit a criminal offence (s.246(3) and (4)). If the Registrar does put a director's residential address on the public record under s.246, that director may not register a service address other than his residential address for a period of five years from the date of the Registrar's decision (s.246(7)).

17.1.5 The board of directors

When the directors act collectively, they act as the board of directors. Unless the company is a single member company, it is the board of directors to whom the articles will have given the right to manage the company. Individual directors have no right to manage unless such a right has been delegated to them. Although the articles will give the board the power to manage the company, it is not uncommon for articles to specify that certain decisions of the board must be approved by the members. The articles of a small company might, for example, say that the company could not borrow more than a certain amount without shareholder approval. The extent to which such a restriction would bind outsiders dealing with the company is considered below at 17.1.8.2. Meetings of the board of directors are known as board meetings and, unless the articles provide otherwise, any director may call a board meeting. A reasonable amount of notice of a board meeting must be given to all of the directors whose whereabouts are known, but there is no need to give notice of matters which may be raised and voted upon. As well as raising matters to be voted upon during the board meeting itself, directors can make informal decisions, without the need for a meeting, if all of the directors agree to this.

One of a director's duties is to attend board meetings, and directors have a right to attend board meetings, and to vote at them. Directors entitled to vote at a board meeting will count towards the quorum of the meeting. The quorum, or the way in which it will be fixed, should be set out in the company's articles. If a meeting is inquorate, any decisions taken at such a meeting will be invalid. Where not all of the directors attend the board meeting, decisions taken at the meeting will nevertheless be valid as long as the meeting was properly convened and was quorate. Article 8 of the Model Articles for Private Companies Limited by Shares also allows directors to make unanimous decisions informally. Article 18 of the Model Articles for Public Companies allows directors to take decisions by a written resolution signed by all of the directors.

The articles of a company may allow any director to appoint an **alternate director** to carry out his duties while he is absent. Companies House must be informed when such an alternate director is both appointed and removed. An alternate director may have all the powers of a director and may count towards a quorum at a board meeting. However, an alternate director will not count towards a quorum if the person who appointed him is also present at the meeting. All the company law requirements which apply to directors also apply to alternate directors.

A board resolution is not passed unless more directors vote in favour than vote against. However, many articles include an article similar to article 88 of Table A, which allows the chairman of the board of directors to have the casting vote where the votes of the directors are equally split. The Model Articles for Public Companies gives the chairman, or other director chairing the meeting, the casting vote. The Model Articles for Private Companies Limited by Shares give the chairman, or some other specified director, the casting vote.

A company's articles might also give weighted voting rights, so that some directors have more votes than others. Articles very commonly provide that a director should not vote on a matter in which he has a personal interest. (As we shall see below at 17.1.9, a director who has a possible conflict between his own interests and those of the company can be absolved from liability for breach of the statutory duty set out in s.175 if the other directors authorise the matter. Also,

s.177 imposes a duty on a director to declare any interest which he might have in a proposed transaction or arrangement with the company.)

Section 248 requires that minutes of board meetings be kept for at least ten years from the date of the meeting. If this is not done, a criminal offence is committed by every company officer in default, although the failure to keep minutes does not render invalid decisions taken. Once the minutes are signed by the chairman, they are evidence of the proceedings at the board meeting (s.249).

A company's articles may allow the directors to delegate any of their powers to a committee as long as the purpose behind this is not to exclude a particular director from participation in board meetings. The Model Articles for Private Companies Limited by Shares and the Model Articles for Public Companies allow the directors, subject to the articles, to delegate any of their powers to any other person and also to allow further delegation from that person. Table A allows delegation to a committee, which may be composed of one or more directors.

A company's articles may allow for the existence of a **managing director** and may allow the managing director to exercise powers of the directors without the need to consult the board of directors. Article 84 of Table A, for example, allows for the appointment of a managing director by the directors. The members of a company with Table A articles would not therefore be allowed themselves to appoint the managing director. The members would, however, be entitled to remove the managing director from office as a director, under s.168(1). This would end his authority to act as managing director but might of course amount to breach of contract. The new Model Articles do not make reference to a managing director. However, companies governed by these articles might nevertheless hold a person out as managing director, a concept explained immediately below.

If a company gives the impression that a person has the necessary authority to make a transaction then the company will be bound by such a transaction, whether or not the person who made it really did have such authority. This is known as **holding out**. The company is said to have held out that the person had authority and is therefore estopped from denying this. In Chapter 11, at 11.2.3, we saw that three requirements are necessary to give rise to such an estoppel:

(i) there must have been a representation that the person was an agent;

(ii) this representation must have been made by the principal or by someone on the principal's behalf;

(iii) the third party must have relied on the representation.

A person who has not validly been appointed managing director may be held out to be managing director, as the following case shows.

Freeman & Lockyer v Buckhurst Park Properties Ltd [1964] 2 QB 480
(Court of Appeal)

A company was formed to buy and resell an estate. The directors had the power to appoint a managing director but they never did so. One of the directors, K, acted as if he had been appointed managing director. K made a contract asking a firm of architects to do work on behalf of the company. The other directors knew that K acted as if he had been appointed managing director and also knew that he had made the contract to employ the architects. When the architects sued the company for their fees, the company argued that K had no authority to employ architects and therefore the contract was not binding on the company.

Held. A managing director would usually have authority to employ architects. The company had given the impression that K was managing director. Therefore, as regards persons dealing with the company in good faith, K had the authority to bind the company as if he really was managing director. The company had held him out to have such powers to bind the company, so as regards persons to whom this representation had been made he did have such powers.

Test your understanding 17.1

1 Can a shareholder in a company also be a director of that company? Can one company be a director of another company?

2 After formation of a company, how are a company's subsequent directors appointed?

3 How may a director be removed from office?

4 Is it possible to give shares weighted voting rights on a resolution to remove a director?

5 Why can a written resolution not be used to dismiss a director under s.168(1)?

6 Are directors required to hold any special qualifications? Are any persons prohibited from holding office as directors?

7 What is meant by the board of directors?

17.1.6 **Remuneration of directors**

Directors will only be entitled to be paid fees for their services if the constitution of the company provides for payment or if the payment is approved by the members. Payments to directors do not depend upon the company having made a profit. As directors stand in a fiduciary position to the company, they are not permitted to make a personal profit which has not been expressly provided for.

The articles of most companies provide that directors should be paid for their services as directors. Article 82 of Table A, for example, provides that:

> 'The directors shall be entitled to such remuneration as the company may by ordinary resolution determine and, unless the resolution provides otherwise, the remuneration shall be deemed to accrue from day to day.'

So if a company has Table A as its articles, a director will not be entitled to any fees for their services except as determined by ordinary resolution of the members. If the members of a company governed by Table A do not resolve to pay the directors anything, then they will not be entitled to any fees. Article 19(2) of the Model Articles for Private Companies Limited by Shares provides that:

> 'Directors are entitled to such remuneration as the directors determine–
> (a) for their services to the company as directors, and
> (b) for any other service which they undertake for the company.'

Article 23(2) of the Model Articles for Public Companies is identically worded.

In Chapter 11 at 11.5.2 we considered *Re Richmond Gate Property Co Ltd* [1965] 1 WLR 335. In that case the company's articles provided that the managing director should receive 'such remuneration (whether by way of salary, commission or participation in profits, or partly in one way and partly in another) as the directors may determine'. At the time of the company going into liquidation the directors had not determined to pay the managing director anything, even though he had put in a considerable amount of work in the performance of his role as managing director.

It was held that the managing director could not be entitled to anything on a *quantum meruit*. No term allowing a *quantum meruit* could be implied. There was an express term dealing with the managing director's remuneration and no implied term of a contract can contradict an express term. Section 15 of the Supply of Goods and Services Act 1982, which implies a term that a person providing a service in the course of a business will be paid a reasonable charge if the price for the service has not been agreed, does not apply to directors of companies.

If a person acting as a director has no contract with the company then he can be paid for his services on a *quantum meruit*.

Craven-Ellis v Canons Ltd
[1936] 2 All ER 1066

The claimant was appointed as managing director of a company and had a contract which entitled him to remuneration. The articles required the claimant to gain qualifying shares within two months of his appointment as managing director. The claimant never acquired such shares and so after two months the claimant was not a director and had no contract with the company. Nevertheless the claimant did considerable work for the company and claimed to be entitled to be paid on a *quantum meruit* for this work.

Held. The claimant was entitled to be paid on a *quantum meruit* because he had worked for the company without a binding contract.

The articles of a company may allow for other payments to be made to directors. Article 83 of Table A, for example, like Article 20 of the Model Articles for Private Companies Limited by Shares, and Article 24 of the Model Articles for Public Companies, allow directors to be paid an indemnity for reasonable expenses properly incurred in connection with the exercise of their powers and the discharge of their responsibilities in relation to the company. The model articles for both public and private companies allow the board of directors to fix the remuneration of individual directors both for their services to the company as directors, and for any other service which they undertake for the company.

Neither directors nor the managing director are automatically regarded as employees of the company. If directors are employees of the company then obviously they will have a contract of employment and if this is breached they may be entitled to remedies for either wrongful or unfair dismissal. However, the mere fact that a person acts as a director does not necessarily mean that that person has any contract with the company. Being a director has traditionally been regarded as 'holding office' rather than as being an employee. A director who does have a contract to supply his services, but who does not supply them as an employee, will supply his services as an independent contractor.

Any voluntary payment to a director in respect of the director's loss of office must be approved by the company. Section 217(1) provides that a company may not make a payment for loss of office to a director of the company unless the payment has been approved by a resolution of members of the company. The members' approval could either be by ordinary or written resolution. If this section is breached the recipient holds the payment made in trust for the company and any director who authorised the payment is jointly and severally liable to indemnify the company that made the payment for any loss resulting from it (s.222(1)). Section 217(1) does not apply to a payment which is *bona fide* made by way of damages for breach of contract or by way of pension for past services. It applies only to payments which the company was under no legal obligation to make (s.220(1)). Nor is approval of the members necessary for payments of £200 or less (s.221(1)).

A company's accounts do not need to show exactly how much each director was paid. However, s.412(1) allows the Secretary of State to make regulations requiring information about directors' remuneration or payment for loss of office to be given in notes to a company's annual accounts.

If a director is employed under a contract of employment, the terms of the contract, or if it was an oral contract a written memorandum setting out the terms, must be made available for inspection by the members at the company's registered office or at a place specified in regulations under s.1136 (s.228(1)). The contract or the memorandum must be kept and made available for one year after the contract terminated (s.228(3)). If the company is listed, the Stock Exchange Listing Rules additionally require the company to make the terms of the contract available at its registered office, for inspection by any person. In addition, the Listing Rules require that the terms of the contract must be available for inspection at the place where the annual meeting is held, for 15 minutes before the meeting.

17.1.7 **Directors' powers**

The powers of the directors will be contained in the company's articles of association. The balance of power between the members and the directors therefore varies from company to company. In many small companies the members and the directors are the same people.

Article 70 of Table A provides that:

'Subject to the provisions of the Act, the memorandum and the articles and to any directions given by special resolution, the business of the company shall be managed by the directors who may exercise all the powers of the company…'

So under Table A the directors are given very wide powers to manage the company, and most companies' articles will contain a provision similar to Table A article 70. Articles 3 and 4 of both the Model Articles for Private Companies Limited by Shares and the Model Articles for Public Companies provide that:

'3. Subject to the articles, the directors are responsible for the management of the company's business, for which purpose they may exercise all the powers of the company.

4. (1) The shareholders may, by special resolution, direct the directors to take, or refrain from taking, specified action.

(2) No such resolution invalidates anything which the directors have already done before the passing of the resolution.'

However, it is possible that the articles will give the directors very much less power, stipulating that a variety of decisions must be made by resolutions of the members. The power conferred on the directors by the articles is subject to the provisions of the Companies Act 2006. The Act provides that several powers can be exercised only by a special resolution of the members. In this and the previous chapter we have already seen that a special resolution is needed to change the company name, to re-register from a public company to a private one and vice versa, and to change unentrenched articles of association. In this chapter we have already seen that the Act provides that compensation paid to directors for loss of office must be approved by an ordinary resolution. We have also seen that the Act provides that directors can be removed from office by an ordinary resolution of which the company has been given special notice,

as long as the resolution is passed at a meeting of the company members. Later in this chapter we shall see that the auditor is appointed by ordinary resolution of the members. In the following two chapters we shall see that the Act provides that a special resolution is needed to reduce the company's share capital or to resolve that the company is voluntarily wound up. Table A allows the members by ordinary resolution to determine the rights which attach to new issues of shares.

As long as the directors stay within the powers conferred by the articles, they need not obey resolutions passed by the members. However, if Table A articles, or the new Model Articles, are adopted the directors must obey directions which they have been given by special resolution. The members of the company own the company's shares but the directors manage the company.

Automatic Self-Cleansing Filter Syndicate Co Ltd v *Cuninghame*
[1906] 2 Ch 34 (Court of Appeal)

The objects of a company gave the company the power to sell the company, or any part of it, to any other company which had similar objects (see below at 17.1.8.1). Article 96 of the company stated that: 'The management of the business and the control of the company shall be vested in the directors, who… may exercise all such powers and do all such acts and things as may be exercised or done by the company…' This article went on to state that the directors would not be able to do an act which was in contravention of an extraordinary [now special] resolution passed by the members. At a general meeting an ordinary resolution was passed, ordering the directors to sell the company's assets to another company which had been recently formed with the purpose of acquiring these assets. The directors did not think that it would be in the best interests of the company to do this, and so they refused to do it.

Held. The directors were within their rights. Whether or not to sell was a question for them and not for the shareholders.

Other articles may confer other, more specific, powers on the directors. We have already seen that articles commonly give the directors the power to appoint a managing director.

However, it must be remembered that a majority of the shareholders have very considerable powers. Subject to a *Bushell* v *Faith* type of clause in the articles, which could now be entrenched, the members can always vote directors out of office under s.168(1).

The members of a company can ratify acts committed by company agents in excess of their actual authority. If this is done the authority which was lacking is supplied retrospectively and the act in question is adopted as an act of the company. An ordinary resolution is needed, unless the act was outside the company's objects, in which case a special resolution is needed. This special resolution would confer retrospective actual authority on the agent, but a separate special resolution would be needed to prevent the agent from incurring personal liability.

17.1.8 Directors as agents

We have already seen that, generally, a company's articles of association will give the board of directors actual authority to exercise all the powers of the company. Under this authority, the board will then commonly give individual directors and employees actual authority to perform certain roles and make certain types of contracts. The people to whom the board have given actual authority might themselves then pass actual authority down the line to others.

The vast majority of individual directors who act on behalf of a company have been given actual authority to do so by the board of directors, the board having been given actual authority by the company's articles. If a director, or the board of directors, with actual authority, make a contract on a company's behalf then the company will be bound by the contract.

Alternatively, a person without actual authority to act on the company's behalf might have apparent authority. This authority would have arisen because the person who acted without actual authority would have been held out by the company, or by a person who could trace a line of actual authority back to the company, as having actual authority to do the act in question, as we saw in *Freeman & Lockyer* v *Buckhurst Park Properties Ltd*. Having held the person out as having authority, the company will be estopped from denying the representation which it has made as regards a third party who has acted on the strength of the representation. However, in *Criterion Properties plc* v *Stratford UK Properties LLC* [2004] UKHL 28, [2004] 1 WLR 1846, Lord Scott explained that if a third party can see that an action of an agent

is against the principal's commercial interests then he will find it very hard to argue that the agent had apparent authority to perform the action.

A company may also ratify an act done on its behalf by a person having no actual or apparent authority. If such a ratification is effective, retrospective actual authority is conferred and so the company is bound by the act as if actual authority had existed all along.

A person who represents that he has authority to act for a company when he does not in fact have such authority can be liable to a person relying on this representation. The liability is for breach of warranty of authority. However, breach of warranty of authority cannot make the company itself liable. Only the person claiming to act for the company, and not the company itself, warranted that he had authority to act for the company. These principles were set out in Chapter 11 at 11.2.

17.1.8.1 Limits on a company's contractual capacity

Before the 2006 Act came into force, all companies had to have an objects clause. This clause, contained in the old-style memorandum of association, set out the 'objects' of the company. It did this by listing the types of contracts which the company had the capacity to make. Section 3A of the Companies Act 1985 allowed a company to state that its objects were to carry on business as a general commercial company. This meant that the company could carry on any trade or business whatsoever. So even before the 2006 Act came into force companies could, in effect, do away with an effective objects clause. Section 31 of the 2006 Act has made it the default position that a newly formed company will not have an objects clause. It states that: 'Unless a company's articles specifically restrict the objects of the company, its objects are unrestricted.' However, an objects clause will be part of the constitution of many companies because they will choose specifically to restrict their objects or because their existing objects clause will be transferred from the old-style memorandum to the articles. (In the previous chapter we saw that s.28 of the 2006 Act provides that provisions of an old-style memorandum are to be treated as provisions of the articles, unless they are the kind of minimal provisions which need to be contained in a new-style memorandum.) If an existing company wishes to make its objects unrestricted, it can do so by amending its articles.

If a company acts for a purpose which is outside the company's objects clause, the contract is said to be *ultra vires*. Prior to the United Kingdom's entry into the EU, an *ultra vires* contract entered into was automatically void, because the company did not have the capacity to make the contract. The contract could not therefore be enforced by the company or by the other contracting party.

For example, in *Ashbury Railway Carriage and Iron Co Ltd* v *Riche* (1875) LR 7 HL 653, the House of Lords held that a company was not liable on a contract it had made to finance one Riche to build a railway line. After Riche had begun work and incurred expenses, the company repudiated the contract. Riche was left without any remedy because the contract was made outside the company's objects clause, which allowed the company to build railway carriages and railway machinery, but not to build a railway line. As the contract was *ultra vires,* the company could not have enforced the contract, and nor could it have been enforced against the company. The *ultra vires* rule may seem strange, but it was felt necessary to protect shareholders. They invested money in the company only to pursue the purposes set out in the objects clause. They did not invest their money to be used for other purposes. The House of Lords also regarded the rule as protecting creditors. Creditors who contracted with the company were deemed to have read the company's constitution and the contents of this would be a factor in their deciding whether or not to extend credit to the company. In fact, very few creditors did read the constitution and the rule usually worked very much against creditors, as the facts of the case demonstrated.

Section 39(1) of the 2006 Act now states: 'The validity of an act done by a company shall not be called into question on the ground of lack of capacity by reason of anything in the company's constitution.'

Section 39(1) therefore has the effect of meaning that an objects clause cannot invalidate a contract made by a company. As we have seen, a contract will be made on behalf of a company when it is made on the company's behalf by a person or persons with authority to make the contract. The act done on the company's behalf does not need to be a contract, it could be the making of a gift. So if the facts of *Ashbury Railway Carriage and Iron Co Ltd* v *Riche* were to arise today, then those who contracted with the company would be protected by s.39(1) and could sue on their contract with the company.

If an *ultra vires* contract causes loss to the company, the director who made the contract is personally liable to reimburse the company for the money lost, as s.171(a) (the duty to act within the company's constitution) will have been breached. The members can excuse the director from making this payment, by passing an ordinary resolution.

17.1.8.2 Constitutional limits on the authority of agents

A contract will not be binding upon the company if the person making the contract on the company's behalf had no actual or apparent authority to do so. This is the case whether or not the contract was within the company's objects clause. Even if the person making the contract has been given authority to do so, it is possible that the contract might contravene the company's constitution. Section 40(1) of the 2006 Act, which replaced s.35A of the 1985 Act, protects third parties by providing that:

> 'In favour of a person dealing with a company in good faith, the power of the directors to bind the company, or authorise others to do so, is deemed to be free of any limitation under the company's constitution.'

We have seen that s.39(1) provides protection where the contract made was a type of contract which the company had no capacity to make, because the contract was outside the company's objects clause. Section 40(1) provides protection where the person who bound the company otherwise contravened the company's constitution by making the contract. For example, we saw that if *Ashbury Railway Carriage and Iron Co Ltd* v *Riche* were to arise today then s.39(1) would protect the people who contracted with the company even though the company had no capacity to make the contract. If, in *Ashbury,* the board of directors had acted in contravention of a limit in the company's constitution, rather than outside the company's objects clause, then s.40(1) would have protected the people with whom the company contracted. This might have happened, for example, if the board had made a contract worth £1 million to build railway carriages but had done so in contravention of one of the articles of association which had said that any contract over £500 000 had to be approved by the members. In making this contract, the board would not have acted outside the objects clause but would have acted outside the constitution. Section 40(1), rather than s.39(1), would therefore have provided the protection.

In summary, s.40(1) therefore protects an unconnected third party dealing with the company in good faith if either: (i) the board of directors made the contract to bind the company, or (ii) the contract was made by others authorised by the board of directors. Even if the board, or the person authorised by the board, acted irregularly in making the contract, the contract will nevertheless be binding upon the company. If the contract was made neither by the board of directors nor by a person authorised by the board, the section will not apply. This is because neither s.39(1) nor s.40(1) can act as a substitute for authority. If a person, acting without actual or apparent authority to do so, makes a contract on behalf of the company, the company will not be bound unless it successfully ratifies the contract.

Section 40(2)(b) states that:

'A person dealing with a company –
(i) is not bound to enquire as to any limitation on the powers of the directors to bind the company or authorize others to do so,
(ii) is presumed to have acted in good faith unless the contrary is proved, and
(iii) is not to be regarded as acting in bad faith by reason only of his knowing that an act is beyond the powers of the directors under the company's constitution.'

Section 40(3) says that the limitations on the powers of the directors under the company's constitution include resolutions of the company or of any class of shareholders, or any agreement between the members of the company or any class of shareholders. Section 40 does not prevent a company member from seeking an injunction to prevent the directors from doing an act which the company constitution does not allow him them to do, but if the directors have made a binding contract the members cannot undo it. (Section 40(4).) Section 40 does not prevent the directors from being liable to the company for having exceeded their powers. (Section 40(5).) As we shall see below (at 17.1.9.1), s.171 imposes a statutory duty on directors to act within their powers. The company members could absolve the directors from liability by passing an ordinary resolution.

Different rules apply when the directors, acting in excess of their constitutional powers, make a contract between the company and a director or between the company and a person connected to a director. Section 41 provides that such a contract is voidable by the company despite s.40. The directors at fault have to account to the company for any gain they have made and indemnify the company for any loss it has suffered. (Section 41(3).) A connected person who does not know that the directors exceeded their powers does not have to do this. The contract ceases to be voidable in four circumstances. First, if it is impossible to restore the money or assets which were the subject of the transaction. Second, if the company is indemnified for any loss. Third, if third parties acting in good faith have acquired rights which would be adversely affected. Fourth, if the company affirms the transaction. (Section 41(4).)

17.1.8.3 Formalities of doing business

Section 43 provides that a company complies with any necessary formalities of doing business by making a contract under its company seal or through a person acting with express or implied actual authority. This section does not act as a substitute for the person using the seal having been granted authority to make the contract in question. Companies do not need to have a company seal but if they do have one, the seal must have the company name engraved upon it in legible characters (s.45). A seal is usually an engraved die which leaves an imprint when pressed onto paper.

A document such as a lease can be executed by a company either by using the company seal, or by two company officers (directors or the company secretary) signing the document or by one director signing and having his signature witnessed (s.44). Again, this does not remove the necessity for the person using the seal to have authority to enter into the lease. This last method is made necessary because a private company might have only one director and no company secretary. The articles may, however, state that the seal may be used only if the directors give authority or only if a director also signs the document. A bill of exchange, such as a cheque, must be signed by a person who has been given authority to sign it. If it is signed in the name of the company or on the company's behalf, by a person with actual authority, it will be binding on the company (s.52).

17.1.9 Directors' duties

The 2006 Act has partially codified the law relating to directors' duties. The new statutory duties, set out in ss.171–177, amend the common law to bring it into line with the expectations of the modern business world. They also attempt to set out in whose interests a company should be run. Broadly speaking, the common law duties of directors were designed to prevent directors from being negligent and to make sure that they put the company's interests ahead of their own interests. The new statutory duties have the same objectives. However, codification was felt to be desirable to make the law more certain and more accessible, and to make future development of the law more predictable. Because directors act as agents of the company, the cases were based on principles derived from the law of agency and the law of trusts.

The duties set out in ss.171–177 are called **general duties**. They are owed by a director to the company (s.170(1)). So if one or more of the duties are breached, the company could bring an action against the director in breach. If the company is unwilling to do this, perhaps because the director in breach controls the company, a member of the company could bring a **derivative claim** under s.260. (Derivative claims are considered in the following chapter at 18.8.2.) Alternatively, members might bring a claim for unfair prejudice. Unfair prejudice is considered in Chapter 18 at 18.8.5.)

Section 170(3) states that the general duties are based on certain common law rules and equitable principles as they apply in relation to directors and have effect in place of those rules and principles. However, s.170(4) says that the general duties shall be interpreted and applied in the same way as common law rules or equitable principles, and regard shall be had to the corresponding common law rules and equitable principles in interpreting and applying the general duties. So when the courts interpret and develop the general duties they will bear in mind the principles of law which they have replaced. The general duties apply to shadow directors to the same extent that the corresponding common law rules or equitable principles would apply to them (s.170(5)). It should be remembered that, in addition to the general duties, legislation imposes many other duties on directors, such as the duty to file accounts.

The seven general statutory duties are as follows.

(1) The duty to act within powers (s.171).
(2) The duty to promote the success of the company (s.172).
(3) The duty to exercise independent judgment (s.173).
(4) The duty to exercise reasonable care, skill and diligence (s.174).
(5) The duty to avoid conflicts of interest (s.175).
(6) The duty not to accept benefits from third parties (s.176).
(7) The duty to declare interest in proposed transaction or arrangement (s.177).

The general duties are of considerable importance and need to be examined individually. However, more than one of the general duties may apply in any given case (s.179). If several duties do apply, then a director must comply with all of the relevant duties.

17.1.9.1 **The duty to act within powers**

Section 171 states that:

> 'A director of a company must –
> (a) act in accordance with the company's constitution; and
> (b) only exercise powers for the purposes for which they are conferred.'

This duty would have been regarded by the old law as two separate duties. Section 257 expands the meaning of a company's constitution in the context of the general duties. It provides that the company's constitution will include not only the articles and resolutions which would have needed to have been passed as special resolutions (the usual meaning) but also any resolution or decision come to by the members, or by a class of members, that is treated by legislation or rule of law as equivalent to a decision by the company. So in this context a unanimous informal decision taken by the members would be regarded as part of the company's constitution, even if it dealt with a matter for which a special resolution would not have been required. Directors might breach the duty set out in s.171(b) by, for example, issuing new shares so as to raise enough capital to prevent a takeover bid from succeeding, without considering whether the members would want the takeover bid to succeed.

17.1.9.2 **The duty to promote the success of the company**

Section 172 states that:

> '(1) A director of a company must act in the way he considers, in good faith, would be most likely to promote the success of the company for the benefit of its members as a whole, and in doing so have regard (amongst other matters) to –
> (a) the likely consequences of any decision in the long term;

(b) the interests of the company's employees;

(c) the need to foster the company's business relationships with suppliers, customers and others;

(d) the impact of the company's operations on the community and the environment;

(e) the desirability of the company maintaining a reputation for high standards of business conduct; and

(f) the need to act fairly as between members of the company.

(2) Where or to the extent that the purposes of the company consist of or include purposes other than the benefit of its members, subsection (1) has effect as if the reference to promoting the success of the company for the benefit of its members were to achieving those purposes.

(3) The duty imposed by this section has effect subject to any enactment or rule of law requiring directors, in certain circumstances, to consider or act in the interests of creditors of the company.'

This section codifies the common law and is intended to promote the concept of 'enlightened shareholder value'. The directors are expected to act in good faith to promote the success of the company. As long as they do this they will not become liable merely because a decision turns out to have been a bad one. However, this section needs to be read in conjunction with s.174, which imposes a duty to exercise reasonable care, skill and diligence.

The list of matters to which the directors must have regard, set out in s.172(1), is not exhaustive. The list does, however, make it quite plain that promoting the success of the company means much more than merely maximising profit.

Subsection 2 applies to charitable companies whose objects are not to benefit the members. Subsection 3 would apply when a company is approaching insolvency. In Chapter 19, at 19.1.4.1, we shall see that s.214 Insolvency Act 1986 can make a director of an insolvent company liable for wrongful trading if he continues to act for a company when he knows, or should have known, that the company had no prospect of avoiding going into insolvent liquidation.

It is hard to predict the impact of s.172. It might significantly alter the approach required of directors so that they do genuinely consider the interests of the listed stakeholder groups. On the other hand, to take a more cynical view, it might amount to little more than a box-ticking exercise.

17.1.9.3 The duty to exercise independent judgment

Section 173 provides that:

'(1) A director of a company must exercise independent judgment.

(2) This duty is not infringed by his acting –

(a) in accordance with an agreement duly entered into by the company that restricts the future exercise of discretion by its directors; or

(b) in a way authorised by the company's constitution.'

The constitution of the company may allow a director to delegate some of his duties. An agreement with the company may prevent the director from acting in a certain way. These matters aside, s.173 requires a director to exercise independent judgment and not merely to obey instructions from other people, such as fellow directors.

17.1.9.4 The duty to exercise reasonable care, skill and diligence

Section 174 states that:

'(1) A director of a company must exercise reasonable care, skill and diligence.

(2) This means the care, skill and diligence that would be exercised by a reasonably diligent person with –

(a) the general knowledge, skill and experience that may reasonably be expected of a person carrying out the functions carried out by the director in relation to the company; and

(b) the general knowledge, skill and experience that the director has.'

This dual objective/subjective standard which applies when considering the level of care, skill and diligence expected is a codification of recent developments in the common law. A director must exercise the standard of care, skill and diligence which could objectively be expected of a director, but if he has any extra skill, knowledge or experience this will raise the standard expected of him.

17.1.9.5 The duty to avoid conflicts of interest

Section 175 sets out the duty to avoid a conflict of interest. It states that:

'(1) A director of a company must avoid a situation in which he has, or can have, a direct or indirect interest that conflicts, or possibly may conflict, with the interests of the company.

(2) This applies in particular to the exploitation of any property, information or opportunity (and it is immaterial whether the company could take advantage of the property, information or opportunity).

(3) This duty does not apply to a conflict of interest arising in relation to a transaction or arrangement with the company.

(4) This duty is not infringed –
   (a) if the situation cannot reasonably be regarded as likely to give rise to a conflict of interest; or
   (b) if the matter has been authorised by the directors.

(5) Authorisation may be given by the directors –
   (a) where the company is a private company and nothing in the company's constitution invalidates such authorisation, by the matter being proposed to and authorised by the directors; or
   (b) where the company is a public company and its constitution includes provision enabling the directors to authorise the matter, by the matter being proposed to and authorised by them in accordance with the constitution.

(6) The authorisation is effective only if –
   (a) any requirement as to the quorum at the meeting at which the matter is considered is met without counting the director in question or any other interested director; and
   (b) the matter was agreed to without their voting or would have been agreed to if their votes had not been counted.

(7) Any reference in this section to a conflict of interest includes a conflict of interest and duty and a conflict of duties.'

Subsection 1 reflects the well-known common law position. It is not enough that the director avoids a situation in which he has a conflict of interest, he must also avoid a situation in which he might have such a conflict. Subsection 2 reflects the common law position that a director must not exploit company property for his own ends and that information which he has gained as a result of being a director is here regarded as company property. However, the words 'in particular' show that this duty is not limited to such matters. Subsection 3 recognises that the duty set out in a different section, s.177, deals with the position where a director deals with the company. Section 175 therefore does not cover such dealings.

Subsections 4–6 allow what would otherwise be a conflict of interest if the directors have properly authorised the act in line with the company's constitution. In a private company it is enough that nothing in the constitution prevents authorisation. In a public company the constitution must positively allow for such authorisation. As regards both public and private companies, the director in question does not count towards the quorum of the meeting which gives authorisation. Nor can that director's vote count in favour of authorisation. The directors who give approval must be genuinely independent of, and unconnected with, the conflict of interest. If s.175 is complied with by authorisation by the directors, the members do not need to give approval or authorisation of the transaction or arrangement unless the constitution of the company requires this (s.180(1)).

Section 180(4)(a) allows the members of the company (not the directors) to authorise any breach of ss.175 or 177. This authorisation may be given specifically or generally. However, s.239(3) and (4), considered below at 17.1.10.2, prevent the director(s) in breach from voting on the resolution which proposes ratification. Section 180(4)(b) provides that where the company's articles contain provision for dealing with conflicts of interest, the general duties are not infringed by anything done or omitted by the directors, or any of them, in accordance with these provisions. A person who ceases to be a director continues to be subject to the duty to avoid a conflict of interest as regards the exploitation of any property, information or opportunity of which he became aware at a time when he was a director (s.170(2)(a)).

17.1.9.6 The duty not to accept benefits from third parties

Section 176 provides that:

'(1) A director of a company must not accept a benefit from a third party conferred by reason of –
   (a) his being a director; or
   (b) his doing (or not doing) anything as director.

(2) A "third party" means a person other than the company, an associated body corporate or a person acting on behalf of the company or an associated body corporate.

(3) Benefits received by a director from a person by whom his services (as a director or otherwise) are provided to the company are not regarded as conferred by a third party.

(4) This duty is not infringed if the acceptance of the benefit cannot reasonably be regarded as likely to give rise to a conflict of interest.

(5) Any reference in this section to a conflict of interest includes a conflict of interest and duty and a conflict of duties.'

Whereas s.175 is primarily concerned with a director using company property to his own advantage, s.176 is concerned with a director receiving a benefit from a person other than the company. The duty is breached if the director receives the benefit either because he is a director or because he does anything, or does not do anything, as a director. Subsection 3 recognises that a person might provide his services as a director through a different company and allows this different company to pay him without the duty being breached.

A person who ceases to be a director continues to be subject to the duty not to accept benefits from third parties as regards things done or omitted by him before he ceased to be a director (s.170(2)(b)). There is no provision for the directors to approve acceptance of a benefit from a third party. However, s.180(4)(a) allows the members of the company to authorise such acceptance. Section 176 will overlap with s.175 where a director receives a benefit, such as a bribe, as an inducement to bring about a conflict of interest.

17.1.9.7 The duty to declare interest in proposed transaction or arrangement

Section 177 provides that:

'(1) If a director of a company is in any way, directly or indirectly, interested in a proposed transaction or arrangement with the company, he must declare the nature and extent of that interest to the other directors.

(2) The declaration may (but need not) be made –
   (a) at a meeting of the directors, or
   (b) by notice to the directors in accordance with –
      (i) section 184 (notice in writing), or
      (ii) section 185 (general notice).

(3) If a declaration of interest under this section proves to be, or becomes, inaccurate or incomplete, a further declaration must be made.

(4) Any declaration required by this section must be made before the company enters into the transaction or arrangement.

(5) This section does not require a declaration of an interest of which the director is not aware or

where the director is not aware of the transaction or arrangement in question.
   For this purpose a director is treated as being aware of matters of which he ought reasonably to be aware.

(6) A director need not declare an interest –
   (a) if it cannot reasonably be regarded as likely to give rise to a conflict of interest;
   (b) if, or to the extent that, the other directors are already aware of it (and for this purpose the other directors are treated as aware of anything of which they ought reasonably to be aware); or
   (c) if, or to the extent that, it concerns terms of his service contract that have been or are to be considered –
      (i) by a meeting of the directors, or
      (ii) by a committee of the directors appointed for the purpose under the company's constitution.'

Section 182(1), considered below, requires a director to declare an interest in any **existing** transaction with the company. Criminal liability is imposed if the section is not complied with. Section 177, by contrast, is a general duty which requires a director to declare any interest in a **proposed** transaction with the company. This section replaces the rule that the members of the company had to authorise a director having an interest in a proposed transaction with the company. (However, the company's articles might still require this.) An interest could be within s.177 even as regards a transaction between the company and a person other than the director. This would be the case if the interest of the other person contracting with the company could also amount to a direct or indirect interest of the director. Subsection 2 provides that the notice can be given at a directors' meeting or by notice to the directors but does not need to be made in these ways. If s.177 is complied with, on account of the director giving notice to the other directors, the members do not need to give approval or authorisation of the proposed transaction unless the constitution of the company requires this (s.180(1)). Subsections (3) and (4) are very straightforward. There are four situations in which a director does not need to declare an interest. First, where he is not aware of the interest or transaction in question. But the director is treated as being aware of matters of which he ought reasonably to be aware (s.177(5)). Second, there is no need to declare an interest if it cannot reasonably be regarded as likely to give rise to a conflict of interest (s.177(6)(a)). Third, if the other directors are, or ought reasonably to be, aware of the interest (s.177(6)(b)). So there is no duty to disclose where a company has only one director. Fourth, if the interest concerns his service contract and this has been approved by the directors (s.177(6)(c)).

Section 180(4), described above at 17.1.9.5 in relation to the duty to avoid to conflicts of interest, applies equally to s.177.

17.1.9.8 Civil consequences of breach of one of the general duties

The consequences of a breach or a proposed breach of any of the general duties set out in ss.171–177 are the same as would apply if the corresponding common law or equitable principle applied (s.178(1)). Section 178(2) provides that a breach of any of the duties except s.174 (the duty to exercise reasonable care, skill and diligence) are enforceable in the same way as any other fiduciary duty owed to a company by its directors. So the remedy for a breach of s.174 would be damages. The possible remedies for breach of one of the other general duties would include damages, avoiding a contract, the restitution of property, an order to account for profits, an injunction and summary dismissal.

The director's duties will generally be enforceable only by the company. This means by the board of directors or by the members in general meeting. However, a member might be able to bring a statutory **derivative claim** on behalf of the company. Derivative claims are considered in detail in the following chapter at 18.8.2. Although s.172 requires the directors to consider the interests of employees, the employees would have no right to bring a civil action under s.172 or any other of the statutory duties.

17.1.9.9 Declaration of interest in existing transaction or arrangement

Section 182 sets out a further duty of a director to declare any interest in a transaction with a company. This duty is not regarded as one of the general duties, as it imposes criminal liability and breach of it has no civil consequences.

Section 182 provides as follows:

'(1) Where a director of a company is in any way, directly or indirectly, interested in a transaction or arrangement that has been entered into by the company, he must declare the nature and extent of the interest to the other directors in accordance with this section.

This section does not apply if or to the extent that the interest has been declared under section 177 (duty to declare interest in proposed transaction or arrangement).

(2) The declaration must be made –
(a) at a meeting of the directors, or
(b) by notice in writing (see section 184), or
(c) by general notice (see section 185).

(3) If a declaration of interest under this section proves to be, or becomes, inaccurate or incomplete, a further declaration must be made.

(4) Any declaration required by this section must be made as soon as is reasonably practicable.

Failure to comply with this requirement does not affect the underlying duty to make the declaration.

(5) This section does not require a declaration of an interest of which the director is not aware or where the director is not aware of the transaction or arrangement in question.

For this purpose a director is treated as being aware of matters of which he ought reasonably to be aware.

(6) A director need not declare an interest under this section –
(a) if it cannot reasonably be regarded as likely to give rise to a conflict of interest;
(b) if, or to the extent that, the other directors are already aware of it (and for this purpose the other directors are treated as aware of anything of which they ought reasonably to be aware); or
(c) if, or to the extent that, it concerns terms of his service contract that have been or are to be considered –
(i) by a meeting of the directors, or
(ii) by a committee of the directors appointed for the purpose under the company's constitution.'

The scope of s.182(1) is very wide. A declaration must be made to the other directors whenever a director is in any way, directly or indirectly, interested in a transaction or arrangement that has been entered into by the company. The director must state the nature and extent of the director's interest in the transaction or arrangement. We saw above that one of the general duties, s.177 (the duty to declare an interest in a proposed transaction or arrangement), applies where the transaction has yet to take place. Section 182 applies when the transaction or arrangement is already existing. If a declaration has been made under s.177 then a further declaration does not need to be made under s.182, unless the director's interest changes from what was proposed.

Section 182(2) sets out the ways in which the declaration must be made. If it is made by notice in writing, s.184 allows the declaration to be made electronically. It also puts the declaration on the agenda of the next meeting of the directors and requires it to be recorded in the minutes of that meeting. If the declaration is made by general notice, s.185(4) provides that the general notice will not be effective unless it is given at a meeting of the directors, or the director takes reasonable steps to secure that it is brought up and read at the next meeting of the directors. Sections 182(3) and (4) are straightforward.

Section 182(5) protects a director who is not aware of an interest which should be declared or not aware of the transaction or arrangement in question. But it also makes a director aware of matters of which he ought reasonably to be aware, so there will be no way out by turning a blind eye. Section 182(6) is straightforward. A director who fails to comply with s.182 commits a criminal offence (s.183). However, a transaction or arrangement which should have been declared cannot be invalidated by s.182. Nor does s.182 impose civil liabilities.

If a company has only one director then s.182 is generally inapplicable. However, s.231 applies where a single-member company makes a contract with the sole member if he is also a director and the contract is not entered into in the ordinary course of the company's business. It requires the contract to be in writing, in a written memorandum or recorded in the minutes of the next directors' meeting. Failure to comply with this section is again a criminal offence but does not invalidate the contract. But if a company with only one director is required to have two directors (generally because it is a plc), then the declaration must be recorded in writing and is deemed to be on the agenda of the next directors' meeting (s.186). Section 187 provides that s.182 applies to shadow directors, except that notice cannot be given at a directors' meeting.

17.1.10 Transactions with directors requiring approval of members

The following four types of transactions with directors must be approved by the members: long-term service contracts; substantial property transactions; loans to directors; and payments of over £200 for loss of office. Failure to gain the members' approval will have civil consequences but will not cause a criminal offence to have been committed.

Section 188 requires that the members give approval when a director is appointed for more than two years under a service contract which the company cannot terminate earlier by giving notice. The section applies if a contract may run for more than two years, even if it will not necessarily do so. An ordinary resolution of the members will suffice unless the company's articles require a higher majority or unanimity (s.281(3)). If the members vote by written resolution, each member must be given a copy of the service contract in question at the same time as, or before, the written resolution is sent to him. If the vote is to be taken at a meeting of members then the service contract must be available for inspection both at the meeting and at the company's registered office for at least 15 days before the meeting. If s.188 is not complied with then the service contract is void, to the extent of the contravention, and is deemed to contain a term allowing the company to terminate it at any time by giving reasonable notice (s.189).

Section 190 requires that substantial property transactions under which a director acquires a non-cash asset must be similarly approved. A 'substantial' non-cash asset is one which exceeds 10 per cent of the company's asset value and is worth more than £5 000 or one which exceeds £10 000 (s.191). If this section is breached, the transaction in question is voidable unless the property has been restored or the company has been indemnified. In addition, the director must account to the company for gains made.

Sections 197–222 require that loans to directors and guarantees of such loans, quasi loans, credit transactions and payment for loss of office must be similarly approved. As regards loans, quasi loans and credit transactions the consequences of breach are that the loan, etc. is voidable unless the money has been repaid or the company has been indemnified. If a payment for loss of office is not properly approved the recipient holds it on trust for the company making it and any director who authorised or approved the payment is jointly and severally liable to indemnify the company for any loss resulting to it.

None of the above contracts will be voidable if a third party in good faith for value and without notice would be affected by the avoidance. All of the matters which require approval of the members apply equally to shadow directors (s.223).

17.1.11 Protecting directors from liability

The company's constitution might contain provisions which seek to protect directors from liability or the members might ratify wrongful acts of directors. In such circumstances ss.232–239 set out safeguards to protect the company.

17.1.11.1 Constitutional provisions protecting directors from liability

Section 232(1) provides that any provision that purports to exempt a director of a company (to any extent) from any liability that would otherwise attach to him in connection with any negligence, default, breach of duty or breach of trust in relation to the company is void. This does not, however, prevent the members from passing a resolution ratifying the negligent conduct of a director.

Section 232(2) provides that any provision by which a company directly or indirectly provides an indemnity (to any extent) for a director of the company, or of an associated company, against any liability attaching to him in connection with any negligence, default, breach of duty or breach of trust in relation to the company of which he is a director is also void. However, as regards this section, exceptions are made in respect of the provision of insurance, certain qualifying provisions to indemnify a third party, or to indemnify a director acting as a trustee of an occupational pension scheme. Section 232 applies to any provision, whether contained in a company's articles or in any contract with the company or otherwise (s.232(3)). However, s.232(4) provides that nothing in s.232 prevents a company's articles from making such provision as has previously been lawful for dealing with conflicts of interest. So a director will be able to have an interest in a transaction which conflicts with the interests of the company as long as the articles permit this, as long as it has been disclosed to the other directors and as long as it would previously have been lawful for dealing with conflicts of interest. This section has to be read in conjunction with s.180(4)(b), which provides that 'the general duties, where the company's articles contain provisions for dealing with conflicts of interest, are not infringed by anything done (or omitted) by the directors, or any of them, in accordance with those provisions'. Both sections were added to the Companies Bill at a very late stage to make sure that the law in this area was not changed. The difficulty is in deciding what provisions in the articles would previously have been lawful for dealing with conflicts of interest. The law here is not at all clear. However, it seems probable that the articles could validly allow for a potential conflict of interest but could not allow for an actual conflict of interest.

17.1.11.2 Ratification of acts giving rise to liability

Section 239 retains the common law right of the members to pass a resolution saying that the company is ratifying conduct by a director amounting to negligence, default, breach of duty or breach of trust in relation to the company. Conduct includes acts and omissions. The section applies to former directors and shadow directors as well as to current directors. The director in question, and any person associated with him, cannot vote on the resolution whether it is proposed as a written resolution or as a resolution proposed at a meeting (s.239(4)). However, the director can count towards the quorum of any meeting and can speak at the meeting. An ordinary resolution of the members is all that is required unless the company's articles require a higher majority or unanimity (s.281(3)). Section 239(6) provides that nothing in s.239 affects the validity of a decision taken by unanimous consent of the members, or any power of the directors to agree not to sue, or to settle or release a claim made by them on behalf of the company. However, s.239(7) limits the power of members to ratify by providing that s.239 does not affect any legislation or rule of law imposing additional requirements for valid ratification or any rule of law as to acts that are incapable of being ratified by the company. So s.239 does not deal with the kinds of acts which can or cannot be ratified. Under the common law, some types of acts can be ratified by ordinary resolution, some by special resolution and some cannot be ratified at all.

Generally, the position is that if the directors do exceed their powers or use them irregularly or negligently, the shareholders may still ratify their acts by passing an ordinary resolution. However, this is not the case if the directors acted fraudulently or if company money or property is misappropriated.

Bamford v Bamford
[1970] Ch 212 (Court of Appeal)

The company was in danger of being taken over. To avoid this the directors issued an extra 500 000 shares to a business which distributed the company's products. This might have been contrary to the articles. (This point was never decided.) The shareholders approved the issue of the shares by passing an ordinary resolution at a general meeting.

Held. Even if the directors had irregularly exercised their powers, the ratification by the shareholders made the contract a good one, and absolved the directors from all liability.

Harman LJ: 'Directors can, by making a full and frank disclosure and calling together the general body of the shareholders, obtain . . . forgiveness of their sins; and . . . everything will go on as if it had been done right from the beginning. I cannot believe that this is not a commonplace of company law. It is done every day. Of course, if the majority of the general meeting will not forgive and approve, the directors must pay for it.'

A director will not be liable to the company for the act of his co-directors if he did not know of the act and should not have suspected it. This is because the other directors are neither his employees nor his agents. However, if a director became aware of serious breaches of duty by fellow directors then he could be liable in negligence if he failed to inform the members or take control of the company's assets. If more than one director is liable for a breach, they are jointly and severally liable. Any of the directors in breach can therefore be sued for the whole amount, but will be able to claim a contribution from the other directors liable.

17.1.11.3 Relief from the court

Section 1157 allows the court to grant relief to a director (or company secretary or auditor) in breach of his duty if the director 'acted honestly and reasonably and ought fairly to be excused'.

Test your understanding 17.2

1 Are directors automatically entitled to be paid for their services?

2 What powers do directors have to manage the company?

3 Can an act done by a company be invalidated on the grounds that it was *ultra vires*?

4 What are the general duties which a director owes to the company?

17.2 THE COMPANY SECRETARY

Section 271 of the Act requires every public company to have a company secretary. Prior to the coming into force of the 2006 Act, private companies also had to have a secretary. Now, however, s.270 provides that a private company is not required to have a secretary. As regards a private company without a secretary, anything which is authorised or required to be sent to the secretary can be sent to the company and anything addressed to the secretary will be regarded as addressed to the company (s.270(3)(a)). When a private company does not have a secretary, anything which is required to be done by the secretary can be done by a director or by a person authorised, generally or specifically, by a director (s.270(3)(b)). When a company does have a company secretary, but the office is vacant or the secretary is unable to act, s.274 similarly allows the directors to authorise any person to do anything which needs to be done by the company secretary. Where there is a legal requirement that something needs to be done by a director and by the secretary, s.280 provides that the thing cannot be done by one person acting both as director and as, or in place of, the secretary.

Section 272 gives the Secretary of State the power to order a public company without a secretary to appoint one. The company has between one and three months to make the appointment and give notice to the Registrar of Companies that this has been done. If the company does not comply with this requirement then the company and every officer in default commits an offence and can be fined.

Section 273 of the Act requires the directors to ensure that the secretary of a public company is a suitably qualified person. This means either that he must hold professionally recognised qualifications, as an accountant or a UK qualified lawyer, or have been a secretary of a public company for three of the past five years. In addition, the directors may appoint a person who appears to them to be capable of discharging the duties and functions of a company secretary, by virtue of holding or having held any other position, or being a member of any other body.

A company secretary can be a corporate body, that is to say a company or an LLP. Partnerships can also act as company secretaries. The articles of a company usually provide that the company secretary is appointed, and can be removed, by the directors. (Article 99 of Table A provides this.) The articles will also usually provide that the directors fix the secretary's conditions of employment and the length of time for which he is to hold office. The secretary is regarded as an employee of the company for the purposes of preferential payments of debts on liquidation, and is also an officer of the company.

In Chapter 16 we saw that when a company is formed the statement of proposed officers must give the name and address of the first company secretary (if the company is to have a company secretary) and the secretary must give consent to acting. The secretary's duties are to look after the administration of the company. This would include keeping the company register up to date, sending information to the Registrar of Companies, arranging meetings, sending notice of meetings and resolutions to members, employing office staff and keeping up to date with legislation which affects the company. The secretary owes the company fiduciary duties which are similar to the fiduciary duties owed by the directors. A few of the secretary's duties, such as the duty to submit the annual return, are imposed by statute, in this case by s.854.

Although concerned in the management of the company's business, the secretary is not a manager of the company and is not concerned in carrying on the business of the company. The company secretary has a limited power to bind the company, but only as regards the type of administrative contracts which a company secretary could be expected to make. He cannot borrow money on the company's behalf, nor sue on the company's behalf, without authority.

Panorama Developments (Guildford) Ltd v *Fidelis Furnishing Fabrics Ltd*
[1971] 3 All ER 16 (Court of Appeal)

B was the secretary of a well-respected company. He used the company's notepaper to order cars from the claimants, a car-hire company. B falsely stated that the cars were needed by the company for business purposes, such as meeting customers at airports. Before supplying the cars, the claimants asked for references about the company, which B provided. In the hire agreements, B was stated to be the hirer, and he was described as 'company secretary'. In fact B used the cars for his own purposes. The company knew nothing about the car hire transactions and when the claimants sent in a bill they refused to pay it.

Held. The company was liable. B, as company secretary, had apparent authority to hire the cars on behalf of the company.

Lord Denning MR: 'A company secretary ... is no longer a mere clerk. He regularly makes representations on behalf of the company and enters into contracts on its behalf which come within the day to day running of the company's business. So much so that he may be regarded as held out as having the authority to do such things on behalf of the company. He is certainly entitled to sign contracts connected with the administrative side of the company's affairs, such as employing staff, and ordering cars, and so forth.'

17.2.1 **Register of secretaries**

Section 275(1) requires every company to keep a register of its secretaries at its registered office or at a place specified in regulations under s.1136. The register must give the following details of the company secretary: his full name, any former name and his address. The address required to be stated is a service address which can be 'The company's registered office'. If the company secretary is changed, s.276(1)(a) requires that notification must be sent to the Registrar within 14 days, along with signed consent by the new secretary appointed. If the details on the register change, s.276(1)(b) requires that the Registrar is informed within 14 days. Members can inspect the register of directors and secretaries free of charge, non-members can be charged a small fee (s.275(5)). If the register is not open to inspection, the company and its officers may be fined (s.275(6)) and the court may order immediate inspection to be allowed (s.275(8)).

17.3 **THE AUDITOR**

Except as regards very small companies, companies will generally need to employ an accountant to prepare the accounts which must be given to members of the company and submitted to Companies House. The accountant will be appointed by the directors of the company. The auditor is not the company accountant, but a different accountant who keeps an eye on the company's accounts and accounting procedures. The auditor is appointed by the members of the company and reports to the members.

17.3.1 The need to have an auditor

Small private companies, but not public companies, are exempt from having to have their accounts audited, by virtue of s.477(1). In this context a company is regarded as small in a particular year if (i) the company's annual turnover is £5.6 million or less, and (ii) the total assets of the company are £2.8 million or less. Dormant companies are exempt from having to appoint an auditor, by virtue of s.480. These two exemptions apart, all companies must have an auditor (s.475(1)). Even as regards these two exemptions, members representing at least 10 per cent of the nominal value of the company's issued share capital or, if the company does not have a share capital, representing at least 10 per cent of the members of the company may give notice requiring an audit (s.476).

The auditor is neither a manager nor an employee of the company. Unlike the directors and the secretary, the auditor is an independent contractor.

17.3.2 Appointment

Officers and employees of the company are prohibited from being appointed as the company auditor or as the auditor of a parent or subsidiary company on the grounds of lack of independence. The business partners and employees of officers and employees of the company are also banned by s.1214. However, members of the company can be appointed as the auditor if they are suitably qualified. With a few minor exceptions, a person can be appointed as an auditor only if he is a chartered or certified accountant. Partnerships and LLPs can be appointed as auditors if the firm is controlled by qualified persons and the individual responsible for the firm's audit work is suitably qualified. A company can be appointed as an auditor as long as qualified persons control the company and its board of directors. A register of persons qualified to act as auditors is kept. It is an offence for a person to describe himself as a registered auditor if his name does not appear on this register.

17.3.2.1 Appointment of auditor of private company

Section 485(1) provides that an auditor or auditors of a private company must be appointed for each financial year of the company, unless the directors reasonably resolve otherwise on the ground that audited accounts are unlikely to be required. The appointment must be made within 28 days of the accounts being circulated to members (s.485(2)) The appointed auditors will take office when the outgoing auditors cease to hold office. The directors can appoint the first auditor of a private company (s.485(3)). If they do not do this, the members appoint the first auditor (s.485(4)). Subsequent auditors are appointed by ordinary resolution of the members (s.485(4)). Section 487 provides that where no auditor has been appointed by the end of the next period for appointing auditors, any auditor in office immediately before that time is deemed to be reappointed at that time, unless: (a) he was appointed by the directors; or (b) the company's articles require actual re-appointment; or (c) the deemed reappointment is prevented by the members under section 488; or (d) the members have resolved that he should not be reappointed, or (e) the directors have resolved that no auditor or auditors should be appointed for the financial year in question. If an auditor is not appointed in accordance with s.485, s.486 gives the Secretary of State the power to appoint one. Section 488 prevents an auditor from being automatically reappointed if members holding at least 5 per cent of the total voting rights give notice that the auditor should not be reappointed.

17.3.2.2 Appointment of auditor of public company

Section 489(1) provides that an auditor or auditors of a public company must be appointed for each financial year of the company, unless the directors reasonably resolve otherwise on the ground that audited accounts are unlikely to be required. The auditor must be appointed before the end of the meeting at which the company accounts are laid before the members (s.489(2)). This is a different rule from the one which applies to private companies because private companies do not need to hold members' meetings.

The first auditor of a public company is appointed by the directors and holds office until the first general meeting at which the accounts are considered (s.489(3)). Section 489(4) provides that subsequent auditors are appointed by ordinary resolution of the members at each general meeting at which the accounts are considered. If an auditor is not appointed in accordance with s.489, s.490 gives the Secretary of State the power to appoint one. The auditors of a public company do not take office until the previous auditors have left office. They cease to hold office at the end of the next meeting at which the accounts are considered (s.491).

17.3.2.3 Leaving office

An auditor can be removed from office, before the expiry of his term of office, at any time (s.510(1)). This can be achieved only by an ordinary resolution at a meeting, and special notice of the resolution proposing to remove the auditor has to be given (s.510(2)). (We have already seen that special notice requires that the company is given 28 days' notice of the resolution. The company will then have to inform members of the notice at the same time and in the same way as it informs them of the meeting.) Section 511 provides that the auditor must be given a copy of the resolution, and has the right to compel the company to circulate written representations of reasonable length to all the members entitled to vote at the meeting. If these representations are received too late by the company to be issued in time, the auditor can require them to be read out at the meeting. However, this right can be disallowed if the company applies to the court and the court finds that the auditor is abusing the right to secure needless publicity for defamatory matter. The written resolution procedure cannot be used to dismiss an auditor. If an auditor is removed, the Registrar must be informed within 14 days (s.512). An auditor removed from office under s.510 is not prevented from claiming damages on account of his contract having been terminated (s.513).

The members of a private company may propose a written resolution to replace an auditor after his term of office has expired (as opposed to removing him from office) (s.514). A copy of the proposed written resolution must be sent to both the outgoing auditor and to his proposed replacement. The outgoing auditor has the right to make written representations, and to have these circulated to members, along with the written resolution. As an alternative to a written resolution, a resolution at a company meeting can propose to replace an auditor after his term of office has expired. Special notice of the resolution must be given to the company and sent to the members. A copy of the proposed written resolution must be sent to both the outgoing auditor and to his proposed replacement. The outgoing auditor has the right to make written representations which should be sent to the members or, if they are not received in time, read out at the meeting (s.515).

An auditor can resign by delivering written notice to the company's registered office (s.516(1)). The company must then send a copy of the auditor's notice of resignation to the Registrar of Companies within 14 days of its being deposited (s.517(1)). In addition, the auditor may require the directors to call a general meeting of the company (s.518(2)). The auditor may deposit with the company an explanation of the circumstances connected with his resignation. Unless this is held by a court to be defamatory, it must be sent to the members along with the notice of the meeting. At the meeting, which must be held within 28 days, the explanation given by the auditor for his resignation must be considered. The auditor has a right to speak at such a meeting (s.518(10)).

As regards companies which are not quoted, whenever an auditor for any reason ceases to hold office he must deposit at the company's registered office a statement of the circumstances connected with his ceasing to hold office, unless he considers that there are no circumstances in connection with his ceasing to hold office that need to be brought to the attention of the members of the company or the creditors (s.519(1)). If he considers that there are no circumstances in connection with his ceasing to hold office that need to be brought to the attention of the members or the creditors of the company, he must deposit at the company's registered office a statement to that effect (s.519(2)). As regards companies which are quoted, whenever an auditor ceases to hold office for any reason he must deposit at the company's registered office a statement of the circumstances connected with his ceasing to hold office (s.519(3)).

Where the statement deposited under s.519 states the circumstances connected with the auditor ceasing to hold office, s.520 requires the company to send a copy to all members and debenture holders within 14 days.

A copy of the auditor's statement must be sent to the Registrar of Companies by the departing auditor (s.521). This must be done within 21 days of its being deposited at the company's registered office under s.519. When an auditor leaves office, s.522 requires that a copy of the statement required under s.519(1) should also be sent to the appropriate audit authority. This copy has to be sent only if the auditor is leaving before the expiry of his term of office or if he has conducted a major audit. A major audit is defined by s.525 as a statutory audit of a listed company or a company in whose financial condition there is a major public interest. Section 523 imposes a duty on a company to notify the appropriate audit authority whenever an auditor leaves office before the expiry of his term of office. If the auditor's statement deposited under s.519 contained a statement of circumstances in connection with his ceasing to hold office, that statement must be sent. If there was no such statement, the company can send its own statement as to why the auditor left office.

17.3.3 Remuneration and duties

Section 492(1) provides that the remuneration which the auditor is to receive must either be fixed by the members at a general meeting, or it must be fixed in such a way as the members in a general meeting determine. In practice, it is usually fixed by the directors, because the members usually determine that the directors should fix it. A note in the accounts must indicate how much the auditors are paid, as well as expenses and benefits.

The auditor has two duties: to audit the accounts and to report to the members regarding the accounts. Auditing of the accounts involves carrying out a series of checks and tests to see that they are fair and accurate. The second duty means that the auditor must certify that in his opinion the books give a true and fair reflection of the company's financial position and have been properly prepared in accordance with the Companies Act 2006. The report is not made to the members directly, but can be delivered to the company secretary. It must, however, be available for inspection by any member. If the directors' report (see below at 17.6.2.1) is inconsistent with the annual accounts, this must be stated in the auditor's report.

Section 499 of the Act provides that the auditors of a company have a right of access at all times to the company's books, accounts and vouchers, and are entitled to require from the company's officers such information and explanations as they think necessary for the performance of their duties as auditors.

It is a criminal offence for any company officer to knowingly or recklessly give false, deceptive or misleading information to an auditor (s.501). Section 502(2) gives auditors the right to attend company meetings and be given notice of them. At a meeting the auditor has a right to speak on any part of the business which concerns him as an auditor. Section 502(1) gives them a right to receive proposed written resolutions. Where the auditor is an individual, the auditor's report must be signed by him. Where the auditor is a

firm, the report must be signed by the senior statutory auditor in his own name, for and on behalf of the auditor (s.503). However, the name of the auditor (or senior statutory auditor) can be omitted from public copies of the report, and from the report delivered to the Registrar, where there are reasonable grounds to believe that statement of the name would create, or be likely to create, a serious risk that the auditor or any other person would be subject to violence or intimidation (s.506).

Lopes LJ described the care and skill required of an auditor in *Re Kingston Cotton Mill Co (No. 2)* [1896] 2 Ch 279 (Court of Appeal):

'An auditor is not bound to be a detective, or, as was said, to approach his work with suspicion or with a foregone conclusion that there is something wrong. He is a watch-dog, but not a bloodhound. He is justified in believing tried servants of the company in whom confidence is placed by the company. He is entitled to assume that they are honest, and to rely upon their representations, provided he takes reasonable care. If there is anything calculated to excite suspicion he should probe it to the bottom; but in the absence of anything of that kind he is only bound to be reasonably cautious and careful.'

The auditor does not guarantee that he will discover all fraud. In *Fomento (Sterling Area) Ltd* v *Selsdon Fountain Pen Co Ltd* [1958] 1 All ER 11 Lord Denning asked, 'What is the proper function of an auditor?' and gave the following explanation:

'It is said that he is bound only to verify the sum, the arithmetical conclusion, by reference to the books and all necessary vouching material and oral explanations . . . I think this is too narrow a view. An auditor is not to be confined to the mechanics of checking vouchers and making arithmetical computations. He is not to be written off as a professional "adder-upper and subtractor". His vital task is to take care to see that errors are not made, be they errors of computation, or errors of omission or commission, or downright untruths. To perform this task properly he must come to it with an inquiring mind – not suspicious of dishonesty, I agree – but suspecting that someone may have made a mistake somewhere and that a check must be made to ensure that there has been none.'

The auditor owes his duty of care and skill to the company and to the membership as a whole. However, the duty is not owed to members of the public nor to individual members of the company.

Caparo Industries plc v Dickman
[1990] 1 All ER 568 (House of Lords)

The claimants owned shares in F plc. After receiving the audited accounts of F plc, the claimants bought more shares in the company and later made a successful take-over bid for the company. Later they sued the auditors of F plc because the accounts had shown a pre-tax profit of £1.2m and the claimants alleged that it should have shown a loss of £0.4m. The claimants alleged that the auditors had owed them a duty of care, which they had breached.

Held. The auditors owed no duty of care to the claimants. The following points were made.

(i) Whether or not a duty of care exists depends upon foreseeability of damage, proximity of relationship and the reasonableness of imposing a duty.

(ii) When a statement was put into more or less general circulation, and the maker had no reason to anticipate that a stranger might rely on it, there was no relationship of proximity between the maker and the person relying on it. This would not be the case if the maker of the statement knew that it would be communicated to the person relying on it specifically in connection with any particular transaction which he was considering entering into.

(iii) The auditors of a company owe no duty to members of the public who relied on the accounts to buy shares in the company. Nor do they owe a duty to individual members of the company who wish to buy more shares in the company.

COMMENT Even where a duty of care is owed by the auditors, it must be shown that the breach of this duty caused the loss in respect of which damages are claimed. In **JEB Fasteners Ltd v Marks, Bloom & Co** [1983] 1 All ER 583 the claimants took over a company after having seen audited accounts which showed an inflated figure for profit. The claimants had no remedy against the auditors, even if a duty of care was owed to them by the auditors, because their real motive in taking over the company was to acquire the services of two directors who worked for the company. They would have taken the company over to acquire the services of these two even if they had not been misled by the accounts, and therefore the auditors' breach of duty did not cause the loss.

Auditors should be familiar with the company's constitution, but have no duty to ensure that the company is well run.

Section 507(1) provides that an auditor commits an offence if he knowingly or recklessly causes an auditor's report on the company's annual accounts to include any matter that is misleading, false or deceptive in a material particular.

Section 507(2) provides that an auditor commits an offence if he knowingly or recklessly causes such a report to omit a statement required by:

(a) s.498(2)(b) (statement that company's accounts do not agree with accounting records and returns);

(b) s.498(3) (statement that necessary information and explanations not obtained); or

(c) s.498(5) (statement that directors wrongly took advantage of exemption from obligation to prepare group accounts).

17.3.4 Auditors' liability

Auditors can be liable to the company either for breach of contract or, if they breach a duty of care owed to the company, in negligence. An auditor who follows accounting standards and guidelines is most unlikely to be in breach of a duty of care.

Section 532 provides that any agreement exempting an auditor from liability is void unless it is within ss.533, or 534–536. This applies whether the agreement was in the articles, or made in a contract with the company or made in any other way. It is therefore necessary to consider the exemptions set out in ss.533–536.

Section 533 merely allows a company to indemnify an auditor against the costs of defending legal proceedings as long as the auditor is acquitted or judgment is given in his favour.

Section 534 is a much more controversial provision which allows for **liability limitation agreements** between companies and their auditors. This provision was brought in under pressure from the four biggest accountancy firms, which argued that without it they would be in danger of going out of business.

Section 534(1) defines a liability limitation agreement as an agreement that purports to limit the amount of a liability owed to a company by its auditor in respect of any negligence, default, breach of duty or breach of trust, occurring in the course of the audit of accounts, of which the auditor may be guilty in relation to the company. Section 534(2) provides that the terms of such an agreement must comply with the requirements of s.535 and must be authorised by the company members in accordance with s.536.

Section 535 requires that the agreement is to apply only to acts and omissions occurring during one financial year, and that the year in question should be specified. It does not matter how the agreement is framed. Nor does the agreement need to specify the limit on the auditor's liability as a sum of money or as a formula.

Section 536(2) sets out the three ways in which the members of a private company can give authorisation:

(a) by the company passing a resolution, before it enters into the agreement, waiving the need for approval;

(b) by the company passing a resolution, before it enters into the agreement, approving the agreement's principal terms; or

(c) by the company passing a resolution, after it enters into the agreement, approving the agreement.

Section 536(3) sets out the two ways in which the members of a public company can give authorisation:

(a) by the company passing a resolution in general meeting, before it enters into the agreement, approving the agreement's principal terms; or

(b) by the company passing a resolution in general meeting, after it enters into the agreement, approving the agreement.

As regards all of the above resolutions, an ordinary resolution will be enough unless the company's articles require a higher threshold. The 'principal terms' of an agreement specify the kinds of acts or omissions covered, the financial year to which the agreement relates and the limit to which the auditor's liability is subject (s.536(4)). Authorisation can be withdrawn by the company passing an ordinary resolution before the company enters into the agreement. If the company has already entered into the agreement, an ordinary resolution withdrawing authorisation must be passed before the beginning of the financial year to which the agreement relates (s.536(5)). Authorisation can always be withdrawn in this way, even if the agreement itself states that it may not.

Section 537(1) limits the effect of a liability limitation agreement by providing that the auditor's liability cannot be limited to less than such amount as is fair and reasonable in all the circumstances, having particular regard to the auditor's responsibilities, the nature and purpose of the auditor's contractual obligations to the company, and the professional standards expected of him. If a liability limitation agreement does attempt to limit the auditor's liability to less than the amount allowed by s.537(1), it will not be rendered completely ineffective but will take effect as if it had limited his liability to the amount allowed by s.537(1).

In determining what is fair and reasonable in all the circumstances of the case, no account is to be taken of matters arising after the loss or damage in question has been incurred, or matters (whenever arising) affecting the possibility of recovering compensation from other persons liable in respect of the same loss or damage. If a company does make a liability limitation agreement s.538 provides that this must be disclosed in a note in the company's annual accounts, in the directors' report and in such other places as the regulations made by the Secretary of State may stipulate.

Section 534(3) provides that a liability limitation agreement is not subject to ss.2 or 3(a) of the Unfair Contract Terms Act 1977 (considered in Chapter 5 at 5.6). This is obviously the case. These sections of UCTA 1977 limit the exclusion of liability for negligence and breach of contract. The whole point of a liability limitation agreement is that it does allow for such a limitation.

17.3.4.1 Web site publication of concerns of members of quoted companies

Section 527 allows the members of quoted companies to require the company to publish concerns which they have about the audit on the company's web site. These concerns can either be about the audit of the company's accounts or about any circumstances connected with an auditor leaving office since the previous accounts meeting (s.527(1)). The company must comply with the request if it is put forward by shareholders holding at least 5 per cent of the voting rights or if it is put forward by at least 100 members with the right to vote, and on average they hold at least £100 of paid up shares. (s.527(2)). The request can be sent in hard copy or electronically (s.527(4)). If the request is not complied with, every company officer in default commits an offence (s.530).

Test your understanding 17.3

1 What is the role of a company secretary?

2 Can a company secretary make contracts which bind the company?

3 Do company secretaries need to hold special qualifications?

4 What is the role of the company auditor? Must all companies have an auditor?

5 Who appoints the auditor?

6 Is it possible to remove an auditor before his term of office has expired?

17.4 COMPANY REGISTERS

A company is obliged to keep certain registers and documents at its registered office. Most of these registers can be inspected by members of the public, although some can only be inspected by company members.

17.4.1 Registers held at the registered office

The following registers and documents must be kept at the registered office of a company, and can be inspected by a member of the public.

(i) The register of directors and the register of secretaries (described above at 17.1.4 and 17.2.1).

(ii) The register of members. Section 113 of the Act requires every company to hold a register of members, giving their names and addresses, the dates on which they became or ceased to be a member, the number of shares held and the amount paid up on each share. Details of a person's membership must be left on the register for ten years after the membership has ceased. If the company has more than 50 members, the company must also keep an up-to-date index of the members. This index can be a part of the register of members. The register must be available for inspection at the company's registered office, or at some other place specified in regulations made by the Secretary of State. If the register of members is not kept at the company's registered office, the Registrar must be notified of where it is kept. Any member has the right to inspect the register of members free of charge; others are also entitled to inspect it but may be charged a small fee. Any person has the right to require the company to supply a copy of the register, or any part of it, within five days, although a fee may be charged for this. A person seeking either to inspect the register or have a copy sent to him must make a request to the company. This request must give his name and address, and the purpose for which the information is to be used. If the request comes from an organisation, the name and address given must be that of the person making the request on behalf of the organisation. A company to which a request has been made can refuse it on the grounds that the request is not sought for a proper purpose. Notice of this must be given to the person who made the request. It is a criminal offence for a person to include in a request to inspect or require a copy of the register a statement that is misleading, false or deceptive in a material particular. A company officer who does not allow inspection of the register, or who refuses to send a copy to a member who has requested one, is guilty of an offence. The court can order the company to allow inspection or to send a copy. Where a person inspects the register or the company provides him with a copy of it, an offence is committed by the company and by every officer in default if the company does not inform the person of the most recent date on which the register was altered and also that there were no further alterations to be made. If the company is a single member company the register of members must state this as well as giving the name and address of the member.

(iii) The register of directors' interests. Section 809 of the Act requires the company to keep a register of any interest which the directors, or their immediate family, have in the company's shares or debentures. The register must show the price paid for shares and any share options which the directors might hold. It must either have an index or be in index form. It is available for inspection in the same way as the register of members. The register must be kept at the registered office or at the place where the register of members is kept. Members can inspect the register free of charge; non-members can be charged a small fee. A copy can be obtained from the company by any person if a fee is paid. The register must be available for inspection at every annual general meeting of the company.

(iv) Section 876 requires that every company keep a register of charges at its registered office. (Charges are explained in Chapter 18 at 18.9.) Section 875 requires that copies of all documents creating a charge are held for inspection at the registered office. The register of charges is therefore a summary giving brief details of each charge (the property charged, the amount of the charge and the person entitled to it). Members and creditors can inspect this register free of charge, others may be charged a small fee. Failure to comply with these requirements mean that the company officers can be fined, but does not make the charge invalid in any way. However, charges must also be registered with the Registrar and if they are not registered with him then they are void against any liquidator or creditor of the company.

(v) A copy of every contract under which a public company bought its own shares must be held at the registered office for ten years after the contract was performed or should have been performed. Any person may inspect this free of charge (s.702).

(vi) A company does not need to hold a register of debenture holders. However, if such a register is kept, it must be kept at the registered office or at some other place specified in regulations made by the Secretary of State. If the register of members is not kept at the company's registered office, the Registrar must be notified of where it is kept (s.743). Debenture holders and company members may inspect this free of charge; others may be charged a small fee. A copy can be obtained from the company on payment of a fee.

(vii) A public company must keep a register of people who hold more than a specified number of the voting rights of its shares (s.808). This register must be kept at the same place as the register of directors' interests. There is no fee for inspection of this register, but a fee may be charged if a copy is obtained from the company. Any report of an investigation of a public company's interests in shares must also be kept and be made available for inspection in the same way.

17.4.2 Documents which can be inspected only by company members

The following documents can be inspected only by members of the company:

(i) A copy of every contract under which a private company buys its own shares must be kept at the registered office for ten years after the purchase (s.702).

(ii) A copy of the contract of service of every director or shadow director, either with the company or with one of its subsidiaries, must be kept for one year after the contract ends (s.228). Where the contract is not in writing, a written memorandum of its terms must be kept available for inspection. The contract, or written memorandum, must be kept at a place where the register of members must be kept. The Registrar must be told where the contract or written memorandum are kept. There is no fee for inspection.

(iii) The minutes of any general meeting must be kept at the registered office for ten years. Copies of resolutions passed otherwise than at general meetings must also be kept for ten years (s.358). Members can inspect the minutes or the copies and there is no fee for inspection. The company can be required to send a copy to a member who pays a small fee.

(iv) The records of written resolutions of a private company which were passed otherwise than as resolutions at a general meeting must be kept at the registered office for ten years (s.358). There is no fee for inspection. The company can be required to send a copy to a member who pays a small fee.

(v) If the member of a single member company takes a decision that takes effect as if agreed by the company in a general meeting, the company must be given details of that decision unless it was taken by written resolution (s.357). These details must be available for inspection for ten years. There is no fee for inspection of these records. The company can be required to send a copy to a member who pays a small fee.

Communications with the Registrar will be able to be made electronically and the registrar will have greater freedom to communicate with companies which have filed inaccurate or incomplete information.

17.4.3 Documents which cannot be inspected by company members or the public

Section 165 requires a company to keep a register of the residential addresses of all directors who are individuals unless his residential address is the same as his service address, in which case there must merely be a note stating that this is the case. This register cannot be inspected by company members or by members of the public. Unless a director gives permission, his residential address is not to be disclosed to anyone except the Registrar. However, the Registrar can communicate a director's residential address to public authorities or in compliance with a court order.

17.5 THE ANNUAL RETURN

Section 854 requires every company to submit an annual return to Companies House. This gives basic information about the company on a particular date, its return date, every year. A company which fails to submit an annual return within 28 days of the return date commits a criminal offence. A company officer who cannot prove that he took all reasonable steps to prevent the commission of the offence is similarly guilty. Persistent failure to supply an annual return can lead to a director being disqualified. Once the annual return becomes 14 days overdue, a member or creditor of the company can apply to the court for an order that an annual return be submitted by the company. The company will have to bear the costs of this application.

Section 855 requires that the following general information must be given in the annual return:

(i) The address of the company's registered office.
(ii) The type of company and its principal business activities.
(iii) The names of the directors and the shadow directors; their service addresses; their countries of residence; their nationalities; their usual business occupations; and their dates of birth.
(iv) The name and address of the company secretary, if the company has one. The address can be a service address.
(v) If either the register of members or the register of debenture holders is not kept at the company's registered office, the address of the place where these registers are kept.

Section 856 requires the following information to be given about share capital and shareholders:

(i) A statement of share capital. This must give the total number of shares in the company; the aggregate nominal value of those shares; and the amounts paid up and unpaid on each share. If there are different classes of shares, the statement must also state the rights attached to the different classes of shares; the total number of shares of each class; and the aggregate nominal value of each class of shares.

(ii) Details of every member of the company or of every person who has ceased to be a member since the previous annual return was submitted.
(iii) The number of shares of each class held by each member.
(iv) The number of shares of each class transferred by each member or former member since the previous annual return was submitted and the dates of transfer.

A £30 annual fee is charged for registration of the annual return. This fee is reduced to £15 if the return is filed electronically. The Registrar operates a shuttle system. This involves sending the company the information contained in the previous year's annual return and asking that changes are notified, or that the company indicates that no changes have been made. The return must be signed by a director or the company secretary. The annual return can be inspected at Companies House without this fact being revealed to the company. If Companies House is visited, there is a charge of £5 to inspect the microfiche and then of 10p per photocopy. Companies House will post a company's annual return for a fee of £9 and fax it for a fee of £12.

17.6 ACCOUNTS AND ACCOUNTING RECORDS

Companies are under a duty to keep accounting records, and to prepare annual accounts.

17.6.1 Accounting records

Section 386 of the Act requires every company to keep accounting records for inspection by the officers of the company. These are not the same as the accounts, but are the documents which enable the accounts to be prepared (ledger, order forms, cash books, receipts, etc.). They must show with reasonable accuracy the financial position of the company at any particular moment. They should be sufficiently detailed to enable the directors to ensure that any balance sheet or profit and loss account prepared gives a true and fair view of the company's affairs. The accounting records must have day-to-day entries of all money spent or received, with details of the transactions, and a record of assets and liabilities. If the company sells goods then:

(i) all sales other than retail sales must be recorded, showing details of buyers and sellers sufficient to identify them; and

(ii) the records must include statements of stock held at the end of the financial year and statements of stocktaking to back these records up.

A public company must hold such records for six years, a private company for three years. Officers in default of the requirement to keep accounting records can be imprisoned for up to two years and/or fined. Members of the company do not have a right to inspect the accounting records, unless they are given such a right by the articles of association or by the directors. Table A articles, like the Model Articles for Private Companies Limited by Shares, and the Model Articles for Public Companies, allow the members to inspect the accounting records if they pass an ordinary resolution to this effect. The auditors do have a right to inspect the accounting records. Accounting records can be, and often are, kept on computer.

17.6.2 **The annual accounts**

A company's annual accounts consist of a balance sheet, a profit and loss account, the directors' report and, if the company is not exempt from audit, the auditor's report. The auditor's report has already been considered above, at 17.3.3.

Section 393 states that the directors must not approve the accounts unless they are satisfied that they give a true and fair view of the assets, liabilities, financial position and profit or loss of the company. If the accounts are for a group of companies then the directors must not approve them unless they are satisfied that they give a true and fair view of the assets etc. of the whole group, so far as this concerns members of the company.

Every company will have an accounting reference date. For a newly formed company this is the last day of the month arising one year after the company was incorporated. For example, if X Ltd was incorporated on 15 November 2008, its first accounting reference date would be 30 November 2009. The accounting reference date will remain the same each successive year, although the directors have a general discretion to move it up to seven days forwards or backwards. The period from one accounting reference date to the next makes up the company's financial year and its accounting reference period. A company may resolve to shorten or extend this period as permitted by s.392. Section 394 requires the directors to prepare accounts for each financial year of the company.

The profit and loss account shows the income and expenses of the company over the financial year. If the income exceeds the expenditure the company will have made a profit, if it is less than the expenditure the company will have made a loss. Capital profits, which arise when the company sells a fixed asset such as land, are generally included as an exceptional item. The balance sheet shows the assets and liabilities of the company on a particular date, its balance sheet date.

A company's annual accounts must be approved by the board of directors and signed by a director on behalf of the board of directors. The signature must be on the company's balance sheet. If the accounts are prepared in accordance with the small companies regime, the balance sheet must contain a statement to that effect in a prominent position above the signature.

17.6.2.1 **The directors' report**

Section 415 requires the directors to prepare a directors' report for each financial year of the company. Failure to do this is a criminal offence. The report must state the names of the directors during the financial year and the principal activities of the company in the course of the year. Unless the company is a small company, it must also state the amount, if any, which the directors recommend should be paid as a dividend. It must be approved by the board of directors and signed by a director or the secretary on behalf of the board of directors.

Unless the company is subject to the small companies regime, the directors' report must contain a **business review**. The definition of a small company was set out earlier in Chapter 16 at 16.4.4. A group of companies is not eligible for the small companies regime if any of the companies is quoted on an EEA stock exchange. The purpose of the business review is to inform the members of the company and to help them assess how the directors have performed their duty, under s.172, to promote the success of the company. The business review must contain a fair review of the company's business and a description of the principal risks and uncertainties facing the company. As regards quoted companies, the business review must contain three additional matters. First, the main trends and factors likely to affect the future development, performance and position of the company's business. Second, information about (a) environmental matters (including the impact of the company's business on the environment), (b) the company's employees, and (c) social and community issues. This information should include any policies of the company in relation to those matters and the effectiveness of those policies. Third, information about persons with whom the company has contractual or other arrangements which are essential to the business of the company.

All of these additional matters which quoted companies need to disclose need be disclosed only to the extent necessary for an understanding of the development, performance or position of the company's business. However, information does not need to be disclosed if, in the opinion of the directors, it would be seriously prejudicial to that person or contrary to the public interest. In addition, nothing in any directors' report need be disclosed about impending developments or matters in the course of negotiation if the disclosure would, in the opinion of the directors, be seriously prejudicial to the interests of the company. However, if the directors' report of a quoted company does not include the three additional matters which it is required to contain, it must state which of the three matters it does not contain. Except as regards medium-sized companies, the review must contain analysis of key financial performance indicators and, if relevant, analysis of other key performance indicators. The indicators must be included to the extent necessary for an understanding of the development, performance or position of the company's business. A company is regarded as a medium-size company if it meets two of the three following requirements:

(1) The company's annual turnover is £22.8 million or less.
(2) The total assets of the company are £11.4 million or less.
(3) The company has 250 or fewer employees.

Unless the company is exempted from having to be audited for the financial year, the directors' report must contain a statement that so far as each director is aware there is no relevant audit information of which the company's auditor is unaware. It must also state that each director has taken all the steps that he ought to have taken as a director to make himself aware of any audit information and to establish that the company's auditor is aware of that information. As regards all types of companies, directors who know or are reckless as to the directors' report containing false or misleading information, or omitting something which is required to be in it, are liable to compensate the company for loss which this causes. The same liability is imposed in respect of the directors' remuneration report and summary financial information derived from either type of report.

Either the company secretary or any director may sign the directors' report, but it must be approved by the board of directors. If the report is prepared in accordance with the small companies regime, it must contain a statement to that effect in a prominent position above the signature.

17.6.2.2 **Distribution and publication of accounts**

Private companies must file their accounts with the Registrar of Companies within nine months of the end of their accounting reference period. Public companies must do so within six months. The corresponding date in the future month is used, so that six months from 20 January is 20 July. However, if the accounting reference period ends at the end of a month the corresponding date is the end of the future month. So six months from 31 August is 28 February (or 29 February in a leap year). Six months from 28 February is 31 August. Small companies must file a balance sheet, a profit and loss account and a directors' report. They do not, however, have to file full accounts. Abbreviated accounts, as defined by Regulations made by the Secretary of State, may be delivered instead. Medium-sized companies must file the company's annual accounts, the directors' report and the auditors' report, unless the company is exempt from audit. However, Regulations made by the Secretary of State allow certain items to be omitted from the accounts. Again, the accounts which must be filed are called abbreviated accounts. Companies other than small or medium-sized companies must file full accounts, the directors' report and a copy of the auditors' report. If the company is quoted it must also file a directors' remuneration report. Such a report must give information about the remuneration of the directors in a manner which complies with Regulations made by the Secretary of State. Unlimited companies do not generally have to file accounts.

Section 423 provides that every company must send its annual accounts and reports for each financial year to all company members, debenture holders and every person who is entitled to receive notice of company general meetings. Public companies must do this at least 21 days before the meeting at which the accounts are laid before members. This rule does not apply to private companies as they are not obliged to hold any meetings of members. Private companies must do it on the date when the accounts have to be filed or on the date when the accounts and reports are actually sent to the registrar of companies if this date is before the filing date. Companies may send a summary financial statement, rather than full accounts, as long as these are in accordance with Regulations made by the Secretary of State. Quoted companies must also publish their accounts on a website which is made available and which names the company in question.

Section 437 requires public companies to lay before the company in general meeting copies of its annual reports and accounts. This must be done before the end of the company's filing period. In addition, quoted companies have to produce a directors' remuneration report for each financial year (s.420). Section 439 requires this report to be sent to the members prior to the meeting, along with an ordinary resolution to approve the report. This resolution has to be put to a vote at the meeting. However, a vote against would not invalidate any payment to any director. It would,

however, strongly indicate shareholder disapproval to the board of directors. Companies are quoted if their shares are quoted on a stock exchange within the European Economic Area or on the New York Stock Exchange or Nasdaq.

If the directors conclude that the accounts did not comply with the Companies Act then they may prepare revised accounts and reports.

Test your understanding 17.4

1 What registers and documents must be held at the registered office and made available for inspection by members of the public?

2 What registers and documents must be held at the registered office and made available for inspection only by company members?

3 What is the annual return?

4 What four documents comprise the company's accounts which must be filed with the Registrar?

Key points

Directors

■ The directors of a company manage the company.

■ A company's articles of association will almost always set out how directors are to be appointed. If the articles do not do this, directors can be appointed by an ordinary resolution of the members.

■ A company's articles usually set out how a director can be removed from office. Such provisions are effective. No matter what the articles say, a director can be removed by an ordinary resolution of which special notice has been given as long as it is passed at a meeting of the members (s.186(1)).

■ On a resolution to remove a director, the shares of the director whose removal is proposed might carry enhanced voting rights.

■ Undischarged bankrupts may not take part in the management of a company without the court's permission. Persons may be disqualified from acting as directors under the CDDA 1986.

■ A register of directors must contain personal details of all of a company's directors and be kept up to date. The Registrar must be informed of changes within 14 days.

■ When directors act collectively, they act as the board of directors. They must act as a board unless a power has been delegated.

■ A company's articles might allow for a managing director to be appointed and for the managing director to exercise the powers of the directors.

■ Directors have no automatic right to be paid a fee for their services. The board of directors usually have the power to employ individual directors to perform duties which exceed their ordinary duties and to pay such salary as they consider fit.

■ The articles will set out the powers of the directors. Usually, the board of directors is given very wide powers to manage the company.

■ Directors will be agents of the company if they have some type of authority to act for the company.

■ An outsider acting in good faith is entitled to assume that the board of directors, or persons appointed by the board, have the power to bind the company.

■ Seven general statutory duties are imposed on directors. These are: to act within powers; to promote the success of the company; to exercise independent judgment; to exercise reasonable

→

care, skill and diligence; to avoid conflicts of interest; not to accept benefits from third parties; and to declare interest in a proposed transaction or arrangement.

Company secretary and auditors

■ All public companies must have a company secretary. Private companies may have a company secretary but they do not have to have one.

■ The secretary is concerned with the day-to-day running of the company.

■ The secretary of a private company needs no special qualifications. The secretary of a public company must be suitably qualified.

■ All companies except certain small companies and dormant companies must have an auditor.

■ The auditor audits the accounts and reports on these to the members of the company.

■ The first auditor is appointed by the directors, subsequent auditors are appointed by the members.

■ Special rules apply when an auditor leaves office.

Company registers and accounts

■ A company must keep certain registers at its registered office. These registers can be inspected free of charge by company members and by outsiders who pay a small fee.

■ Every year a company must send an annual return to the Registrar of Companies. This gives basic information about the company and can be inspected by an outsider without the company being aware of this.

■ A company must keep accounting records which record the day-to-day financial transactions of the company.

■ A company's accounts consist of a directors' report, an auditor's report, a profit and loss account and a balance sheet.

■ Company accounts must be filed with the Registrar and given to members of the company.

■ Small companies may file with the Registrar abbreviated accounts, medium-sized companies may file more detailed abbreviated accounts.

Summary questions

1 Jane Smith owns all the shares in a company registered under the 2006 Act. She wants to leave her shares to her three children, in equal shares. Jane wants all three children to be directors and she wants to ensure that they can all remain directors for as long as they want.

a Advise Jane as to whether it will be possible for her to ensure that the three children each have the right to remain as directors.

b How would your answer be different if Jane owned only 99 per cent of the shares in the company?

2 David is the managing director of Goliath Ltd. There are three other directors, but David has always made whatever decisions he considered necessary and then informed the others at board meetings. Goliath's articles used to provide that the managing director could make any contracts up to the value of £20 000. Recently, the articles were changed so that contracts worth more than £5 000 had to be authorised by the full board.

Yesterday, David saw what seemed like a good business opportunity for the company. He therefore ordered goods worth £17 000 on the company's behalf. The supplier of the goods did not know that

Goliath's articles limited David's authority to make contracts over the value of £5 000. The other directors are convinced that the £17 000 contract is a bad one and are refusing to honour it. Advise the supplier as to whether the company can refuse to honour the contract.

3 Acme Ltd is a medium-sized construction company. The company secretary, without the knowledge of the directors, ordered a new car, a new computer and six pneumatic drills on the company's behalf. None of these items was paid for. The company secretary has subsequently sold the items ordered and disappeared with the money. Advise the company as to whether or not it will have to pay the suppliers of the various items.

4 Arthur, who is neither a shareholder, a creditor nor a company officer of X Co Ltd, wants to find information about X Co Ltd. Will Arthur be able to find the information detailed below? If so, where will it be found? Will Arthur have to make any payment for access to the information?

a The number and nominal value of X Ltd's issued shares.

b Whether or not James held shares in X Ltd four years ago.

c Whether the directors of X Ltd have any interest in X Ltd's debentures.

d Whether or not there are any charges over X Ltd's property.

e The service contracts of the directors of X Ltd.

f The day-to-day expenditure of X Ltd.

5 Some of the shareholders of Y Co Ltd think that the auditor has not performed his duties properly. These shareholders bought additional shares in the company as a result of last year's accounts, which mistakenly stated that the company made a profit when in fact it made a large loss. The directors of the company have faith in the auditors and do not want them to be removed from office. Explain any procedure by which the auditors could be removed from office, and the extent to which the auditors could be liable if the accounts were misleading in the way in which the shareholders allege that they were.

6 Consider the following case.

Regal (Hastings) Ltd v Gulliver
[1942] 1 All ER 378 (House of Lords)

Regal Ltd owned a cinema. It wanted to acquire two more cinemas so that it could sell all three as a going concern. A subsidiary company was formed to make the purchase. The sellers of the cinemas would not go ahead with the deal unless the subsidiary company had at least £5 000 paid-up share capital. Regal could only provide £2 000 of the money which the subsidiary needed. The directors of Regal therefore personally subscribed for a further 3 000 £1 shares in the subsidiary. At the conclusion of the whole business the shares in the subsidiary were sold for £3.80 each. Both Regal and its directors had therefore made a handsome profit. The directors left the company, which was sold to new owners. These new owners sued the former directors, claiming an account of profits.

Held. The former directors had to account to Regal for the profit they had made. It was only because they were directors of Regal that they gained the opportunity to make the profit.

If the case were to come to court today, which of the statutory duties in ss.171–177 might the directors of Regal have breached? What might the consequences of any breach be?

Multiple choice questions

1 Which one of the following statements is true?

a No matter what the articles of a company might say, the members of a company can always dismiss a director if they pass an ordinary resolution to do so, of which special notice has been given, at a general meeting.

b No matter what the articles of a company might say, the members of a private company can always dismiss a director, but only by passing a written ordinary resolution to do so.

c Directors of a company can never be dismissed against their will except by a resolution of the company members.

d In a private limited company a director can always be dismissed by a unanimous written resolution of the members.

2 Which one of the following statements is not true?

a When a resolution to remove a director is voted upon, the articles might validly provide that the shares of any director whose removal is proposed carry weighted voting rights.

b When a director is removed from office under s.168(1), this might amount to breach of contract by the company and the director might be able to claim unfair or wrongful dismissal.

c When a director is removed under s.168(1), a replacement director cannot be voted in at the same meeting unless special notice of the resolution proposing the appointment has been given.

d Shareholders holding 5 per cent of paid up shares can compel the directors to hold an EGM. But the threshold is increased to 10 per cent of paid up shares if the company is a plc.

3 Which one of the following statements is true?

a Directors are always entitled to a salary, and in addition may award themselves such payments as they think fit.

b Directors are always entitled to a salary, and in addition the shareholders may award such payments as they think fit.

c Directors are always entitled to a salary, but may not receive any extra payment from the company.

d Directors have no entitlement to a salary.

4 Which two of the following statements are true?

a All directors whose whereabouts are known must be given 21 days' notice of a board meeting and of motions to be proposed at the meeting.

b If a company holds a person out as having authority to make a contract on the company's behalf then the company will be bound by that contract whether the person held out had actual authority or not.

c All companies must have a managing director, who may exercise the same power as the board of directors.

d If a board meeting is inquorate, any decisions taken at such a meeting will be invalid.

5 Which of the following statements are true?

i All new company secretaries must be 'suitably qualified'.

ii Company secretaries can make contracts concerned with the administration of the company which bind the company.

iii The company secretary is appointed and can be removed by the directors.

iv All companies must have a company secretary.

a ii and iii only.

b ii and iv only.

c ii, iii and iv only.

d i, ii, iii and iv.

6 Which of the following statements are true?

i An auditor owes a duty of care and skill to the company and to the membership as a whole, but not to individual members.

ii All companies other than dormant companies must have their accounts audited every financial year.

iii An LLP can never be appointed the auditor of a company.

iv When an auditor leaves office, he must attach a statement saying that there are no circumstances which ought to be brought to the attention of the members or creditors, or must state what those circumstances are.

a i, ii, iii and iv.

b i, iii and iv only.

c i, ii and iv only.

d i and iv only.

7 Which of the following statements are not true?

i Auditors are appointed annually by the directors.

ii Auditors draw up the company's accounts and must state that these give a true and fair reflection of the company's financial position.

iii All single member companies are exempted from the requirement to appoint an auditor.

iv A member of a company cannot be the auditor of that company.

a i and iii only.

b ii and iv only.

c i and iv only

d i, ii, iii and iv.

8 Which one of the following statements is not true?

a Every company must keep a register of members, which must show the number of shares held by each member and the amount paid up on each share.

b The minutes of any general meeting of a company must be kept at the registered office. Members can inspect these minutes free of charge. Other persons can inspect but must pay a small charge.

c A company has no need to keep a register of debenture holders. If it does keep such a register debenture holders and members may inspect it free of charge.

d Every company must have a register of members, but this does not always need to be kept at the company's registered office.

9 Which one of the following statements is not true?

a Members of a company always have the right to inspect the company's accounting records unless the articles of association say otherwise.

b A company's annual return can be inspected at Companies House without the company knowing this.

c Small companies can file abbreviated accounts with the Registrar, medium-sized companies can file more detailed abbreviated accounts.

d Small private companies do not need to lay the accounts before the members of the company in general meeting.

Task 17

A friend of yours has been offered the chance to buy shares in a small private limited company. Your friend has asked you to write a report, giving details of the following matters:

a The powers of the directors of the company.

b The ways in which directors are appointed and can be removed from office.

c The duties which directors owe to the company.

d The roles of the company secretary and the auditor of the company.

mylawchamber *premium*

Visit **www.mylawchamber.co.uk/macintyre** to access study support resources including interactive multiple-choice questions, weblinks, glossary, glossary flashcards, legal newsfeed, answers to questions in this chapter, legal updates and an overview of this chapter all linked to the **Pearson eText** version of *Business Law* which you can **search**, **highlight** and **personalise** with your **own notes** and **bookmarks**.

Use **Case Navigator** to read in full some of the key cases referenced in this chapter with commentary and questions:

Caparo Industries plc v *Dickman and others* [1990] 1 All ER 568
Freeman & Lockyer (a firm) v *Buckhurst Park Properties (Mangal) Ltd* [1964] 1 All ER 630
Regal (Hastings) Ltd v *Gulliver and others* [1942] 1 All ER 378

18

Shareholders · resolutions · maintenance of capital · minority protection · debentures

Introduction

This chapter considers the following matters:

18.1 SHAREHOLDERS

The shareholders of a company limited by shares are known as the members of the company. As we have seen, the shareholders do not manage the company – that task is delegated to the directors. However, the members of a company have considerable powers, despite the delegation of the powers of management to the directors. The members are given these powers because they have invested money in the company and they hope to profit from the company. While the company exists, the profit to the members might come in the form of a dividend paid on their shares or from their investment increasing in value. A much larger profit might come to them if a solvent company is liquidated. Upon liquidation the surplus assets of the company will be divided amongst some or all of the members.

Section 112 of the Act defines the members of a company:

'(i) The subscribers of a company's memorandum are deemed to have agreed to become members of the company, and on its registration become members and must be entered as such in its register of members.

(ii) Every other person who agrees to become a member of a company, and whose name is registered in its register of members, is a member of the company.'

So s.112(1) provides that the company's first members consist of those who sign the memorandum, a matter we examined in Chapter 16. Section 112(2) provides that subsequent members must not only have their names entered in the register of members, but they must also agree to this. This agreement does not need to amount to a contract. In *Enviroco Ltd* v *Farstad Supply* [2011] UKSC 16 the Supreme Court held that s.112 reflects a fundamental principle of United Kingdom company law, namely that, except where express provision is made to the contrary, the person on the register of the members is the member to the exclusion of any other person, unless and until the register is rectified.

Section 127 provides that the register of members is *prima facie* evidence of any matters which are directed or authorised by the 2006 Act to be inserted in it. In the previous chapter we saw that the register would have to include the names and addresses of members, the dates on which they became or ceased to be a member, the number of shares held and the amount paid up on each share. The register is therefore *prima facie* evidence of all of these matters.

Section 125 allows the register of members to be rectified if anyone's name has either been entered in, or has been omitted from, the register without sufficient cause, or if there is a delay in entering that a person has ceased to be a member. Either the aggrieved person, or any member of the company, or the company itself may apply to the court to have the register rectified. The court has a discretionary power to rectify the register and to order the company to pay damages to an aggrieved party.

18.2 THE NATURE OF SHARES

A share is a type of personal property, known as a thing (or chose) in action. That is to say, it is a form of property which does not have a physical existence of its own, but rather confers certain rights upon the holder. These rights can, ultimately, only be enforced by taking legal action, hence the name a thing in action. (Legal concepts of property are explained in Chapter

23 at 23.1.) Section 540(1) defines a share as a 'share in the company's share capital'. A more detailed definition was given by Farwell J in *Borland's Trustees* v *Steel Brothers & Co Ltd* [1901] 1 Ch 279:

'A share is the interest of a shareholder in the company measured by a sum of money, for the purpose of liability in the first place, and of interest in the second. A share is an interest measured by a sum of money and made up of various rights.'

This definition mentions both liability and rights. The liability of a person taking shares in a limited company is to contribute the amount of capital which he agreed with the company that he would contribute. Generally, this amount is paid when the share is issued. Article 21 of the Model Articles for Private Companies Limited by Shares provides that shares should be fully paid up, but this does not apply to shares taken on formation of the company by subscribers to the memorandum. There is no equivalent article in Table A or in the Model Articles for Public Companies. If the full price is not paid upon issue of the share, the company can ask that it be paid at any time. Beyond this, the shareholders cannot be forced to contribute more capital or to pay the debts of a limited company. If the company is liquidated, the liquidator can insist that members pay any amount of the nominal value of their shares which has not yet been paid. The money raised is used to satisfy the company's debts and liabilities. The liquidator cannot insist that a shareholder pays any amount of a share premium which has not been paid (see the example in Chapter 16 at 16.4.2.2).

Becoming a shareholder will confer several rights, and the articles may provide for different classes of shares, with different rights attaching to the various classes. Members do not have an automatic right to a dividend. A dividend cannot exceed the recommendation made by the directors, who do not have to recommend a dividend. Nor can a dividend be paid if the company has insufficient distributable profit out of which to pay it. Some, if not all, of the company's shares will carry the right to vote at company meetings. If no dividend is paid, the holders of the voting shares might replace the directors with other directors who they see as more capable of making a profit or more willing to declare a dividend. As shares are measured by a sum of money, those who contribute the most capital acquire the most shares. Assuming that a company has only one class of shares, a member with a greater number of shares has more influence in the company, and more of a right to receive any dividends declared, than a member with fewer shares.

18.2.1 Nominal capital and shares issued at a premium

As regards companies having a share capital, s.542(1) of the Act requires every share to have a fixed nominal value. The shares can be denominated in Sterling, Euros or in any other currency. Different classes of shares can be denominated in different currencies (s.542(3)). The nominal value of a share represents the amount which the member and the company have agreed should be paid in return for the share, and it is not possible for them to agree that less should in fact be paid. As we have seen, a shareholder can, however, agree to pay more for the share, the extra payment being a share premium.

The **paid-up** share capital of a company is the amount of the nominal share capital which has been actually paid by the members. Share premiums do not count towards this paid-up share capital. The **called-up** share capital consists of the paid-up share capital and additional amounts which have become due to be paid towards the nominal value by the members.

Section 610(1) requires that amounts received by a company by way of share premium must be paid into **a share premium account**. This requirement exists to prevent the amount paid by way of premium from being distributed as dividends. An amount paid by way of share premium is treated as capital and the balance held in a share premium account must be shown in the balance sheet. Section 610(2) provides that where, on issuing shares, a company has transferred a sum to the share premium account, it may use that sum to write off the expenses of issuing those shares or any commission paid on the issue of those shares. However, money in the share premium account cannot be used to pay off the expenses of issuing other shares or the expenses of forming the company. Section 610(3) allows the company to apply the share premium account in paying up unissued shares which are to be allotted to members as fully paid bonus shares. The share premium account cannot be used to write off expenses incurred when debentures are issued.

18.2.2 Classes of shares

The articles of a company may provide that there shall be different classes of shares, with different rights attaching to the various classes. Table A article 2, for example, provides that: 'Subject to the provisions of the Act and without prejudice to any rights attached to any existing shares, any share may be issued with such rights or restrictions as the company may by ordinary resolution determine.' Article 43 of the Model Articles for Public Companies and article 22 of the Model Articles for Private Companies Limited by Shares are very similar.

Special classes of shares might carry more votes per share than other classes, or might carry the only right to vote, or might effectively have a veto over any proposed change to the company's constitution.

Generally, those who have acquired shares by contributing towards the company's nominal capital will gain the following rights: the right to vote at company meetings; the right to a dividend if one is declared; the right to have their capital returned if the company is solvent when wound up and the right to a share of the company's surplus assets, if any, when the company is wound up.

Although the Act does not use the term, members with these rights are called 'ordinary members' and own 'ordinary shares'.

If a dividend is payable, the size of dividend to which any member is entitled normally depends upon the nominal value of shares held. However, many articles, such as Table A article 104, make the amount of dividend to be paid dependent upon the number of paid-up shares held. Article 73 of the Model Articles for Public Companies allows the directors to deduct from the dividend any amount owing on the shares. As we have seen, the Model Articles for Private Companies Limited by Shares require all shares to be fully paid up.

When a company has only one class of shares, the rights of the members will be set out in the articles of association. If a new class of shares is created, this could be achieved either by altering the articles to cater for such a class or by contractual agreement between the company and those taking the new shares.

Since 1980 companies have been required to register with the Registrar the various rights attaching to different classes of shares if they are not contained in the articles.

18.2.2.1 Alteration of class rights

A company has different classes of shares unless all of the shares carry the same rights. The most important variations are generally concerned with the rights to vote, to receive a dividend if one is declared and to share in surplus assets on dissolution. If a company does have different classes of shares, any definition of the rights attaching to a class of shares will be found in the articles.

Section 630(2) provides that class rights can be altered in only two ways: first, in accordance with a provision for alteration in the articles; second, if there is no provision for alteration in the articles, by the shareholders of the class in question giving consent to the alteration in accordance with s.630.

If the articles are altered by the shareholders giving consent, there are two ways in which this may be done. First, three-quarters of the holders of the nominal value of the issued shares of the class in question can give written consent to the variation. Second, a special resolution may be passed at a separate meeting of members of the class sanctioning the variation (s.630(4)). The articles might specify that a more onerous procedure than the s.630 procedure is required to alter class rights (s.630(3)). So an article might require a higher percentage of votes than the statutory minimum, or an article protecting class rights might be entrenched. If any provision in the articles for the variation of rights attached to a class of shares is amended, the rights attaching to those shares are taken to have been duly altered (s.630(5)).

However an alteration of class rights is achieved, s.633 allows the holders of not less than 15 per cent of the issued shares of the class in question to apply to the court to have the variation cancelled. However, they can do this only if they did not vote in favour of the alteration. If such an application is made, the variation has no effect unless and until it is confirmed by the court (s.633(3)). The court may refuse to allow the variation if it is satisfied that it is unfairly prejudicial to the holders of the class concerned (s.633(5)). The Registrar must be notified of any variation of class rights within one month (s.637).

18.2.2.2 Preference shares

Often a company issues two types of shares, ordinary shares and preference shares. The articles will define the precise rights attaching to preference shares, and obviously these rights will vary from company to company. If the members and the company do not expressly agree with a class of shareholders what their rights should be, then all shares will carry equal rights. Generally, it will be agreed that the rights of preference shares will be as follows.

Preference shares are usually paid a rate of interest per annum as a dividend. For example, the articles might stipulate that preference shares carry a dividend of 7 per cent per annum. If preference shares are not paid a dividend in one year they usually carry a cumulative right to a dividend the following year. This means that the preference share dividend which was not paid in the previous year must be paid before any dividend is paid on ordinary shares. (However, preference shareholders, like ordinary shareholders, have no automatic right to be paid a dividend every year.)

Preference shares will carry the same voting rights as other shares in the absence of agreement to the contrary. (However, articles commonly provide that preference shares do not carry a vote, except when their dividend is in arrears or when the motion to be voted upon proposes to alter their special rights.)

On dissolution of the company, the preference shareholders usually have the right to have their shares repaid in full before the ordinary shares are repaid at all. If this is the case then the preference shares do not have the right to share in the company's surplus assets.

If, after winding up, there is a surplus of assets this will be divided among the shareholders. Whether or not the preference shareholders are entitled to participate in this division will depend upon the provisions of the articles.

Non-voting shares may be issued by a company. These shares would have no right to vote at company meetings but would have a right to a dividend if one is declared and a right to share in the surplus assets on dissolution of the company.

18.3 BECOMING A SHAREHOLDER OF A COMPANY WITH A SHARE CAPITAL

A person might acquire shares either directly from the company (by buying them or through an employees' share scheme), or from an existing member who transfers the shares, or by transmission by operation of law (for example, where shares are inherited). There is no need to inform the Registrar of Companies that shares have been transferred. However, the transfer will be shown in the annual return which requires the company to show the names and addresses of all of the shareholders and the number and class of shares which they hold.

Shares are **issued** when members take them from the company. They are **allotted** when a person acquires an unconditional right to be included in the company's register of members in respect of those shares (s.558).

Section 617 prohibits a limited company from altering its share capital except in the following ways. It may:

(a) increase its share capital by allotting new shares;
(b) reduce its share capital in accordance with the 2006 Act;
(c) sub-divide or consolidate any or all of its share capital;
(d) reconvert stock into shares; or
(e) redenominate any or all of its shares.

If shares are sub-divided they are turned into a greater number of shares, each having a lower nominal value. For example, 100 £10 shares could be sub-divided into 1 000 £1 shares. If they are consolidated they are turned into a smaller number of shares, each having a higher value. For example, 1 000 £20 shares could be consolidated into 100 £200 shares. If they are redenominated they are converted from one currency into another.

Shares can be sub-divided or consolidated only if the members pass a resolution authorising this. The resolution can be an ordinary resolution unless the articles require a higher majority. The Registrar must be given notice of sub-division or consolidation within one month and the notice must be accompanied by a statement of capital. This statement shows the position, immediately after the consolidation or sub-division, as regards: the total number of shares of the company; the aggregate nominal value of those shares; and the amounts paid and unpaid on each share. If there are classes of shares, it must state particulars of the rights attaching to each class, the total number of shares in each class and the aggregate nominal value of each class.

Redenomination is subject to any prohibition or restriction in the company's articles. The members will need to pass a resolution authorising the redenomination and the resolution might set out conditions which have to be fulfilled before it can take effect. The resolution will also need to set out the rate of exchange to be used and will lapse if the redenomination is not made within 28 days of the date on which it was passed. Redenomination does not affect the rights or liabilities of the members. Notice of the redomination must be given to the Registrar within one month and must be accompanied by a statement of capital, as explained in relation to sub-division and consolidation. A copy of the resolution which authorised the redenomination must be sent to the Registrar within 15 days of its being passed.

When shares are allotted, the contract of allotment between the company and the allottee (the person to whom the shares are to be allotted) must state: the amount of capital which is going to be contributed; when it is to be contributed; in what way it is going to be contributed; the time when the allottee will have an unconditional right to the shares; and the rights which attach to each share.

The articles will set out the terms on which a company may allot shares. Apart from allotting shares to employees as part of an employees' share scheme, or converting company securities into shares, s.549 provides that allotment must be in accordance with s.550 or s.551. Section 550 provides that where a private company has only one class of shares the directors may exercise a power of the company to allot shares in the company except to the extent that the company's articles prohibit them from doing so. Before the 2006 Act came into force, a prior resolution of the members was always needed. Section 551 will be needed when the company is a public company or when a private company will have more than one class of shares after the allotment. Section 551 requires a positive authorisation to allot, either in the company's articles or by a resolution of the members. The authorisation may be for a particular power to allot or a general one and may be conditional or unconditional (s.551(2)). Authorisation must state the maximum amount of shares which may be allotted and state the date when it will expire (s.551(3)). A further resolution may revoke the earlier one or extend it for another five years (s.551(4)). This date cannot be more than five years after the resolution was passed or, if the article was in the company's constitution when the company was formed, more than five years after incorporation.

Any further resolution must again state the maximum amount of shares which may be allotted and state the date when it will expire (s.551(5)). An ordinary resolution will suffice for any of the resolutions required by s.551. If the articles require more than an ordinary resolution they will be regarded as having been changed (s.551(8)). This is an exception to the general rule that a special resolution is needed to change the articles. Section 552 generally prohibits the allotment of shares at a discount. Section 554 requires the company to register an allotment of shares as soon as is reasonably practicable and in any event within two months of the date of allotment. Section 555 requires a company to make a return of allotment to the Registrar within one month of the allotment. The return must contain a statement of capital, as described above. As we have seen, shares are regarded as having been allotted when a person acquires an unconditional right to be included in the company's register of members in respect of those shares (s.558).

The shares of public companies cannot be allotted unless the allotment is subscribed in full, unless the offer of allotment was made on the terms that the shares should be allotted anyway or allotted if special conditions were met (s.578). Shares must not be allotted at a discount. If they are the allottee must pay the discount and an appropriate rate of interest (s.580).

18.3.1 Pre-emption rights

Shareholders with pre-emption rights are offered the first chance to buy new shares. This prevents their shareholding in the company from being diluted. Section 561 of the Act provides that equity securities may not be allotted to new company members for cash unless they are first offered to existing members, in proportion to their existing shareholding, on terms which are equally favourable. An equity security is an ordinary share or a right to convert securities into ordinary shares. An ordinary share is one which has full rights to a dividend and a full right to share in the company's assets on dissolution. (It would not therefore include typical preference shares.) The offer can be made in hard copy or electronically (s.562(2)). The offer to existing members must state a period, of at least 21 days, during which it can be accepted and must not be withdrawn before the end of that period (s.562(4)). A right of pre-emption does not exist in relation to bonus shares, shares for which the consideration was not cash or shares held under an employees' share scheme (ss.564–566). A private company's articles can exclude shareholders' rights of pre-emption (s.567). A private company with only one class of shares can allow directors to allot shares without complying with the requirements of ss.561 and 562 (s.569). The company can do this either by excluding the provisions of ss.561 and 562 altogether or by disapplying them in relation to one particular allotment of shares. Exclusion requires a provision in the articles, disapplication requires either a special resolution or a power in the articles.

18.3.2 Payment for shares

Generally, payment for shares may be in money or money's worth and so payment does not have to be in cash. Often shares in a different company or fixed assets are given in return for shares. The court will not usually query the valuation of the consideration received in exchange for shares in a private company. However, shares in public companies can only be sold for cash or for an asset which has been independently valued as being worth at least as much as the amount credited as having been paid up. This valuation must be made by a person qualified as an auditor or by someone appointed by a qualified auditor.

Either a public or a private company which allots shares otherwise than for cash must, in addition to the details of allotment mentioned above, send to the Registrar a copy of the contract of allotment within one month. Public companies also have to send a copy of the valuation report. The Registrar will publish notice of having received this in the *Gazette*.

A public company may not accept promises to perform work or services in return for issuing shares (s.585). If this section is breached, the allottee is regarded as not having paid the amount credited for the shares and remains liable to pay the price and interest at the appropriate rate. A public company must not allot shares unless they are at least one quarter paid up (s.586).

18.3.3 Trading certificates

Section 761(1) provides that a newly incorporated public company may not begin trading or borrow money until it has received a trading certificate (also called a certificate to commence business or a s.761 certificate). The Registrar will issue such a certificate only if satisfied that the company's allotted share capital is not less than the authorised minimum (s.761(2)). This means that the company must have allotted shares with a nominal value of at least £50 000, or the equivalent in Euros, and that each share has been paid up to at least one quarter of the nominal share value plus any premium. In assessing the authorised minimum, shares allotted under employees' share schemes will not count unless one quarter of the nominal value has been paid up.

An application for a certificate must state that at least £50 000 of nominal share capital has been allotted and indicates how much of this has been paid up. It must also state the amount of preliminary expenses, including the amounts to be paid to promoters and the benefits received in return, and be accompanied by a statement of compliance. The application must also be accompanied by a statement of compliance. This states that the company has met all the requirements of s.761. If the application is correctly completed the Registrar must notify receipt of it in the *Gazette* and must issue the certificate. Although the initial application must state the authorised minimum in Sterling or Euros, it can later denominate its share capital in any currency.

A trading certificate is conclusive evidence that a public company is entitled to do business and exercise any borrowing powers. If a public company does conduct business before receiving a certificate, an offence is committed by any company officer who knowingly or wilfully authorised the transaction. The transaction itself is not automatically void. However, the directors will become jointly and severally liable on it if the company does not honour it within 21 days of being asked to do so. A public company can be compulsorily wound up if it does not receive a trading certificate within one year of incorporation.

18.3.3.1 Capital requirements on re-registration as a public company

A private company can re-register as a public company and commence business without a trading certificate. The members will need to pass a special resolution to register as a public company. On the day on which the resolution is passed the company must have allotted at least £50 000 nominal share capital. A quarter of the nominal value of each share and any share premium must have been paid up, and all the requirements regarding allotted capital in a public company must have been complied with. A balance sheet, prepared no more than seven months before the application, must be sent to the Registrar along with the application. An auditor's written statement must say that in their opinion the net assets of the company were not less than the total of called-up share capital and undistributable reserves. If any shares were issued otherwise than for cash, after the preparation of the balance sheet but before the re-registration, then the rules pertaining to the valuation of assets received in return for shares in a public company apply.

The directors must issue a statement that all the requirements relating to capital have been complied with, and that the value of the assets of the company have not fallen since the balance sheet was prepared to less than the total of called-up share capital and undistributable reserves. They will also need to issue a statement of the proposed company secretary if the company does not already have a secretary.

Test your understanding 18.1

1 How does a person become a member of a company?

2 What type of property is a share?

3 What is a company's share premium account?

4 Is it possible for a company to have different classes of shares?

5 What rights usually attach to preference shares?

6 In what three ways may a person acquire shares?

7 What are pre-emption rights?

8 What is a trading certificate?

18.4 COMPANY RESOLUTIONS AND MEETINGS

The members of a company delegate to the directors the task of managing the company. However, the members have the power to take certain decisions themselves by passing resolutions. As regards private companies, a resolution of the members, or of a class of members, may be passed either as a written resolution or at a meeting of the members (s.281(1)). The power to pass written resolutions is necessary because private companies are not required to hold meetings of members. A resolution of the members, or of a class of members, of a public company must be passed at a meeting of the members (s.281(2)). Public companies cannot pass written resolutions.

Most resolutions can be passed as ordinary resolutions, but some must be passed as special resolutions. When the Companies Act requires a resolution of the members to be passed, and does not specify what kind of resolution is required, an ordinary resolution will be sufficient unless the company's articles require a higher majority or unanimity (s.281(3)). Section 281(4) recognises that if all the members entitled to vote take a unanimous decision then the decision is as effective as if it had been passed by a resolution of the members.

Unanimous consent can be substituted for an ordinary resolution and for some types of special resolutions. Buckley J gave the following explanation of this, which has become known as the 'Duomatic principle', in *Re Duomatic Ltd* [1969] 2 Ch 365: 'where it can be shown that all shareholders who have a right to attend and vote at a general meeting of the company assent to some matter which a general meeting of the company could carry into effect, that assent is as binding as a resolution in general meeting would be.' However, unanimous consent could not be used to dismiss a director, or an auditor, before his term of office because of the director or auditor's statutory right to speak at the meeting where his dismissal is proposed.

A special resolution is required by the Companies Act in order to:

(a) alter the articles of the company (s.21(1));
(b) alter the company name (s.77(1));
(c) re-register a company from private to public (s.90(1)), from unlimited to private limited (s.105(1)), or from public to private (s.97(1));
(d) reduce the company's share capital (s.641(1));
(e) authorise the terms on which a company makes an off-market purchase of its own shares, or to vary, revoke or renew any such authority (s.694);
(f) petition for compulsory liquidation of the company (Insolvency Act 1986 s.122(1)).

Members entitled to vote on a resolution proposed at a meeting must be given proper notice of the meeting, and there must be a quorum (minimum number of members present) before a meeting can be properly convened. The notice must be in writing. It can be given in hard copy, electronically or by means of a website (s.308).

Section 282(1) provides that an ordinary resolution of the members, or of a class of members, means a resolution passed by a simple majority, that is to say, by more than 50 per cent. If the resolution is a written resolution, a simple majority of the total voting rights of eligible members is required (s.282(2)). A resolution proposed at a meeting is passed by a simple majority if a majority of those present and voting, in person or by proxy, vote in favour of it (ss.282(3) and (4)). Anything that may be done by ordinary resolution may also be done by special resolution (s.282(5)).

Section 283(1) provides that a special resolution of the members, or of a class of members, means a resolution passed by a majority of not less than 75 per cent. In the case of a written resolution, this means 75 per cent of the total voting rights of eligible members (s.283(2)). In the case of a resolution at a company meeting, it means 75 per cent of those present and voting, in person or by proxy (ss.283(4) and (5)). Where a special resolution of a private company is passed as a written resolution, the resolution must state that it was proposed as a special resolution and if this is stated the resolution may only be passed as a special resolution (s.283(3)). Where a resolution is passed at a meeting of a public or private company, the resolution is not a special resolution unless the notice of the meeting included the text of the resolution and specified the intention to propose the resolution as a special resolution (s.283(6)(a)). If the notice of the meeting specified the intention to propose the resolution as a special resolution, the resolution may only be passed as a special resolution (s.283(6)(b)).

When members vote on a written resolution, each share carries one vote. When a vote on a show of hands is taken at a meeting, each person present, whether a member or a proxy, has one vote. At a vote on a poll taken at a company meeting, each share carries one vote. These rules, contained in s.284, apply unless the articles provide otherwise. Section 321 gives every member the right to demand a poll and this provision cannot be altered by the articles. Section 285 prevents a company's articles from restricting the rights of proxies. A proxy has the same rights to vote at a meeting as the member who appointed him would have had. If a company's articles specify that a member has a certain number of votes when voting on a poll and a different number of votes when voting on a written resolution, the provision relating to the number of votes on a poll is void. The member will have the same number of votes when voting on a poll as he would have when voting on a written resolution (s.285(3)). If shares are held jointly only the senior holder (the person whose name appears first on the register of members) can vote on the shares, unless the articles provide otherwise (s.286). Section 287 allows a company's articles to require that an objection to a person's entitlement to vote be made in a particular way. It also provides that a decision on such an objection can be made final and conclusive. However, if there was fraud the common law would still allow intervention.

18.4.1 Written resolutions

A written resolution may not be used to remove a director, under s.168, before the expiry of his term of office. Nor can a written resolution be used to remove an auditor, under s.510, before the expiry of his term of office (s.288(2)). These two matters aside, a private company may pass any resolution as a written resolution. Public companies cannot pass written resolutions. Written resolutions can be proposed by the directors or by eligible members holding at least 5 per cent of the total voting rights entitled to vote on the resolution (s.288(3)). A written resolution has the same effect, once it is passed, as a resolution at a company meeting (s.288(5)). A written ordinary resolution will be passed as soon as over 50 per cent of eligible members signify agreement to it. A written special resolution will be passed as soon as 75 per cent of eligible members signify agreement. Once agreement has been signified, it cannot be revoked. The eligible members are those members entitled to vote on the circulation date of the written resolution (s.289). The circulation date is defined by s.290 as the date on which copies of the resolution are sent to members in accordance with the Act or, if copies are sent on different days, the first of those days. If the company has different classes of shares, the same rules apply to each class of members.

18.4.1.1 Circulation of written resolution proposed by the directors

When the directors propose a resolution as a written resolution, s.291(2) requires the company to send a copy of the resolution to every eligible member. Section 291(3) sets out the two ways in which this must be done, although it is possible to use a combination of the two methods. First, copies can be sent at the same time in hard copy, or electronically or by means of a website. Second, if it is possible to do so without undue delay, a copy of the resolution can be circulated, in which case the same copy must then be submitted to each eligible member in turn, or different copies must be sent to a number of eligible members in turn. Also, a combination of the two methods may be used. So a hard copy document could be physically circulated or an email could be sent to each individual member or from member to member. The copy of the resolution must be accompanied by a statement telling the member how to signify agreement to the resolution and the date by which the resolution must be passed if it is not to lapse (s.291(4)). If the provisions of s.291 are not complied with, every company officer in default commits an offence. However, the validity of the resolution, if passed, is not affected by failure to comply.

18.4.1.2 Members' power to require circulation of written resolutions

Section 292(1) allows the members of a private company to require the company to circulate a written resolution, as long as the resolution would not be ineffective, defamatory, vexatious or frivolous. The members may also require the company to circulate a statement of not more than 1000 words on the subject matter of the resolution (s.292(3)). This right

to require the company to circulate a written resolution and an accompanying statement is available only if it is requested by the 'requisite percentage' of the voting rights of all members entitled to vote on the resolution (s.292(4)). The requisite percentage is 5 per cent, unless a lower percentage is specified in the company's articles (s.292(5)). This is the same percentage as is needed to require a resolution to be moved at an AGM. The request to circulate a written resolution may be in hard copy or in electronic form, it must identify the resolution and any accompanying statement and it must be authenticated by the person or persons making it (s.292(6)).

18.4.1.3 Circulation of written resolutions proposed by members

If a request to circulate a written resolution is properly made, s.293 requires the company to send the resolution and the accompanying statement to every eligible member. The ways in which the resolution can be circulated, and the ways in which agreement can be signified, are the same as those which would apply if the directors had proposed the written resolution (see above at 18.4.1.1). The resolution must be sent to members within 21 days of the company becoming subject under s. 292 to the requirement to circulate the resolution or, if copies are sent to members on different days, the first copy must be sent by then. Any copy of the resolution must explain how to signify approval and the date by which the resolution is to be passed if it is not to lapse. Section 294 provides that the expenses of the company in complying with s.293 must be paid by the members who request the circulation of the resolution, unless the company resolves otherwise. In addition, the company can demand a deposit of a reasonable sum to meet these expenses, unless the company resolves otherwise. If this deposit is not paid, the company has no obligation to circulate the resolution. The company, or any other person who claims to be aggrieved, can also apply to the court not to have a written resolution requested by members circulated if it thinks that s.292 is being abused. The costs of this application to the court can be ordered against the members requesting circulation of the resolution (s.295).

18.4.1.4 Signifying agreement to written resolutions

Section 296 provides that a member signifies agreement to a proposed written resolution when he sends the company an authenticated document identifying the resolution to which it relates and indicating his agreement to the resolution. This document may generally be sent in hard copy or electronically (s.296(2)). However, it may be sent electronically only if the company has agreed to this or is deemed to have agreed to it (paragraph 6 of Schedule 4). If any document containing or accompanying a proposed written resolution gives an email address, the company is deemed to have agreed that agreement to the resolution can be sent to that address (s.298(1)). Once a member has signified agreement, that agreement may not be revoked (s.296(3)). A written resolution is passed when the required majority of eligible members have signified their agreement to it (s.296(4)). So a simple majority of eligible votes must signify agreement to an ordinary resolution and a 75 per cent majority must signify agreement to a special resolution. The company's articles might specify the time period within which a proposed written resolution must be passed. If the articles do not do this, a proposed written resolution will lapse after 28 days, beginning with the circulation date (s.297). If a proposed written resolution or accompanying statement is sent by publication on a website, the resolution or statement must be available on the website for the whole period from the circulation date to the date on which the resolution lapses (s.299(2)). Any statutory resolution can be proposed and passed by the written resolution procedure. Any provision of the articles which says otherwise is void (s.300).

18.4.2 Resolutions at meetings

The members of both public and private companies can pass resolutions at a company meeting. Private companies do not need to hold any company meetings but may choose to do so. Public companies must hold at least one meeting, the AGM, every financial year and might choose to hold more. A public company must hold its AGM within six months of its accounting reference period. (See 17.6.2.) This is the same time period within which a public company's accounts must be laid before the company members in a general meeting, and so this is normally done at the AGM. Section 301 provides that a resolution of the members can be validly passed at a general meeting only if notice of the meeting and of the resolution were given. Furthermore, it requires that the meeting was held and conducted in accordance with both the Companies Act and the company's articles.

So a resolution can be validly passed only if the correct procedure was followed and mandatory procedural requirements of the Companies Act cannot be removed by the articles.

Section 302 provides that the directors have the power to call a general meeting of the company. Generally, it will be the directors who do call meetings. The members have the power to do so in certain circumstances, as explained below.

18.4.2.1 Members' power to require directors to call meetings

The members may require the directors to call a general meeting of the company under s.303. Section 303(2), as amended, provides that the directors are required to call a general meeting once they have received requests to do so from members holding at least 5 per cent of paid up shares which carry voting rights. As regards public companies, the required percentage is 10 per cent. The members' request must state the general nature of the business to be dealt with at the meeting and may include the text of a resolution to be proposed and voted upon at the meeting (s.303(4)). A resolution cannot be proposed at a meeting if it would be ineffective, defamatory, vexatious or frivolous (s.303(5)). The members' request may be in hard copy or in electronic form and must be authenticated by the person or persons making it (s.303(6)).

If the directors are required to hold a meeting under s.303, then s.304 requires them to call the meeting within 21 days of receiving the request. The meeting must actually be held within 28 days of the notice convening the meeting. If the request for the meeting contained a proposed resolution, notice of the meeting must contain notice of the resolution. If the resolution is to be proposed as a special resolution then the directors must give notice of the special resolution, as required by s.283(6), or they are regarded as not having duly called the meeting. Earlier we saw that s.283(6) provides that when a resolution is passed at a meeting, the resolution is not a special resolution unless the notice of the meeting included the text of the resolution and specified the intention to propose the resolution as a special resolution.

If the directors are requested under s.303 to call a meeting, but do not do so in accordance with s.304, then s.305 allows the members who requested the meeting, or any of them holding at least half of the relevant voting rights, to call a meeting at the company's expense. They must do this within three months of the date on which the directors became subject to the requirement to call a meeting. Any reasonable expenses which the members incurred by requesting a meeting, on account of the directors' failure duly to call the meeting, must be reimbursed by the company. The company will deduct any amount of reimbursement to the members from the directors' fees or remuneration.

18.4.2.2 Meetings ordered by the court

Section 306 gives the court the power to order meetings in any manner it sees fit where it is impracticable for a meeting to be called or properly conducted. The court will do this on the application of a director or a member who is entitled to vote at a company meeting. The court can set the quorum of the meeting at one. This prevents members staying away to make a meeting impossible on the grounds that it is inquorate. The court may also give such other directions as it sees fit.

18.4.3 Notice of meetings

At least 14 days' notice must be given of a meeting of a private company. The same notice period is required of a public company except that at least 21 days' notice must be given of the annual general meeting (s.307(2)). The company's articles might require longer periods of notice (s.307(3)). The members can require a shorter period of notice but this must be agreed by a majority holding not less than the requisite percentage of shares entitled to attend and vote. As regards a private company the requisite percentage is 90 per cent or such higher percentage, not exceeding 95 per cent, as the articles may specify. In the case of a public company, the requisite percentage is 95 per cent. However, the members can reduce the notice required of an annual general meeting of a public company only by unanimous agreement (s.377(2)).

Notice of a general meeting may be given in hard copy, electronically or by means of a website, or by a combination of these methods. Notice must be sent to every member, every director and every person whom the company has been notified is entitled to a share on the death or bankruptcy of a member. However, this is subject to the articles, which might provide that notice should not be sent to a member if their address is unknown. Notice must state the time, date and place of the meeting. Unless the articles provide otherwise,

the notice must also state the general nature of the business to be dealt with at the meeting. If special notice of a resolution is required, notice of the intention to move the resolution must be given to the company at least 28 days before the meeting at which it is to be moved. Such special notice would be required to remove a director or auditor before the expiry of his term of office under s.168 or s.510. Where special notice of a resolution is required, the company must, where practicable, give the members notice of the resolution in the same manner and at the same time as it gives notice of the meeting. Where this is not practicable, 14 days' notice must be given by advertising in an appropriate newspaper or in any other way allowed by the company's articles. Accidental failure to give notice is generally disregarded.

18.4.3.1 Members' power to require circulation of statements

Section 314 provides that the members of a company may require the company to circulate a statement of not more than 1 000 words with respect to a matter referred to in a proposed resolution to be dealt with at a meeting, or with respect to other business to be dealt with at a meeting. This statement must be circulated to all members entitled to receive notice of a general meeting. The company is required to circulate a statement if either members representing at least 5 per cent of the total voting rights of all members who have a relevant right to vote request it, or if at least 100 members with a relevant right to vote, and holding shares having an average sum paid up of £100 each, request it (s.314(2)). In relation to a statement concerning a proposed resolution, 'relevant right to vote' means a right to vote on the resolution at the meeting. In relation to other statements, 'relevant right to vote' means a right to vote at the meeting to which the request relates (s.314(3)). The request may be in hard copy or in electronic form, it must identify the statement to be circulated and it must be authenticated by the person or persons making it. It must also be received by the company at least one week before the meeting to which it relates (s.314(4)).

Section 315(1) provides that when a company is required under s.314 to circulate a statement, it must send a copy of the statement to each member entitled to receive notice of the meeting. This copy must be sent in the same manner as the notice of the meeting and at the same time as, or as soon as reasonably practicable after, the company gives notice of the meeting.

Section 316 provides that the expenses of the company in complying with s.315 do not need to be paid for by the members who requested the circulation if the meeting in question is the AGM of a public company and requests sufficient to require the company to circulate the statement were received before the end of the financial year preceding the meeting. Otherwise, the expenses must be paid by the members who made the request, unless the company resolves otherwise. Furthermore, a company which has not previously resolved otherwise is not bound to comply with the requirements of s.315 unless it has received or been offered a sum reasonably sufficient to meet the expenses of circulation at least one week before the meeting. Section 317 allows a company or other aggrieved person to apply to a court for leave not to circulate a members' statement on the grounds that the rights conferred by s.314 are being abused.

18.4.3.2 Control of political donations and expenditure

A company must not make a political donation to a political party or other political organisation, or to an independent election candidate, unless the members have authorised it to do so by passing an ordinary resolution (s.366). Such a resolution will have effect for four years unless the directors or the articles specify a shorter period. The articles may prevent the directors from shortening the period (s.368). If the company makes an unauthorised donation, s.369 makes the directors jointly and severally liable to make good the loss to the company with interest. There is no prohibition as regards donations and expenditure which does not exceed £5 000 in any 12-month period (s.378).

18.4.4 Procedure at meetings

A company meeting is not properly convened unless a **quorum** (minimum number) of members attend it. Section 318 provides that in single member companies the quorum is one qualifying person. As regards all other companies the quorum is two qualifying people. Both members of a company and proxies are regarded as qualifying persons. However, if one member appoints two proxies then they cannot both count towards the quorum.

The Model Articles for both Public and Private Companies Limited by Shares allow two or more people in different places to be regarded as attending a meeting (articles 29 and 37 respectively). However,

this is the case only as regards a person who can exercise any rights he might have to speak and vote, during the meeting, to all the others attending the meeting. The directors have to make appropriate arrangements to facilitate this and presumably video conferencing and phone conferencing arrangements are envisaged. Both sets of Articles also give directors the right to attend meetings and speak at them whether they are shareholders or not. They also allow the chairman of a meeting to permit other non-members to attend and speak.

Section 319 allows the members at a meeting to elect a **chairman**. However, the articles can restrict who the chairman might be. The chairman supervises the conduct of general meetings and decides matters of procedure. He must act fairly and in good faith, taking into account all of the members' interests and the interest of the company. He cannot stop the meeting because he does not like the way it is going. The articles of many companies give the chairman the casting vote if the votes of the members are equally split. (The Model Articles for Private Companies Limited by Shares, like Table A, give the person chairing the meeting the casting vote, The Model Articles for Public Companies do not.) Section 320 provides that the chairman's declaration of the outcome of a vote on a show of hands is decisive and once entered into the minutes is conclusive proof of the outcome. However, this does not prevent any member from demanding a poll.

Section 321(1) renders void any provision in the articles which excludes **the right to demand a poll** on any question other than the election of the chairman or the adjournment of the meeting. Section 322A allows the articles to provide for poll votes to be cast in advance of a meeting. The articles of many companies restrict, rather than exclude, the right to demand a poll. However, s.321(2) renders void any provision which requires more persons to demand a poll than either: (a) five members entitled to vote on the resolution; or (b) members representing at least 10 per cent of the voting rights on the resolution; or (c) members representing at least 10 per cent of the paid-up capital which confers a right to vote on the resolution. Section 285A provides that in relation to a resolution required or authorised by statute, a member will have the same number of votes on a poll as the articles would have given him on a written resolution.

Section 322 provides that a member entitled to vote on a poll does not need to use all of his votes and can vote different ways with different shares. A member might vote in different ways if he was voting on his own shares and as a proxy. If a company is a member of another company its directors can appoint a representative to vote for it at a meeting of that other company.

A **proxy** is a person entitled to attend a company meeting and to vote on behalf of a company member. Section 324(1) provides that any member of a company is entitled to appoint another person (whether a member or not) as his proxy to attend and to speak and vote instead of him at a meeting of the company. A member of a private company may appoint more than one proxy as long as each proxy is given rights to vote in respect of different shares held by the member (s.324(2)). The Companies (Shareholder's Rights) Regulations 2009 allow a proxy appointed by more than one member of a private company to vote both for and against a motion on a show of hands if this is what he has been instructed to do. The notice of the meeting must inform every member of his rights under s.324. A company's articles can demand 48 hours' notice of the appointment of a proxy but cannot demand more notice. Subject to the articles, a proxy may be elected chairman of a meeting. Any provision in the articles preventing a proxy from demanding a poll is void. Corporate members of companies have the right to appoint a proxy. Section 331 allows a company's articles to confer more extensive rights on members or proxies than those conferred by the Act.

18.4.5 Public companies: additional requirements for AGMs

When the 2006 Act came into force, private companies no longer needed to hold an AGM. Section 336(1) provides that every public company must hold an AGM within six months of its accounting reference date, that is to say within six months of the end of its financial year. Failure to comply is a criminal offence.

A notice calling an AGM of a public company must state that the meeting is an AGM (s.337(1)). Earlier in this chapter, we saw that an AGM of a public company requires 21 days' notice or any longer period specified in the company's articles. Section 337(2) provides that an AGM may be called by shorter notice if all the members entitled to attend and vote at the meeting agree to this.

Section 338(1) allows members of a public company who intend to propose a resolution to be moved at the AGM to require the company to give notice of that resolution to all company members. However, a resolution cannot properly be moved at the AGM if it would be ineffective, defamatory, frivolous or vexatious (s.338(2)). The company is required to give notice of a resolution once it has received requests that it do so from either: (a) members representing at least 5 per cent of the total voting rights of all members who have a relevant right to vote on the resolution at the AGM: or (b) from at least 100 members with a relevant right to vote on the resolution at the AGM, and who hold shares having an average sum paid up of £100 each (s.338(3)). A request by members may be made in hard copy or electronically. It must identify the resolution of which notice is to be given. It must be authenticated by the person or persons making it and must be received by the company not later than six weeks before the AGM or, if later, not later than the time at which notice of the AGM is given (s.338(4)).

A company which is required to give notice of a resolution under s.338 must send a copy of the resolution to each member of the company entitled to receive notice of the AGM. The copy must be sent in the same manner as notice of the meeting and at the same time as notice of the meeting is sent (s.339). The expenses of a company in complying with s.339 need not be paid by the members who requested the circulation of the resolution as long as requests sufficient to require the company to circulate it are received before the end of the financial year preceding the meeting. Otherwise, the members who requested circulation must pay the expenses of the company incurred by complying, unless the company resolves that they need not pay. Unless the company has resolved otherwise, it can refuse to circulate a members' resolution if the members have not deposited or tendered a sum reasonably sufficient to meet the expenses six weeks before the AGM.

18.4.6 Additional requirements for quoted companies

Quoted companies must, of course, comply with the public companies regime but they must also comply with additional requirements.

Where a poll is taken at a general meeting of a quoted company, s.341 requires the company to put the following information on a website: the date of the meeting; the text of the resolution to be voted upon, or, as the case may be, a description of the subject matter of the poll; the number of votes cast in favour;

and the number of votes cast against. Failure to comply is a criminal offence but does not affect the validity of the poll.

Members of a quoted company may require the directors to obtain an independent report on any poll taken or to be taken at a general meeting (s.342(1)). The directors must do this if they receive requests from members either representing at least 5 per cent of the total voting rights of all members who have a right to vote on the matter to which the poll relates, or from at least 100 members with a relevant right to vote on the matter to which the poll relates, and who hold shares having an average sum paid up of £100 each (s.342(2)). A request may be made in hard copy or electronically. It must identify the poll or polls to which it relates, it must be authenticated by the person or persons making it and must be received by the company not later than one week after the poll was taken (s342(4)).

Directors who are required under s.342 to obtain an independent report on a poll must appoint an appropriately qualified 'independent assessor' to prepare a report for the company. This appointment must be made within one week of the company being required to obtain the report. The assessor must be truly independent, that is to say not an officer or employee of that company, or of an associated company, or a partner of such a person. The auditor is regarded as independent. The independent assessor's report must give his opinion as to the following matters: whether the procedures adopted in connection with the poll were adequate; whether the votes cast were fairly and adequately recorded; whether the validity of members' appointment of proxies was properly assessed; and whether notice of the meeting was properly given. He must also give his reasons for his opinions. If he is unable to form an opinion, the report must state this and state why he cannot do so. The report must also name the independent assessor. The independent assessor has the right to attend and be given notice of the meeting at which the poll may be taken and to attend subsequent proceedings in connection with the poll. He also has the right to access the company's records relating to any poll on which he is to report or relating to the meeting at which the poll may be taken. Failure to comply with the requirements regarding independent assessors is a criminal offence. When an independent assessor has been appointed, the company must put on the website the fact of this, his identity, the text of the resolution or a description of the subject matter to which the poll relates and a copy of the independent assessor's report.

Both the result of the poll and the independent assessor's report must be made available on a website which identifies the company. This website must be maintained by or on behalf of the company. Access to the website must be free and unconditional, as must the ability to obtain a hard copy of the information on the website. The information must be made available as soon as reasonably practicable and must be kept on the website for two years.

18.4.7 Records of resolutions and meetings

Section 355 provides that a company must keep records of the following three matters: (a) all resolutions of members passed otherwise than at general meetings; (b) all the minutes of general meetings; and (c) the details provided to the company, under s.357, setting out decisions taken by sole members. These records must be kept for at least ten years. Failure to keep them is a criminal offence.

Section 356 makes the following rules about the extent to which s.355 records can be regarded as evidence. If a director, or the company secretary, signs a record of a resolution which was passed otherwise than at a general meeting this is evidence that the resolution was passed. Where there is a record of a written resolution of a private company the requirements of the 2006 Act as to the passing of the resolution are deemed to have been complied, with unless the contrary is proved. If the minutes of proceedings of a general meeting are signed by the chairman of that meeting, or by the chairman of the next meeting, the minutes are evidence of the proceedings of the meeting. Where there is a record of proceedings of a general meeting of a company, then until the contrary is proved it is taken that the meeting was duly held, that all proceedings duly took place and that all appointments made are valid.

Section 357 applies to records of decisions taken by the sole member of a company. Whenever a sole member takes any decision that may be taken by the company in general meeting, and where the decision has effect as if taken by the company in general meeting, the member must provide the company with details of that decision. However, this does not apply if the decision was taken by written resolution. Failure to comply is a criminal offence but does not invalidate any decision taken by the sole member.

Section 358 provides that the decisions referred to in s.355 must be kept available for inspection at the company's registered office, or at some other place specified in regulations under s.1136, for ten years. The company must notify the Registrar of the place where the records are kept available, and also of any change in this place, unless they have always been kept at the company's registered office. Members may inspect the records without charge. They may also request that a copy of the records be sent to them upon payment of a small fee. The company must comply with these requests within 14 days or a criminal offence is committed. The court also has the power to order inspection or that the records be sent. Section 359 provides that these provisions about records of resolutions and meetings also apply to classes of members if the company has different classes of shares.

Section 30(1) provides that copies of resolutions and agreements affecting a company's constitution must be registered with the Registrar within 15 days of being passed. In Chapter 16 we saw that s.29(1) describes these resolutions and agreements as being either special resolutions or agreements or resolutions which would have needed to have been passed as special resolutions. The full text of s.29(1) is set out in Chapter 16 at 16.6.2.

Section 360 makes a 'clear day' rule in relation to all notice periods applying to meetings, resolutions, circulation of members' statements and deposit or tender of expenses relating to circulation of members' statements. It provides that, when calculating the notice period, the day of the meeting, or the day on which notice was given (or the request received or the sum deposited or tendered) should be disregarded.

Test your understanding 18.2

1 What percentage of votes is required to pass an ordinary or a special resolution?

2 Can any type of resolution be passed as a written resolution?

3 Can the members of a company require the company to circulate a written resolution?

4 Must all companies hold an AGM every year?

5 Can the members of a company require the directors to call a general meeting?

6 How much notice of a company meeting must be given?

7 Can the members require the company to circulate a statement about a proposed resolution to be moved at a meeting?

8 What is a proxy?

9 What is meant by a quorum?

10 Where a poll is taken at a general meeting of a quoted company, what information must the company put on a website?

11 What rights do members of a quoted company have to insist upon the production of an independent report on a poll taken at a general meeting?

12 What records must be kept of decisions taken by the sole member of a company?

18.5 THE LEGAL EFFECT OF THE CONSTITUTION

In Chapter 16, at 16.6, we saw that a company's constitution consists of the company's articles and certain types of resolutions. Section 33(1) of the Act provides that:

'The provisions of a company's constitution bind the company and its members to the same extent as if they were covenants on the part of each member to observe those provisions.'

So the constitution has legal effect to make a contract between each member and the company and between every member and every other member. Section 33(1) of the 2006 Act has replaced s.14(1) of the 1985 Act, which applied to the company's articles rather than to its constitution. So in deciding the effect of the company's constitution, as between the members and the company, it is necessary to consider earlier cases which considered the effect of the articles.

18.5.1 The constitution as a contract between the company and the members

The company can insist that the members stick to the provisions of the constitution.

Hickman v Kent or Romney Marsh Sheep-Breeders' Association [1915] 1 Ch 881

The Sheep-Breeders' Association was registered as a non-profit-making company. One of the Association's articles provided that any dispute between the Association and a member should be referred to ➔

arbitration. The claimant sued the Association in respect of various matters. The Association argued that the court case should be stayed because there was a binding contract to take disputes to arbitration. (Whenever parties have made a valid contract to refer a dispute to arbitration, the court will suspend any proceedings, known as staying the proceedings, on the basis that the dispute should have been taken to arbitration rather than to the court. See Chapter 2 at 2.4.1.)

Held. The proceedings were stayed. The articles form a contract between a company and its members in respect of their ordinary rights as members.

Equally, the members can insist that the company stick to the provisions of the constitution. In *Wood* v *Odessa Waterworks Co* (1889) 42 ChD 636, for example, the company's articles gave the company the power to declare a dividend 'to be paid' to the members. An ordinary resolution was passed to the effect that no dividend should be paid, but that instead members should be given interest-paying debentures. It was held that 'to be paid' meant paid in cash. As the resolution was therefore inconsistent with the articles, a member was granted an injunction to prevent the resolution from being given effect. Another example can be seen in the following case.

Pender v Lushington (1877) 6 ChD 70

The articles of a company provided that every ten shares commanded one vote, as long as the shareholder had possessed the shares for the three months before the meeting, but that no member should be entitled to more than 100 votes. Shareholders who held more than 1 000 shares transferred some of these to Pender and other nominees so that the shares could use their full voting power. The chairman of the company, Lushington, refused to accept the votes of Pender and the nominees, even though their names had been on the register of members as owners of the shares for over three months.

Held. The shares had been properly transferred and so Pender and the other shareholding nominees had a contractual right to have the votes of their shares accepted. Pender was therefore granted an injunction restraining the directors from refusing to count their votes.

It is important to realise that members are only bound to the company in their capacity as members, and that the company is only bound to members in their capacity as members. An example of a member trying to rely on the constitution otherwise than in his capacity as a member can be seen in *Beattie* v *E and F Beattie Ltd* [1938] 3 All ER 214. In that case the defendant, a director who was also a member of the company, was sued by the company for the return of money which had been improperly paid to him as a director. An article similar to that in *Hickman* v *Kent or Romney Marsh Sheep-Breeders' Association* said that disputes between a member and the company should be referred to arbitration. The defendant was not able to rely on this article. He was not attempting to rely on the articles as a contract in his capacity as a member of the company but in his capacity as a director. Lord Greene MR said: 'the contractual force given to the articles of association by [s.33(1)] is limited to such provisions of the articles as apply to the relationship of the members in their capacity as members.' It follows from this that the articles do not create a contract between the company and persons who are not members of it.

18.5.2 The constitution as a contract between the members

Section 33(1) tells us that the constitution creates a contract between the members and other members. However, this is only true in relation to matters concerning membership of the company.

Rayfield v Hands [1960] Ch 1

Article 11 of the company of which the claimant was a member provided that if any member intended to transfer shares in the company he should inform the directors who 'will take the said shares equally between them at a fair price'. The claimant informed the directors that he intended to transfer his shares and they refused to buy them, arguing that the articles imposed no such liability upon them.

Held. The directors were bound by Article 11 and therefore had to take the shares at a fair price. Article 11 was concerned with the relationship between the claimant as a member and the defendants as members of the company.

The constitution does not make any contract with outsiders. Nor does it give outsiders any right to enforce any of its provisions (s.6(2) of the Contracts (Rights of Third Parties) Act 1999). However, outsiders may make a contract in which they expressly or impliedly include the provisions of the constitution.

18.5.3 **Shareholder agreements**

As we have seen, a company must have articles of association. In addition, some or all of a company's members might enter into a shareholder agreement. Such an agreement would not be a part of a company's constitution. A shareholder agreement would form a binding contract between those who enter into it, but would not need to be registered with the Registrar of Companies. Outsiders could not therefore discover what had been agreed. Caution has to be exercised because new members of a company would not be bound by a pre-existing shareholder agreement unless they agreed to be bound by it. Furthermore, if the agreement did not set out the way in which it could be altered, then only a unanimous agreement of all contracting parties could alter the agreement. A company can itself be a party to a shareholder agreement. However, in *Russell* v *Northern Bank Development Corporation Ltd* [1992] 1 WLR 588, the House of Lords held that any agreement by a company that it would not use its statutory power to alter its articles would be unenforceable. This is because s.21 CA 2006 allows a company to alter its articles by special resolution and, as we have seen, this power cannot be contracted out of by the company or the articles. But the House of Lords did accept that a shareholder agreement could bind the shareholders who were party to it to exercise their voting rights in a particular way, even if such an agreement would be unlawful if it was in the articles and therefore binding on the company.

18.6 **MAINTENANCE OF CAPITAL**

The shareholders contribute, or agree to become liable to contribute, the nominal share capital of the company. The company's creditors must accept the risk that the capital will be lost as a result of the company carrying on its business. However, they do not expect the capital to be returned to the members. Companies are therefore prohibited in general from returning capital to their members. It is for this reason that dividends can be paid only out of distributable profits.

The remuneration of directors does not depend on a profit having been made, and the amount paid to directors does not have to be reasonable. But if a payment to a director is in fact a repayment of capital contributed by the director then the amount paid must be returned to the company.

18.6.1 **Reduction of share capital**

The term reduction in capital means that the company's issued share capital is reduced. However, the cancelling of unissued shares is not regarded as a reduction in capital because it does not reduce the amount of capital available to the company in any way. The main reasons for wanting to reduce share capital would be either to reflect the fact that the value of the company's assets had permanently decreased, or to completely extinguish the interests of some members, or to replace share capital with debt capital.

A private company may carry out a reduction of capital under s.641(1)(a), by passing a special resolution supported by a solvency statement. However, there would still have to be at least one member left holding shares other than redeemable shares (s.641(2)). So when capital is reduced under s.641(1)(a), it cannot be reduced to zero.

Both public and private companies may reduce their capital by passing a special resolution confirmed by the court (s.641(1)(b)). Neither s.641(1)(a) nor s.641(1)(b) can override a provision in the articles which prohibits or restricts reduction of the company's share capital (s.641(1)(g)). Section 641(3) allows for a reduction of capital under s.641(1)(a) to be made in any way, and states that this includes reducing or extinguishing liability on share capital not fully paid up, cancelling paid-up share capital which is lost or unrepresented by available assets, or paying off any share capital which is in excess of the company's wants.

If a private company chooses to use the s.641(1)(a) route, s.642(1) requires the directors to make a solvency statement no more than 15 days before the special resolution is passed. Section 642(1) also requires the directors to register the solvency statement with the Registrar. If the special resolution is proposed as a written resolution, a copy of the solvency statement must be sent or submitted to every eligible member at the same time as, or before, the proposed resolution is sent or submitted to him (s.642(2)). If the special resolution is passed at a general meeting, a copy of the solvency statement must be available to members for inspection throughout the meeting (s.642(3)). Failure to comply with s.642(2) or (3) does not invalidate the resolution.

Section 643(1) provides that in the solvency statement each director must state that he has formed the opinion, as regards the company's situation at the date of the statement, that there is no ground on which the company could then be found to be unable to pay (or otherwise discharge) its debts; and that the company will be able to pay (or otherwise discharge) its debts as they fall due during the year immediately following that date. If it is intended to begin to wind the company up within 12 months, the statement must say that each director has formed the opinion that the company will be able to pay its debts in full within 12 months of the commencement of the winding up. In forming these opinions, the directors must take account of all of the company's liabilities (s.643(2)). The statement must be in the form prescribed by Regulations made by the Secretary of State and must state the date on which it is made and the name of each director (s.643(3)). If the directors are not all willing to make the solvency statement then a reduction in capital could be achieved only under s.641(1)(b). If the directors make a solvency statement without having reasonable grounds for the opinions expressed in it, and the statement is delivered to the Registrar, an offence is committed by every director who is in default (s.643(4)).

Within 15 days of the special resolution to reduce capital under s.641(1)(a) being passed, the company must send a copy of the solvency statement, a statement of capital and a copy of the resolution to the Registrar (s.644(1)). The statement of capital shows the position once the capital has been reduced. Section 644(2) requires it to state:

(a) the total number of shares of the company;
(b) the aggregate nominal value of those shares;
(c) for each class of shares – the rights attached to the shares, the total number of shares of that class and the aggregate nominal value of shares of that class; and
(d) the amounts paid and unpaid on each share.

The resolution to reduce capital takes effect when the Registrar registers the documents (s.644(4)). As well as registering the documents required by s.644(2), s.644(5) requires the company to deliver to the Registrar, within 15 days of the resolution being passed, a further statement. This statement must be made by the directors and must confirm that the solvency statement was made not more than 15 days before the resolution was passed and that it has been provided to the members as required by s.642(2) and (3). Failure to comply with any of the registration requirements does not invalidate the resolution. However, the company and every officer

in default would commit an offence. When capital is reduced under s.641(1)(a), the special resolution which authorises the reduction cannot provide that the reduction is to take effect later than the date on which the resolution has effect. So a company could not resolve on 1 March that its capital was to be reduced as from 1 November.

Where capital is to be reduced by a special resolution confirmed by the court, the s.641(1)(b) route, s.645 requires the company to apply to the court for confirmation of the resolution. Section 646 gives the creditors the right to object to the reduction if it involves reducing liability in respect of unpaid share capital or repaying to a shareholder any paid-up share capital. However, the court has the power to direct that s.646 should not apply. If any creditor does object under s.646, a list of all the company's creditors, and details of the amounts owed to them, will be drawn up. The court has the power to publish notices requiring creditors to come forward by a certain date and to exclude creditors who do not do so from objecting to the reduction. The court cannot agree to the reduction until every creditor on the list has either positively consented to the reduction, or had his debt repaid, or the court is satisfied that the company has made adequate provision to ensure that the creditor will be paid. Any company officer who intentionally or recklessly conceals a creditor or misrepresents the amount owed commits an offence under s.647. The court can confirm the reduction on such terms as it sees fit and may order the company to publish the reasons for the reduction in capital. It may also order the company to add the words 'as reduced' to the end of its name for a specified period (s.648). Section 649 requires the Registrar to register the court order and a statement of capital. The statement of capital must give the same details as a statement made under s.644(2). The resolution to reduce capital takes effect when the court order and statement of capital are registered. The court can order that notice of the court order and statement of capital be published in such way as it directs. The Registrar must certify the registration of the court order and statement of capital and this is conclusive evidence that the reduction has been properly made and that the capital is that stated in the statement of capital.

Public companies may not reduce the nominal value of their allotted share capital below £50 000. If the court sanctions a reduction in assets to less than this amount, s.651 sets out an expedited procedure whereby the company can be re-registered as a private company. If a public company loses more than half of its called-up share capital s.656 requires the directors to call a general meeting of the company within 28 days of becoming aware of this. The meeting considers what needs to be done to deal with the problem. It must be held within 56 days of the directors becoming aware of the problem. If the meeting is not convened as required, every director who knowingly and wilfully authorises the failure to convene the meeting, or permits the failure to continue after the meeting should have been convened, commits an offence.

18.6.2 Purchase of own shares

Section 658 makes it a criminal offence for a company to purchase its own shares. However, such a purchase is permitted by s.690 as long as the company's articles do not prohibit it. The members of the company must approve the terms on which the shares are purchased. Shares cannot be purchased by the company unless they are fully paid up. It follows that a company must buy the shares from members to whom they have been issued; they cannot purchase unissued shares. After the purchase of the shares some shares other than redeemable shares must still be held by some members. If the shares are purchased on a recognised stock market, this is known as a market purchase. (Obviously, it is only public companies which are listed on the London Stock Exchange, or admitted to dealings on some other recognised UK investment exchange, which can purchase their own shares in this way.) If the shares are bought in any other way then this is known as an off-market purchase. A company purchasing its own shares must pay for them in full on the date of the purchase. The funds for this must come from company profits or from money raised by issuing new shares.

As long as the company's articles permit for the purchase of its own shares, authority for a market purchase may be given by ordinary resolution of the members. The resolution must state the maximum number of shares which can be purchased, and the maximum and minimum prices which can be paid. The authority given cannot last for longer than 18 months. However, authority to make a market purchase may be renewed, revoked or varied by another ordinary resolution. A copy of the resolution which gives the authority must be registered with the Registrar within 15 days of its being passed. While the authority still exists, a copy

must also be attached to every copy of the articles issued by the company. Once the shares have been purchased, they must be cancelled.

An off-market purchase can be made by either a public or a private company, but only if the company's articles permit this. In addition, the terms of the contract to purchase the shares must be approved by the members of the company in advance of the purchase. The members need to give authority to make the purchase by special resolution. The authority may not be for longer than 18 months if the company is a public company. The votes attaching to the shares which are to be bought are not allowed to vote on the special resolution. If the member whose shares are being bought holds other shares which are not being bought, he may vote with these other shares in a poll, but may not vote at all on a show of hands. If a written resolution is used to give authority, the resolution is passed without the signature of the member whose shares are being bought, who may not vote. Regardless of what the articles might say, any member is entitled to demand a poll if the resolution is proposed at a general meeting. If the resolution is put forward at a general meeting, then a copy of the proposed contract must be available at the meeting, and must have been available for inspection at the company's registered office for 15 days before the meeting. If the resolution is to be adopted by written resolution then every member must be sent a copy of the proposed terms when the resolution is sent for signature. The authority to make an off-market purchase may be renewed, varied or revoked by another special resolution.

Once a company has purchased its own shares, the Registrar must be informed within 28 days. A private company must state the number of shares purchased and their nominal value. A public company must also state the amount paid for the shares. In their annual report the directors must state the number of shares purchased, their nominal value, the price paid, the reason for the purchase and how large a percentage of the paid-up capital of the company the shares purchased represented. For ten years after the purchase, the company must keep a copy of the contract to purchase the shares at its registered office. In a private company this is available for inspection only to members. In a public company it is available for inspection to the public. All shares purchased must be cancelled and the company's issued share capital will be reduced by the nominal value of the cancelled shares.

18.6.2.1 Financial assistance to buy shares

Section 678(1) makes it *prima facie* unlawful for a public company to give financial assistance, direct or indirect, for the acquisition of its own shares or the shares of a holding company, whether before or after or at the same time as the shares are acquired. This prohibition applies whether the shares are being bought from an existing member or whether they are unissued shares. Private companies are not prohibited from giving financial assistance to buy their own shares. Section 678(3) makes it *prima facie* unlawful for a public company to reduce or discharge liability incurred as a consequence of taking shares in the company. Financial assistance is defined by s.677. It includes the company guaranteeing a loan which was taken out by a person buying the company's shares. Gifts, guarantees or indemnities, or the giving of a loan or any other transactions which reduce the company's assets to a material extent, are all also treated as financial assistance.

If a company acts in breach of s.678, it is liable to a fine, and every officer of it who is in default is liable to imprisonment, or a fine, or both. In addition, the directors will incur civil liability for breach of duty and other persons involved in the financial assistance may be liable to the company if they knowingly received company property or knowingly took part in the illegal transaction. Any guarantee or security given in connection with prohibited financial assistance is void. Loans made in the ordinary course of a money-lending business will not be included and nor will money provided in good faith for the purchase of the company's shares under an employee share scheme.

Section 681 provides that the prohibition in s.678 does not extend to the following matters: lawfully distributing dividends; distributions made on the winding up of the company; the allotment of bonus shares; a reduction of capital confirmed by the court under a properly conducted redemption of shares; or a purchase of shares or certain specified arrangements involving creditors of the company.

Section 678(2) does allow financial assistance for the purpose of acquiring shares in the company or in a holding company. But only if the company's principal purpose in giving the assistance is not to give it for the purpose of such acquisition, or the giving of the assistance for that purpose is only an incidental part of some larger purpose of the company. The assistance must also be given in good faith in the interest of the company. It can be difficult to prove that the requirements of s.678(2) have been satisfied, and the fact that the

company benefited from the financial assistance will not necessarily be enough. Often financial assistance is given to facilitate a management buy-out of the company.

18.6.3 Redeemable shares

Redeemable shares are issued by the company on the understanding that they will be bought back by the company on a certain date. The holders of redeemable shares are therefore temporary members of the company. A company may issue redeemable shares as long as its articles permit this. The purchase back of these shares will not contradict the general rule that a company must not acquire its own shares. When the shares are redeemed they must be cancelled. A company may issue redeemable shares only if there will at all times be some members holding shares other than redeemable shares.

18.6.4 Dividends

The members of a company expect to be paid a return on the capital which they invest in the company. This return might come either by sharing in the surplus assets when the company is wound up, by selling their shares at a profit or by way of dividend. Dividends must be paid out of profit, otherwise the payment of them would amount to a reduction of capital. Section 847 makes a dividend repayable to the company if the person receiving it knew or had reasonable grounds to believe that it had been wrongly paid. In *It's a Wrap (UK) Ltd* v *Gula* [2006] EWCA Civ 544, [2006] 2 BCLC 634 the Court of Appeal held that it was no defence to a recipient of an unlawful dividend that he did not know that the Act prevented the payment of the dividend. The relevant question was only whether he knew, or should have known, of the facts which meant that the dividend contravened the Act's requirements. In the case two directors who paid themselves dividends in two years when the company made a loss were liable to repay these dividends to the company, which had since gone into liquidation.

There is no requirement that a company must distribute profit as dividends. It might consider it more prudent to retain the profit for expansion of the company. A dividend only becomes payable if the company declares a dividend. Table A article 102 provides that the members can declare a dividend at a general meeting, but that no dividend can exceed the amount recommended by the directors. (This recommendation is made in the directors' report.) The model articles for both public and private companies include a similar article. The members may reject the directors' recommendation of a dividend, or may declare a dividend smaller than that recommended by the directors. If the directors refuse to recommend a dividend in line with the wishes of the members, the members might begin steps to remove the directors, in order to replace them with directors who would recommend the dividend. Dividends must be paid in cash unless the articles provide otherwise.

Sections 830 and 831 set out the rules on the payment of dividends and other distributions of the company's assets to its members. However, these sections do not apply to a company's purchase of its own shares or to the issue of bonus shares.

Section 830(2) states that:

'A company's profits available for distribution are its accumulated, realised profits, so far as not previously utilised by distribution or capitalisation, less its accumulated, realised losses, so far as not previously written off in a reduction or reorganisation of capital duly made.'

A company's realised profits will be the amount by which income produced by the sale of assets exceeds expenses. (Unrealised profits arise when the assets held by the company increase in value.) A realised loss occurs when expenses exceed the income produced by asset sales.

A dividend is not payable unless the profits made in one year also clear any losses made in previous years. If a dividend is declared but not paid then the member entitled to the dividend has a time limit of 12 years to sue on the debt.

If an illegal distribution is made then the directors who recommended the dividend are liable to repay it to the company. Any of the directors can be sued for the whole amount but, having paid, would then be entitled to a contribution from the other directors. The members receiving the dividend are not obliged to return it, unless they knew or had reasonable grounds to believe that it was paid in contravention of the Act. The rule against payment of dividends out of capital is designed to protect the creditors of the company, but the creditors do not have any power to prevent a proposed dividend out of the company's capital.

18.7 INSIDER DEALING

In order to maintain confidence in stock exchanges it is necessary that all those who might deal on the exchanges have the same information available to them. Those who have special information about a company are prohibited from using this information to deal in the company's securities.

Section 52(1) of the Criminal Justice Act (CJA) 1993 provides that an individual who has information as an insider is guilty of insider dealing if he **deals in securities** that are price-affected securities in relation to the information. The acquisition or disposal which the dealing involves must occur on a regulated stock market, or the person dealing must either be a professional intermediary (a stockbroker) or rely on a professional intermediary. Securities are defined widely to include shares, debentures, options and futures.

Section 52(a) CJA 1993 creates a second offence, whereby an individual who has information as an insider is also guilty of insider dealing if he **encourages another person to deal in price-affected securities** in relation to the information, knowing or having reasonable cause to believe that this would cause insider dealing to take place.

Section 52(b) CJA 1993 creates the third offence of **disclosing the information to another person,** otherwise than in the proper performance of the functions of his employment, office or profession.

Inside information means information which:

(a) relates to particular securities;

(b) is specific or precise;

(c) has not been made public; and

(d) if it were made public would be likely to have a significant effect on the price of the securities (CJA 1993 s.56(1)).

A person has information as an insider if, and only if, he knows that it is inside information and he knows that he has it from an inside source (CJA 1993 s.57(1)). A person has information as an inside source if, and only if, he has it as a consequence of being a director, employee or shareholder of an issuer of securities, or directly or indirectly has the information from such a person, or has access to the information by virtue of his employment, office or profession (CJA 1993 s.57(2)).

Section 53(1) CJA 1993 provides a defendant with a defence to the main offence of dealing in securities if he shows:

(a) that he did not at that time expect the dealing to result in a profit attributable to the fact that the information in question was price-sensitive information in relation to the securities; or

(b) that at the time he believed on reasonable grounds that the information had been disclosed widely enough to ensure that none of those taking part in the dealing would be prejudiced by having the information; or

(c) that he would have done what he did even if he had not had the information.

Very similar defences are provided by s.53(2) and (3) to the other two crimes of encouraging others to deal and disclosing information.

Those convicted can be fined and imprisoned for up to seven years.

The Listing Rules of the London Stock Exchange attempt to reduce insider dealing by requiring that listed companies publish all price-sensitive information as quickly as possible.

Companies which breach the Listing Rules can have their listing suspended and thereby lose a valuable method of raising capital.

18.7.1 **Market abuse**

Section 118 of the Financial Services and Markets Act 2000 creates civil penalties for market abuse. Section 118 defines market abuse as behaviour which is likely to be regarded by a regular user of that market, who is aware of the behaviour, as a failure on the part of the person or persons concerned to observe the standard of behaviour reasonably expected of a person in his or their position in relation to the market. The behaviour can be committed by one or more persons, and must occur in relation to qualifying investments traded on certain markets as defined by the Treasury. Section 118(2) requires that one of three conditions must also be satisfied. The conditions are that:

(a) the behaviour is based on information which is not generally available to those using the market but which, if available to a regular user of the market, would or would be likely to be regarded by him as relevant when deciding the terms on which transactions in investments of the kind in question should be effected;

(b) the behaviour is likely to give a regular user of the market a false or misleading impression as to the supply of, or demand for, or as to the price or value of, investments of the kind in question;

(c) a regular user of the market would, or would be likely to, regard the behaviour as behaviour which would, or would be likely to, distort the market in investments of the kind in question.

If s.118 is breached, a wide range of penalties can be imposed. These include financial penalties and the making of a public statement about the offending behaviour. The FSMA 2000 also creates criminal offences of making a misleading statement and engaging in a course of misleading conduct. The maximum penalty for these offences is seven years imprisonment or an unlimited fine.

Test your understanding 18.3

1 Between whom, if anyone, does a company's constitution create a contract?

2 In what two ways can a company reduce its capital?

3 What is the difference between a market purchase of a company's own shares and an off-market purchase?

4 Can a company's capital be reduced by the payment of a dividend?

5 Can the members of a company governed by Table A articles or the model articles for private and public companies increase the dividend which the directors recommend?

6 What are the three offences of insider dealing?

18.8 PROTECTION OF MINORITY SHAREHOLDERS

A member of a company who owns the majority of the company's voting shares can ensure that an ordinary resolution is passed. A member with 75 per cent of the shares can ensure that a special resolution is passed. Similarly, members who between them can muster over 50 per cent or 75 per cent have the power to see that the two types of resolution are passed.

These percentages can be vitally important when a person is considering whether or not to invest in a company. Let us look at an example. If A invites B to form a company with him, and suggests that B take 49 per cent of the one class of ordinary shares, while A takes 51 per cent, then their investment in the company is almost equal. However, their control of the company is far from equal, and B should be very wary about accepting such a proposition. B's holding of 49 per cent of the voting shares would give him no power to block or pass an ordinary resolution, but would at least give some degree of 'negative control', in that he could block a special resolution. If B was offered only 25 per cent of the shares he would in effect have no control of the company at all, except to prevent the alteration of an entrenched article.

If two shareholders each own 50 per cent of a company's shares then they will both have negative control of the company. Neither member will be able to force through a resolution without the consent of the other. This might sound an ideal way to run a company owned by two people, and while the shareholders are in harmony with each other it probably is. But if complete deadlock is reached then the court may well wind the company up (if either party so requests) on the ground that to do so would be just and equitable. This happened in *Re Yenidje Tobacco Co Ltd* [1916] 2 Ch 426, where the Court of Appeal wound up a profitable company because the two shareholder/directors, Mr Weinberg and Mr Rothman, had reached complete deadlock and only communicated with each other through notes passed via the company secretary. Cozens-Hardy MR said: 'Certainly, having regard to the fact that there are only two directors who will not speak to each other, and no business which deserves the name of business in the affairs of the company can be carried on, I think the company should not be allowed to continue.'

If complete deadlock is reached, a minority shareholder is of course in a far worse position than a 50 per cent shareholder. (One can imagine how Weinberg would have felt if he had owned 49 per cent of the shares to Rothman's 51 per cent.) We have seen that directors can be removed under s.168(1) by an ordinary resolution of which special notice is given. Assuming that there is no *Bushell v Faith* clause in the articles, and no entrenched article gives a minority shareholder the right to remain as a director, a majority shareholder can exclude the minority shareholders both from management of the company and from appointing the managers.

18.8.1 **The rule in *Foss v Harbottle***

The position of minority shareholders is not improved by the rule in *Foss v Harbottle* (1843) 2 Hare 461. This rule provides that if a wrong is done to a company then only the company has the right to sue in respect of that wrong, and that the court will not interfere with the internal management of a company while the company is acting within its powers. The rule in *Foss v Harbottle* is a logical extension of *Salomon v Salomon & Co Ltd*, which established that a company is a legal person in its own right. It follows that if a

company is wronged then it alone has the power to sue in respect of that wrong. So the board of directors would have the power to decide whether or not the company sued.

The main benefit of the rule in *Foss v Harbottle* is that it prevents the huge number of legal actions which would inevitably arise if any member of a company had the power to sue on the company's behalf. The rule also upholds a general principle of company law – that if the members of a company are in disagreement, they should resolve this at a general meeting of the company. If the rule in *Foss v Harbottle* did not exist the courts would constantly be asked to judge whether or not companies were adopting sound business policies. The 2006 Act has, however, made a very significant change to the position of minority shareholders by introducing a statutory derivative claim. Such a claim allows a company member, subject to judicial control, to bring an action on behalf of the company. Such a claim can be brought on account of a director's negligence, default, breach of duty or breach of trust. It can also be brought in pursuance of a court order in proceedings for 'unfair prejudice', a matter considered below at 18.8.5.

18.8.2 **Statutory derivative claims**

Section 260(1) of the 2006 Act allows a member to bring a derivative claim on behalf of the company. Prior to the commencement of the Act, it was possible to bring a derivative claim at common law. However, it was not easy to bring such a claim and the common law derivative claim has effectively been abolished by the new statutory derivative claim.

In Chapter 17, at 17.1.9, we examined the new statutory duties which directors owe to a company. Because these duties are owed to the company, rather than to individual members, they can generally be enforced only by the company or by a liquidator or administrator once insolvency proceedings have commenced. Either the board of directors or the members in general meeting would take the decision to bring proceedings on behalf of the company. The new statutory derivative claim is highly significant because it allows a company member to bring a claim on behalf of the company.

There are, however, safeguards which prevent the bringing of frivolous or unfounded derivative claims. If any member was allowed to pursue a derivative claim whenever he saw fit, there might be a large number of unmeritorious claims. Therefore, a member bringing a derivative claim must gain permission to continue such a claim from the court.

Section 260(1) defines a derivative claim as a claim brought by a member of the company in respect of a cause of action vested in the company and seeking relief on behalf of the company. It is important to remember that the claim is brought on behalf of the company rather than on behalf of the aggrieved member. It is also important to remember that if any remedy is ordered, it will be a remedy in favour of the company. Section 260(2) and (3) then provide that a derivative claim may be brought only in respect of two matters. First, in respect of a cause of action arising from an actual or proposed act or omission which involves negligence, default, breach of duty or breach of trust by a director of the company. Second, in pursuance of a court order in proceedings under s.994 for protection for relief from 'unfair prejudice'. (Unfair prejudice is considered below at 18.8.5.) The first category is the more important and would allow a claim to be brought whenever a director breached any of the general statutory duties set out ss.171–177 (see Chapter 17 at 17.1.9). Section 260(4) provides that it is immaterial whether the cause of action arose before or after the person seeking to bring or continue the claim became a member of the company. So a person who becomes a member will clearly be able to bring a claim in respect of acts which the directors have already committed. Section 260(5)(c) provides that, in this context, a person who is not a member, but to whom shares in the company have been transferred or transmitted by operation of law, is regarded as a member. So this provision protects people who have inherited shares in a company but who have not yet been registered as members. The claim may be brought against a director or another person or against both. In the context of s.260, 'director' includes former directors and shadow directors (s.260(5)(a) and (b)).

Section 261(1) provides that a member of a company who brings a derivative claim must apply to the court for permission to continue it. At this stage the defendant takes no part in the proceedings. The court must dismiss the application if it appears to the court that the application, and the evidence filed by the claimant in support of it, do not disclose a *prima facie* case for giving permission (s.261(2)). If the court does not dismiss the application, it may give directions as to the evidence to be provided by the company and may adjourn the proceedings to enable the evidence

to be obtained (s.261(3)). On hearing the application, s.261(4) gives the court three options:

(a) to give permission for the claim to be continued on such terms as it thinks fit;
(b) to refuse permission and dismiss the claim; or
(c) to adjourn the proceedings and give such directions as it thinks fit.

So if the court does not dismiss the claim, it has considerable power to impose requirements on either side.

Section 262(3) applies where a company has brought a claim and the cause of action is one which could be pursued as a statutory derivative claim brought in respect of a director's breach of duty. It allows a member of the company to apply to the court for permission to continue the claim as a derivative claim if:

(a) the manner in which the company commenced or continued the claim amounts to an abuse of the process of the court;
(b) the company has failed to prosecute the claim diligently; and
(c) it is appropriate for the member to continue the claim as a derivative claim.

This section is necessary because otherwise the directors in breach might cause the company to bring a claim with the intention that the claim could later be abandoned or deliberately made unsuccessful. When a member brings a claim under s.262, the court has the same options to dismiss the claim, or allow continuation of it, as when a claim is brought under s.261.

Section 263(2) deals with whether permission to continue a derivative claim brought in respect of a director's breach of duty should be granted. Under s.263(2), permission must be refused in three circumstances. First, under s. 263(2)(a) if a person acting in accordance with s.172 (duty to promote the success of the company) would not seek to continue the claim. Second, under s.263(2)(b) where the cause of action arises from an act or omission that is yet to occur, and the act or omission has been authorised by the company. Third, under s.263(2)(c) where the cause of action arises from an act or omission that has already occurred but the act or omission was either authorised by the company before it occurred or has been ratified by the company since it occurred. These are important limitations. In Chapter 17 the following rules about authorisation and ratification of acts and omissions were set out. First, s.180(4) allows the members of the company to authorise any breach of duty, including a conflict of interest. Second, s.239 allows the members to pass a resolution saying that the company is ratifying conduct by a director amounting to negligence, default, breach of duty or breach of trust in relation to the company. However, under s.239, the director in question, and any person associated with him, cannot vote on the resolution whether it is proposed as a written resolution or as a resolution proposed at a meeting. Third, s.175(4)–(6) allow what would otherwise be a conflict of interest if the directors have properly authorised the act in line with the company's constitution. However, the director in question does not count towards the quorum of the meeting and cannot vote in favour of authorisation. The members cannot ratify fraud by the directors, nor the misappropriation of company money or property.

Section 263(3) lists six matters which the court should take into account in particular in considering whether to give permission to continue a derivative claim brought in respect of a director's breach of duty. These matters are:

(a) whether the member is acting in good faith in seeking to continue the claim;

(b) the importance that a person acting in accordance with s.172 (the duty to promote the success of the company) would attach to continuing the claim;

(c) where the cause of action results from an act or omission that is yet to occur, whether the act or omission could be, and in the circumstances would be likely to be, either authorised by the company before it occurs or ratified by the company after it has occurred;

(d) where the cause of action arises from an act or omission that has already occurred, whether the act or omission could be, and in the circumstances would be likely to be, ratified by the company;

(e) whether the company has decided not to pursue the claim; and

(f) whether the act or omission in respect of which the claim is brought gives rise to a cause of action that the member could pursue in his own right rather than on behalf of the company.

Section 263(4) provides that the court should have particular regard to the views of members of the company who have no personal interest, direct or indirect, in the matter.

Section 264 allows a second member to continue a derivative claim originally brought by another member. This right can arise either when another member has himself brought a derivative claim or has taken

over a derivative claim brought by the company. Permission from the court must be gained. The court will assess whether or not to grant permission using the same criteria as would apply if the second member had begun the derivative claim.

In the following case the factors to be considered in deciding whether or not to grant permission for a derivative claim to proceed were analysed in detail.

Stainer v Lee [2010] EWHC 1539 (Ch)

Stainer applied to the High Court for permission to continue a derivative claim on behalf of Kerrington Ltd (the company). The claim was brought against two of the company's directors, Lee and Elliott, and against Eldington Holdings Ltd (EH Ltd). EH Ltd was owned and controlled by Lee. Stainer owned 0.08 per cent of the company's issued share capital. At the time of the hearing Lee, either personally or through EH Ltd, held 87 per cent of the company's issued share capital. Stainer had two complaints. First, that the company had lent money to EH Ltd without receiving any interest on the loans. Second, that some of these loans should not have been made at all. He alleged that EH Ltd should hold the loans which should not have been made at all on constructive trust for the company and so should repay the loans to the company. In 2000 Lee had held about 20 per cent of the company's issued share capital of £12.75 million. He had set up EH Ltd to buy all the shares which he did not own, at 90p per share. After EH Ltd made these purchases Lee's holding of the company's share capital rose to 87 per cent. In order to purchase the shares, EH Ltd borrowed £4.3 million from the Royal Bank of Scotland (RBS) at 2 per cent per annum above the RBS base rate. Within about a year, in 2002, EH Ltd repaid the loan to RBS by borrowing £4.7 million from the company. (The loan appears to have been made following the correct procedures and without breaching the financial assistance rules.) The amount of borrowing by EH Ltd from the company increased and by 2008 was £8.1 million. No interest was ever paid on these loans. At all times the company was borrowing very large sums from RBS at commercial rates of interest. Stainer had written to Lee to complain about the loans made by the company, suggesting that there had been a fraud on the minority. Lee dismissed this idea but offered to buy Stainer's shares at 40p per share. Thirty-five other minority shareholders expressly supported Stainer and contributed towards the costs of bringing the derivative claim. Immediately before the court hearing the company called an EGM to consider →

authorising a new loan agreement. This resolution was passed by an 80 per cent majority (excluding the votes of Lee and EH Ltd). The resolution ratified all loans made before April 2010, at a rate of interest which had been agreed between the parties or, alternatively, at 2 per cent above the RBS base rate. The resolution also stated that although the loans had not been repaid, all outstanding interest had been paid. Finally, the resolution stated that interest should be paid in the future on the existing loans. The rate of interest was to be 2 per cent above the base rate on the first loan of £4.7 million and 1.2 per cent above the base rate on loans made after the first loan.

Held. Permission to continue the derivative claim was granted. Roth J noted that although s.263(2) set out the circumstances in which permission to pursue a derivative claim should be refused, it did not set out the circumstances in which it should be granted. He considered s.172, as both ss.262(2) and (3) referred to it. He thought that the mandatory bar to continuation of proceedings in s.263(2)(a) applied only where *no* director, acting in accordance with s.172, would seek to continue the claim. If some directors would seek to continue and others would not s.263(3)(b) should be applied and consideration should be made of the importance that a person acting in accordance with s.172 (the general duty of a director to promote the success of the company) would attach to continuing the claim. Something more than a *prima facie* case was needed but it would be wrong to conduct a mini trial. No particular standard of proof was required but a range of factors had to be considered. If the case was very strong, but the amount to be recovered was small, it might be appropriate to continue because this might provoke a settlement or result in a summary judgment. It might also be in the company's interests to continue if the amount of potential recovery was very large, even if the case was less strong. On the facts, the company had received no interest on its loans for nine years and this strongly indicated that the directors were in breach of their fiduciary duties. The additional lending, after the initial £4.7 million, was not to discharge loans incurred by buying the company's shares and was therefore outside the authority granted in the special resolution. Nor was the ratification in the special resolution effective. The rate of interest which was 'ratified' was not the rate of interest which applied when the loan was made. So it was a new agreement not a ratification. Furthermore, the shareholders who voted in favour of the resolution did not seem to know of Lee's interest in EH Ltd or the reason why EH Ltd wanted the additional loans. It was clear that Stainer was not pursuing a personal vendetta, he was merely trying to protect his interest as a minority shareholder as well as the interests of other minority shareholders. An action for unfair prejudice was less appropriate than continuing the derivative claim because Stainer was not seeking to be bought out. He was seeking financial remedies for misconduct from the directors and an order for restitution from EH Ltd. Although permission to continue was granted, Stainer would have to apply for further permission once all documents had been disclosed. By that time the strength of the case would be much clearer. The costs which Stainer had already incurred were payable by the company. However, further costs in pursuing the claim were limited to £40 000 (reviewable in the future) because the amount which might be recovered was uncertain, and there was a danger that the costs would become disproportionate.

COMMENT Roth J cited with approval Lewison J in *Iesini* v *Westrip Holdings Ltd* [2009] EWHC 2526, [2010] BCC 420 who, considering some of the factors which a director acting in accordance with s.172 would take into account in deciding whether or not to continue a claim, said:

'They include: the size of the claim; the strength of the claim; the cost of the proceedings; the company's ability to fund the proceedings; the ability of the potential defendants to satisfy a judgment; the impact on the company if it lost the claim and had to pay not only its own costs but the defendant's as well; any disruption to the company's activities while the claim is pursued; whether the prosecution of the claim would damage the company in other ways (e.g. by losing the services of a valuable employee or alienating a key supplier or customer) and so on. The weighing of all these considerations is essentially a commercial decision, which the court is ill-equipped to take, except in a clear case.'

This statement of Lewison J has since been approved in several other cases.

18.8.3 Common law exceptions to *Foss* v *Harbottle*

The common law always recognised exceptions to the rule in *Foss* v *Harbottle*. The courts have been prepared to intervene, despite the rule, in four circumstances: if the personal rights of a member are infringed; if the company proposes to enter into an *ultra vires* transaction; if the act confirmed by the majority required a special resolution; or if there has been a fraud on the minority. The last of these exceptions was of considerable significance before the introduction of the statutory derivative claim. However, such a claim can be brought only in respect of a cause of action vested in the company and seeking relief on behalf of the company. In many fraud on the minority cases no wrong was done to the company. Only the minority shareholders were wronged. However, even in these cases the directors would have been in breach of their s.172 duty to act in good faith to promote the success of the company for the benefits of its members as a whole. So even here, a derivative claim would seem to be the most appropriate action.

18.8.3.1 The personal rights of a member have been infringed

In this chapter we have already seen an example of a court holding that a member's personal rights had been infringed in *Pender* v *Lushington* at 18.5.1. It might be remembered that the company chairman refused to accept the votes of Pender's shares, as the articles required him to do, and the court held that this was a breach of Pender's rights as a member. However, this is not a true exception to the rule in *Foss* v *Harbottle*. A member whose constitutional rights have been infringed will have a contractual right to sue on account of the constitution forming a contract between himself and the company and between himself and the other members. Such an action does not allege any wrong done to the company and so a derivative action would not be appropriate.

18.8.3.2 Actions which are *ultra vires*

In Chapter 17 at 17.1.8 we saw that any member of a company has the right to prevent the company from entering into an *ultra vires* transaction, but that if the transaction has already been concluded a member has no power to undo it. We also saw that the members will not have the power to prevent the company entering into an *ultra vires* transaction if the transaction has been approved by special resolution.

18.8.3.3 The act confirmed by the majority required a special resolution

The rule in *Foss* v *Harbottle* does not allow a majority of shareholders sufficient to pass an ordinary resolution to approve a transaction which required approval by a special resolution or by some other special majority vote.

18.8.3.4 Fraud on the minority

At common law, minority shareholders who have been defrauded by a decision of the majority have the right to have the decision overturned. Since the coming into force of the Companies Act 2006, there is no longer much need for an action for fraud on the minority. First, in cases in which the company itself was defrauded, usually by transferring the company's assets to the directors, an aggrieved shareholder could now bring a derivative claim, as explained above at 18.8.2. Second, in cases in which the controlling shareholders and directors defrauded only the minority shareholders, and then passed a resolution to ratify this decision, s.239(4) will allow the ratification to be effective only if it could be achieved without the votes of the directors in question. (See 17.1.10.2.) Nor can this provision be evaded by the board of directors voting to ratify the matter at a board meeting rather than at a company meeting. Section 175(6), considered in the previous chapter at 17.1.9.5, will allow the board of directors to approve a director's conflict of interest only if the vote to approve can be passed without the votes of the errant directors. In any event, where the minority are defrauded the directors are likely to have been in breach of their s.172 duty to act in good faith to promote the success of the company for the benefit of its members as a whole, making a derivative claim the most appropriate action.

18.8.4 Statutory rights to call meetings and propose resolutions

Those with a minority shareholding in a company are given various statutory rights. We have already seen that s.303 allows those holding 10 per cent of the voting shares to require the directors to call a general meeting of the company; that s.292 allows 5 per cent of members entitled to vote on a resolution to require a private company to circulate a written resolution and an accompanying statement; that a public company is required by s.338 to give notice of a resolution to be moved at the AGM once it has received requests to do so from members representing at least 5 per cent of the total voting rights of all members who have a relevant right to vote on the resolution at the AGM, or from at least 100 members with a relevant right to vote on the resolution at the AGM, and who hold shares having an average sum paid up of £100 each; that entrenchment might allow any member to prevent alteration of the articles; that s.633 allows 15 per cent of the holders of a class of shares whose rights are to be varied to apply for a cancellation of the variation. In addition, those who hold 10 per cent of a company's issued share capital can ask for an inspection by the Department of Business, Enterprise and Regulatory Reform, a matter considered below at 18.8.7.

18.8.5 **Protection of members against unfair prejudice**

Section 994 allows any company member, or the personal representative of a deceased member, to petition the court on the grounds that the affairs of the company are being, or have been, or will be, conducted in a manner which is unfairly prejudicial to the interests of the members generally or to the interests of particular members, including himself. (The right of a personal representative is important because after the death of a member directors sometimes refuse to register either the personal representative or the beneficiary as a shareholder. If they are not registered they cannot vote at company meetings, although they would still have a right to dividends declared.) The conduct about which the petitioner complains must relate to the affairs of the company and must affect his interests as a member of the company. The petitioner will not be able to claim the costs of bringing an action from the company, as he would in the case of a derivative claim which was allowed to proceed. As it is the interests of the members, and not merely their rights, which are protected, s.994 can be used to complain of conduct which is technically correct. If the court agrees that the conduct is unfairly prejudicial s.996(1) allows it to make any order it sees fit to give relief from the unfair prejudice. Section 996(2) says that, without prejudice to s.996(1), the court may:

(a) regulate the conduct of the company's affairs in the future;

(b) require the company to refrain from doing or continuing an act complained of, or to do an act that the petitioner has complained it has omitted to do;

(c) authorise civil proceedings to be brought in the name and on behalf of the company by such person or persons and on such terms as the court may direct;

(d) require the company not to make any, or any specified, alterations in its articles without the leave of the court; or

(e) provide for the purchase of the shares of any members of the company by other members or by the company itself and, in the case of a purchase by the company itself, the reduction of the company's capital accordingly.

Section 998 applies where the court orders that the company's constitution be changed or where a court order allows the constitution to be changed by the company. It requires that the company deliver a copy of the court order to the Registrar within 14 days of its being made. Section 999 requires that if the constitution is actually changed a copy of the amended articles (or a copy of the amended Chapter 3 resolutions) must be sent along with the copy of the court order.

Section 994 has replaced s.459 of the 1985 Act.

In *O'Neill* v *Phillips* [1999] 1 WLR 1092 Lord Hoffmann gave the only judgment of the House of Lords and considered unfair prejudice in considerable detail. He made the following points.

(1) Although fairness was the criterion on which relief under [s.994] might be granted, and although the court has a wide power to do whatever it considers just and equitable, the concept must be applied rationally and upon judicial principles.

(2) In deciding what is fair the context and background will be extremely important.

(3) Generally, members will be bound by the articles and any shareholder agreements as these were the terms on which they agreed that the company's affairs should be conducted. However, equitable principles might make it unfair to rely strictly on the articles in a way which equity would regard as contrary to good faith.

(4) The way in which equitable principles are applied is reasonably well settled. These should not be abandoned in favour of some uncertain notion of fairness. Unfair prejudice petitions are often very expensive. If lawyers cannot advise clients of their chances of success this will operate to the detriment of their clients.

(5) Conduct can be unfair under [s.994] even if it would not be sufficient to wind the company up.

(6) In deciding whether conduct is unfair, it should be asked whether the exercise of the power complained of is contrary to what the parties agreed, either by words or conduct.

(7) In quasi-partnership companies what was agreed will usually be found in the understandings

between the members when they entered into association. Promises exchanged in quasi-partnership companies should be binding as a matter of equity even if they are not binding as a matter of law.

(8) Breaching a promise or undertaking is not the only ground on which unfair prejudice may be founded. An analogy could be made with frustration of a contract. (See Chapter 7 at 7.1.3.) The majority might use their powers in a way which the minority can reasonably say that they did not agree to. This might allow winding up of the company or it might afford a remedy for unfair prejudice.

(9) The majority must not use their powers, in breach of equitable considerations, when the articles do not contain the fundamental expectations of the shareholders. For example, if members have entered the company in the understanding that they have all put in capital and will all manage the company, equitable considerations would require that this agreement would be honoured or that a member would be able to withdraw from the company on reasonable terms. A minority shareholder expectation will not give rise to a right to petition merely because the shareholder reasonably and legitimately thought something likely to happen. In fairness or equity the minority shareholder must have a right to expect the thing to happen.

(10) There would be no unfair prejudice if the majority offered to buy the minority's shares at a reasonable price. In a quasi-partnership this price should not be at a discount on account of the shareholding being a minority shareholding, it should amount to the value of the equivalent proportion of the share capital. (In special circumstances a discounted valuation might be appropriate.) An independent expert should usually make this valuation. Both sides should have access to all company information which would affect the value of the shares.

(11) The majority shareholders should be given a reasonable time in which to make the offer to buy out the minority.

In *Re Guidezone Ltd* [2000] BCLC 321, Parker J said that *O'Neill v Phillips* had established that: 'unfairness [for the purposes of s.994] is not to be judged by reference to subjective notions of fairness, but rather by testing whether, applying established equitable principles, the majority has acted, or is proposing to act, in a manner which equity would regard as contrary to good faith.' This statement has since received considerable judicial approval.

In the following case the court did order a purchase of shares at a discount.

Irvine v Irvine [2006] EWHC 1875 Ch, [2006] All ER (D) 329 (Jul)

Two brothers, Malcolm and Ian, had both owned 50 per cent of the shares in a company. When Malcolm died in 1996, he left one share to Ian, and the remainder to his wife, Patricia, and to a trust set up for the benefit of his children. Consequently, Ian owned 50.04 per cent of the shares and Patricia and the trust, who were treated as speaking with one voice, owned the other 49.96 per cent. As from the year 2000 onwards, either no dividends or inadequate dividends were paid. Although Ian and Patricia were both directors, Ian used his control of the company to pay himself excessive amounts as manager of the company. Patricia brought a petition for unfair prejudice under s.459 (now s.994.)

Held. There had been unfair prejudice. It would have been appropriate for Ian to pay himself 40 per cent of the net profits as a salary but he had paid himself far more than that. Ian had also breached the Companies Act in several ways but this was not relevant as it had caused no prejudice to Patricia and the trust, the petitioners. Blackburne J ordered that Ian should buy the shares of Patricia and the trust. However, the shares had to be viewed as a minority holding and valued on that basis. He accepted that Ian, who was approaching 65, was the key to the future trading prospects of the company. He noted that someone holding 49.96 per cent of the shares had no more control than a person holding 30 per cent. (A special resolution could be blocked but not an ordinary one.) He made the point that although the sale he was ordering was to Ian, it was valued on the assumption that it was being made to a willing third party purchaser. The shares to be bought were valued at 70 per cent of what they would have been worth if there had been no discount. (So there was a 30 per cent discount.) The company was taken to be worth £2.53 million and the shares were to be purchased for £884 791 (£2.53 million × 49.96 × 0.7). As regards the excessive salary which Ian had drawn over the years, Ian had to compensate Patricia and the trust for this but the same 30 per cent discount had to be applied. This calculation here was based on a notional repayment of all the excess money →

to the company, interest being added at 8 per cent compound per annum and any amount of corporation tax which would have been payable being deducted. The total amount, added to the cash left in the business, came to £4 387 055. Applying the 30 per cent discount, Patricia and the trust were entitled to £1 534 240 (£4 387 055 × 49.96 × 0.7).

COMMENT (i) Blackburne J stressed that he did not consider the result to be unfair. It was significant that the company was involved in a fast-moving business, the insurance business, which was facing difficult times and that Ian was the main reason why it remained profitable. It was also significant that Ian would probably only stay in the business for another three years and this might make a third party wary of buying the shares.

(ii) Two experts had assessed the appropriate discount. One had thought it should be between 10 per cent and 30 per cent before settling on 20 per cent and the other had thought it should be 35 per cent.

(iii) If the minority shareholding had been 25 per cent or less, so that even a special resolution could not be blocked, then presumably the valuation would have been significantly lower.

(iv) Ian was not to be regarded as a special purchaser of Patricia's shares because he had been given the one share which gave him control. There had been no conditions attached to the gift. The valuation was made on the assumption that the sale was being made to a willing third party purchaser.

In *Exeter City AFC Ltd* v *Football Conference Ltd* [2004] 1 WLR 2910, Judge Weeks QC held that the statutory right to apply for relief under [s.994] was inalienable and could not be removed or diminished by a contract term or otherwise.

18.8.6 Petition for winding up under the Insolvency Act 1986

A court can wind a company up under ss.122–124 of the Insolvency Act 1986 on the grounds that it is just and equitable to do so. Even a single shareholder can petition the court to do this. Whether or not it is just and equitable to wind a company up is a question of fact in every case and will depend upon the circumstances of the case.

In *Loch* v *John Blackwood Ltd* [1924] AC 783 (Privy Council) a profitable company was wound up because the managing director omitted to hold general

meetings, or to submit accounts, or to recommend a dividend. His object was to keep the other shareholders in ignorance of the company's position and to acquire their shares at an undervalue.

In the following case a quasi-partnership company was wound up as if it had been a partnership.

Ebrahimi v Westbourne Galleries
[1973] AC 360 (House of Lords)

Since 1945, E and N had been equal partners in a firm dealing in rugs and carpets. In 1958 they formed a company. The company took the business over. E and N were the first directors, although N's son soon became a third director. The company did not pay any dividends, but the profits were used as directors' remuneration. N and his son held a majority of votes at general meetings and removed E as a director of the company. E applied for the other directors to buy his shares or for the company to be wound up under what is now s.122 Insolvency Act 1986.

Held. The company should be wound up. The corporate veil was lifted and the company was treated as a partnership and wound up on the grounds that it would be just and equitable to do so.

COMMENT (i) It is not clear how the court's decision in this case has been affected by the introduction of the unfair prejudice remedy under what is now s.994. It might be the case that s.994 provides the more appropriate remedy, even as regards quasi-partnership companies. A just and equitable winding up will not be ordered if there is a more appropriate remedy.

(ii) The Court of Appeal had refused to order a winding up.

(iii) The case might have been differently decided if N and his son had offered to buy E's shares.

The winding up of a company on the grounds that it is just and equitable to do so is considered in slightly more detail in Chapter 19 at 19.1.1.2.

18.8.7 Company investigations

Officers of the Department for Business, Innovation and Skills (formerly the Department of Business, Enterprise and Regulatory Reform) have the power to inspect a company's documents. No publicity attaches to this. The Secretary of State also has the power to appoint inspectors (usually a senior accountant and a senior barrister) to investigate a company's affairs.

This is a serious matter as the fact that inspectors have been appointed is publicly announced and the report produced is usually published. These powers of investigation are retained in Part 14 of the Companies Act 1985 instead of being incorporated into the 2006 Act.

Inspectors appointed to inspect a company's documents can inspect any form of information. Any person in possession of the documents who cannot claim privilege may be required to produce them, and this would include the company's bank being required to hand over details of the company bank account. Copies of any documents can be made and any company officer, past or present, can be asked to explain them. If the documents requested cannot be produced, the person required to produce them can be asked to state where they are. It is a criminal offence knowingly or recklessly to give any false explanation. It is not possible to refuse on the grounds of not wanting to give incriminating evidence against oneself, and any response can be used in evidence against its maker. It is an offence not to comply with an order to produce documents and a search warrant may be obtained to find documents. Destroying, mutilating or falsifying documents relating to the company's affairs is an offence. There is, however, a defence that the accused did not intend to conceal the company's affairs or defeat the law.

When inspectors are appointed by the Secretary of State, their function is to investigate the company's affairs and to inquire into them. It is not, however, a judicial role. The investigation is carried on in private but the inspectors produce a report which will usually be published. The company may itself request the investigation, as may the holders of at least 10 per cent of the company's issued share capital or any 200 shareholders. Those requesting the investigation may be required to pay for it and they must provide the Secretary of State with evidence showing that an investigation is required. The Secretary of State may himself decide that a company should be investigated on account of fraud or the company's members not being given all the evidence to which they are entitled. Investigations may be as to ownership or control of the company, directors' share dealings or insider dealing. An investigation may be extended to include inspecting a holding company or subsidiary company.

The Secretary of State may petition for the company to be wound up under the Insolvency Act 1986 on the grounds that this would be just and equitable. He may also sue in the company's name, apply for a disqualification order or make a petition under s.994 to relieve unfair prejudice. If any person is convicted of an offence he may have to pay the expenses of the investigation to the extent which the court orders.

18.9 LOAN CAPITAL

In many cases the members of a company contribute all the capital which the company needs. However, most companies also borrow money, either as a loan or by buying goods on credit.

Providers of credit are likely to want security for the money they are owed. If the security is given by the company, rather than by the directors or shareholders, the document which acknowledges the security, and which undertakes to repay the debt with interest on an ascertainable date, is known as a debenture. Section 738 of the Act defines a debenture as including debenture stock, bonds and any other securities of a company, whether constituting a charge on the company's assets or not. Debenture stocks raise money from a large number of lenders. Each of the lenders is invited to take a holding of a specified value in a large loan made to the company. There must be a trust deed which sets out the terms of the loan and which operates to protect the lenders. Public companies may also offer debentures to the public in a series. Generally, there is an express provision that all the debentures in the series rank equally, that is to say that none of them become payable before any others. If this is the case then any action brought by a debenture holder is regarded as a representative action brought on behalf of all the holders in the series. A bond is a bearer security of a nominal value, issued by the company for cash, which is to be repaid on a certain date. Until that date the bond pays interest.

A company may purchase its own debentures and there is nothing to prevent debentures from being issued at a discount. Private companies are not allowed to offer debentures to the public. Debentures usually have a redemption date, on which the company is bound to repay the debenture. However, some debentures are perpetual. Debenture holders are not members of the company, they are creditors of it. There is nothing to prevent the interest on debentures from being paid out of capital if there is insufficient profit from which to pay it.

The person lending money to a company will want his debenture to be backed up by security. This is commonly provided by a personal guarantee made by a director or shareholder. The company itself can give security by granting a charge over some or all of the company's assets. If the debt is not repaid, the lender will be able to sell the charged assets and take what is owed. Companies can give two types of charges: fixed charges and floating charges.

18.9.1 **Fixed charges**

A company can provide security for a loan by granting a fixed charge on certain assets. In effect, this means that it mortgages those assets to the creditor. Consequently, the company will not be able to dispose of, or change the nature of, the property charged without the permission of the debenture holder.

For example, A Co Ltd wants to borrow £2 000 000 from the bank. The bank lends the money but takes a fixed charge on the company's factory, plant and machinery. As long as the company is repaying the loan as agreed, it will retain possession of the factory, plant and machinery and can use them in the ordinary way. The company cannot, however, sell the factory, plant or machinery without the bank's permission. Furthermore, if the company fails to repay the debt, the bank can sell the factory, plant and machinery and deduct what it is owed from the proceeds of sale.

A charge must be registered with the company and with the Registrar of Companies, within 21 days of the date of its creation (s.860(1)). If a charge is not registered, it will be invalid, although the debenture holder will still be able to sue on the debt as an unsecured creditor. If a fixed charge is properly created and properly registered, its holder will take priority over any subsequent claims to the property charged. If, however, a fixed charge is stated to rank behind an existing floating charge, then it will not only rank behind that floating charge but also behind preferential creditors (*Re Portbase Clothing Ltd* [1993] Ch 388).

A company may grant more than one fixed charge on any particular asset. Let us assume, for example, that a few years ago B Co Ltd borrowed £400 000 from the bank and granted a fixed charge over the company factory, currently worth £2 000 000. If the company now wanted to borrow a further £200 000 from a different creditor then that creditor would be quite happy to register a second fixed charge on the company factory. If the company does not repay its debts, then the factory could be sold by the creditors. The bank would always be entitled to its £400 000 first because it was the first charge registered. But the sale of the factory

would easily realise enough to repay the second charge holder.

In *Re Spectrum Plus Ltd* [2005] UKHL 41, [2005] 3 WLR 58 the House of Lords held that it is conceptually possible to create a fixed charge over book debts. However, this is possible only if the company which granted the charge is not capable of dealing with the debts. (In practice this would be very difficult to achieve, but not impossible.) If the company which granted the charge can draw on the charged accounts then a fixed charge cannot be created over the debts. This case overruled two earlier cases which had held that a fixed charge could more easily be created over book debts.

18.9.2 **Floating charges**

If there were no assets on which a fixed charge could be secured, a creditor might be prepared to accept a floating charge. This means that the creditor would take a class of, or all of, the company's property, both present and future assets, as an equitable security. In *Re Yorkshire Woolcombers' Association Ltd* [1903] 2 Ch 284 Romer LJ said that a floating charge had the three following characteristics:

(i) it is a charge on a class of assets of a company, both present and future;
(ii) that class is one which, in the ordinary course of the company's business, would be changing from time to time; and
(iii) it is contemplated that, until some future step is taken by or on behalf of the charge holder, the company may carry on business in the ordinary way as far as concerns the particular class of assets charged.

In *Buchler and another v Talbot and another* [2004] UKHL 9, [2004] 2 WLR 582 Lord Nicholls described floating charges in the following way:

'They are a means whereby a financier, typically a bank, provides a company with money on the security of the company's assets which continue to be used and turned over in the ordinary course of business until, when certain events happen, the charge "crystallises" into a fixed charge on the assets then within its scope. Notable among crystallising events are the appointment of receivers by the charge holder or the company being wound up.'

A floating charge does not attach to any particular items of property until it crystallises, because it is recognised that the class of assets charged will change from time to time in the ordinary course of the company's business. It is also recognised that a floating charge does not prevent the company from selling the assets over which it is granted. It is particularly useful when a company has a good deal of money tied up in raw materials, stock in trade or book debts. In *Re Spectrum Plus Ltd* [2005] Lord Scott explained these characteristics of a floating charge in the following way.

'In my opinion, the essential characteristic of a floating charge, the characteristic that distinguishes it from a fixed charge, is that the asset subject to the charge is not finally appropriated as a security for the payment of the debt until the occurrence of some future event. In the meantime the chargor is left free to use the charged asset and to remove it from the security.'

In **Buchler v Talbot** Lord Nicholls explained the usefulness of floating charges in the following way:

'Over the years floating charges have played an invaluable role in the development of business. They bridge a gap between businessmen and financiers. Businessmen need money but may have insufficient fixed assets to offer as security. Financiers have money but want security for any loans they make. They wish to rank ahead of the company's unsecured creditors if the business does not prosper. They wish to minimise their risks by having a charge over whatever assets a company may acquire in the course of carrying on its trade. Floating charges have provided a legal mechanism by which in these circumstances capital and business enterprise can be harnessed. Typically, a floating charge extends to substantially all the assets of a company. On its face this gives a charge holder a high degree of control over the assets and fortunes of a company.'

A third party who acquires property which is the subject of a floating charge from the company takes it free of the charge. A third party who acquires property which is the subject of a fixed charge will not gain title to the property as the company had neither actual nor apparent authority to pass title. A fixed charge created on property which is already the subject of a floating charge will take precedence over the floating charge. However, this is not the case if the floating charge has crystallised, because upon crystallisation it will have become a fixed charge on the assets charged. Floating charges commonly provide that any attempt to create a further charge over the property which is the subject

of the floating charge will automatically cause the floating charge to crystallise.

Example

Let us assume that C Co Ltd, which manufactures televisions, has already granted a fixed charge over all those assets, such as its factory, which it does not need to sell. Let us further assume that the company has a warehouse stocked with televisions ready for sale, that it is owed money by various creditors and that it has a large stock of materials with which it makes the televisions. None of these remaining assets could be the subject of a fixed charge without crippling the company's activities. The company would not be able to sell the televisions already manufactured, or work the raw materials into televisions, without the permission of the fixed chargeholder. If such permission was granted the chargeholders would then lose their security.

But the finished televisions, the money owed and the raw materials are worth a great deal. A creditor might well therefore take a floating charge over these assets, secure in the knowledge that if the company did not repay him he could recoup his loan by calling in the charge, selling the assets charged, and deducting what he was owed from the proceeds.

The contract which created the floating charge would state that the company would only use the assets charged in its normal course of business, and that the company would not grant a fixed charge over any such assets.

If more than one floating charge is issued, the charges take priority in the order in which they were created. However, this is not the case if an earlier floating charge provides that the company may create a later floating charge to take priority over it. It would seem unlikely that many floating charges would provide this. A floating charge does not provide the cast-iron security of a fixed charge. It is up to the creditor to ensure that it provides adequate security for the loan. Like a fixed charge, a floating charge must be registered with the Registrar of Companies. It is quite common for a creditor to take both a fixed charge and a floating charge to secure a loan.

In Chapter 19, at 19.1.4.4, we shall see that in some circumstances floating charges created within two years of a company's insolvency can be invalid to the extent that the company did not receive a new benefit in consideration of creating the charge.

18.9.2.1 Rules applying to floating charges created on or after 15 September 2003

The Enterprise Act 2002 came into force on 15 September 2003. In respect of floating charges created on or after this date, the holder of the charge, a 'qualifying holder', does not have the power to appoint an administrative receiver of the company. Instead the charge holder can appoint an administrator. Such an administrator will try to rescue the company as a going concern. Furthermore, a proportion of the assets which are subject to a qualifying floating charge may be 'top sliced' or earmarked for distribution to unsecured creditors.

The holders of fixed charges and holders of floating charges created before September 2003 still have the power to appoint an administrative receiver. In addition, none of the assets secured by such earlier floating charge will be top sliced for distribution to the unsecured creditors. The effect of a company going into administration and the role of an administrative receiver are considered in Chapter 19 at 19.1.4.5. The top slicing of assets for distribution to the unsecured creditors is considered in Chapter 19 at 19.1.3.1.

18.9.3 Crystallisation

A company can continue to sell assets over which a floating charge has been granted up until the time of 'crystallisation'. So in the example just considered, C Co Ltd could still sell the finished televisions even though they were the subject of a floating charge. But when crystallisation occurs the floating charge will become a fixed charge attaching to the assets of the company charged at that time. This, of course, will mean that the company is no longer free to dispose of the assets.

Crystallisation occurs automatically:

(a) When a receiver is appointed.
(b) When the company goes into liquidation.
(c) When the company ceases to carry on business.
(d) On the occurrence of an event which the contract stipulated would lead to automatic crystallisation. (The contract would have been made when the charge was created. It might, for example, state that if the company created another charge over the same class of assets then the first charge should crystallise. Or that it should crystallise if the assets charged are not kept in good repair, or if the stock of assets charged is run down below a certain level, or if an administrator is appointed.)

Crystallisation may also occur when the debenture holder gives notice that he is converting the floating charge into a fixed charge. (This can only be done if the contract which created the charge allows for it.) If the assets which were the subject of the charge are sold after crystallisation then the charge holder can recover them from the party to whom they were sold.

18.9.4 Registration of charges

Section 860 provides that companies must register all charges with the Registrar of Companies within 21 days of the creation of the charge. This registration is necessary so that others who might wish to do business with the company can see what charges exist over the company's property. Although registration confers notice that a charge exists, it does not amount to notice of the charge's terms and conditions. Any person may inspect the register of charges kept by the Registrar. It is possible for any person to register the charge with the Registrar and in practice the lender often registers the charge. If a charge is not registered within 21 days then both the company and any company officer who knowingly or wilfully authorised or permitted the failure to register it are guilty of an offence.

If a charge is not registered it is invalid against a liquidator or any person taking a subsequent charge. In addition, the money lent becomes immediately repayable. Charge holders are allowed to register charges themselves and claim the cost from the company. The details which must be registered set out: the name and number of the company; the date of its creation; the amount secured by the charge; short details of the property charged; the name and addresses of the persons entitled to the charge; and, in the case of a floating charge, a statement of any provisions of the charge which restrict the company's power to grant further charges which are to rank equally or ahead of the charge being registered.

The company must also keep a copy of the documents which created the charge, as well as a register of all the charges affecting its property. This register gives brief details of each charge (the property charged, the amount of the charge and the person entitled to it). Members and creditors can inspect this register free of charge, others may be charged a small fee. If a charge is not entered on the company's register of charges, the directors and secretary may be fined, but the charge will not be rendered invalid.

18.9.5 **Priority of charges**

As regards properly registered charges, the order of priority is as follows.

(i) A fixed charge has immediate effect from the moment it was created. It ranks higher than existing floating charges unless the floating charge expressly prohibits the creation of another charge over the same property and the person taking the later fixed charge knew that this was the case. (Registration is not enough on its own to amount to actual notice of the prohibition.)

(ii) Floating charges only attach to property from the moment of crystallisation.

(iii) Floating charges generally rank amongst themselves in order of priority of creation. This is not the case where the debenture securing the first floating charge provides that a later floating charge may have priority.

Preferential creditors (see Chapter 19 at 19.1.3) take priority over floating charges but not over fixed charges. A valid retention of title clause, even though not registered as a charge, can take effect in priority to a floating charge (see Chapter 9 at 9.2). A company cannot give a fixed charge over property which it has taken subject to an effective retention of title clause. The company does not own the property to which the clause relates, and cannot therefore grant a fixed charge over it.

Test your understanding 18.4

1. What are the two main aspects of the rule in **Foss v Harbottle**?

2. What is a derivative claim?

3. In what four ways can a member with a minority shareholding bring a common law action despite the rule?

4. What two statutory remedies are available to a minority member of a company?

5. What is the difference between a fixed and a floating charge?

6. What is meant by crystallisation of a floating charge?

Key points

Shares

■ A person becomes a member of a company either by subscribing to the memorandum and being entered in the register of members, or by agreeing to become a member and having his name entered in the register of members.

■ A share is a thing in action, conferring certain rights on its holder.

■ A company's articles may allow the company to have different classes of shares, with different rights attaching to the various classes.

■ Preference shares usually have a cumulative right to a dividend which is expressed as a rate of interest per annum.

■ They also usually have a right to be paid in full on dissolution of the company before ordinary shareholders are paid anything. They may or may not carry the same voting rights as the ordinary shares.

■ A person acquires shares in a company by acquiring them from the company, or from an existing member or by transmission by operation of law.

■ A public company will not be able to begin trading or borrow money until it has been issued with a trading certificate. Such a certificate will only be issued if the company has allotted at least £50 000 nominal share capital, at least a quarter of the nominal value of each share being paid up.

Meetings and resolutions

■ Private companies do not need to hold any meetings of members unless they choose to do so.

■ Public companies must hold an AGM every year.

■ An ordinary resolution is passed if more than 50 per cent of eligible members vote in favour of it. A special resolution is passed if at least 75 per cent vote in favour of it. As regards written resolutions, these percentages are of the total voting rights. As regards resolutions passed at meetings, the percentages are of the votes actually cast.

■ Both ordinary resolutions and special resolutions can be passed as written resolutions, but a written resolution cannot be used to remove a director or an auditor before the expiry of his term of office.

■ Generally, written resolutions are proposed by the directors but members who hold at least 5 per cent of the voting rights on the resolution

→

can require the company to circulate a written resolution.

- Generally, the directors will call company meetings. However, members with 10 per cent of the paid-up shares which carry voting rights can compel the directors to hold a meeting. This percentage is reduced to 5 per cent if the company is a private company and 12 months have elapsed since the last meeting at which the members had the right to circulate a resolution.
- 14 days' notice must be given of all company meetings except of the AGM of a public company, when 21 days' notice is required.
- Members holding at least 5 per cent of the total voting rights, or members totalling at least 100, with a right to vote, and holding shares having an average sum paid up of £100, can require the company to circulate a statement of not more than 1 000 words with respect to a matter referred to in a proposed resolution to be voted upon at a meeting.
- A company meeting is not properly convened unless a quorum of members attends it. In single member companies the quorum is one member, in all other companies it is two.
- At a company meeting any member can demand a poll rather than a vote on a show of hands.
- A proxy is a person entitled to attend a company meeting and to vote on behalf of a company member. Any member has the right to appoint a proxy.
- The members of a public company may require the company to give all members notice of a resolution which they intend to propose to be moved at the AGM.
- Where a poll is taken at a general meeting of a quoted company, the company must put on a website the date of the meeting, the text of the resolution voted upon, and the number of votes cast in favour and against.
- The members of a quoted company may require the directors to obtain an independent report on any poll taken or to be taken at a general meeting. This report is prepared by an independent assessor.
- Where the member of a single member company takes any decision which could be taken at a company meeting, and where the decision has effect as if taken by the company in general meeting, the member must provide the company with details of that decision.

Legal effect of the constitution

- A company's constitution forms a contract between the company and every member and between every member and every other member. However, this is only true to the extent that the members are acting in their capacity as members.

Maintenance of capital and insider dealing

- A private company may carry out the reduction of capital by passing a special resolution supported by a solvency statement.
- Both public and private companies may reduce capital by passing a special resolution which is confirmed by the court.
- A company cannot purchase its own shares unless its articles permit this.
- Private companies are not prohibited from giving financial assistance to buy their own shares. It is *prima facie* unlawful for a public company to give financial assistance.
- Dividends can be paid only out of profit.

Minority protection

- The rule in *Foss v Harbottle* provides that only a company can sue in respect of a wrong done to that company and that the court will not interfere with the internal management of a company acting within its powers.
- Despite the rule in *Foss v Harbottle*, a derivative claim is a claim brought by a member of the company in respect of a cause of action vested in the company and seeking relief on behalf of the company.
- A derivative claim can be brought in respect of a cause of action arising from an actual or proposed act or omission which involves negligence, default, breach of duty or breach of trust by a director of the company.
- A member of a company who brings a derivative claim must apply to the court for permission to continue it. This application will be dismissed if the member does not disclose a *prima facie* case.
- A member can take over a derivative claim which has been started by the company or by another member.
- Despite the rule in *Foss v Harbottle*, a member of a company can sue if his personal rights have been infringed, or to prevent the company from entering into an *ultra vires* transaction, or if there has been a fraud on the minority.

→

- The Companies Act 2006 allows any member to sue for unfair prejudice.
- The Insolvency Act 1986 allows any member to petition for the winding up of the company on the grounds that it would be just and equitable to do so.

Fixed and floating charges

- A fixed charge is a mortgage over specific assets of the company, and therefore prevents the company from disposing of the assets charged.

- A floating charge is a security given over a class of assets. It does not prevent the company from disposing of those assets in the ordinary course of its business.
- Once a floating charge crystallises it become a fixed charge on the specific assets of the class of property charged. All charges are void unless registered with the Registrar of Companies.

Summary questions

1 Compare the rights which usually attach to ordinary shares to those which usually attach to preference shares. Are preference shares more similar to ordinary shares than they are to debentures?

2 Len and his sister, Elaine, each own 27.5 per cent of the shares in a private company governed by Table A articles. Their brother, David, owns 45 per cent of the shares and is the sole director. The company made a reasonable profit this year. Len and Elaine believe that this profit should be paid as a dividend. David refuses to recommend a dividend, insisting that the profits should be invested in the company. Advise Len and Elaine as to any powers they might have to force the payment of a dividend.

3 Acme Ltd has five shareholders, Alice, Bertha, Carol, Dinah and Elizabeth, all of whom own 20 per cent of the shares. All of the shares are fully paid up. Alice and Bertha are the only two directors. Carol is the company secretary. Carol wants to see the articles altered so that shareholders can sell their shares only to the company. Dinah, who is much older than the others, is very much opposed to this. Alice, Bertha and Elizabeth are open to persuasion on the matter.

a Explain what support Carol will need in order to achieve the change if the resolution is moved at a company meeting.

b Explain whether Carol could validly propose a written resolution to change the article in question and the procedure which the company would have to follow.

4 Mary holds 14 per cent of the shares in XY plc, a quoted company. She is at odds with the directors who between them hold 55 per cent of the shares. XY plc holds its annual general meeting one week after the end of its financial year. Mary wants to propose a resolution to be moved at the AGM. She will be abroad at the time of the AGM but would like her friend, Nicola, to speak on the resolution on her behalf. Mary does not trust the directors to follow the correct procedures regarding the resolution which she wants to propose. Advise Mary as to whether or not she can ensure that the resolution is proposed at the AGM and as to whether she will have to pay any costs incurred. Advise her also of any safeguards which exist to ensure that the correct procedures were followed when the resolution was voted upon.

5 For several years John and Jack were the sole partners in a successful building firm. Ten years ago they formed a limited company. John and Jack were the only two directors. The company had an issued share capital of 100 £1 ordinary shares, and Jack and John each took 50 of these. Two years ago Jack's son, Alan, was appointed a director of the company and Jack and John each transferred ten shares to Alan.

Last year John discovered that the company had sold building materials to another company in which Jack and Alan are the only shareholders. John brought this matter up at a board meeting. Since this time Alan and Jack have passed an ordinary resolution ratifying the sale of the building materials.

Advise John of any rights which he might have.

6 The firm in which you work is considering lending a large sum of money to Acme Ltd. Acme Ltd is proposing to give a charge over some of its assets as security for the loan. Your employer has asked you to draft a report, dealing briefly with the following matters.

a The nature of a fixed charge.
b The nature of a floating charge.
c The meaning of crystallisation of a floating charge.

d The measures which should be taken to ensure that Acme's assets are not already the subject of an existing charge.

e The steps which should be taken to ensure that the charge granted by Acme Ltd gives adequate security for the loan.

Multiple choice questions

1 Which one of the following statements is not true?

a Shares can be denominated in Sterling, Euros or in any other currency, and different classes of shares can be denominated in different currencies.

b A public company may not accept promises to work or perform services in return for issuing shares.

c If preference shareholders have a right to have their capital repaid ahead of ordinary shareholders, on dissolution of the company, they do not have a right to share in the surplus assets after dissolution.

d Shares can be sub-divided or consolidated by the directors without the need for an authorising resolution of the members.

2 Which one of the following statements is not true?

a Any written resolution will always be passed if more than 50 per cent of all eligible members vote in favour of it.

b A private company may pass either an ordinary or a special resolution by written resolution.

c A special resolution is passed at a company meeting if 75 per cent of those present and voting vote in favour of it, even if the majority of members who could have voted on the resolution do not attend the meeting.

d Every company member has a right to demand that a resolution proposed at a meeting be voted upon by a poll rather than on a show of hands, and this right cannot be taken away by the articles.

3 Which of the following statements are not true?

i Any provision in the articles preventing a proxy from demanding a poll is void.

ii A private company can remove an auditor from office before the expiry of his term of office by passing a unanimous written resolution.

iii As regards either public or private companies, members who hold at least 10 per cent of the paid-up shares which carry voting rights can require the directors to call a general meeting of the company.

iv At least 14 days' notice must be given of a general meeting of a private company.

v Notice of a general meeting of the company may be given in hard copy or electronically but cannot be given by means of a website.

a i, ii and iv only.

b i and v only.

c ii, iii and iv only.

d ii and v only.

4 Which one of the following statements is not true?

a In single member companies the quorum at a company meeting is one qualifying person.

b The members of a company can elect a chairman of a company meeting but the articles can restrict who the chairman might be.

c A company member who votes on a poll cannot vote different ways with different shares.

d A member of a private company can appoint more than one proxy, as long as each proxy is given rights to vote in respect of different shares.

5 Which one of the following statements is not true?

a When a poll is taken at a general meeting of a quoted company, the company is required to put information about the poll on a website.

b The members of a quoted company can require the directors to obtain an independent report on any poll taken or to be taken at a general meeting.

c An independent assessor who reports on a poll of a quoted company must not be a director, the company secretary or the company auditor.

d A private company may carry out a reduction of capital by passing a special resolution supported by a solvency statement.

e Both public and private companies may reduce their capital by passing a special resolution confirmed by the court.

6 Which one of the following statements is not true?

a A derivative claim cannot be brought against the director who has been merely negligent rather than dishonest.

b A person who becomes a member of the company will be able to bring a derivative claim in respect of acts which were committed by the directors before he became a member.

c A member cannot continue a derivative claim unless the court gives permission for this to happen.

d A derivative claim cannot be brought in respect of an act which has already occurred if the act was authorised by the company before it occurred.

7 Which one of the following statements is not true?

a Negligence cannot generally amount to a fraud on the minority, but a minority shareholder may sue if the negligence conferred a benefit on those who controlled the company and committed the negligent act.

b Once inspectors have been appointed by the Secretary of State, it is a criminal offence, to which there is no defence, to destroy company documents.

c The personal representative of a deceased company member can bring an action alleging unfair prejudice under s.994 of the Act.

d Any shareholder may petition the court to wind a company up, under s.122 Insolvency Act 1986, no matter how small the size of his shareholding.

8 Which one of the following statements is not true?

a If a fixed charge is granted over an asset then the company will not be able to dispose of that asset, even in the ordinary course of its business.

b If a floating charge is granted over a class of a company's assets, then even assets subsequently acquired by the company would be charged if they were within the class of assets charged.

c When a floating charge crystallises, it will become a fixed charge attaching to the assets charged at the time of crystallisation.

d Once an asset has become the subject of a fixed or floating charge, a third party who later acquires the asset will always do so subject to the rights of the charge holder.

Task 18

A friend of yours has for many years carried on an unincorporated business as a carpet fitter. Your friend is considering forming a limited company in conjunction with three other carpet fitters. He has asked you to draw up a report, explaining briefly the following matters.

a The nature of shares and the difference between ordinary and preference shares.

b How company resolutions are passed, and the matters for which resolutions are required.

c The legal effect of a company memorandum and articles of association.

d What is meant by the rule in *Foss v Harbottle,* and the way in which the courts and statutes protect minority shareholders.

e The extent to which a company charge provides a creditor with security, and the steps which should be taken by both the company and the creditor when a charge is issued.

mylawchamber *premium*

19

Winding up of companies · limited liability partnerships · benefits of trading as a company, partnership or limited liability partnership

Introduction

19.1 WINDING UP OF COMPANIES

We have already seen that companies have a legal personality of their own. We have also seen that a company's personality is artificially created, by the process of registration with the Registrar of Companies. The legal personality of a company ceases to exist in an artificial way, when the company is liquidated or wound up. (Liquidation and winding up mean the same thing; that the company ceases to exist as a legal entity.) A company liquidation may be brought about by one of two legal processes. Either the court may order a compulsory liquidation of a company, or the members of the company may resolve voluntarily to wind the company up. If the members resolve to wind

up a company which is not solvent the liquidation is known as a creditors' voluntary winding up.

19.1.1 Liquidation by court order

Section 122(1) of the Insolvency Act 1986 lists six grounds for compulsory liquidation of a company. These grounds are that:

(a) The company has by special resolution resolved that the company be wound up by the court.
(b) The company is a public company which has not been issued with a s.761 certificate and more than a year has passed since the company was registered.

(c) The company is an old public company which had not re-registered as a public or private company by March 1982.

(d) The company does not commence its business within a year of its incorporation or suspends its business for a whole year.

(e) The company is unable to pay its debts.

(f) The court is of the opinion that it is just and equitable that the company should be wound up.

The first four of these grounds are essentially straightforward matters of fact. The final two need to be considered in a little detail.

19.1.1.1 The company cannot pay its debts

Either the company itself, the directors, a shareholder or a creditor of the company may petition the court to wind a company up on the grounds that the company cannot pay its debts. In practice such a petition is likely to be made by a creditor.

Section 123(1) of the Insolvency Act states that a company is deemed unable to pay its debts if:

(a) A creditor to whom the company owes more than £750 has served a written demand for payment on the company, by leaving it at the company's registered office, and, three weeks later, the company has neither paid nor given the creditor a security which he finds acceptable; or

(b) Execution issued on a court judgment in favour of a creditor of the company is returned unsatisfied in whole or in part; or

(c) It is proved to the satisfaction of the court that the company is unable to pay its debts as they fall due. Section 123(2) states that a company is deemed unable to pay its debts if it is proved that the value of the company's assets is less than the amount of its liabilities. In making this assessment the court also considers possible liabilities which may arise in the future.

The court does not have to wind the company up, even if it is satisfied that the company cannot pay its debts. If, however, the court does order a winding up then a liquidator is appointed. The liquidator will collect assets owing to the company, sell the assets off, and then distribute the proceeds amongst the creditors according to the specified order. If any surplus did happen to be generated, it would be distributed amongst the company members. As regards all matters relating to the winding up of a company, s.195 of the Insolvency Act gives the court the power to call a meeting of creditors and contributories, if it thinks fit, for the purpose of ascertaining their wishes. (Contributories are liable to contribute to the company's assets when the company is wound up.) Regard is had to the value of each of the creditor's debts and the number of votes conferred on each contributory. If the company is insolvent then only the views of the creditors are considered.

19.1.1.2 The court is of the opinion that it is just and equitable to wind the company up

We shall see that a company may initiate a voluntary winding up by passing a special resolution that the company should be wound up. Also, as we have seen, the company may pass a special resolution that the company be compulsorily wound up by the court. In order for a special resolution to be passed, three-quarters of the votes cast would have to be in favour of the resolution. A petition to wind the company up on the ground that it would be just and equitable to do so can be used by members with insufficient votes to ensure that a special resolution is passed. Even a single member of a company may petition the court to wind the company up on this ground. The petition might alternatively be presented by the company, by the directors, or by a creditor.

In considering whether it would be just and equitable to wind a company up, the court has enormous discretion. Whether or not it is just and equitable to wind the company up is a question of fact, each case depending upon its own circumstances. It is, however, a serious matter to wind up a company which is trading successfully and the courts are reluctant to take such a step. The person petitioning the court for the winding up must have some tangible interest in this happening. A member whose shares are all fully paid up could not have such an interest unless there would be surplus assets available for distribution among the members after the dissolution. As long as the petitioner is acting reasonably, the court can order the winding up even though other remedies (such as relief under s.994 of the 2006 Act) are available to the petitioner. Over the years the courts have wound companies up on the following grounds, amongst others.

(a) That the substratum of the company has failed

The substratum of a company will be regarded as having failed if the main object for which the company was formed fails for some reason. A company's main object is usually to be found in the first article of its objects clause, or in the first few clauses if these are closely related. If there is a main object, which indicates a distinct purpose which is the foundation of the company, other clauses which are unrelated may be regarded as ancillary to the main purpose. If that main purpose cannot be achieved, the substratum of the company may have failed.

Re German Date Coffee Co
(1882) 20 ChD 169 (Court of Appeal)

The company's objects clause had eight articles. The first of these was to acquire a patent on an invention to turn dates into a coffee substitute. The next five articles all concerned exploitation of the patented invention. The seventh article was to acquire patents on similar inventions. The eighth article was more general, allowing importing and exporting of food generally and buying or leasing the means to do this. The founders of the company were sure that they would be granted the necessary patent. In fact the patent was not granted to them.

Held. It was just and equitable to wind the company up as the company substratum had failed.

These days, a company's substratum is much less likely to fail. In Chapter 16 we saw that s.31 of the 2006 Act provides that unless a company's articles specifically restrict the objects of a company, its objects are unrestricted. If a company has no objects clause, or if it has registered its objects as to carry on business as a general company, its substratum cannot disappear. Even as regards companies which do have an objects clause, the objects of most companies tend to be stated in very broad terms, perhaps in recognition that the company might change its line of business.

As Lord Greene put it, in *Re Kitson and Co Ltd* [1946] 1 All ER 435: '. . . a business is a thing which changes. It grows or it contracts. It changes; it disposes of the whole of its plant; it moves its factory; it entirely changes its range of products, and so forth. It is more like an organic thing.'

In *Cotman v Brougham* [1918] AC 514 Lord Parker said: 'The question whether or not a company can be wound up for failure of substratum is a question of equity between a company and its shareholders.'

(b) Where there is deadlock in the management of a small company

A court may consider it just and equitable to wind a small company up if the management of the company

has reached deadlock and is unable to make decisions. An example of such a winding up was seen in *Re Yenidje Tobacco Co Ltd* [1916] 2 Ch 426, considered in Chapter 18 at 18.8. In that case Cozens-Hardy MR said:

'In those circumstances, supposing it had been a private partnership, an ordinary partnership between two people having equal shares, and there being no other provisions to terminate it, what would have been the position? . . . All that is necessary is to satisfy the Court that it is impossible for the partners to place the confidence in each other which each has a right to expect, and that such impossibility has not been caused by the person seeking to take advantage of it . . . I think that in a case like this we are bound to say that circumstances which would justify the winding up of a partnership between these two . . . are circumstances which should induce the Court to exercise its jurisdiction under the just and equitable clause and to wind up the company.'

If the company is a quasi-partnership then it may be just and equitable to wind the company up where one faction excludes another faction from any management of the company. An example was seen in the previous chapter at 18.8.6 in *Ebrahimi v Westbourne Galleries* [1972] 2 All ER 492.

(c) Where there is a justifiable lack of confidence in the management

In order to justify a winding up on this ground the lack of confidence held by the petitioner must be due to a lack of probity (integrity) in the conduct of the company's affairs. This lack of probity must relate to business matters, rather than to personal matters, and must amount to more than merely being outvoted.

In the previous chapter, at 18.8.6, we saw an example of lack of probity in the management of the company's affairs which was sufficient to justify winding up in *Loch v John Blackwood* [1924] AC 783. In that case Lord Shaw said: 'The lack of confidence must spring not from dissatisfaction at being outvoted on the business affairs or on what is called the domestic policy of the company. On the other hand, wherever the lack of confidence is rested on a lack of probity in the conduct of the company's affairs, then the former is justified by the latter, and it is under the statute just and equitable that the company should be wound up.'

(d) Where the company was formed for a fraudulent purpose

If a company is formed for an entirely fraudulent purpose then it will be just and equitable to wind the company up.

> #### Re Thomas Edward Brinsmead and Sons
> [1897] 1 Ch 45 (Court of Appeal)
>
> John Brinsmead and Sons were a well-known firm of piano manufacturers. Three of their former employees, all named Brinsmead, formed the company in question, intending to pass their pianos off as having been produced by the well-established firm. An injunction was granted, preventing the company from the passing off, but the public had already subscribed for a large number of shares in the company.
>
> **Held.** It was just and equitable to wind the company up as this would enable members of the public to get their money back.

19.1.1.3 The petition

Section 124(1) of the Insolvency Act states that a petition for the court to wind the company up may be presented to the court by any of the following:

(a) The company itself.
(b) The directors of the company.
(c) Any creditor of the company (including prospective creditors).
(d) Any contributory (person who might have to contribute when the company is liquidated). Current shareholders are regarded as contributories, even if their shares are fully paid up.
(e) The Secretary of State for Trade and Industry, but only if the reason for the winding up is that the company is a public company which has failed to be issued with a s.761 certificate within one year of its incorporation.
(f) The Official Receiver, if the court is satisfied that a voluntary winding up cannot be continued with due regard to the interests of the creditors or contributories.

Although any of these petitioners may petition the court, in practice it is likely to be a creditor or a contributory who does so. The court may or may not make a winding up order. It may also order the Official Receiver to take over the company's affairs immediately. The court is likely to do this if it considers that the directors might try to dissipate the company's assets.

19.1.1.4 Winding up order

The court does not have to order the company to be wound up, even if a creditor does present a petition showing that he is owed more than £750. If other creditors think that their best chance of being paid lies in allowing the company to continue trading then the court may allow this. Usually, the court will allow this only if the creditors who want to allow the company to continue trading are owed the majority of the money which the company owes. Ultimately, however, the decision is for the court which has a discretion to order the winding up or not.

If the court does order the company to be wound up, the liquidation is deemed to have taken effect from the date when the petition to wind the company up was presented to the court. The Official Receiver becomes the liquidator until another is appointed.

After a winding up order has been made the following rules apply:

(a) Any disposition of the company's property, and any transfer of shares, or alteration of the status of the company members, made after the commencement of the winding up is void, unless authorised by the court (Insolvency Act s.127).
(b) All actions in debt against the company are stopped. If any of the company's assets are seized to satisfy a debt such a seizure will be void (Insolvency Act ss.128 and 130).
(c) The directors' powers cease and are taken over by the liquidator.
(d) The company's employees are dismissed, although the liquidator can re-employ them until the winding up is completed.
(e) Floating charges crystallise.
(f) The business may still be carried on by the liquidator, but only to try to effect the most beneficial realisation of the company's assets.

The liquidator's powers to re-employ the workers and carry on the business are useful in a variety of circumstances, such as where the company has a stock of relatively worthless raw materials which could quickly be manufactured into products of some value.

When a winding up order is made a copy is sent to the Registrar of Companies. He publishes notice of having received the order in the *London Gazette*.

Once the court has made a winding up order, s.131 of the Insolvency Act allows the Official Receiver to require that a statement of the company's affairs is made. The statement would give particulars of the company's assets, debts and liabilities, the names and addresses of the company's creditors, the securities held by the respective creditors, the dates on which the securities were given and such further information as the Official Receiver might require. The statement can be required of past and present company officers, of the promoters if the company was formed within the previous year, and of employees who the Official Receiver thinks might be able to give the information. If another company is an officer of the company which is wound up, those who are similarly connected with the other company can be required to make the statement.

Section 132 of the Insolvency Act provides that where a winding up order is made by the court it is the duty of the Official Receiver to investigate: (a) the causes of failure if the company has failed; and (b) the promotion, formation, business, dealings and affairs of the company generally, and to make such report (if any) to the court as he sees fit. In any proceedings such a report is *prima facie* evidence of the facts stated in it.

Where the court orders a company to be wound up, s.133 of the Insolvency Act gives the Official Receiver the power to conduct a public examination of past and present officers of the company or of a person who has taken part in the promotion, formation or management of the company. The examination is as to that person's role in the promotion, formation or management of the company or as to the conduct of its business and affairs, or his conduct or dealings in relation to the company.

19.1.2 Voluntary liquidation

There are two types of voluntary liquidations; members' voluntary liquidations and creditors' voluntary liquidations. A company will need to pass a special resolution to initiate either type of voluntary winding up, and notice of this resolution must be published in the *Gazette* within 14 days of its being passed.

19.1.2.1 Members' voluntary liquidation

Companies are often wound up when they are solvent. The shareholders might decide that they would rather end the company and share out its assets than continue to own it. A company which can pay its debts can be liquidated by a members' voluntary winding up if the members pass a special resolution that it should be. (A special resolution is a resolution passed by a majority of not less than 75 per cent of votes cast.)

In a members' voluntary winding up the liquidator is appointed by the company in general meeting.

Section 89 of the Insolvency Act says that to effect a members' voluntary winding up the directors (or a majority of them if there are more than two) must make a declaration of solvency within the five weeks before the date on which the resolution to wind the company up is passed.

This declaration of solvency will state that the directors have made a full enquiry into the company's affairs and that, having done so, they have formed the opinion that the company will be able to pay its debts in full, together with interest, within a period specified in the statement (which must not exceed 12 months from the commencement of the winding up). The directors must also attach a statement of liabilities and assets to the declaration, at the latest practicable date before the making of the declaration. The declaration must be delivered to the Registrar of Companies within 15 days of the passing of the resolution to wind the company up, as must a copy of the resolution itself. If any director makes the statement without reasonable grounds, he will commit a criminal offence and be liable to a fine and imprisonment. Section 95 of the Insolvency Act provides that where the liquidator is of the opinion that the company will be unable to pay its debts in full (together with interest at the official rate) within the period stated in the directors' declaration of solvency he shall summon a meeting of creditors within 28 days of forming that opinion. The effect of this is to cause the winding up to proceed as a creditors' voluntary winding up.

As soon as a members' voluntary winding up is completed the liquidator has to make up an account of the winding up, showing how it has been conducted and how the company's property has been disposed of. He must then call a general meeting of the company to lay the account before the meeting and to give an explanation of it.

19.1.2.2 Creditors' voluntary liquidation

This is the method by which the members voluntarily wind a company up when the directors are unable to make a declaration of solvency. The company must pass a special resolution to wind the company up and then, within 14 days, they must call a meeting of creditors. A copy of the reso-lution must be sent to the Registrar of Companies within 15 days.

In addition to calling a meeting of creditors, the company must post notice of the meeting to all creditors at least seven days before the meeting is to be held. Notice of the meeting must also be advertised in the *Gazette* and at least once in two newspapers circulating in the locality in which the company's principal place of business is situated.

The creditors have the choice of who the liquidator should be and fix his remuneration. If they wish to do so, they can approve one nominated by the members of the company at the meeting at which the resolution to wind the company up was proposed.

At their meeting the creditors can appoint a committee of inspection. This will contain no more than five members. This committee does not have all the powers of the liquidator but can make re-commendations, such as to pay a particular class of creditors in full. The liquidator can then act on these recommendations without calling a full meeting of all the creditors.

The directors have to lay a statement of affairs before the creditors. This statement of affairs contains the same information as that which can be required by the Official Receiver under s.131 of the Insolvency Act (see above at 19.1.1.4).

As soon as the company's affairs are fully wound up, the liquidator is required to make up an account of the winding up. This shows how the winding up has been conducted and how the company's property has been disposed of. The liquidator must also call a meeting of the members and the creditors to lay the account before the meeting and to give an explanation of it.

19.1.2.3 **Consequences of a voluntary winding up**

From the time when the resolution to wind the company up is passed, a voluntary winding up has the following consequences:

(1) The company must cease trading immediately, except in so far as may be required for a beneficial winding up.
(2) Shares cannot be transferred without the liquidator's consent, and any alteration in the status of the members is void.
(3) If the company is insolvent its employees are automatically dismissed, although the liquidator has the power to re-employ them.
(4) The directors' powers cease to exist as soon as a liquidator is appointed or nominated, except in so far as the liquidation committee (or, if there is

no such committee, the creditors) sanction their continuance. Before that time, the directors may take such actions as are necessary to protect the company's assets and to dispose of perishable goods.

19.1.2.4 **The liquidator**

Only a person who is a qualified insolvency practitioner may act as a company liquidator. The li-quidator's function is to collect the assets of the company and to distribute the value of these to the company's creditors and members, according to the statutory order for payment. In order to achieve these ends, a liquidator is given the following powers by ss.165–167 of the Insolvency Act.

(1) To pay any class of creditors in full.
(2) To enter into compromises or arrangements with creditors of the company.
(3) To enter into compromises as regards debts owed to the company, and claims of the company.
(4) To defend or bring any action or other legal proceedings in the name of, and on behalf of, the company.
(5) To carry on the business of the company so far as may be necessary for its beneficial winding up.
(6) To sell any of the company's property by public auction or by private contract.
(7) To do all acts in the name of and on behalf of the company, including executing deeds, receipts and other documents, using the company seal where necessary.
(8) To draw and indorse cheques and other bills of exchange in the name of, and on behalf of, the company.
(9) To raise money by giving the company's assets as security.
(10) To appoint an agent to do business which the liquidator is himself unable to do.
(11) To do all such things as may be necessary for winding up the company's affairs and distributing its assets.

In a voluntary winding up the first three of these powers may only be exercised by the liquidator if they are sanctioned: (a) in the case of a members' voluntary winding up, by a special resolution of the company; or (b) in the case of a creditors' voluntary winding up, with the sanction of the court or the liquidation committee or (if there is no liquidation committee) a meeting of the company's creditors. The other powers may be exercised without sanction in either type of voluntary winding up. In a winding up by the court the first five powers may be exercised only with the sanction of the court or the liquidation committee. The sixth to eleventh powers may be exercised without any sanction.

Section 178 of the Insolvency Act gives the liquidator the power to disclaim onerous property. This means that he can release the company from any obligation under an unprofitable contract and disclaim any company property which is unsaleable or which might give rise to a liability to pay money or incur other expenses. A person who incurs loss as a consequence can claim against the company as an unsecured creditor.

19.1.3 Distribution of the company's assets

The order in which the company's assets are distributed is the same whether the winding up is compulsory or voluntary. However, there are now two regimes in place: those which are subject to the amendments made by the Enterprise Act 2002 and those which are not.

When a company is wound up a creditor with a fixed charge will have the right to sell the assets over which he has the charge. The proceeds of the sale will go to the charge holder rather than into the pool of assets, but only to the extent that this is necessary to pay the charge holder what he is owed. Any excess money which is realised goes into the pool of assets. Charges were dealt with in some detail in Chapter 18 at 18.9. We saw that a person with a fixed charge lends money to the company and takes a charge (a mortgage) over specific company assets. If the loan is not repaid the charge holder is entitled to sell those assets and take what he is owed, but only what he is owed, from the proceeds. If the sale of the assets does not yield enough money to pay his debt in full, the holder of a fixed charge can take the amount which is generated and then claim for the rest as an unsecured creditor.

After the holders of fixed charges have called them in, the Insolvency Act sets out the order in which payment must be made. Each class of creditors is paid in full before the class below is paid anything. If there are insufficient funds to pay a class in full, all members of that class receive the same percentage of what they are owed. If some or all of the company's assets are

subject to a floating charge, the order differs depending upon whether the charge was created before or after 15 September 2003. The order of priority is of significance only where there are insufficient assets to pay all of the creditors in full. In such cases the company has usually granted a floating charge over all of its assets which are not the subject of a fixed charge. If the floating charge was created before 15 September 2003, the charge holder still has the power to appoint an administrative receiver and the charge is not subject to 'top slicing' (see below at 19.1.3.1). As regards insolvencies occurring in the next few years, it is likely that many floating charges will have been created before 15 September 2003.

The order of payment is now as follows:

(i) The liquidator's remuneration and the costs and expenses of winding up.

(ii) The preferential creditors at the time of winding up.

(iii) Floating charges created before 15 September 2003.

(iv) Top-sliced assets for distribution to the unsecured creditors (see below at 19.1.3.1).

(v) Floating charges created on or after 15 September 2003.

(vi) The unsecured creditors.

(vii) Sums due to members but not yet paid. For example, dividends declared but not yet paid.

(viii) The members of the company, as set out in the articles of association.

Prior to the commencement of the Companies Act 2006, the general expenses of liquidating the company ranked behind the floating charge holders when applying money which the realisation of floating charges generated. The 2006 Act changed this rule so that floating charge holders rank behind the expenses of winding up and behind preferential creditors. However, the Act has made provision for Regulations to be passed. These Regulations could require floating charge holders, and preferential creditors, to authorise or approve the payment of liquidation expenses in priority to payments to themselves in certain circumstances. At the time of writing, these Regulations have not been drawn up.

As regards floating charges created on or after 15 September 2003, the holders of those charges will lose the right to appoint an administrative receiver but will have the power to appoint an administrator. An administrative receiver realises the property subject to the floating charge in order that the charge holder can be paid from the proceeds. An administrator will generally realise a floating charge but the payment of the charge holder is not his main priority (see below at 19.1.4.5).

In Chapter 9, at 9.2, we considered reservation of title clauses and the circumstances in which they can be effective. It should be borne in mind that goods with which the liquidated company has been supplied will not belong to the company, and will not therefore be available for distribution to the creditors and members, if the goods were supplied subject to a valid reservation of title clause. It should also be borne in mind that goods which the company is hiring or which it has taken on hire-purchase will not belong to the company.

When the winding up process is completed the company can be dissolved.

19.1.3.1 Top slicing

As regards floating charges created on or after 15 September 2003, top slicing, also known as ring fencing, applies. This means that the liquidator must set aside a certain percentage of the assets which would otherwise be payable to floating charge holders so that this amount can be paid to the unsecured creditors. It might take several years for floating charges created after 15 September 2003 to enter the insolvency procedure and so top slicing will not apply immediately in all cases. The amount which must be set aside for the unsecured creditors is 50 per cent if the company's net property (after the payment of the costs of realising the company's assets and the preferential creditors) does not exceed £10 000 in value. If the company's net property exceeds £10 000 then the amount to be set aside is 50 per cent of the first £10 000, then 20 per cent of the remainder. The total amount set aside for the unsecured creditors may not exceed £600 000. If the value of the company's net property (after the payment of those ranking in priority to floating charges) is less than £10 000, the liquidator does not have to distribute the funds to the unsecured creditors if he considers that this would be disproportionate to the costs of doing so. A floating charge holder who is not paid the full amount which the charge secured, on account of there being insufficient funds for full payment to be made, can claim as an unsecured creditor for the amount not paid. However, this does not allow such a floating charge holder to share in the top-sliced fund.

Example

After the costs of realising the company's assets, paying the receiver's expenses and paying the preferential creditors, a company has net assets of £1 010 000. The only floating charge secures a debt of £2 million. If the charge was created before 15 September 2003, all of the £1 010 000 will be used to pay the debt secured by the charge. The charge holder will then be regarded as an unsecured creditor as regards the £990 000 which was not paid. If the charge was created on or after 15 September 2003, £205 000 will be ring-fenced for the unsecured creditors (50 per cent of £10 000 = £5 000 + 20 per cent of £1 million = £200 000, making a total of £205 000). The remaining £805 000 will go to the charge holder. As regards the £1 195 000 which he was not paid, the charge holder will be regarded as an unsecured creditor.

19.1.3.2 Preferential creditors

The Enterprise Act 2002 abolished Crown preference (that is to say, it has removed debts payable to the Government from the list of preferential creditors) and the preferential creditors are now as follows:

- Contributions to occupational pension schemes.
- Payment of wages. Up to £800 wages per employee, earned in the four months prior to the relevant date. (This is either the date of the winding up order, or special resolution in the case of a voluntary winding up, or the date of appointment of a receiver.)
- Any amount of holiday pay accrued before the relevant date.
- Loans made by a third party for the purpose of enabling wages and holiday pay (as specified above) to be paid and which were used for this purpose.
- Any loan used specifically to pay the employee's wages.
- Levies on coal and steel production arising under the European Coal and Steel Community Treaty.

These preferential debts rank equally among themselves. If there are sufficient assets, all of the preferential debts must be repaid before other creditors are paid anything. If there are not sufficient assets to pay all the preferential debts in full, then each of the preferential creditors are paid the same proportion of their claim, for example 10p or 50p in the pound.

Floating charge holders have gained the most from the abolition of Crown preference because after the preferential creditors they are next in line to be paid.

This is particularly true as regards floating charges created before 15 September 2003. Such floating charges rank after the preferential creditors and are not subject to 'top slicing', which was introduced by the Enterprise Act 2002 at the same time as the abolition of Crown preference.

19.1.4 Liability arising from insolvency

In general, a liquidator will not be able to claim assets which do not belong to the company or which are not owed to the company. However, there are certain exceptions to this principle. These exceptions are set out in outline here. It should be noted that these powers can be exercised only by a liquidator or someone acting on behalf of a liquidator.

19.1.4.1 Wrongful trading

Section 214 of the Insolvency Act allows a liquidator to apply to the court to declare that a person who is, or has been, a director should be liable to make such contribution to the company's assets as the court thinks proper. The court may declare a person liable to make a contribution if:

(a) the company has gone into liquidation; and
(b) at some time before the commencement of the winding up of the company, that person knew or ought to have concluded that there was no reasonable prospect that the company would avoid going into insolvent liquidation; and
(c) that person was a director or shadow director of the company at that time.

However, a person shall not be liable for wrongful trading if the court is satisfied that he took every step which he ought to have taken to minimise the potential loss to the company's creditors. The standard expected of the director, both as regards the offence and the defence, is that of a reasonably diligent person who has both the general knowledge, skill and experience which could be objectively expected of such a director and the skill, knowledge and experience which the director in question actually has. An incompetent director will therefore be judged on the standards of a competent one, and a highly competent director will be judged on his own standard. So the director will be judged by whichever standard leads to the higher expectations. The type of company concerned and the functions being carried out by the directors will be relevant considerations in assessing whether or not a director is liable for wrongful trading. A director who can see the inevitability of insolvent liquidation would be well advised to seek advice from a qualified insolvency practitioner before doing anything which could be construed as wrongful trading.

19.1.4.2 Fraudulent trading and misfeasance

Section 213 of the Insolvency Act 1986 provides that if in the course of the winding up of a company it appears than any business of the company has been carried on with the intention of defrauding the creditors of the company, or any other creditors, or for any fraudulent purpose, the court may declare that any persons who were knowingly parties to the fraudulent carrying on of the business are liable to make such contributions to the company's assets as the court thinks proper. In addition, a disqualification order could be made under s.10 of the Company Directors Disqualification Act 1986. In order to be liable under s.213, a person must have deliberately been dishonest by the standards of ordinary business people. It is only the liquidator who can apply to the court for a declaration of fraudulent trading. A separate criminal offence of fraudulent trading is set out by s.993 of the Companies Act 2006. Although both s.993 and s.213 refer to carrying on the business with intent to defraud, the provisions of both sections can be invoked even if there was only one fraudulent transaction defrauding one creditor.

Section 212 of the Insolvency Act 1986 allows the court to examine any person who is or has been an officer of the company, or any other person who has been involved in the promotion, formation or management of the company, in misfeasance proceedings. Such an examination takes place on the application of the Official Receiver, or the liquidator, or any creditor or contributory. Contributories may openly apply to the court with the court's permission, but do not need to benefit from any order the court may make on the application. Misfeasance will have taken place if the officer etc. has misapplied or retained, or become accountable for, any money or other property of the company. It will also have taken place if the officer etc. has been guilty of any misfeasance or breach of any fiduciary or other duty in relation to the company. The court can compel the officer etc. (a) to repay, restore or account for the property or any part of it, with interest at such rates as the court thinks just, or (b) to contribute such sum to the company's assets by way of compensation in respect of the misfeasance or breach of duty as the court thinks just. Liquidators and administrators can also be made liable in misfeasance proceedings. Misfeasance proceedings are important in practice and might be brought to get back from the directors dividends which were paid out of capital.

19.1.4.3 Transactions at undervalue and preferences

Section 238 of the Insolvency Act provides that where the company has gone into liquidation, the liquidator may apply to the court for an order if the company has at a relevant time entered into a transaction with any person at an undervalue. The court has the power to make such order as it thinks fit for restoring the position to what it would have been if the company had not entered into that transaction. A company enters into a transaction at an undervalue with a person if the company (a) makes a gift to that person or (b) enters into a transaction with that person for a consideration which, in money or money's worth, is significantly less than the value of the consideration provided by the company. However, the court will not make the order if satisfied that (a) the company which entered into the transaction did so in good faith and for the purpose of carrying on its business, and (b) that, at the time it did so, there were reasonable grounds for believing that the transaction would benefit the company. The section is therefore intended to prevent the defrauding of creditors and members by giving away the company's assets, or selling them too cheaply, prior to liquidation.

Section 239 of the Insolvency Act allows the court, upon an application by a liquidator, to make an order where the company has given preference to any person at a relevant time. If satisfied that this has happened, the court can make such an order as it sees fit for restoring the position to what it would have been if the company had not given that preference. A company gives a preference to a person if (a) that person is one of the company's creditors or a surety or guarantor for any of the company's debts or other liabilities, and (b) the company does anything, or allows anything to be done, which has the effect of putting that person into a position which, in the event of the company going into insolvent liquidation, will be better than the position he would have been in if the thing had not been done. Although the court will not make the order unless the company which gave the preference was influenced in deciding to give it to put the person to whom it was given into a better position on the company's insolvent liquidation, if the preference is given to a person connected with the company at the time the preference was given it is presumed to have been influenced in deciding to give it for this purpose. A connected person does not include a person whose only connection is that he is an employee of the company. It does include directors and shadow directors, as well as their husbands and wives, their business partners, their employers or their employees.

For the purposes of both ss.238 and 239, the 'relevant time' is defined by s.240 as:

(a) In the case of a transaction at an undervalue or of a preference which is given to a person connected with the company, the time is two years prior to the onset of insolvency.

(b) For preferences in favour of non-connected persons the time period is six months.

The onset of insolvency is either the date of commencement of the winding up, or the date on which an administrator was appointed or the date on which an application for an administrator to be appointed was made. As regards both (a) and (b), it is also a requirement that at the time of entering into the transaction or giving the preference the company was unable to pay its debts, or became unable to do so as a consequence of the transaction or the preference.

Section 423 of the Insolvency Act also confers on the court the power to set aside transactions to defraud creditors by entering into transactions at an undervalue. These powers are not dependent on the company becoming insolvent. A victim of such a transaction may apply to the court, which may make such order as it sees fit to (a) restore the position to what it would have been if the transaction had not been entered into, and (b) protect the interests of persons who are victims of the transaction. A transaction will be regarded as to defraud creditors if the court is satisfied that the person who entered into the transaction did so (a) to put assets beyond the reach of a person who is making, or may at some time make, a claim against him, or (b) to otherwise prejudice the interests of such a person in relation to the claim which he is making or may make. There is no time limit attached to s.423.

19.1.4.4 Invalidity of floating charges

Section 245 of the Insolvency Act renders a floating charge invalid if it was given to a connected person within two years of the commencement of winding up proceedings, whether the company was solvent at the time the charge was created or not. As regards an unconnected person, his charge will be invalid if it was created within 12 months of the commencement of winding up proceedings unless the company was solvent after the creation of the charge. However, in neither case will the charge be invalid to the extent that the company did receive money, or services or goods, or the reduction of a debt, in consideration of the creation of the charge.

This section prevents a company from benefiting an existing creditor by granting him a charge over a previously unsecured debt. The company can still issue valid floating charges to the extent that it receives new funds or assets in return for doing so.

19.1.4.5 Administration and administrative receivership

(a) Administration

Administration is a concept which was introduced by the Insolvency Act 1986. It is a measure short of receivership under which the administrator attempts to rescue an ailing company. So administration may well not lead to the winding up of the company. In recent years, several professional football clubs have gone into administration but have escaped liquidation.

An administrator must be a qualified insolvency practitioner and can be appointed by court order, after an application by the directors, or by a creditor of the company. The Enterprise Act 2002 has also created a new out-of-court mode of appointment of administrators. Such an appointment can be made by either the holder of a qualifying floating charge, or by the company, or by the directors of the company. (As regards floating charges created on or after September 2003, the charge holder can no longer appoint a receiver.) The administrator must perform his functions in the interests of the company's creditors as a whole and has three hierarchical objects. First, to rescue the company as a going concern (the primary purpose). Second, to achieve a better result for the company's creditors than would be achieved if the company was wound up. Third, to realise (sell) property to make a distribution to one or more secured or preferential creditors.

A court will appoint an administrator only if it is satisfied that the company cannot pay its debts or that the administration order is likely to achieve the primary purpose. A floating charge holder can appoint an administrator, but only if his charge or charges relate to substantially the whole of the company's property

(thus making him a 'qualifying' floating charge holder). The company or the directors can appoint an administrator, but not if an administrative receiver has been appointed or a petition for winding up has been presented. Also, if qualifying floating charge holders object, the court will generally allow them, rather than the directors, to appoint the administrator.

An important feature of administration is that it applies a moratorium. The Enterprise Act 2002 has inserted an interim moratorium which comes into force on the date of either the application to the court or, in the case of an out-of-court appointment, the date of the presentation of the notice to appoint an administrator. The interim moratorium gives more limited protection to the company than does the full moratorium which is effective from the date of the administrator's appointment. During the period of the interim moratorium it is still possible for a winding up petition to be presented to the court and a pre-15 September 2003 floating charge holder can apply to the company to appoint an administrative receiver.

Once a company is in administration, any petition to wind the company up will either be dismissed or suspended until the period of administration is over. An administrative receiver who has already been appointed is dismissed. No steps can be taken to enforce any security without the consent of the administrator or the permission of the court. All business documents (invoices, orders for goods or services and business letters) issued by or on behalf of the company must state the name of the administrator and that he is managing the company's affairs. All creditors must be informed that the administrator has been appointed.

As soon as is reasonably practicable after his appointment, the administrator must require an officer or employee of the company to give him a statement of the company's affairs. (If the company had been formed within the previous year a promoter can be required to give the statement.) The statement must be in a prescribed form and state and give details of the company's creditors and the company's property, debts and liabilities. A person requested to submit a statement of affairs has 11 days in which to do so. The administrator then sets out his proposals for achieving the purpose of the administration and sends details to the Registrar of Companies, and all of the company's creditors and members. This must be done as soon as is reasonably practicable and within eight weeks of the company entering administration.

All creditors are invited to a creditors' meeting to consider the administrator's proposals. The creditors can approve the proposals with or without modification. If the creditors approve the proposals, the administrator must manage the company's affairs in accordance with the proposals. If the creditors do not approve the proposals, the administrator might amend the proposals and resubmit them to the creditors who once more might approve them with or without modification. If the creditors still do not approve the proposals, the court may replace the administrator or make any other order which it sees fit. There may be a further creditors' meeting if the court orders one or if creditors holding at least 10 per cent of the company's debt demand one. A creditors' committee may be formed. This committee can demand that the administrator attend a meeting to give information on the way he is performing his role.

The administrator may do anything necessary or expedient for the management of the affairs, business and property of the company, including removing or appointing directors. He takes control of all the property to which he thinks the company is entitled and may pay off creditors. He can sell off property which is subject to a floating charge but the charge holder gets the same priority in respect of any property then acquired. (In effect this reverses the crystallisation of the charge.) By court order he can sell off property subject to a fixed charge, but only if the charge holder is given towards payment of his debt the net proceeds of sale and any other sum which the court thinks would bring the amount up to the market value of the charged property.

A creditor or member can apply to the court challenging the administrator's conduct. The court then has power to make any order which it considers appropriate. An administrator's appointment ends automatically one year after his appointment but can be extended by a further six months. However, this requires the consent of all secured creditors and the consent of creditors holding at least 50 per cent of the company's unsecured debts. Unsecured creditors who do not respond to an invitation to give consent are disregarded.

(b) Administrative receivership

As long as their charges were registered before 15 September 2003, one or more floating charge holders can appoint a receiver to realise the company's property so that the secured debt can be paid. If the charge(s) relate to all or substantially all of the company's assets the receiver is called an administrative receiver. These charge holders can instead appoint an administrator and, as we have seen, holders of floating charges created after 15 September 2003 cannot appoint an administrative receiver but will have to appoint an administrator. The right to appoint an administrative receiver will have been contained in the contract which created the charge. Although administrative receivership is an insolvency procedure, it is not a liquidation procedure. Generally, receivers can be appointed without a court order.

As soon as a receiver is appointed, he, and not the board of directors, has the power to deal with the property which is subject to the floating charge. (Generally, this will be all of the company's property which is not subject to a fixed charge.) An administrative receiver is an agent of the company and his task is to see that the secured creditors get paid. As soon as this is done he will be finished with the company. The floating charge holders will be paid only after the costs of realising the charge and the payment of creditors who were preferential at the date of the receivership. The floating charge holder will also take subject to the general liquidation expenses if the company goes into liquidation. The work of an administrative receiver often causes a company to go into liquidation because once all or most of the company's assets have been sold off to satisfy the secured creditors there is often not much left.

19.1.4.6 Company voluntary arrangement (CVA)

The board of directors of an insolvent company, or the administrator or liquidator, can propose a composition or a scheme of arrangement to be supervised by an insolvency practitioner. Under such an arrangement, which must be agreed by a three-quarters majority of the company's unsecured creditors, all unsecured creditors are paid a proportion of their debts over a period of time. To initiate a CVA, the directors first have to give the nominee a statement of the company's affairs along with any other information which he requires. Within 28 days of receiving notice of the proposal, the nominee has to inform the court whether he thinks the scheme is worth putting to the company's creditors and members, and whether it has a reasonable prospect of being approved by them and put into place. If the company is in liquidation or administration, it is the liquidator or administrator who can propose this, with himself as the nominee, without seeking the court's approval.

Meetings of all company creditors and all members must be called. These meetings can approve the proposal or a modification of it. Approval of the members is by over 50 per cent of votes cast. However, the meetings cannot deprive a secured creditor (floating chargeholder) of the right to enforce his security without that creditor's approval. Nor can the priority of preferential debts be changed without the approval of the preferential creditors who would be affected. If a proposal is approved at the meetings, notice must be given to all the members and creditors who were invited to the meetings and to the court. All members and creditors are then bound by the agreement. If the meetings come to different results, the meeting of the creditors prevails. However, any member then has 28 days to apply to the court to have the decision of the creditors' meeting changed or overruled.

Within 28 days of receiving notice of the proposal, any creditor or member can apply to the court to have the proposal set aside on the grounds that it unfairly prejudices the interests of a creditor or member, or that there was a material irregularity at the meeting. The court then has the power to approve, revoke or suspend the approval and to direct that revised proposals be put to another meeting.

Voluntary arrangement is an insolvency procedure but not a liquidation procedure. It is generally hoped that the company can survive it. Individuals may enter into a similar procedure, known as an individual voluntary arrangement or IVA.

Test your understanding 19.1

1 Can a company be voluntarily wound up by the members?

2 In what circumstances will a company be deemed unable to pay its debts, thereby justifying the court in ordering the company to be wound up?

3 State four grounds on which a court has decided that it is just and equitable to wind a company up.

4 What are the main differences between a members' voluntary liquidation and a creditors' voluntary liquidation?

5 In what order are the creditors of an insolvent company paid?

6 What purposes does an administrator of a company try to achieve? What purpose does an administrative receiver try to achieve?

19.2 LIMITED LIABILITY PARTNERSHIPS

19.2.1 The nature of limited liability partnerships

Since April 2000 it has been possible for two or more persons to trade as a limited liability partnership (LLP). It is important at the outset to realise that an LLP is not an ordinary partnership which has limited liability. Nor is an LLP the same as, or even similar to, a limited partnership registered under the Limited Partnership Act 1907. Indeed, as corporate entities, LLPs have more in common with limited companies than with ordinary or limited partnerships.

Like shareholders in a company, participants in an LLP are known as members and not as partners. It is possible for companies to be members of an LLP, just as it is possible for companies to be members of an ordinary partnership. An LLP can engage in any kind of business. Although an LLP is closer to a limited company than to an ordinary partnership, an LLP does share some of the features of an ordinary partnership. One significant similarity is that the profits of an LLP are not subject to corporation tax. The members of an LLP are taxed on profits in the same way as partners in an ordinary partnership. The members of an LLP will therefore be liable to pay income tax on profits received.

The Limited Liability Partnership Act 2000 (the 2000 Act) created a framework of the law applicable to LLPs, leaving the details to be filled by secondary legislation. The general approach of this legislation has been to apply to LLPs provisions of the Companies Act 2006, the Company Directors Disqualification Act 1986 and the Insolvency Act 1986. Many of these provisions have been modified slightly so that they do not apply in exactly the same way as they apply to companies. Other provisions do apply exactly as they apply to companies. It is because so much company law applies to LLPs, slightly modified or not, that we consider the law relating to LLPs after we have considered the law relating to companies.

Section 1(5) of the 2000 Act provides that, unless the Act provides otherwise, the law relating to partnerships does not apply to an LLP. However, some sections of the Act are obviously based on the Partnership Act 1890. As the law relating to LLPs is an amalgam of company law and partnership law, it would be very difficult to understand it unless one first had an understanding of the law relating to companies and ordinary partnerships.

19.2.2 **Formation of an LLP**

An LLP is created by registration with the Registrar of Companies. A £20 filing fee is payable, or a fee of £50 if the LLP is to be registered the same day. These fees are reduced to £15 and £30 if the filing is done electronically. Once the Registrar has registered an LLP and issued a certificate of incorporation a new corporate body, with a legal personality of its own, is created. The certificate of incorporation will state the name of the LLP, the date on which it was incorporated and whether the registered office is located in England and Wales, (or Wales) or Scotland or Northern Ireland.

Section 2(1) of the 2000 Act sets out three requirements for incorporation. First, s.2(1)(a) requires that two or more persons associated for carrying on a lawful business with a view to profit must have subscribed their names to an incorporation document. Second, s.2(1)(b) requires that this document, or a copy of it, is delivered to the Registrar of Companies. Third, s.2(1)(c) requires that a statement that the requirements of s.2(1)(a) have been complied with is also delivered to the Registrar. This statement must be made by one of the subscribers to the incorporation document or by a solicitor who was engaged in the formation of the LLP. These requirements make it plain that there must be at least two members; there cannot be a single member LLP. If an LLP carries on business with only one member for more than six months, the single member becomes liable for debts incurred while he was the only member. It should also be noticed that, although the business of an LLP must be carried on with a view to profit, there is no requirement that every member should be intended to share in this profit.

Section 2(2) requires the incorporation document to be in a form approved by the Registrar and to state five matters: the name of the LLP; whether the registered office is in England and Wales, in Wales or in Scotland; the actual address of the registered office; the names and addresses of all the members on incorporation; and a statement of who the designated members (see below) are or a statement that all members of the LLP, at any time, are to be designated members. The protection on disclosure of residential address which is available to company directors is also available to members of an LLP. The address of the registered office is important because documents can be served on a LLP by delivering them to the registered office. Form LLIN01, which is available from the Registrar of Companies, is the official form which serves as both the incorporation document and the written statement. As there is no equivalent of an objects clause, questions of *ultra vires* will not arise. When the registration requirements have been satisfied, the Registrar will then issue the LLP with a number and a certificate of incorporation and publish the fact of incorporation in the *London Gazette*.

Section 9 of the 2000 Act provides that when a person becomes or ceases to become a member or a designated member the Registrar must be informed within 14 days. If a member changes his name or address the Registrar must be informed within 28 days.

19.2.3 **The LLP name**

Part 1 of Schedule 1 to the 2000 Act deals with the names of LLPs. It provides that the name of an LLP must end with 'limited liability partnership', 'llp' or 'LLP'. If the registered office is in Wales the Welsh equivalents, 'partneriaeth atebolrwydd cyfyngedig', 'pac' or 'PAC' can be used instead. An LLP must not use the words set out above otherwise than at the end of its name. A name which is identical to that of a registered company or a registered LLP cannot be used. Nor can a name be used if it would constitute a criminal offence or, in the opinion of the Secretary of State, be offensive, indicate a connection with the Government or a local authority or be a name for which a company would need approval. These rules, and the rules relating to a **change of name**, and the circumstances in which the **name must be displayed**, are identical to the rules relating to companies, which were examined in Chapter 16 at 16.9.

19.2.4 **Members and designated members**

Section 4(1) of the 2000 Act provides that on incorporation an LLP's members are the person who subscribed to the incorporation document (unless they have died or, in the case of companies, been dissolved). Section 4(2) provides that any other person may become a member by agreement with all existing members. (Regulation 7(5) of the 2001 Regulations provides that, subject to the terms of any LLP agreement, all existing members must agree to the introduction of a new member.) Section 4(3) of the Act provides that a person may cease to be a member either by agreement with the other members or by giving reasonable notice to the other members. It also makes it plain that a member who has died or, in the case of a company, been dissolved will cease to be a member. Section 4(4) of the Act provides that a member of an LLP should not be regarded as an employee of the LLP unless he would be regarded as an employee of the partnership if the LLP were a partnership. Members of LLPs are therefore self-employed.

Section 8(1) of the 2000 Act deals with the identification of designated members, stating that they may be stated to be designated members in the incorporation document or may become or cease to become designated members by agreement with the other members of the LLP. Section 8(2) provides that where there would otherwise be no designated member, or only one designated member, then every member of the LLP is a designated member. In addition, s.8(3) allows the incorporation document to state that all members of the LLP from time to time are designated members. Section 8(4) provides that an LLP may give notice to the Registrar that a person is a designated member, or that all the members of the LLP are designated members, and that this shall have effect as if stated in the incorporation document. Such a notice has to be signed by a designated member. A person who ceases to be a member of an LLP ceases to be a designated member.

Designated members have certain specific duties such as signing the LLP's accounts and delivering them to the Registrar, giving the Registrar notice that an LLP has changed its name, giving the Registrar notice of who the designated members are, appointing the auditor and signing the annual return form. If company legislation which is applicable to LLPs imposes duties on directors or officers of the company, it is presumed that these duties fall on all members of an LLP unless legislation has allocated the particular duty to designated members.

The rules on approval and removal of auditors, on filing an annual return and on filing of accounts are essentially the same as those which apply to limited companies. These matters were considered in Chapter 17.

An LLP must keep a register of members and a register of members' addresses. For each member the register of members must state his name (or former name), a service address, the country or part of the UK in which he is ordinarily resident, his date of birth and whether or not he is a designated member. The register of members' addresses must state the residential address of each member, if this differs from his service address. If the residential address is the same as the service address this must be stated. In Chapter 17, at 17.1.4.1, we considered the rules which protect the disclosure of company directors' residential addresses. These rules apply equally to the residential addresses of LLP members. LLPs also have duties to keep accounting records, send copies of the annual accounts to members and debenture holders and register charges which the LLP has created.

In Chapter 18, at 18.8.7, we considered the circumstances in which the DBIS can investigate a company's affairs. These rules apply also to LLPs, in a somewhat modified way. Such an investigation can arise if a court orders it or if at least 20 per cent of the members demand it.

19.2.5 Members as agents

An LLP will be bound by a contract if the contract was made by an agent who had authority to make it. So, like a company, an LLP can confer actual authority to make contracts on employees, such as shop assistants and salesmen, or on non-employees. Section 6(1) of the 2000 Act provides that every member of the LLP is an agent of the LLP. But s.6(2) then limits this by stating that an LLP is not bound by anything done by a member in dealing with a person if: (a) the member in fact has no authority to act for the LLP by doing that thing; and (b) the person knows that he has no authority or does not know or believe him to be a member of the LLP. The rules set out in these two subsections are very similar to the rules set out in s.5 of the Partnership Act 1890, which was examined in detail in Chapter 15 at 15.8.1. Whilst the law applicable to s.5 of the Partnership Act 1890 would generally apply to s.6 of the 2000 Act, we should note several points of difference. First, in the case of an LLP the principal is the LLP itself, whereas in the case of an ordinary partnership each of the partners is the principal and is therefore bound by the contract. Second, s.6(1) does not have the s.5 Partnership Act requirement that the partner's act should be done 'for carrying on in the usual way business of the kind carried on by the firm of which he is a member'. Third, in relation to the limitation in s.6(2), it is arguably the case that the requirement that every member of an LLP should be registered on a register which can be inspected by any person means that it might be difficult for a third party to argue that he did not know that the contracting member was a member of the LLP.

Section 6(3) provides that a person dealing with an LLP can still regard a former member of an LLP as a member unless: (a) he has been given notice that the former member has ceased to be a member; or (b) notice that the former member has ceased to be a member has been delivered to the Registrar. These rules on the apparent authority of a former member are similar to the rules applying to former partners in a partnership. However, it seems a little surprising that a third party is regarded as having notice when this is delivered to the Registrar, rather than when the Registrar alters the register.

Section 51(1) of the Companies Act 2006 applies to LLPs, so a person making a pre-incorporation contract on behalf of an LLP will be liable on it (see Chapter 16 at 16.8). If the contract is properly drafted the LLP, once formed, will be able to enforce the contract under the Contract (Rights of Third Parties) Act (C(RTP)A) 1999. Section 6(2A) C(RTP)A 1999 provides that neither an incorporation document of an LLP, nor any LLP agreement, can confer rights on a third party to **enforce** a term.

Section 5(2) of the 2000 Act provides that an agreement made before the incorporation of an LLP, between the subscribers to the incorporation document, may impose obligations on the LLP to take effect at any time after its incorporation.

19.2.6 **Liability in tort**

Section 4(4) of the 2000 Act provides that an LLP will be vicariously liable to outsiders for a wrongful act or omission of a member committed either during the course of the business of the LLP or with the authority of the LLP. This is a partial application of s.10 of the Partnership Act 1890, which was considered in Chapter 15 at 15.8.2. However, it should be noticed that under s.4(4) of the Act it is the LLP, rather than the other members, which becomes liable.

The decision of the House of Lords in *Dubai Aluminium Co Ltd v Salaam and others* [2002] 3 WLR 1913, considered at 15.8.2, would seem to be a starting point for the vicarious liability of LLPs. However, s 4(4) differs from s.10 of the Partnership Act 1890 in that it requires the tort to be committed in the course of business of the LLP, rather than in the ordinary course of business. It therefore seems likely that this will make the liability of an LLP wider than the liability of partners under s.10 of the Partnership Act.

19.2.7 **Members' relationship with each other**

Section 5(1) of the 2000 Act provides that the mutual rights and duties of the members of an LLP as between each other, and as between the members and the LLP, shall be governed by agreement between the members or by agreement between the LLP and the members. In the absence of such agreement, the default provisions set out in reg.7 of the 2001 Regulations apply. Section 5 therefore deals with two different sets of duties. First, the duties which every member owes to every other member. Second, the duties which every member owes to the LLP. Section 5 also makes it plain that a statute, such as the Insolvency Act 1986, may override any agreement made.

When acting as agents of the LLP, members will owe a fiduciary duty to the LLP. This fiduciary duty applies to all agents, including, of course, partners dealing on behalf of their fellow partners and directors dealing on behalf of a company. It is not clear whether members of an LLP will owe a general fiduciary duty to other members. Partners do owe a fiduciary duty to other partners but directors do not generally owe a fiduciary duty to individual shareholders. It seems likely that members of an LLP will not owe a fiduciary duty to other members, as an LLP is a corporate body rather than a relationship between its members. However, there is nothing to prevent the LLP agreement imposing fiduciary duties. Also, the default provision set out in reg.7(8), see immediately below, imposes a fiduciary duty which a member will owe to other members (unless the members have agreed otherwise).

19.2.8 **The default provisions**

Like s.24 of the Partnership Act 1890, reg.7 of the 2001 Regulations set out default provisions which are to apply unless the general law or any LLP agreement provides otherwise. The ten default provisions are as follows:

- Regulation 7(1) – All members are entitled to share equally in the capital and profits of the LLP. (Regulation 7(1) does not refer to losses because such losses will be borne by the LLP rather than by the members.)
- Regulation 7(2) – The LLP must indemnify each member in respect of payments made and liabilities incurred in the ordinary and proper conduct of the business of the LLP or for the preservation of the LLP or its property.

- Regulation 7(3) – Every member may take part in the management of the LLP.
- Regulation 7(4) – No member is entitled to remuneration for acting in the business or management of the LLP.
- Regulation 7(5) – No new member may be introduced, nor may a member voluntarily assign an interest in an LLP, without the consent of all existing members.
- Regulation 7(6) – Differences arising as to ordinary matters may be resolved by a majority vote, but no change may be made in the nature of the business of the LLP without the consent of all of the members.
- Regulation 7(7) – Every member shall have access to the books and records of the LLP and may inspect and make copies of them.
- Regulation 7(8) – Every member shall render true accounts and full information of all things affecting the LLP to any other member or his legal representative.
- Regulation 7(9) – If a member, without the consent of the LLP, carries on any business of the same nature as and competing with the LLP, he must account for and pay over to the LLP all profits made by him in that business.
- Regulation 7(10) – Every member must account to the LLP for any benefit derived by him without the consent of the LLP from any transaction concerning the LLP, or for any use by him of the property of the LLP, name or business connection.

The first seven of these default provisions are modelled very closely on s.24 of the Partnership Act 1890. The last three are modelled on ss.28–30 of the Partnership Act. We examined s.24 in Chapter 15 at 15.5.1 and we examined ss.28–30 in Chapter 15 at 15.7.

Regulation 8 mirrors s.25 of the Partnership Act by providing that no majority can expel any member unless a power to do so has been conferred by express agreement between the members. (This suggests that the matters set out in the reg. 7 default provisions can be altered by express or implied agreement.) If a member is expelled then, at the very least, this power will have to be exercised *bona fide* for the benefit of the LLP. It is not clear whether in exercising such a power the majority would owe fiduciary duties to the expelled member.

19.2.9 Ceasing to be a member

Section 7 of the 2000 Act deals with the position where a member has ceased to be a member, died,

become bankrupt or assigned all or part of his share in the LLP to another person. It provides that neither the member, nor his trustee in bankruptcy, nor his personal representatives, nor the person to whom the share was assigned may interfere in the management or business affairs of the LLP. However, this does not affect any right to receive an amount from the LLP which arose on the member ceasing to be a member, becoming bankrupt etc.

As we have seen, s.4(3) of the 2000 Act allows a member to leave an LLP by agreement with the other members by giving the other members reasonable notice. In Chapter 15 at 15.4.1.4 we saw that only in the case of a partnership at will can a partner give notice to dissolve the firm. If the firm is not a partnership at will no partner has the right to leave by giving notice. So the idea that a member of an LLP can leave by giving reasonable notice is a key difference. Another key difference is that an LLP will not be dissolved when a member leaves. The member who leaves will not therefore have any right to a share of the LLP's assets, unless an agreement has given him such rights. So unless the minority protection provisions (see immediately below) apply, a member of an LLP who wanted to leave might effectively find himself unable to do so.

As we have already seen, s.9 requires that the Registrar is informed within 14 days of a member ceasing to be a member. We have also seen that s.6(3) allows the former member's apparent authority to make contracts to continue until the Registrar is notified that he has ceased to be a member.

19.2.10 **Minority protection**

If a member of an LLP is expelled from the LLP, or is being treated unfairly by a majority of members, or wants to leave the LLP with an appropriate share of the assets having been denied him, the law on minority protection becomes relevant. A derivative claim can be brought only in respect of a wrong done to the LLP, and not in respect of a wrong done to individual members. In company law, common law derivative claims were traditionally very hard to establish in the absence of fraud. If fraud can be established then an individual member can bring a claim for fraud on the minority.

As an LLP is a corporate body the rule in *Foss v Harbottle* applies (*Cablevision Ltd v Feetum* [2005] EWCA Civ 1601, [2006] Ch 585). This rule, set out in Chapter 18 at 18.8.1, holds that if a wrong is done to a company then only the company has the right to sue in respect of that wrong. However, as we saw in Chapter 18, minority shareholders may be given various forms of protection. To what extent do these forms of protection apply to members of an LLP?

First, the common law would give a member the right to bring a derivative claim where the behaviour of the majority amounted to a fraud on the minority (see Chapter 18 at 18.8.3.4). There is no statutory right to bring a derivative claim.

Second, a member may be able to petition the court for a winding up order, under s.122 of the Insolvency Act 1986, on the grounds that this is just and equitable. As we saw earlier, default reg.7(3) gives every member a right to manage the LLP. Such a default term could, of course, be changed by agreement but it would seem unlikely that an agreement would exclude the right of any member to take part in management. A member who was expelled might be able to argue that this breached his right to take part in the management of the LLP and that this would therefore justify a winding up on the just and equitable ground. Winding up under s.122 of the Insolvency Act was examined in Chapter 18 at 18.8.6.

Third, the provisions of s.994 Companies Act 2006 regarding unfair prejudice apply to LLPs. However, the members of a limited liability partnership may by unanimous agreement exclude the right contained in s.994 as long as the agreement is recorded in writing. This potential exclusion of the right to petition the court on the grounds of unfair prejudice seems, at first sight, very significant. However, since the exclusion has to be unanimous and in writing it seems probable that it would apply only where the members had agreed some alternative method of dealing with minority protection. Section 994 was examined in Chapter 18 at 18.8.5.

A member who wants to leave an LLP, but who has been denied an appropriate share of the assets, might gain relief from any of the matters set out above. However, none of these matters provides an easy remedy. Appropriate drafting of the incorporation agreement therefore seems essential when dealing with a leaving member's right to a share of the LLP assets.

19.2.11 Loan capital

As we have seen in the previous five chapters, partnerships cannot issue floating charges but companies can.

The company regime on fixed and floating charges applies to LLPs (see Chapter 18 at 18.9).

19.2.12 Winding up

The Insolvency Act 1986 applies to LLPs in the same way that it applies to companies. Reference should therefore be made to the early part of this chapter, where company winding up was considered.

19.2.13 Members' liability to contribute to the LLP's assets

An LLP is a corporate body and so, as a general principle, it alone will be liable for its debts. If an LLP becomes insolvent the members will lose money which they have invested in the LLP but will not have to pay its debts. However, there are circumstances in which members may have to contribute towards an LLP's debts.

Earlier in this chapter, at 19.1.4.1 and 19.1.4.2, we examined a director's liability for wrongful trading and fraudulent trading under ss.213 and 214 of the Insolvency Act 1986. Both of these sections apply equally to members of an LLP and can make them liable to contribute to the assets when an LLP is wound up. Members can also be made liable by ss.74 and 214A of the Insolvency Act. These two sections do not apply to companies.

Section 74 of the Insolvency Act provides that:

'When a limited liability partnership is wound up every present and past member of the limited liability partnership who has agreed with the other members or with the limited liability partnership that he will, in circumstances which have arisen, be liable to contribute to the assets of the limited liability partnership in the event that the limited liability partnership goes into liquidation is liable, to the extent that he has agreed, to contribute to its assets to any amount sufficient for payment of its debts and liabilities, and for the expenses of the winding up, and for the adjustment of the rights of the contributories amongst themselves.'

It is therefore envisaged that members of an LLP might agree to assume limited liability for the company's debts in the same way that members of a company limited by guarantee might assume limited liability. There are several points to note about s.74. First, a member can only become liable if he has agreed to assume liability. Such an agreement might be with the other members or with the LLP. Second, the liability arises only if the LLP goes into liquidation. Third, the member is liable only to the extent which he has agreed. Fourth, the liability arises only to the extent necessary to pay the LLP's debts, the winding up expenses and to adjust the rights of other members who have agreed to contribute. Fifth, a past member can be liable only if the obligation arising from such an agreement survived his ceasing to be a member of the LLP.

Section 214A of the Insolvency Act 1986 applies to a member of an LLP who, within two years of the commencement of winding up, withdrew LLP property while having reasonable grounds for believing either that the LLP could not pay its debts or would have been unable to pay its debts once the property had been withdrawn. The property withdrawn might be a share of profits, salary, interest on a loan, repayment of a loan or in any other form. On an application by the liquidator, the court can order that the member pay such a contribution to the LLP's assets as the court thinks proper. However, this amount must not be more than the amount of the property withdrawn over the two-year period. The court will make the order only if the member knew or ought to have known, at the time of the relevant withdrawal, that the LLP had no reasonable prospect of avoiding going into insolvent liquidation. When deciding that the member knew or ought to have known that the LLP could not avoid insolvent liquidation, the standards of general knowledge, skill and experience are those which the member actually had **and** those which could reasonably be expected of a person carrying out the functions which the member carried out. Like the test for s.124, then, the test is both objective and subjective. However, this dual standard is not stated to apply when considering whether the member knew that the company could not pay its debts. Section 124A applies to shadow members as well as to members. However, since the section requires the member to know both that the LLP could not pay its debts nor avoid insolvent liquidation, it would seem that it may not be applied much in practice. As we saw at 19.1.4.1, wrongful trading requires a knowledge that the LLP had no reasonable prospect of avoiding insolvent liquidation, but it does not require knowledge that the LLP was unable to pay its debts.

19.2.14 Disqualification of members

Regulation 4(2) applies the Company Directors Disqualification Act 1986 to both members and shadow members of LLPs. (The CDDA 1986 was considered in Chapter 17 at 17.1.3.) Regulation 4 states that references to a company in the CDDA 1986 shall include references to an LLP and references to a director or shadow director shall include reference to a member or a shadow member. Therefore, it seems that a person disqualified from being either a director of a company or a member of an LLP will be disqualified from being a director of any company or a member of any LLP. A person who acts as an LLP member in defiance of a disqualification order commits a crim-inal offence and can be liable without limit for the LLP's debts.

Test your understanding 19.2

1 How is an LLP formed?

2 With what words must the name of an LLP end?

3 How many designated members must an LLP have? What is the significance of being a designated member of an LLP?

4 Is a member of an LLP an agent of the LLP?

5 Is an LLP vicariously liable for the torts of a member of the LLP?

6 How are the rights and duties of one member of an LLP to another member fixed?

7 Is an LLP dissolved when a member leaves?

8 What protection is afforded to a minority member of an LLP?

9 In general, will a member of an LLP be liable to pay the debts of the LLP?

19.3 CHOICE OF LEGAL STATUS

People who intend to go into business together must choose what sort of business organisation they wish to form. Often they might have very clear views. They might be quite sure that they want to trade either as a company, as an LLP or as a partnership. In many other cases, however, the choice may not be so clear cut.

When a business is being set up there are often many matters requiring urgent attention. Perhaps staff must be employed, money borrowed or premises leased. It is easy to regard the decision as to the choice of legal status as less pressing. However, the choice of business status is a very important one. Prospective business people should consider the advantages and disadvantages of trading as a company, a partnership or an LLP in some detail. Even after the initial decision has been made, attention should be given as to whether or not it would be wise to change in the light of changing circumstances, such as rates of taxation.

Most of the matters which follow have been examined in greater detail in previous chapters. Here we are reconsidering such matters solely from the perspective of whether or not they make a company, an LLP or a partnership the most advantageous medium in which to trade.

19.3.1 Limited liability

In Chapter 15 we saw that partners are personally liable, without limit, for the acts of themselves and their fellow partners which were committed in the ordinary course of the firm's business. Cases such as *Mercantile Credit Co* v *Garrod* [1962] 3 All ER 1103 and *Blyth* v *Fladgate* [1891] 1 Ch 337 indicated how great a risk this can be. Although a partner can limit this liability by agreeing a limit on liability with his fellow partners, and informing the third party with whom the firm deals of this limitation, this rarely happens in practice. The partnership agreement may set out how losses are to be borne between the partners, but all partners are jointly and severally liable to outsiders for the firm's debts. If any of the partners are unable to pay their shares then the other partners assume unlimited liability to do so. In Chapter 16 we saw that a company is a legal entity in its own right, and that the members of a limited company have limited liability for the debts of the company. This is, perhaps, the principal advantage of trading as a company rather than as a partnership and it is an advantage also enjoyed by those who trade as an LLP.

However, the extent to which limited liability is a true advantage depends very much upon the circumstances of each individual business. If the business is to engage in a highly speculative line, and can find people willing to provide credit, then limited liability may indeed be a very real advantage. But, as we have seen, the corporate veil can be pierced in certain circumstances, and directors or LLP members who commit wrongful or fraudulent trading can be compelled to contribute towards the company's assets on dissolution. It is also true that many creditors, especially commercial lenders such as banks, are perfectly well aware of a shareholder's limited liability and will not therefore extend any credit to a small limited company or a small LLP unless the loan is personally guaranteed by the company directors or the members.

In business it is not usual to pay for goods and services in advance. If suppliers are eager to do business they will probably accept deferred payment. But suppliers who are aware of the limited liability of shareholders or LLP members might also be unwilling to supply goods or services without first getting personal guarantees. On the other hand, suppliers dealing with a partnership need not have any worries about getting paid as long as they know that some or all of the partners are financially sound.

Many small businesses do not borrow money. Instead, the owners of the business themselves contribute all the capital which the company needs. If such a business should fail, limited liability is not going to prevent the capital which they contributed from being lost.

Despite the matters outlined above, limited liability can be a real advantage to a member of a company or an LLP, especially where the member has considerable personal wealth. Those who spurn the advantage of limited liability should consider the following words of James LJ in *Re Agriculturist Cattle Insurance Co*, *Baird's Case* (1870) LR 5 Ch App 725:

> 'Ordinary partnerships are by the law assumed to be based on the mutual trust and confidence of each partner in the skill, knowledge and integrity of every other partner. As between the partners and the outside world (whatever may be their private arrangements between themselves), each partner is the unlimited agent of every other in every matter connected with the partnership business … A partner who may not have a farthing of capital left may take money or assets of the partnership to the value of millions, may bind the partnership by contracts to any amount … and may even – as has been shewn in many painful instances in this court – involve his innocent partners in unlimited amounts for frauds which he has carefully concealed from them.'

19.3.2 The right to manage

The rights of partners to manage the affairs of the partnership are usually set out in the partnership agreement. In Chapter 15 we saw that partners may be excluded from certain rights of management, but that if a partner is excluded from management without having agreed that he should be, then this is a reason for the court to dissolve the firm. The position regarding members on an LLP is essentially the same.

Shareholders, no matter how large their percentage holding, do not have a right to manage a company. The right to manage is vested in the board of directors, who are elected by a simple majority of the shareholders. A shareholder, or a group of shareholders, with over 50 per cent of the voting shares has the power to change the directors. But, until that power is exercised, the directors in place have the right to manage the company's affairs. *Irvine* v *Irvine* [2006] EWHC 1875 Ch, considered in the previous chapter at 18.8.5, shows how a shareholder can be excluded from management even if he or she owns over 49 per cent of the shares and remains a director. In that case the court found unfair prejudice and ordered that the minority shareholder's shares be bought, but at a significant discount. The company in question, although small, had over £4 million of assets. If the company had been worth much less then seeking a remedy might have incurred costs worth more than the value of the company.

A shareholder with less than 50 per cent of the voting shares can be outvoted on a resolution to appoint or remove a director. Therefore, minority shareholders are in the unfortunate position of having no right to manage the company's affairs, and no power to change this situation. A person going into business with one other person might therefore be very unwilling to form a company unless he was to own 50 per cent of the shares. Similar problems arise when there are several other shareholders. A minority shareholder can find himself in a very precarious position if the other shareholders have a closer relationship with each other than they have with him.

In Chapter 17 we saw that an entrenched article can give protection to a director with less than 50 per cent of the company's shares. Such an entrenched article could provide that a minority shareholder was to remain a director, and it could be made unalterable without the agreement of that minority shareholder. This would now be an effective way of ensuring that a minority shareholder remained a director. A less effective way would be by means of *Bushell* v *Faith* clause, considered in Chapter 17 at 17.1.2. However, when we considered *Bushell* v *Faith* we saw that such clauses can sometimes be circumvented by the majority shareholders.

In small companies the members of the company are often all directors. Often they receive a return by way of director's remuneration rather than as dividends. A member who is removed as a director might therefore not only lose the right to manage the company but might also be financially disadvantaged as well. There is some safeguard in that a court might make an order on the grounds of unfair prejudice or wind the company up in such a situation (as we saw in the previous chapter in *Ebrahimi* v *Westbourne Galleries* and in Lord Hoffmann's speech in *O'Neill* v *Phillips*). However, such a winding up is not readily ordered, and the costs of petitioning the court might well be more than the net assets of many small companies.

In most partnerships and LLPs the partnership or LLP agreement will set out how the profits are to be divided. (If no agreement deals with the matter then the profits will be divided equally.) Once an agreement has been made, it can be altered only by unanimous consent of the partners or LLP members, unless the agreement provides otherwise. Therefore, a partner or LLP member who negotiates an acceptable share of the profits upon joining the firm cannot later be deprived of this share. Nor can a partner or LLP member be dismissed unless there has been an express agreement providing for the dismissal. However, even if there is no express agreement, a partner or LLP member can be dismissed in effect if the other partners dissolve the business and then trade as a new firm or LLP. Upon dissolution, the partner or LLP member would be able to share in the assets of the dissolved firm, and the firm's goodwill might well be a very significant asset.

19.3.3 Withdrawal from the business

Partnerships are either entered into for a fixed period of time or they are partnerships at will (see Chapter 15 at 15.4.1.4). Any partner can withdraw from a partnership at will by giving notice. If a partner does withdraw by giving notice the firm will then be dissolved, and each partner will recover his share of the assets. If a partnership is for a fixed term, a partner wishing to withdraw must wait until the end of that term. Even so, an end is in sight.

It is possible for a partner to assign his share in the firm before the end of the term (unless the partnership deed prevents this). The assignee will receive the share of the profits to which the partner would have been entitled, but will have no right to manage the partnership's affairs. This lack of the right to manage might considerably reduce the value of the share which is assigned.

LLPs will not be dissolved merely because one of the members leaves. As a corporate body, the LLP will continue to exist. Furthermore, members of an LLP have the right to leave the LLP by agreement with the other members or by giving reasonable notice. However, as we have seen, a member leaving an LLP will not have a right to any share of the LLP's assets unless an agreement has given him such rights. Ordinarily, there should be such an agreement. But if there is not, a member might find it impractical to leave an LLP.

Members of companies may or may not have a right to transfer their shares to whoever they wish. It all depends on the articles, which might well say that the board of directors can refuse to register a transfer to persons of whom they disapprove. The articles of many private companies give the directors the power to refuse to register any transfer of shares at their absolute discretion, without giving reasons for their refusal. Although this right has to be exercised *bona fide* for the benefit of the company, if no reasons for the refusal are given it is very difficult to mount a legal challenge to the decision of the directors. So the members of many small companies, no matter how much they dislike the way the company is being run, have no effective right to transfer their shares. If unfair prejudice was proved, the court might order that their shares be purchased at a fair value. But, as we have seen, unfair prejudice is difficult and expensive to prove. Shareholders who are worried about this happening might do well to insist that they will not buy the shares unless a suitably entrenched article allowed them to be freely transferred. Whether or not the other members would agree to include such an article might well depend on how badly they wanted the particular shareholder's investment.

19.3.4 Borrowing power

If sole traders want to borrow money then they will need to provide security for the loan. There are several ways in which they might do this, but generally either they will need to find a guarantor (who agrees to repay the loan if the trader defaults) or they will need to mortgage their own property. Because of the current high level of business failures, banks are demanding very solid security for any money advanced.

Partners are in the same position as sole traders, except that since there are more of them they might well find it easier to find guarantors, or might have more property to mortgage. Creditors who are to be repaid out of partnership profits should make it very clear that they do not intend that this should make them partners.

Members of a company or an LLP can raise money in the same way as partners or sole traders. But companies and LLPs also have additional options.

First, companies can sell shares to people who wish to invest in the company but who have no desire to manage it. Shares in a private limited company cannot be offered to the general public but, subject to the articles, they can be offered to individuals. An investor who is convinced that the company will be a commercial success might be more than willing to pay for shares. Some small companies achieve spectacular success and eventually change into PLCs with enormous assets. If an investor had contributed capital into such a company when it was first formed for, say, 10 per cent of the shares he would have made an outstandingly good bargain. The converse, of course, is that very many small companies go to the wall, in which case the shares become worthless.

Second, companies and LLPs can raise capital by giving a floating charge over their assets. We saw in Chapter 18, at 18.9.2, that a floating charge gives a class or all of the company's assets as security for a loan, while still maintaining the right to use and dispose of those assets. (Assets of the class which are acquired in the future become subject to the charge.) However, many lenders take a particularly jaundiced view of the value of a company's or an LLP's assets. They value them on the basis that everything which could possibly reduce their value will in fact do so. This can make it difficult for companies or LLPs without substantial assets to raise much money by issuing floating charges. Partnership property cannot belong to the partnership because a partnership has no separate legal existence of its own. It therefore belongs to the partners jointly (see Chapter 15 at 15.6). A partnership is not allowed to offer a floating charge over partnership property. The partners can of course mortgage the property, but this will limit the use of the property.

19.3.5 Ease of formation

A business which wants to trade immediately will have to do so as a partnership rather than as a company or an LLP.

A partnership can be created without any formalities. As soon as two people carry on a business in common with a view of profit they will be a partnership, whether they realise this or not.

It is, however, quite likely that partners will want to have a deed of partnership drawn up by a lawyer.

If this is the case, then this is bound to involve some expense and delay. Indeed, the expense of this can be considerably greater than the expense of buying an 'off-the-shelf' company.

Both companies and LLPs are formed by registration, which involves sending documents to the Registrar of Companies and waiting for him to register the company. However, it is possible to buy an 'off-the-shelf' company, that is to say a company which has been formed with the sole purpose of selling it to people who wish to own a company but who do not want to bother with forming one themselves. If the purchasers of the off-the-shelf company wanted to change the articles they would still have to wait for the Registrar to register the alterations. An off-the-shelf company generally costs between £75 and £125.

It is not at all difficult to create a company or an LLP. A fee of £20 is charged to register a company or an LLP. The business will usually be registered within one week. If a fee of £50 is paid, a company will be registered within 24 hours. As regards both the purchase of an off-the-shelf company and the formation of a company it is important to get appropriate articles of association. Advice from an expert in the field, which is bound to incur cost, would be advisable. The same considerations apply when drawing up an LLP agreement. It would also be advisable for those entering a partnership to have an expert draw up a partnership agreement. However, there is the advantage that in the absence of any agreement the Partnership Act provides a default framework which is reasonably suitable for many firms. LLPs also have a statutory framework of default provisions. In the past, small private companies have all too often adopted Table A articles in their entirety, without any regard to their suitability. The new Model Articles for Private Companies, which would now apply to the extent that they are not excluded, are likely to be far more suitable for most small private companies.

19.3.6 Formalities

Partners do not need to adhere to any formalities. There is no need for them to hold meetings. Nor, since the 2006 Act came into force, do private companies need to hold any meetings of members. However, if meetings are held then notice of meetings and of resolutions to be proposed must be given to members, and minutes of meetings must be kept. This can be done electronically. An annual return must be sent to the Registrar of Companies along with a fee, which is currently £30, or £15 if done electronically. LLPs do not have to hold formal meetings of members, but do submit an annual return.

The recent trend is to deregulate companies. The formalities with which they must comply have been greatly reduced in recent years. As a consequence, the advantage which partnerships enjoy by virtue of not having to comply with any formalities is nowadays less marked. Companies House issue excellent leaflets, written in very plain English, which set out the steps which company officers must take. Most people who are competent to run any kind of successful business ought to be able to follow these directions without seeking professional advice.

Small companies and small LLPs will be exempt from having to have their accounts audited if their annual turnover is not more than £1 million and their total assets are not worth more than £1.4 million. However, if a company or an LLP is not entitled to take advantage of this exemption then two accountants will be needed each year, one to draw up the accounts and the other to audit them. A partnership has no duty to have its accounts audited. However, partnerships, like all companies and LLPs, will need to produce accounts which are sufficient to satisfy Revenue and Customs.

19.3.7 Publicity

The affairs of a partnership are completely private. Like anyone else, the partners will, of course, need to declare their earnings to Revenue and Customs. Beyond this, there is no need to reveal details of the firm to anyone.

The affairs of companies and LLPs are much more public. Any member of the public will be able to inspect the annual return, the registered accounts, registers held by the Registrar, and most of the registers which the company is required to keep at its registered office.

The accounts are likely to represent the publicly available information which the company members and directors and LLP members would least like to reveal. However, small companies and small LLPs can deliver abbreviated accounts. These accounts would not reveal the remuneration of the directors or LLP members or the amount of dividend recommended. Nor would they need to include a profit and loss account. An abbreviated balance sheet can be delivered instead. These abbreviated accounts would therefore give only very limited information to outsiders and competitors.

A company or an LLP is regarded as small if it meets two out of the following three requirements:

(i) Its annual turnover is £5.6 million or less.

(ii) Its total assets are £2.8 million or less.

(iii) It has 50 or fewer employees.

Medium-sized companies and LLPs can deliver modified accounts, which conceal information about the breakdown of profit, loss and turnover. A company or LLP is regarded as medium-sized if it meets two of the three following requirements:

(i) Its annual turnover is £22.8 million or less.

(ii) Its total assets are £11.4 million or less.

(iii) It has 250 or fewer employees.

As can be seen, these qualifications are fairly generous. A business which was too large to start trading as a small company or a small LLP might not wish to trade as a partnership. Unlimited companies do not need to deliver any accounts to the Registrar.

19.3.8 **Tax position**

Individuals and companies are not taxed in the same way. Individuals pay Income Tax and National Insurance, companies pay Corporation Tax.

For tax purposes partners, LLP members and sole traders are all treated as individuals, and Income Tax is payable on all of the profits which they make. Even profits which are left in the business are taxed.

However, individuals are given personal allowances for Income Tax purposes. In the tax year April 2012 to April 2013, the single person's allowance is currently £8 105. This means that on the first £8 105 which a single person earns he pays no Income Tax.

Once an individual exceeds his allowance he pays tax at varying rates. A single person pays the basic rate of 20 per cent on the first £34 370 in excess of his allowance and then 40 per cent on anything above this.

National Insurance contributions must also be paid. The self-employed pay a flat rate of £2.50 a week, as long as profits exceed £5 315. A further 9 per cent is payable on profits between £5 315 and £42 475, with 1 per cent payable on profits over £42 475.

It is therefore possible that a self-employed person could be paying a tax rate of 49 per cent on some of his business profits.

Companies, too, are taxed on profits made, in the form of Corporation Tax. Profits of under £300 000 are taxed at 20 per cent. Profits between £300 000 and £1.5 million are taxed on a sliding scale from 20 per cent to 26 per cent. Profits above £1.5 million are taxed at 26 per cent.

Money left in the company is taxed at these rates as Corporation Tax. The owners of the company can withdraw money by paying themselves director's salaries. Corporation Tax would not be paid on such money withdrawn. (Removing the money from the company would reduce the company's profit.) However, self-employed people who wish to trade as a company should bear in mind that if a person arranges to be paid income by a company then they will be an employee of the company. The company will need to pay the employer's National Insurance contribution (13.8 per cent for 2011/12) and the employee's contribution (12 per cent on earnings between £5 304 and £42 484 and 2 per cent on earnings above this amount). This combined rate of 25.8 per cent is well in excess of the rate paid by the self-employed. In addition, Income Tax must be paid by the person receiving the income.

Companies do not receive personal allowances. However, it can be seen that the rates of Corporation Tax can be considerably lower than the rates of tax paid by individuals.

It would therefore seem advantageous for many business people to form a company. They could then pay themselves what they needed to live on as a salary, and leave the rest in the company to grow. However, this is complicated by Capital Gains Tax, which is payable when a person sells assets which have grown in value since he acquired them. If money is left in the company then the value of the company, and therefore the value of the shares, will grow. Ultimately, the owners must sell their shares in order to take the money.

Capital Gains Tax is charged at a flat rate of 18 per cent. So money left in the company is taxed twice (first, it is taxed as company profit, then when the shares are sold it is taxed as a capital gain). Some relief is provided in that individuals are given an annual Capital Gains allowance of £10 600 (for 2011/12) a year.

The rate of Capital Gains Tax is considerably below the combined rates of Income Tax and National Insurance. However, using this method of reducing tax has several disadvantages. First, it means dissolving the company to realise the capital gain. Second, it means that the profits generated by the company cannot be touched until the company is dissolved. Third, it means that as no National Insurance is paid the benefits of having paid National Insurance cannot be claimed.

Before the 2004 Budget there were definite tax advantages attached to trading as a company, and taking money in the form of a dividend, rather than trading as a self-employed person. Since 2004 the tax advantages of trading as a company have been very much reduced. In the light of the changes which were made many companies which were formed to reduce tax have been dissolved. The extra administration involved in running a company does not justify the very marginal tax benefits.

19.3.9 Perpetual succession

Companies continue in existence until they are wound up. The death of a shareholder, or even the death of all the shareholders, will not end the company. In the same way, LLPs stay in existence until they are wound up.

By contrast, the death of a partner will end the partnership. However, the partnership deed might well provide that the surviving partners should carry the business on (in which case they must pay an appropriate amount to the estate of the deceased partner). If the surviving partners do carry the business on, then the dissolution of the partnership will only amount to a technical dissolution.

19.3.10 Sole traders

By definition, a sole trader is in business on his own. However, sole traders should consider the benefits of forming a company. Now that it is possible to have a company with a single shareholder, who can also be the only director, a sole trader can incorporate his business and, in effect, still be in business on his own. Since the 2006 Act came into force, private companies do not need to have a company secretary. So the sole shareholder can also be the sole director. However, a sole director/member must recognise that he is no longer a sole trader and must adhere to certain formalities and procedures.

In this chapter we have considered whether groups of people forming a business should trade as companies or partnerships. Sole traders should consider the same advantages and disadvantages of incorporation.

Key points

Winding up and insolvency

■ A court can order the winding up of a company on seven grounds, if petitioned to do so. The two most important grounds are that the company cannot pay its debts or that the court considers it just and equitable to wind the company up.

■ The petition may be presented to the court by the company itself, the directors, a creditor of the company or a member of the company. In limited circumstances, the Secretary of State for Business, Innovation and Skills or the Official Receiver may present the petition.

■ If a winding up order is made by the court, the company cannot dispose of its property without a court order; actions in debt against the company are stopped; the directors' powers are taken over by the liquidator; floating charges crystallise; and the company's employees are dismissed. The liquidator may re-employ the employees and also carry on the company business, but only in order to effect the most beneficial winding up.

■ A members' voluntarily liquidation is initiated by a special resolution of the company. The directors must be able to file a declaration of solvency. The members appoint the liquidator.

■ A creditors' voluntary liquidation is initiated by a special resolution. The directors do not file a declaration of solvency. The creditors appoint the liquidator.

■ As from the time when the resolution to wind up is passed, the company must cease trading except as may be required for a beneficial winding up; shares cannot be transferred without the liquidator's consent; the company employees are dismissed. The directors' powers are limited and cease when the liquidator is appointed.

■ After liquidation the various classes of creditors are paid. Each class is paid in full before the lower-ranking classes are paid at all. (However, as regards floating charges created on or after 15 September 2003, some of the company's assets may be earmarked for distribution to the unsecured creditors.)

→

If there are insufficient assets to pay a class in full, each member of the class is paid the same percentage of what he is owed.

■ First, the liquidator's remuneration and the costs and expenses of winding up are paid. Then the preferential creditors; then (if appropriate) a top-sliced fund goes to the unsecured creditors; then holders of floating charges are paid what they are owed; then unsecured creditors are paid; finally, any surplus is distributed to members of the company.

■ A director or shadow director can be liable for wrongful trading if he knew that the company could not avoid going into insolvent liquidation, and he did not take all reasonable steps to minimise the potential loss to the company's creditors.

■ After a company has gone into liquidation the liquidator may apply for a court order to avoid transactions entered into at an undervalue or preferences given to creditors.

■ A floating charge will be invalid, to the extent that the company did not receive value in return for creating it, if it was created within 12 months of winding up proceedings, unless the company was solvent after creating the charge.

■ A floating charge created in favour of a connected person within two years of the commencement of winding up proceedings will be invalid, to the extent that the company did not receive value in return for creating it, whether or not the company was solvent at the time the charge was created.

■ When a company is in administration, the administrator has three hierarchical objectives: first, to rescue the company as a going concern (the primary purpose); second, to achieve a better result for the company's creditors than would be achieved if the company was wound up; third, to sell property to pay to the company's secured or preferential creditors.

■ Whilst it is in administration, a petition to wind a company up will be dismissed or suspended.

■ Floating charge holders whose charges were created before 15 September 2003 can appoint an administrative receiver. (If created after this date they can only appoint an administrator.)

■ An administrative receiver realises the charged property so that the floating charge holders can be paid. An administrator also has the power to do this, but it is not his primary purpose.

LLPs

■ Two or more people can trade together as an LLP.

■ An LLP is a corporate body which is created by registration with the Registrar of Companies.

■ The members of an LLP must carry on a lawful business with a view to profit.

■ The name of an LLP must end with the words 'limited liability partnership' or 'llp' or 'LLP' (or their Welsh equivalents). Other than this, the rules relating to the names of LLPs are identical to the rules relating to the names of companies.

■ Every LLP must have at least two designated members. These designated members have certain specified duties, such as signing the LLP's accounts.

■ Every member of an LLP is the agent of the LLP and can therefore make contracts which will bind the LLP.

■ The relationship between one member of an LLP and another member, and between members and the LLP itself, is governed by agreement between the members. In the absence of such agreement, ten default provisions apply.

■ No majority of members can expel any member unless a power to do so has been conferred by express agreement between the members.

■ A member of an LLP can leave by agreement with the other members or by giving the other members reasonable notice. An LLP will not be dissolved when a member leaves.

■ A member may be able to petition the court for a winding up order, under s.122 of the Insolvency Act 1986, on the grounds that this is just and equitable.

■ The provisions of s.994 Companies Act 2006 apply to LLPs, unless the members unanimously agree in writing that they should not.

■ LLPs can issue fixed and floating charges in the same way as companies.

■ In general, members of an LLP will not have any liability to pay the debts of the LLP.

■ Members of an LLP can be liable to pay the debts of an LLP if they have agreed with the other members or with the LLP that they will. They can also be liable for wrongful trading or fraudulent trading, as directors of companies can.

■ Members of an LLP can be liable to make a contribution to the debts of the LLP if they withdrew LLP property within two years of the LLP's insolvency,

→

while having reasonable grounds for believing that the LLP would not be able to pay its debts and should have known that the LLP could not avoid insolvent liquidation.

■ LLP members can be disqualified from becoming LLP members or company directors.

Choice of legal status

■ The members of limited companies, and of LLPs, have limited liability for the debts of the business. Members of ordinary partnerships enjoy no such limited liability.

■ All partners and all LLP members generally have a right to manage the firm or the LLP. The board of directors act as the managers of a company.

■ Depending upon the articles, it can be difficult to withdraw from a company.

■ Companies and LLPs can borrow by giving a floating charge over the company's assets. Companies, but not LLPs, can also raise money by selling shares to investors who do not want to manage the business.

■ Companies are taxed differently from partners, LLP members and sole traders.

Summary questions

1 Benjamin, a building contractor, is owed £2 000 by Acme Ltd. When Benjamin phoned asking for payment, Acme acknowledged the debt and sent him a cheque. Unfortunately, the cheque was dishonoured. A month later, after several promises to pay, Acme sent another cheque. This too was dishonoured. Benjamin discovers that Acme owes money to several other traders. Last week the managing director of Acme wrote to Benjamin, explaining that the Government was due to pay the company £30 000 in 12 weeks' time. The letter promised that as soon as the money was received all of the company's debts would be paid with interest. Advise Benjamin as to:

a The steps he should take if he wants to see the company wound up.

b Whether or not the court would have to order liquidation.

2 On 1 November 2003, following a petition from a creditor, the court ordered that Ace Ltd be wound up. The day before the court order was made, the managing director sold the company car in order to pay his own salary. Ace Ltd's workforce are due to finish a large Government contract on the 5 November. This contract will bring in £20 000. This is not enough money to clear Ace's debts, but it will be a big help. In August the managing director's wife was granted a floating charge to secure a loan of £5 000 which she had made to the company three years earlier. At the same time the company also sold the company's business premises to the managing director's wife for about half of its market value.

Advise the creditors as to:

a Whether the sale of the company car is valid.

b Whether Ace Ltd's workers are still employed.

c Whether Ace Ltd's business can be carried on in order to finish the Government contract.

d Who would have the power to make decisions about re-employing the workers and finishing the contract.

e The legal position as regards the floating charge and the sale of the company's business premises.

3 BrokeCo Ltd was wound up on 2 June 2004. The company has various creditors as follows:

a Arthur is owed £10 000 in respect of goods supplied to BrokeCo and subsequently sold on by BrokeCo.

b Seven employees are each owed four weeks' pay (total £1 000 per employee) and £200 accrued holiday pay.

c The Revenue is owed last month's PAYE bill of £4 000.

d Billy has a floating charge over all of the company's assets, registered two years ago, to secure a debt which currently stands at £5 000.

e The members of the company have not been paid the dividend declared in the previous year (total dividend is £600).

In what order will these creditors be paid? How much will each creditor be paid if, after the costs of winding up, the assets raised by the sale of the company's assets, and available for distribution to creditors and members, amounts to: (a) £10 000; (b) £23 000; (c) £30 000?

4 Three years ago Sarah finished a college course in Health and Beauty Therapy. After a year working in a salon she spent three months in the United States. On a trip to California, Sarah was extremely impressed by some of the alternative beauty treatments available there.

Sarah now wants to market some of the Californian ideas in England, and is worried that if she waits too long others will beat her to it.

Sarah's grandfather, Stanley, has recently retired from the board of a multinational company. He has a variety of interests but, seeing Sarah as a 'chip off the old block', he is prepared to invest in her proposed business and help her in the running of it.

Sarah is very fond of her grandfather but thinks that he is too cautious, not realising that in the modern age opportunities must be seized immediately, before it becomes too late. Stanley is very proud of Sarah but feels that, expert though she might be in the field of beauty therapy, she has a great deal to learn as far as business goes.

Stanley has agreed to invest £25 000 in the business and put in three or four hours' work a week. Sarah is putting in her savings of £3 000 and will devote all of her time to the business.

a Do you think that Stanley would prefer that the business was a company, an LLP or a partnership?

b Which do you think Sarah would prefer?

c As an objective outsider, which type of business organisation do you think they should become?

5 In what ways is an LLP more similar to a limited company than to an ordinary partnership?

6 Steve, Trevor and Ursula are members of an LLP which offers financial advice to small businesses. At the outset each member contributed £30 000 capital to the business. Trevor and Ursula are the designated members. Last year, without any authority from his fellow members, Steve made a contract with a local authority, on behalf of the LLP, to offer financial advice to members of the public for £1 an hour. (Steve thought that this would lead to a good deal of profitable business.) Trevor and Ursula do not regard the LLP as bound by this contract. Steve now wishes to leave the LLP. Trevor and Ursula are happy to see Steve leave, but are not prepared to allow him to take any capital with him. Advise the parties of their legal positions.

Multiple choice questions

1 In which one of the following circumstances would the company be regarded as unable to pay its debts, under s.123 of the Insolvency Act?

a The company has owed Arthur £300 for six months. It has refused to pay, despite Arthur having left a written request for payment at the company's registered office three months ago.

b The company has owed Bill £2 000 for two weeks. It has refused to pay, despite Bill having left a written request for payment at the company's registered office two weeks ago.

c The company owes Charlene £1 000. It has refused to pay, despite Charlene having left a written request for payment at the company's registered office four weeks ago.

d The company owes Derek £4 000. He has phoned once a week, for the past six weeks, demanding payment. Each time the company agreed to pay immediately but, as yet, it has not paid.

2 Which one of the following is unable to petition the court to compulsorily wind up a company which is not defunct?

a The Registrar of Companies.

b A member of the company whose shares are fully paid up.

c The company itself.

d The directors of the company.

3 Caput Ltd has gone into liquidation. The assets have been realised and have generated £20 000. Of this amount, £6 000 came from the sale of the company car over which Charlene had a fixed charge. The following debts and liabilities exist:

i Caput owes Charlene £5 000 (secured by the fixed charge).

ii The three directors are each owed £2 000 a month salary for the past three months.

iii Suppliers of components are owed £20 000.

iv Dividends amounting to £8 000 are owed to shareholders. These dividends were declared three months ago, but have not yet been paid.

v £5 000 is owed to David, a director of Caput, who loaned the money to the company so that the workforce could be paid last month's wages (each worker was owed and paid £750).

vi Three months' VAT, amounting to £1 000, is owed to the Revenue.

vii Costs of winding up, which amount to £1 500.

Which of the creditors will receive payment in full, and which will receive part payment of their debts?

a Charlene, David and the costs of winding up would be paid in full. The supplier of the components, the Revenue and the directors would receive part payment.

b The Revenue, Charlene, the directors, David and the costs of winding up would be paid in full. All the other creditors would receive part payment.

c David and the costs of winding up would be paid in full. Charlene, the directors, and the suppliers of the components would receive part payment.

d The Revenue, David and the costs of winding up would be paid in full. All the other creditors would receive part payment.

4 Jade and Rachel are in partnership as interior designers, sharing profits equally. Jade also owns all of the shares in a mail order company. Which one of the following statements is not true?

a Jade and Rachel will be liable to pay Income Tax on profits which they leave in the partnership.

b If Jade's company pays her a salary, then Jade will have to pay Income Tax on this money. In addition, both Jade and the company will have to pay National Insurance contributions on the salary paid.

c If the assets of the company increase in value then Jade must pay Income Tax on this increase in value.

d If the company makes a profit then the company will have to pay Corporation Tax on this profit. In addition, Jade may become liable to pay Capital Gains Tax when she sells her shares in the company and realises the profit.

5 Consider the following statements. Which of the statements are true?

i As an LLP is a corporate body, it is possible to have a single member LLP.

ii Every LLP must have at least two designated members.

iii Every member of an LLP is the agent of the LLP.

iv Neither an incorporation document, nor an LLP agreement, can confer rights on a third party to enforce a term of the document or agreement.

v An agreement made before the incorporation of an LLP, between the subscribers to the incorporation document, can impose obligations on the LLP to take effect at any time after its incorporation.

a All of the statements.

b All of the statements except i.

c All of the statements except iv.

d Only statements ii and iii.

e None of the statements.

6 Consider the following statements. Which one of the statements is not true?

a When acting as agents of an LLP the members will owe a fiduciary duty to the LLP.

b Unless the members have agreed to the contrary, no member of an LLP is entitled to any remuneration for acting in the business or management of the LLP.

c No majority can expel any member unless a power to do so has been conferred by express agreement between the members.

d If a member of an LLP assigns his share of the LLP to an assignee, the assignee has the right to take part in the management of the LLP, unless there has been an agreement to the contrary.

e The right contained in s.994(1) of the Companies Act 2006 applies to LLPs, unless the members of the LLP have unanimously agreed in writing to exclude the right.

TASK 19

Three friends of yours, who work as builders, are owed money by several companies for which they have worked. One of these companies has now been wound up. Your friends have asked you to draft a report, briefly dealing with the following matters.

a The grounds upon which a company may be compulsorily wound up, and the persons entitled to petition for such a winding up.

b How company members can voluntarily wind the company up.

c The order in which creditors of liquidated companies are paid by the liquidator.

d How the law attempts to ensure that creditors of insolvent companies are not defrauded.

e The main advantages and disadvantages which attach to trading as a company, an LLP or partnership.

mylawchamber *premium*

Visit **www.mylawchamber.co.uk/macintyre** to access study support resources including interactive multiple choice questions, weblinks, glossary, glossary flashcards, legal newsfeed, answers to questions in this chapter, legal updates and an overview of this chapter all linked to the **Pearson eText** version of *Business Law* which you can **search**, **highlight** and **personalise** with your **own notes** and **bookmarks**.

Employment 1 – duties of employer and employee · dismissal · redundancy

Introduction

This chapter considers the following matters:

Courts and tribunals

Before beginning our study of employment law it is necessary to understand the role of the two tribunals which have jurisdiction to hear employment cases and appeals. Almost all claims relating to employment begin in an employment tribunal (previously known as industrial tribunals). In such a tribunal a lawyer who has been qualified for at least seven years sits as chairman, along with two lay members. These lay members generally represent the two 'sides' of industry, one having been nominated by an employers' association whilst the other was nominated by a trade union. Some claims, such as those for breach of a contract, are generally heard by the chairman alone. An employment tribunal has the power to hear any claim based on an employment statute. It also has the power to hear any common law case for breach of a contract of employment, or for breach of most other contracts connected with employment, where the damages claimed are not more than £25 000. (When damages in excess of £25 000 are claimed for breach of a contract of employment the case begins in the ordinary civil courts.) The decision of the tribunal is by a majority. It is possible, although very unusual, for the two lay members to outvote the chairman. Legal aid is not available for a case heard by an employment tribunal. It is not essential to have legal representation and the proceedings are relatively informal. A claim must generally be brought within three months of the effective date of termination of the contract of employment or, if there is no such date, within three months of the last day on which the employee worked. If the claim is for personal injury then it is heard by the ordinary civil courts, rather than by the employment tribunal.

Appeals from an employment tribunal are heard by the Employment Appeal Tribunal (the EAT). This is a wholly appellate court, no cases begin here. The president of the EAT will either be a High Court judge or a Court of Appeal judge. The president sits either alone or with two lay members who are qualified in employment matters. Appeals from cases which were heard by the chairman alone in the employment tribunal are generally heard by the president of the EAT sitting alone. Legal aid is available for appeals heard by the EAT, subject to the usual financial limitations. The Court of Appeal hears appeals from the Employment Appeal Tribunal, but permission to make the appeal must be given by either the EAT or the Court of Appeal. An appeal can be made from the Court of Appeal to the Supreme Court, if either the Court of Appeal or the Supreme Court grants permission. The decisions of an employment tribunal are not binding upon any other courts.

The decisions of the Employment Appeal Tribunal are binding upon employment tribunals, but not upon later sittings of the Employment Appeal Tribunal. They are therefore similar in status to decisions of the High Court. The binding force of decisions of the Court of Appeal and Supreme Court was considered in Chapter 1 at 1.3.2.1.

Much of employment law has an element of EU law, which is supreme over national law (see Chapter 1 at 1.4.4). Any national court may refer a case which involves a matter of EU law to the European Court of Justice (the ECJ). The ECJ gives an opinion and the case then returns to the UK court for this opinion to be applied to the facts of the case. In addition, a Member State can be taken to the European Court for failure to live up to its EU obligations by either the European Commission or a different Member State.

The ECJ does not use a system of precedent, so its own decisions are not binding upon future sittings of the ECJ. However, the decisions of the ECJ are binding upon all of the UK courts, whether the decision in question concerned a UK case or a case from a different Member State. In Chapter 1 at 1.4.3.1 we examined the way in which a case could be sufficiently concerned with EU law for it to be referred to the ECJ. All of the ways which we set out are relevant in employment law. Many cases are referred to the ECJ to give an opinion on an article of a treaty, particularly upon Article 157 of the Treaty on the Functioning of the European Union which provides that men and women should receive equal pay for doing equal work. Many more cases concern UK legislation which was passed in order to give effect to a Directive of the EU. Although UK legislation gives effect to Article 157, the ECJ retains the power to give an opinion as to the interpretation of the Article. Similarly, the ECJ has the power to give opinions on the interpretation of Directives even after the UK has implemented these by legislation.

Codes of practice

Although not sources of law, several codes of practice may be used in evidence in an employment case. These Codes do not have legal force, but failure to observe them will weigh heavily against an employer's argument that he behaved reasonably. Codes have been drawn up by ACAS, the Commission for Racial Equality and Human Rights, the Secretary of State for Employment and the Equal Opportunities Commission.

ACAS conciliation

Before a case is heard by an employment tribunal a conciliation officer from the Advisory, Conciliation and Arbitration Service (ACAS) will try to get the parties to reach an agreement without taking the case further. This procedure has a high success rate and most cases are settled at this stage. If they make an agreement to settle, both employer and employee are bound by it. Matters revealed to the ACAS officer cannot be admitted in evidence without the permission of the party who communicated them. Agreements by which an employee opts out of his statutory rights which were reached otherwise than through ACAS conciliation are only binding upon the employee if they were in writing and the employee received independent legal advice. If conciliation is not reached either party may apply to the employment tribunal for a pre-hearing assessment. This assessment considers the likely outcome of proceedings and can warn an employee with a frivolous or vexatious complaint that costs may be awarded against him.

ACAS has several functions other than conciliation in individual cases. It can give advice to employers, workers or trade unions on matters likely to affect industrial relations. This advice can be given when requested, or ACAS can give it without having been requested to do so. ACAS has a similar role to conciliate when a trade dispute arises. ACAS issues Codes of Practice, as already mentioned. It can in some circumstances refer a trade dispute to arbitration, after all other procedures have been exhausted. ACAS also conducts enquiries into industrial relations. These enquiries may either be of a general nature or they may be into industrial relations within one industry or one undertaking.

20.1 EMPLOYEES CONTRASTED WITH INDEPENDENT CONTRACTORS

People employed under a contract of employment, or a 'contract of service' as such a contract is commonly known, are employees. People who contract to provide services for another otherwise than under a contract of employment are known as independent contractors.

The distinction between employees and independent contractors is an important one for several reasons. First, various terms which are implied into contracts of employment are not implied into contracts under which services are supplied by independent contractors. Second, employers can be vicariously liable for torts committed by employees during the course of their employment, but are not generally liable for the torts of independent contractors who provide a service for them. (Vicarious liability is examined in Chapter 13 at 13.8.) Third, many statutes confer employment protection rights only upon employees. (As we examine the various statutes, we shall see that those which outlaw discrimination also confer protection on independent contractors who personally provide a service.)

Over the years the courts have evolved several tests to distinguish employees and independent contractors. One of the first tests, the control test, held that employees could not only be told what to do but they could also be told how to do it. Independent contractors could be told what purposes to achieve, but it was up to the contractors to use whatever method they thought fit to achieve these purposes. This test did not work particularly well with some skilled employees and so further tests evolved.

In *Stevenson, Jordan and Harrison Ltd* v *MacDonald and Evans* [1952] 1 TLR 101 Denning LJ put forward an integration test.

'One feature which seems to run through the cases is that, under a contract of service [contract of employment], a man is employed as a part of the business and his work is done as an integral part of the business; whereas under a contract for services [contract made by an independent contractor] his work, although done for the business, is not integrated into it but only accessory to it.'

This test worked better than the control test for some skilled employees, such as surgeons. Their employers do not control the way surgeons act when operating upon patients, although they can insist that certain procedures are followed. However, the work of surgeons is done as an integral part of the hospitals in which they work. The work of a roofer, paid £500 to fix the hospital roof, is not done as an integral part of the hospital's business but is only accessory to it. Denning LJ made the point more simply when he said that employees were 'part and parcel of the organisation', whereas independent contractors were not.

Neither the control test nor the integration test seemed to produce entirely satisfactory results, and in *Ready Mixed Concrete (South East) Ltd* v *MPNI* [1968] 2 QB 497 Mackenna J formulated the economic reality test, which held that a worker would be an employee only if three conditions are satisfied. First, the worker must agree to provide his own work and skill in return for a wage or other payment. Second, the worker must agree, expressly or impliedly, that he will be under the control of the person paying for his work. Third, the rest of the terms of the contract must be consistent with a contract of employment. (This would include matters such as who paid the worker's tax, what type of National Insurance contributions were paid and who provided equipment.)

In *Lee Ting Sang* v *Chung Chi-Keung* [1990] 1 RLR 236 the Privy Council held that there is no single test for deciding whether or not a person is working as an employee or as an independent contractor. The fundamental question being, 'Is the person who has engaged himself to perform these services performing them as a person in business on his own account?' This test was first formulated by Cooke J in *Market Investigations* v *Minister of Social Security* [1969] 2 QB 173 and in *Lee v Chung* the Privy Council strongly approved Cooke J's reasoning as to how to answer the question. Cooke J said:

'No exhaustive list has been compiled and perhaps no exhaustive list can be compiled of the considerations which are relevant in determining that question, nor can strict rules be laid down as to the relative weight which the various considerations should carry in particular cases. The most that can be said is that control will no doubt always have to be considered, although it can no longer be regarded as the sole determining factor; and that factors which may be of importance are such matters as whether the man performing the services provides his own equipment, whether he hires his own helpers, what degree of financial risk he takes, what degree of responsibility for investment and management he has, and whether and how far he has an opportunity of profiting from sound management in the performance of his task.'

In *Lee* v *Chung* the Privy Council also stated that the question as to whether or not a person provided services as an employee was a question of fact. (In exceptional cases where the relationship depended solely upon the true construction of a written document it might be a question of law.) As it was a question of fact it was a matter to be decided by the trial court. An appellate court would only interfere with the finding of the trial court if it took 'a view of the facts which could not reasonably be entertained'. (In the case, the Privy Council concluded that the trial court had made such an error and reversed the decision of the trial court.) In *Hall v Lorimer* [1994] IRLR 171 the Court of Appeal warned against the use of 'mechanical tests', indicating that each case should be decided on its own particular facts.

In *Secretary of State for BERR v Neufeld* [2009] EWCA Civ 280, [2009] 3 All ER 790 the Court of Appeal held that there was no reason why a person who was both a director of a company and a major shareholder in it could not also be an employee of the company. Difficult questions arise in respect of agency workers and casual workers. The circumstances in which such workers will be employees are far from being settled, but one important factor is the 'mutuality of obligation' test. If the employer has no duty to provide work, and the worker has no duty to accept work, then it is likely that there will be no contract of employment while the workers are not actually at work. In the following case the House of Lords had to consider whether or not the relationship between casual workers and National Power, for whom they worked as guides, was regulated by a contract of employment when the workers were not working. Making it plain that they were not considering whether or not the workers were employees when actually working as guides, the House of Lords held that the guides were not governed by a contract of employment when they were not working.

Carmichael v National Power
[1999] 4 All ER 897 (House of Lords)

L and C worked as casual guides at a power station. By 1995 they worked up to 25 hours a week, having increased from about 3.75 hours in 1990, and were paid a flat rate for hours worked. Both women claimed to be employees and therefore to be entitled to written particulars of the terms of their employment. (See below at 20.2.1.1.) They claimed that an exchange of correspondence between the parties created a contract of employment. Some of this correspondence referred to guides as being employed. When accepting the work both women signed a pre-typed letter which said, 'I am pleased to accept your offer of employment as a Station Guide on a casual as required basis.' They were both trained, and both worked when they were available and chose to work. When they did work they were on the payroll for PAYE purposes.

Held. There was no contract between the claimants and the defendants. The defendants had no obligation to provide work and the claimants had no duty to accept it. This outcome could be deduced from the following matters: the documents exchanged between the parties did not set out when, how and with what frequency work would be offered; there were no provisions relating to notice or termination; the guides were not part of the full-time employees' sickness, holiday or pension schemes; the usual grievance and disciplinary procedures did not apply; C had not been available for work on 17 occasions and L had not been available on eight occasions, and no question of disciplining them had arisen; when taking the job C had said that the part time/casual arrangement would suit her circumstances ideally. Taking all this into account, the case 'foundered on the rock of absence of mutuality'. All the circumstances indicated that the parties did not intend there to be a contractual relationship while the women were not actually working as guides.

The status of agency workers has continued to cause difficulty. In *Johnson Underwood v Montgomery* [2001] EWCA Civ 318 a telephonist worked for a local firm, through an employment agency which paid her wages, for two and a half years. When she was removed from the job with the local firm she claimed unfair dismissal against both the local firm and the employment agency. Neither claim succeeded as she was not an employee of the agency or of the local firm. The Court of Appeal thought that she was not an independent contractor either, but that she had a special type of contract somewhere between being an employee and an independent contractor.

Dacas v Brook Street Bureau (UK) Ltd
[2004] EWCA Civ 217, [2004] IRLR 190 (Court of Appeal)

Mrs Dacas was registered with the defendants' employment agency and they sent her to a Wandsworth Council residential care home, where she worked as a cleaner for six years. Wandsworth Council exercised day-to-day control over the claimant but the defendants also exercised considerable control in that they paid her wages, deducting tax and National Insurance Contributions, and could discipline her and could terminate her contract. However, the claimant's contract with the defendants clearly stated that she was not employed by them.

Held. The claimant was not employed by the defendants because they had no obligation to provide her with work and she had no obligation to accept work. The defendants paid the claimant but did not control her day-to-day activities. Such control was exercised by the local authority.

COMMENT (i) The Court of Appeal thought that the tribunals should have considered whether or not there was an implied contract of service between the claimant and Wandsworth Council. This question was not relevant in the case only because Wandsworth Council were not a party to the proceedings. However, in future cases tribunals should consider whether or not such an implied contract existed between agency workers and the clients to whom they were sent.

(ii) The decision in this case was approved by the Court of Appeal in *Cable and Wireless plc* **v** *Muscat* [2006] EWCA Civ 220. Arguments that *Dacas* had been decided *per incuriam* were rejected.

Both *Dacas* **v** *Brook Street Bureau* and *Cable and Wireless plc* **v** *Muscat* were reviewed by the Court of Appeal in *James* **v** *London Borough Council* [2008] EWCA Civ 35, [2008] ICR 545. The court stressed that *Dacas* was not an authority that long-term agency workers were always employees of the end user. This was merely a possibility, which depended upon whether, on the facts of the case, a contract could be implied. *Muscat* correctly stated that, in order to imply a contract of employment, this must be *necessary* to give effect to the business reality of the relationship between the worker and the end user. The Court of Appeal also explained the different approaches to be taken when deciding 'agency worker' and 'casual worker' cases. Mummery LJ said: 'The real issue in the "agency worker cases" is whether a contract should be implied between the worker and the end user in a tripartite situation of worker/agency/and end user rather than whether, as in "the casual worker" cases where neither the worker nor the end user has an agency contract, the irreducible minimum of mutual obligations exists.' The point was also made that,

in some very extreme cases, a sham arrangement could be exposed as a contract of employment. The decision in *James* **v** *LBC* has been approved by the Court of Appeal several times. The Agency Workers Regulations 2010, which came into force in October 2011, are considered in Chapter 21 at 21.10. The regulations give rights to equal treatment over matters such as pay, but do not deal with the question as to whether or not an agency worker is an employee or an independent contractor.

The fact that the parties describe the worker as self-employed will not be conclusive if the facts of the case indicate otherwise. The following two cases indicate the matters which must be considered.

Ferguson v *John Dawson & Partners (Contractors) Ltd* [1976] 3 All ER 817 (Court of Appeal)

The claimant was employed as a casual building worker on the defendants' building site under an oral contract. He was told that there were no cards as the labourers were 'purely working as a lump labour force'. The claimant was paid an hourly rate. No tax or National Insurance was deducted from the labourers' pay. The foreman told the labourers what to do and the defendants provided their tools. The claimant was injured while working. He claimed compensation against the defendants under the Construction (Working Place) Regulations 1966. In order to succeed under the Regulations it was essential that the claimant was employed by the defendants. As part of their defence, the defendants argued that the claimant was not employed under a contract of employment.

Held. Even if the parties' true intention was that the claimant was not an employee, this was only a relevant factor rather than a conclusive factor. Regard had to be had to the arrangement as a whole and in particular to the rights and obligations of the parties. The terms of the contract indicated that the claimant was an employee.

Massey v *Crown Life Insurance Co* [1978] ICR 590 (Court of Appeal)

From 1971 to 1973 the claimant worked as a branch manager of an office of the defendant insurance company and was treated as an employee. The claimant also had an agency agreement with the company and in 1973, at his own request, he entered into an agreement whereby he continued to perform the same services as previously, but as self-employed for tax

→

purposes. This agreement was made in the claimant's registered business name. When the agreement was terminated by the company in 1975 the claimant claimed compensation for unfair dismissal. This claim could only succeed if the claimant was an employee.

Held. Although the parties cannot alter the true nature of their relationship by putting a name on it, the 1973 agreement was genuinely intended by the parties to make the claimant an independent contractor rather than an employee. He was therefore an independent contractor and accordingly he could not claim compensation for unfair dismissal. Lord Denning MR said that, 'Having made his bed as "self-employed", he must lie on it.'

COMMENT There were significant differences between this case and *Ferguson*'s case, which was distinguished. The two cases do not necessarily conflict with each other. The important differences were as follows: Massey asked for the change, Ferguson had little choice but to accept it; Massey was a skilled worker, Ferguson was not; the courts are more ready to find employment in cases where a claim for personal injury depends upon such a finding, rather than in cases concerning tax or unfair dismissal.

If an agreement between employer and employee is a sham, designed to indicate falsely that an employee is an independent contractor, the courts will have regard to the reality of the situation. For example, in **Redrow Homes (Yorkshire) Ltd v Buckborough and Sewell** UKEAT/2008/0528/07, [2009] IRLR 34, the EAT held that a clause in a bricklayer's contract which said that he could use substitute labour if necessary was a sham. The bricklayer was therefore an employee and was therefore covered by the Working Time Regulations 1998.

In the light of the above cases, it must be said that the decision as to whether or not a worker is an employee or an independent contractor can be very difficult. The law is still evolving, particularly as employment practices change. It seems likely that many cases involving 'teleworkers', who provide a service from their homes, will soon be before the courts.

Test your understanding 20.1

1 To what extent do decisions of an employment tribunal and the Employment Appeal Tribunal create binding precedents?

2 In what circumstances can questions of employment law be referred to the European Court of Justice? To what extent are decisions of the ECJ binding upon other courts?

3 What is the role of ACAS?

4 Is there any exhaustive list of matters which can determine whether or not a worker is an employee or an independent contractor? Why is the distinction important?

5 Is the question as to whether a worker is an employee or an independent contractor one of law or fact? Why should this matter?

20.2 THE TERMS OF THE CONTRACT OF EMPLOYMENT

Section 230(2) of the Employment Rights Act (ERA) 1996 restates the common law position that a contract of employment may be made expressly or impliedly, and that there is no need for such a contract to be in writing. Generally a contract of employment, like other contracts, will contain both express and implied terms. If any of these terms are breached a remedy will be available for breach of contract.

20.2.1 Express terms

In general, the parties are free to agree whatever express terms they wish. However, several statutes which we study in this and the following chapter confer rights upon employees out of which they may not contract. In addition, s.2(1) of the Unfair Contract Terms Act 1977 renders ineffective any term which seeks to exclude the employer's liability for death or personal injury caused by negligence.

It is obviously desirable that the employer and employee should agree as many express terms as possible when the contract is formed, and that the meaning of these terms should be clear and unambiguous.

20.2.1.1 Written particulars

Section 1 ERA 1996 requires an employer to give an employee a written statement of particulars of the employment. This statement must be given not later than two months after the commencement of the employment. The statement, which can be given in instalments, must contain particulars of the following matters:

(a) The names of the employer and the employee.
(b) The date on which the employment began.

(c) The date on which the employee's continuous employment began and whether any previous employment is to count as continuous employment. (Continuous employment is an important factor in connection with redundancy and unfair dismissal, and is examined later in this chapter at 20.4.1.2.)

(d) The scale and rate of remuneration and the way in which this is calculated.

(e) The intervals at which remuneration is paid (weekly, monthly etc.).

(f) Any terms and conditions relating to hours of work, including any terms and conditions relating to normal working hours.

(g) Any terms and conditions relating to: holiday entitlement and holiday pay; incapacity for work due to sickness and injury, including any provisions for sick pay; pensions and pension schemes.

(h) The length of notice needed to terminate the employment.

(i) The title of the employee's job or a brief description of the work for which he is employed.

(j) If the employment is not intended to be permanent, the period for which it is expected to continue or, if it is for a fixed term, the date on which the term is to end.

(k) Either the place of work or, where the employee is required or permitted to work at various places, an indication of that and of the address of the employer.

(l) Any collective agreements which affect the terms and conditions of the employment.

(m) Where the employee is required to work outside the United Kingdom for a period of more than one month, the period for which he is to work outside the United Kingdom, the currency in which he is to be paid while working outside the United Kingdom, and any additional remuneration or benefits to be paid or provided by reason of his being required to work outside the United Kingdom.

Section 3 ERA 1996 requires that the statement issued under s.1 shall include a note specifying any disciplinary rules applicable to the employee, or referring the employee to the provisions of a document specifying such rules. The document in question must be reasonably accessible to the employee. The note must specify the persons to whom the employee can apply if dissatisfied with any disciplinary decisions relating to him, and the person to whom the employee can apply for the purpose of seeking redress of any grievance relating to his employment. It must also set out the manner in which such an application should be made. However, there is no need to provide these details of workplace disciplinary and grievance procedures if on the date when the employment began the relevant number of employees was fewer than 20.

The employer may refer the employee to other documents, in respect of sick pay and pension schemes, as long as these are reasonably accessible to the employee.

The written particulars which must be provided do not constitute the contract of employment. Unless the employee accepts the offer of employment by signing an agreement which contains all of the written particulars, the contract will have been formed before the employee sees the particulars. However, the written particulars are very strong evidence of the terms of the contract of employment and in the absence of strong conflicting evidence that they were not the terms of the contract a tribunal is likely to conclude that they were. In *Systems Floors v Daniel* [1981] IRLR 475 Browne-Wilkinson J, sitting as President of the EAT, said, 'It seems to us, therefore, that in general the status of the statutory statement is this. It provides very strong *prima facie* evidence of what were the terms of the contract between the parties, but does not constitute a written contract between the parties. Nor are the statements of the terms finally conclusive: at most, they place a heavy burden on the employer to show that the actual terms of the contract are different from those which he has set out in the statutory statement.' In *Southern Cross Healthcare Ltd v Perkins* [2010] EWCA Civ 1442, [2011] IRLR 247 the Court of Appeal held that an employment tribunal does not have the power to interpret the statutory written particulars, as they are not the contract of employment. It did, of course, have the power to see that the written particulars corresponded with the actual terms of the contract of employment.

If the employer does not provide a statement of written particulars, or provides an incomplete statement, an employee can apply to an employment tribunal to decide upon the matters which should have been included. Under s.38 the Employment Act (EA) 2002, the tribunal will make a minimum award of two weeks' pay and a maximum award of four weeks' pay to an employee bringing a case of discrimination, unfair dismissal or redundancy if the employee had not, at the start of proceedings, been given his statement of employment particulars. For these purposes the week's pay is capped at the limit of £400 which applies when calculating a basic award for unfair dismissal. (See below at 20.4.4.2.) If the matters specified in the written particulars change, the employer must give the employee a written statement containing particulars of the change within one month.

20.2.1.2 **Itemised pay statements**

Section 8 ERA 1996 gives an employee the right to be given by his employer, at or before the time at which any payment of wages or salary is made to him, a written itemised pay statement. This must contain particulars of:

(a) the gross amount of the wages or salary;
(b) the amount of any deductions from that gross amount, and the purposes for which they are made;
(c) the net amount of wages and salary payable; and
(d) where different parts of the net amount are paid in different ways, the amount and method of payment of each part-payment.

The total amount of fixed deductions must always be stated. However, rather than give a detailed breakdown of the particulars of these every time wages are paid, the employer may give a detailed breakdown annually.

Where an employee fails to give an employee an itemised pay statement, or where there is a dispute as to the contents of such a statement, the employee can apply to an employment tribunal to determine what matters ought to have been included in an itemised pay statement. Where the employer has made deductions from pay without notifying the employee, the tribunal has the power to award the employee the amount of deductions not notified in the previous 13 weeks.

If an employer has an occupational pension scheme then the Occupational Pension Schemes (Disclosure of Information) Regulations 1986 require that details of the scheme are given to members. The Working Time Regulations 1998 state that if an employer requires holidays to be taken on specified dates, or not to be taken on specified dates, then at least four weeks' notice of these dates must be given to employees.

20.2.2 **Collective agreements as terms**

A collective agreement is defined by s.178 of the Trade Union and Labour Relations (Consolidation) Act 1992 as an agreement or arrangement made by or on behalf of one or more trade unions and one or more employers or employers' associations, and relating to one or more of the following:

(a) terms and conditions of employment, or the physical conditions in which any workers are required to work;
(b) engagement or non-engagement;
(c) allocation of work or the duties of employment between workers or groups of workers;
(d) matters of discipline;
(e) a worker's membership or non-membership of a trade union;
(f) facilities for officials of trade unions; and
(g) machinery for negotiation or consultation, and other procedures, relating to any of the above matters.

Many industries, especially the old-fashioned heavy industries, operate with collective agreements. Collective agreements, or part of them, may be incorporated into a contract by express agreement between the parties to the contract. This is the case whether or not the employee is a member of the union which made the collective agreement. For example if, before agreeing to take a job, an employee was told that the employment was subject to the terms of a collective agreement, then this will be an express term of the contract and the agreement will be binding upon the employee, whether he is in the relevant trade union or not. The written particulars required by s.1 ERA 1996 may also expressly incorporate the terms of a collective agreement into the contract of employment. If not expressly agreed as a term of the contract, the terms of a collective agreement will only be incorporated into the contract if that is what the employer and employee intended.

The terms of collective agreements may be impliedly incorporated into the contracts of members of the union who negotiated the agreement. However, the union member must have had knowledge of the collective agreement, and must have shown in some way that he accepted it. This will not be possible if the employee did not know of the existence or content of the agreement. The terms of a collective agreement will generally not be impliedly incorporated into the contract of an employee who is not a union member. However, they may be if the employee invariably follows them in practice.

Once part of the contract of employment, terms incorporated as part of a collective agreement may only be altered by express agreement by the parties to the contract of employment or under a right to alter contained in the contract of employment. If the trade union unilaterally negotiates a change, they do not do so as agents of the individual employees.

20.2.3 Implied obligations of the employee

At common law, several terms are implied into a contract of employment. As we saw in Chapter 5 at 5.3.2, the courts can imply a term into a contract, as a matter of law, on the basis that the term is generally implied into contracts of the type in question. When examining the terms which are implied into a contract of employment we first consider the terms which impose obligations on the employee, then those which impose obligations on the employer.

20.2.3.1 Duty of mutual respect

Both the employer and the employee owe each other a duty of mutual respect. In *Donovan v Invicta Airways Ltd* [1970] 1 Lloyd's Rep 486 the Court of Appeal held that an airline pilot was entitled to treat his contract of employment as repudiated when he was asked to fly in breach of regulations and was subsequently treated discourteously by his employers. The Court of Appeal held that the correct question to ask was whether the defendants' conduct was such as to make the continuance of the relationship of employer and employee impossible.

20.2.3.2 Duty of faithful service

The employment relationship is one of trust and confidence, and therefore an employee owes a duty faithfully to serve the employer. There have been decisions which indicate that this duty would prevent the employee from competing with the business of the employer whilst the employment continued. In *Hivac Ltd v Park Royal Scientific Instruments Co* [1946] 1 All ER 350 the Court of Appeal granted an injunction preventing employees from working for a competitor of their employer. However, a contractual term might allow such work to be done and there is no reason why an employee should not do work for someone other than a competitor of his employer, as long as doing so does not affect the way in which the employee performs his work.

In *Nottingham University v Fishel* [2000] IRLR 471, Elias J held that an employee's duty not to pursue his own interests at the expense of the employer's interests arose only where there was a definite contractual obligation for the employee to act only in the interests of his employer. The employment relationship was not a typical fiduciary relationship such as that between directors and their companies. As a general proposition a contract of employment did not require an employee to place the employer's interests above his own. It could, however, do so if there was a contractual term to this effect.

The duty of faithful service might be breached in a great number of other ways. In the past the courts have held that the duty was breached by such matters as the employee deliberately obstructing the employer's business, being persistently late, or deliberately falsifying the clocking-in card of a fellow employee.

20.2.3.3 Duty to obey lawful and reasonable orders

An employee is required to obey orders which are lawful and reasonable, but has no obligation to obey orders which are unlawful or unreasonable. The difficulty then is in deciding what amounts to a lawful and reasonable order. There is an abundance of case law on the matter. Each case depends upon its own facts. The express terms of the contract and all the circumstances of the case must be taken into consideration.

If an employee is dismissed for refusing to obey an order, the manner and tone of the refusal may be of relevance in considering whether the dismissal amounted to wrongful dismissal.

Pepper v Webb [1969] 2 All ER 216

A head gardener, who lived in a cottage in the employer's grounds, was required to work from 8 am until noon on Saturdays. He began to fall out with his employer. Between 9 am and 10 am on Saturday the gardener was asked to put some plants in the ground because otherwise they would die. The gardener replied, 'I am leaving at 12 o'clock; you can do what you like about them. If you don't like it you can give me notice.' Shortly before noon further appeals to the gardener to put the plants in, and not to be so awkward, were made. The employer pointed out that it would only take about half an hour to put the plants in. The gardener replied, 'I couldn't care less about your bloody greenhouse and your sodding garden.' The gardener was dismissed immediately, without notice or wages in lieu.

Held. The gardener's action for wrongful dismissal failed. The gardener had repudiated his contract by his refusal to obey the lawful and reasonable order to put the plants in, by his statement that he could not care less about the garden and by his insolence towards the employer.

COMMENT This case arose before the statutory remedy of unfair dismissal became available. Even if the gardener had had the necessary continuous employment to qualify for unfair dismissal, any such claim would have failed on the grounds that the dismissal was fair on the grounds of the employee's conduct.

It is possible for an employee to be fairly dismissed for refusing to obey an order which was outside the requirements of his contract of employment. In *Robinson v Flitwick Frames Ltd* [1975] IRLR 261 a general maintenance fitter refused to work overtime when requested to do so by the management. The overtime became necessary for a two month period and all the employees on the claimant's section agreed that it was necessary. However, on the evening of the meeting which decided this, the claimant made it clear that he would not work after 5 o'clock. The claim for unfair dismissal failed. The variation in working time which the management proposed was reasonable and had been accepted by all the other workers. The claimant had behaved unreasonably in refusing to obey the order and could not give a satisfactory explanation as to why he had refused. (When we study unfair dismissal, below at 20.4, we shall see that a dismissal is unfair unless it is made for one of five specified reasons, or unless it was made, as this dismissal was, for some other substantial reason of a kind such as to justify the dismissal of an employee holding the position which the employee held.)

Several cases have been concerned with whether or not the employee can be required to work elsewhere. In *United Kingdom Atomic Energy Authority v Claydon* [1976] IRLR 6, for example, the EAT had to consider whether an employee of the Atomic Energy Authority in Orfordness could be transferred against his will to the atomic energy site at Aldermaston. A construction of his contract of employment indicated that he could be transferred, and so he could. If the construction of the contract had not indicated this then he could not have been transferred.

Even if an employee can be required to work at a different place of employment, refusal to work at the other place may not always mean that a dismissal is fair, for the purposes of unfair dismissal. In *Wilson v IDR Construction Ltd* [1975] IRLR 260, for example, a bricklayer was unfairly dismissed for failure to work at another site even though the employer had the right to send him to this site. The bricklayer did not want to go because his wife was ill, the trouble having arisen since he last worked away from home, and because his car was in for repairs and an MOT. The bricklayer refused to ring the office to discuss the move. A general manager came to the site to see the bricklayer and, after a slightly rancorous conversation, the bricklayer was dismissed without notice or wages in lieu. The EAT thought that if the bricklayer had been given a proper chance to explain his reasons for not wanting to travel

he would probably not have been unfairly dismissed. On the facts the EAT held that the bricklayer's dismissal was unfair, although his damages were reduced by 25 per cent because he contributed to the dismissal.

20.2.3.4 **Duty to use reasonable care and skill**

An employee agrees to perform his duties using reasonable care and skill. The higher the level of skill which the employee professes to have, the higher the standard expected. Employees who are professionally qualified will be expected to show the care and skill which could reasonably be expected of a member of that profession. Breach of the duty to use reasonable care and skill may give rise to a claim in damages and may also justify dismissal.

The damages claimed for breach of the duty to use reasonable care and skill may be substantial. For example, in *Janata Bank v Ahmed* [1981] IRLR 457 the Court of Appeal held that a bank manager who had cost the bank £34 640 by negligence was liable to pay damages to compensate for this loss. An employee who negligently loses the employer's property may also be in breach of the implied duty to use reasonable care and skill.

20.2.3.5 **Duty not to accept bribes**

In some areas of employment it is well recognised that employees may accept tips. However, an employee should not accept a bribe or secret commission. The mere fact of having received such a payment gives rise to an irrebuttable presumption that it influenced the employee's behaviour in favour of the donor. The employer may recover the amount of the payment from the employee and in many cases the payment will justify the employee's dismissal.

In *Boston Deep Sea Fishing and Ice Co v Ansell* (1888) 39 ChD 339, for example, the managing director of a company ordered two new vessels for the company. The shipbuilder paid the managing director a secret commission. The managing director also placed orders with two companies in which he held shares, and received bonuses from these companies. The Court of Appeal held that the managing director could be dismissed and that he also had to repay the money received, with interest.

20.2.3.6 **Duty not to reveal confidential information**

An employee is under a duty not to reveal confidential information about the employer's business, except where there is a legal duty to do so.

The Public Interest Disclosure Act 1998 protects employees, generally known as 'whistleblowers', who make a 'protected disclosure' of information. A worker protected by the Act cannot suffer a detriment in consequence of the disclosure, nor be dismissed or made redundant. A disclosure is a protected disclosure if, in the reasonable belief of the worker making the disclosure, it tends to show one or more of the following:

(a) that a criminal offence has been committed, is being committed or is likely to be committed;

(b) that a person has failed, is failing or is likely to fail to comply with any legal obligation to which he is subject;

(c) that a miscarriage of justice has occurred, is occurring or is likely to occur;

(d) that the health and safety of an individual has been, is being or is likely to be endangered;

(e) that the environment has been, is being or is likely to be damaged; or

(f) that information tending to show any of the above matters has been, or is likely to be concealed.

20.2.3.7 Patents, inventions and copyright

The extent to which patents, inventions and copyrights which were created by the employee belong to the employer is considered in Chapter 23.

20.2.3.8 Duty of disclosure

Although an employee does not have a duty to disclose his own shortcomings, unless asked about them by the employer, he does have a duty to disclose the shortcomings of his subordinates.

Sybrom Corporation v Rochem Ltd [1983] 2 All ER 707 (Court of Appeal)

The employee was a manager working for the defendant company, and was the overseer of the company's European operations. The employee took early retirement and received a lump sum of £13 200. Other sums were held in trust for him by the company. After paying the £13 200 the company discovered that the employee and his subordinates had committed a massive fraud on the company. The company claimed to be entitled to the £13 200 already paid and also to have no duty to hold the other money on trust for the employee. The employee argued that he had no duty to disclose the fraud and that he was therefore entitled to the pension payment as previously agreed.

Held. The employee had no duty to disclose his own misconduct. However he had breached a duty to disclose the breaches of duty of his subordinates, even if disclosing this would have meant revealing his own breaches of duty. The employee's breach of this duty would have entitled the employer to dismiss the employee summarily and, under the rules of the pension scheme, refuse to make any pension payment. If the employers had known this they could validly have refused to pay under the pension scheme rules. They therefore made the payment under a mistake as to fact which was induced by the employee's breach of duty. The money paid was recoverable and the sums held in trust reverted to the employer.

20.2.4 Implied obligations of the employer

20.2.4.1 Duty of mutual respect

This duty has become increasingly important as the relationship of employer and employee has moved away from the master/servant relationship of Victorian times. The courts have held the duty breached on various grounds, including: failure to provide a grievance procedure, in breach of a statutory obligation to do so; requiring a doctor who was coming back to work after suspension to undergo psychiatric tests when there was no evidence of psychiatric illness; berating an inexperienced employee, in front of his work mates, for incompetence; falsely accusing an employee of theft; and refusing to give one employee a pay rise when all of the other employees were given a rise.

20.2.4.2 Duty to provide work

An employer generally does not have a duty to provide work for an employee, as long as the employee is paid. Asquith J in **Collier v Sunday Referee Publishing Ltd** [1940] 2 KB 647 said: 'It is true that a contract of employment does not necessarily, or perhaps normally, oblige the master to provide the servant with work. Provided I pay my cook her wages regularly she cannot complain if I choose to take any or all of my meals out.' However, in some circumstances there is a duty to provide work. The most notable of these circumstances are as follows: where the work is needed for the employee to maintain his reputation or skill; where the failure to provide work leads to the employee earning less money, as for example where the employee is on piecework; and where the failure to provide work can be taken as a repudiation of the contract of employment.

20.2.4.3 Duty to pay wages

Unless the contract of employment expressly or impliedly provides otherwise, the employer has a duty to pay wages to the employee whether work is provided or not. In *Devonald v Rosser & Sons* [1906] 2 KB 728, for example, a pieceworker who was given one month's notice during which no work was provided was entitled to a payment based on his average monthly earnings. In some circumstances where the lack of work is for a reason beyond the employer's control, there might not be a duty to pay wages.

Wages must be paid in money but not necessarily in cash. The employer must not make any deductions from wages unless the deduction is required to be made by a statutory provision, or a relevant provision of the worker's contract, or unless the worker has previously signified in writing his agreement or consent to the making of the deduction (ERA 1996 s.13(1)). Section 13(1) does not apply to deductions made for over-payment of wages or expenses, or for having taken part in a strike action.

20.2.4.4 Duty of confidentiality

Earlier we saw that employees owe a duty of confidentiality to their employers. The employer owes a similar duty to the employee. In *Dalgleish v Lothian and Borders Police Board* 1992 SLT 721 Lord Cameron of Lochbroom, sitting in the Court of Session, held that an employer asked to provide the names and addresses of employees to the local council, so that they could detect those who had not paid the community charge, was contractually bound not to disclose information held in personal files without the consent of the employees concerned.

20.2.4.5 Duty to indemnify the employee

An employer will be under a duty to indemnify an employee for expenses and costs reasonably incurred in the performance of his employment. In *Re Famatina Development Corporation Ltd* [1914] 2 Ch 271, for example, the claimant was employed under a written contract to go to Argentina and report on some mines which the employer was considering buying. The claimant sent a report saying that the managing director of the company which employed him had committed serious fraud. The claimant was sued for libel. The libel action failed, but the claimant was unable to recover a large part of his costs. The Court of Appeal held that as the report was written in pursuance of the claimant's duties as an agent, and written without malice, he was entitled to an indemnity and reimbursement from the employer.

20.2.4.6 Duty to insure

Employers are required by the Employers' Liability (Compulsory Insurance) Act 1969 to take out insurance for the benefit of employees who are working within the United Kingdom.

20.2.4.7 Duty to provide references

An employer does not have a duty to provide a reference for an employee. There are two reasons why an employer might be reluctant to provide a reference. First, the employer may be sued for defamation if the reference is defamatory. Second, the employer may be liable for negligent misstatement if the reference is so careless or inaccurate that this involves breaching a duty of care owed to the employee. (Negligent misstatement is examined in Chapter 12 at 12.3.)

Spring v Guardian Assurance plc [1994] 3 All ER 129 (House of Lords)

The claimant was employed as sales director and office manager of C Ltd, the second defendants, who were agents for the sale of life assurance policies. C Ltd were taken over by G plc, the first defendants, and the claimant was dismissed. The claimant wanted to work selling the policies of another company. That company was obliged by Lautro rules to to get a reference from the previous employer. The previous employer was required by Lautro rules to provide a reference which made 'full and frank disclosure of all matters which are believed to be true'. G plc provided a very bad reference, which said that the claimant kept the best business for himself, had little integrity, could not be regarded as honest and had mis-sold a policy to make a large commission for himself at the client's expense. Having failed to gain employment with two other members of Lautro, the claimant sued claiming breach of an implied contractual term that the defendants would prepare any reference in regard to him using reasonable care and skill and would provide a reference which was full, frank and truthful. He also sued in negligence, alleging breach of a duty of care.

Held. An employer's duty to take reasonable care and skill in preparing a reference in respect of an employee could, in appropriate circumstances, arise from an implied term of the contract of employment. The employer would therefore have to exercise due care and skill in preparing the reference. However, the duty arising under the implied term did not add anything to the duty arising in negligence.

COMMENT The claimant won the case on the grounds of the defendant's negligence. The employer owed a duty of care to the employee in respect of the preparation of the reference. Having breached this duty, the employer was liable in damages for economic loss suffered by the employee as a consequence. The employer had a duty to avoid negligently making untrue statements or expressing unfounded opinions, even if these were honestly believed to be true or were reasonably held. The duty arose because economic loss, in the form of failure to obtain employment, was clearly foreseeable if a careless reference was given and because there was an obvious proximity of relationship between employer and employee.

Sometimes an employer gives a bad employee an unrealistically good reference to get rid of him. It is possible that such a reference will give the new employer the right to sue for deceit or negligent misstatement if he relied upon the reference to his detriment. The employer writing the reference might be able to protect himself against such liability by means of a disclaimer. However, s.3 Misrepresentation Act 1967 would allow the disclaimer to be effective only if it satisfied the UCTA 1977 requirement of reasonableness. (See Chapter 5 at 5.6.1.7.)

The duty to ensure the employee's safety is considered in Chapter 21 at 21.11.

20.2.5 Terms implied by custom and practice

It is possible for a term to be incorporated into a contract of employment by custom and practice. In order for this to happen, the term must be notorious, certain and reasonable. For example, in *Sagar* v *Ridehalgh & Son Ltd* [1931] Ch 310 a local custom entitled a Lancashire mill owner to deduct wages from a weaver who had spoiled three yards of cloth by defective workmanship. The mill had deducted money in similar circumstances for many years, as had most mills in Lancashire. The importance of terms implied by custom and practice has declined considerably and in modern times the incorporation of terms in this way is of little significance.

20.2.6 Works rule books

An employer's works rule book, or list of rules, may be contractually agreed as being part of the contract of employment. If this is the case then the rules can only be altered by agreement between the parties. If the rules are unilaterally imposed by the employer, rather than being agreed as contractually binding by employer and employee, then failure to observe the rules may be a breach of the duty to obey instructions, and the rules may be unilaterally altered by the employer. However, rules unilaterally imposed would not be able to alter the terms of the contract previously agreed. In the following case the claimant argued that new anti-smoking rules breached her contract of employment.

Dryden v Greater Glasgow Health Board
[1992] IRLR 469

Ms Dryden worked as a nursing auxiliary in the theatre section of a Glasgow infirmary. Her job did not allow her to leave the premises during the day. She smoked 30 cigarettes a day, but until 1991 certain areas of the premises were available for smoking. Then the hospital introduced a no smoking policy. Employees were sent letters giving notice of the change and offered advice and counselling. Ms Dryden resigned and claimed to have been constructively dismissed.

Held. The introduction of the no-smoking policy did not breach Ms Dryden's contract of employment. There was no express or implied term in her contract that smoking would continue to be permitted. Where a new rule was introduced for a legitimate purpose, the fact that the rule works harshly against some employees is not enough to justify an inference that the employer has acted in such a way as to breach the contract with the employee.

Generally, job descriptions are likely to be drawn up unilaterally by the employer. The employee will have a duty to perform the duties set out. The employer will be able to change the job description unilaterally, as long as this does not amount to a breach of contract.

The difficulties in determining the legal effect of rule books are demonstrated by *Secretary of State for Employment* v *ASLEF*, where railwaymen who 'worked to rule', that is to say strictly according to their rule book, were held to be in breach of contract. Lord Denning clearly said that these particular rules were not the terms of the railwaymen's contracts of employment, but merely instructions on how they should do their work. In addition, there was an implied term that the rules would be interpreted reasonably.

In *Keeley* v *Fosroc International Ltd* [2006] EWCA Civ 1277, [2006] IRLR 961 the Court of Appeal held that provisions in a staff handbook, which set out enhanced redundancy payments, were contractual terms and could be relied upon. Auld LJ delivered the only judgment. He found that many parts of the staff handbook were plainly contractual terms. However, he held that even if a contract of employment expressly incorporated a collective agreement or a staff handbook it would not necessarily be the case that everything in the agreement or the handbook would be terms of the contract. 'For example, some provisions, read in their context, may be declarations of an aspiration or policy falling short of a contractual undertaking ... It is necessary to consider in their respective contexts the incorporating words and the provision in question incorporated by them.' The nature of a provision and the language in which it was expressed would indicate whether or not it was a contractual term. The importance of the provision to the overall bargain between employer and employee was highly relevant. Was it part of the employee's overall remuneration package, the consideration for which he undertook to work? Equally important was the wording of the provision. If it was put in clear terms of entitlement it might not be undone by its context in the document in which it appeared. The language of the enhanced redundancy provision, and its inclusion in the 'Employee Benefits and Rights' section of the staff handbook were strong indications that it was to have contractual effect. This was particularly so as the 'Employee Benefits and Rights' section of the staff handbook contained other provisions that were clearly intended to have contractual effect.

20.2.7 ACAS grievance procedure

In October 2004 statutory grievance, disciplinary and dismissal procedures came into force. These statutory procedures were soon found to be too formal and too rigid. It became widely felt that rather than reducing the chances of litigation, as had been intended, they actually made litigation more likely. The Employment Act 2008 abolished these procedures, as from April 2009, and substituted a requirement that the ACAS Code of Practice 1: Discipline and Grievance (the Code) should be followed. Here we consider the Code as it applies to employee grievances. Later in this chapter, at 20.4.3.4, we consider the Code as it applies to dismissal of an employee.

The Code advises that employers and employees should try to resolve disciplinary and grievance matters informally in the workplace, and should consider using independent third parties to help if necessary. However, where this is not possible, the Code sets out procedures which aim to provide basic requirements of fairness and a standard of reasonable behaviour.

The Code defines grievances as concerns, problems or complaints that employees raise with their employers. In the case of a grievance the procedure which the Code requires is as follows:

- First, if the grievance cannot be settled informally, the employee should formally raise the grievance with the employer, via a manager who is not the subject of the grievance. This should be done in writing and without unnecessary delay.
- Second, the employer should hold a formal meeting with the employee, without unreasonable delay, to discuss the nature of the grievance. The employer, the employee and any companion of the employee should make every effort to attend the meeting. The employee should be given a chance to explain the grievance and how he thinks it should be resolved. The employer should consider adjourning the meeting to conduct any necessary investigation.
- Third, the employer should allow the employee to be accompanied at the meeting by a companion, such as a fellow worker or a trade union representative. The employee would have to make a reasonable request to be accompanied, what is reasonable depending upon all the circumstances of the case. The companion would have no right to answer questions on the employee's behalf. However, the companion would have the rights to address the meeting in order to put and sum up the employee's case, to respond on the employee's behalf to any views expressed at the meeting and to confer with the employee during the meeting. There is no right to be accompanied by a legal representative, unless the employer agrees to this.
- Fourth, the employer should decide on appropriate action and communicate this to the employee in writing. The employee should also be told of the right to appeal against the decision.
- Finally, the employer should allow the employee to appeal against the decision if he does not think that the grievance has been satisfactorily resolved. Appeals must be submitted in writing and without reasonable delay. An appeal should be heard without unreasonable delay, preferably by a manager who has not previously been involved. The employee has the right to be accompanied at the appeal. The outcome of the appeal should be communicated in writing without unreasonable delay.

The grievance procedure does not apply when a recognised trade union, or other appropriate workplace representative, raises a grievance on behalf of two or more employees. In such cases the organisation's collective grievance procedures will apply. If an employee raises a grievance during a disciplinary process the disciplinary process can be suspended until the grievance has been dealt with. However, where the disciplinary and grievance cases are related both can be dealt with in the same proceedings. An ACAS Guide provides sample grievance procedures and sample letters which might be used by the employer.

The Code is not legally binding but is admissible as evidence and can be taken into account by the employment tribunal. Section 207A(2) of the Trade Union and Labour Relations (Consolidation) Act 1992 allows the tribunal, if it considers it just and equitable, to increase any award to an employee by up to 25 per cent if it appears to the tribunal that the employer has unreasonably failed to comply with the Code. Section 207A(3) contains a corresponding power to reduce the award by up to 25 per cent where it is the employee who has unreasonably failed to comply with the Code.

20.2.8 **Variation of terms of the contract**

As we saw in Chapter 7 at 7.1.2, a contract cannot be unilaterally varied by one of the parties, but both parties may agree to a variation as long as they both provide some consideration to each other. These general contract principles apply equally to contracts of employment. However, it is clear that employees cannot expect that the conditions of employment will remain unaltered for the whole period of employment, no matter how long that might be.

If the employer unilaterally alters the terms of a contract of employment (other than for a reason which is objectively necessary) and the employee does not accept the variation, then this will amount to a repudiation of the contract and the employee may justifiably regard the contract as terminated. If the employee continues to work without protest this will generally be taken as acceptance of the unilateral change. Whether or not an employee has accepted a unilateral variation of the contract by the employer is a question of fact, to be determined from all the circumstances of the case. In *Marriott v Oxford and District Co-operative Society Ltd* [1969] 3 All ER 1126 a foreman was offered a job as a supervisor, at a reduced wage, because there was insufficient work for

a foreman. The foreman protested about this and tried to find work elsewhere. He received a letter saying that his wages would be reduced by about £1 a week, and again he protested. After three or four weeks of receiving the reduced wage he left to take another job. The Court of Appeal held that the letter terminated his contract unless the foreman chose to accept the terms which it proposed. Even though the foreman continued to work for three or four weeks the circumstances indicated that he did not accept the variation. He was therefore entitled to regard himself as dismissed and claim a redundancy payment.

In *Marriott* it was a reduction in wages which amounted to a variation of the contract. In the same way, demoting an employee, or insisting that he perform duties outside his contract of employment, or withdrawing contractual benefits can amount to a variation of the contract. For example, in *Darby v The Law Society of England and Wales* UKEAT/2008/0447/07, [2008] All ER (D) 129 (Aug) the EAT found that the Law Society had dismissed employees by varying the employees' contract of employment so as to take away their rights to leased cars. The employees were told that they would be dismissed if they did not agree to the variation. This threat caused the employees to sign new contracts. The EAT held that they had been dismissed and immediately re-engaged. The case was referred back to the employment tribunal to see whether or not the dismissal was unfair.

If a repudiation is not accepted by an employee who continues in the employment, the damages are assessed to compensate for the entire period of breach, not merely for the period of notice to which the employee would have been entitled. In *Rigby v Ferodo Ltd* [1987] IRLR 516 the employer unilaterally reduced the employee's wages by £30 a week. The employee did not accept this. The contract could have been terminated by 12 weeks' notice. The claimant continued to work at the lower rate, without accepting the alteration, and then sued for breach of contract. The House of Lords held that he was entitled to the lost wages for the whole of the period of the breach.

An employee who continues to work under protest at a unilateral variation can be regarded as having been dismissed for the purposes of unfair dismissal. (See *Alcan Extrusions v Yates*, below at 20.4.2.1.) An express term of the contract may allow for variation of some of the terms. If the employee consistently works in a manner which is inconsistent with the express terms for a considerable time, then an implied variation can be inferred. When a trade union negotiates a collective agreement which changes the terms of an individual's contract of employment, the change is only effective if it is agreed by the employee individually or if he was collectively represented when the change was agreed. It will not therefore be binding on workers who are not members of the union which negotiated the agreement, unless they expressly agree to it or unless a term of their contracts allowed the terms to be varied by a new collective agreement.

The employer can insist on change if necessary. If the employee refuses to accept such change then the employer should give notice to terminate the employment. This will amount to a dismissal for the purposes of unfair dismissal. However, the dismissal might or might not be regarded as unfair.

Test your understanding 20.2

1 Within what period must an employee be given written particulars of the employment? Are these written particulars the contract of employment itself?

2 What are collective agreements? To what extent are such agreements terms of individual contracts of employment?

3 What duties are impliedly imposed on employees?

4 What duties are impliedly imposed on employers?

5 To what extent are works rule books contractually binding? Can the rules be changed unilaterally by the employer?

6 What is the effect of an employer failing to observe agreed disciplinary and grievance procedures?

7 What is the effect of the employer unilaterally altering the terms of the contract of employment?

20.3 TERMINATION OF EMPLOYMENT

Where a contract of employment is terminated it is possible that the employee might have a remedy for either wrongful or unfair dismissal. Unfair dismissal is a statutory remedy which is considered below at 20.4. Wrongful dismissal is the common law remedy of an employee to sue for contract damages on account of his contract of employment having been breached.

Generally a dismissed employee would prefer to sue for the statutory remedy of unfair dismissal rather than for wrongful dismissal. However, it is sometimes advantageous to sue for wrongful dismissal. This might either be because the damages for wrongful dismissal would be higher than the compensation for unfair dismissal or because the employee is unable to sue for unfair dismissal. It would be unusual for an employee's damages for wrongful dismissal to be higher than the compensation available for unfair dismissal. However, in the case of very highly paid employees who are entitled to long periods of notice, or who are working under a fixed term contract, the damages for wrongful dismissal could well be higher. As we saw in Chapter 7, the purpose of contract damages is to put the injured party in the financial position he would have been in if the breach of contract had not occurred. Certain categories of employees are precluded from claiming unfair dismissal, as we shall see below at 20.4.1. These employees, such as those who have less than two years' continuous employment, might nevertheless be able to bring a claim for wrongful dismissal. Many contracts are terminated by the employer giving notice and this would preclude a claim for wrongful dismissal, although not a claim for unfair dismissal.

A contract of employment may be terminated in several ways. One or other of the parties might give notice to terminate the contract, or both of the parties might agree to end the contract. The employee might complete the task for which he was employed, or might work for the whole of the time period specified in the contract. The contract might become frustrated. The employer might dismiss the employee without notice or might repudiate the contract, thereby entitling the employee to regard the contract as terminated. First, we examine each of these methods by which a contract may be terminated. Then we consider whether or not the termination could give rise to a claim for wrongful or unfair dismissal.

20.3.1 **Termination by notice**

An employment contract can be terminated by either the employer or the employee giving notice. Section 86 ERA 1996 lays down minimum periods of notice which the employer must give in order to terminate the contract. As these statutory notice periods are minimum periods, more notice will be required if there is a term of the contract to this effect. A greater period might also be required by the common law requirement of an employer to give a reasonable period of notice where there is no term as to the period required. The notice which is reasonable will depend upon all the circumstances of the case.

The minimum notice periods set out by s.86 are as follows.

If the employee has been continuously employed for between one month and two years, the minimum period of notice is one week. After the employee has been continuously employed for two years or more the minimum period becomes one week's notice for every year of continuous employment between two and 12 years. If the continuous employment has lasted for more than twelve years the minimum notice period remains 12 weeks.

Section 86 specifies that the notice periods which it sets out are minimum periods. Therefore any agreement that less notice is required will have no effect. If, however, a greater period of notice is agreed then this greater period of notice will be required.

As the employer has no duty to provide work (subject to the exceptions considered above at 20.2.4) an employee cannot insist on a right to work his notice if he is given a payment in lieu of notice.

Often an employee leaves his employment without giving the required period of notice. In such cases the employer could, theoretically, sue the employee for breach of contract. However, such actions are extremely rare. As the employer would be under a duty to mitigate his loss, his damages would generally be limited to the expense of finding another employee.

If a fixed term contract is terminated by the employer before the end of the term then this will amount to a breach of contract. It will also be a breach of contract if an employee is employed to achieve a particular purpose and is dismissed before this purpose has been achieved. If an employee is employed to achieve one specific purpose and the employment is ended as a consequence of this purpose having been achieved, this will not amount to a dismissal. The contract is discharged by performance.

20.3.2 **Summary dismissal**

An employee who is summarily dismissed is dismissed with immediate effect, without being given any notice. If the employee's conduct is a sufficient repudiation of the contract then summary dismissal can be justified and the employer will not have committed a breach of contract. However, summary dismissal is an exceptional measure and only in exceptional circumstances will it be justified. Summary dismissal can be justified for refusal to obey a lawful order, as was seen earlier in this chapter in **Pepper v Webb**. In that case the head

gardener's refusal to obey the lawful order, and the manner of his refusal, caused the employer to summarily dismiss him. The court held that the summary dismissal was justified and so the gardener could not claim wrongful dismissal. Other cases have held that gross misconduct or neglect, or serious breaches of duty can justify summary dismissal. Dishonesty may also justify summary dismissal. In the following case the employee was dishonest, although not dishonest to the point of committing a criminal offence, and summary dismissal was justified.

> ### *Sinclair* v *Neighbour* [1967] 2 QB 279 (Court of Appeal)
>
> The claimant was employed as the manager of a bookmaker's shop. He was paid £22 a week and received 5 per cent commission on the shop's net profits. The claimant took £15 out of the till in order to place a bet at a different betting shop. He left an I.O.U. in the till, but knew that if he had asked for permission to borrow the money this would have been refused. The bet won and the claimant returned the £15 to the till the following day. The employer summarily dismissed the claimant.
>
> **Held.** The summary dismissal was justified. Even if the claimant's behaviour was not dishonest, it was of such a grave and weighty character that it undermined the confidence which should exist between employer and employee.

Whether or not a dismissed employee was given the required period of notice is important for the purposes of wrongful dismissal. But it is not important for the purposes of unfair dismissal, except that it might influence the amount of the discretionary compensatory award.

20.3.3 **Termination by agreement**

The employer and employee may agree to end the contract at any time, with or without notice. If this is a genuine agreement, freely entered into by the employee, then the contract of employment will be discharged and the employee will have no claim for wrongful or unfair dismissal, as there will have been no dismissal. A contract might be terminated by agreement if it was agreed at the outset that the employment was to last merely until some purpose was achieved. However, if the agreement to terminate the contract was entered into as a result of pressure by the employer, the courts may well find that there was no true agreement but rather a dismissal by the employer.

Even if the parties agree that the employment should end on the happening of a certain event this may be a dismissal for the purposes of unfair dismissal and redundancy, although not for the purposes of wrongful dismissal. Section 203 ERA 1996 provides that any provision in an agreement (whether a contract of employment or not) is void in so far as it purports to exclude or limit the operation or provision of any part of ERA 1996. (The ERA confers redundancy rights and the right not to be unfairly dismissed.) In *Igbo v Johnson, Matthey Chemicals Ltd* [1986] IRLR 215 the employee wanted leave to visit Nigeria and it was agreed that if she should fail to return to work on a certain date, for whatever reason, her contract would be terminated. She did not return on the specified date because she was ill. The employer therefore treated the contract as terminated. The Court of Appeal held that the agreement was rendered void by what is now s.203 and so the employee had been dismissed for the purposes of unfair dismissal.

20.3.4 **Termination by frustration**

In Chapter 7 at 7.1.3 we saw that a contract will be frustrated if it becomes impossible to perform, illegal to perform or radically different from what the parties contemplated when they made the contract. We also saw that the frustrating event must not be the fault of either of the parties. If a contract of employment is frustrated it is terminated from the moment of the frustrating event, and the employee is not regarded as dismissed. As a consequence the employee will not be able to claim either unfair or wrongful dismissal. Imprisonment of the employee, or long-term sickness of the employee, may both amount to frustration of the contract. Even though it could be argued that it is the employee's fault that he was imprisoned, the courts have held that the imprisonment of the employee frustrates the contract. If the contract was not frustrated the employer would either have to keep the job open or terminate the contract. Such a termination would amount to a dismissal by the employer and would therefore put the imprisoned employee in a better position than if the contract was not frustrated. (The employee would be able to claim wrongful dismissal and perhaps unfair dismissal.) The argument that imprisonment could not frustrate the contract was described by the Court of Appeal in *Shepherd v Jerrom* [1986] ICR 802 as an 'affront to common sense'.

In *Egg Stores (Stamford Hill) Ltd v Leibovici* [1977] ICR 260 an employee of 15 years' standing was off work for five months after having been injured

in a car crash. The employer continued to pay the employee's wages for two months, but stopped paying when they got another employee to take over his work. When the employee returned to work he was told that his position had been filled. The EAT held that the employer could claim that the contract was frustrated if the employee's injury was such that further performance of his obligations under the contract would be impossible or radically different from what the parties contemplated when they made the contract. As regards a long-standing employee, the question to be asked was 'has the time arrived when the employer can no longer reasonably be expected to keep the absent employee's post open for him?' Phillips J identified nine factors to be taken into account in deciding whether the contract had been frustrated.

(a) the length of the previous employment;
(b) how long it had been expected that the employment would continue;
(c) the nature of the job;
(d) the nature, length and effect of the illness or disabling event;
(e) the need of the employer for the work to be done, and the need for a replacement to do it;
(f) the risk to the employer of acquiring obligations to the replacement employee in respect of redundancy payments or compensation for unfair dismissal;
(g) whether wages have continued to be paid;
(h) the acts and the statements of the employer in relation to the employment, including the dismissal of, or failure to dismiss, the employee; and
(i) whether in all the circumstances a reasonable employer could be expected to wait any longer.

20.3.5 **Repudiation of the contract**

In Chapter 7 we saw that if one party acts in a way which shows that he no longer intends to be bound by the contract, this amounts to a repudiation of the contract and the other party is entitled to accept this repudiation and regard his own contractual obligations as discharged. If, therefore, the employer's behaviour amounts to a repudiation of the contract the employee is entitled to accept this, regard himself as dismissed without notice, and bring a claim for wrongful dismissal. As regards unfair dismissal, an employee who resigns on account of the employer's behaviour may claim to have been constructively dismissed. (Constructive dismissal is examined below at

20.4.2.3.) An employee who resigns otherwise than in response to a repudiatory breach by the employer will have no claim to damages for wrongful dismissal and, unless constructive dismissal can be proved, will not be regarded as dismissed for the purposes of unfair dismissal. Nor will the employee be regarded as dismissed for the purposes of redundancy.

If the employee's behaviour amounts to a repudiation of the contract, and the employer in response dismisses the employee then this will amount to a dismissal. However, if the dismissal is justifiable then the employee will have no claim to damages, as we saw when considering summary dismissal. If the dismissal was fair then there will be no claim for unfair dismissal either. (See, however, **London Transport Executive v Clarke**, below at 20.4.2.6.)

A dismissal also occurs if an employer dismisses an employee without going through the contractually agreed dismissal procedures or makes an employee redundant in breach of contractually agreed redundancy procedures.

20.3.6 **Remedies for wrongful dismissal**

An action for wrongful dismissal is an action for breach of contract. The employee does not need to prove that the employer acted unreasonably, but only that the contract was in fact breached. As an action for wrongful dismissal is an action for breach of contract, the common law rules on quantification of damages apply. As we saw in Chapter 7, contract damages are designed to put the injured party in the position which he would have been in if the breach of contract had not occurred. Damages will be assessed as the amount of wages and other contractual benefits which would have been received if the employee had been given the proper period of notice. Discretionary payments will not be included. Furthermore, the employee will have an obligation to mitigate his loss. If the employer can prove that the employee could have mitigated his loss by earning money at other employment, but has failed to do so, the damages will be reduced accordingly. However, the dismissed employee is only expected to take reasonable steps to mitigate and would therefore only be expected to take a similar type of job at a similar level.

Damages for wrongful dismissal may take into account contractual benefits such as lost pension rights, lost holiday pay, lost share options, lost bonuses or tips, as these would be matters within the two rules in **Hadley v Baxendale**. In **Malik v BCCI SA** [1997] IRLR 462 the House of Lords held that damages for loss of reputation caused by breach of contract may be recoverable, provided that there was a relevant breach of contract and the requirements of causation, remoteness and mitigation were satisfied.

Damages paid for wrongful dismissal are not taxable unless they exceed £30 000, and so the employer only has to pay the net sum which the employee would have received after the payment of tax and National Insurance contributions. If the employee receives benefits, such as unemployment benefit, then the net amount of benefits received will be deducted from the damages. In very limited circumstances, an employee may be entitled to an injunction restraining the employer from breaching the contract of employment. As we saw in Chapter 7, an injunction is only ordered at the court's discretion and would not be ordered to effect specific performance in cases where specific performance would not be ordered. Specific performance is never ordered to enforce a contract of personal service.

The employment tribunal has the power to award up to £25 000 for wrongful dismissal. In **Fraser v HLMAD Ltd** [2006] EWCA Civ 738, [2007] 1 All ER 383, the Court of Appeal held that an employee cannot bring two claims, one before the EAT and one in the High Court, relating to the same dismissal. The dismissed employee claimed wrongful and unfair dismissal in the EAT, stating in his claim that if the damages were over £25 000 he reserved the right to sue for the excess in the High Court. He also brought a claim in the High Court for any damages in excess of £25 000. The EAT assessed the damages at £80 000 but awarded the maximum amount they could award, £25 000. The Court of Appeal held that the claimant could not sue for the excess in the High Court. He had only one cause of action and this was extinguished when the EAT made its final judgment. The employee should have sued only in the High Court.

It would be unusual for an employment tribunal to hear a case of wrongful dismissal if the case could be brought as a claim for unfair dismissal, as the compensatory award available for unfair dismissal would take account of wages lost between the times of dismissal and the hearing. (The two claims are based on different legal rights, but the basis of the complaint often overlaps.) In some limited circumstances it might be possible to bring an action for unfair dismissal at an employment tribunal and an action for wrongful dismissal in the High Court. If this were the case the court could stay one of the actions until the outcome of the other was decided, and the action stayed could only proceed as far as was necessary to resolve matters unde-cided by the first action. An award made by one court would generally be deducted from any award made by the other court to prevent double recovery. An action for wrongful dismissal must be brought within the usual six-year limit laid down by the Limitation Act 1980.

Test your understanding 20.3

1 What is the essential difference between wrongful and unfair dismissal?

2 If an employee is dismissed without having been given the notice to which he was entitled, will damages to compensate for this be awarded on the basis of wrongful or unfair dismissal?

3 How much notice will an employee be entitled to?

4 What is summary dismissal? Can it ever be justified?

5 If an employee agrees to leave the employment, can there be a claim for wrongful dismissal?

6 Can a claim for wrongful dismissal be made if the employer or employee repudiates the contract?

7 How are damages for wrongful dismissal calculated?

20.4 UNFAIR DISMISSAL

Section 94(1) ERA 1996 gives a statutory right not to be unfairly dismissed to employees who have been con-tinuously employed for at least two years. (In addition, certain dismissals are regarded as automatically unfair, in which case there is no qualifying period of continuous employment – see below at 20.4.3.2.) However, certain types of employees are excluded from claiming unfair dismissal. The circumstances in which a person is dis-missed, for the purposes of unfair dismissal, are laid down by ERA 1996. The Act also lays down rules for deciding whether or not a dismissal can be regarded as 'unfair', and sets out a formula for calculating the basic award of compensation. The dismissal will only be unfair if the reason for the dismissal was outside one of the 'fair' reasons set out by the Act and the employer acted unreasonably in deciding to dismiss the employee. It is also necessary that the dismissal is procedurally fair.

It will be seen that unfair dismissal is quite differ-ent from wrongful dismissal and is not based on the general law of contract. Even a person who has been dismissed without any breach of contract may have a claim for unfair dismissal.

20.4.1 Employees excluded from claiming unfair dismissal

Only employees have the right to claim unfair dis-missal. Self-employed workers have no such right. Fishermen who are paid by taking a share of the catch are excluded. If employees are covered by a dismissal procedure designated and approved by the Secretary of State they may not claim unfair dismissal. Such agreements would be made between the employer and the trade unions, substituting their own dismiss-als procedure. There have been few such agreements.

Employees are not generally entitled to claim unfair dismissal unless they have at least two years' con-tinuous employment. Where a dismissal is regarded as automatically unfair then there is no qualifying period of continuous employment. The grounds on which a dismissal is regarded as automatically unfair are set out below at 20.4.3.2.

20.4.1.1 Continuous employment

The concept of continuous employment is important not only because those who have less than two years' continuous employment will not be able to claim unfair dismissal, but also because the amount of the basic award for unfair dismissal will be calculated by reference to the length of the complainant's continu-ous employment.

Section 212(1) ERA 1996 states that:

'Any week during the whole or part of which an employee's relations with his employer are governed by a contract of employment counts in computing the employee's period of employment.'

As continuous employment is only of relevance in a statutory context, it is always calculated according to s.212(1). Any agreement by the parties to count employment as continuous employment will not affect the employee's statutory rights. Section 212(1) does not require that the employee works continuously in the same capacity or at the same place, merely that the employee works for the employer under a continuing contract of employment. In order for con-tinuous employment to be broken the employee must fail to work for the employer for at least one week. Weeks when an employee is off work on account of pregnancy, childbirth, sickness or injury count as continuous employment. Time off for a temporary ces-sation of work also counts. If an employee is on strike this does not break the continuity of employment, but the period on strike does not count as continuous employment. It is presumed that a person's employment is continuous unless the contrary is proved.

Part-time workers are treated in the same way as full-time workers for the purposes of calculating continuous employment, regardless of how many hours a week they work.

If the employer changes, so that the employee becomes employed by a different employer, continuity of employment may be preserved. Section 218 ERA 1996 provides that employment with the old employer will count as continuous employment with the new employer, and there will be no break in the continuity of the employment, if a trade or business is transferred from one employer to another employer as a going concern. The same is true where the employer dies and his personal representatives carry on the business or where there is a change in the partners who constitute the employer. The Transfer of Undertakings (Protection of Employment) Regulations 1981 are considered in the following chapter. Where the Regulations apply, continuity of employment would be preserved despite the transfer.

If an employee is unfairly dismissed and a tribunal orders that the employee be reinstated or re-engaged, the continuity of employment is preserved and the period when the employee was absent after the dismissal will count as continuous employment.

20.4.1.2 **The effective date of termination (EDT)**

In order to calculate the amount of compensation, and in order to know whether or not there is sufficient continuous employment for a claim to be made, it is necessary to know the precise date on which the employment ended. It is also important to know this date because a claim for unfair dismissal must be brought within three months of the termination of the employment. This date is known as the effective date of termination. Section 97 ERA 1996 defines the effective date of termination as being:

(a) Where the contract is terminated by notice, whether given by the employer or the employee, the date on which the notice expires.

(b) Where the contract is terminated otherwise than by notice, the date on which the termination takes effect.

(c) Where the employee is employed under a contract for a fixed term, which expires without being renewed under the same contract, the date on which the fixed term expires.

Where an employee accepts wages in lieu of notice, the effective date of termination will be the date on which the employment ended, not the date on which the notice would have expired. Section 97(2) provides that where a contract of employment is terminated by the employer, the effective date of termination is the date on which the employee's statutory notice would have expired. However, this is only the case for the purpose of seeing if the employee has the necessary two years' continuous employment and for the purpose of calculating the basic award for unfair dismissal. So an employee dismissed after one year and 51 weeks, without notice, would be entitled to two weeks' statutory notice and the effective date of termination, for the purpose of calculating the basic award, would be one week after his actual dismissal. He would therefore have two years' continuous employment. (Section 97(2) only applies as regards statutory notice, not as regards any longer notice agreed by the parties.) If the employee commits a repudiation of the contract which would justify his dismissal without notice the period of notice to which he would otherwise have been entitled will not be regarded as continuous employment, as the provision in s.97(2) will not apply. In *Gisda Cyf v Barratt* [2010] UKSC 41, [2010] IRLR 1073 the Supreme Court reaffirmed that when a dismissal is communicated by letter the contract of employment is not terminated, for the purposes of unfair dismissal, until the employee has either read the letter or had a reasonable opportunity of reading it. The postal rule, a common law concept considered in Chapter 3 at 3.2.1, would not apply as regards unfair dismissal because the common law right not to be wrongfully dismissed is significantly narrower than the statutory right not to be unfairly dismissed. In *Societe Generale v Geys* [2011] EWCA Civ 307, [2011] All ER (D) 350 (Mar) the Court of Appeal emphasised that the decision in *Gisda Cyf* is restricted to the statutory concept of the effective date of termination. The EDT would not necessarily coincide with the date of termination for common law purposes. As regards wrongful dismissal it would be possible for the parties to agree that a contract could be terminated without the employee being given notice of the termination by, for example, placing an agreed payment in lieu of notice into the employee's bank account.

Time limits

Section 111 ERA 1996 requires a claim for unfair dismissal to be brought within three months of the effective date of termination. The tribunal has an option to extend this limit to such period as it considers reasonable where it was satisfied that it was not reasonably practicable for the complaint to be presented within the three-month period. The time limit is not often extended. Even if the late claim is brought in consequence of poor legal advice, this is unlikely to be a sufficient reason to extend the limit. If, however, the lateness was caused by incorrect advice from the Central Office of Industrial Tribunals this may be a good reason for extending the limit.

20.4.2 What amounts to a dismissal?

ERA 1996 provides a statutory definition of dismissal, for the purposes of unfair dismissal. Section 95 provides that an employee is dismissed if: (a) the employer terminates the contract, with or without notice; or (b) a fixed term contract expires; or (c) the employee is constructively dismissed; or (d) an employee who has been given notice by the employer, himself gives the employer a shorter period of notice to end the contract. An employee can also be deemed to have been dismissed. The various methods of dismissal need to be examined individually. It is up to the employee to prove that he was dismissed.

20.4.2.1 Termination by the employer

If the employer terminates the contract unilaterally, with or without notice, then this amounts to a dismissal. If the employee either resigns or agrees to terminate the employment then this will generally not amount to a dismissal. However, if an employee resigns because he is told that if he does not resign he will be dismissed, this amounts to a dismissal. An example can be seen in *Robertson v Securicor Transport Ltd* [1972] IRLR 70, where a guard who had broken the rules by signing for a package he did not have was given the choice of resigning or being sacked. He chose to resign and was held to have been unfairly dismissed.

If the employer radically and unilaterally changes the conditions of employment then this may amount to a dismissal, as it did in the following case.

Alcan Extrusions v Yates [1996] IRLR 327

The employees worked 37 hours a week on a shift system. Work done at the weekend or bank holidays was overtime. The employers introduced a new rolling shift system, which caused the employees to lose money because weekend and holiday work was no longer regarded as overtime. Negotiations with the union failed to achieve acceptance of the new scheme, so the employer imposed it unilaterally. Letters were sent to the employees telling them that the new system would be adopted. The complainant and others stipulated that they would work the new system under protest, reserving their rights to claim unfair dismissal and redundancy. They later lodged unfair dismissal claims, while continuing to work.

Held. The employees had been expressly dismissed by their employers.

COMMENT The dismissal took effect when the employer unilaterally imposed the new conditions. This seems somewhat strange as the complainant continued to work for the employer after this. The explanation is that the old contract was terminated and the complainant then worked under a different, inferior contract.

If the employer's words or actions are ambiguous, so that they might or might not amount to a termination of the contract, the court will ask what the reasonable person would have made of the words. In reaching a decision as to whether or not the employer intended to terminate the employment, the court will consider the context of the employment and the context in which the words were spoken. Words spoken after the dismissal are only relevant in so far as they shed light upon the employer's intention at the time of the dismissal. Once the dismissal has been made it cannot be unilaterally withdrawn, although words spoken in the heat of the moment may sometimes be withdrawn if this is done quickly enough.

20.4.2.2 Expiry of limited term contract

A limited term contract might either be a fixed term contract or one under which some task is to be performed. A fixed term contract of employment has definite dates for both the commencement and the termination of the employment. If such a fixed term contract expires without being renewed under the same contract then the employee is regarded as dismissed, for the purposes of unfair dismissal. Since October 1999 employees can no longer waive their rights to claim unfair dismissal on the expiry of a fixed term contract. However, as regards fixed term contracts entered into before 25 October 1999 an agreement to waive the right to claim unfair dismissal on the expiry of the contract continues to be effective.

20.4.2.3 Constructive dismissal

Section 95(1)(c) ERA 1996 states that an employee is dismissed by his employer, for the purposes of unfair dismissal, if the employee terminates the contract under which he is employed (with or without notice) in circumstances in which the employee is entitled to terminate it without notice by reason of the employer's conduct. This is often known as constructive dismissal. Lord Denning MR gave an explanation of constructive dismissal in **Western Excavating v Sharp** [1978] 1 All ER 713:

'If the employer is guilty of conduct which is a significant breach going to the root of the contract of employment, or which shows that the employer no longer intends to be bound by one or more of the essential terms of the contract, then the employee is entitled to treat himself as discharged from any further performance. If he does so, then he terminates the contract by reason of the employer's conduct. He is constructively dismissed. The employee is entitled in those circumstances to leave at the instant without giving notice at all or, alternatively, he may give notice and say he is leaving at the end of the notice. But the conduct must in either case be sufficiently serious to entitle him to leave at once. Moreover, he must make up his mind soon after the conduct of which he complains: for, if he continues for any length of time without leaving, he will lose his right to treat himself as discharged. He will be regarded as having elected to affirm the contract.'

If the employer unilaterally imposes a change in the essential terms of the contract, the employee is entitled to regard himself as constructively dismissed. It is up to the employee to show that he was constructively dismissed.

Breach of any term of the contract of employment, if sufficiently serious to go to the root of the contract and therefore justify the employee's resignation, will enable the employee to claim constructive dismissal. It is relatively easy to deduce whether or not an express term of the contract has been breached, but can be very difficult to say whether or not an implied term has been breached.

If the conduct of the employer is within the contract of employment then it cannot give rise to a constructive dismissal. However, if the employer invokes a contract term in an unreasonable way then this may be a breach of the implied term of mutual respect and confidence.

The fact that an employee has been constructively dismissed does not necessarily mean that the dismissal was unfair. In the following case the Court of Appeal had to decide two unresolved questions relating to constructive dismissal. First, whether the conduct of the employer was to be judged objectively or by reference to the 'band of reasonable responses' test. (See 20.4.3.3.) Second, whether the employer could cure the breach while the employee was still considering whether to treat it as a dismissal.

Buckland v Bournemouth University Higher Education Corporation
[2010] EWCA Civ 121, [2010] IRLR 445

In September Professor Buckland had to mark the re-sit exams of 16 students who had failed the original exam. He failed 14 out of the 16. The marks were endorsed by a second marker and confirmed by an exam board, chaired by Dr A. The programme leader of the course in question re-marked the papers, without the authority of Dr A. Dr A was concerned about possible appeals and so he asked another member of staff, H, to re-mark the scripts. H raised the marks slightly so that fewer students failed. Professor Buckland continued to protest at what had happened and so in mid-October the University set up an inquiry chaired by Professor V. Professor Buckland refused to attend this inquiry. However, the inquiry vindicated him and said that once his marks had been accepted by the exam board that should have been the end of the matter. It also criticised the way in which the third marking had been done and the lack of suitable benchmarks for second markers. Professor Buckland was not satisfied with this. He was angry because Dr A, in his evidence, had impugned his integrity as an examiner. He also contended, without any justification, that Professor V had supported assaults on his integrity as an examiner and that the inquiry had set out to exonerate the University management. His head of department assured Professor Buckland that this would not happen again and tried to mollify him. Professor Buckland refused to meet H, as Professor V had recommended. On 22 February he sent a letter of resignation, to take effect at the end of July when he would have fulfilled his obligations to the students. The employment tribunal held that the requirement of mutual trust and confidence had been breached. (See above at 20.2.4.1.) The University argued that the real question was whether what it had done was within the band of reasonable responses.

Held. (i) Constructive dismissal can be claimed only in response to a fundamental or repudiatory breach ➜

of contract by the employer. Whether or not there had been such a fundamental breach is an objective test and the 'band of reasonable responses' test is not appropriate here. However, in some cases, reasonableness would be an appropriate factor to consider in deciding whether or not there had been a fundamental breach of contract. But it would still not be a legal requirement. For example, if an employer refused to pay wages because he had no money on account of a major customer defaulting, this would be a reasonable course of action but it would plainly be a fundamental breach of contract. (ii) If, applying the principles set out in **Western Excavating v Sharp**, acceptance of the breach entitled the employee to leave, he has been constructively dismissed. Once a fundamental breach has been committed, rather than merely threatened, the defaulting party can invite affirmation by making amends but cannot withdraw the breach. However, if the wronged party does not make his position clear at the outset he cannot continue with the contract for very long without being regarded as having affirmed the contract. (iii) The employer may be able to show that the dismissal was for a potentially fair reason. (iv) If the employer does show this then in cases of unfair dismissal the employment tribunal must decide whether the dismissal fell within the band of reasonable responses and was fair. However, this could not possibly be shown in this case as the University had not dismissed the employee. Professor Buckland had therefore been constructively dismissed.

There is generally no implied term that an employee will be entitled to an annual pay rise. However, if the employer arbitrarily and capriciously refuses to give an employee a pay rise this may be enough to enable the employee to claim constructive dismissal.

When an employer commits an act which would justify constructive dismissal the employee must leave the employment reasonably soon afterwards. If the employee does not leave reasonably soon, he will be regarded as having waived the right to treat the contract as repudiated. Also, the employee must initiate the ACAS grievance procedure, explained above at 20.2.7, or he will not be able to present a claim of unfair dismissal to a tribunal. In *Buckland v Bournemouth University Higher Education Corporation* the repudiatory breach occurred in September and the claimant did not leave until July. However, he had not affirmed by his delay. First, it was reasonable for him to await the outcome of the inquiry. Second, he was entitled to give the long period of notice as not to do so would have adversely affected his students.

20.4.2.4 Employee gives notice, having already received notice

Section 95(2) provides that an employee shall be taken to be dismissed for the purposes of unfair dismissal if the employer gives notice to terminate the contract and the employee gives notice to terminate on a date earlier than the date on which the employer's notice was to expire. The reason for the dismissal is taken to be the reason for which the employer's notice was given.

20.4.2.5 Deemed dismissal

Section 96 ERA 1996 provides that a woman who is not permitted to return to work after childbirth is deemed to have been dismissed, for the purposes of unfair dismissal. The woman must have properly exercised her right to return to work. The employment is regarded as continuous up until the date on which she would have been due to return to work, and is regarded as terminated from that date.

20.4.2.6 Situations in which there is no dismissal

There will be no dismissal if the contract is frustrated. Nor will there be a dismissal if the employee resigns, unless constructive dismissal can be claimed. (These circumstances in which the contract is frustrated, and in which there is a genuine resignation by the employee were examined above at 20.3.4 and 20.3.5.) Nor will there be a dismissal if the parties mutually agree to end the employment (see above at 20.3.3) nor if the contract is discharged by performance when the employee completes the specific task which he was employed to perform. Nor will there be a dismissal if a woman fails to return to work after maternity leave, although the contract will be terminated.

In the following case the Court of Appeal considered the position where the employer claimed that the contract was terminated by reason of the employee's breach of the contract. (This situation is sometimes referred to as constructive resignation.)

London Transport Executive v Clarke
[1981] IRLR 166 (Court of Appeal)

The complainant, a bus mechanic who had been born in Jamaica, applied for unpaid leave to go back to Jamaica. This request was turned down because he had already exhausted the amount of unpaid leave which the employers allowed. He again applied for leave →

and was again refused. He asked what would happen if he went without permission and was informed that there was a laid down procedure which would be followed and that this procedure would result in his being removed from the books. The complainant took the leave anyway. The employers wrote to the complainant's London address, asking for an explanation. One week later they wrote to say that if he did not respond within 14 days he would be removed from their books. The complainant did not reply within the period. Two weeks later the employers wrote to the complainant, telling him that his name had been permanently removed from the books on that day. When the complainant returned to England he presented himself at work, with a medical certificate which covered the precise period for which he had been absent from work. He claimed that he had sent a medical certificate to the employers, although they did not receive one. The employers refused to take him back and the complainant claimed unfair dismissal.

Held. The contract of employment was not terminated by the complainant's conduct. The complainant had re-pudiated the contract, but the contract was terminated by the employers when they accepted this repudiation. (They did this when they wrote to him telling him that he had been permanently removed from the books.) Therefore, the employers had dismissed the complainant. If an employee walks out of his job and does not thereafter claim to be entitled to resume work, he repudiates his contract of employment and the employer accepts this. There can then be no claim for unfair dismissal unless the worker claims that he was constructively dismissed. But where the worker repudiates his contract, by walking out of his job or otherwise, and later claims to be entitled to resume work, then his contract is only terminated if the employer expressly or impliedly accepts the repudiation. This acceptance of the repudiation by the employer amounts to a dismissal, and refusing to allow the worker to return would be such an acceptance of the repudiation.

COMMENT The dismissal was not unfair. The employment tribunal had held that it was. The Court of Appeal overturned this, regarding the tribunal as having erred in law. The Court of Appeal described the tribunal's finding as to unfairness as one which outraged common sense, being a conclusion which no reasonable tribunal could have reached.

20.4.3 Fair and unfair dismissals

After deciding that an employee has been dismissed, the next step is to consider whether or not the dismissal was unfair.

Section 98 ERA 1996 states that in determining whether or not the dismissal of an employee is fair or unfair, it is for the employer to show the reason for the dismissal, or the principal reason for the dismissal if there was more than one. Section 98 also provides that it is for the employer to show that the reason for the dismissal was either one of the five matters listed, or was for some other substantial reason of a kind such as to justify the dismissal of an employee holding the position which the employee held. The five matters listed are:

(a) the reason for the dismissal relates to the capability or qualifications of the employee for performing work of the kind which he was employed by the employer to do;

(b) the reason for the dismissal relates to the conduct of the employee;

(c) the reason for the dismissal is that the employee was made redundant;

(d) the reason for the dismissal is that the employee could not continue to work in the position which he held without contravention, either by him or by his employer, of a duty or restriction imposed by or under a statute; or

(e) the reason for the dismissal is retirement.

20.4.3.1 Grounds on which dismissal may be fair

As we have seen, the burden of proof is on the employer to show the reason for the dismissal, and that the reason fell within one of the matters listed. We therefore need to consider each of the matters listed. The fact that the dismissal was made on the grounds of one of the matters listed does not necessarily mean that the dismissal was fair. However, if the dismissal was made not on the grounds of one of the matters listed, or for some other substantial reason of a kind such as to justify dismissal, then it will always amount to an unfair dismissal.

Lack of capability or qualifications to do the job
It is obviously fair to dismiss an employee who is inherently incapable of performing the job which he was employed to do. However, the employer is still required to act reasonably and should therefore take steps such as: finding out why the employee has difficulty; providing remedial training; providing warnings in appropriate cases and perhaps offering the employee alternative employment. In **Davison v Kent Meters Ltd** [1975] IRLR 145, for example, an

employee who had incorrectly assembled a large number of components in the wrong way was held to have been unfairly dismissed because she had not been shown how to do the job properly. Generally, a dismissal on the grounds of lack of capability will require more than one act of incompetence.

An employer can dismiss an incompetent employee if, subjectively, the employer considers that the employee was incompetent. There must also be reasonable grounds for such a belief. It is not necessary to prove, objectively, that the employee actually was incompetent. Before dismissing the employee the reasonable employer should first consider other steps, such as warnings. However, a warning is only appropriate if it has some chance of achieving a change in the employee's behaviour.

Earlier in this chapter we considered *Egg Stores (Stamford Hill) Ltd* v *Leibovici* and the circumstances in which a contract of employment is frustrated, rather than terminated by a dismissal, on the grounds of long-term sickness or injury. When an employee is dismissed on the grounds of long-term illness or injury the employer should also consider the Disability Discrimination Act 1995, which is considered in the following chapter at 21.4.

In *International Sports Co Ltd* v *Thomson* [1980] IRLR 340 the EAT considered the position where an employee is off sick due to minor ailments. This case might be better classified as absenteeism, rather than as genuine long-term illness. Over the previous 18 months the complainant had been absent from work for about 25 per cent of the time. She always provided a medical certificate to cover her absences. She suffered from various complaints, including 'dizzy spells, anxiety and nerves, bronchitis, virus infection, althruigra of the left knee and dyspepsia and flatulence'. The employers' medical advisor said that there was no point in examining the complainant because her complaints were all unconnected and none of them amounted to a chronic illness. After several warnings and a final warning, the complainant was dismissed. The EAT held that the dismissal was fair. The EAT held that the procedure required in cases of intermittent absence through minor ailments is similar to the procedure for misconduct. First, the employer should conduct a fair review of the employee's attendance record and the reasons for it. Second, appropriate warnings should be given after the employee has been given an opportunity to make representations. If there is no subsequent improvement in the attendance record, in most cases the employer will be justified in treating the persistent absences as a sufficient reason for dismissing the employee. On the facts of the case the EAT held that this was a case where the reasonable employer was entitled to say 'enough is enough'.

There are very few cases concerning dismissal for lack of qualifications. Generally, those who are not qualified to do the job are not given the job in the first place. If an aptitude test is introduced for all employees, it may be that an employee can be fairly dismissed on account of not being able to pass the test.

Dismissal on the grounds of the employee's conduct

An employee's conduct, either while at work or outside work, may be sufficiently bad for the employer to fairly dismiss the employee. Some misconduct is of such a serious nature that a summary dismissal would be justified. Minor misconduct would not justify a dismissal without warnings and a final warning having been issued. In all cases of misconduct except those which would obviously justify summary dismissal, the employer should not dismiss the employee without giving the employee the chance to explain himself, without gaining evidence as to what happened and without conducting an enquiry into what happened.

Examples of conduct while at work which have been held to justify dismissal include fighting, swearing, theft, dangerous conduct, dishonesty, immorality and refusing to obey orders, to name but a few. Everything depends upon all the facts of the case. A schoolteacher swearing at young children might be fairly dismissed for using language which would not raise an eyebrow if used by one labourer on a building site to another. Again, the question is whether the employer acted reasonably in dismissing the employee.

Conduct outside the employment can be enough to justify dismissal, but only if it would have an sufficiently adverse effect on the employer's business. In *Gardiner* v *Newport County Borough Council* [1974] IRLR 262, for example, a lecturer at a college of art and design, who taught students aged 16–18, was fairly dismissed after having been convicted of gross indecency with another man in a public lavatory.

Dismissal on the grounds of redundancy

Below, at 20.5, we shall consider the circumstances in which a person is made redundant. A person who is made redundant will not be regarded as having been unfairly dismissed. In *Williams v Compair Maxam Ltd* [1982] ICR 156 Browne-Wilkinson J set down five principles which a reasonable employer would be expected to adopt in choosing which employees should be made redundant, when a large number of redundancies were inevitable. The principles were as follows: first, the employees should be given as much warning of redundancy as possible; second, the employer should consult the union to see how the redundancies could be achieved fairly and with as little hardship to the employees as possible; third, criteria which can be objectively checked, such as attendance records, efficiency, experience and length of service should be used rather than subjective criteria; fourth, the employer should consider union representation as to the appropriate criteria; fifth, the employer should consider whether instead of dismissing the employee he could offer him alternative employment.

The principles laid down in *Williams v Compair Maxam Ltd* are less appropriate in relation to small employers. In all cases the employer should consider alternatives to redundancy, should observe the Code of Practice relating to redundancies and should ensure that a proper selection procedure is used.

Dismissal on the grounds of retirement

As from 6 April 2011 employers have no longer been allowed to issue retirement notices, forcing employees to retire on account of their age. Any employee who has become 65 since 30 September 2011 cannot be forcibly retired on account of his age.

Conflict with a statute

An employee might be dismissed fairly on account of the continuing employment conflicting with a statutory provision. For example, if the employee was a driver who was banned from driving, or if a newly passed statute made the employee's further employment unlawful. The employer must still act reasonably. In *Mathieson v Noble & Sons Ltd* [1972] IRLR 76 a salesman, whose job required him to drive, was banned from driving. At his own expense the salesman arranged for a chauffeur to drive him around until his disqualification was over. His employer was not prepared to give this arrangement a try and dismissed him. The dismissal was held to be unfair. The employers had acted unreasonably.

Some other substantial reason

The four factors examined above are not exhaustive. A dismissal may be fair although outside the matters specified if it was for some other substantial reason of a kind such as to justify the dismissal of an employee holding the position which he held. There is no closed list of what might amount to some other substantial reason, but employees have been fairly dismissed under this heading in the following circumstances: a teacher failing to forgo a pay rise when all the other teachers at the school had agreed to this, on account of the financial difficulties which the school was experiencing; deliberate concealment of a history of mental illness by an insurance inspector who had to visit clients' homes; refusing to accept a variation in the terms of the employment which was reasonably made in the commercial interest of the employer; refusing to accept a wage cut which had been negotiated by a trade union; being one of several employees at an off-licence, one of whom had stolen £4 600, where a thorough investigation could not reveal which employee was responsible; being an employee who could not get along with another employee, serious efforts to resolve the situation without the need for a dismissal having been considered.

20.4.3.2 Automatically unfair dismissals

Certain reasons for dismissal are automatically regarded as unfair. These include the following:

Dismissal for claiming a statutory right (ERA 1996 s.104)

Section 104 ERA 1996 provides that an employee is unfairly dismissed if the reason for the dismissal (or the principal reason if there was more than one) was that the employee brought proceedings against the employer to enforce a statutory right, or alleged that the employer had infringed a statutory right. It does not matter whether or not the employee actually had the statutory right, or whether or not it was actually infringed. The statutory rights to which this section applies include all those conferred by ERA 1996.

Leave for family reasons (ERA 1996 s.99)

An employee is automatically unfairly dismissed if the reason for the dismissal, or the principal reason, was a reason relating to: (a) pregnancy, childbirth or maternity; (b) maternity or adoption leave; (c) parental or paternity leave; or (d) statutory time off for dependants.

Health and safety cases (ERA 1996 s.100)

An employee is automatically unfairly dismissed if the reason for the dismissal was that he carried out duties, which the employer had designated him to carry out, in connection with preventing or reducing risks to health and safety at work. If there is no health and safety representative or committee, a dismissal on the grounds of the employee carrying out health and safety duties will similarly be automatically unfair. No qualifying period of employment is necessary. Section 103 makes a similar provision in respect of a dismissal for carrying out duties in connection with the employee's role as trustee of an occupational pension scheme.

Working time cases (ERA 1996 ss.101 and 101A)

A worker who is dismissed for insisting on his rights under the Working Time Regulations 1998 is unfairly dismissed. (These Regulations are considered in the following chapter.) Employees who work in shops or betting offices are automatically unfairly dismissed if they are dismissed for refusing to work on a Sunday.

Retirement of an employee

Dismissing an employee on the grounds of retirement will be automatically unfair if the employee was not informed in writing of the intended date of his retirement and of the right to request to continue to work. Failure to consider an employee's request to continue working beyond the intended date of his retirement will also mean that a dismissal by way of retirement will be automatically unfair. Similarly, an employee dismissed for trying to get a colleague to represent him at the statutory meeting to consider the employee's request, or for trying to represent a colleague at such a meeting, will be an automatically unfair dismissal.

Trade union membership (TULRCA 1992 s.137)

It is automatically unfair to dismiss a person either because he is a member of a trade union or because he is not. There is no qualifying time of employment. If an employee is dismissed on account of having taken official strike action, during the first 12 weeks of such action, this is automatically an unfair dismissal.

Transfer of undertakings

Employees who have at least two years' continuous employment, and who are dismissed in connection with a transfer of undertaking which falls within the 1981 Regulations, are automatically unfairly dismissed. (The circumstances in which employees are protected is considered in Chapter 21.)

Jury service

It is automatically unfair to dismiss an employee for taking time off to perform jury service. No qualification period is necessary.

20.4.3.3 Was the dismissal actually unfair?

If the employer cannot prove that the reason for the dismissal was within the matters listed above at 20.4.3.1, the employee will have been unfairly dismissed. If the employer can show that the employee was dismissed for one of the matters listed, it then needs to be considered whether or not the dismissal actually was unfair. Section 98(4) ERA 1996 states that:

'Where the employer has fulfilled the requirements of [s.98(1)], the determination of the question whether the dismissal is fair or unfair (having regard to the reason shown by the employer) –

(a) depends on whether in the circumstances (including the size and administrative resources of the employer's undertaking) the employer acted reasonably or unreasonably in treating it as a sufficient reason for dismissing the employee, and

(b) shall be determined in accordance with equity and the substantial merits of the case.'

The burden of proof as to whether or not the dismissal actually was unfair is neutral. This is a matter for the tribunal to decide in the light of s.98(4) and all the evidence.

The tribunal is likely to consider the dismissal unfair if the employer cannot show that he went through the proper procedures and then that he acted reasonably, that is to say whether he acted as a reasonable employer would have done. Whether or not the employer actually did act as a reasonable employer would have done is a question to be decided by the tribunal in the light of all the circumstances. An appellate court can only overrule the tribunal's finding if it was perverse or made as a consequence of an error of law.

In **_Willow Oak Developments Ltd_ v _Silverwood_** [2006] EWCA Civ 660, [2006] IRLR 607, employees were dismissed because they would not agree to new terms in their contract which restricted their activities after their employment had ended. The Court of Appeal was prepared to accept that these new terms might have been reasonably necessary to protect the employer's interests and that refusal to accept them could therefore have justified dismissal. However, the dismissals were unfair anyway because the employer did not act reasonably as required by s.98(4), particularly in failing to warn the employees that they could be dismissed if they refused to accept the new terms.

The band of reasonable responses

In *Iceland Frozen Foods* v *Jones* [1983] ICR 17 Browne-Wilkinson J summarised the law in this way:

> 'We consider that the authorities establish that in law the correct approach for the employment tribunal to adopt in answering the question posed by [s.98(4) ERA 1996] is as follows: (1) the starting point should always be the words of [s.98(4) ERA 1996] themselves; (2) in applying the section an employment tribunal must consider the reasonableness of the employer's conduct, not simply whether they (the members of the employment tribunal) consider the dismissal to be fair; (3) in judging the reasonableness of the employer's conduct an employment tribunal must not substitute its decision as to what was the right course to adopt for that of the employer; (4) in many, though not all, cases there is a band of reasonable responses to the employee's conduct within which one employer might reasonably take one view, another quite reasonably take another; (5) the function of the employment tribunal, as an industrial jury, is to determine whether in the particular circumstances of each case the decision to dismiss the employee fell within the band of reasonable responses which a reasonable employer might have adopted. If the dismissal falls within the band the dismissal is fair: if the dismissal falls outside the band the dismissal is unfair.'

This test seems very favourable to the employer. Only if the employer's decision to dismiss could not have been within the band of reasonableness will it be unfair. It will thus be fair even if many employers would have considered the decision to dismiss the employee as an unreasonable response. The band of reasonable responses seems preferable to allowing the tribunal to decide if they, as reasonable employers, would have dismissed the employee. To do this would be to allow a subjective review by the tribunal members to replace the subjective decision of the employer who dismissed the employee. At times the band of reasonable responses test has been doubted, but its validity was approved by the Court of Appeal in *Post Office* v *Foley*; *HSBC Bank* v *Madden* [2000] 1 All ER 550.

In *Claridge* v *Daler Rowney Ltd* UKEAT/0188/08, [2008] IRLR 672, the Employment Appeal Tribunal considered the band of reasonable responses test in relation to constructive dismissal. An employee who had been demoted resigned and claimed constructive dismissal on account of breach of the implied term of trust and confidence. The employment tribunal held that the employer had acted unreasonably but had nevertheless acted within the band of reasonable responses. Not surprisingly, this reasoning was criticised by the EAT. Elias P said that an employer could not be acting reasonably and unreasonably at the same time. Nevertheless, the appeal was dismissed. The correct approach in a case such as this was to ask whether or not the employer's unreasonable conduct was bad enough to amount to a repudiatory breach of contract. This would not be possible unless the employer's behaviour fell outside the band of reasonable responses. In this case the employer's behaviour had not been bad enough to do fall outside the band of reasonable responses, and did not therefore amount to a repudiatory breach of contract, even though the EAT was critical of the employer's behaviour.

Procedural unfairness

Even if a dismissal was for one of the fair reasons specified, and even if it was within the band of reasonable responses, it will be automatically unfair if one of the statutory dismissal and disciplinary procedures was not complied with.

Section 98A(1) ERA 1996 now provides:

> 'An employee who is dismissed shall be regarded for the purposes of this Part as unfairly dismissed if –
>
> (a) one of the procedures set out in Part 1 of Schedule 2 to the Employment Act 2002 (dismissal and disciplinary procedures) applies in relation to the dismissal,
> (b) the procedure has not been completed, and
> (c) the non-completion of the procedure is wholly or mainly attributable to failure by the employer to comply with its requirements.'

As regards dismissal procedures other than the ones set out in Part 1 of Schedule 2 to the Employment Act 2002, s.98A(2) provides that failure to follow such other dismissal procedure shall not be regarded for the purposes of s.98(4)(a) as by itself making the employer's action unreasonable if he shows that he would have decided to have dismissed the employee if he had followed the procedure.

20.4.3.4 **ACAS disciplinary and dismissal procedures**

Earlier in this chapter, at 20.2.7, the new grievance procedures contained in the ACAS Code of Practice 1: Discipline and Grievance (the Code) were considered. The Code also introduced disciplinary and dismissal procedures, which are considered here. These new procedures replaced the statutory procedures, introduced in October 2004, which were found to be too formalistic. The Code provides a framework which will allow employers to take a flexible approach whilst applying the rules of natural justice. As is the case with grievances, both employers and employees should attempt to settle disciplinary matters informally, using outside third parties if necessary. They should also attempt to deal with matters promptly, without undue delay. The Code does not apply to dismissals by way of redundancy or to dismissals which occur when a fixed-term contract is not renewed. The following five stages should be followed when a disciplinary issue cannot be resolved informally:

- The employer should establish the facts of the case. This should be done without undue delay and will involve carrying out necessary investigations. A preliminary investigative meeting with the employee may be required to achieve this. The employee has no statutory right to be accompanied at this meeting, although the employer's own procedure may allow this. No disciplinary action should be taken at this preliminary meeting.
- The employer should inform the employee of the problem. If there is a disciplinary case to answer, the employee should be given details of the case in writing. The details should give the employee enough information for him to prepare an answer, and copies of any written evidence should be provided. As well as setting out the time and place of the disciplinary meeting, the employee should be informed of his right to be accompanied at the meeting.
- The employer should hold a meeting with the employee to discuss the problem. The employee must be given time to prepare his case but the meeting should otherwise be held without unreasonable delay. Employers, employees and the companions of employees should make every effort to attend the meeting. At the meeting the evidence against the employee should be explained and gone over. The employee should be given a chance to set out his own case and answer allegations and should

also be given a reasonable opportunity to ask questions, present evidence and call witnesses. If either side intends to call witnesses, they should give advance notice of this.

- If the meeting could result in a formal warning being issued, or some other disciplinary action taken, the employer must allow the employee to be accompanied at the meeting. However, the employee would have to make a reasonable request to be accompanied. What is reasonable will depend upon all the circumstances of the case. The companion could be a fellow worker, a trade union representative or an official employed by a trade union. The companion would have no right to answer questions on the employee's behalf. However, the companion would have the rights to address the meeting in order to put and sum up the employee's case, to respond on the employee's behalf to any views expressed at the meeting and to confer with the employee during the meeting. There is no right to be accompanied by a legal representative, unless the employer agrees to this.
- The employer must decide upon appropriate action and inform the employee of this decision in writing. As regards most cases of misconduct or unsatisfactory performance, a first written warning would be the usual action taken, with the threat of a final written warning if there was further misconduct or a failure to improve performance. If the misconduct or unsatisfactory performance is sufficiently serious, a final written warning might be appropriate. A written warning should set out the employee's poor performance or misconduct, the change in behaviour or improvement required and the timescale for this. The employee should also be told for how long the warning remains in force and what the consequences of further misconduct or failure to improve might be. Even if there is gross misconduct which would justify dismissal without a warning, the disciplinary process should always be followed. Disciplinary rules should set out examples of gross misconduct. If the employee is persistently unwilling or unable to attend a meeting, without a good reason, the employer should make a decision on the evidence available.
- The employer should provide the employee with an opportunity to appeal. Appeals should be heard without unreasonable delay, preferably by a manager who has not previously been involved.

The employee has the right to be accompanied at the appeal. The outcome of the appeal should be communicated in writing without unreasonable delay.

The Code is not legally binding but is admissible as evidence and can be taken into account by the employment tribunal. Section 207A(2) of Trade Union and Labour Relations (Consolidation) Act 1992 allows the tribunal, if it considers it just and equitable, to increase any award to an employee by up to 25 per cent if it appears to the tribunal that the employer has unreasonably failed to comply with the Code. Section 207A(3) contains a corresponding power to reduce the award by up to 25 per cent where it is the employee who has unreasonably failed to comply with the Code. An ACAS Guide provides rather more detail than the Code. This guide includes sample disciplinary procedures and sample letters which an employer might use when complying with the Code.

Before the Employment Act 2008 changed the law in this area, a dismissal was automatically unfair if the old statutory dismissal procedures were not complied with. This is no longer the case. The law has now reverted to the position it was in before the statutory dismissal procedures were introduced in October 2004. The House of Lords decision in *Polkey v A E Dayton Services Ltd* [1988] AC 344 has once again become the law. Under the *Polkey* ruling, a dismissal might be unfair, even if for one of the fair reasons specified and even if the employer acted within the band of reasonable responses, purely because the correct dismissal procedure was not complied with. However, in such cases the tribunal should reduce or eliminate the compensation payable, other than the basic award (see below at 20.4.4.2), to reflect any likelihood that the employee would have been dismissed even if the correct procedures had been complied with. Despite the *Polkey* ruling, there will have been no unfair dismissal if the tribunal concludes that the employer acted as a reasonable employer would have acted in taking the view that, in the exceptional circumstances of the particular case, the normal procedural steps would have been futile and were dispensed with because they could not have altered the decision to dismiss. The *Polkey* ruling will not apply where the dismissal would have been unfair anyway, despite the failure to follow the correct procedure. In such a case, s.270A(2) of the Trade Union and Labour Relations (Consolidation) Act 1992 would allow the tribunal to increase the amount of any award by up to 25 per cent if the procedure set out in the Code was not complied with.

20.4.4 Remedies for unfair dismissal

ERA 1996 specifies the remedies available for unfair dismissal. These are reinstatement, re-engagement or compensation.

20.4.4.1 Re-engagement and reinstatement

Section 113 ERA 1996 lists re-engagement and reinstatement as remedies for unfair dismissal. If an employee is reinstated he is given his old job back. The employer must treat the complainant in all respects as if he had not been dismissed. The tribunal will specify the amount of back pay he should receive, any rights and privileges (including seniority and pension rights) which must be restored to the employee and the date by which the order must be complied with. If the employee is re-engaged he is taken back in a capacity comparable to that in which he was previously employed, on the terms which the tribunal thinks fit. The tribunal will specify the nature of the employment, the remuneration of the employment, any back pay to which the employee might be entitled, any rights and privileges (including seniority and pension rights) which must be restored to the employee and the date by which the order must be complied with. As regards either type of award the tribunal takes into account any payments made by the employer, and any social security benefits received by the employee, in deciding upon the amount of back pay. Neither of these remedies is awarded very often. Generally, the implied term as to mutual trust and respect has been irrevocably breached by the time of the hearing. For this reason the tribunal is reluctant to make an order of re-engagement or reinstatement. If an employee is re-engaged or reinstated his continuous employment is not broken and the period for which he was absent from work counts as part of his continuous employment.

20.4.4.2 Compensation awards

The basic award

This award is calculated according to a formula set out by s.119 ERA 1996. The formula multiplies the employee's relevant years of continuous employment by his weekly wage. For each year of continuous employment below the age of 22 the employee is awarded half a week's pay. For each year during which the employee was 22 or more but below the age of 41 he gets one week's pay, and for each year of continuous employment during which the employee was 41 or more he gets one and a half weeks' pay. The week's pay is the normal week's pay. Overtime is not included unless there is a contractual provision for the employer to provide it and for the employee to work it. The amount awarded is often severely restricted by two limits. First, an applicant cannot claim for more than 20 years' continuous employment, even if he has worked more. Second, the week's pay which can be claimed is limited to a maximum of £400 per week, no matter how much the employee actually earns. The maximum award is therefore $20 \times 1.5 = 30 \times £400 = £12\,000$. The number of relevant years in each category is calculated by working backwards from the effective date of termination. Only whole years count. The statutory restriction on the maximum week's pay is periodically increased.

The following example shows how the basic award is calculated.

Example

Both Fred and Jill are unfairly dismissed. Fred has 16 years' continuous employment, six of these having been worked since he reached the age of 41. His weekly wage is £200. Jill has 20 years' continuous employment, ten of these having been worked since she reached the age of 41. Jill's weekly wage is £660.

Fred's entitlement will be calculated as 19 weeks' pay, for the purpose of calculating the basic award. (The six years after attaining the age of 41 counting as nine weeks. The ten years before he reached the age of 41 counting as one week per year.) Fred will get a basic award of $19 \times £200 = £3\,800$.

Jill's entitlement will be calculated as 25 weeks' pay for the purpose of calculating the basic award. (The ten years worked after she was 41 count as 15 weeks. The ten years worked before attaining the age of 41 count as one week each.) Jill earns more than the maximum weekly wage of £400, so her weekly wage will be set at £400. Jill will therefore receive a basic award of $25 \times £400 = £10\,000$.

The basic award can be reduced in three circumstances. First, if the employer has made an offer of re-engagement or reinstatement which the employee has refused to take up. The refusal must be unreasonable, in which case the tribunal can reduce the award by the amount which it sees fit. Second, the tribunal may reduce the award if the complainant's conduct before the dismissal was such as to make the reduction equitable. This is similar to contributory negligence, although the conduct of the complainant does not need to have contributed to the employer's decision to dismiss. The award can be dismissed on the grounds of conduct committed before the dismissal, even if this conduct was not discovered until after the dismissal. Third, if the employer claimed that the complainant was dismissed on the grounds of redundancy, when in fact the complainant was unfairly dismissed, the amount of any redundancy payment received by the complainant will be deducted from the basic award for unfair dismissal.

As the basic award is not an award of damages, the complainant has no duty to mitigate the loss.

Automatic entitlement to basic award

Section 138 ERA 1996 provides that an employee who is made redundant, having refused an offer of suitable alternative employment, will not be entitled to a redundancy payment. He will however be entitled automatically to a basic award of two weeks' pay. (The £400 maximum applies.)

Section 141 ERA 1996 entitles an employee who chooses not to accept a renewal of his contract or a re-engagement under a new contract to regard himself as dismissed and take a basic award calculated as two weeks' pay. (Subject to the £400 maximum.) The employee would not be entitled to a redundancy payment, on account of having refused the renewal or re-engagement.

Section 120(1) provides that the amount of the basic award shall be not less than £5 000, subject to any deduction for contributory fault, where the reason, or principal reason, for a dismissal or for selecting a person for redundancy is membership or non-membership of a trade union.

Compensatory awards

Section 123(1) provides that the amount of the compensatory award shall be such amount as the tribunal considers just and equitable in all the circumstances, having regard to the loss sustained by the employee in consequence of the dismissal in so far as that loss is attributable to action taken by the employer. The maximum compensatory award which can be awarded is currently £68 400. (However, in cases where discrimination is proved there is no upper limit on the amount of damages.)

This award is in addition to the basic award. As the purpose of the compensatory award is to compensate the complainant, not to punish the employer, it is only given in respect of financial losses. The tribunal has a wide discretion but should set out the ways in which the award was made up. The usual headings are: immediate and future loss of earnings (the burden of proof as regards these losses is on the complainant but the tribunal speculates as to how long the employee is likely to remain unemployed. There is no upper limit on the weekly pay. The immediate loss of earnings will be the amount lost between the dates of termination and the hearing. If wages were paid in lieu of notice the tribunal will take account of this); expenses; loss of statutory rights, bearing in mind that rights such as not to be unfairly dismissed will not arise until there has been two years continuous employment; loss of pension rights; and a supplementary amount if the employer failed to go through an established appeal procedure. In *Tao Herbs & Acupuncture Ltd v Jin* [2010] UKEAT 1477-09 the EAT held that the ability of the employer to pay should not be taken into account when calculating a compensatory award for unfair dismissal.

The compensatory award will be reduced in respect of losses which the employee could have mitigated. If he therefore turned down suitable employment the amount will be reduced. It is up to the employer to prove that the employee failed to mitigate. It will also be reduced by the amount of job-seeker's allowance which the applicant has received. Section 123(6) provides that where the tribunal finds that the dismissal was to any extent caused or contributed to by any action of the employee, it shall reduce the amount of the compensatory award by such proportion as it considers just and equitable having regard to that finding. Again, this is similar to contributory negligence.

Additional awards

If an employer refuses to comply with a re-engagement or reinstatement order the tribunal may make an additional award. This additional award should be of between 13 and 26 weeks' pay, unless the dismissal was on the grounds of sex or racial discrimination, in which case it could be of between 26 and 52 weeks' pay. (The week's pay is still subject to the £400 maximum.)

Test your understanding 20.4

1 What period of continuous employment must an employee have worked in order to claim unfair dismissal?

2 What is the effective date of termination? In what three ways is it significant?

3 On what grounds may an employee be regarded as having been dismissed, for the purposes of unfair dismissal?

4 On what five grounds might a dismissal be fair, for the purposes of unfair dismissal?

5 On what grounds can a dismissal be automatically unfair?

6 If the employer establishes that the dismissal was for one of the specified fair reasons, does this automatically mean that the dismissal was fair?

7 Can a dismissal be rendered unfair merely because the employer did not follow the correct procedures?

8 What remedies can be awarded for unfair dismissal?

9 How are the basic award and the compensatory award assessed?

20.5 REDUNDANCY

An employee with at least two years' continuous employment who is made redundant is entitled to a statutory payment, as compensation for the loss of his job. Lord Denning MR gave the following explanation of redundancy and the nature of redundancy payments in *Lloyd v Brassey* [1969] 2 QB 98.

'It is as well to remind ourselves of the policy of this legislation [the Redundancy Payments Act 1965, which has been consolidated into the ERA 1996.] ... a worker of long standing is now recognised as having an accrued right in his job; and his right gains in value with the years. So much so that if the job is shut down he is entitled to compensation for loss of the job – just as a director gets compensation for loss of office. The director gets a golden handshake. The worker gets a redundancy payment. It is not unemployment pay. I repeat "not". Even if he gets another job straightaway, he nevertheless is entitled to full redundancy payment. It is, in a real sense, compensation for long service. No man gets it unless he has been employed for at least two years by the employer; and then the amount of it depends solely upon his age and length of service.'

A redundancy payment is therefore aimed at cushioning the blow when workers lose their jobs. Before 1972 there was no statutory payment for unfair dismissal. Employees were therefore keen to prove that a dismissal amounted to redundancy. We saw earlier in this chapter that an employee who is properly made redundant will not be able to claim unfair dismissal. These days, employees commonly argue that they have not been made redundant, as this will entitle them to claim unfair dismissal, which may result in a higher payment being made.

20.5.1 Dismissal by reason of redundancy

Section 139(1) ERA 1996 sets out the circumstances in which an employee will have been made redundant.

'(1) For the purposes of this Act an employee who is dismissed shall be taken to be dismissed by reason of redundancy if the dismissal is wholly or mainly attributable to –
(a) the fact that his employer has ceased or intends to cease –
(i) to carry on the business for the purposes of which the employee was employed by him, or
(ii) to carry on that business in the place where the employee was so employed, or
(b) the fact that the requirements of that business –
(i) for employees to carry out work of a particular kind, or
(ii) for employees to carry out work of a particular kind in the place where the employee was employed by the employer,
have ceased or diminished or are expected to cease or diminish.'

It can be seen from s.139(1) that the meaning of redundancy is not the same as the everyday meaning. Both employers and employees often refer to any dismissal as a redundancy. In fact the situations in which an employee can be dismissed by reason of redundancy are specific. A little needs to be said about each of the possible types of dismissals which can be by reason of redundancy.

20.5.1.1 Cessation of the business

The employees of a business will be dismissed by reason of redundancy if they are dismissed on account of the employer either ceasing or intending to cease to carry on the business for the purposes of which the employee was employed. This is one of the most common redundancy situations, with which most people are probably familiar. It is commonly reported in the newspapers that a particular company has gone into administration and that some or all of the employees have been made redundant.

20.5.1.2 The employer moves the place of the business

If the employer moves the place of work from one place to another the employees may have been made redundant. Whether they have been made redundant is a question of fact, and will depend amongst other things upon the distance moved and the level of inconvenience caused to the employees by the move.

The true place of work of the employee may well cause difficulty if the employee's contract contains a 'mobility clause' requiring him to work anywhere in the country. Is the employee's place of work to be ascertained by the contract test, which would regard the place of work as the place where the employee could be required within his contract to work? Or is it to be ascertained by the geographical test, which would regard the place of work as the place where the employee actually worked? In the following case the Court of Appeal strongly favoured the geographical test.

High Table Ltd v Horst [1997] IRLR 513 (Court of Appeal)

The three applicants worked as waitresses for a firm which provided catering services in London. They were dismissed and the company claimed that this was by reason of redundancy, on the grounds that the employees were no longer needed at the place where they worked. The applicants' contracts of employment contained a mobility clause and so they could therefore have been employed elsewhere. The applicants claimed that as they had not been employed elsewhere they had been unfairly dismissed.

Held. The applicants were made redundant.

Peter Gibson LJ: 'The question [s.139(1)] poses – where was the employee employed by the employer for the purposes of the business? – is one to be →

answered primarily by a consideration of the factual circumstances which obtained until the dismissal. If an employee has worked in only one location under his contract of employment for the purposes of the employer's business, it defies common sense to widen the extent of the place where he was so employed, merely because of the existence of a mobility clause. Of course, the refusal by the employee to obey a lawful requirement under the contract of employment for the employee to move may constitute a valid reason for dismissal, but the issues of dismissal, redundancy and reasonableness in the actions of an employer should be kept distinct. It would be unfortunate if the law were to encourage the inclusion of mobility clauses to defeat genuine redundancy claims.'

20.5.1.3 The employer sheds surplus labour

An employer's need to employ workers may diminish either because there is less work to be done or because the existing work can be performed by fewer employees. Many innovations and new technologies have had the effect of reducing the need for workers of a particular kind. Often a reorganisation by the employer requires employees to work at a different time of day. Employees who refuse to do this and are consequently dismissed will not be entitled to a redundancy payment.

Difficulties have been caused by the meaning of 'work of a particular kind'. Several tests have been used by the courts to discover the meaning of 'work of a particular kind'. In the following case the Employment Appeal Tribunal formulated what has become known as the statutory test.

Safeway Stores plc v Burrell [1997] IRLR 200

A petrol station manager at a Safeway supermarket was dismissed when Safeway carried out a nationwide re-organisation. The post of petrol station manager disappeared and a new post of petrol filling station controller was created. Some redundancies of management employees were inevitable, as there were to be fewer new posts than old posts. The applicant did not apply for the new job of petrol filling station controller as the pay was only £11 000 p.a., whereas previously he had earned £13 052 p.a. The applicant agreed to take a redundancy payment and pay in lieu of notice. Subsequently he claimed unfair dismissal, on the grounds that he had not been made redundant.

Held. The applicant was made redundant. The statutory framework of s.139(1)(b) involved the following three-stage process:

(i) Was the employee dismissed? If so
(ii) Had the requirements of the employer's business for employees to carry out work of a particular kind ceased or diminished, or were they expected to cease or diminish? If so
(iii) Was the dismissal of the employee caused wholly or mainly by the state of affairs identified at stage 2?

COMMENT The test applied in the case is known as the statutory test. Two other tests, the function test and the contract test, have also been used. The statutory test now seems to be the correct one. In **Murray v Foyle Meats** [1999] IRLR 562 the House of Lords strongly approved the decision in **Safeway Stores plc v Burrell**. Lord Irvine of Lairg LC, giving the leading judgment, said that he entirely agreed with the clear reasoning and conclusions of the case. The decision seems to allow for what is known as 'bumping' where one employee, who would otherwise have been made redundant, replaces another and the employee replaced is regarded as having been made redundant. This seems to be allowed because the stage 2 question asks whether the requirements of the employer's business for employees has ceased or diminished, rather than asking whether the need to employ the particular employee had ceased or diminished.

In many cases the fact that a dismissed employee was not replaced will indicate that he was made redundant.

20.5.2 Who can claim redundancy?

Only employees with at least two years' continuous employment are entitled to claim redundancy. Share fishermen and Crown employees are excluded from claiming redundancy. Those ordinarily employed outside Great Britain cannot usually claim. They can, however, claim if they were present in Great Britain on the employer's instructions, on the date when they were made redundant.

We examined the meaning of continuous employment earlier in this chapter at 20.4.1.2. Section 139(2) ERA 1996 provides that for the purposes of redundancy the business of the employer together with the business or businesses of his associated employers shall be treated as one. Associated employers would include companies who control the business of the main employer company or are controlled by it. Two employers are treated as associated if both are companies controlled directly or indirectly by a third person.

Section 218(2) ERA 1996 provides that if a trade or business or undertaking is transferred from one person to another, this does not break the continuity of employment.

Section 163(2) ERA 1996 states that an employee who has been dismissed by his employer shall, unless the contrary is proved, be presumed to have been so dismissed by reason of redundancy.

If upon leaving the employment the employee is immediately entitled to payments under an occupational pension scheme which amount to at least one third of the final salary, the employer may serve notice that he is excluding the right to a redundancy payment. For these purposes the annual salary is set at a maximum of £18 200 (52 weeks × £350). If the amount payable is less than one third of the final salary, or if it is payable not immediately but within 90 weeks, the redundancy payment can be reduced proportionately.

20.5.3 Offer of suitable alternative employment

If an employee is offered suitable alternative employment, and unreasonably refuses to accept it, then he cannot claim to have been dismissed. Whether alternative employment offered is suitable or not is a question to be determined in the light of all the circumstances. Even if the offer of alternative employment is suitable, the employee can still reject it and claim redundancy if this is reasonable in all of the circumstances. The suitable alternative employment must take effect within four weeks of the expiry of the old employment.

20.5.3.1 Trial period of new employment

An employee is entitled to a trial period of four weeks if he is offered employment on terms and conditions which differ from those of the previous employment. If the employer terminates the contract during this four-week period, for a reason connected with the new contract, the employee is regarded as dismissed on the date when the old contract ended and is dismissed for the reason which caused the old contract to end. The same is true if the employee ends the contract within the four-week period unless the employee terminated it unreasonably, in which case he will not be entitled to a redundancy payment. After the statutory four-week period the employee is deemed to have accepted alternative terms regardless of any agreement with the employer and therefore the redundancy claim would be defeated.

20.5.4 Procedure for redundancy

Earlier in this chapter we considered *Williams* v *Compair Maxam Ltd*, in which Browne-Wilkinson J set out the principles which a large employer should adopt for deciding who to make redundant when a large number of redundancies was inevitable. We also considered the dismissal and disciplinary procedures with which an employer must comply before making a dismissal. If these procedures are not followed the dismissal will be unfair. If more than 20 people are being made redundant at the same time the usual procedures are replaced by those set out at 20.5.6 below.

20.5.5 Redundancy payments

A redundancy payment is calculated in the same way as a basic award for unfair dismissal except that the award cannot be reduced on account of the employee's contributory conduct.

The employee must be given a written statement explaining how the redundancy payment was calculated. Failure to do this can result in the employer being fined. The time limit for presenting a claim is six months from the effective date of termination. The tribunal has a discretion to allow a claim to be made within 12 months of the effective date of termination, if it considers it just and equitable to do so, but no claim can be made after 12 months.

If the employer has become insolvent the employee may make a claim to the Department for Work and Pensions, which will pay the statutory redundancy due.

20.5.6 Consultation on redundancies

Section 188 of the Trade Union and Labour Relations (Consolidation) Act 1992 (TULRCA 1992) provides that where an employer is proposing to dismiss as redundant 20 or more employees at one establishment within a period of 90 days or less, the employer shall consult about the dismissals all the persons who are appropriate representatives of any of the employees who may be so dismissed.

These consultations must begin at least 30 days before the dismissals take effect, unless 100 or more dismissals are proposed when they must begin at least 90 days before the dismissals take effect. The consultations must consider ways of avoiding the dismissals, ways of reducing the number of employees to be dismissed and ways of mitigating the consequences of the dismissals. The employer must undertake the consultations with a view to reaching agreement with the appropriate representatives.

The employer has to disclose in writing:

(a) the reason for his proposals,
(b) the number and description of the employees he proposes to make redundant,
(c) the total number of such employees of any such description employed by the employer at the establishment in question,
(d) the proposed method of selecting the employees who are to be dismissed,
(e) the proposed method of carrying out the dismissals, with due regard to any agreed procedure, including the period over which the dismissals are to take effect,
(f) the proposed method of calculating the amount of any redundancy payments to be made to employees who may be dismissed.

The employer has a duty to allow the appropriate representatives access to the employees whom it is proposed to dismiss as redundant and to provide for the representatives such accommodation and other facilities as may be appropriate.

If there are special circumstances which render it not reasonably practicable for the employer to comply with these requirements, the employer must take all steps towards compliance as are reasonably practicable in all the circumstances.

If the employer does not comply with these requirements, a complainant may present a case to an employment tribunal. The tribunal may make a protective award if it considers the case well founded. This award is made in respect of employees dismissed or employees whose dismissal is proposed. The employer is ordered to pay remuneration for the protected period. This period begins on the date when the first of the dismissals to which the complaint relates takes effect, or the date of the award, whichever is earlier. It is of such length as the tribunal considers just and equitable in all the circumstances, having regard to the employer's default in not complying with the requirements to consult. If the employer failed in his duty to consult about avoiding the dismissal, the protected period may not exceed 90 days. In other cases the protected period may not exceed 30 days.

An employer proposing to dismiss as redundant 100 or more employees at one establishment within a period of 90 days or less must **notify the Secretary of State**, in writing, of his proposal at least 90 days before the first of the dismissals take effect. The time limit is 30 days where the redundancy of at least 20 employees is proposed. Failure to give such notification is a criminal offence.

Test your understanding 20.5

1 In what three circumstances will a dismissal be by reason of redundancy?

2 How much continuous employment does an employee need to have in order to claim redundancy?

3 What is the effect of an employer not following the correct procedures when making employees redundant?

4 How is a redundancy payment calculated?

5 In what circumstances will an employer making employees redundant need to consult representatives of the employees concerned?

6 What are the purposes of the consultations?

Key points

■ Although many statutes relate to employment law, and although there is a significant EC element to employment law, the law of contract underpins the employment relationship.

■ Almost all employment cases are heard by an employment tribunal. From there an appeal lies to the Employment Appeal Tribunal and from there to the Court of Appeal and House of Lords.

■ Any UK court can refer an employment case to the European Court of Justice for an opinion on a matter of EC law. The European Court of Justice gives the opinion and the case is then sent back to the court which referred it so that the decision can be applied.

■ Decisions of the European Court of Justice are binding upon all UK courts. The decisions of an employment tribunal are not binding upon other →

courts. The decisions of the Employment Appeal Tribunal are binding upon employment tribunals but not upon subsequent sittings of the Employment Appeal Tribunal.

Employees and independent contractors distinguished

■ Employees are said to be employed under a contract of service. Independent contractors are said to work under a contract for services.

■ There are no absolute tests to be used in distinguishing employees and independent contractors. Generally, the question is one of fact and must be determined by considering all of the relevant facts.

Written particulars and employment terms

■ Employees must be given a written statement of particulars of the employment not later than two months after the commencement of their employment.

■ If expressly agreed as the terms of the contract, the matters set out in the written particulars will be the terms. If not expressly agreed as the terms they are only very strong evidence of the terms of the contract of employment.

■ Collective agreements are made between employers and trade unions. The terms of collective agreements may be expressly accepted by an individual employee as the terms of his contract of employment. The terms of a collective agreement may be impliedly accepted by union members, but not by non-union members.

■ Employees have duties to: show mutual respect; give faithful service; obey lawful and reasonable orders; use reasonable care and skill; not to accept bribes; not to reveal confidential information; and to disclose the shortcomings of their subordinates.

■ Employers have duties to: show mutual respect; pay wages (but not generally to provide work); observe confidentiality; indemnify the employee; ensure the safety of employees; and insure the employee. There is generally no duty to provide references.

■ Terms may be implied into a contract by custom and practice. Such terms are becoming of less importance.

■ A works rule book may provide some of the terms of the contract of employment if there has been an agreement to this effect between employer and employee. Such agreed terms could only be altered by mutual consent.

■ A works rule book may unilaterally impose some of the employees' duties, as long as this is not in conflict with their contract of employment. A unilaterally imposed works rule book could be unilaterally varied by the employer as long as this did not amount to a breach of contract.

■ Failure to observe agreed disciplinary and grievance procedures would amount to a breach of contract and might allow the employee to claim constructive dismissal.

■ Failure to comply with the ACAS dismissal, disciplinary or grievance procedures will mean that any award made to the employee for unfair dismissal may be increased by up to 25 per cent.

■ The terms of a contract of employment can only be varied by agreement between employer and employee. The contract of employment itself might allow for variation.

Termination of employment

■ Either employer or employee can terminate a contract of employment by giving notice.

■ The amount of notice required may be agreed between the parties, or may be the amount which is reasonable. It cannot be less than the statutory minimum period of notice.

■ The statutory minimum period of notice is one week after the employee has been employed for one month. After the employee has been employed for two years this period increases to one week for every year worked. The statutory minimum cannot exceed 12 weeks' notice.

■ An employee is summarily dismissed if he is dismissed without notice. This will only be justifiable in exceptional circumstances where the employee repudiated the contract.

■ If the contract of employment is genuinely terminated by agreement there will be no dismissal.

■ If the contract is frustrated there will be no dismissal.

■ If the employer's behaviour amounts to a repudiation of the contract, the employee is entitled

→

to accept the repudiation and claim to have been wrongfully dismissed.

■ Wrongful dismissal is a common law action for breach of contract and damages are therefore assessed on ordinary contract principles.

Unfair dismissal

■ Employees with at least two years' continuous employment have the right not to be unfairly dismissed.

■ The effective date of termination is the date on which the employment ended. It can be important in determining whether or not the employee has sufficient continuous employment to make a claim for unfair dismissal, in deciding whether the employee has made a claim within the three month time limit and in determining the amount of the employee's basic award. The effective date of termination is also significant in redundancy.

■ For the purposes of unfair dismissal, the employee must show that he was dismissed because the employer terminated the contract, or because a fixed term contract expired without being renewed, or because he was constructively dismissed. A woman who is not allowed to return to work after childbirth is deemed to have been dismissed.

■ An employee who resigns, and who cannot claim constructive dismissal, will not have been dismissed. Nor will there have been a dismissal if the contract of employment is frustrated.

■ The ERA sets out five circumstances in which a dismissal can be fair.

■ Even if the dismissal was on the grounds of one of the five specified circumstances, the dismissal will still be unfair unless the employer acted reasonably in treating the reason for the dismissal as a sufficient reason for dismissing the employee and unless the employer adhered to the statutory dismissal and disciplinary procedures.

■ Remedies for unfair dismissal include re-engagement, reinstatement and compensation. Re-engagement and reinstatement are rarely ordered.

■ The basic award of compensation is calculated according to a statutory formula. The compensatory award is at the discretion of the tribunal, and is designed to compensate the employee for losses sustained as a consequence of having been unfairly dismissed. It cannot exceed £66 200.

Redundancy

■ An employee will have been dismissed by reason of redundancy if the reason for the dismissal was wholly or mainly attributable to: (a) the employer ceasing to carry on the business; or (b) the employer moving the place of business; or (c) the employer shedding surplus labour.

■ Redundancy can only be claimed by those who have two years' continuous employment.

■ If the employer does not follow the correct procedures when making employees redundant then the dismissals are likely to have been unfair, rather than dismissals by reason of redundancy.

■ A redundancy payment is the same as a basic award for unfair dismissal except that the payment cannot be reduced on account of the employee's contributory conduct.

■ If more than 20 employees at one establishment are to be dismissed as redundant within a 90 day period, the employer must consult representatives of the employees concerned about the redundancies.

■ The consultations must consider ways of avoiding the dismissals, reducing the numbers to be dismissed and mitigating the consequences of the dismissals.

Summary questions

1 Brian, a building labourer, has worked for Bigga Builders for the past six years. When Brian took the job he was told that he was self-employed and that he had to look after his own tax and national insurance. Brian's work is not skilled and he uses the tools provided by Bigga Builders. On three occasions when Brian could not work personally his brother did the day's work instead. This situation was accepted, reluctantly, by the foreman. About half of the money which Brian receives from Bigga Builders is by way of bonus. The other half is paid at a flat hourly rate. Consider whether or not Brian is likely to be an employee of Bigga Builders.

2 Charlene has worked as a sales representative of Fancy Products Ltd for 15 years. Every three months the sales representative with the best sales has been

→

given a bonus of £1 000. The office manager has now stuck a notice on the sales representatives' office wall, stating that the bonus will no longer be payable. To what extent will the sales representatives be bound by the provisions of the notice?

3 David, who is 21 years old, has worked as a cocktail barman at a hotel which is part of a large national chain of hotels for the past ten months. His weekly wage is £250 and he averages about £75 a week in tips. Last night, upon arrival for work, David was told by the head waiter that he would not be allowed to work and that he was dismissed with immediate effect. On asking why this had been decided, David is told that one of the tills which he operates was £45 light and that the other three workers with access to the till have worked for years without any problem. After the hotel manager has confirmed that David is dismissed and will not be allowed to work, David swears at both the manager and the head waiter. He is forcibly removed from the hotel premises. The following day the hotel posts a letter to David explaining that he has been dismissed because he is suspected of stealing money and because he assaulted the hotel manager and the head waiter. The letter tells David that he has a right to appeal against this decision but David does not reply to it. Advise David as to whether or not he will have any rights against the hotel.

4 Elaine has worked as a machinist for 22 years at a local factory. She began work on her 18th birthday and earns £300 for a 45 hour week. Two months ago Elaine's supervisor said that Elaine's pay would be subject to a deduction of £40 because a whole batch of clothes which she was meant to stitch had been ruined by Elaine's negligence. Such deductions had been made from other employees' wages, but very rarely. Elaine insists that there was nothing wrong with her work and that she can prove it. She sees the manager who says that he is not prepared to get into arguments about whose defective work caused the problem. Elaine says that she knows whose work it was, but she isn't going to say. The manager says that unless Elaine says whose work it was, the deduction from her wages will stand. In front of all the other machinists, Elaine shouts, 'You know where you can stick your bleeding job' and walks out. The following day Elaine returns and says that she is ready to carry on with her job. The manager, who has subsequently discovered that it was not Elaine's negligence which caused the problem, refuses to take her back. Advise Elaine of any claim which she might make against the employer.

5 Bossco Ltd dismissed three employees, George, Harry and Pritpal, claiming that they had become redundant. All three were dismissed without notice and were given the correct amount of redundancy pay. The employer had no occupational pension scheme. Now a tribunal has held that the workers were unfairly dismissed, not made redundant. At the effective date of termination Harry was aged 62 and had 46 years' continuous employment. His wage as a supervisor was £420 a week. George, aged 53, had 16 years' continuous employment. His weekly wage was £300 a week. Pritpal, aged 40 had 10 years' continuous employment and had a weekly wage of £240. How much redundancy pay would each of the workers have received? How would a finding of unfair dismissal help them?

Multiple choice questions

1 Which one of the following statements is true?

a As all employment law is regarded as having an element of EC law, any national court may refer any question of employment law to the European Court of Justice for a ruling.

b ACAS and other bodies issue Codes of Practice concerning employment law and these Codes have the same legal effect as a statute.

c It is possible for the two lay members sitting in an employment tribunal to outvote the legally qualified chairman.

d Legal aid is available to an employee making a claim in an employment tribunal, but is not available to the employer defending the case.

2 Which one of the following statements is not true?

a There is no single test which is capable of distinguishing employees from independent contractors.

b The question as to whether or not a worker is an employee is, in all but exceptional cases, a question of fact rather than a question of law.

c If an employer has no obligation to employ a casual worker, and the worker has no obligation to accept work offered, the worker is unlikely to be regarded as an employee when not actually working.

d Independent contractors are never protected by employment legislation and can never bring a case alleging discrimination.

3 Which one of the following statements is not true?

a Unless the matters set out in the written particulars are agreed to be the terms of the contract of employment, they are not the terms but only very strong evidence of the terms.

b If a collective agreement is made between an employer and a trade union, all the terms of the agreement will automatically become the terms of all employees.

c Employees have a duty to perform their employment using reasonable care and skill.

d An employee whose negligence causes loss to the employer may be required to pay damages to compensate for the loss.

4 Which one of the following statements is not true?

a An employee who has a valid claim for unfair dismissal must pursue this claim in preference to a claim for wrongful dismissal.

b If a contract of employment is frustrated the employee will not be regarded as having been dismissed.

c Damages for wrongful dismissal are calculated on ordinary common law principles as damages for breach of contract.

d An employee who resigns, otherwise than in response to a repudiation of the contract by the employer, will not be able to claim wrongful dismissal.

5 Which one of the following statements is not true?

a An employee who has less than two years' continuous employment can never claim unfair dismissal.

b Weeks when an employee is off work on account of pregnancy, childbirth, sickness or injury count as continuous employment.

c Even if the employee leaves the job in a manner which amounts to a definite repudiation of the contract, the employer may have dismissed the employee if he is not allowed to return to work.

d If an employee consistently works in a manner which is inconsistent with the express terms of his contract for a considerable time, then an implied variation of the contract can possibly be inferred.

6 Which one of the following statements is not true?

a In some circumstances an employer's conduct is bad enough to entitle the employee to leave the job and nevertheless claim to have been dismissed.

b If an employer has given notice to an employee, and the employee gives counter-notice to expire before the employer's notice would have done so, the employee is taken to be dismissed for the reason for which the employer's notice was given.

c If the employer can prove that the employee's dismissal was within one of the fair reasons specified by the ERA, the dismissal cannot have been unfair.

d If the employer fails to follow the correct procedures when dismissing an employee, a dismissal which would otherwise have been fair will be rendered unfair.

7 John has worked in continuous employment for 22 years and six months. He was unfairly dismissed, the effective date of termination being one week after his 51st birthday. At the time of the dismissal John's weekly wage was £320. How much will John's basic award for unfair dismissal be?

a £9 280.

b £8 640.

c £8 370.

d £6 820.

8 Which one of the following statements is not true?

a An employee can be entitled to a redundancy payment even if he gets another job straightaway.

b An employee who is over 65 can never be unfairly dismissed.

c An employee who unreasonably rejects an offer of suitable alternative employment will not be entitled to claim a redundancy payment.

d A claim for a redundancy payment must be made within six months of the effective date of termination. The tribunal has a discretion to allow a claim to be made within 12 months, but cannot allow a claim after that.

Task 20

A friend of yours visiting the country from the United States has a keen interest in employment rights. She has asked you if you would draw up a report dealing briefly with the following matters.

a How the courts distinguish between employees and independent contractors.

b How the terms of a contract of employment are determined.

c The ways in which a contract of employment can be terminated.

d The differences between unfair and wrongful dismissal and the remedies available for them.

e The meaning of redundancy and the statutory remedies available to an employee who is made redundant.

f The courts and tribunals to which an employment dispute could be taken and the lines of appeal if the case should be appealed as far as possible.

mylawchamber *premium*

Visit **www.mylawchamber.co.uk/macintyre** to access study support resources including interactive multiple-choice questions, weblinks, glossary, glossary flashcards, legal newsfeed, answers to questions in this chapter, legal updates and an overview of this chapter all linked to the **Pearson eText** version of *Business Law* which you can **search**, **highlight** and **personalise** with your **own notes** and **bookmarks**.

Use **Case Navigator** to read in full some of the key cases referenced in this chapter with commentary and questions:

Post Office v *Foley; HSBC Bank* v *Madden* [2000] 1 All ER 550
Western Excavating (ECC) Ltd v *Sharp* [1978] 1 All ER 713

Employment 2 – discrimination · health and safety · rights of employees

Introduction

21.1 OVERVIEW OF THE EQUALITY ACT 2010

The Equality Act 2010 has consolidated much of the law on discrimination. Before the Act came into force the law prohibiting discrimination on account of a personal characteristic, such as sex or race, was contained in a large number of different regulations and statutes. The 2010 Act has replaced all of the previous legislation which outlawed discrimination on account of an employee's personal characteristics. It has therefore replaced statutes such as the Sex Discrimination Act 1975 and the Race Relations Act 1976. However, legislation which prevents discrimination on account of the type of contract on which an employee works, for example on account of an employee being part time or on a fixed-term contract, has not been replaced. The Equality Act was introduced in order to harmonise discrimination law and strengthen progress on equality. It adopts a common approach to outlawing discrimination at work where the discrimination is based on a person's personal characteristics. It also allows positive discrimination to overcome or minimise disadvantage suffered on account of personal characteristics. In addition, certain public bodies are required to consider socioeconomic disadvantage when making strategic decisions.

21.2 THE PROTECTED CHARACTERISTICS

Section 4 of the Act lists nine protected characteristics. Discrimination on the grounds of one or more of these characteristics is outlawed. The protected characteristics are:

- age;
- disability;
- gender reassignment;
- marriage and civil partnership;
- pregnancy and maternity;
- race;
- religion or belief;
- sex; and
- sexual orientation.

As regards each of the protected characteristics, the Act protects those who have the particular characteristic and those who belong to a group which shares the same characteristic.

21.2.1 The protected characteristic of age

Section 5(1)(a) provides that a person has the protected characteristic of age if he belongs to a particular age group, such as being under 18 or over 50. Section 5(1)(b) provides that where people belong to the same age group they share the protected characteristics of age. An age group is a group of persons defined by reference to age, whether by reference to a particular age or to a range of ages. (Section 5(2).) So,

for example, both 18 year-olds and 50 year-olds share the characteristic of being in the 'under 60' age group.

As from October 2011 the Employment Equality (Repeal of Retirement Age Provisions) Regulations 2011 have removed an employers' right to retire employees who have reached the age of 65. Before October 2011 employers could discriminate against employees who had reached the default retirement age by compulsorily retiring them.

Schedule 9 exempts the different national minimum wages. Redundancy schemes are also exempted as long as all employees' redundancy payments are calculated on the same basis. So a person with more years of continuous employment can be given a greater redundancy payment than a person with fewer years.

21.2.2 The protected characteristic of disability

Section 6(1) provides that a person has the protected characteristic of disability, and is known as a disabled person, if he has a physical or mental impairment and the impairment has a substantial and long-term adverse effect on his ability to carry out normal day-to-day activities. Schedule 1 makes the following provisions about disability. An impairment is long term if it has lasted for at least 12 months, or is likely to do so, or is likely to last for the rest of a person's life. If an impairment has ceased to have a substantial adverse effect on a person's ability to carry out normal day-to-day activities it will still be regarded as a disability if it is likely to recur. Severe disfigurement is regarded as having a substantial adverse effect on a person's ability to carry out normal day-to-day activities. Cancer, HIV infection and multiple sclerosis are each regarded as a disability.

21.2.3 The protected characteristic of gender reassignment

A person has the protected characteristic of gender reassignment if he or she is a transsexual person. A transsexual person is a person who is proposing to undergo a process to change sex, or has started or completed such a process. (Section 7(1).)

21.2.4 The protected characteristic of marriage or civil partnership

Section 8(1) provides that a person has the protected characteristic of marriage or civil partnership if he or she is either married or a civil partner. People who are not married and not in a civil partnership do not have this protected characteristic and are not protected by the Act. So people who are engaged to be married or are divorced are not protected.

21.2.5 The protected characteristic of race

Section 9(1) provides that the protected characteristic of race includes colour, nationality or ethnic or national origins. People who share the same colour, nationality or ethnic or national origins share the same racial group. (Section 9(2).) One racial group may comprise two or more distinct racial groups. (Section 9(3).) For example, 'black Britons' are a racial group that comprises the racial group 'black' and the national group 'British'. Caste is currently not an aspect of race, but s.9 allows a Government minister to amend the Act so that caste becomes an aspect of race.

The meaning of 'ethnic' was clarified in the following case.

Mandla v Dowell Lee
[1983] ICR 385 (House of Lords)

A Sikh boy was refused entry to a school because the boy and his father would not agree that the son should cut his hair and cease to wear a turban. The judge who heard the case dismissed the complaint on the grounds that Sikhs were not a racial group.

Held. Sikhs are a racial group defined by ethnic origins and the boy had been indirectly discriminated against.

Lord Fraser thought that in order for a group to constitute an ethnic group in the sense of the Act, it must regard itself, and be regarded by others, as a distinct community by virtue of certain characteristics. Two of the characteristics are essential. Another five characteristics are not essential, but will commonly be found and will help to distinguish the group from the surrounding community.

The two essential characteristics are:

(1) A long-shared history of which the group is conscious as distinguishing it from other groups, and the memory of which it keeps alive.
(2) A cultural tradition of its own, including family and social custom and manners, often but not necessarily associated with religious observance.

The five relevant characteristics are:

(1) Either a common geographical origin, or descent from a small number of ancestors.
(2) A common language, not necessarily peculiar to the group.
(3) A common literature peculiar to the group.
(4) A common religion different from that of neighbouring groups or from the general surrounding community.
(5) Being a minority or being an oppressed or dominant group within a larger community. For example, a conquered people and their conquerors might both be ethnic groups, as would have been the case in England shortly after the Norman Conquest.

21.2.6 The protected characteristics of religion or belief

Section 10(1) provides that the protected characteristic of religion applies to any religion as well as to a lack of religion. Section 10(2) provides that the protected characteristic of belief applies to any religious or philosophical belief, including a lack of belief.

21.2.7 The protected characteristic of sex

Section 11(1) provides that references to the protected characteristic of sex are references to being either a man or a woman.

21.2.8 The protected characteristic of sexual orientation

The protected characteristic of sexual orientation is defined by s.12(1) as a sexual orientation towards persons of the same sex, persons of the opposite sex or persons of either sex.

21.3 TYPES OF PERSONAL CHARACTERISTIC DISCRIMINATION

Direct discrimination, indirect discrimination, harassment and victimisation on account of a protected characteristic all amount to prohibited conduct. Each of these needs to be considered in turn.

21.3.1 **Direct discrimination**

Before the Act came into force there were slightly different definitions of direct discrimination in the previous legislation. Section 13 now applies a uniform definition, which is based on the definition of direct discrimination which used to be contained in the Race Relations Act 1976.

Section 13(1) sets out the meaning of direct discrimination. It says that a person (A) discriminates against another (B) if, because of a protected characteristic, A treats B less favourably that A treats or would treat others.

So it would be direct discrimination, for example, to refuse to employ a person either because he was a Hindu, or because he associated with Hindus or because he was wrongly thought to be a Hindu. It makes no difference that A has the same characteristic. So, for example, a woman can be liable for discriminating against another woman.

In *James v Eastleigh Borough Council* [1990] 2 All ER 607, a case decided under the Sex Discrimination Act 1975, the House of Lords held that the appropriate question to ask to discover whether or not discrimination was on the grounds of sex was objective rather than subjective. That is to say that the motive for the discrimination is not relevant. The case concerned a married couple, both aged 61. The local council had a policy of allowing those who could claim the state old age pension free access to their swimming pools. The wife therefore gained free access but the man did not. The House of Lords held that the man was discriminated against. The question to ask is whether the man would have received the same treatment as his wife but for his sex. As he plainly would, the policy, however well-intentioned, was discriminatory.

Section 13 goes on to make five specific rules which relate to direct discrimination on five of the protected characteristics.

(1) Section 13(2) states that *'if the protected characteristic is age'*, A does not discriminate against B if A can show A's treatment of B to be a proportionate means of achieving a legitimate aim.
(2) Section 13(3) states that *'if the protected characteristic is disability'*, it is not discrimination to treat a disabled person more favourably than a non-disabled person.
(3) Section 13(4) states that *'if the protected characteristic is marriage and civil partnership'*, it is

only a person who is married or in a civil partnership who can be the victim of discrimination.
(4) Section 13(5) states that *'if the protected characteristic is race'*, less favourable treatment includes segregating B from others.
(5) Section 13(6) states that *'if the protected characteristic is sex'* –

   (a) less favourable treatment of a woman includes less favourable treatment of her because she is breast-feeding (but this does not apply for the purposes of employment); and
   (b) a man cannot claim discrimination on account of not being given the special treatment afforded to a woman in connection with pregnancy or childbirth.

Section 14 provides that direct discrimination can be committed by discriminating against a person on account if his or her having two of the relevant protected characteristics. For example, an employer might prohibit Asian women from going on a certain training scheme even though he allows non-Asian women and Asian men to go on the scheme. This would amount to dual discrimination. At the time of writing s.14 is not yet in force and is not due to be brought into force.

21.3.1.1 **Discrimination arising from disability**

Section 15(1) provides that a person (A) discriminates against a disabled person (B) if –

'(a) A treats B unfavourably because of something arising in consequence of B's disability, and
(b) A cannot show that the treatment is a proportionate means of achieving a legitimate aim.

Section 15(2) provides that s.15(1) does not apply if A shows that A did not know, and could not reasonably have been expected to know, that B had the disability.'

So it is not only on account of a person being disabled that direct discrimination can occur. Section 15(1) prohibits unfavourable treatment because of something arising in connection with a person's disability. For example, it would be discriminatory to dismiss a visually impaired person because he could not read as quickly as a normally sighted person or because he needed to attend a large number of hospital appointments. However, it will not be discrimination if the employer can show that his treatment of the disabled person was a proportionate means of achieving a legitimate aim. Nor will it be discriminatory if A shows that

A did not know, and could not reasonably have been expected to know, that B had the disability. Section 15 has effectively overruled the House of Lords decision in *London Borough of Lewisham* v *Malcolm* [2008] UKHL 43, [2008] 1 AC 1399, which had severely restricted the protection available to disabled people.

21.3.1.2 Gender reassignment: cases of absence from work

Section 16 makes it discriminatory to treat a person who is absent from work because of gender reassignment less favourably than that person would be treated if he were absent from work on account of sickness or injury. It is also discrimination to treat the person less favourably than they would be treated if they were off work for some reason other than sickness or injury and it is not reasonable to treat him less favourably.

21.3.1.3 Direct discrimination in pregnancy and maternity cases

Section 18 makes it discriminatory for an employer to treat a woman less favourably because of her pregnancy or because of an illness connected with her pregnancy. It is also discrimination to treat a woman less favourably because she is on maternity leave or is exercising her right to maternity leave or additional maternity leave.

21.3.2 Indirect discrimination

Section 19(1) provides that a person (A) discriminates against another (B) if A applies to B a provision, criterion or practice which is discriminatory in relation to a relevant protected characteristic of B's (except pregnancy and maternity).

A provision, criterion or practice is discriminatory in relation to a relevant protected characteristic of B's if –

'(a) A applies, or would apply, it to persons with whom B does not share the characteristic,
(b) it puts, or would put, persons with whom B shares the characteristic at a particular disadvantage when compared with persons with whom B does not share it,
(c) it puts, or would put, B at that disadvantage, and
(d) A cannot show it to be a proportionate means of achieving a legitimate aim.'

An example might help to show the meaning of this. Let us assume that an employer, A, imposes a pattern of shift working on all employees, and that this pattern would prevent women with young children from continuing in the job. The new shift pattern applies to men as well as women. (Section 19(1)(a).) It puts some women at a particular disadvantage. (Section 19(1)(b).) One particular woman shows that she is put at a disadvantage because she cannot keep the job if the pattern is imposed. (Section 19(1)(c).) This will be indirect discrimination unless the employer can show that imposing the new shift pattern is a proportionate means of achieving a legitimate aim. (Section 19(1)(d).)

Certain parts of the wording of s.19(1) are identical to the wording contained in earlier legislation. Cases on the interpretation of these parts, for example cases on what amounts to a 'provision, criterion or practice', will remain authorities. However, where the wording differs slightly it is hard to say to what extent the old cases will remain authorities.

Section 20 requires employers to make reasonable adjustments to see that disabled employees are not disadvantaged by work practices or by physical features of the workplace. If necessary the employer must also provide auxiliary aids. If the employer fails to comply with this duty then this amounts to discrimination.

Section 23 requires that a person claiming direct, dual or indirect discrimination does so by reference to a **comparator**. The comparator can be a real or a hypothetical person whose circumstances are the same as the claimant's, except that the comparator does not share the claimant's protected characteristic. So, for example, an employee who claimed to be discriminated against on account of being a woman would have to do so by reference to a male comparator whose circumstances were the same as her own. When considering cases of direct or dual discrimination on grounds of disability, the circumstances can include the abilities of the claimant and the comparator to do the job. Section 24 provides that it is no defence that the person committing the discrimination has the same protected characteristic as the person discriminated against.

21.3.3 Harassment

Section 26(1) provides that a person (A) harasses another (B) if –

'(a) A engages in unwanted conduct related to a relevant protected characteristic, or of a sexual nature, and

(b) the conduct has the purpose or effect of –

    (i) violating B's dignity, or

    (ii) creating an intimidating, hostile, degrading, humiliating or offensive environment for B.'

Examples of harassment might include an employer putting up a topless calendar which some employees, male or female, found offensive or a manager making an employee listen to racially offensive jokes. When considering whether or not the conduct has the effect referred to in s.26(1)(b), three matters have to be taken into account. These matters are: the perception of B; the other circumstances of the case; and whether it is reasonable for the conduct to have that effect.

21.3.4 **Victimisation**

Section 27(1) provides that a person (A) victimises another person (B) if A subjects B to a detriment because –

'(a) B does a protected act, or

(b) A believes that B has done, or may do, a protected act.'

Section 27(2) states that each of the following is a protected act –

'(a) bringing proceedings under the Act;

(b) giving evidence or information in connection with proceedings under the Act;

(c) doing any other thing for the purposes of or in connection with the Act;

(d) making an allegation (whether or not express) that A or another person has contravened the Act.'

So if a black employee was not promoted because he had complained about discrimination this would amount to victimisation.

The definition of victimisation in the Sex Discrimination Act 1975 was very similar to that contained in s.27. In *Derbyshire v St Helens MBC* [2007] UKHL 16, [2007] ICR 841 an employer sent letters to employees warning them not to carry on equal pay claims. The purpose of this was to put pressure on the employees to settle. The employment tribunal found that these letters had had an intimidating effect on those employees who had not settled their equal pay claims. The House of Lords was not prepared to change this finding, and held that the employees had been victimised under the SDA 1975.

Section 27(2) provides that giving false evidence or information, or making a false allegation, are not protected acts if they are done in bad faith.

21.3.5 **Discrimination against employees and applicants for employment**

Section 39 states that when selecting employees it is unlawful to discriminate against a person or victimise a person in the following ways:

- by making discriminatory arrangements for the purposes of determining who should be offered employment; or
- by offering discriminatory terms of employment; or
- by refusing or deliberately omitting to offer employment.

As regards existing employees, it is unlawful to discriminate against a person or victimise a person:

- in the terms of the employment;
- in the way access to opportunities for promotion, transfer or training, or to any other benefits are given; or by refusing or deliberately omitting to allow access to these things; or
- by dismissing the employee or subjecting him or her to any other detriment.

Schedule 9 of the Act provides that as regards not offering a person a job, not offering access to promotion etc. or dismissing a person the employer might have the defence of *occupational requirement*. The employer will have to show that, having regard to the nature or context of the work, a requirement imposed by the employer is an occupational requirement which the employee or applicant does not have. The employer will also need to show that the application of the requirement is a proportionate means of achieving a legitimate aim. So, for example, an employer making a film about Nelson Mandela could insist that the actor who was to play Mandela should be both a man and black.

Section 40 requires employees not to harass employees or applicants for employment. Employers also have a duty to make sure, as far as is reasonably practicable, that third parties do not harass either.

Section 60 prevents employers from asking applicants for jobs about their health, except in so far as this is to do with the applicant's ability to do the job or for the purpose of monitoring diversity.

21.4 EQUALITY OF TERMS

The Equality Act 2010 requires that men and women in the same employment should be treated equally by their employer, regardless of their sex, as regards pay and other benefits. It is generally women who have been discriminated against and so when describing the effect of the Act it is convenient to assume that a claim under the Act is brought by a woman. (This is merely as a matter of convenience and there is no reason why a man should not bring a claim.) The sections which require equality of terms apply where a person (A) is employed on work that is equal to the work that a comparator of the opposite sex (B) does. (Section 64(1).) Section 65 provides that A's work is equal to that of B if it is (a) like B's work, (b) rated as equivalent to B's work, or (c) of equal value to B's work. The equal treatment which the Act requires means not only that the woman should receive equal pay, but also that the other benefits of the job, such as pension rights and sick pay, should be equally beneficial. The employer does not need to give equal treatment in so far as he can prove that the difference in treatment was genuinely due to a material factor other than the woman's sex.

21.4.1 The sources of law

The Equality Act 2010 is the main source of law on equal pay. However, Article 157 of the Treaty on the Functioning of the European Union provides that: 'Each Member State shall ensure that the principle of equal pay for male and female workers for equal work or work of equal value is applied.' The Article states that 'pay' includes not only the ordinary basic minimum wage or salary, but also any other consideration, whether in cash or in kind, which the worker receives directly or indirectly, in respect of his employment, from his employer. Two EU Directives passed in 1975 and 1976 (Directives 75/117 and 76/207) make it plain that legislation such as the Equality Act should be interpreted positively with the intention of ending discriminatory treatment of women as regards the conditions of their employment terms. As equal pay is a matter which involves EU law, the European Court of Justice may consider an application that either Article 157 or one of the Directives is not being given effect. If there is a conflict between the UK legislation and Article 157 or the Directives, it is the latter which will prevail.

However, in *Pickstone and others v Freemans plc* [1988] IRLR 357 the House of Lords held that if national legislation gives a sufficient remedy then there is no room for the matter to be pursued through the alternative route of the direct application of European law.

21.4.2 The need for a male comparator

An applicant can only claim equal treatment with a male working in the same employment. (See however, s.71 below at 21.4.6.) The Act does not require that a woman employed by one employer should be treated as favourably as a man doing identical work, or the same type of work, for another employer. In order to gain a remedy under the Act, the woman will therefore need to find a male comparator, that is to say a male working for the same employer who is being treated more favourably. It is not possible to claim equal treatment with a person of the same sex.

Section 79(3) of the Act allows comparison with male employees working for associated employers. (The meaning of this was considered in the previous Chapter 20 at 20.5.2; that one is a company which controls the other, or both are companies controlled by the same third party.) Section 79(4) requires equal treatment not only if the man and the woman are employed at the same establishment, but also if they are employed at different establishments in Great Britain, as long as common terms and conditions apply or are observed at the different establishments. Applying what is now s.79(4), in *Leverton v Clwyd County Council* [1989] ICR 33 the House of Lords held that a nursery nurse employed by the county council could validly compare herself with male clerks who worked for the council in different establishments. The nurse worked 32.5 hours a week and had 70 days' holiday a year, the more highly paid male comparators worked 37 hours a week and had 30 days' holiday a year. (The nurse's claim did not succeed because the House of Lords found that the difference in treatment of her and the men was justified on the grounds of a genuine material factor. However, the principle that the men could be used as comparators was established.) In **British Coal Corporation v Smith** [1996] IRLR 404 the House of Lords allowed female canteen workers and cleaners who were employed at 47 different establishments to compare themselves with male surface workers and clerical staff who worked at four different establishments. The Coal Board's argument that local bargaining accounted for the differences in some terms, as it also accounted for differences between the treatment of miners and clerical workers at different establishments, was rejected. The terms and conditions would be common terms and conditions for the purposes of s.79(4) if they were substantially comparable on a broad basis. They did not have to be identical.

The choice of comparator is a matter for the woman bringing the claim. If the employer were allowed to choose the comparator this would raise the possibility of employers having a 'token man' employed on inferior terms so that the treatment of female employees could be compared with the treatment of the token man. The woman is not confined to one comparator, but may choose multiple comparators.

A former employee may be used as the comparator. In **Macarthys Ltd v Smith** [1980] ICR 672 the European Court of Justice held that a female stockroom manager who was paid £50 a week could compare herself to the male who had previously done the same job at £60 a week. However, it was held that there is a need for a real comparator, the woman cannot compare herself to a hypothetical comparator by asking how a hypothetical man would have been treated.

21.4.3 Like work

In order to succeed under the Act the claimant will need to prove that she does like work, work rated as equivalent, or work of equal value to that of the comparator. Each of these matters needs to be examined in turn.

Section 65(1) of the Act provides that a woman is to be regarded as employed on like work with men if, but only if, her work and theirs is of the same or a broadly similar nature, and the differences (if any) between the things she does and the things they do are not of practical importance in relation to terms and

conditions of employment. Section 65(3) provides that in deciding whether the work is like work regard shall be had to the frequency or otherwise with which any such differences occur in practice as well as to the nature and extent of the differences.

> ### Capper Pass Ltd v Lawton
> [1977] ICR 83 (House of Lords)
>
> The claimant worked 40 hours a week preparing lunches for about 10 to 20 of the company's directors and their guests. She was responsible to the catering manager and was the only cook who worked in the kitchen. The two male comparators were assistant chefs who worked under a head chef in a different kitchen which provided breakfast, lunch and tea in two sittings for the company's workers. The assistant chefs provided about 350 meals each day. They worked 40 hours a week, 5.5 hours overtime and one Saturday in three. When the head chef or catering manager was away, the assistant chefs deputised for the head chef.
>
> **Held.** The work done by the claimant was like work to that done by the assistant chefs.

Work is like work if it is of the same nature as, or of a broadly similar nature to, the work done by the man. In deciding whether work was like work consideration should be given to the type of work involved and the skill and knowledge required to do that work. If there were differences the tribunal should decide whether or not these were of practical importance in relation to the terms and conditions of employment.

In **Shields v E. Coombes (Holdings) Ltd** [1978] ICR 1159, the Court of Appeal demonstrated that practical differences between the duties of the female and the comparators had to be real rather than merely theoretical. The claimant was a counterhand in a betting shop, being paid 92p per hour. The male comparator working in the same shop was a counterhand receiving £1.06 per hour. The employers claimed that the work was not of a broadly similar nature because the shop was in an area where robbery or trouble from customers was expected, and in the event of any such trouble the male was supposed to sort it out, whereas the claimant was not. This argument failed because there had been no trouble for the male to sort out in the previous three years and so the male's additional responsibilities were of no practical importance.

A man can be paid at a higher rate than a woman who does similar work if the man has genuine greater responsibilities than the woman. So in **Eaton Ltd** *v Nuttall* [1977] 1 WLR 549 a man who handled packages worth between £5 and £1 000 could be paid more than a woman who did the same work but only handled packages worth less than £2.50. The man had greater responsibilities because if he made a mistake a much greater loss would be caused to the employer than if the woman did.

If the men and women work different hours, as where only the men work a night shift, this is not a good reason for the basic rate of pay to differ. The men can receive a shift allowance, which will mean that they actually earn more than the women, but this allowance reflects the fact that they worked the night shift. If, however, both men and women work different hours then the basic pay of those working shifts can be higher than the basic pay of those who do not.

21.4.4 Work rated as equivalent

Section 65(4) provides that work is rated as equivalent if a properly conducted job evaluation scheme has been carried out and has found that the work is equivalent. Such a scheme must be analytical in approach, rather than impressionistic. In *Eaton Ltd v Nuttall* [1977] 1 WLR 549 Phillips J reviewed the principal methods of evaluation. He considered the most commonly used system to be one of points assessment, where the job was broken down into component factors with points awarded for each factor according to a predetermined scale. Whatever the method used, the tribunal cannot override the results of a properly conducted job evaluation scheme.

21.4.5 Work of equal value

Work is of equal value to that of a male comparator, if it is equal to his work in terms of demands made on the woman by reference to factors such as effort, skill and decision making. (Section 65(6).) When faced with a claim based on work of equal value the employment tribunal will first decide whether or not there can be grounds for such a complaint. If there cannot, the case will be dismissed. Having decided that there can be grounds, the tribunal can either itself decide whether or not the work was of equal value, or can refer the case for expert evaluation. If the case is referred for expert evaluation, the tribunal cannot come to a decision until the report it has commissioned is received. However, the tribunal can reject part or all of the report's conclusions.

The requirement that a woman should be treated equally for doing work of equal value was introduced by the Equal Pay (Amendment) Regulations 1983. The following case was one of the first major cases to consider the requirements of an equal value claim.

> ### *Hayward v Cammell Laird Shipbuilders Ltd* [1988] 2 All ER 257 (House of Lords)
>
> The claimant worked as a cook at a shipyard. She claimed that her work was of equal value to that of a painter, a joiner and an insulation engineer, all of whom worked at the same shipyard. The employers argued that the claimant was treated as favourably as the men. They claimed that although her basic pay and overtime rates were lower than those of the male comparators her contract as a whole was equally favourable because she enjoyed better sickness benefits, paid meal breaks and better holiday pay. The employment tribunal, the EAT and the Court of Appeal all held that the claim failed because the claimant's conditions were no less favourable when the contract was viewed as a whole. An appeal was made to the House of Lords.
>
> **Held.** Where the woman did equal work to that of a male comparator all the terms of her contract had to be as favourable as the equivalent term in the comparator's contract. This was the case even if she was treated as favourably as the man overall when the whole contract was compared.
>
> **COMMENT** The House of Lords did recognise that this would involve an element of leapfrogging. The claimant's contract was improved so that her basic rate and overtime rates were as favourable as those of the men. The men could then claim the improved sickness, meal and holiday benefits enjoyed by the claimant. In the case the employers did not argue the defence of genuine material factor, which is considered immediately below.

21.4.6 Sex equality clause

If it can be shown that a woman does like work, work rated as equivalent or work which is of equal value to that of a male comparator, s.66(1) provides that the woman's contract of employment should be deemed to include a sex equality clause. Section 66(2) defines an equality clause.

A sex equality clause is a provision that has the following effect –

'(a) if a term of A's is less favourable to A than a corresponding term of B's is to B, A's term is modified so as not to be less favourable;
(b) if A does not have a term which corresponds to a term of B's that benefits B, A's terms are modified so as to include such a term.'

So in essence a sex equality clause would require each of the terms of the woman's contract to be changed so that they became no less favourable than similar terms in the male comparator's contract. In circumstances in which there is no male comparator there can be no claim to equality of terms on the grounds of indirect discrimination. However, s.71 allows a claim to equality of terms to be made in cases of direct sex discrimination, even if there is no male comparator. So in cases of direct sex discrimination s.71 allows a hypothetical comparator to be used. The explanatory notes to the Act give an example of an employer telling a female employee who has no male comparator that he would pay her more if she were a man. It is unlikely that the courts will allow s.71 to be invoked to allow comparison with a successor male comparator.

21.4.7 Defence of material factor

Section 69 gives an employer a defence if he can prove that the different treatment of the woman was due to a material factor which does not directly or indirectly discriminate against the claimant because of her sex. If this can be proved the equality clause will not take effect. If the claimant can show that the factor upon which the employer relies is indirectly discriminatory, the equality clause will not apply if the employer can show that the factor is a proportionate means of achieving a legitimate aim. A long-term objective of reducing inequality between men's and women's terms of work is always to be regarded as a legitimate aim. Section 69 provides as follows:

'(1) The sex equality clause in A's terms has no effect in relation to a difference between A's terms and B's terms if the responsible person shows that the difference is because of a material factor reliance on which –

   (a) does not involve treating A less favourably because of A's sex than the responsible person treats B, and
   (b) if the factor is within subsection (2), is a proportionate means of achieving a legitimate aim.

(2) A factor is within this subsection if A shows that, as a result of the factor, A and persons of the same sex doing work equal to A's are put at a particular disadvantage when compared with persons of the opposite sex doing work equal to A's.
(3) For the purposes of subsection (1), the long-term objective of reducing inequality between men's and women's terms of work is always to be regarded as a legitimate aim …
(4) For the purposes of this section, a factor is not material unless it is a material difference between A's case and B's.'

A wide variety of matters can amount to genuine material factors which would justify different treatment. These matters would include long service increments, academic qualifications, different places of work, perhaps different hours of work, responsibility allowances, and protection of pay for those who were demoted (as long as this treatment was not based on the employee's sex).

In *Redcar and Cleveland BC v Bainbridge* [2008] EWCA Civ 885, [2008] ICR 133 the Court of Appeal held that a local authority scheme designed to end pay discrimination had done so in a discriminatory manner. Under the scheme, and in agreement with the trade unions, the higher discriminatory pay enjoyed by men was to be phased out over a period of time. The higher pay would have been protected for three years on a reducing scale. The claimants argued that it was only the employers' discrimination which meant that they had not been paid at the higher rate of the men, and that if this had not been the case they too would have benefited from the pay protection scheme if their pay had been reduced. Therefore, to exclude them from the pay protection scheme was unlawful sex discrimination. The EAT found that, even though it was a legitimate objective to soften the blow of a wage cut, implementing a scheme which was not open to women was not a proportionate means of achieving that objective. The Court of Appeal upheld the EAT's decision. It stressed that whether or not a legitimate aim is objectively justified is a question of fact for the employment tribunal. Such a finding of fact would not be overturned unless it was perverse. Here there was evidence of a sexual element in the pay disparity and so the disparity had to be justified. The employer had not shown that the pay protection scheme was an appropriate and proportionate means of achieving the legitimate aim of cushioning the blow of those who suffered a wage reduction. The

Court of Appeal did not rule out the possibility that a pay protection scheme which perpetuated historic discrimination could be justified on the facts of the case. However, where the employer knew that the past scheme was discriminatory it would be hard to justify continuing discrimination in a new pay scheme which was trying to rectify the situation. A pay protection scheme might be justified if it was well thought out and well costed and if it could be demonstrated that the scheme had done everything it could to minimise the effects of the discrimination.

It is not easy to state the extent to which market forces will permit the different treatment of female employees. If the difference in treatment is caused by sound economic reasons then the defence of genuine material difference may succeed. In *Rainey v Greater Glasgow Health Board* [1987] 1 All ER 65 the Scottish Health Department employed prosthetists on civil service pay. Twenty employees, who all happened to be men, had previously worked for private contractors. These private contractors paid well above the health service rates. These 20 men were therefore taken on by the Health Department at their old, private practice, rates. The claimant later joined the health service as a prosthetist and was taken on at the health service rate. This meant that she was paid about 72 per cent of the salary paid to the 20 men. The House of Lords held that the employer's defence of genuine material difference succeeded. The 20 men had to be offered their old rates of pay in order to attract them into the Health Department. It was merely fortuitous that the 20 employees taken from private contractors had all been men.

In *Enderby v Frenchay Health Authority* [1994] 1 All ER 495 the ECJ held that the objective of what is now Article 157 of the Treaty on the Functioning of the European Union was equal pay for men and women for work of equal value. Where statistics showed that there were appreciable differences in pay between two jobs of equal value, one of these jobs being carried out exclusively by women and the other predominantly by men, this was *prima facie* discrimination. The onus was therefore on the employer to show that the difference was based on objectively justified factors which were not related to any discrimination on grounds of sex. This was the case even though the rates of pay had been arrived at by a process of collective bargaining. It was for the national courts to decide whether and to what extent the shortage of candidates for a job, and the need to attract them by higher pay,

constituted objectively justified economic grounds for the difference in pay between the jobs in question. The case was brought by a speech therapist working for a health authority on an annual salary of £10 106. She was held to be entitled to compare herself to a clinical psychologist earning £12 527 and to a pharmacist earning £14 106 p.a.

In *Ratcliffe v North Yorkshire County Council* [1995] IRLR 439 the House of Lords held that when women dinner ladies had their wages reduced by a county council, in order that the county council could compete with commercial contractors who paid women employees less than the local government rate, the tribunal could find that this was not a genuine material difference which justified paying the women less than that paid to men engaged on work rated as equivalent. It is plain from this decision that the market forces defence will not be allowed to become too wide.

21.4.8 Discussions about pay and publishing information

Section 77 applies where a term of the contract of employment tries to prevent employees from discussing their pay with others, where the purpose of the discussions is to discover a connection between a difference in pay and a protected characteristic. If an employer takes any action against a person who is protected by this section then this would amount to victimisation. So if a woman thought she was being paid less than a man doing the same type of work, and asked him what he was paid, it would be victimisation of the man if the employer took any action against him for having discussed his pay.

Employers of 250 or more employees may be required by future regulations to publish information relating to differences in the pay of male and female employees.

21.4.9 Remedies

Where a woman does like work, work rated as equivalent or work of equal value with that of a man, s.66(1) of the Equality Act 2010 provides that if the terms of the contract under which the woman is employed do not include *an equality clause* they shall be deemed to include one. An equality clause is a provision which requires that any terms of a woman's contract shall be modified so as to be no less favourable than a term of a similar kind in the contract of a male comparator.

Generally, a claim must be brought before an employment tribunal within six months of the woman leaving the employment, or while she is still in the employment. Back pay and damages can be awarded to a successful complainant. In *Levez v TH Jennings (Harlow Pools) Ltd (No 2)* [1999] IRLR 764 the European Court ruled that up to six years' arrears of pay could be awarded. Before this ruling a claimant could not be awarded more than two years' arrears of pay. The six-year period was necessary to bring the remedies under the Equal Pay Act into line with the remedies under the Race Relations Act and the Disability Discrimination Act. Under both of these Acts unlawful deductions of pay could be claimed for six years before proceedings were begun.

The following matters have all been held to be 'pay' and therefore within the provisions of Article 157: sick pay; compensation for unfair dismissal; redundancy payments; occupational pensions; pay for attending courses; and concessionary travel benefits for employees who have retired. As with all complaints of discrimination, the employee should use the employer's grievance procedure before taking a case to a tribunal. This procedure will have to meet the minimum statutory standards, as explained in the previous chapter at 20.2.7.

21.4.9.1 The burden of proof under the Act

Section 136 provides that a claimant who alleges a contravention of the Act, including a breach of an equality clause, must initially prove his or her case. Once the claimant has proved, in the absence of any other explanation, that a breach of the Act occurred, the burden of proof then shifts on to the employer to show that there was no breach of the Act.

21.5 PUBLIC SECTOR EQUALITY DUTY

Section 149(1) requires public authorities, in the exercise of their functions, to have due regard to the need to:

'(a) eliminate discrimination, harassment, victimisation and any other conduct that is prohibited by or under the Act;

(b) advance equality of opportunity between persons who share a relevant protected characteristic and persons who do not share it; and

(c) foster good relations between persons who share a relevant protected characteristic and persons who do not share it.'

When a major public authority, such as a local authority, makes a decision of a strategic nature about how to exercise its functions it must have due regard to trying to exercise them in such a way that is designed to reduce the inequalities which result from socio-economic disadvantage. This might involve matters such as publicising access to health or educational programmes more widely in disadvantaged areas.

21.6 POSITIVE ACTION

Section 158 allows an employer to discriminate in favour of people who are disadvantaged on account of having a protected characteristic. So particular disadvantaged groups could be targeted for extra training or education. Any such action must be a proportionate means of achieving a positive aim.

Test your understanding 21.2

1 In claims for equality of terms, what is the male comparator?
2 On what three grounds can the applicant claim to be treated as favourably as a male comparator?
3 What is the effect of an equality clause?
4 What defence might an employer have?
5 What remedies can be awarded by the employment tribunal in respect of a claim for equality of terms?

21.7 DISCRIMINATION AGAINST PERSONS WITH CRIMINAL RECORDS

The Rehabilitation of Offenders Act 1974 allows people whose convictions have become **spent** to deny that they have ever been convicted. Furthermore, if a person is dismissed because of a spent conviction this will amount to unfair dismissal. It is, however, permissible for an employer to refuse to employ a person on account of that person's criminal record or to discriminate in other ways such as to refuse promotion. In certain jobs some types of spent convictions will justify dismissal. However, it is up to the employer to check the nature of the spent conviction and whether or not it would make the employee unfit to hold his job.

> ### Brooks v Ladbroke Lucky Seven Entertainment (1977) IRLIB
>
> Ladbrokes dismissed a gaming club employee when they discovered that he had a conviction. They did not know that the conviction was spent and argued that the nature of the work would have justified dismissal anyway. The man claimed unfair dismissal.
>
> **Held.** The dismissal was unfair. The employer should have considered the nature of the conviction and whether or not it made the applicant unsuitable to do the job.

A conviction becomes spent after a length of time which varies with the severity of the sentence passed. The times are:

Over 2.5 years' imprisonment or youth custody	Never spent.
6 months–2.5 years	Spent after 10 years.
Less than 6 months	Spent after 7 years.
Youth custody of less than 2.5 years	Spent after 7 years
Fined/Community Service Order	Spent after 5 years.
Detention Centre	Spent after 3 years.
Probation	Spent after 5 years.
Community service	Spent after 5 years.
Curfew orders	Spent after 5 years.
Drug treatment and testing	Spent after 5 years.
Reparation orders	Spent after 5 years.
Absolute discharge	Spent after 6 months.

The amount of time actually served in prison is not relevant. The time periods begin when the sentence is passed, not when the prisoner is released.

21.8 DISCRIMINATION AGAINST PART-TIME WORKERS

The Part-time Workers (Prevention of Less Favourable Treatment) Regulations 2000 (SI 2000 No. 1551) came into force in July 2000. The main provisions of the Regulations are set out in reg.5(1):

'A part-time worker has the right not to be treated by his employer less favourably than the employer treats a full-time worker –

(a) as regards the terms of his contract; or

(b) by being subjected to any other detriment by any act, or deliberate failure to act, of his employer.'

However, these rights only apply if the treatment of the part-time worker is on the grounds that he is a part-time worker. Nor will the rights apply if the treatment is justified on objective grounds (reg.5(2)(b)).

In assessing whether or not a part-time worker has been treated less favourably the pro-rata principle should be applied unless it is inappropriate. This principle requires that the part-time worker should receive the appropriate proportion of the pay and benefits enjoyed by the full-time worker with whom he compares himself. Part-timers will not be entitled to overtime rates until they have worked for longer than normal full-time hours. Contractual sick pay and maternity pay are covered by the Regulations. Part-timers must have equal access to occupational pension schemes, to training and career breaks. Holiday entitlement should be pro rata the holiday entitlement of full-timers.

Where a part-time worker is given less favourable treatment reg.6 entitles him to a written statement of the reasons for the less favourable treatment. If a worker is dismissed for bringing proceedings under the Regulations, or otherwise in connection with the Regulations, this amounts to automatic unfair dismissal.

A complaint under the Regulations is made to the employment tribunal in the usual way. The tribunal can make a declaration of the claimant's rights, order the employer to pay compensation or recommend that the employer take reasonable action to prevent the discrimination. Compensation cannot include an amount for injured feelings, and the complainant has a duty to mitigate any loss. The Regulations were passed to give effect to EC Directive 98/23/EC.

Regulation 2 defines full-time workers, part-time workers and comparable full-time workers. In *Mathews v Kent and Medway Towns Fire Authority* [2006] UKHL 8, [2006] 2 All ER 171, which will be of significance to many part-time workers, the House of Lords gave reg.2 a very thorough examination. Regulation 2 provides that:

'(1) A worker is a full-time worker for the purpose of these Regulations if he is paid wholly or in part by reference to the time he works and, having regard to the custom and practice of the employer in relation to workers employed by the worker's employer under the same type of contract, is identifiable as a full-time worker.

(2) A worker is a part-time worker for the purpose of these Regulations if he is paid wholly or in part

by reference to the time he works and, having regard to the custom and practice of the employer in relation to workers employed by the worker's employer under the same type of contract, is not identifiable as a full-time worker.

(3) For the purposes of paragraphs (1), (2) and (4), the following shall be regarded as being employed under different types of contract –

   (a) employees employed under a contract that is neither for a fixed term nor a contract of apprenticeship;

   (b) employees employed under a contract for a fixed term that is not a contract of apprenticeship;

   (c) employees employed under a contract of apprenticeship;

   (d) workers who are neither employees nor employed under a contract for a fixed term;

   (e) workers who are not employees but are employed under a contract for a fixed term;

   (f) any other description of worker that it is reasonable for the employer to treat differently from other workers on the ground that workers of that description have a different type of contract.

(4) A full-time worker is a comparable full-time worker in relation to a part-time worker if, at the time when the treatment that is alleged to be less favourable to the part-time worker takes place –

   (a) both workers are –

      (i) employed by the same employer under the same type of contract, and

      (ii) engaged in the same or broadly similar work having regard, where relevant, to whether they have a similar level of qualification, skills and experience; and

   (b) the full-time worker works or is based at the same establishment as the part-time worker or, where there is no full-time worker working or based at that establishment who satisfies the requirements of sub-paragraph (a), works or is based at a different establishment and satisfies those requirements.'

Mathews v Kent and Medway Towns Fire Authority [2006] UKHL 8, [2006] 2 All ER 171

Part-time firefighters claimed equal treatment as regards full-time firefighters under the Regulations. Two questions arose. First, were the part-timers employed under the same type of contracts as the full-timers within the meaning of reg.2(3) and reg.2(4)(a)(i)? Second, if they were employed under the same type of contract, was the work which they did broadly similar to that of the full-timers within reg.2(4)(a)(i)? The employment tribunal and the EAT found against the part-timers on both questions. The Court of Appeal found for the part-timers on the first question but against them on the second. An appeal was made to the House of Lords.

Held (3:2). The part-timers were entitled to equal treatment under the Regulations. On the first question, the House of Lords held that the types of contracts set out in regs.2(3)(a)–(f) were mutually exclusive. Therefore if a firefighter was employed under one of these types of contract he could not be employed under another. Both the part-timers and the full-timers were employed under the type of contract set out in reg.2(3)(a). The part-timers were not therefore employed under the type of contract set out in reg.2(3)(f). So the part-timers could not be denied equal treatment on the grounds that they were employed under a type of contract which was different from the type under which the full-timers were employed. On the second question, the House of Lords held that the work which the part-timers did was 'broadly similar'. The approach under the Regulations is not the same as the approach under the Equal Pay Act 1970. The correct approach under the Regulations is to concentrate on the ways in which the work done by the two groups is similar, rather than to focus on the ways in which it is different. The full-timers did have additional duties. But the main question was the extent to which the duties shared by the two groups were broadly similar. This question was referred back to the employment tribunal for a finding of fact.

COMMENT This case is likely to prove useful to many part-time workers. Each case must be decided on its own facts. However, Baroness Hale said that in assessing whether the work done was broadly similar 'the extent to which the work that they do is exactly the same must be of great importance'. She thought that if the two groups did exactly the same type of work, but the full-timers also did more important work, then the work might not be broadly similar. But if the two groups spent much of the time on the core activity of the enterprise, and the additional work done by the full-timers consisted of extra tasks, then the work would be broadly similar.

The decision in *Mathews* remains good law. However, reg.2(3) has been amended to make sure that employers could not discriminate against fixed term workers by making them part-timers. Regulation 2(3) now reads as follows:

'(3) For the purposes of paragraphs (1), (2) and (4), the following shall be regarded as being employed under different types of contract –

(a) employees employed under a contract that is not a contract of apprenticeship;

(b) employees employed under a contract of apprenticeship;

(c) workers who are not employees;

(d) any other description of worker that it is reasonable for the employer to treat differently from other workers on the ground that workers of that description have a different type of contract.'

21.9 DISCRIMINATION AGAINST FIXED-TERM WORKERS

The Fixed-term Employees (Prevention of Less Favourable Treatment) Regulations 2002 (SI 2002 No. 2034) seek to prevent discrimination against employees working on fixed term contracts. Regulation 3(1) provides that a fixed term employee has the right not to be treated by his employer less favourably than the employer treats a comparable permanent employee: (a) as regards the terms of his contract; or (b) by being subjected to any other detriment by any act, or deliberate failure to act, of his employer. However, these rights apply only if the different treatment was on the grounds that the worker was a fixed term worker and if it was not justified on objective grounds.

Regulation 3(2) specifies that in particular this includes the right not to be treated less favourably in relation to any period of service qualification, the opportunity to receive training or the opportunity to secure any permanent job. In determining whether treatment was less favourable, the pro rata principle is used, as explained above in relation to discrimination against part-time workers. If fixed term workers are treated less favourably as regards particular terms of their contracts, this can be justified on objective grounds if their contracts as a whole are at least as favourable as the terms of the comparable permanent employee's contract of employment (reg.4).

A fixed term employee who thinks that he is being treated less favourably is entitled to a written statement of the reasons for the less favourable treatment

and this is admissible as evidence in any proceedings under the Regulations. It will be automatically unfair dismissal to dismiss an employee on the grounds that he has requested a written statement or brought proceedings under the Regulations. Complaints are made to the tribunal in the usual way. Compensation cannot cover damages for injured feelings. An employee who works on a fixed term contract which is renewed is to be regarded as a permanent employee once he has been continuously employed for at least four years, unless the failure to renew can be justified on objective grounds. However, for this purpose employment before 10 July 2002 does not count as continuous employment.

21.10 THE AGENCY WORKERS REGULATIONS 2010

These regulations protect agency workers. Regulation 3 defines an agency worker as an individual who is supplied by a temporary work agency to work temporarily for and under the direct supervision of a hirer. The individual must also either have a contract of employment with the agency or have a different type of contract to perform work and services personally for the agency. The definition does not cover genuinely self-employed people who provide services for an agency.

Regulation 5 gives an agency worker the right to the same basic working and employment conditions as he would have been entitled to if he had been employed directly by the hirer. There is no need for a comparator. However, reg.6(1) restricts the 'relevant terms and conditions' to the following six matters: pay; the duration of working time; night work; rest periods; rest breaks; and annual leave. Regulation 6(2) defines pay as any sums payable to the worker of a hirer in connection with the worker's employment, including any fee, bonus, commission, holiday pay or other emoluments referable to the employment whether payable under the contract or otherwise. However, reg.6(3) specifically excludes sick pay, pensions, maternity, paternity or adoption leave, redundancy payments and certain other matters. Regulation 7 sets out a qualifying period which must have been worked before reg.5 can apply. Essentially this is a period of 12 continuous calendar weeks, during which the worker must work in the same role for the same hirer during one or more assignments. Any part of a week worked counts as a calendar week. A role is regarded as the same role as long as it is not substantively different from the previous role. Breaks of up to six weeks will not breach the continuity requirement. The regulations also contain anti-avoidance provisions.

Regulation 12(1) provides that as from the first day of working for a hirer an agency worker is entitled to be treated no less favourably than a comparable worker in relation to the collective facilities and amenities provided by the hirer. Regulation 13(1) requires an agency worker to be informed of any relevant vacant posts with the hirer, to give the agency worker the same opportunity as a comparable worker to find permanent employment with the hirer. Regulation 16 gives agency workers the right to request written information from the employer so that they can see if their rights have been infringed. If an agency worker is dismissed on account of bringing proceedings under the regulations, or for doing anything else in connection with the regulations, this is regarded as automatically unfair dismissal.

The rights are enforced through the employment tribunal, which can award compensation to cover the worker's loss. Generally, the minimum award will be two week's pay. A complaint must be presented within three months of the act complained of.

Test your understanding 21.3

1 What protection against discrimination is provided to those who have been convicted of criminal offences?

2 What is the main effect of the Part-time Workers (Prevention of Less Favourable Treatment) Regulations 2000?

3 What rights are given to fixed-term employees by the Fixed-term Employees (Prevention of Less Favourable Treatment) Regulations 2002?

4 What is the main effect of the Agency Workers Regulations 2010?

21.11 HEALTH AND SAFETY

The Health and Safety at Work etc. Act 1974, as amended, imposes duties on employers. Breach of these duties constitutes a criminal offence, but does not necessarily give rise to any civil action. An employee who is injured by an employer's breach of a duty of care can sue in the tort of negligence.

Therefore, for two quite different reasons employers should ensure the health and safety of their workers. First, if they do not they might be convicted of an offence under the Health and Safety at Work Act. Second, they might, additionally or alternatively, be liable to pay compensation to workers who are injured or whose health is adversely affected. First we consider the Act, then the civil position.

In *R v Bristol Magistrates' Court ex parte Junttan Oy* [2003] UKHL 55, [2003] ICR 1475 the House of Lords held that the Health and Safety Executive could choose to prosecute under the 1974 Act rather than under one of the 'six-pack' Regulations considered below at 21.11.6. The maximum sentence under the Act was considerably heavier than that under the Regulations.

21.11.1 The Health and Safety at Work etc. Act 1974

21.11.1.1 Enforcement of the Act

The Health and Safety Executive (HSE) presides over Health and Safety. The HSE is governed by a nine-member Board and a 12-member Senior Management Team. The HSE carries out functions as directed by the Health and Safety Commission. Inspectors are given powers to do the following things:

(a) enter premises where there is a dangerous situation at any reasonable time;
(b) make whatever examinations and investigations as may be necessary;
(c) take samples from within premises or from the atmosphere;
(d) test articles and substances;
(e) dismantle dangerous articles;
(f) take away dangerous articles or substances for examination;
(g) require that books and records are produced;
(h) require that people answer questions and sign a declaration that their answers are true;
(i) require that they are not obstructed in the execution of their powers; and
(j) use any other power necessary to exercise the powers previously listed.

Section 21 allows an inspector to issue an **improvement notice**. Such a notice would be served on an employer, and would require the employer to stop contravening one of the Act's provisions within a period which may not be less than 21 days.

Prohibition notices can be issued under s.22 to prevent, with immediate effect, the carrying on of an activity which involves a risk of serious personal injury. Failure to comply with either an improvement notice or with a prohibition notice is a criminal offence. Where the employee is the Crown, as in many Government departments, improvements and enforcement notices are called **Crown notices**. Breach of these is not a criminal offence, as the Crown cannot be prosecuted, but the publicity engendered would ensure that remedial action is taken.

Section 25 gives an inspector the **power to deal with a cause of imminent danger**. This power allows an inspector to seize and render harmless any article or substance found on any premises which he has the power to enter. The power arises if the inspector has reasonable cause to believe that, in the circumstances in which he finds it, the article or substance is a cause of imminent danger of serious personal injury.

21.11.1.2 **Duties of the employer**

Section 2(1) of the Act states that it shall be the duty of every employer to ensure, so far as is reasonably practicable, the health, safety and welfare at work of all his employees. Without prejudice to this general duty, s.2(2) sets out five matters to which the duty particularly extends. The matters are:

(a) the provision and maintenance of safe plant and safe systems of work;
(b) arrangements for ensuring the safe use, handling, storage and transport of articles and substances;
(c) providing information, instruction, training and supervision as is necessary to ensure the health and safety of employees;
(d) maintaining any place under the employer's control in a safe condition and maintaining safe ways in and out; and
(e) providing and maintaining an overall safe working environment for employees.

It should be emphasised that none of these matters are absolute duties. The employer only has a duty to comply with them so far as is reasonably practicable. However, if a duty is practicable then it will be very likely that failure to carry it out was unreasonable. If the employer argues that it was not reasonably practicable for him to carry out any of his duties under the Act then the burden of proof is on him to prove this.

Section 2(3) provides that it shall be the duty of every employer employing five or more persons to prepare a written statement of his general policy with respect to health and safety at work of his employees. This statement must also be revised as often as is appropriate. The written statement must also set out the organisation and arrangements for the time being in force for carrying out that policy. It is also the duty of the employer to bring the statement and any revision of it to the notice of all of his employees.

Employers may be required to consult with recognised trade unions in order to cooperate effectively in promoting and developing measures to ensure the health and safety at work of the employees, and in checking the effectiveness of such measures. The employer may also be required to set up a safety committee to keep matters under review.

Section 3 requires that employers conduct their undertakings in such a way as to ensure, as far as is reasonably practicable, that non-employees who may be affected by the undertaking are not exposed to risks to their health and safety. Section 4 imposes a similar duty on employers in respect of non-employees who may use the employer's premises.

When we considered unfair dismissal, in the previous chapter, we saw that a dismissal connected with having carried out activities in connection with health and safety could be automatically unfair (ERA ss.44 and 100).

21.11.1.3 **Duties of manufacturers, designers, importers and suppliers**

Section 6(1) imposes a number of duties on employers who design, manufacture, import or supply any article for use at work. The manufacturer etc. must:

(a) ensure, so far as is reasonably practicable, that the article is so designed and constructed that it will be safe and without risk to health at all times when it is being set, used, cleaned or maintained by a person at work;
(b) carry out, or arrange to have carried out, such tests and examinations as are necessary to ensure compliance with requirement (a);
(c) make sure that persons supplied with any article are provided with adequate information about the use for which it is designed and about any conditions required to make sure its use is safe; and
(d) provide revised information to make sure that duty (c) is complied with, as far as is reasonably practicable.

Section 6(4) imposes very similar duties on those who import or supply any substance, rather than manufacture etc. any article.

Section 6(2) imposes a duty upon designers and manufacturers to carry out research with a view to discovering and eliminating risks to health and safety.

Section 6(3) requires those who erect and install equipment at work to ensure, as far as is reasonably practicable, that nothing about the way this is done should make the article unsafe or a risk to health.

The duties imposed by s.6 only extend to things done in the course of a trade or business (whether for profit or not) and also only to matters within the control of the person on whom the duty is imposed.

21.11.1.4 Employees' duties at work

Section 7 provides that it shall be the duty of every employee while at work:

(a) to take reasonable care for the health and safety of himself and of other persons who may be affected by his acts or omissions at work; and

(b) as regards any duty imposed on his employer or anyone else by a statute, to cooperate with him so far as necessary to enable that duty or requirement to be performed or complied with.

21.11.1.5 Other aspects of the Act

Section 8 imposes a duty on all persons not to interfere with or misuse anything provided in the interests of health, safety or welfare in pursuance of the relevant statutory provisions. Both intentional and reckless interference are prohibited.

Section 9 makes it illegal for an employer to charge, or permit to be charged, any employee in respect of anything done or provided in pursuance of any specific requirement of the relevant statutory provisions.

Section 36 provides that where any person commits an offence under the Act due to the act or default of some other person, that other person shall be guilty of the offence. This other person can be convicted even if proceedings are not brought against the person who committed the offence.

Section 37 provides that if a company commits an offence under the Act with the consent or connivance of any director, manager or secretary or other similar officer of the company then both the company and the company officer shall be guilty of the offence. The same is true if the offence was caused by the neglect of the company officer.

The Act also allows Regulations to be made by the Secretary of State or the Health and Safety Commission. There are many Regulations applying either generally or to particular hazards and risks. It is beyond the scope of this book to examine these.

21.11.2 European law

Article 137 of the Treaty of Rome, which used to be Article 118, allows the passing of Directives to improve the working environment to protect workers' health and safety and working conditions. Six new sets of Regulations were passed in 1992. It is probable that these merely state clearly requirements which were previously imposed on employers by the old law. The new law spells out that employers must actively take steps to ensure the health and safety at work of their employees. The six Regulations in question, as amended, are as follows.

The Management of Health and Safety at Work Regulations 1999 require all employers to make an assessment of the risk to health and safety of their employees while at work. An employer must make health and safety arrangements, provide appropriate health surveillance and appoint assistants to help him comply with his statutory duties. The employer must also have procedures to deal with serious and imminent danger and for dealing with danger areas. Information must be given to employees, who must cooperate with the employer. There is also a duty on the employer to provide adequate training of employees.

The Workplace (Health, Safety and Welfare) Regulations 1992 require that employers provide clean, efficient places of work. Sanitary facilities should be provided, safe seats if the workers are to sit down, and also rest facilities where non-smokers are protected from smokers. Suitable facilities for eating meals should also be provided.

The Provision and Use of Work Equipment Regulations 1998 require equipment used at work to be maintained and repaired. They also provide that the equipment must conform to any legislation and that employees should be trained in the use of equipment. In *Stark v The Post Office* (2000) *Times*, 29 March, the Post Office were found to be in breach of these Regulations when a postman suffered injury as a consequence of the front brake of his delivery bike breaking. The duty set out in reg.5(1), that every employer shall ensure that work equipment is maintained in an efficient state, in efficient working order and good repair, was held to be an absolute duty. The Court of Appeal also held that although the EC Directive which gave rise to the Regulations imposed minimum standards to be observed they did not prevent higher standards from being introduced if the Member State chose to introduce higher standards. In *Spencer-Franks* v *Kellogg Brown and Root Ltd* [2008] UKHL 46, the House of Lords held that a device which ensured that a control room door on an oil rig stayed closed was 'work equipment' within the regulations. So a mechanic who was injured while repairing the device could claim under the regulations.

The **Personal Protective Equipment at Work Regulations 1992** provide that personal protective equipment must be supplied to employees where appropriate. The equipment must be kept clean and well repaired and employees must be instructed and trained in the use of it.

The **Manual Handling Operations Regulations 1992** seek to minimise the risk from employees manually handling things in a way which involves the risk of injury.

The **Health and Safety (Display Screen Equipment) Regulations 1992** require that users of work stations must be trained, must be given eye tests and treatment if they request them and must be given breaks and changes of activity.

The Health and Safety Commission may issue **Codes of Practice** in relation to any statutory duties or duties imposed by Regulations. Breach of such a code does not automatically mean that a criminal offence has been committed, but will almost always mean that it has. Adherence to the code will mean that an offence has not been committed.

The **Control of Substances Hazardous to Health Regulations 2002** impose duties on employers to protect employees from hazardous substances used in the workplace. The duties imposed on employers by the Regulations apply not only in respect of employees but also in respect of any person who might be affected by the work carried on by the employer.

The Regulations prohibit the importation or supply for use at work of certain substances. These substances include benzene, sand containing free silica, ground flint or quartz, white phosphorus and certain types of oil. They also require employers to carry out an assessment of the risk to health created by work involving any substances hazardous to health and to make sure that the exposure of employees to substances hazardous to health is prevented.

21.11.3 **Common law health and safety**

A term is implied into a contract of employment requiring an employer to take reasonable care to ensure the safety of his employees. Breach of this term could enable an employee to sue for breach of contract. Generally, however, where an employee is injured at work he will seek to sue the employer in the tort of negligence. As was seen in Chapter 12, a successful claim in negligence will require the claimant to prove three things:

(a) that the defendant (employer) owed the claimant (employee) a duty of care;
(b) that the defendant breached this duty; and
(c) that this breach resulted in the claimant suffering foreseeable injury.

21.11.3.1 **The duty of care**

The circumstances in which a duty of care exists not to cause psychiatric injury through stress at work was considered in detail at 12.2.1.1. Psychiatric injury apart, the duty of care owed by an employer is generally thought to be made up in particular of three matters: to provide safe plant and equipment, to provide a safe system of work and to provide reasonably competent fellow employees. The duty is not an absolute one to see that the employee is not injured, but only a duty to take such care as an ordinary prudent employer would take in all the circumstances. The duty is owed personally by the employer and therefore he cannot escape liability by passing the duty to another person. The duty is also owed to employees personally, rather than to all of the employees collectively. So if the employee has a particular weakness, or is particularly inexperienced, account must be taken of this. An example can be seen in *Paris* v *Stepney Borough Council* [1951] 1 All ER 42. An employee with the use of only one eye was asked to work on the underneath of a vehicle and was not given protective goggles. A shard of metal flew into his good eye and blinded him as he hammered a bolt in an attempt to remove it. The employer was liable for this injury and it was a relevant factor that the employee had the use of only one eye and was therefore particularly vulnerable.

As the general law of negligence is applicable, it is only necessary here to say a little about each of the three matters which apply especially to employers.

21.11.3.2 Safe plant and equipment

An example of an employer being liable in consequence of not providing safe equipment can be seen in the following case.

> #### Bradford v Robinson Rentals
> [1967] 1 All ER 267
>
> The claimant, a 57-year-old man, was employed as a radio service engineer. He generally travelled short distances between customers' houses. In January 1963, when the employer knew that the weather was likely to be very severe, he was ordered to do a round journey of 500 miles to change a colleague's van. This involved about 20 hours' driving. (Motorways were a thing of the future.) Both of the vans were unheated. The employee said that he thought the journey should not be undertaken as it was hazardous. He was ordered to go and suffered frostbite, a very unusual condition in England.
>
> **Held.** The employee was entitled to damages. The employers had exposed him to a reasonable risk of injury. Injury from exposure to cold was foreseeable and so it did not matter that the exact nature of the injury was unusual.

21.11.3.3 Safe system of work

The employer's duty to provide a safe system of work involves all matters relating to the way the work is done. These matters would commonly include whether training was provided, whether the system used was inherently safe, and whether the employee was given special instructions or protective clothing. Problems often arise, as in the case which follows, when employees are provided with protective equipment but choose not to use it.

> #### MacWilliams v Sir William Arrol & Co Ltd
> [1962] 1 All ER 623 (House of Lords)
>
> A steel erector was killed when he fell 70 feet from a steel tower which he was helping to build. His widow sued the employer for negligence. If the worker had been wearing a safety belt he would not have been killed by the fall. The employer had provided safety belts on the site in question until two or three days before the accident when they had been removed. The dead worker was an experienced steel erector and would probably not have worn a safety belt if one had been provided. The employer had never instructed the dead worker to wear a safety belt and it was only in exceptional circumstances that any of the workers did wear them.

> **Held.** The employers were not liable to pay damages. Their breach of duty in not supplying safety belts was not the cause of the damage suffered because the evidence showed that the deceased would not have worn a safety belt and the employer had no duty to exhort or instruct the employee to wear a safety belt.

21.11.3.4 Duty to provide reasonably competent fellow employees

Workers often rely on the competence of other workers for their safety. Several cases, such as the one which follows, have been concerned with injury caused by a practical joker.

> #### Hudson v Ridge Manufacturing Co Ltd
> [1957] 2 QB 348
>
> The claimant was injured by a fellow employee, one Chadwick, who the judge described as 'not over-intelligent and [who] appears to have grown to manhood with childish pranks still part of his make-up'. For some years Chadwick frequently engaged in horseplay and skylarking and often tripped people up. Chadwick frequently teased the claimant. He grabbed the claimant, who was crippled, from behind and forced him down to the ground. The claimant put out his arm to save himself and his wrist was broken in the fall. Chadwick had been warned by the foreman not to indulge in horseplay on many occasions but no further steps had been taken against him.
>
> **Held.** The employers were liable to pay damages to the claimant. They had known about the potentially dangerous behaviour for some time and had failed to prevent it. They had therefore failed to take proper care of the claimant's safety.

An employer who takes all reasonable precautions will not have been negligent and will not therefore be liable to the employee. An example can be seen in *Latimer v AEC Ltd* [1953] AC 643. The floors of a factory became flooded during an unusually heavy rainstorm. The flood caused oil, which normally ran along a channel in the floor, to mix with the flood water on the factory floor. The factory floor was therefore in a slippery state when the flood subsided. Sawdust was spread where possible, but some areas of the floor were still slippery. An employee who was working in an area not treated with sawdust was trying to lift a heavy barrel onto a trolley when he slipped and injured his ankle. The House of Lords held that the employers were not negligent. Having regard to the degree of risk to employees, they had done all that a reasonable employer could be expected to do. The only way to have made sure that the accident did not happen would have been to close the factory down, and this was not reasonable in all the circumstances.

In Chapter 12 at 12.2.6.2 we saw that *volenti non fit injuria* provides a complete defence to negligence and that the contributory negligence of the claimant may result in his damages being reduced to the extent which is just and equitable.

In *ICI Ltd v Shatwell* [1965] AC 656 the employer was able to rely on *volenti non fit injuria* as a complete defence. Experienced and qualified shot firers had been given proper instructions as to how to test detonators. These instructions involved retreating into a shelter before making the tests. In complete contravention of these instructions the claimant and others tested detonators. The claimant was badly injured when testing detonators without retreating to the shelter. The House of Lords held that *volenti non fit injuria* provided the employer with a complete defence.

Test your understanding 21.4

1 Does the Health and Safety at Work etc. Act 1974 impose civil or criminal sanctions against employers who neglect the health and safety of their employees?

2 How is the Act enforced?

3 How is the Act supplemented by European law?

4 What will an injured employee need to prove in order to sue the employer for negligence?

5 What are the three particular aspects of the employer's duty of care to employees?

21.12 MATERNITY AND PATERNITY RIGHTS

Female employees are given several rights in connection with childbirth and pregnancy. The Pregnant Workers Directive (92/85/EEC) required changes to existing law and these changes have been superimposed on the old law. When used in the Employment Rights Act 1996, 'childbirth' means the birth of a living child or the birth of a child whether living or dead after 24 weeks of pregnancy.

21.12.1 Time off for ante-natal care

Section 55(1) ERA 1996 provides that an employee who is pregnant, and who has made an appointment

to attend any place for the purpose of receiving ante-natal care, must be given time off by the employer to keep the appointment. The appointment in question must have been made on the advice of a registered medical practitioner, a registered midwife or a registered health visitor. The employee is also entitled to be paid the appropriate hourly rate for the period when she is absent.

This right is given whether the pregnant employee is full or part-time, and no matter how short her period of continuous employment. If the employee is unreasonably refused the time off work, or is not paid the appropriate amount, she can bring a case before an employment tribunal. The case must be brought within three months of the appointment concerned, although the tribunal has the power to extend this period. The tribunal can make a declaration that the complaint is well founded, and order that the employer pays the amount he should have paid.

Except as regards the first appointment, the pregnant employee must produce a statement from the registered medical practitioner etc. stating that she is pregnant, and an appointment card or some other document showing that an appointment has been made.

21.12.2 Time off for dependants

Section 57A ERA 1996 allows employees to take a reasonable amount of time off, during working hours, to provide assistance to a dependant who gives birth or in other specified circumstances. A dependant is defined as a spouse, a child, a parent or a person who is a live-in lover, as well as any person who reasonably relies on the employee to make arrangements for the provision of care. The entitlement is available if it is necessary:

(1) to make arrangements to provide care for a dependant who is ill, giving birth, injured or assaulted;

(2) in consequence of the death of a dependant;

(3) because of the unexpected disruption or termination of arrangements for the care of a dependant; or

(4) to deal with an incident which involves a child of the employee and which occurs unexpectedly during school hours.

In all these cases the employee must tell the employer the reason for his absence as soon as reasonably practicable. Illness includes mental illness. There is no right to be paid during time off work to look after dependants.

A complaint that time off has not been allowed can be made to an employment tribunal within three months of the refusal. The tribunal has the usual power to extend this period. It can declare the complainant's rights and award compensation, which can take account of any loss to the complainant which is attributable to the matter complained of.

21.12.3 Parental leave

The Maternity and Parental Leave Regulations 1999 give all employees who have one year's continuous employment the right to take parental leave to care for their children. Thirteen weeks' unpaid leave will be allowed in respect of each child or 18 weeks in the case of a disabled child. The leave must be taken before the child's fifth birthday, unless the child is disabled, in which case the leave must be taken before the child's 18th birthday. The employee must give at least 21 days' notice of taking the leave. The employer can postpone the leave, for up to six months, if the needs of the business make this necessary and if it is reasonable to do so.

The employee remains employed during the period of leave and has a right to return to the same job after the leave has ended. Where the leave taken is more than four weeks the employer may offer a similar job instead of the previously held job, as long as the conditions of service are at least as favourable. There is no right to be paid during parental leave.

The Regulations' fallback scheme requires leave to be taken in blocks or multiples of one week and that only four weeks may be taken in any one year. If the employer prevents the employee from taking the leave, or attempts to do so, a complaint can be made to an employment tribunal.

21.12.4 Suspension on maternity grounds

An employee is regarded as suspended from work on maternity grounds if, in consequence of any legislation or official code of practice, the employer suspends her on the ground that she is pregnant, has recently given birth or is breastfeeding a child. However, the woman is only regarded as suspended for as long as she continues to be employed by the employer but is not provided with work or does not perform the work she normally performed before the suspension. The

employee has a right to be offered suitable alternative work if the employer has such work available. Such suitable alternative work must be given on equally favourable terms, must be suitable in relation to the employee, and must not be substantially less favourable than her previous terms. An employee who is suspended on maternity grounds is entitled to be paid the normal weekly wage while she is suspended, unless she unreasonably refused the offer of suitable alternative employment.

Earlier in this chapter we saw that the Management of Health and Safety at Work Regulations 1992 required employers to carry out a risk assessment of the health and safety of employees while they are at work. Such a risk assessment could require the employer to suspend an employee on maternity grounds.

21.12.5 Right to maternity leave of absence

In addition to the two weeks' compulsory maternity leave after the birth of a child, all pregnant employees have the right to a total of at least 26 weeks' maternity leave and 26 weeks' additional maternity leave. A woman who wants to return to work earlier than this must give at least eight weeks' notice to the employer. The employee may choose the date on which the maternity leave period starts. During the maternity leave the employee is entitled to all the benefits of her terms and conditions of employment, except wages or salary, which would have applied if she had not been absent. All employees have the right to return to work after the maternity leave with all seniority rights intact. At the same time the employee is bound by the obligations arising under the terms and conditions of her contract of employment.

The employee is not entitled to remuneration during maternity leave unless her contract provides that she is. However, **statutory maternity pay** is payable for 39 weeks and this period is eventually to be extended to one year. The woman's earnings must be enough for her to pay National Insurance Contributions (she must have earned at least £102 a week) and she must have been continuously employed for 26 weeks by the end of the 14th week before the baby is due. The first six weeks' statutory maternity pay are calculated as 90 per cent of gross average weekly earnings. The other 33 weeks are paid at £128.73 a week or 90 per cent of gross average weekly earnings, whichever is lower. Employers pay the SMP but get a rebate on their National Insurance

Contributions. A woman can return to work for up to ten days, to keep in touch, without losing her right to statutory maternity pay.

Maternity allowance is payable to women who earn at least £30 a week, but who do not qualify for maternity pay from their employer. The amount is £128.73 a week or 90 per cent of the woman's weekly earnings, whichever is smaller, and is payable for nine months.

21.12.5.1 Right to return after maternity leave

If ordinary maternity leave was taken, the employee has a right to return to the same job. If the employee takes additional maternity leave, the employer may provide a suitable alternative job instead if it is not reasonably practicable for the employee to return to her old job. The terms and conditions of this alternative employment must be no less favourable than the terms and conditions of the previous employment.

An employee is **automatically unfairly dismissed** if the reason for the dismissal was connected with pregnancy, childbirth, or the fact that she took or tried to take maternity leave. When calculating a week's pay for the purposes of ERA 1996, any lesser amount paid to an employee who was off work on maternity or parental leave should not be used. Instead the amount the employee would actually have earned if she had worked should be used.

21.12.6 Paternity leave and pay

The Paternity and Adoption Leave Regulations 2002 (SI 2002 No. 2788), give rights to paternity leave and paternity pay. In order to qualify for paternity leave, the employee must satisfy three conditions. First, the employee must have responsibility for the new child's upbringing or expect to have this responsibility. Second, he must either be the biological father of the child or he must be the husband or partner of the child's mother. Third, he must have had at least 26 weeks' continuous employment 15 weeks before the baby is due to be born.

Paternity leave can either be for one week or for two consecutive weeks. It cannot be for parts of a week but it can begin midweek. The leave can begin either from the date of the child's birth or at some later date, but it must be completed 56 days after the child was born. If the mother gives birth to twins no extra paternity leave is available. The rate of statutory paternity pay is currently either £128.73 a

week or, if the average weekly earnings are less than £128.73, 90 per cent of average weekly earnings. Other contractual benefits must also be received. Employees who do not earn enough to pay any National Insurance contributions, that is to say those who earn less than £102 a week, are not entitled to statutory paternity pay.

Employees intending to take statutory paternity leave must inform their employers at least 15 weeks before the baby is expected. They must say when the baby is due, when they want the leave to start, and whether they want one week's leave or two weeks' leave. Employees are obliged to give the employer a completed self-certificate which provides evidence of their entitlement to statutory paternity pay. A model certificate can be found on the DTI website, www.dti.gov.uk. Employees who take statutory paternity leave are entitled to return to work afterwards and must not be discriminated against for having taken the leave. Employers can reclaim from the Government about 90 per cent of the amount which they have paid in statutory paternity pay.

21.13 ADOPTION LEAVE AND PAY

When a couple adopt a child, the Paternity and Adoption Leave Regulations 2002 entitle one member of the couple to time off work with statutory adoption pay. In addition, the other member of the couple, or a partner of an individual who adopts, may be entitled to paternity leave and pay.

In order to claim adoption leave the employee must have worked continuously for the employer for 26 weeks and be newly matched with a child by an adoption agency. Such employees are entitled to 39 weeks' **ordinary adoption leave**, during which they are entitled to statutory adoption pay, and an additional 13 weeks' **additional adoption leave**. The leave can start either on the date of the child's placement or 14 days before the expected date of the placement. The rate of statutory adoption pay is £128.73 a week or 90 per cent of the normal weekly wage if this is less than £128.73. Adopters have to give notice of their intention to take adoption leave. Employers can also ask for a matching certificate from the adoption agency. Those taking time off are entitled to contractual benefits other than pay which they would normally receive and have a right to return to work after the adoption leave. Employers can reclaim about 90 per cent of money paid in adoption leave from the Government. The statutory rates of maternity pay, paternity pay and adoption pay increase periodically.

21.14 FLEXIBLE WORKING FOR PARENTS

Section 80F of the Employment Rights Act 1996 has introduced a right for parents with children under 16 years old to apply for flexible working. In the case of disabled children the age limit is 18. Employers will have a statutory duty to consider these applications seriously but there is no automatic right to work flexibly.

Only employees with at least 26 weeks' continuous employment can apply. They must either be the child's mother, father, adopter, guardian or foster parent or be married to such a person. They must be making the application so that they can care for a child for whom they have, or expect to have, responsibility for bringing up. Only one application can be made every 12 months and agency workers cannot apply.

The application can ask for a change of hours, a change to the times of work or to work from home. If the application is accepted then the change will be permanent unless the parties agree otherwise. As a change in working pattern might involve a drop in pay, applicants need to think things through carefully before applying. Once the employer receives a written application, a meeting with the employee must be arranged within 28 days. At this meeting the application, and other possible solutions, are considered. Within 14 days of the meeting the employer has to write to the employee either agreeing to a new date on which a new work pattern starts or giving reasons why the application has been refused.

21.15 THE NATIONAL MINIMUM WAGE

The National Minimum Wage Act 1998 provides that workers aged 21 or over should be paid a minimum wage of £6.08 an hour, while workers between 18 and 20 are entitled to a minimum wage of £4.98 an hour. 16 and 17 year olds are entitled to a minimum of £3.68 an hour. Apprentices are entitled to at least £2.60 an hour. These rates were set by the Government on the advice of the Low Pay Commission, which consulted various organisations.

The employer is required to keep records relating to pay, and workers are given a right of access to those records. Workers may require the employer to produce the records, and may inspect, examine and copy them. However, these rights are only available if the worker believes, on reasonable grounds, that there has been or will be a breach of the requirement to pay the minimum wage, and the rights are necessary to establish whether or not this is the case. The worker is entitled to exercise the rights accompanied by any other person he sees fit. If the worker is not allowed access to the records an employment tribunal may declare a complaint well founded and award the complainant 80 hours' pay at the minimum wage rate. The burden of proof is on the employer to show that the national minimum wage is being paid. The worker has the right not to suffer any detriment on the grounds of his having taken any action under the Act. A worker who alleges that he has suffered such a detriment may take the case to an employment tribunal. The usual three-month period applies in respect of bringing a claim and the tribunal has the usual power to extend this period. The tribunal can award a payment to an individual to bring the amount he was paid up to the amount he ought to have been paid.

The Act protects all workers, whether they work under a contract of employment or not and no matter what the size of the business for which they work. Workers who do not work under a contract of employment are protected if they contract to perform personally any work or services for another, as long as the other is not a client or customer of any profession or business undertaking carried on by the individual. Those who are genuinely self-employed are therefore not covered by the Act. A worker who is not an employee, but who is dismissed on the grounds of having taken action under the Act, is entitled to a payment which would equal the payment of a basic award for unfair dismissal if the worker had been an employee.

A worker's hourly rate is calculated by reference to a 'relevant pay reference period', which is usually one month. Matters such as incentive bonuses and performance-related pay do count when calculating the hourly rate. But matters such as overtime, tips or shift allowances do not. Therefore, a 22-year-old paid a basic hourly rate of £5.60 per hour plus 20 per cent shift allowance would be being paid less than the minimum wage, even though his pay for hours worked would be £6.72. But a 23-year-old salesman paid a basic rate of £5 an hour would not be paid less than the minimum wage if he always earned an additional £100 commission every week. The only benefit in kind which can be used in calculating the hourly rate is accommodation. Any attempt to contract out of the provisions of the Act is void.

HMRC will be able to enforce the Act on behalf of individual workers and can serve penalty notices on employers who are not complying with the provisions of the Act. The employer has four weeks to appeal against such a notice. The amount of the financial penalty for failure to pay the minimum wage is 50 per cent of the total underpayment, with a minimum payment of £100 and a maximum of £5,000. The burden of proof is on the employer to show that he did pay the minimum wage.

The Act protects not only employees, but also agency workers, home workers and Crown employees. Those serving in the armed forces are not protected, nor are voluntary workers, religious and other community workers, prisoners or employees such as au pairs who work and live as part of a family.

If a worker is dismissed because he has become entitled to the national minimum wage, or to a higher rate of the national minimum wage, this may be unfair dismissal even if the worker has not served the usual qualifying period of one year's continuous employment.

An employer who breaches the Act commits a criminal offence, the maximum fine for which is unlimited.

21.16 THE TRANSFER OF UNDERTAKINGS (PROTECTION OF EMPLOYMENT) REGULATIONS 2006 (TUPE)

At common law the contract of employment is personal between the employer and the employee, and so a worker is dismissed if the employer transfers the undertaking to another employer. The TUPE Regulations were passed to give effect to the Acquired Rights Directive (77/187/EEC). This provided that when a business undertaking is transferred the rights of its employees should be protected and be enforceable against the new employer, the transferee.

The TUPE Regulations apply when an undertaking situated in the UK is transferred to another person and the undertaking retains its identity after the transfer. The Regulations do not apply when a company's shares are bought by new shareholders,

because the company continues to be the employer and there is therefore no transfer of the business undertaking. An 'undertaking' includes any trade or business, and non-profit-making organisations such as charities could be included. Regulation 4(1) provides that a relevant transfer shall not terminate the contract of employment of any person employed by the transferor. The contract continues in effect as if originally made between the employee and the person to whom the undertaking is transferred, the transferee. Regulation 4(2) provides that all the transferor's rights, duties, powers and liabilities are transferred to the transferee. Anything done by the transferor before the transfer is deemed to have been done by the transferee.

Regulation 4(7) allows the employee to object to being transferred. If the employee does object, the contract of employment will be terminated but the employee will not be regarded for any purpose as having been dismissed. However, if substantial and detrimental changes are made in the employee's working conditions the employee can terminate the contract without notice and claim unfair dismissal. The mere fact that the identity of the employer has changed is not enough to amount to a substantial and detrimental change in working conditions.

The only rights which are not transferred are occupational pension rights. Pension rights already accrued are protected but the new employer's occupational pension scheme might be less beneficial than that of the transferor. However, if this is the case it might mean that the overall terms and conditions of the transferee were inferior and the employee might therefore have a claim of unfair dismissal. The new employer can worsen conditions of employment if this is possible under the terms of the contract of employment, but not if this worsening is connected with transfer of the undertaking.

If an employee is dismissed, either before or after a relevant transfer, this will amount to an unfair dismissal as long as the reason or principal reason for the dismissal is the transfer or a reason connected with it. However, this is not the case if the reason for the dismissal, or the principal reason, is an economic, technical or organisational reason entailing changes in either the workforce of the transferor or the transferee before or after a relevant transfer. In such a case the dismissal is regarded as having been for a substantial reason of a kind such as to justify the dismissal of an employee holding the position which the employee held. Continuous employment is preserved, despite the transfer, but an employee will need to have at least one year's continuous employment in order to make a claim for unfair dismissal.

Where a collective agreement exists between the transferor and any trade union which the transferor recognises, then after the transfer the agreement shall be regarded as having been made by the transferee and the trade union. If a trade union is recognised to any extent by the transferor before the transfer then the union will be deemed to have been recognised to the same extent by the transferee. The transferor has a duty to inform employee representatives about the transfer and to consult them about the transfer. If this is not done a complaint may be made to an employment tribunal, which may make a declaration that it has not been done and order the payment of compensation to affected employees.

The Regulations have helped preserve the pay of many groups of employees whose pay was reduced as a result of compulsory competitive tendering and the contracting out of services. It is not possible to make an agreement to contract out of the main provisions of the Regulations.

21.17 THE WORKING TIME REGULATIONS 1998

These Regulations were passed to give effect to the Working Time Directive (93/104/EEC) and the Young Workers Directive (94/33/EC).

Maximum weekly working time

The main provision of the Regulations is that a worker's working time, including overtime, shall not exceed 48 hours for each seven days, averaged out over any period of 17 weeks' employment. The employer has a duty to take all reasonable steps, in keeping with the need to protect the health and safety of workers, to ensure that the limit is complied with. This duty arises in respect of every worker employed by him. Days taken off as annual leave, periods of sick leave and maternity leave are regarded as excluded days. In assessing the average working time of a worker for each seven day period, an appropriate number of days is added on to cater for excluded days. Young workers (aged under 18) are not allowed to work more than eight hours a day or 40 hours a week.

> **Example**
>
> Jim worked in a factory for 50 hours a week for 15 straight weeks. He then took two weeks annual leave and came back to work, doing 46 hours a week for the next two weeks. The days taken as annual leave are excluded. Jim has therefore 750 hours + 92 hours = 842 hours in a 17-week period. This averages out at slightly over 49.5 hours a week and so the Regulations have been breached.

The 48-hour limit does not apply if the worker agrees in writing that it should not. So if in the above example Jim had agreed that the 48-hour limit should not apply, the Regulations would not have been breached.

Protection of night workers

The normal hours of night workers in any 17-week period should not exceed an average of eight hours for each 24 hours. Rest periods do not count as working days.

An employer has a duty to ensure that no night worker employed by him whose work involves special hazards, or heavy physical or mental strain, works for more than eight hours in any 24-hour period in which the worker performs the night work. This differs from the approach on general working hours and general night time working hours in that there is no averaging out over a 17-week period. As regards special hazards or work involving heavy strain, the Regulations are breached if the worker ever works more than eight hours in any 24. Work is to be regarded as involving special hazards or heavy strain if a collective agreement or workforce agreement identifies it as such work.

The employer must not assign a worker to night work unless: (a) the employer has ensured that the worker has the opportunity of a free health assessment before going on to the night work; or (b) the worker has already had an assessment and the employer has no reason to believe that the assessment is no longer valid. In addition, the employer has a duty to ensure that all night workers employed by him have the opportunity of a free health assessment at regular intervals. Young workers, that is to say those under the age of 18, are not allowed to work between 10 pm and 6 am. However, certain types of employment are excluded from this rule. These include working in hospitals, retailing, hotels, catering, agriculture and the delivery of post and newspapers as well as jobs working in cultural, artistic or sporting activities.

Entitlement to daily and weekly rest

Where the **pattern of work** is such as to put the health and safety of a worker at risk, in particular because the work is monotonous or the work-rate is predetermined, the employer must ensure that the worker is given adequate rest breaks.

The employer has a duty to keep records to show that the provisions of the Regulations are being complied with, and to keep such records for two years from the date on which they were made.

An adult worker is entitled to a rest period of at least 11 consecutive hours in each 24-hour period during which he works for the employer. As regards young workers (those under 18 years of age) the entitlement is 12 consecutive hours. The rest periods are not applicable where people work split-shifts or work periods of short duration.

An adult worker is entitled to an uninterrupted rest period of not less than 24 hours in each seven-day period during which he works for his employer. However, the employer can determine that instead an adult worker is entitled to two uninterrupted periods of at least 24 hours in each 14 days, or one uninterrupted period of at least 48 hours in each 14-day period. Young workers are entitled to a rest period of at least 48 hours in each seven-day period. The entitlement of young persons may be interrupted if they work split-shifts or work for periods of short duration. They may also be reduced to 36 consecutive hours where this is justified by technical or organisational reasons.

Entitlement to rest breaks

Where an adult worker's daily working time is more than six hours he is entitled to a rest break. This period, which the employee can spend away from his work station if he has one, must not be of less than 20 minutes. It can be for longer if a collective or workforce agreement provides that it should be. Young workers are entitled to a rest break of 30 minutes, which should be consecutive if possible, if their daily working time is more than 4.5 hours.

Entitlement to annual leave

Workers are entitled to annual leave of at least 5.6 weeks (28 days). If the worker does not work for a full year entitlement is proportional, and any fraction of a day's leave is to count as a full day's leave. However, those with less than 13 weeks' continuous service have no entitlement to annual leave. The leave may

be taken in instalments. However, it can only be taken in respect of the leave year in which it becomes due, and can only be replaced by a payment in lieu where the employment is terminated. If the employment is terminated and the worker has taken less leave than had proportionately become due to him, the employer has to make a payment in lieu of leave.

As a general principle, a worker may take his leave entitlement when he wishes. The worker must give the employer notice of when the leave is to be taken. However, the employer may require that leave is taken, or is not taken, on particular days by giving the worker notice of this before the relevant date. This date is calculated as twice the number of days in advance of the beginning of the leave as the number of days to which the notice relates. In other words, if either an employer or an employee is giving notice of the taking of 15 days' leave, the notice must be given 30 days before the date on which the leave is to commence. The rights as to dates on which leave is to be taken may be varied or excluded by a relevant agreement. (An agreement which is part of a collective agreement, or which is in writing and legally enforceable between the worker and the employee.) The worker is entitled to be paid while on leave.

Who is protected?

The definition of a worker is the same as the definition in the National Minimum Wage Regulations 1998. However, the Regulations do not apply to the police or the armed forces. Domestic servants are protected only as regards daily and weekly rest periods, rest breaks and annual leave. Those who work in transport, or sea fishing, or other activity at sea only gain protection in respect of health assessment for night workers, a safe pattern of work and annual leave.

If the worker's time is not measured or predetermined, most of the Regulations do not apply. The Regulations suggest that this exemption might apply to: (a) managing executives or other persons with autonomous decision-taking powers; or (b) family workers; or (c) workers officiating at religious ceremonies in churches and religious communities.

The Regulations contain other miscellaneous special exemptions, including:

(a) where the worker works at separate places of work which are distant from one another;
(b) where security and surveillance activities require a permanent presence;

(c) where a worker's continuity of presence is needed in relation to hospital services, airport or dock work, media or postal work, work in the industries which provide services to households, industries where there cannot be an interruption for technical reasons, research and development activities and agriculture;

(d) where there is a foreseeable surge of activity in relation to agriculture, tourism or postal services;

(e) where the worker's activities are affected by an occurrence beyond the control of the employer, or exceptional events which could not have been foreseen or an accident or the imminent risk of an accident.

Enforcement of the Regulations

The Health and Safety Executive and local authority inspectors may enforce the Regulations by prosecuting employers who breach them. Employees may bring infringements before an employment tribunal with the usual protection against victimisation on account of having taken action under the Regulations. If an employee is dismissed for having taken action under the Regulations this is automatically unfair dismissal.

21.18 AUTHORISED DEDUCTIONS FROM WAGES

There is no requirement that employees should be paid in cash, rather than into a bank account or by cheque. The way in which an employee is paid is determined by the terms of the contract. However, ERA 1996 makes provisions about protection of wages, and an outline of those provisions is set out below.

Right not to suffer unauthorised deductions

An employer is not allowed to make a deduction from a worker's wages unless: (a) it is authorised or required by a statutory provision or a relevant provision of the worker's contract; or (b) the worker has previously signified in writing his agreement or consent to the making of the deduction. If the deduction is allowed by a written term of the employee's contract, the employee must be given a copy of the term before the deduction is made by the employer. If the deduction is authorised by an implied term of the contract (whether written or not) the existence and effect of the term must be notified to the employee before the deduction is made. Such a notification would usually be in the worker's wage packet. The statutorily allowed deductions will include matters such as tax, National Insurance and deductions made under the Child Support Act 1991.

Whenever the worker is paid less than he should be paid, the missing amount of money is to be treated as a deduction. However, this does not apply if the deficiency was caused by an error, or on account of the employee's conduct, or was in respect of a sum of money which cannot be classed as 'wages'.

The reclaiming of the accidental overpayment of wages is regarded as an excepted deduction and the general provisions do not apply. Deductions made because the employee has been on strike or in consequence of any disciplinary proceedings are also excluded.

The meaning of 'wages'

Section 27(1) ERA 1996 states that 'wages' in relation to a worker, means any sum payable to the worker in connection with his employment, including:

(a) any fee, bonus, commission, holiday pay or other emoluments referable to his employment, whether payable under his contract or otherwise;

(b) statutory sick pay;

(c) statutory maternity pay;

(d) a guarantee payment;

(e) any payment for time off for carrying out trade union activities;

(f) remuneration on suspension on medical or maternity grounds;

(g) any sum payable under a reinstatement or re-engagement order; and

(h) payment under an order for continuance of employment under s.130 of the Act, or under s.164 of the Trade Union and Labour Relations (Consolidation) Act 1992 (TULRCA 1992).

Some of these matters are self-explanatory but others need to be explained. Category (a) is very broad, including overtime pay, shift allowances and bonuses. It does not include payments in lieu of wages, which are damages rather than wages.

A **guarantee payment** entitles an employee to be paid for a day during any part of which he would normally be required to work but on which he is not provided with work due to: (a) a falling off of the employer's need for work to be done; or (b) any other occurrence relating to the employer's business in relation to the need for work of the type in question to be done. The payment is only due to workers who have at least one month's continuous employment. Those employed on a fixed term contract of less than three months' duration are excluded. Seasonal workers are also excluded, as the payment is not due if the employment is expected to last for less than three months. The amount of the payment cannot exceed £17.30 a day and an employee cannot be entitled to be paid for more than five days in any three-month period. There is no entitlement if the employer provides suitable alternative employment.

Suspension on maternity grounds was dealt with above at 21.12.4. Section 64 ERA 1996 provides that an employee who is suspended from work by his employer **on medical grounds** is entitled to be paid while he is suspended for a period not exceeding 26 weeks. The suspension must have arisen as a result of a requirement of a statute or statutory instrument or a recommendation of an approved code of practice. The length of service qualifications are the same as for employees to receive a guarantee payment. The employee is only entitled to the payment if he is fit for work. The provision may seem strange but it applies when a worker is not allowed to work because he has been too exposed to lead, radiation or other specified hazardous substances.

Reinstatement and re-engagement orders were considered in the previous chapter when we considered the remedies for unfair dismissal. We saw that the orders are infrequently made.

An order for **continuance of employment** under s.130 of the Act is a form of interim relief which is applicable when an employee has been unfairly dismissed for an inadmissible reason. The inadmissible reasons in question concern having carried out health and safety duties, or duties as trustee of an occupational pension scheme or as a trade union representative. A similar right exists under TULRCA s.192 when a protective award is made in a redundancy situation.

21.19 TIME OFF WORK

Time off for public duties

Section 50 ERA 1996 provides that an employee who is a magistrate must be given time off during working hours to perform the duties of his office. Time off to attend meetings and otherwise discharge their duties must also be given to employees who are members of the following: a local authority; a statutory tribunal;

a police authority; a Service Authority for National Crime prevention; a board of prison visitors or a prison visiting committee; a relevant health authority; a relevant education body; the Environment Agency; or the Scottish Environment Protection Agency.

The amount of time allowed to be taken is the amount reasonable in all the circumstances. These circumstances include: (a) how much time is needed to perform the duties in question; (b) how much time the employee has already had off for public duties or trade union duties and activities; and (c) the circumstances of the employer's business and the effect which the time off has on the running of that business.

A complaint that time off has not been allowed can be presented to an employment tribunal within the usual time limits. The tribunal may declare the complaint well founded and award the complainant compensation. The amount of compensation should be whatever is just and equitable in all the circumstances, having regard to: (a) the employer's default in not allowing the employee to take the time off; and (b) any loss sustained by the employee which is attributable to the matters to which the complaint relates. The employer does not need to pay the employee for time taken off under s.50.

Time off to look for work or training

Section 52 ERA 1996 allows an employee who is made redundant reasonable time off during the employer's working hours, before the end of his notice, to look for new employment or make arrangements for training for future employment. In order to be afforded this right, the employee must have had two years' continuous employment by the time his notice would have ended. During the time off the employee is entitled to be paid at the usual hourly rate. An employee who is not afforded this right can bring a claim before an employment tribunal in the usual way. The tribunal may declare his complaint well founded and order the employer to pay the employee the amount due to him.

Time off for pension scheme trustees and employee representatives

Employees who are members of a relevant occupational pension scheme are allowed time off, with pay, for performing any of their duties as trustees or undergoing training relevant to the performance of those duties. A very similar right is extended to those employees who are, or who have been elected, employee representatives. The compensation as regards employees not allowed time off for duties as occupational pension scheme trustees is the amount which the tribunal considers just and equitable. As regards employee representatives it is the amount of pay which he would have been entitled to if the employer had allowed him time off with pay. In both cases the tribunal may declare the complaint well founded.

Right to time off for young people for study or training

Employees aged 16 or 17 who are not in full-time education and who have not reached educational standards laid down by the Secretary of State, are entitled to time off, with pay, during working hours, to reach the relevant standard (Level 2). Employees aged 18 or over have the right to time off to complete study or training leading to a relevant qualification if they begun the training before reaching the age of 19. The amount of time is the amount which is reasonable in all of the circumstances having particular regard to: (a) the requirement of the employee's study or training; and (b) the circumstances of the employer's business and the effect of the employee's time off on the running of that business. An employment tribunal can declare the complaint well founded and award the employee the amount of pay he would have been entitled to if he had been given the time off.

Jury service

If an employee is called up for jury service then he has to attend unless he is in one of the excluded categories. The employer must allow the employee time off work to perform jury service. Jurors can be exempted from jury service if they can show a good reason for being excused. The courts are reluctant to allow exemption but if an employee's presence at work was particularly vital this could amount to a good reason.

21.20 PROCEDURE FOR BRINGING A CLAIM BEFORE AN EMPLOYMENT TRIBUNAL

21.20.1 Time limits

A claim to gain a remedy or to enforce a statutory right must be made to an employment tribunal within the appropriate time limit. Generally, this time limit is three calendar months from the date of the act complained of. So if the act complained of occurred on 20 January, the claim would have to be received by the tribunal on or before 19 April. However, where it is not reasonably practicable to present the claim within this period the tribunal can extend the period by the length of time which it considers reasonable. Where the act complained of continues over a period of time, the claim must be brought within three months of the effective date of termination. (See 20.4.2.) In very limited circumstances the tribunal has the power to extend this period. The time limit for a claim to a redundancy payment is six months from the relevant date. Again, the tribunal has a discretion to extend this limit.

21.20.2 Presenting a complaint and conciliation

A complaint must be presented in writing. Most complaints are made by completing Form ET1, which can be obtained from job centres or from the offices of employment tribunals or can be completed online. This relatively short form requires details of the parties involved, the type of complaint being made, the name of anybody representing the employee, the type of work done by the employee, his normal hours and earnings and a brief description of the complaint. If the employer wishes to contest the case he must reply on Form ET3 within 14 days. Form ET3 requires the employer to indicate the grounds on which he intends to resist the application.

The tribunal may conduct a pre-hearing review, either at the request of one of the parties or on its own initiative. At this review a party can be ordered to pay a deposit of £500 if the tribunal considers that he has no reasonable prospect of success. If the party still pursues the case and loses it, he may forfeit the deposit and be ordered to pay costs.

21.20.3 Procedure at the tribunal

The tribunal sets its own procedure but tries to avoid a highly legalistic procedure. It can order a party to produce documents and to reveal more details of his position. The burden of proof is generally upon the applicant. The standard of proof is on a balance of probabilities. Strict rules of evidence may be relaxed. The tribunal's job is to apply the law. The system is adversarial, with the employer and the employee trying to prove their case, but the tribunal members adopt an interventionist approach and may themselves ask questions of witnesses or the parties.

The decisions of employment tribunals are almost always unanimous. When they are not unanimous it is almost always the case that one of the laymen sided with the legally qualified chairman. Very occasionally, the two laymen outvote the chairman. Generally, the tribunal gives an oral decision at the end of the case and follows this up with a written decision at a later date. The written decision should be full enough for the parties to know why they won or lost and for the EAT to see whether a question of law, which might be appealed against, arises.

Generally, the two sides pay their own costs. Costs can be awarded against a party who brought a vexatious or frivolous claim, or if it was that party's fault that the proceedings were postponed. In these circumstances an employment tribunal can award costs of up to £10 000.

21.20.4 Appeals

An appeal can be made to the EAT. Generally, such an appeal must be lodged within 42 days of receiving the full written decision of the employment tribunal. Legal aid may be available for such an appeal. With permission of either the EAT or the Court of Appeal, a further appeal may be made to the Court of Appeal. With permission of the Court of Appeal or the House of Lords, a further appeal may be made to the House of Lords. Where the outcome of an appeal will depend upon the correct application of EC law, and the meaning of the EC law is unclear, any court or tribunal may refer the matter to the ECJ. If the court is the final court of appeal it must make such a reference. Over the next few years it is proposed that Employment Tribunals and the EAT will be part of a unified Tribunal Service.

Test your understanding 21.5

1 What rights in respect of leave and time off work does a pregnant woman have?

2 Do women have the right to be paid while on maternity leave?

3 What is the national minimum wage for adult workers and for those under 20?

4 What are the main rights given to workers by the TUPE Regulations 1981?

5 What is the main provision of the Working Time Regulations 1998?

6 What rights does a worker have in relation to deductions from wages?

7 On what grounds do employees have a right to time off work?

8 In what circumstances will an employee be entitled to paternity leave and pay?

9 In what circumstances will an employee be entitled to adoption leave and pay?

10 What rights does an employee have in respect of flexible working?

Key points

The Equality Act 2010 (Discrimination on the grounds of a personal characteristic)

■ The Equality Act 2010 outlaws direct discrimination, indirect discrimination, victimisation or harassment on the protected characteristics of age; disability; gender reassignment; marriage and civil partnership; pregnancy and maternity; race; religion or belief; sex; and sexual orientation.

■ Direct discrimination occurs when an employer treats a person less favourably than others because of a protected characteristic.

■ Indirect discrimination occurs when an employer applies to an employee a provision, criterion or practice which is discriminatory in relation to a protected characteristic of the employee's.

■ A person harasses another if he engages in unwanted conduct related to a relevant protected characteristic, or of a sexual nature, and the conduct has the purpose or effect of violating the victim's dignity, or creating an intimidating, hostile, degrading, humiliating or offensive environment for the victim.

■ An employer victimises an employee if he subjects the employee to a detriment because the employee has done something for the purposes of or in connection with the Act.

→

Equality Act 2010 (Equality of terms)

■ The Equality Act requires that if a woman does like work, or work rated as equivalent to that of a male comparator her contract of employment should be deemed to include an equality clause.

■ Men can claim equal treatment with a female comparator, but neither men nor women can claim equal treatment with a person of the same sex.

■ An equality clause would modify the woman's contract of employment so that any of the terms of her contract were no less favourable than a similar term in the contract of the male comparator.

■ The male comparator must be a man working for the same employer or an associated employer. The woman's work must be like work to that of the male comparator, or work rated as equivalent or work of equal value.

■ Like work means that the work is broadly similar to that done by the male comparator. Work is rated as equivalent if a properly conducted job evaluation scheme has found it to be equivalent. Work is of equal value if the demands which the work places on the woman are similar to the demands which the male comparator's work places upon him.

■ The employer has a defence if the variation in treatment is due to a genuine material factor which was not the difference in sex.

■ If an applicant's claim is successful under the Act, an employment tribunal can award arrears of pay, backdated for six years, and damages.

Other discrimination legislation

■ The Part-Time Workers (Prevention of Less Favourable Treatment) Regulations 2000 prevent discrimination against part-time workers by applying the pro rata principle.

■ The Fixed-term Employees (Prevention of Less Favourable Treatment) Regulations 2002 prevent discrimination against fixed term workers.

■ The Agency Workers Regulations 2010 give agency workers the right to be treated no less favourably than the hirer's regular workers after a 12-week period of working for the hirer. However, the right to equal treatment is limited to pay; the

duration of working time; night work; rest periods; rest breaks; and annual leave.

Health and safety at work

■ The Health and Safety at Work etc. Act 1974 imposes criminal sanctions on employers who do not look after the health and safety of their employees.

■ The Act is enforced by the Health and Safety Executive and by local authority enforcement officers.

■ The Act imposes particular duties on employers, manufacturers, designers, importers, suppliers and employees.

■ Six directives, all passed in 1992, supplement the Act.

■ An employee will be able to sue his employer in negligence if the employer breached a duty of care owed to that employee and if this breach caused a foreseeable type of loss.

■ The employer's duty of care to employees particularly involves providing safe plant and equipment, a safe system of work and reasonably competent fellow employees.

Maternity rights and rights to time off work

■ Pregnant employees are entitled to paid time off work to attend ante-natal care appointments.

■ Employees are entitled to unpaid time off work to provide necessary assistance to dependants who are ill, giving birth, injured or assaulted. Time off can also be taken in consequence of a dependant's death, or because of unexpected disruption of care arrangements for a dependant, or to deal with an incident which involves the employee's child and which occurs unexpectedly during school hours.

■ Employees are entitled to up to 13 weeks' parental leave in respect of each of their children.

■ An employee who is suspended from work on maternity grounds is entitled to be paid during the period of suspension.

■ All pregnant women are entitled to 26 weeks' maternity leave and 26 weeks' additional maternity leave.

→

■ Women have an entitlement to return to work after their maternity leave.

Other rights to leave or flexible working

■ Employees with 26 weeks' continuous employment are entitled to paternity leave and pay if they are responsible for the child's upbringing, are the biological father of the child or the partner of the child's mother.

■ When a couple adopt a child, one of them, if he or she has 26 weeks' continuous employment, is entitled to 39 weeks' paid adoption leave and another 13 weeks' additional adoption leave.

■ An employee with at least one year's continuous employment can take 13 weeks' parental leave, in respect of each child under five, to look after the child or make arrangements for the child's welfare.

■ Parents of children under six have the right to apply for flexible working and the employer has a duty to consider such an application seriously.

National minimum wage

■ Workers aged 21 or over have a right to be paid the national minimum wage of £6.08 an hour. The rate is £4.98 an hour for those between 18 and 20, and £3.68 for those aged 16 or 17.

■ The hourly rate is calculated by reference to a one-month period.

■ Employers must keep records showing that the national minimum wage is being paid. In certain circumstances employees have a right to access to these records.

■ Workers who are not being paid the national minimum wage can bring a claim before an employment tribunal. In addition, the National Minimum Wage Act 1998 can be enforced by Revenue & Customs.

TUPE

■ When a business undertaking is transferred, and yet retains its identity, employees who work for the undertaking have the same employment rights against the transferee as they had against the transferor.

■ Continuous service worked for the transferor is regarded as having been worked for the transferee.

■ If the employee is dismissed for a reason connected with the transfer this will be an unfair dismissal.

■ Union agreements between the transferor and a trade union which the employer recognised are binding upon the transferee.

Working Time Regulations

■ The normal working week should not exceed 48 hours, averaged out over a 17-week period.

■ Night workers should not work more than eight hours in any 24, averaged out over a 17-week period.

■ Workers are entitled to daily and weekly rest periods.

■ Employees are entitled to 5.6 weeks' (28 days) paid annual leave a year.

Time off work

■ Workers must be given time off work to perform their public duties.

■ Workers who have been made redundant are allowed time off work to look for work or training.

■ Young people who have not reached the Level 2 educational standard are allowed time off to reach this standard.

■ Employees must be allowed time off for jury service. However, it is possible that a court will excuse an employee from jury service if his presence at work is so vital as to amount to a good reason to be excused.

Bringing a claim to a tribunal

■ Generally, a claim to an employment tribunal must be made within three months of the act complained of.

■ The complaint is generally filed by filling in Form ET1. The employer replies on Form ET3 within 14 days if he wishes to contest the claim.

■ ACAS conciliation officers have a duty to attempt conciliation and settlement of the claim before it proceeds to a tribunal hearing.

■ Proceedings at an employment tribunal are relatively relaxed. Each side usually pays their own costs and legal aid is not available.

■ An appeal from the decision of an employment tribunal can be made to the EAT.

Summary questions

1 Alice works as a computer operator for Acme Ltd in Nottingham. She is paid £6.80 an hour. Brian who has worked in the same office as a computer operator for ten years is paid £8.20 an hour. If any of the computer operators experience a problem Brian is required to provide assistance, although such assistance is very rarely in fact required. Alice has heard that computer technicians employed by Acme Ltd in London earn £12 an hour and that female computer operators employed by a subsidiary company of Acme Ltd earn £8.90 an hour.

Advise Alice as to whether or not there are grounds on which she might bring a claim of equal pay and of any defences which Acme Ltd might have. Advise Alice also of the procedure which she would need to follow in order to bring a claim before an employment tribunal.

2 Three years ago Benjamin was injured in a car crash and this has confined him to a wheelchair. Benjamin works as an accounts clerk at a local college. As part of a major reorganisation, the college is moving the accounts department onto the third floor from the ground floor where it is currently situated. The college does not have a lift. Benjamin tells his office manager that he will not be able to work on the third floor as he will not be able to negotiate the stairs. The manager says that if Benjamin could not get to the third floor he would have to leave the job.

Advise Benjamin as to any rights he might have against his employer.

3 Charlie has worked in a bakery for seven years. The work is somewhat monotonous and Charlie seeks to enlighten the atmosphere by playing practical jokes. Charlie climbed into one of the mixing machines so that he could leap out and give a fellow employee, David, a surprise. Charlie has done this type of thing fairly frequently over the years.

The foreman has often told him not to, but rather half-heartedly as he too seems to enjoy Charlie's antics. David is not working on the particular morning when Charlie hides in the mixing machine. Eric, a worker transferred from the cake department, turns on the mixing machine and Charlie is killed. All of the employees in Charlie's department know of the rule that the mixing machines must never be turned on unless they have been checked to see that no one is cleaning them or otherwise too near them. The transferred employee had not been told this. As a result of the accident the transferred employee suffers nervous shock and depression which keep him off work for eight months.

Advise the employers of any civil or criminal liability which they might have incurred.

4 Elaine has been continuously employed for three years. She has recently discovered that she is pregnant. Explain the rights to time off work to which Elaine will become entitled and the benefits which she is entitled to receive during this time off. Explain also any rights to time off work, and the benefits payable, which Elaine's husband might have in connection with the pregnancy, the childbirth and becoming a parent.

5 At Gradgrind Ltd's factory workers work long hours. None of the workers have agreed to give up their rights under the Working Time Regulations. Jim, who is 46, works five consecutive 12-hour day shifts for four weeks in a row and then has a week off. John works five 12-hour night shifts a week every week for five consecutive weeks and then has a week off. The time off taken by John and Jim is not annual leave, but is to compensate for the long hours worked in the previous weeks. Explain whether or not the Regulations have been breached and any entitlement to rest breaks which the two workers are entitled to.

Multiple choice questions

1 Consider the following statements, made in relation to the Equality Act 2010.

i The Equality Act 2010 has replaced all previous legislation dealing with discrimination at work.
ii The Equality Act 2010 has made it illegal for an employer to use the number of years of continuous employment in calculating the size of an employee's redundancy payment.
iii A person who is proposing to undergo a sex change operation is regarded as having the protected characteristic of gender reassignment.
iv The protected characteristic of belief applies to any religious or philosophical belief, including a lack of belief.
v The protected characteristic of sexual orientation includes sexual orientation to persons of the opposite sex.

→

Which of the above statements are true?

a   i, iv and v only.
b   iii, iv and v only.
c   ii and iii only.
d   i and ii only.
e   All of the statements.

2 Consider the following statements, made in relation to the Equality Act 2010.

i   It could be direct discrimination for an employer who was a Sikh to discriminate against a person because he was a Sikh.
ii An employer can legitimately discriminate against a disabled person if he can show that this is a proportionate means of achieving a legitimate aim.
iii The burden of proof is initially on a person who claims a contravention of the Act. But once the claimant has proved that, in the absence of any other explanation, a breach of the Act has occurred, the burden of proof then shifts on to the employer to show that there was no breach of the Act.
iv A person who made a false allegation of discrimination, in bad faith, could not claim victimisation if he suffered a detriment on account of having done so.
v   An employer who claims the defence of occupational requirement will need to show that the application of the requirement is a proportionate means of achieving a legitimate aim.

Which of the above statements are true?

a   i, iv and v only.
b   iii, iv and v only.
c   ii and iii only.
d   i and ii only.
e   All of the statements.

3 Consider the following statements made in relation to the Equality Act 2010.

i   The applicant can choose the comparator, but the comparator must work for the same employer or for an associated employer.
ii If a male comparator working shifts is paid a higher basic hourly rate than a woman in the same employment (ignoring any shift allowance) the woman will always be able to claim that she is doing like work.
iii If a woman does like work to the work done by a male comparator, all of her contract terms must be as beneficial as the equivalent terms in the comparator's contract, even if the woman's contract is more beneficial overall than that of the comparator.

iv The male comparator must be a past or present employee. A woman cannot compare herself to a hypothetical male comparator.

Which of the above statements are true?

a   i and iii only.
b   i, ii and iii only.
c   ii, iii and iv only.
d   All of the statements.

4 Which one of the following statements is not true?

a   Cancer, HIV infection and multiple sclerosis are each regarded as a disability under the Equality Act 2010.
b   Apart from the positive duty set out in (a), employers have no duty to treat disabled persons more favourably than employees who are not disabled.
c   It will always be unfair dismissal to dismiss an employee on account of a spent conviction.
d   If a person sentenced to three years' imprisonment was released after 18 months, his conviction will never become spent.

5 Which one of the following statements is not true?

a   All employers must prepare a written statement on their general policy with respect to the health and safety at work of their employees.
b   Employees have a duty to take reasonable care for the health and safety of themselves and others who may be affected by their acts and omissions at work.
c   The six Regulations passed in 1992 supplement the Health and Safety at Work etc. Act 1974, rather than replace it.
d   The common law duty of care owed by employers is owed to individual employees and therefore account must be taken of their particular weaknesses and inexperience.

6 Which one of the following statements is not true?

a   Women must be allowed paid time off work to attend ante-natal care appointments.
b   Employees are allowed paid time off work if this is necessary to provide care for a dependant who is ill.
c   Parents are allowed up to 13 weeks' unpaid leave in respect of each of their children. If the child is not disabled the leave must be taken before the child's fifth birthday.
d   Parents have no statutory right to flexible working.

→

7 Which one of the following statements is not true?

a There is no national minimum wage for workers under the age of 18.

b A worker dismissed for claiming the national minimum wage can be unfairly dismissed even if he has not been continuously employed for one year.

c The TUPE Regulations only apply where the undertaking retains its identity after the transfer.

d When the TUPE Regulations apply continuous employment worked for the transferor is regarded as having been worked for the transferee.

8 Which one of the following statements is not true?

a A person who has not contracted out of the Working Time Regulations could work 50 hours a week for ten consecutive weeks and yet the Regulations might not have been breached.

b Young workers who work more than 4.5 consecutive hours are entitled to a 30 minute rest break.

c The Working Time Regulations do not apply to workers such as managers whose working time is not measured or predetermined.

d The Working Time Regulations entitle a worker who has been continuously employed for at least four years to six weeks' paid annual leave.

Task 21

A friend of yours visiting the country from Japan has a keen interest in employment rights. Your friend has asked you if you would draw up a report dealing briefly with the following matters.

a The effect of the laws which outlaw discrimination in employment.

b The civil and criminal liability which an employer might be under as regards the health and safety of his employees.

c The maternity rights available to pregnant employees and their relatives.

d Any new types of rights acquired by employees in the past five years.

mylawchamber *premium*

Visit **www.mylawchamber.co.uk/macintyre** to access study support resources including interactive multiple-choice questions, weblinks, glossary, glossary flashcards, legal newsfeed, answers to questions in this chapter, legal updates and an overview of this chapter all linked to the **Pearson eText** version of *Business Law* which you can **search**, **highlight** and **personalise** with your **own notes** and **bookmarks**.

Use **Case Navigator** to read in full some of the key cases referenced in this chapter with commentary and questions:

James v Eastleigh Borough Council [1990] 2 All ER 607

Regulation of business by the imposition of criminal liability

Introduction

22.1 THE NATURE OF A CRIME

It is not the purpose of this book to examine the nature of criminal liability in any degree of detail. However, in order to understand the liability imposed by the legislation considered in this chapter we do need to have some idea of the elements of a crime.

Generally, criminal offences are made up of two elements, an *actus reus* and a *mens rea*. The *actus reus* is often defined as the guilty act, whereas the *mens rea* is defined as the guilty mind. The *actus reus* of each offence is different. The definition of the *actus reus* as the guilty act is essentially correct, but rather too brief. It would be more correct to say that the *actus reus* of an offence is the external element of the definition of the offence which is objectively required before the defendant can be convicted. It might be committed either by mere conduct or by bringing about a prohibited outcome. For example, the *actus reus* of reckless driving is committed by mere conduct, whereas the *actus reus* of causing death by dangerous driving also requires an outcome, namely that

a death is caused. *Mens rea* might be more fully defined as the mental state of the accused which the prosecution will need to prove in order to establish that the offence was committed. Generally, the *mens rea* of a crime will require an intention to do the act which a statute or the common law made illegal, although recklessness as to the circumstances and consequences which amount to the *actus reus* is enough as regards some crimes. The prosecution must prove both the *actus reus* of an offence and the *mens rea* beyond a reasonable doubt.

Homicide provides an easily understood example of what is meant by *actus reus* and *mens rea*. The *actus reus* of both murder and manslaughter is the same. For both crimes the accused must voluntarily and unlawfully cause the death of another human being. It is the different *mens rea* of the two crimes which distinguishes them. The *mens rea* of murder is that the accused either intended to kill or intended to cause grievous bodily harm. The *mens rea* of involuntary manslaughter is that the death was caused by the accused acting in a grossly negligent or reckless manner, but without the *mens rea* necessary for murder. (There are also several defences which reduce murder to voluntary manslaughter.)

So if an accused kills another person by shooting him with a gun, the *actus reus* of both murder and manslaughter is established. Which crime, if either, the accused will have committed will depend upon the accused's state of mind when he pulled the trigger. If the accused intended to kill the victim or intended to cause serious injury then he will be guilty of murder. If the accused was grossly negligent, perhaps pointing the gun at a friend in the grossly negligent belief that it was unloaded, then he will be guilty of manslaughter. If the accused has neither *mens rea* he will not be guilty of either offence. This would be the case, for example, if he shot the victim on a firing range, not knowing that the victim was hiding behind one of the targets.

Actus reus and *mens rea* must coincide

A person can only be guilty of a crime if he commits the *actus reus* of that crime at the same time as he has the *mens rea*. A person who today accidentally ran over his enemy would not be guilty of murder on account of his having unsuccessfully attempted to run him over yesterday. Such a person would have had the *mens rea* of murder yesterday and have committed the *actus reus* today, but that is not enough. The two must coincide.

Similarly, an accused must intend to commit the *actus reus* in the manner in which he did commit it. If an accused was driving around to his enemy's house, with the intention of shooting him dead, he would not be guilty of murder if he accidentally ran over his enemy on the way.

The doctrine of transferred malice holds that a person can be guilty of a crime even if the outcome of his actions was not quite what he expected. If A shoots a gun at B intending to kill him, but misses and kills C, he will still be guilty of murder. He is guilty because he had the *mens rea* for murder at the same time as he had the *actus reus* for murder. Transferred malice will only apply where the accused has the *actus reus* and *mens rea* of the same crime.

R v Pembliton (1874) 17 QBD 359

The defendant and his friends had been thrown out of a pub. They then fought with a crowd of people. After the fight the defendant threw a large stone at the people he had been fighting with, intending to hurt them. The stone missed the people, but broke a large window. The defendant was charged with maliciously damaging the window contrary to the Malicious Damage Act 1861.

Held. The defendant was not guilty of the offence. He had the *actus reus* of malicious damage to property (he broke the window) but he did not have the *mens rea* (he did not intend to break it). Nor would he have been guilty of maliciously wounding the people he threw the stone at. He had the *mens rea* for that crime, but not the *actus reus*.

R v Latimer (1874) LR 2 CCR 119

The defendant had a fight with another man in a pub. Having got the worst of the fight, the defendant went out into the pub yard. He came back into the pub with his belt in his hand and swung it at the man with whom he had been fighting. The belt only grazed this man but it bounced off him and severely wounded the woman he was talking to. The defendant was charged with maliciously wounding the woman.

Held. The defendant was guilty of malicious wounding. He had committed the *actus reus* of that crime (by wounding the woman) at the same time as he had the *mens rea* (by intending to wound the man).

Mens rea will generally consist of either an intention to do the act which is made criminal, or recklessness as to the circumstances and consequences of the action which constitutes the *actus reus* of the crime.

Parliament has created a number of crimes of **strict liability** where the prosecution do not need to prove *mens rea* in respect of one or more elements of the *actus reus*. The two offences set out by reg.8 of the Consumer Protection from Unfair Trading Regulations 2008, considered below at 22.2.1, provide an example of strict liability offences. It is not the case that strict liability offences are offences of absolute liability. Defences may be available, as they are to the reg.8 offences. It is also the case that the accused must know that the acts which he commits are capable of leading to the behaviour which constitutes the offence. Generally, it is presumed that *mens rea* is required in respect of any crime. When it is not required this is because the wording of a statute rebuts this presumption.

22.2 THE CONSUMER PROTECTION FROM UNFAIR TRADING REGULATIONS 2008

The Consumer Protection from Unfair Trading Regulations 2008, which implement Directive 2005/29/EC, create criminal offences relating to unfair business-to-consumer commercial practices. The regulations, which represent a huge change in the criminal law, have as their object the harmonisation of law across the EU. They repeal or amend 40 statutes and 36 statutory instruments. Amongst the statutes repealed are the Trade Descriptions Act 1968 and Part III of the Consumer Protection Act 1987, which previously made it an offence to give misleading price indications.

Before considering the Regulations in detail, it is important to note that they are limited in two ways. First, they create criminal offences but they do not directly give a consumer any right of action. They do not, for example, invalidate any contract which a consumer might have made. Second, the regulations do not cover unfair business-to-business commercial practices. Both of these limitations are addressed by other legislation. First, s.130 of the Powers of Criminal Courts (Sentencing) Act 2000 allows a court to impose a compensation order on a person convicted of a criminal offence. Such an order requires the convicted person to pay compensation for any personal injury, loss or damage resulting from the offence. A court has to give reasons, on passing sentence, if it does not make a compensation order in a case where s.130 empowers it to do so. In the magistrates' court a compensation order may not exceed £5 000. Second, the Business Protection from Misleading Marketing Regulations 2008, considered later in this chapter at 22.3, impose criminal liability in relation to unfair business-to-business advertising.

22.2.1 The structure of the Regulations

The Regulations are set out in four parts. Part 1 deals with definitions. Part 2 describes the acts and omissions which the Regulations prohibit. Part 3 sets out the criminal offences which the Regulations create, as well as the defences available. Part 4 deals with enforcement.

22.2.2 The definition of a commercial practice

At the heart of the Regulations is the idea of a commercial practice. This is defined by reg.2(1) as:

'any act, omission, course of conduct, representation or commercial communication (including advertising or marketing) by a trader, which is directly connected with the promotion, sale or supply of a product to or from consumers, whether occurring before, during or after a commercial transaction (if any) in relation to a product.'

This definition makes it plain that a commercial practice can have occurred even if no commercial transaction has occurred. So if a manufacturer advertised his product to consumers, this would be a commercial practice even if no consumers bought the product or entered into any other commercial transaction. However, as noted above, if one trader merely misdescribed a product to another trader, there would have been no commercial practice. Nor can a commercial practice be engaged in by a consumer. Only a trader can engage in a commercial practice. The width of the definition of a commercial practice is also noteworthy. 'Any act, omission, course of conduct, representation or commercial communication' would encompass just about anything done or not done by a trader. However, the thing done or not done would have to be 'directly connected with the promotion, sale or supply of a product' to or from a consumer. Even the provision of an after-sales service or the collection of a debt would be included. It is plainly the case that a commercial practice could be committed by a trader who buys from a consumer. In *Fletcher v Budgen* [1974] 1 WLR 1056, a motor dealer who was buying a car from a consumer made disparaging remarks about it and falsely said that it was fit only for scrap. Consequently, the consumer sold the car to the dealer for £2. The dealer was convicted of an offence under the Trade Descriptions Act 1968 and, if the case were to arise today, the dealer would plainly have committed an (unfair) commercial practice.

'Consumer' is defined as any individual who in relation to a commercial practice is acting for purposes which are outside his business. This is the usual definition which applies in EU-inspired legislation. Companies are not regarded as individuals and so can never act as consumers. A sole trader or member of a partnership can act as a consumer, but only if he is acting for purposes which are not connected with his business. A 'trader' is defined as any person who, in relation to a commercial practice, is acting for purposes relating to his business, and anyone acting in the name of, or on behalf of, a trader. So employees such as shop assistants are regarded as traders. Whether or not a person acted as a trader will be decided on a case-by-case basis, but it seems likely that regular sellers on the Internet are likely to be regarded as traders. A 'product' is defined as 'any goods or service and includes immoveable property, rights and obligations.' So goods, services, downloaded software, sales of land, premium phone calls and membership of clubs would all be products.

22.2.3 Unfair commercial practices

Regulation 3(1) states that unfair commercial practices are prohibited. Regulations 3(3) and 3(4) then define the circumstances in which a commercial practice is unfair. Regulation 3(3) sets out a general definition, whereas reg.3(4) sets out four, more specific, circumstances in which a commercial practice is unfair. A trader who knowingly or recklessly engages in an unfair commercial practice commits an offence under reg.8.

22.2.3.1 The general definition of an unfair commercial practice

Regulation 3(3) states that:

'A commercial practice is unfair if –

(a) it contravenes the requirements of professional diligence; and
(b) it materially distorts or is likely to materially distort the economic behaviour of the average consumer with regard to the product.'

In order to understand reg.3(3), it is necessary to understand three further definitions: those of 'professional diligence', 'materially distort the economic behaviour' and 'the average consumer'.

Professional diligence is defined as:

'the standard of special skill and care which a trader may reasonably be expected to exercise towards consumers which is commensurate with either –

(a) honest market practice in the trader's field of activity, or
(b) the general principle of good faith in the trader's field of activity.'

So, for example, as regards a plumber, professional diligence is the standard which can reasonably be expected of a plumber exercising honest market practice in the exercise of his trade. Alternatively, it is the standard which would be commensurate with the general principle of good faith in the plumbing trade. The general principle of good faith is not defined by the Regulations.

'Materially distort the economic behaviour' means 'in relation to an average consumer, appreciably to impair the average consumer's ability to make an informed decision thereby causing him to take a transactional decision that he would not have taken otherwise'. A 'transactional decision' is 'any decision taken by a consumer, whether it is to act or to refrain from acting, concerning: (a) whether, how and on what terms to purchase, make payment in whole or in part for, retain or dispose of a product; or (b) whether, how and on what terms to exercise a contractual right in relation to a product'. Although this obviously includes a decision by a consumer to buy or sell a product, it is very much wider than merely that. Decisions taken after a contract has been made are also included. Examples of such decisions would include a decision to pay off a debt, or to follow up an after-sales service, or to make use of a cancellation right or to seek a legal remedy.

An 'average consumer' is not defined as such, but is to be construed in relation to the complex provisions of reg.2(2)–2(6). First, reg.2(2) provides that in determining the effect of a commercial practice on the average consumer where a commercial practice reaches or is addressed to a consumer or consumers, account shall be taken of the material characteristics of such an average consumer including his being reasonably well informed, reasonably observant and reasonably circumspect. Second, reg.2(4) provides that if a commercial practice is aimed at a particular group of consumers, the effect of the commercial practice should be the effect on the average member of that group. Third, reg.2(5) provides that if a clearly identifiable group of consumers is particularly vulnerable to the commercial practice or the underlying product, on account of being mentally or physically infirm, or on account of their age or credulity, the effect on the average consumer shall be the effect on an average member of that group. However, this is the case only if the trader could reasonably be expected to foresee the particular vulnerability and if the commercial practice was likely to materially distort the economic behaviour only of that group. However, reg.2(6) limits reg.2(5) by stating that it is without prejudice to the common and legitimate advertising practice of making exaggerated statements which are not meant to be taken literally. Several points must be made about the average consumer. First, it should be realised that the average consumer is a hypothetical person and there is no need to show that an actual consumer has been affected by an unfair commercial practice. Second, the average consumer may vary, depending upon the trade practices in question and all the surrounding circumstances. Third, there are three different types of average consumer. There is the straightforward reg.2(2) average consumer; the reg.2(4) average member of a targeted group; and the reg.2(5) vulnerable member of a targeted group. As regards this last group, the vulnerability must be on account of mental or physical infirmity, age or credulity.

When faced with these lengthy and complex definitions, it is easy to lose sight of the reg.3(3) definition. Two requirements must be satisfied if a commercial practice is to be unfair. First, the practice must contravene the requirements of professional diligence. Second, the commercial practice must distort, or be likely to distort, the economic behaviour of the average consumer with regard to the product. Some help may be provided by commercial codes of practice, which are to be drawn up. These will indicate whether or not a trader is behaving in a professionally diligent manner. However, the mere fact of compliance with such a code will not automatically mean that a trader has been professionally diligent.

Regulation 3(4) states that a commercial practice is also unfair in four other, more specifically defined, circumstances:

■ if it is a misleading action, as defined by reg.5;
■ if it is a misleading omission, as defined by reg.6;
■ if it is aggressive under reg.7; or
■ if it is listed in Schedule 1.

22.2.3.2 Misleading actions under reg.5

A trader who engages in a misleading action under reg.5 commits an offence under reg.9. Regulation 5(1) provides that a commercial practice can be a misleading action under either reg.5(2) or reg.5(3). Regulation 5(2) deals with misleading actions generally, whereas reg.5(3) deals with two specific types of misleading actions. Regulation 5(2) states that a commercial activity is misleading:

'(a) if it contains false information and is therefore untruthful in relation to any of the matters in paragraph 5(4) (see immediately below) or if it or its overall presentation in any way deceives or is likely to deceive the average consumer in relation to any of the matters in paragraph 5(4), even if the information is factually correct; and

(b) it causes or is likely to cause the average consumer to take a transactional decision he would not have taken otherwise.'

The matters set out in reg.5(4) are very specific, being as follows:

'(a) the existence or nature of the product;
(b) the main characteristics of the product (as defined in paragraph 5);
(c) the extent of the trader's commitments;
(d) the motives for the commercial practice;
(e) the nature of the sales process;
(f) any statement or symbol relating to direct or indirect sponsorship or approval of the trader or the product;
(g) the price or the manner in which the price is calculated;
(h) the existence of a specific price advantage;
(i) the need for a service, part, replacement or repair;
(j) the nature, attributes and rights of the trader (as defined in paragraph 6);
(k) the consumer's rights or the risks he may face.'

In reg.(4)(b), the 'main characteristics of the product' include:

'(a) availability of the product;
(b) benefits of the product;
(c) risks of the product;
(d) execution of the product;
(e) composition of the product;
(f) accessories of the product;
(g) after-sale customer assistance concerning the product;
(h) the handling of complaints about the product;
(i) the method and date of manufacture of the product;
(j) the method and date of provision of the product;
(k) delivery of the product;
(l) fitness for purpose of the product;
(m) usage of the product;
(n) quantity of the product;
(o) specification of the product;
(p) geographical or commercial origin of the product;
(q) results to be expected from use of the product; and
(r) results and material features of tests or checks carried out on the product.'

In reg.(4)(j), the 'nature, attributes and rights' as far as concern the trader include the trader's:

'(a) identity;
(b) assets;

(c) qualifications;

(d) status;

(e) approval;

(f) affiliations or connections;

(g) ownership of industrial, commercial or intellectual property rights; and

(h) awards and distinctions.'

It should be remembered that reg.5(2) states that a commercial activity is misleading only if two requirements are satisfied. First, it must contain false information and be untruthful in relation to the reg.5(4) matters or likely to deceive the average consumer. Second, it must cause or be likely to cause the average consumer to make a transactional decision he would not otherwise have taken. The approach to reg.5(2) is to first find a commercial practice which contains false information. Next, to consider as to which of the matters in reg.5(4) it is untruthful or deceptive. Case law on the Trade Descriptions Act 1968 suggests that it will always be necessary to specify precisely which matters are appropriate. Finally, to show that it caused, or was likely to cause, the average consumer to make a transaction he would not have taken otherwise.

Example

Mrs Smith bought a pair of shoes from Badtrade's shop because she was told by a salesman that the shoes were made of leather. In fact, the shoes were largely made of synthetic materials. Badtrade's commercial practice of describing the shows as leather contains false information. The information is untruthful in relation to reg.5(4)(b), as defined by reg.5(5)(e). This caused an average consumer to buy the shoes. Therefore, Badtrade's description of the shoes was a misleading action and an unfair commercial practice.

Regulation 5(3) provides that a commercial practice is also misleading if:

'(a) it concerns any marketing of a product (including comparative advertising) which creates confusion with any products, trade marks, trade names or other distinguishing marks of a competitor; or

(b) it concerns any failure by a trader to comply with a commitment contained in a code of conduct which the trader has undertaken to comply with, if –

(i) the trader indicates in a commercial practice that he is bound by that code of conduct, and

(ii) the commitment is firm and capable of being verified and is not aspirational,

and it causes or is likely to cause the average consumer to take a transactional decision he would not have taken otherwise, taking account of its factual context and of all its features and circumstances.'

An example of a reg.5(3)(a) misleading action would be marketing a product under a name which is very similar to that of a well-known product. An example of a reg.5(3)(b) misleading action would be advertising adherence to an environmental code of conduct, such as selling only organic meat, and then selling meat which was not organic. As regards both types of misleading action it would also be necessary that the action caused, or would have been likely to cause, the average consumer to take a transactional decision he would not otherwise have taken.

22.2.3.3 Misleading omissions under reg.6

A trader who engages in a commercial practice which is a misleading omission under reg.6 commits an offence under reg.10. Regulation 6 provides that:

'(1) A commercial practice is a misleading omission if, in its factual context, taking account of the matters in paragraph (2) –

(a) the commercial practice omits material information,

(b) the commercial practice hides material information,

(c) the commercial practice provides material information in a manner which is unclear, unintelligible, ambiguous or untimely, or

(d) the commercial practice fails to identify its commercial intent, unless this is already apparent from the context,

and as a result it causes or is likely to cause the average consumer to take a transactional decision he would not have taken otherwise.

(2) The matters referred to in paragraph (1) are–

(a) all the features and circumstances of the commercial practice;

(b) the limitations of the medium used to communicate the commercial practice (including limitations of space or time); and

(c) where the medium used to communicate the commercial practice imposes limitations of space or time, any measures taken by the trader to make the information available to consumers by other means.

(3) In paragraph (1) "material information" means –

(a) the information which the average consumer needs, according to the context, to take an informed transactional decision; and

(b) any information requirement which applies in relation to a commercial communication as a result of a Community obligation.

(4) Where a commercial practice is an invitation to purchase, the following information will be material if not already apparent from the context in addition to any other information which is material information under paragraph (3) –

(a) the main characteristics of the product, to the extent appropriate to the medium by which the invitation to purchase is communicated and the product;

(b) the identity of the trader, such as his trading name, and the identity of any other trader on whose behalf the trader is acting;

(c) the geographical address of the trader and the geographical address of any other trader on whose behalf the trader is acting;

(d) either –

(i) the price, including any taxes; or

(ii) where the nature of the product is such that the price cannot reasonably be calculated in advance, the manner in which the price is calculated;

(e) where appropriate, either –

(i) all additional freight, delivery or postal charges; or

(ii) where such charges cannot reasonably be calculated in advance, the fact that such charges may be payable;

(f) the following matters where they depart from the requirements of professional diligence –

(i) arrangements for payment,
(ii) arrangements for delivery,
(iii) arrangements for performance,
(iv) complaint handling policy;

(g) for products and transactions involving a right of withdrawal or cancellation, the existence of such a right.'

So reg.6 is concerned with omitting or hiding material information, or presenting it in an unclear way. The approach to reg.6 is first to decide which of reg.6(1) (a)–(d) is applicable. Next to find which of the reg.6(2) matters is appropriate. Next, if relevant, to show that the material omitted is material information, and to specify precisely which type of material information it is if the commercial practice is an invitation to purchase. Finally, to show that the commercial practice caused, or was likely to cause, the average consumer to make a transaction he would not have taken otherwise.

> **Example**
>
> Mr Mantle buys a new television from Jones Ltd. He pays by credit card and is charged more than he expected because the price displayed in the shop did not include VAT. Regulation 6(1)(a) is applicable because Jones Ltd have omitted material information, taking account of reg.6(2)(a). The fact that the price did not include VAT was material information within reg.6(3) and, since there was an invitation to purchase, also within reg.6(4)(d)(i). This caused an average consumer to buy the television. Therefore, Jones Ltd's description of the price of the television was a misleading action and an unfair commercial practice.

22.2.3.4 Aggressive commercial practices under reg.7

A trader who engages in a commercial practice which is aggressive under reg.7 commits an offence under reg.11. Regulation 7 provides that:

'(1) A commercial practice is aggressive if, in its factual context, taking account of all of its features and circumstances –

(a) it significantly impairs or is likely significantly to impair the average consumer's freedom of choice or conduct in relation to the product concerned through the use of harassment, coercion or undue influence; and

(b) it thereby causes or is likely to cause him to take a transactional decision he would not have taken otherwise.

(2) In determining whether a commercial practice uses harassment, coercion or undue influence account shall be taken of –

(a) its timing, location, nature or persistence;

(b) the use of threatening or abusive language or behaviour;

(c) the exploitation by the trader of any specific misfortune or circumstance of such gravity as to impair the consumer's judgment, of which the trader is aware, to influence the consumer's decision with regard to the product;

(d) any onerous or disproportionate non-contractual barrier imposed by the trader where a consumer wishes to exercise rights under the contract, including rights to terminate a contract or to switch to another product or another trader; and

(e) any threat to take any action which cannot legally be taken.

(3) In this regulation –

(a) "coercion" includes the use of physical force; and

(b) "undue influence" means exploiting a position of power in relation to the consumer so as to apply pressure, even without using or threatening to use physical force, in a way which significantly limits the consumer's ability to make an informed decision.'

The approach to reg.7 is first to identify a commercial practice which significantly impairs or is likely significantly to impair the average consumer's freedom of choice or conduct in relation to a product. Next to show that the commercial practice used harassment, coercion or undue influence (taking account of the reg.7(2) factors). Finally, to show that the commercial practice caused or was likely to cause the average consumer to take a transactional decision he would not otherwise have taken.

Example

Pressure Ltd invite people who responded to an advertisement to a hotel. Once inside, the customers are told that they cannot leave until they sign a contract to book a holiday. Mr Sharma booked a holiday because he was very frightened to leave without doing so. He tried to leave without booking a holiday but was physically prevented from doing so. Pressure Ltd's commercial practice is aggressive within reg.7(1), taking account of reg.7(2)(a), (b), (c), and (d). This caused an average consumer to book a holiday. Therefore, Pressure Ltd's commercial practice was aggressive and an unfair commercial practice.

22.2.3.5 The unfair commercial practices listed in Schedule 1

Schedule 1 sets out the following 31 commercial practices which are always to be considered unfair. Unlike the other commercial practices, there is here no requirement that a consumer might have been induced to behave differently. As regards all of the prohibited commercial practices except 11 and 28, engaging in them will have caused an offence to be committed under reg.12.

(1) Claiming to be a signatory to a code of conduct when the trader is not.

(2) Displaying a trust mark, quality mark or equivalent without having obtained the necessary authorisation.

(3) Claiming that a code of conduct has an endorsement from a public or other body which it does not have.

(4) Claiming that a trader (including his commercial practices) or a product has been approved, endorsed or authorised by a public or private body when the trader, the commercial practices or the product have not or making such a claim without complying with the terms of the approval, endorsement or authorisation.

(5) Making an invitation to purchase products at a specified price without disclosing the existence of any reasonable grounds the trader may have for believing that he will not be able to offer for supply, or to procure another trader to supply, those products or equivalent products at that price for a period that is, and in quantities that are, reasonable having regard to the product, the scale of advertising of the product and the price offered (bait advertising).

(6) Making an invitation to purchase products at a specified price and then:

(a) refusing to show the advertised item to consumers,

(b) refusing to take orders for it or deliver it within a reasonable time, or

(c) demonstrating a defective sample of it;

with the intention of promoting a different product (bait and switch).

(7) Falsely stating that a product will only be available for a very limited time, or that it will only be available on particular terms for a very

limited time, in order to elicit an immediate decision and deprive consumers of sufficient opportunity or time to make an informed choice.

(8) Undertaking to provide after-sales service to consumers with whom the trader has communicated prior to a transaction in a language which is not an official language of the EEA State where the trader is located and then making such service available only in another language without clearly disclosing this to the consumer before the consumer is committed to the transaction.

(9) Stating or otherwise creating the impression that a product can legally be sold when it cannot.

(10) Presenting rights given to consumers in law as a distinctive feature of the trader's offer.

(11) Using editorial content in the media to promote a product where a trader has paid for the promotion without making that clear in the content or by images or sounds clearly identifiable by the consumer (advertorial).

(12) Making a materially inaccurate claim concerning the nature and extent of the risk to the personal security of the consumer or his family if the consumer does not purchase the product.

(13) Promoting a product similar to a product made by a particular manufacturer in such a manner as deliberately to mislead the consumer into believing that the product is made by that same manufacturer when it is not.

(14) Establishing, operating or promoting a pyramid promotional scheme where a consumer gives consideration for the opportunity to receive compensation that is derived primarily from the introduction of other consumers into the scheme rather than from the sale or consumption of products.

(15) Claiming that the trader is about to cease trading or move premises when he is not.

(16) Claiming that products are able to facilitate winning in games of chance.

(17) Falsely claiming that a product is able to cure illnesses, dysfunction or malformations.

(18) Passing on materially inaccurate information on market conditions or on the possibility of finding the product with the intention of inducing the consumer to acquire the product at conditions less favourable than normal market conditions.

(19) Claiming in a commercial practice to offer a competition or prize promotion without awarding the prizes described or a reasonable equivalent.

(20) Describing a product as 'gratis', 'free', 'without charge' or similar if the consumer has to pay anything other than the unavoidable cost of responding to the commercial practice and collecting or paying for delivery of the item.

(21) Including in marketing material an invoice or similar document seeking payment which gives the consumer the impression that he has already ordered the marketed product when he has not.

(22) Falsely claiming or creating the impression that the trader is not acting for purposes relating to his trade, business, craft or profession, or falsely representing oneself as a consumer.

(23) Creating the false impression that after-sales service in relation to a product is available in an EEA State other than the one in which the product is sold.

(24) Creating the impression that the consumer cannot leave the premises until a contract is formed.

(25) Conducting personal visits to the consumer's home ignoring the consumer's request to leave or not to return, except in circumstances and to the extent justified to enforce a contractual obligation.

(26) Making persistent and unwanted solicitations by telephone, fax, e-mail or other remote media except in circumstances and to the extent justified to enforce a contractual obligation.

(27) Requiring a consumer who wishes to claim on an insurance policy to produce documents which could not reasonably be considered relevant as to whether the claim was valid, or failing systematically to respond to pertinent correspondence, in order to dissuade a consumer from exercising his contractual rights.

(28) Including in an advertisement a direct exhortation to children to buy advertised products or persuade their parents or other adults to buy advertised products for them.

(29) Demanding immediate or deferred payment for or the return or safekeeping of products supplied by the trader, but not solicited by the consumer, except where the product is a substitute supplied in accordance with regulation 19(7) of the Consumer Protection (Distance Selling) Regulations 2000 (inertia selling).

(30) Explicitly informing a consumer that if he does not buy the product or service, the trader's job or livelihood will be in jeopardy.

(31) Creating the false impression that the consumer has already won, will win, or will on doing a particular act win, a prize or other equivalent benefit, when in fact either –

(a) there is no prize or other equivalent benefit; or

(b) taking any action in relation to claiming the prize or other equivalent benefit is subject to the consumer paying money or incurring a cost.

The approach to Schedule 1 is merely to find which of the paragraphs is applicable.

22.2.4 The offences which the Regulations create

22.2.4.1 The reg.8 offence

Regulation 8 sets out the most serious offence, for which *mens rea* is required. If the necessary *mens rea* is present then there are no defences to this offence. Regulation 8 states:

'(1) A trader is guilty of an offence if –

(a) he knowingly or recklessly engages in a commercial practice which contravenes the requirements of professional diligence under regulation 3(3)(a); and

(b) the practice materially distorts or is likely to materially distort the economic behaviour of the average consumer with regard to the product under regulation 3(3)(b).'

If the reg.3(3) definition of an unfair commercial practice has been mastered (see above at 22.3.1), this offence becomes relatively easy to understand. It merely remains to consider the *mens rea*, which can take two forms. The trader must either knowingly or recklessly engage in the relevant commercial practice. Regulation 8(2) deals with the meaning of recklessly. It states that:

'a trader who engages in a commercial practice without regard to whether the practice contravenes the requirements of professional diligence shall be deemed recklessly to engage in the practice, whether or not the trader has reason for believing that the practice might contravene those requirements.'

This definition bears some similarity to the definition of making a statement 'recklessly' under the Trade Descriptions Act 1968. *MFI Warehouses* v *Nattrass* [1973] 1 WLR 307 would suggest that a trader will have behaved recklessly unless he first positively asks himself whether or not a practice contravenes the requirements of professional diligence, and then decides that it does not. This is the case even though the trader might otherwise have behaved honestly and carefully.

22.2.4.2 The reg.9 offence

The strict liability reg.9 offence is committed by engaging in a commercial practice which is misleading under reg.5 otherwise than by reason of the commercial practice satisfying the condition in reg.5(3)(b). As we saw above, reg.5(3)(b) made a commercial practice misleading if it concerned a trader failing to adhere to a code of practice to which he had signed up. So mere failure to do this will not cause the reg.9 offence to have been committed.

22.2.4.3 The reg.10 offence

The strict liability reg.10 offence is committed by engaging in a commercial practice which is a misleading omission under reg.6.

22.2.4.4 The reg.11 offence

The strict liability reg.11 offence is committed by engaging in a commercial practice which is an aggressive omission under reg.7.

22.2.4.5 The reg.12 offence

The strict liability reg.12 offence is committed by engaging in a commercial practice which is set out in Schedule 1, paragraphs 1–10, 12–27 or 29–31. However, it is not an offence under reg.12 to engage in the commercial practices set out in paragraphs 11 or 28 of Schedule 1.

Companies can commit any of the offences and if a company is found guilty, its officers can also be found personally guilty if they connived in the commission of the offence or if their negligence caused the commission of the offence. Prosecutions for all of the offences must be brought within three years of the commission of the offence or within one year of its discovery, whichever is earlier. The maximum penalty is an unlimited fine or two years' imprisonment.

22.2.5 **Defences**

The Regulations set out defences which can apply to the regs.9, 10, 11 or 12 offences, but not to the reg.8 offence.

22.2.5.1 **Due diligence defence**

Regulation 17(1) provides that it is a defence for the person charged under regs.9, 10, 11 or 12 to prove:

(a) that the commission of the offence was due to:
   (i) a mistake; or to
   (ii) reliance on information supplied to him by another person; or to
   (iii) the act or default of another person; or to
   (iv) an accident; or
   (v) some other cause beyond his control; and

(b) that he took all reasonable precautions and exercised all due diligence to avoid the commission of the offence.

The defendant needs to prove both elements of the defence on a balance of probabilities. The Trade Descriptions Act 1968 s.24 contained a defence which was, in all material ways, identically worded. Therefore, cases decided on s.24 TDA can be used to demonstrate the working of the reg.17 defence. If the first limb of the defence is that the offence was committed due to a mistake, then the mistake must be one made by the person charged, not by any other person. In *Birkenhead Co-operative Society v Roberts* [1970] 1 WLR 1497, the defendants, the Co-op, had supplied a customer with a piece of lamb described as English lamb. This was caused by a mistake of one of the supermarket assistants, who had inadvertently used the wrong label on a piece of New Zealand lamb. As the mistake was not their own, the Co-op could not rely on the defence of mistake and were therefore convicted of an offence under s.1(1) TDA 1968. If the first limb of the defence is either that the offence was committed in reliance on information supplied by another or that it was committed on account of the act or default of another person, reg.17(2) requires the defendant to give the prosecution seven days' clear notice identifying this other person. If this is not done, the defences cannot be relied upon. (The prosecution might prosecute the other person under the reg.16 by-pass provision, which is considered below.)

As regards companies, it can be difficult to decide which employees can be regarded as another person and which can be regarded as the company itself. In *Tesco Supermarkets v Nattrass* [1971] 2 All ER 127, the House of Lords held that the very senior managers of a company might be regarded as the controlling mind and will of the company, and therefore as its alter ego. A mere supermarket manager could not be so regarded and was therefore another person. The defendants, Tesco Ltd, were charged under a section of the Act concerning the giving of misleading price indications. The offence had been committed when a shop assistant had put out ordinary packets of Radiant washing powder, which cost 3s 11d. Posters in the shop stated that 'flash packs' of Radiant were available at 2s 11d. The shop assistant did not tell the supermarket manager that the wrong packets had been put out and a customer paid 3s 11d for a packet of Radiant. The responsibility of seeing that the correct packets were put out was that of the supermarket manager, who had been trained to do this properly. The defendants argued that the offence was committed because of the act of another person, the supermarket manager. Holding that the offence had been committed on account of the act of another person, the supermarket manager, the House of Lords recognised that very senior managers might be regarded as the alter ego of the company.

Whichever of the aspects of the reg.17 defence is being relied upon, the defendant will always need to prove that he took all reasonable precautions and exercised all due diligence to prevent the commission of the offence. Whether or not this has been done will be an objective question of fact, to be decided by examining all the circumstances of the case. In *Tesco Supermarkets Ltd v Nattrass*, Lord Morris thought that a company would have satisfied the requirement if it had created a system which could be rationally said to be so designed that the commission of offences would be avoided.

22.2.5.2 **The by-pass provision**

Regulation 16 deals with the situation where the offence was committed due to the act or default of another person. A person who uses the reg.17(1)(a)(ii) or (iii) defence, must give the name of the person at fault to the prosecution. Regulation 16 provides that the person at fault can then be guilty of an offence, even if he is not a trader. For example, in *Olgiersson v Kitching* [1986] a private motorist sold a car to a garage saying that it had done 38 000 miles, even though he knew that this was not true. The owner of the garage sold the car on, applying the 38 000-mile description. The purchaser found out that the description was false. The private motorist was guilty of an offence, under the by-pass provision in the Trade Descriptions Act 1968. He could not have been guilty of any other offence under that Act, as these other offences could be committed only by a person who made a false description in the course of a trade or in business. In the same way, a person who is not a trader cannot be guilty of any of the main offences under the 2008 Regulations.

22.2.5.3 Innocent publication of advertisement defence

Regulation 18 provides a defence to a person who is in business to publish or to arrange for the publication of advertisements if he received an advertisement for publication in the ordinary course of business and he did not know and had no reason to suspect that its publication would amount to an offence.

22.2.6 Enforcement of the Regulations

The Office of Fair Trading and local authority trading standards departments have a duty to enforce the regulations. These enforcers are given wide powers to make test purchases, enter premises, carry out investigations and seize goods or documents. Enforcement does not necessarily mean bringing prosecutions. The main aim of enforcement is to ensure compliance through the most appropriate methods. These include the use of codes of conduct and of existing enforcement procedures, as well as education, advice and guidance. Any action taken should aim to change the offender's behaviour, eliminate any benefit gained by non-compliance, restore the harm caused by non-compliance and deter further non-compliance. Where established systems of regulation already exist to deal with specific areas, enforcement authorities can refer a complaint to the already existing relevant bodies. So, for example, advertising complaints might be referred to the Advertising Standards Authority or complaints about premium telephone services might be referred to PhonepayPlus. Enforcers can also apply to a court for enforcement orders to prevent further infringements anywhere in the EC. Generally, however, an enforcer should seek prevention through consultation with the trader and by acceptance of undertakings not to infringe. The EC Regulation on Consumer Protection Cooperation (2006/2004) allows enforcement authorities in different Member States to share information and to request that breaches in other Member States be dealt with.

22.3 THE BUSINESS PROTECTION FROM MISLEADING MARKETING REGULATIONS 2008

These regulations make it a criminal offence to engage in advertising which misleads a trader. Only a trader can commit the offence. The standard EC definition of a trader, considered above in relation to the Consumer Protection from Unfair Trading Regulations 2008, applies. This definition is important in the Business Protection from Misleading Marketing (BPMM) Regulations in two different ways. First, only a trader can commit the main offence which the regs create. Second, the offence is committed only if a trader is, or is likely to be, influenced by the advertising. If a consumer is likely to be influenced by misleading advertising then an offence would have been committed under the Consumer Protection from Unfair Trading Regulations 2008.

22.3.1 The reg.6 offence

Regulation 6 provides that a trader is guilty of an offence if he engages in advertising which is misleading under reg.3. It is therefore necessary to understand reg.3. First, reg.3(1) states that advertising which is misleading is prohibited. Regulation 3(2)–(5) then give a lengthy definition of what is meant by misleading advertising, as follows:

'(2) Advertising is misleading which –

(a) in any way, including its presentation, deceives or is likely to deceive the traders to whom it is addressed or whom it reaches; and by reason of its deceptive nature, is likely to affect their economic behaviour; or

(b) for those reasons, injures or is likely to injure a competitor.

(3) In determining whether advertising is misleading, account shall be taken of all its features, and in particular of any information it contains concerning –

(a) the characteristics of the product (as defined in paragraph (4));

(b) the price or manner in which the price is calculated;

(c) the conditions on which the product is supplied or provided; and

(d) the nature, attributes and rights of the advertiser (as defined in paragraph (5)).

(4) In paragraph (3)(a) the "characteristics of the product" include –

(a) availability of the product;

(b) nature of the product;

(c) execution of the product;

(d) composition of the product;

(e) method and date of manufacture of the product;

(f) method and date of provision of the product;

(g) fitness for purpose of the product;

(h) uses of the product;

(i) quantity of the product;

(j) specification of the product;

(k) geographical or commercial origin of the product;

(l) results to be expected from use of the product; or

(m) results and material features of tests or checks carried out on the product.

(5) In paragraph (3)(d) the "nature, attributes and rights" of the advertiser include the advertiser's –

(a) identity;

(b) assets;

(c) qualifications;

(d) ownership of industrial, commercial or intellectual property rights; or

(e) awards and distinctions.'

Regulation 3(2) requires that the deceptive advertising should be likely either to affect the economic behaviour of the traders to whom it is addressed, or that it should injure or be likely to injure a competitor. These regulations are not, therefore, trying to extend consumer protection but are trying to prevent a competitor from gaining an unfair advantage by means of misleading advertising. The Trade Descriptions Act 1968 aimed both to protect consumers and prevent one trader from gaining an unfair advantage over another. Case law on the TDA 1968 suggests that it will always be necessary to specify precisely which matters set out in reg.3(3)–(5) are appropriate.

Regulation 11 sets out a due diligence defence and reg.12 sets out an innocent publication defence. Regulation 9 sets out a by-pass offence which can be committed by a person who is not a trader. The two defences, and the by-pass provision, are identical to those in the Consumer Protection from Unfair Trading Regulations 2008 (considered above at 22.2.5).

22.3.2 Prohibition of comparative advertising

Regulation 4 prohibits comparative advertising, that is to say advertising which compares products, unless certain conditions are met. However, no criminal offence is created. Instead, enforcement authorities will take action against offending advertising. Product is defined in the same way as in the Consumer Protection from Unfair Trading Regulations 2008 and means any goods or services and includes immovable property, rights and obligations.

Regulation 4 provides as follows:

'(4) Comparative advertising shall, as far as the comparison is concerned, be permitted only when the following conditions are met –

(a) it is not misleading under regulation 3;

(b) it is not a misleading action under regulation 5 of the Consumer Protection from Unfair Trading Regulations 2008(5) or a misleading omission under regulation 6 of those Regulations;

(c) it compares products meeting the same needs or intended for the same purpose;

(d) it objectively compares one or more material, relevant, verifiable and representative features of those products, which may include price;

(e) it does not create confusion among traders –

(i) between the advertiser and a competitor, or

(ii) between the trade marks, trade names, other distinguishing marks or products of the advertiser and those of a competitor;

(f) it does not discredit or denigrate the trade marks, trade names, other distinguishing marks, products, activities, or circumstances of a competitor;

(g) for products with designation of origin, it relates in each case to products with the same designation;

(h) it does not take unfair advantage of the reputation of a trade mark, trade name or other distinguishing marks of a competitor or of the designation of origin of competing products;

    (i) it does not present products as imitations or replicas of products bearing a protected trade mark or trade name.'

Regulation 5 provides that a trader or trade body which is responsible for drawing up codes of conduct should not promote advertising which is misleading under reg.3 or comparative advertising which contravenes reg.4.

The Regulations are enforced in the same way as the Consumer Protection from Unfair Trading Regulations 2008.

Test your understanding 22.1

1 How is a commercial practice defined in the Unfair Trading Regulations 2008?

2 In what circumstances will a commercial practice be unfair?

3 What offences are created by regs.8, 9, 10, 11 and 12?

4 How does the reg.8 offence differ from the other offences?

5 What defences are available under the Regulations?

22.4 PRODUCT SAFETY

Criminal liability as regards unsafe products is imposed by the General Product Safety Regulations 2005.

The general safety requirement

Regulation 5 sets out the general safety requirement:

'(1) No producer shall place a product on the market unless the product is a safe product.

(2) No producer shall offer or agree to place a product on the market or expose or possess a product for placing on the market unless the product is a safe product.

(3) No producer shall offer or agree to supply a product or expose or possess a product for supply unless the product is a safe product.

(4) No producer shall supply a product unless the product is a safe product.'

Regulation 2, the interpretation Regulation, defines a 'producer' as:

'(a) the manufacturer of a product, when he is established in a Member State and any other person presenting himself as the manufacturer by affixing to the product his name, trade mark or other distinctive mark, or the person who reconditions the product;

(b) when the manufacturer is not established in a Member State –

  (i) if he has a representative established in a Member State, the representative;

  (ii) in any other case, the importer of the product from a state that is not a Member State into a Member State.

(c) other professionals in the supply chain, insofar as their activities may affect the safety properties of a product.'

It should be noted that retailers are not included in this definition unless their activities affect the safety properties of a product. However, distributors can commit two separate offences under reg.8, as we shall see.

Regulation 2 defines 'product' as a product which is intended for consumers or likely, under reasonably foreseeable conditions, to be used by consumers, even if not intended for them. The product must be supplied in the course of a commercial activity but there is no requirement that the consumer pays for it. Both new and used goods are included. However, equipment used by service providers themselves to provide a service is not included. Transport services provided by suppliers, such as buses and trains, are specifically excluded.

Regulation 2 also defines a 'safe product':

'"safe product" means any product which, under normal or reasonably foreseeable conditions of use including duration, ... does not present any risk or only the minimum risks compatible with the product's use, considered to be acceptable and consistent with a high level of protection for the safety and health of persons. In determining the foregoing, the following shall be taken into account in particular –

(a) the characteristics of the product, including its composition, packaging, instructions for assembly and, where applicable, instructions for installation and maintenance,

(b) the effect of the product on other products, where it is reasonably foreseeable that it will be used with other products,

(c) the presentation of the product, the labelling, any warnings and instructions for its use and disposal and any other indication or information regarding the product, and

(d) the categories of consumers at risk when using the product, in particular children and the elderly.'

A product is not to be considered dangerous just because it would be possible to make it safer, nor just because other products are safer.

The Regulations do not apply to: antiques; second-hand products supplied for repair or reconditioning before use, provided the supplier clearly informs the person to whom he supplies the product to that effect; or any product where there are specific provisions in rules of European Community law or British standards governing all aspects of the safety of the product.

Regulation 7(1) requires a producer, within the limits of his activity, to provide consumers with the relevant information to enable them: (a) to assess the risks inherent in a product throughout the normal or reasonably foreseeable period of its use, where such risks are not immediately obvious without adequate warnings, and (b) to take precautions against those risks. Regulation 7(2) provides that the presence of a warning does not exempt a person from complying with the requirements of the Regulations. Regulation 7(3) requires a producer, within the limits of his activity, to adopt measures commensurate with the characteristics of the products which he supplies, to enable him to:

(a) be informed of the risks which those products might pose; and

(b) to take appropriate action, including, where necessary to avoid such risks, withdrawal, adequately and effectively warning consumers as to the risk or, as last resort, recalling the product.

The appropriate measures might include, except where it is not reasonable to do so –

(a) marking of their products or product batches in such a way that they and the producer can be identified;

(b) sample testing of marketed products;

(c) investigating complaints; and

(d) keeping distributors informed of such monitoring.

Regulation 8 requires that distributors act with due care in order to help ensure compliance with the applicable safety requirements. (A distributor is defined as any professional in the supply chain whose activity does not affect the safety properties of a product. It would generally therefore include retailers.) In particular distributors are required not to expose or possess for supply or agree to supply, or supply products which they know, or should have presumed on the basis of information in their possession as a professional, are dangerous products. It is an offence for a distributor to do this. Distributors are also particularly required, within the limits of their activities, to participate in monitoring the safety of products placed on the market, in particular by passing on information on the product risks and cooperating in the action taken to avoid those risks.

Regulation 9 requires producers and distributors who know that they have placed an unsafe product on the market or supplied an unsafe product to notify the authorities in writing. If the risk is serious they must identify the product, fully describe the risk, give all information needed to trace the product and describe the action they have taken to prevent risks to the consumer.

Regulation 29 sets out the standard defence of due diligence. Regulation 31 sets out a by-pass procedure.

Local authority enforcement authorities are given very wide powers, including issuing suspension notices, withdrawal notices and recall notices. They can require that products are marked or warnings are issued. Products can be forfeited and test purchases can be made. Authorities are also given the power to enter premises and carry out searches.

22.5 THE COMPUTER MISUSE ACT 1990

The Computer Misuse Act 1990 was passed to deal with computer hacking. Since 1968 the Theft Act could deal adequately with computer crime where money was stolen or where property or a pecuniary advantage were obtained by deception. But no statute dealt with computer hacking, that is to say with accessing another's computer system without that person's express or implied permission. The need for a new statute was made plain by the House of Lords decision in *R v Gold* [1988] 2 WLR 984. In that case two journalists gained access to BT's computer network and altered some data. One of the journalists also gained access to the Duke of Edinburgh's PC and left the message: 'GOOD AFTERNOON. HRH DUKE OF EDINBURGH'. The journalists, who claimed to have acted to demonstrate how easy hacking was, were charged with an offence under the Forgery and Counterfeiting Act

1981. The House of Lords held that the defendants had committed no offence under that Act and so the need for new legislation was made apparent.

22.5.1 The unauthorised access offence

Section 1(1) of the Computer Misuse Act makes hacking a criminal offence. It provides that:

'A person is guilty of an offence if –

(a) he causes a computer to perform any function with intent to secure access to any program or data held in any computer;
(b) the access he intends to secure is unauthorised; and
(c) he knows at the time when he causes the computer to perform the function that this is the case.'

The *actus reus* of the s.1 offence is causing a computer to perform any function, which could merely meaning turning a computer on. Section 1(1)(c) makes it plain that *mens rea* is needed and s.1(2) provides that:

'The intent a person has to have to commit an offence under this section need not be directed at –

(a) any particular program or data;
(b) a program or data of any particular kind; or
(c) a program or data held in any particular computer.'

The s.1 offence is punishable by six months' imprisonment. The offence does not require that the defendant succeeds in securing unauthorised access, it is enough that he intends to do this.

Section 17(2) defines securing access to a program or data as causing a computer to perform any function so as to alter or erase the program or data, or copy or move it, or use it or have it output from the computer. So downloading music or copying software would be within s.1 as long as this was unauthorised. Although hackers generally use one computer to gain access to another, this is not necessary. In *Attorney-General's Reference (No. 1 of 1991)* [1992] 3 WLR 432 a customer who had been left alone in a shop caused the shop owner's computer to give him a discount on the goods he was buying. The Court of Appeal held that he was rightly convicted under s.1.

Section 17(5) defines the meaning of unauthorised access:

'Access of any kind by any person to any program or data held in a computer is unauthorised if –

(a) he is not entitled to control access of the kind in question to the program or data; and
(b) he does not have consent to access by him of the kind in question to the program or data from any person who is so entitled.'

This definition was interpreted in a very limited way in *DPP v Bignell* [1988] 1 Cr App R 1. In that case two police officers who did have authorised access to the national police computer used a computer operator to gain information for personal purposes, misrepresenting the reason why they wanted the information. The Divisional Court held that the officers were not guilty, as 'access of the kind in question' (in s.17(5)(a)) meant only the type of access defined in s.17(2), that is to say altering, erasing, copying or moving it. The court thought that the Act was designed to protect the integrity of computer systems themselves rather than to protect the integrity of the information stored on such computer systems. In *R v Bow Street Magistrates and Allison, ex parte US Government* [1999] 3 WLR 620 the House of Lords agreed that the decision in *Bignell* was probably correct on the grounds that the computer operator did not exceed his authority. (This seems somewhat surprising, as it would be easy to regard the computer operator as an innocent agent through whom the police officers exceeded their authority.) However, their Lordships indicated that the Divisional Court had been wrong to interpret s.17(5) as it did. Lord Hobhouse said that s.1 was concerned with authority to access the actual data involved, rather than with authority to access kinds of data. In *Bignell* the Divisional Court thought that there was no problem in acquitting the officers as they would anyway have committed an offence under the Data Protection Act. However, this would not have been the case if the information retrieved had not been personal data (see Chapter 23 at 23.5.1).

A circuit judge who is satisfied that there are reasonable grounds for believing that a s.1 offence has been or is about to be committed in any premises can issue a search warrant for those premises to be searched. The police can then seize any article if they believe that it is evidence that a s.1 offence has been or is about to be committed. So a computer could be seized in order that its hard disk could be examined.

22.5.2 Intent to commit a further offence

The second offence under the Act is contained in s.2(1). This section makes it an offence to commit the s.1 offence with the intention of committing, or facilitating the commission of, murder or a further offence which carries a sentence of at least five years' imprisonment.

There is no requirement that the further offence should be committed at the same time as the s.1 offence. Indeed, the s.2 offence can be committed even though it was impossible to commit the further offence. The sentence for the s.2 offence is five years' imprisonment. So the s.2 offence will not generally be used where the defendant succeeds in committing the further offence, because the defendant could anyway be sentenced to at least five years for having committed that offence. The s.2 offence is therefore useful when the defendant does not succeed in committing the further offence. For example, it would be useful where a defendant hacked into a computer to try to commit blackmail but failed so abysmally that he could not be convicted of blackmail or attempted blackmail.

22.5.3 Unauthorised modification of computer material

Section 3 makes it an offence to modify computer material without authorisation, by providing that:

'A person is guilty of an offence if –

(a) he does any act which causes an unauthorised modification of the contents of any computer; and

(b) at the time when he does the act he has the requisite intent and the requisite knowledge.'

The requisite intent is defined by s.3(2) as an intent to cause a modification of the contents of any computer program and by so doing: impair the operation of any computer; or prevent or impair access to any program or data held on any computer; or impair the operation of any such program or reliability of such data. The requisite knowledge is defined by s.3(4) as knowledge that any modification the defendant intends to cause is unauthorised. Section 3(3) provides that the intent does not need to be directed at any particular computer, program, data or modification.

Section 17(7) defines modification as using any computer so as to alter, add to or erase any program or data. Therefore, sending computer viruses is clearly within s.3. The maximum sentence is five years. In the following case the Divisional Court considered whether 'mail-bombing' a computer amounted to an unauthorised modification of its contents.

DPP v David Lennon [2006] EWHC 1201

The defendant, a 16-year-old who had been sacked after three months' employment, used an Avalanche V3.6 programme to send half a million emails to his former employer. These purported to come from the employer's Human Resources Manager. The emails were sent from different email addresses to try and prevent the employer from stopping the emails. Section 17(8) of the CMA provides that a modification of the contents of a computer is unauthorised if: (a) the person whose act causes it is not himself entitled to determine whether the modification should be made; and (b) he does not have consent to the modification from any person who is so entitled. The main argument of the defence was that the employer's servers consented to receiving emails.

Held. Clearly, the defendant was not the person who was entitled to determine whether the modification should be made. That person was the owner of the computer. It would generally be implied that a computer owner would consent to receiving emails. However, an owner did not impliedly consent to emails which were designed to interrupt the proper operation and functioning of his system. Jack J drew an analogy with a householder. He would consent to people walking up his drive or posting a letter through his letter box. He would not consent to a burglar walking up his drive or to a person choking his letter box with rubbish. The defendant was therefore guilty of the s.3 offence.

22.6 ENFORCEMENT OF CONSUMER LAW

The Enterprise Act 2002 has replaced the Stop Now Orders (EC Directive) Regulations 2001 and Part III of the Fair Trading Act 1973 by setting up an enforcement procedure which is based on the one created by the 2001 Regulations. The powers set out in the Act can be exercised by the OFT and other bodies responsible for enforcing consumer legislation. However, before seeking an enforcement order against a trader, the enforcing body will always give the trader a chance to respond to allegations against him and the option of giving a binding undertaking instead of being taken to court.

The OFT has a coordinating role to see that it is the most appropriate enforcement authority which takes action in any particular case. There are three types of enforcer. First, there are general enforcers, namely the OFT, trading standards departments and the Department of Enterprise, Trade and Investment in Northern Ireland. Second, there are EC based community enforcers. Third, there are bodies designated by the Secretary of State. At the time of writing these are the Civil Aviation Authority, the Director General of Electricity Supply for Northern Ireland, the Director General of Gas for Northern Ireland, the Director General of Telecommunications, the Director General of Water Services, the Information Commissioner and the Office of the Rail Regulator. However, enforcers other than the OFT must consult the OFT before taking any action to prevent a breach of consumer protection law.

Before taking action against a business any enforcer must give the business a notice period during which the business can give written undertakings, to either the OFT or a court, that it will voluntarily stop the offending behaviour and in future comply with the law. This notice period is generally two weeks but can be a short period if the interests of consumers are threatened to the extent that a shorter period is appropriate. An enforcement order will indicate the nature of the conduct which amounts to an infringement and direct the perpetrator not to continue with the conduct or repeat it. The court can also order that a corrective statement be published by the perpetrator in order to eliminate any continuing effects of the infringement. If undertakings are given but then ignored, action can be taken for contempt of court.

A domestic infringement of consumer law occurs when an act or omission is done or made by a person in business and this harms the collective interests of consumers within the UK. However, the act or omission in question must be a criminal offence, a breach of contract or some other civil wrong with a remedy which would be legally enforceable. It must also be within a certain range of trading activities. The OFT gives the following examples: misleading advertising, lotteries, credit, underage sales, sale of goods laws, misleading health claims, trade descriptions and mock auctions. A community infringement is an act or omission which harms the collective interests of consumers and which contravenes a Directive which has been given effect by a European Economic Area State. The OFT gives as examples: timeshare, unfair terms in consumer contracts, doorstep selling, distance selling, package travel and consumer credit. The OFT has the power to take action in other EC States but if a business in another country harms the collective interests of UK consumers then, generally, the OFT would ask the appropriate community enforcer to take enforcement action. If it is a UK-based business which is harming the collective interest of consumers in another EC State then a community enforcer could either ask the OFT to take action in the UK courts or could take such action himself, in consultation with the OFT.

22.7 COMPETITION LAW

It is generally accepted that competition amongst businesses produces better results than monopoly. Free competition leads to lower prices, better goods and services and more choice for consumers as producers are forced to work with ever greater efficiency to maintain their position. Consequently, a body of competition law has been created. This body of law aims to protect consumers and businesses and to ensure that no one producer can take advantage of its dominant position in the market place. Small producers are given some protection from their most powerful competitors and mergers may be forbidden. In the United Kingdom there are three main sources of competition law; Articles 81–82 of the EC Treaty, the Competition Act 1998 and the Enterprise Act 2002. Firms which engage in anti-competitive behaviour may find that their agreements are unenforceable. They also risk being fined up to 10 per cent of group global turnover for particularly damaging behaviour. In addition, customers might be able to claim damages. It is not possible in a book of this nature to examine these matters in any depth, but it is possible to give an outline explanation of their effect and the connection between the three sources of competition law.

22.7.1 Articles 101 and 102 of the TFEU

Article 101 of the Treaty on the Functioning of the European Union renders void all agreements between undertakings, decisions by associations of undertakings and concerted practices which may affect trade between Member States and which have as their object or effect the prevention, restriction or distortion of competition within the EU. All of the elements of Article 101 have to be satisfied or the prohibition will not apply. Nor will the prohibition apply unless the effect of the agreement is significant enough to be appreciable. The word 'undertaking' in Article 101 is not defined by the Treaty but includes any entity engaged in economic activity, regardless of its legal status. State-owned and state-financed bodies can be undertakings if they provide services of general economic interest. If two companies are sufficiently closely related, for example one owns all of the shares in the other, they may be regarded as one undertaking. If they are, an agreement between them could not be covered by Article 101. Associations of undertakings means trade associations. Agreement is widely interpreted to include both formal and informal agreements. Concerted practices exist where there is evidence of collusion, in the absence of being able to point to an actual agreement. If competitors inform each other in advance about future price rises this is likely to be a concerted practice. The agreement etc. does not actually need to prevent, restrict or distort competition, it will be caught if it aims to do this or actually does it. Agreements etc. are also caught if they are capable of affecting trade between Member States of the EU. Even actions carried out solely within one Member State could be caught as they might, for example, make it more difficult for another Member State to enter into a particular market.

Article 101(1)(a)–(e) provides some examples of the types of activity caught by this provision, listing agreements etc. which:

'(a) directly or indirectly fix purchase or selling prices or any other trading conditions;
(b) limit or control production, markets, technical development, or investment;
(c) share markets or sources of supply;
(d) apply dissimilar conditions to equivalent transactions with other trading parties, thereby placing them at a competitive disadvantage;
(e) make the conclusion of contracts subject to the acceptance by other parties of supplementary obligations which, by their nature or according to commercial usage, have no connection with the subject of such contracts.'

It is important to remember that the above lists examples of the type of 'behaviour' that contravenes Article 101 and is not intended to be exhaustive.

Article 101(2) provides that any agreement or decision prohibited under Article 101(1) is automatically void.

Article 101(3) provides that the provisions of Article 101 are inapplicable if the 'agreement' meets specified criteria, namely:

'– any agreement or category of agreements between undertakings;

– any decision or category of decisions by associations of undertakings;
– any concerted practice or category of concerted practices

which contributes to improving the production or distribution of goods or to promoting technical economic progress, while allowing consumers a fair share of the resulting benefit, and which does not:

(a) impose on the undertakings concerned restrictions which are not indispensable to the attainment of these objectives;
(b) afford such undertakings the possibility of eliminating competition in respect of a substantial part of the products in question.'

Prior to the Modernisation Regulation (Regulation 1/2003), which came into effect on 1 May 2004, the European Commission had sole power to grant an exemption under Article 101(3).

The Modernisation Regulation completely changes the procedural rules underlying Article 101, whilst at the same time transferring the power to deal with 'run of the mill' cases to the Member States (i.e. away from the Commission).

Before 1 May 2004 it was possible to apply to the Commission, prior to any agreement being entered into, for individual exemption under Article 101(3). This is no longer possible.

Instead, the undertakings will proceed on the basis that the 'agreement' falls outside Article 101 until being challenged by the national competition authority (NCA).

In the United Kingdom the NCA is the Office of Fair Trading (together with the courts).

Once challenged by the NCA, the burden falls upon the undertaking concerned to argue convincingly that the 'agreement' satisfies the Article 101(3) criteria.

In addition to the Article 101(3) exemption, the Commission has drafted a significant number of Block Exemptions that allow undertakings to enter into very specific agreements which meet requisite criteria.

Detailed consideration of the Block Exemptions falls outside the scope of this text. By way of very general summary, the Block Exemptions allow undertakings to enter into certain agreements providing the agreement does not contain 'hardcore' (i.e. absolutely prohibited) terms (e.g. price fixing, partitioning of territory etc.).

It is crucial, therefore, to scrutinise any proposed agreement between undertakings in order to be completely sure that either a Block Exemption will apply, or, in the event of being challenged by the NCA, that the agreement is covered by the Article 101(3) exemption.

An example of the effect of what is now Article 101 can be seen in *ICI* v *Commission (Dyestuffs)* [1972] ECR 619. Leading producers of aniline dye introduced identical price increases at identical times for the three years 1964, 1965 and 1967. The Commission found that the businesses had colluded amongst themselves so that the prices were increased at the same time. Customers therefore had no choice but to pay the increased prices. The businesses were 'substituting co-operation for the risks of competition'.

Whereas Article 101 is concerned with 'agreements' between undertakings (etc.) that may distort competition, Article 102 aims to prevent dominant undertakings from acting unilaterally in an abusive way.

Article 102 provides that:

'Any abuse by one or more undertakings of a dominant position within the internal market or in a substantial part of it shall be prohibited as incompatible with the internal market in so far as it may affect trade between Member States. Such abuse may, in particular, consist in:

(a) directly or indirectly imposing unfair purchase or selling prices or other unfair trading conditions;

(b) limiting production, markets, or technical development to the prejudice of consumers;

(c) applying dissimilar conditions to equivalent transactions with other trading parties, thereby placing them at a competitive disadvantage;

(d) making the conclusion of contracts subject to acceptance by the other parties of supplementary obligations which, by their nature or according to commercial usage, have no connection with the subject of such contracts.'

In *United Brands Co* v *Commission* [1978] ECR 207 the ECJ said that the term 'a dominant position' in what is now Article 102 'relates to a position of economic strength enjoyed by an undertaking which enables it to prevent effective competition being maintained on the relevant market by affording it the power to behave to an appreciable extent independently of its competitors, customers and ultimately of its consumers'. Article 102 does not define exactly what is meant by 'abuse' and conduct can be abusive even if it is not within the particular examples set out in paragraphs (a)–(d).

United Brands Co v *Commission* gives an example of the effect of what is now Article 102. United Brands, an American undertaking, was dominant with respect to production, distribution and retailing of bananas within the EC. They were found to be in breach of Article 102 as a result of abusing their dominant position on a number of counts, including refusal to supply to an individual wholesaler and operating discriminatory pricing between customers.

It is crucial to recognise that an undertaking will not breach Article 102 simply by being dominant in a particular product market. It is only where an undertaking abuses its dominant position (i.e. takes advantage of the fact) that it will be in breach of Article 102. Also the effect of the abuse must be capable of affecting trade between Member States, although any act which affects the overall structure of the market will be enough.

22.7.1.1 Enforcement

Article 6 of the Modernising Regulation gives NCAs the power to enforce Articles 101 and 102.

The Modernisation Regulation also sets out fines that can be imposed by NCAs for both procedural (i.e. failing to supply information when requested) and substantive contraventions of Articles 101 and 102.

Procedural infringements now carry a potential fine up to 1 per cent of the previous year's turnover. Much harsher fines will be imposed for substantive breaches (i.e. where undertakings, etc. act in a way that contravenes the anti-competitive rules contained in Articles 81 or 82 EC). Fines for substantive breaches can amount to up to 10 per cent of the undertaking's turnover in the previous year.

22.7.2 The Competition Act 1998

The Competition Act 1998 is comprised of four parts. Part 1 is divided into five chapters. Chapter I contains prohibitions which are similar to Article 101 of the Treaty on the Functioning of the European Union. Chapter II contains prohibitions which are similar to Article 82. However, the provisions of the Competition Act apply to practices affecting competition within the UK, rather than within the EU.

Section 2(1) sets out the Chapter I prohibition:

'Subject to subsection 3, agreements between undertakings, decisions by associations of undertakings or concerted practices which –

(a) may affect trade within the UK, and

(b) have as their object or effect the prevention, restriction or distortion of competition within the UK,

are prohibited unless they are exempt in accordance with the provisions of this Part.'

Section 2(3) provides that s.2(1) applies only if the agreement, decision or practice is, or is intended to be, implemented in the United Kingdom. Section 2(2) sets out examples of practices which would infringe s.2(1) and these examples are identical to those set out in Article 101(1) TFEU. They are not exhaustive. If an agreement or decision does infringe s.2(1), it is rendered void and illegal. It follows that a party who has made a payment under such an agreement may not be able to recover it. However, severance, considered earlier in Chapter 6 at 6.4.3.5, may be allowed.

The Office of Fair Trading (OFT) has issued Guidelines on the Chapter I prohibitions and these make it plain that s.2(1) will apply only where the impact on competition is appreciable.

Certain types of agreements are exempt from s.2(1), generally because they are already covered by some other statute. In addition, s.9 sets out block exemptions which are virtually identical to those found in the criteria for Article 101(3) TFEU.

Section 18(1) EC sets out the Chapter II prohibition. It provides:

'Subject to subsection 19, any conduct on the part of one or more undertakings which amounts to the abuse of a dominant position in a market is prohibited if it may affect trade within the UK.'

Section 18(2) sets out specific examples of such abuse and is identical to Article 102 TFEU. Section 18(3) provides that dominant position means a dominant position within the United Kingdom; and 'the UK' means the United Kingdom or any part of it. So a local undertaking not represented elsewhere in the country could infringe s.18(1). The Act does not specifically say so, but it seems that any agreement which infringes s.18(1) will be void. Section 19 exempts merger situations and certain other technical situations.

The Competition Act gives wide enforcement powers to the OFT, who can conduct inquiries and investigations. The OFT can also authorise officers of the OFT to enter premises without a warrant. Those who do not comply with investigations can commit criminal offences. The OFT can order that infringements cease and impose penalties.

22.7.3 **The Enterprise Act 2002**

The Enterprise Act 2002 does not replace the Competition Act 1998 but rather it complements it. The Act has 11 parts.

Part 1 abolishes the position of Director General of Fair Trading, transferring his duties to the Office of Fair Trading (OFT). Previously, the OFT had not existed as a legal entity in its own right but had given administrative support to the Director General. The OFT tries to promote good consumer practice and to make the public aware of how competition may benefit consumers. It also gives advice to Ministers and investigates a market which it does not think is working well for consumers. It has a board consisting of a chairman and at least four other members.

Part 2 provides for a new Competition Appeal Tribunal (CAT).

Part 3 provides a framework for controlling UK mergers and acquisitions. Decisions on whether mergers need to be controlled have been taken away from the Secretary of State and are to be taken by the OFT or the Competition Commission (CC). Furthermore, mergers will be prohibited on the basis that they would cause a substantial lessening of competition, rather than on the previous basis that they were contrary to the public interest. The OFT has a duty to investigate if a company targeted for merger has a UK turnover of over £70 million. It also has a duty to investigate if the merged companies would between them supply at least 25 per cent of either goods or services of a particular description in the UK or in a substantial part of the UK. If the OFT considers that a merger may result in a substantial lessening of competition it must either refer the matter to the CC or get appropriate assurances from the companies which propose to merge. But the OFT does not have to refer if the market is not important enough to justify a reference or if the obvious benefits to consumers would outweigh the adverse effect on competition. If the CC considers that there will be a substantial lessening of competition it can either prohibit the merger, impose remedies or seek assurances. Special rules apply to newspaper and water company mergers. The CAT has the right to review decisions on mergers taken by the OFT, the CC or the Secretary of State if such a review is applied for.

Part 4 allows the CC to investigate markets where it appears that competition is being harmed by the structure of the market or the conduct of suppliers or customers. Either the OFT or the regulators of industries which were previously nationalised, such as the Rail Regulator, can refer a market to the CC for investigation. The OFT can do this on the grounds that one or more features of the market prevents, restricts or distorts competition in relation to the supply or acquisition of goods or services in the United Kingdom or a part of it. Ministers have a similar power. If the CC finds that competition is being prevented, restricted or distorted it can take remedies to rectify the situation. An appeal can be made to the CAT, asking it to review a decision of the OFT, the CC or the Secretary of State.

Part 6 creates a new cartel offence. Section 188 of the Enterprise Act provides that an individual is guilty of an offence if he or she dishonestly agrees with one or more other persons that undertakings will engage in one or more of the following prohibited cartel activities: price-fixing; limitation of supply or production; market-sharing; or bid-rigging. The offence is committed by the mere fact of agreement, there is no need that the agreement should be implemented. However, the offence applies only to horizontal agreements, that is to say to agreements between individuals at the same level in the supply chain. It does not apply to vertical agreements, that is to say to agreements between individuals at different levels of the supply chain. There is a requirement for dishonesty but there is no requirement that the agreement be actually implemented. On conviction on indictment, offenders can be sentenced to five years' imprisonment and an unlimited fine. The OFT has the power to grant a 'no-action letter' to give immunity to prosecution to individuals who admit participation in the criminal offence. Such a letter will be granted to individuals who provide the OFT with all information which they have about the cartel if they maintain cooperation throughout the investigation, did not coerce another undertaking to take part in the cartel and refrain from participating in the cartel. If these conditions are subsequently breached, the no-action letter can be revoked. Further offences can be committed by: unreasonably failing to comply with a requirement to answer questions or provide information or documents (maximum sentence six months); making false or misleading statements (maximum sentence two years); and destroying, concealing or falsifying documents which are relevant to an investigation (five years' imprisonment). As regards all of these offences the offender can be fined instead of, or as well as, imprisoned.

Part 7 gives the OFT the power to ask the High Court to make a Competition Disqualification Order. Such an order would be granted, and would disqualify an individual from being a director of a company, if the court was satisfied that his conduct as an individual makes him unfit to be concerned in the management of a company. Such conduct might have arisen in connection with the cartel offence, or infringements of Articles 101 or 102 TFEU, or Chapter I or Chapter II of the Competition Act prohibitions.

Part 8 allows designated consumer bodies to make 'super complaints' about market features which relate to markets as a whole.

Part 9 sets out new rules on the enforcement of certain consumer regulations. (See this chapter at 22.6.)

Part 10 changes insolvency law. (See Chapter 19 at 19.1.4.5.)

Part 11 deals with several technical matters.

22.8 THE BRIBERY ACT 2010

The Bribery Act 2010 has reformed the law by creating new offences relating to bribery. The previous law was contained in several statutes that were over 100 years old. These statutes no longer adequately dealt with modern business practices. However, the Act has been criticised on the grounds that it is vague and that it will unnecessarily hamper British companies that operate abroad. As a consequence of these criticisms the Act's implementation was delayed until late 2011, and the Ministry of Justice has set out guidelines as to what British businesses must do to conform to the Act.

22.8.1 The offences

The Bribery Act 2010 has created four new offences relating to bribery. **Section 1 creates the offence of bribing another person.** This offence can be committed in two different ways, known as Case 1 and Case 2. The *actus reus* of both Case 1 and Case 2 is committed by offering, promising or giving a financial or other advantage to another person. The *mens rea* of the Case 1 offence requires that the accused intends the advantage given (i) to induce a person to perform improperly a relevant activity or function, or (ii) to reward a person for the improper performance of such a function or activity. It does not matter whether the person bribed is the same person as the person who is to improperly perform the activity or function. For example, the offence would be committed by paying a firm's manager to make sure that a buying clerk placed an order for goods with a particular supplier.

The *actus reus* of the Case 2 offence has already been set out: offering, promising or giving a financial or other advantage to another person. The *mens rea* is that the accused knows or believes that the acceptance of the advantage would itself constitute the improper performance of a relevant function or activity. As regards both Case 1 and Case 2 it does not matter whether the advantage is offered, promised or given by the accused directly or through a third party.

Section 2 creates several offences relating to being bribed. These offences are called Case 3, Case 4, Case 5 and Case 6. The Case 3 offence is committed by an accused who requests, agrees to receive or accepts a financial or other advantage, intending that, in consequence, a relevant function or activity should be performed improperly. The improper performance can be by the accused or by another person. The Case 4 offence is committed by an accused who requests, agrees to receive or accepts a financial or other advantage, and the request, agreement or acceptance itself constitutes the improper performance by the accused of a relevant function or activity. The Case 5 offence is committed by an accused who requests, agrees to receive or accepts a financial or other advantage as a reward for the improper performance (by the accused or by another person) of a relevant function or activity. The Case 6 offence is committed where, in anticipation of or in consequence of the accused requesting, agreeing to receive or accepting a financial or other advantage, a relevant function or activity is performed improperly. The improper performance can be either by the accused or by another person with the accused's assent or acquiescence. As regards Cases 3–6 it does not matter whether the accused requests, agrees to receive or accepts the advantage directly or through a third party. Not does it matter whether the advantage is for the benefit of the accused or for the benefit of another person. As regards Cases 4–6, it does not matter whether the accused knew or believed that the performance of the function or activity was improper. In Case 6, where a person other than the accused is performing the function or activity, it does not matter whether the person knows or believes that the performance of the function or activity is improper.

Section 6 makes it an offence **to bribe foreign officials.** The accused must intend to influence the foreign official in his capacity as a foreign official. The accused must also intend to obtain or retain business, or intend to obtain or retain an advantage in the conduct of business. Furthermore, the offence is committed only if the accused, directly or through a third party, promises or gives any financial or other advantage to the foreign official or gives it to another person at the foreign official's request or with his assent or acquiescence.

Section 7 makes it an offence **for a commercial organisation to fail to prevent bribery.** This offence is committed by a commercial organisation (C) if a person connected with C bribes another person intending to obtain or retain business for C, or intending to obtain or retain an advantage in the conduct of business for C. However, it is a defence for C to prove that C had in place adequate protection procedures to prevent persons connected with C from undertaking such conduct.

22.8.1.1 A relevant function or activity

Both ss.1 and 2 refer to the improper performance of a relevant function or activity. A relevant function or activity is defined by s.3 as one which is either:

'(a) of a public nature;
(b) any activity connected with a business;
(c) any activity performed in the course of a person's employment; or
(d) any activity performed by or on behalf of a body of persons such as a company or a partnership.'

However, a function can be a relevant function only if the person performing it is expected to perform it in good faith, or impartially or if the person performing it is in a position of trust by virtue of performing it. The function or activity does not need to be performed in the UK or to have a connection with the UK.

22.8.1.2 Improper performance to which the bribe relates

Section 4 provides that a relevant function or activity is performed improperly if it is performed in breach of a relevant expectation, or if there is a failure to perform the function or activity and that failure is itself a breach of a relevant expectation. **Section 5 sets out an expectation test.** For the purposes of ss.3 and 4 the test of what is expected is a test of what a reasonable person in the UK would expect in relation to the performance of the type of function or activity concerned. For example, it would be expected that a police officer should not take money to overlook a crime. Where the function or activity is not subject to the law of the UK, any local custom or practice is to be disregarded unless it is permitted or required by the written law of the country concerned.

22.8.1.3 Defences and penalties

It is a defence for an accused to prove that his conduct was required by the armed forces or the intelligence services. The maximum penalty for offences under ss.1, 2 or 6 is ten years imprisonment or a fine. The section 7 offence is punishable only by a fine.

Test your understanding 22.2

1 In broad terms, how can a producer commit an offence under the General Product Safety Regulations 2005?

2 What three offences are created by the Computer Misuse Act 1990?

3 What powers does the OFT have to ensure that consumer protection legislation is complied with?

4 What is the effect of Articles 101 and 102 TFEU?

5 What is the effect of the Chapter I and Chapter II prohibitions in the Competition Act 1998?

6 On what basis can mergers be prohibited under the Enterprise Act 2002?

7 On what basis can the OFT refer a market to the CC for investigation?

8 How is the cartel offence in s.188 of the Enterprise Act committed?

9 What offences are created by ss.1, 6 and 7 of the Bribery Act 2010?

Key points

The nature of criminal liability

■ The *actus reus* of an offence is the external element of the definition of the offence which is objectively required before the crime can be committed. The *mens rea* is the mental state of the accused which the prosecution will need to prove in order to establish that the offence was committed.

■ A crime of strict liability is one which does not require the prosecution to prove *mens rea* in respect of one or more elements of the *actus reus*.

The Consumer Protection from Unfair Trading Regulations 2008

■ The Consumer Protection from Unfair Trading Regulations 2008 prohibit unfair commercial practices.

■ A commercial practice is generally unfair if: (a) it contravenes the requirements of professional diligence; and (b) it materially distorts or is likely to materially distort the economic behaviour of the average consumer with regard to the product.

■ It is an offence knowingly or recklessly to engage in a commercial practice which is generally unfair.

■ A commercial practice is also unfair if it is: (a) a misleading action; (b) a misleading omission; (c) an aggressive commercial action; or (d) it is listed in Schedule 1 of the Regulations. It is an offence of strict liability to commit a commercial practice which is unfair in one of these ways.

The Business Protection from Misleading Marketing Regulations 2008

■ The Business Protection from Misleading Marketing Regulations 2008 prohibit deceptive advertising by a trader if it is likely to affect the economic behaviour of another trader or to injure a competitor.

Product safety

■ The General Product Safety Regulations 2005 impose criminal liability in respect of unsafe products.

■ Regulation 5 provides that a producer would commit an offence by: placing an unsafe product on the market; offering or agreeing to place an unsafe product on the market; exposing or possessing an unsafe product for placing on the market; offering or agreeing to supply an unsafe product; or supplying an unsafe product.

■ An unsafe product is one which does not present any risk or only the minimum risks compatible with the product's use, considered to be acceptable and consistent with a high level of protection for the safety and health of persons.

■ A product is defined as any product intended for consumers or likely to be used by consumers and which was supplied in the course of a commercial activity. However, products used exclusively in the context of a commercial activity are excluded.

→

- Regulation 13 of the General Product Safety Regulations 2005 makes it an offence for a producer or distributor to:
  a offer or agree to place on the market any dangerous product or expose or possess any such product on the market; or
  b offer or agree to supply any dangerous product or expose or possess any such product for supply.

Misuse of computers

- Section 1 of the Computer Misuse Act makes it an offence to cause a computer to perform any function with the intention of securing access to a program or data where this access is known to be unauthorised.
- Section 2 of the Computer Misuse Act makes it an offence to commit the s.1 offence with the intention of committing, or facilitating the commission of, an offence which carries a sentence of at least five years' imprisonment.
- Section 3 of the Computer Misuse Act makes it an offence to intentionally modify computer material while knowing that this is unauthorised.

Competition law

- Article 101 TFEU renders void all agreements between undertakings, decisions by associations of undertakings and concerted practices which may affect trade between Member States which have as their object or effect the prevention, restriction or distortion of competition within the EC.
- Article 102 TFEU prevents dominant undertakings from acting in an abusive way.
- The Competition Act 1998 Chapter I prohibits agreements between undertakings, decisions by associations of undertakings or concerted practices which may affect trade within the United Kingdom, and which have as their object or effect the prevention, restriction or distortion of competition within the United Kingdom.

- The Chapter II prohibition prohibits any conduct on the part of one or more undertakings which amounts to the abuse of a dominant position in a market if it may affect trade within the United Kingdom.
- The Enterprise Act 2002 abolished the office of Director General of Fair Trading, his duties passing to the Office of Fair Trading (OFT).
- Under the Enterprise Act mergers will be prohibited if they would cause a substantial lessening of competition.
- The OFT has a duty to investigate if a company targeted for merger has a United Kingdom turnover of over £70 million.
- The Competition Commission can investigate markets where it appears that competition is being harmed by the structure of the market or the conduct of suppliers or customers.
- Section 188 of the Enterprise Act provides that an individual is guilty of an offence if he dishonestly agrees with one or more other persons that undertakings will engage in one or more of the following prohibited cartel activities: price-fixing; limitation of supply or production; market-sharing; or bid-rigging.
- The High Court can make a Competition Disqualification Order, disqualifying an individual from being a director of a company, if it was satisfied that his conduct as an individual makes him unfit to be concerned in the management of a company. Such conduct might have arisen in connection with the cartel offence, or infringements of Articles 81 or 82 EC, or the Chapter I or Chapter II Competition Act prohibitions.

Bribery

- The Bribery Act 2010 has created offences of bribing another person, taking or asking for bribes, bribing foreign officials and failure to prevent bribery.

Summary questions

1 Consider whether or not an offence had been committed under the Consumer Protection from Unfair Trading Regulations 2008 in the following circumstances:

a A representative from a holiday company drives consumers to a remote area of Dartmoor and refuses to bring them back until they agree to take out extra holiday insurance.

b A trader increases his prices by more than the rate of inflation.

c A debt collector threatens a debtor with imprisonment for debt if he does not settle the debt immediately. (It is not possible to be imprisoned for debt.)

d A car dealer reduces the allowance on a car which a consumer is trading in by untruthfully saying that the car has no chance of passing its MOT.

e A postman sells potatoes which he has grown in his garden, describing them as organically grown, which they are not.

f A manufacturer of furniture, who never sells direct to consumers, falsely describes his beds, in a newspaper advertisement, as made from oak.

g A holiday company advertises that a hotel has a swimming pool when it does not.

h A trader advertises televisions which are for sale as 'new', without revealing that they have been reconditioned.

i An estate agent describes a house as having three double bedrooms when the third 'bedroom' is too small to fit a bed in.

2 In February 1999 Jim booked a holiday in Scotland with AB Holidays Ltd. The holiday was booked after Jim read AB's 1998 holiday brochure at a 'selected customer event' for old-age pensioners at a hotel some 50 miles from where he lived. AB's brochure stated that the hotel which Jim had chosen was 'within a stone's throw of the beach'. The brochure also said that the hotel had its own 18-hole golf course, and that this was reserved solely for the hotel's guests. Jim booked the holiday only because those at the 'selected customer event' were told that they could not leave the hotel where the event was held until they had booked a holiday.

When he returned from his holiday, Jim complained to his local trading standards department that the hotel was at the top of a sheer 300 foot cliff, that it took 35 minutes to walk to the beach, and that the golf course was closed while its greens were being re-laid. At the time when Jim booked the holiday, AB Holidays Ltd knew that the golf course greens were to be re-laid but it was believed that the job would have been completed by the time of Jim's holiday.

Advise AB Holidays Ltd of any liability they may have under the Consumer Protection from Unfair Trading Regulations 2008.

3 The Nottville Leisure Centre (NLC) advertised a series of tennis lessons in the local newspaper. The advertisement stated that the first person to sign up to the lessons would be provided with a free Slazenger tennis racquet. Alonso, who wrote the advertisement, had intended that it should say that the first person to sign up would get a free box of Slazenger tennis balls. Alonso had checked the advertisement over before sending it to the newspaper. Elspeth was the first person to sign up for the lessons. When she received the free tennis balls, rather than the free racquet, she complained to her local Trading Standards Officer. This officer threatened NLC with prosecution and so Alonso gave Elspeth a free Slazenger tennis racquet. Trading Standards Officers are also threatening NLC with prosecution in respect of an offer to reduce the price of gym membership. The offer was made by leaflet to all the members of a local hostel for adults with learning difficulties. The leaflet said that the price of membership was, in effect, £30. The leaflet went on to explain that although the normal annual subscription of £60 had to paid at the outset, £30 would be refunded if a questionnaire was completed within six weeks of joining the gym. Several members of the hostel joined and paid the £60 but did not complete a questionnaire in time and therefore did not receive the refund.

Advise NLC of any criminal liability which might have been incurred in respect of the free tennis racquet and the offer of reduced rate gym membership.

4 Susan buys an electric hedge-cutter from Blunder Ltd DIY store. The hedge-cutters are part of a consignment which were manufactured in the United Kingdom by Cutcost Co Ltd. Blunder's manager saw a documentary on television which revealed that two people in Scotland have been severely electrocuted while using this type of hedge-cutter on damp hedges. As the documentary made clear, the instructions which come with the hedge-cutters clearly state that they should never be used on wet hedges and never used without a circuit breaker. Blunder Ltd do not make any attempt to recall hedge-cutters already sold, but do decide not to order any more.

While cutting the hedge after a heavy shower, Susan's gardener, Henry, is electrocuted by the hedge-cutter and suffers severe burns.

Explain any criminal liability which either Blunder Ltd or Cutcost Co Ltd might be under.

Multiple choice questions

1 Consider the following statements, made in relation to the Consumer Protection from Unfair Trading Regulations 2008.

a An unfair commercial practice can have occurred even if no commercial transaction has occurred.

b Only a trader can engage in a commercial practice.

c A trader could engage in an unfair commercial practice when buying goods from a consumer.

d A shop assistant can be regarded as a trader.

Which of the above statements are true?

i (a), (b) and (c) only.

ii (a) and (b) only.

iii (a), (d) and (c) only.

iv (b), (c) and (d) only.

v All of the statements.

2 Which one of the following statements, made in relation to the Consumer Protection from Unfair Trading Regulations 2008, is not true?

a A commercial practice cannot be unfair under reg.3 unless it materially distorts or is likely to materially distort the economic behaviour of the average consumer with regard to a product.

b A consumer's decision not to enforce a guarantee given with a product could be a 'transactional decision', even if the decision was made three months after the product was bought.

c A trader who adheres to an approved code of practice will always be regarded as having been professionally diligent.

d The offence created by reg.8 requires *mens rea*, but the offences created by regs.9–12 do not.

3 Which one of the following statements, made in relation to the Consumer Protection from Unfair Trading Regulations 2008, is not true?

a A commission of any of the 31 commercial practices set out in Schedule 1 will always be considered unfair, even if no consumer might have been induced to behave differently.

b If any of the 31 commercial practices set out in Schedule 1 are committed then an offence will always have been committed under reg.12.

c A consumer can be convicted of an offence under reg.16, the by-pass provision.

d A special defence is available to advertisers who innocently publish advertisements.

4 Which one of the following statements, made in relation to the Business Protection from Misleading Marketing Regulations 2008, is not true?

a The aim of the Regulations is not consumer protection.

b The Regulations do not create an offence of issuing comparative advertising.

c If advertising misleads, or is likely to mislead, only consumers no offence will have been created under the Regulations.

d A consumer can never be guilty of an offence under the Regulations.

Task 22

Your employer has asked you to draft a report briefly outlining the following matters.

a The main effect of the Consumer Protection from Unfair Trading Regulations 2008.

b The main effect of the Business Protection from Misleading Marketing Regulations 2008.

c The offences relating to the supply of unsafe products created by the General Product Safety Regulations 2005.

d The offences created by the Computer Misuse Act 1990.

e An overview of competition law.

f The main offences created by the Bribery Act 2010.

23

Business property

Introduction

23.1 LEGAL CONCEPTS OF PROPERTY

The common law categorises all property as either real property or as personal property. Real property is comprised of all freehold interests in land. Personal property is comprised of all other property, including leasehold interests in land. This distinction arose because historically a person who was dispossessed of real property could bring what was known as a real action to regain possession of the land. A person dispossessed of personal property could only bring a personal action, that is to say that he could only bring an action against the person who had dispossessed him, rather than an action which gave him a right to recover the property itself. Although leasehold interests in land are classed as personal property rather than as real property, most businesses would regard freehold and leasehold interests in land as much the same type of property. For most practical purposes leasehold interests in land have much more in common with real property than with other types of personal property (such as goods) or intangible rights (such as copyright).

Personal property is itself classified as either chattels real or chattels personal. Chattels real consist of leasehold interests in land. Chattels personal consist of all the remaining types of personal property. Chattels personal are divided into choses in possession, choses in action and intangible personal property. Choses in possession are movable things of which physical possession can be taken, for example goods. Choses in action are intangible property rights which can only be enforced by taking legal action, for example the rights attaching to shares in a company. Finally, choses in action may be split into documentary and non-documentary choses in action. Documentary choses in action are represented by documents, such as bills of lading, which give a tangible form to a right to money or goods. The rights represented by the document can be transferred to a third party by delivering the document to him, and if necessary by endorsing the document. Choses in action other than documentary choses are non-documentary choses and consist of absolutely intangible rights such as a debt. These rights can be transferred to another by assignment. Intellectual property such as patents, copyright

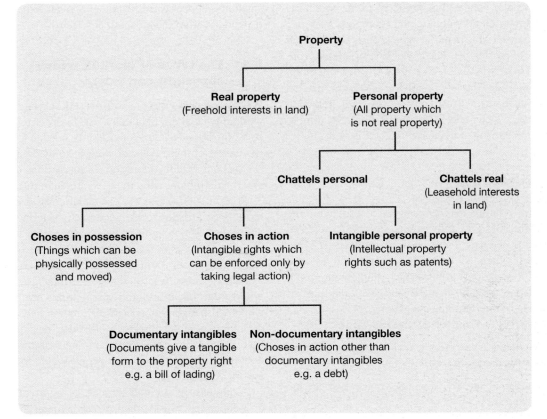

Figure 23.1 The legal classification of property

and trade marks are best regarded as intangible personal property, as various statutes indicate that they are not choses in action.

The different types of property can be seen in Figure 23.1.

At common law personal property can either be owned or possessed. No other rights regarding property are recognised. But equity recognises other rights, such as a beneficiary's rights under a trust. Equity also recognises powers concerning property, these powers only being exercisable against certain other people. A good example is provided by the power of a person to rescind a voidable contract and thereby regain ownership of property which passed under the contract. (Rescission is examined in Chapter 6 at 6.1.3.) It should also be realised that property rights are not absolute. For example, we saw in Chapter 9, at 9.3.8, that until January 1995 a person who bought goods in good faith in a market overt could defeat any claim to ownership by a person from whom the goods had been stolen. The person from whom the goods had

been stolen might have considered his ownership total, but his inability to regain the goods would reveal that this was not in fact the case.

Generally, a person who owns property will have both legal and equitable ownership. However, this is not necessarily the case. For example, when a trust exists the trustees have legal ownership of the property whilst the beneficiaries have equitable ownership.

Both the common law and equity recognise co-ownership of personal chattels. The common law recognises that a chattel might be co-owned either by joint tenants or by tenants in common. Equity has always recognised that chattels may be the subject of several equitable interests. Statutes too recognise co-ownership. For example, in Chapter 9 at 9.1.3, we saw that s.20A of the Sale of Goods Act 1979 allows a person who has bought a specified quantity of uncertained goods which form part of a bulk to become an owner in common of the bulk, even though his share of the bulk has not been ascertained.

The major intellectual property rights are fairly well known. These would include copyright, patents, trade marks, rights in performance, design rights, and the law of passing-off. The law of passing-off was considered briefly in Chapter 15 at 15.4.1.3. In this chapter we consider the law relating to copyright, patents and trade marks. We also consider the Data Protection Act 1998, which seeks to ensure that data relating to identifiable living individuals are not misused.

23.2 COPYRIGHT

The law relating to copyright is governed by the Copyright, Designs and Patents Act 1988, referred to in this section of the book as the Act. The Act has been amended by the Copyright and Related Rights Regulations 2003, which implemented the Information Society Directive (2001/39) and fulfilled a number of international obligations.

Section 1(1) of the Act defines copyright:

'Copyright is a property right which subsists . . . in the following descriptions of work –

(a) original literary, dramatic, musical or artistic works,
(b) sound recordings, films, or broadcasts and
(c) the typographical arrangements of published editions.'

Copyright protects the way in which ideas are expressed, rather than the ideas themselves. The matters listed in s.1(1)(a) must be original. In *University of London Press Ltd* v *University Tutorial Press Ltd* [1916] 2 Ch 601 Peterson J said: 'The word original does not in this connection mean that the work must be the expression of original or inventive thought. Copyright Acts are not concerned with the originality of ideas, but with the expression of thought, and in the case of a literary work, with the expression of thought in print, writing or recorded spoken words. The originality which is required relates to the expression of the thought.' In the case it was decided that mathematics exams which drew on the stock of knowledge common to mathematicians were literary works. In other words what is required is that the copyright work must originate from the author and not have been copied from someone else.

It is not essential that the work must have taken a long time to complete, but the *de minimis* principle will prevent single words, such as brand names, or very small numbers of words from being regarded as artistic works, within the meaning of s.1(1)(a).

23.2.1 The types of work in which copyright can exist

We have seen that s.1(1) of the Act sets out the types of work in which copyright can exist. In order to understand the boundaries of copyright we need to examine the nature of these types of work in some detail. The Act sets out specific definitions of the various matters and the definitions need to be examined in turn.

Section 1(1)(a) refers to original literary, dramatic, musical or artistic works. Section 3(1) defines both 'literary work' and 'musical work'. This rather lengthy definition tells us that a literary work might be written, spoken or sung and therefore classifies song lyrics as literary works. It also tells us that databases, computer programs, tables and compilations are literary works. Although not specifically mentioned in the definition, a street directory has been held to be a literary work. It is therefore plain that a literary work does not have to be what most people would regard as a work of literature.

A database is defined by s.3A(1) as a collection of independent works, data or other material which (a) are arranged in a systematic or methodical way, and (b) are individually accessible by electronic or other means. However, a database can only be regarded as a literary work under the Act if the content of the database is original work and the database is creative (as regards matters such as layout or method of delivery). So it is the intellectual creativity of the author which is being protected. However, if the database content is original work but the database is not creative, for example if it consists of a list of UK companies, the content will retain full copyright protection as a literary work but the database will hold a separate 'database right'. This right will arise if there has been a substantial investment in obtaining, verifying or presenting the contents of the database. The database right arises automatically as soon as the database is put into a recorded form. As is the case with copyright, there is no need to register it. However, the database right lasts for only 15 years after the end of the year in which the database was completed or first made available to the public.

A musical work is defined as a work consisting of music, exclusive of any words or action intended to be sung, spoken or performed with the music. A dramatic work is not defined, but includes a work of dance or mime as well as the more obvious example of a script for a play. Artistic work is not concerned with artistic quality at all where photographs, graphic works, sculptures and collages are concerned. However, works of architecture and of artistic craftsmanship do require artistic quality.

Section 3(2) of the 1988 Act provides that copyright does not exist in a literary, dramatic or musical work until it is recorded, in writing or otherwise. However, the recording does not need to be done by the author or with the author's permission.

The matters set out in s.1(1)(a) need to be original works in the sense that they must involve an original expression of an idea. The matters listed in s.1(1)(b) and (c) are derivative. They are based upon and derived from an original work. For example, most popular films are derivative works which are based upon an original work, the film script.

Sound recordings are defined by s.5A(1) of the Act. They mean (a) a recording of sounds, from which the sounds may be reproduced, or (b) a recording of the whole or any part of a literary, dramatic or musical work, from which sounds reproducing the work or part may be produced. Recordings can be sound recordings regardless of the medium on which they are made or the method by which the sounds are reproduced or produced. Copyright does not exist to the extent that a sound recording is a copy taken from a previous sound recording. The use of the word 'sound' means that speech and other noises are included, and that any musical quality or other quality of the sounds is not a factor.

Films are defined by s.5B(1) as recordings on any medium from which a moving image may by any means be reproduced. An accompanying sound track is treated as part of the film. Copyright does not exist in a film to the extent that it is a copy of a previous film.

Section 6(1) has been amended by the 2003 Regulations to give a new definition of 'broadcasts':

'A broadcast is an electronic transmission of visual images, sounds or other information which –

(a) is transmitted for simultaneous reception by members of the public and is capable of being lawfully received by them, or
(b) is transmitted at a time determined solely by the person making the transmission for presentation to members of the public.'

Section 6(1A) provides that Internet transmissions are not broadcasts unless they are one of the following:

'(a) a transmission taking place simultaneously on the internet and by other means;
(b) a concurrent transmission of a live event; or
(c) a transmission of recorded moving images or sounds forming part of a programme service offered by the person responsible for making the transmission, being a service in which programmes are transmitted at scheduled times determined by that person.'

Section 6(2) provides that an encrypted transmission (such as pay-per-view tv) shall be regarded as capable of being lawfully received by members of the public only if decoding equipment has been made available to members of the public by or with the authority of the person making the transmission or the person providing the contents of the transmission.

Section 1(1)(c) provided that copyright could subsist in the typographical arrangements of published editions. Typography is the art of planning and setting out type so that a work may be printed. Section 8(1) states that 'published edition' in the context of copyright in the typographical arrangement of a published edition, means a published edition of the whole or any part of one or more literary, dramatic or musical works. Although most readers of a book would recognise that the author had copyright in the words, they might not realise that the publisher has copyright in the typographical arrangement of the book.

23.2.2 Authorship and ownership of copyright

The Act defines the author of a work as the person who created it. In the case of a film the authors will be taken to be the producer and principal director, who will be joint owners if they are not the same person. As regards the typographical arrangements of published editions, the publisher is regarded as the author. The author of a work will be the first owner of it. However, s.11(2) provides that where a literary, dramatic, musical or artistic work, or a film, is made by an employee in the course of his employment, the employer is the first owner of any copyright in the work subject to any agreement to the contrary.

23.2.3 Duration of copyright

Copyright exists for different lengths of time, depending upon the type of work concerned. As regards the copyright in literary, dramatic, musical or artistic works, the copyright expires at the end of 70 years from the end of the calendar year in which the author dies. However, if the work is computer-generated, copyright expires at the end of the period of 50 years from the end of the calendar year in which the work was made. A work will not be a computer-generated work merely because it was produced on a word processor. Section 178 provides that a work is computer-generated if it is generated by computer in circumstances such that there is no human author of the work. There is considerable debate as to the circumstances in which this might happen. One pos-sible example might be provided by weather reports produced by a computer which automatically took information from various weather centres.

Section 13A provides that copyright in a sound recording expires:

'(a) at the end of the period of 50 years from the end of the calendar year in which the recording is made, or

(b) if during that period it is published, 50 years from the end of the calendar year in which it is first published; or

(c) if during that period the recording is not published but is made available to the public by being played in public or communicated to the public, 50 years from the end of the calendar year in which it is first so made available,

but in determining whether a sound recording has been published, played in public or communicated to the public, no account shall be taken of any unauthorised act.'

It would therefore be possible for the copyright in a sound recording to exist for 100 years after it was made, if the sound recording was not published until 50 years after it was made.

The copyright in films expires 70 years from the end of the calendar year in which the death occurs of the last to die of:

(a) the principal director;

(b) the author of the screenplay;

(c) the author of the dialogue; or

(d) the composer of music specially created for and used in the film.

Copyright in a broadcast expires at the end of the period of 50 years from the end of the calendar year in which the broadcast was made. Copyright in typographical arrangements of published editions expires at the end of 25 years from the end of the calendar year in which the edition was first published.

Special rules apply to Crown and Parliamentary copyright. As regards literary, dramatic, musical or artistic work, Crown or Parliamentary copyright does not expire until 125 years from the end of the calendar year in which the work was created. As regards Acts of Parliament, copyright expires 50 years after the end of the year in which the Act was given the Royal Assent.

23.2.4 **Rights of copyright owners**

Section 16(1) gives the copyright owner the exclusive right to:

(a) copy the work;

(b) issue copies of the work to the public;

(c) rent or lend the work to the public;

(d) perform, show or play the work in public;

(e) communicate the work to the public;

(f) make an adaptation of the work or do any of the above in relation to an adaptation.

If any person does any of the above restricted acts without the licence of the copyright holder, or authorises anyone else to do this, copyright in the work is infringed. It is important to remember that what is protected is not an idea, but the way in which an idea is expressed. It is also important to realise that infringement does not need to be intentional and can be committed subconsciously. There must, however, be a causal connection. The work must be copied.

A little needs to be said about the various matters in respect of which the copyright owner has exclusive rights. Copying the work can be done by storing the work electronically, for example by downloading material onto a computer, CD or DVD. In relation to a film or broadcast, copying can be done by making a photograph of the whole or any substantial part of any image forming part of the film or broadcast. Making a video recording of a film would probably be the most common way in which this is done. In relation to typographical arrangements of published editions, copying can only be done by making a facsimile copy of the arrangement, for example by photocopying it.

A new section, s.28A, allows the making of temporary copies in certain circumstances such as browsing on the Internet. It provides that copyright in a literary work, other than a computer program or a database, or in a dramatic, musical or artistic work, the typographical arrangement of a published edition, a sound recording or a film, is not infringed by the making of a temporary copy which is transient or incidental, which is an integral and essential part of a technological process and the sole purpose of which is to enable: (a) a transmission of the work in a network between third parties by an intermediary; or (b) a lawful use of the work; and which has no independent economic significance.

Section 16(3)(a) provides that restricted acts must relate to the work as a whole or to any substantial part of it. This creates a difficulty in that the Act does not define what is meant by a substantial part. Each case is decided on its own facts, and there is no given percentage above which a substantial part is reached. It is not the quantity of the work copied which is relevant, but the quality. If the most 'important' part of a work was copied this might be a substantial part even if it was not a large percentage of the work. An important factor for consideration, but only a factor, is whether the work alleged to have been copied is in competition with the copyrighted work.

Infringement by issuing copies to the public would be committed by putting into circulation copies which had not previously been put into circulation by or with the consent of the copyright owner. The right of the copyright owner to issue works to the public for the first time is known as the 'distribution right'. Once copies have been put on the market in the EEA, this right is exhausted.

Copyright can be infringed by renting the work for commercial gain. Lending of the work to the public without gaining any commercial advantage can also infringe copyright. The performance of a literary, dramatic or musical work in public includes delivery in a lecture or speech and any mode of visual or acoustic presentation. If the copyright is infringed by being shown by electronic means, the person by whom the visual images or sounds are sent is not regarded as responsible for the infringement. Section 182 of the Act deals with performers' rights. It provides that a performer's rights are infringed if a person (without consent) makes a recording of the whole or any substantial part of a qualifying performance directly from a live performance, broadcasts the performance live or makes a recording from a broadcast of the live performance.

Section 16(1)(e) gives the copyright owner the exclusive right to make an adaptation of a literary, dramatic or musical work. Adaptations of works include translations, conversions of a dramatic work into a non-dramatic work and vice versa, and conveying the work in pictures. In relation to computer programs and databases, adaptation includes making an arrangement or altered version of the work. A computer program is regarded as having been translated if it is converted into or out of a computer language or code, or into a different computer language or code.

Section 23 provides that:

'The copyright in a work is infringed by a person who, without the licence of the copyright owner –

(a) possesses in the course of a business;
(b) sells or lets for hire, or offers or exposes for sale or hire;
(c) in the course of a business exhibits in public or distributes; or
(d) distributes otherwise than in the course of a business to such an extent as to affect prejudicially the owner of the copyright,

an article which is, and which he knows or has reason to believe is, an infringing copy of the work.'

This is known as secondary infringement, whereby the perpetrator does not himself copy the work but rather he exploits it commercially. It can be seen from the definition that secondary infringement can only be committed when the perpetrator knows or has reason to believe that copyright is being infringed. This is in contrast to primary infringement which, as we have seen, can be committed subconsciously.

The Act lists at great length various acts which are permitted in relation to copyright works. The more important of these relate to the following: 'Fair dealing with a literary work (other than a database), or a dramatic, musical or artistic work for the purposes of research or private study does not infringe copyright.' The Act does not define the meaning of fair dealing. In *Hubbard v Vosper* [1972] 2 QB 84 at 94 Lord Denning MR said:

'It is impossible to define what is "fair dealing". It must be a question of degree. You must consider first the number and extent of the quotations and extracts. Are they altogether too many and too long to be fair? Then you must consider the use made of them. If they are used as a basis for comment, criticism or review, that may be fair dealing. If they are used to convey the same information as the author, for a rival purpose, that may be unfair. Next, you must consider the proportions. To take long extracts and attach short comments may be unfair. But short extracts and long comments may be fair. Other considerations may come to mind also. But, after all is said and done, it must be a matter of impression.'

As regards a database, fair dealing for the purposes of research and private study will not infringe copyright as long as the source is indicated. In the cases of criticism, review and news reporting, fair dealing does not infringe copyright provided that it is accompanied by a sufficient acknow-ledgement. Where a work is incidentally included in an artistic work, sound recording, film, broadcast or cable programme, copyright in the work is not infringed.

As well as these generally permitted acts, special exemptions also apply as regards things done for the purpose of education, as regards libraries and archives, and as regards things done for the purposes of Parliamentary or judicial proceedings.

If the copyright is transferred by the author to another by way of assignment then the transferee takes over from the author all rights in respect of infringement. The assignment may be partial, in that it may apply to only some of the things which the copyright holder has the exclusive right to do. It may also be partial in that it may be for a shorter period of time than that for which the copyright is to exist. An assignment of copyright will only be effective if it is signed by or on behalf of the assignor.

As an alternative to assignment, the proprietor might grant a licence in respect of the work. This licence might be exclusive, in which case the assignee is granted rights in the work to the exclusion of all other people, including the person granting the licence. An exclusive licence can only be transferred in writing signed by or on behalf of the copyright owner. A licence granted by a copyright owner will bind all successors in title to his interest in the copyright, except a purchaser in good faith for valuable consideration who had no actual or constructive notice of the assignment, or a person deriving title from such a purchaser. At first sight this seems a major exception. However, once a work has been exploited commercially by the licensee it will be very difficult for anyone to argue that he had no constructive notice of the licence.

The Digital Economy Act 2010 places new obligations on Internet Service Providers (ISPs) to monitor and report upon online copyright infringement by subscribers (such as illegal peer to peer sharing and illegal downloading of copyright material). New sanctions for online copyright infringement include ISPs adopting 'technical measures' against some or all subscribers to deter copyright infringement. Sanctions include reducing the quality of a subscriber's Internet connection and there is a graduated 'three strikes and you're out' rule under which the ISP may block the infringing content from a subscriber's web site for an indefinite period.

23.2.4.1 Moral rights

Authors are given several moral rights in respect of their works. If these rights are infringed then a remedy for breach of statutory duty will be available. Damages are therefore available. An injunction will be the appropriate remedy to prevent derogatory treatment of the work.

There are five moral rights. First, an author who asserts his right to be identified as the author of a literary, dramatic, musical or artistic work has the moral right to be identified as the author of the work whenever the work is performed commercially, performed in public or communicated to the public (the paternity right). Regardless of whether or not the author asserted any rights, he is also given a second moral right to object to any derogatory treatment of the work, and a third right not to have literary, dramatic, musical or artistic works falsely attributed to him as author. (This particular right subsists only for 20 years after the author's death, the other moral rights subsist for as long as the copyright itself subsists.) A fourth moral right gives a person who commissions the taking of a photograph or the making of a film for private purposes not to have the work, or copies of it, exhibited, broadcast or shown in public. Arguably, a fifth artist's resale, the right or *droit de suite*, has been created. This came into effect under the Artist's Resale Rights Regulations 2006 and gives an artist a percentage of the selling price when certain types of works of art, which are within copyright, are sold. The seller of the work of art pays the money to the artist or to his heirs and apply only in respect of graphic or plastic art, such as painting, sculptures or photographs. It does not apply when the work is first sold by the artist or to sales between private individuals. The rate is 4 per cent of the selling price on the first £50 000, and then 3 per cent above that. The money due under a single sale cannot exceed £12 500, and is collected and distributed by a collecting society.

Generally, copyright can be transmitted by assignment, by leaving it in a will, by operation of law or as personal or movable property. The moral rights cannot be assigned, but some moral rights can be inherited. (The paternity right, the right to object to derogatory treatment and the right to privacy regarding photographs or films.) The moral rights cannot be infringed if the author has consented to the infringement or has waived his moral rights.

23.2.5 Remedies for infringement

Section 96 provides that an infringement of copyright is actionable by the copyright owner, and that all the remedies which would be available in respect of the infringement of any other property right should be available. However, the remedy of damages is not available if the defendant, at the time of infringement, did not know, and had no reason to believe, that copyright subsisted in the work. The other remedies, such as injunction, would be available. When a court does award damages it may award additional damages if the justice of the case so requires. In assessing this, s.97 requires the court to have regard to all the circumstances, but particularly to (a) the flagrancy of the infringement, and (b) any benefits accruing to the defendant by reason of that infringement.

An owner of copyright may apply for a court order that a person deliver up an infringing copy of a work in his possession, custody or control. This right also exists in respect of articles specifically designed or adapted for making copies of a particular copyright work. An owner of copyright may seize and detain infringing copies of works which are exposed for sale or hire. A court order is not necessary, but the owner, or a person authorised by him to do the seizing, must notify a local police station of the time and place of the proposed seizure. Where a person has been granted an exclusive licence in respect of the work he has the same rights as the copyright owner.

Various criminal offences are created in relation to articles which are, and which the defendant knows or has reason to believe are, infringements of copyright. These offences relate to making copies of the work for sale or hire, importing them for business purposes, possessing them for business purposes with a view to committing a copyright infringement and selling, exhibiting or distributing them. The criminal law here is enforced by local weights and measures authorities. The 2003 Regulations have created new criminal offences of infringing a work by communicating it to the public to such an extent as to affect prejudicially the owner of the copyright (while knowing or believing that by so doing he is infringing copyright in the

work). It is also now an offence to manufacture or import, sell, advertise, possess or distribute any device which is primarily designed to facilitate the circumvention of technological measures which are designed to protect copyright holders against infringement and unauthorised use.

Copyright licensing schemes exist whereby the owners of copyright give permission to do certain acts on standard terms. An example is provided by the Authors' Licensing and Collecting Society Limited. This society runs a scheme which raises money, to be distributed to authors, when copies of works are made by licensees.

Civil copyright cases are heard in the county court or the Chancery Division of the High Court. If the infringement of copyright constitutes a criminal offence a case can be brought in either the magistrates' court or the Crown Court.

Test your understanding 23.1

1 What are choses in action?
2 What is the difference between a documentary intangible and a non-documentary intangible?
3 What three descriptions of work in which copyright might subsist are set out in s.1(1)(a)–(c) of the Copyright, Designs and Patents Act 1988?
4 To what extent is copyright concerned with the protection of ideas?
5 For how long does copyright in a literary, dramatic, musical or artistic work subsist?
6 Does copyright have to be registered?
7 What are the five moral rights given to an author of copyright?

23.3 PATENTS

Patents can be taken out only in respect of inventions which are capable of having industrial application. A patent must be applied for and, as we shall see, is not easily granted. Patents law is governed by the Patents Act 1977, as amended by the Patent Act 2004, which in this section of this book is referred to as the Act. Patents have a twofold purpose. They encourage innovation by granting monopoly rights in respect of inventions, while at the same time making access to technological advances publicly available.

23.3.1 **Patentable inventions**

Section 1(1) of the Patents Act 1977 provides that a patent can only be granted for an invention in respect of which four conditions are satisfied. These conditions are:

(a) that the invention is new;
(b) that it involves an inventive step;
(c) that it is capable of industrial application;
(d) that the grant of a patent is not excluded by s.1(2) or s.1(3).

Section 1(2) provides that the following matters are not inventions and that there can therefore be no patenting of them:

(a) discoveries, scientific theories or mathematical methods;
(b) aesthetic creations and literary, dramatic, musical or artistic works;
(c) ways of performing a mental act, playing a game, or doing business;
(d) a program for a computer; or
(e) the presentation of information.

Section 1(3) provides that a patent shall not be granted for an invention the commercial exploit-ation of which would be contrary to public policy or moral-ity (which means that the exploitation is prohibited by any law in force in the United Kingdom or part of it). Plant varieties are protected by the Plant Varieties Act 1997.

An invention can only be regarded as new if it does not form part of the state of the prior art, which includes all matters that have at any time before the date of the invention been made available to the public in any way. This can include matters contained in an application for another patent.

An invention can only be regarded as an inventive step if it was not obvious to a person who was skilled in the art. An invention is capable of having industrial application if it can be made or used in any kind of industry, including agriculture. New methods of sur-gery, therapy or diagnosis which are to be practised on humans or animals cannot be taken to be of industrial application.

A patent does not have to apply to a new item, it can apply to the way an existing item is used or to the way in which an existing item is produced. For example, a new way of manufacturing paper could be patentable.

23.3.2 **Making an application**

Applications for a patent are made to the Patent Office, to whom a fee must be paid. The application must contain a specification containing a description of the invention, as well as a claim for the patent and any drawing referred to in the description or the claim. An abstract, meaning a concise summary of the speci-fication, must also be submitted. Generally, a specifi-cation would contain complex drawings.

Section 14(3) provides that the specification must disclose the invention in a manner which is clear enough and complete enough for the invention to be performed by a person skilled in the art. It must there-fore be comprehensive and exact enough to be capable of being used by a person skilled in the art to produce the invention. Section 14(5) provides that the claim must: (a) define the matter for which the applicant seeks protection; (b) be clear and concise; (c) be sup-ported by the description; and (d) relate to one inven-tion or to a group of inventions which are so linked as to form a single inventive concept.

The date of filing an application will arise as soon as the documents filed at the Patent Office contain an indication that a patent is being sought. These docu-ments must identify the applicant and a description of the invention, and the date will not arise until the fee is paid.

Once the application has acquired a date of filing it is then referred to an examiner for a preliminary application and search. The purpose of this examina-tion is to determine whether or not the application complies with the Act's requirements. If this stage is satisfied, the application then goes for a substantive examination. If this substantive examination reveals that any of the Act's requirements have not been met the applicant is given an opportunity, within a speci-fied time, to make observations on the report and to amend the application. If the examiner is not satisfied with the amendments the application for a patent may be refused. If the examiner is satisfied that the applica-tion does satisfy the Act's requirements then a patent can be granted.

An applicant has a general power to amend an application of his own volition before a patent is granted. A patent must comply with all of the Act's requirements within a prescribed period or the appli-cation will be regarded as having been refused.

If a patent is granted this fact is published as soon as is practicable in a notice in the *Patents and Designs*

Journal. The notice contains the name of the inventor, the names of the proprietor and any other matters which the comptroller thinks it desirable to publish. A patent can continue in force for 20 years from the date of filing the application for the patent. Initially patents last for four years. After this they can be renewed annually on payment of a fee.

Patent attorneys (also known as patent agents) commonly act for people applying for a patent. A patent attorney's role is to prepare the specification and the claim. Only those who are registered with the Chartered Institute of Patents Agents can call themselves patent attorneys.

All patent attorneys have the right to conduct litigation. They have rights of audience in the Patents County Court and in the Patents Court, which is part of the Chancery Division.

23.3.3 Property in patents

The proprietor of a patent has a monopoly right to exploit it. This is the case even if it could be shown that someone else had independently reached the same inventive step. Both patents and applications for patents are personal property but s.30(1) of the Act states that they are not things in action. This seems surprising but it is a technicality which allows patents to be reached in bankruptcy proceedings. Anyway, it is of little importance as patents can be transferred by way of assignment or mortgaged. A patent may also be inherited in the same way as any other personal property. When two or more people are granted a patent they are granted equal co-ownership unless there is an indication to the contrary.

A patent can be licensed to another so that this other may exploit the patent without infringing the rights of the proprietor. Rights are commonly granted in this way.

23.3.4 Employees' inventions

Section 39(1) states that an invention made by an employee shall be taken as belonging to his employer in two circumstances. These circumstances are that:

(a) the invention was made in the course of the normal duties of the employee, or in the course of other duties which were specifically assigned to him, and the circumstances in either case were such that an invention might reasonably be expected to result from the carrying out of his duties; or

(b) the invention was made in the course of the duties of the employee and, at the time of making the invention, because of the nature of his duties and the particular responsibilities arising from the nature of his duties, he had a special obligation to further the interests of the employer's undertaking.

Where the conditions in s.39(1) are not satisfied, s.39(2) provides that any other invention made by an employee shall be taken as belonging to the employee.

Section 40, as amended by the Patents Act 2004, allows a court or the comptroller to award compensation to an employee who makes an invention belonging to the employer for which a patent has been granted. This will be done if the invention or the patent for it, or the combination of both, is (having regard among other things to the size and nature of the employer's undertaking) of outstanding benefit to the employer and that by reason of those facts it is just that the employee should be paid compensation by the employer. Section 41 provides that the amount of the compensation should be such as will secure for the employee a fair share, having regard to all the circumstances, of the benefits which the employer has derived or can be expected to derive from the patent. The court or comptroller also has the power to award compensation where the patent was assigned by the employee to the employer for less than it was worth. Contract terms which seek to restrict these rights will be unenforceable.

23.3.5 Compulsory licences

Subject to provisions of EC law, three years after a patent has been granted, any person may apply to the comptroller for a licence under the patent on the following grounds:

(a) that the patented invention is not being worked commercially in the United Kingdom, although it could be, or is not being worked to the fullest extent that is reasonably practicable;

(b) in the case of a patented product, that UK demand for the product is either not being met on reasonable terms, or is being met to a substantial extent by imports;

(c) in the case of patented inventions, that they are not being commercially worked in the United Kingdom, although they could be, and that they are being prevented or hindered from being so worked by imports;

(d) that on account of the proprietor's refusal to grant a licence on reasonable terms, an export market for the patented product is not being supplied, or that commercial or industrial activities in the United Kingdom are unfairly prejudiced from being established or developed, or that the working in the United Kingdom of any other patented invention is prevented or hindered;

(e) that the manufacture, use or disposal of materials which are not protected by the patent, or commercial or industrial development in the United Kingdom, is unfairly prejudiced by conditions imposed by the proprietor of the patent.

If satisfied that any of these conditions are being fulfilled the comptroller may either grant a licence in respect of the patent on any terms which he sees fit, or may make an entry in the register to the effect that licences under the payment are available as of right. The Secretary of State may also make such an entry on the register if the Competition Commission lay a report before Parliament to the effect that a monopoly situation exists. When a compulsory licence is granted the patentee will generally be compensated.

Section 55 allows any Government department to take over a patent for the services of the Crown. When the Crown exercises this right compensation is payable to the proprietor of the patent. The compensation is for any loss resulting from the proprietor not being awarded a contract to supply the patented product or to perform the patented process or supply a thing made by means of the patented process.

23.3.6 Infringement of patents

Section 60(1) sets out three ways in which a patent can be infringed. These are as follows:

(a) In respect of patented products infringement is committed by making, disposing of, offering to dispose of, using or importing the product or keeping it whether for disposal or otherwise.

(b) In respect of patented processes, infringement is committed by using the process or offering it for use in the United Kingdom when the person who does this knows, or where it is obvious to a reasonable person in the circumstances, that its use there without the consent of the proprietor would be an infringement of the patent.

(c) In respect of patented process infringement can be committed by disposing of, offering to dispose of, using or importing any product obtained directly by means of that process or by keeping any such product whether for disposal or otherwise.

Section 60(5) provides that acts done privately and for purposes which are not commercial will not constitute infringement, nor will acts done for purely experimental purposes.

Section 61(1) provides that the following civil remedies may be claimed for infringement:

(a) an injunction restraining the defendant from any apprehended act of infringement;

(b) an order to destroy or deliver up any patented product or any product in which a patented product is incorporated;

(c) damages;

(d) an account of the profits derived from the infringement;

(e) a declaration that the patent is valid and has been infringed.

A court will not award both damages and an order for an account of profits. A person who was not aware, and had no reasonable grounds to suppose, that the patent existed will not be ordered to pay damages or ordered to make an account of profits. It is up to the defendant relying on either of these two matters to prove them. The word patent on the product will not be enough to mean that the defendant should have been aware that a patent existed unless it is accompanied by the appropriate patent number.

If a patentee brings groundless claims for infringement then any aggrieved person who has suffered more than minimal damage may sue for a declaration that the threats are groundless, or an injunction to prevent further groundless threats and damages to compensate for losses caused by the groundless threats.

The court or comptroller may revoke a patent for an invention on grounds which equate approximately to the grounds on which an application for a patent could have been refused in the first place. The comptroller can exercise this power on his own initiative.

It is a criminal offence either to represent falsely that a thing disposed of for value is a patented product, or to claim falsely that a patent has been applied for in respect of any article disposed of for value. The Patents County Court deals with matters relating to intellectual property, in particular patent law matters.

23.4 TRADE MARKS

The Trade Marks Act 1994 (which in this section of the book is called 'the Act') replaced the Trade Marks Act 1938. The Act, and the accompanying Trade Mark Rules 1994, have updated the law and given effect to an EC Directive which sought to harmonise the law throughout the EC.

23.4.1 Meaning of trade marks and registration of trade marks

A trade mark is given a wide definition by s.1(1):

'In this Act a "trade mark" means any sign capable of being represented graphically which is capable of distinguishing goods or services of one undertaking from those of another undertaking. A trade mark may, in particular, consist of words (including personal names), designs, letters, numerals or the shape of goods or their packaging.'

It can be seen that a trade mark is widely defined and can consist of almost any visual representation, including a shape. The only two requirements in s.1(1) are that the sign should be capable of being represented graphically and that it should be capable of distinguishing one person's products from another person's. However, registration of a trade mark can be refused on either absolute or relative grounds.

The absolute grounds for refusal of registration, set out in s.3, are as follows:

(a) the sign does not satisfy the definition set out in s.1(1);
(b) that the trade mark is devoid of any distinctive character;
(c) that the trade mark consists exclusively of signs which may serve in trade to indicate matters such as kind, quality, quantity, intended purpose, value, geographical origin, the time of production or other characteristics of goods or services;
(d) that the trade mark consists exclusively of signs or indications which have become customary in the current language or established practices of the trade;
(e) that it consists exclusively of a shape which results from the very nature of the goods, or a shape necessary to obtain technical results, or a shape which gives substantial value to the goods;
(f) that the trade mark is contrary to public policy or is of a nature intended to deceive the public;

(g) that the trade mark is illegal or the application was made in bad faith.

The matters set out in (b), (c) and (d) will not prevent registration if the trade mark has acquired a distinctive character as a result of the use which is made of it. A large number of national and international emblems are prohibited from being trade marks by s.4.

The relative grounds for refusing registration, set out in s.5, are as follows:

(a) identical marks on identical goods and services;
(b) identical marks on similar goods and services (and there exists a likelihood of confusion on the part of the public, which includes the likelihood of association with the earlier mark);
(c) similar marks on identical or similar goods and services (and there exists a likelihood of confusion on the part of the public, which includes the likelihood of association with the earlier mark);
(d) an identical or similar trade mark to an earlier trade mark shall not be registered, if the earlier mark has a reputation in the United Kingdom and the use of the mark without due cause would take unfair advantage of the earlier mark or be detrimental to it.

An identical or similar mark can be registered, but not if the earlier mark has a reputation in the United Kingdom and the later mark would take unfair advantage of this or be detrimental to it. An earlier trade mark is one which has been registered in the United Kingdom or the EC or has an earlier date of application to be registered.

The rights under the Act are only conferred once the trade mark, which is a property right, is registered. As regards an unregistered trade mark an action for passing off may lie, but the Act will provide no remedies.

23.4.2 Effect of registered trade mark

The proprietor of a registered trade mark is given exclusive rights in the trade mark. If the trade mark is used in the UK without his consent these rights are infringed. Section 10 sets out the various ways in which infringement might occur. These might be summarised as:

(a) using a sign in the course of a trade or business which is identical to the trade mark and is used in relation to identical goods or products;

(b) using a sign which is similar to the trade mark, in relation to similar or identical goods, thereby creating the likelihood of confusion on the part of the public;

(c) using a sign which is similar or identical to a trade mark where the trade mark has a reputation in the United Kingdom and the use of the sign takes unfair advantage of, or is detrimental to, the distinctive character or the repute of the trade mark.

A sign is used in various ways, including by: fixing it onto a package; putting goods under the sign; importing or exporting under the sign; or using the sign on business paper or in advertising.

Trade marks are not infringed by a person using his own name and address as long as the use is in accordance with honest practices in industrial or commercial matters. This is an objective test and is not the same as asking whether or not the defendant acted honestly.

An action for infringement is brought by the proprietor of the trade mark and all remedies which would be available in respect of any other property right are available. In addition the court may: order offending signs to be erased or removed; order infringing goods, materials or articles to be delivered up to the proprietor; and order that these may be destroyed or forfeited to such person as the court thinks fit. If a groundless threat of infringement proceedings is made any aggrieved person who has suffered more than minimal damage may apply to a court for a declaration that the threats are unjustifiable or for damages or for an injunction.

A registered trade mark is personal property which can be co-owned or assigned to another. Licences permitting their use may be granted to others.

23.4.3 Procedure for registration

An application for registration of a UK trade mark has to include the following four matters: a request for registration; the name and address of the applicant; a statement of the goods or services to which the trade mark is to apply; and a representation of the trade mark itself. A system of classification exists, for more than 40 classes of goods and services, under which the applicant applies for registration.

The Registrar decides whether or not an application should be granted. In order to make this decision he will carry out a search of earlier trade marks. If the Registrar decides that the requirements are met he will accept the application. If the Registrar decides that the requirements are not met he will give the applicant an opportunity to amend the application within a given period. Failure to amend the application adequately within this period will mean that the Registrar will refuse the application.

Where the Registrar decides that the application for registration has been accepted he publishes this in the *Trade Marks Journal*. Any person may then make a written objection or make written observations to the Registrar. The applicant may amend or withdraw his application at any time. If, after considering any objections and observations, the Registrar is satisfied, and if the appropriate fee has been paid, the trade mark is registered as of the date when the application was filed.

Many trade mark owners prefer to register an EU-wide mark known as a CTM or Community Trade Mark. This done by registering the mark with OHIM, the Office for Harmonisation in the Internal Market. A CTM is valid in all of the 27 signatory countries of the EU, including the UK. There is therefore no need for a separate UK registration.

Initially, trade marks are registered for a ten-year period from the date of registration (the date of filing). Registration may be renewed for further periods of ten years ad infinitum if the proprietor so requests and pays the appropriate fee. Generally, trade marks cannot be altered in the register either during the period of registration or renewal. However, if the trade mark includes the proprietor's name and address alteration of this may be allowed as long as this does not substantially affect the identity of the trade mark.

A trade mark may be surrendered by the proprietor. It may also be revoked on the following grounds:

(a) it has, without good reason, not been put to genuine use in the UK within five years of completion of the registration procedure;

(b) that its use has become suspended for a five-year period, without good reason;

(c) that the proprietor's acts or omissions have allowed it to become the common name in the trade for a service or product for which it is registered;

(d) that the way it has been used, or been allowed to be used, by the proprietor has made it liable to mislead the public.

A trade mark can be declared invalid on the ground that it was wrongly registered. If the proprietor of a trade mark acquiesces in another's use of the trade mark for a continuous period of five years he loses any entitlement to oppose the use of that trade mark by

the other or to apply for a declar-ation that its registration is invalid. However, this is not the case if the later registration was applied for in bad faith.

Collective marks, which distinguish the goods or services of members of an association, are covered by the Act.

A register of trade mark attorneys is kept. These agents act for others for the purpose of obtaining the registration of trade marks. Once a person's name is on the register he is known as a 'registered trade mark attorney'. It is an offence for any other person to claim to be a registered trade mark attorney.

In any civil proceedings the burden of proof is on the proprietor to show any use to which a registered trade mark has been put.

The unauthorised use of a trade mark can amount to a criminal offence. It is also a criminal offence to falsely represent that a trade mark has been registered. Counterfeit goods which misuse trade marks can be forfeited and destroyed.

Test your understanding 23.2

1 How is a patent acquired?

2 What three conditions relating to an invention must be satisfied before a patent can be granted?

3 How can a person other than the patentee acquire the right to exploit the patent?

4 What rights are available if a patent is infringed?

5 What is a trade mark?

6 Does a trade mark have to be registered?

7 What rights does registration give to the proprietor of a trade mark?

23.5 THE DATA PROTECTION ACT 1998

The Data Protection Act 1998 was passed to give effect to the EC Data Protection Directive (94/46/EC), which strengthened the regime imposed by the Data Protection Act 1984. The 1998 Act (which in this section of the book is called 'the Act'), applied the rules on data protection to some manual files and strengthened the rights available to individuals. The Act imposes criminal liability on those who breach its provisions.

The holding of data banks has increased in a way which was unimaginable 40 years ago. The Younger Committee's Report in 1972 found that the public felt very concerned about the possible misuse of data. Without protective legislation these fears would have increased as the amount of data held multiplied and became a commodity. There are nowadays few businesses which do not hold and process personal data.

23.5.1 The definitions in the Act

The Act begins with certain definitions. These definitions need to be considered carefully because the provisions of the Act can only be understood in the light of the definitions.

Section 1(1) defines 'data' as information which:

'(a) is being processed by means of equipment operating automatically in response to instructions given for that purpose,

(b) is recorded with the intention that it should be processed by means of such equipment,

(c) is recorded as part of a relevant filing system or with the intention that it should form part of a relevant filing system, or

(d) does not fall within paragraph (a), (b) or (c) but forms part of an accessible [health, educational or publicly accessible] record.'

A data controller is defined by s.1(1) as a person who determines the purposes for which and the manner in which any personal data are, or are to be, processed.

In relation to personal data, a 'data processor' is defined as any person (other than an employee of the data controller) who processes the data on behalf of the data controller. A 'data subject' is an individual who is the subject of personal data.

Personal data must relate to a living individual who can be identified either from the data itself or from the data and other information which is, or which is likely to come into, the possession of the data controller. Both expressions of opinion about the individual and indications of the intentions of the data controller or other person are included. In ***Durant v The Financial Services Authority*** [2003] EWCA Civ 1746, [2004] FSR 28 the Court of Appeal held that data is personal data only if it affects a person's privacy, whether this be in his personal or family life or in a business or commercial capacity. The court also held that a 'relevant filing system' is a system if two conditions are met. First, the system must be structured or referenced in such a way as to clearly indicate at the start of a search whether specific information which could amount to personal data is held within the system and, if it is, the files in which it is held. Second, the system must be sophisticated and detailed enough to indicate readily whether and where in a file specific criteria or information about a person making an application under s.7 of the Act can be located.

'Processing' in relation to information or data is defined as obtaining, recording or holding the information or data or carrying out any operation or set of operations on the information or data. Specifically included are:

(a) organising, adapting or altering the information or data;

(b) retrieving, consulting or using the information or data;

(c) disclosing the information or data by transmitting it, disseminating it or otherwise making it available;

(d) aligning, combining, blocking, erasing or destroying the information or data. There is no requirement that processing should be done electronically. The Act will apply even if it is done manually.

Special rules apply to 'sensitive personal data' which is defined as personal data consisting of information as to:

(a) the racial or ethnic origin of the data subject;

(b) his political beliefs;

(c) his religious beliefs or other beliefs of a similar nature;

(d) whether he is a member of a trade union;

(e) his physical or mental health or condition;

(f) his sexual life;

(g) the commission or alleged commission by him of any offence; or

(h) any proceedings for any offence committed or alleged to have been committed by him, the disposal of such proceedings or the sentence of any court in such proceedings.

The Act is enforced by the Information Commissioner.

23.5.2 **The rights conferred on data subjects**

Section 7 of the Act gives individuals the right of access to their personal data. This right entitles individuals to be informed by a data controller whether personal data of which the individual is a data subject is being processed by or on behalf of the data controller. If this is happening the individual is entitled to a description of the data, the purpose for which it was processed and the recipients to whom it was disclosed. The individual is also entitled to be given a copy of any personal data of which the individual is a data subject and any information which the data controller has as to the source of those data. If personal data relating to the individual are processed automatically in order to evaluate the individual (perhaps in relation to his work, creditworthiness, reliability or conduct) and this is the sole basis of any decision taken in respect of him, the individual is entitled to be informed of the logic involved in the decision-taking. The data controller is only obliged to supply the information described above if he receives a request in writing and a fee. Nor is the data controller obliged to comply unless he is given enough information as he may reasonably require to satisfy himself as to the identity of the person making the request and to locate the information which that person requests. In certain circumstances the data controller can refuse the request if it would be impossible to comply with it without revealing information about another identifiable person.

Section 10 gives an individual the right to give a data controller written notice requiring the data controller to stop processing personal data of which the individual is the data subject. This right only arises if the processing of the data, or the way in which it is processed, is likely to cause substantial unwarranted damage or distress to the individual. The data controller then has 21 days in which to give the individual notice either that he has complied or the reasons why he considers compliance unjustified.

Section 11 gives an individual the right to give written notice requiring the data controller, at the end of a reasonable period, to stop processing personal data for the purposes of direct marketing.

Section 12 gives an individual a right to give written notice to a data controller preventing him from taking an evaluating decision which significantly affects the individual if the decision is based solely on the processing by automatic means of personal data in respect of which that individual is the data subject. Even where no notice is given by the individual, a data controller who takes an evaluating decision which significantly affects an individual, and which was based solely on the processing by automatic means of personal data, must as soon as is reasonably practicable notify the individual that the decision was taken on that basis. The individual then has 21 days in which to require the data controller to reconsider the decision. If the individual does this the data controller has 21 days in which to give a written notification of the steps which he intends to take in order to comply with the request.

If any of the requirements of the Act are contravened by a data controller, an individual who suffers damage as a consequence is entitled to damages.

Section 14 gives a court, upon application by a data subject, the power to order inaccurate personal data to be rectified, blocked, erased or destroyed.

Subject to certain exceptions, personal data must not be processed unless an entry in respect of the data controller is included in the register maintained by the Commissioner. Data controllers who want to be included in the register give a notification to the Commissioner. A person who processes personal data without an entry in respect of the data being included in the register commits an offence. Data does not have to be notified unless it is in relation to personal data, or if it appears to the Secretary of State that processing of a particular description is unlikely to prejudice the rights and freedoms of data subjects and regulations have done away with the need to notify. Nor is there a need to notify in relation to any processing whose sole purpose is the maintenance of a public register. The Secretary of State may also make Regulations under which a data controller may appoint a person to act as data protection supervisor to monitor the data controller's compliance with the Act in an independent manner. A data controller who did this might then be able to take advantage of exemptions or other modifications such as the Regulations might specify.

23.5.3 The data protection principles

Schedule 1 to the Act sets out eight data protection principles, which apply to all non-exempt processing. The eight principles are as follows:

(1) Personal data shall be processed fairly and lawfully and, in particular, shall not be processed unless:
(a) at least one of the conditions in Schedule 2 is met, and
(b) in the case of sensitive personal data, at least one of the conditions in Schedule 3 is also met.

(Schedules 1 and 2 are considered after the eight data protection principles are set out.)

(2) Personal data shall be obtained only for one or more specified and lawful purposes, and shall not be further processed in any manner incompatible with that purpose or those purposes.

(3) Personal data shall be adequate, relevant and not excessive in relation to the purpose or purposes for which they are processed.

(4) Personal data shall be accurate and, where necessary, kept up to date.

(5) Personal data processed for any purpose or purposes shall not be kept for longer than is necessary for that purpose or those purposes.

(6) Personal data shall be processed in accordance with the rights of data subjects under this Act.

(7) Appropriate technical and organisational measures shall be taken against unauthorised or unlawful processing of personal data and against accidental loss or destruction of, or damage to, personal data.

(8) Personal data shall not be transferred to a country or territory outside the European Economic Area unless that country or territory ensures an adequate level of protection for the rights and freedoms of data subjects in relation to the processing of data.

The European Economic Area is made up of the Member States of the EC and Iceland, Norway and Liechtenstein.

Schedule 2 provides that for the purposes of the first data principle, in regard to determining whether personal data are fairly processed, regard should be had to the method by which the data are obtained, including in particular whether any person from whom they were obtained was deceived or misled as to the purposes for which they were to be processed. It also provides that, as regards the first principle, data are not to be treated as fairly processed unless the data subject is provided with information as to the identity of the controller and the purposes for which the data are to be processed, or unless this information is made readily available to him. The first principle is not breached if the data subject has given his consent to the processing. Nor is it breached if the processing is necessary for: functions of a judicial or public nature; or for the performance of a contract to which the data subject is a party; or to comply with a legal obligation to which the data controller is subject; or to protect the vital interests of the data subject.

The fourth principle is not to be regarded as having been contravened by reason of inaccuracy in personal data which accurately record information obtained by the data controller where the data controller had taken reasonable steps to ensure the accuracy of the data. Where the data subject has notified the data controller that the data are inaccurate the data must either be made accurate or indicate that this notification has been made.

The sixth principle can only be committed by a person who breaches ss.7, 10, 11 or 12.

As regards the seventh principle, in order to decide whether the measures ensure a level of security appropriate to the harm which might be done and the nature of the data to be protected, regard must be had to the technological development and the cost of implementing any measures. The data controller must take reasonable steps to ensure the reliability of any employees of his who have access to personal data. He must also take reasonable steps to ensure that any data processor he appoints gives sufficient guarantees in respect of organisational security measures governing the processing to be carried out and also take reasonable steps to ensure compliance with those measures. The seventh principle also requires that a data controller employing a data processor must ensure that the processing is carried out under a contract which is evidenced in writing and under which the data processor is to act only on instructions from the data controller. In addition, the contract must require the data processor to comply with obligations equivalent to those which the seventh principle imposes on a data controller.

As regards the eighth principle an adequate level of protection is a level which is adequate in all the circumstances of the case. The nature of the data and the the laws of the countries of destin-ation and origin are particularly important. Schedule 4 provides that the eighth principle does not apply if the transfer is necessary for the performance of a contract between the data subject and the data controller, or where the transfer is necessary for reasons of substantial public interest. Nor does it apply where the transfer is necessary in respect of legal proceedings, or to protect the vital interests of the data subject or where the transfer is authorised by the Commissioner as being made in a manner which will ensure adequate safeguards for the rights and freedoms of data subjects.

As regards sensitive personal data, Schedule 3 provides that the following are relevant conditions for assessing the extent to which the first principle's requirements that data should be processed fairly and lawfully have been met:

(1) The data subject has given his explicit consent to the processing of the personal data.
(2) The processing is necessary for the data controller to exercise or perform a right or obligation conferred or imposed on him in connection with employment.
(3) The processing is necessary to protect the vital interest of the data subject.
(4) The processing is carried out in the course of legitimate activities by a non-profit-making body which exists for political, philosophical, religious or trade union purposes. The processing must be carried out with appropriate safeguards for the rights and freedoms of data subjects and relate only to members of the body or association in question and must not involve disclosure of the personal data to a third party without the consent of the data subject.
(5) The information in the personal data has been made public as a result of steps deliberately taken by the data subject.
(6) The processing is necessary for the purposes of legal proceedings or the administration of justice.
(7) The processing is necessary for medical purposes and is undertaken by a health professional or some other person who owes a duty of confidentiality which is the equivalent of that owed by a health professional.
(8) The processing is of sensitive data relating to racial or ethnic origin and is necessary to make sure that unequal treatment in these fields does not occur.
(9) The processing is necessary for other purposes set out in Regulations made by the Secretary of State.

The Act contains various exemptions in respect of: confidential references given by the data controller; the armed forces; judicial appointments and honours; Crown employment and Ministerial appointment; managment forecasts; corporate finance; exam marks and scripts; legal professional privilege; and self-incrimination.

Exemptions in respect of the data protection principles, or the data protection rights, or the need to register also exist in relation to: national security; crime and taxation; health education and social work; journalism, literature or art; and domestic purposes.

The Act is enforced by the Information Commissioner. A circuit judge can issue a search warrant to the Commissioner if the Commissioner satisfies him that there are reasonable grounds for suspecting that a data controller has contravened, or is contravening, any of the data protection principles or that an offence under the Act has been or is being committed. Intentionally obstructing a person executing such a warrant is an offence. It is also an offence to fail to give any person executing a warrant such assistance as he may reasonably require, without reasonable excuse. The main offences created by the Act are: failure to specify changes in contravention of a notice to do this; failure to comply with an enforcement notice; deliberately or recklessly making a false statement while purporting to comply with an enforcement notice; and unlawfully obtaining, selling or offering to sell personal data.

The Commissioner has the power to serve enforcement notices which give a person a reasonable time to stop contravening the data protection principles. The Commissioner also has the function of promoting good practice by data controllers and ensuring that data controllers comply with the Act. On its website, the Information Commissioner's Office publishes details of the enforcement notices which it has served.

Test your understanding 23.3

1 What rights does the Data Protection Act 1998 confer on data subjects?

2 What are the eight data protection principles?

Key points

The nature of property

■ Intellectual property rights are concerned with rights in intangible property.

■ Choses in action may be documentary or non-documentary. The documentary rights can be transferred to another by delivering the document which embodies the right. Non-documentary rights can be transferred to another by assignment.

Copyright

■ Copyright is concerned with protecting the expression of ideas, rather than with protecting ideas themselves.

■ There is no need to register copyright.

■ Copyright may exist in: (a) original literary, dramatic, musical or artistic works; (b) sound recordings, films, broadcasts or cable programmes; and (c) the typographical arrangements of published editions.

■ As regards literary, dramatic, musical and artistic works, copyright subsists for 70 years after the end of the calendar year in which the author dies.

■ Authors of copyright are given moral rights in respect of the work. These rights are the paternity right; the right to object to derogatory treatment of the work; the right not to have work falsely attributed to them; and a right of privacy relating to photographs and films.

■ If copyright is infringed the copyright holder will have all the remedies available to him which would be available in respect of infringement of any other property right.

Patents

■ A patent can only exist if it is granted by the Patent Office.

■ An invention can only be patented if it is new, involves an inventive step and is capable of industrial application.

■ Animals and plants may not be patented.

■ Patents may be assigned or mortgaged. Licences to exploit a patent may be granted.

■ Inventions made by employees will belong to the employer if they were made in the normal course of the employment.

■ A compulsory licence may be granted if a patent is not being fully exploited in the United Kingdom.

■ A person whose patent is being infringed can bring an action for an injunction, an order to deliver up or destroy a product, damages, an account of profits or a declaration that the patent has been infringed.

Trade marks

■ A trade mark is a sign capable of being represented graphically which is capable of distinguishing

→

the goods or services of one undertaking from those of another.

■ The Trade Marks Act 1994 gives the proprietor of a registered trade mark exclusive rights in the trade mark. Before a trade mark is registered the Act will confer no rights, although a passing off action may be possible.

■ There are a number of absolute and relative grounds for refusing registration of a trade mark.

■ If the rights of a proprietor of a trade mark are infringed any civil remedy which would ordinarily be available for infringement of a property right will be available to the proprietor.

The Data Protection Act 1998

■ The 1998 Act confers upon data subjects the rights to:

a access to personal data;

b prevent processing which is likely to cause distress or damage;

c prevent processing for the purposes of direct marketing;

d prevent evaluation by automatic decision-taking;

e compensation if certain requirements are not complied with; and

f have inaccurate data rectified or erased.

■ The eight data protection principles are as follows:

– that personal data should be processed lawfully and fairly;

– that personal data should be obtained for one or more specified and lawful purposes and not be used for other purposes;

– that personal data should be adequate, relevant and not excessive;

– that personal data should be accurate and kept up to date;

– that personal data should not be kept for longer than is necessary to process it;

– that personal data should be processed in accordance with the rights given to data subjects by the Act;

– that appropriate measures should be taken against unauthorised processing, and against loss or destruction of personal data;

– that personal data should not be transferred to a country outside the EEA, unless that country ensures an adequate level of protection for the rights and freedoms of data subjects.

Summary questions

1 In 2001 Angus MacSpiers wins the most prestigious prize for any work of art, the Rembrandt prize, with his photograph of two haggises in a butcher's shop. The photograph is lavishly praised by the Rembrandt prize judges as a highly significant comment on the pressures of 21st-century life. John Doe writes an article in a national newspaper which is highly critical of MacSpiers' work. This article falsely shows a variety of everyday photographs and claims that they are 'other works of genius by Angus MacSpiers'. A University lecturer photocopies Doe's article and gives a copy to 250 of his students. A local printer incorporates a copy of the prize-winning photograph into a poster which also shows a piece of tripe. The poster is entitled, 'Spot the difference'. The printer sells this poster in several newsagents. Advise the parties as to whether or not any of them have infringed copyright and of any remedies which may be available.

2 John thinks he has invented a new mousetrap which is superior to any mousetrap he has ever seen or heard of. Explain to John what a patent is, the steps which he will need to take in order to acquire a patent and the rights which a patent would confer upon him.

3 Acme Ltd, a manufacturer of footballs, wants to register a trade mark under which its goods are sold. Explain the process of registration, the tests the mark will have to satisfy in order to be capable of being a trade mark and the benefits of registering the mark as a trade mark.

4 Try to think of two persons who hold personal data on you or a member of your family. Is the data held personal data? Outline the data protection principles which would apply in respect of this data and the rights conferred on the data subject.

Multiple choice questions

1 Which one of the following statements is not true?

a Copyright does not exist in a literary, dramatic, or musical work until that work is recorded.

b Copyright in a literary, dramatic, musical or artistic work subsists for 70 years after the end of the calendar year in which the author died.

c The mere act of down-loading work from the Internet could amount to an infringement of copyright.

d The five moral rights can be enforced by injunction but damages cannot be claimed in respect of a breach of a moral right.

2 Which one of the following statements is not true?

a A patent can only be granted in respect of an invention which is new, which involves an inventive step and which is capable of industrial application.

b If a patent is registered the patentee is granted an absolute right to prevent the use of the patented invention for 20 years.

c A person can be sued for bringing a groundless claim for infringement of a patent.

d A patent can be assigned to another person, and another person can be granted a licence to exploit a patent.

3 Which one of the following statements is not true?

a Only a sign which is capable of being represented graphically can be a trade mark.

b Shapes cannot be registered as trade marks.

c A court may order the destruction of goods which infringe a trade mark.

d Trade marks are initially registered for a ten-year period and registration can be renewed at ten-yearly intervals.

4 Which one of the following statements is not true?

a The Data Protection Act 1998 applies only to electronically processed data.

b Upon making a written request and paying a fee, individuals have a right to receive a copy of personal data relating to them.

c Personal data held by a data controller must be accurate and, where necessary, kept up to date.

d A circuit judge has the power to issue a search warrant if the Commissioner satisfies him that a person is contravening any of the data principles.

Task 23

Your employer has recently become concerned with the infringement of intellectual property rights. Write a report for him, briefly explaining the following matters:

a The meaning of copyright, the ways in which copyright is created and the remedies available for infringement of copyright.

b The meaning of a patent, how a patent is acquired and the remedies of infringement of a patent.

c The meaning of a trade mark, the way in which a trade mark is acquired and the remedies for infringement of a trade mark.

d The effect of the Data Protection Act 1998.

mylawchamber *premium*

Appendix:
Answers to Test your understanding questions

Chapter 1

Answers to 1.1

1 Under the adversarial system of trial the lawyers act as adversaries. One party's lawyers try to establish a case, the other party's lawyers use whatever means permissible to deny that there is a case.

2 The distinction between common law and equity is concerned with whether legal rules originated in the King's (or Queen's) courts or whether they originated in the courts of equity. The two systems of common law and equity have been merged but the distinction is still significant today. Some matters are still equitable and in such cases equitable rules and principles will be applied. Any court can apply both common law and equitable rules.

3 A criminal case has the purpose of punishing a wrongdoer who has committed a criminal offence. A civil case has the purpose of compensating a person wrongly caused to suffer a loss or injury.

4 In civil cases the burden of proof is on the claimant, in criminal cases it is on the prosecution. The civil standard of proof requires the claimant to prove his case on a balance of probabilities. The criminal standard of proof requires the prosecution to prove the accused's guilt beyond reasonable doubt.

5 The distinction between law and fact can be important because: only statements of law can become precedents; an appeal may only be available against a statement of law, or the appeal might have to be made to different courts depending upon whether it was against a statement of law or a statement of fact; and in Crown Court cases the jury decide the facts, whereas the judge decides the law.

Answers to 1.2

1 In order to become a statute a Bill will need to pass through both Houses of Parliament and gain the Royal Assent.

2 A codifying Act puts all the existing law into one comprehensive statute, perhaps making some changes to the law at the same time. A consolidating Act re-enacts several existing statutes into one new Act. An amending Act makes minor amendments to an existing Act.

3 Delegated legislation is legislation passed otherwise than by statute. Statutory instruments are introduced by Government Ministers, the power to create the instruments having been conferred by an enabling Act. Orders in Council are introduced by the Privy Council, which is made up of eminent parliamentarians. Bye-laws are local laws passed by local authorities.

4 The three main rules of statutory interpretation are the literal rule, the golden rule and the mischief rule. The literal rule holds that if the words in a statute are not ambiguous they should be given their ordinary literal meaning. The golden rule requires a judge to give the words in a statute their ordinary, literal meaning as far as possible, but only to the extent that this would not produce an absurd result or, where the words are ambiguous, to prefer the meaning which would give the least absurd or undesirable result. The mischief rule allows the court to be guided by the 'mischief' or problem which the statute sought to address.

5 The *ejusdem generis rule* is that where specific words are followed by general words, the general words must be given the same type of meaning as the specific words. The rule *expressio unius est exclusio alterius* is to the effect that where specific words are not followed by any general words then the statute only applies to the specific words included.

6 Intrinsic aids to interpretation include interpretation sections, the Act's title and punctuation and probably also marginal notes and headings. External aids include dictionaries, previous statutes on the same subject and the Interpretation Act 1978. In the limited circumstances specified in **Pepper v Hart,** Parliamentary materials may be considered.

Answers to 1.3

1 The doctrine of judicial precedent requires lower-ranking courts to follow legal principles previously formulated in higher-ranking courts.

2 The Supreme Court is the highest ranking court. Its precedents bind all lower courts but not future sittings of the Supreme Court. The Court of Appeal ranks below the Supreme Court. Decisions of the Court of Appeal are binding on all inferior courts and, almost always, upon future sittings of the Court of Appeal. Decisions of Divisional Courts of the High Court are binding upon future sittings of the High Court and upon inferior courts. Decisions of ordinary courts of the High Court are binding upon inferior courts but not upon other High Court judges. Decisions of inferior courts are not binding.

3 The *ratio decidendi* of a case could be defined as any statement of law which the judge applied to the facts of the case and upon which the decision in the case is based. *Obiter dicta* would include other statements of law made by the judge. Only the *ratio decidendi* of a case can be

a binding precedent. *Obiter dicta* can be of persuasive authority only.

4 When a precedent is overruled it is changed by a higher-ranking court or by a statute. A case is reversed when an appeal is successful so that the party who won in the lower court loses the appeal. An apparently binding precedent can be distinguished by a judge who refuses to follow it on the grounds that the facts of the case he is considering are materially different from the facts of the case he is distinguishing.

Answers to 1.4

1 The Council, which is not a permanent body but is made up of the relevant Ministers from Member States, is the main policy-making body of the EU. It passes legislation by a system of qualified majority-voting.

2 The European Commission is a permanent institution which makes broad EU policy, drafts secondary legislation and ensures that the Treaty is observed. It also prepares reports on EU matters and negotiates with Member States on these matters.

3 The European Parliament does not pass legislation but has important powers in its capacity as part of the legislative process. It has the power to approve or amend the EU budget, to approve the accounts of the European Commission and to dismiss the entire Commission.

4 If EU legislation is directly applicable it automatically forms part of the domestic law of Member States.

5 EU legislation which has direct effect can be relied upon directly by an individual in a legal action in the domestic courts.

6 If EU legislation has only direct vertical effect, it can only be relied upon by an individual against the State or against an emanation of the State. If the legislation has direct horizontal effect, one individual can invoke it against another individual.

7 Articles of the EC Treaty and Regulations are directly applicable. Whether or not they have direct effect will depend upon whether or not they satisfy the *Van Gend* criteria of being sufficiently clear, precise and unconditional.

8 Before its implementation date, a Directive has no legal effect (subject to the *Wallonie* principle). Once it has been implemented, the UK legislation which implemented the Directive can be relied upon like any other UK law. If the Directive is not properly implemented by the implementation date it can have direct vertical effect, but not direct horizontal effect. Domestic courts are under a duty to try to give indirect effect as far as possible.

9 As a last resort this can be allowed, if the criteria set out in the *Francovich* case (as refined by the *Brasserie de Pêcheur* case) are satisfied.

10 The ECJ expresses authoritative rulings on the interpretation of EC legislation when such interpretations are sought by national courts. It reviews acts adopted by the European Parliament and the other EC institutions. It can also hear cases which the Commission brings against Member States to make sure that they fulfil their EC obligations.

Answers to 1.5

1 Any precedent-making court can make a declaration of incompatibility during legal proceedings. Such a declaration would be to the effect that UK legislation is incompatible with a Convention right. The relevant Minister may revoke or amend the legislation in question, but has the power to leave it unamended.

2 Parliament still has the power to pass legislation which is incompatible with the Convention. However, before the second reading of a Bill the relevant Minister will have to make a written statement saying whether or not the legislation is compatible or incompatible.

3 It is unlawful for public authorities to act in a way which is incompatible with a Convention right. (Unless this was unavoidable as a result of UK legislation.) Public authorities are defined so as to include any person certain of whose functions are of a public nature. Individuals are given the power to bring proceedings against public authorities which breach Convention rights.

4 An individual can only bring a case before the Court of Human Rights as a last resort. The complaint must involve a breach of the Convention by a country which has ratified the Convention. All domestic remedies must have been exhausted and the complaint must be brought within six months of these remedies having been exhausted.

Chapter 2

Answers to 2.1

1 A civil case might be tried in either the county court or the High Court.

2 The county court has unlimited jurisdiction to hear contract and tort cases, as does the High Court, subject to the claim being for a large enough sum of money. If the claim is sufficiently large the claimant can issue his claim in either court. However, there is a presumption that the case will be heard in the county court, this presumption being rebuttable if the case is for a particularly large amount of money, is particularly complex or of particular importance to the general public.

3 The Court of Appeal (Civil Division) hears appeals from the High Court. It also hears appeals from the county court, but only if the appeal was against a final decision in a multi-track case or if it was itself an appeal from a district judge.

4 The Supreme Court hears appeals from the Court of Appeal (Civil Division) and, very occasionally, from the High Court when the leapfrog procedure is invoked.

5 Criminal cases might be tried in either the magistrates' court or in the Crown Court. Summary offences are tried in the magistrates' court, as are the majority of either way offences.

6 The Crown Court tries indictable offences and some either way offences.

7 The Queen's Bench Divisional Court can hear appeals by way of case stated from the magistrates' court or from the

Crown Court if the case was appealed to the Crown Court from the magistrates' court. The appeal can only be made on a point of law or on the grounds of the magistrates having exceeded their powers.

8 The Crown Court hears appeals against conviction by the magistrates and against sentences imposed by the magistrates. The Court of Appeal (Criminal Division) hears appeals from the Crown Court. The Supreme Court hears appeals from the Court of Appeal (Criminal Division) and from the Queen's Bench Divisional Court.

Answers to 2.2

1 The overriding objective of both the Act and the Procedure Rules is that the courts should be enabled to deal with cases justly.

2 A case might be allocated to the small claims track, to the fast track or to the multi-track. This allocation will be done by a master or a district judge, who will take into account the size of the claim, the complexity of the case and the amount of expert evidence which may be needed.

3 The defendant may ignore the claim (and thereby lose the case); admit the claim in full; admit part of the claim; admit the claim but dispute the amount claimed; gain an extra 14 days by filing an acknowledgement of service; or file a defence and/or a counterclaim.

4 The scheme means that a party will not be liable to pay his lawyer if he does not win the case. However, the loser is likely to have to pay the costs of the successful party and should insure against such a possibility.

5 Litigation has the disadvantages of being costly, lengthy, complex, stressful, likely to destroy any business relationship with the other party and conducted in public.

6 Arbitration is the process in which disputes are resolved by an arbitrator rather than by a court. A dispute may be referred to arbitration by the parties themselves, by a term of a contract between the parties, by a court or by an Act of Parliament.

7 Mediation and conciliation do not involve a third party having the power to resolve a dispute. Mediation allows a third party to communicate between the parties, in an attempt to get them to agree to a resolution. Conciliation envisages that a third party will suggest the basis on which a dispute might be resolved.

8 A tribunal is a body which, although technically not a court, acts as a court to resolve certain types of disputes within its ambit. Generally, a tribunal is made up of a legally qualified chairman and two lay members who have expert knowledge of the appropriate field.

Answers to 2.3

1 Barristers act as advocates in all courts. They also draft opinions and statements of case.

2 Solicitors act as the first point of contact for a person seeking professional legal advice. They advise clients, enter into correspondence on their behalf, draft wills, draw up documents which transfer ownership of land and, if necessary, engage the services of a barrister. Solicitors may

act as advocates in the magistrates' court and the county court and also in higher courts if they gain the qualifications needed to do this.

3 Barristers can only be engaged through solicitors. The public may not engage them directly.

4 Only High Court judges, Court of Appeal judges and Supreme Court justices make precedents. Circuit judges try cases but do not make precedents.

5 A district judge (magistrates' court) is a professional magistrate who tries the case on his own. Lay magistrates are not legally qualified and sit with other magistrates as a bench when deciding cases.

6 Judicial review is the process by which the High Court considers whether a decision of public law or the exercise of a discretionary power by a public body was legally taken.

7 In the Crown Court juries decide whether the accused is guilty or not guilty. The decision is based on the judge's summing up of the law. Juries are very rarely used in civil cases.

8 The Law Commission, which has some full-time commissioners, keeps certain areas of the law under review, with a view to systematic development and reform. The Law Reform Committee is a part-time body which considers civil law matters which have been referred to it by the Lord Chancellor. The Criminal Law Revision Committee is a part-time body which has a similar role as regards matters of criminal law referred to it by the Home Secretary.

9 The Law Reports are published by the Incorporated Council for Law Reporting for England and Wales. They report cases in four series. The All England Law Reports report major decisions on any subject. Specialist and electronic law reports also exist.

Chapter 3

Answers to 3.1

1 An offeror makes an offer by proposing a set of terms with the intention that these terms will form a legally binding agreement if they are accepted by the person to whom they are proposed, the offeree.

2 As soon as an offer is accepted a contract is made.

3 An invitation to treat is an invitation to negotiate or an invitation to bargain. It is not an offer.

4 A bilateral contract is one under which both sides exchange promises.

5 The offer of a unilateral contract is made when the offeror gives a definite promise to be bound if the offeree performs some specified action.

Answers to 3.2

1 An acceptance is effective when it is communicated to the offeror. As soon as acceptance is received by the offeror a contract is created. (Communication of acceptance is not necessary when the offer was of a unilateral contract.)

2 When the postal rule applies an acceptance by letter is effective as soon as it is properly posted. The rule will not

be applied where to do so would produce a manifestly absurd result. Nor will it be applied if the circumstances indicated that the parties did not intend there to be a binding contract until acceptance of the offer was received.

3 A counter offer revokes the offer to which it is a response.

4 If an auction is advertised as being 'without reserve' this means that if the auction of a particular lot actually starts the auctioneer makes an offer of a unilateral contract, promising that he will sell to the highest genuine bidder, no matter how low that bid might be. However, the auctioneer does not make a definite offer that particular goods will be included in the auction or that the auction will actually take place.

5 An invitation to submit tenders will generally only be an invitation to treat. However, an invitation to submit tenders will amount to an offer if it states that the highest or lowest tender will definitely be accepted.

6 In ascertaining whether or not an agreement was sufficiently certain to constitute a contract the court considers the objective meaning of what was agreed.

7 A meaningless term will generally not affect the validity of a contract. If a term is meaningless it can generally be ignored.

Answers to 3.3

1 A revocation of an offer will be effective once it is received by the offeree. This is the case whether or not the revocation was posted.

2 In all but exceptional cases it will not be possible to revoke an offer of a unilateral contract once an offeree has begun to perform the act requested in the offer.

3 Unless an offer is revoked, it will remain open for a stipulated time, or if no time was stipulated for a reasonable time.

4 The courts will solve 'battle of the forms' cases by applying the ordinary rules of offer and acceptance. Generally, the person who makes the last counter offer will win as long as it can be inferred that this was accepted by the other party.

Chapter 4

Answers to 4.1

1 When an agreement is made in a business or commercial context the courts will presume that the parties did intend to create legal relations. This presumption can be rebutted by the evidence.

2 When an agreement is made in a social or domestic context the courts will presume that the parties did not intend to create legal relations. This presumption can be rebutted by the evidence.

3 A letter of comfort is a letter designed to give reassurance. It might or might not give rise to contractual liability depending upon the words used and the circumstances of the case.

4 Any contractual term which excludes the jurisdiction of the courts will be void. (A term providing that disputes

should be referred to arbitration is the only exception to this principle.)

Answers to 4.2

1 Consideration consists either in the giving of a benefit or the suffering of a loss. An agreement will only amount to a contract if both parties give some consideration to the other. A contract is a bargain under which the parties exchange their respective considerations.

2 The rule that past consideration is no consideration means that a party cannot give as consideration some act which he has already performed. A past act can amount to consideration for a promise if the act was performed at the request of the promisor and if both parties all along contemplated that payment would be made.

3 The rule means that consideration must be of some recognisable economic value (sufficient), but it does not need to be equal in value to the other party 's consideration (adequate).

4 Privity of contract holds that a person who is not a party to a contract can neither sue to enforce the contract nor be sued on the contract. There are several exceptions to this rule.

5 Generally, the common law will not allow a third party to sue to enforce a contract made on his behalf. The Contracts (Rights of Third Parties) Act 1999 may allow a third party to sue to enforce a term of a contract made on his behalf, but only if the third party was expressly identified in the contract. A term can be enforced by the third party if the term expressly provides that it may be enforced by him. If a term purports to confer a contractual benefit on a third party the term will be enforceable by the third party unless the parties to the contract did not intend it to be enforceable by the third party. There is therefore a rebuttable presumption that a third party can enforce a term which purports to confer a benefit upon him.

6 It is not good consideration to promise to perform a duty imposed by the general law.

7 A promise to perform an existing duty which arose under a contract with a third party can be given as good consideration. A promise to perform an existing duty which arose under a previous contract with the same promisee may possibly be good consideration if performance of the duty confers a benefit on the promisee.

8 The rule in *Pinnel's Case* is that a lesser sum of money paid on the date when a greater sum is owed cannot be good consideration for the greater sum.

9 Promissory estoppel is an equitable doctrine which prevents a claimant from breaking a promise not to insist on his strict legal rights if the promise was intended to create legal relations, if the claimant knew that the promise was going to be acted upon and if the defendant did act upon the promise. The doctrine only applies where it would be inequitable for the claimant to break his promise.

Answers to 4.3

1 A deed is necessary to convey a legal estate in land. A lease of over three years' duration must also be made by a deed

or no legal estate will be created. A promise of a gift will not be enforceable unless made by a deed.

2 Contracts for the sale or other disposition of an interest in land must be made in writing. Regulated consumer credit agreements will be unenforceable without a court order if not made in writing and signed by the debtor.

3 Contracts of guarantee must be evidenced in writing or they will be unenforceable.

4 A minor will be bound to pay a reasonable price for necessary goods delivered or necessary services supplied. Beneficial contracts of employment, and analogous contracts, will also be binding upon a minor.

5 Contracts giving an interest in property, which also impose a continuing liability on a minor, are voidable by the minor.

Chapter 5

Answers to 5.1

1 Express terms are specifically agreed upon by the parties. Implied terms are put into the contract, either by the courts or by a statute, without the parties needing to expressly agree them.

2 An express statement will be a term of a contract if the court infers that the parties intended the statement to be a term of the contract.

3 **a** If the maker of the statement was much better placed to know whether or not it was true, the statement is likely to be a term. If the person to whom the statement was made was much better placed to know whether or not it was true, the statement is likely to be a representation.

b If the party to whom the statement was made indicated that he considered the statement to be vitally important to him then it is likely to be a term.

c A statement which is made very strongly is likely to be a term. A statement made very weakly is likely to be a representation.

d The longer the time lapse between the making of the statement and the making of the contract the more likely it is that the statement is not a term. The shorter the time lapse between the making of the statement and the formation of the contract the more likely it is that the statement is a term.

4 The parol evidence rule is that extrinsic (outside) evidence cannot be introduced to add to or vary a written contract. There are several exceptions to the rule.

Answers to 5.2

1 A court will imply a term as a matter of fact to give business efficacy to a contract. The term is implied because the court considers that the parties obviously intended the term to be a part of the contract.

2 A court will imply a term as a matter of law when the contract is of a sufficiently recognisable type, the parties have not dealt with the matter and it is necessary to imply the term to make the contract work.

3 A customary term can be implied by the courts on the grounds that it is customary in a particular locality, or customary in a particular trade, or customary between the parties themselves.

4 In deciding whether a term is a condition or a warranty a court will look at all the evidence to see if the parties considered the term to be vitally important, a term which went to the root of the contract, at the time when the contract was made. If the parties would have considered the term vitally important the term will be a condition. If the parties would not have considered the term to be vitally important it will only be a warranty.

5 Breach of a condition allows the injured party to treat the contract as repudiated and/or claim damages. Breach of a warranty allows the injured party to claim damages but not to treat the contract as repudiated.

6 Breach of an innominate term will always allow the injured party to claim damages. The injured party will be entitled to treat the contract as repudiated only if he was deprived of substantially the whole benefit of the contract.

Answers to 5.3

1 If an exclusion clause is not incorporated as a term of a contract then it cannot affect liability arising under the contract, in which case there is no need to consider the effect of the 1977 Act or the 1999 Regulations.

2 In order for an exclusion clause to be a term of a contract it must have been agreed upon, or reasonable notice of it have been given, before the contract was made.

3 As regards business liability, a contract term or notice cannot exclude liability for death or personal injury caused by negligence (UCTA s.2(1)). A contract term can only exclude liability for other types of loss caused by negligence in so far as the term satisfies UCTA's requirement of reasonableness (UCTA s.2(2)).

4 Liability for breach of the terms implied by SGA 1979, and the corresponding terms implied by SGITA 1973 and SGSA 1982 can never be excluded where the buyer deals as a consumer. Where the buyer does not deal as a consumer liability for breach of the implied terms can be excluded by a term which satisfies UCTA's requirement of reasonableness. However, liability for breach of the terms as to the right to sell can never be excluded.

5 The 1999 Regulations apply only to terms in contracts between a consumer and a seller or supplier.

6 The main effect of the 1999 Regulations is that consumers will not be bound by unfair terms, that is to say by terms which were not individually negotiated and which, contrary to the requirement of good faith, cause a significant imbalance between the rights and obligations under the contract to the detriment of the consumer.

Chapter 6

Answers to 6.1

1 A voidable contract is a valid contract, but one of the parties has the option to avoid the contract (call it off). A void

contract is a nullity, and confers no legal rights on either party.

2 An actionable misrepresentation is an untrue statement of fact made by one of the parties to a contract which induced the other party to make the contract.

3 Silence is not generally capable of amounting to an actionable misrepresentation. It can however do so, (i) where there has been a change of circumstances, (ii) where the contract is of the utmost good faith, (iii) where there is a fiduciary relationship between the parties or (iv) where the silence makes a statement misleading.

Answers to 6.2

1 A fraudulent misrepresentation is an actionable misrepresentation made either knowing that it was false, or without belief in its truth or recklessly, carelessly whether it was true or false.

2 A non-fraudulent misrepresentation will be a negligent misrepresentation unless the maker of the misrepresentation can prove that he had reasonable grounds for believing that it was true and did hold such a belief up until the time of the contract. If these matters can be proved then the misrepresentation will have been made wholly innocently.

3 A fraudulent misrepresentation makes the contract voidable and gives rise to an action for damages for the tort of deceit.

4 Section 2(1) of the Misrepresentation Act 1967 gives a right to damages for negligent misrepresentation. These damages are assessed on the tort of deceit basis. The contract will be voidable, but the court may award damages in lieu of rescission under s.2(2) of the Misrepresentation Act 1967.

5 There is no right to damages for wholly innocent misrepresentation. The contract will be voidable, but the court may award damages in lieu of rescission under s.2(2) of the Misrepresentation Act 1967. Such awards of damages are very rare.

6 Under s.2(2) of the 1967 Act damages may be awarded in lieu of rescission for either negligent or wholly innocent misrepresentation. These damages are assessed on the breach of warranty basis.

7 The right to rescind can be lost if the contract has been affirmed, if restitution is impossible or if a third party in good faith has acquired ownership of the subject matter of the contract.

Answers to 6.3

1 A contract which is held to be void for a mistake is a nullity. It cannot give rise to contractual rights or obligations. If goods are sold under a contract which is void for mistake ownership will not pass to the buyer and the seller will have to refund the purchase price.

2 A common mistake might be either as to the existence of the subject matter of the contract, or as to its ownership or as to its quality. Mistake as to existence or ownership can make the contract void. Mistake as to quality is most unlikely to make the contract void.

3 A mutual mistake will render the contract void if it could not be objectively inferred that either of the views held by the parties, as to the terms of the contract, was what the parties intended. If either view could be inferred as objectively reflecting the intention of the parties then there will be a contract on those terms.

4 A unilateral mistake might be made either as to the identity of the other contracting party, or as to the terms of the contract.

5 Mistake as to the identity of the other contracting party will make a contract void if the parties made a written contract without meeting face to face, if the mistake was as to the identity of the other party and not just as to his attributes, and if the mistake was a material mistake which was known to the other party.

6 A unilateral mistake as to the terms of the contract will make a contract void only if the party who is not mistaken could not reasonably have supposed that the other party intended to contract on the terms which were agreed.

7 A person can escape a contract on the grounds of *non est factum* if he signed a document, without being careless in so doing, while under a complete misapprehension as to its effect.

Answers to 6.4

1 Historically, the common law held a contract voidable for duress only if the contract was entered into as a consequence of physical violence or the threat of it.

2 A contract can be voidable for economic duress if it was entered into as a consequence of commercial pressure which coerced the other party's will so as to vitiate consent. Generally, a threat to commit a lawful act cannot amount to economic duress.

3 Equity will hold a contract voidable on the grounds of actual undue influence without the need to prove a special relationship between the parties. The party claiming to have been unduly influenced must prove that undue influence was in fact exerted.

4 In certain types of relationships undue influence is automatically presumed. Contracts made between parties in such relationships will be voidable at the option of the influenced party unless the other party can prove that there was no undue influence. The relationships are solicitor and client, doctor and patient, parent and child, guardian and ward, trustee and beneficiary, and religious advisor and disciple. The victim will need to prove that the contract was manifestly to his disadvantage.

5 In relationships other than those where undue influence is automatically presumed, it may still be presumed if the influenced party proves that the relationship was such that he placed great trust and confidence in the other party. It must also be proved that the contract entered into could not easily be explained by the relationship between the parties.

Answers to 6.5

1 The following contracts are illegal at common law: contracts tending to promote corruption in public life;

contracts tending to impede the administration of justice; contracts to trade with enemy nations; contracts to commit a tort, fraud or crime; contracts tending to promote sexual immorality; contracts to defraud the Revenue.

2 Contracts damaging to the institution of marriage, to oust the jurisdiction of the courts or in restraint of trade are void at common law.

3 A contract in restraint of trade will be void unless it can be proved to be reasonable as between the parties and as regards the public interest.

4 Where severance is allowed the unreasonable part of a contract in restraint of trade can be severed from the reasonable part, leaving the reasonable part to stand. Severance will only be permitted if the unreasonable parts of the contract could be crossed out with a blue pencil, leaving the reasonable parts: unaffected.

Chapter 7

Answers to 7.1

1 A breach of condition will allow the injured party to treat his further contractual obligations as discharged, whereas a breach of warranty will not. A breach of an innominate term will allow the injured party to treat his further contractual obligations as discharged only if the breach deprived the injured party of substantially the whole benefit of the contract.

2 If a contractual obligation is held to be entire, then the general rule is that it is a condition precedent of the other party's performance of the contract that the entire obligation be fully performed.

3 A contractual obligation will be entire if the construction of the contract indicates that this is what the parties to the contract intended. If the contract was intended to be divisible or severable then it will consist of a number of separate obligations rather than of one entire obligation. Where the contract is divisible or severable a party who performs some of the obligations will be entitled to payment for the obligations performed but will be liable in damages for the obligations not performed.

4 Failure to perform an entire obligation will not discharge the other party from performing his own contractual obligations in three circumstances: where partial performance was genuinely accepted by the other contracting party; where the other party prevented performance of the entire obligation; or where the contract was substantially performed.

5 Tendering delivery of goods discharges the seller from further liability to deliver. If the tender is not accepted the seller will be entitled to damages for non acceptance.

6 Tendering the price does not discharge the buyer from liability to pay it. However, if the buyer pays the money into court this acts as a defence to being sued on the contract.

7 A contract can be discharged or varied by accord and satisfaction. Accord means that both parties must agree to the discharge or variation. Satisfaction means that both

parties must give some consideration in return for their liabilities being discharged or varied.

Answers to 7.2

1 A contract can be frustrated if, after the contract has been created but before it has been performed, any of the following matters occur: the subject matter of the contract ceases to exist; a person who was to perform personally has become unavailable; an event which was central to the contract has not occurred; the contract cannot be performed in the manner agreed in the contract; or the contract has become illegal to perform.

2 If the frustrating event is the fault of one of the parties, that party cannot claim that the contract was frustrated.

3 A *force majeure* clause is a clause in the contract which provides what should happen if the 'frustrating' event occurs. Such clauses are given legal effect.

4 If only one of the parties foresaw, or should have foreseen, the frustrating event then that party cannot claim that the contract was frustrated.

5 The Law Reform (Frustrated Contracts) Act 1943 provides that when a contract is frustrated: money owing ceases to be due; money paid is recoverable, although the court has a power to allow some money paid or payable to be retained to cover expenses; a party who has received a valuable benefit may be ordered to pay a just amount to compensate for this.

6 An anticipatory breach occurs when a party expressly or impliedly indicates an unwillingness to perform the contract before the time for performance has become due.

7 A party faced with a repudiatory anticipatory breach can treat the contract as discharged and sue for damages. Alternatively, he may affirm the contract and sue for damages when an actual breach occurs. If the contract can still be performed without the cooperation of the party committing the anticipatory breach, the injured party may be able to perform the contract and then sue for the contract price.

Answers to 7.3

1 The two rules in *Hadley* v *Baxendale* are used to assess whether or not a loss caused by a breach of contract is too remote for damages to be claimed in respect of it. The first rule is that damages can be claimed in respect of a loss if the loss arose naturally from the breach according to the usual course of things. The second rule is that damages can be claimed in respect of a loss if both of the parties would have contemplated that the loss would be the probable result of breach, at the time when they made the contract.

2 Damages for wasted expenditure can generally be claimed as an alternative to damages for loss of the bargain.

3 The injured party will not be able to claim damages in respect of losses which could have been mitigated by taking reasonable steps.

4 When the parties specify in the contract itself the amount of damages payable in the event of breach this amount may be either a penalty or liquidated damages. If the

amount is a genuine pre-estimate of the loss it will be regarded as liquidated damages and applied no matter what the actual loss. If the amount specified is a large sum designed to warn the other party against breaching the contract it will be ignored as a penalty and damages will be assessed in the usual way.

Answers to 7.4

1 An action for an agreed sum is not the same as an action for damages. It is an action in debt. Hence the rules on remoteness, quantification and mitigation of damage do not apply.

2 A claim on a *quantum meruit* is a claim for reasonable remuneration for work performed. Such a claim can be made: if the other party prevented completion of the contract; or if work has been done and accepted under a void or partially performed contract; or where the contract does not expressly provide what the remuneration should be.

3 Specific performance is a discretionary equitable remedy ordering a party to actually do what he agreed in the contract that he would do. Failure to comply with the order will be contempt of court.

4 An injunction is a court order requiring a person to do or not to do a certain act. It can be used to prevent a party from breaking the terms of his contract.

Chapter 8

Answers to 8.1

1 A contract of sale of goods is a contract by which the seller transfers or agrees to transfer the property in goods to the buyer for a money consideration, called the price.

2 Goods are defined as all personal chattels other than things in action. A thing in action is a right which can only be enforced by suing. A personal chattel is a physical object which can be touched and moved.

3 a Not a contract of sale of goods. A contract for the supply of a service.

   b Not a contract of sale of goods. A patent is a thing in action.

   c A contract of sale of goods.

   d A contract of sale of goods.

   e Not a contract of sale of goods. The customer's consideration is not money, but rather the act of purchasing the £20 worth of groceries.

   f Not a contract of sale of goods. A contract to sell land.

   g An agreement to sell future goods. The agreement is governed by the 1979 Act.

   h Not a contract of sale of goods. The sale of copyright is the sale of a thing in action.

   i A contract of sale of goods.

   j Not a contract of sale of goods. A contract of barter.

   k Not a contract of sale of goods. A contract for work and materials.

   l Not a contract of sale of goods. The ticket is a thing in action.

m Not a contract of sale of goods. A contract of hire-purchase.

n Not a contract of sale of goods. A share is a thing in action.

Answers to 8.2

1 Section 12(1) implies a condition on the part of the seller that in the case of a sale he has a right to sell the goods, and in the case of an agreement to sell he will have such a right at the time when the property is to pass.

2 Section 12(2) implies warranties as to quiet possession and freedom from encumbrances.

3 Section 12(1) says that it is a condition that the seller must have the right to sell the goods. In *Rowland* v *Divall* the defendant thought that he had the right to sell, but this was no defence.

4 There is no breach of s.12(1). This is an agreement to sell in the future, and s.12(1) only requires that the seller will have the right to sell at the time when the property is to pass.

5 Because although the buyer had actual possession he never had what he paid for: the right to legal possession and ownership of the car.

6 a Ownership remained throughout with the person from whom the thief stole the batteries.

   b The customer did have actual possession of the batteries.

   c The customer never had legal possession, as per Lord Atkin in *Rowland* v *Divall* (1923).

   d The customer will be able to claim all of his money back from the shop. This involves an element of unjust enrichment, but the Law Commission Report 160 saw no way around this problem.

Answers to 8.3

1 SGA s.13(1) implies a term that where there is a contract for the sale of goods by description, then the goods will correspond with the description.

2 Unascertained future goods are always sold by description.

3 Specific goods are sold by description where the description was an essential term of the contract on which the buyer relied, and where the descriptive words are a substantial part of the identity of what is being bought.

4 Section 13(1) is always regarded as a condition when the buyer deals as a consumer. Therefore the shopper would be entitled to treat the contract as repudiated and/or claim damages. The supermarket, although not dealing as a consumer, would generally be entitled to the same remedies, for breach of condition. However, if the breach was so slight as to make rejection of the goods unreasonable, the supermarket would only be able to claim damages and would not be entitled to treat the contract as repudiated.

Answers to 8.4

1 a The term as to satisfactory quality will not be implied at all, as the sale was not made in the course of a business.

   b If, as seems highly likely, the examination by Adam should have revealed the rust, then the fact of the car being rusty will not make the quality of the car unsatisfactory. Adam's examination of the car ought to have revealed this defect. The car will be unsatisfactory on account of the brakes being so poor. It is not the case that Adam's examination ought to have revealed this defect.

c The damage to the fuel tank will not cause the bike to be of unsatisfactory quality. The defect was specifically pointed out to Charlene.

d The bicycle would not be of satisfactory quality, as the gears would not work. No defect was specifically pointed out to David.

2 Section 14(3) provides that where the seller sells goods in the course of a business and the buyer, expressly or by implication, makes known ... to the seller ... any particular purpose for which the goods are being bought, there is an implied [term] that the goods supplied under the contract are reasonably fit for that purpose, whether or not that is a purpose for which such goods are commonly supplied, except where the circumstances show that the buyer does not rely, or that it is unreasonable for him to rely, on the skill or judgment of the seller.

3 Those who purchase privately will not be protected by either s.14(2) or s.14(3) SGA, whereas those who purchase from a garage will be protected by both implied terms.

4 David might be unwise to behave in this way because the protection conferred by s.14(2) will be lost as regards defects which the examination ought to have revealed. Furthermore, it is possible that the examination might indicate that David did not reasonably rely on the seller's skill and judgment that the car was fit for any particular purpose. This might happen if defects were particularly apparent and the seller gave no assurances about these defects.

Answers to 8.5

1 a This is quite likely to be a sale by sample. It seems highly likely that the buyer would have insisted on examining a sample before making the purchase. Alternatively, or in addition, it might be a sale by description.

b This would be a sale by sample.

c This is not a sale by sample as there is no bulk and no sample. It is a sale by model. There is no SGA term requiring correspondence with the model, but there would be a common law term to this effect.

d This could well be a sale by sample. When selling to retailers salesmen often bring samples of new products. (As was the case in *Godley v Perry*.) If the retailer examined such a sample and then placed the order in reliance on the examination the sale would be by sample.

e This would be a sale by description rather than a sale by sample.

2 The two implied terms are that the bulk will correspond with the sample in quality; and that the goods will be free from any defect, making their quality unsatisfactory, which would not be apparent on reasonable examination of the sample.

3 The boy would sue the shop under s.14(2) and (3) SGA. The catapult was plainly not of satisfactory quality. Nor was it fit for the boy's purpose. (As this purpose was the usual purpose, it would have impliedly been made known to the shopkeeper.) Both s.14(2) and (3) would therefore have been breached.

Answers to 8.6

1 a SGSA 1982 s.9(2). (Only if the owner of the goods is acting in the course of a business.)

b SGSA 1982 s.2(1).

c SGA 1979 s.13(1).

d SGSA 1982 s.13. (Only if the supplier of the service is acting in the course of a business.)

e SGITA 1973 s.10(3).

2 a A condition.

b Warranties.

c An innominate term.
Breach of warranty will entitle the buyer/hirer to damages but not to treat the contract as repudiated. Breach of a statutory condition as to correspondence with description, satisfactory quality, fitness for purpose or correspondence with sample will entitle the buyer/hirer to damages and to treat the contract as repudiated unless the buyer was not a consumer, and the breach was so slight as to make rejection of the goods unreasonable, and no term gave the right to reject the goods for such a breach. Breach of an innominate term will entitle the injured party to treat the contract as repudiated only if the breach deprived of substantially the whole benefit of the contract. Damages for breach will always be available.

Answers to 8.7

1 s.12(1) UCTA provides that a person deals as a consumer if: (a) he neither makes the contract in the course of a business nor holds himself out as doing so; and (b) the other party does make the contract in the course of a business; and (c) (which applies only in cases where the potential consumer is a company rather than an individual) the goods supplied under the contract are of a type ordinarily supplied for private use or consumption.

2 a As Jemima deals as a consumer, s.7 UCTA 1977 provides that liability for breach of s.9(2) SGSA 1982 cannot be excluded by any contract term.

b As the shop owner did not deal as a consumer, s.6 UCTA 1977 provides that liability for breach of the terms implied by s.14(2) and (3) SGA 1979 can be excluded only in so far as the term excluding liability satisfies UCTA's requirement of reasonableness.

c If the failure to supply the service using reasonable care and skill caused death or personal injury to any person then s.2(1) UCTA 1977 provides that no term can exclude liability for this. If the failure to supply the service using reasonable care and skill caused other loss or damage, s.2(2) UCTA 1977 provides that liability for this can be excluded to the extent that the term which excludes liability satisfies UCTA's requirement of reasonableness.

Chapter 9

Answers to 9.1

1 The passing of the property in the goods means the passing of the ownership of the goods.
2 In this context, the risk means the risk of the goods becoming lost, damaged or destroyed.
3 Specific goods are defined as goods which are identified and agreed on at the time a contract of sale is made.
4 Unascertained goods are not defined by the Act, but would include all goods which are not specific.
5 Future goods are goods which have yet to be acquired or manufactured by the seller. In this context future goods are always regarded as unascertained goods.
6 (a) Specific goods. (b) Unascertained goods. (c) The sale from David to Charles would be a sale of specific goods. The sale by Charles to Edward would be a sale of future goods and would therefore be treated, for the purposes of discovering when the property passed, as unascertained goods.

Answers to 9.2

1 Section 17 provides that the property in specific goods passes when the parties to the contract intend it to pass, and this intention can either be a term of the contract or can be inferred from the conduct of the parties and the circumstances of the case.
2 Section 17 takes precedence over s.18. The Rules in s.18 are to apply only if the parties have not expressly or impliedly shown an intention as to when the property is to pass.
3 The property in the haystack would have passed to the buyer when the contract was made. Risk would also have passed at this time. The buyer would therefore be obliged to pay the full price for what he received – ownership of the haystack. (This case was codified by the 1893 Act, and so the outcome was the same in 1827.)
4 Goods are in a deliverable state, for the purpose of s.18, when the seller has no more obligation to do anything to the goods as an article.
5 The property will pass to the buyer at such time as the parties expressly or impliedly agreed (s.17). Assuming no agreement, the property will pass when the goods are put into a deliverable state and the buyer has notice of this (s.18 Rule 2).

Answers to 9.3

1 Subject to s.20A, it is not possible for the property in unascertained goods to pass to the buyer before the goods have become ascertained.
2 Unascertained goods will become ascertained when they are identified in accordance with the agreement after the contract of sale has been made.
3 As long as the goods have become ascertained, the intention shown will dictate when the property in the goods passes (s.17). However, if the goods have not become ascertained then, subject to s.20A, no property can pass to the buyer.
4 Where s.18 Rule 5 applies, it will pass the property in the goods when goods which match the contract description and which are in a deliverable state are unconditionally appropriated to the contract, either by the seller with the assent of the buyer or by the buyer with the assent of the seller.
5 The three conditions are that: (i) A specified quantity of unascertained goods must have been bought. (ii) These goods must form part of a bulk which is identified in the contract or by subsequent agreement between the parties. (iii) The buyer must have paid the price for some or all of the goods which are the subject of the contract and which form part of the bulk.
6 In this context the risk means the risk of the goods becoming lost, damaged or destroyed.
7 Risk will usually pass with the property in the goods, but not if the parties have expressly or impliedly agreed that it should not (s.20) or if the buyer deals as a consumer and property passes before delivery.
8 A bailee is a person who has possession of property which he does not own. The two main duties of a bailee are to take reasonable care of the goods and to return them to the owner if asked to do so.

Answers to 9.4

1 A reservation of title clause reserves the title in goods sold until the price is paid. If the clause is effective, the seller therefore owns the goods until such time as the buyer pays the price.
2 A company charge which has not been registered with the Registrar of Companies is void under s.874 of the Companies Act 2006.
3 Belinda will be able to keep the goods as long as she acted in good faith and in ignorance of the reservation of title clause. Brian would have passed title to Belinda under s.25 SGA as a buyer in possession of the goods.

Answers to 9.5

1 The maxim means that a person who is not the owner of goods cannot pass ownership to another person, unless he does so as the agent of the owner.
2 A mercantile agent is an agent who has in the customary course of his business as such an agent authority to sell goods, to buy goods or to raise money on the security of goods.
3 If a mercantile agent has possession of goods, or of documents of title to goods, with the consent of the owner, for a purpose connected with his business as a mercantile agent, a sale or other disposition by the mercantile agent made in the ordinary course of business as a mercantile agent can pass title to the goods to a third party acting in good faith and without notice of the mercantile agent's lack of authority.

4 Section 21 SGA provides that an owner of goods who makes a representation to a third party that a seller of goods has the right to sell the goods will be estopped (prevented) from later denying the truth of the representation.

5 Section 23 provides that where a seller of goods has a voidable title to the goods, and this title has not been avoided at the time of the sale, a buyer who buys the goods in good faith and without notice of the seller's defect of title will acquire a good title to the goods.

6 Section 24 provides that if a seller (a seller in possession) sells goods to one person, but retains possession of the goods, and then sells or disposes of the same goods to a second person who takes delivery of the goods or of documents of title to the goods, the second buyer acquires title to the goods even if title had already passed to the first buyer.

7 Section 25 allows a person who has bought or agreed to buy goods (a buyer in possession) to pass title to the goods to a third party, as if the buyer in possession were acting as a mercantile agent on behalf of the owner of the goods. The buyer in possession must have obtained the goods, or documents of title to the goods, with the owner's consent. The third party must act in good faith and the goods, or documents of title, must be delivered to the third party under a contract of sale or other disposition of the goods.

8 The Hire Purchase Act 1964 Part III provides that a private purchaser acting in good faith who agrees to buy a motor vehicle which is the subject of a hire-purchase agreement, or who agrees to take the motor vehicle on hire-purchase, while acting in ignorance of the hire-purchase agreement, acquires title to the motor vehicle.

Chapter 10

Answers to 10.1

1 The seller would not have to actually deliver the goods. He could sue for damages for non-acceptance as long as he could show that he had been ready and willing to deliver the goods. Section 28 makes it plain that the duty of the seller to deliver the goods and of the buyer to pay for them are concurrent conditions.

2 (a) and (b) the place of delivery is the seller's place of business or, if he has not got a place of business, his home (s.29(2)). (c) The place of delivery will be the place where both of the parties know the goods to be (s.29(2)).

3 If time of delivery is of the essence then the time of delivery is a condition. Consequently the buyer can treat the contract as repudiated, and/or claim damages, if the goods are delivered late. If time was not of the essence then the buyer will only be able to claim damages. Whether or not time is of the essence depends upon the intentions of the parties (s.10(2)).

4 (a) If the seller delivers too large a quantity of goods then the buyer may accept the correct quantity of goods and reject the rest, or he may reject the whole (s.30(2)). Or the buyer may accept the whole of the goods delivered and pay for them at the contract rate (s.30(3)). (b) If the seller delivers too small a quantity then the buyer may reject the goods, or accept the goods delivered and pay for them at the contract rate (s.30(1)).

5 The buyer will be able to treat the whole contract as repudiated only if the breach by the seller amounted to a repudiation of the whole contract. It is a question in each case depending on the terms of the contract and the circumstances of the case whether the breach of contract is a repudiation of the whole contract or whether it is a severable breach giving rise to a claim for compensation but not a right to treat the whole contract as repudiated (s.31(2)).

Answers to 10.2

1 The price of the goods can be fixed by the contract, or by a manner agreed by the contract, or may be determined by a course of dealing between the parties (s.8(1)). If the price is not fixed in any of these ways then the buyer must pay a reasonable price (s.8(2)). What amounts to a reasonable price is a question of fact dependent on the circumstances of each particular case (s.8(3)).

2 An unpaid seller is a seller to whom the whole of the price has not been paid or tendered, or a seller who has taken a negotiable instrument as conditional payment and the condition on which this was taken has not been fulfilled (s.38(1)).

3 The three remedies available only to an unpaid seller are: the unpaid seller's lien; stoppage in transit and the right of resale.

4 The seller can only sue for the price if the property in the goods has passed to the buyer or if the contract fixed a definite date for payment (s.49).

5 There will be an available market if the goods were not unique, if a different buyer of the goods could be found, and if the price of the goods could be fixed by the prevailing conditions of supply and demand. Where there is such an available market the court will *prima facie* assess the loss directly and naturally flowing from the breach as the difference between the contract price and the price at the time when the goods ought to have been accepted or, if the time for acceptance was not fixed, at the time when the buyer refused to accept (s.50(3)).

Answers to 10.3

1 a Where there is no available market for the goods the buyer's damages will be quantified as the estimated loss directly and naturally resulting in the ordinary course of events from the seller's breach of contract (s.51(2)).

b Where there is an available market for the goods the measure of damages is *prima facie* to be ascertained by the difference between the contract price and the market price of the goods at the time or times when they ought to have been delivered or (if no time was fixed) at the time of the refusal to deliver (s.51(3)).

2 In the case of a breach of warranty of quality the buyer's loss is *prima facie* the difference between the value of the

goods in the state they were in and the value which they would have had if the warranty had not been breached (s.53(3)).

3 The buyer will have the right to reject the goods if the seller has breached a condition of the contract; if the seller has breached an innominate term and this breach has deprived the buyer of substantially the whole benefit of the contract; if the express or implied terms of the contract conferred upon the buyer a right to reject; or if the seller has repudiated the contract.

4 Once the buyer has accepted the goods he will no longer be able to reject, even for breach of condition. The buyer will still be entitled to sue for damages.

5 The buyer can be deemed to have accepted the goods when he intimates to the seller that he has accepted them; when the goods have been delivered to him and he does any act in relation to them which is inconsistent with the ownership of the seller; or when after the lapse of a reasonable time the buyer retains the goods without intimating to the seller that he is rejecting them.

6 The property in the goods passes to the buyer at the fall of the hammer.

Answers to 10.4

1 The bill of lading is only evidence of the contract of carriage, rather than being the contract of carriage itself. However, as between the shipowner and a third party to whom the bill of lading has been transferred, the bill becomes conclusive evidence of the contract of carriage.

2 As a document of title, the bill transfers constructive possession of the goods to the holder of the bill.

3 a A clean bill of lading will certify that the goods were shipped in apparent good order and condition.

b A claused bill will specify in what way the goods shipped were not in apparent good order and condition.

4 The seller has the duties to put the goods on board ship and pay the loading charges. The buyer has the duties to nominate an effective ship and pay the shipping costs. It is generally also the buyer's duty to make the contract of carriage.

5 The seller has the duties to present to the buyer a clean bill of lading, a policy of insurance and an invoice for the goods. The buyer must take these documents and pay for them if they are in order. If the goods do not conform to the contract the buyer will be able to reject the goods. However, the buyer must accept the three documents and pay for them even if he knows that the goods have been lost or damaged.

Chapter 11

Answers to 11.1

1 Belinda, the auctioneer is Alice's agent. Denise is Celia's agent.

2 Both express and actual authority arise by agreement between principal and agent. Express actual authority

arises where the principal and agent agree in words that the agent shall have the authority. Implied actual authority arises where this is agreed otherwise than in words.

3 Apparent authority arises when a principal represents to a third party that someone is his agent. Once the third party has acted on the representation the principal will be estopped from denying its truth. Actual authority does not arise on account of a representation to a third party, but by agreement between principal and agent.

4 (a) The manager did not have actual authority because the hotel owner had not agreed with the manager that the manager had authority to buy tobacco on credit. (b) The manager did not have apparent authority because the hotel owner had not made a representation to the third party that the manager was his agent.

5 Agency by ratification can arise when a principal agrees to adopt a transaction conducted on his behalf by an agent who had no authority to bind the principal. Retrospective actual authority is conferred.

Answers to 11.2

1 Agency is undisclosed where the agent does not reveal that he is acting as an agent. Agency is disclosed where the agent reveals that he is acting as an agent.

2 a Where the agency is disclosed then the principal will be liable on the contract only if the agent had some type of authority to act for the principal.

b The agent will have no liability on the contract, unless the circumstances show that he intended to be personally liable on it. However, the agent might be liable to the third party for breach of warranty of authority. This liability would arise if the agent warranted that he had authority which he did not have, and if reliance on this warranty caused a loss to the third party.

3 a The principal will be liable on the contract as long as the agent acted within the scope of his actual authority.

b The agent will be liable on the contract, whether or not the principal is also liable on it.

4 An undisclosed principal cannot sue on the contract:

a where a term of the contract excluded agency;

b where the third party would have refused to contract with the undisclosed principal;

c where the third party made the contract with the agent because he particularly wanted to contract with the agent personally.

Answers to 11.3

1 The non-fiduciary duties imposed on an agent are: to obey instructions, to use an appropriate amount of care and skill, and to perform personally.

2 The fiduciary duties imposed on an agent are: to avoid a conflict of interest, not to make a secret profit, not to take a bribe and to account to the principal. These duties are imposed because the very nature of agency causes the principal to place great trust and confidence in the agent.

3 An agent might have the right to an indemnity to cover expenses necessarily incurred in performing the agency.

An express or implied term of the contract between principal and agent might entitle an agent to remuneration. An agent might have a particular lien over the principal's goods until some claim has been satisfied.

4 An agent whose authority has been withdrawn could continue to have apparent authority to bind the principal to third parties who do not know that the authority has been withdrawn.

5 Agency may be terminated by operation of law by: frustration, the death of either party, the insanity of either party, the bankruptcy of the principal or by the bankruptcy of the agent if this would render him unfit to perform his duties.

Chapter 12

Answers to 12.1

1 Contractual liability is voluntarily undertaken, tortious liability is imposed by the courts; contractual liability is generally strict, tortious liability is generally based on fault; contract damages are designed to put the party in the position he would have been in if the contract had been properly performed, tort damages are designed to put the injured party in the position he would have been in if the tort had never been committed.

2 In order to establish that the tort of negligence has been committed the claimant will need to prove that the defendant owed him a duty of care, that the defendant breached that duty and that a foreseeable type of injury was caused by this breach.

3 A duty of care owed by a defendant to a claimant will have been breached if the defendant did not take the care which a reasonable person would have taken in all the circumstances of the case.

4 The four factors which are likely to be of particular significance in deciding whether or not a duty of care was breached are: the likelihood of harm being caused to the claimant; the potential seriousness of injury; the cost of making sure that injury was not caused; and the usefulness of the objectives which the defendant was trying to achieve.

5 The 'but for' test asks whether the claimant would have suffered the same damage but for the defendant's actions. If the claimant would have suffered the same loss anyway, damages can generally not be recovered in respect of the loss.

6 The claimant will only be able to succeed in respect of loss or damage of a type which was a reasonably foreseeable consequence of the defendant's breach of duty.

7 Damages in respect of psychiatric injury can only be claimed if there is a sufficient proximity based on ties of love and affection between the claimant and the injured loved one. The claimant would also have to be sufficiently close in terms of time and space. The death or injury of the loved one must be caused by a sudden horrific event.

8 Damages cannot be claimed for pure economic loss. Damages can however be claimed for financial loss which was a direct consequence of a foreseeable type of damage to goods or a foreseeable type of physical injury.

9 Contributory negligence on the claimant's part entitles the court to reduce the claimant's damages to the extent which the court considers just and equitable, having regard to the claimant's share in responsibility for the damage which he has suffered.

10 *Volenti non fit injuria* is a complete defence. It allows the defendant to escape liability where the claimant voluntarily consented to running the risk which injured him or where the claimant agreed that liability should be excluded.

Answers to 12.2

1 Liability for negligent misstatements can only be incurred where there is a special relationship between the defendant and the claimant. A special relationship will only arise where the defendant gives a response to an inquiry made by the claimant, it will not arise where advice is volunteered. In order for the special relationship to arise there must be a very proximate relationship between the claimant and the defendant. Appropriately worded disclaimers of responsibility might mean that a duty of care does not arise.

2 The Consumer Protection Act 1987 Part I allows a person injured by an unsafe product to sue the manufacturers, extractors of raw materials, own branders and importers into the EC (and possibly others in the chain of supply), who can be liable even if they were not at fault.

3 Under the 1987 Act a claim can be made for death or personal injury. A claim can also be made for damage to property as long as the property was not business property and as long as the damage to property amounted to more than £275.

4 An occupier of premises is a person who has any degree of control over the state of the premises.

5 Section 2(2) of the Occupiers' Liability Act 1957 provides that an occupier has a duty to take such care as in all the circumstances of the case is reasonable to see that the visitor will be reasonably safe in using the premises for the purposes for which he is invited or permitted by the occupier to be there.

6 Section 1(4) of the Occupiers' Liability Act 1984 provides that an occupier of premises has a duty to take such care as is reasonable in all the circumstances of the case to see that a trespasser does not suffer injury on the premises by reason of a danger of which the occupier is aware. The duty only arises if the occupier knows or has reasonable grounds to believe that the trespasser is in the vicinity of the danger concerned and the risk is one in respect of which he might reasonably be expected to offer some protection.

Chapter 13

Answers to 13.1

1 A private nuisance is an indirect unlawful interference with another person's land or his use or enjoyment of his land.

2 The tort can be committed even if the defendant does not act negligently, but an action can only be brought in respect of a type of damage which was a foreseeable consequence of the nuisance.

3 Damages or an injunction will be the usual remedies. Abatement of the nuisance is a possibility.

4 Public nuisance is very hard to define. It has, however, been defined as any nuisance which materially affects the reasonable comfort and convenience of life of a class of Her Majesty's subjects.

5 The tort of strict liability is committed by allowing a dangerous thing, which has deliberately been brought on to the defendant 's land or allowed to settle there, to escape. The defendant can be liable for damage caused by this escape even if he has not been negligent. However, damages can only be recovered in respect of losses which are a foreseeable type of consequence.

6 Trespass to land is an unauthorised, direct interference with another person's land.

7 The three forms of trespass to the person are: battery, the direct and intentional infliction of unlawful force on another person; assault, directly and reasonably making another feel frightened that he is about to be immediately battered; and false imprisonment, wrongfully depriving another person of his personal liberty.

8 The tort of conversion is committed by intentionally dealing with goods in a way which is inconsistent with the right of another to possess those goods. It is not necessary that the defendant should know that another has the right to possess the goods.

Answers to 13.2

1 Defamation is committed by publishing a statement which lowers the claimant in the estimation of right-thinking people generally or causes the claimant to be shunned and avoided.

2 Libel is committed when the defamatory statement is published in some permanent form, slander when it is published in a non-permanent form.

3 Employers are vicariously liable for the torts of their employees which are committed during the course of their employment. This means that although the employee committed the tort the employer can be sued.

4 The four 'economic torts' are: interfering with a subsisting contract, intimidation, conspiracy and interference with trade by unlawful means.

Chapter 14

Answers to 14.1

1 A regulated agreement is a consumer credit agreement, or consumer hire agreement, other than an exempt agreement.

2 The definition of a regulated agreement is significant because most of the Act's provisions apply only to regulated agreements.

3 Running-account credit is given under a master agreement which allows for separate credit agreements to be made under it. Fixed-sum credit fixes the amount of credit in the agreement or allows the amount of credit to be calculated by reference to the agreement.

4 Restricted-use credit is transferred directly from the creditor to the supplier of the goods or services being acquired by the debtor, or is provided by the supplier. Any credit actually received by the debtor is unrestricted-use credit.

5 Under a debtor–creditor–supplier agreement the creditor is either the legal supplier of the goods or services or has an existing or future contemplated connection with the legal supplier. Any agreement other than a debtor–creditor– supplier agreement is a debtor–creditor agreement.

6 A non-commercial agreement is one made by the creditor or owner otherwise than in the course of a business carried on by him. A small agreement is one where the credit extended is less than £50 or one where the hirer does not need to make payments exceeding £50.

Answers to 14.2

1 If an unexecuted document is presented personally to the debtor or hirer for signature he must there and then be given a copy of the agreement and of any document referred to in it (s.62(1)). Within seven days of the making of the agreement the creditor or owner must send a copy of the executed agreement, and of any other document referred to in it, to the debtor or hirer (s.63(2)). If the agreement is cancellable notice of the right to cancel and how to cancel must be included in the copy of the regulated agreement (s.64(1)(a)).

2 If an unexecuted agreement is sent to the debtor or hirer for signature, a copy of the agreement and of any document referred to in it must also be sent (s.62(2)). Within seven days of the making of the agreement the creditor or owner must send a copy of the executed agreement, and of any other document referred to in it, to the debtor or hirer (s.63(2)). If the agreement is cancellable notice of the right to cancel and how to cancel must be included in the copy of the regulated agreement (s.64(1)(a)).

3 If the creditor has already signed a document which is presented personally to the debtor for signature then the debtor or hirer must there and then be given a copy of the executed agreement and any documents referred to in it (s.63(1)). There is no need to send another copy later (s.63(2)(a)). However, s.64(1)(b) requires that if the agreement is a cancellable agreement the debtor or hirer must be sent notice of the right to cancel and how to cancel within seven days of making the agreement.

4 Where the creditor has already signed a document which is sent to the debtor for signature then a copy of the unexecuted document and of any document referred to in it must also be sent at the same time (s.62(2)). There is no need to send another copy later (s.63(2)(a)). However, s.64(1)(b) requires that if the agreement is a cancellable agreement the debtor or hirer must be sent notice of the

right to cancel and how to cancel within seven days of making the agreement.

5 If the debtor or hirer is not given his cancellation rights, as required by s.64, the court has the option to refuse enforcement or to order it under s.127(1) and (2).

Answers to 14.3

1 Section 56(2) can help a debtor because it provides that in two and three party debtor–creditor–supplier agreements a person who conducts negotiations on behalf of the creditor is deemed to do so as the agent of the creditor.

2 Section 75(1) can help a debtor because it provides that in debtor–creditor–supplier agreements where the creditor is not also the supplier of the goods the creditor assumes joint and several liability for breaches of contract or misrepresentations made by the supplier.

3 A credit token is a card etc. provided by a person carrying on a consumer credit business who undertakes that on production of it he will supply cash, goods or services on credit or that on production of it to a third party he will pay the third party for cash, goods or services in return for payment to him by the individual.

4 A credit-token agreement is a regulated agreement for the provision of credit in connection with the use of a credit token.

5 A debtor whose credit token is stolen is not liable to the creditor for losses over £50 arising from unauthorised misuse of the credit card.

Answers to 14.4

1 If a debtor or hirer is liable to make payments to the same person under two or more regulated agreements, and sends less than the total sums due, he can allocate the payments towards one or more of the agreements as he sees fit (s.81(1)). Appropriation of payments to a particular transaction might protect the debtor against the creditor snatching back the goods, by making the goods protected goods, on account of the debtor having paid more than one third of the total price.

2 The debtor under a regulated consumer credit agreement is entitled to discharge the debt at any time by giving the creditor notice in writing and by repaying the whole debt (s.94(1)).

3 If a debtor terminates a regulated hire-purchase or conditional sale agreement early, arrears must be paid. The debtor may also be required to bring payments made (including arrears) up to half of the total price. If the debtor has failed to take reasonable care of the goods, the amount payable should be increased to compensate the creditor for this.

4 If a debtor repudiates a hire-purchase agreement the creditor will be able to sue for arrears and for damages for the whole loss of the bargain. If the creditor terminates a hire-purchase agreement on account of a breach by the debtor which did not amount to a repudiation the creditor will be entitled to arrears (plus interest) but not to damages for the loss of the bargain.

Answers to 14.5

1 A hire-purchase agreement is an agreement under which a debtor hires goods for a fixed period, and has an option to buy the goods for a nominal sum at the end of that period. The debtor has no obligation to continue with the agreement for the whole of the fixed period.

2 Under a conditional sale a buyer agrees to buy goods but the ownership of the goods is not to pass to the buyer until all of the price has been paid. Usually the price is to be paid by instalments, in which case a conditional sale agreement is very similar to hire-purchase. However, under a conditional sale agreement there is an agreement to sell from the outset and the buyer agrees to make all of the payments. Under a hire-purchase contract the debtor has no obligation to continue paying instalments until the end of the agreement.

Chapter 15

Answers to 15.1

1 Section 1(1) of the Partnership Act 1890 defines a partnership as 'the relation which subsists between persons carrying on a business in common with a view of profit'.

2 A partnership does not have a legal identity of its own. A partnership is only a relationship between the partners. (Limited liability partnerships are different and do have a separate legal identity of their own.)

3 People can be in partnership with each other without having agreed that they should be. They must however make a contract with each other, agreeing to carry on a business together with the intention of making a profit.

4 A company can be a partner in a firm. A company cannot be a partnership.

5 A partnership can exist even though no profit was ever made. However, a partnership can only exist if the partners intended to make a profit for themselves.

6 An unincorporated association differs from a partnership in that its members do not have the intention of making a profit which they will share amongst themselves.

7 The receipt by a person of a share of the profits of a business is only *prima facie* evidence that he is a partner. The Partnership Act lists five situations where it is presumed that a person receiving a share of the profits is not a partner. Even in other situations the decision as to whether or not a person receiving a share of the profits is a partner must be based on all of the evidence to see if what was agreed fits within s.1(1)'s definition of a partnership.

Answers to 15.2

1 People can become partners without making any formal agreement. They will be partners if they carry on a business in common with the intention of making a profit.

2 The 13 'universal' articles deal with: the parties to the agreement; the nature of the business; the name of the firm; the dates of commencement and dissolution; the capital of the

firm and of the individual partners; the salary and profit entitlement of the partners; the management of the firm; the banking arrangements; the firm's accounts; admission and expulsion of partners; death and retirement of partners; valuation of the goodwill; and reference of disputes to arbitration.

3 The Companies Act 2006 makes it a criminal offence to use certain words in the firm's name and to use other specified words without gaining permission from the Secretary of State. It also requires that the names of all the partners, and an address at which they can be served with documents, be clearly displayed at the firm's place of business and on the firm's business documents.

4 A passing-off action can be brought to prevent a firm from using a name which is likely to cause confusion with another business, or to deceive the public, so as to divert trade from that other business.

5 A partner can only terminate a partnership by giving notice if the partnership is a partnership at will. A partnership at will arises when the partners have not themselves agreed a fixed term for the duration of the partnership.

6 A formal partnership agreement can be varied by the agreement of all the partners. This agreement does not need to be express and can arise from the partners' course of dealing.

7 Minors can become partners, but cannot become liable for debts of the firm which were incurred while they were minors.

Answers to 15.3

1 All of the terms implied by s.24 are to apply only if the partners do not expressly or impliedly agree to exclude them. Plainly, the partners can contract out of them.

2 A majority of partners can only expel a partner if a power to do so has been conferred by express agreement between all of the partners.

3 Partnership property is held on trust by the partners for the benefit of each other. Prior to dissolution a partner does not personally own any particular item of partnership property.

4 Property will be partnership property if the partners have expressly or impliedly agreed that it should be. Section 20(1) provides that property can become partnership property either if it was originally brought into the partnership; or if the property was acquired on behalf of the firm; or if the property was acquired for the purposes of and in the course of the partnership business. Section 21 provides that unless a contrary intention appears, property bought with money belonging to the firm is also deemed to be partnership property.

5 The three fiduciary duties specified by the Act are: to render accounts; to account for profits; and not to compete with the firm. These duties are not intended to be exhaustive. The fiduciary duties cannot be contracted out of, but it is a defence to breach of a fiduciary duty that the act complained of was consented to.

Answers to 15.4

1 Partners are agents of their firms and of their fellow partners if: (i) the act done was done as a partner; (ii) the act was the type of act which would ordinarily be done by a partner in the firm; and (iii) the act was done in the way in which it ordinarily would be done. However, there is no liability if the outsider either knows that the partner has no authority to do the act, or does not know or believe him to be a partner.

2 All of the partners will be liable for the torts of an individual partner if the tort was committed while the partner was doing an act which he had actual, apparent or usual authority to do.

3 A person who represents himself as a partner, or who knowingly allows himself to be represented as a partner, will become liable as if he was a partner to anyone who relied on the representation to give credit to the firm.

4 A partner coming into the firm is not liable for debts which had previously arisen.

5 A retiring partner can be discharged from liability by a novation (a contract to that effect) between himself, the firm as newly constituted and the creditors.

6 A firm can be dissolved under a provision of the Act if: (i) a fixed term has expired or a single purpose been achieved; (ii) a partner has died or become bankrupt; (iii) a partner has assigned his share of the partnership assets to a creditor in order to satisfy a private debt; (iv) an event has happened which makes it unlawful to carry on the business of the firm.

7 Any partner can apply for a court order to dissolve the partnership on the following grounds: (i) a partner has become permanently incapable of performing his role in the partnership; (ii) a partner has been guilty of conduct which prejudicially affects the carrying on of the business; (iii) a partner has wilfully or persistently breached the partnership agreement or acted in such a way that it is not reasonably practicable for the other partners to carry on in partnership with him; (iv) the business can only be carried on at a loss; (v) the court considers it just and equitable to wind the firm up.

8 In the absence of agreement to the contrary, the partners are to bear the losses in the same ratio as they were to share the profits.

9 First outsiders are paid, then loans from partners are repaid, then capital contributions of partners are repaid. Any remaining assets are shared by the partners in the ratio in which they were to share profits.

10 Individual partners can have limited liability for the firm's debts if they register as limited partners under the Limited Partnerships Act 1907. The Act requires that at least one general partner must have unlimited liability. If a business is registered as a limited liability partnership, under the Limited Liability Partnerships Act 2000, then all of the members can have limited liability for the firm's debts. However, an LLP is quite different to a partnership.

Chapter 16

Answers to 16.1

1 It is true to state that a company has a separate legal identity of its own.
2 The concept of limited liability means that the members of a limited company do not become liable to pay the debts of the company. The company itself does not have limited liability.
3 Perpetual succession, a consequence of a company being a legal person in its own right, means that a company can continue in existence indefinitely, even though its shareholders and officers either leave the company or die.
4 As a company is a legal person, it can both own property and make contracts.
5 A company can be guilty of a crime which requires a *mens rea* if a person who is sufficiently senior to be regarded as the mind of the company acts on the company's behalf with the necessary *mens rea*. The *mens rea* of the person who can be regarded as the mind of the company is attributable to the company.
6 The corporate veil is an image used to demonstrate that the company cannot be regarded in law as its members: a veil separates them. The veil can be lifted in a variety of situations, including: if the company was formed for a fraudulent purpose; if the company can be characterised as an enemy in time of war; in exceptional circumstances groups of companies may be regarded as one; small companies which are like partnerships may be wound up as partnerships; various statutory provisions may look behind incorporation.

Answers to 16.2

1 Public companies can advertise their shares for sale and their shares may be quoted on the London Stock Exchange; public companies need at least two directors, private companies need have only one; public companies must have at least £50 000 allotted share capital, one quarter of which must be paid up; public companies must have 'public limited company' or 'plc' as the end of their names, private companies must have 'limited' or 'Ltd', unless they are unlimited; public companies cannot be unlimited; public companies cannot pass written resolutions or elect to dispense with the holding of an AGM; a public company must have a company secretary and this person must be suitably qualified.
2 An unlimited company is regarded as having a legal personality of its own. However, the members of the company have agreed with the company that they will have unlimited liability to pay the debts of the company in the event of the company being wound up.
3 A share premium is an additional amount, over and above the nominal value of a share, which a person taking the share from a company agrees that he will pay for the share. A member of a company who has agreed to pay a share premium can be called upon by the company to pay that premium. However, on liquidation the creditors cannot insist that a share premium is paid. (They can insist that any unpaid amount of the nominal share value be paid.)
4 The members of a company limited by guarantee agree with the company that on liquidation they will contribute the amount which they have guaranteed, towards payment of the company's debts and the costs of winding up. Usually this amount is small.
5 Companies can also be created by Royal Charter or by statute.
6 A corporation sole is an office or position which can only be held by one person at a time, and which is regarded as having a legal personality of its own.

Answers to 16.3

1 In order to form a company, promoters must send to the Registrar of Companies: a new-style memorandum of association; an application for registration; a statement of share capital and initial share holdings; a statement of the company's proposed officers; a statement of the intended address of the company's registered office, and a statement of any proposed articles of association, to the extent that default articles are not being used. A fee of £20 will also be payable.
2 Before the 2006 Act came into force, the Registrar would incorporate a company if he received a £20 fee and: (i) the company's old-style memorandum of association; (ii) the company's articles of association; (iii) a statement giving the names of the company's first directors and of the company secretary; and (iv) a statement that all the statutory requirements of registration have been complied with.
3 Once a certificate of incorporation is issued, the company comes into existence.
4 A new-style memorandum of association states that the subscribers wish to form a company under the Act and that they agree to become members of the company by taking at least one share each.
5 An old-style memorandum of association had to contain five clauses which stated: (i) the name of the company; (ii) the jurisdiction of the registered office; (iii) the objects of the company; (iv) that the liability of the members of the company was limited (if it was); and (v) the amount of share capital and how it was divided into shares. Every subscriber to the memorandum had to sign it, indicating how many shares he had taken, and that the subscribers wished to be formed into a company.
6 A company's articles of association are the rules of the company. Companies can either write their own articles or adopt, wholly or in part, model articles contained in a statutory instrument.

Answers to 16.4

1 A company cannot ratify a contract which was made before the company was formed.
2 Under s.51(1) a promoter will be personally liable on a pre-incorporation contract made on the company's behalf unless there is an agreement to the contrary.

3 The Registrar will refuse to register a name if it would constitute a criminal offence or be offensive, if it is identical to a name already on the register, or if the name is prohibited by Regulations made by the Secretary of State. The Registrar can also refuse to register a company if it is not being formed for a lawful purpose.

4 A passing-off action is an action in tort to prevent a business from trading under a name which is too similar to the name of an existing business. If trading under the new company name would be likely to divert customers away from the existing business, or cause confusion between the two businesses, an injunction can be granted to prevent this. However, a complaint to a company names adjudicator would be an easier way to prevent a company registering a name which is either likely to divert goodwill or likely to mislead by suggesting a connection between the company and the business which is objecting.

5 The company name must be published, clearly and conspicuously: (i) outside all places of business; (ii) on all letters, invoices, notices, cheques, order forms and receipts; (iii) on the company seal, if the company has a seal.

6 The Registrar issues certificates of incorporation and of re-registration; keeps a list of the names of registered companies; keeps basic information on all registered companies; and strikes companies off the Register of Companies when they are wound up.

Chapter 17

Answers to 17.1

1 There is no requirement that a director should be a shareholder in the company but there is no reason why a director should not be a shareholder. One company can act as the director of another company.

2 A company's directors are appointed according to the rules set out in the company's articles of association. If no article deals with the matter, the directors are appointed by an ordinary resolution of the members.

3 A director may resign from his office at any time. The articles of the company may set out other ways in which a director can be removed. No matter what the articles say, s.168(1) allows the members of the company to remove a director by passing at a meeting an ordinary resolution of which special notice has been given.

4 It is possible for some of the shares to carry weighted voting rights, as happened in *Bushell* v *Faith*.

5 A written resolution cannot be used to dismiss a director under s.168(1) because that section says that the resolution must be passed at a company meeting. The purpose of this rule is to allow the director to address the members at the meeting which considers the resolution proposing to dismiss him.

6 No special qualifications are needed by directors except that they must be at least 16 years old. Undischarged bankrupts may not hold office as directors without the permission of the court which heard the bankruptcy proceedings. Persons disqualified under CDDA 1986 may not hold office as directors.

7 Directors are known as the board of directors when they act collectively. Unless a power has been delegated it must be exercised by the board of directors rather than by individual directors.

Answers to 17.2

1 Directors can be paid fees for their services only if the company's constitution allows for such payments or if these are approved by the members. Most articles (Table A article 84, for example), allow the directors to be paid for their services.

2 The powers of the directors will be set out in the company's articles of association and therefore differ from company to company. Generally, the directors are given very wide powers to manage the company's affairs.

3 Section 39(1) provides that an act done by a company cannot be invalidated by reason of anything in the company's constitution.

4 The seven general statutory duties are: to act within powers (s.171); to promote the success of the company (s.172); to exercise independent judgment (s.173); to exercise reasonable care, skill and diligence (s.174); to avoid conflicts of interest (s.175); not to accept benefits from third parties (s.176); and to declare interest in a proposed transaction or arrangement (s.177).

Answers to 17.3

1 The company secretary looks after the administration of the company.

2 A company secretary has apparent authority to make contracts which are concerned with the day to day administration of the company.

3 Secretaries of private companies need have no special qualifications. Secretaries of public companies must be suitably qualified.

4 The auditor audits the company accounts and reports to the members that these give a true and fair reflection of the company's position and have been properly prepared. All companies except for dormant companies and some small companies will need to have an auditor.

5 The first auditor is appointed by the directors of the company. As regards private companies, subsequent auditors are appointed by ordinary resolution of the members, except that if there is no such resolution, the auditors are generally deemed to have been reappointed. As regards public companies, subsequent auditors are appointed by the members at the general meeting at which the accounts are considered.

6 An auditor can be removed from office, before the expiry of his term of office, at any time. However, this can be achieved only by an ordinary resolution at a meeting, and special notice of the resolution proposing to remove the auditor has to be given.

Answers to 17.4

1 The following documents and registers must be held at the registered office and made available for inspection by members of the public: the register of directors; the register of secretaries; the register of members; the register of directors' interests; the register of charges; a copy of every contract under which a public company bought its own shares; the register of debenture holders, if the company has such a register; and a public company must keep a register of people who hold more than a specified number of the voting rights of its shares.

2 The following documents and registers must be held at the registered office and made available for inspection by members of the company: a copy of every contract under which a private company bought its own shares; a copy of the service contract of every director or shadow director; the minutes of general meetings; the records of written resolutions of a private company which were passed otherwise than as resolutions at a general meeting; the records of written resolutions which were agreed as if they were resolutions at a company meeting; and decisions of single member companies that takes effect as if agreed by the company in a general meeting, unless they were taken by written resolution.

3 The annual return must be completed once a year, on the return date, and sent to the Registrar. It gives basic information about the company.

4 The accounts which a company must file consist of the balance sheet, a profit and loss account, the directors' report and, if the company is not exempt from audit, the auditor's report.

Chapter 18

Answers to 18.1

1 A person becomes a member of a company either by subscribing to the company's memorandum and on registration being entered on the register of members, or by agreeing to become a member and his name being registered on the register of members.

2 A share is a type of personal property, known as a thing in action.

3 A share premium account is an account into which share premiums are paid. Rules governing such an account require the company to treat the money in the account as capital, and therefore prevent its distribution as dividends.

4 The articles of a company may allow for different classes of shares, with different rights attaching to the various classes.

5 Generally, it is agreed that preference shares carry a cumulative right to a dividend expressed as a rate of interest per annum, and the right to be paid ahead of the ordinary shareholders on dissolution of the company. Preference shares might or might not have the same voting rights as the ordinary shares.

6 A person may acquire shares from the company, by a transfer from an existing member, or by transmission by operation of law.

7 Pre-emption rights give existing shareholders the right to have new shares offered to them in proportion to their existing shareholdings before they are allotted for cash to new members.

8 A trading certificate must be issued by the Registrar before a public company can commence trading or borrow money. The certificate will only be issued if the Registrar is satisfied that the company has allotted shares with a nominal value of at least £50 000, and that a quarter of the nominal value of each share and any share premium has been paid up.

Answers to 18.2

1 An ordinary resolution is passed if a simple majority vote in favour. A special resolution is passed if at least 75 per cent vote in favour. If the resolution is a written resolution, these percentages are of the total voting rights on the resolution. If the resolution is passed at a company meeting, the percentages are of the members who actually vote on the resolution.

2 Both ordinary and special resolutions of private companies can be passed as written resolutions. However, a written resolution cannot be used to remove an auditor or a director before the expiry of his term of office.

3 Section 292 allows the members to require the company to circulate a written resolution, and a statement of not more than 1 000 words on the subject matter of the resolution. However, unless the articles set a lower figure, the request must be made by at least 5 per cent of the members who could vote on the resolution.

4 Private companies do not need to hold an AGM but might choose to do so. A public company must hold an AGM every year, within six months of the end of its financial year.

5 The members of a company can require the directors to call a general meeting if they hold the required percentage of paid-up shares which carry voting rights. The percentage is 10 per cent unless the company is a private company and 12 months have elapsed since the last meeting at which members could circulate a resolution, in which case the percentage is 5 per cent.

6 If the meeting is an AGM of a public company 21 days' notice must be given. As regards all other meetings, 14 days' notice must be given.

7 Section 314 allows the members to require the company to circulate a statement of not more than 1 000 words with respect to a matter referred to in a proposed resolution. However, the request to do this must be made either by members representing at least 5 per cent of the total voting rights, or by at least 100 members with the right to vote who hold shares having an average sum paid up of at least £100 each.

8 A proxy is a person entitled to attend and vote at a company meeting on behalf of a company member who has appointed him.

9 A quorum is a minimum number of members who must be present before a company meeting can validly be commenced. If the articles do not provide otherwise, two persons will constitute a quorum. In single member companies one person constitutes a quorum notwithstanding any provision to the contrary in the articles.

10 Where a poll is taken at a general meeting of a quoted company, s.341 requires the company to put the following information on a website: the date of the meeting; the text of the resolution to be voted upon; the number of votes cast in favour and cast against.

11 Section 342 allows the members of a quoted company to require the directors to obtain an independent report on a poll taken at a general meeting. However, the members must either hold at least 5 per cent of the total voting rights of all members who have a right to vote on the matter to which the poll relates, or they must total 100 members with a relevant right to vote who between them hold shares having an average sum paid up of £100 each.

12 Where the sole member of a company takes a decision otherwise than by written resolution, and where the decision has effect as if taken by the company in general meeting, the member must provide the company with details of that decision.

Answers to 18.3

1 The constitution creates a contract between the company and the members, in their capacity as members. It also creates a contract between each member and every other member, in their capacity as members. It does not create a contract between the company and outsiders.

2 A private company can carry out a reduction of capital by passing a special resolution supported by a solvency statement. Both public and private companies can reduce their capital by passing a special resolution confirmed by the court.

3 A market purchase of a company's own shares is made on a recognised stock market and can therefore only be made by a public company which is listed or a member of a UK recognised investment exchange. An off-market purchase is one made in any other way.

4 A company cannot reduce its capital by paying a dividend. Dividends must be paid out of profits.

5 The members of a company governed by Table A cannot increase the dividend recommended by the directors. They can reduce the dividend or declare that no dividend should be paid. The position is the same as regards companies governed by the new draft model articles.

6 The three offences relating to insider dealing are: using inside information to deal in price-affected securities; encouraging others to do this; or disclosing inside information.

Answers to 18.4

1 The rule in *Foss v Harbottle* is to the effect that only the company can sue for a wrong done to the company and the court will not interfere with the internal management of a company acting within its powers.

2 A derivative claim is a claim brought by a member of the company in respect of a cause of action vested in the company and seeking relief on behalf of the company. A derivative claim can be brought in respect of a cause of action arising from an actual or proposed act or omission which involves negligence, default, breach of duty or breach of trust by a director of the company. The court must give permission for a derivative claim to be continued.

3 The rule in *Foss v Harbottle* does not prevent a minority shareholder from bringing an action: which alleges that his personal rights have been infringed; or which prevents the company from entering into an *ultra vires* contract; or if an act confirmed by the majority required a special resolution; or which alleges fraud on the minority.

4 A member can claim unfair prejudice under s.994 of the 2006 Act, or may petition for the winding up of the company under ss.122–124 of the Insolvency Act 1986.

5 A fixed charge is a mortgage over specific assets belonging to the company. The company may not therefore dispose of those assets once the charge has been created. A floating charge gives a lender security over a class of assets, but does not prevent the company from dealing with those assets in the course of its business.

6 When a floating charge crystallises, it becomes a fixed charge on the assets charged.

Chapter 19

Answers to 19.1

1 A company can be voluntarily wound up by the members, or compulsorily wound up by order of the court.

2 A company is deemed unable to pay its debts if: (a) a creditor who has properly demanded payment of more than £750 has not been paid within three weeks; (b) execution of a court's judgment against the company in favour of a creditor is returned unsatisfied; or (c) it is proved to the satisfaction of the court that the company is unable to pay its debts as they fall due.

3 The courts have wound companies up on the grounds that this is just and equitable for the following reasons: (a) the substratum of the company has failed; (b) there is deadlock in the management of a company; (c) there is a justifiable lack of confidence in the management of a company; (d) the company was formed for a fraudulent purpose. There is no closed list of grounds on which a court might consider it just and equitable to wind a company up.

4 A members' voluntary liquidation is initiated by a special resolution. The directors must file a declaration of solvency and the members appoint the liquidator. A creditors' voluntary liquidation is also initiated by a special resolution. The directors do not have to file a declaration of solvency and the creditors appoint the liquidator.

5 First, the liquidator's remuneration and the costs and expenses of winding up are paid, then the preferential

creditors at the date of winding up, then top-sliced assets for distribution to the unsecured creditors (if a floating charge was created on or after 15 September 2003); then floating charge holders, then the unsecured creditors, and finally sums due to members are paid.

6 An administrator of a company tries primarily to rescue the company as a going concern, secondarily to achieve a better result for the company's creditors than would be achieved by a winding up, thirdly to realise property to distribute to secured or preferential creditors. An administrative receiver realises company property to pay the debts of the floating charge holder who appointed him.

Answers to 19.2

1 An LLP is formed by registration with the Registrar of Companies. Two or more persons associated for carrying on a lawful business must subscribe to a registration document and send it to the Registrar.

2 The name of an LLP must end with the words 'limited liability partnership' or 'llp' or 'LLP' (or their Welsh equivalents).

3 Every LLP must have at least two designated members, who have certain specified duties such as signing the LLP's accounts and delivering them to the Registrar.

4 Every member of an LLP is an agent of the LLP. However, an LLP is not bound by anything done by a member in dealing with a person if: (a) the member in fact has no authority to act for the LLP by doing that thing; and (b) the person knows that he has no authority or does not know or believe him to be a member of the LLP.

5 An LLP will be vicariously liable to outsiders for the tort of a member if the tort was committed either during the course of the business of the LLP or with the authority of the LLP.

6 The rights and duties of the members between themselves are fixed by agreement. However, in the absence of agreement ten default provisions apply.

7 An LLP is not dissolved when a member leaves.

8 A member of an LLP can petition the court for a just and equitable winding up under s.122 of the Insolvency Act 1986. A member can also claim unfair prejudice under s.994 of the Companies Act 2006, unless the right to do so has been excluded by unanimous written agreement. It seems likely that a member can bring a derivative claim where the behaviour of the majority amounts to a fraud on the minority.

9 In general, members will not have to pay the debts of an LLP.

Chapter 20

Answers to 20.1

1 The decisions of employment tribunals are not binding upon any other courts. The decisions of the Employment Appeal Tribunal are binding upon employment tribunals, but not upon later sittings of the Employment Appeal Tribunal.

2 Any UK court can refer a case to the ECJ if the case involves a matter of European law. Member States of the EC can also be taken to the European Court by other Member States of the European Community. The decisions of the ECJ are binding upon all UK courts.

3 ACAS attempts conciliation before a case is taken to an employment tribunal. It also advises employers, workers and trade unions on matters likely to affect industrial relations, attempts to settle trade disputes, conducts enquiries into industrial relations, has the power to refer disputes to arbitration and issues Codes of Practice.

4 There is no exhaustive list of matters which can determine whether or not a worker is an employee or an independent contractor. A wide variety of factors needs to be considered in every case. The distinction between employees and independent contractors is important because terms which are implied into contracts of employment are not implied into contracts with independent contractors, because employers can be vicariously liable for the torts of their employees and because many employment rights are afforded only to employees.

5 The question as to whether a worker is an employee or an independent contractor is generally a question of fact. Consequently, an appellate court will only overturn the decision of the trial court if that court took a view of the facts which could not reasonably be entertained. An appellate court overturns a decision of law made by an inferior court whenever it considers that the decision was wrong.

Answers to 20.2

1 An employee must be given written particulars of the contract of employment not later than two months after the commencement of the employment. The written particulars are not the contract of employment itself, unless expressly agreed as such, but are very strong evidence of the terms of the contract.

2 Collective agreements are agreements negotiated between employers and trade unions which set out terms and conditions of employment. They can become terms of an individual contract of employment if expressly agreed as terms of the contract by an individual employee. They can impliedly become the terms of the contracts of union members who knew of the terms and accepted them.

3 The following duties are impliedly imposed on employees: the duty of mutual respect; the duty to give faithful service; the duty to obey lawful and reasonable orders; the duty to use reasonable care and skill; the duty not to accept bribes; the duty not to disclose confidential information; and the duty to disclose the shortcomings of subordinates.

4 The following duties are impliedly imposed on employers: the duty of mutual respect; the duty to pay wages; the duty of confidentiality; the duty to indemnify the employee; the duty to take out insurance for the benefit of the employee; and the duty to ensure the employee's safety. There is generally no duty to provide references or to provide the employee with work.

5 The parties may agree that a works rule book is incorporated as part of the contract of employment. If a works rule book is agreed as part of the contract of employment it can only be altered by agreement. An employer may unilaterally impose duties by means of a works rule book as long as the duties do not alter the terms of the employment previously agreed. Rules unilaterally imposed can be altered unilaterally by the employer as long as this does not amount to a breach of contract.

6 If the employer does not follow agreed disciplinary and grievance procedures this will be a breach of contract. The breach may entitle the employee to claim constructive dismissal. If the employer does not comply with the statutory grievance procedure set out in Part 2 of Schedule 2 to the Employment Act 2002 then any award for unfair dismissal will be increased by between 10 per cent and 50 per cent.

7 If the employer unilaterally alters the terms of the contract of employment, the employee may accept this in which case the contract will be varied by mutual agreement. If the employee does not accept the variation the employee may regard the contract as terminated on the grounds of the employer's repudiation of it.

Answers to 20.3

1 Wrongful dismissal is a common law action for breach of contract. Unfair dismissal is a statutory concept and if unfair dismissal is substantiated compensation is awarded on a statutory basis.

2 An employee dismissed without having been given the proper amount of notice will be entitled to sue for damages for wrongful dismissal.

3 Employees will be entitled to the notice agreed with their employers or, if there was no agreement, to a reasonable period of notice. Statute lays down minimum periods of notice, which may well exceed the amount agreed or the amount which the common law would require. The minimum periods are one week for every year's continuous employment where the employee has worked for between two and 12 years. Where the employee has worked for more than 12 years the statutory minimum remains 12 weeks. Employees who have worked for more than one month but less than two years are entitled to one week's statutory minimum notice.

4 An employee is summarily dismissed if he is dismissed on the spot, without notice. This can be justified if the employee's behaviour was a sufficient repudiation of the contract of employment.

5 If the agreement to leave was freely entered into by the employee there can be no claim for wrongful dismissal. If the employee left in response to the employer's repudiation of the contract, there could be a claim for wrongful dismissal.

6 If the employer's conduct amounts to a repudiation of the contract, the employee is entitled to accept this, leave the job and claim wrongful dismissal. An employee who repudiates the contract cannot claim wrongful dismissal.

7 Damages for wrongful dismissal are calculated on ordinary contract principles. The employee can claim for foreseeable losses and has a duty to mitigate.

Answers to 20.4

1 Except as regards dismissals which are automatically unfair, only employees with at least two years' continuous employment will be able to claim unfair dismissal.

2 The effective date of termination is the date at which the employment is taken to have ended, for the purposes of unfair dismissal and redundancy. In relation to unfair dismissal, it is significant in deciding: whether or not a claimant has enough continuous employment to make a claim; whether the claim is made in time; and the amount of the complainant's basic award.

3 An employee can only be regarded as having been dismissed, for the purposes of unfair dismissal if: (a) the employer terminates the contract, with or without notice; or (b) a fixed term contract expires; or (c) the employee is constructively dismissed; or (d) an employee who has been given notice by the employer, himself gives the employer a shorter period of notice to end the contract. An employee who is not allowed to return to work after childbirth can be deemed to have been dismissed. There is a dismissal if the employer accepts a repudiatory breach by the employee (because the employer terminates the contract by accepting the breach) but not if the contract is frustrated.

4 The employee's dismissal can only be regarded as fair if the employer shows that the dismissal was for one of the five following reasons: (a) the reason for the dismissal relates to the capability or qualifications of the employee for performing work of the kind which he was employed by the employer to do; (b) the reason for the dismissal relates to the conduct of the employee; (c) the reason for the dismissal is that the employee was made redundant; (d) the reason for the dismissal is that the employee could not continue to work in the position which he held without contravention, either by him or by his employer, of a duty or restriction imposed by or under a statute; (e) a dismissal can also be regarded as fair if the employer shows that the dismissal was for some other substantial reason of a kind such as to justify the dismissal of an employee holding the position which the employee held.

5 A dismissal can be automatically unfair if it was: on the grounds of the employee claiming a statutory right; or in connection with pregnancy and childbirth; or for pursuing health and safety issues; or for failing to observe the procedure required in cases of compulsory retirement; or for causing shop assistants to work on Sundays; or connected with trade union membership or because the employer's statutory dismissal and disciplinary procedures were not complied with.

6 Even if the employer proves that the dismissal was for one of the specified fair reasons, the dismissal may still be unfair. This will depend upon whether in the circumstances the employer acted reasonably or unreasonably in

treating the reason shown for the dismissal as a sufficient reason for dismissing the employee. This matter will be determined by the tribunal in accordance with equity and the substantial merits of the case.

7 Even if a dismissal is for one of the fair reasons specified, and was within the band of reasonable responses, it will be rendered unfair if the employer's statutory dismissal and disciplinary procedures were not complied with.

8 The possible remedies for unfair dismissal are: re-engagement or reinstatement; a basic award; and a compensatory award.

9 The basic award is calculated according to a formula set out in the ERA. The complainant has no duty to mitigate his loss. The compensatory award is at the tribunal's discretion. It is designed to compensate the complainant for financial losses and therefore the complainant has a duty to mitigate these.

Answers to 20.5

1 A dismissal will be by reason of redundancy if it is wholly or mainly attributable to: (a) the employer ceasing to carry on the business; or (b) the employer moving the place of business; or (c) the employer shedding surplus labour.

2 Only employees with at least two years' continuous employment can claim redundancy.

3 If the employer's statutory dismissal and disciplinary procedures are not followed an employee will have been unfairly dismissed, rather than made redundant.

4 Redundancy payments are calculated on the same basis as the basic award for unfair dismissal, except that the payment will not be reduced on account of the employee's contributory conduct.

5 An employer proposing to make 20 or more employees at one establishment redundant within a 90 day period must consult appropriate representatives of any of the employees who may be made redundant.

6 The consultations must consider ways of avoiding the dismissals, reducing the number of employees to be dismissed and mitigating the consequences of the dismissals. Also, the employer must undertake the consultations with a view to reaching agreement with the appropriate representatives.

Chapter 21

Answers to 21.1

1 The nine protected characteristics are: age; disability; gender reassignment; marriage and civil partnership; pregnancy and maternity; race; religion or belief; sex; and sexual orientation.

2 Section 13(1) provides that a person (A) discriminates against another (B) if, because of a protected characteristic, A treats B less favourably than A treats or would treat others.

3 Section 19(1) provides that a person (A) discriminates against another (B) if A applies to B a provision, criterion or practice which is discriminatory in relation to a relevant protected characteristic of B's (except pregnancy and maternity). A provision, criterion or practice is discriminatory in relation to a relevant protected characteristic of B's if–

a A applies, or would apply, it to persons with whom B does not share the characteristic,

b it puts, or would put, persons with whom B shares the characteristic at a particular disadvantage when compared with persons with whom B does not share it,

c it puts, or would put, B at that disadvantage, and

d A cannot show it to be a proportionate means of achieving a legitimate aim.

4 Section 26(1) provides that a person (A) harasses another (B) if–

a A engages in unwanted conduct related to a relevant protected characteristic, or of a sexual nature, and

b the conduct has the purpose or effect of–

i violating B's dignity, or

ii creating an intimidating, hostile, degrading, humiliating or offensive environment for B.

5 Section 27(1) provides that a person (A) victimises another person (B) if A subjects B to a detriment because–

a B does a protected act, or

b A believes that B has done, or may do, a protected act.

Answers to 21.2

1 The male comparator is the man with whom the woman wishes to compare herself. He must be employed by the same employer or by an associated employer.

2 Under the Act, a woman can claim equal treatment to that afforded the male comparator if she does like work to his work, or work rated as equivalent or work of equal value.

3 An equality clause modifies the terms of the applicant's contract of employment so that any term of that contract is no less favourable than a similar term in the contract of the male comparator.

4 The employer will have a defence if he can prove that the unequal treatment was due to a genuine material factor which was not the difference of sex.

5 The employment tribunal can award arrears of pay, backdated for six years, and damages.

Answers to 21.3

1 A person whose conviction is spent can deny having been convicted. If dismissed on account of the conviction this will amount to unfair dismissal. However, several types of employment are exempted from these provisions.

2 The Regulations insist that part-time workers should be treated no less favourably than comparable full-time workers unless the less favourable treatment is justified on objective grounds.

3 The Fixed-term Employees (Prevention of Less Favourable Treatment) Regulations 2002 provide that a fixed term employee has the right not to be treated by his employer less favourably than the employer treats a comparable permanent employee.

4 The regulations give agency workers the right to be treated no less favourably than the hirer's regular workers after a 12-week period of working for the hirer. However, the right to equal treatment is limited to pay, the duration of working time; night work; rest periods; rest breaks; and annual leave.

Answers to 21.4

1 The Health and Safety at Work etc. Act 1974 imposes criminal sanctions on employers who neglect the health and safety of their employees.
2 The Act is enforced by the Health and Safety Executive and by local authority enforcement officers.
3 Article 137 of the Treaty of Rome allows the passing of Directives to improve the working environment and to protect workers' health and safety and working conditions. Six important Regulations were passed in 1992.
4 The employee will need to prove that the employer owed him a duty of care, that this duty was breached and that he suffered a foreseeable type of damage as a consequence.
5 The three particular aspects of the employer's duty of care are to provide safe plant and equipment, a safe system of work and reasonably competent fellow employees.

Answers to 21.5

1 A pregnant woman is entitled to paid time off work to attend ante-natal appointments. In addition, all pregnant employees are entitled to up to 26 weeks' maternity leave. Additional maternity leave is available to women who have been continuously employed for one year by the beginning of the 11th week before the expected date of childbirth.
2 Women on maternity leave are entitled to all the benefits of their contract of employment except pay. However statutory maternity pay can be claimed for the 26 week ordinary maternity leave period.
3 For workers 22 or over the national minimum wage is £5.80 an hour. For those between 18 and 21 it is £4.83 an hour. For those aged 16 or 17 it is £3.57 an hour. There is no entitlement to the minimum wage for those under the age of 18.
4 The TUPE Regulations provide that where a business undertaking is transferred to a transferee and it retains its identity, the contractual right of the workers should be enforceable against the transferee. In addition, continuous service worked for the transferor should be regarded as having been worked for the transferee.
5 Although they can be contracted out of, the Working Time Regulations provide that workers should not work more than 48 hours a week, averaged out over a 17-week period. Other rights relating to rest breaks and annual leave are conferred. Special rights are conferred on night workers.
6 Unauthorised deductions cannot be made from a worker's wages.
7 Workers must be allowed time off work for public duties. Those made redundant must be allowed a reasonable amount of time off work to look for work or training.

Pensions scheme trustees and employee representatives must be given time off work to perform their duties. Young people are allowed time off for study and training if they have not reached the Level 2 educational standard. Workers are also allowed time off for jury service. Time may also be taken off to look after dependants or as parental leave.

8 Employees with 26 weeks' continuous employment are entitled to paternity leave and pay if they are responsible for the child's upbringing, are the biological father of the child or the partner of the child's mother.
9 When a couple adopt a child, one of them, if he or she has 26 weeks' continuous employment, is entitled to 39 weeks' paid adoption leave and another 13 weeks' additional adoption leave.
10 Parents of children under six have the right to apply for flexible working and the employer has a duty to consider such an application seriously.

Chapter 22

Answers to 22.1

1 A commercial practice is any act, omission, course of conduct, representation or commercial communication (including advertising or marketing) by a trader, which is directly connected with the promotion, sale or supply of a product to or from consumers, whether occurring before, during or after a commercial transaction (if any) in relation to a product.
2 A commercial practice will be unfair if: (a) it contravenes the requirements of professional diligence; and (b) materially distorts or is likely to materially distort the economic behaviour of the average consumer with regard to the product. A commercial practice will also be unfair if it is a misleading action, as defined by reg.5; if it is a misleading omission, as defined by reg.6; if it is aggressive under reg.7; or if it is listed in Schedule 1.
3 Regulation 8 creates the offence of knowingly or recklessly engaging in a commercial practice which contravenes the requirements of professional diligence under reg.3(3)(a); as long as the practice materially distorts or is likely to materially distort the economic behaviour of the average consumer with regard to the product under reg.3(3)(b). Regulation 9 creates the offence of engaging in a commercial practice which is misleading under reg.5. Regulation 10 creates the offence of engaging in a commercial practice which is misleading omission under reg.6. Regulation 11 creates the offence of engaging in a commercial practice which is aggressive omission under reg.7. Regulation 12 creates the offence of engaging in a commercial practice which is set out in Schedule 1.
4 The reg.8 offence requires *mens rea,* and the due diligence defence has no application to it.
5 The due diligence defence is available to an offence under regs.9–12 if the person charged can prove:
   a that the commission of the offence was due to a mistake, or to reliance on information supplied to him by another

person, or to the act or default of another person, or to an accident or some other cause beyond his control; **and**

b that he took all reasonable precautions and exercised all due diligence to avoid the commission of the offence. A special defence is available to advertisers who innocently publish advertisements.

Answers to 22.2

1 A producer would commit an offence under the 2005 Regulations by: placing an unsafe product on the market; offering or agreeing to place an unsafe product on the market; exposing or possessing an unsafe product for placing on the market; offering or agreeing to supply an unsafe product; or supplying an unsafe product. An unsafe product is one which does not present any risk or only the minimum risks compatible with the product's use, considered to be acceptable and consistent with a high level of protection for the safety and health of persons.

2 Section 1 of the Computer Misuse Act makes it an offence to cause a computer to perform any function with the intention of securing access to a program or data where this access is known to be unauthorised. Section 2 of the Computer Misuse Act makes it an offence to commit the s.1 offence with the intention of committing, or facilitating the commission of, an offence which carries a sentence of at least five years' imprisonment. Section 3 of the Computer Misuse Act makes it an offence to intentionally modify computer material while knowing that this is unauthorised.

3 The OFT has a coordinating role to ensure that the most appropriate enforcement authority takes action against a trader who is breaching consumer protection legislation. The OFT itself might be the most appropriate authority, in which case it could seek an enforcement order against a trader.

4 Article 81 renders void all agreements between undertakings, decisions by associations of undertakings and concerted practices which may affect trade between Member States which have as their object or effect the restriction or distortion of competition within the EC. Article 82 tries to prevent dominant undertakings from acting unilaterally in an abusive way.

5 The Competition Act 1998 Chapter I prohibition prohibits agreements between undertakings, decisions by associations of undertakings or concerted practices which may affect trade within the United Kingdom, and which have as their object or effect the prevention, restriction or distortion of competition within the United Kingdom. The Chapter II prohibition prohibits any conduct on the part of one or more undertakings which amounts to the abuse of a dominant position in a market if it may affect trade within the United Kingdom.

6 Mergers can be prohibited on the basis that they would cause a substantial lessening of competition.

7 The OFT can refer a market to the CC for investigation on the grounds that one or more features of the market prevents, restricts or distorts competition in relation to

the supply or acquisition of goods or services in the United Kingdom or a part of the United Kingdom.

8 Section 188 of the Enterprise Act provides that an individual is guilty of an offence if he dishonestly agrees with one or more other persons that undertakings will engage in one or more of the following prohibited cartel activities: price-fixing; limitation of supply or production; market-sharing; or bid-rigging.

9 The Bribery Act 2010 creates four offences in relation to bribery. These are bribing another person; requesting, agreeing to receive or requesting a bribe; bribing a foreign official; and failure by a commercial organisation to prevent a bribe.

Chapter 23

Answers to 23.1

1 A chose in action is an intangible form of personal property which cannot be physically possessed or touched.

2 A documentary intangible is a form of intangible property represented by and embodied in a document. A non-documentary intangible is an intangible property right which is not represented by and embodied in a document.

3 The three types of work in which copyright may exist, as set out by s.1(1) of the Act are: (a) original literary, dramatic, musical or artistic works; (b) sound recordings, films or broadcasts; and (c) the typographical arrangements of published editions.

4 Copyright is not concerned with the protection of ideas themselves, but with the protection of the way in which ideas are expressed.

5 Copyright in a literary, dramatic, musical or artistic work subsists for 70 years after the end of the calendar year in which the author died.

6 Copyright does not have to be registered.

7 The five moral rights given to an author of copyright are: the right to be identified as the author of the work; the right to object to derogatory treatment of the work; the right not to have literary, dramatic, musical or artistic work falsely attributed to him; the right of a person who commissions the taking of a photograph or making of a film for private purposes not to have the work or copies of it exhibited, broadcast or shown in public; and the right to have a percentage of the selling price when certain types of art within copyright are sold (resale right).

Answers to 23.2

1 Patents are granted by the Patent Office if they approve an application for a patent.

2 A patent can be granted only if the invention is new, if the invention involves an inventive step and if the invention is capable of industrial application.

3 Patents may be assigned to another or a licence to exploit the patent may be granted.

4 If a patent is infringed the following remedies are available: an injunction, an order to destroy or deliver up any

patented product, damages, an account of profit, and a declaration that the patent is valid and has been infringed.

5 A trade mark is a sign capable of being represented graphically which is capable of distinguishing goods or services of one undertaking from those of another undertaking.

6 No rights under the Trade Marks Act 1994 are gained until a trade mark is registered. Prior to registration a passing-off action may be possible.

7 The proprietor of a registered trade mark is given exclusive rights in the trade mark. If these rights are infringed the proprietor may bring an action for any civil remedy which would be available in respect of infringement of any other property right.

Answers to 23.3

1 The 1998 Act confers upon data subjects the following rights: to access to personal data; to prevent processing which is likely to cause distress or damage; to prevent processing for the purposes of direct marketing; to prevent evaluation by automatic decision taking; to compensation if certain requirements are not complied with; and to have inaccurate data rectified or erased.

2 The eight data protection principles are that: personal data should be processed lawfully and fairly; that personal data should be obtained for one or more specified and lawful purposes and not be used for other purposes; that personal data should be adequate, relevant and not excessive; that personal data should be accurate and kept up to date; that personal data should not be kept for longer than is necessary to process it; that personal data should be processed in accordance with the rights which the Act gives to data subjects; that appropriate measures should be taken against unauthorised processing and against loss or destruction of personal data; and that personal data should not be transferred to a country outside the EEA, unless its laws are sufficiently robust to ensure protection for the rights and freedoms of data subjects.

Bibliography

Chapters 1 and 2

Smith, Bailey and Gunn on the Modern English Legal System (5th edition) Sweet and Maxwell deals very comprehensively with all the matters considered in these two chapters. Despite the scope of the book and the detailed approach, the book remains fairly easy to read.

Chapter 3

The Law of Contract by Paul Richards (10th edition) Pearson/Longman is a detailed book which is easy to read. A short is devoted to the evolution and definition of a contract. A lengthy chapter deals with offer, acceptance, termination of offers and certainty. Despite being aimed primarily at LLB students, this is a useful book for anyone who wants a good understanding of the law of contract.

Chapter 4

Richards has a lengthy chapter on consideration and shorter chapters on intention to create legal relations, capacity and formalities. Again, plenty of detail while remaining easily readable.

Chapter 5

In *Richards* one chapter deals with terms generally (express and implied terms and the classification of terms) while another chapter is devoted to exemption clauses, which are considered in considerable detail.

Chapter 6

Richards devotes a chapter to misrepresentation, another to mistake, another to duress, undue influence and inequality of bargaining power and yet another to illegality. The detail here might be excessive for readers other than LLB students. *Davies on Contract by Robert Upex (10th edition) Sweet and Maxwell* might be preferable. *Davies* is very easy to read, but lacks the detailed analysis to be found in *Richards*.

Chapter 7

Again *Richards* might be too detailed here. Three separate chapters deal with discharge of contracts while three more deal with remedies for breach of contract. Again, *Davies* is an excellent alternative. *Contract Law: Text, Cases and Materials by Professor Ewan McKendrick (4th edition) Oxford University Press* is an outstanding case book on the whole of the law of contract. The materials reproduced are well chosen and the author's detailed comments are very useful.

Chapter 8

Commercial Law by Robert Bradgate (4th edition) LexisNexis UK has one chapter devoted to the classification of transactions and another to the substance of the statutory implied terms to be found in the Sale of Goods Act 1979. Yet another chapter deals with contracts for the supply of services. *Bradgate* is a well-written book which deals with the various matters convincingly. Some students might find it rather difficult to read, but it is much easier to read than most of its competitors.

Chapter 9

Bradgate considers the matters covered in this chapter in great detail, taking four chapters to do so. Again, preferable to most of its competitors.

Chapter 10

The matters covered in this chapter are dealt with more briefly by *Bradgate*. Complex issues are not avoided, and yet the style remains readable.

Chapter 11

Bradgate deals with agency over four relatively short chapters, providing an excellent treatment of the subject, once the basic concepts have been mastered. *Agency* by R. Munday (1st edition) OUP is a short but interesting book which deals with some of the more complex aspects of the law of agency. However, at times this book can be rather difficult to read.

Chapters 12 and 13

The Law of Torts Learning Text by John Hodgson and John Lewthwaite (2nd edition) Blackstone Press leads the reader through this difficult subject. The text is designed to be used with a companion text containing Cases and Materials. The complexity of the subject is never avoided and yet the style remains clear and readable. For those who prefer a more conventional approach, *Street on Torts (12th edition) LexisNexis UK* is an excellent book.

Chapter 14

The law on credit is highly complex and maintaining a readable style is a struggle for any author dealing with the subject. *Bradgate* explores the subject in great detail and is as readable as any other book which does so.

Chapter 15

There are few books which deal convincingly with the law of partnership. *Partnership Law by Geoffrey Morse (7th edition) Oxford University Press* is probably the best. The book is academic in its approach but remains reasonably easy to read.

Chapter 16

Mayson, French and Ryan on Company Law (27th edition) Blackstone Press is an excellent book. It deals with all aspects of company law in great detail and yet remains clear, practical and comprehensible. Several chapters are devoted to corporate personality and the registration of companies.

Chapters 17 to 19

Again, *Mayson, French and Ryan* seems the pick of the bunch. It is updated annually and is therefore always up to date. Much of company law is changing rapidly and the book explains these changes in a readable style. The policy behind the law is also considered critically and convincingly.

Chapters 20 and 21

Selwyn's Law of Employment (16th edition) LexisNexis UK is an excellent conventional textbook. The text is broken down into easily manageable chunks and the style of the writing is clear. Employment law is changing at a phenomenal rate and the Department for Business Innovation & Skills web site (www.bis.gov.uk) provides excellent summaries of all new legislation. *Tolley's Employment Handbook by Elizabeth Slade (25th edition) LexisNexis UK* is the most authoritative book on employment law. It is clear and accurate, but very expensive.

Chapter 22

Textbook on Consumer Law by David Oughton and John Lowry (2nd edition) Oxford University Press is a good book but is somewhat out of date. The text is detailed and authoritative but reasonably easy to read.

Chapter 23

Intellectual Property by David Bainbridge (8th edition) Financial Times Prentice Hall/Pearson Education is a comprehensive work which deals with all aspects of intellectual property. The book is well written and detailed.

Index

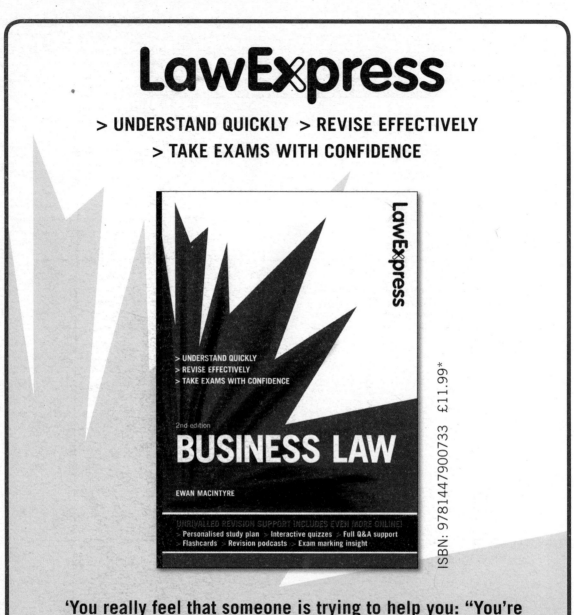